Official

BASEBALL GUIDE

1985 EDITION

Editor/Baseball Guide
DAVE SLOAN

Associate Editor/Baseball Guide
MIKE NAHRSTEDT

Contributing Editors/Baseball Guide
CRAIG CARTER
CARL CLARK
LARRY WIGGE

President-Chief Executive Officer
RICHARD WATERS

Editor
DICK KAEGEL

Director of Books and Periodicals
RON SMITH

Published by

The Sporting News

1212 North Lindbergh Boulevard
P.O. Box 56 — St. Louis, MO 63166

Copyright © 1985
The Sporting News Publishing Company
a Times Mirror company

IMPORTANT NOTICE

ISBN 0-89204-178-1   ISSN 0078-3838

TABLE OF CONTENTS

REVIEW OF 1984—Ueberroth Takes Over as Commissioner, Most Valuable Player Tables, Cy Young Tables 3

AMERICAN LEAGUE—Team Reviews of '84 Season, Day-by-Day Scores, Official Batting, Fielding and Pitching Averages 31

NATIONAL LEAGUE—Team Reviews of '84 Season, Day-by-Day Scores, Official Batting, Fielding and Pitching Averages 113

AMERICAN LEAGUE CHAMPIONSHIP SERIES—Tigers-Royals Series Review, Box Scores, Composite Box Scores 189

NATIONAL LEAGUE CHAMPIONSHIP SERIES—Padres-Cubs Series Review, Box Scores, Composite Box Scores 195

WORLD SERIES—Tigers-Padres Series Review, Official Box Scores, Play-by-Play 203

ALL-STAR GAME—1984 Game Review, Official Box Score, Play-by-Play, Results of Previous Games 219

BATTING AND PITCHING FEATURES—No-Hit and Low-Hit Games, Top Strikeout Performances, Top Firemen, Pitchers Winning 1-0 Games, Multi-Homer Games, Grand Slam Hitters, One-Game Hitting Feats, Top Pinch-Hitters, Top Debut Performances, Homers by Parks, Award Winners, Hall of Fame Electees, List ... 225

1984 RE-ENTRY DRAFT, MINOR LEAGUE DRAFT, MAJOR LEAGUE TRANSACTIONS, NECROLOGY 263

INFORMATION ON LEAGUES AND CLUBS—Major League and Minor League Directories, American League Directory, American League Club Directories, National League Directory, National League Club Directories, Players Association Directory, Major League Farm Systems, Minor League Presidents 285

OFFICIAL 1984 MINOR LEAGUE AVERAGES 319

1985 AMERICAN LEAGUE SCHEDULE 490

1985 NATIONAL LEAGUE SCHEDULE 492

For Index to Contents See Page 495

(Index to Minor League Cities on Page 496)

ON THE COVER: During the 1984 season, it was Cub second baseman Ryne Sandberg's 19 homers, 84 runs batted in and .314 average that led Chicago to its first championship of any kind in 39 years and won him National League Most Valuable Player honors.
—Photo by Janis Rettaliata

Selection of Commissioner Highlights Year in Baseball

By CLIFFORD KACHLINE

In baseball, as in life, the expression "If it isn't one thing, it's another" seems to hold true. The sport's powers-that-be addressed two major issues confronting them in 1984—the selection of a new commissioner and the drug problem. But, as the year closed and 1985 gave birth to spring fever, they still were wrestling with an equally weighty subject: Renewal of the Basic Agreement with the players, which expired on December 31, 1984.

That was the key issue facing baseball as Peter V. Ueberroth entered his first full year as the sport's sixth commissioner.

Ueberroth's impressive start gave quick rise to thoughts that he could help provide a solution to any player-management stalemate. While a majority of baseball officials and close observers had nothing but praise for the job done by outgoing Commissioner Bowie Kuhn during his 16-year tenure, the increased authority vested in Ueberroth led to the feeling that he might be able to produce solutions to some issues that Kuhn often was forced to view from a distance.

Ueberroth's remarkable business background and his successful leadership of the 1984 Summer Olympics in Los Angeles also spurred hopes that he could provide answers to some of the game's other problems. The hottest issue immediately facing him was the economic viability of the baseball industry. Some insiders claimed the 26 major league clubs experienced a deficit of more than $100 million over the last two years.

By contrast, on the field the sport was probably never healthier. Attendance was down slightly but still reached the second highest figure ever. Veterans such as Pete Rose, Phil Niekro and Tony Armas continued to make headlines in a positive way, and youngsters like Dwight Gooden, Alvin Davis, Don Mattingly and Tony Gwynn grabbed their share of the spotlight. For the first time since 1945, the Chicago Cubs and their fans enjoyed the heady experience of a first-place finish, only to be upset by the San Diego Padres, who captured the first pennant in their 16-year existence. And, for the sixth consecutive year, a new world champion was crowned when the Detroit Tigers capped a spectacular season by winning the World Series.

Peter V. Ueberroth, president of the Los Angeles Olympic Organizing Committee, answers questions at the March 3 press conference announcing his selection as the new commissioner of baseball.

From a long-range viewpoint, the election and installation of Ueberroth as commissioner has to rate as the year's most important baseball development. The game's high command had been functioning in something of a twilight zone since November 1, 1982, when five National League owners blocked Kuhn's re-election. Shortly thereafter, the owners talked of slicing up the commissioner's job among several specialists, with boards, commissions and councils to oversee the office as a whole. But in the end, they went the opposite direction, agreeing to broaden the commissioner's authority in order to convince Ueberroth to accept the job.

The long search for a successor to Kuhn came to an end on Saturday, March 3. Meeting in Tampa, Fla., the club owners unanimously elected Ueberroth, a 47-year-old, self-made millionnaire, at an annual salary of $300,000. Because of his role as president and chief executive officer of the Los Angeles Olympic Organizing Committee, he stipulated that he would not take office until October 1, seven weeks after the conclusion of the Summer Olympics. His first term was set at five years and three months, extending through December 31, 1989.

Kuhn, whose contract expired on August 12, 1983, agreed to a third interim appointment, this one for seven months. It meant he would remain in office through September 30, the final day of the regular 1984 season.

"I congratulate the owners on making a decision that I feared they might not make," Kuhn said after Ueberroth's selection. "Peter is uniquely qualified for the position." Even Yankees Owner George Steinbrenner, a man not easily impressed, voiced nothing but compliments. "Ueberroth is a very impressive man," he said.

Ueberroth's selection climaxed a long, wearing experience for Bud Selig, president and chief executive officer of the Milwaukee Brewers and chairman of the eight-man Commissioner Search Committee. Some 15 months earlier, at the 1982 winter meetings in Hawaii, he said he felt the task would not be too difficult.

"There ought to be hundreds of dynamic men out there in the business world who are qualified for the commissioner's job," he commented at the time. But after the process was completed, he admitted his role as head of the Search Committee "became a totally time-consuming, overriding passion. I forgot about my car business and I paid little attention to my ball club. I would never undertake anything like it again."

At the same time, Selig denied reports published prior to the 1983 winter meetings that the position of commissioner had been offered to James Baker, the White House chief of staff under President Ronald Reagan. Selig added that while the committee had interviewed more than 30 men and had reviewed more than 100 applications, only Ueberroth had been offered the job.

Originally, it was revealed, Ueberroth resisted baseball's blandishments, telling Selig that he "was convinced the best man

(Kuhn) already was on the job." But later he expressed interest when it became apparent that Kuhn could not win re-election and was on his way out. Selig and other members of the Search Committee flew to Monterrey, Calif., to meet with Ueberroth on February 3-4 during the Bing Crosby Golf Tournament. "The discussions became very serious at that point," Ueberroth said.

The spectacular results he achieved as head of the Los Angeles Olympic Organizing Committee were what first caught Selig's eye. In 1982, Ueberroth helped to negotiate a $225 million Olympic television contract with ABC-TV. He then personally went around the country on a selling trip that yielded nearly $120 million worth of "official Olympic sponsorships" from 30 corporations.

To induce him to accept the role of commissioner, baseball's owners had to make a string of important concessions designed to strengthen the position. As a result, he has been given greater freedom to act than any commissioner since the game's first czar, Judge Kenesaw M. Landis. "Ueberroth knew how badly baseball wanted him, and he would have been dumb if he hadn't demanded the right to dictate the terms under which he would accept," remarked Jerry Reinsdorf, co-owner of the Chicago White Sox. "He is a man of affluence and doesn't need the job from a financial standpoint."

Ironically, Ueberroth's principal adviser on the matter of contract terms was Kuhn. Although the outgoing commissioner had been unsuccessful in getting the changes for himself, he at least had the pleasure of seeing to it that his successor was so privileged. "I didn't create the changes; they were Bowie's recommendations," Ueberroth conceded.

Foremost among the changes was one providing for the commissioner to be formally recognized as baseball's chief executive officer. The new setup provides that all departments must report directly to him. Earlier, the major league's Committee on Restructuring had proposed that the new commissioner would be third in the power structure behind a 26-man board of directors and an eight-man Executive Council. That plan was unacceptable to Ueberroth.

He also insisted on a major revision of re-election procedures. Instead of a three-fourth majority in each league (the rule that toppled Kuhn), Ueberroth will require the approval of only a simple majority of the 26 teams, including at least five from each league, to gain a second term.

Peter Ueberroth, the newly elected commissioner of baseball, posed with outgoing Commissioner Bowie Kuhn before the March 3 press conference to announce his selection in Tampa, Fla.

Other key changes dictated by the new commissioner at Kuhn's urging included:

• Both the American and National League presidents will report directly to the commissioner on matters pertaining to the overall administration of baseball.

• The commissioner will be able to fine a team a maximum of $250,000 instead of the former limit of $5,000 and is empowered to deny or transfer a club's amateur or minor league draft choices if such a penalty is deemed appropriate.

• Strengthening of the Major League Agreement's provisions involving the club's waiver of legal action against decisions by the commissioner.

At a media conference after his election, Ueberroth commented: "I am not anywhere near an expert, but from afar it appears to me that baseball lacks economic viability. My accounting background tells me that. For now, though, my only baseball duty will be to learn as much as I can. I will not participate in any decision-making processes before October 1."

Born on September 2, 1937, at Evanston, Ill., the new commissioner was christened Peter Victor Ueberroth. He also lived in Wisconsin, Iowa and Pennsylvania before his family moved to California, where he lettered in baseball, football and swimming at Fremont High. He subsequently attended San Jose State University on an athletic scholarship, captaining the water polo team as a freshman and then leading the conference in scoring in both his junior and senior years. In between, he had a tryout with the 1956 Olympic water polo team, but didn't make the squad.

After graduating from San Jose State with a degree in business, he married Virginia (Ginny) Nicolaus and moved to Hawaii. In recent years, the Ueberroths have lived in Laguna Beach, Calif., with their four children.

While living in Hawaii, Ueberroth launched his career in the travel industry. He served as vice-president of Trans International Airlines for several years and then in 1963 founded a small company—First Travel Corp. Starting with capital of $5,000 and one employee, he developed the firm into a giant. By 1980, when he sold out, it was the second largest travel business in North America. As of early 1984, it had 1,500 employees and $300 million in annual revenues.

When plans for the 1984 Summer Olympics were first being formulated, an executive talent search company recommended Ueberroth to head up the operation. He started his job as president and chief executive officer of the Los Angeles Olympic Organizing Committee on April 1, 1979. Under his leadership and management, the '84 Summer Games were proclaimed the best-run Olympics in history. Attendance was reported as a record 5.8 million, and his great organizational and marketing skills helped the first-time privately financed Games to produce a surplus of more than $200 million.

During an interview a few months after his selection to the baseball post, Ueberroth said he felt he would be bringing a high degree of much-needed business acumen to the sport and agreed that he thrived on solving problems and making decisions, but added: "The critical thing in the future is going to be the will of the people in baseball to make it better. The commissioner alone is not going to make it better. It's up to the will of the owners, players, managers and the Players' Association."

Ueberroth will long remember his first week on the job. Besides trips to the four League Championship Series cities and his New York office, it included an umpires' strike, charges of mistreatment of a woman sportswriter covering the N.L. Championship Series and an important scheduling conflict.

On October 1, his first day in office, the new commissioner was greeted by an announcement by Richie Phillips, general counsel for the Major League Baseball Umpires Association, that the arbiters would refuse to officiate in the playoffs barring a last-minute agreement. After three months, Phillips said, negotiations with the two league presidents had broken down. The dispute centered around postseason pay and job security. After winning big financial concessions following a strike in 1979, the umpires had signed a new four-year contract in 1982, but it provided that after two years Phillips could reopen the issues of postseason competition and selection of umpires for postseason games.

According to Phillips, the umpires were seeking a slice of gate receipts, the same as the players receive. He said they were asking for 6 percent of the live gate from the first three games of each Championship Series and the first four games of the World Series as well as 2 percent of the national television package for those games. In addition, he revealed they wanted to add outside arbitration to the process by which umpires are dismissed.

The umpires' latest demand represented a package estimated at $340,000. Because arbiters were selected for postseason games on merit rather than on a rotating basis, as once was the practice, the Umpires Association revealed it intended to distribute the additional compensation among all 60 umpires on the two league staffs, not just those who worked postseason games.

Ueberroth's initial responses to media queries about the umpire strike produced groans among many observers. He said he was leaving the matter in the hands of the league presidents, Dr. Bobby Brown of the American League and Chub Feeney of the National. The comments prompted recollections of the negative "It's a league matter" response often given by the late former commissioner Ford Frick. A few days later, however, Ueberroth entered the fray as an arbitrator, and major league umpires replaced the stand-ins for the final game of the National League Championship Series and for the World Series.

The National League Championship Series opened at Wrigley Field on October 2 with four Chicago-area college and high school umpires on the job instead of the six N.L. umpires who had been assigned. The replacements were Dick Cavanaugh, an airplane salesman; Dave Slickenmeyer, a food salesman, and Joe Pomponi and Joe Maher, both physical education teachers.

Later that day at Kansas City, the American League playoff got underway with six umpire replacements on the field. Bill Deegan, who umpired 10 years in the American League before retiring in 1980, was behind the plate. Joining him were Jon Bible, Randy Christal, Larry Zirdel, Harold Jordan and Mike O'Dell. Bible and Christal were college umpires imported from Texas. Zirdel was a 62-year-old high school counselor; Jordan an assembly-line worker for General Mills and O'Dell a postman.

Deegan, who remained behind the plate for the entire A.L. Series, was joined in Game 2 by Bible, Christal and three new locals—Bob Jones, Rick Denny and Carl Nothnagel. Deegan, Bible and Christal all traveled to Detroit for Game 3 and were joined by locals Doug Cossey, Dick Runchey and Dick Zivic.

When the National League playoff switched to San Diego, four umpires from Yuma, Ariz., were recruited for duty. The crew, which had worked together during the 1979 umpire strike, consisted of Terry Bovey, Frank Campagna, Frank Fisher and John Stewart.

The short-lived umpire walkout came to an end on October 7. Although the two sides still were far apart, the league presidents and Phillips agreed to submit the dispute to binding arbitration with the new commissioner as the arbitrator. One condition of the agreement was that the umpires would return to work immediately.

Four N.L. arbiters residing in the San Diego area—John Kibler, Paul Runge, John McSherry and Doug Harvey—quickly were rounded up and handled the final contest of the Padres-Cubs series that afternoon. Of the four, only Kibler originally had been scheduled to work the playoff.

As if the umpire work stoppage wasn't headache enough, Ueberroth found himself drawn into two other incidents during the playoffs. The one involving the female writer occurred at the opening game in Chicago. Claire Smith, who covered the Yankees during the season for the Hartford (Conn.) Courant, claimed she was denied access to the San Diego Padres' dressing room after the contest. Her paper immediately sent telegrams of protest to the commissioner, Feeney and Jack McKeon, Padres general manager. Smith was granted access to the dressing room at ensuing games.

The first of two nationally-televised debates between the two candidates for U.S. President—incumbent Ronald Reagan and challenger Walter Mondale—figured in the scheduling conflict. The debate was set to begin at 9 p.m. (EDT) on October 7 in Louisville. All three major networks arranged to televise it live. Meanwhile, the fifth game of the American League Series, if needed, was scheduled to start at 8:25—or 35 minutes earlier—in Detroit. ABC-TV had television rights to all of the playoff games.

After a request from the League of Women Voters, which sponsored the debates, Ueberroth announced on October 5 that the Detroit game would be switched to a 1 p.m. starting time. "This will necessitate a change in plans for the fans planning to attend the game, and we are apologetic for any inconvenience to them," the commissioner said. "But the decision on the leadership of the country is the most important one the American public will make." Several hours after the announcement was made, the Tigers defeated the Royals for the third time, making games four and five unnecessary.

Ueberroth handed down his ruling in the umpire arbitration on October 15, and the decision reportedly stunned the club owners and league presidents. It awarded the umpires a boost of more than 100 percent in postseason compensation. The ruling stipulated that remuneration would remain at $2,500 per umpire for the All-Star Game, $10,000 for the playoffs and $15,000 for the World Series, but provided for an increase of nearly $1.12 million in payments over the three-year period of 1984-86. A sum of $720,000 was earmarked for All-Star Game and postseason compensation over the three years and $400,000 for regular-season salary increases in 1986. The decision also granted the umpires full pay for the 1984 playoff games they missed and permitted them to divide the pooled money among all umpires, including those not selected for the All-Star contest or postseason games.

Under the old agreement, the arbiters' postseason and All-Star remuneration had amounted to $225,000 a year and only those who worked were paid. The new contract calls for an increase to $405,000 in 1984, to $465,000 in 1985 and to $525,000 in 1986. The hikes amount to about $4,000 per man in 1984 and $5,000 in 1986, exclusive of the '86 salary boost.

The new commissioner continued to make a strong impression in succeeding weeks and forcefully demonstrated his independence. At the general managers' meeting in Austin, Tex., late in October and then again at the winter meetings in Houston early in December, he made it clear that he saw cable TV superstations and the ability of owners to work together as baseball's most serious concerns. He further showed his independence by arranging to meet with Don Fehr, Marvin Miller and other leaders of the Players Association and by blocking, at least temporarily, one player trade and plans by a club to sell a block of stock to a broadcasting firm.

The explosive superstation situation focused on WTBS of Atlanta, WGN of Chicago and WOR and WPIX of New York. The four stations have been beaming games of the Braves, Cubs, Mets and Yankees, respectively, into living rooms throughout the U.S. WTBS is owned by Ted Turner, owner of the Braves, while the Chicago Tribune Co. owns both WGN and the Cubs.

"They are telecasting into territories of other major league teams, and it is blatantly unfair," Ueberroth said. He added that the saturation created by the superstations could impair future contractual dealings with the commercial TV networks. In addition, the TV profits were enabling the Braves and Cubs, in particular, to pour huge sums into contracts for free-agent players.

At their Houston meetings, the owners voted 25-1 in favor of a resolution authorizing Ueberroth to find a "business solution" to the superstations problem. Potential solutions included getting the superstations to turn over a share of the advertising revenues gleaned from other teams' territories to a communal baseball fund and inducing them to reduce the number of games they televise.

Prior to the winter meetings, Ueberroth had nixed a proposal by Eddie Chiles, owner of the Texas Rangers, to sell the team's TV rights as well as a one-third interest in the club to Gaylord Broadcasting. Gaylord's superstation potential was said to present the stumbling block. However, the commissioner later indicated the transaction might be approved.

Ueberroth also refused to sanction a player swap in which the Yankees were to send outfielder Steve Kemp, shortstop Tim Foli and $800,000 to the Pittsburgh Pirates for shortstop Dale Berra and rookie pitchers Alfonso Pulido and Jay Buhner. As part of the deal the Yankees agreed to pick up an $800,000 portion of Kemp's contract. The commissioner ruled the deal violated established guidelines calling for a $400,000 limit on player transactions. The deal later was approved as an exception to the $400,000 guideline. The commissioner made it clear, however, that the guideline remains in force and can be circumvented only at his discretion.

Prior to the winter meetings, the new commissioner revealed that he intended to conduct a fan survey on the designated hitter rule. He said he was opposed to having the two leagues operate under different sets of rules. Ever since being adopted by the American League as an experiment in 1973, the DH has been a source of controversy, with the National League continuing to reject it. Meanwhile, the designated hitter has become entrenched in the minor leagues and in college, high school and amateur programs. Ueberroth said he planned to hire a professional polling organization to determine whether there was a "significant preference" among the fans.

Kuhn's final nine months in the top baseball post were not without controversy. His rulings in several drug cases were challenged by an arbitrator and he came in for considerable criticism over the World Series schedule. The latter, of course, was arranged well before his successor took office.

The Chicago Cubs' rise to the National League East title created a dilemma because of the absence of lights at Wrigley Field. With the World Series due to open in the National League park, it would have meant playing the first two games and also the sixth and seventh games, if needed, on weekday afternoons if the Cubs qualified—unless temporary lights were installed. Under its contract with NBC-TV, midweek daytime games would have cost baseball millions of dollars in television revenue because of the reduced advertising income that would have been realized by the network.

To solve the situation Kuhn arranged for alternate schedules. They provided for the Series to open in the National League city if the San Diego Padres won the pennant whereas the Series would start in the American League city if the Cubs captured the pennant.

"We analyzed any number of possibilities for the World Series, including the installation of temporary lights at Wrigley Field and moving to another stadium," Kuhn said. "We settled on this schedule because of baseball's commitment for weekday night games to both fans and the television networks. While not ideal, the schedule arrived at is the best alternative."

The setup drew sharp criticism in some quarters and, in the view of many observers, reinforced the argument that television dominates sports. Several media members charged Kuhn had compromised his integrity, but others suggested he willingly took the heat for the owners to preserve the TV income. One Cubs season ticket holder filed a lawsuit in Cook County Circuit Court seeking $1 million in damages from Kuhn and NBC because he might miss a fourth home game if the Series went the limit. The suit was dismissed.

The arrangement also did not sit well with Cubs Manager Jim Frey. "I'd be a fool to say it's OK," he commented. "I want this team to have every possible advantage wherever it plays, and playing away from Wrigley Field in the first and last games definitely is not an advantage. It's not right."

As it turned out, the entire matter became moot when the Padres whipped the Cubs in the Championship Series.

Kuhn himself passed up the World Series. After clearing out his office, he departed on September 27 for Seoul, South Korea, to represent baseball at the Korean championship Series. Although he was due back in time for the Series, he said he told

Ueberroth that he "thought it would be better if I didn't come." He added: "This is Peter's first time (running the World Series). He should be there without the old Commish at his side."

Despite having been rebuffed in his re-election bid, Kuhn said he was leaving the game without rancor.

"When you've been commissioner almost 16 years, that's long enough," he said. "It's a very tough, demanding job."

Before heading for South Korea, he was honored at a $250-a-plate charity dinner in New York. After the trip, the 58-year-old outgoing commissioner returned to his old law firm of Willkie Farr and Gallagher, which serves as counsel to baseball. There were indications, however, that he had hopes of returning to baseball at some future date in an ownership-executive role.

The end of Kuhn's reign coincided with the retirement of his secretary, Mary Sotos Anargeros. She rounded out 48 years in baseball. Starting as secretary to the late Ford Frick when he was National League president, she moved with him when he became commissioner. She later served as secretary to Commissioner William Eckert until he was succeeded by Kuhn.

When Kuhn became commissioner early in 1969 after the sudden ouster of William Eckert, he was accepted as a popular figure. He was a tall, articulate lawyer with an impressive record. During those litigious times, baseball seemed to need someone with Kuhn's credentials. But within a few years, the situation began to change. The revolution wrought by the Players' Association resulted in striking down the old reserve clause, the shift of power from management to the players' union and battles with several of the new breed of owners. These factors eventually combined to turn the pendulum against Kuhn.

The swing in power was emphasized anew in 1984 by developments in several drug-related cases. Acting on grievances filed by the Players' Association, arbitrator Richard I. Bloch nullified entirely or in part Kuhn's suspensions of three players. Bloch, a Tampa, Fla., lawyer, was chosen to handle grievances under the collective bargaining provision of the Basic Agreement.

Willie Wilson, Jerry Martin, Willie Aikens and Pascual Perez were the central figures in the grievances.

In December of 1983, Kunn banned Kansas City players Wilson, Martin and Willie Aikens and Los Angeles pitcher

Atlanta pitcher Pascual Perez had plenty of reason to smile after leaving the Dominican Republic prison where he spent three months on drug charges during the 1983-84 off-season.

Steve Howe from baseball for the 1984 season because of alleged drug involvement, with the proviso that the suspensions of all but Howe might be lifted pending a May 15 review. Perez was arrested early in January in his native Dominican Republic on drug charges, and the commissioner subsequently placed him under suspension through May 15.

However, in a decision handed down on April 3, the day after the season opened, Bloch modified the year-long bans on Wilson and Martin. While acknowledging the commissioner's disciplinary authority, the arbitrator ruled the pair must be reinstated on May 15. This ruling subsequently was applied to Aikens as well. And on April 29, Bloch threw out Perez's suspension because of a lack of evidence that the player had been involved with cocaine. He also rescinded all other conditions imposed on the Atlanta pitcher by the commissioner.

Kuhn did emerge victorious in one other drug-related grievance. It involved Vida Blue, who drew his release from Kansas City shortly before the 1983 drug inquiry became public. Like ex-teammates Wilson, Martin and Aikens, Blue was convicted late in the year of cocaine possession and was sentenced to three months in jail. In midsummer, the 35-year-old lefty indicated an interest in returning to baseball. But Kuhn notified him on July 13 that he was barred for the remainder of the 1984 season. Kuhn said his decision was based not only on the pitcher's conviction, but also on the results of an investigation that showed "substantial use of and involvement with cocaine during the 1982 and 1983 seasons." The Players' Association promptly challenged the ruling. After a grievance hearing on July 16, Bloch sustained the commissioner's decision.

The Perez episode had its comic as well as serious aspects. Arrested outside a bar in Santiago on January 9, the Braves' pitcher gave Dominican police several conflicting versions of how he came into possession of the half gram of cocaine found in his wallet. At the same time he insisted he never used the substance. One prosecutor, contending the player was a drug trafficker, called for him to be jailed "for at least two years." It later became apparent that rival political factions in the Dominican Republic were using Perez in a tug of war.

During his three months in Fort San Luis Prison in Santiago, Perez was permitted to engage in regular baseball workouts. He was tried in late March and let off with mild punishment. Found guilty of a reduced charge of possession of cocaine, he was fined $1,000 and made eligible for release on bond, but an appeal by the prosecutor delayed his discharge for several additional weeks.

When he arrived in the U.S., Perez met with a Kuhn aide before the commissioner's April 17 announcement that he was suspended without pay. The suspension, retroactive to the season opener, was to extend through May 15, costing the pitcher an estimated $50,000 in salary. In additon, he was placed on probation until May 15, 1985. Arbitrator Bloch's ruling on the subsequent grievance, of course, nullified the Kuhn decree, and on May 2 Perez made his debut. He pitched three perfect innings against San Diego before rain washed out the game. A 15-game winner the previous season, he went on to chalk up a 14-8 record for Atlanta.

Bloch's ruling in the Perez case drew a sharp blast from Kuhn. "The decision is inexplicable, indefensible and highly destructive of baseball's efforts to deal with its serious drug problem," the commissioner declared. "I will decide shortly what further action is appropriate in this case." No additional disciplinary measures were taken.

On May 15, as instructed, Wilson, Martin and Aikens reported to the commissioner's office in New York. Kuhn told them they were free to resume playing the next day, but he cautioned they must continue their community work and submit to periodic urinalysis. Each had served a three-month sentence in Forth Worth Correctional Institute, but then had been working out with their teams since their discharge. After having missed the first 44 days of the season, Wilson was back in the Kansas City lineup on May 16. Aikens, traded by the Royals to Toronto during the winter, made his debut with the Blue Jays the same day, while Martin, who was released by Kansas City after the 1983 season, broke in with the New York Mets on May 18.

Meanwhile, Howe continued on a drug rehabilitation program and opted not to challenge his year-long suspension. Four days before a scheduled grievance hearing, the Los Angeles Dodgers pitcher, his attorney and officials of the Dodgers and Players' Association held a meeting in California on June 1. At the conclusion of the session, the player's attorney, Jim Hawkins, disclosed that an out-of-court settlement had been reached, and Kuhn announced that Howe would remain out of baseball for the entire 1984 season.

As part of the agreement, Howe's one-year suspension was lifted. Barring any recurrence of drug problems, he was slated to rejoin the Dodgers in spring training of 1985.

"It was entirely Steve's decision," Hawkins said. He revealed that Howe made the decision based on the advice of Dr. Forrest Tennant, under whose care he had been placed. The Los Angeles club had hired Dr. Tennant the previous December as a consultant to the entire organization on drug abuse. In a statement released by the Dodgers after the meeting, Howe said: "I must face up to reality—that if I truly want to put my recovery first, then I should not return to baseball this year. My doctor, my therapist and fellow members in my recovery program have urged me to take more time before subjecting myself to the high emotions and stress of a pennant race. I am following their advice."

Howe resumed pitching briefly in the Arizona Instructional League in October and later in the Puerto Rican Winter League. Blue, likewise, began his comeback in the Puerto Rican League.

No additional suspensions for drug involvement were meted out in 1984, but several other players were revealed to have experienced problems with the use of drugs and/or alcohol.

Two days after Perez's arrest, Atlanta newspapers published stories that two other Braves—outfielder Claudell Washington and pitcher Steve Bedrosian—had sought help during the off-season. Washington reportedly spent 28 days in a California clinic undergoing therapy for cocaine use. Bedrosian allegedly admitted he had experimented with cocaine and visited a professional counselor but was found to have no serious problem.

During spring training Dennis Martinez, Baltimore pitcher, revealed he had attended an eight-week program designed to combat alcohol dependency during the winter.

Rod Scurry, Pittsburgh reliever, disclosed his drug dependency April 7 while the Pirates were in Los Angeles. Two days earlier at San Diego he had faced two batters, walking them on eight pitches. After spending 30 days in Gateway Rehabilitation Center near Pittsburgh, he returned to action with the Pirates on May 13. Because Scurry was a first-time offender who came forward voluntarily under baseball's amnesty program, Kuhn took no disciplinary action.

Willie Wilson (above) and former Kansas City teammate Jerry Martin served three-month sentences in the Fort Worth Correctional Institute and then resumed their baseball careers in mid-May, Martin with the New York Mets.

Oakland pitcher Mike Norris, recovering from off-season nerve surgery on his shoulder, was arrested on May 6 along with a female companion in an Oakland motel. Police reportedly found $20 worth of cocaine in the room. Two days later, the Alameda County prosecutors dropped the case for lack of evidence.

A story in Milwaukee newspapers early in May stated that a man on trial as alleged head of a cocaine ring indicated that his customers included five major league players. Those named in the story were Mike Caldwell and Paul Molitor of the Milwaukee Brewers; Dick Davis, a former Brewer who was released during spring training by the Philadelphia Phillies; Len Barker of the Atlanta Braves and Joe Charboneau, former Cleveland Indians outfielder. After investigating the case, the commissioner's office announced that no disciplinary action would be taken, thus supporting the players' contention that they were not involved.

On May 24, the St. Louis Cardinals placed first baseman-outfielder David Green on the disabled list to undergo med-

ical evaluation. He subsequently underwent rehabilitation and returned to the lineup on June 15.

Late in the year, Brian Giles, former New York Mets infielder who was claimed in the draft by Milwaukee, was found guilty of possession of 12 grams of marijuana in the Dominican Republic. He had just arrived in Santo Domingo to play in the Dominican Winter League.

Drug incidents propelled four other former major leaguers into the news.

Denny McLain, the majors' last 30-game winner, was named in what was potentially the most serious. He and six other persons were listed in a five-count federal indictment issued in Tampa, Fla., on March 19. They were accused of possession and distribution of cocaine, conspiracy to import cocaine, loan sharking, bookmaking, accepting kickbacks and extortion. McLain's bond originally was set at $500,000, but later was reduced to $200,000.

McLain's trial began in November and was expected to last six to eight weeks. McLain also figured in another legal action.

In July, the U.S. District Court of Appeals in Cincinnati handed down a ruling holding the 40-year-old former pitcher liable for an estimated $20,000 in back taxes owed by the 1976 Memphis team of the Southern Association. McLain served as general manager of that club.

Maury Wills, former Los Angeles Dodgers shortstop, pleaded not guilty to one count of possession of cocaine in Municipal Court in Compton, Calif., in January and was released on $1,000 bail. Several months later, the charge was dropped for lack of evidence.

Dock Ellis, former Pittsburgh pitcher who was working as a drug counselor in Los Angeles, told a Pittsburgh writer that he was under the influence of LSD when he pitched a no-hitter in San Diego in 1970. Although Ellis reportedly once was a drug addict, some scoffed at his story.

The year's biggest drug flap occurred in February. It resulted from comments made by Ken Moffett, former executive director of the Major League Players Association. In an interview printed in the February 22 issue of the Washington Post, Moffett charged that drug abuse by baseball players was widespread.

That same day Moffett appeared before an assemblage of newspaper columnists and reporters attending a conference on sports issues in Washington. The session, held at the Watergate Hotel, was sponsored by the Washington Journalism Center. His theme was that drugs were a big problem in baseball and that he had been trying to deal with the issue in a cooperative effort with management, but that his stance conflicted with the view of Marvin Miller and Don Fehr and led to his dismissal as head of the Players' Association in November of 1983.

During his talk, Moffett jolted the journalists by tossing out several names—Keith Hernandez, Doug Bair and Dusty Baker—and implying they might have been traded or released because of drug involvement. Moffett said Hernandez, the Cardinals' player representative at the time, informed him of a meeting called by Whitey Herzog early in the 1983 season at which the St. Louis manager allegedly told his players that he knew three of them were on drugs and asked them to step forward. None did, Moffett related, but shortly thereafter Lonnie Smith admitted to drug addiction and Hernandez and Bair were traded to the New York Mets and Detroit, respectively.

Upon learning of Moffett's comments, Hernandez immediately called a press conference, denied the implications and threatened a suit. Moffett then recanted a day later, saying: "There was never any feeling on my part that Keith or Doug Bair was involved in any way with the drug thing." Some observers felt Moffett's bitterness over his ouster by the Players' Association contributed to his indiscriminate aspersions. A few weeks prior to making his remarks, he had reached a settlement with the players' union on the last two years of his contract.

The concern over drug use prompted many teams to resort to sophisticated, intricate tests in the mandatory preseason physical exams at the minor league level. It also led to stepped-up drug education programs both at the major and minor league levels. Several clubs retained psychologists or psychiatrists and enrolled some of their executives in courses designed to teach how to spot behavior patterns of possible drug users.

Declaring drugs could "ruin our industry," General Manager Dallas Green of the Chicago Cubs tried to insert a drug-testing clause in some of his club's player contracts, but the players balked. He especially wanted long-term pacts to include provisions allowing for urinalysis and blood tests any time the team chose. A handful of major league players reportedly agreed to clauses in their 1984 contracts accepting random testing.

After more than five months of negotiations, attempts by a union/management

Joint Drug Committee to formulate a drug treatment program acceptable to both sides finally met with success. On May 23 it was announced the players had approved the tentative agreement by a 97 percent majority. However, an owners' ratification meeting set for the next day was cancelled when some clubs expressed objections to the terms. The program, which emphasized education and rehabilitation and disputes resolution procedures, eventually was accepted at a meeting of the magnates in Kansas City on June 21.

"I think that, given the history of oftentimes little cooperation between the Players' Association and major league clubs, this is a dramatic breakthrough in labor relations and sports," Kuhn said. Coincidentally, he had paid his first-ever visit to the Players' Association office the previous day.

The four management members of the committee that hammered out the agreement were Lee MacPhail, Player Relations Committee president; John McHale of Montreal, Roy Eisenhardt of Oakland and PRC attorney Barry Rona. The Players' Association was represented by Don Fehr, acting executive director; Mark Belanger, his assistant, and consultant Marvin Miller.

Basic terms of the program, which was to run through the 1984 season and could be terminated by either party, included the following:

• If a club suspects a player has a drug problem but he declines to undergo treatment, a three-man board of professionals in the field of drug matters will review the case; should the board recommend treatment and the player still refuse, he would be subject to discipline by the commissioner.

• While undergoing treatment, the player is to receive full pay for the first 30 days, half pay for the next 30 days and thereafter be paid at the rate of the minimum major league salary of $40,000.

• The commissioner has authority to discipline a player—and the players' union retains the right to challenge with a grievance—if the player pleads guilty to or is convicted of a drug charge, if he distributes drugs or if he uses them at the ball park.

A week after the agreement went into effect, Kuhn issued guidelines for dealing with cases not covered by the joint program. While the latter did not cover such substances as marijuana, amphetamines and alcohol, Kuhn's rules extended to those substances and included the possibility of permanent disbarment from baseball.

The guidelines stipulate that:

• Players who are convicted of or plead guilty to a crime related to the distribution of a controlled substance and those who facilitate the use by others of a controlled substance will be suspended without pay for a minimum of one year and could be declared permanently ineligible.

• Players convicted of pleading guilty to any crime related to possession or use of a controlled substance and those found in possession of or using any controlled substance on the playing field or premises of a stadium will be suspended for one year without pay.

• Any player disciplined under these rules and later caught violating any of them will be subject to such discipline as in the opinion of the commissioner may be appropriate under the circumstances, which could include permanent ineligibility.

• If a player voluntarily seeks assistance for his problem, he will be granted amnesty on the first occasion and not be subject to discipline but will be subject to probation, which could include testing, aftercare and community service.

While the transition in commissioners and the drug situation dominated off-the-field developments, fan attention as usual was focused primarily on action on the diamond. Extra zest was added to the pennant chases when all four divisions crowned new champions. Both of the American League's 1983 leaders slipped to fifth place and the National League's 1983 champs each finished fourth to round out a rare turnabout.

The spectacular start of Sparky Anderson's Detroit Tigers stole the early spotlight. With Jack Morris tossing a no-hitter in Chicago on the first Saturday of the season, the Tigers roared away to 35 victories in 40 games through May 24. It was one of the best getaways in major league history. As a result, even though the Toronto Blue Jays played at a remarkable .659 clip over the same period, they found themselves already 8½ games behind.

The Tigers went on to win 104 games and finish 15 lengths ahead of the runner-up Blue Jays in the American League East. Anderson thus gained the distinction of being the first manager to lead teams to 100 victories in both leagues. He also became only the fourth pilot to gain a pennant in each circuit.

The Chicago Cubs, who entered the campaign owning the longest run of seasons (38) without a first-place finish, quickly emerged as a solid contender in the National League East. General Manager Dallas Green's deals gave new Manager Jim Frey a total of 11 former Philadelphia Phillies on his roster, but probably Green's most important trade came on June 13 when he acquired Rick Sutcliffe from Cleveland. The big righthander proceeded to post a 16-1 record for the Cubs.

The surprising New York Mets, with new Manager Dave Johnson relying on a mostly young, inexperienced pitching staff, gave Chicago a scare in July by surging into the lead. But the Cubs won 10 of 14 encounters with the Mets in their last four series and went on to finish 6½ games in front of the New Yorkers.

Only one team in the West Division of each league wound up above .500. The San Diego Padres won easily in the National League West, winding up 12 lengths ahead of their nearest rivals. Their success enabled Dick Williams to join Anderson in the ranks of managers who led teams to first-place finishes in both leagues.

In the A.L. West, the Kansas City Royals limped off to a 12-20 start while Willie Wilson sat out his suspension and George Brett was shelved by injury. After the return of the two stars, Dick Howser's crew began the long road back and passed the California Angels and Minnesota Twins down the stretch, finishing three games in front of their two rivals.

The Tigers made quick work of the Royals in the League Championship Series, polishing them off in three games.

When Chicago won the first two contests of the National League playoff, it appeared Wrigley Field would play host to a World Series for the first time since the 1945 Tigers-Cubs confrontation. But the Padres erased those prospects by sweeping three straight after the series shifted to San Diego. The stunning turnaround enabled the Padres to become the fourth expansion team to reach the fall classic.

The World Series featured teams owned by two fast-food magnates—Joan Kroc, widow of the founder of the McDonald's hamburger chain, and Tom Monaghan of Domino's pizza. The Tigers, of course, downed the Padres handily, four games to one. Ironically, the Detroit loss in Game 2 came on the first anniversary of the date on which John Fetzer announced he was selling the Detroit club to Monaghan for an estimated $43 million. Terms of the agreement provided Fetzer would retain control of the club for at least two years.

San Diego's pennant success likewise had an ironic twist. Ray Kroc, who bought the team in 1974 when the fledgling franchise appeared headed for Washington, wasn't around to enjoy the heady experience. He died on January 14 at age 81. The Padres dedicated the season to his memory by wearing the initials "RAK" on the left sleeve of their uniforms.

The Chicago White Sox similarly dedicated the campaign to a pair of deceased members of their organization. Coach Loren Babe died of lung cancer on February 14, and the team's noted hitting instructor, Charley Lau, succumbed to cancer on March 18. To honor their memories the White Sox wore patches with the inscription "6/46"—the uniform numbers of Lau and Babe, respectively—in black on their left sleeve.

The season was replete with remarkable individual as well as team achievements.

Besides Morris' opening-week no-hitter, there were two other notable pitching gems. Montreal's Dave Palmer, attempting a comeback after missing all of 1983 because of arm surgery, tossed a five-inning perfect game in a rain-curtailed contest at St. Louis on April 21. Mike Witt of California topped that by pitching a nine-inning perfect game to beat Texas, 1-0, in closing out the regular season on September 30. It was just the 13th perfect game of nine or more innings in major league history.

An unusual number of newcomers—either rookies or players in their first full major league campaign—captured batting and pitching laurels.

Probably the biggest surprise was Dwight Gooden, the New York Mets' 19-year-old righthander. With barely two seasons of Class A experience, he celebrated his promotion to the major leagues by establishing several strikeout records and leading the upstart Mets with a 17-9 record. Gooden topped all pitchers in strikeouts with 276, smashing the previous rookie record of 245 set by Cleveland's Herb Score in 1955. He averaged an amazing 11.39 strikeouts per nine innings and finished second in ERA among National League pitchers at 2.60.

Mark Langston, a 24-year-old Seattle rookie lefthander, fanned 204 to lead American League pitchers in that department.

Outfielder Tony Gwynn, another 24-year-old playing his first full season in the majors, compiled a .351 batting average for San Diego to top all hitters and win the National League crown. He finished 30 points ahead of his nearest rival.

In the American League, the New York Yankees produced their first batting champion since 1956 when 23-year-old Don Mattingly capped his first full year in

San Diego Owner Ray Kroc (left), founder of the McDonald's hamburger chain, and White Sox batting coach Charley Lau were two notable baseball personalities who died in 1984.

the majors by edging teammate Dave Winfield, .343 to .340. Going into the last day of the season, Mattingly trailed by .341 to .339, but he went 4-for-5 in the final game while Winfield was being limited to one hit in four at-bats. Gwynn and Mattingly also paced their leagues in hits with 213 and 207, respectively, while Mattingly's 44 doubles were tops in the A.L.

Juan Samuel, Philadelphia second baseman, set a modern major league record for rookies by stealing 72 bases. His league-leading totals of 701 at-bats and 168 strikeouts represented all-time rookie marks.

Tim Raines of Montreal led the National League in stolen bases with 75 and in the process became the first big leaguer to register 70 or more thefts for four consecutive seasons. Rickey Henderson of Oakland paced the American League for the fifth straight year by stealing 66 bases.

Tony Armas of Boston captured American League honors in home runs (43), total bases (339) and runs batted in (123) and tied with teammate Dwight Evans for most extra-base hits (77). Evans led in runs scored with 121. Baltimore's Eddie Murray was tops in on-base percentage (.410), walks (107) and game-winning

RBIs (19), while Harold Baines of the Chicago White Sox had the best slugging percentage, .541, four points ahead of batting champ Mattingly.

Dale Murphy of Atlanta topped the National League in total bases (332) and slugging percentage (.547) and tied Philadelphia's Mike Schmidt for most home runs at 36. Schmidt and Gary Carter of Montreal deadlocked for RBI honors at 106. Gary Matthews, obtained by Chicago in a preseason trade with Philadelphia, led in on-base percentage (.410), bases on balls (103) and game-winning RBIs (19), while another ex-Phil with the Cubs, Ryne Sandberg, scored the most runs, 114, and tied Samuel for the lead in triples with 19.

Only three pitchers reached the 20-victory circle. Mike Boddicker, who attained stardom a year earlier with Baltimore, capped what actually was his first full year in the majors by posting a 20-11 record and leading the American League with a 2.79 ERA. Joaquin Andujar turned in a 20-14 ledger for the St. Louis Cardinals to rank as the National League's biggest winner. Andujar also was the workhorse of the N.L., pitching 261⅓ innings, and tied for most shutouts with four.

The third 20-game winner was Sutcliffe, who went 4-5 with Cleveland before compiling his amazing 16-1 record with the Cubs. He was only the fourth pitcher in modern history to notch 20 victories while performing in both major leagues in the same season.

In keeping with the trend of recent years, relievers almost overshadowed starting pitchers. Cardinals ace Bruce Sutter registered 45 saves to equal the major league record set by Dan Quisenberry of Kansas City in 1983. Quisenberry again led the American League with 44, giving him the distinction of being the first pitcher ever to have back-to-back seasons of 40 or more saves. Hernandez was even more impressive than his Cardinals and Royals counterparts. The lefthanded relief specialist accounted for 32 saves in 33 save opportunities and had a 1.92 ERA in his 140⅓ innings while leading both leagues in mound appearances with 80.

Sutcliffe's .941 winning percentage for the Cubs was easily the best in the National League, and Doyle Alexander of Toronto boasted the American League's best percentage on his 17-6 record. Charlie Hough of Texas tied for the A.L. lead in games started (36) and led in complete games (17), Dave Stieb of Toronto worked the most innings (267) and Bob Ojeda of Boston and Geoff Zahn of California led in shutouts with five.

In the National League, Alejandro Pena of Los Angeles captured the earned-run title with 2.48 and tied with teammate Orel Hershiser and Andujar for most shutouts (four). Houston's Joe Niekro made the most pitching starts (38), Mario Soto of Cincinnati had the most complete games (13) and Ted Power, also of the Reds, led in mound appearances with 78.

Several veterans achieved new milestones. They included Pete Rose, Phil Niekro, Mike Schmidt, Joe Morgan, Cliff Johnson, Reggie Jackson, Rusty Staub, Nolan Ryan, Steve Carlton and Don Sutton.

Rose, who signed a one-year, $700,000 contract as a free agent with Montreal in January, joined Ty Cobb as the only players ever to attain the 4,000-hit class. When Rose delivered Nos. 3,998 and 3,999 at Cincinnati on April 10, the Reds' management had 28,000 certificates printed saying, "I was there for Pete Rose's 4,000th hit," anticipating he would do it in the April 11 series finale. Instead, after being married in the morning, Rose went hitless that afternoon—and the Reds were stuck with the certificates. But a fourth-inning double off southpaw Jerry Koosman in Montreal's home opener on April 13 lifted Rose to the magic mark just one day ahead of his 43rd birthday.

Rose returned to Cincinnati as player-manager in mid-August and closed out the season with 107 hits, making him the first man to collect 100 or more safeties for 22 consecutive seasons. He also broke Carl Yastrzemski's record when he played in his 3,309th major league game on June 29, erased Cobb's mark of 3,052 singles on July 27 and surpassed Stan Musial in career doubles with No. 726 in the September 30 season finale.

Like Rose, Phil Niekro was released at the close of the '83 season but refused to call it quits. The Yankees signed him on January 5 to a two-year, $1.4 million contract. The majors' oldest player at 45, the knuckleballer demonstrated that he still could do the job. At the All-Star break he boasted an 11-4 record and led American League pitchers with a 1.84 ERA. Although he slipped during the second half, he wound up being the Yankees' biggest winner with a 16-8 ledger.

Niekro achieved two other distinctions. On July 4 against Texas, he became only the ninth pitcher to register 3,000 career strikeouts. And on August 6 his former club, the Atlanta Braves, staged a Phil Niekro Night and retired his No. 35 as a tribute to his 20 years with the team.

Schmidt, the Phillies' slugging third baseman, reached the 400-homer plateau with a blast on May 15 in Los Angeles, while Morgan, picked up as a free agent by Oakland during the winter, gained the distinction of being the career home run leader among second basemen when he belted No. 265 on June 24. This surpassed Rogers Hornsby's long-time record. Toronto's Johnson set a major league record for pinch-homers by hitting his 19th. It came off Baltimore's Tippy Martinez on August 5.

Jackson became only the 13th player to join the 500-homer club when the California Angels' slugger connected against Bud Black of Kansas City at Anaheim Stadium on September 17. The historic blast came 17 years to the day after Reggie's first major league round-tripper. Despite batting a meager .223, he finished the year with 25 homers and a career total of 503.

Another feat performed previously only by Cobb—hitting a home run in the majors before his 20th and after his 40th birthday—was equalled by Staub when the New York Mets' pinch-hitter walloped a game-winning, two-run pinch-homer for a 6-4 victory over the Phillies at Shea Stadium on September 25.

Ryan, the fireballing Houston right-hander, closed out the season as the all-time strikeout king among pitchers with 3,874. The Phillies' Carlton, who began the campaign as the career leader, was only two behind at 3,872. Sutton, pitching for Milwaukee, established a major league record by chalking up at least 100 strike-outs for the 19th season, and Carlton moved into a second-place tie by reaching the 100-whiff mark for the 18th time.

At the team level, the Tigers became only the fourth club in modern major league history—and the first since the 1955 Brooklyn Dodgers—to occupy first place from start to finish. Their 35-5 start, which included a record-tying 17 consecutive victories on the road, also was the best mark ever at the 40-game mark.

The Boston Red Sox were the first team since the 1929 Chicago Cubs to have three outfielders—Armas, Evans and Jim Rice —with 100 or more RBIs each. With a season total of 220 stolen bases, the St. Louis Cardinals became the first team since the 1914-15-16 St. Louis Browns to swipe 200 or more bases for three consecutive seasons.

Seven teams established attendance records in '84. Although the two-league total of 44,739,427 represented a drop of 801,451 from the previous year's all-time high, it still was the second-best total ever. The 14 American League clubs attracted 23,961,427, down 29,626 from the prior season, while the draw of 20,778,000 in the 12-team National League was off 771,285.

The Detroit Tigers led the turnstile record-breakers with a gate of 2,704,794, an increase of 875,158 over the previous season and the second best in American League history next to the California Angels' 1982 total. Four other American League clubs broke their former crowd marks—the Chicago White Sox with 2,136,988; Toronto Blue Jays, 2,110,009; Baltimore Orioles, 2,045,784, and Minnesota Twins, 1,598,692. In the case of both the White Sox and Blue Jays, it was the first time they reached the two-million mark. The Twins showed the year's biggest increase, 739,753.

The two National League teams that set attendance records were the division champion Chicago Cubs and San Diego Padres. Enjoying a 624,502 rise over '83, the Cubs drew 2,104,219, while the Padres finished with 1,983,904. The Mets enjoyed the largest gain in the National League, 729,921.

Three teams failed to reach the million figure at the gate. They were the Seattle Mariners, who drew 870,372; Pittsburgh

Pirates, 773,500, and Cleveland Indians, 734,079. Excluding the strike-shortened 1981 season, it was the Pirates' worst gate since 1969 and the Indians' lowest since 1973.

Attendance at spring training games rose to a record 1,710,305, a 17 percent increase. The first game of the Freeway Series between the Dodgers and Angels at Anaheim Stadium drew 62,921, the largest crowd ever for a preseason contest, while a three-game series between the Brewers and Blue Jays at the new domed B. C. Place in Vancouver attracted 106,328. Counting the spring exhibitions, All-Star Game, regular season and the postseason series, the majors attracted 47,246,990. Excluding the Mexican League, the minors played to 14,753,093 customers.

The 37th annual attendance survey conducted by Daily Racing Form, Inc., which was released in April, showed that baseball surged ahead of horse racing in 1983 as America's No. 1 spectator sport. The '83 total for the major and minor leagues and college baseball was 78,051,343 compared to 75,784,430 for horse racing. Automobile racing was third with 55,122,329, followed by college and pro football at 54,417,705.

Three veterans hung up their spikes during spring training, and four others saw their names removed from the active list, presumably for the last time, during the first half of the season.

Southpaw Jim Kaat, 45, called it quits after failing to catch on in a spring trial with the Pittsburgh Pirates, and right-hander Fergy Jenkins, 40, was cut loose by the Chicago Cubs. A week before the season opened, the Houston Astros dropped pitcher J. R. Richard. The 34-year-old hurler, who suffered a near-fatal stroke in July of 1980, had pitched the last two seasons in the Astros' farm system, never regaining his old form.

Pitcher Jim Palmer, 38, was handed his release by the Baltimore Orioles on May 16. Exactly one month later, 40-year-old outfielder Lou Piniella made his farewell appearance as a player before switching to a full-time coaching role with the New York Yankees. The Los Angeles Dodgers released 38-year-old outfielder Rick Monday on June 22 and 37-year-old Kansas City Royals southpaw Paul Splittorff retired on July 1. Kaat, Palmer and Splittorff all moved up to the broadcasting booth.

For the third consecutive year, Jim Eisenreich's bid with the Minnesota Twins was stalled by a nervous disorder. Treated by a hypnotist during the off-season, the young outfielder began the campaign in center field, but shortly thereafter he went to the bench. The Twins removed him from the active list in late April, and after coming back to start one more game, he again sat out the balance of the season.

The year's most serious casualty was Dickie Thon. In Houston's fifth game of the season on April 8, the 25-year-old Astros shortstop was struck by a pitch thrown by the Mets' Mike Torrez. The blow caused a tripod fracture near Thon's left eye, necessitating surgery. The mishap left him with blurred vision that sidelined him the remainder of the season and placed his career in jeopardy.

Two pitchers staged remarkable comebacks after being sidelined all of 1983 because of arm surgery.

Rollie Fingers resumed his role as Milwaukee's ace reliever, appearing in 33 games and posting 23 saves before a herniated disc forced him out of action again on July 24 for the balance of the season. Joe Sambito, who hadn't pitched since April of 1982 because of an elbow injury, worked in 32 games with Houston.

Five clubs began the season with new managers, but two of them—Vern Rapp of Cincinnati and Rene Lachemann of Milwaukee—were dismissed before the campaign ended. A third, Yogi Berra, beginning his second hitch at the Yankee helm, reportedly came close to being fired at midseason. The two other newcomers were Jim Frey of the Cubs and Dave Johnson, who was making his major league piloting debut with the Mets.

The year witnessed another heavy managerial turnover as 10 teams changed skippers. The first casualty was Steve Boros. Just 44 games into his second season at the Oakland helm, he was given his walking papers on May 24 in a surprise move. The decision was announced following a victory over Baltimore in an afternoon game that brought the A's record to 20-24. First base coach Jackie Moore replaced Boros. The A's dropped pitching coach Ron Schueler at the same time and brought in Wes Stock.

The Bay Area's other team, the San Francisco Giants, made the second switch. Shortly after a 9-2 victory at Atlanta on August 4, Frank Robinson was informed of his dismissal. The Giants were in last place with a 42-64 record. Third base coach Danny Ozark took over the reins. Ironically, in February the Giants had extended Robinson's contract, which called for approximately $200,000 per season, for two years through 1986. Less than a week after his ouster he joined the Milwaukee Brewers as a coach.

In what probably was the most unexpected shift, Rose returned to the Cincinnati Reds on August 16 after a nearly six-year absence and became baseball's first player-manager since Don Kessinger guided the White Sox in 1979. The Reds obtained him from Montreal, where he had recently been relegated to pinch-hitting duty, in exchange for infielder Tom Lawless. Rose replaced Rapp, who was in the first season of a two-year contract. The Reds were 51-70 at that juncture. In his initial series as skipper, Rose started at first base in all three games against the Cubs and went 8 for 15. He proceeded to hit .365 in 26 games with the Reds. Six days after assuming the helm, Rose brought in Jim Kaat as his pitching coach, replacing Stan Williams.

When Bill Virdon was released as Montreal manager on August 30, Jim Fanning moved from the front office on an interim basis, the same as he had done three years previously. The Expos decided to make the change after Virdon informed President John McHale that he did not intend to return for another season. The club had lost its last six games, all at home and all by one run or in extra innings, to slip to 64-67.

Two weeks after receiving a vote of confidence from Owner George Argyros, Del Crandall of Seattle was fired on September 1. Also dismissed was one of his close friends, batting coach Ben Hines. The Mariners were ensconced in the cellar with a 59-76 ledger. A week earlier, Crandall had fired pitching coach Frank Funk and replaced him with Phil Regan. Third base coach Chuck Cottier was named to pilot the team for the balance of the season.

Boston's Ralph Houk, dean of the major league managers, disclosed on September 25 that he intended to retire at the end of the season. Co-owner Haywood Sullivan tried to talk him into staying, but Houk refused, saying: "There was a big temptation to give it one more shot, but that wasn't as strong as the temptation to enjoy myself and have my wife enjoy things while we were still young enough to do so." The 65-year-old Houk had previously called it quits in 1978, but was lured back two years later by the Red Sox. His four-year hitch in Boston rounded out a 43-year career in the game.

On September 27, with three games remaining in the season, the Milwaukee Brewers announced the ouster of Rene Lachemann and the return of George Bamberger for a second term as manager in 1985. Under Lachemann, who finished out the season, the Brewers wound up in last place for the first time since 1976. The 56-year-old Bamberger piloted the Brewers in 1978, 1979 and 1980, but then retired after undergoing open-heart surgery and suffering health problems. He came back a year later to manage the New York Mets, only to quit again in June of 1983.

Paul Owens resigned as manager of the Philadelphia Phillies after a September 30 season-ending doubleheader loss to Pittsburgh, and the next day Atlanta Owner Ted Turner announced the firing of Joe Torre.

The 60-year-old Owens, who guided the Phillies into the 1983 World Series, cited declining health as his reason for stepping down. Coach John Felske was appointed to succeed him. The fact that two other clubs had asked to interview Felske for managerial openings also figured in the decision, President Bill Giles admitted. Giles promptly gave Owens a five-year contract as his assistant in the evaluation of player personnel. The switch came some two months after a July 27 announcement by Giles that Owens and his entire coaching staff would return in '85.

Boston Manager Ralph Houk (above) called it quits after a 43-year baseball career while 60-year-old Paul Owens turned over the Phillies reins to John Felske.

Like Owens, Torre seemed assured of returning as Atlanta manager. Early in July his contract, calling for around $125,000 per season, was extended two years through 1986 at a hefty increase by Turner. However, a few weeks later, ominous signs developed when Eddie Haas, manager of the Braves' Richmond (International League) farm team, was promoted to the Atlanta coaching staff and then Johnny Sain, the organization's roving pitching instructor, also was ordered to join the Braves. Despite a disappointing 80-82 record, the Braves tied for second place in the N.L. West. This gave Torre a record of one division championship and two second-place finishes in his three years at the Atlanta helm. The Braves' loss of appeal on cable-TV and a rift between Sain and pitching coach Bob Gibson reportedly spurred Turner to make the change.

To replace Torre, the Braves signed Haas to a one-year contract. Ironically, Haas was the unanimous recommendation of a five-man Braves' search committee for the Atlanta managerial vacancy in 1981, but at the urging of his cable-TV advisers Turner opted for a better-known name—Torre.

Berra almost walked the plank in June. With the Yankees already far off the pace, he and Owner George Steinbrenner engaged in a shouting match during a June

17 postgame meeting attended by the club's coaches and front-office staff. Newspaper reports disclosed that at one point the owner asked Berra if he wanted to quit and the manager replied: "I'm not going to quit. You'll have to fire me." Queried about the story, Steinbrenner admitted he was considering a change and that Billy Martin, who had been dismissed the previous December, was "at the top of my list." The Yankees boss did order his annual coaching change, demoting Sammy Ellis to the role of minor league instructor—and later firing him—and promoting Mark Connor from Columbus (International). Connor became the 20th pitching coach in Steinbrenner's 12-year regime. The Yankees' strong second-half showing eased the pressure on Berra, and on October 25 the Yankees owner announced that Yogi would return in '85. It was the earliest he had resolved the club's managerial situation since 1978.

John McNamara became the last of the '84 pilots to move on. His two-year contract as manager of the California Angels having expired, he disclosed on October 9 that he would not return. A week later the Angels announced that Gene Mauch had agreed to resume command of the team he led to the 1982 A.L. West title. Mauch resigned later that year to be with his terminally-ill wife, but rejoined the Angels' front office in September of 1983.

McNamara's unemployment was shortlived. On October 18, the Red Sox unveiled him as their new manager. He was signed to a two-year contract. As one of his first moves he hired Rene Lachemann as his third base coach.

After Danny Ozark turned down an offer to return as San Francisco manager and decided instead to retire, the Giants named coach Jim Davenport as their new skipper on October 30. The Seattle Mariners' search ended on November 9 when they announced that Chuck Cottier would continue as manager, and the Montreal Expos filled their vacancy on November 14 by giving a two-year contract to Bob (Buck) Rodgers, who had led their Indianapolis (American Association) farm to the pennant. Before settling on Rodgers, the Expos tried to lure Earl Weaver from his ABC-TV booth. Jeff Torborg, the Yankees' co-pitching coach, reportedly was Seattle's top candidate before the Mariners settled on Cottier.

Despite the volatile nature of baseball, the value of major league franchises continued to skyrocket and there was no shortage of potential purchasers. A statement by Steinbrenner that he probably could sell the Yankees for close to $100 million and the sale of the Minnesota Twins for approximately $47 million pointed up the escalating values. Following a rumor that the Yankees were about to be sold, Steinbrenner issued a May 13 pronouncement that declared, "The Yankees have not been and are not now for sale" and added the reference to "close to $100 million," which would be 10 times the price that he and his group paid to buy the club from CBS in 1973.

Baseball's longest family ownership reign came to a close when Calvin Griffith and his sister, Thelma Haynes, sold their majority interest in the Twins to Minneapolis banker Carl Pohlad. The Griffiths had headed up the Twins and the predecessor Washington Senators for 65 years, or ever since Clark (The Old Fox) Griffith was named president in 1920. Upon Clark's death in 1955, Calvin, Clark's adopted son, ascended to the presidency and eventually moved the team to the Twin Cities after the 1960 season.

The sale to Pohlad ended threats that the Twin Cities might lose the team. Poor attendance and an escape clause in their 30-year lease with the Metrodome had led the Griffith family to entertain bids to move the Twins or sell them to interests in another city. Under terms of the Metrodome pact, unless the Twins attracted a three-year average of 1.4 million fans, they could terminate the contract and move after the 1985 season.

The 68-year-old Pohlad was rated by Fortune magazine as one of the 100 wealthiest men in the U.S. Newspaper accounts pegged his worth at $500 million. The business empire of banks and corporations he heads does $3 billion a year in business. Besides being president of MEI Corp., the nation's third largest Pepsi-Cola bottler, he is an executive officer of Bank Shares, Inc., a holding company that owns 35 banks, most of them in the upper Midwest.

Pohlad began negotiating to buy the Twins early in the year, but Gabe Murphy, the club's only minority partner, further muddled the situation when he sold his 42 percent interest to a Tampa, Fla., group for $11.5 million.

A letter-of-intent binding Calvin Griffith and his sister to sell their 52 percent share to Pohlad for $32 million was signed in an emotional pregame home-plate ceremony on June 22. Three weeks later, Pohlad bought the Tampa purchasers' 42 percent share for the same $11.5 million they paid Murphy plus about $1 million in costs they incurred. By the time the long-term deal for the Griffith-Haynes shares was finalized on July 31, the Twins had climbed into first place in the A.L. West and the purchase price had risen to an estimated $35 million. It included $10 million up front and the remainder over 10 years. In addition, Calvin Griffith and five other family members received five-year contracts with the club. Clark Griffith, who was on leave while attending law school, was one of those given a five-year contract but later was notified there was no job for him. Calvin, 72, was named chairman of the board. Howard Fox, who had been an executive vice-president, was chosen by Pohlad to succeed Calvin as president.

The only other major change in ownership involved the Cincinnati Reds. Late in the year Marge Schott, a local automobile dealer, arranged to purchase a majority interest in the club from brothers James and William Williams. The transaction was subject to approval by owners of the other clubs.

At least three other teams—the San Francisco Giants, Pittsburgh Pirates and Cleveland Indians—were on the block, and Eddie Chiles of the Texas Rangers was trying to get approval to sell some stock to Gaylord Broadcasting of Oklahoma City. Chiles, who bought out his minority partners during the summer, saw the Rangers experience their fifth straight year of red ink since he became majority owner in 1980. It was estimated that the sale of stock and TV rights to Gaylord would mean as much as $15 to $20 million for the Rangers.

Shortly after the season ended Bob Lurie, owner of the Giants since 1976, disclosed he was putting the club up for sale. He cited continuing financial losses as the reason. The Giants' poor performance coupled with the fact that Candlestick Park is regarded as the worst in the majors and plans for a new downtown stadium fell through contributed to the dismal picture. Lurie's decision raised anew the old question of whether the Bay Area can support two teams. Several groups expressed interest in buying and moving the Giants, but Lurie, a San Francisco native, insisted the team must remain in San Francisco.

Pittsburgh President Dan Galbreath announced on November 20 that Warner Communications, owner of 48 percent of the Pirates' stock, wanted out and that he and his father also had decided to sell. He said his family was not in position to buy back the Warner stock and "because of that situation we (he and his father John)

have concluded reluctantly . . . that we sell our interest in the Pirates." According to General Manager Pete Peterson, the Galbreath's losses since the club moved into Three Rivers Stadium in 1970 had approached $20 million. The club was bound to the stadium by an iron-clad 40-year lease. The Galbreaths retained a 51 percent interest in the club after selling a 48 percent share to Warner early in 1983 for $10 million. A group of individuals owned the remaining 1 percent.

A deal that would have infused the Cleveland Indians with new ownership fell through, temporarily at least. In January, President Gabe Paul revealed that the financial firm of E. F. Hutton had made inquiries about buying the team. Several weeks later, David LeFevre, a New York attorney, sold his 10 percent holdings in the Houston Astros and began serious negotiations to purchase the Indians. A native of Cleveland and the grandson of Cyrus Eaton, late Cleveland industrialist, LeFevre had been considered the frontrunner among prospective buyers ever since the death of principal Owner F. J. (Steve) O'Neill in August of 1983.

After months of speculation and fears the city might lose the team, LeFevre announced on June 21 that he had arranged to buy the 53 percent share of Indians' stock held by the O'Neill estate for $16.5 million. He also offered to purchase the remaining equity from the minority partners for an additional $14 million. The entire transaction was contingent upon LeFevre's ability to negotiate a lease with the Cleveland Stadium Corporation, which is operated by Art Modell, owner of the football Browns. Several minority owners filed suit, claiming they weren't being treated fairly, and the ensuing legal entanglements led LeFevre to withdraw his bid on November 14. "The year is almost over and my group needs a place to put its money for tax purposes," he declared.

For the second time in three years John McMullen of the Houston Astros had to survive an uprising by a group of minority owners. They sought to force major changes in the power structure of the Houston Sports Association, parent company of the Astros. McMullen, who owned a 34 percent share, eventually gained majority control when he and several other minority owners purchased the interests of 10 dissident shareholders. Five Houstonians retained shares, with E. F. Hutton executive Don Sanders owning about 13 percent and Mrs. R. E. (Bob) Smith, widow of one of the franchise's original owners, controlling about 12 percent.

The feud among Boston Red Sox owners was in and out of the court several times during the year. Buddy LeRoux, one of three original partners, filed an appeal of the 1983 decision that barred him and two limited partners, Kentucky coal baron Rogers Badgett and Al Curran, from taking over control of the club. The ruling was upheld by both the Massachusetts Superior Court and the Massachusetts Appeals Court, and LeRoux's group was ordered to sell its 16 limited partnership shares to the two other general partners, Haywood Sullivan and Mrs. Jean Yawkey.

Sullivan and Mrs. Yawkey hired Tal Smith, former major league executive whose consulting firm represents numerous clubs in salary arbitration cases, as their appraiser in the buyout. LeRoux countered by employing Marvin Miller, former executive director of the Major League Players Association, as his appraiser. The selection of Miller, who fought for 15 years as head of the players' union to examine club financial records, was expected to slow the appraisal process because other clubs are reluctant to allow him to see certain financial information.

Another magnate faced a legal challenge when Avron Fogelman, co-owner of the Kansas City Royals, was named in a $1.54 million suit on October 23. In a 14-page complaint filed in U.S. District Court in Trenton, N.J., real-estate broker Gerald M. Sherman of West Long Branch, N.J., claimed he represented Fogelman for five years in his efforts to buy into a major league club and acted as his broker in the 1983 deal in which Fogelman acquired a 49 percent interest in the Royals. Besides claiming he was never paid for his services, Sherman contended Fogelman promised him a position with the Royals in the "salary range of $250,000."

During the course of the season it was revealed that one manager had become a part owner of his team. He was Sparky Anderson. Detroit's new owner, Tom Monaghan, admitted he permitted the Tigers manager to purchase 400 shares in the club.

The retirement of two of the game's best-known executives highlighted a series of changes in front-office personnel. Buzzie Bavasi, executive vice-president of the California Angels, announced on August 31 that he was retiring at season's end, and Gabe Paul, president of the Cleveland Indians, retired at the close of the year. Bavasi, 68, had served at the top level of major league management since being named general manager of the Brooklyn Dodgers in 1951. Paul, 74, spent 56 years in professional baseball, the last 48 as a major league official. His contract called for him to serve as a consultant to the Indians from his Tampa, Fla., home.

By coincidence, Paul's departure and the aborted sale of the Cleveland club paved the way for another Bavasi to return to the baseball executive ranks. Late in the year Patrick J. O'Neill, who headed the Cleveland ownership since the death of his uncle, named Peter Bavasi as president and chief operating officer of the Indians. The 42-year-old son of Buzzie had previously directed establishment of the expansion Toronto Blue Jays and more recently operated his own consulting firm.

Bavasi immediately restructured the Indians' front office into four divisions. General Manager Phil Seghi was put in charge of baseball operations and Jason Rosenthal of the finance division. Dan O'Brien, former Seattle Mariners president, was brought in as Bavasi's assistant and head of the revenue production department, and Terry Barthelmas was hired as director of operations and administration. Barthelmas had served as vice-president of business operations of the Chicago Cubs before relinquishing the position in midsummer.

As usual, the Yankees were involved in a series of unusual front-office shifts. On the eve of their April 10 home opener, Clyde King was appointed general manager. He replaced Murray Cook, who was demoted to scouting director just nine months after being named to the G.M. post. King, Steinbrenner's long-time friend and adviser, received a five-year, $750,000 contract. Vice-President Bill Bergesch was designated as his assistant, but in mid-June coach Roy White was elevated to the front office to serve as King's assistant. Another early-season Yankee administrative casualty was Dave Hersh, who was dismissed as farm director.

Cook subsequently resigned from the Yankees on August 20 and less than two weeks later was hired by the Montreal Expos as general manager to relieve President John McHale of some responsibilities. Bergesch quit the Yankees shortly after the season ended and on October 19 joined the Cincinnati Reds as general manager. Three days later, Woody Woodward, who had been the Reds' assistant G.M. the past four years, was hired by the Yankees to fill Bergesch's former role of vice-president, baseball administration.

Buzzie Bavasi, executive vice-president of the California Angels, retired after the 1984 season. The 68-year-old Bavasi had served in baseball management since 1951.

Early in the year, Lou Gorman resigned as vice-president, baseball operations with the New York Mets to accept a similar position with the Boston Red Sox. Five months later the Red Sox also underwent a major front-office shakeup. With the courts having thwarted the LeRoux takeover attempt, Haywood Sullivan was elected chief executive officer/chief operating officer and Gorman was named to succeed him as general manager. Other changes in the June 5 shakeup resulted in the dismissal of Public Relations Director George Sullivan and Treasurer James Olivier, Jr., while Dick Bresciani was elevated to P.R. director, Robert Furbush was named treasurer and John Reilly was promoted from assistant treasurer to the comptroller's spot formerly held by Furbush.

Two other clubs named new general managers. After the resignation of Joe Klein on September 1 amid speculation he was about to be fired, farm director Tom Grieve was appointed general manager of the Texas Rangers and, at 36, became the majors' youngest G.M. Vice-President Mike Port, 39, took over as the Angels' G.M. upon the retirement of Buzzie Bavasi.

In Chicago, Jim Finks resigned as president of the Cubs on December 18 and was replaced by Dallas Green.

A pair of pitchers—veteran Tom Seaver and newcomer Tim Belcher, who had yet to play a game of professional baseball—became causes celebre early in the year. To the great consternation of the New York teams, the two hurlers were snatched by rival clubs under the free-agent compensation rules. The Chicago White Sox' selection of Seaver from the Mets on January 20 and the Oakland A's choice of Belcher from the Yankee organization on February 8 caused tremendous uproars, especially from the front offices of the New York clubs. The moves also produced surprising agreement among both the players' union and management that changes were needed in the compensation rule.

The White Sox and A's each lost a Type-A player to free agency during the winter and thus were the only teams to qualify for compensation. The White Sox became eligible when Toronto signed pitcher Dennis Lamp, while Oakland qualified when pitcher Tom Underwood came to terms with Baltimore. Lamp and Underwood earned Type-A status on the basis of finishing in the top 20 percent of statistical rankings of pitchers for the two prior seasons.

In what the New York media labeled "a terrible blunder," the Mets left Seaver off the protected player list they submitted. Chairman of the Board Nelson Doubleday and his partner, Fred Wilpon, were devastated by the White Sox's choice of the 39-year-old righthander, with Doubleday accusing the Sox of dirty tactics. General Manager Frank Cashen, who was roundly praised 13 months earlier for bringing Seaver back to New York from Cincinnati, confessed to miscalculating the White Sox's needs when he decided not to protect Seaver. Before turning in their list, the Mets tried to get sore-armed pitcher Craig Swan to waive the no-trade clause in his contract, but, when he refused, he had to be included on the protected list.

Like the Mets, Seaver also was deeply upset by the situation. But eventually everything worked out well for both Seaver and the Mets. The veteran righthander went on to win 15 games for the

White Sox, while the loss of Seaver forced the Mets to bring along young Dwight Gooden quicker than planned and he developed into their ace.

The Belcher case was even more unusual. He declined to sign with the Minnesota Twins after being the No. 1 pick in the previous summer's amateur draft, but the Yankees made him the No. 1 choice in the January 17 draft. They signed the 22-year-old righthander on February 2 to a contract with their Greensboro (South Atlantic) farm team, giving him a reported $125,000 bonus. Six days later, after Baltimore's signing of Underwood, the A's grabbed Belcher as their compensation pick.

Under the rules, the Yankees received $150,000 from the compensation fund for losing Belcher, but that hardly soothed their feelings. The New York club immediately filed a protest with the Player Relations Committee, claiming Belcher should not have been eligible because he was not a member of the Yankee organization when the protected lists were submitted and pointing out that the Yankees never had a chance to protect him. The Major League Players' Association joined in the protest. After studying the case, President Lee MacPhail of the Player Relations Committee denied the Yankee protest and ruled Belcher belonged to Oakland.

The loss of Belcher led to repercussions on the Yankees. Murray Cook, then general manager, came under severe criticism from Owner George Steinbrenner because of the situation. Cook later was ordered to remain at home, rather than go to spring training, and subsequently was demoted.

Fifty-six players went through the 1984 free-agent re-entry draft on November 8, including one—Oscar Gamble of the Yankees—for the third time. Despite the presence of such names as Rick Sutcliffe and Bruce Sutter, the player chosen by the greatest number of teams was Steve Trout. The Chicago Cubs southpaw was picked by 17 clubs. Lee Lacy of Pittsburgh was next, being selected by 14, followed by Don Aase of the California Angels (13) and Ed Whitson of the San Diego Padres (11).

The Texas Rangers and Pittsburgh Pirates made the most selections, 16 each, while the Detroit Tigers, Chicago Cubs and New York Mets did not select anyone.

Among the 56 free agents were five who qualified as Type-A players. They were Sutcliffe, Sutter, Fred Lynn of California, Andre Thornton of Cleveland and Cliff

Johnson of Toronto. The only player who qualified as a Type-B player was Steve Henderson of Seattle.

Thirty-seven players were picked by fewer than four teams and consequently, under the rules, became free to negotiate with any team.

The full list of players involved in the re-entry process, with the number of teams selecting them in parentheses and an asterisk indicating the player's own team retained negotiating rights to him, follow:

AMERICAN LEAGUE

Baltimore—Benny Ayala (0), Al Bumbry (2), Ken Singleton (0); Boston—Gary Allenson (1), Rich Gale (0); California—Don Aase (13*), John Curtis (0), Bruce Kison (1), Fred Lynn (5*), Craig Swan (0), Derrel Thomas (0), Rob Wilfong (7*); Chicago—Greg Luzinski (1); Cleveland—Andre Thornton (7*); Detroit —John Grubb (4*), Ruppert Jones (5*), Dave Rozema (2); Kansas City—Greg Pryor (4*); Milwaukee—Jerry Augustine (0), Rollie Fingers (3), Jim Kern (0); Minnesota—Bobby Castillo (5), Pat Putnam (0), Chris Speier (0); New York—Oscar Gamble (4), Rudy May (0); Oakland—Bill Almon (1), Dave Kingman (1), Dan Meyer (0), Mark Wagner (0); Seattle—Steve Henderson (0); Texas—None; Toronto—Cliff Johnson (3).

NATIONAL LEAGUE

Atlanta—Jerry Royster (2); Chicago—Dennis Eckersley (5*), Rick Reuschel (0), Tim Stoddard (9*), Rick Sutcliffe (8*), Steve Trout (17*); Cincinnati—Bob Owchinko (0), Tony Perez (0); Houston—Mike LaCoss (0), Vern Ruhle (0); Los Angeles—Burt Hooton (5); Montreal—Miguel Dilone (1), Jim Wohlford (1); New York—John Stearns (3); Philadelphia—Sixto Lezcano (7), Tug McGraw (1); Philadelphia—Lee Lacy (14*), Milt May (0); St. Louis—Bruce Sutter (6*); San Diego—Champ Summers (0), Ed Whitson (11*); San Francisco—Steve Nicosia (5*), Randy Lerch (0), Gene Richards (0).

Goose Gossage had emerged with the most lucrative contract given to a pitcher up to that point when he signed with the San Diego Padres as a free agent in January. He was given a five-year package worth $6.25 million. That figure, however, was dwarfed in December when another free-agent pitcher, Bruce Sutter, inked a six-year, $10 million contract with Atlanta. Based on compound interest at an assumed 12 percent annual rate, it was estimated Sutter's pact would be worth $43.6

million over a 36-year period. The agreement calls for the relief ace to receive $750,000 per season for six years, with the remaining $5.5 million to be turned over to an insurance company to cover a plan that could pay Sutter approximately $1.3 million a year for 30 years starting in 1991.

Several other '84 free agents pocketed fat contracts. Sutcliffe opted to remain with the Cubs when they offered him a five-year, $9.6 million deal, and Andre Thornton decided to stay in Cleveland in return for a four-year, $4.4 million contract. On the other hand, Fred Lynn accepted a five-year, $6.8 million offer from Baltimore and Whitson agreed to a five-year, $4.25 million pact with the Yankees.

Eighty players filed for salary arbitration early in '84, but all except 10 reached contract agreements without the need of an arbitrator. Although it was generally conceded that arbitration was a more significant factor in rising salaries than free agency, the fact that so many contract disputes were resolved without the need of arbitration led both labor and management to agree that the arbitration process was working.

Some of the contract settlements worked out in advance of arbitration involved hefty, long-term guaranteed contracts. According to Murray Chass of the New York Times, they included: Pedro Guerrero of Los Angeles, $7 million for five years; Cal Ripken of Baltimore, $4 million for four years; Ryne Sandberg of the Cubs, $3.97 million for six years; Tony Pena of Pittsburgh, $3.55 million for four years; Bill Gullickson of Montreal, $3 million for four years; Jeff Reardon of Montreal, $2,975,000 for four years; Lee Smith of the Cubs, $3.7 million for five years; Willie Upshaw of Toronto, $2.5 million for three years; Damaso Garcia of Toronto, $2.15 million for three years; Keith Moreland, Cubs, $2 million for three years; Ron Oester, Cincinnati, $2,475,000 for four years; Johnny Ray, Pittsburgh, $2.91 million for five years, and Dale Berra, Pittsburgh, $2,820,000 for five years.

In the arbitration hearings, four players emerged victorious and six lost. That brought the nine-year total to management 96, players 80.

The salaries awarded the four players who won their cases, with the club's offer in parentheses, were: George Frazier, Cleveland, $425,000 ($325,000); Juan Bonilla, San Diego, $325,000 ($185,000); Paul Householder, Cincinnati, $200,000 ($120,000), and Ron Roenicke, Seattle, $125,000 ($80,000).

The six who had to settle for the club's offer, with the player's requested figure in parentheses, were: Pat Putnam, Seattle, $280,000 ($425,000); Joe Price, Cincinnati, $330,000 ($495,000); Tim Wallach, Montreal, $360,000 ($500,000); Gary Ward, Texas, $450,000 ($559,000); Rafael Ramirez, Atlanta, $500,000 ($625,000), and Rickey Henderson, Oakland, $950,000 ($1,200,000).

The average major league player salary in 1984 was $329,408, according to figures Chass obtained from the Major League Players' Association. This represented almost a 300 percent increase since 1979, when the average was $113,558. It rose to $143,756 in 1980, to $185,651 in 1981, $241,497 in 1982 and $289,194 in 1983.

The data showed the Yankees had the highest average salary for the sixth time in seven years at $458,544. This was slightly under the club's $463,687 figure of the previous year because of the departure of such high-paid performers as Gossage, Graig Nettles, Roy Smalley and Shane Rawley. With Tom Seaver collecting $1,066,017, including $241,017 in bonuses, and LaMarr Hoyt and Rich Dotson drawing $900,000 and $800,000, respectively, the White Sox moved into second place in average salary at $447,281.

The average player salaries for all teams in 1983 and 1984, as compiled by the Major League Players' Association, were as follows:

Team	1984	1983
New York Yankees	$458,544	$463,687
Chicago White Sox	447,281	291,114
California Angels	431,431	389,833
Chicago Cubs	422,194	268,947
Atlanta Braves	402,689	347,620
Philadelphia Phillies	401,476	442,165
Milwaukee Brewers	385,215	352,061
Oakland A's	384,027	266,815
Houston Astros	382,991	364,825
Detroit Tigers	371,332	263,899
Montreal Expos	368,557	353,357
Baltimore Orioles	360,204	305,305
Pittsburgh Pirates	330,661	314,769

Team	1984	1983
Los Angeles Dodgers	$316,530	$288,555
San Diego Padres	311,199	261,820
Boston Red Sox	297,878	264,833
Toronto Blue Jays	295,632	213,087
Kansas City Royals	291,160	309,962
St. Louis Cardinals	290,886	259,393
New York Mets	282,952	306,253
San Francisco Giants	282,132	248,204
Cincinnati Reds	269,019	239,068
Texas Rangers	247,081	180,848
Minnesota Twins	172,024	97,980
Seattle Mariners	168,505	118,875
Cleveland Indians	159,774	242,134

Beanballs produced several serious episodes during the 1984 campaign. The most violent occurred in Atlanta on August 12.

It resulted in two free-for-alls and led to fines and/or suspensions for 18 individuals, including the heaviest fine and longest suspension handed a manager in many years. The frightening melee was touched off at game's start when Atlanta pitcher Pascual Perez hit San Diego leadoff batter Alan Wiggins with his first pitch. Wiggins had bunted twice for hits the previous day against the Braves. Padres pitchers subsequently threw at Perez on each of his four plate appearances.

Ed Whitson and Manager Dick Williams both were ejected in the third inning after an earlier warning by umpire John McSherry. When Craig Lefferts hit Perez with a pitch in the eighth inning, the first fight broke out. In the top of the ninth, Atlanta reliever Donnie Moore hit Graig Nettles with a pitch, sparking a fierce fight. Several fans charged onto the field during the melee, and five were arrested. Altogether, 14 Braves and Padres were ejected from the game, and after the second fight in the ninth inning, the umpires cleared both benches and both bullpens, and police lined both dugouts for the remainder of the game. "It was the worst thing I have ever seen," said McSherry afterward. "It took baseball down 50 years."

The incident led league President Chub Feeney to hand Padres Manager Dick Williams a $10,000 fine and 10-day suspension while Manager Joe Torre of the Braves was docked $1,000 and suspended three days. Perez was let off with a $300 fine, but teammates Gerald Perry, Rick Mahler and Steve Bedrosian were banned three days each and docked $700 (Perry and Mahler) and $600, respectively, while Donnie Moore drew a $350 fine. The Padres' Champ Summers was suspended three days and fined an amount that the San Diego front office refused to divulge.

In addition, two more Braves players, six more Padres players and two Padres coaches were fined, bringing the grand total of players, managers and coaches fined and/or suspended to 18.

An earlier brawl precipitated by an alleged beanball incident in Atlanta on June 16 resulted in Mario Soto, Cincinnati pitcher, drawing a $5,000 fine and five-day suspension and Claudell Washington of the Braves being docked $1,000 and set down for three days. It was a second offense for Soto, who had been fined $1,000 and suspended for five days after a May 27 brawl in Chicago.

Willie Hernandez, Detroit's spectacular relief ace, and a pair of Chicago Cubs, Ryne Sandberg and Rick Sutcliffe, dominated postseason honors. Hernandez won

Cincinnati ace Mario Soto served two suspensions last season for his part in alleged beanball incidents.

both the Most Valuable Player and Cy Young awards in the American League, while Sandberg was an overwhelming choice as MVP and Sutcliffe was a unanimous pick for the Cy Young prize in the National League voting by members of the Baseball Writers' Association of America.

Sandberg collected 22 of 24 first-place votes in the MVP poll in the senior circuit to finish far ahead of runnerup Keith Hernandez of the Mets. In the American League voting, Willie Hernandez was the top choice on 16 of 28 ballots to edge Minnesota's Kent Hrbek, 306 points to 247, for Most Valuable Player honors. The results of the voting in the two MVP polls, with each first-place vote worth 14 points, second-place nine, and on down to one for 10th:

American League

Player—Club	1	2	3	4	5	6	7	8	9	10	Pts.
Willie Hernandez	16	4	3	2	—	—	2	—	—	—	306
Kent Hrbek	5	7	10	3	2	—	—	—	—	1	247
Dan Quisenberry	5	10	2	4	2	3	1	—	—	—	235
Eddie Murray	2	5	4	8	2	3	1	1	1	—	197
Don Mattingly	—	—	1	2	6	3	6	4	2	—	113
Kirk Gibson	—	1	3	2	3	2	3	3	—	—	96
Tony Armas	—	—	1	1	3	4	3	3	6	1½	87½
Dave Winfield	—	—	1	2	2	2	4	5	3	2	83
Alan Trammell	—	1	—	3	2	2	2	1	4	5½	76½
Willie Wilson	—	—	3	1	3	—	1	1	1	3	61
Dwight Evans	—	—	—	—	1	3	—	3	3	3	39
Alvin Davis	—	—	—	—	—	2	1	1	3	3	26
Jim Rice	—	—	—	—	—	1	—	1	1	—	10
Harold Baines	—	—	—	—	—	—	1	1	—	3	10
Dave Kingman	—	—	—	—	—	—	1	1	—	3	10
Lance Parrish	—	—	—	—	1	—	—	—	1	—	8
Willie Upshaw	—	—	—	—	—	1	—	1	—	—	8
Brain Downing	—	—	—	—	1	—	—	—	—	—	6
Steve Balboni	—	—	—	—	—	1	—	—	—	—	5
Andre Thornton	—	—	—	—	—	1	—	—	—	—	5
George Bell	—	—	—	—	—	—	—	1	1	—	5
Buddy Bell	—	—	—	—	—	—	1	—	—	—	4
Dave Stieb	—	—	—	—	—	—	1	—	—	—	4
Lloyd Moseby	—	—	—	—	—	—	—	1	—	1	4
Juan Beniquez	—	—	—	—	—	—	—	—	1	—	2
Mike Boddicker	—	—	—	—	—	—	—	—	1	—	2
Doyle Alexander	—	—	—	—	—	—	—	—	—	1	1
Cal Ripken	—	—	—	—	—	—	—	—	—	1	1

National League

Player—Club	1	2	3	4	5	6	7	8	9	10	Pts.
Ryne Sandberg	22	2	—	—	—	—	—	—	—	—	326
Keith Hernandez	1	12	2	5	3	—	1	—	—	—	195
Tony Gwynn	1	7	8	4	1	1	1	—	—	—	184
Rick Sutcliffe	—	2	8	6	3	1	1	—	—	—	151
Gary Matthews	—	—	1	3	—	3	1	4	5	—	70
Bruce Sutter	—	—	3	2	2	1	1	—	3	2	67
Mike Schmidt	—	—	1	1	2	2	—	2	5	2½	55½
Jose Cruz	—	—	1	—	—	2	4	4	2½	2	53
Dale Murphy	—	—	—	—	—	5	2	4	1	5½	52½
Jody Davis	—	—	—	1	2	2	2	3	1	1	49
Tim Raines	—	—	—	1	2	1	2	2	1½	—	41
Leon Durham	—	—	—	1	4	—	1	—	1	1	38
Rich Gossage	—	1	—	—	2	1	—	2	—	2	34
Gary Carter	—	—	—	—	1	—	3	3	1	3	32
Dwight Gooden	—	—	—	—	—	3	2	—	2	1	28
Alan Wiggins	—	—	—	—	—	2	1	—	—	—	14
Ron Cey	—	—	—	—	1	—	—	—	—	—	6
Kevin McReynolds	—	—	—	—	1	—	—	—	—	—	6
Bob Dernier	—	—	—	—	—	—	1	—	1	—	6
Steve Garvey	—	—	—	—	—	—	1	—	—	1	5
Bob Brenly	—	—	—	—	—	—	—	—	—	1	1
Juan Samuel	—	—	—	—	—	—	—	—	—	1	1
Jeff Leonard	—	—	—	—	—	—	—	—	1	1	1

Chicago's Jim Frey (above) was honored as TSN's Manager of the Year while Seattle's Mark Langston was named A.L. Rookie Pitcher of the Year.

Sutcliffe joined Sandy Koufax, Bob Gibson and Steve Carlton as the only National League pitchers to win the N.L. Cy Young Award by acclamation. Hernandez edged another reliever, Dan Quisenberry of Kansas City, for the American League prize. A breakdown of the Cy Young Award voting, with five points awarded for a first-place vote, three for a second and one for third:

American League

Pitcher—Team	1	2	3	Pts.
Willie Hernandez, Det.....	12	7	7	88
Dan Quisenberry, K.C.....	9	8	2	71
Bert Blyleven, Cleveland	4	6	7	45
Mike Boddicker, Balt......	3	6	8	41
Dan Petry, Detroit	—	1	—	3
Frank Viola, Minnesota .	—	—	—	2
Jack Morris, Detroit	—	—	1	1
Dave Stieb, Toronto	—	—	1	1

National League

Pitcher—Team	1	2	3	Pts.
Rick Sutcliffe, Chicago...	24	—	—	120
Dwight Gooden, N.Y.	—	12	9	45
Bruce Sutter, St. Louis....	—	9	6½	33½
Joaquin Andujar, St.L. ...	—	2	6½	12½
Rich Gossage, San Diego	—	1	—	3
Mario Soto, Cincinnati....	—	—	2	2

Members of the Baseball Writers' Association also selected Sparky Anderson and Jim Frey as American League and National League Manager of the Year, respectively. With two writers from each city participating, Anderson collected 96 points on 13 first-place votes, nine seconds and four thirds to edge Kansas City's Dick Howser by a single point. Billy Gardner of Minnesota was third with 48 points. Frey was a decisive winner in the N.L., gaining 16 first-place votes and seven seconds for 101 points as compared to 72 for runnerup Dave Johnson of the Mets.

The BBWAA's choices for Rookies of the Year were Alvin Davis of the Seattle Mariners in the American League and Dwight Gooden of the Mets in the National. Davis received 25 of 28 first-place votes and 134 points to win easily over teammate Mark Langston, who was second with 82 points. Gooden was the top choice of 23 of the 24 writers participating in the N.L. balloting and wound up with 118 points compared to 67 for runnerup Juan Samuel of Philadelphia.

A poll of major league managers conducted by The Sporting News resulted in Jim Frey being named as Manager of the Year. He received 10 votes, doubling the totals of Dick Howser and Billy Gardner, who tied for second.

Tigers relief ace Willie Hernandez capped his sensational season by capturing American League MVP and Cy Young honors.

Other choices by The Sporting News included the designation of Don Mattingly of the Yankees and Willie Hernandez of Detroit as Player and Pitcher of the Year in the American League and Ryne Sandberg and Rick Sutcliffe of the Cubs as Player and Pitcher of the Year in the National League. Dan Quisenberry of Kansas City was named Fireman of the Year in the American League on the basis of 44 saves and six relief victories for 50 points, five ahead of runnerup Bill Caudill of Oakland, while Bruce Sutter of St. Louis gained National League Fireman of the Year honors with 45 saves and five relief wins for 50 points, eight more than runnerup Lee Smith of the Cubs registered.

Davis and Langston, both of Seattle, were selected by The Sporting News as Rookie Player and Rookie Pitcher of the Year in the A.L., while Samuel of Philadelphia and Gooden of the Mets were chosen for similar honors in the N.L. Dave Kingman of Oakland and Joaquin Andujar were tabbed as Comeback Players of the Year in the American and National Leagues, respectively.

The annual All-Star Teams selected by The Sporting News for the two leagues lined up as follows:

American League: 1B—Don Mattingly, New York; 2B—Lou Whitaker, Detroit; SS —Cal Ripken, Baltimore; 3B—Buddy Bell, Texas; OF—Dave Winfield, New York;

Tony Armas, Boston, and Dwight Evans, Boston; C—Lance Parrish, Detroit; DH—Dave Kingman, Oakland; RHP—Mike Boddicker, Baltimore; LHP—Willie Hernandez, Detroit.

National League: 1B—Keith Hernandez, New York; 2B—Ryne Sandberg, Chicago; SS—Ozzie Smith, St. Louis; 3B—Mike Schmidt, Philadelphia; OF—Tony Gwynn, San Diego; Dale Murphy, Atlanta, and Jose Cruz, Houston; C—Gary Carter, Montreal; RHP—Rick Sutcliffe, Chicago, and LHP—Mark Thurmond, San Diego.

The Hillerich & Bradsby Silver Slugger Awards for the best offensive player at each position, as selected by the managers and coaches in a poll conducted by The Sporting News, consisted of the following: 1B—Eddie Murray, Baltimore, in the American League and Hernandez in the National; 2B—Whitaker and Sandberg; SS —Ripken and Garry Templeton, San Diego; 3B—Bell and Schmidt; OF—Winfield, Armas and Jim Rice, Boston, in the American and Gwynn, Murphy and Cruz in the National; C—Parrish and Carter; DH—Andre Thornton, Cleveland, and pitcher in the National—Rick Rhoden, Pittsburgh.

The Rawlings Gold Glove winners for fielding excellence were: 1B—Murray in the American League and Hernandez in the National: 2B—Whitaker and Sandberg; SS—Alan Trammell, Detroit, and Smith; 3B—Bell and Schmidt; OF-Winfield, Dwight Evans and Dwayne Murphy, Oakland, in the American and Dale Murphy, Bob Dernier, Chicago, and Andre Dawson, Montreal, in the National; C—Parrish and Tony Pena, Pittsburgh; P —Ron Guidry, New York, and Andujar, St. Louis.

Ueberroth was chosen as The Sporting News Man of the Year in sports for his brilliant leadership of the Summer Olympics. At the minor league level, The Sporting News honored the following: Player of the Year—Alan Knicely, first baseman-catcher for Wichita (American Association); Manager of the Year—Bob Rodgers of Indianapolis (American Association), and Executives of the Year—Mike Tamburro, Pawtucket (International), in Class AAA, Bruce Baldwin, Greenville (Southern), in Class AA and Dave Tarrolly, Beloit (Midwest), in Class A.

The Baltimore Orioles staged a 14-game exhibition tour during a 22-day trip to Japan after the close of the season. Unloading 35 homers in the 14 games, the Orioles won eight contests, lost five and had one end in a tie. They won four of five games from both the Hiroshima Carp,

Japanese champions, and the Yomiuri Giants, sponsors of the tour. Two of the losses came at the hands of the Japan All-Stars and the other defeat and the tie were against a combined team. Eddie Murray paced the Orioles with nine homers while rookie Nate Snell was Baltimore's top pitcher with a 4-0 record and 1.08 ERA.

At baseball's annual winter meetings, besides the decisions mentioned earlier, major league owners met with representatives of eight cities bidding for expansion franchises—Denver, Tampa, St. Petersburg, Vancouver, Washington, Buffalo, Indianapolis and Miami. "We told them there is no time frame for expanding, but that we are likely to move along on this issue before next summer," Ueberroth announced, adding: "The financial difficulties of an existing club will have no effect on any of the expansion candidates. Each will be judged on its individual merits."

In other action at the meetings, the owners approved a resolution providing that any motions concerning TV can be passed by a simple majority in both leagues rather than the former three-fourths requirement, thus giving Ueberroth greater freedom in dealing with superstations, and voted another year of existence to the Major League Scouting Bureau, with all 26 clubs participating. Ueberroth also asked the owners to get involved with ending bench-clearing brawls, which increased in number in 1984. In individual league meetings, the National League extended President Feeney's contract one year through 1986 and chose Charles Bronfman to succeed Dan Galbreath on the Executive Council, while the American League named Peter Hardy to fill the Executive Council seat vacated by Bud Selig.

Late in the year it was disclosed that CBS Radio and the major leagues had negotiated a new five-year contract. The pact is worth about $31 million, according to estimates. Besides covering the All-Star Game, League Championship Series and World Series, the arrangement contains a Game of the Week package, marking the first time in nearly 30 years that network radio will carry major league games during the regular season. The plan calls for one day game and one night contest to be aired on Saturdays during the regular season over a 20-week period beginning late in May. CBS Radio also will carry some key weekday games late in the season. The previous four-year deal with CBS Radio covered only the All-Star Game and postseason play.

AMERICAN LEAGUE

Including

Team Reviews of 1984 Season

Team Day-by-Day Scores

1984 Standings, Home-Away Records

1984 Official A.L. Batting Averages

1984 Official A.L. Fielding Averages

1984 Official A.L. Pitching Averages

1984 Pitching Against Each Club

Jack Morris pitched his first career no-hitter, won 19 games and anchored a strong Tigers starting rotation.

Tigers Enjoy a Dream Season

By TOM GAGE

What a difference a trade makes.

The Detroit Tigers didn't try to conceal their confidence when they arrived in Florida to begin 1984 spring training. They were coming off a 92-victory, second-place 1983 season, their best finish since winning the American League East in 1972, and the future looked bright. But there still was a potential problem.

Somewhere along the way, the Tigers had to find a lefthanded pitcher, preferably for the bullpen. After failing in the winter meetings, the Tigers found who they were looking for during spring training: Willie Hernandez.

The Tigers acquired Hernandez along with first baseman Dave Bergman from the Philadelphia Phillies in exchange for outfielder Glenn Wilson and catcher-first baseman John Wockenfuss. Hernandez was the last piece to the Tigers' puzzle, and behind the 1984 A.L. Most Valuable Player and Cy Young Award winner the Tigers went from contenders to front-runners.

Front-runners, indeed. The way Detroit burst out of the starting gate, no team ever had a chance to look back at the Tigers. Not once.

Detroit won its first nine games of the season, including a no-hit victory by Jack Morris over the Chicago White Sox on April 7. The 4-0 shutout at Comiskey Park was the first no-hitter thrown by a Tiger pitcher since Jim Bunning did it in 1958.

By May 24 the club had posted a 35-5 mark, the best 40-game start in major league history. The Tigers went on to finish at 104-58, 15 games ahead of the second-place Toronto Blue Jays. Then by sweeping the Kansas City Royals in the A.L. playoffs and defeating the San Diego Padres, four games to one, in the World Series, the Tigers became the first team since the 1955 Brooklyn Dodgers to win the Series after holding first place from their season opener to season finale.

Despite their incredible start, the Tigers felt pressure all season.

"If we don't win it now," Manager Sparky Anderson told his players during a team meeting, "they'll lynch us."

"We would have been labeled as chokers," shortstop Alan Trammell said.

Not to worry. The Tigers never let up, and never did they lose more than four games in succession. An all-out consistent effort from the entire club kept the momentum going throughout the season.

Catcher Lance Parrish dropped 30 points below his career average but still powered 33 home runs and drove in 98 runs.

"Everybody says there are heroes and magic on this club," said Bergman, who hit .273 in a part-time role. "I don't see any magic, and I don't believe in heroes. What I see is a team playing tough baseball every day, and busting its gut to do so."

Still, pitching had a lot to do with Detroit's success. The Tigers led all American League clubs with a 3.49 earned-run average and 51 saves. The bullpen duo of Hernandez and Aurelio Lopez was, perhaps, the most consistently effective segment of that pitching staff.

Between them, Hernandez and Lopez were 19-4 with 46 saves and a 2.43 ERA. Hernandez alone (1.92 ERA) had 32 saves in 33 save situations as he broke the team record for pitching appearances with 80.

"I can tell you the difference between

SCORES OF DETROIT TIGERS' 1984 GAMES

APRIL

Date	W/L	Score	Winner	Loser
3—At Minn.	W	8-1	Morris	Williams
5—At Minn.	W	7-3	Petry	Viola
6—At Chicago	W	3-2	Wilcox	Dotson
7—At Chicago	W	4-0	Morris	Bannister
8—At Chicago	W	7-3	Lopez	Seaver
10—Texas	W	5-1	Petry	Stewart
12—Texas	W	9-4	Morris	Tanana
13—At Boston	W	13-9	Bair	Hurst
18—Kan. City	W	4-3†	Hernandez	Beckwith
19—Kan. City	L	2-5	Saberhagen	Petry
20—Chicago	W	3-2	Lopez	Reed
21—Chicago	W	4-1	Rozema	Hoyt
22—Chicago	W	9-1	Berenguer	Brennan
24—Minnesota	W	6-5	Morris	Davis
24—Minnesota	W	4-3	Abbott	Viola
25—At Texas	W	9-4	Wilcox	Stewart
26—At Texas	W	7-5	Bair	Tanana
27—Cleveland	L	4-8y	Aponte	Abbott
28—Cleveland	W	6-2	Morris	Behenna
29—Cleveland	W	6-1	Petry	Spillner

Won 18, Lost 2

MAY

Date	W/L	Score	Winner	Loser
1—Boston	W	11-2	Wilcox	Hurst
2—Boston	L	4-5	Brown	Berenguer
3—Boston	L	0-1	Ojeda	Morris
4—At Cleve.	W	9-2	Petry	Spillner
5—At Cleve.	W	6-5	Abbott	Heaton
6—At Cleve.	W	6-5§	Lopez	Camacho
7—At Kan. C.	W	10-3	Berenguer	Gubicza
8—At Kan. C.	W	5-2	Morris	Black
9—At Kan. C.	W	3-1	Petry	Jackson
11—California	W	8-2	Wilcox	Witt
12—California	L	2-4	John	Berenguer
14—Seattle	W	7-5	Lopez	Vande Berg
15—Seattle	W	6-4	Morris	Thomas
16—Seattle	W	10-1	Wilcox	Young
18—Oakland	W	8-4*	Petry	Krueger
19—Oakland	W	5-4	Morris	McCatty
20—Oakland	W	4-3	Wilcox	Sorensen
22—At Calif.	W	3-1	Berenguer	Witt
23—At Calif.	W	4-2	Petry	LaCorte
24—At Calif.	W	5-1	Morris	Slaton
25—At Seattle	L	3-7	Vande Berg	Wilcox
26—At Seattle	L	5-9	Moore	Berenguer
27—At Seattle	L	1-6	Young	Petry
28—At Oak.	W	6-2	Morris	Codiroli
29—At Oak.	L	5-8	Krueger	Wilcox
30—At Oak.	W	2-1	Hernandez	McCatty

Won 19, Lost 7

JUNE

Date	W/L	Score	Winner	Loser
1—Baltimore	W	14-2	Petry	McGregor
2—Baltimore	L	0-5	Davis	Morris
3—Baltimore	L	1-2	Flanagan	Wilcox
4—Toronto	W	6-3†	Lopez	Key
5—Toronto	L	4-8	Acker	Abbott
6—Toronto	L	3-6	Leal	Petry
7—Toronto	W	5-3	Morris	Clancy
8—At Balt.	W	3-2	Wilcox	Davis
9—At Balt.	L	0-4	Flanagan	Berenguer
10—At Balt.	W	10-4	Bair	Boddicker
10—At Balt.	W	8-0	Petry	D. Martinez
11—At Toronto	W	5-4	Rozema	Leal
12—At Toronto	L	3-12	Clancy	Morris
13—At Toronto	L	3-7	Stieb	Wilcox
15—At Milw.	W	3-2	Petry	Cocanower
16—At Milw.	W	6-0	Berenguer	Sutton
17—At Milw.	W	7-4	Rozema	McClure
18—New York	L	1-2	Niekro	Wilcox
19—New York	W	7-6	Lopez	Guidry
20—New York	W	6-9x	Bair	Rijo
21—Milwaukee	L	3-4	Sutton	Berenguer
22—Milwaukee	W	7-3	Rozema	McClure
23—Milwaukee	W	5-1	Wilcox	Porter
24—Milwaukee	W	7-1	Morris	Haas
25—At N.Y.	L	3-7	Guidry	Bair
26—At N.Y.	W	9-7†	Hernandez	Christiansen
27—At N.Y.	L	4-5	Howell	Willis
29—Minnesota	L	3-5	Williams	Morris
29—Minnesota	W	7-5	Hernandez	Filson
30—Minnesota	W	4-3	Petry	Schrom

Won 18, Lost 12

JULY

Date	W/L	Score	Winner	Loser
1—Minnesota	L	0-9	Viola	Berenguer
2—At Chicago	L	1-7	Bannister	Rozema
3—At Chicago	L	5-9	Seaver	Morris
4—At Chicago	L	2-8	Dotson	Wilcox
5—At Texas	W	7-4	Lopez	Hough
6—At Texas	L	3-5	Mason	Berenguer
7—At Texas	W	5-2	Rozema	Darwin
8—At Texas	L	7-9	Tanana	Bair
12—At Minn.	L	2-4	Viola	Petry
13—At Minn.	W	5-3‡	Hernandez	Lysander
14—At Minn.	W	6-5§	Hernandez	Walters
15—At Minn.	W	6-2	Rozema	Schrom
16—Chicago	W	7-1	Abbott	Hoyt
17—Chicago	W	3-2	Petry	Nelson
18—Chicago	L	6-10	Bannister	Morris
19—Texas	W	9-2	Wilcox	Stewart
20—Texas	W	3-1	Rozema	Tanana
21—Texas	W	7-6	Monge	Noles
22—Texas	W	2-0	Petry	Hough
23—At Cleve.	W	4-1	Morris	Blyleven
24—At Cleve.	W	9-5	Wilcox	Farr
25—At Cleve.	L	1-4	Smith	Rozema
27—Boston	W	9-1	Petry	Hurst
27—Boston	L	0-4	Ojeda	Abbott
28—Boston	L	2-3	Stanley	Morris
29—Boston	W	3-0	Wilcox	Boyd
31—Cleveland	W	5-1	Berenguer	Smith
31—Cleveland	L	4-6	Heaton	Rozema

Won 16, Lost 12

AUGUST

Date	W/L	Score	Winner	Loser
1—Cleveland	L	2-4	Farr	Petry
2—Cleveland	W	2-1	Morris	Blyleven
3—Kan. City	L	6-9	Saberhagen	Wilcox
4—Kan. City	L	5-9	Beckwith	Bair
5—Kan. City	L	4-5	Saberhagen	Hernandez
5—Kan. City	L	0-4	Leibrandt	Berenguer
6—At Boston	W	9-7	Lopez	Ojeda
6—At Boston	L	2-10	Clemens	Willis
7—At Boston	L	7-12	Hurst	Morris
7—At Boston	W	7-5‡	Lopez	Gale
8—At Boston	L	0-8	Boyd	Abbott
10—At Kan. C.	W	5-4	Lopez	Beckwith
11—At Kan. C.	W	9-5	Morris	Leibrandt
12—At Kan. C.	W	8-4	Wilcox	Saberhagen
14—California	L	4-6	Aase	Hernandez
14—California	L	1-12	Kison	Rozema
15—California	W	8-3	Petry	John
16—California	W	8-7§	Hernandez	Curtis
17—Seattle	W	6-2	Wilcox	Moore
18—Seattle	W	4-3	Berenguer	Geisel
19—Seattle	L	1-4	Langston	Petry
20—Oakland	W	14-1	Morris	Young
21—Oakland	W	12-6	Wilcox	Sorensen
22—Oakland	W	11-4	Berenguer	Krueger
24—At Calif.	L	3-5	Witt	Petry
25—At Calif.	W	5-1	Morris	Kison
26—At Calif.	W	12-6	Wilcox	John
28—At Seattle	W	5-4	Hernandez	Stanton
29—At Seattle	L	1-5	Langston	Petry
30—At Seattle	L	1-2	Beattie	Morris
31—At Oak.	L	6-7x	Atherton	Rozema

Won 16, Lost 15

SEPTEMBER

Date	W/L	Score	Winner	Loser
1—At Oak.	L	5-7	Young	Berenguer
2—At Oak.	W	6-3	Petry	Conroy
3—Baltimore	L	4-7	Stewart	Morris
4—Baltimore	L	1-4	Boddicker	Rozema
5—Baltimore	W	1-0	Berenguer	Flanagan
7—At Toronto	W	7-4†	Hernandez	Musselman
8—At Toronto	W	10-4	Scherrer	Leal
9—At Toronto	W	7-2	Wilcox	Clancy
10—At Balt.	L	1-3	Flanagan	Berenguer
11—At Balt.	W	9-2	Petry	Swaggerty
12—At Balt.	L	1-3	D. Martinez	Mason
14—Toronto	L	2-7	Clancy	Morris
15—Toronto	W	2-1	Wilcox	Stieb
16—Toronto	W	8-3	Berenguer	Clark
17—Milwaukee	W	7-3	Mason	Waits
18—Milwaukee	W	3-0	O'Neal	McClure
19—Milwaukee	W	4-2	Morris	Candiotti
21—New York	L	3-5	Montefusco	Wilcox
22—New York	W	6-0	Petry	Christiansen
23—New York	W	4-1	Morris	Fontenot
24—At Milw.	W	7-3	Berenguer	Hartzell
25—At Milw.	W	9-1	O'Neal	Gibson
26—At Milw.	L	5-7	Searage	Lopez
27—At N.Y.	L	1-2	Shirley	Hernandez
28—At N.Y.	W	4-2§	Bair	Cowley
29—At N.Y.	W	11-3	Berenguer	Guidry
30—At N.Y.	L	2-9	Rasmussen	O'Neal

Won 17, Lost 10

*5 innings.　†10 innings.　‡11 innings.　§12 innings.　x13 innings.　y19 innings.

Kirk Gibson came of age with 27 homers and 91 RBIs.

Detroit and Toronto in two words," Anderson said just before the Tigers clinched the A.L. East. "Hernandez and Lopez. If Toronto had them instead of us, we'd be trailing by as many games, if not more, than the Blue Jays are now."

The starting rotation, which did not include a single 20-game winner, also was a big plus for Detroit. The trio of Morris (19-11, 3.60 ERA), Dan Petry (18-8, 3.24) and Milt Wilcox (17-8, 4.00) combined for 54 victories and 411 strikeouts. Juan Berenguer, the other regular starter, was 11-10 with a 3.48 ERA.

Wilcox almost had left the Tigers as a free agent during the off-season despite his desire to re-sign with the club. He had received a letter from the team after the 1983 season saying his services no longer were needed, but the club wound up offering him a contract after failing to trade for another pitcher. Wilcox responded with his best major league season ever.

On offense, Detroit's main weapon was power. The Tigers hit 187 home runs, most in the majors, while scoring a major league-high 829 runs and pounding out a .271 batting average (fourth in the league).

Catcher Lance Parrish, whose 1984 average (.237) was 30 points lower than his career average entering the season, led the power assault with team highs of 33 homers and 98 runs batted in.

Another long-ball threat for Detroit was Kirk Gibson, whose determination to turn his slumping career around was a big boost for the Tigers in 1984.

"I needed to make more of a commitment to the game," Gibson said. "I wasn't fooling anyone but myself. I could either have gone the way I was going and been a bad baseball player, or I could get my act together and make something of myself. I decided to get my act together."

Gibson, coached by Hall of Famer and former Tiger Al Kaline, learned to play right field without embarrassing himself, but most of his contributions were at the plate, where he hit .282 with 27 homers and 91 RBIs. Gibson also led the club with 10 triples, 274 total bases, 92 runs scored, 29 stolen bases and 17 game-winning RBIs, many of them in dramatic late-inning situations.

The Tigers had baseball's strongest team up the middle, both offensively and defensively, with Parrish, Trammell, second baseman Lou Whitaker and center fielder Chet Lemon. Trammell, the No. 5 hitter in the league at .314, played despite suffering from torn ligaments in his left knee and a superficial tear of the rotator cuff in his right shoulder. When soreness in his shoulder made it impossible for him to play shortstop, Trammell became the team's designated hitter for a month until he returned to the infield. He went on to earn Most Valuable Player honors in the World Series, after which he underwent surgery on both his knee and his shoulder.

Whitaker hit .289 with 13 homers, while Lemon hit .287 with 20 homers. Lemon tied Trammell for the team high in doubles (34).

Several players performed well in part-time roles. Ruppert Jones hit .284 with 12 homers in 215 at-bats, Howard Johnson batted .248 with 12 homers in 355 at-bats, and rookie Barbaro Garbey hit .287 in 327 at-bats. Veteran Larry Herndon, platooning in left field, batted .280 but managed only seven homers and 43 RBIs.

Anderson notched a couple of spots for himself in the record books in 1984. The former manager of the Cincinnati Reds during their glory years in the 1970s became the first skipper ever to win 100 games in a season in both leagues as well as the first to win the World Series in both leagues.

Detroit's incredible season brought more than 2.7 million fans to Tiger Stadium, by far the best season attendance in the club's history. The Tigers, who only once before had drawn more than 2 million fans at home and never had done it on the road, also played before more than 2.1 million spectators at their opponents' stadiums.

Outfielder George Bell blossomed in 1984, hitting .292, driving in 87 runs and leading the Blue Jays with 26 home runs.

Bullpen Lets Down Blue Jays

By NEIL MacCARL

A strong bullpen probably would have done it. If the Toronto Blue Jays had known how to spell "relief," the Detroit Tigers might not have won the American League East, much less gone on to win the World Series.

Forget the Tigers' unprecedented start, in which they lost only five of their first 40 games and were leading the division by 8½ games on May 24. Toronto was hanging tough at 27-14, and at that time the Tigers and the Blue Jays had not yet played each other. When the two clubs finally met in early June for a four-game series, Toronto won two of the first three games. On June 6, the Blue Jays trailed the incredible Tigers by a mere 3½ games.

But that was as close as Toronto ever came to catching Detroit. Though they never relinquished the No. 2 spot in the division, the Jays went 53-56 after June 6, and Detroit went on to win the division by 15 games.

Some semblance of order in the Blue Jay bullpen could have made Toronto a contender in the division rather than simply the leading runner-up. But the relief corps, despite logging a team-record 33 saves, was charged with 28 losses. The Blue Jays won only six of 18 extra-inning games, with relief pitchers bearing the responsibility for all 12 of those losses. Relievers were credited with only five of the six victories, however; Dave Stieb went the distance to win one 10-inning game.

Only one Toronto reliever, Jim Gott, had a winning record (7-6), and he began the season as a starter. Gott, who finished 1984 with a 4.02 earned-run average, posted a 2-1 record with just two saves in 23 relief appearances.

Gott was moved to the bullpen, however, only out of desperation because Toronto's projected stopper, Dennis Lamp, failed to live up to high-priced expectations. Lamp, who signed a multimillion-dollar contract with Toronto as a free agent three days after the Blue Jays failed to win the Goose Gossage sweepstakes, was a major disappointment. He managed only one save after May 23, and his overall 8-8 record included three wins as a starter late in the year. Lamp finished with nine saves in 52 relief appearances and a 4.55 ERA.

The other relievers fared little better. Roy Lee Jackson was 6-1 with a 2.44 ERA at the All-Star break but finished at 7-8 with a 3.56 ERA. Jackson shared the team

Veteran Doyle Alexander surprised everybody by winning a team-leading 17 games.

high in saves (10) with rookie Jimmy Key (4-5, 4.65 ERA). Bryan Clark, who was supposed to provide valuable lefthanded relief after being obtained from Seattle in a trade for outfielder Barry Bonnell, pitched in just 20 games and had a 1-2 record, no saves and the team's highest ERA (5.91).

The starting rotation was far more solid. Veteran Doyle Alexander was the biggest surprise, pacing the staff with a career-high 17 victories and ranking among the league leaders in ERA (3.13), innings pitched (261⅔) and complete games (11).

Stieb (16-8) still was the ace of the staff. His 198 strikeouts and 2.83 ERA were second in the league, while his 267 innings pitched was a league high. He pitched 11 complete games.

Luis Leal enjoyed a remarkable start and was 12-2 on August 1. He fizzled in the last two months, however, and wound up at 13-8 with a 3.89 ERA. Jim Clancy (13-15, 5.12 ERA) had a losing season for the first time since 1981.

Offensively, the Blue Jays were dynamite. Toronto led the league in doubles

SCORES OF TORONTO BLUE JAYS' 1984 GAMES

APRIL			Winner	Loser
4—At Seattle	L	2-3†	Stanton	Lamp
5—At Seattle	W	13-5	Leal	Beattie
6—At Calif.	W	11-5	Key	Brown
7—At Calif.	W	3-1	Stieb	Forsch
8—At Calif.	L	3-4	Sanchez	Jackson
9—At Oak.	L	3-4	Caudill	Lamp
10—At Oak.	W	3-0	Leal	Sorensen
13—At Texas	W	3-2	Lamp	Tobik
14—At Texas	L	2-6	Hough	Clancy
15—At Texas	W	2-1	Lamp	Stewart
17—Baltimore	W	3-2	Key	T. Martinez
18—Baltimore	W	7-1	Stieb	Palmer
19—Baltimore	W	2-1	Clancy	McGregor
20—California	L	6-10x	Sanchez	Acker
21—California	L	4-8	Romanick	Gott
22—California	L	6-9	Slaton	Key
23—Seattle	W	8-5	Stieb	Langston
24—Seattle	L	2-4	Beard	Clancy
25—Oakland	W	11-0	Leal	Conroy
26—Oakland	L	4-7	Warren	Gott
27—At Kan. C.	W	1-0	Alexander	Gubicza
28—At Kan. C.	W	6-0	Stieb	Saberhagen
			Won 13, Lost 9	
MAY				
1—Texas	W	10-4	Leal	Tanana
1—Texas	L	1-4	Darwin	Alexander
2—Texas	W	7-6	Clancy	Hough
4—Kan. City	W	4-3†	Stieb	Huismann
5—Kan. City	W	10-1	Gott	Jackson
6—Kan. City	W	2-1	Jackson	Gura
9—At Balt.	L	4-7	McGregor	Clancy
9—At Balt.	L	3-7	T. Martinez	Key
10—At Balt.	W	4-3†	Jackson	D. Martinez
12—At Cleve.	L	4-8	Blyleven	Acker
13—At Cleve.	T	4-4*	....	....
15—At Minn.	W	5-2†	Jackson	Davis
16—At Minn.	W	8-7	Alexander	Filson
17—Chicago	W	3-2	Jackson	Hoyt
18—Chicago	W	4-3	Clancy	Burns
19—Chicago	W	1-0	Gott	Seaver
20—Chicago	L	0-3	Dotson	Stieb
21—Minnesota	W	3-2	Alexander	Davis
22—Minnesota	W	3-2	Jackson	Smithson
23—Minnesota	W	4-1	Clancy	Viola
25—Cleveland	W	5-1	Stieb	Heaton
26—Cleveland	W	2-1	Alexander	Farr
27—Cleveland	W	6-1	Leal	Sutcliffe
27—Cleveland	W	6-5	Jackson	Camacho
29—At Chicago	L	1-8	Hoyt	Clancy
30—At Chicago	W	2-1	Stieb	Burns
			Won 19, Lost 6	
JUNE				
1—New York	W	10-2	Alexander	Fontenot
2—New York	W	9-8†	Lamp	Christiansen
3—New York	L	2-15	Niekro	Clancy
4—At Detroit	L	3-6†	Lopez	Key
5—At Detroit	W	8-4	Acker	Abbott
6—At Detroit	W	6-3	Leal	Petry
7—At Detroit	L	3-5	Morris	Clancy
8—At N.Y.	L	3-4‡	Righetti	Acker
9—At N.Y.	L	1-2	Guidry	Stieb
10—At N.Y.	L	3-5	Christiansen	Alexander
11—Detroit	L	4-5	Rozema	Leal
12—Detroit	W	12-3	Clancy	Morris
13—Detroit	W	7-3	Stieb	Wilcox
15—Boston	W	4-3‡	Lamp	Clear
16—Boston	W	7-0	Leal	Hurst
17—Boston	W	5-3	Clancy	Gale
19—Milwaukee	L	5-6	Fingers	Key
20—Milwaukee	L	4-5	Tellmann	Alexander
21—At Boston	W	5-2	Leal	Nipper
22—At Boston	L	1-8	Clemens	Clancy
23—At Boston	W	9-3	Gott	Gale
24—At Boston	L	3-5†	Stanley	Lamp
25—At Milw.	L	1-2	Cocanower	Alexander
25—At Milw.	L	4-9	McClure	Acker
26—At Milw.	L	3-6	Sutton	Leal
27—At Milw.	L	1-5	Porter	Clancy
28—Oakland	W	9-6	Gott	Atherton
29—Oakland	L	1-2	Burris	Stieb
30—Oakland	W	6-1	Alexander	Krueger
			Won 13, Lost 16	
JULY				
1—Oakland	W	7-6	Acker	Atherton
2—California	L	3-6	Witt	Clancy
3—California	W	4-0	Gott	John
4—California	W	6-3	Stieb	Romanick

JULY			Winner	Loser
5—Seattle	W	10-8	Alexander	Beattie
6—Seattle	W	9-2	Leal	Langston
7—Seattle	L	4-8	Moore	Clancy
8—Seattle	L	1-7	Beattie	Gott
12—At Oak.	L	4-7	Krueger	Lamp
13—At Oak.	W	6-3	Leal	Burris
14—At Oak.	W	2-1	Stieb	Caudill
15—At Oak.	W	6-3	Clancy	Young
16—At Calif.	L	0-3	Slaton	Gott
17—At Calif.	L	3-5	Witt	Acker
18—At Calif.	W	8-2	Leal	Zahn
19—At Seattle	W	8-1	Stieb	Vande Berg
20—At Seattle	W	12-7	Acker	Mirabella
21—At Seattle	L	3-9	Barojas	Lamp
22—At Seattle	W	5-3	Alexander	Langston
23—At Kan. C.	W	8-9	Beckwith	Jackson
23—At Kan. C.	L	2-7	Wills	Gott
24—At Kan. C.	L	4-5	Gubicza	Stieb
25—At Kan. C.	L	4-5x	Quisenberry	Clark
27—Texas	L	2-4	Hough	Alexander
28—Texas	L	4-5	Mason	Jackson
29—Texas	W	6-2	Stieb	Darwin
30—Kan. City	L	4-7	Leibrandt	Clancy
31—Kan. City	W	6-5	Alexander	Wills
			Won 14, Lost 14	
AUGUST				
1—Kan. City	W	4-1	Leal	Gura
3—At Balt.	W	5-2	Jackson	McGregor
4—At Balt.	W	6-2	Clancy	Flanagan
5—At Balt.	W	4-3	Key	T. Martinez
6—At Texas	L	4-5	Mason	Jackson
7—At Texas	L	6-7†	Schmidt	Lamp
8—At Texas	W	7-2	Clancy	Darwin
10—Baltimore	W	2-0	Alexander	D. Martinez
11—Baltimore	W	3-2	Gott	Davis
12—Baltimore	L	4-5	McGregor	Jackson
13—Baltimore	L	1-2	Boddicker	Clancy
14—At Cleve.	W	8-1	Alexander	Heaton
14—At Cleve.	W	9-5	Lamp	Waddell
15—At Cleve.	L	1-16	Schulze	Leal
15—At Cleve.	L	3-4x	Jeffcoat	Key
16—At Cleve.	L	5-6	Waddell	Lamp
17—At Chicago	W	4-3	Clancy	Hoyt
18—At Chicago	L	6-7	Roberge	Jackson
19—At Chicago	W	7-4	Key	Agosto
21—Cleveland	L	1-3	Smith	Stieb
22—Cleveland	L	3-13	Blyleven	Clancy
23—Cleveland	W	6-1	Alexander	Schulze
24—At Minn.	W	6-2	Leal	Lysander
25—At Minn.	L	4-5§	Castillo	Gott
26—At Minn.	W	2-1	Stieb	Schrom
27—At Minn.	W	5-2	Lamp	Smithson
28—Chicago	W	7-6‡	Clark	Reed
29—Chicago	L	5-8	Bannister	Leal
30—At Chicago	W	4-3	Gott	Seaver
31—Minnesota	W	7-0	Stieb	Castillo
			Won 18, Lost 12	
SEPTEMBER				
1—Minnesota	W	12-4	Lamp	Smithson
2—Minnesota	W	6-0	Alexander	Viola
3—At N.Y.	L	0-2	Cowley	Leal
4—At N.Y.	W	6-4	Clancy	Armstrong
5—At N.Y.	L	3-4†	Righetti	Jackson
7—Detroit	L	4-7†	Hernandez	Musselman
8—Detroit	L	4-10	Scherrer	Leal
9—Detroit	L	2-7	Wilcox	Clancy
10—New York	L	2-6	Montefusco	Stieb
11—New York	W	10-3	Lamp	Rasmussen
12—New York	W	2-1	Alexander	Niekro
13—New York	L	1-6	Fontenot	Leal
14—At Detroit	W	7-2	Clancy	Morris
15—At Detroit	L	1-2	Wilcox	Stieb
16—At Detroit	L	3-8	Berenguer	Clark
17—Boston	W	5-4	Alexander	Ojeda
18—Boston	L	3-10	Gale	Leal
19—Boston	L	4-10	Hurst	Clancy
20—Milwaukee	W	6-4	Stieb	Gibson
21—Milwaukee	L	1-5	Sutton	Lamp
22—Milwaukee	W	2-1	Alexander	Haas
23—Milwaukee	L	5-8	Kern	Jackson
24—At Boston	W	9-8	Clancy	Hurst
25—At Boston	L	6-14	Nipper	Stieb
26—At Boston	W	8-4	Alexander	Boyd
28—At Milw.	L	3-4‡	Searage	Musselman
29—At Milw.	W	5-4	Stieb	Cocanower
30—At Milw.	L	0-4	Gibson	Alexander
			Won 12, Lost 16	

*7 innings. †10 innings. ‡11 innings. §12 innings. x13 innings.

After winning 12 of his first 14 decisions, Luis Leal battled a slump and ended up 13-8.

(275, tied with New York), triples (68) and stolen bases (193) while compiling a .273 team batting average, third in the league.

Outfielders George Bell, Dave Collins and Lloyd Moseby were among the leaders at the plate for Toronto. Bell, who earned a starting job as Bonnell's replacement in right field, became the team's new hitting hero with a .292 average, 87 runs batted in and a club-leading 26 home runs. He hit 39 doubles (third in the league) to set a team record and tallied 302 total bases, another team record.

Collins and Moseby were dual threats at the plate and on the basepaths. They tied for the league lead in triples with 15 each and combined for 99 stolen bases. Collins, with 60 of those steals, set a new team high. (Second baseman Damaso Garcia, a .284 hitter in '84, added 46 more stolen bases.) Moseby hit .280, 35 points below his 1983 average, but led the Blue Jays with 92 RBIs, and Collins batted .308.

Outfielder Jesse Barfield saw less action than in previous years with Toronto but contributed a .284 average and 14 homers.

Third baseman Rance Mulliniks, who set a team record by slapping eight consecutive hits in a series at Minnesota, led the Blue Jays with his .324 average. Mulliniks shared his position with Garth Iorg, who struggled at the plate, hitting .227.

Manager Bobby Cox also juggled shortstops, using veteran Alfredo Griffin and Tony Fernandez. After missing spring training with a thumb injury, Fernandez joined the team in May as a much-heralded rookie. Though he didn't play regularly, he batted .270 in 233 at-bats and showed signs of becoming the Blue Jays' shortstop of the future. Griffin, who also was used at second, hit .241 and often was pulled for a pinch-hitter.

At catcher, another platoon position for Toronto, both Buck Martinez and Ernie Whitt dropped in their offensive production. Whitt had the better season, hitting .238 with 15 homers.

In 1983, Cliff Johnson and Jorge Orta had given the Blue Jays a productive designated hitter combination. Toronto traded Orta, however, to Kansas City for long-ball threat Willie Aikens before the 1984 season, and the new DH duo was not nearly as devastating. Aikens, who served a drug-related suspension through May 15, batted a disappointing .205 and knocked in only 26 runs, despite hitting 11 homers.

Johnson had a strong second half to finish with a .304 average and 16 homers. He also tied a team record with 11 pinch hits, including the 19th pinch-hit homer of his career, a major league record.

First baseman Willie Upshaw (.278, 19 homers, 84 RBIs), who seemed headed for record totals in home runs and RBIs in late June, slumped in the second half. He hit only six homers after the All-Star break. Upshaw also drew a fine and three-game suspension for charging the mound and knocking down New York's Dennis Rasmussen, who had thrown near Upshaw's head after giving up two two-run homers.

Overall, it was an upbeat season for the Blue Jays. They won 89 games, the same total as in 1983 (when they finished fourth), but it was enough for second place, their first finish ever in the upper half of the division. They won more one-run games (34) than any other team in the league, including a stretch of 19 consecutive victories in one-run games.

Baseball fever continued to spread in Toronto as 2,110,009 fans, an average of 26,709 per date, visited Exhibition Stadium. It was the first time the Blue Jays had drawn more than 2 million fans in one season.

Yankees slugger Dave Winfield battled teammate Don Mattingly all season long for the A.L. batting title, but finally fell three points short.

Bad First Half Kills Yankees

By MOSS KLEIN

Even Yogi Berra, whose philosophy has always been "It ain't over till it's over," knew that the New York Yankees realistically were finished as 1984 contenders in the American League East before June. But that didn't stop the lovable manager from leading his team to a dramatic second-half turnaround that produced a "Wait till next year" enthusiasm.

The Yankees' season was a play in two acts. The first act could have been called "The Bronx Bomb" as the team staggered to the All-Star break in sixth place in the division with a 36-46 record, 20 games behind the runaway Detroit Tigers.

The second act, however, became "The Greatest Show on Earth." The Yankees, aided by a group of young, enthusiastic reinforcements from Columbus (International), were the best team in the major leagues after the All-Star break with a 51-29 second-half record.

By the time the Yankees finished the season in third place, Berra was a proud manager. "Right now, we're as good as the Tigers," he said. "If only we didn't have that awful start. But there's nothing we can do about that."

Berra, returning as the Yankees' manager after a 20-year gap (he also managed the New York Mets in the mid-1970s), watched helplessly as the Yankees skidded 10½ games from first place by the end of April and 17½ behind by the end of May. "I just look at the standings and it's incredible," designated hitter Don Baylor said in early June. "It's hard to believe we could be this far out this soon."

But the standings didn't lie. The Yankees' slow start and the Tigers' record-setting 35-5 getaway reduced New York to an also-ran long before summer officially arrived.

The primary constants in the diverse halves of the season were right fielder Dave Winfield and first baseman Don Mattingly. They had a season-long duel for the American League batting title before Mattingly won in his final at-bat, his .343 average edging Winfield by three points. Mattingly, a 23-year-old lefthanded hitter, became the first Yankee to win a batting title since Mickey Mantle in 1956.

In his first full season following a part-time role as a rookie in 1983, Mattingly hit 23 home runs, drove in 110 runs and led the league with 44 doubles and 207 hits, the most by a Yankee since Bobby Richardson's 209 in 1962. Mattingly also was

Ageless Phil Niekro got off to a blazing start and gave the Yankees 16 victories.

among the league leaders in slugging percentage (.537) and on-base percentage (.381). Berra, when asked if Mattingly had exceeded his expectations, said, "Not only that, he's done better."

Winfield, the 12-year veteran in his fourth season as a Yankee, had 19 homers, 100 runs batted in, 106 runs scored and 193 hits. His on-base percentage of .393 was fourth in the league.

Phil Niekro, the 45-year-old knuckleballer who had signed with the Yankees after 20 seasons with the Milwaukee and Atlanta Braves, was the brightest development during the otherwise dull early months. Niekro, who finished with a 16-8 record, ran up an 11-4 mark and a league-leading 1.84 earned-run average at the All-Star break. In the second half, however, Niekro slumped to a 5-4 record and a 5.06 ERA and was sidelined most of the last month because of a pulled muscle.

Dave Righetti's shift to the bullpen was a major controversy early in the season.

SCORES OF NEW YORK YANKEES' 1984 GAMES

APRIL

Date	W/L	Score	Winner	Loser
3—At Kan. C.	L	2-4	Black	Guidry
4—At Kan. C.	W	4-3	Niekro	Splittorff
5—At Kan. C.	L	4-15	Gura	Rawley
6—At Texas	L	6-7	Tobik	Murray
7—At Texas	L	5-8*	Mason	Fontenot
8—At Texas	W	4-3x	Murray	Tobik
10—Minnesota	W	4-1	Niekro	Viola
12—Minnesota	L	0-3	Smithson	Fontenot
13—Chicago	L	3-5	Bannister	Montefusco
15—Chicago	W	2-1†	Righetti	Burns
18—At Cleve.	W	5-0	Niekro	Sutcliffe
20—Texas	W	4-1	Guidry	Stewart
21—Texas	L	0-1	Tanana	Fontenot
22—Texas	L	0-4	Darwin	Rijo
24—Kan. City	W	4-0	Niekro	Black
25—At Minn.	L	6-8	Filson	Howell
26—At Minn.	L	2-4	Filson	Rijo
27—Milwaukee	L	0-12	Caldwell	Rawley
28—Milwaukee	L	0-8	Porter	Montefusco
29—Milwaukee	W	6-5x	Howell	McClure
30—At Chicago	L	3-5	Bannister	Guidry

Won 8, Lost 13

MAY

Date	W/L	Score	Winner	Loser
1—At Chicago	L	5-7	Barojas	Fontenot
2—At Chicago	L	0-3	Hoyt	Rijo
4—At Milw.	L	0-1	Porter	Niekro
5—At Milw.	L	1-2†	Ladd	Brown
6—At Milw.	W	8-4†	Brown	Ladd
7—Cleveland	W	5-2	Rawley	Behenna
9—Cleveland	W	11-4	Niekro	Sutcliffe
10—Cleveland	W	7-6y	Rijo	Waddell
11—Seattle	L	3-4z	Thomas	Christiansen
12—Seattle	L	0-5	Beattie	Rawley
13—Seattle	W	7-0	Shirley	Langston
14—Oakland	W	3-1	Niekro	Sorensen
15—Oakland	W	9-6	Guidry	Burris
16—Oakland	W	7-6†	Christiansen	Caudill
18—California	L	3-4†	Sanchez	Howell
19—California	L	0-4	Zahn	Niekro
20—California	L	0-3	Romanick	Guidry
22—At Seattle	L	3-5	Young	Rijo
23—At Seattle	W	3-0	Rasmussen	Beattie
24—At Seattle	W	2-0	Niekro	Langston
25—At Oak.	L	7-10	Atherton	Guidry
26—At Oak.	W	8-4	Fontenot	Sorensen
27—At Oak.	L	1-7	Burris	Rijo
28—At Calif.	L	2-6	Corbett	Rasmussen
29—At Calif.	L	5-6	LaCorte	Niekro
30—At Calif.	W	10-1	Guidry	Romanick

Won 12, Lost 14

JUNE

Date	W/L	Score	Winner	Loser
1—At Toronto	L	2-10	Alexander	Fontenot
2—At Toronto	L	8-9†	Lamp	Christiansen
3—At Toronto	W	15-2	Niekro	Clancy
4—Boston	W	8-3	Guidry	Ojeda
5—Boston	L	4-5	Clear	Howell
6—Boston	L	3-5	Hurst	Rijo
8—Toronto	W	4-3‡	Righetti	Acker
9—Toronto	W	2-1	Guidry	Stieb
10—Toronto	W	5-3	Christiansen	Alexander
11—At Boston	L	6-9	Clear	Howell
12—At Boston	L	8-9	Crawford	Righetti
13—At Boston	W	4-2	Niekro	Boyd
14—At Boston	W	12-11†	Fontenot	Stanley
15—Baltimore	L	1-2	Boddicker	Shirley
16—Baltimore	W	8-3	Howell	McGregor
17—Baltimore	L	2-6	Flanagan	Rasmussen
18—At Detroit	W	2-1	Niekro	Wilcox
19—At Detroit	L	6-7	Lopez	Guidry
20—At Detroit	L	6-9x	Bair	Rijo
21—At Balt.	W	5-3	Rawley	McGregor
22—At Balt.	L	4-5	Flanagan	Rasmussen
23—At Balt.	W	5-4‡	Rijo	T. Martinez
25—Detroit	W	7-3	Guidry	Bair
26—Detroit	L	7-9†	Hernandez	Christiansen
27—Detroit	W	5-4	Howell	Willis
29—At Kan. C.	L	2-3	Black	Niekro
30—At Kan. C.	L	2-6	Gubicza	Guidry

Won 13, Lost 14

JULY

Date	W/L	Score	Winner	Loser
1—At Kan. C.	L	0-8	Leibrandt	Shirley
2—At Texas	L	6-7	Noles	Rijo
3—At Texas	W	5-4	Bystrom	Tanana
4—At Texas	W	5-0	Niekro	Stewart
5—At Minn.	L	4-5	Schrom	Guidry
6—At Minn.	L	4-9	Viola	Shirley
7—At Minn.	W	11-4	Rasmussen	Butcher
8—At Minn.	L	3-4†	Davis	Righetti
12—Kan. City	W	5-2	Niekro	Gura
13—Kan. City	W	7-1	Guidry	Black
13—Kan. City	W	8-1	Bystrom	Saberhagen
14—Kan. City	W	4-1	Rasmussen	Gubicza
15—Kan. City	W	4-1	Fontenot	Leibrandt
16—Texas	W	9-8	Armstrong	Schmidt
17—Texas	L	4-10	Hough	Niekro
18—Texas	W	3-1	Guidry	Mason
19—Minnesota	L	1-2	Whitehouse	Righetti
20—Minnesota	W	4-3	Howell	Davis
21—Minnesota	L	2-5	Smithson	Fontenot
22—Minnesota	W	6-5	Cowley	Viola
23—At Milw.	L	4-6	Sutton	Guidry
24—At Milw.	L	1-2‡	Ladd	Cowley
25—At Milw.	W	3-0	Rasmussen	Caldwell
27—At Chicago	W	8-6	Armstrong	Hoyt
28—At Chicago	W	3-2	Guidry	Nelson
29—At Chicago	L	4-5	Bannister	Bystrom
30—Milwaukee	W	4-3	Rasmussen	Caldwell
31—Milwaukee	W	7-4	Fontenot	Beene

Won 17, Lost 11

AUGUST

Date	W/L	Score	Winner	Loser
1—Milwaukee	W	7-3	Niekro	Cocanower
2—Milwaukee	W	6-4	Howell	Tellmann
3—Cleveland	W	9-0	Cowley	Comer
3—Cleveland	W	3-2	Armstrong	Camacho
4—Cleveland	W	8-5	Ramussen	Smith
5—Cleveland	W	4-0	Fontenot	Heaton
7—Chicago	L	3-6	Hoyt	Deshaies
7—Chicago	W	7-0	Guidry	Gleaton
8—Chicago	L	4-5	Bannister	Niekro
9—Chicago	W	7-6	Rasmussen	Seaver
10—At Cleve.	W	6-4	Cowley	Schulze
10—At Cleve.	W	10-1	Fontenot	Heaton
11—At Cleve.	W	10-1	Niekro	Farr
12—At Cleve.	L	0-6	Blyleven	Guidry
13—At Cleve.	L	5-6‡	Farr	Righetti
14—Seattle	L	1-2	Langston	Rasmussen
15—Seattle	W	3-2	Cowley	Beattie
16—Seattle	L	4-5	Barojas	Niekro
17—Oakland	L	3-7	Krueger	Fontenot
18—Oakland	W	8-0	Montefusco	McCatty
19—Oakland	W	9-6	Howell	Caudill
20—California	W	8-4	Cowley	John
21—California	W	8-2	Niekro	Romanick
22—California	L	1-2	Slaton	Fontenot
24—At Seattle	W	6-4†	Righetti	Stanton
25—At Seattle	W	14-1	Rasmussen	Beattie
26—At Seattle	W	7-2	Niekro	Barojas
27—At Oak.	W	8-7	Righetti	Caudill
28—At Oak.	L	3-4§	Caudill	Murray
29—At Oak.	W	4-1	Montefusco	McCatty
31—At Calif.	L	3-4	Curtis	Armstrong

Won 21, Lost 10

SEPTEMBER

Date	W/L	Score	Winner	Loser
1—At Calif.	L	6-11	Corbett	Righetti
2—At Calif.	W	5-3	Howell	Curtis
3—Toronto	W	2-0	Cowley	Leal
4—Toronto	L	4-6	Clancy	Armstrong
5—Toronto	W	4-3†	Righetti	Jackson
7—At Boston	W	4-2	Howell	Ojeda
8—At Boston	W	12-6	Cowley	Hurst
9—At Boston	L	1-10	Nipper	Bystrom
10—At Toronto	W	6-2	Montefusco	Stieb
11—At Toronto	L	3-10	Lamp	Rasmussen
12—At Toronto	L	1-2	Alexander	Niekro
13—At Toronto	W	6-1	Fontenot	Leal
14—Boston	W	7-1	Cowley	Hurst
15—Boston	L	3-4	Nipper	Montefusco
16—Boston	L	3-5	Boyd	Rasmussen
17—Baltimore	W	12-7	Howell	Pacella
18—Baltimore	W	10-2	Fontenot	D. Martinez
19—Baltimore	W	6-5	Cowley	Boddicker
21—At Detroit	W	5-3	Montefusco	Wilcox
22—At Detroit	L	0-6	Petry	Christiansen
23—At Detroit	L	1-4	Morris	Fontenot
24—At Balt.	L	1-8	Boddicker	Guidry
24—At Balt.	L	6-7	Snell	Righetti
25—At Balt.	W	6-5	Shirley	Brown
26—At Balt.	W	3-1	Montefusco	Davis
27—Detroit	W	2-1	Shirley	Hernandez
28—Detroit	L	2-4§	Bair	Cowley
29—Detroit	L	3-11	Berenguer	Guidry
30—Detroit	W	9-2	Rasmussen	O'Neal

Won 16, Lost 13

*5 innings.   †10 innings.   ‡11 innings.   §12 innings.   x13 innings.   y16 innings.   z17 innings.

Dave Righetti responded to his bullpen shift with 31 saves.

The 25-year-old lefthander had a 14-8 record as a starter in 1983, including a no-hitter against Boston, but the departure of free agent Goose Gossage to San Diego left a gaping hole in the bullpen, and Berra, despite opposition from Owner George Steinbrenner, selected Righetti as his new stopper. Righetti, initially reluctant, warmed to his new role and finished with 31 saves, fourth in the league and the third-highest single-season total ever by a Yankee.

Righetti was aided by hard-throwing Jay Howell, who registered a 9-4 record, seven saves and a 2.69 ERA while emerging as an ideal setup man. The new combination reminded many observers of the Gossage-Ron Davis duo of 1980-81.

It was during the first-half struggles that Berra was forced to resist putting Righetti back in the starting rotation, which was, except for Niekro, flat.

Ron Guidry, who finished with a 10-11 record and a 4.51 ERA, the worst season by far of his eight-year major league career, was rocked frequently in the first half. John Montefusco (5-3, 3.58 ERA) spent more than three months on the disabled list before finishing strong in September. Shane Rawley (2-3, 6.21) was ineffective when he wasn't injured, and he was traded on June 30 to the Phillies for Marty Bystrom. Ray Fontenot, 8-2 as a

1983 rookie, was inconsistent and finished at 8-9.

After the All-Star break, however, the pitching—and everything else—changed for the better. The Yankees took off with six straight victories, including a five-game sweep of the Kansas City Royals. As if that wasn't enough of a boost for team spirit, the establishment of a kangaroo court kept the players hopping and laughing. Headed by Baylor, the court imposed fines for on-the-field blunders and clubhouse violations and became a source of rollicking humor.

The major transfusion of spirit, however, came in the form of new blood from Columbus, the club's Triple-A affiliate. Third baseman Mike Pagliarulo, shortstop Bobby Meacham, outfielders Brian Dayett and Vic Mata and pitchers Joe Cowley and Dennis Rasmussen completed the transformation of the Yankees.

Pagliarulo replaced Roy Smalley, who was traded to the Chicago White Sox in July. He was platooned with Toby Harrah at third and quickly proved to be a vast defensive improvement over Smalley. The rookie also surprised the Yankees with his bat, hitting only .239 but pounding seven homers and knocking in 34 runs in 201 at-bats.

Meacham had been banished to the minors by Steinbrenner after a game-losing error in the fourth game of the season. But he returned in mid-June to replace Andre Robertson, who still was not fully recovered from injuries he received in a 1983 car accident. Meacham became the everyday shortstop and was impressive offensively and defensively.

Left fielder Dayett and center fielder Mata became platoon players who provided fine defense. Rasmussen, a lefthander promoted in late May, had a 9-6 record and was especially effective during the second half. Cowley, a righthander called up at the All-Star break, ran up a 9-2 record and was 8-0 as a starter.

Veterans who made solid contributions included second baseman Willie Randolph, a .287 hitter who was among the league leaders in on-base percentage (.377) and walks (86); Baylor, who led the team with 27 homers and drove in 89 runs; catcher Butch Wynegar, who hit .267 with 45 RBIs, and part-time outfielders Ken Griffey (.273, 56 RBIs) and Steve Kemp (.291, 41 RBIs).

By the time the season ended, the first half had become a distant memory. "I wish we could start next season right away," said Berra, obviously anticipating a strong 1985 start for the Yankees.

Boston center fielder Tony Armas enjoyed a banner season, leading both leagues with 43 homers and 123 RBIs.

Red Sox Put On Power Display

By JOE GIULIOTTI

An awesome display of power, signs of pitching potential, a fourth-place finish and the end of a 40-year baseball career.

That basically sums up 1984 for the Boston Red Sox, who were far more exciting than in 1983 but were not much different as far as the final standings were concerned. They finished with a respectable 86-76 record, but with Detroit's strong start and their own weak one, they were all but eliminated from the American League East race by Memorial Day.

Manager Ralph Houk decided to call it quits after the season, his fourth in Boston, ending a long baseball career that began when he first played professionally in 1939. Houk, who won 1,619 games in 20 seasons as a major league manager, said that he wanted to spend more time with his family but that it still was not easy to decide to retire.

"One reason I hate to leave is we never went all the way," said Houk, 65. "I thought we had a legitimate shot this year, but the Tigers broke out to that 35-5 start and nobody could catch up. But the one thing I'm proud of is the team is a much better one than it was when I took over. And I hope the new manager can get the job done and win a pennant next year because I really think this team has a chance."

The Red Sox will have a chance only if their pitching improves. The club's 4.18 earned-run average was fourth from the bottom in the league, and no pitcher won more than 12 games. But the biggest culprit was the bullpen, which earned only 32 saves all season.

Bob Stanley, the club's bullpen ace in '83, had 22 saves and a 3.54 ERA but posted a 9-10 record and was inconsistent. Mark Clear (8-3, 4.03 ERA, eight saves) was tough to hit but was plagued by wildness, surrendering 70 walks in 67 innings. John Henry Johnson (1-2, 3.53) had three good spot starts and some fair middle-inning performances but could not get batters out in the short role. Steve Crawford (5-0, 3.34) finished 19 games but managed only one save.

The starters were not much better. Dennis (Oil Can) Boyd had a terrible start and was sent to Boston's Triple-A affiliate in Pawtucket in early May after going 0-3 with a 7.36 ERA. He returned for his first start in early June to improve his record to 12-12 with a 4.37 ERA and 10 complete games.

Jim Rice (above) and Dwight Evans completed Boston's 100-RBI outfield.

SCORES OF BOSTON RED SOX' 1984 GAMES

APRIL

Date		Score	Winner	Loser
2—At Calif.	L	1-2	Forsch	Hurst
4—At Calif.	W	2-1	Clear	Sanchez
5—At Calif.	W	7-4	Stanley	Kaufman
6—At Oak.	L	1-3	Sorensen	Boyd
7—At Oak.	W	3-0	Hurst	Warren
8—At Oak.	L	2-14	McCatty	Brown
10—At Seattle	L	1-5	Beattie	Ojeda
11—At Seattle	L	4-5	Young	Eckersley
13—Detroit	L	9-13	Bair	Hurst
17—Texas	L	4-8	Tanana	Eckersley
18—Texas	L	3-4	Darwin	Ojeda
19—Texas	L	4-7	Jones	Boyd
20—Oakland	W	3-1	Hurst	Conroy
21—Oakland	L	2-5	Warren	Brown
22—Oakland	W	12-8	Eckersley	McCatty
23—California	W	2-0*	Ojeda	Zahn
24—California	L	7-8	Sanchez	Stanley
25—Seattle	W	2-1	Hurst	Beattie
26—Seattle	L	5-6†	Vande Berg	Stanley
27—At Chicago	W	5-3	Eckersley	Hoyt
28—At Chicago	W	8-7	Clear	Reed
29—At Chicago	L	4-6	Dotson	Nipper

Won 9, Lost 13

MAY

Date		Score	Winner	Loser
1—At Detroit	L	2-11	Wilcox	Hurst
2—At Detroit	W	5-4	Brown	Berenguer
3—At Detroit	W	1-0	Ojeda	Morris
4—Chicago	L	3-5	Seaver	Eckersley
5—Chicago	L	5-8	Dotson	Boyd
6—Chicago	W	3-1	Hurst	Bannister
8—At Texas	L	3-4	Hough	Brown
9—At Texas	W	2-0	Ojeda	Mason
11—At Kan. C.	L	4-6	Gura	Eckersley
12—At Kan. C.	L	0-3	Gubicza	Hurst
13—At Kan. C.	L	1-5	Black	Brown
14—At Cleve.	W	6-1	Ojeda	Behenna
15—At Cleve.	L	5-7	Waddell	Johnson
16—At Cleve.	W	5-2	Eckersley	Farr
17—At Cleve.	W	11-10†	Crawford	Camacho
18—At Minn.	L	3-8	Smithson	Brown
19—At Minn.	L	0-7	Viola	Ojeda
20—At Minn.	W	5-4	Clemens	Butcher
21—Cleveland	W	6-3	Eckersley	Farr
22—Cleveland	W	7-1	Hurst	Sutcliffe
23—Cleveland	L	4-5	Waddell	Stanley
25—Kan. City	L	5-8	Saberhagen	Ojeda
26—Kan. City	L	7-11	Splittorff	Stanley
27—Kan. City	W	6-0	Hurst	Beckwith
30—Minnesota	W	2-0	Ojeda	Butcher

Won 12, Lost 13

JUNE

Date		Score	Winner	Loser
1—At Milw.	W	3-1	Hurst	Sutton
2—At Milw.	W	6-3	Clemens	Porter
3—At Milw.	W	6-3	Clear	Ladd
4—At N.Y.	L	3-8	Guidry	Ojeda
5—At N.Y.	W	5-4	Clear	Howell
6—At N.Y.	W	5-3	Hurst	Rijo
7—Milwaukee	L	3-6	McClure	Clemens
8—Milwaukee	W	11-3	Boyd	Haas
9—Milwaukee	W	15-6	Ojeda	Gibson
10—Milwaukee	W	5-4	Gale	Waits
11—New York	W	9-6	Clear	Howell
12—New York	W	9-8	Crawford	Righetti
13—New York	L	2-4	Niekro	Boyd
14—New York	L	11-12†	Fontenot	Stanley
15—At Toronto	L	3-4‡	Lamp	Clear
16—At Toronto	L	0-7	Leal	Hurst
17—At Toronto	L	3-5	Clancy	Gale
19—Baltimore	L	7-9	Swaggerty	Stanley
20—Baltimore	L	1-4	Boddicker	Boyd
21—Toronto	L	2-5	Leal	Nipper
22—Toronto	W	8-1	Clemens	Clancy
23—Toronto	L	3-9	Gott	Gale
24—Toronto	W	5-3†	Stanley	Lamp
25—At Balt.	W	7-4	Boyd	Davis
26—At Balt.	W	5-2	Nipper	Boddicker
27—At Balt.	L	1-3	McGregor	Clemens
28—Seattle	W	9-6†	Stanley	Mirabella
29—Seattle	L	3-5	Vande Berg	Ojeda
30—Seattle	L	1-2	Beattie	Boyd

Won 15, Lost 14

JULY

Date		Score	Winner	Loser
1—Seattle	L	0-1	Langston	Nipper
2—Oakland	L	6-9‡	Caudill	Clear
3—Oakland	W	6-5	Stanley	Sorensen
4—Oakland	W	13-9†	Crawford	Heimueller
5—California	W	12-7	Boyd	Zahn

JULY

Date		Score	Winner	Loser
6—California	W	8-7	Nipper	Slaton
8—California	W	3-2†	Stanley	Sanchez
8—California	L	0-4	John	Clemens
12—At Seattle	L	2-3	Langston	Ojeda
13—At Seattle	W	9-5	Boyd	Moore
14—At Seattle	L	4-5	Vande Berg	Clemens
15—At Seattle	W	11-3	Nipper	Beattie
16—At Oak.	W	4-1	Hurst	Sorensen
17—At Oak.	W	6-1	Ojeda	Krueger
18—At Oak.	L	2-7	Burris	Boyd
20—At Calif.	W	4-3†	Hurst	Aase
21—At Calif.	W	16-4	Hurst	John
22—At Calif.	W	3-0	Ojeda	Slaton
24—Chicago	W	3-2	Boyd	Bannister
25—Chicago	W	3-2§	Clear	Gleaton
26—Chicago	W	7-0	Clemens	Dotson
27—At Detroit	L	1-9	Petry	Hurst
27—At Detroit	W	4-0	Ojeda	Abbott
28—At Detroit	W	3-2	Stanley	Morris
29—At Detroit	L	0-3	Wilcox	Boyd
30—At Chicago	L	0-7	Seaver	Nipper
31—At Chicago	W	14-4	Clemens	Dotson

Won 18, Lost 9

AUGUST

Date		Score	Winner	Loser
1—At Chicago	L	3-5	Hoyt	Ojeda
3—Texas	L	3-4†	Schmidt	Stanley
4—Texas	W	5-2	Boyd	Tanana
5—Texas	W	4-2	Nipper	Hough
6—Detroit	L	7-9	Lopez	Ojeda
6—Detroit	W	10-2	Clemens	Willis
7—Detroit	W	12-7	Hurst	Morris
7—Detroit	L	5-7‡	Lopez	Gale
8—Detroit	W	8-0	Boyd	Abbott
9—At Texas	L	3-7	Tanana	Nipper
10—At Texas	L	4-8	Hough	Ojeda
11—At Texas	W	5-4	Clemens	Stewart
12—At Texas	W	3-2‡	Clear	Schmidt
13—At Kan. C.	L	1-6	Black	Boyd
14—At Kan. C.	W	8-2	Nipper	Gubicza
15—At Kan. C.	L	8-13	Beckwith	Stanley
16—Minnesota	W	7-5	Crawford	Davis
17—Minnesota	L	5-6	Viola	Hurst
18—Minnesota	L	4-6	Davis	Stanley
18—Minnesota	L	1-3	Castillo	Johnson
19—Minnesota	W	5-4	Crawford	Whitehouse
20—Kan. City	L	5-8	Gubicza	Brown
21—Kan. City	W	11-1	Clemens	Leibrandt
22—Kan. City	L	2-6	Beckwith	Hurst
24—Cleveland	W	7-6	Boyd	Comer
25—Cleveland	W	11-6	Nipper	Farr
26—Cleveland	W	4-2	Clemens	Smith
28—At Minn.	L	1-2	Davis	Stanley
29—At Minn.	W	4-0	Boyd	Butcher
30—At Minn.	W	9-3	Nipper	Hodge
31—At Cleve.	W	8-7	Stanley	Camacho

Won 17, Lost 14

SEPTEMBER

Date		Score	Winner	Loser
1—At Cleve.	W	4-1	Ojeda	Blyleven
2—At Cleve.	L	3-8	Waddell	Clear
3—At Milw.	W	8-5	Boyd	Cocanower
4—At Milw.	W	3-1	Nipper	Sutton
5—At Milw.	L	5-7	Haas	Brown
7—New York	L	2-4	Howell	Ojeda
8—New York	L	6-12	Cowley	Hurst
9—New York	W	10-1	Nipper	Bystrom
10—Milwaukee	L	4-7	Sutton	Brown
11—Milwaukee	L	6-14	Haas	Boyd
12—Milwaukee	W	5-4	Ojeda	McClure
14—At N.Y.	L	1-7	Cowley	Hurst
15—At N.Y.	W	4-3	Nipper	Montefusco
16—At N.Y.	W	5-3	Boyd	Rasmussen
17—At Toronto	L	4-5	Alexander	Ojeda
18—At Toronto	W	10-3	Gale	Leal
19—At Toronto	W	10-4	Hurst	Clancy
20—At Balt.	L	1-15	Flanagan	Nipper
21—At Balt.	W	8-0	Boyd	Davis
22—At Balt.	W	4-2	Ojeda	Dixon
23—At Balt.	W	6-2	Johnson	D. Martinez
24—Toronto	L	8-9	Clancy	Hurst
25—Toronto	W	14-6	Nipper	Stieb
26—Toronto	L	4-8	Alexander	Boyd
27—Baltimore	W	4-3	Clear	Stewart
28—Baltimore	W	5-4	Stanley	Snell
29—Baltimore	L	3-6	Boddicker	Hurst
30—Baltimore	L	3-5	Brown	Boyd

Won 15, Lost 13

*6 innings.　†10 innings.　‡11 innings.　§12 innings.

Rookie Roger Clemens pitched well before suffering a season-ending injury.

Also going 12-12 were lefthanders Bruce Hurst and Bob Ojeda. Hurst, however, was only 4-8 after June 6, and Ojeda, while tying for the league lead in shutouts with five, had a 3.99 ERA.

Righthander Mike Brown, who started the season in the rotation, was another disappointment, being sent to the minors after posting a 1-5 record through mid-May. Used only sparingly after being called back in August, Brown lost three more games.

There were two bright spots in Boston's pitching situation that bode well for the future: rookies Roger Clemens and Al Nipper.

Clemens, who was called up from Pawtucket in mid-May, won nine games in 13 decisions and averaged just under nine strikeouts per nine innings pitched. He was lost for the season, however, after suffering a slight muscle tear in his right (pitching) arm on August 31.

Nipper became the team's most consistent starter after joining the rotation in June. He finished at 11-6 with a 3.89 ERA.

Fielding, like pitching, was not a strong point for Boston. The Red Sox committed 143 errors, only three fewer than the league's most error-prone teams (Oakland and Cleveland), and turned only 128 double plays, the lowest total in the league.

An infield that was 75 percent new by June was largely responsible for the defensive breakdown. Rookie Jackie Gutierrez replaced Glenn Hoffman at shortstop and showed potential but left plenty

of room for improvement by making 31 errors, the second-highest total by an American League player. Veteran Bill Buckner, who was acquired in a trade for pitcher Dennis Eckersley in May, provided some stability at first base. A season-ending injury to Jerry Remy in May made room for Marty Barrett, who committed only nine errors (while hitting .303) and made second base the most solid point in the infield. But third baseman Wade Boggs, the only infielder who was a regular on the '83 team, made 20 errors.

Obviously, a team with these weaknesses that won 10 more games than it lost had to be doing something right, and the Red Sox were. They were hitting up a storm.

The Red Sox were at or near the top of almost every club and individual offensive category. The team's .283 batting average, 1,598 hits and 2,490 total bases all were league-leading totals.

Boston's outfield provided the club's most devastating assault on opposing pitchers. Center fielder Tony Armas led both leagues with 43 home runs and 123 runs batted in while hitting .268. Left fielder Jim Rice's statistics were down slightly from his incredible 1983 season, but his .280 average, 28 homers and 122 RBIs still were among the best all-around totals in the league. And right fielder Dwight Evans was right up there among the leaders with a .295 average, 32 homers, 104 RBIs, 37 doubles, eight triples, 96 walks and 121 runs scored (first in the league).

Boggs, the A.L. batting champion in '83 with a .361 average, pounded out more than 200 hits for the second consecutive year and finished at .325, No. 3 in the league.

Designated hitter Mike Easler, who was obtained in an off-season trade for pitcher John Tudor, did what he was hired to do, hitting .313 with 27 homers and 91 RBIs.

A final indicator of Boston's strength at the plate is the fact that no starter for the Red Sox batted below .260. Buckner (.278), Gutierrez (.263) and catcher Rich Gedman (.269) completed the Red Sox lineup.

Boston's only offensive weakness was basestealing, in which the Red Sox ranked last in the league with 38. Gutierrez, with just 12 stolen bases, was the team leader.

The Red Sox played better on the road, where they were 45-36, than they did at home (41-40). Home attendance also was down as 1,661,618 fans visited Fenway Park, about 120,000 fewer than the year before.

Baltimore first baseman Eddie Murray was his usual devastating self, hitting .306 with 29 homers and 110 RBIs.

Offensive Problems Plague O's

By JIM HENNEMAN

Entering the 1984 season, five consecutive World Series championship teams had failed to successfully defend their league titles.

The Baltimore Orioles made it six.

From the start, nothing went right for Manager Joe Altobelli's team. That in itself wasn't unusual because the Orioles are known for their sluggish starts. This time, however, the Detroit Tigers and Toronto Blue Jays put so much distance between themselves and the rest of the division so fast that the Orioles never were in the American League East race.

Thanks to brilliant performances by first baseman Eddie Murray and pitcher Mike Boddicker and a solid season from shortstop Cal Ripken, the Orioles ran third most of the season. But they never were able to mount a sustained drive, and eventually the Orioles were overtaken by both the Yankees and the Red Sox.

The fifth-place finish was the club's lowest since 1967, and its 85-77 record, though respectable, marked only the third time in that span that the Orioles had failed to win 90 games in a full season. The club's nosedive in the tough A.L. East standings triggered a few late-season moves that hinted there would be several roster changes for the 1985 team.

Designated hitter Ken Singleton and outfielder Al Bumbry, two principals since the early 1970s with the Orioles, were informed that they would not be offered contracts for 1985. The same was true for Benny Ayala, who served more than five years as a righthanded hitting specialist, and Tom Underwood, who had an undistinguished year (one win and one save in 37 appearances) after being signed as a free agent to bolster the bullpen.

The problem was primarily offensive. The pitchers, overall, were solid if not spectacular, but their performance alone was not enough to carry a team that scored 118 fewer runs than the year before and batted only .252, 17 points below its 1983 average.

Murray and Ripken were the only consistent hitters in Baltimore's lineup.

Murray batted .306, hit 29 home runs, drove in 110 runs and received 107 walks, all team-leading figures. The switch-hitter also led the league in on-base percentage (.410) and game-winning runs batted in (19).

Ripken, the league's Most Valuable Player in '83, posted another strong sea-

Shortstop Cal Ripken hit .304 and enjoyed another solid season.

son, batting .304 with 27 homers and 86 RBIs. In his third full season in the majors, Ripken also led the Orioles in runs scored (103), hits (195) and several other categories.

The loss of outfielder Dan Ford, a .280 hitter in 1983, for all but 25 games in '84 because of knee problems left a void in the second spot in the batting order. But that didn't explain the offensive declines by the rest of the Orioles.

John Lowenstein and Gary Roenicke, who combined for 34 home runs and 124 RBIs while sharing left field in '83, managed only 18 homers and 72 RBIs while batting under .240. Singleton went from .276 and 84 RBIs to .215 and 36 RBIs. Outfielder John Shelby went from .258 to .209. Bumbry, hitting .270, had only 24 RBIs. And catcher Rick Dempsey and second baseman Rich Dauer both hit below their career averages.

The downward trend also was evident in the bullpen. Tippy Martinez, the Orioles' ace reliever, was troubled by a sore shoulder and suffered through the worst year of his career. After going 9-3 with 21 saves and a 2.35 earned-run average in '83, Martinez stumbled to 4-9, only the second losing season in his 10-year major league career. The lefthander did lead the club with 17 saves, but his 3.91 ERA was a better indication of his overall season.

Sammy Stewart, Martinez's righthanded counterpart, avoided a dropoff with a

SCORES OF BALTIMORE ORIOLES' 1984 GAMES

APRIL

Date		Score	Winner	Loser
2—Chicago	L	2-5	Hoyt	McGregor
6—At Minn.	L	4-9	Smithson	Boddicker
7—At Minn.	L	4-13	Butcher	Flanagan
8—At Minn.	L	3-7	Williams	Palmer
10—Kan. City	W	6-3	McGregor	Splittorff
11—Kan. City	L	2-5	Gura	Boddicker
14—At Cleve.	L	2-8	Sutcliffe	McGregor
15—At Cleve.	W	6-5	Stewart	Frazier
16—At Cleve.	L	3-4	Blyleven	Flanagan
17—At Toronto	L	2-3	Key	T. Martinez
18—At Toronto	L	1-7	Stieb	Palmer
19—At Toronto	L	1-2	Clancy	McGregor
20—Minnesota	W	4-2*	Stewart	Davis
21—Minnesota	W	5-3	Flanagan	Smithson
22—Minnesota	L	1-6	Butcher	Boddicker
23—At Chicago	L	6-7*	Burns	T. Martinez
24—At Chicago	W	8-3	McGregor	Dotson
25—At Kan. C.	L	2-3	Quisenberry	T. Martinez
26—At Kan. C.	W	11-3	Flanagan	Jackson
27—Texas	W	4-3†	Stewart	Tobik
28—Texas	W	6-1	McGregor	Hough
29—Texas	W	3-2	Davis	Stewart
30—Cleveland	W	6-3	Stewart	Camacho

Won 10, Lost 13

MAY

Date		Score	Winner	Loser
1—Cleveland	W	3-0	Boddicker	Blyleven
2—Cleveland	L	7-9‡	Frazier	Palmer
4—At Texas	W	2-0	Davis	Schmidt
5—At Texas	W	7-5	D. Martinez	Wright
6—At Texas	W	6-1	Boddicker	Tanana
9—Toronto	W	7-4	McGregor	Clancy
9—Toronto	W	7-3	T. Martinez	Key
10—Toronto	L	3-4*	Jackson	D. Martinez
11—Oakland	W	4-3	Boddicker	Warren
12—Oakland	L	2-12	Krueger	D. Martinez
13—Oakland	W	5-1	Davis	McCatty
14—California	W	4-1	McGregor	Zahn
15—California	L	2-5	Romanick	Flanagan
16—California	W	5-0	Boddicker	Witt
18—Seattle	W	4-1	Davis	Beattie
19—Seattle	L	5-6*	Vande Berg	T. Martinez
20—Seattle	W	5-1	Flanagan	Moore
22—At Oak.	L	4-6	Burris	Boddicker
23—At Oak.	W	9-5	Swaggerty	Warren
24—At Oak.	L	2-3	Krueger	Davis
25—At Calif.	L	2-10	Romanick	Flanagan
26—At Calif.	W	9-5	Boddicker	Swan
27—At Calif.	W	8-0	McGregor	Witt
28—At Seattle	W	7-4	Davis	Beattie
29—At Seattle	W	3-2	T. Martinez	Mirabella
30—At Seattle	W	8-2	Boddicker	Vande Berg

Won 18, Lost 8

JUNE

Date		Score	Winner	Loser
1—At Detroit	L	2-14	Petry	McGregor
2—At Detroit	W	5-0	Davis	Morris
3—At Detroit	W	2-1	Flanagan	Wilcox
4—Milwaukee	W	6-2	Boddicker	Ladd
5—Milwaukee	L	3-8	Cocanower	Swaggerty
6—Milwaukee	W	3-0	McGregor	Sutton
8—Detroit	L	2-3	Wilcox	Davis
9—Detroit	W	4-0	Flanagan	Berenguer
10—Detroit	L	4-10	Bair	Boddicker
10—Detroit	L	0-8	Petry	D. Martinez
11—At Milw.	W	3-1	McGregor	Sutton
12—At Milw.	W	5-4	T. Martinez	Fingers
13—At Milw.	L	1-6	Haas	Flanagan
14—At Milw.	L	2-3	Waits	Davis
15—At N.Y.	W	2-1	Boddicker	Shirley
16—At N.Y.	L	3-8	Howell	McGregor
17—At N.Y.	W	6-2	Flanagan	Rasmussen
19—At Boston	W	9-7	Swaggerty	Stanley
20—At Boston	W	4-1	Boddicker	Boyd
21—New York	L	3-5	Rawley	McGregor
22—New York	W	5-4	Flanagan	Rasmussen
23—New York	L	4-5†	Rijo	T. Martinez
25—Boston	L	4-7	Boyd	Davis
26—Boston	L	2-5	Nipper	Boddicker
27—Boston	W	3-1	McGregor	Clemens
28—At Chicago	W	2-0	Flanagan	Seaver
29—At Chicago	L	1-2	Dotson	D. Martinez
30—At Chicago	L	4-5†	Jones	Stewart

Won 14, Lost 14

JULY

Date		Score	Winner	Loser
1—At Chicago	W	8-3	Boddicker	Hoyt
2—At Minn.	L	4-6	Butcher	McGregor
3—At Minn.	L	1-3	Smithson	Flanagan
4—At Minn.	W	6-4	D. Martinez	Williams
6—Kan. City	L	2-6	Leibrandt	Boddicker
7—Kan. City	W	6-2	McGregor	Gura
7—Kan. City	W	8-0	Flanagan	Jones
8—Kan. City	L	1-6	Black	D. Martinez
12—Chicago	W	2-1	Davis	Hoyt
12—Chicago	W	3-0	McGregor	Nelson
13—Chicago	W	7-5†	T. Martinez	Reed
14—Chicago	L	2-3	Seaver	Flanagan
15—Chicago	W	6-4	D. Martinez	Dotson
16—Minnesota	W	3-1	Davis	Smithson
17—Minnesota	W	3-1	McGregor	Viola
18—Minnesota	L	1-3	Butcher	Boddicker
19—At Kan. C.	L	3-6	Gubicza	Flanagan
20—At Kan. C.	L	3-4	Saberhagen	T. Martinez
21—At Kan. C.	W	4-3	Davis	Huismann
22—At Kan. C.	L	4-8	Gura	McGregor
23—At Texas	W	9-5	Boddicker	Mason
24—At Texas	L	2-3	Darwin	Flanagan
25—At Texas	W	3-1	D. Martinez	Tanana
27—Cleveland	W	4-3	Davis	Heaton
28—Cleveland	L	3-6	Blyleven	McGregor
29—Cleveland	W	3-1	Boddicker	Comer
30—Texas	L	1-5	Tanana	Flanagan
31—Texas	L	6-7	Jones	T. Martinez

Won 15, Lost 13

AUGUST

Date		Score	Winner	Loser
1—Texas	W	7-2	Davis	Hough
3—Toronto	L	2-5	Jackson	McGregor
4—Toronto	L	2-6	Clancy	Flanagan
5—Toronto	L	3-4	Key	T. Martinez
6—At Cleve.	W	4-2	Davis	Farr
7—At Cleve.	L	4-5	Blyleven	McGregor
8—At Cleve.	W	7-4	Boddicker	Comer
9—At Cleve.	L	5-7	Easterly	Brown
10—At Toronto	L	0-2	Alexander	D. Martinez
11—At Toronto	L	2-3	Gott	Davis
12—At Toronto	W	5-4	McGregor	Jackson
13—At Toronto	W	2-1	Boddicker	Clancy
14—Oakland	L	3-4	Burgmeier	Stewart
15—Oakland	L	1-6	Young	D. Martinez
16—Oakland	L	1-8	Sorensen	Davis
17—California	W	6-5	McGregor	Slaton
18—California	W	1-0	Boddicker	Witt
19—California	W	10-4	Flanagan	Kison
20—Seattle	W	5-4	D. Martinez	Beattie
21—Seattle	L	3-4	Barojas	Davis
22—Seattle	W	4-0	McGregor	Moore
24—At Oak.	W	4-2	Boddicker	McCatty
25—At Oak.	W	4-2	Flanagan	Burris
26—At Oak.	W	13-6	Underwood	Young
27—At Calif.	W	7-6*	Stewart	Sanchez
28—At Calif.	L	2-4	Slaton	McGregor
29—At Calif.	L	5-7	Corbett	Boddicker
31—At Seattle	W	11-7	Stewart	Mirabella

Won 15, Lost 13

SEPTEMBER

Date		Score	Winner	Loser
1—At Seattle	L	9-10	Vande Berg	T. Martinez
2—At Seattle	W	4-3	Swaggerty	Moore
3—At Detroit	W	7-4	Stewart	Morris
4—At Detroit	W	4-1	Boddicker	Rozema
5—At Detroit	L	0-1	Berenguer	Flanagan
7—Milwaukee	L	8-10	Tellmann	Stewart
8—Milwaukee	W	5-3	Davis	Lazorko
9—Milwaukee	W	4-0	Boddicker	Gibson
10—Detroit	W	3-1	Flanagan	Berenguer
11—Detroit	L	2-9	Petry	Swaggerty
12—Detroit	W	3-1	D. Martinez	Mason
14—At Milw.	L	2-4	Candiotti	Boddicker
15—At Milw.	L	0-7	Gibson	Flanagan
16—At Milw.	W	11-8	Davis	Sutton
17—At N.Y.	L	7-12	Howell	Pacella
18—At N.Y.	L	2-10	Fontenot	D. Martinez
19—At N.Y.	L	5-6	Cowley	Boddicker
20—Boston	W	15-1	Flanagan	Nipper
21—Boston	L	0-8	Boyd	Davis
22—Boston	L	2-4	Ojeda	Dixon
23—Boston	L	2-6	Johnson	D. Martinez
24—New York	W	8-1	Boddicker	Guidry
24—New York	W	7-6	Snell	Righetti
25—New York	L	5-6	Shirley	Brown
26—New York	L	1-3	Montefusco	Davis
27—At Boston	L	3-4	Clear	Stewart
28—At Boston	L	4-5	Stanley	Snell
29—At Boston	W	6-3	Boddicker	Hurst
30—At Boston	W	5-3	Brown	Boyd

Won 13, Lost 16

*10 innings.   †11 innings.   ‡16 innings.

A sore shoulder contributed to the worst season in relief ace Tippy Martinez' career.

7-4 record, 13 saves and a 3.29 ERA, but the bullpen as a whole never established any consistency.

In addition to Ford, the Orioles suffered three other costly injuries: to catcher Joe Nolan (knee), who accumulated only 62 at-bats, outfielder Jim Dwyer (knee), who missed more than half the season, and pitcher Scott McGregor, who was 15-12 despite missing the last month with a broken finger.

Veteran infielder Wayne Gross and rookie outfielder Mike Young picked up some of the slack, but not enough to offset the general decline. Despite hitting just .216, Gross was about as effective as the Orioles had expected when they acquired him from Oakland to platoon with Todd Cruz at third base. Gross hit 22 home runs and drove in 64 runs, and his 68 walks gave him a respectable on-base percentage of .346.

After failing to make the club during spring training, Young capitalized on Ford's injury to stake his claim to a piece of the club's future. He started slowly but finished with a respectable .252 batting average.

Led by Boddicker, the Orioles' starting pitchers earned mostly high grades. Boddicker, who went 16-8 as a rookie the year before, was the league's only 20-game winner (20-11) as well as the league's ERA champ with a 2.79 mark. The right-hander also logged 16 complete games, second best in the league, and finished with four shutouts, giving him nine in the last two years.

Storm Davis posted a 14-9 record and a 3.12 ERA but struggled after winning six of his first seven decisions. He started the season in the bullpen but earned a regular spot in the rotation after Jim Palmer retired. Palmer had been in the Baltimore organization since 1963 and ended his major league career with a 268-152 record.

Lefty Mike Flanagan finished with a mediocre 13-13 record and a 3.53 ERA. Flanagan, who was sidelined with a knee injury for three months in 1983, discarded his protective brace six weeks into the season and started 34 games, matching Boddicker for the team lead.

Dennis Martinez, who went 6-9 with a 5.02 ERA and started 20 games, was the only disappointment among the regulars in the rotation.

An attendance record was set at Memorial Stadium as 2,045,784 fans watched the Orioles play at home in 1984. That was 3,713 more spectators than the year before, when the 2 million level was reached in Baltimore for the first time.

Designated hitter Andre Thornton led the Indians with 33 homers and 99 RBIs.

Indians Finally Show Punch

By SHELDON OCKER

The 1984 Cleveland Indians actually were two teams.

The first group won just 17 of 50 games through June 5. After that, an oddly different gathering of Indians began flexing new muscle as the run-starved Tribe went on a power binge. Despite shaky starting pitching, Cleveland went on to post a 58-54 record in the final 112 games.

The reason for this turnabout was simple: The Tribe suddenly went from bunting and stealing and scratching for runs to scoring in bunches. In early June, Cleveland was languishing near the bottom of the American League in runs, yet the Tribe finished the year as the third-best run producer in the league. Over the last 112 games, the Indians hit 102 home runs, compared with just 21 in the first 50 games.

The culmination of this transformation came on September 28, when Cleveland was ending its season with a four-game home stand against the Minnesota Twins. The Twins, who were fighting to stay alive in the A.L. West race with Kansas City, hammered out 10 runs in the first three innings.

No problem. With the help of a seven-run sixth inning, Cleveland went on to win, 11-10, thanks largely to two homers by rookie Joe Carter and one by designated hitter Andre Thornton. The Indians also won the last two games against Minnesota to finish the season with a six-game winning streak and a 75-87 record, good for sixth place in the A.L. East.

"You know, there are still people around who don't know we can score," Manager Pat Corrales said the next day. Corrales was not talking about the casual fan; he meant hardened baseball professionals.

The change in the character of the Indians came suddenly. Corrales had planned to surround Thornton, the Tribe's only legitimate power threat—he finished 1984 with 33 homers, 99 runs batted in and a .271 batting average—with players whose forte was supposed to be reaching base in any way possible. Corrales' grand design was for a speedy foursome of Otis Nixon, Brett Butler, Tony Bernazard and Julio Franco to set the table for Thornton and infielder Pat Tabler. But Nixon was unable to raise his average above .160, and Bernazard was struggling below .220 entering the middle of June. It was obvious that changes were necessary.

The front office made a key trade June

Shortstop Julio Franco (above) enjoyed his second straight productive season while Joe Carter arrived late and hit 13 home runs.

SCORES OF CLEVELAND INDIANS' 1984 GAMES

APRIL			Winner	Loser
3—At Texas	W	9-1	Sutcliffe	Hough
5—At Texas	W	7-3	Heaton	Stewart
6—At Kan. C.	W	2-0	Blyleven	Gubicza
8—At Kan. C.	L	4-5	Black	Frazier
10—At Chicago	L	3-7	Hoyt	Heaton
11—At Chicago	L	1-6	Dotson	Blyleven
14—Baltimore	W	8-2	Sutcliffe	McGregor
15—Baltimore	L	5-6	Stewart	Frazier
16—Baltimore	W	4-3	Blyleven	Flanagan
18—New York	L	0-5	Niekro	Sutcliffe
20—Kan. City	L	4-6	Gura	Heaton
21—Kan. City	W	3-2	Blyleven	Jackson
23—Texas	W	3-1	Sutcliffe	Hough
25—Chicago	W	9-2	Heaton	Bannister
26—Chicago	W	5-4	Frazier	Reed
27—At Detroit	W	8-4z	Aponte	Abbott
28—At Detroit	L	2-6	Morris	Behenna
29—At Detroit	L	1-6	Petry	Spillner
30—At Balt.	L	3-6	Stewart	Camacho
Won 10, Lost 9				

MAY				
1—At Balt.	L	0-3	Boddicker	Blyleven
2—At Balt.	W	9-7y	Frazier	Palmer
4—Detroit	L	2-9	Petry	Spillner
5—Detroit	L	5-6	Abbott	Heaton
6—Detroit	L	5-6§	Lopez	Camacho
7—At N.Y.	L	2-5	Rawley	Behenna
9—At N.Y.	L	4-11	Niekro	Sutcliffe
10—At N.Y.	L	6-7y	Rijo	Waddell
12—Toronto	W	8-4	Blyleven	Acker
13—Toronto	T	4-4*	......	......
14—Boston	L	1-6	Ojeda	Behenna
15—Boston	W	7-5	Waddell	Johnson
16—Boston	L	2-5	Eckersley	Farr
17—Boston	L	10-11†	Crawford	Camacho
18—At Milw.	W	8-4	Jeffcoat	Ladd
19—At Milw.	L	0-3	Cocanower	Spillner
20—At Milw.	W	3-2	Camacho	Sutton
21—At Bos.	L	3-6	Eckersley	Farr
22—At Bos.	L	1-7	Hurst	Sutcliffe
23—At Bos.	W	5-4	Waddell	Stanley
25—At Toronto	L	1-5	Stieb	Heaton
26—At Toronto	L	1-2	Alexander	Farr
27—At Toronto	L	1-6	Leal	Sutcliffe
27—At Toronto	L	5-6	Jackson	Camacho
29—Milwaukee	L	3-5	Haas	Spillner
30—Milwaukee	W	9-1	Heaton	Caldwell
30—Milwaukee	L	2-3†	Cocanower	Waddell
Won 7, Lost 19				

JUNE				
1—California	L	2-5	Witt	Sutcliffe
2—California	L	4-6	Sanchez	Camacho
3—California	L	4-7	Kaufman	Spillner
4—Oakland	L	3-7	Krueger	Heaton
5—Oakland	L	2-4†	Atherton	Jeffcoat
6—Oakland	W	7-6	Jeffcoat	Jones
8—Seattle	W	4-3	Comer	Beattie
9—Seattle	W	8-7	Frazier	Langston
10—Seattle	W	3-1	Heaton	Vande Berg
10—Seattle	L	3-4	Langston	Camacho
12—At Oak.	W	11-5	Sutcliffe	Conroy
13—At Oak.	L	1-3	Caudill	Blyleven
14—At Oak.	L	6-7	Atherton	Camacho
15—At Calif.	L	2-5	Zahn	Heaton
16—At Calif.	L	2-7	Slaton	Farr
17—At Calif.	W	4-3	Camacho	Witt
19—At Minn.	W	7-4	Blyleven	Schrom
20—At Minn.	L	2-8	Viola	Comer
21—At Minn.	W	7-0	Heaton	Butcher
22—At Seattle	W	13-3	Jeffcoat	Vande Berg
23—At Seattle	W	11-4	Smith	Moore
24—At Seattle	W	5-0	Blyleven	Stoddard
26—Minnesota	L	3-8	Viola	Comer
27—Minnesota	W	6-4†	Camacho	Davis
28—Texas	L	6-10	Schmidt	Schulze
28—Texas	W	7-2	Smith	Tanana
29—Texas	W	13-12x	Easterly	Tobik
30—Texas	L	1-2	Hough	Comer
Won 14, Lost 14				

JULY				
1—Texas	W	13-5	Schulze	Mason
2—Kan. City	L	3-9	Gura	Heaton
2—Kan. City	L	3-4	Huismann	Smith
3—Kan. City	W	15-3	Blyleven	Black
4—Kan. City	L	0-4	Saberhagen	Comer
5—At Chicago	L	6-7	Nelson	Heaton
6—At Chicago	L	6-11	Hoyt	Schulze

JULY			Winner	Loser
7—At Chicago	L	2-4	Bannister	Smith
8—At Chicago	L	8-9	Agosto	Farr
12—At Texas	L	2-7	Hough	Heaton
13—At Texas	W	5-0	Blyleven	Mason
14—At Texas	W	5-0	Farr	Stewart
15—At Texas	W	5-4‡	Camacho	Jones
16—At Kan. C.	L	1-3	Jones	Schulze
17—At Kan. C.	W	9-7	Heaton	Gura
17—At Kan. C.	W	6-2	Comer	Wills
18—At Kan. C.	W	2-1	Blyleven	Black
19—Chicago	L	0-3	Seaver	Farr
20—Chicago	W	6-3	Smith	Dotson
21—Chicago	L	3-4	Gleaton	Waddell
22—Chicago	W	4-1	Heaton	Nelson
23—Detroit	L	1-4	Morris	Blyleven
24—Detroit	L	5-9	Wilcox	Farr
25—Detroit	W	4-1	Smith	Rozema
27—At Balt.	L	3-4	Davis	Heaton
28—At Balt.	W	6-3	Blyleven	McGregor
29—At Balt.	L	1-3	Boddicker	Comer
31—At Detroit	L	1-5	Berenguer	Smith
31—At Detroit	W	6-4	Heaton	Rozema
Won 13, Lost 16				

AUGUST				
1—At Detroit	W	4-2	Farr	Petry
2—At Detroit	L	1-2	Morris	Blyleven
3—At N.Y.	L	0-9	Cowley	Comer
3—At N.Y.	L	2-3	Armstrong	Camacho
4—At N.Y.	L	5-8	Rasmussen	Smith
5—At N.Y.	L	0-4	Fontenot	Heaton
6—Baltimore	L	2-4	Davis	Farr
7—Baltimore	W	5-4	Blyleven	McGregor
8—Baltimore	L	4-7	Boddicker	Comer
9—Baltimore	W	7-5	Easterly	Brown
10—New York	L	4-6	Cowley	Schulze
10—New York	L	1-10	Fontenot	Heaton
11—New York	L	1-10	Niekro	Farr
12—New York	W	6-0	Blyleven	Guidry
13—New York	W	6-5‡	Farr	Righetti
14—Toronto	L	1-8	Alexander	Heaton
14—Toronto	L	5-9	Lamp	Waddell
15—Toronto	W	16-1	Schulze	Leal
15—Toronto	W	4-3x	Jeffcoat	Key
16—Toronto	W	6-5	Waddell	Lamp
17—Milwaukee	W	5-3	Blyleven	Cocanower
19—Milwaukee	W	8-6	Waddell	Ladd
19—Milwaukee	W	2-1	Comer	Waits
21—At Toronto	W	3-1	Smith	Stieb
22—At Toronto	W	13-3	Blyleven	Clancy
23—At Toronto	L	1-6	Alexander	Schulze
24—At Boston	L	6-7	Boyd	Comer
25—At Boston	L	6-11	Nipper	Farr
26—At Boston	L	2-4	Clemens	Smith
27—At Milw.	W	7-1	Blyleven	Caldwell
28—At Milw.	W	8-5	Heaton	McClure
29—At Milw.	W	5-2	Jeffcoat	Cocanower
30—At Milw.	L	6-7	Tellmann	Farr
31—Boston	L	7-8	Stanley	Camacho
Won 16, Lost 18				

SEPTEMBER				
1—Boston	L	1-4	Ojeda	Blyleven
2—Boston	W	8-3	Waddell	Clear
3—California	W	6-5	Comer	Slaton
4—California	L	3-5§	Aase	Easterly
5—California	L	4-11	Kison	Roman
7—Oakland	W	13-2	Blyleven	Conroy
8—Oakland	L	5-9	Codiroli	Heaton
9—Oakland	W	7-5	Easterly	McCatty
11—At Calif.	W	4-2	Schulze	Romanick
12—At Calif.	W	7-1	Blyleven	Kison
13—At Calif.	L	3-7	Slaton	Roman
14—At Oak.	W	6-1	Heaton	Codiroli
15—At Oak.	W	6-3	Ujdur	Burris
16—At Oak.	W	8-4	Waddell	Atherton
17—At Seattle	L	2-3‡	Geisel	Jeffcoat
18—At Seattle	L	3-6	Moore	Ujdur
19—At Seattle	L	3-4	Langston	Heaton
21—At Minn.	L	3-7	Butcher	Schulze
22—At Minn.	L	1-4	Schrom	Blyleven
23—At Minn.	L	1-5	Lysander	Ujdur
25—Seattle	W	13-5	Heaton	Langston
26—Seattle	W	1-0	Blyleven	Beattie
27—Minnesota	W	4-3	Camacho	Davis
28—Minnesota	W	11-10	Waddell	Davis
29—Minnesota	W	6-4	Heaton	Butcher
30—Minnesota	W	7-4	Blyleven	Schrom
Won 15, Lost 11				

*7 innings. †10 innings. ‡11 innings. §12 innings. x13 innings. y16 innings. z19 innings.

Bert Blyleven put together an amazing 19-7 season with 170 strikeouts and a 2.87 ERA.

13. Cleveland sent pitchers Rick Sutcliffe and George Frazier and catcher Ron Hassey to the Chicago Cubs for outfielders Mel Hall and Carter plus rookie pitchers Don Schulze and Darryl Banks.

"When you surround Andy Thornton with players who can drive in runs, it makes a world of difference," Corrales said.

To say the least. Hall and Carter began to make immediate contributions—as did Chris Bando, who was recalled from Maine (International) to share catching duties with Jerry Willard after Hassey's departure—and opposing pitchers were forced to pitch to Thornton. Thus began Cleveland's scoring bonanza.

Hall hit seven home runs and drove in 30 runs in 257 at-bats as an Indian; Carter smacked 13 homers and tallied 41 RBIs in 244 at-bats; Bando collected 12 homers and 41 RBIs while hitting .291 in 220 at-bats, and Willard finished his rookie season with 10 homers and 37 RBIs in 246 at-bats.

Meanwhile, Corrales' decision to platoon George Vukovich and Carmen Castillo in right field produced 19 homers and 96 RBIs. Vukovich wound up as Cleveland's top hitter with a .304 average.

Franco, as expected, followed an excellent rookie season with a .286 average, 79 RBIs and 19 stolen bases. The shortstop was less impressive defensively, however, tallying 36 errors, the most by an Indian in 1984.

Among the other offensive producers for Cleveland were Butler, who batted .269 and was among the league leaders in stolen bases (52), walks (86), runs scored (108) and triples (nine); Tabler, who hit .290, pounded 10 home runs and collected 68 RBIs, and third baseman Brook Jacoby, who had seven homers and 40 RBIs before missing the last month of the season with a broken hand.

The Indians' basic problem last season was starting pitching. Aside from Bert Blyleven, Cleveland was unable to come up with any stable starters.

But Blyleven was a marvel. In addition to his 19-7 record, 170 strikeouts, four shutouts and 2.87 earned-run average (No. 3 in the league), he lasted seven innings or more in 26 of his 32 starts and allowed three or fewer runs 22 times. Though his first complete game did not come until June 24, he finished with 12.

Neal Heaton had a disappointing sophomore season, posting a 12-15 record and a 5.21 ERA. Except for Steve Comer (4-8, 5.68 ERA), the remaining starters were rookies: Roy Smith (5-5, 4.59 ERA), Steve Farr (3-11, 4.58), who finished the year as a reliever, and Schulze (3-6, 4.83).

In the bullpen, an attempt to turn Frazier into a stopper was unsuccessful, and Dan Spillner was traded to the White Sox in June after he failed to regain the fine form he displayed in 1982, when he had 21 saves.

But Ernie Camacho came from nowhere to set a club record of 23 saves while posting a 2.43 ERA, and rookie Tom Waddell was 7-4 with six saves and a 3.06 ERA. Waddell finished the season by pitching 22⅓ scoreless innings.

Inasmuch as the core of the club was young, the Indians were looking to 1985 with optimism. Carter, Willard and Jacoby all were rookies, while Bando, Tabler, Hall, Butler and Franco all will be less than 30 when the 1985 campaign begins.

Milwaukee relief ace Rollie Fingers was his old self in 1984 before back problems forced him back to the bench.

Injured Brewers Hit Bottom

By TOM FLAHERTY

The Milwaukee Brewers opened the 1984 season with a new manager and high hopes. They finished it six months later with a last-place finish in the American League East and the return of an old manager.

In between there were very few victories, a bundle of injuries and a lot of grief.

Manager Rene Lachemann was fired three days before the Brewers finished with a 67-94 record, 36½ games out of first place. It was the first time they had wound up on the bottom since 1976. George Bamberger, Milwaukee's favorite adopted son and the manager who had directed the Brewers' climb out of the second division in 1978, was rehired.

The Brewers, however, needed more than Bamberger's magic and wide smile in the dugout. Milwaukee's problems extended beyond simply the field manager, and General Manager Harry Dalton promised—without being specific—that there would be other changes before the 1985 season.

Lachemann's one season at the Brewer helm started out on troubled waters, and the sailing was rough all year. Injuries were his largest albatross.

The first bit of bad news came in the middle of spring training. Pitcher Pete Vuckovich, who had missed most of the 1983 season with a rotator cuff injury and was expected to make a comeback, suffered new shoulder problems that required surgery to remove a bone spur. He did not throw a pitch for the Brewers in 1984.

Third baseman Paul Molitor tore a muscle in his right elbow later in spring training and had to undergo surgery after playing in only 13 games.

"After a very enjoyable spring training, this is the worst moment I've had this spring," Lachemann said after Molitor suffered his injury.

Unfortunately for the new manager, that was only the beginning.

Even the brightest story of the year had a bad ending. Rollie Fingers, who had missed the 1983 season with a variety of arm problems that eventually required surgery, appeared to be headed for Comeback Player of the Year honors after compiling 23 saves and a 1.96 earned-run average by July 23. Then disaster struck again. He was rushed to the hospital on July 24 after experiencing severe pain in

First baseman Cecil Cooper (above) and outfielder Ben Oglivie suffered through below-par offensive seasons.

SCORES OF MILWAUKEE BREWERS' 1984 GAMES

APRIL

Date	W/L	Score	Winner	Loser
3—At Oak.	L	5-6	Burgmeier	Fingers
4—At Oak.	L	3-4	Burris	Caldwell
6—At Seattle	L	3-6	Young	Haas
7—At Seattle	L	2-3	Langston	Tellmann
8—At Seattle	L	4-5	Moore	Sutton
10—At Calif.	W	10-1	Caldwell	Witt
11—At Calif.	L	5-9	Romanick	Haas
13—At Kan. C.	L	3-6	Black	Cocanower
14—At Kan. C.	W	8-4	Sutton	Huismann
15—At Kan. C.	W	3-2	Caldwell	Quisenberry
17—Chicago	W	7-3	Haas	Seaver
19—Chicago	L	1-3	Dotson	Cocanower
20—Seattle	L	0-5	Beattie	Sutton
21—Seattle	W	6-2	Caldwell	Young
24—Oakland	W	3-2	Ladd	Sorensen
25—California	L	1-5	Witt	Cocanower
26—California	W	2-1	Sutton	John
27—At N.Y.	W	12-0	Caldwell	Rawley
28—At N.Y.	W	8-0	Porter	Montefusco
29—At N.Y.	L	5-6‡	Howell	McClure

Won 9, Lost 11

MAY

Date	W/L	Score	Winner	Loser
1—Kan. City	L	0-3	Gura	Cocanower
3—Kan. City	W	6-5*	Tellmann	Quisenberry
4—New York	W	1-0	Porter	Niekro
5—New York	W	2-1*	Ladd	Brown
6—New York	L	4-8*	Brown	Ladd
7—At Chicago	W	7-3	Cocanower	Hoyt
8—At Chicago	L	6-7§x	Seaver	Porter
9—At Chicago	L	4-5	Seaver	Caldwell
11—Minnesota	W	4-1	Haas	Hodge
12—Minnesota	L	2-4	Smithson	Caldwell
13—Minnesota	W	4-1	Cocanower	Viola
15—Texas	W	3-2	Sutton	Mason
16—Texas	W	5-1	Porter	Darwin
17—Texas	L	1-4	Tanana	Haas
18—Cleveland	L	4-8	Jeffcoat	Ladd
19—Cleveland	W	3-0	Cocanower	Spillner
20—Cleveland	L	2-3	Camacho	Sutton
22—At Texas	W	7-1	Porter	Darwin
23—At Texas	L	1-6	Tanana	Haas
24—At Texas	L	3-4	Stewart	Caldwell
25—At Minn.	L	4-7	Butcher	Cocanower
26—At Minn.	L	6-7	Filson	Waits
27—At Minn.	W	5-4	Porter	Smithson
29—At Cleve.	W	5-3	Haas	Spillner
30—At Cleve.	L	1-9	Heaton	Caldwell
30—At Cleve.	W	3-2*	Cocanower	Waddell

Won 13, Lost 13

JUNE

Date	W/L	Score	Winner	Loser
1—Boston	L	1-3	Hurst	Sutton
2—Boston	L	3-6	Clemens	Porter
3—Boston	L	3-6	Clear	Ladd
4—At Balt.	L	2-6	Boddicker	Ladd
5—At Balt.	W	8-3	Cocanower	Swaggerty
6—At Balt.	L	0-3	McGregor	Sutton
7—At Boston	W	6-3	McClure	Clemens
8—At Boston	L	3-11	Boyd	Haas
9—At Boston	L	6-15	Ojeda	Gibson
10—At Boston	L	4-5	Gale	Waits
11—Baltimore	L	1-3	McGregor	Sutton
12—Baltimore	L	4-5	T. Martinez	Fingers
13—Baltimore	W	6-1	Haas	Flanagan
14—Baltimore	W	3-2	Waits	Davis
15—Detroit	L	2-3	Petry	Cocanower
16—Detroit	L	0-6	Berenguer	Sutton
17—Detroit	L	4-7	Rozema	McClure
19—At Toronto	W	6-5	Fingers	Key
20—At Toronto	W	5-4	Tellmann	Alexander
21—At Detroit	W	4-3	Sutton	Berenguer
22—At Detroit	L	3-7	Rozema	McClure
23—At Detroit	L	1-5	Wilcox	Porter
24—At Detroit	L	1-7	Morris	Haas
25—Toronto	W	2-1	Cocanower	Alexander
25—Toronto	W	9-4	McClure	Acker
26—Toronto	W	6-3	Sutton	Leal
27—Toronto	W	5-1	Porter	Clancy
28—California	L	3-7	John	Gibson
29—California	W	1-0	Haas	Romanick
30—California	L	0-2	Zahn	Cocanower

Won 12, Lost 18

JULY

Date	W/L	Score	Winner	Loser
1—California	L	6-7	Kison	McClure
2—Seattle	W	3-2	Sutton	Moore
2—Seattle	W	6-4	Tellmann	Barojas
3—Seattle	W	11-6	Ladd	Young
4—Seattle	W	4-2	Haas	Vande Berg
5—Oakland	W	7-5	Cocanower	Krueger
6—Oakland	L	6-7	Burris	Ladd
6—Oakland	L	0-11	Young	Caldwell
7—Oakland	L	2-8	McCatty	Sutton
8—Oakland	L	1-4	Sorensen	Porter
12—At Calif.	L	2-5	Witt	Cocanower
13—At Calif.	W	5-4	Sutton	Zahn
14—At Calif.	L	1-2*	Romanick	Tellmann
15—At Calif.	L	6-7	Sanchez	McClure
16—At Seattle	L	2-11	Barojas	Candiotti
17—At Seattle	L	1-3	Langston	Cocanower
18—At Seattle	W	5-2	Sutton	Moore
19—At Oak.	L	1-4	McCatty	Haas
20—At Oak.	W	9-7	Tellmann	Caudill
21—At Oak.	W	7-4*	Waits	Rainey
22—At Oak.	L	4-5	Krueger	Caldwell
23—New York	W	6-4	Sutton	Guidry
24—New York	W	2-1†	Ladd	Cowley
25—New York	L	0-3	Rasmussen	Caldwell
27—Kan. City	L	8-12	Gura	Cocanower
27—Kan. City	W	3-1	Candiotti	Jones
28—Kan. City	W	3-2	Sutton	Black
29—Kan. City	L	1-5	Gubicza	Haas
30—At N.Y.	L	3-4	Rasmussen	Caldwell
31—At N.Y.	L	4-7	Fontenot	Beene

Won 13, Lost 17

AUGUST

Date	W/L	Score	Winner	Loser
1—At N.Y.	L	3-7	Niekro	Cocanower
2—At N.Y.	L	4-6	Howell	Tellmann
3—Chicago	L	1-5	Bannister	Sutton
4—Chicago	L	3-7	Seaver	Haas
5—Chicago	L	0-7	Dotson	Caldwell
6—Chicago	L	3-5	Nelson	Cocanower
7—At Kan. C.	L	5-8	Beckwith	Ladd
8—At Kan. C.	W	3-2	Sutton	Black
9—At Kan. C.	L	4-5	Huismann	Ladd
10—At Chicago	W	4-2	Caldwell	Dotson
11—At Chicago	W	10-5	Cocanower	Nelson
12—At Chicago	W	8-1	McClure	Hoyt
13—At Minn.	L	1-5	Butcher	Sutton
14—At Minn.	L	2-3	Hodge	Haas
15—At Minn.	W	8-4	Caldwell	Schrom
17—At Cleve.	L	3-5	Blyleven	Cocanower
19—At Cleve.	L	6-8	Waddell	Ladd
19—At Cleve.	L	1-2	Comer	Waits
22—Minnesota	L	2-5	Smithson	Caldwell
22—Minnesota	L	3-4	Lysander	Searage
23—Minnesota	W	5-2	McClure	Viola
24—Texas	L	3-10	Tanana	Beene
25—Texas	W	7-6	Sutton	Hough
26—Texas	W	6-3	Haas	Mason
27—Cleveland	L	1-7	Blyleven	Caldwell
28—Cleveland	L	5-8	Heaton	McClure
29—Cleveland	L	2-5	Jeffcoat	Cocanower
30—Cleveland	W	7-6	Tellmann	Farr
31—At Texas	L	6-7	McLaughlin	Ladd

Won 9, Lost 20

SEPTEMBER

Date	W/L	Score	Winner	Loser
1—At Texas	L	4-8	Stewart	Caldwell
3—Boston	L	5-8	Boyd	Cocanower
4—Boston	L	1-3	Nipper	Sutton
5—Boston	W	7-5	Haas	Brown
7—At Balt.	W	10-8	Tellmann	Stewart
8—At Balt.	L	3-5	Davis	Lazorko
9—At Balt.	L	0-4	Boddicker	Gibson
10—At Boston	W	7-4	Sutton	Brown
11—At Boston	W	14-6	Haas	Boyd
12—At Boston	L	4-5	Ojeda	McClure
14—Baltimore	W	4-2	Candiotti	Boddicker
15—Baltimore	W	7-0	Gibson	Flanagan
16—Baltimore	L	8-11	Davis	Sutton
17—At Detroit	L	3-7	Mason	Waits
18—At Detroit	L	0-3	O'Neal	McClure
19—At Detroit	L	2-4	Morris	Candiotti
20—At Toronto	L	4-6	Stieb	Gibson
21—At Toronto	W	5-1	Sutton	Lamp
22—At Toronto	L	1-2	Alexander	Haas
23—At Toronto	W	8-5	Kern	Jackson
24—Detroit	L	3-7	Berenguer	Hartzell
25—Detroit	L	1-9	O'Neal	Gibson
26—Detroit	W	7-5	Searage	Lopez
28—Toronto	W	4-3†	Searage	Musselman
29—Toronto	L	4-5	Stieb	Cocanower
30—Toronto	W	4-0	Gibson	Alexander

Won 11, Lost 15

*10 innings. †11 innings. ‡13 innings. §25 innings. xSuspended game, completed May 9.

Steady shortstop Robin Yount hit .298 with 16 homers and 80 RBIs.

his back. The injury, diagnosed as a herniated disc and irritation of the sciatic nerve, sidelined Fingers for the rest of '84.

On the same day that Fingers was stricken, the Brewers received additional bad news, this time about Chuck Porter, who had been the Brewers' most consistent starter early in the season. After suffering a torn ligament in his elbow, Porter was lost for the season.

In all, the Brewers placed 12 players on the disabled list, one of them twice. But these medical problems, troublesome though they were, did not give the Brewers their biggest headaches. Their worst problem was an anemic offense.

Milwaukee, which had hit 216 home runs just two years before while slugging its way into the World Series, hit only 96 homers, last in the league, and scored only

641 runs, also last in the league.

First baseman Cecil Cooper, who had never hit under .300 in seven previous seasons as a Brewer, batted only .275 with 11 homers and 67 runs batted in. Several other key players had off seasons, including first baseman-designated hitter Ted Simmons, who hit .221 with four homers and 52 RBIs, and outfielder Ben Oglivie, who batted .262 with 12 homers and 60 RBIs.

Shortstop Robin Yount led the team in almost every offensive category, including batting average (.298), homers (16), RBIs (80) and runs scored (105). He was troubled by shoulder problems, however, and had to finish the season as the team's designated hitter.

Second baseman Jim Gantner was one of the few Brewers to have a virtually injury-free season and was the club's most consistent performer, batting a solid .282.

There were some impressive newcomers. Catcher Jim Sundberg, obtained during the off-season from the Texas Rangers, batted .261 and was outstanding defensively, but he spent a month on the disabled list with back problems. Rookie Bill Schroeder filled in and was the team leader with 14 home runs until a hand injury benched him late in the season.

Dion James, a rookie outfielder, finished strong with a .295 average and showed great promise for the future.

On the pitching staff, Don Sutton finished with a 14-12 record and a 3.77 ERA. The 39-year-old righthander was the team's only consistent starter all season and easily could have been a 20-game winner with any kind of offensive support.

Rookie Jaime Cocanower got off to an impressive start and was 7-7 at the All-Star break but fell apart in the second half. He finished at 8-16 with a 4.02 ERA. Moose Haas (9-11, 3.99 ERA) and Mike Caldwell (6-13, 4.64) also were disappointing.

In the bullpen, Pete Ladd, who had earned 25 saves in '83, saved only three games and had a 4-9 record and a 5.24 ERA. But the late-season discovery of lefthander Ray Searage, a 29-year-old rookie who saved six games in the final five weeks of the season and posted a 0.70 ERA in 38⅓ innings, was encouraging for the Brewers.

The Brewers' problems were reflected in the attendance totals at Milwaukee County Stadium. After drawing almost 2.4 million fans to set an all-time Milwaukee baseball attendance record in 1983, the Brewers attracted only 1,608,509 fans in '84.

Lefthander Bud Black asserted himself as the ace of a young Royals' staff.

Young Royals Mature Quickly

By MIKE FISH

Everybody—management, players, media—said before the season that it would be a few years until the Kansas City Royals appeared in postseason competition again.

The Royals' front-office people talked up "transition" from the first day of spring training. Yes, they said, they would like for the club to be competitive. But win the American League West? Well, that might be a different story. An all-rookie outfield would have to start the season, there was no reliable veteran pitching and worst of all, the club was suffering from the effects of a nasty drug investigation that put center fielder Willie Wilson and three other Royals (who later were released or traded from the team) in federal prison.

Besides, nobody expected the Royals to make up 20 games on the Chicago White Sox. Some oddsmakers even had Kansas City as a 100-to-1 longshot to win the division.

So much for low expectations. The Royals turned what was supposed to be a rebuilding year into a championship season.

Some of the cornerstones of Kansas City's past division title teams—George Brett, Hal McRae, Frank White, Dan Quisenberry and Wilson—were familiar names in the Royals' lineup. But the bulk of the cast was new on the scene.

There were guys like Darryl Motley, who came to spring training as the No. 9 outfielder on a team that planned to carry only six but who wound up playing in more games (146) than any other Royal; like Bud Black, who went 17-12 with a 3.12 earned-run average and 140 strikeouts in his first full season in the majors and became the ace of a rebuilt starting rotation in which not one member was with the team on opening day in 1983, and like Greg Pryor, a journeyman utility infielder who filled several vacancies caused by injuries, batted .263 and was recognized by many teammates as the club's most valuable player.

The 1984 season saw the birth of a new generation of Royals pitchers, including Black, Charlie Leibrandt, Bret Saberhagen, Mark Gubicza, Mark Huismann, Danny Jackson and Frank Wills. It also saw ex-Dodger Joe Beckwith (8-4, 3.40 ERA) fit comfortably into a bullpen role as a strong middle reliever.

Leibrandt, a veteran who was obtained from Cincinnati in a 1983 trade but began the '84 season with Kansas City's Triple-A team in Omaha, posted an 11-7 record (his career high) and a 3.63 ERA. Rookies Saberhagen and Gubicza combined for 20 victories. The young pitchers carried the team while veterans Larry Gura (12-9, 5.18 ERA) and Paul Splittorff (1-3, 7.71) struggled. Both Gura and Splittorff wound up in the bullpen, and Splittorff, the winningest pitcher in Royals history, decided to retire July 1.

For his part, Quisenberry offered his colleagues the security of knowing that any leads they could produce would, in all likelihood, be protected. The righthanded relief ace led the league with 44 saves, thus becoming the first pitcher ever to record 40-plus saves in consecutive seasons, and earned his fourth Fireman of the Year award in the last five seasons.

"I didn't have any expectations when I went to spring training," Quisenberry said. "I thought . . . that it was going to be a real pain. Then I saw some of the young guys. They were like frisky puppies, and it rubbed off on the older pitchers. It is fun again."

It wasn't fun at the start. The Royals were playing without Wilson, who was suspended through May 15 by former Commissioner Bowie Kuhn for his drug violations, and Brett, who underwent arthroscopic surgery on his knee after being injured at the end of spring training and missed the first 33 games of the season.

The Royals began to win more games upon the return of the two leaders in mid-May, but by the All-Star break they were languishing in fifth place with a 39-43 record. Kansas City then lost eight of its next nine games to reach its low point of the season on July 18: a 40-51 record, sixth place and eight games behind the division-leading California Angels.

But no team in baseball won more games than the Royals after July 18. Kansas City went 44-27 to finish at 84-78, three games in front of the Twins and the Angels. The Royals were back in the playoffs for the fifth time in nine years.

Kansas City's storybook season came to a quick and painful conclusion, however, in the A.L. Championship Series. The Detroit Tigers swept the Royals, who never held a lead in any game during the playoffs. But the Royals, while disappointed, seemed happy just to have made it as far as they did.

SCORES OF KANSAS CITY ROYALS' 1984 GAMES

APRIL

Date	W/L	Score	Winner	Loser
3—New York	W	4-2	Black	Guidry
4—New York	L	3-4	Niekro	Splittorff
5—New York	W	15-4	Gura	Rawley
6—Cleveland	L	0-2	Blyleven	Gubicza
8—Cleveland	W	5-4	Black	Frazier
10—At Balt.	L	3-6	McGregor	Splittorff
11—At Balt.	W	5-2	Gura	Boddicker
13—Milwaukee	W	6-3	Black	Cocanower
14—Milwaukee	L	4-8	Sutton	Huismann
15—Milwaukee	L	2-3	Caldwell	Quisenberry
18—At Detroit	L	3-4*	Hernandez	Beckwith
19—At Detroit	W	5-2	Saberhagen	Petry
20—At Cleve.	W	6-4	Gura	Heaton
21—At Cleve.	L	2-3	Blyleven	Jackson
24—At N.Y.	L	0-4	Niekro	Black
25—Baltimore	W	3-2	Quisenberry	T. Martinez
26—Baltimore	L	3-11	Flanagan	Jackson
27—Toronto	L	0-1	Alexander	Gubicza
28—Toronto	L	0-6	Stieb	Saberhagen

Won 8, Lost 11

MAY

Date	W/L	Score	Winner	Loser
1—At Milw.	W	3-0	Gura	Cocanower
3—At Milw.	L	5-6*	Tellmann	Quisenberry
4—At Toronto	L	3-4*	Stieb	Huismann
5—At Toronto	L	1-10	Gott	Jackson
6—At Toronto	L	1-2	Jackson	Gura
7—Detroit	L	3-10	Berenguer	Gubicza
8—Detroit	L	2-5	Morris	Black
9—Detroit	L	1-3	Petry	Jackson
11—Boston	W	6-4	Gura	Eckersley
12—Boston	W	3-0	Gubicza	Hurst
13—Boston	W	5-1	Black	Brown
14—At Chicago	L	0-2	Seaver	Saberhagen
15—At Chicago	L	2-3	Dotson	Jackson
16—At Chicago	W	7-6	Beckwith	Barojas
18—Texas	L	1-2	Stewart	Black
19—Texas	W	6-2	Gubicza	Hough
20—Texas	L	2-3	Mason	Saberhagen
21—Chicago	L	4-8	Bannister	Gura
22—Chicago	W	7-6	Beckwith	Barojas
23—Chicago	W	1-0	Black	Burns
25—At Boston	W	8-5	Saberhagen	Ojeda
26—At Boston	W	11-7	Splittorff	Stanley
27—At Boston	L	0-6	Hurst	Beckwith
28—At Texas	W	6-1	Gura	Tanana
29—At Texas	W	7-5*	Quisenberry	Schmidt
30—At Texas	L	3-7	Hough	Saberhagen
31—At Minn.	L	2-7	Hodge	Gubicza

Won 12, Lost 15

JUNE

Date	W/L	Score	Winner	Loser
1—At Minn.	W	7-1	Leibrandt	Smithson
2—At Minn.	W	7-6*	Quisenberry	Whitehouse
3—At Minn.	W	5-2	Black	Viola
4—Seattle	L	1-7	Langston	Saberhagen
5—Seattle	W	4-3	Gubicza	Vande Berg
6—Seattle	W	5-2	Leibrandt	Moore
7—Seattle	W	9-8	Jackson	Beard
9—California	L	1-4	Romanick	Black
10—California	L	0-2	Zahn	Gubicza
12—At Seattle	L	2-3*	Moore	Saberhagen
13—At Seattle	W	6-4	Gura	Young
14—At Seattle	L	1-4	Beattie	Black
15—Minnesota	L	0-3	Butcher	Gubicza
16—Minnesota	L	1-6	Williams	Saberhagen
17—Minnesota	L	1-3	Smithson	Leibrandt
18—At Oak.	L	2-10	Burris	Gura
19—At Oak.	W	6-2	Black	Codiroli
20—At Oak.	L	1-8	Krueger	Gubicza
22—At Calif.	L	1-8	Witt	Leibrandt
23—At Calif.	W	6-5	Gura	Kison
24—At Calif.	W	3-2	Black	Romanick
25—Oakland	W	16-0	Gubicza	Krueger
26—Oakland	L	4-8	Sorensen	Splittorff
26—Oakland	L	1-6	Young	Leibrandt
27—Oakland	L	5-9	McCatty	Gura
29—New York	W	3-2	Black	Niekro
30—New York	W	6-2	Gubicza	Guidry

Won 13, Lost 14

JULY

Date	W/L	Score	Winner	Loser
1—New York	W	8-0	Leibrandt	Shirley
2—At Cleve.	W	9-3	Gura	Heaton
2—At Cleve.	W	4-3	Huismann	Smith
3—At Cleve.	L	3-15	Blyleven	Black
4—At Cleve.	W	4-0	Saberhagen	Comer
6—At Balt.	W	6-2	Leibrandt	Boddicker
7—At Balt.	L	2-6	McGregor	Gura
7—At Balt.	L	0-8	Flanagan	Jones

JULY

Date	W/L	Score	Winner	Loser
8—At Balt.	W	6-1	Black	D. Martinez
12—At N.Y.	L	2-5	Niekro	Gura
13—At N.Y.	L	1-7	Guidry	Black
13—At N.Y.	L	1-8	Bystrom	Saberhagen
14—At N.Y.	L	1-4	Rasmussen	Gubicza
15—At N.Y.	L	1-4	Fontenot	Leibrandt
16—Cleveland	W	3-1	Jones	Schulze
17—Cleveland	L	7-9	Heaton	Gura
17—Cleveland	L	2-6	Comer	Wills
18—Cleveland	L	1-2	Blyleven	Black
19—Baltimore	W	6-3	Gubicza	Flanagan
20—Baltimore	W	4-3	Saberhagen	T. Martinez
21—Baltimore	L	3-4	Davis	Huismann
22—Baltimore	W	8-4	Gura	McGregor
23—Toronto	W	9-8	Beckwith	Jackson
23—Toronto	W	7-2	Wills	Gott
24—Toronto	W	5-4	Gubicza	Stieb
25—Toronto	W	5-4§	Quisenberry	Clark
27—At Milw.	W	12-8	Gura	Cocanower
27—At Milw.	L	1-3	Candiotti	Jones
28—At Milw.	L	2-3	Sutton	Black
29—At Milw.	W	5-1	Gubicza	Haas
30—At Toronto	W	7-4	Leibrandt	Clancy
31—At Toronto	L	5-6	Alexander	Wills

Won 17, Lost 15

AUGUST

Date	W/L	Score	Winner	Loser
1—At Toronto	L	1-4	Leal	Gura
3—At Detroit	W	9-6	Saberhagen	Wilcox
4—At Detroit	W	9-5	Beckwith	Bair
5—At Detroit	W	5-4	Saberhagen	Hernandez
5—At Detroit	W	4-0	Leibrandt	Berenguer
7—Milwaukee	W	8-5	Beckwith	Ladd
8—Milwaukee	L	2-3	Sutton	Black
9—Milwaukee	W	5-4	Huismann	Ladd
10—Detroit	L	4-5	Lopez	Beckwith
11—Detroit	L	5-9	Morris	Leibrandt
12—Detroit	L	4-8	Wilcox	Saberhagen
13—Boston	W	6-1	Black	Boyd
14—Boston	L	2-8	Nipper	Gubicza
15—Boston	W	13-8	Beckwith	Stanley
16—At Texas	W	6-3	Leibrandt	Mason
17—At Texas	L	6-8	Schmidt	Quisenberry
18—At Texas	W	5-4	Black	Darwin
19—At Texas	L	4-6	Tanana	Gura
20—At Boston	W	8-5	Gubicza	Brown
21—At Boston	L	1-11	Clemens	Leibrandt
22—At Boston	W	6-2	Beckwith	Hurst
24—Chicago	W	5-2	Black	Bannister
25—Chicago	L	0-3	Seaver	Gubicza
26—Chicago	W	6-5x	Gura	Roberge
27—Chicago	W	7-4	Saberhagen	Hoyt
28—Texas	L	0-6	Darwin	Wills
29—Texas	W	4-1	Black	Tanana
30—Texas	L	3-4	Hough	Gubicza
31—At Chicago	W	3-1	Leibrandt	Dotson

Won 17, Lost 12

SEPTEMBER

Date	W/L	Score	Winner	Loser
1—At Chicago	L	1-6	Hoyt	Saberhagen
2—At Chicago	W	6-4*	Quisenberry	Burns
3—Minnesota	L	1-4	Butcher	Black
4—Minnesota	W	4-1	Gubicza	Schrom
5—Minnesota	W	4-1	Leibrandt	Smithson
7—Seattle	W	5-4	Saberhagen	Young
8—Seattle	W	5-4	Beckwith	Moore
9—Seattle	W	6-5	Huismann	Nunez
10—At Minn.	L	3-7	Smithson	Gubicza
11—At Minn.	L	1-5	Viola	Leibrandt
12—At Minn.	W	3-2	Black	Lysander
14—At Seattle	L	1-2	Langston	Jackson
15—At Seattle	W	8-5	Jones	Best
16—At Seattle	W	4-2	Leibrandt	Barojas
17—At Calif.	W	10-1	Black	Kison
18—At Calif.	W	10-0	Saberhagen	Slaton
19—At Calif.	L	3-4†	Aase	Beckwith
20—At Calif.	L	0-2	Witt	Gubicza
21—Oakland	W	7-4	Wills	Sorensen
22—Oakland	W	4-2	Black	Burris
23—Oakland	L	1-5	Codiroli	Jones
24—California	W	4-0	Saberhagen	Zahn
24—California	W	12-4	Jackson	Steirer
25—California	W	6-5‡	Quisenberry	Kaufman
26—California	L	0-2	Romanick	Black
28—At Oak.	W	6-5	Leibrandt	Burris
29—At Oak.	L	2-6	Codiroli	Saberhagen
30—At Oak.	L	2-8	Krueger	Gubicza

Won 17, Lost 11

*10 innings. †11 innings. ‡12 innings. §13 innings. z16 innings.

Willie Wilson couldn't play until May 16, but the veteran speedster made up for lost time.

"We weren't much credit to the American League West," Brett said after the playoffs. "In a way, we should be embarrassed, but the way our young pitchers pitched, we've a lot to look forward to."

Brett, who missed several games down the stretch with a hamstring injury, can hope for a healthier, more productive 1985 season. The two-time A.L. batting champion hit .284, his lowest average since his 1974 rookie season, and added 13 home runs and 69 runs batted in.

Brett wasn't the only Royal bitten by the injury bug. White, who batted .271 and hit a career-high 17 homers, missed a month in the middle of the season because of a pulled left hamstring. Shortstop Onix Concepcion, who hit .282 and established himself as the club's best all-around shortstop since Fred Patek, was on the disabled list twice. Steve Balboni, the club leader in homers (28), RBIs (77) and walks (45), missed several games because of a bruised left arch and then a pulled rib cage muscle.

Designated hitter McRae hit .303 but was unable to drive in many runs and was benched against most righthanded pitchers. Jorge Orta, who came to Kansas City from Toronto in exchange for Willie Aikens (one of the four Royals players sentenced in the drug scandal), was effective as the other half of the DH platoon situation, hitting .298 with nine homers and 50 RBIs.

Wilson came back from his imprisonment and suspension with tremendous motivation and again became the club's offensive catalyst from his leadoff spot. He hit .301 and led the Royals in hits (163), runs scored (81), triples (nine) and stolen bases (47).

The young outfield packed an offensive punch, with right fielder Pat Sheridan hitting .283 and left fielder Motley collecting the best all-around numbers on the club—.284, 15 homers and 70 RBIs.

Manager Dick Howser earned the accolades of his peers by taking a team steeped in adversity and loaded with rookies to the top of its division. He guided the club with a calm, steady hand, through the good times and the bad. Only once did he lose his temper, and it was not at his players, but at umpires Joe Brinkman and Vic Voltaggio.

Howser was ejected from games on June 23 and 24 in Anaheim. The Royals won both games, but several close calls went against Kansas City. The ejections touched off a classic postgame tirade in which Howser blasted the umpires for incompetence as well as for pointing out that the Royals were in last place in the division.

"They may not believe we are in a pennant race, but I do, and so do our players," Howser said.

The Royals made believers out of everybody—including themselves.

California righthander Mike Witt closed out his 15-victory campaign with a perfect game against Texas on the final day of the season.

Fallen Angels Look for Revival

By TOM SINGER

It was a season of phases for the California Angels, and ultimately they were phased out of the American League West race.

First, a makeshift but surprising pitching staff overcame a punchless attack as the Angels led the division for a 52-day stretch that ended July 5.

Then, when the arms waned, the hitting awoke to pace a surge back into contention.

Finally, both barrels misfired. California lost seven of its last 10 games to limp home with a .500 (81-81) record and a second-place tie with Minnesota, three games behind Kansas City.

"Since spring training, all we wanted was to be in a position to take a shot at it," said Manager John McNamara, who resigned after the season. "We just couldn't pull it off."

The Angels definitely had their shot. But their last hurrah was sharing the lead for a few hours following a September 15 afternoon victory. It was downhill from there.

Several critics blamed the team's season-ending collapse on the Angels' collective age. They said that a lack of team spirit was at least partly responsible and that younger clubs such as the Royals and Twins did not suffer from that problem.

Several Angels such as Doug DeCinces disagreed.

"This team isn't old," the third baseman said. "That had no bearing on the race. Sure, some spots can be shored up. But they've written about us being too old before. And I don't think this team is in decline."

If the team is in decline, it is up to Mike Port to pick up the pieces. Port took over as the club's executive vice president when E.J. (Buzzie) Bavasi resigned after more than 50 years of front-office work.

Fortunately for Port, there were enough pleasant surprises to inspire hope for the future.

Mike Witt blossomed into a dominant 15-game winner, punctuating his rise by pitching the 13th nine-inning perfect game in baseball history on the final day of the season. Witt finished with a 15-11 record, a 3.47 earned-run average and 196 strikeouts (third in the league).

Ron Romanick, who had posted a losing record as a Double-A pitcher in 1983, produced a 12-12 rookie season and a 3.76 ERA. And relievers Doug Corbett (5-1,

Rookie Ron Romanick was impressive enough to raise the hopes of Angels fans.

2.12 ERA) and Don Aase (4-1, 1.62, eight saves) made convincing comebacks, Aase from an injury and Corbett from a season spent mostly in the minor leagues.

Rookie Gary Pettis played beautifully in center field and stole 48 bases (fourth in the league) even though at midseason he lost his starting job to Juan Beniquez, a journeyman who led the team with a .336 batting average.

But for the most part, the expected offense wasn't there. The Angels' .249 batting average was the club's lowest since 1976 and was 13th in the league, ranking ahead only of Chicago.

SCORES OF CALIFORNIA ANGELS' 1984 GAMES

APRIL

Date		Score	Winner	Loser
2—Boston	W	2-1	Forsch	Hurst
4—Boston	L	1-2	Clear	Sanchez
5—Boston	L	4-7	Stanley	Kaufman
6—Toronto	L	5-11	Key	Brown
7—Toronto	L	1-3	Stieb	Forsch
8—Toronto	W	4-3	Sanchez	Jackson
10—Milwaukee	L	1-10	Caldwell	Witt
11—Milwaukee	W	9-5	Romanick	Haas
12—At Oak.	W	3-2	Zahn	Warren
13—At Oak.	L	1-2	Caudill	John
14—At Oak.	L	3-4	Caudill	Kaufman
15—At Oak.	W	12-8	Witt	Sorensen
16—At Minn.	L	2-9	Smithson	Romanick
17—At Minn.	W	6-3	John	Butcher
18—At Minn.	W	9-2	Zahn	Williams
20—At Toronto	W	10-6x	Sanchez	Acker
21—At Toronto	W	8-4	Romanick	Gott
22—At Toronto	W	9-6	Slaton	Key
23—At Boston	L	0-2*	Ojeda	Zahn
24—At Boston	W	8-7	Sanchez	Stanley
25—At Milw.	W	5-1	Witt	Cocanower
26—At Milw.	L	1-2	Sutton	John
27—Seattle	W	9-3	Romanick	Stoddard
28—Seattle	W	10-1	Zahn	Langston
29—Seattle	L	6-9†	Thomas	LaCorte
30—Seattle	W	8-1	Witt	Mirabella

Won 15, Lost 11

MAY

Date		Score	Winner	Loser
1—Oakland	W	4-1	John	Warren
2—Oakland	L	6-7	Atherton	Romanick
4—At Seattle	W	4-1	Zahn	Moore
5—At Seattle	W	3-1	Witt	Beattie
6—At Seattle	L	1-3	Vande Berg	John
7—Minnesota	L	1-11	Smithson	Romanick
8—Minnesota	L	0-5	Viola	Slaton
9—Minnesota	L	2-5	Filson	Zahn
11—At Detroit	L	2-8	Wilcox	Witt
12—At Detroit	W	4-2	John	Berenguer
14—At Balt.	L	1-4	McGregor	Zahn
15—At Balt.	W	5-2	Romanick	Flanagan
16—At Balt.	L	0-5	Boddicker	Witt
18—At N.Y.	W	4-3†	Sanchez	Howell
19—At N.Y.	W	4-0	Zahn	Niekro
20—At N.Y.	W	3-0	Romanick	Guidry
22—Detroit	L	1-3	Berenguer	Witt
23—Detroit	L	2-4	Petry	LaCorte
24—Detroit	L	1-5	Morris	Slaton
25—Baltimore	W	10-2	Romanick	Flanagan
26—Baltimore	L	5-9	Boddicker	Swan
27—Baltimore	L	0-8	McGregor	Witt
28—New York	W	6-2	Corbett	Rasmussen
29—New York	W	6-5	LaCorte	Niekro
30—New York	L	1-10	Guidry	Romanick

Won 11, Lost 14

JUNE

Date		Score	Winner	Loser
1—At Cleve.	W	5-2	Witt	Sutcliffe
2—At Cleve.	W	6-4	Sanchez	Camacho
3—At Cleve.	W	7-4	Kaufman	Spillner
4—At Chicago	L	4-6	Hoyt	Romanick
5—At Chicago	W	6-1	Zahn	Burns
6—At Chicago	L	0-4	Seaver	Witt
7—At Chicago	L	10-11	Roberge	John
9—At Kan. C.	W	4-1	Romanick	Black
10—At Kan. C.	W	2-0	Zahn	Gubicza
12—Chicago	W	3-2†	Corbett	Jones
13—Chicago	L	1-2	Dotson	John
14—Chicago	W	9-3	Romanick	Burns
15—Cleveland	W	5-2	Zahn	Heaton
16—Cleveland	W	7-2	Slaton	Farr
17—Cleveland	L	3-4	Camacho	Witt
18—Texas	L	2-6	Tanana	John
19—Texas	L	2-4	Stewart	Romanick
20—Texas	L	2-3	Hough	Zahn
22—Kan. City	W	8-1	Witt	Leibrandt
23—Kan. City	L	5-6	Gura	Kison
24—Kan. City	L	2-3	Black	Romanick
25—At Texas	L	4-5‡	Schmidt	Corbett
26—At Texas	W	3-2y	Kison	Jones
27—At Texas	W	2-1	Witt	Mason
28—At Milw.	W	7-3	John	Gibson
29—At Milw.	L	0-1	Haas	Romanick
30—At Milw.	W	2-0	Zahn	Cocanower

Won 15, Lost 12

JULY

Date		Score	Winner	Loser
1—At Milw.	W	7-6	Kison	McClure
2—At Toronto	W	6-3	Witt	Clancy
3—At Toronto	L	0-4	Gott	John
4—At Toronto	L	3-6	Stieb	Romanick
5—At Boston	L	7-12	Boyd	Zahn
6—At Boston	L	7-8	Nipper	Slaton
8—At Boston	L	2-3†	Stanley	Sanchez
8—At Boston	W	4-0	John	Clemens
12—Milwaukee	W	5-2	Witt	Cocanower
13—Milwaukee	W	4-5	Sutton	Zahn
14—Milwaukee	W	2-1†	Romanick	Tellmann
15—Milwaukee	W	7-6	Sanchez	McClure
16—Toronto	W	3-0	Slaton	Gott
17—Toronto	W	5-3	Witt	Acker
18—Toronto	L	2-8	Leal	Zahn
20—Boston	L	3-4†	Stanley	Aase
21—Boston	L	4-16	Hurst	John
22—Boston	L	0-3	Ojeda	Slaton
23—Seattle	W	7-1	Witt	Moore
24—Seattle	L	3-4	Vande Berg	Zahn
25—Seattle	W	1-0†	Sanchez	Beattie
27—At Minn.	L	0-2	Smithson	John
28—At Minn.	L	1-6	Viola	Slaton
29—At Minn.	L	5-6†	Lysander	Sanchez
30—At Oak.	W	5-4§	Corbett	Caudill
31—At Oak.	W	7-3	Romanick	Sorensen

Won 12, Lost 14

AUGUST

Date		Score	Winner	Loser
1—At Oak.	W	6-4	John	Krueger
2—Minnesota	W	14-2	Slaton	Viola
3—Minnesota	L	2-4	Butcher	Witt
4—Minnesota	W	4-2	Zahn	Filson
5—Minnesota	L	2-4	Schrom	Romanick
6—At Seattle	W	8-4	John	Barojas
7—At Seattle	W	7-6	Aase	Stanton
8—At Seattle	L	2-7	Langston	Witt
9—Oakland	L	4-5	Young	Zahn
10—Oakland	L	6-7†	Atherton	Sanchez
11—Oakland	L	2-3†	Burgmeier	Sanchez
12—Oakland	W	10-9	Sanchez	Caudill
14—At Detroit	W	6-4	Aase	Hernandez
14—At Detroit	W	12-1	Kison	Rozema
15—At Detroit	L	3-8	Petry	John
16—At Detroit	L	7-8§	Hernandez	Curtis
17—At Balt.	L	5-6	McGregor	Slaton
18—At Balt.	L	0-1	Boddicker	Witt
19—At Balt.	L	4-10	Flanagan	Kison
20—At N.Y.	L	4-8	Cowley	John
21—At N.Y.	L	2-8	Niekro	Romanick
22—At N.Y.	W	2-1	Slaton	Fontenot
24—Detroit	W	5-3	Witt	Petry
25—Detroit	L	1-5	Morris	Kison
26—Detroit	L	6-12	Wilcox	John
27—Baltimore	L	6-7†	Stewart	Sanchez
28—Baltimore	W	4-2	Slaton	McGregor
29—Baltimore	W	7-5	Corbett	Boddicker
31—New York	W	4-3	Curtis	Armstrong

Won 13, Lost 16

SEPTEMBER

Date		Score	Winner	Loser
1—New York	W	11-6	Corbett	Righetti
2—New York	L	3-5	Howell	Curtis
3—At Cleve.	L	5-6	Comer	Slaton
4—At Cleve.	W	5-3§	Aase	Easterly
5—At Cleve.	W	11-4	Kison	Roman
7—At Chicago	W	16-8	Zahn	Burns
8—At Chicago	W	6-5	Sanchez	Reed
9—At Chicago	L	2-8	Seaver	Witt
11—Cleveland	L	2-4	Schulze	Romanick
12—Cleveland	L	1-7	Blyleven	Kison
13—Cleveland	W	7-3	Slaton	Roman
14—Chicago	W	5-0	Zahn	Bannister
15—Chicago	W	11-2	Witt	Seaver
16—Chicago	W	4-2	Romanick	Dotson
17—Kan. City	L	1-10	Black	Kison
18—Kan. City	L	0-10	Saberhagen	Slaton
19—Kan. City	W	4-3‡	Aase	Beckwith
20—Kan. City	W	2-0	Witt	Gubicza
21—Texas	W	5-4	Kaufman	Wright
22—Texas	L	7-9	McLaughlin	Sanchez
23—Texas	L	1-2†	Stewart	Slaton
24—At Kan. C.	L	0-4	Saberhagen	Zahn
24—At Kan. C.	L	4-12	Jackson	Steirer
25—At Kan. C.	L	5-6§	Quisenberry	Kaufman
26—At Kan. C.	W	2-0	Romanick	Black
27—At Texas	L	1-2	Noles	John
28—At Texas	L	1-4	Stewart	Slaton
29—At Texas	W	4-0	Zahn	Tanana
30—At Texas	W	1-0	Witt	Hough

Won 15, Lost 14

*6 innings. †10 innings. ‡11 innings. §12 innings. x13 innings. y14 innings.

Reggie Jackson bounced back to hit 25 home runs, including the 500th of his career.

First baseman Rod Carew began the season aiming for 3,000 hits but, often injured, fell 71 short and batted .295, narrowly missing .300 for the first time since 1968.

Reggie Jackson bounced back from a frustrating 1983 season with 25 home runs and 81 runs batted in. But the 38-year-old designated hitter's .223 average made his comeback less than complete.

And two players who barely batted their weight, 36-year-old catcher Bob Boone (.202) and rookie shortstop Dick Schofield (.193), had to be used daily for their defense, despite their quiet bats.

But the biggest blow for California came on April 7, when righthander Ken Forsch, considered the club's ace, dislocated his shoulder in a play at first base and was lost for the season. McNamara shuffled to round out his starting rotation all year, and Forsch's consistency was missed.

Consistency. That was the problem; no one had it.

Not the starters. They tied for second in the league with 12 shutouts but went from August 3 through September 13 without completing a win.

Not the venerable sluggers. The Angels fell two Bobby Grich homers shy of a quintet of 20-homer men, but Jackson (25), DeCinces (20), Brian Downing (23) and Fred Lynn (23) either hit them in unison or didn't hit them at all.

Not the relievers. Aase, returning from a nearly two-year layoff following elbow surgery, and Corbett eased the sting of the club's off-season inability to land free agent Goose Gossage, but the rest of the bullpen combined for only 14 saves, and the club total of 26 saves ranked next to last in the league.

Not the front office. Bavasi & Co., which had re-signed all six Angels who had played out their options the year before, stood by helplessly while injuries riddled the cast.

For instance, veteran lefty Geoff Zahn scattered five shutouts around three disabling leg injuries, the last of which kept him out from August 10 until September 1, but the club offered no reinforcements. When it was speculated that the Angels were neglecting a strong shot at the flag by refusing to offer top minor league prospects in exchange for proven pitching, Bavasi said: "We haven't by any means given up on this season. But if the price is too high, we aren't going to give away our kids."

The lack of front-office support appeared to demoralize the team, and in the end, management was among the critics charging the players with complacency.

Only fleeting moments of individual triumph tempered the bitter end.

There was Witt's 16-strikeout effort against Seattle on July 23 and his 27-up, 27-down masterpiece in Texas on September 30. . . . Tommy John's 250th career victory, against Oakland on May 1. . . . Jackson passing Lou Gehrig with his 494th homer on July 31, then becoming the 13th member of the 500 club on September 17 with a seventh-inning solo shot off Kansas City's Bud Black.

And as a team, there were high notes as well for the Angels. California won 11 more games than in 1983 and rose three notches in the division standings. About 152,000 fewer fans visited Anaheim Stadium than in '83, but the Angels still drew 2.4 million, the highest attendance figure for any team in the league except the Detroit Tigers.

First baseman Kent Hrbek hit .311 with 27 homers and 107 RBIs and keyed Minnesota's surprising run at the A.L. West title.

Young Twins Fall Just Short

By PATRICK REUSSE

The 1984 season started amid speculation that the Minnesota Twins were on their way to Tampa-St. Petersburg, and it ended on a dreary weekend in Cleveland. But in between, local ownership acquired the Twins and Minnesotans rediscovered baseball.

For good reason. The Twins played good baseball for the first time in years and stayed in the American League West title race until the final weekend of the season. The fans responded, and a franchise attendance record of 1,598,422 was established. It was the first time Minnesota's home attendance had surpassed 1 million in a season since 1979.

Part of that total—150,000—came during an early-season ticket buyout intended to prevent the Twins from using an escape clause in their 30-year lease with the Metrodome. The buyout lasted for a couple of weeks and included an announced crowd of 51,863 on May 16, when only 6,346 ticket purchasers actually showed up. The buyout was dropped as the Griffith family, the longtime owners of the Washington Senators-Twins franchise, neared completion of a sale agreement with Minnesota businessman Carl Pohlad.

In late June, Calvin Griffith and his sister, Thelma Griffith Haynes, signed a letter of agreement to sell their 52 percent share of the Twins to Pohlad for $35 million. That sale was finalized in late July, and as the season ended, Pohlad was on his way to buying out the rest of the minority partners.

During all of the front-office maneuvering, the Twins, who had gone 70-92 and finished tied for fifth the year before, stayed among the leaders in the congested A.L. West. Never in 1984 were the Twins more than 4½ games out of first place, and on July 28 they moved into the lead. The Twins put together a sprint in mid-August, and after sweeping a doubleheader in Milwaukee on August 22, Minnesota held a 5½-game lead in the division.

The Twins were nine games over .500 (67-58) at the time, the most games they had been on the plus side since 1979. But then they lost 11 of their next 14 games to drop back near the .500 level and turn the final three weeks of the season into a race with Kansas City and California.

Entering the final week—a seven-game trip to Chicago and Cleveland—Minnesota was tied for first with Kansas City. The Twins won the first game in Chicago, then lost their last six games to finish at 81-81, tied for second with the Angels.

Minnesota's elimination became official in Cleveland on September 28, when the Twins blew a 10-0 lead and lost, 11-10, to the Indians. It was the largest lead ever blown by the Twins—not to mention a bitter way for the pennant race to end for Minnesota's improbable contenders.

"You play 160 games and then it just goes pffft . . . you know what I mean?" first baseman Kent Hrbek said.

Hrbek was the main reason the Twins didn't go "pffft" much earlier. In his third full season in the majors, Hrbek finished with 27 home runs and team-leading totals in batting average (.311), runs batted in (107), runs scored (80) and total bases (292), among other categories.

"It's more than his offense," Twins Manager Billy Gardner pointed out. "Hrbek is the best defensive first baseman I've seen in my 39 years in pro baseball."

Hrbek was the single-most important key to Minnesota's sudden rise to respectability, but the improvement in the club's starting pitching, the clutch hitting of outfielders Mickey Hatcher and Tom Brunansky and the May arrival of rookie center fielder Kirby Puckett also were crucial factors.

Considerable controversy surrounded the December 1983 trade of outfielder Gary Ward to Texas for pitchers Mike Smithson and John Butcher. As it turned out, the trade was a bonanza for the Twins. "If we hadn't made the deal for Smithson and Butcher, I would have been back home in Connecticut in June, selling sausage," Gardner said.

Smithson pitched 252 innings and struck out 144 batters en route to a 15-13 record and a 3.68 earned-run average with the Twins. Butcher was 13-11 with a 3.44 ERA in 225 innings of work. In 1983, no Twins starter worked more than the 210 innings of Frank Viola.

Viola led the Twins in innings pitched again in 1984, but he had to work 257⅔ innings to do it. In the process, Viola became one of the top lefthanded starters in the league. After posting a combined record of 11-25 and ERAs of 5.21 and 5.49 in his first two years, respectively, in the majors, Viola went 18-12 with a 3.21 ERA, four shutouts and 149 strikeouts to lead the Twins' staff in '84.

Left fielder Hatcher, who had been shopped around to no avail in the spring of 1983, had his second consecutive over-.300

SCORES OF MINNESOTA TWINS' 1984 GAMES

APRIL

Date	W/L	Score	Winner	Loser
3—Detroit	L	1-8	Morris	Williams
5—Detroit	L	3-7	Petry	Viola
6—Baltimore	W	9-4	Smithson	Boddicker
7—Baltimore	W	13-4	Butcher	Flanagan
8—Baltimore	W	7-3	Williams	Palmer
10—At N.Y.	L	1-4	Niekro	Viola
12—At N.Y.	W	3-0	Smithson	Fontenot
13—Seattle	W	4-3	Davis	Stanton
14—Seattle	W	4-3†	Davis	Stoddard
15—Seattle	L	4-5	Thomas	Walters
16—California	W	9-2	Smithson	Romanick
17—California	L	3-6	John	Butcher
18—California	L	2-9	Zahn	Williams
20—At Balt.	L	2-4*	Stewart	Davis
21—At Balt.	L	3-5	Flanagan	Smithson
22—At Balt.	W	6-1	Butcher	Boddicker
24—At Detroit	L	5-6	Morris	Davis
24—At Detroit	L	3-4	Abbott	Viola
25—New York	W	8-6	Filson	Howell
26—New York	W	4-2	Filson	Rijo
27—At Oak.	L	3-5	McCatty	Pashnick
28—At Oak.	L	0-7	Burris	Williams
29—At Oak.	W	5-2	Viola	Sorensen
29—At Oak.	L	0-3	Codiroli	Smithson

Won 11, Lost 13

MAY

Date	W/L	Score	Winner	Loser
1—At Seattle	L	8-11	Beard	Walters
2—At Seattle	W	8-6	Pashnick	Vande Berg
3—At Seattle	L	2-6	Langston	Smithson
4—Oakland	W	3-1	Viola	Burris
5—Oakland	W	5-4	Pashnick	Codiroli
6—Oakland	W	4-3	Hodge	Warren
7—At Calif.	W	11-1	Smithson	Romanick
8—At Calif.	W	5-0	Viola	Slaton
9—At Calif.	W	5-2	Filson	Zahn
11—At Milw.	L	1-4	Haas	Hodge
12—At Milw.	W	4-2	Smithson	Caldwell
13—At Milw.	L	1-4	Cocanower	Viola
15—Toronto	L	2-5*	Jackson	Davis
16—Toronto	L	7-8	Alexander	Filson
18—Boston	W	8-3	Smithson	Brown
19—Boston	W	7-0	Viola	Ojeda
20—Boston	L	4-5	Clemens	Butcher
21—At Tor.	L	2-3	Alexander	Davis
22—At Tor.	L	2-3	Jackson	Smithson
23—At Tor.	L	1-4	Clancy	Viola
25—Milwaukee	W	7-4	Butcher	Cocanower
26—Milwaukee	W	7-6	Filson	Waits
27—Milwaukee	L	4-5	Porter	Smithson
30—At Boston	L	0-2	Ojeda	Butcher
31—Kan. City	W	7-2	Hodge	Gubicza

Won 13, Lost 12

JUNE

Date	W/L	Score	Winner	Loser
1—Kan. City	L	1-7	Leibrandt	Smithson
2—Kan. City	L	6-7*	Quisenberry	Whitehouse
3—Kan. City	L	2-5	Black	Viola
4—Texas	W	6-2	Butcher	Stewart
5—Texas	L	1-2	Hough	Hodge
6—Texas	W	2-1	Smithson	Mason
7—Texas	W	5-4	Davis	Darwin
8—At Chicago	L	1-6	Bannister	Viola
9—At Chicago	L	4-8	Hoyt	Butcher
10—At Chicago	W	12-5	Hodge	Burns
12—At Texas	L	2-6	Darwin	Smithson
13—At Texas	L	0-3	Tanana	Schrom
14—At Texas	W	3-2	Viola	Stewart
15—At Kan. C.	W	3-0	Butcher	Gubicza
16—At Kan. C.	W	6-1	Williams	Saberhagen
17—At Kan. C.	W	3-1	Smithson	Leibrandt
19—Cleveland	L	4-7	Blyleven	Schrom
20—Cleveland	W	8-2	Viola	Comer
21—Cleveland	L	0-7	Heaton	Butcher
22—Chicago	L	6-8	Spillner	Davis
23—Chicago	W	4-3	Whitehouse	Seaver
24—Chicago	W	3-2	Schrom	Dotson
26—At Cleve.	W	8-3	Viola	Comer
27—At Cleve.	L	4-6*	Camacho	Davis
29—At Detroit	W	5-3	Williams	Morris
29—At Detroit	L	5-7	Hernandez	Filson
30—At Detroit	L	3-4	Petry	Schrom

Won 13, Lost 14

JULY

Date	W/L	Score	Winner	Loser
1—At Detroit	W	9-0	Viola	Berenguer
2—Baltimore	W	6-4	Butcher	McGregor
3—Baltimore	W	3-1	Smithson	Flanagan
4—Baltimore	L	4-6	D. Martinez	Williams
5—New York	W	5-4	Schrom	Guidry
6—New York	W	9-4	Viola	Shirley
7—New York	L	4-1	Rasmussen	Butcher
8—New York	W	4-3*	Davis	Righetti
12—Detroit	W	4-2	Viola	Petry
13—Detroit	L	3-5†	Hernandez	Lysander
14—Detroit	L	5-6‡	Hernandez	Walters
15—Detroit	L	2-6	Rozema	Schrom
16—At Balt.	L	1-3	Davis	Smithson
17—At Balt.	L	1-3	McGregor	Viola
18—At Balt.	W	3-1	Butcher	Boddicker
19—At N.Y.	W	2-1	Whitehouse	Righetti
20—At N.Y.	L	3-4	Howell	Davis
21—At N.Y.	W	5-2	Smithson	Fontenot
22—At N.Y.	L	5-6	Cowley	Viola
23—Oakland	W	14-4	Butcher	Burris
24—Oakland	W	6-4	Filson	McCatty
25—Oakland	L	0-1	Young	Schrom
27—California	W	2-0	Smithson	John
28—California	W	6-1	Viola	Slaton
29—California	W	6-5*	Lysander	Sanchez
30—Seattle	W	9-5	Filson	Beattie
31—Seattle	W	9-2	Schrom	Vande Berg

Won 17, Lost 10

AUGUST

Date	W/L	Score	Winner	Loser
1—Seattle	L	1-5	Barojas	Smithson
2—At Calif.	L	2-14	Slaton	Viola
3—At Calif.	W	4-2	Butcher	Witt
4—At Calif.	L	2-4	Zahn	Filson
5—At Calif.	W	4-2	Schrom	Romanick
6—At Oak.	W	7-4	Smithson	Krueger
7—At Oak.	W	2-1	Viola	McCatty
8—At Oak.	L	0-5	Burris	Butcher
9—At Seattle	L	5-6*	Stanton	Davis
10—At Seattle	W	13-7	Lysander	Vande Berg
11—At Seattle	L	4-5*	Nunez	Filson
12—At Seattle	W	3-0	Viola	Moore
13—Milwaukee	W	5-1	Butcher	Sutton
14—Milwaukee	W	3-2	Hodge	Haas
15—Milwaukee	L	4-8	Caldwell	Schrom
16—At Boston	L	5-7	Crawford	Davis
17—At Boston	W	6-5	Viola	Hurst
18—At Boston	W	6-4	Davis	Stanley
18—At Boston	W	3-1	Castillo	Johnson
19—At Boston	L	4-5	Crawford	Whitehouse
22—At Milw.	W	5-2	Smithson	Caldwell
22—At Milw.	W	4-3	Lysander	Searage
23—At Milw.	L	2-5	McClure	Viola
24—Toronto	L	2-6	Leal	Lysander
25—Toronto	W	5-4‡	Castillo	Gott
26—Toronto	L	1-2	Stieb	Schrom
27—Toronto	L	2-5	Lamp	Smithson
28—Boston	W	2-1	Davis	Stanley
29—Boston	L	0-4	Boyd	Butcher
30—Boston	L	3-9	Nipper	Hodge
31—At Toronto	L	0-7	Stieb	Castillo

Won 15, Lost 16

SEPTEMBER

Date	W/L	Score	Winner	Loser
1—At Toronto	L	4-12	Lamp	Smithson
2—At Toronto	L	0-6	Alexander	Viola
3—At Kan. C.	W	4-1	Butcher	Black
4—At Kan. C.	L	1-4	Gubicza	Schrom
5—At Kan. C.	L	1-4	Leibrandt	Smithson
7—Texas	W	7-3	Viola	Mason
8—Texas	W	5-4	Butcher	Noles
9—Texas	L	3-9	Hough	Schrom
10—Kan. City	W	7-3	Smithson	Gubicza
11—Kan. City	W	5-1	Viola	Leibrandt
12—Kan. City	L	2-3	Black	Lysander
14—At Texas	L	2-9	Hough	Williams
15—At Texas	W	1-0	Smithson	Darwin
16—At Texas	W	2-0	Viola	Stewart
17—Chicago	L	3-7	Hoyt	Butcher
18—Chicago	L	3-5	Nelson	Filson
19—Chicago	L	3-7	Bannister	Smithson
20—Chicago	W	5-4§	Davis	Roberge
21—Cleveland	W	7-3	Butcher	Schulze
22—Cleveland	W	4-1	Schrom	Blyleven
23—Cleveland	W	5-1	Lysander	Ujdur
24—At Chicago	W	8-4	Viola	Bannister
25—At Chicago	L	4-8	Seaver	Butcher
26—At Chicago	L	3-9	Dotson	Schrom
27—At Cleve.	L	3-4	Camacho	Davis
28—At Cleve.	L	10-11	Waddell	Davis
29—At Cleve.	L	4-6	Heaton	Butcher
30—At Cleve.	L	4-7	Blyleven	Schrom

Won 12, Lost 16

*10 innings.   †11 innings.   ‡12 innings.   §13 innings.

Frank Viola won 18 games and developed into one of the best lefthanders in the A.L.

season. The righthanded batter hit .302, tied for the team lead in hits with 174 and delivered 69 RBIs. Hatcher provided a tremendous run of clutch hits over the second half of the season as the Twins moved into contention.

Right fielder Brunansky also warmed up in the second half and finished with 85 RBIs and a team-high 32 home runs.

The Twins' outfield came together on May 8, when Puckett—in only his third professional season—entered the lineup with a 4-for-5 hitting performance and a stolen base against the Angels in Anaheim. It was a sign of things to come.

Puckett wound up batting .296, with 165 hits in 128 games. The 23-year-old rookie led the Twins with 14 stolen bases and tied for the team lead in triples with five. Puckett also proved himself an outstanding defensive player, making only three errors all year.

Puckett's achievements were all the more astonishing considering the fact that he was not even invited to the club's spring training camp in '84. Officials in the Twins' farm system believed that Puckett needed another year in the minors to develop, but Gardner's lobbying on the youngster's behalf led to his recall from Toledo (International) when a roster position in center field opened up.

That roster vacancy was created by the retirement of Jim Eisenreich, who was attempting a comeback after leaving the club two games into the 1983 season. The same nervous disorder that forced his retirement in '83 prevented the 25-year-old from making a successful return.

There were other disappointments for the Twins in '84. Ken Schrom, the club's winningest pitcher with 15 victories in '83, slumped to a 5-11 record and a 4.47 ERA. The shortstop situation remained a mystery as Houston Jimenez (.201, 19 RBIs) and Ron Washington (.294 but only 23 RBIs) both were inconsistent and unproductive. At catcher, neither Dave Engle (.266, 38 RBIs) nor backup Tim Laudner (.206, 10 homers, 35 RBIs) provided much punch. Third baseman Gary Gaetti batted .262, 25 points above his career average, but fell from 21 homers and 78 RBIs to five homers and 65 RBIs.

There also were disappointing results from the two players—infielder John Castino and reliever Ron Davis—Griffith had signed to long-term contracts (a rarity with Griffith) before the 1984 season.

Castino had a recurrence of a previous back problem and was able to play in only eight games. It was believed that the injury may force Castino to retire. Davis, meanwhile, had an off season, finishing with a 7-11 record, a 4.55 ERA and 29 saves in 44 save opportunities.

Still, the contributions of such players as Hrbek, Puckett and Viola put the Twins in the pennant race and generated enthusiasm among fans in the Twin Cities for the first time in a long while.

Veteran slugger Dave Kingman returned to old form and gave Oakland a 35-homer, 118-RBI season.

Pieces Don't Fit A's Puzzle

By KIT STIER

The 1984 Oakland A's might be likened to a complicated puzzle where all the pieces don't fit.

In the winter of 1983, A's management was among the busiest in the game. It wheeled and dealed and was happy with its moves. There were many new faces in Phoenix when spring training opened, including Joe Morgan, Dave Kingman, Bill Caudill, Bruce Bochte, Ray Burris, Lary Sorensen and Jim Essian.

During the spring, all the pieces—pitching, defense, offense—appeared to be in place. But when summer arrived it became quickly and painfully evident that something was amiss.

The problem was not the new acquisitions.

Reliever Caudill, obtained from Seattle during the off-season, earned a club-record 36 saves to rank second in the American League and posted a 2.71 earned-run average. Caudill also notched a spot for himself in All-Star Game history by striking out Tim Raines, Ryne Sandberg and Keith Hernandez—the only three batters he faced—to retire the side in the seventh inning.

New York Mets castoff Kingman appeared to find happiness on a new coast and in a new league. The 35-year-old veteran hit .268, provided 35 home runs (second in the league) and tied a team record by driving in 118 runs.

Burris, brought in from Montreal, became Oakland's No. 1 starter, finishing at 13-10 with a 3.15 ERA.

Trouble was, some of the puzzle's parts, mostly those already in the box, lost their shape. The inevitable result was a jumbled picture in Oakland.

Young pitching hopefuls such as Tim Conroy (1-6, 5.23 ERA), Bill Krueger (10-10, 4.75), Chris Codiroli (6-4, 5.84) and Mike Warren (3-6, 4.90) struggled throughout the season.

Veteran Steve McCatty (8-14, 4.76) started strong but lost eight of his last nine starts. Lefthanded reliever Tom Burgmeier appeared in just 17 games all season because of injuries. Newcomer Sorensen, whom the A's had hoped would win at least half of his decisions, wound up at 6-13 with a 4.91 ERA.

Rookie lefthander Curt Young was a bright spot for the season and for the future, finishing with a 9-4 mark. Middle reliever Keith Atherton (7-6, 4.33) was inconsistent, pitching well at times, giving up homers by the bushel at others.

The result of these pitching woes was that the A's spent most of the summer unsuccessfully trying to play catch-up. "Whatever we gained, we gave it right back," Caudill said after the season. "You've got to get to .500 and go from there. We never took the ball and ran with it. We fumbled, and it's sad. And I think everybody in this clubhouse knows it."

The A's finished the year in fourth place with a 77-85 record, seven games off the pace in the American League West. That marked only a minor improvement over the 74-88 finish in 1983. The team now has had just two winning seasons since 1976, and one of the over-.500 years was strike-shortened 1981.

The A's continually flirted with .500 but never managed to catch up to it after May 14. One game following the All-Star break, Oakland was 44-45. The team then lost five straight.

The A's made another run in August, improving from a 48-60 record to 60-63. Then they lost nine straight, and any pennant hopes—even in the weak A.L. West—were squashed.

The A's never could put together a winning streak, especially at the beginning of the year. Oakland won its first three games, then repeated that streak only once before Steve Boros on May 24 became the first manager to get the ax during the 1984 season. His replacement, assistant coach Jackie Moore, fared little better, achieving a five-game winning stretch only once.

"Mercy," Moore often said. "We've got to turn some of these seven-game losing streaks into seven-game winning streaks."

Boros, then Moore, spent most of the season juggling the pitching staff. Nine players were used as starters, while everyone worked out of the bullpen at one time or another.

If not for Caudill, the A's might have found themselves floundering in the cellar with Texas. The club's 4.48 ERA and 695 strikeouts ranked last in the league, and its totals in walks (592) and home runs allowed (155) also were near the bottom.

And it seemed that every time the pitching staff would start to get hot, the offense would go on ice.

Two key disappointments at the plate were Morgan, who ended his fine 20-year major league career, and young right fielder Mike Davis.

SCORE OF OAKLAND ATHLETICS' 1984 GAMES

APRIL

Date	W/L	Score	Winner	Loser
3—Milwaukee	W	6-5	Burgmeier	Fingers
4—Milwaukee	W	4-3	Burris	Caldwell
6—Boston	W	3-1	Sorensen	Boyd
7—Boston	L	0-3	Hurst	Warren
8—Boston	W	14-2	McCatty	Brown
9—Toronto	W	4-3	Caudill	Lamp
10—Toronto	L	0-3	Leal	Sorensen
12—California	L	2-3	Zahn	Warren
13—California	W	2-1	Caudill	John
14—California	W	4-3	Caudill	Kaufman
15—California	L	8-12	Witt	Sorensen
16—At Seattle	W	9-6	Warren	Young
17—At Seattle	W	6-2	McCatty	Moore
18—At Seattle	L	4-5	Mirabella	Atherton
20—At Boston	L	1-3	Hurst	Conroy
21—At Boston	W	5-2	Warren	Brown
22—At Boston	L	8-12	Eckersley	McCatty
24—At Milw.	L	2-3	Ladd	Sorensen
25—At Toronto	L	0-11	Leal	Conroy
26—At Toronto	W	7-4	Warren	Gott
27—Minnesota	W	5-3	McCatty	Pashnick
28—Minnesota	W	7-0	Burris	Williams
29—Minnesota	L	2-5	Viola	Sorensen
29—Minnesota	W	3-0	Codiroli	Smithson

Won 14, Lost 10

MAY

Date	W/L	Score	Winner	Loser
1—At Calif.	L	1-4	John	Warren
2—At Calif.	W	7-6	Atherton	Romanick
4—At Minn.	L	1-3	Viola	Burris
5—At Minn.	L	4-5	Pashnick	Codiroli
6—At Minn.	L	3-4	Hodge	Warren
7—Seattle	W	6-5	Caudill	Thomas
8—Seattle	W	3-2	Caudill	Beard
9—Seattle	L	1-4	Stanton	Atherton
11—At Balt.	L	3-4	Boddicker	Warren
12—At Balt.	W	12-2	Krueger	D. Martinez
13—At Balt.	L	1-5	Davis	McCatty
14—At N.Y.	L	1-3	Niekro	Sorensen
15—At N.Y.	L	6-9	Guidry	Burris
16—At N.Y.	L	6-7†	Christiansen	Caudill
18—At Detroit	L	4-8*	Petry	Krueger
19—At Detroit	L	4-5	Morris	McCatty
20—At Detroit	L	3-4	Wilcox	Sorensen
22—Baltimore	W	6-4	Burris	Boddicker
23—Baltimore	L	5-9	Swaggerty	Warren
24—Baltimore	W	3-2	Krueger	Davis
25—New York	W	10-7	Atherton	Guidry
26—New York	L	4-8	Fontenot	Sorensen
27—New York	W	7-1	Burris	Rijo
28—Detroit	L	2-6	Morris	Codiroli
29—Detroit	W	8-5	Krueger	Wilcox
30—Detroit	L	1-2	Hernandez	McCatty

Won 9, Lost 17

JUNE

Date	W/L	Score	Winner	Loser
1—At Chicago	L	4-6	Agosto	Sorensen
2—At Chicago	W	6-3	Burris	Dotson
3—At Chicago	L	2-3	Roberge	Jones
4—At Cleve.	W	7-3	Krueger	Heaton
5—At Cleve.	W	4-2†	Atherton	Jeffcoat
6—At Cleve.	L	6-7	Jeffcoat	Jones
8—At Texas	L	4-8	Tanana	Burris
9—At Texas	L	3-4§	Schmidt	Atherton
10—At Texas	L	1-3	Hough	Krueger
11—At Texas	L	3-6	Mason	McCatty
12—Cleveland	L	5-11	Sutcliffe	Conroy
13—Cleveland	W	3-1	Caudill	Blyleven
14—Cleveland	W	7-6	Atherton	Camacho
15—Chicago	W	2-1	Atherton	Hoyt
16—Chicago	W	6-4	McCatty	Bannister
17—Chicago	L	4-9	Seaver	Jones
18—Kan. City	W	10-2	Burris	Gura
19—Kan. City	L	2-6	Black	Codiroli
20—Kan. City	W	8-1	Krueger	Gubicza
22—Texas	L	0-4	Mason	McCatty
23—Texas	W	5-1	Conroy	Darwin
24—Texas	W	4-2	Caudill	Tobik
25—At Kan. C.	L	0-16	Gubicza	Krueger
26—At Kan. C.	W	8-4	Sorensen	Splittorff
26—At Kan. C	W	6-1	Young	Leibrandt
27—At Kan. C.	W	9-5	McCatty	Gura
28—At Toronto	L	6-9	Gott	Atherton
29—At Toronto	W	2-1	Burris	Stieb
30—At Toronto	L	1-6	Alexander	Krueger

Won 15, Lost 14

JULY

Date	W/L	Score	Winner	Loser
1—At Toronto	L	6-7	Acker	Atherton
2—At Boston	W	9-6‡	Caudill	Clear
3—At Boston	L	5-6	Stanley	Sorensen
4—At Boston	L	9-13†	Crawford	Heimueller
5—At Milw.	L	5-7	Cocanower	Krueger
6—At Milw.	W	7-6	Burris	Ladd
6—At Milw.	W	11-0	Young	Caldwell
7—At Milw.	W	8-2	McCatty	Sutton
8—At Milw.	W	4-1	Sorensen	Porter
12—Toronto	W	7-4	Krueger	Lamp
13—Toronto	L	3-6	Leal	Burris
14—Toronto	L	1-2	Stieb	Caudill
15—Toronto	L	3-6	Clancy	Young
16—Boston	L	1-4	Hurst	Sorensen
17—Boston	L	1-6	Ojeda	Krueger
18—Boston	W	7-2	Burris	Boyd
19—Milwaukee	W	4-1	McCatty	Haas
20—Milwaukee	L	7-9	Tellmann	Caudill
21—Milwaukee	L	4-7†	Waits	Rainey
22—Milwaukee	W	5-4	Krueger	Caldwell
23—At Minn.	L	4-14	Butcher	Burris
24—At Minn.	L	4-6	Filson	McCatty
25—At Minn.	W	1-0	Young	Schrom
27—At Seattle	L	2-12	Barojas	Krueger
28—At Seattle	L	1-2	Langston	Burris
29—At Seattle	L	1-4	Moore	McCatty
30—California	L	4-5§	Corbett	Caudill
31—California	L	3-7	Romanick	Sorensen

Won 10, Lost 18

AUGUST

Date	W/L	Score	Winner	Loser
1—California	L	4-6	John	Krueger
3—Seattle	W	5-3	Burris	Moore
3—Seattle	W	11-7	Rainey	Langston
4—Seattle	W	4-2	Young	Beattie
5—Seattle	W	5-4	Sorensen	Vande Berg
6—Minnesota	L	4-7	Smithson	Krueger
7—Minnesota	L	1-2	Viola	McCatty
8—Minnesota	W	5-0	Burris	Butcher
9—At Calif.	W	5-4	Young	Zahn
10—At Calif.	W	7-6†	Atherton	Sanchez
11—At Calif.	W	3-2†	Burgmeier	Sanchez
12—At Calif.	L	9-10	Sanchez	Caudill
14—At Balt.	W	4-3	Burgmeier	Stewart
15—At Balt.	W	6-1	Young	D. Martinez
16—At Balt.	W	8-1	Sorensen	Davis
17—At N.Y.	W	7-3	Krueger	Fontenot
18—At N.Y.	L	0-8	Montefusco	McCatty
19—At N.Y.	W	6-9	Howell	Caudill
20—At Detroit	L	1-14	Morris	Young
21—At Detroit	L	6-12	Wilcox	Sorensen
22—At Detroit	L	4-11	Berenguer	Krueger
24—Baltimore	L	2-4	Boddicker	McCatty
25—Baltimore	L	2-4	Flanagan	Burris
26—Baltimore	L	6-13	Underwood	Young
27—New York	L	7-8	Righetti	Caudill
28—New York	W	4-3§	Caudill	Murray
29—New York	L	1-4	Montefusco	McCatty
31—Detroit	W	7-6x	Atherton	Rozema

Won 14, Lost 14

SEPTEMBER

Date	W/L	Score	Winner	Loser
1—Detroit	W	7-5	Young	Berenguer
2—Detroit	L	3-6	Petry	Conroy
3—At Chicago	W	8-2	Codiroli	Bannister
4—At Chicago	L	2-12	Seaver	McCatty
5—At Chicago	W	5-4	Burris	Dotson
6—At Chicago	L	3-7	Hoyt	Young
7—At Cleve.	L	2-13	Blyleven	Conroy
8—At Cleve.	W	9-5	Codiroli	Heaton
9—At Cleve.	L	5-7	Easterly	McCatty
10—Chicago	W	1-0	Burris	Dotson
11—Chicago	W	4-1	Young	Hoyt
12—Chicago	L	2-4	Burns	Conroy
14—Cleveland	L	1-6	Heaton	Codiroli
15—Cleveland	L	3-6	Ujdur	Burris
16—Cleveland	L	4-8	Waddell	Atherton
17—Texas	W	5-4	Krueger	Mason
18—Texas	W	5-2	Codiroli	Tanana
19—Texas	W	8-7	McCatty	Henke
21—At Kan. C.	L	4-7	Wills	Sorensen
22—At Kan. C.	L	2-4	Black	Burris
23—At Kan. C.	W	5-1	Codiroli	Jones
24—At Texas	W	10-6	Sorensen	Henry
25—At Texas	W	7-5	Young	Hough
26—At Texas	W	7-5	Leiper	Darwin
28—Kan. City	L	5-6	Leibrandt	Burris
29—Kan. City	W	6-2	Codiroli	Saberhagen
30—Kan. City	W	8-2	Krueger	Gubicza

Won 15, Lost 12

*5 innings. †10 innings. ‡11 innings. §12 innings. x13 innings.

Center fielder Dwayne Murphy hit a career-high 33 home runs and continued his usual defensive wizardry.

Morgan, who turned 41 in September, was continually hampered by minor injuries. He hit just .244 with six homers but did surpass Rogers Hornsby to become the all-time leading home run hitter among second basemen with 268. He also wound up ranked third in career walks with 1,865 and as the leading active basestealer with 689.

Davis, who hit .275 with 62 runs batted in a year earlier, batted around .200 until finally waking up in September to finish at .230 with 46 RBIs.

First baseman Bochte, who took a year off from the game in 1983, found it difficult coming back. His batting average dropped to .264, 33 points below his '82 mark.

Kingman virtually carried the club for the first half of the season, but a few players came on later to post respectable

years. Center fielder Dwayne Murphy hit a career-high 33 homers and batted .256, his best average since 1980. Third baseman Carney Lansford also got off to a poor start but surged to finish with a .300 average, his fourth consecutive season at or above that mark. In addition, infielder Tony Phillips appeared to have found a home at second base after hitting .266. Phillips, however, made a team-high 28 errors, contributing to the team total of 146, tied for worst in the league.

Left fielder Rickey Henderson won his fifth basestealing title with 66 steals, hit .293 with 16 homers and was among the league leaders in runs scored (113), walks (86) and on-base percentage (.399). However, his totals fell short of the club's high expectations for him.

All in all, it was a season of many high hopes gone sour for the A's in 1984.

Right fielder Harold Baines was the one consistent piece in the White Sox' otherwise confusing puzzle.

Major Flop Stuns White Sox

By DAVE van DYCK

If there ever was a study in contrasts, it was the 1983 Chicago White Sox and the 1984 version of the same team. The White Sox went from American League West champions, 99 victories and 800 runs scored in 1983 to fifth place, 74 victories and 679 runs a year later.

It was the biggest flop by a division champion since divisional play began in 1969. The previous record drop-off (in terms of victories) was by the Minnesota Twins, who went from 98 wins in 1970 (when they won the A.L. West) to 74 wins in 1971. (The strike-shortened 1981 season throws a kink into the computation of this record. It could be argued that Oakland, which went 64-45 overall in the '81 split season but managed only 68 victories in a full 162-game schedule in '82, offered the most disastrous defense of its title.)

So, with basically the same personnel they had in '83, the White Sox won 25 fewer games in '84.

What happened?

"Probably the worst thing that happened was the seven-game winning streak right before the All-Star break," White Sox Chairman of the Board Jerry Reinsdorf said.

That winning streak, which put Chicago in sole possession of first place for the first time all season and gave the club a one-game lead in the tight A.L. West, apparently convinced the players, the manager, the coaches and the front office that the White Sox finally had found the groove. All of the prognosticators had predicted the White Sox would successfully defend their title, and there they were in first place at the halfway point. What was there to worry about?

"The intensity was lost," Reinsdorf said. And with that relaxed attitude, so was the season.

The White Sox lost 13 of their next 17 games. They followed that with a 9-2 spurt, but then came a 36-game stretch when they won only 10 games, none of them in succession. By mid-September, Chicago was out of the race.

"I'm glad the season is over," Manager Tony LaRussa, the 1983 Major League Manager of the Year, said after the season. "As soon as I knew we couldn't win the division, I was ready to start a new year."

The White Sox finished 1984 with the second-worst road record (31-50) in the league. They also doubled their number of

Veteran Tom Seaver recorded 15 victories, high on Chicago's staff.

one-run losses (32, the highest total in the league) from the year before.

"A lot of things pyramided," Reinsdorf said. "The hitting was so bad it caused pitchers to think they had to pitch a shutout. Then the pitching went to pot."

That it did. The staff earned-run average of 4.13 was a far cry from the 3.67 figure of a year earlier.

LaMarr Hoyt, the 1983 Cy Young Award winner, went from 24-10 and a 3.66 ERA to 13-18 and a 4.47 ERA. Though he pitched 11 complete games he often had first-inning trouble, once leaving a game against New York after getting only two outs and giving up five runs.

Richard Dotson, who went from 22-7 to 14-15, mirrored the second-half collapse of the entire team. The righthander, the only White Sox player to make the All-Star team, was 3-11 in the second half. Britt Burns (4-12, 5.00 ERA) started 16 games

SCORES OF CHICAGO WHITE SOX' 1984 GAMES

APRIL

Date		Score	Winner	Loser
2—At Balt.	W	5-2	Hoyt	McGregor
6—Detroit	L	2-3	Wilcox	Dotson
7—Detroit	L	0-4	Morris	Bannister
8—Detroit	L	3-7	Lopez	Seaver
10—Cleveland	W	7-3	Hoyt	Heaton
11—Cleveland	W	6-1	Dotson	Blyleven
13—At N.Y.	W	5-3	Bannister	Montefusco
15—At N.Y.	L	1-2*	Righetti	Burns
17—At Milw.	L	3-7	Haas	Seaver
19—At Milw.	W	3-1	Dotson	Cocanower
20—At Detroit	L	2-3	Lopez	Reed
21—At Detroit	L	1-4	Rozema	Hoyt
22—At Detroit	L	1-9	Berenguer	Brennan
23—Baltimore	W	7-6*	Burns	T. Martinez
24—Baltimore	L	3-8	McGregor	Dotson
25—At Cleve.	L	2-9	Heaton	Bannister
26—At Cleve.	L	4-5	Frazier	Reed
27—Boston	L	3-5	Eckersley	Hoyt
28—Boston	L	7-8	Clear	Reed
29—Boston	W	6-4	Dotson	Nipper
30—New York	W	5-3	Bannister	Guidry

Won 8, Lost 13

MAY

Date		Score	Winner	Loser
1—New York	W	7-5	Barojas	Fontenot
2—New York	W	3-0	Hoyt	Rijo
4—At Boston	W	5-3	Seaver	Eckersley
5—At Boston	W	8-5	Dotson	Boyd
6—At Boston	L	1-3	Hurst	Bannister
7—Milwaukee	L	3-7	Cocanower	Hoyt
8—Milwaukee	W	7-6yz	Seaver	Porter
9—Milwaukee	W	5-4	Seaver	Caldwell
10—Texas	W	8-6	Barojas	Jones
11—Texas	L	1-6	Tanana	Bannister
12—Texas	L	4-6	Stewart	Hoyt
13—Texas	W	8-1	Burns	Hough
14—Kan. City	W	2-0	Seaver	Saberhagen
15—Kan. City	W	3-2	Dotson	Jackson
16—Kan. City	L	6-7	Beckwith	Barojas
17—At Toronto	L	2-3	Jackson	Hoyt
18—At Toronto	L	3-4	Clancy	Burns
19—At Toronto	L	0-1	Gott	Seaver
20—At Toronto	W	3-0	Dotson	Stieb
21—At Kan. C.	W	8-4	Bannister	Gura
22—At Kan. C.	L	6-7	Beckwith	Barojas
23—At Kan. C.	L	0-1	Black	Burns
25—At Texas	L	0-11	Hough	Seaver
26—At Texas	W	5-1	Dotson	Mason
27—At Texas	L	3-11	Darwin	Bannister
29—Toronto	W	8-1	Hoyt	Clancy
30—Toronto	L	1-2	Stieb	Burns

Won 14, Lost 13

JUNE

Date		Score	Winner	Loser
1—Oakland	W	6-4	Agosto	Sorensen
2—Oakland	L	3-6	Burris	Dotson
3—Oakland	W	3-2	Roberge	Jones
4—California	W	6-4	Hoyt	Romanick
5—California	L	1-6	Zahn	Burns
6—California	W	4-0	Seaver	Witt
7—California	W	11-10	Roberge	John
8—Minnesota	W	6-1	Bannister	Viola
9—Minnesota	W	8-4	Hoyt	Butcher
10—Minnesota	L	5-12	Hodge	Burns
12—At Calif.	L	2-3*	Corbett	Jones
13—At Calif.	W	2-1	Dotson	John
14—At Calif.	L	3-9	Romanick	Burns
15—At Oak.	L	1-2	Atherton	Hoyt
16—At Oak.	L	4-6	McCatty	Bannister
17—At Oak.	W	9-4	Seaver	Jones
18—At Seattle	W	8-4	Dotson	Young
19—At Seattle	L	2-8	Beattie	Burns
20—At Seattle	W	5-4	Hoyt	Langston
22—At Minn.	W	8-6	Spillner	Davis
23—At Minn.	L	3-4	Whitehouse	Seaver
24—At Minn.	L	2-3	Schrom	Dotson
25—Seattle	L	1-6	Beattie	Burns
26—Seattle	L	0-5	Langston	Hoyt
27—Seattle	W	9-7	Barojas	Nunez
28—Baltimore	L	0-2	Flanagan	Seaver
29—Baltimore	W	2-1	Dotson	D. Martinez
30—Baltimore	W	5-4†	Jones	Stewart

Won 15, Lost 13

JULY

Date		Score	Winner	Loser
1—Baltimore	L	3-8	Boddicker	Hoyt
2—Detroit	W	7-1	Bannister	Rozema
3—Detroit	W	9-5	Seaver	Morris
4—Detroit	W	8-2	Dotson	Wilcox
5—Cleveland	W	7-6	Nelson	Heaton
6—Cleveland	W	11-6	Hoyt	Schulze
7—Cleveland	W	4-2	Bannister	Smith
8—Cleveland	W	9-8	Agosto	Farr
12—At Balt.	L	1-2	Davis	Hoyt
12—At Balt.	L	0-3	McGregor	Nelson
13—At Balt.	L	5-7†	T. Martinez	Reed
14—At Balt.	W	3-2	Seaver	Flanagan
15—At Balt.	L	4-6	D. Martinez	Dotson
16—At Detroit	L	1-7	Abbott	Hoyt
17—At Detroit	L	2-3	Petry	Nelson
18—At Detroit	W	10-6	Bannister	Morris
19—At Cleve.	W	3-0	Seaver	Farr
20—At Cleve.	L	3-6	Smith	Dotson
21—At Cleve.	W	4-3	Gleaton	Waddell
22—At Cleve.	L	1-4	Heaton	Nelson
24—At Boston	L	2-3	Boyd	Bannister
25—At Boston	L	2-3‡	Clear	Gleaton
26—At Boston	L	0-7	Clemens	Dotson
27—New York	L	6-8	Armstrong	Hoyt
28—New York	L	2-3	Guidry	Nelson
29—New York	W	5-4	Bannister	Bystrom
30—Boston	W	7-0	Seaver	Nipper
31—Boston	L	4-14	Clemens	Dotson

Won 13, Lost 15

AUGUST

Date		Score	Winner	Loser
1—Boston	W	5-3	Hoyt	Ojeda
3—At Milw.	W	5-1	Bannister	Sutton
4—At Milw.	W	7-3	Seaver	Haas
5—At Milw.	W	7-0	Dotson	Caldwell
6—At Milw.	W	5-3	Nelson	Cocanower
7—At N.Y.	W	6-3	Hoyt	Deshaies
7—At N.Y.	L	0-7	Guidry	Gleaton
8—At N.Y.	W	5-4	Bannister	Niekro
9—At N.Y.	L	6-7	Rasmussen	Seaver
10—Milwaukee	L	2-4	Caldwell	Dotson
11—Milwaukee	L	5-10	Cocanower	Nelson
12—Milwaukee	L	1-8	McClure	Hoyt
13—Texas	W	5-3	Bannister	Darwin
14—Texas	L	3-9	Tanana	Seaver
15—Texas	L	5-6*	Hough	Dotson
17—Toronto	L	3-4	Clancy	Hoyt
18—Toronto	W	7-6	Roberge	Jackson
19—Toronto	L	4-7	Key	Agosto
20—At Texas	W	7-5	Dotson	Hough
21—At Texas	L	3-4*	Henke	Roberge
22—At Texas	L	1-3	Darwin	Hoyt
24—At Kan. C.	L	2-5	Black	Bannister
25—At Kan. C.	W	3-0	Seaver	Gubicza
26—At Kan. C.	L	5-6x	Gura	Roberge
27—At Kan. C.	L	4-7	Saberhagen	Hoyt
28—At Toronto	L	6-7†	Clark	Reed
29—At Toronto	W	8-5	Bannister	Leal
30—Toronto	L	3-4	Gott	Seaver
31—Kan. City	L	1-3	Leibrandt	Dotson

Won 12, Lost 17

SEPTEMBER

Date		Score	Winner	Loser
1—Kan. City	W	6-1	Hoyt	Saberhagen
2—Kan. City	L	4-6*	Quisenberry	Burns
3—Oakland	L	2-8	Codiroli	Bannister
4—Oakland	W	12-2	Seaver	McCatty
5—Oakland	L	4-5	Burris	Dotson
6—Oakland	W	7-3	Hoyt	Young
7—California	L	8-16	Zahn	Burns
8—California	L	5-6	Sanchez	Reed
9—California	W	8-2	Seaver	Witt
10—At Oak.	L	0-1	Burris	Dotson
11—At Oak.	L	1-4	Young	Hoyt
12—At Oak.	W	4-2	Burns	Conroy
14—At Calif.	L	0-5	Zahn	Bannister
15—At Calif.	L	2-11	Witt	Seaver
16—At Calif.	L	2-4	Romanick	Dotson
17—At Minn.	W	7-3	Hoyt	Butcher
18—At Minn.	W	5-3	Nelson	Filson
19—At Minn.	W	7-3	Bannister	Smithson
20—At Minn.	L	4-5§	Davis	Roberge
21—Seattle	L	1-5	Beattie	Dotson
22—Seattle	L	1-7	Young	Hoyt
23—Seattle	W	4-0	Burns	Moore
24—Minnesota	L	4-8	Viola	Bannister
25—Minnesota	W	8-4	Seaver	Butcher
26—Minnesota	W	9-3	Dotson	Schrom
27—At Seattle	L	2-7	Young	Hoyt
28—At Seattle	L	1-7	Moore	Burns
29—At Seattle	W	6-2	Bannister	Barojas
30—At Seattle	L	3-5	Langston	Seaver

Won 12, Lost 17

*10 innings. †11 innings. ‡12 innings. §13 innings. x16 innings. y25 innings. zSuspended game, completed May 9.

Young Greg Walker (above) took over first base duties and contributed 24 home runs while left fielder Ron Kittle dropped off to 32 homers and 74 RBIs.

but found himself working out of the bullpen much of the time.

The bullpen, which sent Salome Barojas (who had posted only one 1984 save) to Seattle in a June trade and which lost Dennis Lamp to free agency in the off-season, had 32 saves, 16 fewer than the year before. Ron Reed, a newcomer acquired from the Phillies, led the relievers with 12 saves and a 3.08 ERA but was 0-6. Lefty Juan Agosto had a 2-1 record and a 3.09 ERA but only seven saves in 55⅓ innings.

In the batting department, designated hitter Greg Luzinski dropped from a .255 average, 32 home runs and 95 runs batted in to .238, 13 homers and 58 RBIs. Left fielder Ron Kittle's Rookie of the Year statistics of a .254 average, 35 homers and 100 RBIs fell to .215, 32 and 74, respectively. Catcher Carlton Fisk, who hit .289 with 26 homers and 86 RBIs in '83, fought injuries much of the season and contributed only 21 homers and 43 RBIs while batting .231.

Every phase of the game suffered. Center fielder Rudy Law stole 77 bases in '83 but only 29 in '84; second baseman Julio Cruz stole 24 bases in 99 White Sox games in '83 (after being obtained from Seattle) but only 14 in 143 games in '84. The reason? Law dropped 32 points off his '83 batting average (to .251) and Cruz 29 points (to .222), and it's hard to steal bases when you're not on base. The team batting average ranked last in the league, falling from .262 to .247.

There were some bright spots.

Right fielder Harold Baines hit .304, the first time in his five-year major league career he had batted over .300. He also swatted a career-high 29 homers and led Chicago with 94 RBIs and 72 runs scored while ranking among the league leaders in slugging percentage (.541, tops in the league), triples (10) and game-winning RBIs (17).

Second-year man Greg Walker took over first base on a permanent basis behind the strength of his .294 average, 24 homers and 75 RBIs.

And there was Tom Seaver, the pitcher acquired during the off-season from the New York Mets in the free-agent compensation draft. At 39, Seaver led the Chicago staff with 15 victories and finished with a 3.95 ERA while never missing a turn.

Reinsdorf and co-Owner Eddie Einhorn had to be pleased with a Chicago attendance record for the second straight year. More than 2.1 million fans came to Comiskey Park, an average attendance of 26,383 per date.

Young Mariners Show Promise

By BILL PLASCHKE

So what if the Seattle Mariners finished tied for fifth out of seven teams in the American League West, the weakest division in baseball. Some very good things happened in Seattle in 1984, and the Mariners appeared to be making strides toward respectability.

The Mariners had their best start in club history at 6-1. They had their best finish, too, going 15-12 in September. Overall, the young team wound up with the second-best record in club history, 74-88, two games behind a 1982 team filled with veterans.

But more importantly for Seattle, the Mariners produced two rookie stars—first baseman Alvin Davis and pitcher Mark Langston—who became the city's first true baseball heroes.

Davis, the A.L. Rookie of the Year, hit .284 while leading his teammates in home runs (27), runs batted in (116, fourth in the league), doubles (34), total bases (282), walks (97, second in the league) and on-base percentage (.391, fifth in the league). Davis set a number of rookie and overall team records as well as major league marks for intentional walks (16) and game-winning RBIs (13) in a rookie season.

Langston was the American League's answer to Dwight Gooden, the Mets' rookie pitching sensation. The lefthander struck out nine batters in the season finale against Chicago to finish with 204, making him the first rookie since Cleveland's Herb Score in 1955 to lead the American League in strikeouts. Langston was the ace of Seattle's staff, posting a 17-10 record with a 3.40 earned-run average.

Another rookie, outfielder Phil Bradley, showed promise for the future by hitting .349 after the All-Star break and raising his season batting average to .301. Bradley also was outstanding in the field, making only two errors all season.

"You're never satisfied, but it's safe to say I'm pleased with things," General Manager Hal Keller said after the season. "We have several pennant-type ball players around here. The biggest thing this club needs is experience."

Experience and a stable managerial situation—if such a situation is possible on a club that has never posted a winning season—would benefit the Mariners. Despite starting and finishing well, Seattle sputtered in between, and the administration of Manager Del Crandall was blamed for the team's mounting losses. Several players said Crandall failed to spell out their roles on the team, a problem that caused "confusion in the clubhouse."

Crandall was fired September 1. A sigh of relief could be heard throughout the clubhouse as the tension of the final month under Crandall—when the Mariners lost 18 of 28 games—finally was broken.

The worst episode during that irritable month was an on-field fistfight between catcher Bob Kearney and pitching coach Frank Funk, who was well liked by the Seattle pitchers. Crandall fired Funk shortly thereafter, and a week after that, Crandall was gone.

"We just felt it was time for a change," Keller said. "We felt something else was needed."

Third base coach Chuck Cottier became that "something else." Cottier was named manager for the remainder of the season and led Seattle to its strong September finish.

The team earlier had been taken aback by the loss of slugger Gorman Thomas for the season. Thomas, who had been acquired during the off-season from Cleveland, left the club in mid-May for surgery on a torn rotator cuff but hoped to return as a designated hitter in 1985.

The Mariners also were hurt by the failure of pitcher Matt Young to match the achievements of his strong rookie season in 1983. Young was suffering from a sore back, and when he finally went on the disabled list July 4 he had a 4-6 record with a 7.66 ERA. He subsequently was sent to the club's Triple-A affiliate in Salt Lake City, where he managed to regain his old form. Young returned to Seattle in September and threw effectively, allowing only two runs over 17 innings in his final two starts. He finished at 6-8 with a 5.72 ERA.

Young was not the only pitcher who struggled. Mike Moore struck out 158 batters but went 7-17 with a 4.97 ERA. Ed Vande Berg (8-12, 4.76 ERA), working as a starter and reliever, allowed a team-high 18 home runs. Salome Barojas (6-5, 3.97), who was acquired from the Chicago White Sox in June, and Jim Beattie (12-16, 3.41) were effective, although their records did not reflect it because of a lack of offensive support.

One pleasant surprise was reliever Edwin Nunez. The righthander went 2-2 with a 3.19 ERA and seven saves. Mike Stanton (4-4, 3.54) was the team leader with just eight saves.

Rookie Alvin Davis came out of nowhere to hit 27 home runs, drive in 116 runs and capture TSN A.L. Rookie Player of the Year honors.

Overall, Seattle pitchers had the league's second-worst team ERA (4.31) and threw fewer shutouts (four) and allowed more walks (619) than any other club in the league. On a positive note, they did throw 972 strikeouts, No. 2 in the league.

Seattle was among the lightest-hitting teams in the league despite the contributions of Davis and Bradley. The Mariners batted .258 and hit 129 homers, both figures ranking near the bottom of the league.

A couple of other players, however, made strong showings. Second baseman Jack Perconte, who came over from Cleveland with Thomas, batted .294, stole 29 bases and tied the club record for hits (180) in the season finale. Outfielder Al Cowens raised his batting average 72 points over his 1983 mark to .277 and added 15 homers and 78 R.BIs.

Though Seattle fans had the opportunity to watch two rookie sensations (Davis and Langston) in 1984, their response in terms of ticket sales was less than overwhelming. Attendance at the Kingdome was up only slightly, rising from 813,537 in '83 to 870,372, an average of 10,745 fans per date.

SCORES OF SEATTLE MARINERS' 1984 GAMES

Date	W/L	Score	Winner	Loser
APRIL				
4—Toronto	W	3-2*	Stanton	Lamp
5—Toronto	L	5-13	Leal	Beattie
6—Milwaukee	W	6-3	Young	Haas
7—Milwaukee	W	3-2	Langston	Tellmann
8—Milwaukee	W	5-4	Moore	Sutton
10—Boston	W	5-1	Beattie	Ojeda
11—Boston	W	5-4	Young	Eckersley
13—At Minn.	L	3-4	Davis	Stanton
14—At Minn.	L	3-4†	Davis	Stoddard
15—At Minn.	W	5-4	Thomas	Walters
16—Oakland	L	6-9	Warren	Young
17—Oakland	L	2-6	McCatty	Moore
18—Oakland	W	5-4	Mirabella	Atherton
20—At Milw.	W	5-0	Beattie	Sutton
21—At Milw.	L	2-6	Caldwell	Young
23—At Toronto	L	5-8	Stieb	Langston
24—At Toronto	W	4-2	Beard	Clancy
25—At Boston	L	1-2	Hurst	Beattie
26—At Boston	W	6-5*	Vande Berg	Stanley
27—At Calif.	L	3-9	Romanick	Stoddard
28—At Calif.	L	1-10	Zahn	Langston
29—At Calif.	W	9-6*	Thomas	LaCorte
30—At Calif.	L	1-8	Witt	Mirabella
Won 12, Lost 11				
MAY				
1—Minnesota	W	11-8	Beard	Walters
2—Minnesota	L	6-8	Pashnick	Vande Berg
3—Minnesota	W	6-2	Langston	Smithson
4—California	L	1-4	Zahn	Moore
5—California	L	1-3	Witt	Beattie
6—California	W	3-1	Vande Berg	John
7—At Oak.	L	5-6	Caudill	Thomas
8—At Oak.	L	2-3	Caudill	Beard
9—At Oak.	W	4-1	Stanton	Atherton
11—At N.Y.	W	4-3§	Thomas	Christiansen
12—At N.Y.	W	5-0	Beattie	Rawley
13—At N.Y.	L	0-7	Shirley	Langston
14—At Detroit	L	5-7	Lopez	Vande Berg
15—At Detroit	L	4-6	Morris	Thomas
16—At Detroit	L	1-10	Wilcox	Young
18—At Balt.	L	1-4	Davis	Beattie
19—At Balt.	W	6-5*	Vande Berg	T. Martinez
20—At Balt.	L	1-5	Flanagan	Moore
22—New York	W	5-3	Young	Rijo
23—New York	L	0-3	Rasmussen	Beattie
24—New York	L	0-2	Niekro	Langston
25—Detroit	W	7-3	Vande Berg	Wilcox
26—Detroit	W	9-5	Moore	Berenguer
27—Detroit	W	6-1	Young	Petry
28—Baltimore	L	4-7	Davis	Beattie
29—Baltimore	L	2-3	T. Martinez	Mirabella
30—Baltimore	L	2-8	Boddicker	Vande Berg
Won 11, Lost 16				
JUNE				
1—At Texas	W	5-3	Beard	Tobik
2—At Texas	W	10-7	Stoddard	Schmidt
3—At Texas	W	10-4	Beattie	Tanana
4—At Kan. C.	W	7-1	Langston	Saberhagen
5—At Kan. C.	L	3-4	Gubicza	Vande Berg
6—At Kan. C.	L	2-5	Leibrandt	Moore
7—At Kan. C.	L	8-9	Jackson	Beard
8—At Cleve.	L	3-4	Comer	Beattie
9—At Cleve.	L	7-8	Frazier	Langston
10—At Cleve.	L	1-3	Heaton	Vande Berg
10—At Cleve.	W	4-3	Langston	Camacho
12—Kan. City	W	3-2*	Moore	Saberhagen
13—Kan. City	L	4-6	Gura	Young
14—Kan. City	W	4-1	Beattie	Black
15—Texas	W	4-3*	Nunez	McLaughlin
16—Texas	L	1-5	Mason	Vande Berg
17—Texas	W	5-2	Stanton	Jones
18—Chicago	L	4-8	Dotson	Young
19—Chicago	W	8-2	Beattie	Burns
20—Chicago	L	4-5	Hoyt	Langston
22—Cleveland	L	3-13	Jeffcoat	Vande Berg
23—Cleveland	L	4-11	Smith	Moore
24—Cleveland	L	0-5	Blyleven	Stoddard
25—At Chicago	W	6-1	Beattie	Burns
26—At Chicago	W	5-0	Langston	Hoyt
27—At Chicago	L	7-9	Barojas	Nunez
28—At Boston	L	6-9†	Stanley	Mirabella
29—At Boston	W	5-3	Vande Berg	Ojeda
30—At Boston	W	2-1	Beattie	Boyd
Won 14, Lost 15				
JULY				
1—At Boston	W	1-0	Langston	Nipper
2—At Milw.	L	2-3	Sutton	Moore
JULY				
2—At Milw.	L	4-6	Tellmann	Barojas
3—At Milw.	L	6-11	Ladd	Young
4—At Milw.	L	2-4	Haas	Vande Berg
5—At Toronto	L	8-10	Alexander	Beattie
6—At Toronto	L	2-9	Leal	Langston
7—At Toronto	W	8-4	Moore	Clancy
8—At Toronto	W	7-1	Beattie	Gott
12—Boston	W	3-2	Langston	Ojeda
13—Boston	L	5-9	Boyd	Moore
14—Boston	W	5-4	Vande Berg	Clemens
15—Boston	L	3-11	Nipper	Beattie
16—Milwaukee	W	11-2	Barojas	Candiotti
17—Milwaukee	W	3-1	Langston	Cocanower
18—Milwaukee	L	2-5	Sutton	Moore
19—Toronto	L	1-8	Stieb	Vande Berg
20—Toronto	L	7-12	Acker	Mirabella
21—Toronto	W	9-3	Barojas	Lamp
22—Toronto	L	3-5	Alexander	Langston
23—At Calif.	L	1-7	Witt	Moore
24—At Calif.	W	4-3	Vande Berg	Zahn
25—At Calif.	L	0-1*	Sanchez	Beattie
27—Oakland	W	12-2	Barojas	Krueger
28—Oakland	W	2-1	Langston	Burris
29—Oakland	W	4-1	Moore	McCatty
30—At Minn.	L	5-9	Filson	Beattie
31—At Minn.	L	2-9	Schrom	Vande Berg
Won 12, Lost 16				
AUGUST				
1—At Minn.	W	5-1	Barojas	Smithson
3—At Oak.	L	3-5	Burris	Moore
3—At Oak.	L	7-11	Rainey	Langston
4—At Oak.	L	2-4	Young	Beattie
5—At Oak.	L	4-5	Sorensen	Vande Berg
6—California	L	4-8	John	Barojas
7—California	L	6-7	Aase	Stanton
8—California	W	7-2	Langston	Witt
9—Minnesota	W	6-5*	Stanton	Davis
10—Minnesota	L	7-13	Lysander	Vande Berg
11—Minnesota	W	5-4*	Nunez	Filson
12—Minnesota	L	0-3	Viola	Moore
14—At N.Y.	W	2-1	Langston	Rasmussen
15—At N.Y.	L	2-3	Cowley	Beattie
16—At N.Y.	L	5-4	Barojas	Niekro
17—At Detroit	L	2-6	Wilcox	Moore
18—At Detroit	L	3-4	Berenguer	Geisel
19—At Detroit	W	4-1	Langston	Petry
20—At Balt.	L	4-5	D. Martinez	Beattie
21—At Balt.	W	4-3	Barojas	Davis
22—At Balt.	L	0-4	McGregor	Moore
24—New York	L	4-6*	Righetti	Stanton
25—New York	L	1-14	Rasmussen	Beattie
26—New York	L	2-7	Niekro	Barojas
28—Detroit	L	4-5	Hernandez	Stanton
29—Detroit	W	5-1	Langston	Petry
30—Detroit	W	2-1	Beattie	Morris
31—Baltimore	L	7-11	Stewart	Mirabella
Won 10, Lost 18				
SEPTEMBER				
1—Baltimore	W	10-9	Vande Berg	T. Martinez
2—Baltimore	L	3-4	Swaggerty	Moore
3—At Texas	W	7-3	Langston	Tanana
4—At Texas	W	6-3‡	Stoddard	Schmidt
5—At Texas	W	6-5*	Mirabella	Stewart
7—At Kan. C.	L	4-5	Saberhagen	Young
8—At Kan. C.	L	4-5	Beckwith	Moore
9—At Kan. C.	L	5-6	Huismann	Nunez
10—Texas	W	7-3	Beattie	Darwin
11—Texas	W	4-3	Best	Noles
12—Texas	L	1-8	Mason	Young
13—Texas	L	7-9	Tanana	Moore
14—Kan. City	W	2-1	Langston	Jackson
15—Kan. City	L	5-8	Jones	Best
16—Kan. City	L	2-4	Leibrandt	Barojas
17—Cleveland	W	3-2†	Geisel	Jeffcoat
18—Cleveland	W	6-3	Moore	Ujdur
19—Cleveland	W	4-3	Langston	Heaton
21—At Chicago	W	5-1	Beattie	Dotson
22—At Chicago	W	7-1	Young	Hoyt
23—At Chicago	L	0-4	Burns	Moore
25—At Cleve.	L	5-13	Heaton	Langston
26—At Cleve.	L	0-1	Blyleven	Beattie
27—Chicago	W	7-2	Young	Hoyt
28—Chicago	W	7-1	Moore	Burns
29—Chicago	L	2-6	Bannister	Barojas
30—Chicago	W	5-3	Langston	Seaver
Won 15, Lost 12				

*10 innings.   †11 innings.   ‡13 innings.   §17 innings.

Bottom Drops Out on Rangers

By JIM REEVES

There was no in-between for the Texas Rangers in 1984, not even the mediocrity for which they have become famous.

Two years after the 98-loss disaster of 1982, the bottom again dropped out for the Rangers as they sank all the way to the basement of baseball's weakest division. For the first time since they lost 105 games in 1973, the Rangers finished last in the American League West, this time with a dismal 69-92 record. They never stood higher than fourth in the division, and they spent all but 40 days of the season in the bottom spot.

As proof that individual achievements and team success do not necessarily go hand in hand, 1984 was a banner season statistically for many Texas players.

Third baseman Buddy Bell batted .315 to rank fourth in the league and had 11 home runs, 83 runs batted in and 36 doubles in his best overall season since 1980.

Right fielder-designated hitter Larry Parrish hit .285 with a club-high 22 homers and had career bests as well as team-leading totals in hits (175), doubles (42, second in the league), and RBIs (101, ninth in the league).

Second-year first baseman Pete O'Brien, who had a disappointing rookie season, rewarded the Rangers for their patience by batting .287 with 18 homers and 80 RBIs.

Even outfielder Gary Ward, who had been acquired in an off-season trade with Minnesota, overcame a horrendous first half and finished with a .284 average, 21 homers, 79 RBIs and a club-leading 97 runs scored.

The pitching staff had its bright spots, too. Knuckleballer Charlie Hough led the league with 17 complete games while pacing the Texas staff with a 16-14 record, 266 innings pitched and 164 strikeouts. Lefthander Frank Tanana posted a 15-15 record, his best since 1978, and compiled a team-leading 3.25 earned-run average.

Righthander Dave Schmidt (6-6, 2.56 ERA) got into the act, too. His 12 saves were the most by a Ranger reliever since Jim Kern's 29 in 1979.

With so many things going right, how did the season go so wrong?

"Too many holes," said second-year Manager Doug Rader, who came out of the season with a two-year contract extension (through 1987) despite the team's poor performance. "We had too many other people who just didn't produce at all."

Exactly. For every positive there was a negative—and then some.

At catcher, the Rangers were simply awful. Ned Yost, rookie Donnie Scott and journeyman Marv Foley combined for a .204 batting average. In addition, only 40 of 167 would-be basestealers were thrown out by the Rangers—and some of those runners were erased on pickoff moves by pitchers. The catchers' success rate for throwing out runners was the worst in the league.

Second baseman Wayne Tolleson, who hit .213, and rookie shortstop Curtis Wilkerson, who batted .248, combined for just 24 extra-base hits and 35 RBIs in 822 at-bats. Leadoff man Billy Sample batted .247, his worst average ever in professional baseball.

The bullpen saved a league-low 21 games, while the Rangers' opponents more than doubled that figure with 47 saves.

Injuries that kept outfielder George Wright out for most of the first half of the season and poor performances by pitchers Dave Stewart (7-14, 4.73 ERA) and Danny Darwin (8-12, 3.94) also hurt.

"It was a weird year," Parrish said. "We had a bunch of guys who had really good years. And we had some more guys that didn't, guys at key positions."

Said Hough: "At one time or another, we fouled up every phase of the game."

Bell, who was named team captain for 1985 just before the end of the season, cautioned his teammates not to go home and spend the winter admiring personal statistics.

"That's why statistics don't mean anything," Bell said. "You can look back and say some guys had good years, but the bottom line is we didn't win, so nobody can be happy. . . . We've got to shore up some spots."

Tom Grieve, who became the youngest general manager in the major leagues when he took over after the September 1 resignation of Joe Klein, said he would look for more pitching depth, particularly in the bullpen, a middle infielder with some offensive punch and a strong catcher during the off-season.

But that was for the future. The Rangers had a long winter to mull over the immediate past.

"You try to put winning in perspective," Bell said, "but that's hard to do when winning is really the only thing."

SCORES OF TEXAS RANGERS' 1984 GAMES

APRIL

Date		Score	Winner	Loser
3—Cleveland	L	1-9	Sutcliffe	Hough
5—Cleveland	L	3-7	Heaton	Stewart
6—New York	W	7-6	Tobik	Murray
7—New York	W	8-5*	Mason	Fontenot
8—New York	L	3-4x	Murray	Tobik
10—At Detroit	L	1-5	Petry	Stewart
12—At Detroit	L	4-9	Morris	Tanana
13—Toronto	L	2-3	Lamp	Tobik
14—Toronto	W	6-2	Hough	Clancy
15—Toronto	L	1-2	Lamp	Stewart
17—At Boston	W	8-4	Tanana	Eckersley
18—At Boston	W	4-3	Darwin	Ojeda
19—At Boston	W	7-4	Jones	Boyd
20—At N.Y.	L	1-4	Guidry	Stewart
21—At N.Y.	W	1-0	Tanana	Fontenot
22—At N.Y.	W	4-0	Darwin	Rijo
23—At Cleve.	L	1-3	Sutcliffe	Hough
25—Detroit	L	4-9	Wilcox	Stewart
26—Detroit	L	5-7	Bair	Tanana
27—At Balt.	L	3-4‡	Stewart	Tobik
28—At Balt.	L	1-6	McGregor	Hough
29—At Balt.	L	2-3	Davis	Stewart

Won 8, Lost 14

MAY

Date		Score	Winner	Loser
1—At Toronto	L	4-10	Leal	Tanana
1—At Toronto	W	4-1	Darwin	Alexander
2—At Toronto	L	6-7	Clancy	Hough
4—Baltimore	L	0-2	Davis	Schmidt
5—Baltimore	L	5-7	D. Martinez	Wright
6—Baltimore	L	1-6	Boddicker	Tanana
8—Boston	W	4-3	Hough	Brown
9—Boston	L	0-2	Ojeda	Mason
10—At Chicago	L	6-8	Barojas	Jones
11—At Chicago	W	6-1	Tanana	Bannister
12—At Chicago	W	6-4	Stewart	Hoyt
13—At Chicago	L	1-8	Burns	Hough
15—At Milw.	L	2-3	Sutton	Mason
16—At Milw.	L	1-5	Porter	Darwin
17—At Milw.	W	4-1	Tanana	Haas
18—At Kan. C.	W	2-1	Stewart	Black
19—At Kan. C.	L	2-6	Gubicza	Hough
20—At Kan. C.	W	3-2	Mason	Saberhagen
22—Milwaukee	L	1-7	Porter	Darwin
23—Milwaukee	W	6-1	Tanana	Haas
24—Milwaukee	W	4-3	Stewart	Caldwell
25—Chicago	W	11-0	Hough	Seaver
26—Chicago	L	1-5	Dotson	Mason
27—Chicago	W	11-3	Darwin	Bannister
28—Kan. City	L	1-6	Gura	Tanana
29—Kan. City	L	5-7†	Quisenberry	Schmidt
30—Kan. City	W	7-3	Hough	Saberhagen

Won 12, Lost 15

JUNE

Date		Score	Winner	Loser
1—Seattle	L	3-5	Beard	Tobik
2—Seattle	L	7-10	Stoddard	Schmidt
3—Seattle	L	4-10	Beattie	Tanana
4—At Minn.	L	2-6	Butcher	Stewart
5—At Minn.	W	2-1	Hough	Hodge
6—At Minn.	L	1-2	Smithson	Mason
7—At Minn.	L	4-5	Davis	Darwin
8—Oakland	W	8-4	Tanana	Burris
9—Oakland	W	4-3§	Schmidt	Atherton
10—Oakland	W	3-1	Hough	Krueger
11—Oakland	W	6-3	Mason	McCatty
12—Minnesota	W	6-2	Darwin	Smithson
13—Minnesota	W	3-0	Tanana	Schrom
14—Minnesota	L	2-3	Viola	Stewart
15—At Seattle	L	3-4†	Nunez	McLaughlin
16—At Seattle	W	5-1	Mason	Vande Berg
17—At Seattle	L	2-5	Stanton	Jones
18—At Calif.	W	6-2	Tanana	John
19—At Calif.	W	4-2	Stewart	Romanick
20—At Calif.	W	3-2	Hough	Zahn
22—At Oak.	W	4-0	Mason	McCatty
23—At Oak.	L	1-5	Conroy	Darwin
24—At Oak.	L	2-4	Caudill	Tobik
25—California	W	5-4‡	Schmidt	Corbett
26—California	L	2-3y	Kison	Jones
27—California	L	1-2	Witt	Mason
28—At Cleve.	W	10-6	Schmidt	Schulze
28—At Cleve.	L	2-7	Smith	Tanana
29—At Cleve.	L	12-13x	Easterly	Tobik
30—At Cleve.	W	2-1	Hough	Comer

Won 15, Lost 15

JULY

Date		Score	Winner	Loser
1—At Cleve.	L	5-13	Schulze	Mason
2—New York	W	7-6	Noles	Rijo

JULY

Date		Score	Winner	Loser
3—New York	L	4-5	Bystrom	Tanana
4—New York	L	0-5	Niekro	Stewart
5—Detroit	L	4-7	Lopez	Hough
6—Detroit	W	5-3	Mason	Berenguer
7—Detroit	L	2-5	Rozema	Darwin
8—Detroit	W	9-7	Tanana	Bair
12—Cleveland	W	7-2	Hough	Heaton
13—Cleveland	L	0-5	Blyleven	Mason
14—Cleveland	L	0-5	Farr	Stewart
15—Cleveland	L	4-5‡	Camacho	Jones
16—At N.Y.	L	8-9	Armstrong	Schmidt
17—At N.Y.	W	10-4	Hough	Niekro
18—At N.Y.	L	1-3	Guidry	Mason
19—At Detroit	L	2-9	Wilcox	Stewart
20—At Detroit	L	1-3	Rozema	Tanana
21—At Detroit	L	6-7	Monge	Noles
22—At Detroit	L	0-2	Petry	Hough
23—Baltimore	L	5-9	Boddicker	Mason
24—Baltimore	W	3-2	Darwin	Flanagan
25—Baltimore	L	1-3	D. Martinez	Tanana
27—At Toronto	W	4-2	Hough	Alexander
28—At Toronto	W	5-4	Mason	Jackson
29—At Toronto	L	2-6	Stieb	Darwin
30—At Balt.	W	5-1	Tanana	Flanagan
31—At Balt.	W	7-6	Jones	T. Martinez

Won 10, Lost 17

AUGUST

Date		Score	Winner	Loser
1—At Balt.	L	2-7	Davis	Hough
3—At Boston	W	4-3†	Schmidt	Stanley
4—At Boston	L	2-5	Boyd	Tanana
5—At Boston	L	2-4	Nipper	Hough
6—Toronto	W	5-4	Mason	Jackson
7—Toronto	W	7-6†	Schmidt	Lamp
8—Toronto	L	2-7	Clancy	Darwin
9—Boston	W	7-3	Tanana	Nipper
10—Boston	W	8-4	Hough	Ojeda
11—Boston	L	4-5	Clemens	Stewart
12—Boston	L	2-3‡	Clear	Schmidt
13—At Chicago	L	3-5	Bannister	Darwin
14—At Chicago	W	9-3	Tanana	Seaver
15—At Chicago	W	6-5†	Hough	Dotson
16—Kan. City	L	3-6	Leibrandt	Mason
17—Kan. City	W	8-6	Schmidt	Quisenberry
18—Kan. City	L	4-5	Black	Darwin
19—Kan. City	W	6-4	Tanana	Gura
20—Chicago	L	5-7	Dotson	Hough
21—Chicago	W	4-3†	Henke	Roberge
22—Chicago	W	3-1	Darwin	Hoyt
24—At Milw.	W	10-3	Tanana	Beene
25—At Milw.	L	6-7	Sutton	Hough
26—At Milw.	L	3-6	Haas	Mason
28—At Kan. C.	W	6-0	Darwin	Wills
29—At Kan. C.	L	1-4	Black	Tanana
30—At Kan. C.	W	4-3	Hough	Gubicza
31—Milwaukee	W	7-6	McLaughlin	Ladd

Won 15, Lost 13

SEPTEMBER

Date		Score	Winner	Loser
1—Milwaukee	W	8-4	Stewart	Caldwell
3—Seattle	L	3-7	Langston	Tanana
4—Seattle	L	3-6x	Stoddard	Schmidt
5—Seattle	L	5-6†	Mirabella	Stewart
7—At Minn.	L	3-7	Viola	Mason
8—At Minn.	L	4-5	Butcher	Noles
9—At Minn.	W	9-3	Hough	Schrom
10—At Seattle	L	3-7	Beattie	Darwin
11—At Seattle	L	3-4	Best	Noles
12—At Seattle	W	8-1	Mason	Young
13—At Seattle	W	9-7	Tanana	Moore
14—Minnesota	W	9-2	Hough	Williams
15—Minnesota	L	0-1	Smithson	Darwin
16—Minnesota	L	0-1	Viola	Stewart
17—At Oak.	L	3-5	Krueger	Mason
18—At Oak.	L	2-5	Codiroli	Tanana
19—At Oak.	L	7-8	McCatty	Henke
21—At Calif.	L	4-5	Kaufman	Wright
22—At Calif.	W	9-7	McLaughlin	Sanchez
23—At Calif.	W	2-1†	Stewart	Slaton
24—Oakland	L	6-10	Sorensen	Henry
25—Oakland	L	5-7	Young	Hough
26—Oakland	L	5-7	Leiper	Darwin
27—California	W	2-1	Noles	John
28—California	W	4-1	Stewart	Slaton
29—California	L	0-4	Zahn	Tanana
30—California	L	0-1	Witt	Hough

Won 9, Lost 18

*5 innings.   †10 innings.   ‡11 innings.   §12 innings.   x13 innings.   y14 innings.

Right fielder Larry Parrish led the Rangers with 22 homers and 101 RBIs.

American League Averages for 1984

CHAMPIONSHIP WINNERS IN PREVIOUS YEARS

1900—Chicago*	.607	1928—New York	.656	1956—New York	.630
1901—Chicago	.610	1929—Philadelphia	.693	1957—New York	.636
1902—Philadelphia	.610	1930—Philadelphia	.662	1958—New York	.597
1903—Boston	.659	1931—Philadelphia	.704	1959—Chicago	.610
1904—Boston	.617	1932—New York	.695	1960—New York	.630
1905—Philadelphia	.622	1933—Washington	.651	1961—New York	.673
1906—Chicago	.616	1934—Detroit	.656	1962—New York	.593
1907—Detroit	.613	1935—Detroit	.616	1963—New York	.646
1908—Detroit	.588	1936—New York	.667	1964—New York	.611
1909—Detroit	.645	1937—New York	.662	1965—Minnesota	.630
1910—Philadelphia	.680	1938—New York	.651	1966—Baltimore	.606
1911—Philadelphia	.669	1939—New York	.702	1967—Boston	.568
1912—Boston	.691	1940—Detroit	.584	1968—Detroit	.636
1913—Philadelphia	.627	1941—New York	.656	1969—Baltimore (East)	.673
1914—Philadelphia	.651	1942—New York	.669	1970—Baltimore (East)	.667
1915—Boston	.669	1943—New York	.636	1971—Baltimore (East)	.639
1916—Boston	.591	1944—St. Louis	.578	1972—Oakland (West)	.600
1917—Chicago	.649	1945—Detroit	.575	1973—Oakland (West)	.580
1918—Boston	.595	1946—Boston	.675	1974—Oakland (West)	.556
1919—Chicago	.629	1947—New York	.630	1975—Boston (East)	.594
1920—Cleveland	.636	1948—Cleveland†	.626	1976—New York (East)	.610
1921—New York	.641	1949—New York	.630	1977—New York (East)	.617
1922—New York	.610	1950—New York	.636	1978—New York (East)	.613
1923—New York	.645	1951—New York	.636	1979—Baltimore (East)	.642
1924—Washington	.597	1952—New York	.617	1980—Kansas City (West)	.599
1925—Washington	.636	1953—New York	.656	1981—New York (East)	.551
1926—New York	.591	1954—Cleveland	.721	1982—Milwaukee (East)	.586
1927—New York	.714	1955—New York	.623	1983—Baltimore (East)	.605

*Not recognized as major league in 1900. †Defeated Boston in one-game playoff for pennant.

STANDING OF CLUBS AT CLOSE OF SEASON

EAST DIVISION

Club	Det.	Tor.	N.Y.	Bos.	Balt.	Cle.	Mil.	Cal.	Chi.	K.C.	Min.	Oak.	Sea.	Tex.	W.	L.	Pct.	G.B.
Detroit	..	8	7	6	6	9	11	8	8	7	9	9	6	10	104	58	.642	......
Toronto	5	..	5	8	9	7	3	5	8	7	11	8	7	6	89	73	.549	15
New York	6	8	..	6	8	11	7	4	5	7	4	8	7	6	87	75	.537	17
Boston	7	5	7	..	7	10	9	9	7	3	6	7	4	5	86	76	.531	18
Baltimore	7	4	5	6	..	7	7	8	7	5	5	6	9	9	85	77	.525	19
Cleveland	4	6	2	3	6	..	9	4	4	6	7	7	8	9	75	87	.463	29
Milwaukee	2	10	6	4	6	4	..	4	5	6	5	4	6	5	67	94	.416	36½

WEST DIVISION

Club	K.C.	Cal.	Min.	Oak.	Chi.	Sea.	Tex.	Balt.	Bos.	Cle.	Det.	Mil.	N.Y.	Tor.	W.	L.	Pct.	G.B.
Kansas City	..	7	6	5	8	9	6	7	9	6	5	6	5	5	84	78	.519	......
California	6	..	4	7	8	9	5	4	3	8	4	8	8	7	81	81	.500	3
Minnesota	7	9	..	8	5	7	8	7	6	5	3	7	8	1	81	81	.500	3
Oakland	8	6	5	..	7	8	8	6	5	5	3	8	4	7	77	85	.475	7
Chicago	5	5	8	6	..	5	5	5	5	8	4	7	7	4	74	88	.457	10
Seattle	4	4	6	5	8	..	10	3	8	4	6	6	5	5	74	88	.457	10
Texas	7	8	5	5	8	3	..	3	7	3	2	6	6	6	69	92	.429	14½

Tie Game—Toronto vs. Cleveland.
Championship Series—Detroit defeated Kansas City, three games to none.

RECORD AT HOME

EAST DIVISION

Club	Det.	N.Y.	Tor.	Balt.	Clv.	Bos.	Mil.	Min.	K.C.	Oak.	Chi.	Sea.	Cal.	Tex.	W.	L.	Pct.
Detroit	......	4-2	4-3	2-4	4-3	3-4	6-1	4-2	1-5	6-0	5-1	5-1	3-3	6-0	53	29	.646
New York	4-3	......	5-1	4-2	7-0	2-4	5-2	3-3	6-0	5-1	3-3	2-4	2-4	3-3	51	30	.630
Toronto	2-4	4-3	......	5-2	5-2	4-2	2-4	6-0	5-1	4-2	4-2	3-3	4-2	3-3	49	32	.605
Baltimore	3-4	3-4	2-4	......	4-2	2-5	4-2	4-2	3-3	2-4	4-2	4-2	5-1	4-2	44	37	.543
Cleveland	1-5	2-4	4-2	4-3	......	2-5	4-2	5-1	2-4	3-3	4-2	5-1	1-5	4-2	41	39	.513
Boston	3-3	3-4	3-4	2-4	5-1	......	4-3	3-3	2-4	4-2	4-2	4-2	2-4	4-2	41	40	.506
Milwaukee	1-5	4-2	6-1	4-3	2-5	1-5	......	3-3	3-3	2-4	1-5	5-1	2-4	4-2	38	43	.469

WEST DIVISION

Club	Min.	K.C.	Oak.	Chi.	Sea.	Cal.	Tex.	Det.	N.Y.	Tor.	Balt.	Clv.	Bos.	Mil.	W.	L.	Pct.
Minnesota	......	3-4	5-1	3-4	4-2	4-2	5-2	1-5	5-1	1-5	5-1	4-2	3-3	4-2	47	34	.580
Kansas City	2-4	......	3-4	5-2	6-1	3-3	2-4	0-6	5-1	4-2	4-2	2-4	5-1	3-3	44	37	.543
Oakland	4-3	4-2	......	4-2	6-1	2-5	5-1	3-3	3-3	2-4	2-4	4-2	3-3	4-2	44	37	.543
Chicago	4-2	3-3	4-3	......	2-4	4-3	3-4	3-3	4-2	2-4	3-3	6-0	3-3	2-4	43	38	.531
Seattle	4-3	3-3	4-2	4-3	......	2-4	4-3	5-1	1-5	2-4	1-5	3-3	4-2	5-1	42	39	.519
California	2-5	3-4	2-4	5-1	5-2	......	1-5	1-5	4-2	3-3	3-3	1-5	4-2	......	37	44	.457
Texas	3-3	3-4	4-3	4-2	0-6	3-4	......	2-4	3-3	3-3	1-5	1-5	3-3	4-1	34	46	.425

RECORD ABROAD

EAST DIVISION

Club	Det.	Bos.	Balt.	Tor.	N.Y.	Clv.	Mil.	Cal.	K.C.	Tex.	Min.	Oak.	Sea.	Chi.	W.	L.	Pct.
Detroit	.....	3-3	4-3	4-2	3-4	5-1	5-1	5-1	6-0	4-2	5-1	3-3	1-5	3-3	51	29	.638
Boston	4-3	.....	5-2	2-4	4-2	5-2	5-1	5-1	1-5	3-3	3-3	3-3	2-4	3-3	45	36	.556
Baltimore	4-2	4-2	.....	2-5	2-4	3-4	3-4	3-3	2-4	5-1	1-5	4-2	5-1	3-3	41	40	.506
Toronto	3-4	4-3	4-2	.....	1-5	2-4	1-6	3-3	2-4	3-3	5-1	4-2	4-2	4-2	40	41	.494
New York	2-4	4-3	4-3	3-4	.....	4-2	2-4	2-4	1-5	3-3	1-5	3-3	5-1	2-4	36	45	.444
Cleveland	3-4	1-5	2-4	2-5	0-7	.....	5-2	3-3	4-2	5-1	2-4	4-2	3-3	0-6	34	48	.415
Milwaukee	1-6	3-4	2-4	4-2	2-5	2-4	.....	2-4	3-3	1-4	2-4	2-4	1-5	4-2	29	51	.363

WEST DIVISION

Club	Cal.	K.C.	Tex.	Min.	Oak.	Sea.	Chi.	Det.	Bos.	Balt.	Tor.	N.Y.	Clv.	Mil.	W.	L.	Pct.
California	.....	3-3	4-3	2-4	5-2	4-2	3-4	3-3	2-4	1-5	4-2	4-2	5-1	4-2	44	37	.543
Kansas City	4-3	.....	4-3	4-3	2-4	3-3	3-3	5-1	4-2	3-3	1-5	0-6	4-2	3-3	40	41	.494
Texas	5-1	4-2	.....	2-5	1-5	3-4	4-0	0-6	4-2	2-4	3-3	3-3	2-4	2-4	35	46	.432
Minnesota	5-2	4-2	3-3	.....	3-4	3-4	2-4	2-4	3-3	2-4	0-6	3-3	1-5	3-3	37	47	.420
Oakland	4-2	4-3	3-4	1-5	.....	2-4	3-4	0-6	2-4	4-2	2-4	1-5	3-3	4-2	33	48	.407
Seattle	2-5	1-6	6-0	2-4	1-6	.....	4-2	1-5	4-2	2-4	3-3	4-2	1-5	1-5	32	49	.395
Chicago	1-5	2-5	2-4	4-3	2-4	3-4	.....	1-5	2-4	2-4	2-4	3-3	2-4	5-1	31	50	.383

SHUTOUT GAMES

Club	Balt.	Tor.	Bos.	Det.	Cal.	Clv.	Oak.	N.Y.	Min.	Chi.	Mil.	K.C.	Tex.	Sea.	W.	L.	Pct.
Baltimore	..	0	0	2	3	1	0	0	0	2	2	1	1	1	13	5	.722
Toronto	1	..	1	0	1	0	2	0	2	1	0	2	0	0	10	4	.714
Boston	1	0	..	3	2	0	1	0	2	1	0	1	1	0	12	7	.632
Detroit	2	0	1	..	0	0	0	1	0	1	2	0	1	0	8	7	.533
California	0	1	1	0	..	0	0	2	0	1	1	3	2	1	12	12	.500
Cleveland	0	0	0	0	0	..	0	1	1	0	0	1	2	2	7	7	.500
Oakland	0	0	0	0	0	0	..	0	4	1	1	0	0	0	6	6	.500
New York	0	1	0	0	0	3	1	..	0	1	1	1	1	3	12	13	.480
Minnesota	0	0	1	1	2	0	0	1	..	0	0	1	2	1	9	10	.474
Chicago	0	1	1	0	1	1	0	1	0	..	1	2	0	1	9	11	.450
Milwaukee	1	1	0	0	1	0	3	0	0	0	..	0	0	0	7	10	.412
Kansas City	0	0	1	1	2	1	1	1	0	1	1	..	0	0	9	13	.409
Texas	0	0	0	0	0	0	1	2	1	1	0	1	..	0	6	10	.375
Seattle	0	0	1	0	0	0	0	1	0	1	1	0	0	..	4	9	.308

OFFICIAL AMERICAN LEAGUE BATTING AVERAGES

Compiled by Sports Information Center

CLUB BATTING

Club	Pct.	G.	AB.	R.	OR.	H.	TB.	2B.	3B.	HR.	RBI.	SH.	SF.	SB.	CS.	LOB.
Boston	.283	162	5648	810	764	1598	2490	259	45	181	767	36	46	38	25	1128
New York	.276	162	5661	758	679	1560	2289	275	32	130	725	64	59	62	38	1217
Toronto	.273	163	5687	750	696	1555	2395	275	46	143	702	35	49	193	67	1177
Detroit	.271	162	5644	829	643	1529	2436	254	46	187	788	48	45	106	68	1214
Kansas City	.268	162	5543	673	686	1487	2211	269	52	117	639	41	55	106	64	1071
Cleveland	.265	163	5643	761	766	1498	2167	222	39	123	704	37	67	126	77	1185
Minnesota	.265	162	5562	673	675	1473	2140	259	33	114	636	26	58	39	30	1125
Milwaukee	.262	161	5511	641	734	1446	2038	232	36	96	598	42	46	52	57	1087
Texas	.261	161	5569	656	714	1452	2097	227	29	120	618	47	43	81	50	1090
Oakland	.259	162	5457	738	796	1415	2204	257	29	158	697	37	77	145	64	1115
Seattle	.258	162	5546	682	774	1429	2128	244	34	129	635	66	38	116	62	1184
Baltimore	.252	162	5456	681	667	1374	2134	234	23	160	647	45	43	51	36	1203
California	.249	162	5470	696	697	1361	2084	211	30	150	649	65	46	80	51	1098
Chicago	.247	162	5513	679	736	1360	2177	225	38	172	640	37	44	109	49	1097
Totals	.264	1134	77910	10027	10027	20539	30990	3443	534	1980	9445	626	716	1304	738	15991

INDIVIDUAL BATTING

(Top Fifteen Qualifiers for Batting Championship—502 or More Plate Appearances)

*Bats lefthanded. †Switch-hitter.

Player and Club	Pct.	G.	AB.	R.	H.	TB.	2B.	3B.	HR.	RBI.	GW.	SH.	SF.	SB.	CS.
Mattingly, Donald, New York*	.343	153	603	91	207	324	44	2	23	110	12	8	9	1	1
Winfield, David, New York	.340	141	567	106	193	292	34	4	19	100	13	0	6	6	4
Boggs, Wade, Boston*	.325	158	625	109	203	260	31	4	6	55	5	8	4	3	2
Bell, David, Texas	.315	148	553	88	174	253	36	5	11	83	10	2	9	2	1
Trammell, Alan, Detroit	.314	139	555	85	174	260	34	5	14	69	5	6	2	19	13
Easler, Michael, Boston*	.313	156	601	87	188	310	31	5	27	91	11	1	2	1	1
Hrbek, Kent, Minnesota*	.311	149	559	80	174	292	31	3	27	107	11	1	6	1	1
Murray, Eddie, Baltimore†	.306	162	588	97	180	299	26	3	29	110	19	0	8	10	2
Ripken, Calvin, Baltimore	.304	162	641	103	195	327	37	7	27	86	11	0	2	2	1
Baines, Harold, Chicago*	.304	147	569	72	173	308	28	10	29	94	17	1	5	1	2
Barrett, Martin, Boston	.303	139	475	56	144	182	23	3	4	45	3	4	5	4	5
Hatcher, Michael, Minnesota	.302	152	576	61	174	234	35	5	5	69	7	1	8	0	1
Wilson, Willie, Kansas City†	.301	128	541	81	163	211	24	9	2	44	7	2	3	47	5
Lansford, Carney, Oakland	.300	151	597	70	179	262	31	5	14	74	8	2	9	9	3
Yount, Robin, Milwaukee	.298	160	624	105	186	275	27	7	16	80	9	1	9	14	4

DEPARTMENTAL LEADERS: G—Ripken, Dw. Evans, Gaetti, Murray, 162; AB—Franco, 658; R—Dw. Evans, 121; H—Mattingly, 207; TB—Armas, 339; 2B—Mattingly, 44; 3B—Collins, Moseby, 15; HR—Armas, 43; RBI—Armas, 123; GW—Murray, 19; SH—Meacham, 14; SF—Kingman, 14; SB—Henderson, 66; CS—Butler, 22.

(All Players—Listed Alphabetically)

Player and Club	Pct.	G.	AB.	R.	H.	TB.	2B.	3B.	HR.	RBI.	GW.	SH.	SF.	SB.	CS.
Aikens, Willie, Toronto*	.205	93	234	21	48	88	7	0	11	26	3	0	0	0	0
Allen, Roderick, Detroit	.296	15	27	6	8	9	1	0	0	3	0	1	0	1	0
Allenson, Gary, Boston	.229	35	83	9	19	27	2	0	2	8	1	0	0	0	0
Almon, William, Oakland	.223	106	211	24	47	79	11	0	7	16	3	0	4	5	7
Anderson, James, Texas	.106	39	47	2	5	5	0	0	0	1	0	2	0	0	0
Armas, Antonio, Boston	.268	157	639	107	171	339	29	5	43	123	8	0	7	1	3
Ashford, Thomas, Kansas City	.154	9	13	1	2	3	1	0	0	0	0	0	0	0	0
Ayala, Benigno, Baltimore	.212	60	118	9	25	43	6	0	4	24	4	0	2	1	1
Baines, Harold, Chicago*	.304	147	569	72	173	308	28	10	29	94	17	1	5	1	2
Baker, Douglas, Detroit†	.185	43	108	15	20	26	4	1	0	12	1	2	0	3	0
Balboni, Stephen, Kansas City	.244	126	438	58	107	218	23	2	28	77	8	0	1	0	0
Bando, Christopher, Cleveland†	.291	75	220	38	64	111	11	0	12	41	2	3	4	1	2
Bannister, Alan, Texas	.295	47	112	20	33	43	2	1	2	9	2	0	1	3	0
Bannister, Floyd, Chicago*	.000	34	1	0	0	0	0	0	0	0	0	0	0	0	0
Barfield, Jesse, Toronto	.284	110	320	51	91	149	14	1	14	49	3	1	2	8	2
Barrett, Martin, Boston	.303	139	475	56	144	182	23	3	3	45	3	4	4	5	3
Baylor, Donald, New York	.262	134	493	84	129	241	29	1	27	89	13	1	3	1	1
Bell, David, Texas	.315	148	553	88	174	253	36	5	11	83	10	2	9	2	1
Bell, George, Toronto	.292	159	606	85	177	302	39	4	26	87	11	0	3	11	2
Beniquez, Juan, California	.336	110	354	60	119	160	17	0	8	39	4	4	3	0	3
Bergman, David, Detroit*	.273	120	271	42	74	113	8	5	7	44	5	3	6	3	4
Bernazard, Antonio, Cleveland†	.221	140	439	44	97	126	15	4	2	38	4	7	6	20	13
Biancalana, Roland, Kansas City†	.194	66	134	18	26	40	6	1	2	9	0	5	0	1	2
Bochte, Bruce, Oakland*	.264	148	469	58	124	162	23	0	5	52	9	4	8	2	5
Boddicker, Michael, Baltimore	.000	35	0	1	0	0	0	0	0	0	0	0	0	0	0
Boggs, Wade, Boston*	.325	158	625	109	203	260	31	4	6	55	5	8	4	3	2
Bonnell, R. Barry, Seattle	.264	110	363	42	96	143	15	4	8	48	7	5	0	5	2
Boone, Robert, California	.202	139	450	33	91	118	16	1	3	32	3	6	5	3	3
Boston, Daryl, Chicago*	.169	35	83	8	14	19	3	1	0	3	0	0	0	6	0
Bradley, Philip, Seattle	.301	124	322	49	97	117	12	4	0	24	1	11	0	21	8
Bradley, Scott, New York*	.286	9	21	3	6	7	1	0	0	2	1	0	0	0	0
Brett, George, Kansas City*	.284	104	377	42	107	173	21	3	13	69	9	0	7	0	2
Brookens, Thomas, Detroit	.246	113	224	32	55	89	11	4	5	26	0	8	1	6	6
Brouhard, Mark, Milwaukee	.239	66	197	20	47	72	7	0	6	22	3	0	3	0	3
Brown, Darrell, Minnesota†	.273	95	260	36	71	89	9	3	1	19	1	4	1	4	1
Brown, Michael, California	.284	62	148	19	42	77	8	3	7	22	4	2	0	0	2
Brunansky, Thomas, Minnesota	.254	155	567	75	144	261	21	0	32	85	11	0	4	4	5
Buckley, Kevin, Texas	.286	5	7	1	2	3	1	0	0	0	0	0	0	0	0
Buckner, William, Boston*	.278	114	439	51	122	180	21	2	11	67	4	0	3	2	2
Bumbry, Alonza, Baltimore*	.270	119	344	47	93	116	12	1	3	24	2	2	3	9	5
Burleson, Richard, California	.000	7	4	2	0	0	0	0	0	0	0	1	0	0	0
Burris, B. Ray, Oakland	.000	37	0	1	0	0	0	0	0	0	0	0	0	0	0
Burroughs, Jeffrey, Oakland	.211	58	71	5	15	22	1	0	2	8	0	0	1	0	0
Bush, R. Randall, Minnesota*	.222	113	311	46	69	121	17	1	11	43	3	0	10	1	2
Butler, Brett, Cleveland*	.269	159	602	108	162	214	25	9	3	49	5	11	6	52	22
Calderon, Ivan, Seattle	.208	11	24	2	5	9	1	0	1	1	0	0	0	1	0
Carew, Rodney, California*	.295	93	329	42	97	116	8	1	3	31	2	5	4	4	3
Carter, Joseph, Cleveland	.275	66	244	32	67	114	6	1	13	41	8	0	1	2	4
Castillo, Martin, Detroit	.234	70	141	16	33	54	5	2	4	17	1	4	0	1	0
Castillo, M. Carmelo, Cleveland	.261	87	211	36	55	98	9	2	10	36	4	0	3	1	3
Castino, John, Minnesota	.444	8	27	5	12	13	1	0	0	3	1	0	0	0	0
Caudill, William, Oakland	.000	68	1	0	0	0	0	0	0	0	0	0	0	0	0
Cerone, Richard, New York	.208	38	120	8	25	34	3	0	2	13	2	2	0	1	0
Chambers, Albert, Seattle*°	.224	22	49	4	11	15	1	0	1	4	0	0	0	2	1
Christmas, Stephen, Chicago*	.364	12	11	1	4	8	1	0	1	4	1	0	0	0	0
Clark, Robert, Milwaukee	.260	58	169	17	44	61	7	2	2	16	1	2	1	1	5
Coles, Darnell, Seattle	.161	48	143	15	23	28	3	1	0	6	2	3	0	2	1
Collins, David, Toronto†	.308	128	441	59	136	196	24	15	2	44	11	6	3	60	14
Concepcion, Onix, Kansas City	.282	90	287	36	81	97	9	2	1	23	2	4	3	9	6
Cooper, Cecil, Milwaukee*	.275	148	603	63	166	233	28	3	11	67	5	0	3	8	2
Cowens, Alfred, Seattle	.277	139	524	60	145	228	34	2	15	78	10	1	5	5	5
Cruz, Julio, Chicago†	.222	143	415	42	92	129	14	4	5	43	6	4	5	14	6
Cruz, Todd, Baltimore	.218	96	142	15	31	44	4	0	3	9	1	2	1	1	4
Dauer, Richard, Baltimore	.254	127	397	29	101	133	26	0	2	24	4	3	2	1	3
David, Andre, Minnesota*	.250	33	48	5	12	17	2	0	1	5	1	0	1	0	0
Davis, Alvin, Seattle*	.284	152	567	80	161	282	34	3	27	116	13	0	7	5	4
Davis, Michael, Oakland*	.230	134	382	47	88	139	18	3	9	46	2	2	7	14	9
Davis, Wallace, Kansas City	.147	41	116	11	17	26	3	0	2	12	1	0	2	4	3
Dayett, Brian, New York	.244	64	127	14	31	51	8	0	4	23	0	0	2	0	0
DeCinces, Douglas, California	.269	146	547	77	147	236	23	3	20	82	12	0	12	4	1
Dempsey, J. Rikard, Baltimore	.230	109	330	37	76	120	11	0	11	34	3	5	4	1	2
Dent, Russell, Kansas City	.333	11	9	2	3	3	0	0	0	1	0	0	0	0	0
Dotson, Richard, Chicago	.000	33	0	1	0	0	0	0	0	0	0	0	0	0	0
Downing, Brian, California	.275	156	539	65	148	249	28	2	23	91	11	3	6	0	4
Dunbar, Thomas, Texas*	.258	34	97	9	25	33	2	0	2	10	1	0	1	0	0

Player and Club	Pct.	G.	AB.	R.	H.	TB.	2B.	3B.	HR.	RBI.	GW.	SH.	SF.	SB.	CS.
Dwyer, James, Baltimore*	.255	76	161	22	41	58	9	1	2	21	4	5	6	0	2
Dybzinski, Jerome, Chicago	.235	94	132	17	31	41	5	1	1	10	1	4	1	7	2
Earl, W. Scott, Detroit	.114	14	35	3	4	6	0	1	0	1	0	2	0	1	0
Easler, Michael, Boston*	.313	156	601	87	188	310	31	5	27	91	11	1	2	1	1
Eisenreich, James, Minnesota*	.219	12	32	1	7	8	1	0	0	3	0	0	2	2	0
Engle, R. David, Minnesota	.266	109	391	56	104	138	20	1	4	38	5	2	5	0	1
Essian, James, Oakland	.235	63	136	17	32	47	9	0	2	10	1	1	1	1	1
Evans, Darrell, Detroit*	.232	131	401	60	93	154	11	1	16	63	7	1	4	2	2
Evans, Dwight, Boston	.295	162	630	121	186	335	37	8	32	104	15	1	7	3	1
Faedo, Leonard, Minnesota	.250	16	52	6	13	17	1	0	1	6	0	0	0	0	0
Fernandez, O. Antonio, Toronto†	.270	88	233	29	63	83	5	3	3	19	3	2	2	5	7
Fischlin, Michael, Cleveland	.226	85	133	17	30	41	4	2	1	14	0	5	0	2	2
Fisk, Carlton, Chicago	.231	102	359	54	83	168	20	1	21	43	3	1	4	6	0
Fletcher, Scott, Chicago	.250	149	456	46	114	142	13	3	3	35	10	9	2	10	4
Foley, Marvis, Texas*	.217	63	115	13	25	45	2	0	6	19	4	0	3	0	0
Foli, Timothy, New York	.252	61	163	8	41	52	11	0	0	16	2	6	0	0	0
Ford, Darnell, Baltimore	.231	25	91	7	21	28	4	0	1	5	0	2	0	1	0
Franco, Julio, Cleveland	.286	160	658	82	188	229	22	5	3	79	8	1	10	19	10
Gaetti, Gary, Minnesota	.262	162	588	55	154	206	29	4	5	65	5	3	5	11	5
Gagne, Gregory, Minnesota	.000	2	1	0	0	0	0	0	0	0	0	0	0	0	0
Gamble, Oscar, New York*	.184	54	125	17	23	55	2	0	10	27	3	0	1	1	0
Gantner, James, Milwaukee*	.282	153	613	61	173	211	27	1	3	56	7	2	10	6	5
Garbey, Barbaro, Detroit	.287	110	327	45	94	128	17	1	5	52	4	0	2	6	7
Garcia, Damaso, Toronto	.284	152	633	79	180	237	32	5	5	46	8	3	4	46	12
Gedman, Richard, Boston*	.269	133	449	54	121	227	26	4	24	72	9	2	5	0	0
Gibson, Kirk, Detroit*	.282	149	531	92	150	274	23	10	27	91	17	3	6	29	9
Grich, Robert, California	.256	116	363	60	93	164	15	1	18	58	8	6	4	2	5
Griffin, G. Kenneth, New York*	.273	120	399	44	109	152	20	1	7	56	5	3	4	2	2
Griffin, Alfredo, Toronto†	.241	140	419	53	101	125	8	2	4	30	2	13	4	11	3
Gross, Wayne, Baltimore*	.216	127	342	53	74	151	9	1	22	64	7	1	2	1	2
Grubb, John, Detroit*	.267	86	176	25	47	76	5	0	8	17	5	1	1	1	0
Gruber, Kelly, Toronto	.063	15	16	1	1	4	0	0	1	2	0	0	0	0	0
Gutierrez, Joaquin, Boston	.263	151	449	55	118	142	12	3	2	29	1	12	4	12	5
Hairston, Jerry, Chicago†	.260	115	227	41	59	91	13	2	5	19	2	0	2	2	1
Hall, Melvin, Cleveland*	.257	83	257	43	66	102	13	1	7	30	3	0	5	1	1
Hancock, R. Garry, Oakland*	.217	51	60	2	13	15	2	0	0	8	1	1	0	0	0
Hargrove, D. Michael, Cleveland*	.267	133	352	44	94	118	14	2	2	44	5	3	2	2	0
Harrah, Colbert, New York	.217	88	253	40	55	75	9	4	1	26	2	0	2	3	0
Hart, Michael, Minnesota*	.172	13	29	0	5	5	0	0	0	5	1	0	1	0	1
Hassey, Ronald, Cleveland*	.255	48	149	11	38	45	5	1	0	19	2	0	1	0	1
Hatcher, Michael, Minnesota	.302	152	576	61	174	234	35	5	5	69	7	1	8	0	1
Heath, Michael, Oakland	.248	140	475	49	118	188	21	5	13	64	4	2	4	7	4
Henderson, David, Seattle	.280	112	350	42	98	163	23	0	14	43	6	2	1	5	5
Henderson, Rickey, Oakland	.293	142	502	113	147	230	27	4	16	58	4	1	3	66	18
Henderson, Stephen, Seattle	.262	109	325	42	85	133	12	3	10	35	2	0	2	4	4
Hernandez, Tobias, Toronto	.500	3	2	1	1	1	0	0	0	0	0	0	0	0	0
Herndon, Larry, Detroit	.280	125	407	52	114	163	18	5	7	43	4	1	3	6	2
Hill, Donald, Oakland†	.230	73	174	21	40	52	6	0	2	16	1	4	2	1	1
Hill, Marc, Chicago	.233	77	193	15	45	72	10	1	5	20	1	0	1	1	1
Hoffman, Glenn, Boston	.189	64	74	8	14	18	4	0	0	4	0	1	0	0	1
Hostetler, David, Texas	.220	37	82	7	18	31	2	1	3	10	0	0	0	0	0
Howell, Roy, Milwaukee*	.232	68	164	12	38	57	5	1	4	17	1	0	0	0	1
Hrbek, Kent, Minnesota*	.311	149	559	80	174	292	31	3	27	107	11	1	6	1	1
Hudler, Rex, New York	.143	9	7	2	1	2	1	0	0	0	0	0	0	0	0
Hulett, Timothy, Chicago	.000	8	7	1	0	0	0	0	0	0	0	0	0	1	0
Iorg, Dane, Kansas City*	.255	78	235	27	60	95	16	2	5	30	6	0	6	0	1
Iorg, Garth, Toronto	.227	121	247	24	56	75	10	3	1	25	4	3	1	1	3
Jackson, Reginald, California*	.223	143	525	67	117	213	17	2	25	81	11	1	0	8	4
Jackson, Ronnie, Cal.-Balt.	.193	45	119	5	23	29	4	1	0	7	1	1	1	0	2
Jacoby, Brook, Cleveland	.264	126	439	64	116	162	19	3	7	40	4	2	7	3	2
James, Dion, Milwaukee*	.295	128	387	52	114	146	19	5	1	30	3	6	3	10	10
Javier, Stanley, New York†	.143	7	7	1	1	1	0	0	0	0	0	0	0	0	0
Jimenez, Alfonso, Minnesota	.201	108	298	28	60	73	11	1	0	19	3	2	2	0	1
Johnson, Clifford, Toronto	.304	127	359	51	109	182	23	1	16	61	7	0	3	0	1
Johnson, Howard, Detroit†	.248	116	355	43	88	140	14	1	12	50	8	4	2	10	6
Jones, Lynn, Kansas City	.301	47	103	11	31	40	6	0	1	10	2	0	1	3	3
Jones, Robert, Texas*	.259	64	143	14	37	53	4	0	4	22	3	0	2	1	1
Jones, Ruppert, Detroit*	.284	79	215	26	61	111	12	1	12	37	6	0	1	2	4
Jurak, Edward, Boston	.242	47	66	6	16	24	3	1	1	7	1	1	0	0	0
Kearney, Robert, Seattle	.225	133	431	39	97	144	24	1	7	43	3	9	4	7	5
Kemp, Steven, New York*	.291	94	313	37	91	126	12	1	7	41	3	3	4	4	1
Kiefer, Steven, Oakland	.175	23	40	7	7	12	1	2	0	2	0	2	1	2	1
Kingman, David, Oakland	.268	147	549	68	147	277	23	1	35	118	14	0	14	2	1
Kittle, Ronald, Chicago	.215	139	466	67	100	211	15	0	32	74	3	0	4	3	6
Kunkel, Jeffrey, Texas	.204	50	142	13	29	46	2	3	3	7	0	3	2	4	3
Kuntz, Russell, Detroit	.286	84	140	32	40	58	12	0	2	22	4	0	2	2	2
Laga, Michael, Detroit*	.545	9	11	1	6	6	0	0	0	1	0	0	0	0	0
Lansford, Carney, Oakland	.300	151	597	70	179	262	31	5	14	74	8	2	9	9	3
Laudner, Timothy, Minnesota	.206	87	262	31	54	102	16	1	10	35	4	1	2	0	0
Law, Rudy, Chicago	.251	136	487	68	122	168	14	7	6	37	1	4	1	29	17

Player and Club	Pct.	G.	AB.	R.	H.	TB.	2B.	3B.	HR.	RBI.	GW.	SH.	SF.	SB.	CS.
Law, Vance, Chicago	.252	151	481	60	121	194	18	2	17	59	5	6	4	4	1
Leach, Richard, Toronto*	.261	65	88	11	23	33	6	2	0	7	1	0	1	0	0
Leeper, David, Kansas City*	.000	4	6	1	0	0	0	0	0	0	0	0	0	0	0
Lemon, Chester, Detroit	.287	141	509	77	146	252	34	6	20	76	5	2	4	5	5
Loman, Douglas, Milwaukee*	.276	23	76	13	21	31	4	0	2	12	0	1	0	0	2
Lopes, David, Oakland	.257	72	230	32	59	99	11	1	9	36	3	2	3	12	0
Lowenstein, John, Baltimore*	.237	105	270	34	64	101	13	0	8	28	3	0	3	1	0
Lowry, Dwight, Detroit*	.244	32	45	8	11	19	2	0	2	7	1	4	0	0	0
Lozado, William, Milwaukee	.271	43	107	15	29	44	8	2	1	20	2	3	2	0	3
Luzinski, Gregory, Chicago	.238	125	412	47	98	150	13	0	13	58	11	0	6	5	1
Lynn, Fredric, California*	.271	142	517	84	140	245	28	4	23	79	10	2	2	2	2
Manning, Richard, Milwaukee*	.249	119	341	53	85	126	10	5	7	31	3	3	1	5	7
Manrique, Fred, Toronto	.333	10	9	0	3	3	0	0	0	1	1	0	0	0	0
Martinez, John, Toronto	.220	102	232	24	51	81	13	1	5	37	3	1	9	0	3
Mata, Victor, New York	.329	30	70	8	23	31	5	0	1	6	1	4	1	1	1
Mattingly, Donald, New York*	.343	153	603	91	207	324	44	2	23	110	12	8	9	1	1
McRae, Harold, Kansas City	.303	106	317	30	96	126	13	4	3	42	3	0	9	0	3
Meacham, Robert, New York†	.253	99	360	62	91	118	13	4	2	25	4	14	9	9	5
Meier, David, Minnesota	.238	59	147	18	35	45	8	1	0	13	5	3	1	0	1
Mercado, Orlando, Seattle	.218	30	78	5	17	22	3	1	0	5	0	1	0	1	0
Meyer, Daniel, Oakland*	.318	20	22	1	7	12	3	1	0	4	0	0	0	0	0
Milbourne, Lawrence, Seattle†	.265	79	211	22	56	66	5	1	1	22	3	11	1	0	2
Miller, Darrell, California	.171	17	41	5	7	7	0	0	0	1	0	0	0	0	0
Miller, Richard, Boston*	.260	95	123	17	32	39	5	1	0	12	2	0	1	1	1
Molitor, Paul, Milwaukee	.217	13	46	3	10	11	1	0	0	6	0	1	1	1	0
Moore, Charles, Milwaukee	.234	70	188	13	44	59	7	1	2	17	0	3	1	0	4
Moreno, Omar, New York*	.259	117	355	37	92	128	12	6	4	38	1	4	4	20	11
Morgan, Joe, Oakland*	.244	116	365	50	89	128	21	0	6	43	5	0	6	8	3
Moronko, Jeffrey, Cleveland	.158	7	19	1	3	4	1	0	0	3	0	1	0	0	0
Moseby, Lloyd, Toronto*	.280	158	592	97	166	278	28	15	18	92	8	3	7	39	9
Moses, John, Seattle*	.343	19	35	3	12	15	1	1	0	2	0	1	0	1	0
Motley, Darryl, Kansas City	.284	146	522	64	148	230	25	6	15	70	6	2	4	10	12
Mulliniks, S. Rance, Toronto*	.324	125	343	41	111	151	21	5	3	42	6	0	2	2	3
Murphy, Dwayne, Oakland*	.256	153	559	93	143	264	18	2	33	88	9	4	7	4	5
Murray, Eddie, Baltimore†	.306	162	588	97	180	299	26	3	29	110	19	0	8	10	2
Nahorodny, William, Seattle	240	12	25	2	6	9	0	0	1	3	0	0	1	0	1
Narron, Jerry, California*	.247	69	150	9	37	51	5	0	3	17	0	1	2	0	0
Nelson, Ricky, Seattle*	.200	9	15	2	3	6	0	0	1	2	0	0	0	0	0
Newman, Jeffrey, Boston	.222	24	63	5	14	19	2	0	1	3	0	2	1	0	0
Nichols, T. Reid, Boston	.226	74	124	14	28	38	5	1	1	14	1	1	1	2	1
Nixon, Otis, Cleveland†	.154	49	91	16	14	14	0	0	0	1	0	3	1	12	6
Noboa, Milciades, Cleveland	.364	23	11	3	4	4	0	0	0	0	0	0	0	0	0
Nolan, Joseph, Baltimore*	.290	35	62	2	18	24	1	1	1	9	0	0	1	0	0
O'Berry, P. Michael, New York	.250	13	32	3	8	10	2	0	0	5	0	0	0	0	0
O'Brien, Peter, Texas*	.287	142	520	57	149	233	26	2	18	80	8	1	7	3	5
Oglivie, Benjamin, Milwaukee*	.262	131	461	49	121	177	16	2	12	60	5	1	2	0	6
O'Malley, Thomas, Chicago*	.125	12	16	0	2	2	0	0	0	3	0	0	0	0	0
Orta, Jorge, Kansas City*	.298	122	403	50	120	184	23	7	9	50	5	1	4	0	1
Owen, Spike, Seattle†	.245	152	530	67	130	173	18	8	3	43	5	9	2	16	8
Paciorek, Thomas, Chicago	.256	111	363	35	93	130	21	2	4	29	3	1	4	6	0
Pagliarulo, Michael, New York	.239	67	201	24	48	90	15	3	7	34	5	0	3	0	0
Pagliarulo, Michael, New York*	.237	147	578	75	137	256	16	2	33	98	12	2	6	2	3
Parrish, Lance, Detroit	.285	156	613	72	175	285	42	1	22	101	11	0	3	2	4
Parrish, Larry, Texas	.000	1	1	0	0	0	0	0	0	0	0	0	0	0	0
Perconte, John, Seattle*	.294	155	612	93	180	212	24	4	0	31	3	11	3	29	6
Perkins, Broderick, Cleveland*	.197	58	66	5	13	14	1	0	0	4	1	0	2	0	0
Petralli, Eugene, Toronto†	.000	3	3	0	0	0	0	0	0	0	0	0	0	0	0
Pettis, Gary, California†	.227	140	397	63	90	119	11	6	2	29	3	5	1	48	17
Phelps, Kenneth, Seattle*	.241	101	290	52	70	151	9	0	24	51	7	0	4	3	3
Phillips, K. Anthony, Oakland†	.266	154	451	62	120	162	24	3	4	37	1	7	5	10	6
Picciolo, Robert, California	.202	87	119	18	24	33	6	0	1	9	2	8	1	0	1
Piniella, Louis, New York	.302	29	86	8	26	35	4	1	1	6	2	0	0	0	0
Presley, James, Seattle	.227	70	251	27	57	101	12	1	10	36	0	0	1	1	1
Pryor, Gregory, Kansas City	.263	123	270	32	71	96	11	1	4	25	3	2	1	0	3
Puckett, Kirby, Minnesota	.296	128	557	63	165	187	12	5	0	31	3	4	2	14	7
Pujols, Luis, Kansas City	.200	4	5	0	1	1	0	0	0	1	0	0	0	0	0
Putnam, Patrick, Sea.-Minn.*	.176	78	193	12	34	47	7	0	2	20	1	0	3	3	0
Quirk, James, Chi.-Clev.*	.333	4	3	1	1	4	0	0	1	2	2	0	1	0	0
Ramos, Domingo, Seattle	.185	59	81	6	15	17	2	0	0	2	1	1	0	2	2
Randolph, William, New York	.287	142	564	86	162	196	24	2	2	31	5	7	7	10	6
Rayford, Floyd, Baltimore	.256	86	250	24	64	90	14	0	4	27	3	2	2	0	3
Ready, Randy, Milwaukee	.187	37	123	13	23	40	6	1	3	13	2	3	0	0	0
Reed, Jeffrey, Minnesota*	.143	18	21	3	3	6	3	0	0	1	0	1	0	0	0
Reed, Ronald, Chicago	.000	51	1	0	0	0	0	0	0	0	0	0	0	0	0
Remy, Gerald, Boston*	.250	30	104	8	26	29	1	1	0	8	0	2	0	4	3
Reynolds, Harold, Seattle	.300	10	10	3	3	3	0	0	0	0	0	1	0	1	0
Rhomberg, Kevin, Cleveland	.250	13	8	0	2	2	0	0	0	0	0	0	0	0	0
Rice, James, Boston	.280	159	657	98	184	307	25	7	28	122	17	0	6	4	0
Richardt, Michael, Texas	.111	6	9	0	1	1	0	0	0	0	0	0	0	0	1
Ripken, Calvin, Baltimore	.304	162	641	103	195	327	37	7	27	86	11	0	2	2	1

Player and Club	Pct.	G.	AB.	R.	H.	TB.	2B.	3B.	HR.	RBI.	GW.	SH.	SF.	SB.	CS.
Rivers, John, Texas*	.300	102	313	40	94	121	13	1	4	33	3	4	0	5	5
Roberts, Leon, Kansas City	.222	29	45	4	10	13	1	1	0	3	1	0	0	0	0
Robertson, Andre, New York	.214	52	140	10	30	37	5	1	0	6	1	8	0	0	1
Rodriguez, Victor, Baltimore	.412	11	17	4	7	10	3	0	0	2	0	0	0	0	0
Roenicke, Gary, Baltimore	.224	121	326	36	73	124	19	1	10	44	4	3	2	1	2
Romero, Edgardo, Milwaukee	.252	116	357	36	90	105	12	0	1	31	3	6	4	3	3
Sakata, Lenn, Baltimore	.191	81	257	23	30	40	1	0	3	11	3	5	0	4	1
Sample, William, Texas	.247	130	489	67	121	160	20	2	5	33	1	4	6	18	6
Sanchez, Orlando, K.C.-Balt.*	.167	14	18	0	3	4	1	0	0	3	1	0	0	0	0
Schofield, Richard, California	.193	140	400	39	77	105	10	3	4	21	1	13	0	5	2
Schroeder, A. William, Milwaukee	.257	61	210	29	54	102	6	0	14	25	2	4	2	0	1
Sconiers, Daryl, California*	.244	57	160	14	39	55	4	0	4	17	1	0	0	1	2
Scott, Donald, Texas†	.221	81	235	16	52	70	9	0	3	20	1	6	2	0	1
Scranton, James, Kansas City	.000	2	2	0	0	0	0	0	0	0	0	0	0	0	0
Sheets, Larry, Baltimore*	.438	8	16	3	7	11	1	0	1	2	0	0	0	0	0
Shelby, John, Baltimore†	.209	128	383	44	80	120	12	5	6	30	4	12	0	12	4
Shepherd, Ronald, Toronto	.000	12	4	0	0	0	0	0	0	0	0	0	0	0	1
Sheridan, Patrick, Kansas City*	.283	138	481	64	136	192	24	4	8	53	13	5	3	19	6
Simmons, Nelson, Detroit†	.433	9	30	4	13	15	2	0	0	3	0	0	1	0	
Simmons, Ted, Milwaukee†	.221	132	497	44	110	149	23	2	4	52	8	1	1	3	0
Singleton, Kenneth, Baltimore†	.215	111	363	28	78	105	7	1	6	36	2	1	2	0	0
Skinner, Joel, Chicago	.213	43	80	4	17	19	2	0	0	3	0	1	1	0	
Slaught, Donald, Kansas City	.264	124	409	48	108	155	27	4	4	42	4	8	7	0	0
Smalley, Roy, New York-Chicago†	.212	114	344	32	73	120	12	1	11	39	5	0	4	3	2
Smith, P. Keith, New York	.000	2	4	0	0	0	0	0	0	0	0	0	0	0	0
Speier, Chris, Minnesota	.212	12	33	2	7	7	0	0	0	1	1	1	0	0	0
Spillner, Daniel, Clev.-Chicago	.000	37	0	1	0	0	0	0	0	0	0	0	0	0	0
Squires, Michael, Chicago*	.183	104	82	9	15	16	1	0	0	6	1	1	0	2	2
Stapleton, David, Boston	.231	13	39	4	9	11	2	0	0	1	1	1	0	0	0
Stegman, David, Chicago	.261	55	92	13	24	35	1	2	2	11	0	1	2	3	0
Stein, William, Texas	.279	27	43	3	12	13	1	0	0	3	0	0	0	0	0
Sullivan, Marc, Boston	.500	2	6	1	3	3	0	0	0	1	0	0	0	0	0
Sundberg, James, Milwaukee	.261	110	348	43	91	139	19	4	7	43	8	6	3	1	1
Swaggerty, William, Baltimore	.000	24	0	1	0	0	0	0	0	0	0	0	0	0	0
Tabler, Patrick, Cleveland	.290	144	473	66	137	194	21	3	10	68	7	0	5	3	1
Tartabull, Danilo, Seattle	.300	10	20	3	6	13	1	0	2	7	3	0	1	0	0
Tettleton, Mickey, Oakland†	.263	33	76	10	20	27	2	1	1	5	0	1	0	0	
Teufel, Timothy, Minnesota	.262	157	568	76	149	227	30	3	14	61	10	2	4	1	3
Thomas, Derrel, California†	.138	14	29	3	4	6	0	1	0	2	0	1	0	0	0
Thomas, J. Gorman, Seattle	.157	35	108	6	17	23	3	0	1	13	2	0	6	0	3
Thornton, Andre, Cleveland	.271	155	587	91	159	284	26	0	33	99	11	0	9	6	5
Tolleson, J. Wayne, Texas†	.213	118	338	35	72	85	9	2	0	9	2	9	1	22	4
Traber, James, Baltimore*	.238	10	21	3	5	5	0	0	0	2	0	0	1	0	0
Trammell, Alan, Detroit	.314	139	555	85	174	260	34	5	14	69	5	6	2	19	13
Upshaw, Willie, Toronto*	.278	152	569	79	158	264	31	9	19	84	9	3	3	10	4
Valle, David, Seattle	.296	13	27	4	8	12	1	0	1	4	0	0	0	0	0
Vande Berg, Edward, Seattle	.000	51	0	1	0	0	0	0	0	0	0	0	0	0	0
Vukovich, George, Cleveland*	.304	134	437	38	133	192	22	5	9	60	5	0	2	1	4
Wagner, Mark, Oakland	.230	82	87	8	20	27	5	1	0	12	3	5	1	2	0
Walker, Cleotha, Boston†	.000	3	2	0	0	0	0	0	0	1	1	0	1	0	0
Walker, Gregory, Chicago*	.294	136	442	62	130	235	29	2	24	75	5	0	3	8	5
Ward, Gary, Texas	.284	155	602	97	171	269	21	7	21	79	9	1	1	7	5
Washington, Ronald, Minnesota	.294	88	197	25	58	88	11	5	3	23	3	1	3	1	1
Washington, U.L., Kansas City†	.224	63	170	18	38	47	6	0	1	10	1	4	1	4	6
Wathan, John, Kansas City	.181	97	171	17	31	46	7	1	2	10	1	4	0	6	6
Webster, Mitchell, Toronto†	.227	26	22	9	5	9	2	1	0	4	0	0	0	0	0
Whitaker, Louis, Detroit*	.289	143	558	90	161	227	25	1	13	56	12	4	5	6	5
White, Frank, Kansas City	.271	129	479	58	130	213	22	5	17	56	9	4	3	5	5
Whitt, L. Ernest, Toronto*	.238	124	315	35	75	134	12	1	15	46	6	0	5	0	3
Wilfong, Robert, California*	.248	108	307	31	76	111	13	2	6	33	2	6	2	3	2
Wilkerson, Curtis, Texas†	.248	153	484	47	120	135	12	0	1	26	3	12	2	12	10
Willard, Gerald, Cleveland*	.224	87	246	21	55	95	8	1	10	37	3	0	3	1	0
Wilson, Willie, Kansas City†	.301	128	541	81	163	211	24	9	2	44	7	2	3	47	5
Winfield, David, New York	.340	141	567	106	193	292	34	4	19	100	13	0	6	6	4
Wright, George, Texas†	.243	101	383	40	93	147	19	4	9	48	2	1	3	0	2
Wynegar, Harold, New York†	.267	129	442	48	118	151	13	1	6	45	5	4	1	1	4
Yost, Edgar, Texas	.182	80	242	15	44	66	4	0	6	25	3	2	1	1	2
Young, Michael, Baltimore†	.252	123	401	59	101	173	17	2	17	52	7	2	2	6	2
Yount, Robin, Milwaukee	.298	160	624	105	186	275	27	7	16	80	9	1	9	14	4

The following pitchers neither had a plate appearance nor scored a run, but made appearances in addition to their games pitched as indicated: Ronald Guidry, New York—one game as a pinch-runner; D. LaMarr Hoyt, Chicago—one game in the outfield but did not pitch; Bret Saberhagen, Kansas City—one game as a pinch-runner.

AWARDED FIRST BASE ON INTERFERENCE—Bradley, Sea. 3 (Hill, Dempsey, Castillo); Bell, Tor. 2 (Slaught, Castillo); Herndon, Det. (Hill); Thornton, Clev. (Kearney); Lemon, Det. (Dempsey); Singleton, Balt. (Allenson); Perconte, Sea. (Essian); Griffin, Tor. (Scott); G. Wright, Tex. (Slaught); Slaught, K.C. (Laudner); Owen, Sea. (Scott); Sheridan, K.C. (Scott); Buckner, Bos. (Rayford).

PLAYERS WITH TWO OR MORE CLUBS
(Alphabetically Arranged With Player's First Club on Top)

Player and Club	Pct.	G.	AB.	R.	H.	TB.	2B.	3B.	HR.	RBI.	GW.	SH.	SF.	Tot. BB.	Int. BB.	HP.	SO.	SB.	CS.	GI. DP.
Jackson, Cal.	.165	33	91	5	15	19	2	1	0	5	0	1	1	7	1	0	13	0	0	3
Jackson, Balt.	.286	12	28	0	8	10	2	0	0	2	1	0	0	0	0	0	4	0	2	0
Putnam, Sea.	.200	64	155	11	31	43	6	0	2	16	0	0	2	12	1	0	27	3	0	5
Putnam, Minn.	.079	14	38	1	3	4	1	0	0	4	1	0	1	4	0	0	12	0	0	0
Quirk, Chi.	.000	3	2	0	0	0	0	0	0	1	1	0	1	0	0	0	2	0	0	0
Quirk, Clev.	1.000	1	1	1	1	4	0	0	1	1	1	0	0	0	0	0	0	0	0	0
Sanchez, K.C.	.100	10	10	0	1	2	1	0	0	2	1	0	0	0	0	0	2	0	0	1
Sanchez, Balt.	.250	4	8	0	2	2	0	0	0	1	0	0	0	0	0	0	2	0	0	0
Smalley, N.Y.	.239	67	209	17	50	81	8	1	7	26	4	0	3	15	2	0	35	2	1	5
Smalley, Chi.	.170	47	135	15	23	39	4	0	4	13	1	0	1	22	1	0	30	1	1	1
Spillner, Clev.	.000	14	0	0	0	0	0	0	0	0	0	0	0	0	0	0	0	0	0	0
Spillner, Chi.	.000	23	0	1	0	0	0	0	0	0	0	0	0	0	0	0	0	0	0	0

OFFICIAL MISCELLANEOUS AMERICAN LEAGUE BATTING RECORDS

CLUB MISCELLANEOUS BATTING RECORDS

Club	Slg. Pct.	OB Pct.	Tot. BB.	Int. BB.	HP.	SO.	GIDP.	ShO.
Boston	.441	.341	500	48	20	842	148	7
Detroit	.432	.342	602	51	34	941	102	7
Toronto	.421	.331	460	46	52	816	91	4
New York	.404	.339	534	41	38	673	147	13
Oakland	.404	.327	568	29	22	871	116	6
Kansas City	.399	.317	400	39	24	832	128	13
Chicago	.395	.314	523	43	39	883	111	11
Baltimore	.391	.328	620	48	22	888	133	5
Minnesota	.385	.318	437	45	24	735	138	10
Cleveland	.384	.335	600	34	27	815	137	7
Seattle	.384	.324	519	35	42	871	101	9
California	.381	.319	556	33	29	928	140	12
Texas	.377	.313	420	36	20	807	130	10
Milwaukee	.370	.317	432	35	26	673	152	10
Totals	.398	.326	7171	562	419	11575	1774	124

INDIVIDUAL MISCELLANEOUS BATTING RECORDS
(Top Ten Qualifiers for Slugging Championship)

Player—Club	Slg. Pct.	OB Pct.	Tot. BB.	Int. BB.	HP.	SO.	GI DP.
Baines, Chi.	.541	.361	54	9	0	75	12
Mattingly, N.Y.	.537	.381	41	8	1	33	15
Evans, Bos.	.532	.388	96	2	4	115	19
Armas, Bos.	.531	.300	32	9	1	156	13
Hrbek, Minn.	.522	.383	65	15	4	87	17
Gibson, Det.	.516	.363	63	6	8	103	4
Easler, Bos.	.516	.376	58	4	4	134	8
Winfield, N.Y.	.515	.393	53	9	0	71	14
Ripken, Balt.	.510	.374	71	1	2	89	16
Murray, Balt.	.509	.410	107	25	2	87	9

DEPARTMENTAL LEADERS: OBP—Murray, .410; Tot. BB—Murray, 107; Int. BB—Murray, 25; HP—Baylor, 23; SO—Armas, 156; GIDP—Rice, 36.

Player—Club	Slg. Pct.	OB Pct.	Tot. BB.	Int. BB.	HP.	SO.	GI DP.
Aikens, Tor.	.376	.298	29	1	2	56	6
Allen, Det.	.333	.367	2	0	1	8	0
Allenson, Bos.	.325	.304	9	2	0	14	5
Almon, Oak.	.374	.253	10	0	0	42	3
Anderson, Tex.	.106	.176	4	0	0	7	0
Armas, Bos.	.531	.300	32	9	1	156	13
Ashford, K.C.	.231	.214	1	0	0	2	1
Ayala, Balt.	.364	.258	8	0	0	24	4
Baines, Chi.	.541	.361	54	9	0	75	12
Baker, Det.	.241	.241	7	0	1	22	1
Balboni, K.C.	.498	.320	45	5	4	139	9
Bando, Clev.	.505	.377	33	5	0	35	8
Bannister, Tex.	.384	.407	21	0	1	17	1
Bannister, Chi.	.000	.000	0	0	0	0	0
Barfield, Tor.	.466	.357	35	5	2	81	5
Barrett, Bos.	.383	.358	42	2	1	25	9
Baylor, N.Y.	.489	.341	38	6	23	68	10

Player—Club	Slg. Pct.	OB Pct.	Tot. BB.	Int. BB.	HP.	SO.	GI DP.
Bell, Tex.	.458	.382	63	8	3	54	21
Bell, Tor.	.498	.326	24	2	8	86	14
Beniquez, Cal.	.452	.370	18	0	3	43	12
Bergman, Det.	.417	.351	33	2	3	40	4
Bernazard, Clev.	.287	.290	43	0	2	70	10
Biancalana, K.C.	.299	.229	6	0	0	44	2
Bochte, Oak.	.345	.333	52	3	0	59	12
Boddicker, Balt.	.000	.000	0	0	0	0	0
Boggs, Bos.	.416	.407	89	6	0	44	13
Bonnell, Sea.	.394	.315	25	3	2	51	10
Boone, Cal.	.262	.242	25	1	0	45	11
Boston, Chi.	.229	.207	4	0	0	20	0
Bradley, Sea.	.363	.373	34	2	3	61	6
Bradley, N.Y.	.333	.318	1	0	0	1	0
Brett, K.C.	.459	.344	38	6	0	37	11
Brookens, Det.	.397	.306	19	0	1	33	2
Brouhard, Milw.	.365	.298	16	3	2	36	3
Brown, Minn.	.342	.309	14	1	0	16	5
Brown, Cal.	.520	.342	13	1	0	23	8
Brunansky, Minn.	.460	.320	57	2	0	94	15
Buckley, Tex.	.429	.444	2	0	0	4	0
Buckner, Bos.	.410	.321	24	5	5	38	11
Bumbry, Balt.	.337	.317	25	0	0	35	11
Burleson, Cal.	.000	.000	0	0	0	2	0
Burris, Oak.	.000	.000	0	0	0	0	0
Burroughs, Oak.	.310	.367	18	0	0	23	2
Bush, Minn.	.389	.292	31	6	4	60	1
Butler, Clev.	.355	.361	86	1	4	62	6
Calderon, Sea.	.375	.269	2	0	0	5	3
Carew, Cal.	.353	.367	40	1	0	39	8
Carter, Clev.	.467	.307	11	0	1	48	2
Castillo, Det.	.383	.285	10	0	0	33	4
Castillo, Clev.	.464	.329	21	0	2	32	7

Player—Club	Slg. Pct.	OB Pct.	Tot. BB.	Int. BB.	HP.	SO.	GI DP.
Castino, Minn.	.481	.531	5	2	0	2	2
Caudill, Oak.	.000	.000	0	0	0	1	0
Cerone, N.Y.	.283	.269	9	0	1	15	5
Chambers, Sea.	.306	.269	3	0	0	12	0
Christmas, Chi.	.727	.364	0	0	0	2	0
Clark, Milw.	.361	.326	16	0	1	35	9
Coles, Sea.	.196	.259	17	0	2	26	5
Collins, Tor.	.444	.366	33	0	9	41	0
Concepcion, K.C.	.338	.319	14	0	3	33	3
Cooper, Milw.	.386	.307	27	6	2	59	12
Cowens, Sea.	.435	.312	27	2	2	83	18
Cruz, Chi.	.311	.295	45	0	0	58	9
Cruz, Balt.	.310	.263	8	0	1	33	2
Dauer, Balt.	.335	.296	24	1	0	23	15
David, Minn.	.354	.351	7	2	1	11	2
Davis, Sea.	.497	.391	97	16	7	78	7
Davis, Oak.	.364	.285	31	2	1	66	5
Davis, K.C.	.224	.211	10	0	0	19	2
Dayett, N.Y.	.402	.295	9	0	1	14	3
DeCinces, Cal.	.431	.327	53	4	0	79	16
Dempsey, Balt.	.364	.312	40	0	1	58	11
Dent, K.C.	.333	.400	1	0	0	2	0
Dotson, Chi.	.000	.000	0	0	0	0	0
Downing, Cal.	.462	.361	70	3	7	66	18
Dunbar, Tex.	.340	.301	6	1	0	16	1
Dwyer, Balt.	.360	.337	23	0	0	24	2
Dybzinski, Chi.	.311	.311	13	0	2	12	3
Earl, Det.	.171	.114	0	0	0	9	0
Easler, Bos.	.516	.376	58	4	4	134	8
Eisenreich, Minn.	.250	.250	2	1	0	4	1
Engle, Minn.	.353	.308	26	3	0	22	18
Essian, Oak.	.346	.348	23	0	1	17	3
Evans, Det.	.384	.353	77	10	0	70	7
Evans, Bos.	.532	.388	96	2	4	115	19
Faedo, Tor.	.327	.304	4	0	0	3	1
Fernandez, Tor.	.356	.317	17	0	0	15	3
Fischlin, Clev.	.308	.290	12	0	0	20	2
Fisk, Chi.	.468	.289	26	4	5	60	7
Fletcher, Chi.	.311	.328	46	2	8	46	5
Foley, Tex.	.391	.306	15	1	1	24	1
Foli, N.Y.	.319	.265	2	0	1	16	4
Ford, Balt.	.308	.286	7	0	0	13	3
Franco, Clev.	.348	.331	43	1	6	68	23
Gaetti, Minn.	.350	.315	44	1	4	81	9
Gagne, Minn.	.000	.000	0	0	0	0	0
Gamble, N.Y.	.440	.318	25	0	0	18	1
Gantner, Milw.	.344	.314	30	0	3	51	16
Garbey, Det.	.391	.325	17	2	2	35	8
Garcia, Tor.	.374	.310	16	1	9	46	6
Gedman, Bos.	.506	.312	29	8	1	72	5
Gibson, Det.	.516	.363	63	6	8	103	4
Grich, Cal.	.452	.357	57	3	2	70	11
Griffey, N.Y.	.381	.321	29	2	1	32	7
Griffin, Tor.	.298	.248	4	0	1	33	5
Gross, Balt.	.442	.346	68	4	1	69	6
Grubb, Det.	.432	.395	36	5	2	36	1
Gruber, Tor.	.250	.063	0	0	0	5	1
Gutierrez, Bos.	.316	.284	15	0	0	49	18
Hairston, Chi.	.401	.373	41	3	1	29	3
Hall, Clev.	.397	.344	35	5	2	55	3
Hancock, Oak.	.250	.217	0	0	0	1	4
Hargrove, Clev.	.335	.361	53	3	0	38	12
Harrah, N.Y.	.296	.331	42	2	2	28	9
Hart, Minn.	.172	.194	1	0	0	2	0
Hassey, Clev.	.302	.321	15	2	0	26	4
Hatcher, Minn.	.406	.342	37	3	2	34	17
Heath, Oak.	.396	.287	26	2	1	72	14
D. Henderson, Sea.	.466	.320	19	0	2	56	4
Henderson, Oak.	.458	.399	86	1	5	81	7
S. Henderson, Sea.	.409	.341	38	4	1	62	6
Hernandez, Tor.	.500	.500	0	0	0	0	0
Herndon, Det.	.400	.333	32	1	2	63	8
Hill, Oak.	.299	.249	5	0	0	12	3
Hill, Chi.	.373	.275	9	0	2	26	12
Hoffman, Bos.	.243	.241	5	0	0	10	3
Hostetler, Tex.	.378	.326	13	0	0	27	5
Howell, Milw.	.348	.284	8	1	4	32	9
Hrbek, Minn.	.522	.383	65	15	4	87	17
Hudler, N.Y.	.286	.333	1	0	1	5	0
Hulett, Chi.	.000	.125	1	0	0	4	0
Iorg, K.C.	.404	.287	13	3	0	15	7
Iorg, Tor.	.304	.244	5	0	1	16	7
Jackson, Calif.	.406	.300	55	7	3	141	10
Jackson, Cal.-Balt.	.244	.236	7	1	0	17	3
Jacoby, Clev.	.369	.314	32	0	3	73	13
James, Milw.	.377	.351	32	1	3	41	7
Javier, N.Y.	.143	.143	0	0	0	1	0
Jimenez, Minn.	.245	.238	15	0	0	34	7
Johnson, Tor.	.507	.390	50	4	3	62	9
Johnson, Det.	.394	.324	40	1	1	67	6
Jones, K.C.	.388	.330	4	0	1	9	4
Jones, Tex.	.371	.308	10	1	1	19	0
Jones, Det.	.516	.346	21	0	0	47	5
Jurak, Bos.	.364	.359	12	0	0	12	1
Kearney, Sea.	.334	.257	18	0	2	72	7
Kemp, N.Y.	.403	.369	40	0	1	54	12
Kiefer, Oak.	.300	.209	2	0	0	10	0
Kingman, Oak.	.505	.321	44	8	6	119	7
Kittle, Chi.	.453	.295	49	5	6	137	7
Kunkel, Tex.	.324	.218	2	0	1	35	2
Kuntz, Det.	.414	.393	25	1	1	28	2
Laga, Det.	.545	.583	1	0	0	2	0
Lansford, Oak.	.439	.342	40	6	3	62	12
Laudner, Minn.	.389	.258	18	0	1	78	4
R. Law, Chi.	.345	.309	39	6	3	42	9
V. Law, Chi.	.403	.309	41	2	1	75	13
Leach, Tor.	.375	.320	8	0	0	14	3
Leeper, K.C.	.000	.000	0	0	0	1	0
Lemon, Det.	.495	.357	51	9	7	83	16
Loman, Milw.	.408	.402	15	2	1	7	0
Lopes, Oak.	.430	.343	31	1	1	36	8
Lowenstein, Balt.	.374	.319	33	3	1	54	5
Lowry, Det.	.422	.292	3	0	0	11	3
Lozado, Milw.	.411	.339	12	0	0	23	1
Luzinski, Chi.	.364	.329	56	3	3	80	11
Lynn, Calif.	.474	.366	77	8	2	97	14
Manning, Milw.	.370	.318	34	1	1	32	7
Manrique, Tor.	.333	.333	0	0	0	1	1
Martinez, Tor.	.349	.301	29	0	2	49	2
Mata, N.Y.	.443	.333	0	0	1	12	1
Mattingly, N.Y.	.537	.381	41	8	1	33	15
McRae, K.C.	.397	.363	34	3	1	47	10
Meacham, N.Y.	.328	.312	32	0	3	70	2
Meier, Minn.	.306	.271	6	0	1	9	5
Mercado, Seattle	.282	.265	4	0	1	12	1
Meyer, Oak.	.545	.318	0	0	0	2	2
Milbourne, Sea.	.313	.304	12	0	0	16	7
Miller, Calif.	.171	.244	4	0	0	9	0
Miller, Bos.	.317	.348	17	0	0	22	3
Molitor, Milw.	.239	.245	2	0	0	8	0
Moore, Milw.	.314	.275	10	0	1	26	6
Moreno, N.Y.	.361	.294	18	1	1	48	3
Morgan, Oak.	.351	.356	66	4	1	39	6
Moronko, Clev.	.211	.273	3	0	0	5	0
Moseby, Tor.	.470	.368	78	9	8	122	8
Moses, Sea.	.429	.395	2	0	1	5	0
Motley, K.C.	.441	.319	28	2	1	73	23
Mulliniks, Tor.	.440	.383	33	3	1	44	5
Murphy, Oak.	.472	.342	74	1	3	111	15
Murray, Balt.	.509	.410	107	25	2	87	9
Nahorodny, Sea.	.360	.310	1	0	2	7	0
Narron, Calif.	.340	.286	8	1	1	12	7
Nelson, Sea.	.400	.294	2	0	0	4	0
Newman, Bos.	.302	.275	5	0	0	16	1
Nichols, Bos.	.306	.307	12	1	3	18	0
Nixon, Clev.	.154	.220	8	0	0	11	2
Noboa, Clev.	.364	.364	0	0	0	2	1
Nolan, Balt.	.387	.400	12	4	0	10	0
O'Berry, N.Y.	.313	.294	2	0	0	2	0
O'Brien, Tex.	.448	.348	53	8	0	50	11
Ogilvie, Milw.	.384	.327	44	5	1	56	12
O'Malley, Chi.	.125	.125	0	0	0	5	1
Orta, K.C.	.457	.343	28	8	2	39	6
Owen, Sea.	.326	.308	46	0	3	63	5
Paciorek, Chi.	.358	.308	25	4	4	69	5
Pagliarulo, N.Y.	.448	.288	15	0	0	46	5
Parrish, Det.	.443	.287	41	6	2	120	12
Parrish, Tex.	.465	.336	42	7	6	116	20

Player—Club	Slg. Pct.	OB Pct.	Tot. BB.	Int. BB.	HP.	SO.	GI DP.
Parsons, Chi.	.000	.000	0	0	0	1	0
Perconte, Sea.	.346	.357	57	1	5	47	5
Perkins, Clev.	.212	.276	7	1	1	10	3
Petralli, Tor.	.000	.000	0	0	0	0	0
Pettis, Calif.	.300	.332	60	1	3	115	4
Phelps, Sea.	.521	.378	61	5	5	73	1
Phillips, Oak.	.359	.325	42	1	0	86	5
Picciolo, Calif.	.277	.200	0	0	0	21	2
Piniella, N.Y.	.407	.355	7	1	0	5	7
Presley, Sea.	.402	.247	6	1	1	63	4
Pryor, K.C.	.356	.301	12	0	3	28	9
Puckett, Minn.	.336	.320	16	1	4	69	11
Pujols, K.C.	.200	.200	0	0	0	0	0
Putnam, Sea.-Minn.	.244	.236	16	1	0	39	5
Quirk, Chi.-Clev.	1.333	.250	0	0	0	2	0
Ramos, Sea.	.210	.233	5	0	0	12	4
Randolph, N.Y.	.348	.377	86	4	0	42	15
Rayford, Balt.	.360	.296	12	0	3	51	5
Ready, Milw.	.325	.270	14	0	0	18	2
Reed, Minn.	.286	.217	2	0	0	6	0
Reed, Chi.	.000	.000	0	0	0	0	0
Remy, Bos.	.279	.297	7	0	0	11	1
Reynolds, Sea.	.300	.364	0	0	1	1	0
Rhomberg, Clev.	.250	.250	0	0	0	3	0
Rice, Bos.	.467	.323	44	8	1	102	36
Richardt, Tex.	.111	.200	1	0	0	1	0
Ripken, Balt.	.510	.374	71	1	2	89	16
Rivers, Tex.	.387	.320	9	1	0	23	1
Roberts, K.C.	.289	.300	4	0	1	3	1
Robertson, N.Y.	.264	.236	4	0	0	20	11
Rodriguez, Balt.	.588	.412	0	0	0	2	0
Roenicke, Balt.	.380	.346	58	1	4	43	10
Romero, Milw.	.294	.307	29	2	1	25	12
Sakata, Minn.	.255	.221	6	2	0	15	4
Sample, Tex.	.327	.286	29	1	0	46	9
Sanchez, K.C.-Balt..	.222	.167	0	0	0	4	1
Schofield, Calif.	.263	.264	33	0	6	79	7
Schroeder, Milw.	.486	.288	8	2	2	54	6
Sconiers, Calif.	.344	.301	13	2	0	17	6
Scott, Tex.	.298	.280	20	1	0	44	5
Scranton, K.C.	.000	.000	0	0	0	0	0
Sheets, Balt.	.688	.471	1	0	0	3	0
Shelby, Balt.	.313	.248	20	0	0	71	4
Shepherd, Tor.	.000	.000	0	0	0	3	0
Sheridan, K.C.	.399	.338	41	3	1	91	6
Simmons, Det.	.500	.469	2	1	0	5	2
Simmons, Milw.	.300	.269	30	3	3	40	23
Singleton, Balt.	.289	.286	37	5	0	60	20
Skinner, Chi.	.238	.273	7	0	0	19	2
Slaught, K.C.	.379	.297	20	4	2	55	8
Smalley, N.Y.-Chi.	.349	.286	37	3	0	65	6
Smith, N.Y.	.000	.200	0	0	1	2	0
Speier, Minn.	.212	.278	3	0	0	7	1
Spillner, Clev.-Chi.	.000	.000	0	0	0	0	0
Squires, Chi.	.195	.239	6	1	0	7	1
Stapleton, Bos.	.282	.286	3	1	0	3	2
Stegman, Chi.	.380	.306	4	0	2	18	1
Stein, Tex.	.302	.354	5	2	0	9	1
Sullivan, Bos.	.500	.571	1	0	0	0	0
Sundberg, Milw.	.399	.332	38	2	0	63	5
Swaggerty, Balt.	.000	.000	0	0	0	0	0
Tabler, Clev.	.410	.354	47	2	3	62	16
Tartabull, Sea.	.650	.375	2	0	1	3	0
Tettleton, Oak.	.355	.352	11	0	0	21	3
Teufel, Minn.	.400	.349	76	8	2	73	18
Thomas, Calif.	.207	.219	3	0	0	4	1
G. Thomas, Sea.	.213	.322	28	0	1	27	3
Thornton, Clev.	.484	.366	91	11	2	79	9
Tolleson, Tex.	.251	.276	27	0	3	47	12
Traber, Balt.	.238	.292	2	0	0	4	1
Trammell, Det.	.468	.382	60	2	3	63	8
Upshaw, Tor.	.464	.345	55	14	5	86	8
Valle, Sea.	.444	.321	1	0	0	5	0
Vande Berg, Sea.	.000	.000	0	0	0	0	0
Vukovich, Clev.	.439	.354	34	3	1	61	10
Wagner, Oak.	.310	.284	7	0	0	11	5
Walker, Bos.	.000	.000	0	0	0	1	0
Walker, Chi.	.532	.346	35	3	2	66	9
Ward, Tex.	.447	.343	55	3	0	95	22
Washington, Minn.	.447	.307	4	0	1	31	4
Washington, K.C.	.276	.281	14	0	0	31	1
Wathan, K.C.	.269	.271	21	0	0	34	6
Webster, Tor.	.409	.261	1	0	0	7	1
Whitaker, Det.	.407	.357	62	5	0	63	9
White, K.C.	.445	.311	27	3	2	72	11
Whitt, Tor.	.425	.327	43	7	1	49	7
Wilfong, Calif.	.362	.296	20	0	2	53	2
Wilkerson, Tex.	.279	.282	22	0	2	72	7
Willard, Clev.	.386	.295	26	0	0	55	6
Wilson, K.C.	.390	.350	39	2	3	56	7
Winfield, N.Y.	.515	.393	53	9	0	71	14
G. Wright, Tex.	.384	.273	15	2	2	54	6
Wynegar, N.Y.	.342	.360	65	6	0	35	18
Yost, Tex.	.273	.201	6	0	0	47	5
Young, Balt.	.431	.355	58	2	7	110	5
Yount, Milw.	.441	.362	67	7	1	67	22

OFFICIAL AMERICAN LEAGUE DESIGNATED HITTING

CLUB DESIGNATED HITTING

Club	Pct.	AB	R	H	TB	2B	3B	HR	RBI	SH	SF	BB	HP	SO	SB	CS	GI DP.
Boston	.306	637	93	195	328	36	5	29	97	1	1	53	3	137	0	1	8
Kansas City	.305	623	77	190	273	33	10	10	81	1	12	54	2	72	0	3	14
Texas	.272	635	80	173	255	29	1	17	81	3	3	45	5	95	2	4	12
Toronto	.270	612	91	165	280	32	1	27	93	0	4	79	5	121	4	4	14
Detroit	.263	616	98	162	269	24	1	27	87	6	5	75	5	123	7	1	11
Oakland	.261	618	80	161	297	23	2	37	122	0	15	60	7	132	5	1	10
Cleveland	.251	621	94	156	271	25	0	30	92	0	11	92	3	91	7	7	12
New York	.250	623	98	156	291	31	1	34	111	2	5	58	0	93	1	1	11
Chicago	.246	605	72	149	231	24	2	18	79	0	8	78	3	110	10	1	11
Milwaukee	.244	644	70	157	219	22	5	10	76	1	5	42	4	78	8	2	18
Minnesota	.234	610	73	143	212	29	2	12	71	4	15	56	5	94	3	2	13
Seattle	.233	597	89	139	252	20	0	31	82	1	4	95	4	128	6	6	12
California	.230	613	76	141	253	21	2	29	96	2	1	69	3	152	8	4	12
Baltimore	.219	607	58	133	189	19	2	11	68	2	8	67	0	107	1	1	26
Totals	.256	8661	1149	2220	3620	368	33	322	1236	23	97	923	72	1533	62	38	181

INDIVIDUAL DESIGNATED HITTING
(Listed Alphabetically)

Player and Club	Pct.	G.	AB.	R.	H.	TB.	2B.	3B.	HR.	RBI.	SH.	SF.	BB.	HP.	SO.	SB.	CS.	GI DP.
Aikens, Tor.	.194	81	222	19	43	77	7	0	9	21	0	0	27	2	54	0	0	6
Allen, Det.	.280	11	25	6	7	8	1	0	0	3	1	0	2	1	7	1	0	0
Almon, Oak.	.000	12	2	1	0	0	0	0	0	0	0	0	0	1	0	1	0	0
Armas, Bos.	.228	31	123	16	28	50	5	1	5	15	0	0	5	0	30	0	1	2

Player and Club	Pct.	G.	AB.	R.	H.	TB.	2B.	3B.	HR.	RBI.	SH.	SF.	BB.	HP.	SO.	SB.	CS.	GIDP.
Ayala, Balt.	.235	34	81	7	19	33	5	0	3	19	0	2	4	0	14	1	1	4
Baker, Det.	.000	1	0	0	0	0	0	0	0	0	0	0	0	0	0	0	0	0
Balboni, K.C.	.250	1	4	1	1	4	0	0	1	1	0	0	0	0	0	0	0	0
Bando, Clev.	.333	1	3	1	1	1	0	0	0	0	0	0	0	0	1	0	0	0
Bannister, Tex.	.318	9	22	4	7	10	0	0	1	4	0	1	2	0	3	0	0	0
Barfield, Tor.	.000	9	7	2	0	0	0	0	0	1	0	0	1	0	3	0	0	0
Baylor, N.Y.	.262	127	477	81	125	230	28	1	25	85	1	3	35	23	68	1	1	9
Bell, Tor.	.292	7	24	4	7	14	1	0	2	7	0	1	2	0	5	1	1	9
Bernazard, Clev.	.000	1	0	0	0	0	0	0	0	0	0	0	0	0	0	0	0	0
Biancalana, K.C.	.000	1	0	0	0	0	0	0	0	0	0	0	0	0	0	0	1	0
Bochte, Oak.	.333	2	3	0	1	1	0	0	0	0	0	0	0	0	0	0	0	0
Boddicker, Balt.	.000	1	0	1	0	0	0	0	0	0	0	0	0	0	0	0	0	0
Boggs, Bos.	.500	2	6	0	3	4	1	0	0	0	0	0	0	0	0	0	0	0
Bonnell, Sea.	.111	8	9	1	1	4	0	0	1	3	0	0	1	0	1	0	0	1
Boston, Chi.	.000	1	0	0	0	0	0	0	0	0	0	0	0	0	4	0	0	0
Bradley, Sea.	.000	3	2	0	0	0	0	0	0	0	0	0	0	0	0	0	0	0
Brookens, Det.	.000	1	0	0	0	0	0	0	0	0	0	0	0	0	1	0	0	0
Brouhard, Milw.	.348	8	23	4	8	13	2	0	1	5	0	1	5	0	5	0	0	1
Brown, Minn.	.280	13	25	4	7	7	0	0	0	2	3	0	2	0	2	0	0	2
Brown, Cal.	.222	3	9	1	2	3	1	0	0	2	3	0	2	0	2	0	0	2
Brunansky, Minn.	.333	1	3	0	1	1	0	0	0	1	0	0	0	0	2	0	0	0
Buckley, Tex.	.400	3	5	1	2	3	1	0	0	0	0	0	0	0	1	0	0	0
Bumbry, Balt.	.000	9	4	2	0	0	0	0	0	0	0	0	2	0	2	0	0	0
Burris, Oak.	.000	3	0	1	0	0	0	0	0	0	0	0	0	0	1	0	0	0
Burroughs, Oak.	.261	23	46	4	12	19	1	0	2	6	0	1	11	0	15	0	0	2
Bush, Minn.	.212	89	292	44	62	110	16	1	10	36	0	8	29	4	58	1	0	2
Carew, Cal.	.500	1	4	0	2	2	0	0	0	0	0	0	1	0	0	0	2	1
Castillo, Det.	.500	1	4	0	2	3	1	0	0	1	0	0	0	0	0	0	0	0
Castillo, Clev.	.000	2	2	0	0	0	0	0	0	0	0	0	0	0	2	0	0	0
Chambers, Sea.	.000	1	2	0	0	0	0	0	0	0	0	0	0	0	0	0	0	0
Coles, Sea.	.000	3	0	3	0	0	0	0	0	0	0	0	0	0	1	0	0	0
Collins, Tor.	.750	4	8	1	6	6	0	0	0	2	0	0	0	0	0	0	0	0
Cooper, Milw.	.259	26	112	10	29	39	4	0	2	14	0	2	3	0	11	2	0	2
Cowens, Sea.	.278	7	18	2	5	6	1	0	0	5	0	0	4	0	3	0	0	1
Cruz, Balt.	.000	1	0	0	0	0	0	0	0	0	0	0	0	0	0	0	0	0
David, Minn.	.333	2	6	0	2	2	0	0	0	0	0	0	1	0	2	0	0	0
Davis, Oak.	.000	4	1	2	0	0	0	0	0	0	0	0	1	0	1	0	0	0
Davis, K.C.	.000	2	0	1	0	0	0	0	0	0	0	0	1	0	0	2	0	0
Davis, Sea.	.222	7	27	4	6	10	1	0	1	3	0	1	3	0	8	0	1	0
Dayett, N.Y.	1.000	1	1	1	1	2	1	0	0	0	0	0	0	0	0	0	0	0
DeCinces, Cal.	.353	5	17	1	6	7	1	0	0	1	0	0	5	0	5	0	0	0
Downing, Cal.	.222	21	72	8	16	32	4	0	4	15	1	1	7	0	9	0	0	0
Dunbar, Tex.	.235	6	17	3	4	4	0	0	0	1	0	0	3	0	2	0	0	0
Dwyer, Balt.	.000	3	5	0	0	0	0	0	0	0	0	0	1	0	4	0	0	0
Dybzinski, Chi.	.000	1	0	0	0	0	0	0	0	0	0	0	0	0	0	0	0	0
Easler, Bos.	.330	126	491	75	162	269	30	4	23	79	1	1	48	3	103	0	0	3
Eisenreich, Minn.	.263	6	19	1	5	6	1	0	0	2	0	2	0	0	2	2	0	3
Engle, Minn.	.288	22	73	14	21	26	3	1	0	9	0	2	6	0	2	0	0	2
Essian, Oak.	.000	1	0	0	0	0	0	0	0	0	0	0	1	0	0	0	0	0
Evans, Bos.	.000	1	4	0	0	0	0	0	0	0	0	0	0	0	0	0	0	1
Evans, Det.	.246	62	199	31	49	81	8	0	8	35	1	2	35	0	32	1	1	2
Faedo, Minn.	.000	1	2	0	0	0	0	0	0	0	0	0	0	0	0	0	0	0
Fernandez, Tor.	.000	1	0	0	0	0	0	0	0	0	0	0	0	0	0	0	1	0
Fisk, Chi.	.211	5	19	2	4	8	1	0	1	1	0	0	1	0	3	0	1	0
Foley, Tex.	.308	4	13	1	4	4	0	0	0	1	0	0	1	0	0	0	0	0
Ford, Balt.	.226	8	31	2	7	8	1	0	0	1	0	0	3	0	7	0	0	1
Franco, Clev.	.000	1	1	0	0	0	0	0	0	0	1	0	1	0	1	0	0	1
Gamble, N.Y.	.211	28	76	10	16	38	1	0	7	19	0	1	17	0	10	0	0	1
Garbey, Det.	.283	17	53	12	15	25	1	0	3	9	0	0	1	1	6	2	0	4
Garcia, Tor.	.000	1	0	0	0	0	0	0	0	0	0	0	0	0	0	0	0	0
Gibson, Det.	.263	6	19	6	5	11	0	0	2	4	1	0	0	0	0	0	1	0
Griffey, N.Y.	.750	2	4	0	3	3	0	0	0	1	1	1	3	1	8	2	0	0
Griffin, Tor.	1.000	5	1	3	1	1	0	0	0	1	0	0	0	0	0	3	0	0
Gross, Balt.	.000	1	5	0	0	0	0	0	0	0	0	0	0	0	0	0	0	0
Grubb, Det.	.250	33	80	11	20	38	3	0	5	10	1	1	14	2	19	0	0	0
Hairston, Chi.	.270	20	74	14	20	28	4	2	0	9	0	2	12	0	6	2	0	1
Hall, Clev.	.242	9	33	5	8	11	0	0	1	2	0	2	2	1	9	0	1	0
Hancock, Oak.	.250	5	4	0	1	1	0	0	0	0	0	1	2	1	0	0	1	0
Harrah, N.Y.	.000	2	1	0	0	0	0	0	0	0	0	0	1	0	0	0	0	0
Hassey, Clev.	.000	1	4	0	0	0	0	0	0	0	0	0	0	0	0	0	0	0
Hatcher, Minn.	.267	37	135	7	36	49	7	0	2	15	0	2	11	0	12	0	0	8
D. Henderson, Sea.	.379	10	29	5	11	20	3	0	2	15	0	0	2	0	2	0	0	1
S. Henderson, Sea.	.245	51	143	17	35	55	5	0	5	16	0	0	20	0	27	1	3	3
Herndon, Det.	.100	4	10	1	1	1	0	0	0	0	0	0	0	0	2	0	0	0
Hill, Oak.	.000	2	1	0	0	0	0	0	0	0	0	0	0	0	0	0	0	0
Hostetler, Tex.	.158	13	38	3	6	13	1	0	2	5	0	0	6	0	15	0	0	2
Howell, Milw.	.217	8	23	0	5	5	0	0	0	3	0	0	0	2	5	0	0	2
Hrbek, Minn.	.000	1	2	0	0	0	0	0	0	0	0	0	0	0	0	0	0	0
Iorg, Tor.	1.000	1	1	0	1	1	0	0	0	0	0	0	0	0	0	0	0	0

Player and Club	Pct.	G.	AB.	R.	H.	TB.	2B.	3B.	HR.	RBI.	SH.	SF.	BB.	HP.	SO.	SB.	CS.	GI DP.
Iorg, K.C.	.400	5	15	2	6	10	2	1	0	4	0	0	0	0	1	0	0	0
Re. Jackson, Cal.	.225	134	507	66	114	208	15	2	25	80	1	0	55	3	136	8	4	9
Johnson, Det.	.077	4	13	2	1	1	0	0	0	0	0	0	1	0	5	0	0	0
Johnson, Tor.	.303	109	337	50	102	174	22	1	16	60	0	3	47	3	58	0	1	8
Jones, Det.	.000	2	8	0	0	0	0	0	0	1	0	1	0	0	2	0	0	0
B. Jones, Tex.	.182	4	11	2	2	2	0	0	0	2	0	0	0	0	2	0	0	1
Kemp, N.Y.	.146	12	41	3	6	7	1	0	0	4	1	1	2	0	10	0	0	0
Kiefer, Oak.	.000	3	0	1	0	0	0	0	0	0	0	0	0	0	0	1	0	0
Kingman, Oak.	.264	139	518	68	137	265	21	1	35	112	0	14	41	6	112	2	0	7
Kittle, Chi.	.200	7	25	0	5	5	0	0	0	1	0	0	3	1	12	0	0	0
Kunkel, Tex.	.000	1	0	0	0	0	0	0	0	0	0	0	0	0	0	0	0	0
Kuntz, Det.	.200	10	10	3	2	2	0	0	0	3	0	0	1	0	3	0	0	0
Laga, Det.	.800	4	5	1	4	4	0	0	0	1	0	0	1	0	1	0	0	0
Laudner, Minn.	.000	2	1	0	0	0	0	0	0	0	0	0	0	0	1	0	0	0
Leach, Tor.	.500	6	6	4	3	4	1	0	0	0	0	0	1	0	0	0	0	0
Leeper, K.C.	.000	1	0	1	0	0	0	0	0	0	0	0	0	0	0	0	0	0
Lemon, Det.	.000	1	1	0	0	0	0	0	0	0	0	0	0	0	0	0	0	0
Lopes, Oak.	.300	9	30	2	9	10	1	0	0	4	0	1	9	1	3	0	0	0
Lowenstein, Balt.	.215	22	65	11	14	25	5	0	2	6	0	1	9	0	12	0	0	0
Lozado, Milw.	.000	1	0	1	0	0	0	0	0	0	0	0	0	0	0	0	0	0
Luzinski, Chi.	.241	114	403	46	97	146	13	0	12	56	0	5	56	2	76	5	1	11
Manning, Milw.	.000	1	0	0	0	0	0	0	0	0	0	0	0	0	0	0	0	0
Manrique, Tor.	.000	1	1	0	0	0	0	0	0	0	0	0	0	0	0	0	0	0
Martinez, Tor.	.000	1	0	1	0	0	0	0	0	0	0	0	1	0	0	0	0	0
McRae, K.C.	.309	94	307	30	95	125	13	4	3	42	0	9	32	1	46	0	3	9
Meier, Minn.	.200	4	5	0	1	2	1	0	0	1	1	0	0	0	0	0	0	0
Meyer, Oak.	.000	2	2	0	0	0	0	0	0	0	0	0	0	0	2	0	0	0
Milbourne, Sea.	.000	6	7	1	0	0	0	0	0	0	1	0	1	0	0	0	0	2
Molitor, Milw.	.154	4	13	2	2	2	0	0	0	1	0	0	1	0	4	0	0	0
Moreno, N.Y.	.000	1	0	0	0	0	0	0	0	0	0	0	0	0	0	0	0	0
Morgan, Oak.	.091	5	11	0	1	1	0	0	0	0	0	0	2	0	1	0	0	0
Moronko, Clev.	.000	1	1	0	0	0	0	0	0	0	0	0	0	0	0	0	0	0
Moses, Sea.	.000	1	0	0	0	0	0	0	0	0	0	0	0	0	0	0	0	0
Murray, Balt.	.286	3	7	3	2	2	0	0	0	2	0	2	6	0	1	0	0	0
Nelson, Sea.	.000	3	8	0	0	0	0	0	0	0	0	0	0	0	1	0	0	0
Nichols, Bos.	.000	1	1	0	0	0	0	0	0	0	0	0	0	0	1	0	0	0
Noboa, Clev.	.000	1	1	0	0	0	0	0	0	0	0	0	0	0	1	1	0	0
Nolan, Balt.	.303	11	33	1	10	13	1	1	0	4	0	0	5	0	6	0	0	0
Oglivie, Milw.	.500	1	4	0	2	2	0	0	0	2	0	0	0	0	0	0	1	0
Orta, K.C.	.289	83	294	40	85	131	18	5	6	32	1	2	22	1	24	0	0	6
Parrish, Det.	.235	22	85	13	20	40	2	0	6	9	0	0	5	0	16	1	0	1
Parrish, Tex.	.263	63	243	17	64	93	12	1	5	23	0	1	16	3	39	0	1	8
Perkins, Clev.	.200	10	25	3	5	5	0	0	0	0	0	0	2	0	3	0	0	0
Petralli, Tor.	.000	1	1	0	0	0	0	0	0	0	0	0	0	0	0	0	0	0
Phelps, Sea.	.235	84	255	47	60	130	7	0	21	45	0	3	54	4	63	3	2	1
Piniella, N.Y.	.000	2	1	0	0	0	0	0	0	0	0	0	1	0	1	0	0	0
Presley, Sea.	.000	1	1	0	0	0	0	0	0	0	0	0	0	0	0	0	0	0
Pryor, K.C.	1.000	1	1	1	1	1	0	0	0	0	0	0	0	0	0	0	0	0
Putnam, Sea.-Minn.	.186	41	129	8	24	31	4	0	1	11	0	1	11	0	27	2	0	3
Rhomberg, Clev.	.000	1	0	0	0	0	0	0	0	0	0	0	0	0	0	0	0	0
Rice, Bos.	.250	2	8	2	2	5	0	0	1	3	0	0	0	0	1	0	0	1
Rivers, Tex.	.285	48	186	27	53	72	10	0	3	20	2	0	7	0	14	2	3	1
Roberts, K.C.	1.000	3	2	1	2	2	0	0	0	1	0	0	0	0	0	0	0	0
Rodriguez, Balt.	.000	1	0	0	0	0	0	0	0	0	0	0	0	0	0	0	0	0
Romero, Milw.	.143	2	7	0	1	1	0	0	0	0	0	0	0	0	0	0	0	0
Sample, Tex.	.000	2	4	1	0	0	0	0	0	0	0	0	1	0	0	0	0	0
Schroeder, Milw.	.111	3	9	0	1	1	0	0	0	0	0	0	1	0	3	0	0	0
Sconiers, Cal.	.250	1	4	0	1	1	0	0	0	0	0	0	0	0	0	0	1	0
Shepherd, Tor.	.000	4	0	0	0	0	0	0	0	0	0	0	0	0	0	0	0	0
Simmons, Milw.	.210	77	295	26	62	79	10	2	1	28	1	1	18	2	27	2	0	11
Simmons, Det.	.455	4	11	3	5	7	2	0	0	0	0	0	2	0	1	0	0	2
Singleton, Balt.	.217	103	355	28	77	104	7	1	6	35	1	2	37	0	58	0	0	20
Slaught, K.C.	.000	1	0	0	0	0	0	0	0	1	0	1	0	0	0	0	0	0
Smalley, N.Y.-Chi.	.185	7	27	4	5	11	0	0	2	3	0	1	4	0	5	0	0	0
Stapleton, Bos.	.000	1	4	0	0	0	0	0	0	0	0	0	0	0	1	0	0	0
Stegman, Chi.	.000	3	6	1	0	0	0	0	0	0	0	0	0	0	4	0	0	0
Stein, Tex.	.286	4	7	2	2	2	0	0	0	0	0	0	1	0	1	0	0	0
Tabler, Clev.	.000	1	4	0	0	0	0	0	0	0	0	0	0	0	0	0	0	0
Thomas, Sea.	.000	1	2	1	0	0	0	0	0	0	0	0	3	0	0	0	0	0
Thornton, Clev.	.259	144	544	84	141	253	25	0	29	89	0	9	86	2	75	6	5	10
Tolleson, Tex.	.000	1	1	0	0	0	0	0	0	0	0	0	0	0	1	0	0	0
Traber, Balt.	.200	9	20	3	4	4	0	0	0	2	0	1	2	0	4	0	0	1
Trammell, Det.	.333	23	93	9	31	48	6	1	3	11	2	0	10	0	20	0	0	1
Upshaw, Tor.	.000	1	0	1	0	0	0	0	0	0	0	0	0	0	0	0	0	0
Vande Berg, Sea.	.000	1	0	1	0	0	0	0	0	0	0	0	0	0	0	0	0	0
Wagner, Oak.	.000	3	0	1	0	0	0	0	0	0	0	0	0	0	0	3	0	0
Walker, Chi.	.315	21	73	8	23	44	6	0	5	11	0	0	4	0	9	0	0	0
Ward, Tex.	.250	5	20	9	5	11	0	0	2	8	0	0	4	0	1	0	0	0
Washington, Minn.	.417	4	12	1	5	5	0	0	0	1	0	0	1	0	0	0	0	0

Player and Club	Pct.	G.	AB.	R.	H.	TB.	2B.	3B.	HR.	RBI.	SH.	SF.	BB.	HP.	SO.	SB.	CS.	GI DP.
Wathan, K.C.	.000	4	0	0	0	0	0	0	0	0	0	0	0	0	0	0	0	0
Webster, Tor.	.500	9	4	6	2	3	1	0	0	1	0	0	0	0	1	0	0	0
Wilfong, Cal.	.000	1	0	0	0	0	0	0	0	0	0	0	0	0	0	0	0	0
Willard, Clev.	.333	1	3	1	1	1	0	0	0	1	0	1	0	0	0	0	0	0
G. Wright, Tex.	.353	18	68	9	24	41	5	0	4	17	1	1	2	2	14	0	0	1
Young, Balt.	.000	1	1	0	0	0	0	0	0	0	0	0	0	0	1	0	0	0
Yount, Milw.	.297	39	158	27	47	77	6	3	6	23	0	1	14	0	23	4	1	2

OFFICIAL AMERICAN LEAGUE FIELDING AVERAGES

CLUB FIELDING

Club	Pct.	G.	PO.	A.	E.	TC.	DP.	TP.	PB.
Baltimore	.981	162	4318	1910	123	6351	166	0	9
Chicago	.981	162	4363	1796	122	6281	160	0	4
Minnesota	.980	162	4313	1678	120	6111	134	1	4
Toronto	.980	163	4392	1669	123	6184	166	0	9
California	.980	162	4374	1803	128	6305	170	0	4
Detroit	.979	162	4392	1667	127	6186	162	0	16
Kansas City	.979	162	4332	1860	131	6323	157	0	3
Seattle	.979	162	4326	1700	128	6154	143	0	17
Milwaukee	.978	161	4299	1812	136	6247	156	0	8
Texas	.977	161	4316	1671	138	6125	138	0	33
New York	.977	162	4396	1750	142	6288	177	0	8
Boston	.977	162	4326	1737	143	6206	128	0	10
Cleveland	.977	163	4403	1719	146	6268	163	0	14
Oakland	.975	162	4290	1508	146	5944	159	0	9
Totals	.979	1134	60840	24280	1853	86973	2179	1	148

INDIVIDUAL FIELDING

*Throws lefthanded.

FIRST BASEMEN

Leader—Club	Pct.	G.	PO.	A.	E.	DP.
MATTINGLY, N.Y.*	.996	133	1107	124	5	135

Player—Club	Pct.	G.	PO.	A.	E.	DP.
Almon, Oak.	.990	44	184	13	2	18
Balboni, K.C.	.987	125	1102	79	15	102
Bergman, Det.*	.989	114	657	75	8	63
Bochte, Oak.*	.993	144	1048	66	8	119
Buckner, Bos.*	.986	113	974	96	15	75
Carew, Cal.	.981	83	724	59	15	73
Cooper, Milw.*	.991	122	1061	98	10	106
Davis, Sea.	.992	147	1271	94	11	108
Easler, Bos.	.976	29	256	29	7	21
Evans, Det.	.997	47	324	44	1	33
Garbey, Det.	.989	65	391	42	5	50
Grich, Cal.	.977	25	120	10	3	18
Griffey, N.Y.*	.959	27	241	16	11	23
Hargrove, Clev.*	.991	124	790	83	8	86
Hatcher, Minn.	.984	17	115	9	2	9
Hostetler, Tex.	1.000	14	90	8	0	9
Hrbek, Minn.	.990	148	1320	99	14	113
Iorg, K.C.	.995	43	357	22	2	33
Ro. Jackson, Cal.	.990	21	186	13	2	17
B. Jones, Tex.*	.990	15	97	5	1	7
Jurak, Bos.	1.000	19	72	10	0	8
Leach, Tor.*	1.000	15	69	13	0	9
Mattingly, N.Y.*	.996	133	1107	124	5	135
Miller, Cal.	.990	16	92	7	1	12
Murray, Balt.	.992	159	1538	143	13	152
O'Brien, Tex.*	.992	141	1270	105	11	103
Paciorek, Chi.	.993	67	532	23	4	50
Sconiers, Cal.*	.990	41	355	26	4	27
Simmons, Milw.	.995	37	346	27	2	35
Squires, Chi.*	1.000	77	226	16	0	29
Stapleton, Bos.	1.000	10	86	8	0	5
Tabler, Clev.	.998	67	433	39	1	46
Thornton, Clev.	.979	11	86	9	2	11
Upshaw, Tor.*	.990	151	1246	103	14	133
Walker, Chi.	.995	101	791	51	4	66
Wathan, K.C.	1.000	33	91	10	0	8

TRIPLE PLAY: Hrbek.

(Fewer Than Ten Games)

Player—Club	Pct.	G.	PO.	A.	E.	DP.
Aikens, Tor.	1.000	2	12	1	0	1
Bando, Clev.	1.000	1	2	0	0	0
Bannister, Tex.	1.000	1	12	0	0	0
Bonnell, Sea.	1.000	5	15	2	0	1
Bush, Minn.*	1.000	2	5	0	0	1
Carter, Clev.	1.000	7	47	2	0	4
Collins, Tor.	1.000	6	34	3	0	4
Foley, Tex.	.000	1	0	0	0	0
Foli, N.Y.	1.000	2	2	0	0	0
Gross, Balt.	1.000	3	5	0	0	0
Hancock, Oak.*	1.000	4	5	0	0	1
Hassey, Clev.	.889	1	7	1	1	0
Hill, Chi.	1.000	2	7	0	0	2
Howell, Milw.	1.000	4	19	2	0	4
Johnson, Det.	1.000	2	1	0	0	1
Johnson, Tor.	1.000	2	26	0	0	0
Kingman, Oak.	1.000	9	55	2	0	3
Laga, Det.*	1.000	4	12	1	0	1
Lowenstein, Balt.	1.000	2	19	0	0	2
Meyer, Oak.	.944	3	15	2	1	1
Miller, Bos.	1.000	8	44	4	0	1
Nahorodny, Sea.	1.000	1	3	0	0	2
Narron, Cal.	1.000	7	38	2	0	5
Perkins, Clev.*	1.000	2	8	0	0	2
Phelps, Sea.*	.987	9	72	4	1	7
Pryor, K.C.	1.000	1	0	1	0	0
Putnam, Sea.	.974	6	32	6	1	7
Ramos, Sea.	1.000	5	14	1	0	4
Rayford, Balt.	1.000	1	6	0	0	1
Rhomberg, Clev.	.000	1	0	0	0	0
Romero, Milw.	1.000	4	24	4	0	2
Schroeder, Milw.	1.000	1	3	0	0	0
Smalley, N.Y.-Chi.	.981	6	51	1	1	8
Stein, Tex.	1.000	3	4	0	0	1
Webster, Tor.*	1.000	1	2	0	0	1

FIRST BASEMAN WITH TWO OR MORE CLUBS

Player—Club	Pct.	G.	PO.	A.	E.	DP.
Smalley, N.Y.	.978	5	44	0	1	7
Smalley, Chi.	1.000	1	7	1	0	1

SECOND BASEMEN

Leader—Club	Pct.	G.	PO.	A.	E.	DP.
BARRETT, Bos.	.987	136	245	417	9	67

Player—Club	Pct.	G.	PO.	A.	E.	DP.
Bannister, Tex.	.959	25	40	30	3	4
Barrett, Bos.	.987	136	245	417	9	67
Bernazard, Clev.	.971	136	264	397	20	85
Biancalana, K.C.	.988	29	34	50	1	15
Brookens, Det.	.950	26	28	48	4	14
Cruz, Chi.	.976	141	273	452	18	92
Dauer, Balt.	.980	123	225	325	11	76
Earl, Det.	.959	14	23	24	2	9
Fischlin, Clev.	.981	55	90	115	4	25
Fletcher, Chi.	.969	28	39	56	3	13
Foli, N.Y.	1.000	21	39	43	0	12
Gantner, Milw.	.985	153	362	469	13	111
Garcia, Tor.	.980	149	267	427	14	90
Grich, Cal.	.982	91	182	249	8	65
Griffin, Tor.	.968	21	41	51	3	7
Jurak, Bos.	.960	14	12	12	1	4
V. Law, Chi.	.973	22	29	42	2	6
Lopes, Oak.	.948	17	20	35	3	8
Milbourne, Sea.	.964	14	25	29	2	8
Morgan, Oak.	.977	100	201	229	10	62
Noboa, Clev.	1.000	19	7	13	0	4
Perconte, Sea.	.981	150	303	438	14	90
Phillips, Oak.	.982	90	121	156	5	36
Pryor, K.C.	.975	22	28	49	2	14
Randolph, N.Y.	.983	142	334	419	13	112
Remy, Bos.	.973	24	40	70	3	13
Romero, Milw.	.981	11	19	33	1	5
Sakata, Balt.	.988	76	80	161	3	33
Stein, Tex.	.967	11	12	17	1	3
Teufel, Minn.	.984	157	315	485	13	81
Tolleson, Tex.	.979	109	191	276	10	61
Whitaker, Det.	.979	142	290	405	15	83

Player—Club	Pct.	G.	PO.	A.	E.	DP.
White, K.C.	.985	129	299	425	11	97
Wilfong, Cal.	.975	97	161	266	11	48
Wilkerson, Tex.	.978	47	76	106	4	23

TRIPLE PLAY: Teufel.

(Fewer Than Ten Games)

Player—Club	Pct.	G.	PO.	A.	E.	DP.
Anderson, Tex.	1.000	1	0	1	0	0
Baker, Det.	.944	5	10	7	1	2
Concepcion, K.C.	1.000	6	11	15	0	6
Dybzinski, Chi.	.000	1	0	0	0	0
Garbey, Det.	1.000	3	2	2	0	2
Harrah, N.Y.	1.000	4	1	4	0	0
Hill, Oak.	1.000	4	3	3	0	0
Hoffman, Bos.	1.000	2	3	0	0	0
Hudler, N.Y.	1.000	9	4	7	0	1
Hulett, Chi.	1.000	3	4	12	0	2
Iorg, Tor.	1.000	7	3	6	0	2
Lozado, Milw.	1.000	1	0	3	0	0
Manrique, Tor.	.938	9	5	10	1	3
Meacham, N.Y.	1.000	2	4	3	0	0
Mulliniks, Tor.	.000	1	0	0	0	0
Orta, K.C.	.000	1	0	0	0	0
Picciolo, Cal.	.975	9	14	25	1	5
Ramos, Sea.	1.000	3	4	5	0	0
Reynolds, Sea.	1.000	6	8	12	0	3
Rhomberg, Clev.	1.000	1	0	1	0	0
Richardt, Tex.	1.000	4	5	6	0	4
Robertson, N.Y.	.917	6	5	6	1	2
Rodriguez, Balt.	.958	7	8	15	1	1
Tabler, Clev.	.000	1	0	0	0	0
Tartabull, Sea.	1.000	1	1	1	0	1
Wagner, Oak.	1.000	8	3	4	0	0
Walker, Bos.	1.000	1	0	1	0	0
Washington, Minn.	1.000	9	17	17	0	5

THIRD BASEMEN

Leader—Club	Pct.	G.	PO.	A.	E.	DP.
MULLINIKS, Tor.	.968	119	65	148	7	13

(Listed Alphabetically)

Player—Club	Pct.	G.	PO.	A.	E.	DP.
Bell, Tex.	.958	147	129	323	20	28
Boggs, Bos.	.959	156	141	330	20	30
Bonnell, Sea.	.762	10	3	13	5	0
Brett, K.C.	.949	101	59	201	14	18
Brookens, Det.	.969	68	32	63	3	10
Castillo, Det.	.950	33	12	26	2	1
Coles, Sea.	.918	42	28	62	8	10
Cruz, Balt.	.955	89	23	104	6	10
DeCinces, Cal.	.964	140	107	266	14	22
Dybzinski, Chi.	.875	14	1	6	1	0
Evans, Det.	.962	19	7	18	1	1
Fernandez, Tor.	.952	10	3	17	1	1
Fischlin, Clev.	.933	17	3	11	1	0
Foli, N.Y.	.968	10	10	20	1	3
Gaetti, Minn.	.960	154	142	334	20	26
Garbey, Det.	.750	20	7	14	7	1
Grich, Cal.	.970	21	9	23	1	1
Gross, Balt.	.937	117	64	205	18	13
Gruber, Tor.	.933	12	4	10	1	0
Harrah, N.Y.	.968	74	51	128	6	17
Howell, Milw.	.907	46	21	67	9	7
Iorg, Tor.	.945	112	62	110	10	15
Ro. Jackson, Cal-Balt	.956	19	21	22	2	5
Jacoby, Clev.	.951	126	86	187	14	17
Johnson, Det.	.944	108	58	143	12	16
Lansford, Oak.	.957	151	137	268	18	27
V. Law, Chi.	.955	137	79	199	13	24
Lozado, Milw.	.925	36	23	51	6	7
Milbourne, Sea.	.900	40	22	50	8	6
Mulliniks, Tor.	.968	119	65	148	7	13
Pagliarulo, N.Y.	.955	67	44	106	7	16
Parrish, Tex.	.967	12	2	27	1	3
Picciolo, Cal.	.933	13	3	11	1	0
Presley, Sea.	.958	69	48	113	7	12
Pryor, K.C.	.970	105	59	138	6	13
Ramos, Sea.	.911	38	18	23	4	4

Player—Club	Pct.	G.	PO.	A.	E.	DP.
Rayford, Balt.	.942	22	17	32	3	2
Ready, Milw.	.946	36	29	76	6	4
Romero, Milw.	.943	59	38	111	9	13
Simmons, Milw.	.838	14	6	25	6	2
Smalley, N.Y.-Chi.	.923	73	32	135	14	14
Squires, Chi.*	1.000	13	3	9	0	0
Tabler, Clev.	.950	36	27	49	4	7
Wagner, Oak.	1.000	15	17	16	0	1

TRIPLE PLAY: Gaetti.

(Fewer Than Ten Games)

Player—Club	Pct.	G.	PO.	A.	E.	DP.
Almon, Oak.	1.000	4	1	0	0	0
Anderson, Tex.	1.000	6	2	4	0	0
Ashford, K.C.	.909	9	2	8	1	1
Bando, Clev.	.000	1	0	0	0	0
Bannister, Tex.	.500	1	1	0	1	0
Bell, Tor.	1.000	3	0	2	0	0
Castino, Minn.	1.000	8	8	12	0	1
Concepcion, K.C.	.000	1	0	0	0	0
Dauer, Balt.	1.000	3	0	4	0	0
Dent, K.C.	1.000	2	2	1	0	0
Essian, Oak.	.667	1	0	2	1	0
Fletcher, Chi.	1.000	3	2	2	0	1
Foley, Tex.	1.000	1	1	1	0	0
Hatcher, Minn.	.000	1	0	0	0	0
Heath, Oak.	1.000	2	1	1	0	0
Hill, Oak.	.000	2	0	0	0	0
Hoffman, Bos.	1.000	4	1	3	0	1
Hulett, Chi.	1.000	4	0	3	0	0
Iorg, K.C.	.000	1	0	0	0	0
Jurak, Bos.	.929	9	8	18	2	0
Kiefer, Oak.	1.000	2	1	2	0	0
Lopes, Oak.	1.000	5	1	8	0	0
Meier, Minn.	1.000	1	0	0	0	0
Molitor, Milw.	.933	7	7	21	2	3
Moronko, Clev.	.895	6	10	7	2	2
O'Berry, N.Y.	.000	1	0	0	0	0
O'Malley, Chi.	1.000	6	2	1	0	0
Quirk, Chi.	1.000	1	1	0	0	0

THIRD BASEMEN—Continued

Player—Club	Pct.	G.	PO.	A.	E.	DP.
Scranton, K.C.	.000	1	0	0	0	0
Stein, Tex.	.000	3	0	0	0	0
Thomas, Cal.	1.000	3	1	0	0	0
Tolleson, Tex.	1.000	5	2	3	0	0
Washington, Minn.	1.000	2	0	3	0	0

THIRD BASEMAN WITH TWO OR MORE CLUBS

Player—Club	Pct.	G.	PO.	A.	E.	DP.
Ro. Jackson, Cal.	.950	9	9	10	1	1
Ro. Jackson, Balt.	.960	10	12	12	1	4
Smalley, N.Y.	.905	35	17	78	10	8
Smalley, Chi.	.947	38	15	57	4	6

SHORTSTOPS

Leader—Club	Pct.	G.	PO.	A.	E.	DP.
SCHOFIELD, Cal.	.982	140	218	420	12	95

Player—Club	Pct.	G.	PO.	A.	E.	DP.
Anderson, Tex.	.989	31	35	53	1	13
Baker, Det.	.969	39	46	79	4	18
Biancalana, K.C.	.946	33	28	94	7	13
Brookens, Det.	.958	28	38	76	5	11
Concepcion, K.C.	.972	85	105	280	11	53
Dybzinski, Chi.	.974	76	68	154	6	32
Faedo, Minn.	.968	15	22	39	2	4
Fernandez, Tor.	.974	73	116	178	8	40
Fischlin, Clev.	.912	15	11	20	3	5
Fletcher, Chi.	.973	134	193	381	16	75
Foli, N.Y.	.950	28	37	59	5	17
Franco, Clev.	.955	159	280	481	36	116
Griffin, Tor.	.962	115	189	269	18	65
Gutierrez, Bos.	.949	150	228	347	31	60
Hill, Oak.	.949	66	99	125	12	28
Hoffman, Bos.	.957	56	39	71	5	17
Jimenez, Minn.	.959	107	145	273	18	59
Kiefer, Oak.	.904	17	14	33	5	5
Kunkel, Tex.	.922	48	81	120	17	22
Meacham, N.Y.	.955	96	136	269	19	52
Owen, Sea.	.977	151	245	463	17	86
Phillips, Oak.	.941	91	133	235	23	54
Picciolo, Cal.	.974	66	51	99	4	17
Ramos, Sea.	.972	13	15	20	1	2
Ripken, Balt.	.971	162	297	583	26	122
Robertson, N.Y.	.930	49	63	136	15	34
Romero, Milw.	.955	39	60	108	8	15
Schofield, Cal.	.982	140	218	420	12	95
Smalley, N.Y.-Chi.	.967	16	7	22	1	2
Speier, Minn.	.977	12	14	28	1	6
Trammell, Det.	.980	114	180	314	10	71

Player—Club	Pct.	G.	PO.	A.	E.	DP.
Wagner, Oak.	.951	57	53	63	6	14
Washington, Minn.	.978	71	60	114	4	19
Washington, K.C.	.961	61	81	166	10	40
Wilkerson, Tex.	.944	116	151	285	26	50
Yount, Milw.	.971	120	199	402	18	80

(Fewer Than Ten Games)

Player—Club	Pct.	G.	PO.	A.	E.	DP.
Almon, Oak.	1.000	1	0	1	0	0
Dent, K.C.	1.000	9	2	5	0	0
Gaetti, Minn.	.750	2	2	1	1	1
Gruber, Tor.	.667	1	0	2	1	0
Heath, Oak.	.000	1	0	0	0	0
Iorg, Tor.	1.000	2	1	1	0	1
Jacoby, Clev.	1.000	1	0	1	0	0
Johnson, Det.	.833	9	3	7	2	4
Jurak, Bos.	.000	2	0	0	0	0
V. Law, Chi.	1.000	4	0	4	0	1
Lozado, Milw.	.909	6	3	7	1	0
Milbourne, Sea.	.867	5	6	7	2	0
Mulliniks, Tor.	.857	3	2	4	1	2
Pryor, K.C.	1.000	2	0	2	0	0
Scranton, K.C.	1.000	1	0	1	0	1
Smith, N.Y.	.923	2	2	10	1	1
Tartabull, Sea.	.931	8	7	20	2	4
Thomas, Cal.	1.000	4	3	1	0	1
Tolleson, Tex.	1.000	7	2	8	0	1
Wilfong, Cal.	.750	4	1	2	1	0

SHORTSTOP WITH TWO OR MORE CLUBS

Player—Club	Pct.	G.	PO.	A.	E.	DP.
Smalley, N.Y.	.963	13	5	21	1	2
Smalley, Chi.	1.000	3	2	1	0	0

OUTFIELDERS

Leader—Club	Pct.	G.	PO.	A.	E.	DP.
DOWNING, Cal.	1.000	131	272	5	0	0

Player—Club	Pct.	G.	PO.	A.	E.	DP.
Almon, Oak.	1.000	48	70	1	0	1
Armas, Bos.	.974	126	329	4	9	2
Ayala, Balt.	1.000	13	10	0	0	0
Baines, Chi.*	.981	147	307	8	6	1
Barfield, Tor.	.952	88	190	9	10	5
Bell, Tor.	.971	147	289	11	9	1
Beniquez, Cal.	.971	98	197	5	6	1
Bonnell, Sea.	.994	94	153	8	1	0
Boston, Chi.*	.910	34	59	2	6	1
Bradley, Sea.	.992	117	235	3	2	1
Brouhard, Milw.	.983	52	107	6	2	2
Brown, Minn.	.993	55	144	4	1	0
Brown, Cal.	.968	44	57	4	2	0
Brunansky, Minn.	.984	153	304	13	5	6
Bumbry, Balt.	.988	99	230	7	3	1
Butler, Clev.*	.991	156	448	13	4	3
Calderon, Sea.	1.000	11	22	0	0	0
Carter, Clev.	.956	59	122	9	6	0
Castillo, Clev.	.933	70	123	2	9	0
Chambers, Sea.*	.947	13	18	0	1	0
Clark, Milw.	.981	56	106	0	2	0
Collins, Tor.	.991	108	203	8	2	3
Cowens, Sea.	.987	130	228	8	3	0
David, Minn.*.	1.000	14	14	0	0	0
Davis, K.C.	.959	35	69	2	3	1
Davis, Oak.*	.961	127	287	6	12	4
Dayett, N.Y.	.988	62	80	3	1	0
Downing, Cal.	1.000	131	272	5	0	0

Player—Club	Pct.	G.	PO.	A.	E.	DP.
Dunbar, Tex.*	.939	20	31	0	2	0
Dwyer, Balt.*	.966	52	83	3	3	1
Evans, Bos.	.994	161	311	7	2	2
Ford, Balt.	1.000	15	36	1	0	0
Gamble, N.Y.	1.000	12	15	1	0	0
Garbey, Det.	1.000	10	11	0	0	0
Gibson, Det.*	.954	139	245	4	12	2
Griffey, N.Y.*	.974	82	181	6	5	0
Grubb, Det.	1.000	36	47	0	0	0
Hairston, Chi.	.967	37	57	2	2	0
Hall, Clev.*	.993	69	143	3	1	0
Hancock, Oak.*	1.000	18	19	0	0	0
Hart, Minn.*	1.000	11	24	1	0	0
Hatcher, Minn.	.974	100	249	11	7	1
Heath, Oak.	.986	45	71	1	1	1
Henderson, Oak.*	.969	140	341	7	11	1
D. Henderson, Sea.	.988	97	242	11	3	5
S. Henderson, Sea.	.936	53	84	4	6	0
Herndon, Det.	.986	117	199	7	3	0
Iorg, K.C.	.977	22	42	0	1	0
James, Milw.*	.989	118	252	7	3	1
B. Jones, Tex.*	1.000	22	42	2	0	1
Jones, Det.*	1.000	73	150	4	0	1
L. Jones, K.C.	.962	45	51	0	2	0
Kemp, N.Y.*	.972	75	138	2	4	0
Kittle, Chi.	.972	124	226	14	7	2
Kuntz, Det.	.987	67	74	2	1	1
R. Law, Chi.	.985	130	322	5	5	0
Leach, Tor.*	1.000	23	23	1	0	0
Lemon, Det.	.995	140	427	6	2	1
Loman, Milw.*	.967	23	54	4	2	0

OUTFIELDERS—Continued

Player—Club	Pct.	G.	PO.	A.	E.	DP.
Lopes, Oak.	.965	42	78	4	3	2
Lowenstein, Balt.	.971	67	94	5	3	0
Lynn, Cal.*	.982	140	321	12	6	5
Manning, Milw.	.987	114	231	2	3	2
Mata, N.Y.	.942	28	49	0	3	0
Mattingly, N.Y.*	.974	19	36	2	1	1
Meier, Minn.	.978	50	87	2	2	0
Miller, Bos.*	.974	31	36	1	1	0
Moore, Milw.	.984	61	119	2	2	0
Moreno, N.Y.*	.985	108	262	9	4	2
Moseby, Tor.	.990	156	473	8	5	2
Moses, Sea.*	1.000	19	26	1	0	0
Motley, K.C.	.984	138	301	7	5	2
Murphy, Oak.	.988	153	474	14	6	2
Nichols, Bos.	.988	48	79	3	1	0
Nixon, Clev.	1.000	46	81	3	0	0
Oglivie, Milw.*	.970	125	256	6	8	1
Orta, K.C.	.980	26	48	0	1	0
Paciorek, Chi.	.971	41	64	2	2	0
Parrish, Tex.	.982	81	153	8	3	3
Pettis, Cal.	.983	134	337	11	6	4
Piniella, N.Y.	1.000	24	40	3	0	0
Puckett, Minn.	.993	128	438	16	3	4
Putnam, Sea.	1.000	13	14	0	0	0
Rice, Bos.	.989	157	336	12	4	3
Rivers, Tex.*	1.000	30	49	3	0	2
Roberts, K.C.	1.000	16	24	0	0	0
Roenicke, Balt.	.995	117	197	6	1	0
Sample, Tex.	.986	122	285	3	4	2
Shelby, Balt.	.993	124	261	9	2	1
Sheridan, K.C.	.986	134	273	8	4	1
Stegman, Chi.	.985	46	65	1	1	0
Tabler, Clev.	.973	43	72	1	2	1
G. Thomas, Sea.	1.000	34	45	2	0	0
Vukovich, Clev.	.994	130	316	13	2	5
Ward, Tex.	.987	148	376	11	5	1
Webster, Tor.*	.875	10	14	0	2	0
Wilson, K.C.	.990	128	383	6	4	2
Winfield, N.Y.	.994	140	306	3	2	1

Player—Club	Pct.	G.	PO.	A.	E.	DP.
G. Wright, Tex.	.983	80	175	3	3	0
Young, Balt.	.982	115	216	4	4	0

(Fewer Than Ten Games)

Player—Club	Pct.	G.	PO.	A.	E.	DP.
Allen, Det.	1.000	2	2	0	0	0
Bannister, Tex.	1.000	3	7	0	0	0
Baylor, N.Y.	.889	5	8	0	1	0
Bergman, Det.*	1.000	2	1	0	0	0
Bradley, N.Y.	1.000	5	8	0	0	0
Burroughs, Oak.	1.000	4	1	0	0	0
Coles, Sea.	1.000	3	3	1	0	0
Eisenreich, Minn.*	1.000	3	5	0	0	0
Gaetti, Minn.	1.000	8	19	0	0	0
Gruber, Tor.	1.000	2	2	0	0	0
Harrah, N.Y.	.000	1	0	0	0	0
Hoyt, Chi.	.000	1	0	0	0	0
Ro. Jackson, Cal.	1.000	1	1	0	0	0
Re. Jackson, Cal.*	1.000	3	7	0	0	0
Javier, N.Y.	1.000	5	3	0	0	0
Johnson, Det.	1.000	1	1	0	0	0
V. Law, Chi.	.923	5	11	1	1	1
Leeper, K.C.*	1.000	2	4	0	0	0
Miller, Cal.	.000	1	0	0	0	0
Nelson, Sea.	1.000	2	2	0	0	0
O'Brien, Tex.*	1.000	1	1	0	0	0
Phillips, Oak.	1.000	1	1	0	0	0
Picciolo, Cal.	1.000	1	1	0	0	0
Rhomberg, Clev.	1.000	7	7	0	0	0
Romero, Milw.	.000	1	0	0	0	0
Sakata, Balt.	.000	1	0	0	0	0
Sheets, Balt.	1.000	7	12	1	0	0
Shepherd, Tor.	1.000	5	2	1	0	0
Simmons, Det.	1.000	5	8	0	0	0
Squires, Chi.*	1.000	3	5	0	0	0
Thomas, Cal.	.889	7	8	0	1	0
Tolleson, Tex.	.000	1	0	0	0	0
Wathan, K.C.	.000	1	0	0	0	0

CATCHERS

Leader—Club	Pct.	G.	PO.	A.	E.	DP.	PB.
SUNDBERG, Milw.	.995	109	556	55	3	6	2

Player—Club	Pct.	G.	PO.	A.	E.	DP.	PB.
Allenson, Bos.	.987	35	135	12	2	4	1
Bando, Clev.	.982	63	305	30	6	4	5
Boone, Calif.	.984	137	660	71	12	10	4
Castillo, Det.	.970	36	149	11	5	2	5
Cerone, N.Y.	.996	38	230	9	1	1	1
Dempsey, Balt.	.992	108	453	43	4	5	4
Engle, Minn.	.981	86	376	34	8	3	3
Essian, Oak.	.985	59	229	28	4	6	1
Fisk, Chi.	.987	90	421	38	6	4	2
Foley, Tex.	.988	36	147	13	2	3	3
Gedman, Bos.	.977	125	693	58	18	5	8
Hassey, Clev.	1.000	44	203	15	0	1	1
Heath, Oak.	.986	108	423	54	7	7	7
Hill, Chi.	.991	72	308	17	3	4	0
Kearney, Sea.	.988	133	823	63	11	9	11
Laudner, Minn.	.978	81	362	38	9	2	0
Lowry, Det.	1.000	31	87	8	0	2	0
Martinez, Tor.	.995	98	360	34	2	5	3
Mercado, Sea.	.992	29	118	10	1	0	3
Nahorodny, Sea.	.976	10	38	2	1	0	1
Narron, Calif.	.994	46	146	10	1	1	0
Newman, Bos.	.992	24	118	8	1	0	1
O'Berry, N.Y.	1.000	12	53	5	0	1	1
Parrish, Det.	.991	127	720	67	7	11	11
Rayford, Balt.	.991	66	287	35	3	2	4
Reed, Minn.	.977	18	41	1	1	1	1
Schroeder, Milw.	.987	58	274	24	4	2	4

Player—Club	Pct.	G.	PO.	A.	E.	DP.	PB.
Scott, Tex.	.974	80	400	41	12	9	18
Skinner, Chi.	.989	43	171	11	2	1	2
Slaught, K.C.	.982	123	547	44	11	8	2
Sundberg, Milw.	.995	109	556	55	3	6	2
Tettleton, Oak.	.992	32	112	10	1	1	1
Valle, Sea.	1.000	13	56	5	0	0	2
Wathan, K.C.	.975	59	213	21	6	2	1
Whitt, Tor.	.994	118	583	40	4	8	6
Willard, Clev.	.981	76	335	35	7	7	8
Wynegar, N.Y.	.993	126	757	59	6	9	6
Yost, Tex.	.995	78	368	20	2	1	12

(Fewer Than Ten Games)

Player—Club	Pct.	G.	PO.	A.	E.	DP.	PB.
Almon, Oak.	.000	1	0	0	0	0	0
Bradley, N.Y.	1.000	3	2	0	0	0	0
Christmas, Chi.	1.000	1	2	0	0	0	0
Hernandez, Tor.	1.000	3	1	0	0	0	0
Moore, Milw.	.964	7	26	1	1	0	2
Nolan, Balt.	.962	6	22	3	1	0	1
Petralli, Tor.	1.000	1	1	0	0	0	0
Pujols, K.C.	1.000	4	9	0	0	0	0
Quirk, Clev.	.000	1	0	0	0	0	0
Sanchez, K.C.-Balt.	1.000	5	10	1	0	0	0
Sullivan, Bos.	.950	2	19	0	1	0	0

CATCHER WITH TWO OR MORE CLUBS

Player—Club	Pct.	G.	PO.	A.	E.	DP.	PB.
Sanchez, K.C.	1.000	1	1	1	0	0	0
Sanchez, Balt.	1.000	4	9	1	0	0	0

PITCHERS

Leader—Club	Pct.	G.	PO.	A.	E.	DP.
SEAVER, Chi.	1.000	34	16	40	0	2

Player—Club	Pct.	G.	PO.	A.	E.	DP.
Aase, Calif.	.857	23	1	5	1	0

Player—Club	Pct.	G.	PO.	A.	E.	DP.
Abbott, Det.	.857	13	4	8	2	1
Acker, Tor.	.938	32	7	8	1	0
Agosto, Chi.*	.958	49	7	16	1	5
Alexander, Tor.	.962	36	18	33	2	4

PITCHERS—Continued

Player—Club	Pct.	G.	PO.	A.	E.	DP.
Aponte, Clev.	1.000	25	1	5	0	0
Armstrong, N.Y.	.917	36	7	4	1	0
Atherton, Oak.	.909	57	5	5	1	0
Bair, Det.	1.000	47	12	11	0	2
Bannister, Chi.*	.963	34	3	23	1	0
Barojas, Chi.-Sea.	1.000	43	8	27	0	1
Beard, Sea.	.933	43	2	12	1	0
Beattie, Sea.	1.000	32	13	33	0	2
Beckwith, K.C.	1.000	49	10	12	0	1
Berenguer, Det.	.929	31	11	15	2	0
Black, K.C.*	.970	35	13	51	2	2
Blyleven, Clev.	.962	33	21	30	2	2
Boddicker, Balt.	.933	34	49	49	7	6
Boyd, Bos.	.962	29	20	31	2	3
Brown, Bos.	.905	15	11	8	2	1
Brown, N.Y.	1.000	13	2	2	0	0
Burgmeier, Oak.*	1.000	17	3	3	0	1
Burns, Chi.*	.905	34	2	17	2	0
Burris, Oak.	1.000	34	5	16	0	2
Butcher, Minn.	.938	34	25	20	3	5
Caldwell, Milw.*	.912	26	7	24	3	2
Camacho, Clev.	1.000	69	1	15	0	0
Castillo, Minn.	1.000	10	2	2	0	1
Caudill, Oak.	1.000	68	4	4	0	0
Christiansen, N.Y.	.889	24	5	3	1	0
Clancy, Tor.	.978	36	15	30	1	4
Clark, Tor.*	1.000	20	1	13	0	0
Clear, Bos.	1.000	47	4	8	0	0
Clemens, Bos.	1.000	21	11	14	0	0
Cocanower, Milw.	.887	33	15	32	6	0
Codiroli, Oak.	.941	28	5	11	1	1
Comer, Clev.	.964	22	7	20	1	1
Conroy, Oak.*	1.000	38	0	7	0	1
Corbett, Calif.	1.000	45	4	13	0	0
Cowley, N.Y.	.905	16	7	12	2	0
Crawford, Bos.	1.000	35	4	8	0	1
Curtis, Calif.*	1.000	17	2	4	0	0
Darwin, Tex.	.919	35	13	21	3	2
Davis, Balt.	.943	35	15	18	2	1
Davis, Minn.	1.000	64	4	8	0	0
Dotson, Chi.	.978	32	8	36	1	3
Easterly, Clev.*	1.000	26	6	10	0	0
Farr, Clev.	.926	31	7	18	2	1
Filson, Minn.*	.938	55	2	13	1	0
Fingers, Milw.	1.000	33	3	3	0	0
Flanagan, Balt.*	1.000	34	3	33	0	2
Fontenot, N.Y.*	.919	35	6	28	3	1
Frazier, Clev.	.857	22	3	3	1	0
Gale, Bos.	1.000	13	4	3	0	0
Geisel, Sea.*	1.000	20	2	2	0	0
Gibson, Milw.	1.000	18	11	7	0	0
Gleaton, Chi.*	.667	11	1	1	1	0
Gott, Tor.	.938	35	6	9	1	0
Gubicza, K.C.	.962	29	19	31	2	1
Guidry, N.Y.*	1.000	29	8	24	0	3
Gura, K.C.*	1.000	31	6	30	0	1
Haas, Milw.	1.000	31	19	36	0	2
Heaton, Clev.*	.933	38	9	19	2	0
Henke, Tex.	1.000	25	1	2	0	0
Hernandez, Det.*	1.000	80	5	14	0	1
Hodge, Minn.*	1.000	25	2	6	0	0
Hough, Tex.	.984	36	12	51	1	2
Howell, N.Y.	.964	61	11	16	1	3
Hoyt, Chi.	.942	34	12	37	3	2
Huismann, K.C.	.850	38	7	10	3	0
Hurst, Bos.*	1.000	33	10	30	0	1
Jackson, Tor.	1.000	54	5	11	0	0
Jackson, K.C.*	.929	15	6	7	1	2
Jeffcoat, Clev.*	1.000	63	2	13	0	3
John, Calif.*	1.000	32	15	27	0	1
Johnson, Bos.*	1.000	30	0	8	0	0
O. Jones, Tex.	1.000	33	5	10	0	1
Jones, Chi.	1.000	13	0	3	0	0
Jones, Oak.	1.000	13	2	3	0	2
M. Jones, Oak.*	1.000	23	2	7	0	0
Kaufman, Calif.	1.000	29	1	12	0	1
Key, Tor.*	.952	63	9	11	1	0
Kison, Calif.	.833	20	7	3	2	1
Krueger, Oak.*	1.000	26	6	12	0	1
LaCorte, Calif.	.800	13	0	4	1	0
Ladd, Milw.	.900	54	5	4	1	0
Lamp, Tor.	.923	56	9	15	2	3
Langston, Sea.*	.957	35	15	30	2	2
Lazorko, Milw.	1.000	15	3	5	0	0
Leal, Tor.	1.000	35	12	30	0	3
Leibrandt, K.C.*	.889	23	9	15	3	1
Lopez, Det.	.895	71	6	11	2	2
Lysander, Minn.	.933	36	8	6	1	1
J. D. Martinez, Balt.	.947	34	17	19	2	4
F. Martinez, Balt.*	.889	55	2	14	2	0
Mason, Tex.*	1.000	36	4	22	0	0
McCatty, Oak.	.939	33	15	16	2	1
McClure, Milw.*	.926	39	4	21	2	2
McGregor, Balt.*	.980	30	14	35	1	2
McLaughlin, Tor.-Tex.	.889	21	3	5	1	2
Mirabella, Sea.*	1.000	52	4	11	0	1
Mitchell, Bos.	.800	10	1	3	1	0
Monge, Det.*	.667	19	0	2	1	0
Montefusco, N.Y.	.889	11	1	7	1	1
Moore, Sea.	.894	34	18	41	7	0
Morris, Det.	.953	35	29	32	3	4
Murray, N.Y.	.800	19	0	4	1	0
Musselman, Tor.	1.000	11	0	3	0	0
Nelson, Chi.	1.000	20	11	8	0	1
Niekro, N.Y.	.980	32	13	36	1	4
Nipper, Bos.	.983	29	28	31	1	0
Noles, Tex.	.750	18	1	2	1	0
Nunez, Sea.	.909	37	4	6	1	0
Ojeda, Bos.*	.955	33	10	32	2	3
Pashnick, Minn.	1.000	13	3	6	0	0
Petry, Det.	.986	35	38	34	1	4
Porter, Milw.	.944	17	7	10	1	2
Quisenberry, K.C.	1.000	72	15	29	0	1
Rainey, Oak.	1.000	16	3	2	0	1
Rasmussen, N.Y.*	.913	24	7	14	2	1
Rawley, N.Y.	.857	11	1	5	1	0
Reed, Chi.	.929	51	2	11	1	3
Righetti, N.Y.*	.882	64	2	13	2	0
Rijo, N.Y.	.933	24	2	12	1	0
Roberge, Chi.	1.000	21	5	9	0	1
Romanick, Cal.	.875	33	18	24	6	3
Rozema, Det.	1.000	29	17	10	0	3
Saberhagen, K.C.	.974	38	15	22	1	1
Sanchez, K.C.	.867	49	3	10	2	2
Scherrer, Det.*	1.000	18	0	1	0	0
Schmidt, Tex.	.950	43	6	13	1	2
Schrom, Minn.	.944	25	8	9	1	0
Schulze, Clev.	1.000	19	9	9	0	0
Searage, Milw.*	.857	21	1	5	1	0
Seaver, Chi.	1.000	34	11	40	0	2
Shirley, N.Y.*	.957	41	6	16	1	4
Slaton, Cal.	1.000	32	9	25	0	3
Smith, Clev.	.769	22	4	6	3	0
Smithson, Minn.	.958	36	17	29	2	2
Sorensen, Oak.	.971	46	15	18	1	3
Spillner, Clev.-Chi.	1.000	36	11	16	0	0
Splittorff, K.C.*	1.000	12	2	9	0	0
Stanley, Bos.	.946	57	7	28	2	0
Stanton, N.Y.	.889	54	4	4	1	0
Stewart, Balt.	1.000	60	2	14	0	0
Stewart, Tex.	.909	32	11	19	3	2
Stieb, Tor.	.982	35	22	34	1	4
Stoddard, Sea.	1.000	27	3	14	0	1
Sutcliffe, Clev.	.947	15	7	11	1	1
Sutton, Milw.	.968	33	11	19	1	1
Swaggerty, Balt.	.818	23	3	6	2	0
Tanana, Tex.*	1.000	35	18	35	0	2
Tellmann, Milw.	1.000	50	4	15	0	0
R. Thomas, Sea.	1.000	21	4	7	0	1
Tobik, Tex.	1.000	24	3	7	0	1
Underwood, Balt.*	1.000	37	5	12	0	2
Vande Berg, Sea.*	.920	50	3	20	2	0
Viola, Minn.*	.970	35	6	26	1	1
Waddell, Clev.	1.000	58	8	9	0	1
Waits, Milw.*	1.000	47	2	12	0	0
Walters, Minn.	1.000	23	1	2	0	1

PITCHERS—Continued

Player—Club	Pct.	G.	PO.	A.	E.	DP.
Warren, Oak.	.714	24	1	4	2	0
Whitehouse, Minn.*	1.000	30	2	3	0	0
Wilcox, Det.	.941	33	20	28	3	4
Williams, Minn.	1.000	17	4	10	0	1
Willis, Det.	1.000	10	1	2	0	1
Wills, K.C.	.714	10	3	2	2	0
Witt, Cal.	.956	34	16	27	2	0
Young, Sea.*	.923	22	3	21	2	3
Young, Oak.*	1.000	20	6	13	0	1
Zahn, Cal.*	.979	28	14	33	1	1

(Fewer Than Ten Games)

Player—Club	Pct.	G.	PO.	A.	E.	DP.
Augustine, Milw.*	1.000	4	1	1	0	0
Barkley, Clev.	1.000	3	0	1	0	0
Beene, Milw.	1.000	5	1	4	0	1
Behenna, Clev.	1.000	3	3	0	0	0
Best, Sea.	.000	5	0	0	0	0
Bettendorf, Oak.	.000	3	0	0	0	0
Bibby, Tex.	1.000	8	1	2	0	0
Brennan, Chi.	1.000	4	0	3	0	0
Brown, Cal.	1.000	3	0	1	0	0
Brown, Balt.	1.000	9	0	2	0	0
Bystrom, N.Y.	1.000	7	4	2	0	0
Candiotti, Milw.	1.000	8	3	1	0	0
Cliburn, Cal.	1.000	1	1	1	0	0
Comstock, Minn.*	1.000	4	1	2	0	0
Cruz, Balt.	.000	1	0	0	0	0
Deshaies, N.Y.*	1.000	2	0	1	0	0
Dixon, Balt.	1.000	2	2	2	0	0
Dorsey, Bos.	1.000	2	0	1	0	0
Eckersley, Bos.	.957	9	11	11	1	2
Fallon, Chi.*	1.000	3	1	3	0	0
Forsch, Cal.	1.000	2	1	6	0	1
Guetterman, Sea.*	1.000	3	0	1	0	1
Hancock, Oak.*	.000	1	0	0	0	0

Player—Club	Pct.	G.	PO.	A.	E.	DP.
Hartzell, Milw.	1.000	4	0	2	0	0
Heimueller, Oak.*	1.000	6	1	3	0	1
Henry, Tex.	.000	3	0	0	0	0
Kern, Milw.	1.000	6	1	0	0	0
Langford, Oak.	.000	3	0	0	0	0
Leach, Tor.*	.000	1	0	0	0	0
Leiper, Oak.*	1.000	8	1	2	0	0
Mason, Det.	1.000	5	5	1	0	0
Niemann, Chi.*	1.000	5	2	1	0	0
O'Connor, Minn.*	.000	2	0	0	0	0
O'Neal, Det.	.750	4	2	1	1	0
Pacella, Balt.	.500	6	0	1	1	0
Palmer, Balt.	1.000	5	1	3	0	1
Roberts, K.C.	.000	1	0	0	0	0
Roman, Clev.	.000	3	0	0	0	0
Romero, Clev.*	.000	1	0	0	0	0
Siwy, Chi.	1.000	1	0	1	0	0
Smith, Cal.	.000	1	0	0	0	0
Snell, Balt.	1.000	5	1	0	0	0
Squires, Chi.*	.000	1	0	0	0	0
Steirer, Cal.	1.000	1	1	0	0	1
Swan, Cal.	1.000	2	0	1	0	0
Torrez, Oak.	.000	2	0	0	0	0
Ujdur, Clev.	.000	4	0	0	1	0
Wagner, Oak.	.000	1	0	0	0	0
Wardle, Minn.*	1.000	2	0	1	0	0
R. Wright, Tex.*	1.000	8	1	4	0	0

PITCHERS WITH TWO OR MORE CLUBS

Player—Club	Pct.	G.	PO.	A.	E.	DP.
Barojas, Chi.	1.000	24	4	10	0	0
Barojas, Sea.	1.000	19	4	17	0	1
McLaughlin, Tor.	.800	6	0	4	1	1
McLaughlin, Tex.	1.000	15	3	1	0	1
Spillner, Clev.	1.000	14	9	10	0	0
Spillner, Chi.	1.000	22	2	6	0	0

OFFICIAL AMERICAN LEAGUE PITCHING AVERAGES

CLUB PITCHING

Club	ERA.	G.	CG.	ShO.	Sv.	IP.	H.	BFP.	R.	ER.	HR.	SH.	SF.	HB.	Tot. BB.	Int. BB.	SO.	WP.	Bk.
Detroit	3.49	162	19	8	51	1464.0	1358	6127	643	568	130	41	42	30	489	41	914	47	6
Baltimore	3.71	162	48	13	32	1439.1	1393	6065	667	594	137	42	52	23	512	46	714	58	6
New York	3.78	162	15	12	43	1465.1	1485	6262	675	615	120	46	56	20	518	28	992	33	8
Minnesota	3.85	162	32	9	38	1437.2	1429	6078	679	615	159	31	44	35	463	50	713	38	7
Toronto	3.86	163	34	10	33	1464.0	1433	6235	696	628	140	54	45	34	528	40	875	42	2
Texas	3.91	161	38	6	21	1438.2	1443	6188	714	625	148	45	39	34	518	37	863	62	7
Kansas City	3.92	162	18	9	50	1444.0	1426	6076	686	629	136	37	52	27	433	20	724	31	11
California	3.96	162	36	12	26	1458.0	1526	6234	697	641	143	48	54	27	474	59	754	44	8
Milwaukee	4.06	161	13	7	41	1433.0	1532	6202	734	646	137	56	58	22	480	44	785	45	3
Chicago	4.13	162	43	18	32	1433.1	1416	6143	736	668	155	50	49	35	483	26	840	39	10
Boston	4.18	162	40	12	32	1442.0	1524	6271	764	669	141	37	40	30	517	38	927	37	3
Cleveland	4.26	163	21	7	35	1467.2	1523	6360	766	694	141	55	73	27	545	47	803	46	7
Seattle	4.31	162	26	6	35	1442.0	1497	6302	774	690	138	44	56	40	619	53	972	47	11
Oakland	4.48	162	15	6	44	1430.0	1554	6315	796	712	155	40	56	35	592	34	695	47	7
Totals	3.99	1134	398	124	513	20280.0	20539	86858	10027	8994	1980	626	716	419	7171	563	11571	616	100

NOTE—Totals for earned runs for several clubs do not agree with the composite totals for all pitchers of each respective club due to instances in which provisions of Section 10.18 (i) of the Scoring Rules were applied. The following differences are to be noted: Boston pitchers add to 672 earned runs, Chicago pitchers add to 669, Cleveland pitchers add to 695, Milwaukee pitchers add to 647, Minnesota pitchers add to 616, New York pitchers add to 618, Seattle pitchers add to 693, Toronto pitchers add to 630.

PITCHERS' RECORDS

(Top Fifteen Qualifiers for Earned-Run Leadership—162 or More Innings)

* Throws lefthanded.

Pitcher and Club	W.	L.	Pct.	ERA.	G.	GS.	CG.	ShO.	GF.	Sv.	IP.	H.	BFP.	R.	ER.	HR.	SH.	SF.	HB.	Tot. BB.	Int. BB.	SO.	WP.	Bk.
Boddicker, Michael, Baltimore	20	11	.645	2.79	34	34	16	4	0	0	261.1	218	1051	95	81	23	2	7	5	81	1	128	6	1
Stieb, David, Toronto	16	8	.667	2.83	35	35	11	2	0	0	267.0	215	1085	87	84	19	8	6	11	88	1	198	2	0
Blyleven, Rikalbert, Cleveland	19	7	.731	2.87	33	32	12	4	1	0	245.0	204	1004	86	78	19	5	8	6	74	4	170	6	0
Niekro, Philip, New York	16	8	.667	3.09	32	31	5	1	1	0	215.2	219	916	85	74	15	5	11	3	76	4	136	6	0
Zahn, Geoffrey, California*	13	10	.565	3.12	28	27	9	1	0	0	199.1	200	821	78	69	11	6	6	1	48	0	61	3	0
Black, Harry, Kansas City*	17	12	.586	3.12	35	35	8	3	0	0	257.0	226	1045	89	89	22	7	1	4	64	4	140	5	2
Davis, George, Baltimore	14	9	.609	3.12	35	31	10	2	1	0	225.0	205	923	86	78	7	9	4	0	62	2	105	6	1
Alexander, Doyle, Toronto	17	6	.739	3.13	36	35	11	2	1	0	261.2	238	1061	99	91	21	5	12	5	59	1	139	2	0
Burris, B. Ray, Oakland	13	10	.565	3.15	36	28	5	1	3	0	212.2	193	900	84	74	15	8	4	8	73	1	93	1	2
Viola, Frank, Minnesota*	18	12	.600	3.21	35	35	10	4	0	0	257.2	225	1047	101	92	28	4	5	4	90	1	149	6	1
Petry, Daniel, Detroit	18	8	.692	3.24	35	35	7	2	0	0	233.1	231	968	94	84	21	1	2	3	66	0	144	6	0
Tanana, Frank, Texas*	15	15	.500	3.25	35	33	5	0	0	0	246.1	234	1054	117	89	30	6	5	6	81	3	141	7	1
Langston, Mark, Seattle*	17	10	.630	3.40	35	33	5	2	0	0	225.0	188	965	99	85	16	13	7	8	118	5	204	12	4
Beattie, James, Seattle	12	16	.429	3.41	32	32	12	2	0	0	211.0	206	882	86	80	13	1	4	1	75	6	119	6	0
Butcher, John, Minnesota	13	11	.542	3.44	34	34	8	1	0	0	225.0	242	944	98	86	18	5	4	5	53	5	83	3	0

DEPARTMENTAL LEADERS: W—Boddicker, Michael, 20; L—Hoyt, 18; Pct.—Alexander, .739; G—Hernandez, 80; GS—Hough, Clancy, Smithson, 36; CG—Hough, 17; ShO—Ojeda, Zahn, 5; GF—Hernandez, 68; Sv—Quisenberry, 44; IP—Stieb, 267.0; H—Hough, 260; BFP —Hough, 1133; R—Clancy, 132; ER—Clancy, 125; HR—Smithson, 35; SH—Langston, 13; SF—Romanick, 12; HB—Stieb, 11; Tot. BB—Langston, 118; Int. BB—F. Martinez, 13; SO—Langston, 204; WP—Morris, 14; Bk—Sorensen, Tanana, 4.

(All Pitchers—Listed Alphabetically)

Pitcher and Club	W.	L.	Pct.	ERA.	G.	GS.	CG.	ShO.	GF.	Sv.	IP.	H.	BFP.	R.	ER.	HR.	SH.	SF.	HB.	Tot. BB.	Int. BB.	SO.	WP.	Bk.
Aase, Donald, California	4	1	.800	1.62	23	0	0	0	17	8	39.0	30	160	7	7	1	3	2	2	19	5	28	0	0
Abbott, W. Glenn, Detroit	3	4	.429	5.93	13	8	0	0	1	0	44.0	62	205	39	29	9	1	2	0	8	1	8	1	0
Acker, James, Toronto	3	5	.375	4.38	32	3	0	0	9	1	72.0	79	312	35	35	3	4	1	6	25	8	33	5	0
Agosto, Juan, Chicago*	2	1	.667	3.09	49	0	0	0	18	7	55.1	54	243	20	19	2	5	1	1	34	5	26	1	1
Alexander, Doyle, Toronto	17	6	.739	3.13	36	35	11	2	0	0	261.2	238	1061	99	91	21	4	12	3	59	0	139	3	1
Aponte, Luis, Cleveland	1	0	1.000	4.11	25	0	0	0	14	0	50.1	53	218	25	23	6	2	4	1	15	4	25	2	0
Armstrong, Michael, New York	3	2	.600	3.48	36	0	0	0	15	2	54.1	47	229	21	21	13	4	0	1	26	8	43	3	0
Atherton, Keith, Oakland	7	6	.538	4.33	57	0	0	0	24	4	104.0	110	453	51	50	10	2	6	3	39	0	58	1	1
Augustine, Gerald, Milwaukee*	0	0	.000	0.00	4	0	0	0	1	0	5.1	4	24	1	0	0	0	0	0	5	2	3	0	0
Bair, C. Douglas, Detroit*	5	3	.625	3.75	47	0	0	0	12	0	93.2	82	388	42	39	10	3	0	2	36	2	57	3	1
Bannister, Floyd, Chicago*	14	11	.560	4.83	34	33	4	0	0	0	218.0	211	936	127	117	30	8	0	6	80	0	152	10	0
Barkley, Jeffrey, Cleveland	0	0	.000	6.75	3	0	0	0	1	0	4.0	6	19	5	3	1	0	1	0	1	0	4	0	0
Barojas, Salome, Chicago-Seattle	9	7	.563	4.14	43	3	0	0	11	2	134.2	136	577	70	62	15	5	2	5	60	5	55	4	2
Beard, David, Seattle	3	2	.600	5.80	43	14	0	0	27	5	76.0	88	350	56	49	13	5	6	5	33	6	40	3	0
Beattie, James, Seattle	12	16	.429	3.41	32	32	12	2	0	0	211.0	206	882	86	80	13	5	6	4	75	0	119	6	1
Beckwith, T. Joseph, Kansas City	8	4	.667	3.40	49	1	0	0	24	2	100.2	92	410	39	38	13	5	4	6	25	6	75	4	1
Beene, R. Andrew, Milwaukee	0	0	.000	11.09	5	1	0	0	0	0	18.2	28	92	23	23	5	1	0	1	9	2	11	4	0
Behenna, Richard, Cleveland	0	3	.000	13.97	3	3	0	0	0	0	9.2	17	54	15	15	5	1	2	0	8	0	6	1	0
Berenguer, Juan, Detroit	11	10	.524	3.48	31	27	2	1	2	0	168.1	146	720	75	65	14	6	2	6	79	2	118	0	0
Best, Karl, Seattle	0	0	.000	3.00	5	0	0	0	2	0	6.0	7	25	5	2	2	2	0	0	5	0	6	0	0
Bettendorf, Jeffrey, Oakland	0	0	.000	4.66	3	0	0	0	2	0	9.2	19	42	5	5	3	1	1	0	10	0	5	5	1
Bibby, James, Texas	0	0	.000	4.41	8	0	0	0	5	0	16.1	9	75	9	8	1	0	0	0	4	0	5	0	0
Black, Harry, Kansas City*	17	12	.586	3.12	35	35	8	1	0	0	257.0	226	1045	99	89	22	9	6	6	64	2	140	6	1
Blyleven, Rikalbert, Cleveland	19	7	.731	2.87	33	32	12	4	0	0	245.0	204	1004	86	78	19	6	8	5	74	4	170	6	1
Boddicker, Michael, Baltimore	20	11	.645	2.79	34	34	16	4	0	0	261.1	218	1051	95	81	23	2	7	5	81	5	128	5	0
Boyd, Dennis, Boston	12	12	.500	4.37	29	26	3	3	0	0	197.2	207	835	109	96	18	4	8	1	53	0	134	3	1
Brennan, Thomas, Chicago	0	1	.000	4.05	4	0	0	0	3	0	16.2	8	71	5	3	1	0	0	0	4	0	3	0	0
Brown, Curtis, New York	1	2	.500	2.70	13	0	0	0	7	0	23.0	18	94	11	10	2	3	0	1	7	0	10	3	1
Brown, Mark, Baltimore	1	1	.333	3.91	9	0	0	0	0	0	11.0	22	57	11	10	9	1	3	0	19	1	10	1	0
Brown, Michael, Boston	1	8	.111	6.85	15	11	0	0	3	0	67.0	104	326	63	51	9	0	0	2	9	1	32	4	0
Brown, Steven, California	1	0	1.000	9.00	3	0	0	0	0	0	23.0	16	57	13	13	2	2	1	0	8	0	5	1	2
Burgmeier, Thomas, Oakland*	3	3	.500	2.35	34	0	0	0	8	0	23.0	15	89	6	6	7	1	3	1	8	4	8	1	0
Burns, R. Britt, Chicago*	4	12	.250	5.00	34	16	2	1	0	0	117.0	130	519	74	65	7	3	6	1	45	1	85	2	0
Burris, B. Ray, Oakland	13	10	.565	3.15	34	28	8	0	6	0	211.2	193	900	84	74	15	6	9	4	90	5	93	4	1
Butcher, John, Minnesota	13	11	.542	3.44	34	34	5	1	0	0	225.0	242	944	98	86	18	9	8	4	53	4	83	4	0
Bystrom, Martin, New York*	2	2	.500	2.97	7	7	0	0	1	0	39.1	34	164	16	13	3	0	1	0	13	0	24	0	1
Caldwell, R. Michael, Milwaukee*	6	13	.316	4.64	26	19	0	0	0	0	126.0	160	545	76	65	11	4	4	3	21	5	34	3	1
Camacho, Ernie, Cleveland	5	9	.357	2.43	69	0	0	0	62	23	100.0	83	411	31	27	6	2	0	1	37	5	48	1	0
Candiotti, Thomas, Milwaukee	2	2	.500	5.29	8	6	0	0	0	0	32.1	38	147	21	19	5	0	3	0	10	0	23	0	0
Castillo, Robert, Minnesota	2	2	.667	1.78	10	0	0	0	8	0	38.2	14	101	7	7	4	0	5	1	19	4	7	1	0
Caudill, William, Oakland	9	7	.563	2.71	68	0	0	0	49	36	96.1	77	394	30	29	9	5	5	2	31	2	89	1	0
Christiansen, Clay, New York	2	4	.333	6.05	24	6	0	0	0	0	38.2	50	178	28	26	4	1	4	1	12	2	27	7	1
Clancy, James, Toronto*	13	15	.464	5.12	36	34	5	0	0	0	219.2	249	966	132	125	25	6	1	6	88	3	118	4	0
Clark, Bryan, Toronto*	1	3	.333	5.91	20	3	0	0	8	0	67.0	66	318	33	30	6	4	6	1	22	3	21	6	0
Clear, Mark, Boston	8	3	.727	4.03	47	0	0	0	27	8	133.1	47	575	38	30	13	1	3	2	70	3	76	3	0
Clemens, W. Roger, Boston	9	4	.692	4.32	21	20	5	1	0	0	133.1	146	575	67	64	11	3	6	3	29	0	126	4	0
Cliburn, Stewart, California	0	0	.000	13.50	1	1	0	0	0	0	2.0	3	10	9	3	1	1	0	0	1	3	6	9	3
Cocanower, James, Milwaukee*	8	16	.333	4.02	33	27	1	0	6	0	174.2	188	771	99	78	13	2	5	9	78	4	65	3	0
Codiroli, Christopher, Oakland	6	8	.600	5.84	28	14	1	0	5	1	89.1	111	406	67	58	16	3	2	3	34	4	44	2	3
Comer, Steven, Cleveland	4	8	.333	5.68	22	20	1	0	0	0	117.1	146	530	80	74	11	5	9	4	39	2	39	2	0

Pitcher and Club	W.	L.	Pct.	ERA.	G.	GS.	CG.	ShO.	GF.	Sv.	IP.	H.	BFP.	R.	ER.	HR.	SH.	SF.	HB.	Tot. BB.	Int. BB.	SO.	WP.	Bk.
Comstock, Keith, Minnesota*	0	0	.000	8.53	4	0	0	0	2	0	6.1	6	28	6	6	0	0	0	0	4	0	8	0	0
Conroy, Timothy, Oakland*	1	6	.143	5.23	38	14	0	0	6	0	93.0	82	417	58	54	11	4	4	2	63	0	69	8	1
Corbett, Douglas, California	5	1	.833	2.12	45	0	0	0	30	4	85.0	76	353	22	20	2	2	4	2	30	12	48	2	1
Cowley, Joseph, New York	9	2	.818	3.56	16	11	3	1	1	0	85.1	75	356	34	33	12	3	2	2	31	5	71	2	0
Crawford, Steven, Boston	9	0	1.000	3.34	35	0	0	0	19	1	83.1	69	268	31	23	6	4	0	0	21	5	21	0	1
Cruz, Todd, Baltimore	0	0	.000	0.00	1	0	0	0	1	0	1.0	0	3	0	0	0	0	0	0	0	0	0	0	0
Curtis, John, California*	0	2	.333	4.40	17	0	0	0	6	0	28.2	30	127	16	14	4	0	1	1	11	1	18	3	0
Darwin, Danny, Texas	8	12	.400	3.94	35	32	5	1	2	0	223.2	249	955	110	98	19	3	9	3	54	2	123	0	0
Davis, George, Baltimore	14	9	.609	3.12	35	31	10	2	2	0	225.0	205	923	86	78	17	7	3	5	71	6	105	6	0
Davis, Ronald, Minnesota	7	11	.389	4.55	64	0	0	0	57	29	83.0	79	364	44	42	11	7	6	0	41	9	74	8	1
Deshaies, James, New York*	0	1	.000	11.57	2	2	0	0	0	0	7.0	14	40	9	9	1	0	0	0	7	0	5	2	0
Dixon, Kenneth, Baltimore	0	0	.000	4.15	2	2	0	0	0	0	13.0	14	56	6	6	1	1	0	0	4	0	8	1	0
Dorsey, James, Boston	0	0	.000	10.13	2	0	0	0	0	0	2.2	6	15	6	3	0	0	0	0	2	0	4	1	0
Dotson, Richard, Chicago	14	15	.483	3.59	32	32	14	1	0	0	245.2	216	1035	110	98	24	3	10	7	103	5	120	4	1
Easterly, James, Cleveland*	3	1	.750	3.38	26	1	0	0	11	2	69.1	74	300	31	26	3	8	3	0	23	3	42	4	0
Eckersley, Dennis, Boston	4	4	.500	5.01	9	9	0	0	0	0	64.2	71	270	38	36	10	3	3	0	13	3	33	2	0
Fallon, Robert, Chicago*	0	0	.000	3.68	3	0	0	0	0	0	14.2	12	62	7	10	2	2	3	0	6	2	10	2	0
Farr, Steven, Cleveland	3	11	.214	4.58	31	16	0	0	4	1	116.0	106	488	61	59	14	3	3	2	46	3	83	2	2
Filson, W. Peter, Minnesota*	6	5	.545	4.10	55	7	0	0	13	0	118.2	106	514	56	54	14	5	3	2	54	7	59	2	0
Fingers, Roland, Milwaukee	1	2	.333	1.96	33	0	0	0	30	23	46.0	38	193	13	10	5	4	0	0	13	5	40	4	2
Flanagan, Michael, Baltimore*	13	13	.500	3.53	34	34	10	2	0	0	226.2	213	947	103	89	24	8	6	8	81	5	115	0	1
Fontenot, S. Ray, New York*	8	9	.471	3.61	35	24	4	1	0	0	169.1	189	721	77	68	8	8	4	6	58	4	85	4	0
Forsch, Kenneth, California	0	0	.500	2.20	2	0	0	0	1	1	16.1	14	62	4	4	3	0	0	0	3	0	10	0	0
Frazier, George, Cleveland	3	2	.600	3.65	22	0	0	0	17	3	44.1	45	190	19	18	6	2	0	3	14	4	24	3	2
Gale, Richard, Boston	1	3	.400	5.56	13	2	0	0	4	0	43.2	57	200	27	27	3	2	2	0	18	3	28	0	0
Geisel, J. David, Seattle*	1	1	.500	4.15	20	0	0	0	9	1	43.1	47	185	20	20	10	0	2	2	19	0	28	4	0
Gibson, Robert, Milwaukee	2	2	.500	4.96	18	3	0	1	4	0	69.0	61	312	43	38	6	5	2	2	47	2	54	5	0
Gleaton, Jerry, Chicago*	1	2	.286	3.44	11	0	0	0	5	0	18.1	20	81	8	7	3	2	0	0	6	2	4	1	0
Gott, James, Toronto	7	6	.538	4.02	35	28	2	0	1	1	109.2	93	464	54	49	7	4	3	7	49	3	73	3	1
Gubicza, Mark, Kansas City	10	14	.417	4.05	29	29	0	0	0	0	189.0	172	800	90	85	13	7	6	9	75	3	111	3	0
Guetterman, A. Lee, Seattle*	0	0	.000	4.15	5	3	0	0	1	0	4.1	9	22	2	2	0	0	0	0	2	0	2	1	0
Guidry, Ronald, New York*	10	11	.476	4.51	29	30	4	2	0	0	195.2	223	841	102	98	24	4	2	2	44	3	127	0	0
Gura, Lawrence, Kansas City*	12	9	.571	5.18	31	34	4	0	0	0	168.2	175	732	102	97	26	4	6	0	67	3	68	3	1
Haas, Bryan, Milwaukee	9	11	.450	3.99	31	31	4	0	0	0	189.1	205	793	91	84	15	7	9	0	43	3	84	3	0
Hancock, R. Garry, Oakland*	0	0	.000	7.84	1	0	0	0	5	2	11.1	17	54	11	9	0	0	0	0	6	0	0	0	0
Hartzell, Paul, Milwaukee	0	0	.000	7.84	4	0	0	0	1	0	10.1	5	54	6	9	0	1	0	0	6	0	3	2	1
Heaton, Neal, Cleveland*	12	15	.444	5.21	38	34	4	0	0	0	198.2	231	880	128	115	21	6	2	6	75	5	75	3	0
Heimueller, Gorman, Oakland*	0	0	.000	6.14	6	0	0	0	3	0	14.2	21	72	21	10	2	1	4	0	7	2	8	0	0
Henke, Thomas, Texas	1	1	.500	6.35	25	0	0	0	13	2	28.1	36	141	24	20	6	0	0	1	20	0	25	2	2
Henry, Dwayne, Texas	0	1	.000	8.31	3	0	0	0	0	0	4.1	7	25	5	4	0	0	0	0	7	0	3	2	0
Hernandez, Guillermo, Detroit*	9	3	.750	1.92	80	0	0	0	68	32	140.1	96	548	30	30	6	9	3	6	36	8	112	3	2
Hodge, Ed, Minnesota*	4	3	.571	4.77	25	15	0	0	3	0	100.0	116	432	59	53	13	5	3	1	29	1	59	3	0
Hough, Charles, Texas	16	14	.533	3.76	36	36	17	4	0	0	266.0	260	1133	111	111	26	5	3	3	94	3	164	12	2
Howell, Jay, New York	9	4	.692	2.69	61	1	0	0	23	7	103.2	86	426	33	31	7	4	5	5	34	3	109	3	2
Hoyt, D. LaMarr, Chicago	13	18	.419	4.47	34	34	11	0	0	0	235.2	244	975	127	117	31	3	4	7	43	3	126	1	2
Huismann, Mark, Kansas City	3	3	.500	4.20	38	0	0	0	23	3	75.0	84	324	38	35	7	5	5	6	21	6	54	6	2
Hurst, Bruce, Boston*	12	12	.500	3.92	33	33	9	2	0	0	218.0	232	958	106	95	25	3	4	4	88	3	136	4	1
Jackson, Danny, Kansas City*	2	6	.250	4.26	15	11	1	0	0	0	76.0	84	338	41	36	4	3	2	6	35	4	40	3	2
Jackson, Roy Lee, Toronto	7	8	.467	3.56	54	0	0	0	29	10	86.0	73	355	34	34	12	4	1	2	31	7	58	4	0
Jeffcoat, J. Michael, Cleveland*	5	2	.714	2.99	63	1	0	0	12	1	75.1	82	327	28	25	7	3	7	1	24	7	41	8	1

Pitcher and Club	W.	L.	Pct.	ERA.	G.	GS.	CG.	ShO.	GF.	Sv.	IP.	H.	BFP.	R.	ER.	HR.	SH.	SF.	HB.	Tot. BB.	Int. BB.	SO.	WP.	Bk.
John, Thomas, California°	7	13	.350	4.52	32	29	4	0	1	0	181.1	223	797	97	91	15	3	6	4	56	3	47	11	0
Johnson, John Henry, Boston°	1	1	.500	3.53	30	3	0	0	14	1	63.2	64	275	26	25	5	2	2	0	27	3	57	4	1
Jones, Alfornia, Chicago	1	2	.333	4.43	20	0	0	0	8	5	20.1	23	93	10	10	3	2	2	1	11	1	15	2	0
Jones, Jeffrey, Oakland°	0	3	.000	3.55	13	0	0	0	4	0	33.0	31	135	14	13	4	2	1	1	12	1	19	2	0
Jones, Michael, Kansas City°	0	0	.000	4.89	23	12	0	0	8	0	81.0	86	359	48	44	10	6	3	1	36	3	43	2	0
Jones, Odell, Texas	2	4	.333	3.64	33	1	0	0	24	2	59.1	62	254	28	24	7	2	2	1	23	4	28	3	1
Kaufman, Curt, California	2	3	.400	4.57	29	9	0	0	11	1	69.0	68	292	37	35	13	0	0	0	20	0	41	0	0
Kern, James, Milwaukee	2	0	1.000	0.00	6	0	0	0	3	1	4.2	6	23	0	0	0	1	1	0	3	0	4	1	0
Key, James, Toronto°	4	5	.444	4.65	63	0	0	0	24	10	62.0	70	285	37	32	8	6	2	2	32	8	44	4	0
Kison, Bruce, California	4	5	.444	5.37	13	7	0	0	8	2	65.1	72	294	42	39	10	1	8	2	28	2	66	3	1
Krueger, William, Oakland°	10	10	.500	4.75	26	24	0	0	0	0	142.0	156	647	95	75	9	4	8	2	85	4	61	5	0
LaCorte, Frank, California	1	2	.333	7.06	54	0	0	0	5	2	29.1	33	131	26	23	9	7	0	2	13	6	13	2	0
Ladd, Peter, Milwaukee	4	9	.308	5.24	56	1	0	0	37	3	91.0	94	397	58	53	9	10	1	1	38	7	75	2	0
Lamp, Dennis, Toronto	8	8	.500	4.55	56	1	0	0	37	9	85.0	97	387	53	43	9	7	4	0	38	0	45	4	0
Langford, J. Rick, Oakland	0	0	.000	8.31	3	1	0	0	0	0	8.2	15	43	8	8	2	0	1	0	2	0	2	0	0
Langston, Mark, Seattle°	17	10	.630	3.40	35	35	5	2	0	0	225.0	188	965	99	85	16	13	7	8	118	5	204	4	2
Lazorko, Jack, Milwaukee	0	1	.000	4.31	15	0	0	0	3	1	39.2	37	175	19	19	7	4	0	8	22	2	24	0	0
Leach, Richard, Toronto°	0	0	.000	27.00	1	0	0	0	0	0	1.0	2	9	3	3	0	0	1	0	1	0	0	0	0
Leal, Luis, Toronto	13	8	.619	3.89	35	35	4	0	0	0	222.1	221	949	106	96	27	5	8	0	77	6	134	5	1
Leibrandt, Charles, Kansas City°	11	7	.611	3.63	23	23	2	1	0	0	143.2	158	621	65	58	11	8	7	0	38	2	53	1	1
Leiper, David, Oakland°	0	1	.000	9.00	8	0	0	0	2	1	7.0	12	39	7	7	1	0	0	1	5	0	1	1	0
Lopez, Aurelio, Detroit	10	1	.909	2.94	71	0	0	0	41	14	137.2	109	559	51	45	16	6	6	0	52	6	94	3	1
Lysander, Richard, Minnesota	4	3	.571	3.49	36	0	0	0	14	5	56.2	62	252	24	22	2	2	3	0	27	2	22	3	1
Martinez, Felix, Baltimore°	4	9	.308	3.91	55	0	0	0	42	17	89.2	88	402	42	39	9	7	5	1	51	4	72	7	0
Martinez, J. Dennis, Baltimore	6	9	.400	5.02	34	20	2	0	0	0	141.2	145	599	81	79	26	5	5	5	37	5	77	5	1
Mason, Michael, Texas°	9	13	.409	3.61	36	30	4	2	0	0	184.1	159	750	78	74	18	6	9	5	51	13	113	5	0
Mason, Roger, Detroit	1	1	.500	4.50	11	0	0	0	6	1	22.0	23	97	11	11	1	0	2	0	10	0	15	1	0
McCatty, Steven, Oakland	8	14	.364	4.76	33	30	4	0	1	0	179.2	206	793	101	95	24	8	6	1	71	5	63	5	0
McClure, Robert, Milwaukee°	4	8	.333	4.38	39	18	1	0	5	1	139.2	154	616	76	68	8	4	8	1	52	4	68	5	0
McGregor, Scott, Baltimore°	15	12	.556	3.94	30	30	10	2	0	0	196.1	216	840	86	86	18	8	5	2	54	2	67	1	3
McLaughlin, Joey, Toronto-Texas	2	5	.286	3.95	21	0	0	0	10	3	43.1	45	192	23	19	4	0	2	2	20	6	24	7	0
Mirabella, Paul, Seattle°	0	0	.000	4.37	52	1	0	0	18	0	68.0	74	303	39	33	6	3	2	2	32	3	41	0	0
Mitchell, Charles, Boston	0	0	.000	2.76	10	0	0	0	9	0	16.1	14	71	7	5	1	0	3	0	6	0	19	1	0
Monge, Isidro, Detroit°	1	0	1.000	4.25	19	0	0	0	6	0	36.0	40	159	21	17	5	3	2	3	12	2	23	1	0
Montefusco, John, New York	5	3	.625	3.58	11	11	0	0	0	0	55.1	55	234	26	22	5	1	5	2	13	2	23	7	0
Moore, Michael, Seattle	7	17	.292	4.97	34	33	6	0	0	0	212.0	236	937	127	117	16	5	3	1	85	10	158	14	2
Morris, John, Detroit	19	11	.633	3.60	35	35	9	2	0	0	240.1	221	1015	108	96	20	6	5	5	87	7	148	0	0
Murray, Dale, New York	0	2	.000	4.94	19	0	0	0	12	4	23.2	30	106	15	13	2	5	2	0	5	2	13	0	0
Musselman, R. Ronald, Toronto	2	1	.667	2.11	11	0	0	0	0	1	21.1	18	93	7	5	1	0	2	2	17	0	9	5	0
Nelson, W. Eugene, Chicago	3	5	.375	4.46	20	9	0	0	4	1	74.2	72	304	38	37	9	4	2	2	17	0	36	1	0
Niekro, Philip, New York	16	8	.667	3.09	32	32	5	1	0	0	215.2	219	916	85	74	15	7	11	7	76	1	136	7	1
Niemann, Randy, Chicago°	0	0	.000	1.69	5	0	0	0	4	0	5.1	5	24	1	1	0	0	0	0	7	0	5	3	0
Nipper, Albert, Boston	11	6	.647	3.89	29	24	2	0	1	0	182.2	183	777	86	79	18	3	2	7	52	0	84	9	1
Noles, Dickie, Texas	2	3	.400	5.15	18	6	0	0	6	0	57.2	60	264	38	33	6	0	7	0	38	2	39	3	1
Nunez, Edwin, Seattle	2	2	.500	3.19	37	0	0	0	23	7	67.2	55	280	26	24	8	5	3	3	21	0	57	1	1
O'Connor, Jack, Minnesota°	0	0	.000	1.93	2	0	0	0	0	0	4.2	5	19	4	1	1	1	0	0	4	2	5	0	0
Ojeda, Robert, Boston°	12	12	.500	3.99	33	32	5	2	0	0	216.2	211	928	106	96	17	6	8	6	96	2	137	1	1
O'Neal, Randall, Detroit	2	1	.667	3.38	4	3	0	0	0	0	18.2	16	78	13	7	0	0	0	0	6	0	12	2	1
Pacella, John, Baltimore	0	0	.000	6.75	6	1	0	0	5	0	14.2	15	66	13	11	2	1	1	0	9	2	8	1	0
Palmer, James, Baltimore	0	3	.000	9.17	5	3	0	0	0	0	17.2	22	89	19	18	2	0	2	0	17	1	4	2	0

Pitcher and Club	W.	L.	Pct.	ERA.	G.	GS.	CG.	ShO.	GF.	Sv.	IP.	H.	BFP.	R.	ER.	HR.	SH.	SF.	HB.	Tot. BB.	Int. BB.	SO.	WP.	Bk.
Pashnick, Larry, Minnesota	2	1	.667	3.52	13	1	1	0	4	0	38.1	38	160	19	15	3	1	0	2	11	1	10	0	1
Petry, Daniel, Detroit	18	8	.692	3.24	35	35	7	2	0	0	233.1	231	968	94	84	21	5	2	3	66	4	144	7	0
Porter, Charles, Milwaukee	6	4	.600	3.87	17	12	1	0	1	0	81.1	92	339	37	35	8	2	1	0	12	2	48	4	0
Quisenberry, Daniel, Kansas City	6	3	.667	2.64	72	0	0	0	67	44	129.1	121	506	39	38	10	2	3	0	12	4	41	0	0
Rainey, Charles, Oakland	1	1	.500	6.75	16	0	0	0	8	1	30.2	43	151	27	23	2	2	3	0	17	4	10	2	0
Rasmussen, Dennis, New York*	9	6	.600	4.57	24	24	1	0	0	0	147.2	127	616	79	75	16	4	7	4	60	0	110	8	2
Rawley, Shane, New York*	2	3	.400	6.21	11	0	0	0	1	0	42.0	46	198	33	29	0	0	0	0	27	2	24	5	0
Reed, Ronald, Chicago	3	6	.000	3.08	51	0	0	0	38	12	73.0	67	293	29	25	5	2	4	2	14	7	57	3	0
Righetti, David, New York*	5	6	.455	2.34	64	0	0	0	53	31	96.1	79	400	29	25	5	4	2	0	37	1	90	2	2
Rijo, Jose, New York	2	8	.200	4.76	24	5	0	0	8	2	62.1	74	289	40	33	5	6	2	1	33	0	47	2	1
Roberge, Bertrand, Chicago	3	3	.500	3.76	21	0	0	0	10	0	40.2	36	172	18	17	2	4	1	3	15	1	25	2	0
Roberts, Leon, Kansas City	0	0	.000	27.00	1	0	0	0	0	0	1.0	4	9	3	3	1	6	0	0	1	0	1	0	0
Roman, Jose, Cleveland	0	2	.000	18.00	3	2	0	0	0	0	6.0	9	37	12	12	1	3	0	0	11	0	3	1	0
Romanick, Ronald, California	12	12	.500	3.76	33	33	8	2	0	0	229.2	240	973	107	96	23	8	3	4	61	3	87	3	0
Romero, Ramon, Cleveland*	0	0	.000	0.00	1	0	0	0	0	0	3.0	0	9	0	0	0	0	0	0	3	0	3	0	0
Rozema, David, Detroit	0	6	.538	3.74	29	16	2	0	6	0	101.0	110	425	49	42	13	8	2	2	18	4	48	3	1
Saberhagen, Bret, Kansas City	10	11	.476	3.48	38	18	0	0	9	1	157.2	138	634	71	61	13	6	2	2	36	4	73	7	1
Sanchez, Luis, California	9	7	.563	3.33	49	0	0	0	44	11	83.2	84	359	34	31	6	8	3	5	33	9	62	1	0
Scherrer, William, Detroit*	1	0	1.000	1.89	18	0	0	0	2	0	19.0	14	77	4	4	1	1	3	2	8	1	16	0	0
Schmidt, David, Texas	5	5	.500	2.56	43	0	0	0	37	12	70.1	69	293	30	20	3	7	0	3	20	4	46	4	0
Schrom, Kenneth, Minnesota	5	11	.313	4.47	25	21	3	2	1	0	137.0	156	596	75	68	15	5	3	1	41	2	49	4	2
Schulze, Donald, Cleveland	2	6	.333	4.83	19	14	2	0	2	0	85.2	105	380	53	46	9	2	3	0	27	0	39	2	0
Searage, Raymond, Milwaukee*	2	1	.667	0.70	21	0	0	0	16	6	38.1	20	149	3	3	0	2	0	1	16	3	29	5	0
Seaver, G. Thomas, Chicago	15	11	.577	3.95	34	33	10	4	0	0	236.2	216	978	108	104	27	8	7	0	61	3	131	5	0
Shirley, Robert, New York*	3	3	.500	3.38	41	7	1	0	11	1	114.1	119	477	47	43	8	3	2	2	38	7	48	1	0
Siwy, James, Chicago	0	0	.000	2.08	32	0	0	0	11	0	4.1	3	17	2	1	0	1	0	0	2	0	1	1	0
Slaton, James, California	7	10	.412	4.97	22	22	5	0	0	0	163.0	192	722	95	90	22	7	6	7	56	5	67	5	0
Smith, David, California	0	0	.000	18.00	1	0	0	0	0	0	1.0	4	7	2	2	0	0	0	0	0	0	0	0	0
Smith, Leroy, Cleveland	5	5	.500	4.59	22	14	2	0	2	0	86.1	91	382	49	44	14	1	3	6	40	5	55	6	0
Smithson, B. Mike, Minnesota	15	13	.536	3.68	36	36	10	1	0	0	252.0	246	1047	113	103	35	5	3	3	54	7	144	0	2
Snell, Nathaniel, Baltimore	6	1	.316	2.35	46	0	0	0	36	2	7.2	6	33	2	2	0	1	0	0	1	0	7	3	0
Sorensen, Lary, Oakland	6	13	.316	4.91	36	21	2	0	5	0	183.1	240	818	117	100	21	4	7	8	44	4	63	7	2
Spillner, Daniel, Clev.-Chi.	5	11	.167	4.89	12	8	0	0	1	2	99.1	121	444	61	54	10	4	7	6	36	2	49	3	0
Splittorff, Paul, Kansas City*	1	5	.250	7.71	21	3	0	0	9	0	28.0	47	138	30	24	3	7	0	0	10	0	0	4	4
Squires, Michael, Chicago*	0	0	.000	0.00	2	0	0	0	0	0	0.1	1	3	0	0	0	0	0	0	0	0	0	0	0
Stanley, Robert, Boston	9	10	.474	3.54	57	0	0	0	47	22	106.2	113	455	57	42	9	6	1	2	23	9	52	1	1
Stanton, Michael, Seattle	4	4	.500	3.54	54	0	0	0	31	8	61.0	55	256	28	24	0	3	2	1	22	1	55	3	0
Steirer, Ricky, California	0	1	.000	16.88	3	1	0	0	0	0	2.2	3	14	5	5	0	0	0	0	1	0	2	0	0
Stewart, David, Texas	7	14	.333	4.73	32	27	2	0	2	0	192.1	193	847	106	101	26	6	5	4	87	3	119	12	1
Stewart, Samuel, Baltimore	16	8	.636	3.29	60	0	0	0	39	13	93.0	81	395	42	34	4	8	5	11	47	1	56	5	0
Stieb, David, Toronto	16	8	.667	2.83	35	35	11	2	0	0	267.0	215	1085	87	84	19	8	6	8	88	7	198	5	0
Stoddard, Robert, Seattle	2	3	.400	5.13	27	6	0	0	7	0	79.0	86	352	51	45	10	8	6	1	37	1	39	3	1
Sutcliffe, Richard, Cleveland	4	5	.444	5.15	15	15	2	0	0	0	94.1	111	428	60	54	7	3	2	3	46	2	58	6	0
Sutton, Donald, Milwaukee	14	12	.538	3.77	33	33	9	0	0	0	212.2	224	912	103	89	24	4	3	1	51	2	143	3	1
Swaggerty, William, Baltimore	3	2	.600	5.21	23	2	0	1	6	0	57.0	68	251	41	33	7	4	11	3	21	1	18	4	1
Swan, Craig, California	0	1	.000	10.80	2	1	0	0	0	0	5.0	8	23	6	6	3	0	0	0	3	0	1	1	1
Tanana, Frank, Texas*	15	15	.500	3.25	35	35	9	0	0	0	246.1	234	1054	117	89	30	6	5	6	81	3	141	12	0
Tellmann, Thomas, Milwaukee	6	2	.667	2.78	50	0	0	0	25	4	81.0	82	344	28	25	8	7	6	4	31	10	28	4	4
Thomas, Roy, Seattle	3	2	.600	5.26	21	1	0	0	4	1	49.2	52	233	33	29	6	0	6	4	37	2	42	4	0
Tobik, David, Texas	1	6	.143	3.61	24	0	0	0	19	5	42.1	44	186	20	17	5	2	0	1	17	6	30	5	0

Pitcher and Club	W.	L.	Pct.	ERA.	G.	GS.	CG.	ShO.	GF.	Sv.	IP.	H.	BFP.	R.	ER.	HR.	SH.	SF.	HB.	Tot. BB.	Int. BB.	SO.	WP.	Bk.
Torrez, Michael, Oakland	0	0	.000	27.00	2	0	0	0	0	0	2.1	9	19	14	7	0	0	1	0	3	0	2	0	0
Ujdur, Gerald, Cleveland	1	2	.333	6.91	4	1	0	0	0	0	14.1	22	72	14	11	1	1	1	1	6	0	6	1	1
Underwood, Thomas, Baltimore*	2	0	1.000	3.52	37	1	0	0	10	0	71.2	78	316	33	28	8	5	3	0	31	5	39	4	1
Vande Berg, Edward, Seattle*	8	12	.400	4.76	50	8	2	0	13	7	130.1	165	588	76	69	18	3	5	4	50	1	71	5	2
Viola, Frank, Minnesota*	18	12	.600	3.21	35	35	4	0	0	0	257.2	225	1047	101	92	28	1	9	4	73	4	149	6	2
Waddell, Thomas, Cleveland	7	4	.636	3.06	58	0	0	0	26	6	97.0	68	390	35	33	12	6	3	0	37	4	59	0	0
Wagner, Mark, Oakland	0	4	.000	0.00	1	0	0	0	0	0	1.2	0	7	0	0	0	0	0	0	0	0	1	0	0
Waits, M. Richard, Milwaukee*	2	4	.333	3.58	47	1	0	0	16	3	73.0	84	316	32	29	7	6	3	1	24	3	49	0	0
Walters, Michael, Minnesota	0	3	.000	3.72	23	0	0	0	13	2	29.0	31	126	14	12	1	3	2	0	14	4	10	0	0
Wardle, Curtis, Minnesota*	0	3	.000	4.50	24	0	0	0	2	0	4.0	3	15	2	2	2	0	0	0	0	1	5	0	0
Warren, Michael, Oakland	3	6	.333	4.90	30	12	0	0	5	1	90.0	104	411	52	49	11	3	3	3	44	1	61	3	0
Whitehouse, Leonard, Minnesota*	1	1	.500	3.16	33	0	0	0	10	0	31.1	29	136	11	11	3	5	1	0	17	5	18	2	0
Wilcox, Milton, Detroit	17	8	.680	4.00	33	33	1	1	0	0	193.2	183	814	99	86	13	3	9	8	66	1	119	3	3
Williams, Alberto, Minnesota	3	5	.375	5.77	17	11	0	0	3	0	68.2	75	297	46	44	9	9	3	0	22	2	22	3	0
Willis, Carl, Detroit	0	3	.000	7.31	10	0	0	0	4	0	16.0	25	74	13	13	1	3	4	0	5	0	4	0	0
Wills, Frank, Kansas City	2	3	.400	5.11	10	5	0	0	2	0	37.0	39	161	21	21	3	0	7	0	13	0	21	2	0
Witt, Michael, California	15	11	.577	3.47	34	34	9	2	0	0	246.2	227	1032	103	95	17	7	5	5	84	3	196	7	2
Wright, J. Richard, Texas*	0	4	.000	6.14	8	0	0	0	3	0	14.2	20	69	10	10	3	1	4	0	11	0	6	1	0
Young, Curtis, Oakland*	9	4	.692	4.06	20	17	1	1	0	0	108.2	118	475	53	49	9	4	8	8	31	4	41	3	1
Young, Matthew, Seattle*	6	8	.429	5.72	22	22	2	0	0	0	113.1	141	524	81	72	11	5	1	1	57	4	73	3	1
Zahn, Geoffrey, California*	13	10	.565	3.12	28	27	5	0	1	0	199.1	200	821	78	69	11	6	1	1	48	4	61	3	0

NOTE— Following pitchers combined to pitch shutout games: Baltimore (2)—McGregor, Underwood and Swaggerty, Flanagan, Stewart and F. Martinez; Boston (1)—Ojeda and Stanley; California (1)—Romanick and Sanchez; Chicago (3)—Seaver and Gleaton, Dotson and Reed, Burns and Reed; Cleveland (2)—Blyleven and Frazier, Farr and Camacho; Detroit (4)—Petry and Hernandez, Wilcox and Hernandez, Berenguer and Hernandez, O'Neal and Hernandez; Kansas City (5)—Leibrandt and Quisenberry 2, Gura and Quisenberry, Saberhagen and Quisenberry, Saberhagen, Beckwith and Quisenberry; Milwaukee (5)—Porter and McClure, Porter and Fingers, Cocanower and Fingers, Haas and Fingers, Gibson and Searage; Minnesota (3)—Smithson and Davis, Smithson, Whitehouse and Davis, Viola and Davis; New York (9)—Niekro and Rijo, Shirley, Rijo and Righetti, Rasmussen and Righetti, Niekro, Howell and Righetti, Niekro and Howell, Rasmussen, Howell and Righetti, Fontenot, Armstrong and Niekro, Montefusco and Armstrong, Cowley and Righetti; Oakland (4)—Burris and Caudill 2, Codiroli, Burgmeier and Caudill, Young and Caudill; Texas (3)—Tanana and Tobik, Darwin and Mason, Mason and Tobik; Toronto (3)—Leal and Jackson, Alexander and Lamp, Gott, Jackson, Clark and Lamp.

PITCHERS WITH TWO OR MORE CLUBS

(Alphabetically Arranged With Pitcher's First Club on Top)

Pitcher and Club	W.	L.	Pct.	ERA.	G.	GS.	CG.	ShO.	GF.	Sv.	IP.	H.	BFP.	R.	ER.	HR.	SH.	SF.	HB.	Tot. BB.	Int. BB.	SO.	WP.	Bk.
Barojas, Salome, Chicago	3	2	.600	4.58	24	0	0	0	10	1	39.1	48	177	24	20	3	3	2	0	19	1	18	0	0
Barojas, Salome, Seattle	6	5	.545	3.97	19	14	0	0	5	1	95.1	88	400	46	42	12	1	2	3	41	1	37	3	0
McLaughlin, Joey, Toronto	0	1	.000	2.53	6	0	0	0	5	0	10.2	12	50	6	3	0	1	1	0	7	1	3	1	0
McLaughlin, Joey, Texas	2	1	.667	4.41	15	0	0	0	5	0	32.2	33	142	17	16	4	0	0	1	13	1	21	0	1
Spillner, Daniel, Cleveland	0	5	.000	5.65	14	8	0	0	3	1	51.0	70	241	36	32	3	2	6	0	22	2	23	0	1
Spillner, Daniel, Chicago	1	0	1.000	4.10	22	0	0	0	9	1	48.1	51	203	25	22	7	2	1	1	14	0	26	1	1

1984 A.L. Pitching Against Each Club

BALTIMORE—85-77

Pitcher	Bos. W-L	Cal. W-L	Chi. W-L	Clev. W-L	Det. W-L	K.C. W-L	Mil. W-L	Min. W-L	N.Y. W-L	Oak. W-L	Sea. W-L	Tex. W-L	Tor. W-L	Totals W-L
Boddicker...	2-1	3-1	1-0	3-0	1-1	0-2	2-1	0-3	2-1	2-1	1-0	2-0	1-0	20-11
Brown........	1-0	0-0	0-0	0-1	0-0	0-0	0-0	0-0	0-1	0-0	0-0	0-0	0-0	1- 2
Davis........	0-2	0-0	1-0	2-0	1-1	1-0	2-1	1-0	0-1	1-2	2-1	3-0	0-1	14- 9
Dixon	0-1	0-0	0-0	0-0	0-0	0-0	0-0	0-0	0-0	0-0	0-0	0-0	0-0	0- 1
Flanagan	1-0	1-2	1-1	0-1	3-1	2-1	0-2	1-2	2-0	1-0	1-0	0-2	0-1	13-13
D. Martinez	0-1	0-0	1-1	0-0	1-1	0-1	0-0	1-0	0-1	0-2	1-0	2-0	0-2	6- 9
T. Martinez	0-0	0-0	1-1	0-0	0-0	0-2	1-0	0-0	0-1	0-0	1-2	0-1	1-2	4- 9
McGregor...	1-0	3-1	2-1	0-3	0-1	2-1	2-0	1-1	0-2	0-0	1-0	1-0	2-2	15-12
Pacella	0-0	0-0	0-0	0-0	0-0	0-0	0-0	0-0	0-1	0-0	0-0	0-0	0-0	0- 1
Palmer	0-0	0-0	0-0	0-1	0-0	0-0	0-0	0-1	0-0	0-0	0-0	0-0	0-1	0- 3
Snell	0-1	0-0	0-0	0-0	0-0	0-0	0-0	0-0	1-0	0-0	0-0	0-0	0-0	1- 1
Stewart	0-1	1-0	0-1	2-0	1-0	0-0	0-1	1-0	0-0	0-1	1-0	1-0	0-0	7- 4
Swaggerty .	1-0	0-0	0-0	0-0	0-1	0-0	0-0	0-1	0-0	0-0	1-0	1-0	0-0	3- 2
Underwood.	0-0	0-0	0-0	0-0	0-0	0-0	0-0	0-0	0-0	1-0	0-0	0-0	0-0	1- 0
Totals	6-7	8-4	7-5	7-6	7-6	5-7	7-6	5-7	5-8	6-6	9-3	9-3	4-9	85-77

No Decisions—Cruz.

BOSTON—86-76

Pitcher	Balt. W-L	Cal. W-L	Chi. W-L	Clev. W-L	Det. W-L	K.C. W-L	Mil. W-L	Min. W-L	N.Y. W-L	Oak. W-L	Sea. W-L	Tex. W-L	Tor. W-L	Totals W-L
Boyd..........	2-2	1-0	1-1	1-0	1-1	0-1	2-1	1-0	1-1	0-2	1-1	1-1	0-1	12-12
Brown........	0-0	0-0	0-0	0-0	1-0	0-2	0-2	0-1	0-0	0-2	0-0	0-1	0-0	1- 8
Clear..........	1-0	1-0	2-0	0-1	0-0	0-0	1-0	0-0	2-0	0-1	0-0	1-0	0-1	8- 3
Clemens.....	0-1	0-1	2-0	1-0	1-0	1-0	1-1	1-0	0-0	0-0	0-1	1-0	1-0	9- 4
Crawford....	0-0	0-0	0-0	1-0	0-0	0-0	0-0	2-0	1-0	1-0	0-0	0-0	0-0	5- 0
Eckersley ...	0-0	0-0	1-1	2-0	0-0	0-1	0-0	0-0	0-0	1-0	0-1	0-1	0-0	4- 4
Gale	0-0	0-0	0-0	0-0	0-1	0-0	1-0	0-0	0-0	0-0	0-0	1-2	0-0	2- 3
Hurst	0-1	1-1	1-0	1-0	1-3	1-2	1-0	0-1	1-2	3-0	1-0	0-0	1-2	12-12
Johnson......	1-0	0-0	0-0	0-1	0-0	0-0	0-0	0-1	0-0	0-0	0-0	0-0	0-0	1- 2
Nipper........	1-1	1-0	0-2	1-0	0-0	1-0	1-0	1-0	2-0	0-0	1-1	1-1	1-1	11- 6
Ojeda.........	1-0	2-0	0-1	2-0	2-1	0-1	2-0	1-1	0-2	1-0	0-3	1-2	0-1	12-12
Stanley.......	1-1	3-1	0-0	1-1	1-0	0-2	0-0	0-2	0-1	1-0	1-1	0-1	1-0	9-10
Totals	7-6	9-3	7-5	10-3	7-6	3-9	9-4	6-6	7-6	7-5	4-8	5-7	5-8	86-76

No Decisions—Dorsey, Mitchell.

CALIFORNIA—81-81

Pitcher	Balt. W-L	Bos. W-L	Chi. W-L	Clev. W-L	Det. W-L	K.C. W-L	Mil. W-L	Min. W-L	N.Y. W-L	Oak. W-L	Sea. W-L	Tex. W-L	Tor. W-L	Totals W-L
Aase	0-0	0-1	0-0	1-0	1-0	1-0	0-0	0-0	0-0	0-0	1-0	0-0	0-0	4- 1
Brown........	0-0	0-0	0-0	0-0	0-0	0-0	0-0	0-0	0-0	0-0	0-0	0-0	0-1	0- 1
Corbett	1-0	0-0	1-0	0-0	0-0	0-0	0-0	0-0	2-0	1-0	0-0	0-1	0-0	5- 1
Curtis.........	0-0	0-0	0-0	0-0	0-1	0-0	0-0	0-0	1-1	0-0	0-0	0-0	0-0	1- 2
Forsch........	0-0	1-0	0-0	0-0	0-0	0-0	0-0	0-0	0-0	0-0	0-0	0-0	0-1	1- 1
John...........	0-0	1-1	0-2	0-0	1-2	0-0	1-1	1-1	0-1	2-1	1-1	0-2	0-1	7-13
Kaufman	0-0	0-1	0-0	1-0	0-0	0-1	0-0	0-0	0-0	0-1	1-0	0-0	0-0	2- 3
Kison	0-1	0-0	0-0	1-1	1-1	0-2	1-0	0-0	0-0	0-0	1-0	0-0	0-0	4- 5
LaCorte......	0-0	0-0	0-0	0-0	0-1	0-0	0-0	0-0	1-0	0-0	0-1	0-0	0-0	1- 2
Romanick ...	2-0	0-0	2-1	0-1	0-0	2-1	2-1	0-3	1-2	1-1	1-0	0-1	1-1	12-12
Sanchez......	0-1	1-2	1-0	1-0	0-0	0-0	0-0	0-1	0-1	1-2	1-0	0-1	2-0	9- 7
Slaton........	1-1	0-2	0-0	2-1	0-1	0-1	0-0	1-2	1-0	0-0	0-0	0-2	2-0	7-10
Steirer	0-0	0-0	0-0	0-0	0-0	0-0	0-0	0-0	0-0	0-0	0-0	0-0	0-0	0- 1
Swan..........	0-1	0-0	0-0	0-0	0-0	0-0	0-0	0-0	0-0	0-0	0-0	0-0	0-0	0- 1
Witt...........	0-3	0-0	1-2	1-1	1-2	2-0	2-1	0-1	0-0	1-0	3-1	2-0	2-0	15-11
Zahn...........	0-1	0-2	3-0	1-0	0-0	1-1	1-1	2-1	1-0	1-1	2-1	1-1	0-1	13-10
Totals	4-8	3-9	8-5	8-4	4-8	6-7	8-4	4-9	8-4	7-6	9-4	5-8	7-5	81-81

No Decisions—Cliburn, Smith.

CHICAGO—74-88

Pitcher	Balt. W-L	Bos. W-L	Cal. W-L	Clev. W-L	Det. W-L	K.C. W-L	Mil. W-L	Min. W-L	N.Y. W-L	Oak. W-L	Sea. W-L	Tex. W-L	Tor. W-L	Totals W-L
Agosto........	0-0	0-0	0-0	1-0	0-0	0-0	0-0	0-0	0-0	1-0	0-0	0-0	0-1	2- 1
Bannister....	0-0	0-2	0-1	1-1	2-1	1-1	1-0	2-1	4-0	0-2	1-0	1-2	1-0	14-11
Barojas.......	0-0	0-0	0-0	0-0	0-0	0-2	0-0	0-0	1-0	0-0	1-0	1-0	0-0	3- 2
Brennan......	0-0	0-0	0-0	0-0	0-1	0-0	0-0	0-0	0-0	0-0	0-0	0-0	0-0	0- 1
Burns..........	1-0	0-0	0-3	0-0	0-0	0-2	0-0	0-1	0-1	1-0	1-3	1-0	0-2	4-12
Dotson........	1-2	2-2	1-1	1-1	1-1	1-1	2-1	1-1	0-0	0-3	1-1	2-1	1-0	14-15
Gleaton.......	0-0	0-1	0-0	1-0	0-0	0-0	0-0	0-0	0-1	0-0	0-0	0-0	0-0	1- 2
Hoyt...........	1-2	1-1	1-0	2-0	0-2	1-1	0-2	2-0	2-1	1-2	1-3	0-2	1-2	13-18
Jones..........	1-0	0-0	0-1	0-0	0-0	0-0	0-0	0-0	0-0	0-0	0-0	0-0	0-0	1- 1
Nelson........	0-1	0-0	0-0	1-1	0-1	0-0	1-1	0-0	0-1	0-0	0-0	0-0	0-0	3- 5
Reed..........	0-1	0-1	0-1	0-1	0-1	0-0	0-0	0-0	0-0	0-0	0-0	0-0	0-1	0- 6
Roberge......	0-0	0-0	1-0	0-0	0-0	0-0	0-0	0-0	0-1	0-0	1-0	0-1	1-0	3- 3
Seaver........	1-1	2-0	2-1	1-0	1-1	2-0	3-1	1-1	0-1	2-0	0-1	0-2	0-2	15-11
Spillner	0-0	0-0	0-0	0-0	0-0	0-0	0-0	1-0	0-0	0-0	0-0	0-0	0-0	1- 0
Totals	5-7	5-7	5-8	8-4	4-8	5-8	7-5	8-5	7-5	6-7	5-8	5-8	4-8	74-88

No Decisions—Fallon, Niemann, Siwy, Squires.

CLEVELAND—75-87

Pitcher	Balt. W-L	Bos. W-L	Cal. W-L	Chi. W-L	Det. W-L	K.C. W-L	Mil. W-L	Min. W-L	N.Y. W-L	Oak. W-L	Sea. W-L	Tex. W-L	Tor. W-L	Totals W-L
Aponte	0-0	0-0	0-0	0-0	1-0	0-0	0-0	0-0	0-0	0-0	0-0	0-0	0-0	1-0
Behenna	0-0	0-1	0-0	0-0	0-1	0-0	0-0	0-0	0-1	0-0	0-0	0-0	0-0	0-3
Blyleven	3-1	0-1	1-0	0-1	0-2	4-0	2-0	2-1	1-0	1-1	2-0	1-0	2-0	19-7
Camacho	0-1	0-2	1-1	0-0	0-1	0-0	1-0	2-0	0-1	0-1	0-1	1-0	0-1	5-9
Comer	0-2	0-1	1-0	0-0	0-0	1-1	1-0	0-2	0-1	0-0	1-0	0-1	0-0	4-8
Easterly	1-0	0-0	0-1	0-0	0-0	0-0	0-0	0-0	0-0	1-0	0-0	1-0	0-0	3-1
Farr	0-1	0-3	0-1	0-0	1-1	0-0	0-1	0-0	1-1	0-0	0-0	0-0	0-1	3-11
Frazier	1-1	0-0	0-0	1-0	0-0	0-1	0-0	0-0	0-0	0-0	1-0	0-0	0-0	3-2
Heaton	0-1	0-0	0-1	2-2	1-1	1-2	2-0	2-0	0-2	1-2	2-1	1-1	0-2	12-15
Jeffcoat	0-0	0-0	0-0	0-0	0-0	0-0	2-0	0-0	0-0	1-1	1-1	0-0	1-0	5-2
Roman	0-0	0-0	0-2	0-0	0-0	0-0	0-0	0-0	0-0	0-0	0-0	0-0	0-0	0-2
Schulze	0-0	0-0	1-0	0-1	0-0	0-0	0-0	0-1	0-1	0-0	0-0	1-1	1-1	3-6
Smith	0-0	0-1	0-0	1-1	1-1	0-1	0-0	0-0	0-0	0-0	1-0	1-0	0-0	5-5
Spillner	0-0	0-0	0-1	0-0	0-2	0-0	0-2	0-0	0-0	0-0	0-0	0-0	0-0	0-5
Sutcliffe	1-0	0-1	0-1	0-0	0-0	0-0	0-0	0-0	0-2	1-0	0-0	2-0	0-1	4-5
Ujdur	0-0	0-0	0-0	0-0	0-0	0-0	0-0	0-1	0-0	1-0	0-1	0-0	0-0	1-2
Waddell	0-0	3-0	0-0	0-1	0-0	0-0	1-1	1-0	0-1	1-0	0-0	0-0	1-1	7-4
Totals	6-7	3-10	4-8	4-8	4-9	6-6	9-4	7-5	2-11	7-5	8-4	9-3	6-7	75-87

No Decisions—Barkley, Romero.

DETROIT—104-58

Pitcher	Balt. W-L	Bos. W-L	Cal. W-L	Chi. W-L	Clev. W-L	K.C. W-L	Mil. W-L	Min. W-L	N.Y. W-L	Oak. W-L	Sea. W-L	Tex. W-L	Tor. W-L	Totals W-L
Abbott	0-0	0-2	0-0	1-0	1-1	0-0	0-0	1-0	0-0	0-0	0-0	0-0	0-1	3-4
Bair	1-0	1-0	0-0	0-0	0-0	0-1	0-0	0-0	2-1	0-0	0-0	1-1	0-0	5-3
Berenguer	1-2	0-1	1-1	1-0	1-0	1-1	2-1	0-1	1-0	1-1	1-1	0-1	1-0	11-10
Hernandez	0-0	0-0	1-1	0-0	0-0	1-1	0-0	3-0	1-1	1-0	1-0	0-0	1-0	9-3
Lopez	0-0	2-0	0-0	2-0	1-0	1-0	0-1	0-0	1-0	0-0	0-0	1-0	1-0	10-1
Mason	0-1	0-0	0-0	0-0	0-0	0-0	1-0	0-0	0-0	0-0	0-0	0-0	0-0	1-1
Monge	0-0	0-0	0-0	0-0	0-0	0-0	0-0	0-0	0-0	0-0	1-0	0-0	0-0	1-0
Morris	0-2	0-3	2-0	1-2	3-0	2-0	2-0	2-1	1-0	3-0	1-1	0-0	1-2	19-11
O'Neal	0-0	0-0	0-0	0-0	0-0	0-0	2-0	0-0	0-1	0-0	0-0	0-0	0-0	2-1
Petry	3-0	1-0	2-1	1-0	2-1	1-1	1-0	2-1	1-0	2-0	0-3	2-0	0-1	18-8
Rozema	0-1	0-0	0-1	1-1	0-2	0-0	2-0	1-0	0-0	0-1	0-0	2-0	1-0	7-6
Scherrer	0-0	0-0	0-0	0-0	0-0	0-0	0-0	0-0	0-0	0-0	0-0	0-0	1-0	1-0
Wilcox	1-1	2-0	2-0	1-1	1-0	1-1	1-0	0-0	0-2	2-1	2-1	2-0	2-1	17-8
Willis	0-0	0-1	0-0	0-0	0-0	0-0	0-0	0-0	0-1	0-0	0-0	0-0	0-0	0-2
Totals	6-7	6-7	8-4	8-4	9-4	7-5	11-2	9-3	7-6	9-3	6-6	10-2	8-5	104-58

KANSAS CITY—84-78

Pitcher	Balt. W-L	Bos. W-L	Cal. W-L	Chi. W-L	Clev. W-L	Det. W-L	Mil. W-L	Min. W-L	N.Y. W-L	Oak. W-L	Sea. W-L	Tex. W-L	Tor. W-L	Totals W-L
Beckwith	0-0	2-1	0-1	2-0	0-0	1-2	1-0	0-0	0-0	0-0	1-0	0-0	1-0	8-4
Black	1-0	2-0	2-2	2-0	1-2	0-1	1-2	2-1	2-2	2-0	0-1	2-1	0-0	17-12
Gubicza	1-0	2-1	0-2	0-1	0-1	0-1	1-0	1-3	1-1	1-2	1-0	1-1	1-1	10-14
Gura	2-1	1-0	1-0	1-1	2-1	0-0	2-0	0-0	0-2	1-1	1-1	0-2	0-2	12-9
Huismann	0-1	0-0	0-0	0-0	1-0	0-0	1-1	0-0	0-0	1-0	1-0	0-0	0-1	3-3
Jackson	0-1	0-0	1-0	0-1	0-1	0-1	0-0	0-0	0-0	0-0	1-1	0-0	0-1	2-6
M. Jones	0-1	0-0	0-0	0-0	1-0	0-0	0-1	0-0	0-1	1-0	1-0	0-0	0-0	2-3
Leibrandt	1-0	0-1	0-1	1-0	0-0	1-1	0-0	2-2	1-1	1-1	2-0	1-0	1-0	11-7
Quisenberry	1-0	0-0	1-0	1-0	0-0	0-0	0-2	1-0	0-0	0-0	0-0	1-1	1-0	6-3
Saberhagen	1-0	1-0	2-0	1-2	1-0	3-1	0-0	0-1	0-1	0-1	1-2	0-2	0-1	10-11
Splittorff	0-1	1-0	0-0	0-0	0-0	0-0	0-0	0-0	0-1	0-1	0-0	0-0	0-0	1-3
Wills	0-0	0-0	0-0	0-0	0-1	0-0	0-0	0-0	0-0	1-0	0-0	0-1	1-1	2-3
Totals	7-5	9-3	7-6	8-5	6-6	5-7	6-6	6-7	5-7	5-8	9-4	6-7	5-7	84-78

No Decisions—Roberts.

MILWAUKEE—67-94

Pitcher	Balt. W-L	Bos. W-L	Cal. W-L	Chi. W-L	Clev. W-L	Det. W-L	K.C. W-L	Min. W-L	N.Y. W-L	Oak. W-L	Sea. W-L	Tex. W-L	Tor. W-L	Totals W-L
Beene	0-0	0-0	0-0	0-0	0-0	0-0	0-0	0-0	0-1	0-0	0-0	0-1	0-0	0-2
Caldwell	0-0	0-0	1-0	1-2	0-2	0-0	1-0	1-2	1-2	0-3	1-0	0-2	0-0	6-13
Candiotti	1-0	0-0	0-0	0-0	0-0	0-1	1-0	0-0	0-0	0-1	0-0	0-0	0-0	2-2
Cocanower	1-0	0-1	0-3	2-2	2-2	0-1	0-3	1-1	0-1	1-0	0-1	0-0	0-1	8-16
Fingers	0-1	0-0	0-0	0-0	0-0	0-0	0-0	0-0	0-0	0-1	0-0	0-0	1-0	1-2
Gibson	1-1	0-1	0-1	0-0	0-0	0-1	0-0	0-0	0-0	0-0	0-0	0-0	1-1	2-5
Haas	1-0	2-1	1-1	1-1	1-0	0-1	0-1	1-1	0-0	0-1	1-1	1-2	0-1	9-11
Hartzell	0-0	0-0	0-0	0-0	0-0	0-1	0-0	0-0	0-0	0-0	0-0	0-0	0-0	0-1
Kern	0-0	0-0	0-0	0-0	0-0	0-0	0-0	0-0	0-0	0-0	0-0	0-0	1-0	1-0
Ladd	0-1	0-1	0-0	0-0	0-2	0-0	0-2	0-0	2-1	1-1	1-0	0-1	0-0	4-9
Lazorko	0-1	0-0	0-0	0-0	0-0	0-0	0-0	0-0	0-0	0-0	0-0	0-0	0-0	0-1
McClure	0-0	1-1	0-2	1-0	0-1	0-0	1-0	0-0	0-0	0-0	0-0	0-0	1-0	4-8
Porter	0-0	0-1	0-0	0-0	0-1	0-0	0-0	1-0	2-0	0-0	0-0	2-0	1-0	6-4
Searage	0-0	0-0	0-0	0-0	0-0	1-0	0-0	0-1	0-0	0-0	0-0	0-0	1-0	2-1
Sutton	0-3	1-2	2-0	0-1	0-1	1-1	3-0	0-1	1-0	0-1	2-2	2-0	2-0	14-12
Tellmann	0-0	0-0	0-1	0-0	1-0	0-0	1-0	0-0	0-1	1-0	1-1	0-0	1-0	6-3
Waits	1-0	0-1	0-0	0-0	0-1	0-1	0-0	0-1	0-0	1-0	0-0	0-0	0-0	2-4
Totals	6-7	4-9	4-8	5-7	4-9	2-11	6-6	5-7	6-7	4-8	6-6	5-6	10-3	67-94

No Decisions—Augustine.

MINNESOTA—81-81

Pitcher	Balt. W-L	Bos. W-L	Cal. W-L	Chi. W-L	Clev. W-L	Det. W-L	K.C. W-L	Mil. W-L	N.Y. W-L	Oak. W-L	Sea. W-L	Tex. W-L	Tor. W-L	Totals W-L
Butcher	4-0	0-3	1-1	0-3	1-2	0-0	2-0	2-0	0-1	1-1	0-0	2-0	0-0	13-11
Castillo	0-0	1-0	0-0	0-0	0-0	0-0	0-0	0-0	0-0	0-0	0-0	0-0	1-1	2- 1
Davis	0-1	2-1	0-0	1-1	0-3	0-1	0-0	0-0	1-1	0-0	2-1	1-0	0-2	7-11
Filson	0-0	0-0	1-1	0-1	0-0	0-1	0-0	1-0	2-0	1-0	1-1	0-0	0-1	6- 5
Hodge	0-0	0-1	0-0	1-0	0-0	0-0	1-0	1-1	0-0	1-0	0-0	0-1	0-0	4- 3
Lysander	0-0	0-0	1-0	0-0	1-0	0-1	0-1	1-0	0-0	0-0	1-0	0-0	0-1	4- 3
Pashnick	0-0	0-0	0-0	0-0	0-0	0-0	0-0	0-0	0-0	1-1	0-0	0-0	0-0	2- 1
Schrom	0-0	0-0	1-0	1-1	1-2	0-2	0-1	0-1	1-0	0-1	1-0	0-2	0-1	5-11
Smithson	2-2	1-0	3-0	0-1	0-0	0-0	2-2	2-1	2-0	1-1	0-2	2-1	0-3	15-13
Viola	0-1	2-0	2-1	1-1	2-0	2-2	1-1	0-2	1-2	3-0	1-0	3-0	0-2	18-12
Walters	0-0	0-0	0-0	0-0	0-0	0-1	0-0	0-0	0-0	0-0	0-2	0-0	0-0	0- 3
Whitehouse	0-0	0-1	0-0	1-0	0-0	0-0	0-1	0-0	1-0	0-0	0-0	0-0	0-0	2- 2
Williams	1-1	0-0	0-1	0-0	0-0	1-1	1-0	0-0	0-0	0-1	0-0	0-0	0-1	3- 5
Totals	7-5	6-6	9-4	5-8	5-7	3-9	7-6	7-5	8-4	8-5	7-6	8-5	1-11	81-81

No Decisions—Comstock, O'Connor, Wardle.

NEW YORK—87-75

Pitcher	Balt. W-L	Bos. W-L	Cal. W-L	Chi. W-L	Clev. W-L	Det. W-L	K.C. W-L	Mil. W-L	Min. W-L	Oak. W-L	Sea. W-L	Tex. W-L	Tor. W-L	Totals W-L
Armstrong	0-0	0-0	0-1	1-0	1-0	0-0	0-0	0-0	0-0	0-0	0-0	1-0	0-1	3- 2
Brown	0-0	0-0	0-0	0-0	0-0	0-0	0-0	1-1	0-0	0-0	0-0	0-0	0-0	1- 1
Bystrom	0-0	0-1	0-0	0-1	0-0	0-0	1-0	0-0	0-0	0-0	1-0	0-0	0-0	2- 2
Christiansen	0-0	0-0	0-0	0-0	0-0	0-2	0-0	0-0	0-0	1-0	0-1	0-0	1-1	2- 4
Cowley	1-0	2-0	1-0	0-0	2-0	0-1	0-0	0-1	1-0	0-0	1-0	0-0	1-0	9- 2
Deshaies	0-0	0-0	0-0	0-0	0-0	0-0	0-0	0-0	0-0	0-0	0-0	0-0	0-0	0- 1
Fontenot	1-0	1-0	0-1	0-1	2-0	0-1	1-0	1-0	0-2	1-1	0-0	0-2	1-1	8- 9
Guidry	0-1	1-0	1-1	2-1	0-1	1-2	1-2	0-1	0-1	1-1	0-0	2-0	1-0	10-11
Howell	2-0	1-2	1-1	0-0	1-0	0-0	0-0	2-0	1-1	0-0	0-0	0-0	0-0	9- 4
Montefusco	1-0	0-1	0-0	0-0	1-0	0-0	1-0	0-0	0-1	2-0	0-0	0-0	0-0	5- 3
Murray	0-0	0-0	0-0	0-0	0-0	0-0	0-0	0-0	0-0	0-1	1-0	1-1	0-0	1- 2
Niekro	0-0	1-0	1-2	0-1	3-0	1-0	3-1	1-1	1-0	1-0	2-1	1-1	1-1	16- 8
Rasmussen	0-2	0-1	0-1	1-0	1-0	1-0	1-0	2-0	1-0	0-0	2-1	0-0	0-0	9- 6
Rawley	1-0	0-0	0-0	0-0	1-0	0-0	0-1	0-0	0-0	0-1	0-0	0-0	0-0	2- 3
Righetti	0-1	0-1	0-1	1-0	0-1	0-0	0-0	0-0	0-2	1-0	1-0	0-0	2-0	5- 6
Rijo	1-0	0-1	0-0	0-1	1-0	0-1	0-0	0-0	0-1	0-1	0-1	0-2	0-0	2- 8
Shirley	1-1	0-0	0-0	0-0	0-0	1-0	0-1	0-0	0-1	0-0	1-0	0-0	0-0	3- 3
Totals	8-5	6-7	4-8	5-7	11-2	6-7	7-5	7-6	4-8	8-4	7-5	6-6	8-5	87-75

OAKLAND—77-85

Pitcher	Balt. W-L	Bos. W-L	Cal. W-L	Chi. W-L	Clev. W-L	Det. W-L	K.C. W-L	Mil. W-L	Min. W-L	N.Y. W-L	Sea. W-L	Tex. W-L	Tor. W-L	Totals W-L
Atherton	0-0	0-0	2-0	1-0	2-1	1-0	0-0	0-0	0-0	1-0	0-2	0-1	0-2	7- 6
Burgmeier	1-0	0-0	1-0	0-0	0-0	0-0	0-0	1-0	0-0	0-0	0-0	0-0	0-0	3- 0
Burris	1-1	1-0	0-0	3-0	0-1	0-0	1-2	2-0	2-2	1-1	1-1	0-0	1-1	13-10
Codiroli	0-0	0-0	0-0	1-0	1-1	0-1	2-1	0-0	1-0	0-0	0-0	1-0	0-0	6- 4
Conroy	0-0	0-1	0-0	0-1	0-2	0-1	0-0	0-0	0-0	0-0	0-0	1-0	0-1	1- 6
Caudill	0-0	1-0	2-2	0-0	1-0	0-0	0-0	0-1	0-0	1-3	2-0	1-0	1-1	9- 7
Heimueller	0-0	0-1	0-0	0-0	0-0	0-0	0-0	0-0	0-0	0-0	0-0	0-0	0-0	0- 1
Jones	0-0	0-0	0-0	0-2	0-1	0-0	0-0	0-0	0-0	0-0	0-0	0-0	0-0	0- 3
Krueger	2-0	0-1	0-1	0-0	1-0	1-2	2-1	1-1	0-1	1-0	0-1	1-1	1-1	10-10
Leiper	0-0	0-0	0-0	0-0	0-0	0-0	0-0	0-0	0-0	0-0	0-0	1-0	0-0	1- 0
McCatty	0-2	1-1	0-0	1-1	0-1	0-2	1-0	2-0	1-2	0-2	1-1	1-2	0-0	8-14
Rainey	0-0	0-0	0-0	0-0	0-0	0-0	0-0	0-1	0-0	0-0	1-0	0-0	0-0	1- 1
Sorensen	1-0	1-2	0-2	0-1	0-0	0-2	1-1	1-1	0-1	0-2	1-0	1-0	0-1	6-13
Warren	0-2	1-1	0-2	0-0	0-0	0-0	0-0	0-0	0-1	0-0	1-0	0-0	1-0	3- 6
Young	1-1	0-0	1-0	1-1	0-0	1-1	1-0	1-0	1-0	0-0	1-0	1-0	0-1	9- 4
Totals	6-6	5-7	6-7	7-6	5-7	3-9	8-5	8-4	5-8	4-8	8-5	8-5	4-8	77-85

No Decisions—Bettendorf, Hancock, Langford, Torrez, Wagner.

SEATTLE—74-88

Pitcher	Balt. W-L	Bos. W-L	Cal. W-L	Chi. W-L	Clev. W-L	Det. W-L	K.C. W-L	Mil. W-L	Min. W-L	N.Y. W-L	Oak. W-L	Tex. W-L	Tor. W-L	Totals W-L
Barojas	1-0	0-0	0-1	0-1	0-0	0-0	0-1	1-1	1-0	1-1	1-0	0-0	1-0	6- 5
Beard	0-0	0-0	0-0	0-0	0-0	0-0	0-1	0-0	1-0	0-0	0-1	1-0	1-0	3- 2
Beattie	0-3	2-2	0-2	3-0	0-2	1-0	1-0	1-0	0-1	1-3	0-1	2-0	1-2	12-16
Best	0-0	0-0	0-0	0-0	0-0	0-0	0-1	0-0	0-0	0-0	0-0	1-0	0-0	1- 1
Geisel	0-0	0-0	0-0	0-0	1-0	0-1	0-0	0-0	0-0	0-0	0-0	0-0	0-0	1- 1
Langston	0-0	2-0	1-1	2-1	2-2	2-0	2-0	2-0	1-0	1-2	1-1	1-0	0-3	17-10
Mirabella	0-2	0-1	0-1	0-0	0-0	0-0	0-0	0-0	0-0	1-0	1-0	0-1	0-0	2- 5
Moore	0-3	0-1	0-2	1-1	1-1	1-1	1-2	1-2	0-1	0-0	1-2	0-1	1-0	7-17
Nunez	0-0	0-0	0-0	0-1	0-0	0-0	0-0	0-1	0-0	1-0	0-0	1-0	0-0	2- 2
Stanton	0-0	0-0	0-1	0-0	0-0	0-1	0-0	0-0	1-1	0-1	1-0	1-0	1-0	4- 4
Stoddard	0-0	0-0	0-1	0-0	0-1	0-0	0-0	0-0	0-1	0-0	2-0	0-0	0-0	3- 2
Thomas	0-0	0-0	1-0	0-0	0-0	0-1	0-0	0-0	1-0	1-0	0-1	0-0	0-0	3- 2
Vande Berg	2-1	3-0	2-0	0-0	0-2	1-1	0-1	0-1	0-3	0-0	0-1	0-1	0-1	8-12
Young	0-0	1-0	0-0	2-1	0-0	1-1	0-2	1-2	0-0	1-0	0-1	0-1	0-0	6- 8
Totals	3-9	8-4	4-9	8-5	4-8	6-6	4-9	6-6	6-7	5-7	5-8	10-3	5-7	74-88

No Decisions—Guetterman.

TEXAS—69-92

Pitcher	Balt. W-L	Bos. W-L	Cal. W-L	Chi. W-L	Clev. W-L	Det. W-L	K.C. W-L	Mil. W-L	Min. W-L	N.Y. W-L	Oak. W-L	Sea. W-L	Tor. W-L	Totals W-L
Darwin	1-0	1-0	0-0	2-1	0-0	0-1	1-1	0-2	1-2	1-0	0-2	0-1	1-2	8-12
Henke	0-0	0-0	0-0	1-0	0-0	0-0	0-0	0-0	0-0	0-0	0-1	0-0	0-0	1-1
Henry	0-0	0-0	0-0	0-0	0-0	0-0	0-0	0-0	0-0	0-0	0-1	0-0	0-0	0-1
Hough	0-2	2-1	1-1	2-2	2-2	0-2	2-1	0-1	3-0	1-0	1-1	0-0	2-1	16-14
Jones	1-0	1-0	0-1	0-1	0-1	0-0	0-0	0-0	0-0	0-0	0-0	0-1	0-0	2-4
Mason	0-1	0-1	0-1	0-1	0-2	1-0	1-1	0-2	0-2	1-1	2-1	2-0	2-0	9-13
McLaughlin.	0-0	0-0	1-0	0-0	0-0	0-0	0-0	1-0	0-0	0-0	0-0	0-1	0-0	2-1
Noles	0-0	0-0	1-0	0-0	0-0	0-1	0-0	0-0	0-1	1-0	0-0	0-1	0-0	2-3
Schmidt	0-1	1-1	1-0	0-0	1-0	0-0	1-1	0-0	0-0	0-1	1-0	0-2	1-0	6-6
Stewart	0-1	0-1	3-0	1-0	0-2	0-3	1-0	2-0	0-3	0-2	0-0	0-1	0-1	7-14
Tanana	1-2	2-1	1-1	2-0	0-1	1-3	1-2	3-0	1-0	1-1	1-1	1-2	0-1	15-15
Tobik	0-1	0-0	0-0	0-0	0-1	0-0	0-0	0-0	0-0	1-1	0-0	0-1	0-1	1-6
Wright	0-1	0-0	0-1	0-0	0-0	0-0	0-0	0-0	0-0	0-0	0-0	0-0	0-0	0-2
Totals	3-9	7-5	8-5	8-5	3-9	2-10	7-6	6-5	5-8	6-6	5-8	3-10	6-6	69-92

No Decisions—Bibby.

TORONTO—89-73

Pitcher	Balt. W-L	Bos. W-L	Cal. W-L	Chi. W-L	Clev. W-L	Det. W-L	K.C. W-L	Mil. W-L	Min. W-L	N.Y. W-L	Oak. W-L	Sea. W-L	Tex. W-L	Totals W-L
Acker	0-0	0-0	0-2	0-0	0-1	1-0	0-0	0-1	0-0	0-1	1-0	1-0	0-0	3-5
Alexander...	1-0	2-0	0-0	0-0	3-0	0-0	2-0	1-3	3-0	2-1	1-0	2-0	0-2	17-6
Clancy	2-2	2-2	0-1	2-1	0-1	2-2	0-1	0-1	1-0	1-1	1-0	0-2	2-1	13-15
Clark	0-0	0-0	0-0	1-0	0-0	0-1	0-1	0-0	0-0	0-0	0-0	0-0	0-0	1-2
Gott	1-0	1-0	1-2	2-0	0-0	0-0	1-1	0-0	0-1	0-0	1-1	0-1	0-0	7-6
Jackson	2-1	0-0	0-1	1-1	1-0	0-0	1-1	0-1	2-0	0-1	0-0	0-0	0-2	7-8
Key	2-1	0-0	1-1	1-0	0-1	0-1	0-0	0-1	0-0	0-0	0-0	0-0	0-0	4-5
Lamp	0-0	1-1	0-0	0-0	1-1	0-0	0-0	0-1	2-0	2-0	0-2	0-2	2-1	8-8
Leal	0-0	2-1	1-0	0-1	1-1	1-2	1-0	0-1	1-0	0-2	3-0	2-0	1-0	13-8
Musselman .	0-0	0-0	0-0	0-0	0-0	0-1	0-0	0-1	0-0	0-0	0-0	0-0	0-0	0-2
Stieb	1-0	0-1	2-0	1-1	1-1	1-1	2-1	2-0	2-0	0-2	1-1	2-0	1-0	16-8
Totals	9-4	8-5	5-7	8-4	7-6	5-8	7-5	3-10	11-1	5-8	8-4	7-5	6-6	89-73

No Decisions—Leach, McLaughlin.

NATIONAL LEAGUE

Including

Team Reviews of 1984 Season

Team Day-by-Day Scores

1984 Standings, Home-Away Records

1984 Official N.L. Batting Averages

1984 Official N.L. Fielding Averages

1984 Official N.L. Pitching Averages

1984 Pitching Against Each Club

Outfielder Tony Gwynn captured the N.L. batting title (.351) and led the Padres to their first-ever World Series.

Padres Finally Come of Age

By PHIL COLLIER

Spending their first 15 seasons in the second division of the National League West didn't prepare the San Diego Padres or their fans for what happened in 1984.

In mid-September, several players complained about relatively small home crowds of 13,000 to 14,000. Within a month, however, the Padres were the darlings of San Diego.

The turnaround began when the team clinched its first N.L. West championship on September 20. Fan interest reached a crescendo on October 7 when the underdog Padres, beaten at Chicago in the first two games of the National League Championship Series, rebounded for their third straight victory over the Cubs to capture the league pennant. No National League team ever before had won the playoffs after losing the first two games.

That feverish support continued in the first two games of the World Series as the Padres narrowly lost Game 1, 3-2, and then won Game 2 thanks to a three-run home run by Kurt Bevacqua, who had had only one homer and nine runs batted in during the regular season. The Tigers swept the next three games in Detroit to win the Series, but nevertheless, almost 40,000 fans turned out at San Diego Jack Murphy Stadium to honor the Padres upon their return.

If San Diego fans were late in discovering the Padres, who set a club record by drawing 1,983,904 spectators at home during the regular season, the main reason was because they felt cheated not to have experienced the pennant race they had been looking forward to since the club's inception in 1969.

It was like waiting 16 years for a coming-out party and having no one show up.

"We won the games we had to win, but we never had a crucial game or series until we got to the playoffs," General Manager Jack McKeon said.

The Padres never relinquished first place after taking command of the division June 9. Their lead grew steadily after that, hovering around nine games much of the season and removing most of the suspense from the pennant race. In addition, they spent most of the second half of the season on the road, giving the hometown fans fewer opportunities to watch them.

The Padres finished the regular season with a 92-70 record, 12 games ahead of the Houston Astros and Atlanta Braves. The first-place finish followed two consecutive

81-81, fourth-place finishes in Dick Williams' first two years as manager. The only previous San Diego team to finish above .500 was the 1978 club (84-78).

"Our young players matured in the playoffs; there are no unseasoned players on this team anymore," Williams said.

Williams labeled the Padres as definite National League contenders in 1984 when they signed free-agent reliever Goose Gossage in January. The Padres' preseason stock took another jump in late March when McKeon traded promising rookie lefthander Dennis Rasmussen to the New York Yankees for Graig Nettles. The Gold Glove third baseman, who turned 40 in August, solidified the San Diego infield and provided the club with much-needed power. He hit a team-high 20 home runs (tied with Kevin McReynolds).

Veteran first baseman Steve Garvey, who came to San Diego as a free agent in 1983, looked at the mixture of youngsters and veterans McKeon had assembled for 1984 and began to refer to the group as "Team Padres." Garvey talked about synergism, about how the Padres were greater than the sum of their parts.

But despite all of Garvey's optimism, this was a team loaded with question marks.

One was the outfield. The Padres were frighteningly dependent upon 24-year-olds in all three spots: rookie Carmelo Martinez in left, McReynolds in center and Tony Gwynn in right.

Another was starting pitching. The Padres' season-opening rotation of Eric Show, Mark Thurmond, Andy Hawkins, Ed Whitson and Tim Lollar had a combined 105-113 lifetime record in the big leagues, a mark that reflected both losing and inexperience.

Other question marks surrounded Garvey, who was coming back from a thumb injury that caused him to miss the last two months of the 1983 season, and catcher Terry Kennedy, who underwent arthroscopic knee surgery in February. In addition, lefthander Craig Lefferts, who was acquired with Martinez in a winter trade with the Chicago Cubs, was such an uncertain commodity that Dave Dravecky, a proven starter coming off a 1983 shoulder injury, was consigned to the bullpen in April to help out Gossage.

The biggest gamble of all, however, concerned the move of fleet Alan Wiggins from the outfield to second base. The spring training release of incumbent Juan

SCORES OF SAN DIEGO PADRES' 1984 GAMES

APRIL

Opp	W/L	Score	Winner	Loser
3—Pittsburgh	W	5-1	Show	Rhoden
5—Pittsburgh	W	8-6	DeLeon	Scurry
6—Chicago	W	3-2	Monge	Smith
7—Chicago	W	7-6	Dravecky	Trout
8—Chicago	L	5-8†	Smith	Thurmond
10—St. Louis	W	7-3	Hawkins	Forsch
11—St. Louis	W	7-5	Lollar	Andujar
12—Atlanta	W	6-1	Whitson	Falcone
13—Atlanta	W	5-2	Show	Barker
14—Atlanta	L	1-5	Camp	Thurmond
15—Atlanta	W	6-4	Monge	McMurtry
17—At S. Fran.	W	2-1	Lollar	Davis
19—At L.A.	L	0-4	Pena	Whitson
20—At L.A.	L	2-8	Valenzuela	Show
21—At L.A.	W	9-6	Thurmond	Reuss
22—At L.A.	L	7-15	Honeycutt	Lollar
23—San Fran.	W	8-2	Hawkins	Robinson
24—San Fran.	W	6-1	Whitson	Krukow
25—San Fran.	W	3-0	Show	Laskey
26—Los Ang.	L	5-6	Diaz	Dravecky
27—Los Ang.	L	0-1*	Honeycutt	Lollar
28—Los Ang.	W	5-1	Hawkins	Welch
29—Los Ang.	L	0-6	Pena	Whitson

Won 15, Lost 8

MAY

Opp	W/L	Score	Winner	Loser
1—At Atlanta	W	3-2	Show	McMurtry
3—At Atlanta	L	5-6	Bedrosian	Gossage
4—At Chicago	L	6-7	Smith	Monge
5—At Chicago	L	5-6†	Brusstar	Lefferts
6—At Chicago	W	8-5	Show	Ruthven
9—At St. L.	W	3-2	Thurmond	Stuper
10—At St. L.	L	0-7	Andujar	Lollar
11—Phila.	L	4-6	Holland	Dravecky
12—Phila.	L	2-3	Campbell	Hawkins
13—Phila.	L	3-8	Denny	Whitson
14—Montreal	L	6-7†	Reardon	Dravecky
15—Montreal	L	4-6	Smith	Lollar
16—Montreal	L	2-3	Lea	Show
17—Montreal	W	5-4	Gossage	McGaffigan
18—New York	W	5-4	Whitson	Gooden
19—New York	W	8-3	Thurmond	Lynch
20—New York	L	2-4†	Orosco	Lefferts
22—At Mon.	L	2-3	Lea	Show
23—At Mon.	W	2-1‡	Dravecky	McGaffigan
25—At Phila.	W	7-3	Whitson	Hudson
26—At Phila.	L	2-7	Bystrom	Thurmond
27—At Phila.	W	4-0	Lollar	Koosman
28—At N.Y.	W	5-4	Show	Gaff

Won 10, Lost 13

JUNE

Opp	W/L	Score	Winner	Loser
1—At S. Fran.	L	7-11	Williams	Hawkins
2—At S. Fran.	W	3-2†	Gossage	Garrelts
3—At S. Fran.	W	7-5	Lollar	Cornell
3—At S. Fran.	W	7-6	Show	Lavelle
4—Houston	W	3-0	Whitson	Scott
5—Houston	W	3-0	Hawkins	Ruhle
6—Houston	W	4-3†	Gossage	Smith
7—Cincinnati	L	1-12	Berenyi	Show
8—Cincinnati	W	6-0	Lollar	Price
9—Cincinnati	W	12-2	Whitson	Russell
10—Cincinnati	W	7-5	Chiffer	Hume
11—Atlanta	W	5-4	Dravecky	Bedrosian
12—Atlanta	W	7-6§	Lefferts	Bedrosian
14—San Fran.	L	2-5	Davis	Lollar
15—San Fran.	W	3-2	Whitson	Robinson
16—San Fran.	L	3-6	Laskey	Hawkins
17—San Fran.	L	3-5y	Williams	Lefferts
19—At Hous.	W	2-0	Show	Knepper
20—At Hous.	W	6-2	Lollar	Madden
21—At Hous.	L	5-11	Niekro	Whitson
22—At Cinn.	L	7-8	Franco	Gossage
23—At Cinn.	W	5-2	Thurmond	Puleo
24—At Cinn.	W	8-3x	Dravecky	Hume
25—At L.A.	W	9-4	Lollar	Zachry
26—At L.A.	W	5-0	Whitson	Welch
27—At L.A.	L	4-5	Valenzuela	Dravecky
28—St. Louis	W	7-3	Thurmond	Dayley
29—St. Louis	L	0-5	Horton	Show
30—St. Louis	L	1-4	Andujar	Lollar

Won 19, Lost 10

JULY

Opp	W/L	Score	Winner	Loser
1—St. Louis	W	3-1	Whitson	LaPoint
2—Chicago	W	5-1	Dravecky	Reuschel
3—Chicago	L	2-3	Trout	Thurmond
4—Chicago	L	1-2	Sutcliffe	Show
5—Pittsburgh	W	2-1	Gossage	Scurry
6—Pittsburgh	W	7-3	Whitson	Rhoden
7—Pittsburgh	W	1-0	Dravecky	McWilliams
8—Pittsburgh	L	3-4	Candelaria	Thurmond
12—At St. L.	W	4-1	Show	Andujar
13—At St. L.	L	4-7†	Allen	DeLeon
14—At St. L.	L	6-7	LaPoint	Lollar
15—At St. L.	W	6-1	Dravecky	Kepshire
16—At Chicago	W	4-0	Thurmond	Ruthven
17—At Chicago	W	6-5	Show	Trout
18—At Chicago	L	1-4	Sutcliffe	Whitson
19—At Pitts.	L	1-5	Candelaria	Lollar
20—At Pitts.	L	3-4	Rhoden	Dravecky
20—At Pitts.	W	3-2	Hawkins	Tudor
21—At Pitts.	W	6-4	Thurmond	Walk
22—At Pitts.	W	5-1	Whitson	DeLeon
22—At Pitts.	L	2-3‡	Winn	Gossage
24—Cincinnati	L	2-4	Soto	Lollar
25—Cincinnati	W	6-5	Gossage	Owchinko
26—Cincinnati	W	8-2	Thurmond	Russell
27—Houston	W	7-3	Whitson	Ruhle
28—Houston	L	1-3	Niekro	Hawkins
28—Houston	W	1-0	Show	Ryan
29—Houston	W	9-0	Lollar	LaCoss
30—Los Ang.	W	12-0	Dravecky	Valenzuela
31—Los Ang.	W	1-0	Thurmond	Honeycutt

Won 19, Lost 11

AUGUST

Opp	W/L	Score	Winner	Loser
1—Los Ang.	W	4-3	Lefferts	Pena
3—At Hous.	L	2-6	Ryan	Show
4—At Hous.	W	5-2	Lollar	LaCoss
5—At Hous.	W	9-5	Hawkins	Niekro
6—At Cinn.	W	1-0	Gossage	Price
7—At Cinn.	L	7-8	Power	Harris
8—At Cinn.	L	2-4	Soto	Gossage
9—At Cinn.	L	0-8	Russell	Lollar
10—At Atlanta	L	1-3	Bedrosian	Dravecky
10—At Atlanta	W	10-4	Hawkins	Falcone
11—At Atlanta	W	4-1	Thurmond	Mahler
12—At Atlanta	L	3-5	Perez	Whitson
14—Phila.	W	3-2	Show	Koosman
15—Phila.	W	4-3	Gossage	Holland
16—Phila.	L	3-8	Denny	Hawkins
17—Montreal	L	4-8	Rogers	Thurmond
19—Montreal	L	0-3	Hesketh	Whitson
20—New York	W	3-1	Show	Fernandez
21—New York	W	7-4	Lollar	Lynch
22—New York	L	2-5	Gooden	Hawkins
24—At Mon.	L	1-4	Rogers	Thurmond
24—At Mon.	W	5-4	Gossage	Reardon
25—At Mon.	W	4-3x	Harris	Reardon
26—At Mon.	W	2-1	Show	Schatzeder
27—At Phila.	L	1-9	Koosman	Lollar
28—At Phila.	L	8-11	Rawley	Hawkins
29—At Phila.	W	2-0	Thurmond	Denny
31—At N.Y.	W	5-1	Whitson	Fernandez
31—At N.Y.	L	0-4	Berenyi	Dravecky

Won 15, Lost 14

SEPTEMBER

Opp	W/L	Score	Winner	Loser
1—At N.Y.	L	4-7	Gooden	Hawkins
1—At N.Y.	L	6-10	Gorman	Show
2—At N.Y.	L	2-3§	Gaff	Gossage
3—At L.A.	W	4-3	Thurmond	Reuss
4—At L.A.	L	1-2	Howell	Hawkins
5—Cincinnati	W	15-11	Lefferts	Hume
6—Cincinnati	L	3-10	Price	Show
7—Houston	L	4-6	Niekro	Lollar
9—Houston	W	8-4	Thurmond	LaCoss
11—Los Ang.	L	2-5	Valenzuela	Whitson
12—Los Ang.	L	1-8	Hooton	Dravecky
14—At Hous.	W	4-2	Gossage	DiPino
15—At Hous.	L	2-3	Dawley	Lefferts
16—At Hous.	L	9-10	Smith	Gossage
17—At Cinn.	W	3-2‡	Gossage	Power
18—At Cinn.	W	2-0	Dravecky	Price
19—San Fran.	W	5-4†	Hawkins	Garrelts
20—San Fran.	W	5-4	Lollar	Krukow
21—Atlanta	L	1-3	Mahler	Thurmond
22—Atlanta	L	2-5	Perez	DeLeon
23—Atlanta	W	2-1‡	Booker	Moore
24—At S. Fran.	W	7-1	Harris	Robinson
24—At S. Fran.	W	8-6‡	DeLeon	Lacey
25—At S. Fran.	L	3-4	Krukow	Lollar
26—At S. Fran.	W	4-0	Show	Laskey
28—At Atlanta	W	4-2	Thurmond	McMurtry
29—At Atlanta	W	6-2	Whitson	Mahler
30—At Atlanta	L	3-4	Perez	Booker

Won 14, Lost 14

*6 innings. †10 innings. ‡11 innings. §12 innings. x13 innings. y15 innings.

Goose Gossage came via the free-agent draft and provided some much-needed late-inning relief.

Bonilla necessitated that move.

Fortunately for San Diego, many of these question marks became distinct pluses.

In the outfield, Gwynn became the major league batting champion, hitting .351 with five homers and 71 RBIs. Gwynn also topped the league in hits (213) and on-base percentage (.410) while pacing his teammates with 10 triples and 269 total bases. He was a threat on the basepaths as well, stealing 33 bases, and he struck out only 23 times in 606 at-bats.

McReynolds (.278 batting average, 20 homers, 75 RBIs) and Martinez (.250, 13 homers, 66 RBIs) also posted good seasons. The loss of McReynolds during the N.L. playoffs because of a fractured wrist was a big blow to the Padres in the World Series.

The starting pitching also dealt San Diego a big blow in the Series when it utterly collapsed, allowing 16 earned runs in just 10⅓ innings for a composite 13.94 earned-run average in the five games. But the results during the regular season were impressive.

Show was the club's winningest pitcher in 1984 with a 15-9 record and a 3.40 ERA. Thurmond and Whitson both exceeded expectations by posting identical 14-8 records and a 2.97 and a 3.24 ERA, respectively. Lollar led the club in strikeouts with 131 but was only 11-13. Hawkins (8-9, 4.68 ERA) was a disappointment as a starter but was fairly effective as a reliever later in the season.

In the bullpen, Lefferts (3-4, 2.13 ERA, 10 saves) and Dravecky (9-8, 2.93, eight saves) were nice complements to the staff ace, Gossage. The Goose, who went 10-6 with a 2.90 ERA and 25 saves, provided the expected late-inning relief that contributed to the Padres' 34-24 record in one-run games, an improvement in that department from 29-30 a year earlier.

Wiggins' performance at second base, a position he had played when he entered the minor leagues but only occasionally since then, was good but not great. His 32 errors was a team high. However, he also led the team in stolen bases (70), walks (75) and runs scored (106) while batting .258. The switch-hitting leadoff man combined with Gwynn to give the Padres a dangerous one-two punch.

A few players had off years, including Kennedy (.240, 14 homers, 57 RBIs) and shortstop Garry Templeton (.258, two homers, 35 RBIs). Garvey's home run production (eight) was down from recent years, but his .284 average and 86 RBIs were quite respectable.

Overall, the Padres improved in many team statistical categories such as batting average (.250 in 1983 to .259 in '84), homers (93 to 109), ERA (3.62 to 3.48) and shutouts (five to a league-leading 17).

Fittingly, the Padres dedicated the season to the late Ray Kroc, the club owner and McDonald's restaurant founder who died in January. His widow, Joan Kroc, took over as the Padres' owner and board chairwoman.

Atlanta center fielder Dale Murphy had some offensive problems, but still finished with 36 home runs and 100 RBIs.

Disappointing Braves Stagnate

By GERRY FRALEY

In 1982, he commanded a large presence. By September 30, 1984, he had prepared himself for the worst.

It happened October 1. Saying "it was time for a change," Atlanta Braves Owner Ted Turner dismissed Manager Joe Torre and named Eddie Haas to replace him.

"I had myself conditioned to expect what I got," Torre said. "The thing that hurt is that I feel this club is getting ready to do something."

It did little in 1984. After winning the National League West in '82, Torre's first season, and leading the pack through most of '83, the Braves flopped to an 80-82 record and a second-place tie with Houston. Rather than collapsing, the Braves simply stagnated in '84.

One factor in Torre's firing was a perceived inability to work with and develop younger players. That problem became evident in his final season as promising rookies Brad Komminsk and Gerald Perry both struggled. Both players are expected to start in '85 under Haas, who has spent 20 years working with young players in the minors.

But unfulfilled high expectations were, most likely, Torre's undoing.

"Probably the worst thing that happened to me was winning the first year we were here," Torre said. "It got people's mouths watering for what's next."

The Braves plodded through the '84 season. They emerged from a lethargic training camp with the first three of the 11 players who eventually would find their way to the disabled list: pitcher Terry Forster, outfielder Terry Harper and infielder Randy Johnson. For the first time in three years under Torre, they did not start explosively, failing to rise above .500 until May 11.

Without warning, the Braves hit their one dynamic stretch of the year. A nine-game winning streak put them in the division lead by 1½ games on June 7. That became the season's high-water mark.

After June 7, the Braves were 46-59 and never won more than three games in succession. They still were only five games behind San Diego at the All-Star break, but for the third time under Torre the club had a second-half losing record (34-41 in '84) and could not pressure the Padres.

"We never really played very well," said outfielder Dale Murphy, whose own statistics were impressive but did not bring him a third consecutive N.L. Most Valu-

Pascual Perez started late but still led the Braves with 14 victories.

able Player award. "I can't say we were better than our record, because we weren't. We never got anything going. A lot of things went against us."

The factors in the Braves' downfall:

● Injuries. The Braves had 43 injuries that cost them the use of at least one regular player for each game. Torre thus was forced to use more than 100 different lineups that featured seven left fielders, five leadoff men and a variety of pitchers in different roles.

The most significant injury occurred May 29. Third baseman Bob Horner broke his right wrist diving for a foul ball and, after playing the next day, missed the rest of the season. Horner also had sat out the last seven weeks of the '83 season with the same injury.

Horner's absence sent a damaging ripple effect through the Braves' lineup. Chris Chambliss, who lost his first base position to Perry by the end of the year, could not provide suitable protection while batting behind Murphy in the lineup.

"I've been telling people this, but nobody seemed to want to listen: The loss of Horner devastated this team," General Manager John Mullen said. "He changes

SCORES OF ATLANTA BRAVES' 1984 GAMES

APRIL

Date	W/L	Score	Winner	Loser
3—Phila.	L	0-5	Carlton	Barker
4—Phila.	W	4-0	McMurtry	Denny
6—Montreal	L	5-8	Smith	Dayley
7—Montreal	L	2-7	Palmer	Falcone
8—Montreal	W	6-2	Barker	Lea
10—New York	L	2-4	Swan	McMurtry
11—New York	L	1-6	Terrell	Dayley
12—At S. Diego	L	1-6	Whitson	Falcone
13—At S. Diego	L	2-5	Show	Barker
14—At S. Diego	W	5-1	Camp	Thurmond
15—At S. Diego	L	4-6	Monge	McMurtry
18—Cinn.	W	5-4‡	Bedrosian	Hume
20—Houston	W	8-7	Garber	Ruhle
21—Houston	L	3-4	Dawley	Bedrosian
22—Houston	L	1-3	Niekro	Falcone
24—Cincinnati	W	4-2	Barker	Hume
25—Cincinnati	L	3-4	Soto	Dayley
26—Cincinnati	W	2-1	McMurtry	Russell
27—At Hous.	W	6-0	Falcone	Niekro
28—At Hous.	W	5-3	Camp	Knepper
29—At Hous.	L	5-8	Scott	Barker

Won 9, Lost 12

MAY

Date	W/L	Score	Winner	Loser
1—San Diego	L	2-3	Show	McMurtry
3—San Diego	W	6-5	Bedrosian	Gossage
5—At Mon.	L	1-2‡	McGaffigan	Garber
6—At Mon.	W	2-0	McMurtry	Lea
6—At Mon.	W	9-8	Dedmon	James
7—At Phila.	W	8-6	Perez	Bystrom
8—At Phila.	W	8-2	Falcone	Denny
9—At N.Y.	L	1-3	Darling	Mahler
10—At N.Y.	W	7-3	Barker	Terrell
11—Pittsburgh	W	4-2‡	Forster	Tekulve
12—Pittsburgh	W	4-3	Perez	Guante
13—Pittsburgh	W	9-8‡	Dedmon	Candelaria
15—At St. L.	L	1-9	Andujar	Barker
16—At St. L.	L	2-4	LaPoint	McMurtry
17—At St. L.	W	7-2	Perez	Cox
18—At Pitts.	L	0-6	McWilliams	Falcone
19—At Pitts.	W	4-2*	Mahler	Tudor
20—At Pitts.	W	5-1	Bedrosian	Tekulve
23—At Chicago	L	1-3	Trout	McMurtry
24—At Chicago	L	7-10	Rainey	Perez
24—At Chicago	L	5-7	Reuschel	Falcone
25—St. Louis	W	8-4	Barker	LaPoint
26—St. Louis	W	7-3	Mahler	Allen
27—St. Louis	L	9-12	Andujar	McMurtry
28—St. Louis	W	6-2	Falcone	Cox
29—Chicago	W	7-4	Perez	Brusstar
30—Chicago	L	2-6	Trout	Barker
31—At Cinn.	W	7-1	Mahler	Pastore

Won 17, Lost 11

JUNE

Date	W/L	Score	Winner	Loser
1—At Cinn.	W	4-2	McMurtry	Berenyi
1—At Cinn.	W	7-3	Falcone	Power
2—At Cinn.	W	9-3	Perez	Owchinko
3—At Cinn.	W	4-0	Forster	Power
4—At S. Fran.	W	2-1	Mahler	Davis
5—At S. Fran.	W	8-3	McMurtry	Krukow
6—At S. Fran.	W	5-4§	Bedrosian	Lavelle
7—At L.A.	W	8-1	Perez	Hershiser
8—At L.A.	L	3-5	Welch	Barker
9—At L.A.	L	3-4	Valenzuela	Bedrosian
10—At L.A.	L	2-3	Pena	McMurtry
11—At S. Diego	L	4-5	Dravecky	Bedrosian
12—At S. Diego	L	6-7x	Lefferts	Bedrosian
14—Cincinnati	W	3-0	Barker	Russell
15—Cincinnati	W	6-1	Mahler	Pastore
16—Cincinnati	L	1-2	Power	Bedrosian
17—Cincinnati	W	6-5	Perez	Owchinko
19—San Fran.	W	11-6	Camp	Cornell
20—San Fran.	W	6-5	Barker	Robinson
21—San Fran.	L	3-5	Laskey	Mahler
22—Los Ang.	L	4-10	Welch	Falcone
23—Los Ang.	L	2-10	Valenzuela	Perez
24—Los Ang.	L	2-5	Pena	McMurtry
25—Houston	L	5-8	LaCoss	Barker
25—Houston	W	6-4	Mahler	Madden
26—Houston	L	5-10	Niekro	Camp
27—Houston	W	6-4	Perez	Scott
28—At N.Y.	W	5-3	McMurtry	Berenyi
29—At N.Y.	W	5-3	Bedrosian	Lynch

Won 17, Lost 12

JULY

Date	W/L	Score	Winner	Loser
1—At N.Y.	L	1-2	Darling	Mahler
1—At N.Y.	L	2-3	Leary	Dedmon
2—Montreal	L	4-5	Palmer	Perez
3—Montreal	W	5-3	McMurtry	Gullickson
4—Montreal	L	4-7	Lea	Bedrosian
5—At Phila.	L	0-1*	Hudson	Mahler
6—At Phila.	W	5-0	Perez	Gross
7—At Phila.	W	5-2	Camp	Rawley
8—At Phila.	L	0-7	Koosman	McMurtry
12—New York	L	6-8	Orosco	Moore
13—New York	L	4-5	Terrell	Perez
14—New York	L	0-7	Berenyi	McMurtry
15—New York	W	8-3	Moore	Gooden
16—At Mon.	L	1-3	Schatzeder	Camp
17—At Mon.	L	0-2	Smith	Mahler
18—At Mon.	W	3-2‡	Bedrosian	Gullickson
19—Phila.	L	1-9	Koosman	McMurtry
20—Phila.	W	13-1	Barker	Hudson
21—Phila.	W	5-3	Camp	Gross
22—Phila.	L	2-6	Carlton	Mahler
24—At L.A.	W	4-2	Bedrosian	Hershiser
25—At L.A.	L	1-2	Valenzuela	Barker
26—At L.A.	W	5-1	McMurtry	Honeycutt
27—At S.F.	L	0-6	Krukow	Camp
28—At S.F.	W	4-3	Mahler	Davis
29—At S.F.	W	4-3	Perez	Calvert
30—At Hous.	L	3-4	Smith	Moore
31—At Hous.	W	6-3	Dedmon	DiPino

Won 12, Lost 16

AUGUST

Date	W/L	Score	Winner	Loser
1—At Hous.	W	6-5	Falcone	Solano
3—San Fran.	W	2-1§	Moore	Minton
4—San Fran.	L	2-9	Calvert	McMurtry
5—San Fran.	L	4-7	Lavelle	Garber
6—Los Ang.	W	2-0	Mahler	Honeycutt
7—Los Ang.	L	1-2§	Howell	Moore
8—Los Ang.	L	1-5	Welch	Brizzolara
9—Los Ang.	L	0-1	Hershiser	Camp
10—San Diego	W	3-1	Bedrosian	Dravecky
10—San Diego	L	4-10	Hawkins	Falcone
11—San Diego	L	1-4	Thurmond	Mahler
12—San Diego	W	5-3	Perez	Whitson
14—Pittsburgh	W	3-1	Camp	Candelaria
15—Pittsburgh	W	7-3	Bedrosian	Rhoden
16—Pittsburgh	L	2-5	Tudor	Mahler
17—At. St. L.	L	1-3	Andujar	Perez
18—At St. L.	W	8-3	Brizzolara	Cox
19—At St. L.	L	5-8	Horton	Camp
20—At Pitts.	W	4-1‡	Garber	Tekulve
21—At Pitts.	L	4-5	Robinson	Dedmon
22—At Pitts.	L	2-7	McWilliams	Payne
24—At Chicago	L	0-3	Sutcliffe	Camp
25—At Chicago	W	3-2	Mahler	Sanderson
26—At Chicago	L	0-5	Trout	Perez
28—St. Louis	L	3-5‡	Sutter	Garber
29—St. Louis	L	6-10	Allen	McMurtry
30—Chicago	L	3-8‡	Smith	Garber
31—Chicago	W	3-2 .	Moore	Smith

Won 11, Lost 17

SEPTEMBER

Date	W/L	Score	Winner	Loser
1—Chicago	L	1-4	Bordi	McMurtry
2—Chicago	L	2-4	Ruthven	Mahler
3—Houston	W	6-4	McMurtry	Ruhle
4—Houston	W	8-7	Moore	DiPino
5—At L.A.	L	3-4	Hooton	Dedmon
6—At L.A.	W	3-2y	Dedmon	White
7—At S. Fran.	L	4-5	Grant	Garber
8—At S. Fran.	L	0-4	Laskey	McMurtry
9—At S. Fran.	L	4-6	Davis	Brizzolara
10—At Hous.	W	3-1	Smith	Ryan
11—At Hous.	W	6-4	Mahler	Solano
12—At Hous.	W	4-1	Perez	Smith
14—San Fran.	L	0-3	Minton	Moore
15—San Fran.	W	4-1	Camp	Krukow
16—San Fran.	W	7-5	Mahler	Laskey
17—Los Ang.	L	0-9	Welch	Perez
18—Los Ang.	W	6-5	Garber	Hooton
19—Cincinnati	L	2-4	Tibbs	McMurtry
20—Cincinnati	W	9-3	Camp	Russell
21—At S. Diego	W	3-1	Mahler	Thurmond
22—At S. Diego	W	5-2	Perez	DeLeon
23—At S. Diego	L	1-2§	Booker	Moore
25—At Cinn.	W	4-2†	Mahler	Willis
26—At Cinn.	L	3-6	Soto	Perez
27—At Cinn.	L	1-2‡	Franco	Garber
28—San Diego	L	2-4	Thurmond	McMurtry
29—San Diego	L	2-6	Whitson	Mahler
30—San Diego	W	4-3	Perez	Booker

Won 14, Lost 14

*7 innings. †8 innings. ‡10 innings. §11 innings. x12 innings. y18 innings.

A broken wrist sidelined third baseman Bob Horner and curtailed Atlanta's offensive production.

everything. He makes everybody in the lineup better. He gets Murphy better pitches. That, to me, is the primary reason behind what happened."

There were other significant injuries. Ken Oberkfell, acquired in a trade with St. Louis to replace Horner, did not play after August 26 because of a broken thumb. Len Barker, the projected ace of the pitching staff, went 7-8 with a 3.85 earned-run average and pitched in only three games after the All-Star break because of elbow problems. Steve Bedrosian, who had an outstanding season as a reliever, going 9-6 with a 2.37 ERA and 11 saves, did not pitch after August 15 because of tendinitis. Forster, the hefty lefthanded force in the bullpen, pitched only two innings after June 20 because of a damaged hamstring muscle. In all, eight Braves suffered season-ending injuries.

• Offense. In 1983, the Braves led the league with a .272 average and scored 746 runs. Without Horner, Atlanta dropped to a .247 average (third worst in the league) and scored 632 runs. The Braves collected 111 home runs, 11 fewer than their opponents.

"The great mystery to me," Torre said, "is what happened to the offense." Other than Murphy and right fielder Claudell Washington, no one approached his previous statistics.

Murphy, despite having problems at the plate with runners in scoring position, led the team in almost every offensive category. He tied Philadelphia's Mike Schmidt for the league lead in homers with 36, was first in slugging percentage (.547) and was third in runs batted in (100), marking the third straight season he had knocked in 100 or more runs. Murphy also amassed a whopping 332 total bases while batting .290.

Washington, who slumped after the All-Star break, finished with a .286 average, 17 homers, 61 RBIs and a team-high 21 stolen bases.

No other Atlanta player had more than nine homers or 48 RBIs.

The catchers, Bruce Benedict and Alex Trevino (the latter obtained in an April deal with Cincinnati), batted a combined .233 with seven homers and 53 RBIs.

Chambliss had no homers and only four extra-base hits in his final 100 at-bats. After driving in at least 72 runs in the previous three full seasons, he finished 1984 with only 44 RBIs.

Like Washington, second baseman Glenn Hubbard and shortstop Rafael Ramirez slipped in the second half. Hubbard went from .253 at the All-Star break to .194 afterward to finish at .234, while Ramirez dropped from .303 to .217 for an overall .266 average.

• Pitching. In a sense, the Braves' pitching exceeded expectations. The team ERA dropped from 3.67 to 3.57, and righthander Rick Mahler (13-10, 3.12 ERA) had a solid year after Torre's staff nearly released him.

The Braves, however, never filled the void caused by Phil Niekro's departure. The starters, in search of a leader, were left stranded.

Pascual Perez, who served a drug-related suspension through May 6 (although there was some doubt about the guilty verdict rendered by Dominican Republic courts), paced the staff with 14 victories and 145 strikeouts but saw his ERA rise to 3.74. Both Craig McMurtry (9-17, 4.32 ERA) and Pete Falcone, who divided his time between starting and relieving and went 5-7, were unimpressive. Rick Camp was 8-6.

The bullpen provided 49 saves, one more than the year before, but that number is deceptive because relievers blew several late-inning leads. Righthander Donnie Moore topped the Braves with 16 saves.

The Braves were more successful on the road (42-39) than at home (38-43) in 1984. Home attendance also was a disappointment as 1.7 million fans visited Atlanta Stadium, down from 2.1 million in '83.

Astros left fielder Jose Cruz ranked among the top 10 N.L. hitters in average, runs scored, RBIs, on-base percentage, walks, hits and triples.

Inconsistency Kills Astros

By HARRY SHATTUCK

Probably no other team in the 23-year history of the Houston franchise defies analysis so much as the 1984 Astros.

Consider first their performance compared with the National League champion San Diego Padres:

Hitting? Houston's team average was .264; the Padres hit .259. Houston scored 693 runs, San Diego 686.

Pitching? The Astros' team earned-run average was 3.32; San Diego's ERA was 3.48.

Fielding? The Astros committed 133 errors, the Padres 138. Houston turned 160 double plays, San Diego 144.

Indeed, the Astros fared better in all of those categories. But there was one not-so-slight problem. While the Padres finished 22 games above the .500 mark, the Astros funneled all of their impressive statistics into an 80-82 record, 12 games out of first place in the N.L. West.

How could this happen?

There were two main reasons. One, the Astros lost too many close games, especially early in the season when they dug themselves a hole so deep they never could climb all the way out. Houston was 27-28 in one-run games, compared with San Diego's 34-24 mark.

And two, though the Astros compiled losing records against only three teams, they were 6-12 head to head with both San Diego and Atlanta.

The Astros did tie Atlanta for second place in the division, showing continued improvement over their third-place standing the previous year and their fifth-place finish in 1982.

But this upward trend in the standings, which actually is misleading in that the Astros lost five more games in 1984 than the year before, offered little solace to Houston fans, who indicated their displeasure by staying away from the Astrodome. Attendance was down 122,000 from the 1983 total of 1.35 million. Since 1980, when the Astros earned their only division championship, home attendance has declined more than 1 million.

This lack of interest may be partially a result of the Astros' second consecutive miserable start. They opened 1983 with nine straight losses and improved only to 1-6 in the first seven games of '84. Even during their best moments, they never offered any real hope of a pennant race.

High expectations also may have dulled fans' interest as the Astros struggled early

An eye injury to shortstop Dickie Thon proved to be a crippling blow to the Astros.

on. Several Houston players and front-office people as well as local sportswriters had billed the team as a champion before the season.

Actually, the Astros did have excuses for faltering early this time.

Foremost was an eye injury to All-Star

SCORES OF HOUSTON ASTROS' 1984 GAMES

APRIL

Date		Score	Winner	Loser
3—Montreal	L	2-4	Lea	Niekro
4—Montreal	W	8-2	Ryan	Gullickson
6—New York	L	1-8	Terrell	Scott
7—New York	L	2-3	Gooden	Knepper
8—New York	L	1-3	Leary	Niekro
10—At Phila.	L	1-3	Denny	Ryan
11—At Phila.	L	6-7	Campbell	Dawley
13—Cincinnati	W	1-0	Niekro	Soto
14—Cincinnati	W	9-1	Knepper	Russell
15—Cincinnati	W	6-5	DiPino	Hume
16—Los Ang.	L	4-5	Zachry	DiPino
17—Los Ang.	L	0-1	Honeycutt	Niekro
18—Los Ang.	W	3-0	Knepper	Welch
20—At Atlanta	L	7-8	Garber	Ruhle
21—At Atlanta	W	4-3	Dawley	Bedrosian
22—At Atlanta	W	3-1	Niekro	Falcone
23—At L.A.	L	1-2	Welch	Knepper
24—At L.A.	L	3-5	Pena	Madden
25—At L.A.	L	2-4	Valenzuela	Ryan
27—Atlanta	L	0-6	Falcone	Niekro
28—Atlanta	L	3-5	Camp	Knepper
29—Atlanta	W	8-5	Scott	Barker

Won 8, Lost 14

MAY

Date		Score	Winner	Loser
1—At Cinn.	L	1-2	Franco	Dawley
2—At Cinn.	L	2-3	Soto	Niekro
4—At N.Y.	L	0-2	Darling	Knepper
5—At N.Y.	W	10-6	Dawley	Orosco
6—At N.Y.	W	10-1	Ryan	Gooden
7—At Mon.	L	1-4	Rogers	Niekro
9—Phila.	W	7-1	Knepper	Hudson
10—Phila.	W	4-2	Scott	Koosman
11—Chicago	W	3-1	Ryan	Ruthven
12—Chicago	L	4-5	Noles	DiPino
13—Chicago	W	1-0	Madden	Reuschel
14—At Pitts.	L	2-3	DeLeon	Knepper
15—At Pitts.	L	2-3*	Guante	DiPino
16—At Pitts.	W	1-0	Ryan	Candelaria
18—At Chicago	L	6-7	Stoddard	Smith
19—At Chicago	L	4-5	Reuschel	Dawley
20—At Chicago	L	3-10	Bordi	Scott
21—At St. L.	W	3-2	Ryan	Forsch
22—At St. L.	W	4-3†	Dawley	Sutter
23—At St. L.	W	4-0	Knepper	Andujar
25—Pittsburgh	L	2-6	Tudor	Scott
26—Pittsburgh	W	2-0	Ryan	DeLeon
27—Pittsburgh	L	1-2	Rhoden	Niekro
28—Pittsburgh	L	0-7	Candelaria	Ruhle
29—St. Louis	W	1-0	Knepper	LaPoint
30—St. Louis	L	4-6	Horton	DiPino

Won 12, Lost 14

JUNE

Date		Score	Winner	Loser
1—At L.A.	L	2-6	Honeycutt	Ruhle
2—At L.A.	W	9-3	Niekro	Reuss
3—At L.A.	W	5-3	Knepper	Welch
4—At S. Diego	L	0-3	Whitson	Scott
5—At S. Diego	L	0-3	Hawkins	Ruhle
6—At S. Diego	L	3-4*	Gossage	Smith
7—At S. Fran.	W	14-5	Niekro	Laskey
8—At S. Fran.	L	4-5	Lerch	Knepper
9—At S. Fran.	L	5-6	Williams	Dawley
10—At S. Fran.	W	7-4	Ruhle	Robinson
11—Cincinnati	W	3-2x	LaCoss	Power
12—Cincinnati	W	7-0	Niekro	Berenyi
13—Cincinnati	L	4-5†	Owchinko	DiPino
14—Los Ang.	W	3-1	Scott	Valenzuela
15—Los Ang.	W	3-2	Dawley	Hershiser
16—Los Ang.	W	7-5	Madden	Hooton
17—Los Ang.	W	1-0	Ryan	Welch
19—San Diego	L	0-2	Show	Knepper
20—San Diego	W	2-6	Lollar	Madden
21—San Diego	W	11-5	Niekro	Whitson
22—San Fran.	W	10-3	Scott	Krukow
23—San Fran.	L	5-7	Williams	Ruhle
24—San Fran.	W	8-3	Knepper	Robinson
25—At Atlanta	W	8-5	LaCoss	Barker
25—At Atlanta	L	4-6	Mahler	Madden
26—At Atlanta	W	10-5	Niekro	Camp
27—At Atlanta	L	4-6	Perez	Scott
28—At Phila.	W	7-6	Dawley	Holland
29—At Phila.	L	2-7	Carlton	Knepper
30—At Phila.	W	7-0	LaCoss	Hudson

Won 17, Lost 13

JULY

Date		Score	Winner	Loser
1—At Phila.	W	13-1	Niekro	Gross
2—At N.Y.	L	2-4	Gooden	Scott
3—At N.Y.	L	3-4	Berenyi	Ryan
4—At N.Y.	W	10-5	Knepper	Lynch
5—At Mon.	W	2-1	LaCoss	Smith
6—At Mon.	W	8-2	Niekro	Rogers
6—At Mon.	L	5-7	Schatzeder	Ruhle
7—At Mon.	W	3-2	DiPino	James
8—At Mon.	L	5-8	Gullickson	Ryan
12—Phila.	L	3-5	Carlton	Niekro
13—Phila.	L	3-7	Rawley	Ryan
14—Phila.	L	3-4	Koosman	Ruhle
15—Phila.	W	3-2y	DiPino	Carman
16—New York	L	3-13	Fernandez	Scott
17—New York	W	3-2	DiPino	Sisk
18—New York	L	1-3	Terrell	Ryan
19—Montreal	W	3-2	LaCoss	Lucas
20—Montreal	W	8-4	Knepper	Rogers
21—Montreal	L	2-4	Palmer	Scott
22—Montreal	W	6-1	Niekro	Smith
24—At S. Fran.	W	10-3	Ryan	Davis
25—At S. Fran.	L	3-7	Robinson	LaCoss
26—At S. Fran.	L	2-3	Laskey	Scott
27—At S. Diego	L	3-7	Whitson	Ruhle
28—At S. Diego	W	3-1	Niekro	Hawkins
28—At S. Diego	L	0-1	Show	Ryan
29—At S. Diego	L	0-9	Lollar	LaCoss
30—Atlanta	W	4-3	Smith	Moore
31—Atlanta	L	3-6	Dedmon	DiPino

Won 13, Lost 16

AUGUST

Date		Score	Winner	Loser
1—Atlanta	L	5-6	Falcone	Solano
3—San Diego	W	6-2	Ryan	Show
4—San Diego	L	2-5	Lollar	LaCoss
5—San Diego	L	5-9	Hawkins	Niekro
6—San Fran.	W	8-0	Knepper	Laskey
7—San Fran.	L	2-9	Krukow	Scott
8—San Fran.	W	7-6‡	Dawley	Calvert
9—San Fran.	W	6-0	LaCoss	Robinson
10—At Cinn.	L	4-5‡	Franco	Solano
10—At Cinn.	W	11-7	Knepper	Pastore
11—At Cinn.	W	8-2	Scott	Price
12—At Cinn.	W	6-1	Ryan	McGaffigan
13—Chicago	W	2-1	Dawley	Sanderson
14—Chicago	W	7-6	Solano	Frazier
15—Chicago	W	6-2	Knepper	Eckersley
17—At Pitts.	W	7-4*	Dawley	Tekulve
18—At Pitts.	W	5-0	LaCoss	DeLeon
19—At Pitts.	W	4-3	Niekro	Candelaria
20—At Chicago	L	1-6	Trout	Knepper
21—At Chicago	L	5-11	Eckersley	Scott
22—At Chicago	W	8-3	Ryan	Ruthven
23—St. Louis	W	9-6	Smith	Rucker
24—St. Louis	W	7-2	Niekro	Horton
25—St. Louis	W	5-2	Knepper	LaPoint
26—St. Louis	L	2-3	Kepshire	Ryan
28—Pittsburgh	W	3-2	Smith	Tudor
29—Pittsburgh	L	2-4	Robinson	DiPino
31—At St. L.	L	5-7	Allen	Ryan

Won 18, Lost 10

SEPTEMBER

Date		Score	Winner	Loser
1—At St. L.	W	8-4	Ross	Kepshire
2—At St. L.	L	1-4	Horton	Niekro
3—At Atlanta	L	4-6	McMurtry	Ruhle
4—At Atlanta	L	7-8	Moore	DiPino
5—At S. Fran.	W	4-1	Ryan	Lerch
6—At S. Fran.	W	14-2	Knepper	Laskey
7—At S. Diego	W	6-4	Niekro	Lollar
9—At S. Diego	L	4-8	Thurmond	LaCoss
10—Atlanta	L	1-3	Smith	Ryan
11—Atlanta	L	4-6	Mahler	Solano
12—Atlanta	L	1-4	Perez	Smith
14—San Diego	L	2-4	Gossage	DiPino
15—San Diego	W	3-2	Dawley	Lefferts
16—San Diego	W	10-9	Smith	Gossage
17—San Fran.	W	5-3	Niekro	Grant
18—San Fran.	W	5-4*	Smith	Garrelts
19—Los Ang.	L	1-3	Reuss	Knepper
20—Los Ang.	L	2-6	Hershiser	Ryan
21—Cincinnati	L	2-5	Soto	Niekro
22—Cincinnati	L	1-2§	Power	Smith
23—Cincinnati	W	2-1	Knepper	Price
24—At L.A.	L	1-5	Reuss	LaCoss
25—At L.A.	W	12-6	Niekro	Zachry
26—At L.A.	W	3-1	Dawley	Valenzuela
28—At Cinn.	W	6-3*	Dawley	Power
29—At Cinn.	L	1-4	Tibbs	Niekro
30—At Cinn.	L	6-7	Soto	Calhoun

Won 12, Lost 15

*10 innings. †11 innings. ‡12 innings. §13 innings. x14 innings. y16 innings.

shortstop Dickie Thon, whose season ended abruptly in the fifth game. A pitch thrown by the New York Mets' Mike Torrez hit Thon in the head April 8, causing severe damage near his left eye. Thon experienced impaired vision all summer, and his career is in jeopardy.

"I don't like to make excuses, but Dickie Thon is a franchise player," General Manager Al Rosen said. "I don't know of any team that could lose a player of his stature and not be seriously affected."

The Astros also lost right fielder Terry Puhl for most of April because of an elbow injury. Three separate ailments sidelined pitcher Nolan Ryan for a combined six weeks.

But the Braves and Dodgers had similar problems (though San Diego escaped severe physical blows). The point is that despite losing key players, the Astros—on paper—played well enough to give San Diego a good scare.

But they didn't.

"We weren't consistent," Manager Bob Lillis said. "We can't have everyone cold all at once and then everyone hot for a while. You can't be a streaky club and expect to contend."

Especially amazing was the inconsistency of Houston's offense. Through June 5, the Astros were batting .237, worst in the league. By the finish, however, they were at .264, a club record and only two points behind league-leader Philadelphia.

Houston's pitching was inconsistent, too, but in a different sense. Among starters, knuckleballer Joe Niekro (16-12, 3.04 ERA) and Bob Knepper (15-10, 3.20) almost always were good, and Mike LaCoss (7-5, 4.02) had a brief flurry of excellence before fading in September. Ryan, despite his injuries, was 12-11 with a 3.04 ERA and 197 strikeouts, giving him 3,874 for his career, two more than the No. 2 man on the all-time strikeout list, Philadelphia's Steve Carlton.

But Mike Scott won only five of 29 starts, absorbing 11 defeats and a rather incredible 13 no-decisions. Mike Madden (2-3, 5.53 ERA), given seven starts, had problems with control, and veteran Vern Ruhle spent most of his time in the bullpen and finished at 1-9.

The combined result was a lack of depth in the rotation, an unusual problem for a team that for many years has been built on pitching.

The bullpen was difficult to evaluate. On the one hand, the relievers' ERAs were eye-popping: Bill Dawley was at 1.93, Dave Smith 2.21, Julio Solano 1.95, Joe Sambito 3.02 and Frank DiPino 3.35. But on the other hand, the bullpen recorded only 29 saves, fewer than the totals for many individual relief aces on other staffs.

Inconsistency affected this area, too. DiPino, the team leader with 14 saves, was superb early but then struggled. Dawley (11-4, five saves) began slowly, then emerged into the team's stopper.

Several individual performances merit attention:

Left fielder Jose Cruz continued to rank among the best, albeit unheralded, players in baseball. He hit .312, tied for fifth in the league, and finished among the top 10 in runs scored (96), runs batted in (95), on-base percentage (.381), walks (73), hits (187) and triples (13). Not surprisingly, after also leading the Astros with 22 stolen bases, 12 home runs, 28 doubles and 277 total bases, he was voted the club's most valuable player for the second consecutive season and the fourth time since 1977.

Center fielder Jerry Mumphrey made the All-Star team and carried the team's offense for the first three months. The switch-hitter finished with 83 RBIs and a solid .290 average.

Enos Cabell, counted on as a pinch-hitter and utility player, earned a starting job at first base and hit .310.

Puhl enjoyed one of his best seasons, batting .301 with a .380 on-base percentage.

Craig Reynolds, a two-time All-Star who lost his starting shortstop job to Thon two years earlier, was ready to fill in when Thon was injured. He responded by batting .260 and driving in 60 runs, No. 3 on the club.

Also contributing offensively were second baseman Bill Doran (.261) and infielders Phil Garner (.278) and Denny Walling (.281). At catcher, rookie Mark Bailey, who was called up from Houston's Double-A club in Columbus when veteran Alan Ashby went on the disabled list in late April, batted only .212 but provided some power with nine homers.

Finally, if Thon's story was the saddest of the Astros' season, Sambito provided the happiest development.

Sambito, who was sidelined all of 1983 and most of 1982 because of an elbow injury that required three operations, returned to pitch in 32 games. Lillis, taking no chances, never used Sambito with the Astros ahead or with a game on the line, and so Sambito's record shows no victories, no losses and no saves. But with only 39 hits allowed in 47⅔ innings, Sambito indicated he may be ready to play an important role in the Astros' future.

Rookie Orel Hershiser established his credentials as a future Dodgers star.

Dodgers Tumble to Fourth

By GORDON VERRELL

The Los Angeles Dodgers were one of several teams this year—Pittsburgh and Montreal were two other notable examples—that proved that pitching is not 75 percent of the game.

If it were, the Dodgers would have been solidly in the scramble for the National League West flag they were trying to defend. But as it was, Los Angeles wound up fourth, its first second-division finish since 1969. The Dodgers' 79-83 record marked only the second time since 1968 that the team had fallen below .500. (The other time was in 1979, when, coincidentally, the Dodgers finished at 79-83.)

Los Angeles was second in the league in staff earned-run average (3.17), first in complete games (39), second in shutouts (16) and first, by a good margin, in home runs allowed (76, compared with 91 for No. 2 Houston). Alejandro Pena was the league's ERA champion with a 2.48 mark, while rookie Orel Hershiser was third (2.66), Rick Honeycutt was sixth (2.84) and Fernando Valenzuela was 10th (3.03).

The problem, obviously, was hitting. The Dodgers were tied for last in team batting (.244), the lowest club average since 1968, and last in runs scored (580). And after leading the league in home runs six times in the previous seven years, the Dodgers finished eighth with 102.

Why were the Dodgers so cold at the plate?

One reason was injuries. Fifteen Dodgers were placed on the disabled list at some time during the season. "The number of injuries we had was totally incomprehensible," Dodgers Vice President Al Campanis said.

Another reason was the failure of several players—many of whom had been rewarded earlier with generous long-term contracts—to perform up to expectations.

Pedro Guerrero is a prime example. After hitting 64 home runs and knocking in 203 runs over the previous two summers, Guerrero received a five-year, $7 million contract before the start of the '84 season, making him the highest-paid Dodger ever.

By the All-Star break, when the Dodgers were well into their skid and in need of an offensive leader, Guerrero was hitting .287 but had only seven home runs and 31 runs batted in. At the break in 1983 he was hitting .301 with 17 homers and 50 RBIs.

The club's decision before the season to release veteran outfielder Dusty Baker, who still had two years remaining on his contract, was partly responsible for Guerrero's slump. Baker's departure left Guerrero as the only proven player in the middle of the Los Angeles lineup.

"He's trying to do everything himself, and he's putting too much pressure on himself," Manager Tom Lasorda said at the time, attempting to explain Guerrero's slow start. The six-year veteran improved somewhat in the second half, finishing at .303 with 16 homers and a team-leading 72 RBIs.

Mike Marshall started the season well enough as Baker's replacement in left field, hitting .282 with 14 home runs by the All-Star break. But he was hampered in the second half, first by a foot ailment that required surgery and then by a knee injury. He finished with a .257 average and a team-high 21 home runs.

Greg Brock had another disappointing season as Steve Garvey's successor at first base, even having to spend a month in the minors. He returned from Albuquerque (Pacific Coast) with a renewed enthusiasm but with the same ineffective bat. He finished the season at .225, one point better than his 1983 rookie average.

Second baseman Steve Sax, who just about tossed himself out of the league with his errant throws in 1983, encountered a momentary relapse in 1984 but brought his error total down to 21 from a league-high 30 a year earlier. Sax suffered at the plate, however, hitting only .243, 38 points below his career mark for his first two-plus seasons.

Third base was the Dodgers' real bugaboo. Lasorda started with German Rivera, but the rookie ended up with only two more RBIs (17) than errors. Guerrero (the team leader in errors with 22), shortstop Dave Anderson, outfielder Candy Maldonado and utilityman Bob Bailor also were tried at third, but no one was an adequate replacement for Ron Cey, who was traded to the Cubs early in 1983.

Ken Landreaux started the year in center field and finished in right, moving over for Guerrero, whose days as a third baseman appear to be over. Landreaux, playing under a new long-term contract, was another disappointment, both offensively and defensively. He hit only .251, a 30-point dropoff from 1983, and knocked in only 47 runs.

The bright spots were few but notable. One, of course, was Hershiser. Brought out

SCORES OF LOS ANGELES DODGERS' 1984 GAMES

APRIL			Winner	Loser
3—St. Louis	L	7-11	Cox	Valenzuela
5—St. Louis	W	5-2§	Hershiser	Lahti
6—Pittsburgh	L	1-3	Tudor	Welch
7—Pittsburgh	L	0-3	Candelaria	Pena
8—Pittsburgh	L	2-5	Rhoden	Valenzuela
9—Chicago	W	4-2	Reuss	Rainey
11—Chicago	W	2-1	Honeycutt	Sanderson
13—San Fran.	W	2-0	Welch	Robinson
14—San Fran.	W	8-4	Pena	Krukow
15—San Fran.	L	6-8‡	Lerch	Niedenfuer
16—At Hous.	W	5-4	Zachry	DiPino
17—At Hous.	W	1-0	Honeycutt	Niekro
18—At Hous.	L	0-3	Knepper	Welch
19—San Diego	W	4-0	Pena	Whitson
20—San Diego	W	8-2	Valenzuela	Show
21—San Diego	L	6-9	Thurmond	Reuss
22—San Diego	W	15-7	Honeycutt	Lollar
23—Houston	W	2-1	Welch	Knepper
24—Houston	W	5-3	Pena	Madden
25—Houston	W	4-2	Valenzuela	Ryan
26—At S. Diego	W	6-5	Diaz	Dravecky
27—At S. Diego	L	1-0*	Honeycutt	Lollar
28—At S. Diego	L	1-5	Hawkins	Welch
29—At S. Diego	W	6-0	Pena	Whitson
30—At S. Fran.	W	1-0	Valenzuela	Laskey

Won 17, Lost 8

MAY				
1—At S. Fran.	W	3-2‡	Hershiser	Lavelle
2—At S. Fran.	L	3-4	Lavelle	Niedenfuer
5—At Pitts.	L	7-8†	Tekulve	Hershiser
6—At Pitts.	W	6-4†	Niedenfuer	Tekulve
6—At Pitts.	L	1-2	Tudor	Valenzuela
7—At St. L.	L	1-5	LaPoint	Honeycutt
8—At St. L.	W	2-1	Reuss	Cox
9—At Chicago	L	0-7	Sanderson	Hooton
10—At Chicago	W	5-1	Welch	Trout
11—New York	L	0-2	Gooden	Valenzuela
12—New York	L	3-4	Lynch	Pena
13—New York	W	5-3	Honeycutt	Torrez
14—Phila.	L	2-3	Hudson	Reuss
15—Phila.	L	1-12	Koosman	Welch
16—Phila.	L	2-7	Carlton	Valenzuela
18—Montreal	L	4-5‡	McGaffigan	Niedenfuer
19—Montreal	W	5-1	Honeycutt	Gullickson
20—Montreal	W	3-2	Zachry	Smith
22—At Phila.	L	1-3	Koosman	Welch
23—At Phila.	W	1-0	Valenzuela	Carlton
24—At Phila.	L	3-4	Holland	Zachry
25—At N.Y.	L	1-2	Gooden	Honeycutt
26—At N.Y.	L	1-2	Leary	Niedenfuer
27—At N.Y.	W	3-2	Welch	Torrez
28—At Mon.	W	6-1	Valenzuela	Rogers
30—At Mon.	W	4-1	Pena	Smith

Won 11, Lost 15

JUNE				
1—Houston	W	6-2	Honeycutt	Ruhle
2—Houston	L	3-9	Niekro	Reuss
3—Houston	L	3-5	Knepper	Welch
4—Cincinnati	L	1-3	Pastore	Valenzuela
5—Cincinnati	W	2-1	Pena	Russell
6—Cincinnati	W	3-2x	Zachry	Hume
7—Atlanta	L	1-8	Perez	Hershiser
8—Atlanta	W	5-3	Welch	Barker
9—Atlanta	W	4-3	Valenzuela	Bedrosian
10—Atlanta	W	3-2	Pena	McMurtry
11—San Fran.	L	4-8	Laskey	Honeycutt
12—San Fran.	W	8-7	Zachry	Minton
13—San Fran.	L	5-10	Cornell	Hooton
14—At Hous.	L	1-3	Scott	Valenzuela
15—At Hous.	L	2-3	Dawley	Hershiser
16—At Hous.	L	5-7	Madden	Hooton
17—At Hous.	L	0-1	Ryan	Welch
19—At Cinn.	L	4-10	Price	Valenzuela
20—At Cinn.	L	2-4	Russell	Pena
21—At Cinn.	W	9-7	Hooton	Power
22—At Atlanta	W	10-4	Welch	Falcone
23—At Atlanta	W	10-2	Valenzuela	Perez
24—At Atlanta	W	5-2	Pena	McMurtry
25—San Diego	L	4-9	Lollar	Zachry
26—San Diego	L	0-5	Whitson	Welch
27—San Diego	W	5-4	Valenzuela	Dravecky
28—Chicago	L	3-5	Trout	Pena
29—Chicago	W	7-1	Hershiser	Sutcliffe
30—Chicago	L	4-14	Frazier	Howell

Won 13, Lost 16

JULY				
1—Chicago	L	3-4	Eckersley	Valenzuela
2—Pittsburgh	W	5-4	Pena	McWilliams

JULY			Winner	Loser
3—Pittsburgh	L	0-6	Candelaria	Howell
4—Pittsburgh	W	9-0	Hershiser	Tudor
5—St. Louis	L	0-3	Allen	Welch
6—St. Louis	W	3-2§	Howell	Allen
7—St. Louis	W	3-0	Pena	Ownbey
8—St. Louis	L	6-8§	Sutter	Zachry
12—At Chicago	L	2-3†	Stoddard	Niedenfuer
13—At Chicago	L	5-7	Sutcliffe	Welch
14—At Chicago	W	8-0	Hershiser	Sanderson
15—At Chicago	L	1-4	Eckersley	Valenzuela
16—At Pitts.	L	1-4	Walk	Honeycutt
17—At Pitts.	W	5-0	Pena	DeLeon
18—At Pitts.	L	2-5	McWilliams	Reuss
19—At St. L.	W	10-0	Hershiser	LaPoint
20—At St. L.	L	5-10	Kepshire	Valenzuela
21—At St. L.	W	3-1	Honeycutt	Andujar
22—At St. L.	L	6-7	Cox	Welch
24—Atlanta	L	2-4	Bedrosian	Hershiser
25—Atlanta	W	2-1	Valenzuela	Barker
26—Atlanta	L	1-5	McMurtry	Honeycutt
27—Cincinnati	L	0-4	Price	Pena
28—Cincinnati	W	1-0	Welch	Hume
29—Cincinnati	W	1-0	Hershiser	Soto
30—At S. Diego	L	0-12	Dravecky	Valenzuela
31—At S. Diego	L	0-1	Thurmond	Honeycutt

Won 11, Lost 16

AUGUST				
1—At S. Diego	L	3-4	Lefferts	Pena
3—At Cinn.	W	5-2	Welch	Soto
4—At Cinn.	W	5-3‡	Zachry	Hume
5—At Cinn.	L	1-2‡	Power	Reuss
6—At Atlanta	L	0-2	Mahler	Honeycutt
7—At Atlanta	W	2-1‡	Howell	Moore
8—At Atlanta	W	5-1	Welch	Brizzolara
9—At Atlanta	W	1-0	Hershiser	Camp
10—At S. Fran.	L	1-4	Calvert	Valenzuela
11—At S. Fran.	W	4-2	Honeycutt	Laskey
12—At S. Fran.	W	5-4†	Pena	Davis
13—New York	W	9-2	Welch	Terrell
14—New York	L	0-4	Berenyi	Hershiser
15—New York	L	2-3	Fernandez	Valenzuela
17—Phila.	W	2-1	Honeycutt	Carlton
18—Phila.	L	5-6	Koosman	Howell
19—Phila.	L	3-6	Rawley	Welch
20—Montreal	L	1-3	Gullickson	Hershiser
21—Montreal	W	4-3	Valenzuela	Schatzeder
22—Montreal	L	3-5‡	James	Howell
24—At Phila.	L	5-6†	Gross	Reuss
25—At Phila.	W	7-4	Welch	Denny
26—At Phila.	L	8-10	Campbell	Hooton
27—At N.Y.	L	1-5	Gooden	Valenzuela
28—At N.Y.	L	1-5	Terrell	Honeycutt
29—At N.Y.	L	2-3	Orosco	Zachry
30—At Mon.	L	2-5	Gullickson	Welch
31—At Mon.	L	2-5	Schatzeder	Hershiser

Won 11, Lost 17

SEPTEMBER				
1—At Mon.	W	4-3	Valenzuela	Lea
2—At Mon.	L	0-4	Smith	Honeycutt
3—San Diego	L	3-4	Thurmond	Reuss
4—San Diego	W	2-1	Howell	Hawkins
5—Atlanta	W	4-3	Hooton	Dedmon
6—Atlanta	L	2-3y	Dedmon	White
7—Cincinnati	L	0-1	Franco	Howell
8—Cincinnati	W	6-3	Reuss	Russell
9—Cincinnati	L	1-5	Browning	Hershiser
11—At S. Diego	W	5-2	Valenzuela	Whitson
12—At S. Diego	W	8-1	Hooton	Dravecky
14—At Cinn.	W	6-5	Howell	Franco
15—At Cinn.	W	5-2	Hershiser	Robinson
16—At Cinn.	W	7-5†	Howell	Franco
17—At Atlanta	W	9-0	Welch	Perez
18—At Atlanta	L	5-6	Garber	Hooton
19—At Hous.	W	3-1	Reuss	Knepper
20—At Hous.	W	6-2	Hershiser	Ryan
21—At S. Fran.	L	1-5	Laskey	Valenzuela
22—At S. Fran.	L	7-8	Garrelts	Zachry
23—At S. Fran.	L	2-4	Riley	Hooton
24—Houston	W	5-1	Reuss	LaCoss
25—Houston	L	6-12	Niekro	Zachry
26—Houston	L	1-3	Dawley	Valenzuela
28—San Fran.	W	4-3	Welch	Williams
29—San Fran.	W	4-3‡	Niedenfuer	Williams
30—San Fran.	W	7-2	Hershiser	Davis

Won 16, Lost 11

*6 innings.   †10 innings.   ‡11 innings.   §12 innings.   x14 innings.   y18 innings.

A strong finish helped Pedro Guerrero rebound from an early season slump.

of the bullpen in early June, the 25-year-old blossomed into the hottest pitcher in the league in July with four shutouts and a string of 33⅔ scoreless innings. He finished with an 11-8 record and 150 strikeouts. Another was catcher Mike Scioscia, who missed all but six weeks of the 1983 season because of an injury but came back to hit a respectable .273.

Valenzuela pitched well, but the lack of offensive support left the four-year veteran with his first losing record (12-17) in the major leagues. Valenzuela was second in the league in complete games (12), innings pitched (261) and strikeouts (240). The top winner for Los Angeles was Bob Welch (13-13).

The bullpen was socked especially hard by injuries. Big Tom Niedenfuer went down no less than four times with assorted elbow and shoulder problems, and once he passed out in a hotel coffee shop and had to be rushed to the hospital to treat a kidney stone condition. The Dodgers already were strapped for short relief without left-hander Steve Howe, who was suspended for a year because of repeated drug troubles. His replacement, Carlos Diaz, posted a 5.49 ERA in 37 games and was shipped to the minors for several weeks at midseason.

The Dodgers did manage to discover 23-year-old Ken Howell, who was thrust onto the hot seat almost immediately and responded with five wins and six saves in 32 appearances.

After going 17-8 in April, the Dodgers followed with four successive losing months, the first time in more than 15 years they had suffered four losing months in a row. The Dodgers also lost at the gate, their one source of pride even in the worst of years. Attendance dropped 375,489 in 1984 from the previous year, but the Dodgers were still far and away baseball's biggest draw at 3,134,824.

Rose Revives Cincinnati Fans

By EARL LAWSON

"Pete's back!"

That joyous cry was heard throughout Cincinnati on August 16, a memorable day for Reds fans because it marked the first time in a long while that they had had anything to be joyous about.

Their hero, Pete Rose, was coming back to town.

It was on August 16 that Reds President Bob Howsam held a news conference at Riverfront Stadium announcing Rose as the club's new player-manager, replacing Vern Rapp, who was in his first year as Reds manager. Rose thus became the first player-manager in the major leagues since Don Kessinger performed both roles for the Chicago White Sox in 1979.

From a public relations standpoint, at least, Howsam couldn't have made a wiser move.

Reds fans never had forgiven the club's management for permitting the popular Rose to leave Cincinnati after opting for free agency in November of 1978. Rose, who spent the next five seasons playing for the Philadelphia Phillies and the first 4½ months of 1984 with the Montreal Expos, offered the Reds more than box-office appeal, however. As a manager, he lacks only experience. He is loaded with baseball tactical knowledge, and above all, he commands respect from players.

"Instant respect," pitcher Joe Price said. "Not many guys command it. Pete is one who does."

Shortly after taking the helm, Rose vowed that the Reds would not finish last in the National League West again, as they had the previous two seasons. They didn't in 1984, despite the fact that they were 19 games under .500 when Rose took over. The Reds started poorly, going 4-10 under Rose in August, but they won 15 of 27 games in September to finish fifth in the division with a 70-92 record (19-22 during Rose's 41 games as manager).

"Finishing the season on a positive note was one of my goals when I took over as manager," Rose said. "I wanted the guys returning home wishing the start of a new season was just a few weeks away."

At season's end, Rose was not predicting a division title for the Reds in 1985. "But I didn't see any club in the West that scares me," he said.

That was a pretty bold statement coming from a skipper whose team batted a mere .244 (tied for last in the league) and whose pitching staff had a composite earned-run average of 4.16 (second worst in the league) while posting fewer saves (25) and issuing more walks (578) than any other National League team.

But Rose saw several reasons for optimism, including the performances of some young pitchers brought up from the Reds' farm system during the season.

"Guys like Jay Tibbs, Tom Browning and Ron Robinson are more than prospects," Rose said.

Tibbs, a 22-year-old righthander acquired in a June 15 trade that sent Bruce Berenyi to the New York Mets, compiled a 6-2 record with a 2.86 ERA in 14 starts after joining the Reds for the second half of the season. Robinson, another 22-year-old righthander called up in August, was 1-2 with a 2.72 ERA in 12 appearances, five as a starter. Browning, a 24-year-old lefthander, was 1-0 with a 1.54 ERA in three starts covering a span of 23⅓ innings in September.

The only other bright spots on Cincinnati's pitching staff were relievers Ted Power and John Franco and starter Mario Soto.

Power, a big righthander, topped the league with 78 appearances and went 9-7 with 11 saves and a 2.82 ERA. Franco, a rookie lefthander, was 6-2 with four saves and a 2.61 ERA in 54 relief appearances.

Soto and the Reds beat the Houston Astros in the season finale, giving the righthander his 18th victory, a career high, against seven losses. The Reds' ace also racked up 185 strikeouts, topping the 150 mark for the fifth straight year, and he led the league with 13 complete games.

Soto, who received two five-day suspensions plus fines from National League President Chub Feeney for his part in two bench-clearing brawls in 1984, came within one out of posting a no-hit shutout against the St. Louis Cardinals. He earned the 2-1 victory but lost the no-hitter and the shutout when George Hendrick homered with two out in the top of the ninth inning.

That May 12 no-hitter marked the high point of the Reds' season. It was their 13th victory in a 14-game span and raised their record to 19-14, placing them half a game out of first. The rest of the season was practically all downhill.

Several pitchers were major disappointments. Price, who was 10-6 with a 2.88 ERA in '83, slumped to 7-13 and a 4.19 ERA. Tom Hume, one of baseball's top relief pitchers just a few years ago, experi-

The return of Pete Rose to Cincinnati rekindled interest in an otherwise dismal season.

enced another dismal season with a 4-13 record, a 5.64 ERA and only three saves. Starters Jeff Russell (6-18, 4.26 ERA) and Frank Pastore (3-8, 6.50) also had off years.

A number of players were disappointments at the plate, too. Leadoff man Eddie Milner hit just .232 with 29 runs batted in. Outfielder Gary Redus stole a club-leading 48 bases but produced only 22 RBIs while batting .254.

Infielder Nick Esasky offered 10 home runs and 45 RBIs in 322 at-bats but hit a lowly .193, while second baseman Ron Oester (.242, 38 RBIs) had his worst season ever with the Reds.

At catcher, Brad Gulden, Dann Bilardello and Dave Van Gorder combined for a .221 average and only 49 RBIs.

But Rose's optimism was not entirely unwarranted. A couple of players—infielder Wayne Krenchicki and outfielder Duane Walker—compiled their best statistics ever in part-time roles.

Krenchicki, a .264 career hitter, batted .298 with six homers in 181 at-bats. Walker, who was batting .226 after two major league seasons, hit .292 with 10 homers in 195 at-bats.

In addition, Rose was encouraged by the performances of three veterans—Dave Parker, Cesar Cedeno and Dave Concepcion.

Parker, who signed with the Reds as a free agent in December of 1983, hit .285 and led Cincinnati in almost every offensive category, including homers (16), RBIs (94), runs scored (73) and hits (173). It was Parker's most productive season since 1980.

After Rose joined the Reds, Cedeno, playing on a regular basis, collected 51 hits in 165 at-bats for a .309 average to finish with an overall .276 average. He also drove in 21 runs and scored 25 in those 40 games.

Though Concepcion wound up with a disappointing .245 average, Rose was pleased with the shortstop's strong finish. Concepcion rapped out 14 hits in 36 at-bats and knocked in seven runs in his last 10 games of the season.

"Young players watch veterans play," Rose said, "so you want the type of veterans youngsters will look up to."

Rose himself set a good example for young players when he came to Cincinnati in August.

While playing in 26 of the Reds' last 41 games, Rose contributed 35 hits and 11 RBIs in 96 at-bats for a .365 average. He finished 1984 with an overall .286 average on 107 hits, leaving him 94 short of tying Ty Cobb's career record of 4,191 hits.

Depending on how often Rose the manager lets Rose the player play, that half-century-old mark could tumble during the 1985 season.

SCORES OF CINCINNATI REDS' 1984 GAMES

APRIL

Date	W/L	Score	Winner	Loser
2—New York	W	8-1	Soto	Torrez
4—New York	L	0-2	Darling	Berenyi
6—Phila.	L	4-8	Hudson	Price
7—Phila.	L	1-9	Koosman	Pastore
8—Phila.	W	8-7‡	Smith	Anderson
9—Montreal	W	9-6	Russell	Gullickson
10—Montreal	W	8-6	Price	James
11—Montreal	L	3-9	Smith	Berenyi
13—At Hous.	L	0-1	Niekro	Soto
14—At Hous.	L	1-9	Knepper	Russell
15—At Hous.	L	5-6	DiPino	Hume
18—Atlanta	L	4-5†	Bedrosian	Hume
19—At S. Fran.	L	1-3	Robinson	Berenyi
20—At S. Fran.	L	4-6	Minton	Russell
21—At S. Fran.	W	5-4	Power	Minton
22—At S. Fran.	L	5-9	Martin	Pastore
24—At Atlanta	L	2-4	Barker	Hume
25—At Atlanta	W	4-3	Soto	Dayley
26—At Atlanta	L	1-2	McMurtry	Russell
27—San Fran.	W	9-3	Price	Grant
28—San Fran.	W	7-6x	Hume	Lerch
29—San Fran.	W	8-1	Berenyi	Robinson
29—San Fran.	W	7-3	Owchinko	Krukow

Won 10, Lost 13

MAY

Date	W/L	Score	Winner	Loser
1—Houston	W	2-1	Franco	Dawley
2—Houston	W	3-2	Soto	Niekro
4—At Phila.	W	9-5	Pastore	Hudson
5—At Phila.	L	2-11	Koosman	Berenyi
6—At Phila.	W	5-3	Franco	Carlton
7—At N.Y.	W	11-2	Soto	Leary
9—At Mon.	W	6-4	Hume	Gullickson
10—At Mon.	W	2-1	Pastore	Smith
11—St. Louis	W	4-3	Russell	LaPoint
12—St. Louis	W	2-1	Soto	Sutter
13—St. Louis	L	2-6	Stuper	Owchinko
15—Chicago	L	3-6	Noles	Pastore
16—Chicago	L	4-10	Trout	Russell
17—Chicago	W	5-3	Soto	Ruthven
18—At St. L.	L	3-5	Stuper	Price
19—At St. L.	L	1-9	Andujar	Berenyi
20—At St. L.	L	2-3	Allen	Hume
22—At Pitts.	W	5-3	Soto	Scurry
23—At Pitts.	L	2-7	Candelaria	Russell
24—At Pitts.	L	1-5	McWilliams	Price
25—At Chicago	W	3-0	Hume	Noles
26—At Chicago	W	7-6	Scherrer	Trout
27—At Chicago	W	4-3	Berenyi	Eckersley
29—Pittsburgh	W	5-4†	Power	Tekulve
30—Pittsburgh	W	6-4y	Owchinko	Robinson
31—Atlanta	L	1-7	Mahler	Pastore

Won 16, Lost 10

JUNE

Date	W/L	Score	Winner	Loser
1—Atlanta	L	2-4	McMurtry	Berenyi
1—Atlanta	L	3-7	Falcone	Power
2—Atlanta	L	3-9	Perez	Owchinko
3—Atlanta	L	0-4	Forster	Power
4—At L.A.	W	3-1	Pastore	Valenzuela
5—At L.A.	L	1-2	Pena	Russell
6—At L.A.	L	2-3y	Zachry	Hume
7—At S. Diego	W	12-1	Berenyi	Show
8—At S. Diego	L	0-6	Lollar	Price
9—At S. Diego	L	2-12	Whitson	Russell
10—At S. Diego	L	5-7	Chiffer	Hume
11—At Hous.	L	2-3y	LaCoss	Power
12—At Hous.	L	0-7	Niekro	Berenyi
13—At Hous.	W	5-4‡	Owchinko	DiPino
14—At Atlanta	L	0-3	Barker	Russell
15—At Atlanta	L	1-6	Mahler	Pastore
16—At Atlanta	W	2-1	Power	Bedrosian
17—At Atlanta	L	5-6	Perez	Owchinko
19—Los Ang.	W	10-4	Price	Valenzuela
20—Los Ang.	W	4-2	Russell	Pena
21—Los Ang.	L	7-9	Hooton	Power
22—San Diego	W	8-7	Franco	Gossage
23—San Diego	L	2-5	Thurmond	Puleo
24—San Diego	L	3-8x	Dravecky	Hume
25—At S. Fran.	W	2-1	Power	Laskey
26—At S. Fran.	W	4-2	Soto	Williams
27—At S. Fran.	L	9-14	Lerch	Owchinko
29—Montreal	L	3-7	Lea	Scherrer
30—Montreal	W	4-1	Soto	Smith

Won 10, Lost 19

JULY

Date	W/L	Score	Winner	Loser
1—Montreal	W	4-1	Russell	Rogers
2—At Phila.	L	0-4	Rawley	Hume
3—At Phila.	W	6-5	Puleo	Koosman
4—At Phila.	W	5-4†	Power	Holland
5—At N.Y.	L	3-4	Terrell	Price
6—At N.Y.	L	0-1	Darling	Russell
6—At N.Y.	L	5-6	Orosco	Power
7—At N.Y.	L	4-14	Gooden	Soto
8—At N.Y.	L	3-7	Berenyi	Puleo
12—At Mon.	L	1-3	Smith	Price
13—At Mon.	L	2-7	Gullickson	Russell
14—At Mon.	L	2-6	Lea	Soto
15—At Mon.	W	3-2	Tibbs	Rogers
16—Phila.	L	2-7	Gross	Hume
17—Phila.	L	3-4	Carlton	Price
18—Phila.	L	5-7	Rawley	Russell
19—New York	W	9-6	Soto	Berenyi
20—New York	L	2-3‡	Orosco	Lesley
21—New York	L	1-2	Fernandez	Hume
22—New York	W	6-7	Gorman	Cato
24—At S. Diego	W	4-2	Soto	Lollar
25—At S. Diego	L	5-6	Gossage	Owchinko
26—At S. Diego	L	2-8	Thurmond	Russell
27—At L.A.	W	4-0	Price	Pena
28—At L.A.	L	0-1	Welch	Hume
29—At L.A.	L	0-1	Hershiser	Soto
31—San Fran.	W	3-0	Tibbs	Robinson

Won 8, Lost 19

AUGUST

Date	W/L	Score	Winner	Loser
1—San Fran.	W	6-3	Price	Lavelle
2—San Fran.	L	2-5	Krukow	Pastore
3—Los Ang.	L	2-5	Welch	Soto
4—Los Ang.	L	3-5‡	Zachry	Hume
5—Los Ang.	W	2-1‡	Power	Reuss
6—San Diego	L	0-1	Gossage	Price
7—San Diego	W	8-7	Power	Harris
8—San Diego	W	4-2	Soto	Gossage
9—San Diego	W	8-0	Russell	Lollar
10—Houston	W	5-4§	Franco	Solano
10—Houston	L	7-11	Knepper	Pastore
11—Houston	L	2-8	Scott	Price
12—Houston	L	1-6	Ryan	McGaffigan
13—At St. L.	L	3-5	Horton	Soto
14—At St. L.	L	2-8	LaPoint	Russell
15—At St. L.	W	3-2‡	Hume	Sutter
17—Chicago	W	6-4	Soto	Ruthven
18—Chicago	L	11-13	Sutcliffe	Robinson
19—Chicago	L	6-9	Frazier	Russell
20—St. Louis	L	7-9	Lahti	Tibbs
21—St. Louis	W	4-1	Price	Kepshire
22—St. Louis	L	3-6	Andujar	Soto
24—At Pitts.	W	2-0	Russell	DeLeon
25—At Pitts.	L	3-5	Candelaria	Tibbs
26—At Pitts.	L	1-7	Rhoden	Price
28—At Chicago	L	2-5	Eckersley	McGaffigan
28—At Chicago	L	2-5	Ruthven	Pastore
29—At Chicago	L	2-7	Sutcliffe	Russell
30—Pittsburgh	W	4-1	Tibbs	DeLeon
31—Pittsburgh	L	2-6	Candelaria	Price

Won 11, Lost 19

SEPTEMBER

Date	W/L	Score	Winner	Loser
1—Pittsburgh	W	7-5‡	Power	Robinson
2—Pittsburgh	W	7-1	Robinson	Tudor
3—At S. Fran.	L	3-4	Minton	Russell
4—At S. Fran.	W	8-3	Soto	Minton
5—At S. Diego	L	11-15	Lefferts	Hume
6—At S. Diego	W	10-3	Price	Show
7—At L.A.	W	1-0	Franco	Howell
8—At L.A.	L	3-6	Reuss	Russell
9—At L.A.	W	5-1	Browning	Hershiser
11—San Fran.	W	7-3	Soto	Lerch
12—San Fran.	W	7-4	Tibbs	Grant
14—Los Ang.	L	5-6	Howell	Franco
15—Los Ang.	L	2-5	Hershiser	Robinson
16—Los Ang.	L	5-7†	Howell	Franco
17—San Diego	L	2-3‡	Gossage	Power
18—San Diego	L	0-2	Dravecky	Price
19—At Atlanta	W	4-2	Tibbs	McMurtry
20—At Atlanta	L	3-9	Camp	Russell
21—At Hous.	W	5-2	Soto	Niekro
22—At Hous.	W	2-1x	Power	Smith
23—At Hous.	L	1-2	Knepper	Price
25—Atlanta	L	2-4*	Mahler	Willis
26—Atlanta	W	6-3	Soto	Perez
27—Atlanta	W	2-1†	Franco	Garber
28—Houston	L	3-6†	Dawley	Power
29—Houston	W	4-1	Tibbs	Niekro
30—Houston	W	7-6	Soto	Calhoun

Won 15, Lost 12

*8 innings.   †10 innings.   ‡11 innings.   §12 innings.   x13 innings.   y14 innings.

Defenseless Giants Fall Apart

By NICK PETERS

By posting the worst record in the team's 27-year San Francisco history, the Giants fell far short of their preseason expectations. The club managed only 66 victories, the fewest in the major leagues in 1984, after finishing spring training with the best record in the National League.

Nothing seemed to develop as anticipated. Off-season acquisitions Al Oliver and Manny Trillo were supposed to solidify the defense, yet the Giants made the most errors in the league.

Joel Youngblood was expected to fill a hole at third base, but he had made a major league-leading 37 errors with one month to go when that experiment was scrapped. Fielding problems also drained his offensive production, which slumped to a .254 average with 51 runs batted in.

The pitching rotation, contributing to the highest staff earned-run average in the league (4.39), was a disaster. Mike Krukow (11-12, 4.56 ERA), Bill Laskey (9-14, 4.33) and Mark Davis (5-17, 5.36) were major disappointments. Rookie righthander Jeff Robinson was promoted from Class-AA Shreveport before the opener to help out the rotation, but he fared no better, posting a 7-15 record and a 4.56 ERA in 33 starts.

The pitching weaknesses placed a burden on the offense, which ranked first in the league in hits (1,499), second in batting (.265) and fifth in runs scored (682) but had problems producing in the clutch. A 7-16 April gave an indication of what was to come, and there was only one non-losing month, a 16-16 standoff in August.

"Pitching was a question mark from the start of spring training, but I felt we started the season with the best overall talent since I came to San Francisco," said Frank Robinson, who was dismissed as manager August 4, when the Giants were 42-64. He was replaced by third base coach Danny Ozark, who stepped down after the season.

Robinson helped dig his own grave by extolling the club's virtues after a solid spring. As losses mounted and he took away privileges and imposed fines, some of the players became discouraged. The team's attitude was more relaxed under Ozark, although it failed to show any drastic improvement on the field. The club perked during a 9-3 August swing through the East but reverted to its losing ways in September.

Nevertheless, there were some positive aspects of the Giants' disappointing season. Several players responded with dazzling individual performances, and a number of rookies gave hope for the future.

Right fielder Jack Clark, whose attitude became a major question mark after he made it clear that he would rather be playing elsewhere following a slump-torn 1983, came to spring camp a new man. He displayed a positive attitude and was named team captain by Robinson. Clark jumped out to a great start, hitting .320 with 11 home runs in late June. Knee surgery, however, limited his season to 57 games.

Bob Brenly blossomed into the regular catcher, hit above .300 most of the season, reached career highs in most offensive categories, made the All-Star team and was voted most valuable player by his teammates. Brenly finished 1984 hitting .291 with 20 homers and 80 RBIs.

Three-year veteran Chili Davis also had his best season in the major leagues and was named to the All-Star team for the first time. The switch-hitting outfielder batted .315 to rank third in the league and was among the leaders in homers (21), slugging percentage and on-base percentage.

Jeff Leonard enjoyed another outstanding season in left field, continuing to excel defensively and joining Davis among the league offensive leaders (.302, 21 homers and a team-high 86 RBIs). Still, he was one of the most underrated players in the league.

Trillo was a tremendous addition, giving San Francisco superb defense at second base and serving as an ideal No. 2 hitter. He was off to a solid start offensively, but a broken bone in his right hand kept him out of the lineup for two months before the All-Star break, and he finished the season hitting .254.

Clark and Trillo were among nine Giants who spent time on the disabled list. Injuries hit the pitching staff hardest, the main victim being lefthander Atlee Hammaker, the league ERA champ in 1983. Hammaker underwent rotator cuff surgery the previous winter and had approached his rehabilitation cautiously. He pitched well in his only six appearances (all starts), going 2-0 with a 2.18 ERA, but his comeback was slowed by elbow surgery to remove bone spurs and a chip.

Reliever Greg Minton had his second consecutive mediocre season (4-9, 3.76

Outfielder Chili Davis put together the best season of his three-year career.

ERA, 19 saves) after signing a fat contract and was upstaged by rookie right-hander Frank Williams, a sidearmer who went 9-4 with a 3.55 ERA. Gary Lavelle (5-4, 2.76, 12 saves) was the most reliable reliever, but he suffered from arm and knee problems.

San Francisco's most pleasant surprise was rookie center fielder Dan Gladden, who joined the club at midseason. After batting .397 at Phoenix (Pacific Coast), Gladden hit .351, scored 71 runs and stole a team-leading 31 bases for the Giants.

September trials suggested that third baseman Chris Brown, pitcher George Riley and outfielders Alejandro Sanchez

and Rob Deer may have a future with the Giants.

Oliver, who hit .298 but produced only 34 RBIs and no homers, was traded in late August, a move that was expected to start a chain reaction for a club in need of change to improve and to revive fan interest.

Attendance barely reached 1 million on the final day of the home season, leaving Owner Bob Lurie far short of the 1.8 million he said he needed to break even. Lurie also was disappointed when plans for a new downtown stadium fell through, and he announced after the season that he was putting the team up for sale.

SCORES OF SAN FRANCISCO GIANTS' 1984 GAMES

APRIL

Date	W/L	Score	Winner	Loser
3—Chicago	L	3-5	Ruthven	Davis
5—Chicago	L	7-11	Rainey	Krukow
6—St. Louis	L	0-2	Anujar	Laskey
7—St. Louis	W	11-0	Robinson	LaPoint
8—St. Louis	L	3-9	Allen	Davis
10—Pittsburgh	W	4-3	Krukow	McWilliams
11—Pittsburgh	W	2-1†	Lavelle	Guante
13—At L.A.	L	0-2	Welch	Robinson
14—At L.A.	L	4-8	Pena	Krukow
15—At L.A.	W	8-6‡	Lerch	Niedenfuer
17—San Diego	L	1-2	Lollar	Davis
19—Cincinnati	W	3-1	Robinson	Berenyi
20—Cincinnati	W	6-4	Minton	Russell
21—Cincinnati	L	4-5	Power	Minton
22—Cincinnati	W	9-5	Martin	Pastore
23—At S. Diego	L	2-8	Hawkins	Robinson
24—At S. Diego	L	1-6	Whitson	Krukow
25—At S. Diego	L	0-3	Show	Laskey
27—At Cinn.	L	3-9	Price	Grant
28—At Cinn.	L	6-7x	Hume	Lerch
29—At Cinn.	L	1-8	Berenyi	Robinson
29—At Cinn.	L	3-7	Owchinko	Krukow
30—Los Ang.	L	0-1	Valenzuela	Laskey

Won 7, Lost 16

MAY

Date	W/L	Score	Winner	Loser
1—Los Ang.	L	2-3‡	Hershiser	Lavelle
2—Los Ang.	W	4-3	Lavelle	Niedenfuer
4—At St. L.	W	2-0	Robinson	Cox
5—At St. L.	W	7-0*	Williams	Forsch
6—At St. L.	W	3-2	Laskey	Andujar
7—At Chicago	L	7-10	Rainey	Davis
8—At Chicago	L	11-12	Smith	Minton
10—At Pitts.	L	2-4	Rhoden	Robinson
11—Montreal	L	5-7	Lea	Laskey
12—Montreal	W	8-7	Krukow	Rogers
13—Montreal	W	4-3	Garrelts	McGaffigan
15—New York	L	6-7‡	Orosco	Davis
16—New York	W	4-3	Davis	Terrell
18—Phila.	L	0-1	Bystrom	Krukow
19—Phila.	L	2-6	Denny	Martin
20—Phila.	L	4-7	Hudson	Robinson
22—At N.Y.	W	5-4	Davis	Darling
24—At N.Y.	W	3-2	Krukow	Terrell
25—At Mon.	L	2-3	Reardon	Minton
26—At Mon.	L	2-4	Gullickson	Laskey
27—At Mon.	L	2-6	Lea	Grant
30—At Phila.	L	2-3	Holland	Minton

Won 9, Lost 13

JUNE

Date	W/L	Score	Winner	Loser
1—San Diego	W	11-7	Williams	Hawkins
2—San Diego	L	2-3†	Gossage	Garrelts
3—San Diego	L	5-7	Lollar	Cornell
3—San Diego	L	6-7	Show	Lavelle
4—Atlanta	L	1-2	Mahler	Davis
5—Atlanta	L	3-8	McMurtry	Krukow
6—Atlanta	L	4-5‡	Bedrosian	Lavelle
7—Houston	L	5-14	Niekro	Laskey
8—Houston	W	5-4	Lerch	Knepper
9—Houston	W	6-5	Williams	Dawley
10—Houston	L	4-7	Ruhle	Robinson
11—At L.A.	W	8-4	Laskey	Honeycutt
12—At L.A.	L	7-8	Zachry	Minton
13—At L.A.	W	10-5	Cornell	Hooton
14—At S. Diego	W	5-2	Davis	Lollar
15—At S. Diego	L	2-3	Whitson	Robinson
16—At S. Diego	W	6-3	Laskey	Hawkins
17—At S. Diego	W	5-3y	Williams	Lefferts
19—At Atlanta	L	6-11	Camp	Cornell
20—At Atlanta	L	5-6	Barker	Robinson
21—At Atlanta	W	5-3	Laskey	Mahler
22—At Hous.	L	3-10	Scott	Krukow
23—At Hous.	W	7-5	Williams	Ruhle
24—At Hous.	L	3-8	Knepper	Robinson
25—Cincinnati	L	1-2	Power	Laskey
26—Cincinnati	L	2-4	Soto	Williams
27—Cincinnati	W	14-9	Lerch	Owchinko
28—Pittsburgh	W	4-3‡	Lavelle	Robinson
29—Pittsburgh	W	3-0	Robinson	Tudor
30—Pittsburgh	W	7-5	Williams	Guante

Won 14, Lost 16

JULY

Date	W/L	Score	Winner	Loser
1—Pittsburgh	W	7-4	Hammaker	Rhoden
3—St. Louis	W	6-2	Krukow	Allen
4—St. Louis	L	3-4	Horton	Davis
4—St. Louis	L	1-5	Kepshire	Robinson
5—Chicago	L	3-9	Sanderson	Laskey
6—Chicago	L	4-5	Stoddard	Minton
7—Chicago	W	7-2	Krukow	Reuschel
8—Chicago	L	3-6	Sutcliffe	Davis
12—At Pitts.	L	3-6	DeLeon	Laskey
13—At Pitts.	L	2-8	Candelaria	Krukow
13—At Pitts.	L	3-4z	Scurry	Cornell
14—At Pitts.	L	2-6	Rhoden	Davis
15—At Pitts.	L	3-9	Tudor	Robinson
16—At St. L.	W	7-6	Laskey	Ownbey
17—At St. L.	W	7-2	Krukow	Andujar
18—At St. L.	L	4-8‡	Von Ohlen	Lacey
19—At Chicago	L	4-6	Frazier	Davis
20—At Chicago	W	3-2	Robinson	Eckersley
21—At Chicago	L	3-4‡	Bordi	Minton
22—At Chicago	W	11-5	Krukow	Trout
24—Houston	L	3-10	Ryan	Davis
25—Houston	W	7-3	Robinson	LaCoss
26—Houston	W	3-2	Laskey	Scott
27—Atlanta	W	6-0	Krukow	Camp
28—Atlanta	L	3-4	Mahler	Davis
29—Atlanta	L	3-4	Perez	Calvert
31—At Cinn.	L	0-3	Tibbs	Robinson

Won 10, Lost 17

AUGUST

Date	W/L	Score	Winner	Loser
1—At Cinn.	L	3-6	Price	Lavelle
2—At Cinn.	W	5-2	Krukow	Pastore
3—At Atlanta	L	1-2‡	Moore	Minton
4—At Atlanta	W	9-2	Calvert	McMurtry
5—At Atlanta	W	7-4	Lavelle	Garber
6—At Hous.	L	0-8	Knepper	Laskey
7—At Hous.	W	9-2	Krukow	Scott
8—At Hous.	L	6-7§	Dawley	Calvert
9—At Hous.	L	0-6	LaCoss	Robinson
10—Los Ang.	W	4-1	Calvert	Valenzuela
11—Los Ang.	L	2-4	Honeycutt	Laskey
12—Los Ang.	L	4-5†	Pena	Davis
14—Montreal	L	6-7	Gullickson	Davis
15—Montreal	L	3-8	Schatzeder	Calvert
16—Montreal	L	3-11	Lea	Lacey
17—New York	L	0-2†	Gooden	Krukow
18—New York	W	6-5	Lerch	Gaff
19—New York	W	7-6	Lavelle	Orosco
19—New York	L	2-4	Berenyi	Davis
20—Phila.	L	4-6	Denny	Calvert
21—Phila.	L	5-12	Gross	Williams
22—Phila.	W	7-5	Davis	Holland
24—At N.Y.	W	7-6	Williams	Orosco
24—At N.Y.	W	6-5	Williams	Terrell
25—At N.Y.	W	5-4	Lerch	Berenyi
26—At N.Y.	L	6-11	Gaff	Krukow
27—At Mon.	W	5-4‡	Williams	Reardon
28—At Mon.	W	3-2	Robinson	Smith
29—At Mon.	W	4-3‡	Minton	Grapenthin
30—At Phila.	W	6-5	Lacey	Holland
30—At Phila.	L	5-6	Andersen	Davis
31—At Phila.	W	6-5	Laskey	Koosman

Won 16, Lost 16

SEPTEMBER

Date	W/L	Score	Winner	Loser
1—At Phila.	W	7-2	Hammaker	Hudson
2—At Phila.	L	3-8	Rawley	Robinson
3—Cincinnati	W	4-3	Minton	Russell
4—Cincinnati	L	3-8	Soto	Minton
5—Houston	L	1-4	Ryan	Lerch
6—Houston	L	2-14	Knepper	Laskey
7—Atlanta	W	5-4	Grant	Garber
8—Atlanta	W	4-0	Laskey	McMurtry
9—Atlanta	W	6-4	Davis	Brizzolara
11—At Cinn.	L	3-7	Soto	Lerch
12—At Cinn.	L	4-7	Tibbs	Grant
14—At Atlanta	W	3-0	Minton	Moore
15—At Atlanta	L	1-4	Camp	Krukow
16—At Atlanta	L	5-7	Mahler	Laskey
17—At Hous.	L	3-5	Niekro	Grant
18—At Hous.	L	4-5†	Smith	Garrelts
19—At S. Diego	L	4-5†	Hawkins	Garrelts
20—At S. Diego	L	4-5	Lollar	Krukow
21—Los Ang.	W	5-1	Laskey	Valenzuela
22—Los Ang.	W	8-7	Garrelts	Zachry
23—Los Ang.	W	4-2	Riley	Hooton
24—San Diego	L	1-7	Harris	Robinson
24—San Diego	L	6-8‡	DeLeon	Lacey
25—San Diego	W	4-3	Krukow	Lollar
26—San Diego	L	0-4	Show	Laskey
28—At L.A.	L	3-4	Welch	Williams
29—At L.A.	L	3-4‡	Niedenfuer	Williams
30—At L.A.	L	2-7	Hershiser	Davis

Won 10, Lost 18

*5 innings.   †10 innings.   ‡11 innings.   §12 innings.   x13 innings.   y15 innings.   z18 innings.

Rick Sutcliffe compiled an amazing 16-1 record after joining the Cubs and earned N.L. Cy Young honors.

Chicago Catches 'Cub Fever'

By JOE GODDARD

Most people were shocked by the Chicago Cubs' meteoric rise from fifth place to the top of the National League East. Bob Marks wasn't. He said it was written in the stars.

Marks, a San Francisco astrologer, studied the universe and came up with this startling prediction: "The Cubs will start slowly. They'll fight among themselves but make their move August 18 and be totally awesome."

Hire that man!

Marks missed his mark by only 2½ weeks. The Cubs moved into first place on August 1 and stayed there the last 61 days of the season to bring Chicago's North Side its first baseball crown in 39 years.

The ingredients for a championship team were not evident in spring training, which first-year Manager Jim Frey referred to as "horrendous." It included the release of veteran pitcher Fergie Jenkins, two intrasquad brawls and a 7-20 exhibition record.

The regular season was a different matter. The Cubs were in the race from the start as they finished April tied for the division lead with the New York Mets. They led or were tied for the lead on 11 different occasions, the longest being a 13-day stretch in May, before capturing the top spot for good with two months to go.

Thanks in part to the club's long (but recently undistinguished) heritage and in larger part to the superstation (WGN) that fed Cubs games into the homes of millions of cable television subscribers, "Cub Fever" soon became a nationwide epidemic. The Atlanta Braves, another club with national appeal thanks to cable TV, found that they were upstaged—for 1984, at least—as "America's Team."

The Cubs also were a big hit at home. By drawing more than 2.1 million fans, the Cubs smashed their home attendance record (set in 1969) by almost 430,000. And Chicago played well at Wrigley Field, going 51-29 there in '84. The team's success let the '69 Cubs, who had blown a big lead in September to the Miracle Mets, off the hook.

Ironically, New York was Chicago's principal foe in '84, but the Mets lost 12 of 18 games between the two clubs and finished 6½ games out.

The Cubs' improvement from 71-91 in 1983 to 96-65 was built on astute trades by General Manager Dallas Green and steady, relaxed guidance from Frey, who

Gary Matthews came in a preseason trade and provided some much-needed leadership.

became the first manager ever to win a divisional title in his first season in each league. (Frey led Kansas City to the World Series in 1980, his first season in the American League.)

Frey and Green worked well in tandem. Every time Frey expressed a need, Green

SCORES OF CHICAGO CUBS' 1984 GAMES

APRIL

Date		Score	Winner	Loser
3—At S. Fran.	W	5-3	Ruthven	Davis
5—At S. Fran.	W	11-7	Rainey	Krukow
6—At S. Diego	L	2-3	Monge	Smith
7—At S. Diego	L	6-7	Dravecky	Trout
8—At S. Diego	W	8-5*	Smith	Thurmond
9—At L.A.	L	2-4	Reuss	Rainey
11—At L.A.	L	1-2	Honeycutt	Sanderson
13—New York	W	11-2	Trout	Gooden
14—New York	W	5-2	Ruthven	Leary
18—St. Louis	L	0-5	Andujar	Rainey
18—St. Louis	W	6-1	Sanderson	LaPoint
19—St. Louis	W	6-1	Trout	Cox
20—Pittsburgh	W	5-4*	Stoddard	Tekulve
21—Pittsburgh	L	5-8	DeLeon	Noles
23—At St. L.	W	6-2	Sanderson	LaPoint
24—At St. L.	W	3-2	Stoddard	Sutter
25—At St. L.	L	5-7	Lahti	Ruthven
27—At Pitts.	L	2-3	Rhoden	Rainey
28—At Pitts.	W	7-1	Sanderson	McWilliams
29—At Pitts.	W	2-1	Trout	Candelaria

Won 12, Lost 8

MAY

Date		Score	Winner	Loser
1—At N.Y.	L	1-8	Gooden	Ruthven
2—At N.Y.	L	3-4	Lynch	Smith
4—San Diego	W	7-6	Smith	Monge
5—San Diego	W	6-5*	Brusstar	Lefferts
6—San Diego	L	5-8	Show	Ruthven
7—San Fran.	W	10-7	Rainey	Davis
8—San Fran.	W	12-11	Smith	Minton
9—Los Ang.	W	7-0	Sanderson	Hooton
10—Los Ang.	L	1-5	Welch	Trout
11—At Hous.	L	1-3	Ryan	Ruthven
12—At Hous.	W	5-4	Noles	DiPino
13—At Hous.	L	0-1	Madden	Reuschel
15—At Cinn.	W	6-3	Noles	Pastore
16—At Cinn.	W	10-4	Trout	Russell
17—At Cinn.	L	3-5	Soto	Ruthven
18—Houston	W	7-6	Stoddard	Smith
19—Houston	W	5-4	Reuschel	Dawley
20—Houston	W	10-3	Bordi	Scott
23—Atlanta	W	3-1	Trout	McMurtry
24—Atlanta	W	10-7	Rainey	Perez
24—Atlanta	W	7-5	Reuschel	Falcone
25—Cincinnati	L	0-3	Hume	Noles
26—Cincinnati	L	6-7	Scherrer	Trout
27—Cincinnati	L	3-4	Berenyi	Eckersley
29—At Atlanta	L	4-7	Perez	Brusstar
30—At Atlanta	W	6-2	Trout	Barker
31—At Phila.	L	2-10	Hudson	Rainey

Won 15, Lost 12

JUNE

Date		Score	Winner	Loser
1—At Phila.	W	12-3	Reuschel	Bystrom
2—At Phila.	L	2-3	Holland	Smith
3—At Phila.	W	11-2	Trout	Gross
5—At Mon.	W	3-2	Rainey	Smith
6—At Mon.	L	1-8	Gullickson	Reuschel
7—At Mon.	L	1-2	Lea	Eckersley
8—At St. L.	L	4-5	Lahti	Stoddard
9—At St. L.	W	5-0	Bordi	Stuper
10—At St. L.	W	2-0	Rainey	Andujar
11—Montreal	L	1-2	James	Smith
12—Montreal	W	11-4	Eckersley	Lea
13—Montreal	W	7-4	Stoddard	Lucas
14—Phila.	L	2-11	Carlton	Bordi
15—Phila.	L	2-5	Hudson	Rainey
16—Phila.	L	2-8	Bystrom	Reuschel
17—Phila.	L	7-9	Gross	Eckersley
19—At Pitts.	W	4-3	Sutcliffe	Tudor
20—At Pitts.	L	1-5	DeLeon	Rainey
21—At Pitts.	L	6-8	Rhoden	Eckersley
22—St. Louis	W	9-3	Reuschel	Stuper
23—St. Louis	W	12-11†	Smith	Rucker
24—St. Louis	W	5-0	Sutcliffe	Horton
25—Pittsburgh	L	0-3	DeLeon	Rainey
26—Pittsburgh	L	0-9	Rhoden	Eckersley
26—Pittsburgh	W	9-8	Bordi	McWilliams
27—Pittsburgh	W	8-7†	Stoddard	Scurry
28—At L.A.	W	5-3	Trout	Pena
29—At L.A.	L	1-7	Hershiser	Sutcliffe
30—At L.A.	W	14-4	Frazier	Howell

Won 15, Lost 14

JULY

Date		Score	Winner	Loser
1—At L.A.	W	4-3	Eckersley	Valenzuela
2—At S. Diego	L	1-5	Dravecky	Reuschel
3—At S. Diego	W	3-2	Trout	Thurmond
4—At S. Diego	W	2-1	Sutcliffe	Show
5—At S. Fran.	W	9-3	Sanderson	Laskey

JULY

Date		Score	Winner	Loser
6—At S. Fran.	W	5-4	Stoddard	Minton
7—At S. Fran.	L	2-7	Krukow	Reuschel
8—At S. Fran.	W	6-3	Sutcliffe	Davis
12—Los Ang.	W	3-2*	Stoddard	Niedenfuer
13—Los Ang.	W	7-5	Sutcliffe	Welch
14—Los Ang.	L	0-8	Hershiser	Sanderson
15—Los Ang.	W	4-1	Eckersley	Valenzuela
16—San Diego	L	0-4	Thurmond	Ruthven
17—San Diego	L	5-6	Show	Trout
18—San Diego	W	4-1	Sutcliffe	Whitson
19—San Fran.	W	6-4	Frazier	Davis
20—San Fran.	L	2-3	Robinson	Eckersley
21—San Fran.	W	4-3†	Bordi	Minton
22—San Fran.	L	5-11	Krukow	Trout
23—At Phila.	W	3-2	Sutcliffe	Rawley
24—At Phila.	L	2-3	Koosman	Stoddard
25—At Phila.	W	9-4	Eckersley	Hudson
27—At N.Y.	L	1-2	Gooden	Ruthven
28—At N.Y.	W	11-4	Smith	Sisk
29—At N.Y.	W	3-0	Trout	Terrell
29—At N.Y.	W	5-1	Sanderson	Berenyi
30—Phila.	W	3-2	Eckersley	Hudson
31—Phila.	L	1-2‡	Holland	Stoddard

Won 18, Lost 10

AUGUST

Date		Score	Winner	Loser
1—Phila.	W	5-4	Smith	Holland
2—Montreal	W	3-2	Sutcliffe	Smith
3—Montreal	L	5-6	Reardon	Stoddard
4—Montreal	W	4-1	Eckersley	Schatzeder
5—Montreal	W	4-3	Reuschel	Grapenthin
6—New York	W	9-3	Ruthven	Gooden
7—New York	W	8-6	Sutcliffe	Darling
7—New York	W	8-4	Stoddard	Lynch
8—New York	W	7-6	Smith	Gardner
9—At Mon.	L	0-1*	Schatzeder	Frazier
10—At Mon.	L	2-4	James	Stoddard
11—At Mon.	W	2-1	Smith	Lea
12—At Mon.	W	7-3	Sutcliffe	Rogers
13—At Hous.	L	1-2	Dawley	Sanderson
14—At Hous.	L	6-7	Solano	Frazier
15—At Hous.	L	2-6	Knepper	Eckersley
17—At Cinn.	L	4-6	Soto	Ruthven
18—At Cinn.	W	13-11	Sutcliffe	Robinson
19—At Cinn.	W	9-6	Frazier	Russell
20—Houston	W	6-1	Trout	Knepper
21—Houston	W	11-5	Eckersley	Scott
22—Houston	L	3-8	Ryan	Ruthven
24—Atlanta	W	3-0	Sutcliffe	Camp
25—Atlanta	L	2-3	Mahler	Sanderson
26—Atlanta	W	5-0	Trout	Perez
28—Cincinnati	W	5-2	Eckersley	McGaffigan
28—Cincinnati	W	5-2	Ruthven	Pastore
29—Cincinnati	W	7-2	Sutcliffe	Russell
30—At Atlanta	W	8-3*	Smith	Garber
31—At Atlanta	L	2-3	Moore	Smith

Won 20, Lost 10

SEPTEMBER

Date		Score	Winner	Loser
1—At Atlanta	W	4-1	Bordi	McMurtry
2—At Atlanta	W	4-2	Ruthven	Mahler
3—At Phila.	W	4-3‡	Frazier	Martin
4—At Phila.	W	7-2	Sanderson	Carlton
5—At Mon.	L	1-3	Palmer	Trout
6—At Mon.	W	4-1	Frazier	Lea
7—At N.Y.	L	0-10	Gooden	Ruthven
8—At N.Y.	W	6-0	Sutcliffe	Terrell
9—At N.Y.	L	1-5	Darling	Frazier
10—Phila.	W	3-2	Stoddard	Koosman
11—Phila.	L	3-6	Hudson	Smith
12—Montreal	W	11-5	Stoddard	Smith
14—New York	W	7-1	Sutcliffe	Darling
15—New York	W	5-4	Sanderson	Fernandez
16—New York	L	3-9	Berenyi	Trout
18—Pittsburgh	L	2-6	Tudor	Eckersley
19—Pittsburgh	L	6-11	McWilliams	Stoddard
20—Pittsburgh	L	6-7	Tekulve	Smith
21—At St. L.	L	0-8	Kepshire	Sanderson
23—At St. L.	W	8-1	Trout	Ownbey
23—At St. L.	W	4-2	Eckersley	Andujar
24—At Pitts.	W	4-1	Sutcliffe	McWilliams
25—At Pitts.	L	1-7	DeLeon	Patterson
26—At Pitts.	W	5-2	Ruthven	Tunnell
28—St. Louis	L	1-4*	Andujar	Bordi
29—St. Louis	W	9-5	Eckersley	Cox
30—St. Louis	W	2-1	Frazier	Sutter

Won 16, Lost 11

*10 innings. †11 innings. ‡12 innings.

satisfied it with a deal.

At the end of spring training, Green gave Frey a leadoff man and center fielder in Bob Dernier and an experienced leader in Gary Matthews. All Philadelphia got in return was overworked reliever Bill Campbell and minor league catcher Mike Diaz.

And when injuries struck starting pitchers Dick Ruthven and Scott Sanderson, the latter an acquisition from Montreal in a three-team winter trade, Green brought in Dennis Eckersley from Boston for the popular-but-benched Bill Buckner, plus Rick Sutcliffe (and pitcher George Frazier and catcher Ron Hassey) from Cleveland for young outfielders Mel Hall and Joe Carter (and two minor leaguers).

"When we got Dernier and Matthews, I felt we had become a .500 team," Frey said. "Getting Eckersley and Sutcliffe made us contenders."

Sutcliffe, who lost 15 pounds while recovering from root-canal surgery, was 4-5 with the Indians but was virtually unbeatable with the Cubs. He compiled a 2.69 earned-run average and went 16-1, including victories in all three of his decisions against New York, and won the National League Cy Young Award. The righthander also became only the fourth pitcher to win 20 games in a season in different leagues. (Another irony is that the last person to do it was Chicago's Hank Borowy in 1945, the Cubs' last championship season.)

Eckersley, another righthander, was 10-8 with a 3.03 ERA for Chicago. Lefthander Steve Trout had his best season ever with a 13-7 record and a 3.41 ERA, while Sanderson (3.14 ERA) went 8-5 despite back problems. Only Ruthven (6-10) had a losing record among the regular starters.

Strapping Lee Smith led the relief corps with 33 saves, second in the league to St. Louis' record-setting Bruce Sutter. The bullpen also was strengthened by the acquisition from Oakland of Tim Stoddard, who won 10 games and earned seven saves. Frazier, Rich Bordi and Warren Brusstar combined for 10 more saves to give the bullpen a total of 50, one below the league high.

While Sutcliffe led the Cubs on the mound, Ryne Sandberg led the team at the plate. Sandberg, who was voted the league's Most Valuable Player in 1984, came within one triple and one home run of being the first player ever to collect 200 hits, 20 doubles, 20 triples, 20 homers and 20 stolen bases in a year. The Gold Glove second baseman also sparkled in the field, enjoying an errorless streak of 62 games

and making only six errors, one over the major league season record for second basemen.

Batting second, Sandberg teamed with his former partner in the Phillies' chain, Dernier, to form what announcer Harry Caray called the Cubs' "Daily Double." He hit .314 (fourth in the league), Dernier .278, while the two combined for 77 stolen bases, 349 hits, 62 doubles and 208 runs scored. Sandberg led the league in that last category by scoring 114 runs, and he knocked in 84 more.

Several other Cubs had good years offensively. Third baseman Ron Cey led the team in homers with 25 and in runs batted in with 97. Leon Durham, who turned in another good season at first base by making just seven errors, batted .279 with 23 homers and 96 RBIs. Left fielder Matthews hit .291 with 14 homers and 82 RBIs and led the league in walks (103), on-base percentage (.410) and game-winning RBIs (19). Catcher Jody Davis hit 19 homers and drove in 94 runs, while right fielder Keith Moreland added 16 homers and 80 RBIs while batting .279.

The only regular who had an off season at the plate was shortstop Larry Bowa (.223, 17 RBIs), but his experience and leadership were invaluable down the stretch.

As a team, the Cubs batted .260 to rank fourth in the league and finished first in runs scored (762) and walks (567) and second in home runs (136). Defensively, the Cubs made 121 errors, just three more than St. Louis, the league's least error-prone team.

"I felt very good about the way in which our ball club went out on the field and played from April to October," Frey said. "I never got the feeling a player wasn't giving 100 percent."

The Cubs played above .500 every month during the regular season. Unfortunately for the North Siders, that was not true in October, when Chicago was 2-3. Those five playoff games determined the National League representative in the World Series, and it appeared after the first two games, which Chicago won by 13-0 and 4-2 scores, that the Cubs were a shoo-in. But the unthinkable occurred as the San Diego Padres stormed back to sweep the next three games at home and win the playoffs.

Cubs players and fans alike were crushed, dumbfounded. What had seemed all but theirs—the club's first N.L. pennant since 1945—suddenly slipped through their grasp.

Thirty-nine years . . . and counting.

Dwight Gooden, a 19-year-old rookie, led the major leagues with 276 strikeouts and gave Mets fans plenty of reasons for optimism.

Young Pitchers Spark Mets

By JACK LANG

When Frank Cashen announced the appointment of Dave Johnson as manager of the Mets in October of 1983, the executive vice president and general manager called Johnson a "proven winner, as a player and as a manager." Cashen added: "It's exciting to have him managing the Mets. Our club is ready to make a move, and Johnson can be the catalyst."

Six months later, when Johnson expressed a commitment to youth and decided to go with an almost all-rookie pitching staff, Cashen still was confident. "We can win," he said. "I don't see a standout team in our division."

Forgive Cashen for his apparent lack of foresight. When he made the remark one week before the end of spring training, the Chicago Cubs had not yet acquired Rick Sutcliffe or Dennis Eckersley, and the deals for Bob Dernier and Gary Matthews were only in the talking stage. The Cubs' roster at that time did not feature many of the key players who helped bring Chicago its first National League East crown ever and its first opportunity for postseason play since 1945.

So, the emergence of the Cubs was a surprise. There was a "standout team" in the division. But Cashen wasn't far off in his lofty projections for the Mets. New York won 90 games—22 more than in 1983 —and finished second in the division, 6½ games behind Chicago. With a rookie manager, a rookie pitching staff and a rookie catcher (Mike Fitzgerald), the Mets were as much of a surprise as the Cubs.

Good pitching was largely responsible for the Mets' success. After veterans Craig Swan, Dick Tidrow and Mike Torrez were released early in the season, New York was left with a pitching staff that featured no one in his 30s (until August), and this group of young pitchers quickly became the talk of the league.

Dwight Gooden clearly ranked at the top of his class. The 19-year-old rookie demonstrated remarkable control and poise, not to mention an uncanny ability to strike out batters. While walking only 73 men, Gooden recorded a major league-leading 276 strikeouts in 218 innings, breaking Herb Score's major league rookie record of 245 strikeouts in one season. He became the youngest player in All-Star Game history in July and proceeded to baffle American League batters by striking out the side in the first of his two

First baseman Keith Hernandez hit .311 and provided leadership for the youthful Mets.

innings on the mound. Gooden, who ranked second in the league with a 2.60 earned-run average, wound up with a 17-9 record to lead the Mets' staff and was named the league's Rookie of the Year.

Among the other starters, Ron Darling was 12-9 with a 3.81 ERA. The rookie enjoyed a great first half that included seven straight wins. Walt Terrell was a solid starter who finished with an 11-12 record and a 3.52 ERA in his second year in the majors. Bruce Berenyi, who turned 30 in August, two months after he was traded to New York from Cincinnati, was 9-6 with the Mets after going 3-7 for the Reds before the trade.

The bullpen, led by Jesse Orosco and Doug Sisk, was superb until Sisk suffered a shoulder ailment in late July. Sisk was virtually useless for the next month, which Johnson said was the most difficult period of the year for the Mets. Though their second-half efforts did not match

SCORES OF NEW YORK METS' 1984 GAMES

APRIL

Date	W/L	Score	Winner	Loser
2—At Cinn.	L	1-8	Soto	Torrez
4—At Cinn.	W	2-0	Darling	Berenyi
6—At Hous.	W	8-1	Terrell	Scott
7—At Hous.	W	3-2	Gooden	Knepper
8—At Hous.	W	3-1	Leary	Niekro
10—At Atlanta	W	4-2	Swan	McMurtry
11—At Atlanta	W	6-1	Terrell	Dayley
13—At Chicago	L	2-11	Trout	Gooden
14—At Chicago	L	2-5	Ruthven	Leary
17—Montreal	L	0-10	Smith	Darling
18—Montreal	W	5-4	Lynch	Reardon
19—Montreal	W	7-6	Orosco	Schatzeder
20—At Phila.	W	3-1*	Sisk	Holland
21—At Phila.	L	2-12	Denny	Torrez
22—At Phila.	L	5-12	Hudson	Darling
23—At Mon.	L	4-6	Lea	Terrell
25—At Mon.	W	2-1†	Orosco	Harris
27—Phila.	L	3-8	Campbell	Sisk
28—Phila.	W	4-3	Lynch	Holland
29—Phila.	W	6-2	Terrell	Koosman

Won 12, Lost 8

MAY

Date	W/L	Score	Winner	Loser
1—Chicago	W	8-1	Gooden	Ruthven
2—Chicago	W	4-3	Lynch	Smith
4—Houston	W	2-0	Darling	Knepper
5—Houston	L	6-10	Dawley	Orosco
6—Houston	L	1-10	Ryan	Gooden
7—Cincinnati	L	2-11	Soto	Leary
9—Atlanta	W	3-1	Darling	Mahler
10—Atlanta	L	3-7	Barker	Terrell
11—At L.A.	W	2-0	Gooden	Valenzuela
12—At L.A.	W	4-3	Lynch	Pena
13—At L.A.	L	3-5	Honeycutt	Torrez
15—At S. Fran.	W	7-6†	Orosco	Davis
16—At S. Fran.	L	3-4	Davis	Terrell
18—At S. Diego	L	4-5	Whitson	Gooden
19—At S. Diego	L	3-8	Thurmond	Lynch
20—At S. Diego	W	4-2*	Orosco	Lefferts
22—San Fran.	L	4-5	Davis	Darling
24—San Fran.	L	2-3	Krukow	Terrell
25—Los Ang.	W	2-1	Gooden	Honeycutt
26—Los Ang.	W	2-1	Leary	Niedenfuer
27—Los Ang.	L	2-3	Welch	Torrez
28—San Diego	L	4-5	Show	Gaff
31—St. Louis	L	2-5	Forsch	Terrell

Won 10, Lost 13

JUNE

Date	W/L	Score	Winner	Loser
1—St. Louis	L	1-5	Andujar	Orosco
2—St. Louis	W	5-2	Lynch	Cox
3—St. Louis	L	0-1	LaPoint	Torrez
4—At Pitts.	W	4-2	Darling	Robinson
5—At Pitts.	W	3-0	Terrell	DeLeon
6—At Pitts.	W	2-1§	Gorman	Scurry
8—At Mon.	W	4-1	Lynch	Rogers
9—At Mon.	W	5-3	Darling	Palmer
9—At Mon.	W	6-5	Torrez	McGaffigan
10—At Mon.	L	2-3	Schatzeder	Terrell
11—Pittsburgh	W	3-1	Gooden	Rhoden
12—Pittsburgh	L	3-6	McWilliams	Leary
13—Pittsburgh	W	2-0	Lynch	Tunnell
14—At St. L.	W	6-0	Darling	Stuper
15—At St. L.	W	5-0	Terrell	Andujar
16—At St. L.	W	4-1	Gooden	Cox
17—At St. L.	L	3-6	Horton	Berenyi
19—Phila.	L	4-6	Koosman	Lynch
20—Phila.	W	7-4	Darling	Carlton
21—Phila.	W	10-7	Orosco	Campbell
22—Montreal	L	1-2	Gullickson	Gooden
23—Montreal	W	2-0	Berenyi	Lea
24—Montreal	L	3-5	Smith	Lynch
25—At Phila.	W	10-5	Darling	Hudson
26—At Phila.	L	0-3	Gross	Terrell
27—At Phila.	L	1-5	Bystrom	Gooden
28—Atlanta	L	3-5	McMurtry	Berenyi
29—Atlanta	L	3-5	Bedrosian	Lynch

Won 16, Lost 12

JULY

Date	W/L	Score	Winner	Loser
1—Atlanta	W	2-1	Darling	Mahler
1—Atlanta	W	3-2	Leary	Dedmon
2—Houston	W	4-2	Gooden	Scott
3—Houston	W	4-3	Berenyi	Ryan
4—Houston	L	5-10	Knepper	Lynch
5—Cincinnati	W	4-3	Terrell	Price
6—Cincinnati	W	1-0	Darling	Russell
6—Cincinnati	W	6-5	Orosco	Power
7—Cincinnati	W	14-4	Gooden	Soto
8—Cincinnati	W	7-3	Berenyi	Puleo
12—At Atlanta	W	8-6	Orosco	Moore
13—At Atlanta	W	5-4	Terrell	Perez
14—At Atlanta	W	7-0	Berenyi	McMurtry
15—At Atlanta	L	3-8	Moore	Gooden
16—At Houston	W	13-3	Fernandez	Scott
17—At Houston	L	2-3	DiPino	Sisk
18—At Houston	W	3-1	Terrell	Ryan
19—At Cinn.	L	6-9	Soto	Berenyi
20—At Cinn.	W	3-2†	Orosco	Lesley
21—At Cinn.	W	2-1	Fernandez	Hume
22—At Cinn.	W	7-6	Gorman	Cato
23—St. Louis	W	4-3‡	Lynch	Allen
24—St. Louis	W	9-8*	Gaff	Allen
25—St. Louis	W	9-3	Fernandez	Kepshire
27—Chicago	W	2-1	Gooden	Ruthven
28—Chicago	L	4-11	Smith	Sisk
29—Chicago	L	0-3	Trout	Terrell
29—Chicago	L	1-5	Sanderson	Berenyi
30—At St. L.	L	1-3*	Lahti	Orosco
31—At St. L.	L	3-6	Kepshire	Lynch

Won 21, Lost 9

AUGUST

Date	W/L	Score	Winner	Loser
1—At St. L.	L	2-11	Andujar	Gooden
2—At Pitts.	L	4-6	Robinson	Darling
3—At Pitts.	W	4-1	Terrell	Candelaria
4—At Pitts.	W	4-3	Gorman	Scurry
5—At Pitts.	W	3-1*	Gardner	Robinson
6—At Chicago	L	3-9	Ruthven	Gooden
7—At Chicago	L	6-8	Sutcliffe	Darling
7—At Chicago	L	4-8	Stoddard	Lynch
8—At Chicago	L	6-7	Smith	Gardner
9—Pittsburgh	L	0-11	Rhoden	Berenyi
10—Pittsburgh	L	1-4	Tudor	Fernandez
11—Pittsburgh	W	3-1	Gooden	McWilliams
12—Pittsburgh	W	6-3	Darling	DeLeon
13—At L.A.	L	2-9	Welch	Terrell
14—At L.A.	W	4-0	Berenyi	Hershiser
15—At L.A.	W	3-2	Fernandez	Valenzuela
17—At S. Fran.	W	2-0*	Gooden	Krukow
18—At S. Fran.	L	5-6	Lerch	Gaff
19—At S. Fran.	L	6-7	Lavelle	Orosco
19—At S. Fran.	W	4-2	Berenyi	Davis
20—At S. Diego	L	1-3	Show	Fernandez
21—At S. Diego	L	4-7	Lollar	Lynch
22—At S. Diego	W	5-2	Gooden	Hawkins
24—San Fran.	L	6-7	Williams	Orosco
24—San Fran.	L	5-6	Williams	Terrell
25—San Fran.	L	4-5	Lerch	Berenyi
26—San Fran.	W	11-6	Gaff	Krukow
27—Los Ang.	W	5-1	Gooden	Valenzuela
28—Los Ang.	W	5-1	Terrell	Honeycutt
29—Los Ang.	W	3-2	Orosco	Zachry
31—San Diego	L	1-5	Whitson	Fernandez
31—San Diego	W	4-0	Berenyi	Dravecky

Won 15, Lost 17

SEPTEMBER

Date	W/L	Score	Winner	Loser
1—San Diego	W	7-4	Gooden	Hawkins
1—San Diego	W	10-6	Gorman	Show
2—San Diego	W	3-2‡	Gaff	Gossage
3—At St. L.	L	3-7	Andujar	Darling
4—At St. L.	L	2-12	Cox	Fernandez
5—At Pitts.	W	4-2	Berenyi	Tunnell
6—At Pitts.	L	2-7	Rhoden	Schiraldi
7—Chicago	W	10-0	Gooden	Ruthven
8—Chicago	L	0-6	Sutcliffe	Terrell
9—Chicago	W	5-1	Darling	Frazier
10—St. Louis	L	2-3	LaPoint	Fernandez
11—St. Louis	L	5-9	Allen	Orosco
12—Pittsburgh	W	2-0	Gooden	Tudor
13—Pittsburgh	L	4-14	McWilliams	Terrell
14—At Chicago	L	1-7	Sutcliffe	Darling
15—At Chicago	L	4-5	Sanderson	Fernandez
16—At Chicago	W	9-3	Berenyi	Trout
17—At Phila.	L	1-2	Rawley	Gooden
18—At Phila.	W	8-5	Gorman	Andersen
19—At Phila.	L	5-13	Carlton	Darling
21—Montreal	W	6-2	Fernandez	Schazeder
22—Montreal	W	4-2	Gorman	James
23—Montreal	W	6-1	Gooden	Hesketh
24—Phila.	W	7-5	Orosco	Andersen
25—Phila.	W	6-4	Lynch	Andersen
26—Phila.	W	7-1	Fernandez	Koosman
28—At Mon.	L	0-7	Hesketh	Schiraldi
29—At Mon.	W	8-4	Terrell	Smith
30—At Mon.	L	4-5	Gullickson	Darling

Won 16, Lost 13

*10 innings.   †11 innings.   ‡12 innings.   §13 innings.

Jesse Orosco anchored the Mets bullpen with 31 saves and a 2.59 ERA.

their stellar performances before the All-Star break, Orosco still wound up with a club-record 31 saves and a 2.59 ERA, and Sisk chipped in with 15 saves and a 2.09 ERA. Only the Willie Hernandez-Aurelio Lopez duo in Detroit combined for as many saves as Orosco and Sisk.

As good as the Mets were, they were unable to win the crucial games, namely the ones against the Cubs. In late July, the Mets led the division by 3½ games when the Cubs visited Shea Stadium. New York won the opener but lost the next three, and the Cubs left town 1½ games out. The Mets went to Chicago a week later and were swept in four straight. By that time they were 4½ games behind the Cubs, who never relinquished their lead. Overall, New York lost 12 of 18 games with Chicago.

Darryl Strawberry, the 1983 National League Rookie of the Year, was spectacular at times but ordinary at others. He ranked fourth in the league with 26 home runs and tied for fourth with 97 runs bat-

ted in, both team-leading figures. He hit no home runs in either May or August, however, and though he closed strong with nine homers and 30 RBIs in September, the race by then was all but over for the Mets. Strawberry's .251 batting average also was below expectations, and twice he had to be lectured by Johnson for reporting late for practice. In addition, his effort in the outfield often was lackadaisical.

While Strawberry was alternately up and down, first baseman Keith Hernandez provided consistent leadership the entire season. The 30-year-old veteran was superb defensively as well as at the plate, where he produced a .311 average, seventh in the league. Hernandez also ranked among the leaders in RBIs (94), game-winning RBIs (17), walks (97) and on-base percentage (.409).

Left fielder George Foster had his best season since being traded to the Mets in 1982, hitting .269 with 24 homers and 86 RBIs. Switch-hitting center fielder Mookie Wilson was a threat from either side of the plate, batting .276 lefthanded and .275 righthanded. Wilson contributed a team-high 46 stolen bases.

Shortstop was a problem for New York in 1984. Johnson tried Jose Oquendo and Rafael Santana at the position but settled on neither player. Santana swung a hotter bat (.276), but Oquendo (.222) was the slicker fielder. When Santana went on the disabled list and Ray Knight was acquired from Houston in late August, however, third baseman Hubie Brooks was moved to short. Knight hit .280 in 93 at-bats for the Mets, and as both players performed admirably in the field, it appeared as if Johnson might stay put with the new left side of his infield.

Brooks, who had a 24-game hitting streak from May 1 through June 1, was another of New York's offensive leaders, hitting .283 with 16 homers and 73 RBIs. Second basemen Wally Backman (.280) and rookie Kelvin Chapman (.289 in 197 at-bats) also contributed to the Mets' team batting average of .257, an increase of 16 points over 1983.

Though several players had good years, only Gooden was exceptional, which may explain why the Mets had to settle for runner-up status.

"Nobody on my team is having a better year than we might have expected," Johnson said during the season. "The Cubs have several players who are having their best years."

Still, the jump from last to second place was better than almost anyone predicted —except Cashen.

Cardinals center fielder Willie McGee took over the leadoff spot and responded with a .291 average and 43 stolen bases.

Offensive Woes Hurt Cards

By RICK HUMMEL

The St. Louis Cardinals staged a strong September finish to wind up in third place in the National League East, which was rather remarkable considering that there was a three-way race for the division title —and they weren't in it.

The Cubs, Mets and Phillies provided all the excitement in the N.L. East while the Cardinals spent most of their season in fourth or fifth place. A customary slide by Montreal, a late-season collapse by Philadelphia, which lost its last nine games, and a 17-13 September by St. Louis made it possible for the Cards to slip into the first division by season's end with an 84-78 record.

A benign offensive attack that hit a league-low 75 home runs while batting a paltry .252 as a team (compared with a .270 mark the year before) was the main reason for the Cardinals' poor showing.

After a season that included more valleys than mountaintops, Manager Whitey Herzog was asked to determine the highlights of 1984. Herzog replied that only rookie third baseman Terry Pendleton, among the everyday players, had exceeded expectations.

Pendleton, a second baseman in his first two seasons of professional baseball, was expected to spend '84 in the minors. But when Andy Van Slyke didn't satisfy Herzog at third base after Ken Oberkfell was traded to Atlanta, Pendleton was recalled from the club's Triple-A affiliate in Louisville in mid-July. Pendleton promptly batted .430 for his first three weeks in the majors while playing marvelously at third base. The switch-hitter finished with a .324 batting average, 33 runs batted in and 20 stolen bases in 67 games.

On the other hand, outfielders Lonnie Smith and George Hendrick were huge disappointments, and catcher Darrell Porter wasn't much better.

Smith, a .316 lifetime hitter, slumped to an even .250 although he led the club with 50 stolen bases and 70 walks. Hendrick, one of the Cards' few power hitters, raised his average to .277 with a late surge before missing the last three weeks of the season to undergo thyroid surgery. But he hit just nine home runs, and his team-leading 69 RBIs was his second-lowest season total since 1974.

Porter started quickly but drove in only 18 runs in the last two months of the season. He wound up at .232 with 68 RBIs and 11 home runs.

Ozzie Smith continued to display his defensive wizardry and contributed 35 stolen bases.

"There were five guys who didn't do it," said Herzog, adding first baseman David Green and utilityman Van Slyke to the list of disappointments. "Greenie did come back (after alcohol-abuse treatment). But I really did think he'd drive in 90 runs."

Green, who missed three weeks after he followed the club's suggestion to seek help for drinking problems, hit 13 homers after returning on June 15, giving him a club-high 15 for the season. He drove in 65 runs while batting .268.

Van Slyke, who drifted between the infield, the outfield and the bench, batted just .244 but was one of the team's best hitters with men in scoring position, driving in 50 runs on just 88 hits.

The Cardinals undoubtedly would have been in the division race if those five players had not had subpar seasons. But a number of other players made solid contributions all season and helped the Cardinals avoid a second consecutive second-division finish since winning the World Series in 1982.

SCORES OF ST. LOUIS CARDINALS' 1984 GAMES

APRIL

Date	W/L	Score	Winner	Loser
3—At L.A.	W	11-7	Cox	Valenzuela
5—At L.A.	L	2-5§	Hershiser	Lahti
6—At S. Fran.	W	2-0	Andujar	Laskey
7—At S. Fran.	L	0-11	Robinson	LaPoint
8—At S. Fran.	W	9-3	Allen	Davis
10—At S. Diego	L	3-7	Hawkins	Forsch
11—At S. Diego	L	5-7	Lollar	Andujar
13—Pittsburgh	W	4-1	LaPoint	Candelaria
14—Pittsburgh	W	7-5	Cox	Rhoden
15—Pittsburgh	W	1-0	Rucker	McWilliams
18—At Chicago	W	5-0	Andujar	Rainey
18—At Chicago	L	1-6	Sanderson	LaPoint
19—At Chicago	L	1-6	Trout	Cox
21—Montreal	L	3-6	Rogers	Stuper
21—Montreal	L	0-4*	Palmer	Forsch
22—Montreal	L	2-4	Smith	Andujar
23—Chicago	L	2-6	Sanderson	LaPoint
24—Chicago	L	3-2	Stoddard	Sutter
25—Chicago	W	7-5	Lahti	Ruthven
27—At Mon.	W	8-2	Andujar	Rogers
28—At Mon.	W	6-1	LaPoint	Smith
29—At Mon.	L	2-6	Lea	Cox
30—At Pitts.	W	5-3	Sutter	Tunnell

Won 11, Lost 12

MAY

Date	W/L	Score	Winner	Loser
1—At Pitts.	W	10-5	Andujar	DeLeon
2—At Pitts.	W	3-1	LaPoint	Rhoden
4—San Fran.	L	0-2	Robinson	Cox
5—San Fran.	L	0-7*	Williams	Forsch
6—San Fran.	L	2-3	Laskey	Andujar
7—Los Ang.	W	5-1	LaPoint	Honeycutt
8—Los Ang.	L	1-2	Reuss	Cox
9—San Diego	L	2-3	Thurmond	Stuper
10—San Diego	W	7-0	Andujar	Lollar
11—At Cinn.	L	3-4	Russell	LaPoint
12—At Cinn.	L	1-2	Soto	Sutter
13—At Cinn.	W	6-2	Stuper	Owchinko
15—Atlanta	W	9-1	Andujar	Barker
16—Atlanta	W	4-2	LaPoint	McMurtry
17—Atlanta	L	2-7	Perez	Cox
18—Cincinnati	W	5-3	Stuper	Price
19—Cincinnati	W	9-1	Andujar	Berenyi
20—Cincinnati	W	3-2	Allen	Hume
21—Houston	L	2-3	Ryan	Forsch
22—Houston	L	3-4‡	Dawley	Sutter
23—Houston	L	0-4	Knepper	Andujar
25—At Atlanta	L	4-8	Barker	LaPoint
26—At Atlanta	L	3-7	Mahler	Allen
27—At Atlanta	W	12-9	Andujar	McMurtry
28—At Atlanta	L	2-6	Falcone	Cox
29—At Hous.	L	0-1	Knepper	LaPoint
30—At Hous.	W	6-4	Horton	DiPino
31—At N.Y.	W	5-2	Forsch	Terrell

Won 13, Lost 15

JUNE

Date	W/L	Score	Winner	Loser
1—At N.Y.	W	5-1	Andujar	Orosco
2—At N.Y.	L	2-5	Lynch	Cox
3—At N.Y.	W	1-0	LaPoint	Torrez
4—Phila.	W	4-3‡	Sutter	Holland
5—Phila.	W	5-3	Andujar	Hudson
6—Phila.	W	4-3	Allen	Campbell
8—Chicago	W	5-4	Lahti	Stoddard
9—Chicago	L	0-5	Bordi	Stuper
10—Chicago	L	0-2	Rainey	Andujar
11—At Phila.	W	6-4	Cox	Bystrom
12—At Phila.	W	7-2	Horton	Gross
13—At Phila.	L	1-4	Koosman	LaPoint
14—New York	L	0-6	Darling	Stuper
15—New York	L	0-5	Terrell	Andujar
16—New York	L	1-4	Gooden	Cox
17—New York	W	6-3	Horton	Berenyi
19—At Mon.	L	3-6	Rogers	Dayley
20—At Mon.	W	2-0	Andujar	Reardon
22—At Chicago	L	3-9	Reuschel	Stuper
23—At Chicago	L	11-12‡	Smith	Rucker
24—At Chicago	L	0-5	Sutcliffe	Horton
25—Montreal	W	5-4	Andujar	Rogers
26—Montreal	W	6-3	Stuper	Palmer
27—Montreal	L	2-4	Gullickson	Citarella
28—At S. Diego	L	3-7	Thurmond	Dayley
29—At S. Diego	W	5-0	Horton	Show
30—At S. Diego	W	4-1	Andujar	Lollar

Won 14, Lost 13

JULY

Date	W/L	Score	Winner	Loser
1—At S. Diego	L	1-3	Whitson	LaPoint
3—At S. Fran.	L	2-6	Krukow	Allen
4—At S. Fran.	W	4-3	Horton	Davis
4—At S. Fran.	W	5-1	Kepshire	Robinson
5—At L.A.	W	3-0	Allen	Welch
6—At L.A.	L	2-3§	Howell	Allen
7—At L.A.	L	0-3	Pena	Ownbey
8—At L.A.	W	8-6§	Sutter	Zachry
12—San Diego	L	1-4	Show	Andujar
13—San Diego	W	7-4†	Allen	DeLeon
14—San Diego	W	7-6	LaPoint	Lollar
15—San Diego	L	1-6	Dravecky	Kepshire
16—San Fran.	L	6-7	Laskey	Ownbey
17—San Fran.	L	2-7	Krukow	Andujar
18—San Fran.	W	8-4‡	Von Ohlen	Lacey
19—Los Ang.	L	0-10	Hershiser	LaPoint
20—Los Ang.	W	10-5	Kepshire	Valenzuela
21—Los Ang.	L	1-3	Honeycutt	Andujar
22—Los Ang.	W	7-6	Cox	Welch
23—At N.Y.	L	3-4§	Lynch	Allen
24—At N.Y.	L	8-9†	Gaff	Allen
25—At N.Y.	L	3-9	Fernandez	Kepshire
27—At Pitts.	W	3-2†	Andujar	Tekulve
28—At Pitts.	W	5-1	Cox	DeLeon
29—At Pitts.	W	4-3	Allen	Candelaria
30—New York	W	3-1†	Lahti	Orosco
31—New York	W	6-3	Kepshire	Lynch

Won 14, Lost 13

AUGUST

Date	W/L	Score	Winner	Loser
1—New York	W	11-2	Andujar	Gooden
2—Phila.	L	2-3	Rawley	Cox
3—Phila.	W	4-3	Horton	Koosman
4—Phila.	W	3-2	LaPoint	Andersen
5—Phila.	L	3-6	Campbell	Lahti
6—Pittsburgh	L	2-3	McWilliams	Andujar
7—Pittsburgh	W	2-1	Cox	DeLeon
8—Pittsburgh	L	4-6	Candelaria	Horton
9—At Phila.	L	1-2x	Campbell	Rucker
10—At Phila.	W	3-0†	Sutter	Andersen
11—At Phila.	L	1-6	Carlton	Andujar
13—Cincinnati	W	5-3	Horton	Soto
14—Cincinnati	W	8-2	LaPoint	Russell
15—Cincinnati	L	2-3‡	Hume	Sutter
17—Atlanta	W	3-1	Andujar	Perez
18—Atlanta	L	3-8	Brizzolara	Cox
19—Atlanta	W	8-5	Horton	Camp
20—At Cinn.	W	9-7	Lahti	Tibbs
21—At Cinn.	L	1-4	Price	Kepshire
22—At Cinn.	W	6-3	Andujar	Soto
23—At Hous.	L	6-9	Smith	Rucker
24—At Hous.	L	2-7	Niekro	Horton
25—At Hous.	L	2-5	Knepper	LaPoint
26—At Hous.	W	3-2	Kepshire	Ryan
28—At Atlanta	W	5-3†	Sutter	Garber
29—At Atlanta	W	10-6	Allen	McMurtry
31—Houston	W	7-5	Allen	Ryan

Won 15, Lost 12

SEPTEMBER

Date	W/L	Score	Winner	Loser
1—Houston	L	4-8	Ross	Kepshire
2—Houston	W	4-1	Horton	Niekro
3—New York	W	7-3	Andujar	Darling
4—New York	W	12-2	Cox	Fernandez
5—Phila.	W	6-5	Rucker	Holland
6—Phila.	W	6-5	Forsch	Campbell
7—At Pitts.	L	1-4	Tudor	Horton
8—At Pitts.	W	9-2	Andujar	McWilliams
9—At Pitts.	W	2-1	Cox	DeLeon
10—At N.Y.	W	3-2	LaPoint	Fernandez
11—At N.Y.	W	9-5	Allen	Orosco
12—At Phila.	L	1-3	Rawley	Kepshire
12—At Phila.	L	5-6	McGraw	Sutter
13—At Phila.	L	2-10	Denny	Andujar
14—Pittsburgh	L	7-8§	Robinson	Sutter
15—Pittsburgh	W	8-3	LaPoint	Candelaria
16—Pittsburgh	W	8-7†	Hassler	Tunnell
18—Montreal	L	4-7	Smith	Andujar
19—Montreal	W	1-0	Cox	Rogers
20—Montreal	W	3-2	LaPoint	Gullickson
21—Chicago	W	8-0	Kepshire	Sanderson
23—Chicago	L	1-8	Trout	Ownbey
23—Chicago	L	2-4	Eckersley	Andujar
24—At Mon.	L	1-2	Reardon	Allen
25—At Mon.	W	6-4	Hagen	Gullickson
26—At Mon.	W	5-0	Kepshire	Schatzeder
27—At Mon.	L	3-6	Palmer	Forsch
28—At Chicago	W	4-1†	Andujar	Bordi
29—At Chicago	L	5-9	Eckersley	Cox
30—At Chicago	L	1-2	Frazier	Sutter

Won 17, Lost 13

*5 innings.   †10 innings.   ‡11 innings.   §12 innings.   x13 innings.

One bright spot for the Cardinals was Terry Pendleton, who took over third base duties and hit .324.

Center fielder Willie McGee became a consistent leadoff man for St. Louis, batting a point above his career average of .290 and pacing his teammates with 166 hits, 11 triples, 225 total bases and 82 runs scored. McGee also was second on the team in steals with 43.

The Cardinals stole a club-record and major league-high 220 bases, marking the third year in a row they had equaled or surpassed 200. That made them the first team in more than 60 years to steal 200 or more bases in three straight years. (The last previous team to do that, the St. Louis Browns, stole 200 or more bases in the four seasons from 1913 to 1916.)

Shortstop Ozzie Smith was his normally splendid self in the field as the Cardinals led the league with 184 double plays and committed the fewest errors (118). He also stole 35 bases, batted .257 (a point below his major league career high) and drove in 44 runs despite missing five weeks because of a broken wrist he suffered when he was hit by a pitch from San Diego's Ed Whitson.

Second baseman Tom Herr answered any questions about his ability to overcome knee surgery by making just six errors, stealing 13 bases and batting .276 with a career-high 49 RBIs.

Outfielder Tito Landrum batted over .300 most of the season and was the Cardinals' best player off the bench. Landrum, who started several games when Lonnie Smith was in a slump, finished at .272 with 26 RBIs in 173 at-bats. Steve Braun, though suffering through a drought of his own most of the year, collected his 100th career pinch-hit the last week of the season at Montreal.

The Cardinals' pitching staff, led by Joaquin Andujar and Bruce Sutter, was surprisingly effective in 1984.

Sutter had the best year of his career with a tidy 1.54 earned-run average and a National League-record 45 saves, which tied Kansas City's Dan Quisenberry for the major league record.

Andujar, coming off a miserable 6-16 season in '83, had the first 20-victory season of his career. The righthander went 20-14 with a 3.34 ERA while regaining his form of 1982, when he was a World Series hero.

Lefthander Dave LaPoint, who never has had a losing season in eight years of professional baseball, contributed 12 victories, while rookies Rick Horton and Kurt Kepshire were pleasant surprises.

Horton, originally programmed for relief duty, gained eight of his nine victories as a starter and flirted with a no-hitter at San Diego on June 29 before allowing a two-out, eighth-inning double to Kevin McReynolds and settling for a two-hit shutout. Kepshire, a righthander called up in July, was 6-5 and finished with two straight shutouts.

Another young righthander, Danny Cox, was 9-11 but was 6-3 after being recalled from Louisville in July. Neil Allen, a righthander with enormous potential, had a roller-coaster season pitching mostly long relief but wound up with a 9-6 record, a 3.55 ERA and three saves.

One veteran who was expected to be part of the starting rotation, Bob Forsch, was lost for most of the season with a back injury. Forsch was placed on the disabled list June 1 but returned to win one more game, doubling his season victory total.

Attendance at Busch Stadium was not as anemic as the Cardinals' offense in 1984. More than 2 million fans watched the Cardinals at home for the third consecutive year, although the '84 total of 2,037,448 was about 280,000 less than the year before.

Second baseman Juan Samuel was an offensive sparkplug, but hurt the Phillies by committing 33 errors.

Bad Second Half Ruins Phillies

By PETER PASCARELLI

Ever notice how a company with a successful product will add a couple of new ingredients, label the product "new and improved" and hope for even better market results?

The Philadelphia Phillies tried that in 1984. After winning the National League pennant the year before, the Phils dispensed with several key players—Pete Rose and Joe Morgan were released, while Bob Dernier, Gary Matthews, Tony Perez, Willie Hernandez and Ron Reed were dealt in trades—then added such players as Glenn Wilson, John Wockenfuss, Jerry Koosman, Bill Campbell and Mike Diaz. Presto, there were the "new and improved" Phillies.

The team didn't sell. Oh, the Phils drew more than 2 million fans to Veterans Stadium for the eighth time in the last nine years, but they didn't cut it in the most important market: The N.L. East standings. They finished fourth with an 81-81 record, 15½ games behind the Chicago Cubs (who were pleased to add Dernier and Matthews to their roster).

The Phils were in the hunt for a while. It was a nip-and-tuck three-way race in the East Division through the All-Star break, and Philadelphia was on top in early July. But the Phils tumbled in the second half and never seriously challenged for the title again.

Instead, the Phillies finished the season with a nine-game losing streak. On the last day of the season, Manager Paul Owens resigned to become the assistant to Phils President Bill Giles. Owens was replaced by coach John Felske, who became Philly's fourth manager in the last four years.

But no one pretended that managing—despite the short tenure of recent skippers—was the major reason for the Phils' collapse. Nor were the personnel moves necessarily to blame, even though Dernier and Matthews were stars for Chicago and Hernandez won the American League Cy Young Award with the world champion Detroit Tigers. Many factors were involved, with injuries ranking near the top of the list.

Thirteen Phillies went on the disabled list at one time or another in 1984. Several other players were nagged by injuries but remained on the list of active players.

The biggest blow was the loss of pitcher John Denny for more than two months because of elbow problems. Denny, the 1983 Cy Young Award winner, was leading the National League in earned-run average when he damaged the radial nerve in his elbow in late May. The right-hander missed more than a dozen starts and finished with a 7-7 record and a 2.45 ERA.

As a result, the Phils' bullpen lost effective long reliever Kevin Gross (8-5, 4.12 ERA), who had to start in Denny's place. That stretched the bullpen thin, and by season's end, the entire staff had notched only 35 saves.

Lefty Al Holland broke his own club record for saves with 29, but only four of them came after August 7. Plagued by overwork earlier in the season, Holland saw his record drop from 5-5 at the end of July to a final 5-10 mark.

Another key injury was to outfielder Joe Lefebvre, whose season-ending knee injury in June deprived the Phils of a potentially effective run producer. Also included in the glut of injuries were front-line catcher Bo Diaz, first baseman Len Matuszek (.248 batting average, 43 runs batted in and 12 home runs in 262 at-bats) and outfielder Garry Maddox (.282, five homers and 19 RBIs in 241 at-bats). Though reserves such as catcher Ozzie Virgil (.261, 18 homers, 68 RBIs) and first baseman Tim Corcoran (.341 in 208 at-bats) surfaced to become key players, the series of injuries robbed the Phils of their depth, which was to have been their biggest strength.

The other dominant Phillie theme (along with injuries) was errors. The Phils committed more miscues than any team in the league for most of the season before the Dodgers and Giants out-blundered the Phils near the end of the season to rank 11th and 12th, respectively, in that category. Philadelphia also allowed the league's most unearned runs (104) while turning the fewest double plays (112).

The club's defensive problems constantly defused its occasional stabs at consistency on the mound. "It killed us in an awful lot of games, especially in the first 100 games or so," Owens said. "We wasted a lot of good pitching because of defense."

Some of the Phils' worst performances were saved for Veterans Stadium, where they finished with a 39-42 record. They were 42-39 on the road.

Despite these problems, the division title still was within reach in early August. It was then that a team batting slump took over, wasting an amazing string of consis-

SCORES OF PHILADELPHIA PHILLIES' 1984 GAMES

APRIL

Date	W/L	Score	Winner	Loser
3—At Atlanta	W	5-0	Carlton	Barker
4—At Atlanta	L	0-4	McMurtry	Denny
6—At Cinn.	W	8-4	Hudson	Price
7—At Cinn.	W	9-1	Koosman	Pastore
8—At Cinn.	L	7-8‡	Smith	Andersen
10—Houston	W	3-1	Denny	Ryan
11—Houston	W	7-6	Campbell	Dawley
13—At Mon.	L	1-5	Lea	Koosman
14—At Mon.	W	4-3	Andersen	Schatzeder
17—At Pitts.	W	4-1	Hudson	Tudor
18—At Pitts.	L	3-6	Candelaria	Koosman
20—New York	L	1-3†	Sisk	Holland
21—New York	W	12-2	Denny	Torrez
22—New York	W	12-5	Hudson	Darling
24—Pittsburgh	L	2-3	Candelaria	Koosman
25—Pittsburgh	W	8-7	McGraw	Tunnell
27—At N.Y.	W	8-3	Campbell	Sisk
28—At N.Y.	L	3-4	Lynch	Holland
29—At N.Y.	L	2-6	Terrell	Koosman
30—Montreal	L	2-5	McGaffigan	Carlton

Won 11, Lost 9

MAY

Date	W/L	Score	Winner	Loser
1—Montreal	W	7-4	Gross	James
2—Montreal	L	2-3	James	Denny
4—Cincinnati	L	5-9	Pastore	Hudson
5—Cincinnati	W	11-2	Koosman	Berenyi
6—Cincinnati	L	3-5	Franco	Carlton
7—Atlanta	L	6-8	Perez	Bystrom
8—Atlanta	L	2-8	Falcone	Denny
9—At Hous.	L	1-7	Knepper	Hudson
10—At Hous.	L	2-4	Scott	Koosman
11—At S. Diego	W	6-4	Holland	Dravecky
12—At S. Diego	W	3-2	Campbell	Hawkins
13—At S. Diego	W	8-3	Denny	Whitson
14—At L.A.	W	3-2	Hudson	Reuss
15—At L.A.	W	12-1	Koosman	Welch
16—At L.A.	W	7-2	Carlton	Valenzuela
18—At S. Fran.	W	1-0	Bystrom	Krukow
19—At S. Fran.	W	6-2	Denny	Martin
20—At S. Fran.	W	7-4	Hudson	Robinson
22—Los Ang.	W	3-1	Koosman	Welch
23—Los Ang.	L	0-1	Valenzuela	Carlton
24—Los Ang.	W	4-3	Holland	Zachry
25—San Diego	L	3-7	Whitson	Hudson
26—San Diego	W	7-2	Bystrom	Thurmond
27—San Diego	L	0-4	Lollar	Koosman
30—San Fran.	W	3-2	Holland	Minton
31—Chicago	W	10-2	Hudson	Rainey

Won 16, Lost 10

JUNE

Date	W/L	Score	Winner	Loser
1—Chicago	L	3-12	Reuschel	Bystrom
2—Chicago	W	3-2	Holland	Smith
3—Chicago	L	2-11	Trout	Gross
4—At St. L.	L	3-4‡	Sutter	Holland
5—At St. L.	L	3-5	Andujar	Hudson
6—At St. L.	L	3-4	Allen	Campbell
8—Pittsburgh	W	5-4	Koosman	Candelaria
8—Pittsburgh	W	2-1	Gross	McWilliams
9—Pittsburgh	W	6-5	Carlton	Tudor
10—Pittsburgh	L	6-12§	Guante	Kern
11—St. Louis	L	4-6	Cox	Bystrom
12—St. Louis	L	2-7	Horton	Gross
13—St. Louis	W	4-1	Koosman	LaPoint
14—At Chicago	W	11-2	Carlton	Bordi
15—At Chicago	W	5-2	Hudson	Rainey
16—At Chicago	W	8-2	Bystrom	Reuschel
17—At Chicago	W	9-7	Gross	Eckersley
19—At N.Y.	W	6-4	Koosman	Lynch
20—At N.Y.	L	4-7	Darling	Carlton
21—At N.Y.	L	7-10	Orosco	Campbell
22—At Pitts.	L	3-10	McWilliams	Bystrom
22—At Pitts.	L	6-7x	Scurry	Campbell
23—At Pitts.	W	7-5	Koosman	Candelaria
24—At Pitts.	W	4-2	Carlton	Tudor
25—New York	L	5-10	Darling	Hudson
26—New York	W	3-0	Gross	Terrell
27—New York	W	5-1	Bystrom	Gooden
28—Houston	L	6-7	Dawley	Holland
29—Houston	W	7-2	Carlton	Knepper
30—Houston	L	0-7	LaCoss	Hudson

Won 15, Lost 15

JULY

Date	W/L	Score	Winner	Loser
1—Houston	L	1-13	Niekro	Gross
2—Cincinnati	W	4-0	Rawley	Hume
3—Cincinnati	L	5-6	Puleo	Koosman
4—Cincinnati	L	4-5†	Power	Holland
5—Atlanta	W	1-0*	Hudson	Mahler
6—Atlanta	L	0-5	Perez	Gross
7—Atlanta	L	2-5	Camp	Rawley
8—Atlanta	W	7-0	Koosman	McMurtry
12—At Hous.	W	5-3	Carlton	Niekro
13—At Hous.	W	7-3	Rawley	Ryan
14—At Hous.	W	4-3	Koosman	Ruhle
15—At Hous.	L	2-3y	DiPino	Carman
16—At Cinn.	W	7-2	Gross	Hume
17—At Cinn.	W	4-3	Carlton	Price
18—At Cinn.	W	7-5	Rawley	Russell
19—At Atlanta	W	9-1	Koosman	McMurtry
20—At Atlanta	L	1-13	Barker	Hudson
21—At Atlanta	L	3-5	Camp	Gross
22—At Atlanta	W	6-2	Carlton	Mahler
23—Chicago	L	2-3	Sutcliffe	Rawley
24—Chicago	W	3-2	Koosman	Stoddard
25—Chicago	L	4-9	Eckersley	Hudson
27—Montreal	L	1-6	Palmer	Carlton
28—Montreal	L	1-4	Smith	Rawley
29—Montreal	W	6-4	Gross	Reardon
30—At Chicago	L	2-3	Eckersley	Hudson
31—At Chicago	W	2-1§	Holland	Stoddard

Won 14, Lost 13

AUGUST

Date	W/L	Score	Winner	Loser
1—At Chicago	L	4-5	Smith	Holland
2—At St. L.	W	3-2	Rawley	Cox
3—At St. L.	L	3-4	Horton	Koosman
4—At St. L.	L	2-3	LaPoint	Andersen
5—At St. L.	W	6-3	Campbell	Lahti
6—At Mon.	W	4-1	Carlton	Lea
7—At Mon.	W	6-2	Rawley	Smith
7—At Mon.	L	2-3	Reardon	Campbell
8—At Mon.	L	1-3	Gullickson	Koosman
9—St. Louis	W	2-1x	Campbell	Rucker
10—St. Louis	L	0-3†	Sutter	Andersen
11—St. Louis	W	6-1	Carlton	Andujar
14—At S. Diego	L	2-3	Show	Koosman
15—At S. Diego	L	3-4	Gossage	Holland
16—At S. Diego	W	8-3	Denny	Hawkins
17—At L.A.	L	1-2	Honeycutt	Carlton
18—At L.A.	W	6-5	Koosman	Howell
19—At L.A.	W	6-3	Rawley	Welch
20—At S.F.	W	6-4	Denny	Calvert
21—At S.F.	W	12-5	Gross	Williams
22—At S.F.	L	5-7	Davis	Holland
24—Los Ang.	W	6-5†	Gross	Reuss
25—Los Ang.	L	4-7	Welch	Denny
26—Los Ang.	W	10-8	Campbell	Hooton
27—San Diego	W	9-1	Koosman	Lollar
28—San Diego	W	11-8	Rawley	Hawkins
29—San Diego	L	0-2	Thurmond	Denny
30—San Fran.	L	5-6	Lacey	Holland
30—San Fran.	W	6-5	Andersen	Davis
31—San Fran.	L	5-6	Laskey	Koosman

Won 16, Lost 14

SEPTEMBER

Date	W/L	Score	Winner	Loser
1—San Fran.	L	2-7	Hammaker	Hudson
2—San Fran.	W	8-3	Rawley	Robinson
3—Chicago	L	3-4§	Frazier	Martin
4—Chicago	L	2-7	Sanderson	Carlton
5—At St. L.	L	5-6	Rucker	Holland
6—At St. L.	L	5-6	Forsch	Campbell
7—At Mon.	L	1-7	Smith	Rawley
8—At Mon.	L	0-4	Rogers	Denny
9—At Mon.	W	6-5‡	Andersen	Hesketh
10—At Chicago	L	2-3	Stoddard	Koosman
11—At Chicago	W	6-3	Hudson	Smith
12—St. Louis	W	3-1	Rawley	Kepshire
12—St. Louis	W	6-5	McGraw	Sutter
13—St. Louis	W	10-2	Denny	Andujar
14—Montreal	W	9-5	Carlton	Rogers
15—Montreal	L	3-4	Gullickson	Koosman
16—Montreal	L	4-8	Reardon	Martin
17—New York	W	2-1	Rawley	Gooden
18—New York	L	5-8	Gorman	Andersen
19—New York	W	13-5	Carlton	Darling
21—At Pitts.	L	1-5	Scurry	Koosman
22—At Pitts.	L	1-2§	Robinson	Andersen
23—At Pitts.	L	2-4	Tudor	Rawley
24—At N.Y.	L	5-7	Orosco	Andersen
25—At N.Y.	L	4-6	Lynch	Andersen
26—At N.Y.	L	1-7	Fernandez	Koosman
29—Pittsburgh	L	0-4	Rhoden	Hudson
30—Pittsburgh	L	0-2	Tudor	Denny
30—Pittsburgh	L	2-7	McWilliams	Rawley

Won 9, Lost 20

*7 innings.　†10 innings.　‡11 innings.　§12 innings.　x13 innings.　y16 innings.

Von Hayes rebounded from a shaky 1983 by hitting .292 with 16 homers and 67 RBIs.

tent pitching performances. The Phils were unable to gain any ground on Chicago, suffering through one stretch when they lost eight straight times on days when the Cubs also lost.

But overall, several players had fine years at the plate. The Phillies led the league in team batting average (.266), total bases (2,285) and homers (147) while ranking second in runs scored (720) and stolen bases (186).

Mike Schmidt batted .277 and ended up tied for the league lead in home runs with 36 and RBIs with 106. The All-Star third baseman also was among the leaders in walks (92) and slugging percentage (.536) despite suffering a hamstring injury that limited his effectiveness in several games.

Second baseman Juan Samuel shined offensively in his rookie season, hitting .272 with 15 homers and 69 RBIs and leading the club in several categories such as stolen bases (72) and runs scored (105). However, he also led the Phils with 168 strikeouts and was a disaster in the field, making 33 errors, the second-highest total in the league. (San Francisco's Joel Youngblood committed 37 errors.)

Another key offensive leader was outfielder Von Hayes, who rebounded from a shaky 1983 National League debut to hit .292 with 16 homers, 67 RBIs and 48 steals.

That performance quieted the critics who had scoffed at the trade in which five players, including several top prospects, were sent to Cleveland for Hayes.

Philadelphia's other offensive contributors included Greg Gross (.322 in 202 at-bats) and Wockenfuss (.289 in 180 at-bats).

Koosman and Shane Rawley proved to be key pitching acquisitions. Koosman's 14-15 record would have been much better with some offensive support, and he posted an impressive 3.25 ERA with 137 strikeouts. Rawley, who was obtained from the Yankees in a trade, went 10-6 in Philadelphia. Among the other starters, Steve Carlton (13-7, 3.58 ERA, 163 strikeouts) was the most effective, while Charles Hudson struggled to a 9-11 mark.

The 1984 season was a big disappointment for the Phillies, but the club did get a chance to watch several young players whose performances bode well for the team's future.

Outfielder Jeff Stone hit .362 in 185 at-bats while stealing 27 bases. Shortstop Steve Jeltz played the entire month of September and displayed excellent defensive skills—an obvious strong point for the young Phillie—while outfielder John Russell (.283) and third baseman Rick Schu (.276) looked promising.

Tim Raines took over center-field duties for Montreal and hit a team-leading .309 while stealing a league-leading 75 bases.

Expos Drop Out of Contention

By IAN MacDONALD

For the first time in six years, the Montreal Expos were not contenders in the National League East.

When the Expos burst into prominence with a 95-65 record in 1979, they were hailed as the team of the '80s. For five years they were in the race into the final week of the schedule, making the playoffs in 1981 and being eliminated in the final weekend twice.

But the Expos were eliminated on September 14 in 1984. They spent all but 21 days of the season in the bottom half of the division, most often in fifth place, where they finished with a 78-83 record, 18 games behind the Chicago Cubs.

It was no big surprise when Manager Bill Virdon was fired August 30, but Expos President and General Manager John McHale said he had not planned to dismiss Virdon until the latter said he did not want to return in 1985. Expos Vice President Jim Fanning was named interim manager to evaluate the talent available to the team's next skipper.

Shortly after Virdon was fired, McHale relinquished his duties as general manager and hired Murray Cook to fill that role. McHale remained the club's chief executive officer.

The Expos entered the 1984 season loaded with talent and, as always, high expectations. This time, however, the Expos added one player with a winning mystique who they hoped would be the missing ingredient in their championship formula: veteran free agent Pete Rose.

Rose, with his positive attitude, hustle and excellent work habits, was an exciting addition from the start. Tremendous media attention surrounded the Expos as they went into Cincinnati for their third series of the season and Rose prepared to collect the 4,000th hit of his career.

Rose pounded out two hits in each of the first two games of the series to leave him one short of the 4,000-hit plateau. But in the series finale, the Cincinnati fans booed boisterously as Reds pitchers walked Rose four times—he grounded out in his only other plate appearance—and deprived him of the chance to reach the mark in the city where he had spent most of his long career.

Two days later and one day before his 43rd birthday, Rose highlighted the Expos' April 13 home-opening victory over the Phillies with the milestone hit, a double to right field. He joined Ty Cobb to become only the second player in the 4,000-hit club.

Rose began the season playing left field, but when it was decided that his throwing arm was not up to the task, Rose was relegated to spot starts at first base and pinch-hitting. Still, he provided his share of hits—72 in 278 at-bats for a .259 average—and any blame for the Expos' poor showing in '84 did not belong to him.

Rather, the Expos failed, despite excellent overall pitching and All-Star seasons from catcher Gary Carter and outfielder Tim Raines, because they could not survive injuries to three key players: pitcher Steve Rogers, outfielder Andre Dawson and outfielder-first baseman Terry Francona.

Rogers reported to spring training with a twinge in his shoulder and started the season on the disabled list. By the halfway mark he was 3-8 with a 5.73 earned-run average. The year before, Rogers was 12-3 at the break. The righthander had his worst season ever as a major leaguer, finishing with a 6-15 record, a 4.31 ERA and only 64 strikeouts.

Dawson, one of the top center fielders in baseball, was hampered by knee problems all season. The Gold Glover had to be rested periodically, and he was moved to right field to lessen the strain caused by running. Dawson struggled for the first three months of the season, batting .217 through July 5, before he started to resemble the All-Star Dawson of old. He batted .275 after July 5 and finished with 17 home runs and 86 runs batted in.

Francona was the league's second-ranked batter with a .346 mark when he damaged his knee June 14 while trying to dodge a tag on the way to first base. Surgery wiped out the rest of his season.

Another offensive problem for Montreal was the middle part of the infield.

Derrel Thomas, who won the shortstop job after the Expos gave up on their experiment with Doug Flynn and rookie Argenis Salazar, batted .255 and knocked in only 20 runs. Thomas was traded to the California Angels in early September. At second base, Flynn and Bryan Little combined for a .244 average and only 26 RBIs.

Overall, Montreal batted .251, 13 points lower than in '83, and scored 593 runs, the second-lowest total in the league. But there were some bright lights at the plate for the Expos in '84.

Carter, who batted .294, tied Philadelphia's Mike Schmidt for the league lead in

SCORES OF MONTREAL EXPOS' 1984 GAMES

APRIL

Date	W/L	Score	Winner	Loser
3—At Hous.	W	4-2	Lea	Niekro
4—At Hous.	L	2-8	Ryan	Gullickson
6—At Atlanta	W	8-5	Smith	Dayley
7—At Atlanta	W	7-2	Palmer	Falcone
8—At Atlanta	L	2-6	Barker	Lea
9—At Cinn.	L	6-9	Russell	Gullickson
10—At Cinn.	L	6-8	Price	James
11—At Cinn.	W	9-3	Smith	Berenyi
13—Phila.	W	5-1	Lea	Koosman
14—Phila.	L	3-4	Andersen	Schatzeder
17—At N.Y.	W	10-0	Smith	Darling
18—At N.Y.	L	4-5	Lynch	Reardon
19—At N.Y.	L	6-7	Orosco	Schatzeder
21—At St. L.	W	6-3	Rogers	Stuper
21—At St. L.	W	4-0*	Palmer	Forsch
22—At St. L.	W	4-2	Smith	Andujar
23—New York	W	6-4	Lea	Terrell
25—New York	L	1-2‡	Orosco	Harris
27—St. Louis	L	2-8	Andujar	Rogers
28—St. Louis	L	1-6	LaPoint	Smith
29—St. Louis	W	6-2	Lea	Cox
30—At Phila.	W	5-2	McGaffigan	Carlton

Won 12, Lost 10

MAY

Date	W/L	Score	Winner	Loser
1—At Phila.	L	4-7	Gross	James
2—At Phila.	W	3-2	James	Denny
5—Atlanta	W	2-1†	McGaffigan	Garber
6—Atlanta	L	0-2	McMurtry	Lea
6—Atlanta	L	8-9	Dedmon	James
7—Houston	W	4-1	Rogers	Niekro
9—Cincinnati	L	4-6	Hume	Gullickson
10—Cincinnati	L	1-2	Pastore	Smith
11—At S. Fran.	W	7-5	Lea	Laskey
12—At S. Fran.	L	7-8	Krukow	Rogers
13—At S. Fran.	L	3-4	Garrelts	McGaffigan
14—At S. Diego	W	7-6†	Reardon	Dravecky
15—At S. Diego	W	6-4	Smith	Lollar
16—At S. Diego	W	3-2	Lea	Show
17—At S. Diego	L	4-5	Gossage	McGaffigan
18—At L.A.	W	5-4‡	McGaffigan	Niedenfuer
19—At L.A.	L	1-5	Honeycutt	Gullickson
20—At L.A.	L	2-3	Zachry	Smith
22—San Diego	W	3-2	Lea	Show
23—San Diego	L	1-2‡	Dravecky	McGaffigan
25—San Fran.	W	3-2	Reardon	Minton
26—San Fran.	W	4-2	Gullickson	Laskey
27—San Fran.	W	6-2	Lea	Grant
28—Los Ang.	L	1-6	Valenzuela	Rogers
30—Los Ang.	L	1-4	Pena	Smith
31—At Pitts.	L	1-2	DeLeon	Gullickson

Won 12, Lost 14

JUNE

Date	W/L	Score	Winner	Loser
1—At Pitts.	W	2-0	Lea	Rhoden
2—At Pitts.	L	1-2	Tunnell	Rogers
3—At Pitts.	L	0-4	Tudor	Palmer
5—Chicago	L	2-3	Rainey	Smith
6—Chicago	W	8-1	Gullickson	Reuschel
7—Chicago	W	2-1	Lea	Eckersley
8—New York	L	1-4	Lynch	Rogers
9—New York	L	3-5	Darling	Palmer
9—New York	L	5-6	Torrez	McGaffigan
10—New York	W	3-2	Schatzeder	Terrell
11—At Chicago	W	2-1	James	Smith
12—At Chicago	L	4-11	Eckersley	Lea
13—At Chicago	L	4-7	Stoddard	Lucas
14—Pittsburgh	L	2-3	Tekulve	Lucas
15—Pittsburgh	W	1-0	Schatzeder	DeLeon
16—Pittsburgh	W	3-2‡	Reardon	Tekulve
17—Pittsburgh	W	5-3	Lea	McWilliams
19—St. Louis	W	6-3	Rogers	Dayley
20—St. Louis	L	0-2	Andujar	Reardon
22—At N.Y.	W	2-1	Gullickson	Gooden
23—At N.Y.	L	0-2	Berenyi	Lea
24—At N.Y.	W	5-3	Smith	Lynch
25—At St. L.	L	4-5	Andujar	Rogers
26—At St. L.	L	3-6	Stuper	Palmer
27—At St. L.	W	4-2	Gullickson	Citarella
29—At Cinn.	W	7-3	Lea	Scherrer
30—At Cinn.	L	1-4	Soto	Smith

Won 13, Lost 14

JULY

Date	W/L	Score	Winner	Loser
1—At Cinn.	L	1-4	Russell	Rogers
2—At Atlanta	W	5-4	Palmer	Perez
3—At Atlanta	L	3-5	McMurtry	Gullickson
4—At Atlanta	W	7-4	Lea	Bedrosian
5—Houston	L	1-2	LaCoss	Smith
6—Houston	L	2-8	Niekro	Rogers

JULY

Date	W/L	Score	Winner	Loser
6—Houston	W	7-5	Schatzeder	Ruhle
7—Houston	L	2-3	DiPino	James
8—Houston	W	8-5	Gullickson	Ryan
12—Cincinnati	W	3-1	Smith	Price
13—Cincinnati	W	7-2	Gullickson	Russell
14—Cincinnati	W	6-2	Lea	Soto
15—Cincinnati	L	2-3	Tibbs	Rogers
16—Atlanta	W	3-1	Schatzeder	Camp
17—Atlanta	W	2-0	Smith	Mahler
18—Atlanta	L	2-3†	Bedrosian	Gullickson
19—At Hous.	L	2-3	LaCoss	Lucas
20—At Hous.	L	4-8	Knepper	Rogers
21—At Hous.	W	4-2	Palmer	Scott
22—At Hous.	L	1-6	Niekro	Smith
24—Pittsburgh	L	5-12‡	Scurry	Reardon
25—Pittsburgh	L	1-3	Rhoden	Lea
26—Pittsburgh	W	5-4	James	Robinson
27—At Phila.	W	6-1	Palmer	Carlton
28—At Phila.	W	4-1	Smith	Rawley
29—At Phila.	L	4-6	Gross	Reardon
30—At Pitts.	W	3-1	James	Rhoden
31—At Pitts.	L	3-5	Tudor	Rogers

Won 14, Lost 14

AUGUST

Date	W/L	Score	Winner	Loser
1—At Pitts.	L	0-4	McWilliams	Lea
2—At Chicago	L	2-3	Sutcliffe	Smith
3—At Chicago	W	6-5	Reardon	Stoddard
4—At Chicago	L	1-4	Eckersley	Schatzeder
5—At Chicago	L	3-4	Reuschel	Grapenthin
6—Phila.	L	1-4	Carlton	Lea
7—Phila.	L	2-6	Rawley	Smith
7—Phila.	W	3-2	Reardon	Campbell
8—Phila.	W	3-1	Gullickson	Koosman
9—Chicago	W	1-0†	Schatzeder	Frazier
10—Chicago	W	4-2	James	Stoddard
11—Chicago	L	1-2	Smith	Lea
12—Chicago	L	3-7	Sutcliffe	Rogers
14—At S. Fran.	W	7-6	Gullickson	Davis
15—At S. Fran.	W	8-3	Schatzeder	Calvert
16—At S. Fran.	W	11-3	Lea	Lacey
17—At S. Diego	W	8-4	Rogers	Thurmond
19—At S. Diego	W	3-0	Hesketh	Whitson
20—At L.A.	W	3-1	Gullickson	Hershiser
21—At L.A.	L	3-4	Valenzuela	Schatzeder
22—At L.A.	W	5-3‡	James	Howell
24—San Diego	W	4-1	Rogers	Thurmond
24—San Diego	L	4-5	Gossage	Reardon
25—San Diego	L	3-4§	Harris	Reardon
26—San Diego	L	1-2	Show	Schatzeder
27—San Fran.	L	4-5‡	Williams	Reardon
28—San Fran.	L	2-3	Robinson	Smith
29—San Fran.	L	3-4‡	Minton	Grapenthin
30—Los Ang.	W	5-2	Gullickson	Welch
31—Los Ang.	W	5-2	Schatzeder	Hershiser

Won 15, Lost 15

SEPTEMBER

Date	W/L	Score	Winner	Loser
1—Los Ang.	L	3-4	Valenzuela	Lea
2—Los Ang.	W	4-0	Smith	Honeycutt
3—Pittsburgh	L	0-3	McWilliams	Rogers
4—Pittsburgh	L	3-5	Scurry	James
5—Chicago	W	3-1	Palmer	Trout
6—Chicago	L	1-4	Frazier	Lea
7—Phila.	W	7-1	Smith	Rawley
8—Phila.	W	4-0	Rogers	Denny
9—Phila.	L	5-6‡	Andersen	Hesketh
10—At Pitts.	W	8-5	Grapenthin	Tunnell
11—At Pitts.	L	1-5	Rhoden	Bargar
12—At Chicago	L	5-11	Stoddard	Smith
14—At Phila.	L	5-9	Carlton	Rogers
15—At Phila.	W	4-3	Gullickson	Koosman
16—At Phila.	W	8-4	Reardon	Martin
18—At St. L.	W	7-4	Smith	Andujar
19—At St. L.	L	0-1	Cox	Rogers
20—At St. L.	L	2-3	LaPoint	Gullickson
21—At N.Y.	L	2-6	Fernandez	Schatzeder
22—At N.Y.	L	2-4	Gorman	James
23—At N.Y.	L	1-6	Gooden	Hesketh
24—St. Louis	W	2-1	Reardon	Allen
25—St. Louis	L	4-6	Hagen	Gullickson
26—St. Louis	L	0-5	Kepshire	Schatzeder
27—St. Louis	W	6-3	Palmer	Forsch
28—New York	W	7-0	Hesketh	Schiraldi
29—New York	L	4-8	Terrell	Smith
30—New York	W	5-4	Gullickson	Darling

Won 12, Lost 16

*5 innings.   †10 innings.   ‡11 innings.   §13 innings.

RBIs with 106, a career high. The catcher also hit 27 homers to rank third in the league and was named the club's most valuable player.

The switch-hitting Raines, moved from left field to center after Dawson was shifted, hit a team-high .309 with 60 RBIs. He stole 75 bases to capture the league's basestealing title for the fourth time in his four-year major league career and was caught stealing only 10 times. Raines also was among the league leaders in runs scored (106), doubles (38), hits (192) and walks (87).

Third baseman Tim Wallach hit just .246 but provided tremendous run production with 18 homers and 72 RBIs, while outfielder Jim Wohlford batted .300 in 213 at-bats.

Pitching was a strong point for the Expos. The staff's 3.31 ERA was third in the league.

Led by veteran righthander Jeff Reardon with 23, the Expos' bullpen posted a club-record 48 saves. With his final save on the last day of the season, Reardon (7-7, 2.90 ERA) became the Expos' career saves leader with 76. Bob James survived a shaky start to finish at 6-6 with 10 saves.

Charlie Lea (above) paced the Expos with 15 victories while Tim Wallach contributed 18 home runs.

Among the starters, Charlie Lea paced the staff with a 15-10 record, a 2.89 ERA and 123 strikeouts. The righthander was the National League's starting and winning pitcher in the All-Star Game after posting a 13-4 record in the first half of the season. Lea was only 2-6 after that, despite his 2.86 ERA in the second half. In Lea's 10 losses, Montreal supported him with just 13 runs.

Righthander Bill Gullickson was "Mr. Control" for the Expos, walking only 37 batters in 226⅔ innings. He tallied 100 strikeouts, and after losing his first four decisions, Gullickson won 12 of his last 17 decisions to finish at 12-9.

Lefthander Dan Schatzeder split his time between the bullpen and the starting rotation and had an even 7-7 record and a 2.71 ERA. Rounding out the rotation were Bryn Smith (12-13, 3.32 ERA) and David Palmer (7-3, 3.84). The highlight of Palmer's season was a five-inning perfect game April 21 at St. Louis. The game was called because of rain.

Effective pitching, however, was not enough to offset the club's run-scoring lethargy, and the Expos' season dwindled away. Fans in Montreal, perhaps disillusioned with the team's repeated failure to reach its potential, were scarce at Olympic Stadium. The Expos drew only 1.6 million fans at home in '84, compared with 2.3 million the year before.

**Second baseman Johnny Ray hit .312 for a Pirates team that had
trouble scoring runs.**

Pitching Can't Save Pirates

By CHARLEY FEENEY

The Pittsburgh Pirates proved in 1984 that effective pitching does not always lead to a winning record.

The Pirates finished last in the National League East with a 75-87 record while their pitching staff led the major leagues with a composite earned-run average of 3.11. Three Pirates pitchers were among the top eight in the league ERA rankings.

Pittsburgh's problem in 1984 obviously was not pitching, although the bullpen did struggle at times, especially in the first two months of the season. The problem was run production.

The offense scratched and clawed for runs from day one, and when the season ended, there was no one on the team with either 20 home runs or 80 runs batted in. (First baseman Jason Thompson led the club with 17 homers, and catcher Tony Pena was the RBI leader with 78.) The Pirates scored only 615 runs, the third-lowest total in the league, and hit just 98 homers, marking the first time since 1968 that the club had not hit at least 100 homers in a full season. Pittsburgh also was shut out 14 times, more than any other team in the league except Los Angeles.

The problems began when third baseman Bill Madlock, a four-time National League batting champion, opened the season with a sore right shoulder and a spur in his right elbow. He batted .253, his lowest average ever in the major leagues, and underwent season-ending surgery on his elbow and shoulder in mid-August.

Madlock's replacement, Jim Morrison, batted over .320 during the last seven weeks of the season and finished at .286 with 11 homers and 45 RBIs. Second baseman Johnny Ray, a switch-hitter, batted .312 and was equally effective from both sides of the plate. Ray also led the Pirates with 241 total bases and tied for the league lead in doubles with 38.

Left fielder Lee Lacy was the runner-up in the race for the league batting title with a .321 average. He also drove in a career-high 70 runs and hit 12 homers. Center fielder Marvell Wynne, the Pirates' lead-off man, batted .266, led the club in hits (174), runs scored (77, a tie) and stolen bases (24) and gave the Pirates quality defense.

Pena (who batted .286), Ray, Lacy and Wynne deserved high marks as everyday players. But Madlock's ineffectiveness due to his injury and poor production from

Center fielder Marvell Wynne (above) was an offensive plus while veteran Bill Madlock struggled through an injury-riddled season.

SCORES OF PITTSBURGH PIRATES' 1984 GAMES

APRIL

Date		Score	Winner	Loser
3—At S. Diego	L	1-5	Show	Rhoden
5—At S. Diego	L	6-8	DeLeon	Scurry
6—At L.A.	W	3-1	Tudor	Welch
7—At L.A.	W	3-0	Candelaria	Pena
8—At L.A.	W	5-2	Rhoden	Valenzuela
10—At S. Fran.	L	3-4	Krukow	McWilliams
11—At S. Fran.	L	1-2†	Lavelle	Guante
13—At St. L.	L	1-4	LaPoint	Candelaria
14—At St. L.	L	5-7	Cox	Rhoden
15—At St. L.	L	0-1	Rucker	McWilliams
17—Phila.	L	1-4	Hudson	Tudor
18—Phila.	W	6-3	Candelaria	Koosman
20—At Chicago	L	4-5†	Stoddard	Tekulve
21—At Chicago	W	8-5	DeLeon	Noles
24—At Phila.	W	3-2	Candelaria	Koosman
25—At Phila.	L	7-8	McGraw	Tunnell
27—Chicago	W	3-2	Rhoden	Rainey
28—Chicago	L	1-7	Sanderson	McWilliams
29—Chicago	L	1-2	Trout	Candelaria
30—St. Louis	L	3-5	Sutter	Tunnell

Won 7, Lost 13

MAY

Date		Score	Winner	Loser
1—St. Louis	L	5-10	Andujar	DeLeon
2—St. Louis	L	1-3	LaPoint	Rhoden
5—Los Ang.	W	8-7†	Tekulve	Hershiser
6—Los Ang.	L	4-6†	Niedenfuer	Tekulve
6—Los Ang.	W	2-1	Tudor	Valenzuela
10—San Fran.	W	4-2	Rhoden	Robinson
11—At Atlanta	L	2-4†	Forster	Tekulve
12—At Atlanta	L	3-4	Perez	Guante
13—At Atlanta	L	8-9†	Dedmon	Candelaria
14—Houston	W	3-2	DeLeon	Knepper
15—Houston	W	3-2†	Guante	DiPino
16—Houston	L	0-1	Ryan	Candelaria
18—Atlanta	W	6-0	McWilliams	Falcone
19—Atlanta	L	2-4*	Mahler	Tudor
20—Atlanta	L	1-5	Bedrosian	Tekulve
22—Cincinnati	L	3-5	Soto	Scurry
23—Cincinnati	W	7-2	Candelaria	Russell
24—Cincinnati	W	5-1	McWilliams	Price
25—At Hous.	W	6-2	Tudor	Scott
26—At Hous.	L	0-2	Ryan	DeLeon
27—At Hous.	W	2-1	Rhoden	Niekro
28—At Hous.	W	7-0	Candelaria	Ruhle
29—At Cinn.	L	4-5†	Power	Tekulve
30—At Cinn.	L	4-6y	Owchinko	Robinson
31—Montreal	W	2-1	DeLeon	Gullickson

Won 12, Lost 13

JUNE

Date		Score	Winner	Loser
1—Montreal	L	0-2	Lea	Rhoden
2—Montreal	W	2-1	Tunnell	Rogers
3—Montreal	W	4-0	Tudor	Palmer
4—New York	L	2-4	Darling	Robinson
5—New York	L	0-3	Terrell	DeLeon
6—New York	L	1-2x	Gorman	Scurry
8—At Phila.	L	4-5	Koosman	Candelaria
8—At Phila.	L	1-2	Gross	McWilliams
9—At Phila.	L	5-6	Carlton	Tudor
10—At Phila.	W	12-6§	Guante	Kern
11—At N.Y.	L	1-3	Gooden	Rhoden
12—At N.Y.	W	6-3	McWilliams	Leary
13—At N.Y.	L	0-2	Lynch	Tunnell
14—At Mon.	W	3-2	Tekulve	Lucas
15—At Mon.	L	0-1	Schatzeder	DeLeon
16—At Mon.	L	2-3‡	Reardon	Tekulve
17—At Mon.	L	3-5	Lea	McWilliams
19—Chicago	L	3-4	Sutcliffe	Tudor
20—Chicago	W	5-1	DeLeon	Rainey
21—Chicago	W	8-6	Rhoden	Eckersley
22—Phila.	W	10-3	McWilliams	Bystrom
22—Phila.	W	7-6x	Scurry	Campbell
23—Phila.	L	5-7	Koosman	Candelaria
24—Phila.	L	2-4	Carlton	Tudor
25—At Chicago	W	3-0	DeLeon	Rainey
26—At Chicago	W	9-0	Rhoden	Eckersley
26—At Chicago	L	8-9	Bordi	McWilliams
27—At Chicago	L	7-8‡	Stoddard	Scurry
28—At S. Fran.	L	3-4‡	Lavelle	Robinson
29—At S. Fran.	L	0-3	Robinson	Tudor
30—At S. Fran.	L	5-7	Williams	Guante

Won 11, Lost 20

JULY

Date		Score	Winner	Loser
1—At S. Fran.	L	4-7	Hammaker	Rhoden
2—At L.A.	L	4-5	Pena	McWilliams
3—At L.A.	W	6-0	Candelaria	Howell
4—At L.A.	L	0-9	Hershiser	Tudor
5—At S. Diego	L	1-2	Gossage	Scurry
6—At S. Diego	L	3-7	Whitson	Rhoden
7—At S. Diego	L	0-1	Dravecky	McWilliams
8—At S. Diego	W	4-3	Candelaria	Thurmond
12—San Fran.	W	6-3	DeLeon	Laskey
13—San Fran.	W	8-2	Candelaria	Krukow
13—San Fran.	W	4-3z	Scurry	Cornell
14—San Fran.	W	6-2	Rhoden	Davis
15—San Fran.	W	9-3	Tudor	Robinson
16—Los Ang.	W	4-1	Walk	Honeycutt
17—Los Ang.	L	0-5	Pena	DeLeon
18—Los Ang.	W	5-2	McWilliams	Reuss
19—San Diego	W	5-1	Candelaria	Lollar
20—San Diego	W	4-3	Rhoden	Dravecky
20—San Diego	L	2-3	Hawkins	Tudor
21—San Diego	L	4-6	Thurmond	Walk
22—San Diego	L	1-5	Whitson	DeLeon
22—San Diego	W	3-2‡	Winn	Gossage
24—At Mon.	W	12-5‡	Scurry	Reardon
25—At Mon.	W	3-1	Rhoden	Lea
26—At Mon.	L	4-5	James	Robinson
27—St. Louis	L	2-3†	Andujar	Tekulve
28—St. Louis	L	1-5	Cox	DeLeon
29—St. Louis	L	3-4	Allen	Candelaria
30—Montreal	L	1-3	James	Rhoden
31—Montreal	W	5-3	Tudor	Rogers

Won 15, Lost 15

AUGUST

Date		Score	Winner	Loser
1—Montreal	W	4-0	McWilliams	Lea
2—New York	W	6-4	Robinson	Darling
3—New York	L	1-4	Terrell	Candelaria
4—New York	L	3-4	Gorman	Scurry
5—New York	L	1-3†	Gardner	Robinson
6—At St. L.	W	3-2	McWilliams	Andujar
7—At St. L.	L	1-2	Cox	DeLeon
8—At St. L.	W	6-4	Candelaria	Horton
9—At N.Y.	W	11-0	Rhoden	Berenyi
10—At N.Y.	W	4-1	Tudor	Fernandez
11—At N.Y.	L	1-3	Gooden	McWilliams
12—At N.Y.	L	3-6	Darling	DeLeon
14—At Atl.	L	1-3	Camp	Candelaria
15—At Atl.	L	3-7	Bedrosian	Rhoden
16—At Atl.	W	5-2	Tudor	Mahler
17—Houston	L	4-7†	Dawley	Tekulve
18—Houston	L	0-5	LaCoss	DeLeon
19—Houston	L	3-4	Niekro	Candelaria
20—Atlanta	L	1-4†	Garber	Tekulve
21—Atlanta	W	5-4	Robinson	Dedmon
22—Atlanta	W	7-2	McWilliams	Payne
24—Cincinnati	L	0-2	Russell	DeLeon
25—Cincinnati	W	5-3	Candelaria	Tibbs
26—Cincinnati	W	7-1	Rhoden	Price
28—At Hous.	L	2-3	Smith	Tudor
29—At Hous.	W	4-2	Robinson	DiPino
30—At Cinn.	L	1-4	Tibbs	DeLeon
31—At Cinn.	W	6-2	Candelaria	Price

Won 13, Lost 15

SEPTEMBER

Date		Score	Winner	Loser
1—At Cinn.	L	5-7‡	Power	Robinson
2—At Cinn.	L	1-7	Robinson	Tudor
3—At Mon.	W	3-0	McWilliams	Rogers
4—At Mon.	W	5-3	Scurry	James
5—New York	L	2-4	Berenyi	Tunnell
6—New York	W	2-0	Rhoden	Schiraldi
7—St. Louis	W	4-1	Tudor	Horton
8—St. Louis	L	2-9	Andujar	McWilliams
9—St. Louis	L	1-2	Cox	DeLeon
10—Montreal	L	5-8	Grapenthin	Tunnell
11—Montreal	W	5-1	Rhoden	Bargar
12—At N.Y.	L	0-2	Gooden	Tudor
13—At N.Y.	W	14-4	McWilliams	Terrell
14—At St. L.	W	8-7§	Robinson	Sutter
15—At St. L.	L	3-8	LaPoint	Candelaria
16—At St. L.	L	7-8†	Hassler	Tunnell
18—At Chicago	W	6-2	Tudor	Eckersley
19—At Chicago	W	11-6	McWilliams	Stoddard
20—At Chicago	W	7-6	Tekulve	Smith
21—Phila.	W	5-1	Scurry	Koosman
22—Phila.	W	2-1§	Robinson	Andersen
23—Phila.	W	4-2	Tudor	Rawley
24—Chicago	L	1-4	Sutcliffe	McWilliams
25—Chicago	W	7-1	DeLeon	Patterson
26—Chicago	L	2-5	Ruthven	Tunnell
29—At Phila.	W	4-0	Rhoden	Hudson
30—At Phila.	W	2-0	Tudor	Denny
30—At Phila.	W	7-2	McWilliams	Rawley

Won 17, Lost 11

*7 innings. †10 innings. ‡11 innings. §12 innings. x13 innings. y14 innings. z18 innings.

Rick Rhoden led the Pirates with a 14-9 record and 2.72 ERA.

several other players were too much for good pitching and a few good offensive efforts to overcome.

Rookie Doug Frobel was supposed to be free agent Dave Parker's replacement in right field. He flopped. Frobel hit just .203 in 276 at-bats with 28 RBIs, barely double the number of his home runs (12).

Dale Berra was supposed to improve defensively at shortstop. He didn't. He committed a team-high 30 errors, and his .222 batting average was 20 points below his career average.

Thompson was supposed to swing the biggest bat for the Pirates. He didn't. While batting .254, 11 points below his career average, Thompson knocked in 74 runs, his lowest run production in a full major league season since his rookie year in 1976.

When these players slumped, Manager Chuck Tanner had few good backups to turn to. Outfielders Amos Otis (who was released in August after being signed before the season as a free agent and batted .165 in 40 games), Lee Mazzilli (.237), Benny Distefano (.167) and Joe Orsulak (.254) and infielders Denny Gonzalez

(.183), Ron Wotus (.218) and Hedi Vargas (.226) were no better than the regulars they were replacing. Berra's backup, Rafael Belliard, missed most of the season with a broken leg.

Considering the Pirates' lack of run production and the club's overall losing record, it was amazing that four of the starting pitchers in Tanner's season-long rotation wound up with winning records.

Righthander Rick Rhoden led the staff with a 14-9 record, a 2.72 ERA and three shutouts. Posting identical 12-11 records were lefthanders John Candelaria, who tied Rhoden for the team lead in ERA at 2.72, Larry McWilliams (149 strikeouts, 2.93 ERA) and John Tudor (3.27 ERA).

Second-year man Jose DeLeon was the only disappointment among the regular starters. The righthander went 7-13 with a 3.74 ERA and had a stretch of nine consecutive losses. Surprisingly, he paced the staff with 153 strikeouts.

In the bullpen, veteran Kent Tekulve was expected to be the team's righthanded stopper while Rod Scurry would be his lefthanded counterpart. Six games into the season, however, Scurry entered a rehabilitation center near Pittsburgh because of a drug problem and did not return until mid-May. He was inconsistent until the last three weeks of the season, when he put together several strong performances. Scurry finished with a 5-6 record, four saves and a 2.53 ERA.

Tekulve, as usual, was the most active of the Pittsburgh relievers, working in 72 games, but he was not his usual effective self. His 2.66 ERA did not reflect the fact that he often allowed runs that were charged to other pitchers, and the sidearmer finished at 3-9 with only 13 saves.

With Scurry and Tekulve both struggling, the bullpen provided only 34 saves all season. But it would have been worse if not for the contributions of righthander Don Robinson, who made a strong comeback as a reliever after recovering from several shoulder operations that limited him to nine games in '83. Robinson worked a career-high 51 games and posted a 5-6 record with 10 saves and a 3.02 ERA in 1984, making him the most pleasant surprise of the Pirates' season.

Valiant efforts by the pitchers were not enough, however, as the club collected loss after loss. The season was frustrating for the players, not to mention the fans, who stayed away from Three Rivers Stadium in droves. Pittsburgh's home attendance of 773,500 was the lowest of any team in the league.

National League Averages for 1984

CHAMPIONSHIP WINNERS IN PREVIOUS YEARS

1876—Chicago	.788	1912—New York	.682	1948—Boston	.595
1877—Boston	.646	1913—New York	.664	1949—Brooklyn	.630
1878—Boston	.683	1914—Boston	.614	1950—Philadelphia	.591
1879—Providence	.705	1915—Philadelphia	.592	1951—New York†	.624
1880—Chicago	.798	1916—Brooklyn	.610	1952—Brooklyn	.627
1881—Chicago	.667	1917—New York	.636	1953—Brooklyn	.682
1882—Chicago	.655	1918—Chicago	.651	1954—New York	.630
1883—Boston	.643	1919—Cincinnati	.686	1955—Brooklyn	.641
1884—Providence	.750	1920—Brooklyn	.604	1956—Brooklyn	.604
1885—Chicago	.777	1921—New York	.614	1957—Milwaukee	.617
1886—Chicago	.726	1922—New York	.604	1958—Milwaukee	.597
1887—Detroit	.637	1923—New York	.621	1959—Los Angeles‡	.564
1888—New York	.641	1924—New York	.608	1960—Pittsburgh	.617
1889—New York	.659	1925—Pittsburgh	.621	1961—Cincinnati	.604
1890—Brooklyn	.667	1926—St. Louis	.578	1962—San Francisco§	.624
1891—Boston	.630	1927—Pittsburgh	.610	1963—Los Angeles	.611
1892—Boston	.680	1928—St. Louis	.617	1964—St. Louis	.574
1893—Boston	.662	1929—Chicago	.645	1965—Los Angeles	.599
1894—Baltimore	.695	1930—St. Louis	.597	1966—Los Angeles	.586
1895—Baltimore	.669	1931—St. Louis	.656	1967—St. Louis	.627
1896—Baltimore	.698	1932—Chicago	.584	1968—St. Louis	.599
1897—Boston	.705	1933—New York	.599	1969—New York (East)	.617
1898—Boston	.685	1934—St. Louis	.621	1970—Cincinnati (West)	.630
1899—Brooklyn	.677	1935—Chicago	.649	1971—Pittsburgh (East)	.599
1900—Brooklyn	.603	1936—New York	.597	1972—Cincinnati (West)	.617
1901—Pittsburgh	.647	1937—New York	.625	1973—New York (East)	.509
1902—Pittsburgh	.741	1938—Chicago	.586	1974—Los Angeles (West)	.630
1903—Pittsburgh	.650	1939—Cincinnati	.630	1975—Cincinnati (West)	.667
1904—New York	.693	1940—Cincinnati	.654	1976—Cincinnati (West)	.630
1905—New York	.686	1941—Brooklyn	.649	1977—Los Angeles (West)	.605
1906—Chicago	.763	1942—St. Louis	.688	1978—Los Angeles (West)	.586
1907—Chicago	.704	1943—St. Louis	.682	1979—Pittsburgh (East)	.605
1908—Chicago	.643	1944—St. Louis	.682	1980—Philadelphia (East)	.562
1909—Pittsburgh	.724	1945—Chicago	.636	1981—Los Angeles (West)	.573
1910—Chicago	.675	1946—St. Louis*	.628	1982—St. Louis (East)	.568
1911—New York	.647	1947—Brooklyn	.610	1983—Philadelphia (East)	.556

*Defeated Brooklyn, two games to none, in playoff for pennant. †Defeated Brooklyn, two games to one, in playoff for pennant. ‡Defeated Milwaukee, two games to none, in playoff for pennant. §Defeated Los Angeles, two games to one, in playoff for pennant.

STANDING OF CLUBS AT CLOSE OF SEASON

EAST DIVISION

Club	Chi.	N.Y.	St.L.	Phil.	Mon.	Pitt.	Atl.	Cin.	Hou.	L.A.	S.D.	S.F.	W.	L.	Pct.	G.B.
Chicago	..	12	13	9	10	8	9	7	6	7	6	9	96	65	.596	....
New York	6	..	7	10	11	12	8	9	8	9	6	4	90	72	.556	6½
St. Louis	5	11	..	10	9	14	7	8	4	6	5	5	84	78	.519	12½
Philadelphia	9	8	8	..	7	7	5	7	6	9	7	8	81	81	.500	15½
Montreal	7	7	9	11	..	7	7	5	5	6	7	7	78	83	.484	18
Pittsburgh	10	6	4	11	11	..	4	5	6	8	4	6	75	87	.463	21½

WEST DIVISION

Club	S.D.	Atl.	Hou.	L.A.	Cin.	S.F.	Chi.	Mon.	N.Y.	Phil.	Pitt.	St.L.	W.	L.	Pct.	G.B.
San Diego	..	11	12	8	11	13	6	5	6	5	8	7	92	70	.568	....
Atlanta	7	..	12	6	13	10	3	5	4	7	8	5	80	82	.494	12
Houston	6	6	..	9	10	12	6	7	4	6	6	8	80	82	.494	12
Los Angeles	10	12	9	..	11	10	5	6	3	3	4	6	79	83	.488	13
Cincinnati	7	5	8	7	..	12	5	7	3	5	7	4	70	92	.432	22
San Francisco	5	8	6	8	6	..	3	5	8	4	6	7	66	96	.407	26

Championship Series—San Diego defeated Chicago, three games to two.

RECORD AT HOME

EAST DIVISION

Club	Chi.	N.Y.	St.L.	Pitt.	Mon.	Phil.	S.D.	Hou.	L.A.	Cin.	Atl.	S.F.	W.	L.	Pct.
Chicago	......	8-1	7-2	3-6	6-2	3-6	3-3	5-1	4-2	3-3	5-1	4-2	51	29	.638
New York	5-4		4-5	5-4	6-3	7-2	4-2	3-3	5-1	5-1	3-3	1-5	48	33	.593
St. Louis	3-6	6-3	......	6-3	4-5	7-2	3-3	2-4	3-3	5-1	4-2	1-5	44	37	.543
Pittsburgh	4-5	2-7	1-8	......	6-3	6-3	3-3	2-4	4-2	4-2	3-3	6-0	41	40	.506
Montreal	5-4	4-5	4-5	4-5	......	5-4	2-4	3-3	3-3	3-3	3-3	3-3	39	42	.481
Philadelphia	3-6	6-3	6-3	4-5	3-6	......	3-3	3-3	4-2	2-4	2-4	3-3	39	42	.481

WEST DIVISION

Club	S.D.	Hou.	L.A.	Cin.	Atl.	S.F.	Chi.	N.Y.	St.L.	Pitt.	Mon.	Phil.	W.	L.	Pct.
San Diego	....	7-2	4-5	6-3	6-3	6-3	3-3	4-2	4-2	5-1	1-5	2-4	48	33	.593
Houston	4-5	....	5-4	6-3	2-7	7-2	5-1	1-5	4-2	2-4	4-2	3-3	43	38	.531
Los Angeles	5-4	5-4	....	5-4	5-4	6-3	3-3	2-4	3-3	2-4	3-3	1-5	40	41	.494
Cincinnati	4-5	5-4	3-6	....	2-7	8-1	2-4	2-4	3-3	5-1	4-2	1-5	39	42	.481
Atlanta	4-5	5-4	2-7	6-3	....	5-4	2-4	1-5	3-3	3-3	2-4	3-3	38	43	.469
San Francisco	2-7	4-5	5-4	5-4	4-5	....	1-5	3-3	2-4	6-0	2-4	1-5	35	46	.432

RECORD ABROAD

EAST DIVISION

Club	Chi.	N.Y.	Phil.	St.L.	Mon.	Pitt.	S.D.	Atl.	L.A.	Hou.	Cin.	S.F.	W.	L.	Pct.
Chicago	....	4-5	6-3	6-3	4-5	5-4	3-3	4-2	3-3	1-5	4-2	5-1	45	36	.556
New York	1-8	....	3-6	3-6	5-4	7-2	2-4	5-1	4-2	5-1	4-2	3-3	42	39	.519
Philadelphia	6-3	2-7	....	2-7	4-5	3-6	4-2	3-3	5-1	3-3	5-1	5-1	42	39	.519
St. Louis	2-7	5-4	3-6	....	5-4	8-1	2-4	3-3	3-3	2-4	3-3	4-2	40	41	.494
Montreal	2-6	3-6	6-3	5-4	....	3-6	5-1	4-2	3-3	2-4	2-4	4-2	39	41	.488
Pittsburgh	6-3	4-5	5-4	3-6	5-4	....	1-5	1-5	4-2	4-2	1-5	0-6	34	47	.420

WEST DIVISION

Club	S.D.	Atl.	L.A.	Hou.	Cin.	S.F.	Chi.	N.Y.	Phil.	St. L.	Mon.	Pitt.	W.	L.	Pct.
San Diego	....	5-4	4-5	5-4	5-4	7-2	3-3	2-4	3-3	3-3	4-2	3-3	44	37	.543
Atlanta	3-6	....	4-5	7-2	7-2	5-4	1-5	3-3	4-2	2-4	3-3	3-3	42	39	.519
Los Angeles	5-4	7-2	....	4-5	6-3	4-5	2-4	1-5	2-4	3-3	3-3	2-4	39	42	.481
Houston	2-7	4-5	4-5	....	4-5	5-4	1-5	3-3	3-3	4-2	3-3	4-2	37	44	.457
Cincinnati	3-6	3-6	4-5	3-6	....	4-5	3-3	1-5	4-2	1-5	3-3	2-4	31	50	.383
San Francisco	3-6	4-5	3-6	2-7	1-8	....	2-4	5-1	3-3	5-1	3-3	0-6	31	50	.383

SHUTOUT GAMES

Club	S.D.	N.Y.	Hou.	Mon.	L.A.	Pitt.	St.L.	Chi.	S.F.	Phil.	Atl.	Cin.	W.	L.	Pct.
San Diego	..	0	5	0	3	1	0	1	2	2	0	3	17	8	.680
New York	1	..	1	1	2	3	2	1	1	0	1	2	15	8	.652
Houston	0	0	..	0	2	3	1	2	1	0		2	13	9	.591
Montreal	1	2	0	..	1	2	1	1	0	1	1	0	10	8	.556
Los Angeles	3	0	1	0	..	2	2	1	2	1	2	2	16	15	.516
Pittsburgh	0	2	1	3	2	..	0	2	0	2	1	0	13	14	.481
St. Louis	2	1	0	3	1	1	..	2	1	1	0	0	12	13	.480
Chicago	0	2	0	0	1	0	3	..	0	0	2	0	8	10	.444
San Francisco	0	0	0	0	0	1	3	0	..	0	3	0	7	10	.412
Philadelphia	0	1	0	0	0	0	0	0	1	..	3	1	6	10	.375
Atlanta	0	0	1	1	1	0	0	0	0	2	..	2	7	13	.350
Cincinnati	1	0	0	2	1	0	1	1	1	0	0	..	6	12	.333

OFFICIAL NATIONAL LEAGUE BATTING AVERAGES

Compiled by Elias Sports Bureau

CLUB BATTING

Club	Pct.	G.	AB.	R.	OR.	H.	TB.	2B.	3B.	HR.	RBI.	SH.	SF.	SB.	CS.	LOB.
Philad'phia	.266	162	5614	720	690	1494	2285	248	51	147	673	39	46	186	60	1187
San Fran.	.265	162	5650	682	807	1499	2116	229	26	112	646	51	44	126	76	1188
Houston	.264	162	5548	693	630	1465	2058	222	67	79	640	87	55	105	61	1160
Chicago	.260	161	5437	762	658	1415	2157	240	47	136	703	59	51	154	66	1118
San Diego	.259	162	5504	686	634	1425	2043	207	42	109	629	64	55	152	68	1086
New York	.257	162	5438	652	676	1400	2006	235	25	107	607	59	49	149	54	1107
Pittsburgh	.255	162	5537	615	567	1412	2009	237	33	98	586	81	44	96	62	1084
St. Louis	.252	162	5433	652	645	1369	1907	225	44	75	610	68	46	220	71	1101
Montreal	.251	162	5439	593	585	1367	1969	242	36	96	553	74	34	131	38	1149
Atlanta	.247	162	5422	632	655	1338	1959	234	27	111	578	64	45	140	85	1137
Cincinnati	.244	162	5498	627	747	1342	1958	238	30	106	578	71	53	160	63	1148
Los Angeles	.244	162	5399	580	600	1316	1881	213	23	102	530	92	48	109	69	1075
Totals	.255	971	65919	7894	7894	16842	24348	2770	451	1278	7333	809	570	1728	773	13540

INDIVIDUAL BATTING

(Top Fifteen Qualifiers for Batting Championship—502 or More Plate Appearances)

*Bats lefthanded.   †Switch-hitter.

Player and Club	Pct.	G.	AB.	R.	H.	TB.	2B.	3B.	HR.	RBI.	GW.	SH.	SF.	SB.	CS.
Gwynn, Anthony, San Diego*	.351	158	606	88	213	269	21	10	5	71	10	6	2	33	18
Lacy, Leondaus, Pittsburgh	.321	138	474	66	152	220	26	3	12	70	9	12	2	21	11
Davis, Charles, San Francisco†	.315	137	499	87	157	253	21	6	21	81	7	2	2	12	8
Sandberg, Ryne, Chicago	.314	156	636	114	200	331	36	19	19	84	9	5	4	32	7
Ray, Johnny, Pittsburgh†	.312	155	555	75	173	241	38	6	6	67	9	2	6	11	6
Cruz, Jose, Houston*	.312	160	600	96	187	277	28	13	12	95	8	2	10	22	8
Hernandez, Keith, New York*	.311	154	550	83	171	247	31	0	15	94	17	0	9	2	3
Raines, Timothy, Montreal†	.309	160	622	106	192	272	38	9	8	60	13	3	4	75	10
Guerrero, Pedro, Los Angeles	.303	144	535	85	162	247	29	4	16	72	8	1	8	9	8

Player and Club	Pct.	G.	AB.	R.	H.	TB.	2B.	3B.	HR.	RBI.	GW.	SH.	SF.	SB.	CS.
Leonard, Jeffrey, San Francisco	.302	136	514	76	155	249	27	2	21	86	9	0	5	17	7
Puhl, Terrance, Houston*	.301	132	449	66	135	195	19	7	9	55	10	6	4	13	8
Carter, Gary, Montreal	.294	159	596	75	175	290	32	1	27	106	16	0	3	2	2
Hayes, Von, Philadelphia*	.292	152	561	85	164	251	27	6	16	67	3	0	2	48	13
Matthews, Gary, Chicago..................	.291	147	491	101	143	210	21	2	14	82	19	1	10	17	8
McGee, Willie, St. Louist	.291	145	571	82	166	225	19	11	6	50	7	0	3	43	10

DEPARTMENTAL LEADERS: G—Murphy, 162; AB—Samuel, 701; R—Sandberg, 114; H—Gwynn, 213; TB—Murphy, 332; 2B—Raines, Ray, 38; 3B—Samuel, Sandberg, 19; HR—Murphy, Schmidt, 36; RBI—Carter, Schmidt, 106; GW—Matthews, 19; SH—G.C. Reynolds, 16; SF—Cruz, Garvey, Martinez, Matthews, 10; SB—Raines, 75; CS—Wiggins, 21.

(All Players—Listed Alphabetically)

Player and Club	Pct.	G.	AB.	R.	H.	TB.	2B.	3B.	HR.	RBI.	GW.	SH.	SF.	SB.	CS.
Aguayo, Luis, Philadelphia................	.278	58	72	15	20	33	4	0	3	11	0	0	0	0	0
Allen, Neil, St. Louis	.240	57	25	0	6	8	0	1	0	4	0	0	0	0	0
Altamirano, Porfirio, Chicago.............	.000	5	2	0	0	0	0	0	0	0	0	0	0	0	0
Amelung, Edward, Los Angeles*	.217	34	46	7	10	10	0	0	0	4	1	1	0	3	2
Andersen, Larry, Philadelphia............	.000	64	4	0	0	0	0	0	0	0	0	0	0	0	0
Anderson, David, Los Angeles	.251	121	374	51	94	123	16	2	3	34	1	7	5	15	5
Andujar, Joaquin, St. Louist	.131	36	84	8	11	18	1	0	2	8	1	7	0	1	1
Ashby, Alan, Houstont	.262	66	191	16	50	69	7	0	4	27	2	4	3	0	0
Backman, Walter, New Yorkt	.280	128	436	68	122	148	19	2	1	26	7	5	2	32	9
Bailey, J. Mark, Houstont	.212	108	344	38	73	118	16	1	9	34	4	1	3	0	1
Bailor, Robert, Los Angeles	.275	65	131	11	36	40	4	0	0	8	2	3	0	3	1
Baker, Johnnie, San Francisco	.292	100	243	31	71	91	7	2	3	32	4	0	4	4	1
Bannister, Alan, Houston	.200	9	20	2	4	6	2	0	0	0	0	0	0	0	0
Bargar, Gregory, Montreal	.000	3	1	0	0	0	0	0	0	0	0	0	0	0	0
Barker, Leonard, Atlanta	.053	21	38	2	2	3	1	0	0	1	0	4	0	0	0
Barnes, William, Cincinnati...............	.119	32	42	5	5	8	0	0	1	3	1	0	0	0	0
Bass, Kevin, Houstont	.260	121	331	33	86	119	17	5	2	29	3	2	0	5	5
Beane, William, New York	.100	5	10	0	1	1	0	0	0	0	0	0	0	0	1
Bedrosian, Stephen, Atlanta	.118	40	17	0	2	2	0	0	0	0	0	1	0	0	0
Belliard, Rafael, Pittsburgh	.227	20	22	3	5	5	0	0	0	0	0	0	0	4	1
Benedict, Bruce, Atlanta	.223	95	300	26	67	89	8	1	4	25	2	1	4	1	2
Berenyi, Bruce, Cin.-New York	.189	32	53	3	10	11	1	0	0	3	0	7	1	0	0
Berra, Dale, Pittsburgh	.222	136	450	31	100	143	16	0	9	52	9	6	9	1	3
Bevacqua, Kurt, San Diego	.200	59	80	7	16	22	3	0	1	9	2	0	0	0	0
Bielecki, Michael, Pittsburgh	.000	4	0	0	0	0	0	0	0	0	0	0	0	0	0
Bilardello, Dann, Cincinnati	.209	68	182	16	38	51	7	0	2	10	0	4	0	0	1
Bochy, Bruce, San Diego	.228	37	92	10	21	40	5	1	4	15	2	1	1	0	1
Booker, Gregory, San Diego	.286	32	7	1	2	3	1	0	0	0	0	0	0	0	0
Bordi, Richard, Chicago	.053	31	19	0	1	1	0	0	0	0	0	0	0	0	0
Bosley, Thaddis, Chicago*	.296	55	98	17	29	41	2	2	2	14	2	0	1	5	1
Bowa, Lawrence, Chicagot	.223	133	391	33	87	105	14	2	0	17	1	3	1	10	4
Braun, Stephen, St. Louis*	.276	86	98	6	27	32	3	1	0	16	3	0	0	0	0
Bream, Sidney, Los Angeles*	.184	27	49	2	9	12	3	0	0	6	2	1	2	1	0
Breining, Fred, Montreal...................	.000	4	1	0	0	0	0	0	0	0	0	0	0	0	0
Brenly, Robert, San Francisco	.291	145	506	74	147	235	28	0	20	80	7	4	6	6	9
Brewer, Anthony, Los Angeles	.108	24	37	3	4	8	1	0	1	4	0	0	0	1	0
Brizzolara, Anthony, Atlanta	.000	10	7	0	0	0	0	0	0	0	0	2	0	0	0
Brock, Gregory, Los Angeles*	.225	88	271	33	61	109	6	0	14	34	3	0	3	8	0
Brooks, Hubert, New York	.283	153	561	61	159	234	23	2	16	73	15	0	2	6	5
Brown, J. Christopher, San Fran......	.286	23	84	6	24	34	7	0	1	11	0	0	1	2	1
Brown, Rogers, San Diegot	.251	85	171	28	43	63	7	2	3	29	3	2	3	16	4
Browning, Thomas, Cincinnati*	.143	3	7	0	1	1	0	0	0	0	0	0	0	0	0
Brummer, Glenn, St. Louis	.207	28	58	3	12	15	0	0	1	3	0	0	0	0	0
Brusstar, Warren, Chicago	.200	41	5	1	1	1	0	0	0	1	0	1	0	0	0
Buckner, William, Chicago*	.209	21	43	3	9	9	0	0	0	2	1	0	1	0	0
Butera, Salvatore, Montreal	.000	3	3	0	0	0	0	0	0	0	0	0	0	0	0
Bystrom, Martin, Philadelphia	.158	11	19	1	3	4	1	0	0	0	0	3	0	0	0
Cabell, Enos, Houston	.310	127	436	52	135	182	17	3	8	44	5	3	3	8	11
Calhoun, Jeffrey, Houston*	.000	9	0	0	0	0	0	0	0	0	0	0	0	0	0
Calvert, Mark, San Francisco	.000	10	8	0	0	0	0	0	0	0	0	0	0	0	0
Camp, Rick, Atlanta	.111	31	45	0	5	6	1	0	0	3	0	3	0	0	0
Campbell, William, Philadelphia	.000	57	1	0	0	0	0	0	0	0	0	0	0	0	0
Candelaria, John, Pittsburght	.129	33	62	6	8	13	2	0	1	2	0	4	0	0	1
Carlton, Steven, Philadelphia*	.190	34	84	8	16	21	2	0	1	10	1	3	0	0	0
Carman, Donald, Philadelphia*	.000	11	1	0	0	0	0	0	0	0	0	0	0	0	0
Carter, Gary, Montreal	.294	159	596	75	175	290	32	1	27	106	16	0	3	2	2
Cato, J. Keefe, Cincinnati	.500	8	4	1	2	2	0	0	0	1	0	0	0	0	0
Cedeno, Cesar, Cincinnati	.276	110	380	59	105	163	24	2	10	47	4	4	2	19	3
Cey, Ronald, Chicago	.240	146	505	71	121	223	27	0	25	97	8	0	8	3	2
Chambliss, C. Christopher, Atl.*	.257	135	389	47	100	141	14	0	9	44	3	0	6	1	2
Chapman, Kelvin, New York	.289	75	197	27	57	79	13	0	3	23	3	4	1	8	7
Chiffer, Floyd, San Diego	.000	15	3	0	0	0	0	0	0	0	0	0	0	0	0
Christensen, John, New York	.273	5	11	2	3	5	2	0	0	3	1	0	1	0	1
Citarella, Ralph, St. Louis	.250	10	4	1	1	1	0	0	0	1	0	0	0	0	0
Clark, Jack, San Francisco................	.320	57	203	33	65	109	9	1	11	44	4	0	3	1	1
Concepcion, David, Cincinnati...........	.245	154	531	46	130	170	26	1	4	58	4	8	9	22	6

Player and Club	Pct.	G.	AB.	R.	H.	TB.	2B.	3B.	HR.	RBI.	GW.	SH.	SF.	SB.	CS.
Corcoran, Timothy, Philadelphia*	.341	102	208	30	71	101	13	1	5	36	1	0	2	0	1
Cornell, Jeffery, San Francisco†	.000	23	4	0	0	0	0	0	0	0	0	0	0	0	0
Cotto, Henry, Chicago	.274	105	146	24	40	45	5	0	0	8	1	3	0	9	3
Cox, Danny, St. Louis	.132	31	53	4	7	7	0	0	0	1	0	1	0	0	0
Cruz, Jose, Houston*	.312	160	600	96	187	277	28	13	12	95	8	2	10	22	8
Darling, Ronald, New York	.149	39	67	7	10	11	1	0	0	3	0	6	1	0	0
Davis, Charles, San Francisco†	.315	137	499	87	157	253	21	6	21	81	7	2	2	12	8
Davis, Eric, Cincinnati	.224	57	174	33	39	81	10	1	10	30	0	0	1	10	2
Davis, Glenn, Houston	.213	18	61	6	13	24	5	0	2	8	2	2	1	0	0
Davis, Jody, Chicago	.256	150	523	55	134	220	25	2	19	94	6	1	7	5	6
Davis, Mark, San Francisco*	.130	46	46	4	6	10	0	2	0	4	0	6	0	0	0
Dawley, William, Houston	.333	60	9	2	3	5	0	1	0	3	0	2	0	0	0
Dawson, Andre, Montreal	.248	138	533	73	132	218	23	6	17	86	13	1	6	13	5
Dayley, Kenneth, Atlanta-St. L.*	.500	8	4	1	2	2	0	0	0	0	0	1	0	0	0
Dedmon, Jeffrey, Atlanta*	.000	54	6	0	0	0	0	0	0	0	0	1	0	0	0
Deer, Robert, San Francisco	.167	13	24	5	4	13	0	0	3	3	0	0	0	1	1
DeJesus, Ivan, Philadelphia	.257	144	435	40	112	133	15	3	0	35	3	1	3	12	5
DeLeon, Jose, Pittsburgh	.085	30	59	0	5	5	0	0	0	2	0	4	1	0	0
DeLeon, Luis, San Diego	.000	32	4	0	0	0	0	0	0	0	0	1	0	0	0
Denny, John, Philadelphia	.191	22	47	3	9	9	0	0	0	4	0	5	1	0	0
Dernier, Robert, Chicago	.278	143	536	94	149	194	26	5	3	32	5	11	4	45	17
Diaz, Baudilio, Philadelphia	.213	27	75	5	16	23	4	0	1	9	0	1	2	0	0
Diaz, Carlos, Los Angeles	.000	37	1	0	0	0	0	0	0	0	0	0	0	0	0
Dilone, Miguel, Montreal†	.278	88	169	28	47	62	8	2	1	10	0	1	1	27	2
DiPino, Frank, Houston*	.000	57	10	0	0	0	0	0	0	0	0	0	0	0	0
Distefano, Benito, Pittsburgh*	.167	45	78	10	13	27	1	2	3	9	0	2	0	0	1
Doran, William, Houston†	.261	147	548	92	143	195	18	11	4	41	2	7	3	21	12
Dravecky, David, San Diego	.098	50	41	3	4	6	2	0	0	3	1	5	0	0	0
Driessen, Daniel, Cin.-Montreal*	.269	132	387	47	104	176	24	0	16	60	8	1	5	2	2
Durham, Leon, Chicago*	.279	137	473	86	132	239	30	4	23	96	14	0	5	16	8
Eckersley, Dennis, Chicago	.109	24	55	1	6	6	0	0	0	1	0	1	0	0	0
Esasky, Nicholas, Cincinnati	.193	113	322	30	62	112	10	5	10	45	4	3	5	1	2
Falcone, Peter, Atlanta*	.212	35	33	2	7	9	2	0	0	2	0	3	0	0	0
Fernandez, C. Sid, New York*	.179	15	28	0	5	5	0	0	0	1	0	3	0	0	0
Fimple, John, Los Angeles	.192	12	26	2	5	6	1	0	0	3	1	0	1	0	0
Fireovid, Stephen, Philadelphia*	.000	6	0	0	0	0	0	0	0	0	0	0	0	0	0
Fitzgerald, Michael, New York	.242	112	360	20	87	110	15	1	2	33	6	5	4	1	0
Flannery, Timothy, San Diego*	.273	86	128	24	35	50	3	3	2	10	2	2	1	4	1
Flynn, R. Douglas, Montreal	.243	124	366	23	89	103	12	1	0	17	3	4	0	0	0
Foley, Thomas, Cincinnati*	.253	106	277	26	70	99	8	3	5	27	2	1	2	3	2
Forsch, Robert, St. Louis	.250	16	16	1	4	5	1	0	0	3	0	1	0	0	0
Forster, Terry, Atlanta*	.667	25	3	1	2	2	0	0	0	1	0	0	0	0	0
Foster, George, New York	.269	146	553	67	149	245	22	1	24	86	7	0	6	2	2
Franco, John, Cincinnati*	.000	54	3	0	0	0	0	0	0	0	0	1	0	0	0
Francona, Terry, Montreal*	.346	58	214	18	74	100	19	2	1	18	1	1	2	0	0
Frazier, George, Chicago	.286	37	7	0	2	2	0	0	0	0	0	0	0	0	1
Frobel, Douglas, Pittsburgh*	.203	126	276	33	56	107	9	3	12	28	2	3	1	7	5
Fuentes, Michael, Montreal	.250	3	4	0	1	1	0	0	0	0	0	0	0	0	0
Gaff, Brent, New York	.000	47	6	0	0	0	0	0	0	0	0	0	0	0	0
Garber, H. Eugene, Atlanta	.143	62	14	1	2	2	0	0	0	0	0	0	0	0	0
Garcia, Alfonso, Philadelphia	.233	57	60	6	14	16	2	0	0	5	3	0	0	0	0
Gardenhire, Ronald, New York	.246	74	207	20	51	63	7	1	1	10	0	1	1	6	1
Gardner, Wesley, New York	.000	21	1	1	0	0	0	0	0	0	0	0	0	0	0
Garner, Philip, Houston	.278	128	374	60	104	145	17	6	4	45	9	5	4	3	2
Garrelts, Scott, San Francisco	.100	21	10	0	1	1	0	0	0	0	0	0	0	0	0
Garvey, Steven, San Diego	.284	161	617	72	175	230	27	2	8	86	15	1	10	1	2
Gibbons, John, New York	.065	10	31	1	2	2	0	0	0	1	0	0	0	0	0
Gladden, C. Daniel, San Francisco	.351	86	342	71	120	153	17	2	4	31	3	6	1	31	16
Gomez, Randall, San Francisco	.167	14	30	0	5	6	1	0	0	0	0	3	0	0	0
Gonzales, Rene, Montreal	.233	29	30	5	7	8	1	0	0	2	0	0	0	0	0
Gonzalez, Denio, Pittsburgh	.183	26	82	9	15	20	3	1	0	4	0	2	0	1	1
Gonzalez, Jose, St. Louis†	.211	8	19	4	4	4	0	0	0	3	0	1	0	1	0
Gooden, Dwight, New York	.200	31	70	5	14	14	0	0	0	3	0	10	2	0	0
Gorman, Thomas, New York*	.000	36	3	0	0	0	0	0	0	0	0	0	0	0	0
Gossage, Richard, San Diego	.182	62	22	0	4	4	0	0	0	0	0	2	0	0	0
Grant, Mark, San Francisco	.000	11	17	0	0	0	0	0	0	0	0	3	0	0	0
Grapenthin, Richard, Montreal	.200	13	5	1	1	1	0	0	0	0	0	0	0	0	0
Green, Christopher, Pittsburgh*	.000	4	0	0	0	0	0	0	0	0	0	0	0	0	0
Green, David, St. Louis	.268	126	452	49	121	188	14	4	15	65	10	0	5	17	9
Gross, Gregory, Philadelphia*	.322	112	202	19	65	76	9	1	0	16	2	0	2	1	0
Gross, Kevin, Philadelphia	.067	44	30	0	2	2	0	0	0	0	0	2	0	1	0
Guante, Cecilio, Pittsburgh	.000	27	4	0	0	0	0	0	0	0	0	1	0	0	0
Guerrero, Pedro, Los Angeles	.303	144	535	85	162	247	29	4	16	72	8	1	8	9	8
Gulden, Bradley, Cincinnati*	.226	107	292	31	66	90	8	2	4	33	4	3	2	2	2
Gullickson, William, Montreal	.110	32	73	1	8	8	0	0	0	1	0	6	1	0	1
Gwosdz, Douglas, San Diego	.250	7	8	0	2	2	0	0	0	1	0	0	0	0	0
Gwynn, Anthony, San Diego*	.351	158	606	88	213	269	21	10	5	71	10	6	2	33	18
Hagen, Kevin, St. Louis	.000	4	0	0	0	0	0	0	0	0	0	0	0	0	0
Hall, Albert, Atlanta†	.261	87	142	25	37	48	6	1	1	9	2	1	0	6	4
Hall, Melvin, Chicago*	.280	48	150	25	42	71	11	3	4	22	1	0	2	2	1

Player and Club	Pct.	G.	AB.	R.	H.	TB.	2B.	3B.	HR.	RBI.	GW.	SH.	SF.	SB.	CS.
Hammaker, C. Atlee, San Francisco	.182	6	11	1	2	2	0	0	0	1	0	0	0	0	0
Harper, Brian, Pittsburgh	.259	46	112	4	29	39	4	0	2	11	1	1	1	0	0
Harper, Terry, Atlanta	.157	40	102	4	16	21	3	1	0	8	2	0	1	4	1
Harris, Greg, Mtl.-S.D.†	.333	34	9	3	3	4	1	0	0	0	0	0	0	0	0
Hassey, Ronald, Chicago*	.333	19	33	5	11	17	0	0	2	5	0	0	0	0	1
Hassler, Andrew, St. Louis*	.000	3	0	0	0	0	0	0	0	0	0	0	0	0	0
Hatcher, William, Chicago	.111	8	9	1	1	1	0	0	0	0	0	0	0	2	0
Hawkins, M. Andrew, San Diego	.195	36	41	2	8	8	0	0	0	1	0	3	0	0	0
Hayes, Von, Philadelphia*	.292	152	561	85	164	251	27	6	16	67	3	0	2	48	13
Hebner, Richard, Chicago*	.333	44	81	12	27	36	3	0	2	8	2	0	0	1	0
Heep, Daniel, New York*	.231	99	199	36	46	62	9	2	1	12	0	1	5	3	1
Hendrick, George, St. Louis	.277	120	441	57	122	179	28	1	9	69	16	0	5	0	2
Hernandez, Keith, New York*	.311	154	550	83	171	247	31	0	15	94	17	0	9	2	3
Herr, Thomas, St. Louis†	.276	145	558	67	154	193	23	2	4	49	2	10	3	13	7
Hershiser, Orel, Los Angeles	.200	45	50	4	10	10	0	0	0	2	0	8	0	0	0
Hesketh, Joseph, Montreal*	.100	11	10	1	1	1	0	0	0	0	0	1	0	0	0
Hodges, Ronald, New York*	.208	64	106	5	22	28	3	0	1	11	0	1	1	1	1
Holland, Alfred, Philadelphia	.000	68	5	0	0	0	0	0	0	0	0	0	0	0	0
Honeycutt, Frederick, Los Angeles*	.143	29	56	1	8	8	0	0	0	1	0	9	0	1	0
Hooton, Burt, Los Angeles	.071	54	14	0	1	1	0	0	0	1	0	3	0	0	0
Horner, J. Robert, Atlanta	.274	32	113	15	31	48	8	0	3	19	3	0	2	0	0
Horton, Ricky, St. Louis*	.065	39	31	2	2	2	0	0	0	0	0	6	0	0	0
Householder, Paul, Cin.-St. L.†	.115	27	26	4	3	4	1	0	0	0	0	0	0	1	1
Howe, Arthur, St. Louis	.216	89	139	17	30	41	5	0	2	12	1	1	3	0	2
Howell, Kenneth, Los Angeles	.000	32	5	0	0	0	0	0	0	0	0	1	0	0	0
Hubbard, Glenn, Atlanta	.234	120	397	53	93	151	27	2	9	43	6	2	3	4	1
Hudson, Charles, Philadelphia†	.089	30	56	3	5	8	3	0	0	4	0	4	1	0	0
Hume, Thomas, Cincinnati	.136	54	22	1	3	3	0	0	0	1	0	0	0	0	0
Iorg, Dane, St. Louis*	.143	15	28	3	4	6	2	0	0	3	0	0	0	0	0
James, Robert, Montreal	.143	62	14	0	2	2	0	0	0	1	0	0	0	0	0
Jeltz, L. Steven, Philadelphia	.206	28	68	7	14	19	0	1	1	7	0	1	1	2	1
Johnson, Randall, Atlanta	.279	91	294	28	82	110	13	0	5	30	5	6	0	4	7
Johnson, Ronald, Montreal	.200	5	5	0	1	1	0	0	0	1	0	0	0	0	0
Johnson, Roy, Montreal*	.152	16	33	2	5	10	2	0	1	2	0	0	0	1	0
Johnson, Wallace, Montreal†	.208	17	24	3	5	5	0	0	0	4	0	0	0	0	0
Johnson, William, Chicago	.000	4	0	0	0	0	0	0	0	0	0	0	0	0	0
Johnstone, John, Chicago*	.288	52	73	8	21	27	2	2	0	3	0	0	0	0	0
Jones, Ross, New York	.100	17	10	2	1	2	1	0	0	1	1	0	0	0	0
Jorgensen, Michael, Atl.-St. L.*	.250	90	124	9	31	43	5	2	1	17	3	0	1	0	1
Kennedy, Terrence, San Diego*	.240	148	530	54	127	187	16	1	14	57	7	0	5	1	2
Kepshire, Kurt, St. Louis*	.056	17	36	0	2	3	1	0	0	0	0	5	0	0	0
Kern, James, Philadelphia	.000	8	1	0	0	0	0	0	0	0	0	0	0	0	0
Knepper, Robert, Houston*	.171	35	76	6	13	18	2	0	1	8	0	6	0	1	0
Knicely, Alan, Cincinnati	.138	10	29	0	4	4	0	0	0	5	1	0	3	0	0
Knight, C. Ray, Hou.-N.Y.	.237	115	371	28	88	111	14	0	3	35	2	0	4	0	3
Komminsk, Brad, Atlanta	.203	90	301	37	61	95	10	0	8	36	9	1	1	18	8
Koosman, Jerry, Philadelphia	.108	36	74	2	8	8	0	0	0	3	0	14	0	0	0
Krawczyk, Raymond, Pittsburgh	.000	4	0	0	0	0	0	0	0	0	0	0	0	0	0
Krenchicki, Wayne, Cincinnati*	.298	97	181	18	54	85	9	2	6	22	5	0	4	0	1
Krukow, Michael, San Francisco	.139	36	72	5	10	11	1	0	0	2	1	2	1	0	0
Kuiper, Duane, San Francisco*	.200	83	115	8	23	24	1	0	0	11	0	2	1	0	1
Lacey, Robert, San Francisco	.333	34	6	1	2	2	0	0	0	1	0	0	0	0	0
LaCoss, Michael, Houston	.129	39	31	1	4	5	1	0	0	1	0	6	1	0	0
Lacy, Leondaus, Pittsburgh	.321	138	474	66	152	220	26	3	12	70	9	12	2	21	11
Lahti, Jeffrey, St. Louis	.167	63	6	0	1	1	0	0	0	0	0	1	0	0	0
Lake, Steven, Chicago	.222	25	54	4	12	22	4	0	2	7	0	1	1	0	0
Landestoy, Rafael, Los Angeles†	.185	53	54	10	10	13	0	0	1	2	1	2	0	2	1
Landreaux, Kenneth, Los Angeles*.	.251	134	438	39	110	164	11	5	11	47	5	3	6	10	9
Landrum, Terry, St. Louis	.272	105	173	21	47	67	9	1	3	26	3	1	3	3	4
LaPoint, David, St. Louis*	.068	33	59	3	4	4	0	0	0	3	1	9	1	0	0
Laskey, William, San Francisco	.063	35	63	3	4	4	0	0	0	0	0	4	0	0	0
Lavalliere, Michael, Philadelphia*	.000	6	7	0	0	0	0	0	0	0	0	0	0	0	0
Lavelle, Gary, San Francisco	.000	77	5	0	0	0	0	0	0	0	0	0	0	0	0
Lawless, Thomas, Cin.-Mtl.	.237	54	97	11	23	29	3	0	1	2	0	1	0	7	3
Lea, Charles, Montreal	.111	30	72	3	8	8	0	0	0	2	0	12	0	0	0
Leary, Timothy, New York	.300	20	10	2	3	6	0	0	1	1	0	3	0	1	0
Lefebvre, Joseph, Philadelphia*	.250	52	160	22	40	58	9	0	3	18	2	0	2	0	2
Lefferts, Craig, San Diego*	.294	62	17	1	5	6	1	0	0	0	0	1	0	0	0
LeMaster, Johnnie, San Francisco.	.217	132	451	46	98	127	13	2	4	32	2	7	4	17	5
Leonard, Jeffrey, San Francisco	.302	136	514	76	155	249	27	2	21	86	9	0	5	17	7
Lerch, Randy, San Francisco*	.133	37	15	2	2	2	0	0	0	1	0	0	0	0	0
Lesley, Bradley, Cincinnati	.500	16	2	0	1	1	0	0	0	1	0	0	0	0	0
Lezcano, Sixto, Philadelphia	.277	109	256	36	71	123	6	2	14	40	5	0	0	0	1
Linares, Rufino, Atlanta	.207	34	58	4	12	18	3	0	1	10	1	0	2	0	0
Little, R. Bryan, Montreal†	.244	85	266	31	65	78	11	1	0	9	2	8	0	2	3
Lollar, W. Timothy, San Diego*	.221	31	68	6	15	27	1	1	3	15	0	1	1	0	0
Lopes, David, Chicago	.235	16	17	5	4	5	1	0	0	0	0	0	0	3	0
Lucas, Gary, Montreal*	.000	55	4	0	0	0	0	0	0	0	0	0	0	0	0
Lynch, Edward, New York	.222	40	27	0	6	7	1	0	0	1	0	3	0	0	0
Lyons, William, St. Louis	.219	46	73	13	16	19	3	0	0	3	0	1	0	3	1

Player and Club	Pct.	G.	AB.	R.	H.	TB.	2B.	3B.	HR.	RBI.	GW.	SH.	SF.	SB.	CS.
Madden, Michael, Houston*	.333	17	6	1	2	2	0	0	0	0	0	0	0	0	0
Maddox, Garry, Philadelphia	.282	77	241	29	68	94	11	0	5	19	3	1	2	3	2
Madlock, Bill, Pittsburgh	.253	103	403	38	102	130	16	0	4	44	7	1	4	3	1
Mahler, Richard, Atlanta	.296	38	71	6	21	24	3	0	0	3	1	3	0	0	0
Maldonado, Candido, Los Angeles	.268	116	254	25	68	97	14	0	5	28	5	1	3	0	3
Marshall, Michael, Los Angeles	.257	134	495	68	127	217	27	0	21	65	10	1	2	4	3
Martin, D. Renie, S.F.-Phila	.375	21	8	0	3	3	0	0	0	0	0	0	0	0	0
Martin, Jerry, New York	.154	51	91	6	14	24	1	0	3	5	2	0	0	0	0
Martinez, Carmelo, San Diego	.250	149	488	64	122	193	28	2	13	66	11	0	10	1	3
Matthews, Gary, Chicago	.291	147	491	101	143	210	21	2	14	82	19	1	10	17	8
Matuszek, Leonard, Philadelphia*	.248	101	262	40	65	120	17	1	12	43	7	0	4	4	3
May, Milton, Pittsburgh*	.177	50	96	4	17	23	3	0	1	8	0	1	0	0	1
Mazzilli, Lee, Pittsburgh†	.237	111	266	37	63	88	11	1	4	21	2	1	1	8	1
McGaffigan, Andrew, Mont-Cin	.000	30	10	0	0	0	0	0	0	0	0	3	0	0	0
McGee, Willie, St. Louis†	.291	145	571	82	166	225	19	11	6	50	7	0	3	43	10
McGraw, Frank, Philadelphia	.333	25	3	0	1	1	0	0	0	0	0	0	0	0	0
McMurtry, J. Craig, Atlanta	.115	40	52	4	6	8	0	1	0	1	0	8	0	1	0
McReynolds, W. Kevin, San Diego	.278	147	525	68	146	244	26	6	20	75	10	3	9	3	6
McWilliams, Larry, Pittsburgh*	.122	36	74	1	9	9	0	0	0	4	0	12	0	0	1
Melendez, Francisco, Philadelphia*	.130	21	23	0	3	3	0	0	0	2	0	0	0	0	0
Meridith, Ronald, Chicago*	.000	3	0	0	0	0	0	0	0	0	0	0	0	0	0
Miller, Edward, San Diego†	.286	13	14	4	4	9	0	1	1	2	0	0	0	4	0
Miller, Lemmie, Los Angeles	.167	8	12	1	2	2	0	0	0	0	0	0	0	0	0
Milner, Eddie, Cincinnati*	.232	117	336	44	78	115	8	4	7	29	5	4	4	21	13
Minton, Gregory, San Francisco†	.048	74	21	0	1	1	0	0	0	0	0	1	0	0	0
Mitchell, Kevin, New York	.214	7	14	0	3	3	0	0	0	1	0	0	0	0	1
Monday, Robert, Los Angeles*	.191	31	47	4	9	14	2	0	1	7	1	2	0	0	0
Monge, Isidro, San Diego†	.000	13	1	0	0	0	0	0	0	0	0	0	0	0	0
Moore, Donnie, Atlanta*	.000	47	3	0	0	0	0	0	0	0	0	0	0	0	0
Morales, Jose, Los Angeles	.158	22	19	0	3	3	0	0	0	0	0	0	0	0	0
Moreland, B. Keith, Chicago	.279	140	495	59	138	209	17	3	16	80	11	2	5	1	4
Morrison, James, Pittsburgh	.286	100	304	38	87	138	14	2	11	45	3	2	4	0	1
Mullins, Francis, San Francisco	.218	57	110	8	24	38	8	0	2	10	1	1	0	3	1
Mumphrey, Jerry, Houston†	.290	151	524	66	152	205	20	3	9	83	7	0	6	15	7
Murphy, Dale, Atlanta	.290	162	607	94	176	332	32	8	36	100	13	0	3	19	7
Nettles, Graig, San Diego*	.228	124	395	56	90	163	11	1	20	65	8	0	7	0	0
Nicosia, Steven, San Francisco	.303	48	132	9	40	61	11	2	2	19	2	1	3	1	1
Niedenfuer, Thomas, Los Angeles	.000	33	3	0	0	0	0	0	0	0	0	1	0	0	0
Niekro, Joseph, Houston	.133	38	83	4	11	11	0	0	0	6	0	11	0	0	0
Nieto, Thomas, St. Louis	.279	33	86	7	24	37	4	0	3	12	2	0	2	0	0
Noles, Dickie, Chicago	.000	21	10	0	0	0	0	0	0	0	0	0	0	0	0
Oberkfell, Kenneth, St.L-Atl*	.269	100	324	38	87	113	19	2	1	21	3	3	3	2	5
Oester, Ronald, Cincinnati†	.242	150	553	54	134	175	26	3	3	38	2	5	1	7	2
Oliver, Albert, S.F.-Phil*	.301	119	432	36	130	160	26	2	0	48	5	0	3	0	4
O'Malley, Thomas, San Francisco*	.120	13	25	2	3	3	0	0	0	0	0	0	0	0	0
Oquendo, Jose, New York	.222	81	189	23	42	47	5	0	0	10	0	3	2	10	1
Orosco, Jesse, New York	.250	60	4	1	1	1	0	0	0	1	0	1	0	0	0
Orsulak, Joseph, Pittsburgh*	.254	32	67	12	17	22	1	2	0	3	0	3	1	3	1
Ortiz, Adalberto, New York	.198	40	91	6	18	21	3	0	0	11	1	0	2	1	0
Otis, Amos, Pittsburgh	.165	40	97	6	16	20	4	0	0	10	0	1	4	0	0
Owchinko, Robert, Cincinnati*	.167	49	12	2	2	3	1	0	0	0	0	1	0	0	0
Owen, Dave, Chicago†	.194	47	93	8	18	27	2	2	1	10	2	1	1	1	2
Ownbey, Richard, St. Louis	.000	5	4	1	0	0	0	0	0	0	0	2	0	0	0
Page, Mitchell, Pittsburgh*	.333	16	12	2	4	5	1	0	0	0	0	0	0	0	0
Palmer, David, Montreal	.152	20	33	2	5	9	1	0	1	3	1	6	0	0	0
Pankovits, James, Houston	.284	53	81	6	23	33	7	0	1	14	2	1	1	2	1
Parker, David, Cincinnati*	.285	156	607	73	173	249	28	0	16	94	13	0	6	11	10
Pastore, Frank, Cincinnati	.071	24	28	2	2	2	0	0	0	1	0	2	0	0	0
Patterson, Reginald, Chicago*	.000	3	2	0	0	0	0	0	0	0	0	0	0	0	0
Payne, Michael, Atlanta	.000	3	1	0	0	0	0	0	0	0	0	0	0	0	0
Pena, Adalberto, Houston	.205	24	39	3	8	12	1	0	1	4	0	0	0	0	0
Pena, Alejandro, Los Angeles	.121	28	66	5	8	11	3	0	0	1	1	4	0	0	0
Pena, Antonio, Pittsburgh	.286	147	546	77	156	232	27	2	15	78	7	4	2	12	8
Pendleton, Terry, St. Louis†	.324	67	262	37	85	110	16	3	1	33	4	0	5	20	5
Perez, Atanasio, Cincinnati	.241	71	137	9	33	47	6	1	2	15	5	0	1	0	0
Perez, Pascual, Atlanta	.076	32	66	5	5	8	1	1	0	3	0	6	0	1	0
Perry, Gerald, Atlanta*	.265	122	347	52	92	129	12	2	7	47	4	2	7	15	12
Pittman, Joseph, San Francisco	.227	17	22	2	5	5	0	0	0	2	0	0	1	1	1
Pocoroba, Biff, Atlanta*	.000	4	2	1	0	0	0	0	0	0	0	0	0	0	0
Porter, Darrell, St. Louis*	.232	127	422	56	98	153	16	3	11	68	7	0	6	5	3
Power, Ted, Cincinnati	.000	78	5	2	0	0	0	0	0	0	0	1	0	0	0
Price, Joseph, Cincinnati	.146	30	48	3	7	8	1	0	0	2	0	9	0	0	0
Puhl, Terrance, Houston*	.301	132	449	66	135	195	19	7	9	55	10	6	4	13	8
Puleo, Charles, Cincinnati	.200	5	5	1	1	2	1	0	0	2	0	2	0	0	0
Pulido, Alfonso, Pittsburgh*	.000	1	0	0	0	0	0	0	0	0	0	0	0	0	0
Rabb, John, San Francisco	.195	54	82	10	16	26	1	0	3	9	0	0	1	1	1
Raines, Timothy, Montreal†	.309	160	622	106	192	272	38	9	8	60	13	3	4	75	10
Rainey, Charles, Chicago	.097	17	31	2	3	3	0	0	0	3	1	1	0	0	0
Rajsich, Gary, St. Louis*	.143	7	7	1	1	1	0	0	0	2	0	0	1	0	0
Ramirez, Mario, San Diego	.119	48	59	12	7	14	1	0	2	9	1	1	0	0	0

Player and Club	Pct.	G.	AB.	R.	H.	TB.	2B.	3B.	HR.	RBI.	GW.	SH.	SF.	SB.	CS.
Ramirez, Rafael, Atlanta	.266	145	591	51	157	193	22	4	2	48	5	5	6	14	17
Ramos, Roberto, Montreal	.193	31	83	8	16	23	1	0	2	5	0	1	1	0	0
Ramsey, Michael, St.L-Mont†	.188	58	85	3	16	18	2	0	0	3	0	2	0	0	0
Rawley, Shane, Philadelphia*	.116	19	43	3	5	5	0	0	0	1	0	1	0	1	0
Ray, Johnny, Pittsburgh†	.312	155	555	75	173	241	38	6	6	67	9	2	6	11	6
Reardon, Jeffrey, Montreal	.000	68	9	0	0	0	0	0	0	0	0	0	0	0	0
Redus, Gary, Cincinnati	.254	123	394	69	100	148	21	3	7	22	2	3	5	48	11
Reuschel, Ricky, Chicago	.241	20	29	2	7	10	3	0	0	3	0	4	1	0	0
Reuss, Jerry, Los Angeles*	.167	30	24	2	4	5	1	0	0	2	0	2	0	0	0
Reyes, Gilberto, Los Angeles	.000	4	5	0	0	0	0	0	0	0	0	0	0	0	0
Reynolds, G. Craig, Houston*	.260	146	527	61	137	192	15	11	6	60	9	16	6	7	1
Reynolds, Robert, Los Angeles†	.258	73	240	24	62	84	12	2	2	24	4	4	2	7	5
Rhoden, Richard, Pittsburgh	.333	35	84	9	28	34	6	0	0	4	1	5	1	0	0
Richards, Eugene, San Francisco*	.252	87	135	18	34	38	4	0	0	4	0	0	0	5	3
Richardt, Michael, Houston	.267	16	15	1	4	5	1	0	0	2	1	0	0	0	0
Riley, George, San Francisco*	.100	5	10	1	1	1	0	0	0	0	0	1	0	0	0
Rivera, German, Los Angeles	.260	94	227	20	59	81	12	2	2	17	1	2	3	1	0
Robinson, Don, Pittsburgh	.290	53	31	6	9	12	0	0	1	5	1	0	0	0	0
Robinson, Jeffrey, San Francisco	.115	34	61	0	7	7	0	0	0	2	1	1	0	0	0
Robinson, Ronald, Cincinnati	.000	12	8	0	0	0	0	0	0	0	0	1	0	0	0
Rodas, Richard, Los Angeles*	.000	3	1	0	0	0	0	0	0	0	0	0	0	0	0
Roenicke, Ronald, San Diego†	.300	12	20	4	6	10	1	0	1	2	0	0	0	0	0
Rogers, Stephen, Montreal	.143	31	49	2	7	10	1	1	0	1	1	4	0	0	0
Rohn, Daniel, Chicago*	.129	25	31	1	4	7	0	0	1	3	0	0	1	0	0
Rose, Peter, Mont–Cin†	.286	121	374	43	107	126	15	2	0	34	0	3	1	1	1
Ross, Mark, Houston	.000	2	0	0	0	0	0	0	0	0	0	0	0	0	0
Rowdon, Wade, Cincinnati	.286	4	7	0	2	2	0	0	0	0	0	0	0	0	0
Royster, Jeron, Atlanta	.207	81	227	22	47	67	13	2	1	21	1	2	2	6	4
Rucker, David, St. Louis*	.143	50	7	0	1	1	0	0	0	0	0	0	0	0	0
Ruhle, Vernon, Houston	.083	40	12	0	1	1	0	0	0	0	0	5	0	0	0
Runge, Paul, Atlanta	.267	28	90	5	24	29	3	1	0	3	0	3	0	5	3
Russell, Jeffrey, Cincinnati	.140	34	57	2	8	10	2	0	0	7	1	5	1	0	0
Russell, John, Philadelphia	.283	39	99	11	28	44	8	1	2	11	1	0	3	0	1
Russell, William, Los Angeles	.267	89	262	25	70	84	12	1	0	19	4	9	2	4	4
Ruthven, Richard, Chicago	.159	25	44	2	7	10	3	0	0	2	0	5	0	0	0
Ryan, L. Nolan, Houston	.098	30	61	3	6	8	2	0	0	1	0	5	0	1	0
St. Claire, Randy, Montreal	.000	4	0	0	0	0	0	0	0	0	0	0	0	0	0
Salas, Mark, St. Louis*	.100	14	20	1	2	3	1	0	0	1	0	1	0	0	0
Salazar, Argenis, Montreal	.155	80	174	12	27	35	4	2	0	12	1	4	1	1	1
Salazar, Luis, San Diego	.241	93	228	20	55	75	7	2	3	17	2	2	0	11	7
Sambito, Joseph, Houston*	.000	32	2	0	0	0	0	0	0	0	0	0	0	0	0
Samuel, Juan, Philadelphia	.272	160	701	105	191	310	36	19	15	69	13	0	1	72	15
Sanchez, Alejandro, San Francisco	.195	13	41	3	8	10	0	1	0	2	1	0	0	2	3
Sandberg, Ryne, Chicago	.314	156	636	114	200	331	36	19	19	84	9	5	4	32	7
Sanderson, Scott, Chicago	.119	24	42	3	5	5	0	0	0	5	1	4	1	0	0
Santana, Rafael, New York	.276	51	152	14	42	58	11	1	1	12	2	1	0	0	3
Sax, Stephen, Los Angeles	.243	145	569	70	138	173	24	4	1	35	5	2	3	34	19
Schatzeder, Daniel, Montreal*	.314	37	35	2	11	15	2	1	0	3	2	5	0	0	0
Scherrer, William, Cincinnati*	.000	36	3	0	0	0	0	0	0	0	0	1	0	0	0
Schiraldi, Calvin, New York	.000	5	3	0	0	0	0	0	0	0	0	0	0	0	0
Schmidt, Michael, Philadelphia	.277	151	528	93	146	283	23	3	36	106	13	0	8	5	7
Schu, Richard, Philadelphia	.276	17	29	12	8	18	2	1	2	5	0	0	1	0	0
Schulze, Donald, Chicago	.000	1	0	0	0	0	0	0	0	0	0	0	0	0	0
Scioscia, Michael, Los Angeles*	.273	114	341	29	93	126	18	0	5	38	8	1	4	2	1
Scott, Anthony, Hou–Mont†	.239	70	92	10	22	27	5	0	0	5	2	1	1	1	1
Scott, Michael, Houston	.128	31	47	3	6	8	2	0	0	3	0	6	0	0	0
Scurry, Rodney, Pittsburgh*	.000	43	2	0	0	0	0	0	0	0	0	0	0	0	0
Shines, A. Raymond, Montreal†	.300	12	20	0	6	7	1	0	0	2	0	0	1	0	0
Show, Eric, San Diego	.246	32	69	7	17	29	3	0	3	10	0	6	0	0	0
Sinatro, Matthew, Atlanta	.000	2	4	0	0	0	0	0	0	0	0	0	0	0	0
Sisk, Douglas, New York	.091	50	11	0	1	1	0	0	0	0	2	0	0	0	0
Smith, Bryn, Montreal	.132	28	53	9	7	10	3	0	0	1	0	7	0	0	0
Smith, David, Houston	.000	53	4	1	0	0	0	0	0	0	0	1	0	0	0
Smith, Lee, Chicago	.077	69	13	0	1	1	0	0	0	1	0	1	0	0	0
Smith, Lonnie, St. Louis	.250	145	504	77	126	172	20	4	6	49	4	3	4	50	13
Smith, Michael, Cincinnati	.000	8	0	0	0	0	0	0	0	0	0	1	0	0	0
Smith, Osborne, St. Louis†	.257	124	412	53	106	139	20	5	1	44	5	11	3	35	7
Smith, Zane, Atlanta*	.556	3	9	1	5	5	0	0	0	0	0	0	0	0	0
Solano, Julio, Houston	.333	31	3	1	1	1	0	0	0	0	0	0	0	0	0
Soto, Mario, Cincinnati	.207	33	87	5	18	26	5	0	1	9	2	4	1	0	0
Speier, Chris, Mont.–St.L.	.171	63	158	10	27	45	7	1	3	9	3	3	0	0	0
Spilman, W. Harry, Houston*	.264	32	72	14	19	27	2	0	2	15	3	0	3	0	0
Staub, Daniel, New York*	.264	78	72	2	19	26	4	0	1	18	3	0	3	0	0
Stearns, John, New York	.176	8	17	6	3	4	1	0	0	1	0	0	0	1	0
Stenhouse, Michael, Montreal*	.183	80	175	14	32	52	8	0	4	16	2	1	2	0	0
Stoddard, Timothy, Chicago	.091	58	11	0	1	1	0	0	0	0	0	0	1	0	0
Stone, Jeffery, Philadelphia*	.362	51	185	27	67	86	4	6	1	15	3	1	2	27	5
Strawberry, Darryl, New York*	.251	147	522	75	131	244	27	4	26	97	8	1	4	27	8
Stubbs, Franklin, Los Angeles*	.194	87	217	22	42	74	2	3	8	17	3	3	1	2	2
Stuper, John, St. Louis	.063	15	16	0	1	1	0	0	0	1	0	3	0	0	0

Player and Club	Pct.	G.	AB.	R.	H.	TB.	2B.	3B.	HR.	RBI.	GW.	SH.	SF.	SB.	CS.
Summers, John, San Diego*	.185	47	54	5	10	16	3	0	1	12	3	0	0	0	0
Sutcliffe, Richard, Chi.*	.250	20	56	3	14	17	3	0	0	6	1	5	0	0	0
Sutter, H. Bruce, St. Louis	.000	71	10	0	0	0	0	0	0	0	0	0	0	0	0
Swan, Craig, New York	.000	10	0	0	0	0	0	0	0	0	0	1	0	0	0
Tekulve, Kenton, Pittsburgh	.000	72	7	0	0	0	0	0	0	0	0	0	0	0	0
Templeton, Garry, San Diego†	.258	148	493	40	127	158	19	3	2	35	6	0	2	8	3
Terrell, C. Walter, New York*	.080	33	75	3	6	8	2	0	0	0	0	1	0	0	0
Thomas, Derrel, Montreal†	.255	108	243	26	62	78	12	2	0	20	0	3	3	0	4
Thompson, Jason, Pittsburgh*	.254	154	543	61	138	211	22	0	17	74	11	0	4	0	0
Thompson, Milton, Atlanta*	.303	25	99	16	30	37	1	0	2	4	1	1	0	14	2
Thompson, V. Scot, San Fran.*	.306	120	245	30	75	87	7	1	1	31	1	1	4	5	3
Thon, Richard, Houston	.353	5	17	3	6	8	0	1	0	1	0	0	0	0	1
Thurmond, Mark, San Diego*	.190	32	58	1	11	12	1	0	0	4	0	7	0	0	0
Tibbs, Jay, Cincinnati	.139	14	36	1	5	5	0	0	0	1	0	1	0	0	0
Tidrow, Richard, New York	.000	11	0	0	0	0	0	0	0	0	0	0	0	0	0
Toliver, Freddie, Cincinnati	.000	3	1	0	0	0	0	0	0	0	0	1	0	0	0
Tolman, Timothy, Houston	.176	14	17	2	3	4	1	0	0	0	0	0	0	0	0
Torrez, Michael, New York	.300	9	10	0	3	3	0	0	0	1	0	0	0	0	0
Trevino, Alejandro, Cin.-Atl.	.243	85	272	36	66	91	16	0	3	28	5	5	1	5	2
Trillo, J. Manuel, San Francisco	.254	98	401	45	102	137	21	1	4	36	3	4	4	0	0
Trout, Steven, Chicago*	.131	32	61	4	8	8	0	0	0	3	0	5	1	0	0
Tudor, John, Pittsburgh*	.211	36	76	3	16	17	1	0	0	2	0	4	0	1	0
Tunnell, B. Lee, Pittsburgh	.083	26	12	0	1	1	0	0	0	0	0	3	0	0	0
Vail, Michael, Los Angeles	.063	16	16	1	1	1	0	0	0	2	1	0	0	0	0
Valenzuela, Fernando, Los Angeles*	.190	35	79	5	15	27	3	0	3	7	2	9	0	0	0
Van Gorder, David, Cincinnati	.228	38	101	10	23	25	2	0	0	6	0	0	0	0	0
Van Slyke, Andrew, St. Louis*	.244	137	361	45	88	133	16	4	7	50	3	0	2	28	5
Vargas, Hediberto, Pittsburgh	.226	18	31	3	7	9	2	0	0	2	0	0	0	0	0
Venable, W. McKinley, Montreal*	.239	38	71	7	17	25	2	0	2	7	2	0	1	1	0
Veryzer, Thomas, Chicago	.189	44	74	5	14	15	1	0	0	4	0	2	0	0	0
Virgil, Osvaldo, Philadelphia	.261	141	456	61	119	198	21	2	18	68	4	1	5	1	1
Von Ohlen, David, St. Louis*	1.000	27	1	0	1	1	0	0	0	0	0	0	0	0	0
Walk, Robert, Pittsburgh	.000	2	3	0	0	0	0	0	0	0	0	0	0	0	0
Walker, Duane, Cincinnati*	.292	83	195	35	57	103	10	3	10	28	3	1	2	7	3
Wallach, Timothy, Montreal	.246	160	582	55	143	230	25	4	18	72	8	0	4	3	7
Walling, Dennis, Houston*	.281	87	249	37	70	100	11	5	3	31	6	0	2	7	1
Washington, Claudell, Atlanta*	.286	120	416	62	119	195	21	2	17	61	9	0	3	21	9
Watson, Robert, Atlanta	.212	49	85	4	18	28	4	0	2	12	0	0	0	0	0
Wehrmeister, David, Philadelphia	.000	7	2	0	0	0	0	0	0	0	0	0	0	0	0
Welch, Robert, Los Angeles	.078	32	51	0	4	4	0	0	0	3	0	8	0	0	0
Wellman, Brad, San Francisco	.226	93	265	23	60	77	9	1	2	25	2	3	4	10	5
White, Larry, Los Angeles	.000	7	1	0	0	0	0	0	0	0	0	0	0	0	0
Whitfield, Terry, Los Angeles*	.244	87	180	15	44	64	8	0	4	18	1	2	0	1	4
Whitson, Eddie, San Diego	.049	36	61	0	3	3	0	0	0	1	0	6	0	0	0
Wieghaus, Thomas, Houston	.000	6	10	0	0	0	0	0	0	1	0	0	1	0	0
Wiggins, Alan, San Diego†	.258	158	596	106	154	196	19	7	3	34	0	14	4	70	21
Williams, Frank, San Francisco	.222	61	18	1	4	4	0	0	0	1	0	0	0	0	0
Willis, Carl, Cincinnati*	.000	7	0	0	0	0	0	0	0	0	0	0	0	0	0
Wilson, Glenn, Philadelphia	.240	132	341	28	82	127	21	3	6	31	5	1	3	7	1
Wilson, William, New York†	.276	154	587	88	162	240	28	10	10	54	7	2	2	46	9
Winn, James, Pittsburgh	.000	9	1	0	0	0	0	0	0	0	0	0	0	0	0
Winningham, Herman, New York*	.407	14	27	5	11	14	1	1	0	5	0	0	0	2	1
Wockenfuss, Johnny, Philadelphia	.289	86	180	20	52	75	3	1	6	24	2	1	0	1	0
Wohlford, James, Montreal	.300	95	213	20	64	96	13	2	5	29	2	0	1	3	0
Woods, Gary, Chicago	.235	87	98	13	23	38	4	1	3	10	1	2	1	2	1
Wotus, Ronald, Pittsburgh	.218	27	55	4	12	18	6	0	0	2	0	2	1	0	0
Wynne, Marvell, Pittsburgh*	.266	154	653	77	174	220	24	11	0	39	7	5	2	24	19
Yeager, Stephen, Los Angeles	.228	74	197	16	45	61	4	0	4	29	5	1	3	1	2
Youngblood, Joel, San Francisco	.254	134	469	50	119	168	17	1	10	51	5	3	0	5	6
Zachry, Patrick, Los Angeles	.333	58	6	0	2	2	0	0	0	0	0	0	0	0	0
Zaske, L. Jeffrey, Pittsburgh	.000	3	0	0	0	0	0	0	0	0	0	0	0	0	0
Zuvella, Paul, Atlanta	.200	11	25	2	5	6	1	0	0	1	0	0	0	0	0

AWARDED FIRST BASE ON INTERFERENCE: Van Slyke, St.L. 4 (Bailey 2, Gulden, Kennedy); Wellman, S.F. 2 (Wockenfuss, Kennedy); Baker, S.F. (Wockenfuss), Chambliss, Atl. (Kennedy), Hendrick, St.L. (Hodges), Householder, Cin. (Rabb), Maddox, Phila. (Bailey), Reynolds, L.A. (Kennedy).

PLAYERS WITH TWO OR MORE CLUBS
(Alphabetically Arranged With Player's First Club on Top)

Player and Club	Pct.	G.	AB.	R.	H.	TB.	2B.	3B.	HR.	RBI.	GW.	SH.	SF.	Tot. BB.	Int. BB.	HP.	SO.	SB.	CS.	GI. DP.
Berenyi, Cin.	.063	13	16	0	1	1	0	0	0	0	0	2	0	0	0	0	5	0	0	0
Berenyi, N.Y.	.243	19	37	3	9	10	1	0	0	3	0	5	1	0	0	0	5	0	0	1
Dayley, Atl.	.500	5	4	1	2	2	0	0	0	0	0	0	0	0	0	0	2	0	0	0
Dayley, St.L.	.000	3	0	0	0	0	0	0	0	0	0	1	0	0	0	0	0	0	0	0
Driessen, Cin.	.280	81	218	27	61	95	13	0	7	28	3	0	4	37	2	0	25	2	1	5
Driessen, Mtl.	.254	51	169	20	43	81	11	0	9	32	5	1	1	17	6	0	15	0	1	5
Harris, Mtl.	.000	15	1	0	0	0	0	0	0	0	0	0	0	0	0	0	1	0	0	0
Harris, S.D.	.375	19	8	3	3	4	1	0	0	0	0	0	0	0	0	0	1	0	0	0

Player and Club	Pct.	G.	AB.	R.	H.	TB.	2B.	3B.	HR.	RBI.	GW.	SH.	SF.	Tot. BB.	Int. BB.	HP.	SO.	SB.	CS.	GI. DP.
Householder, Cin....	.083	14	12	3	1	2	1	0	0	0	0	0	0	3	1	0	3	1	1	0
Householder, St.L..	.143	13	14	1	2	2	0	0	0	0	0	0	0	0	0	0	3	0	0	1
Jorgensen, Atl.	.269	31	26	4	7	8	1	0	0	5	2	0	1	3	1	0	6	0	1	0
Jorgensen, St.L.....	.245	59	98	5	24	35	4	2	1	12	1	0	0	10	1	0	17	0	0	1
Knight, Hou.	.223	88	278	15	62	78	10	0	2	29	1	0	4	14	1	1	30	0	3	4
Knight, N.Y.	.280	27	93	13	26	33	4	0	1	6	1	0	0	7	1	1	13	0	0	1
Lawless, Cin.	.250	43	80	10	20	25	2	0	1	2	0	1	0	8	1	0	12	6	3	1
Lawless, Mtl..........	.176	11	17	1	3	4	1	0	0	0	0	0	0	0	0	0	4	1	0	3
Martin, S.F.	.500	12	6	0	3	3	0	0	0	0	0	0	0	0	0	0	2	0	0	0
Martin, Phil.	.000	9	2	0	0	0	0	0	0	0	0	0	0	0	0	0	0	0	0	0
McGaffigan, Mtl.	.000	21	8	0	0	0	0	0	0	0	1	0	0	0	0	0	7	0	0	0
McGaffigan, Cin....	.000	9	2	0	0	0	0	0	0	0	0	2	0	0	0	0	0	0	0	0
Oberkfell, St.L.......	.309	50	152	17	47	60	11	1	0	11	3	0	0	16	2	1	10	1	2	3
Oberkfell, Atl.........	.233	50	172	21	40	53	8	1	1	10	0	3	3	15	1	0	17	1	3	4
Oliver, S.F.	.298	91	339	27	101	124	19	2	0	34	5	0	0	20	4	1	27	2	2	19
Oliver, Phila.	.312	28	93	9	29	36	7	0	0	14	0	0	0	7	2	0	9	1	2	4
Ramsey, St.L.........	.067	21	15	1	1	2	1	0	0	0	0	2	0	1	0	0	3	0	0	0
Ramsey, Mtl..........	.214	37	70	2	15	16	1	0	0	3	0	0	0	0	0	0	13	0	0	2
Rose, Mtl................	.259	95	278	34	72	82	6	2	0	23	0	3	1	31	3	1	20	1	1	10
Rose, Cin...............	.365	26	96	9	35	44	9	0	0	11	0	0	0	9	1	2	7	0	0	1
T. Scott, Hou.	.190	25	21	2	4	5	1	0	0	0	0	1	0	4	1	0	3	0	0	0
Scott, Mtl...............	.254	45	71	8	18	22	4	0	0	5	2	0	1	7	1	0	21	1	1	1
Speier, Mtl.............	.150	25	40	1	6	6	0	0	0	1	0	2	0	1	0	0	8	0	0	1
Speier, St.L............	.178	38	118	7	21	39	7	1	3	8	3	1	0	9	1	1	19	0	0	4
Trevino, Cin...........	.167	6	6	0	1	1	0	0	0	0	0	0	0	0	0	0	2	0	0	0
Trevino, Atl...........	.244	79	266	36	65	90	16	0	3	28	5	5	1	16	1	1	27	5	2	4

OFFICIAL MISCELLANEOUS NATIONAL LEAGUE BATTING RECORDS

CLUB MISCELLANEOUS BATTING RECORDS

Club	Slg. Pct.	OB Pct.	Tot. BB.	Int. BB.	HP.	SO.	GIDP.	ShO.
Philadelphia	.407	.333	555	60	29	1084	140	10
San Francisco	.375	.328	528	44	17	980	141	10
Houston	.371	.323	494	57	17	837	88	9
Chicago	.397	.331	567	69	29	967	102	10
San Diego	.371	.317	472	70	24	810	132	8
New York	.369	.320	500	73	20	1001	132	8
Pittsburgh	.363	.310	438	47	19	841	131	14
St. Louis	.351	.317	516	49	23	924	120	13
Montreal	.362	.312	470	50	25	782	101	8
Atlanta	.361	.317	555	70	20	896	113	13
Cincinnati	.356	.313	566	62	12	978	99	12
Los Angeles	.348	.306	488	56	14	829	120	15
Totals	.369	.319	6149	707	249	10929	1419	130

INDIVIDUAL MISCELLANEOUS BATTING RECORDS
(Top Ten Qualifiers for Slugging Championship)

Player—Club	Slg. Pct.	OB Pct.	Tot. BB.	Int. BB.	HP.	SO.	GI DP.
Murphy, Atl.	.547	.372	79	20	2	134	13
Schmidt, Phila.	.536	.383	92	14	4	116	15
Sandberg, Chi.	.520	.367	52	3	3	101	7
C. Davis, S.F.	.507	.368	42	6	1	74	13
Durham, Chi.	.505	.369	69	11	1	86	8
Carter, Mtl.	.487	.366	64	9	6	57	8
Leonard, S.F.	.484	.357	47	3	0	123	13
Strawberry, N.Y.	.467	.343	75	15	0	131	8
McReynolds, S.D.	.465	.317	34	8	0	69	14
Brenly, S.F.	.464	.352	48	3	5	52	14

DEPARTMENTAL LEADERS: OB Pct.—Matthews, Gwynn, .410; TBB—Matthews, 103; IBB—Templeton, 23; HP—Lo. Smith, 9; SO—Samuel, 168; GIDP—Garvey, 25.

(All Players—Listed Alphabetically)

Player—Club	Slg. Pct.	OB Pct.	Tot. BB.	Int. BB.	HP.	SO.	GI DP.
Aguayo, Phila.	.458	.350	8	2	0	16	1
Allen, St.L.	.320	.240	0	0	0	8	0
Altamirano, Chi.	.000	.000	0	0	0	0	0
Amelung, L.A.	.217	.250	2	0	0	4	1
Andersen, Phila.	.000	.000	0	0	0	3	0

Player—Club	Slg. Pct.	OB Pct.	Tot. BB.	Int. BB.	HP.	SO.	GI DP.
Anderson, L.A.	.329	.331	45	4	2	55	8
Andujar, St.L.	.214	.215	9	0	0	47	0
Ashby, Hou.	.361	.330	20	2	1	22	4
Backman, N.Y.	.339	.360	56	2	0	63	13
Bailey, Hou.	.343	.318	53	4	2	71	7
Bailor, L.A.	.305	.317	8	1	0	1	3
Baker, S.F.	.374	.387	40	1	0	27	5
Bannister, Hou.	.300	.273	2	0	0	2	0
Bargar, Mtl.	.000	.000	0	0	0	1	0
Barker, Atl.	.079	.182	6	0	0	19	1
Barnes, Cin.	.190	.196	4	1	0	6	1
Bass, Hou.	.360	.279	6	1	3	57	2
Beane, N.Y.	.100	.100	0	0	0	2	0
Bedrosian, Atl.	.118	.118	0	0	0	9	0
Belliard, Pitt.	.227	.227	0	0	0	1	0
Benedict, Atl.	.297	.301	34	3	1	25	9
Berenyi, Cin.-N.Y.	.208	.185	0	0	0	10	1
Berra, Pitt.	.318	.273	34	8	1	78	11
Bevacqua, S.D.	.275	.326	14	1	1	19	6
Bielecki, Pitts.	.000	.000	0	0	0	0	0
Bilardello, Cin.	.280	.287	19	3	1	34	6
Bochy, S.D.	.435	.250	3	0	0	21	2
Booker, S.D.	.429	.286	0	0	0	2	0
Bordi, Chi.	.053	.100	1	0	0	7	1
Bosley, Chi.	.418	.375	13	2	0	22	1

Player—Club	Slg. Pct.	OB Pct.	Tot. BB.	Int. BB.	HP.	SO.	GI DP.
Bowa, Chi.	.269	.274	28	5	0	24	4
Braun, St.L.	.327	.383	17	0	0	17	0
Bream, L.A.	.245	.263	6	2	0	9	1
Breining, Mtl.	.000	.000	0	0	0	1	0
Brenly, S.F.	.464	.352	48	3	3	52	14
Brewer, L.A.	.216	.195	4	1	0	9	1
Brizzolara, Atl.	.000	.000	0	0	0	2	0
Brock, L.A.	.402	.319	39	3	0	37	6
Brooks, N.Y.	.417	.341	48	15	2	79	17
Brown, S.F.	.405	.358	9	0	1	19	4
Brown, S.D.	.368	.292	11	0	0	33	6
Browning, Cin.	.143	.143	0	0	0	3	0
Brummer, St.L.	.259	.246	3	0	0	7	5
Brusstar, Chi.	.200	.429	2	0	0	1	0
Buckner, Chi.	.209	.239	1	1	1	1	1
Butera, Mtl.	.000	.250	1	0	0	0	0
Bystrom, Phila.	.211	.158	0	0	0	7	0
Cabell, Hou.	.417	.341	21	5	1	47	12
Calhoun, Hou.	.000	.000	0	0	0	0	0
Calvert, S.F.	.000	.000	0	0	0	5	0
Camp, Atl.	.133	.130	0	0	1	20	1
Campbell, Phila.	.000	.000	0	0	0	0	0
Candelaria, Pitt.	.210	.182	4	0	0	25	3
Carlton, Phila.	.250	.209	2	0	0	20	1
Carman, Phila.	.000	.000	0	0	0	1	0
Carter, Mtl.	.487	.366	64	9	6	57	8
Cato, Cin.	.500	.500	0	0	0	0	0
Cedeno, Cin.	.429	.321	25	4	1	54	11
Cey, Chi.	.442	.324	61	10	6	108	10
Chambliss, Atl.	.362	.350	58	12	1	54	10
Chapman, N.Y.	.401	.356	19	0	2	30	7
Chiffer, S.D.	.000	.000	0	0	0	1	0
Christensen, N.Y.	.455	.308	1	0	0	2	0
Citarella, St.L.	.250	.250	0	0	0	2	0
Clark, S.F.	.537	.434	43	7	0	29	9
Concepcion, Cin.	.320	.307	52	5	0	72	9
Corcoran, Phila.	.486	.440	37	5	1	27	6
Cornell, S.F.	.000	.000	0	0	0	3	0
Cotto, Chi.	.308	.325	10	2	1	23	1
Cox, St.L.	.132	.207	5	0	0	22	2
Cruz, Hou.	.462	.381	73	10	0	68	8
Darling, N.Y.	.164	.159	1	0	0	19	1
C. Davis, S.F.	.507	.368	42	6	1	74	13
Davis, Cin.	.466	.320	24	0	1	48	1
Davis, Hou.	.393	.258	4	0	0	12	0
Davis, Chi.	.421	.315	47	15	1	99	20
M. Davis, S.F.	.217	.167	2	0	0	16	0
Dawley, Hou.	.556	.333	0	0	0	3	0
Dawson, Mtl.	.409	.301	41	2	2	80	12
Dayley, Atl.-St.L.	.500	.500	0	0	0	2	0
Dedmon, Atl.	.000	.000	0	0	0	1	0
Deer, S.F.	.542	.375	7	0	1	10	0
DeJesus, Phila.	.306	.325	43	7	2	76	13
DeLeon, Pitt.	.085	.083	0	0	0	25	1
DeLeon, S.D.	.000	.000	0	0	0	3	0
Denny, Phila.	.191	.204	1	0	0	11	0
Dernier, Chi.	.362	.356	63	0	2	60	5
Diaz, Phila.	.307	.256	5	0	0	13	4
Diaz, L.A.	.000	.000	0	0	0	1	0
Dilone, Mtl.	.367	.346	17	0	1	18	4
DiPino, Hou.	.000	.000	0	0	0	5	0
Distefano, Pitt.	.346	.226	5	1	1	13	3
Doran, Hou.	.356	.341	66	7	2	69	6
Dravecky, S.D.	.146	.159	3	0	0	8	0
Driessen, Cin.-Mtl.	.455	.354	54	8	0	40	10
Durham, Chi.	.505	.369	69	11	1	86	8
Eckersley, Chi.	.109	.125	1	0	0	25	1
Esasky, Cin.	.348	.301	52	3	0	103	6
Falcone, Atl.	.273	.212	0	0	0	14	0
Fernandez, N.Y.	.179	.179	0	0	0	9	0
Fimple, L.A.	.231	.214	1	0	0	6	3
Fireovid, Phila.	.000	.000	0	0	0	0	0
Fitzgerald, N.Y.	.306	.288	24	7	1	71	17
Flannery, S.D.	.391	.347	12	1	3	17	1
Flynn, Mtl.	.281	.267	12	6	0	41	5
Foley, Cin.	.357	.310	24	7	0	36	2
Forsch, St.L.	.313	.250	0	0	0	3	1
Forster, Atl.	.667	.667	0	0	0	1	0
Foster, N.Y.	.443	.311	30	9	6	122	14
Franco, Cin.	.000	.000	0	0	0	2	0
Francona, Mtl.	.467	.360	5	3	1	12	4
Frazier, Chi.	.286	.286	0	0	0	1	0
Frobel, Pitt.	.388	.271	24	2	2	84	7
Fuentes, Mtl.	.250	.400	1	0	0	2	0
Gaff, N.Y.	.000	.000	0	0	0	2	0
Garber, Atl.	.143	.143	0	0	0	5	1
Garcia, Phila.	.267	.281	4	1	0	11	4
Gardenhire, N.Y.	.304	.276	9	1	0	43	7
Gardner, N.Y.	.000	.000	0	0	0	0	0
Garner, Hou.	.388	.355	43	2	4	63	9
Garrelts, S.F.	.100	.100	0	0	0	3	0
Garvey, S.D.	.373	.307	24	3	1	64	25
Gibbons, N.Y.	.065	.171	3	1	1	11	0
Gladden, S.F.	.447	.410	33	2	2	37	3
Gomez, S.F.	.200	.342	8	0	0	3	2
Gonzales, Mtl.	.267	.303	2	0	1	5	0
Gonzalez, Pitt.	.244	.247	7	1	0	21	4
Gonzalez, St.L.	.211	.211	0	0	0	2	1
Gooden, N.Y.	.200	.205	1	0	0	14	3
Gorman, N.Y.	.000	.000	0	0	0	1	0
Gossage, S.D.	.182	.217	1	0	0	8	0
Grant, S.F.	.000	.056	0	0	1	10	0
Grapenthin, Mtl.	.200	.200	0	0	0	1	0
Green, Pitt.	.000	.000	0	0	0	0	0
Green, St.L.	.416	.297	20	4	1	105	8
G. Gross, Phila.	.376	.393	24	3	1	11	4
K. Gross, Phila.	.067	.097	1	0	0	21	1
Guante, Pitt.	.000	.000	0	0	0	3	0
Guerrero, L.A.	.462	.358	49	7	1	105	7
Gulden, Cin.	.308	.307	33	2	2	35	7
Gullickson, Mtl.	.110	.143	3	0	0	22	0
Gwosdz, S.D.	.250	.400	2	0	0	5	0
Gwynn, S.D.	.444	.410	59	13	2	23	15
Hagen, St.L.	.000	.000	0	0	0	0	0
Hall, Atl.	.338	.309	10	0	0	18	2
Hall, Chi.	.473	.329	12	3	0	23	2
Hammaker, S.F.	.182	.308	2	0	0	3	0
Harper, Pitt.	.348	.300	5	0	2	11	4
Harper, Atl.	.206	.194	4	0	1	21	6
Harris, Mtl.-S.D.	.444	.333	0	0	0	2	0
Hassey, N.Y.	.515	.405	4	1	0	6	1
Hassler, St.L.	.000	.000	0	0	0	0	0
Hatcher, Chi.	.111	.200	1	1	0	0	0
Hawkins, S.D.	.195	.214	1	0	0	14	1
Hayes, Phila.	.447	.359	59	41	0	84	10
Hebner, Chi.	.444	.407	10	2	0	15	2
Heep, N.Y.	.312	.319	27	3	1	22	9
Hendrick, St.L.	.406	.324	32	2	1	75	13
Hernandez, N.Y.	.449	.409	97	12	1	89	9
Herr, St.L.	.346	.335	49	2	2	56	11
Hershiser, L.A.	.200	.259	3	0	1	14	0
Hesketh, Mtl.	.100	.250	2	0	0	4	1
Hodges, N.Y.	.264	.351	23	0	1	18	3
Holland, Phila.	.000	.000	0	0	0	4	0
Honeycutt, L.A.	.143	.186	3	0	0	17	1
Hooton, L.A.	.071	.071	0	0	0	3	0
Horner, Atl.	.425	.349	14	2	0	17	3
Horton, St.L.	.065	.094	1	0	0	13	0
Householder, Ci-StL	.154	.207	3	1	0	6	1
Howe, St.L.	.295	.300	18	1	0	18	6
Howell, L.A.	.000	.000	0	0	0	3	0
Hubbard, Atl.	.380	.331	55	6	4	61	8
Hudson, Phila.	.143	.088	0	0	0	27	0
Hume, Cin.	.136	.174	1	0	0	8	1
Iorg, St.L.	.214	.200	2	1	0	6	2
James, Mtl.	.143	.143	0	0	0	11	0
Jeltz, Phila.	.279	.276	7	1	0	11	3
Johnson, Atl.	.374	.329	21	6	1	21	2
Rn. Johnson, Mtl.	.200	.200	0	0	0	2	0
Ry. Johnson, Mtl.	.303	.300	7	0	0	10	0
W. Johnson, Mtl.	.208	.345	5	0	0	4	0
Johnson, Chi.	.000	.000	0	0	0	0	0
Johnstone, Chi.	.370	.350	7	4	0	18	2
Jones, N.Y.	.200	.308	3	0	0	4	0
Jorgensen, At-StL.	.347	.319	13	2	0	23	1
Kennedy, S.D.	.353	.284	33	8	2	99	16
Kepshire, St.L.	.083	.081	1	0	0	23	0
Kern, Phila.	.000	.000	0	0	0	1	0

Player—Club	Slg. Pct.	OB Pct.	Tot. BB.	Int. BB.	HP.	SO.	GI DP.
Knepper, Hou.	.237	.241	7	0	0	28	1
Knicely, Cin.	.138	.200	3	0	0	6	1
Knight, Hou.-N.Y.	.299	.279	21	2	2	43	5
Komminsk, Atl.	.316	.276	29	0	2	77	5
Koosman, Phila.	.108	.120	1	0	0	23	3
Krawczyk, Pitt.	.000	.000	0	0	0	0	0
Krenchicki, Cin.	.470	.358	19	3	0	23	4
Krukow, S.F.	.153	.149	1	0	0	19	1
Kuiper, S.F.	.209	.273	12	5	0	10	2
Lacey, S.F.	.333	.333	0	0	0	2	0
LaCoss, Hou.	.161	.125	0	0	0	16	1
Lacy, Pitt.	.464	.362	32	2	0	61	10
Lahti, St.L.	.167	.167	0	0	0	2	0
Lake, Chi.	.407	.232	0	0	1	7	0
Landestoy, L.A.	.241	.200	1	0	0	6	1
Landreaux, L.A.	.374	.295	29	3	1	35	7
Landrum, St.L.	.387	.306	10	1	0	27	8
LaPoint, St.L.	.068	.097	2	0	0	19	2
Laskey, S.F.	.063	.119	4	0	0	26	1
Lavalliere, Phila.	.000	.222	2	0	0	2	0
Lavelle, S.F.	.000	.167	1	0	0	4	0
Lawless, Cin.-Mtl.	.299	.295	8	1	0	16	4
Lea, Mtl.	.111	.123	1	0	0	24	2
Leary, N.Y.	.600	.300	0	0	0	2	0
Lefebvre, Phila.	.363	.348	23	4	2	37	5
Lefferts, S.D.	.353	.294	0	0	0	6	0
LeMaster, S.F.	.282	.265	31	5	0	97	6
Leonard, S.F.	.484	.357	47	3	0	123	13
Lerch, S.F.	.133	.278	3	0	0	5	0
Lesley, Cin.	.500	.500	0	0	0	0	0
Lezcano, Phila.	.480	.371	38	1	0	43	11
Linares, Atl.	.310	.273	6	0	0	12	1
Little, Mtl.	.293	.332	34	0	1	19	3
Lollar, S.D.	.397	.280	6	0	0	21	1
Lopes, Chi.	.294	.435	6	0	0	5	0
Lucas, Mtl.	.000	.000	0	0	0	2	0
Lynch, N.Y.	.259	.222	0	0	0	9	1
Lyons, St.L.	.260	.305	9	1	0	13	0
Madden, Hou.	.333	.429	1	0	0	3	0
Maddox, Phila.	.390	.316	13	1	0	29	2
Madlock, Pitt.	.323	.297	26	5	1	29	11
Mahler, Atl.	.338	.315	2	0	0	8	1
Maldonado, L.A.	.382	.318	19	0	1	29	6
Marshall, L.A.	.438	.315	40	6	3	93	12
Martin, S.F.-Phil.	.375	.375	0	0	0	2	0
Martin, N.Y.	.264	.206	6	0	0	29	5
Martinez, S.D.	.395	.340	68	4	4	82	7
Matthews, Chi.	.428	.410	103	2	3	97	10
Matuszek, Phila.	.458	.350	39	4	4	54	7
May, Pitt.	.240	.255	10	1	0	15	3
Mazzilli, Pitt.	.331	.338	40	2	1	42	5
McGaffigan, Mt-Ci..	.000	.000	0	0	0	7	0
McGee, St.L.	.394	.325	29	2	1	80	12
McGraw, Phila.	.333	.333	0	0	0	0	0
McMurtry, Atl.	.154	.148	2	0	0	27	0
McReynolds, S.D.	.465	.317	34	8	0	69	14
McWilliams, Pitt.	.122	.122	0	0	0	22	0
Melendez, Phila.	.130	.167	1	0	0	5	1
Meridith, Chi.	.000	.000	0	0	0	0	0
Miller, S.D.	.643	.286	0	0	0	4	0
Miller, L.A.	.167	.231	1	0	0	2	0
Milner, Cin.	.342	.333	51	3	2	50	2
Minton, S.F.	.048	.091	1	0	0	7	1
Mitchell, N.Y.	.214	.214	0	0	0	3	0
Monday, L.A.	.298	.309	8	3	0	16	0
Monge, S.D.	.000	.000	0	0	0	0	0
Moore, Atl.	.000	.000	0	0	0	1	0
Morales, L.A.	.158	.200	1	1	0	2	0
Moreland, Chi.	.422	.326	34	5	3	71	16
Morrison, Pitt.	.454	.328	20	1	1	52	9
Mullins, S.F.	.345	.277	9	0	0	29	3
Mumphrey, Hou.	.391	.355	56	7	0	79	12
Murphy, Atl.	.547	.372	79	20	2	134	13
Nettles, S.D.	.413	.329	58	4	5	55	12
Nicosia, S.F.	.462	.336	8	0	0	14	3
Niedenfuer, L.A.	.000	.000	0	0	0	3	0
Niekro, Hou.	.133	.153	2	0	0	21	0
Nieto, St.L.	.430	.312	5	2	0	18	3
Noles, Chi.	.000	.091	1	0	0	6	0
Oberkfell, St.L.-Atl.	.349	.331	31	3	1	27	7
Oester, Cin.	.316	.295	41	7	1	97	16
Oliver, S.F.-Phil.	.370	.343	27	6	1	36	23
O'Malley, S.F.	.120	.185	2	0	0	2	0
Oquendo, N.Y.	.249	.284	15	2	2	26	2
Orosco, N.Y.	.250	.571	3	0	0	2	0
Orsulak, Pitt.	.328	.271	1	0	1	7	0
Ortiz, N.Y.	.231	.235	5	0	0	15	2
Otis, Pitt.	.206	.213	7	0	0	15	4
Owchinko, Cin.	.250	.333	3	0	0	5	2
Owen, Chi.	.290	.269	8	1	2	15	0
Ownbey, St.L.	.000	.000	0	0	0	2	0
Page, Pitt.	.417	.467	3	0	0	4	0
Palmer, Mtl.	.273	.152	0	0	0	12	0
Pankovits, Hou.	.407	.298	2	0	0	20	1
Parker, Cin.	.410	.328	41	10	1	89	8
Pastore, Cin.	.071	.103	1	0	0	11	0
Patterson, Chi.	.000	.000	0	0	0	0	0
Payne, Atl.	.000	.000	0	0	0	1	0
Pena, Hou.	.308	.262	3	1	0	8	3
Pena, L.A.	.167	.147	2	0	0	26	1
Pena, Pitt.	.425	.333	36	5	4	79	14
Pendleton, St.L.	.420	.357	16	3	0	32	7
Perez, Cin.	.343	.295	11	2	0	21	8
Perez, Atl.	.121	.164	6	0	1	29	0
Perry, Atl.	.372	.372	61	5	2	38	9
Pittman, S.F.	.227	.217	0	0	0	6	1
Pocoroba, Atl.	.000	.500	2	0	0	0	0
Porter, St.L.	.363	.331	60	12	5	79	10
Power, Cin.	.000	.167	1	0	0	4	0
Price, Cin.	.167	.180	2	0	0	16	0
Puhl, Hou.	.434	.380	59	12	1	45	5
Puleo, Cin.	.400	.200	0	0	0	2	0
Pulido, Pitt.	.000	.000	0	0	0	0	0
Rabb, S.F.	.317	.283	10	0	0	33	0
Raines, Mtl.	.437	.393	87	7	2	69	7
Rainey, Chi.	.097	.152	2	0	0	12	0
Rajsich, St.L.	.143	.300	2	0	0	1	0
Ramirez, N.Y.	.237	.278	13	1	0	14	2
Ramirez, Atl.	.327	.295	26	1	1	70	9
Ramos, Mtl.	.277	.244	6	1	0	13	5
Ramsey, St.L.-Mtl.	.212	.198	1	0	0	16	2
Rawley, Phila.	.116	.133	1	0	0	17	0
Ray, Pitt.	.434	.354	37	2	3	31	16
Reardon, Mtl.	.000	.000	0	0	0	7	0
Redus, Cin.	.376	.338	52	3	1	71	4
Reuschel, Chi.	.345	.281	2	0	0	8	1
Reuss, L.A.	.208	.259	3	0	0	9	1
Reyes, L.A.	.000	.000	0	0	0	3	0
Reynolds, Hou.	.364	.286	22	2	0	53	4
Reynolds, L.A.	.350	.300	14	0	1	38	6
Rhoden, Pitt.	.405	.345	2	0	0	10	1
Richards, S.F.	.281	.340	18	2	0	28	3
Richardt, Hou.	.333	.267	0	0	0	1	0
Riley, S.F.	.100	.100	0	0	0	5	1
Rivera, L.A.	.357	.321	21	5	1	30	15
Robinson, Pitt.	.387	.371	4	1	0	9	0
Robinson, S.F.	.115	.143	2	0	0	23	2
Robinson, Cin.	.000	.000	0	0	0	5	0
Rodas, L.A.	.000	.000	0	0	0	0	0
Roenicke, S.D.	.500	.364	2	1	0	5	0
Rogers, Mtl.	.204	.176	2	0	0	15	1
Rohn, Chi.	.226	.152	1	0	0	6	1
Rose, Mtl.-Cin.	.337	.359	40	4	3	27	11
Ross, Hou.	.000	.000	0	0	0	0	0
Rowdon, Chi.	.286	.286	0	0	0	1	0
Royster, Atl.	.295	.257	15	1	1	41	8
Rucker, St.L.	.143	.143	0	0	0	3	0
Ruhle, Hou.	.083	.214	2	0	0	7	0
Runge, Atl.	.322	.340	10	0	0	14	2
Russell, Cin.	.175	.194	4	0	0	27	0
Russell, Phil.	.444	.351	12	2	0	33	2
Russell, L.A.	.321	.329	25	1	0	24	7
Ruthven, Chi.	.227	.178	1	0	0	18	0
Ryan, Hou.	.131	.127	2	0	0	26	1
St. Claire, Mtl.	.000	.000	0	0	0	0	0
Salas, St.L.	.150	.100	0	0	0	3	0
Salazar, Mtl.	.201	.178	4	0	1	38	2
Salazar, S.D.	.329	.261	6	1	0	38	5

Player—Club	Slg. Pct.	OB Pct.	Tot. BB.	Int. BB.	HP.	SO.	GI DP.
Sambito, Hou.	.000	.000	0	0	0	0	0
Samuel, Phila.	.442	.307	28	2	7	168	6
Sanchez, S.F.	.244	.195	0	0	0	12	0
Sandberg, Chi.	.520	.367	52	3	3	101	7
Sanderson, Chi.	.119	.191	3	0	1	18	0
Santana, N.Y.	.382	.317	9	0	0	17	3
Sax, L.A.	.304	.300	47	3	1	53	12
Schatzeder, Mtl.	.429	.351	2	0	0	10	0
Scherrer, Cin.	.000	.000	0	0	0	2	0
Schiraldi, N.Y.	.000	.000	0	0	0	0	0
Schmidt, Phila.	.536	.383	92	14	4	116	15
Schu, Phila.	.621	.389	6	0	0	6	0
Schulze, Chi.	.000	.000	0	0	0	0	0
Scioscia, L.A.	.370	.367	52	10	1	26	10
A. Scott, Hou.-Mtl.	.293	.317	11	2	0	24	1
M. Scott, Hou.	.170	.163	2	0	0	26	1
Scurry, Pitt.	.000	.000	0	0	0	1	0
Shines, Mtl.	.350	.286	0	0	0	3	0
Show, S.D.	.420	.257	0	0	1	23	4
Sinatro, Atl.	.000	.000	0	0	0	0	0
Sisk, N.Y.	.091	.167	1	0	0	6	1
Smith, Mtl.	.189	.207	5	0	0	18	0
Smith, Hou.	.000	.200	1	0	0	2	0
Smith, Chi.	.077	.077	0	0	0	8	0
L. Smith, St.L.	.341	.349	70	0	9	90	7
Smith, Cin.	.000	.000	0	0	0	0	0
O. Smith, St.L.	.337	.347	56	5	2	17	8
Smith, Atl.	.556	.556	0	0	0	1	0
Solano, Hou.	.333	.333	0	0	0	2	0
Soto, Cin.	.299	.205	0	0	0	28	0
Speier, Mtl.-St.L.	.285	.225	10	1	1	27	5
Spilman, Hou.	.375	.356	12	0	0	10	1
Staub, N.Y.	.361	.291	4	3	0	9	1
Stearns, N.Y.	.235	.333	4	0	0	2	0
Stenhouse, Mtl.	.297	.289	26	4	1	32	5
Stoddard, Chi.	.091	.091	0	0	0	5	0
Stone, Phila.	.465	.394	9	0	2	26	2
Strawberry, N.Y.	.467	.343	75	15	0	131	8
Stubbs, L.A.	.341	.273	24	3	0	63	0
Stuper, St.L.	.063	.118	1	0	0	8	0
Summers, S.D.	.296	.254	4	1	1	15	2
Sutcliffe, Chi.	.304	.276	2	0	0	18	1
Sutter, St.L.	.000	.000	0	0	0	3	0
Swan, N.Y.	.000	.000	0	0	0	0	0
Tekulve, Pitt.	.000	.000	0	0	0	4	0
Templeton, S.D.	.320	312	39	23	1	81	10
Terrell, N.Y.	.107	.092	1	0	0	33	1
Thomas, Mtl.	.321	.308	20	1	0	33	7
Thompson, Pitt.	.389	.357	87	14	2	73	13
Thompson, Atl.	.374	.373	11	1	0	11	1
Thompson, S.F.	.355	.376	30	5	0	26	11
Thon, Hou.	.471	.389	0	0	1	4	1
Thurmond, S.D.	.207	.230	3	0	0	10	1
Tibbs, Cin.	.139	.162	1	0	0	13	0
Tidrow, N.Y.	.000	.000	0	0	0	0	0
Toliver, Cin.	.000	.000	0	0	0	0	0
Tolman, Hou.	.235	.176	0	0	0	3	0
Torrez, N.Y.	.300	.364	1	0	0	1	1
Trevino, Cin.-Atl.	.335	.286	16	1	1	29	4
Trillo, S.F.	.342	.300	25	0	3	55	8
Trout, Chi.	.131	.182	4	0	0	21	1
Tudor, Pitt.	.224	.241	3	0	0	24	0
Tunnell, Pitt.	.083	.083	0	0	0	6	0
Vail, L.A.	.063	.118	1	0	0	7	0
Valenzuela, L.A.	.342	.200	1	0	0	11	2
Van Gorder, Cin.	.248	.310	12	2	0	17	2
Van Slyke, St.L.	.368	.354	63	9	0	71	5
Vargas, Pitt.	.290	.294	3	0	0	5	0
Venable, Mtl.	.352	.287	3	1	1	7	0
Veryzer, Chi.	.203	.259	3	1	4	11	3
Virgil, Phila.	.434	.331	45	5	5	91	19
Von Ohlen, St.L.	1.000	1.000	0	0	0	0	0
Walk, Pitt.	.000	.000	0	0	0	2	0
Walker, Cin.	.528	.391	33	2	0	35	1
Wallach, Mtl.	.395	.311	50	6	7	101	12
Walling, Hou.	.402	.325	16	2	1	28	4
Washington, Atl.	.469	.374	59	8	1	77	11
Watson, Atl.	.329	.287	9	2	0	12	2
Wehrmeister, Phila.	.000	.000	0	0	0	1	0
Welch, L.A.	.078	.113	2	0	0	15	1
Wellman, S.F.	.291	.274	19	0	0	41	8
White, L.A.	.000	.000	0	0	0	0	0
Whitfield, L.A.	.356	.313	17	2	1	35	5
Whitson, S.D.	.049	.065	1	0	0	12	0
Wieghaus, Hou.	.000	.083	1	0	0	3	1
Wiggins, S.D.	.329	.342	75	1	3	57	2
Williams, S.F.	.222	.333	3	0	0	7	0
Willis, Cin.	.000	.000	0	0	0	0	0
Wilson, Phila.	.372	.276	17	1	1	56	12
Wilson, N.Y.	.409	.308	26	2	2	90	5
Winn, Pitt.	.000	.000	0	0	0	0	0
Winningham, N.Y.	.519	.429	1	0	0	7	0
Wockenfuss, Phila.	.417	.390	30	1	0	24	4
Wohlford, Mtl.	.451	.342	14	0	0	19	1
Woods, Chi.	.388	.333	15	0	0	21	3
Wotus, Pitt.	.327	.290	6	2	0	8	4
Wynne, Pitt.	.337	.310	42	0	0	81	8
Yeager, L.A.	.310	.295	20	1	0	38	2
Youngblood, S.F.	.358	.328	48	1	4	86	8
Zachry, L.A.	.333	.333	0	0	0	1	1
Zaske, Pitt.	.000	.000	0	0	0	0	0
Zuvella, Atl.	.240	.259	2	0	0	3	0

OFFICIAL NATIONAL LEAGUE FIELDING AVERAGES

CLUB FIELDING

Club	Pct.	G.	PO.	A.	E.	TC.	DP.	TP.	PB.
St. Louis	.982	162	4347	2001	118	6466	184	0	14
Chicago	.981	161	4302	1850	121	6273	137	0	10
Pittsburgh	.980	162	4410	1792	128	6330	142	0	6
Houston	.979	162	4348	1844	133	6325	160	0	38
New York	.979	162	4328	1632	129	6089	154	0	14
Atlanta	.978	162	4341	1963	139	6443	153	0	7
Montreal	.978	161	4293	1663	132	6088	147	0	8
San Diego	.978	162	4381	1633	138	6152	144	0	12
Cincinnati	.977	162	4384	1629	139	6152	116	0	18
Los Angeles	.975	162	4382	1918	163	6463	146	0	11
Philadelphia	.975	162	4375	1792	161	6328	112	0	10
San Francisco	.973	162	4383	1843	173	6399	134	0	18
Totals	.978	971	52274	21560	1674	75508	1729	0	166

INDIVIDUAL FIELDING

*Throws lefthanded.

FIRST BASEMEN

Leader—Club	Pct.	G.	PO.	A.	E.	DP.
GARVEY, S.D.	1.000	159	1232	87	0	117

(Listed Alphabetically)

Player—Club	Pct.	G.	PO.	A.	E.	DP.
Bevacqua, S.D.	1.000	20	66	5	0	8
Bream, L.A.*	1.000	14	95	11	0	9
Brenly, S.F.	.983	22	171	7	3	17
Brock, L.A.	.995	83	703	65	4	61
Buckner, Chi.*	1.000	7	66	5	0	5
Cabell, Hou.	.993	112	971	66	7	97
Carter, Mtl.	.996	25	218	13	1	19
Cedeno, Cin.	.983	44	215	14	4	16
Chambliss, Atl.	.993	109	996	70	8	84
Clark, S.F.	.970	4	26	6	1	3
Concepcion, Cin.	.941	6	29	3	2	2
Corcoran, Phil.*	.997	51	318	21	1	20
Davis, Hou.	.988	16	151	15	2	13
Distefano, Pitt.*	.984	17	55	7	1	5
Driessen, Cin.-Mtl.	.992	115	870	52	7	69
Durham, Chi.*	.994	130	1162	96	7	96
Esasky, Cin.	1.000	25	169	7	0	11
Francona, Mtl.*	.994	50	427	49	3	43
Garvey, S.D.	1.000	159	1232	87	0	117
Green, St.L.	.991	117	1088	69	10	98
G. Gross, Phila.*	.993	28	128	11	1	9
Guerrero, L.A.	.957	16	129	6	6	12
Hassey, Chi.	.960	4	23	1	1	2
Hebner, Chi.	1.000	3	35	2	0	4
Heep, N.Y.*	.983	10	51	6	1	3
Hendrick, St.L.	1.000	1	1	0	0	0
Hernandez, N.Y.*	.994	153	1214	142	8	127
Howe, St.L.	.979	11	45	2	1	6
Iorg, St.L.	1.000	6	30	1	0	4
Rn. Johnson, Mtl.	1.000	2	5	0	0	0
W. Johnson, Mtl.*	.968	4	27	3	1	3
Jorgensen, Atl.-St.L.*	.992	47	219	19	2	30
Knicely, Cin.	.984	8	58	5	1	5
Knight, Hou.-N.Y.	1.000	27	205	10	0	17
Krenchicki, Cin.	.900	3	9	0	1	1
Kuiper, S.F.	1.000	1	3	0	0	0
Madlock, Pitt.	1.000	1	10	0	0	0
Marshall, L.A.	.993	15	131	8	1	11
Martin, N.Y.	1.000	3	16	1	0	4
Martinez, S.D.	1.000	2	5	0	0	0

Player—Club	Pct.	G.	PO.	A.	E.	DP.
Matuszek, Phila.	.990	81	643	55	7	40
Mazzilli, Pitt.	1.000	5	11	0	0	0
Melendez, Phila.*	1.000	10	37	4	0	1
Monday, L.A.*	.987	10	72	4	1	3
Moreland, Chi.	.977	29	230	20	6	18
Morrison, Pitt.	1.000	1	3	0	0	0
Oliver, S.F.-Phila.*	.985	101	814	60	13	58
Perez, Cin.	.990	31	186	12	2	17
Perry, Atl.	.988	64	476	26	6	41
Rabb, S.F.	.988	13	79	6	1	3
Rajsich, St.L.*	1.000	3	13	0	0	2
Rose, Mtl.-Cin.	.989	63	479	51	6	36
Schmidt, Phila.	1.000	2	8	1	0	1
Shines, Mtl.	1.000	3	26	0	0	2
Spilman, Hou.	.978	18	130	6	3	14
Staub, N.Y.	1.000	3	13	0	0	2
Stearns, N.Y.	1.000	2	8	1	0	3
Stenhouse, Mtl.	.981	14	51	1	1	6
Stubbs, L.A.*	.993	51	395	37	3	31
Summers, S.D.	1.000	8	53	1	0	8
Thomas, Mtl.	.000	1	0	0	0	0
Thompson, Pitt.*	.990	152	1337	74	14	111
Thompson, S.F.*	.998	87	555	36	1	48
Tolman, Hou.	1.000	1	2	0	0	0
Van Gorder, Cin.	.000	1	0	0	0	0
Van Slyke, St.L.	.996	30	245	9	1	30
Vargas, Pitt.	.982	13	51	4	1	6
Walling, Hou.	.988	16	83	2	1	7
Watson, Atl.	.983	19	165	12	3	17
Wockenfuss, Phila.	.996	39	231	13	1	20

FIRST BASEMEN WITH TWO OR MORE CLUBS

Player—Club	Pct.	G.	PO.	A.	E.	DP.
Driessen, Cin.	.991	70	507	29	5	31
Driessen, Mtl.	.995	45	363	23	2	38
Jorgensen, Atl.	1.000	8	25	0	0	0
Jorgensen, St.L.	.991	39	194	19	2	30
Knight, Hou.	1.000	24	199	9	0	16
Knight, N.Y.	1.000	3	6	1	0	1
Oliver, S.F.	.985	82	665	55	11	50
Oliver, Phila.	.987	19	149	5	2	8
Rose, Mtl.	.988	40	298	42	4	22
Rose, Cin.	.990	23	181	9	2	14

SECOND BASEMEN

Leader—Club	Pct.	G.	PO.	A.	E.	DP.
SANDBERG, Chi.	.993	156	314	550	6	102

(Listed Alphabetically)

Player—Club	Pct.	G.	PO.	A.	E.	DP.
Aguayo, Phila.	1.000	12	14	28	0	5
Backman, N.Y.	.981	115	218	294	10	72
Bailor, L.A.	.944	23	38	47	5	8
Belliard, Pitt.	1.000	1	1	0	0	0
Chapman, N.Y.	.979	57	104	131	5	32

Player—Club	Pct.	G.	PO.	A.	E.	DP.
Doran, Hou.	.986	139	261	419	10	83
Flannery, S.D.	.944	22	17	34	3	4
Flynn, Mtl.	.979	88	148	223	8	47
Foley, Cin.	1.000	10	15	31	0	5
Garcia, Phila.	1.000	1	2	1	0	0
Gardenhire, N.Y.	1.000	18	18	43	0	5
Garner, Hou.	.956	35	65	88	7	26
Gonzalez, St.L.	1.000	1	0	1	0	0
Herr, St.L.	.992	144	328	452	6	106

SECOND BASEMEN—Continued

Player—Club	Pct.	G.	PO.	A.	E.	DP.
Howe, St.L.	1.000	8	3	4	0	2
Hubbard, Atl.	.988	117	237	405	8	78
Jones, N.Y.	1.000	1	0	2	0	1
Krenchicki, Cin.	1.000	3	1	1	0	0
Kuiper, S.F.	.969	31	59	66	4	14
Lacy, Pitt.	.875	2	4	3	1	0
Landestoy, L.A.	.886	14	15	16	4	4
Lawless, Cin.-Mtl.	1.000	32	43	47	0	7
Little, Mtl.	.982	77	137	197	6	44
Lopes, Chi.	1.000	2	0	2	0	0
Lyons, St.L.	.991	25	52	58	1	18
Morrison, Pitt.	1.000	26	49	44	0	13
Mullins, S.F.	1.000	4	2	4	0	0
Oberkfell, St.L.-Atl.	1.000	6	4	6	0	0
Oester, Cin.	.980	147	357	388	15	75
Owen, Chi.	.571	4	1	3	3	0
Pankovits, Hou.	.925	15	17	20	3	7
Pittman, S.F.	1.000	5	3	6	0	1
Raines, Mtl.	.000	2	0	0	1	0
Ramirez, S.D.	1.000	2	2	0	0	1
Ramsey, St.L.-Mtl.	.972	19	13	22	1	4
Ray, Pitt.	.984	149	331	400	12	90
Rohn, Chi.	1.000	5	3	4	0	0
Royster, Atl.	.973	29	51	95	4	15
Runge, Atl.	.970	22	46	82	4	15
Russell, L.A.	1.000	5	3	7	0	0
Samuel, Phila.	.962	160	388	438	33	77
Sandberg, Chi.	.993	156	314	550	6	102
Sax, L.A.	.973	141	318	450	21	99
Thomas, Mtl.	.925	15	16	21	3	6
Trillo, S.F.	.988	96	215	287	6	67
Veryzer, Chi.	.957	4	7	15	1	3
Wellman, S.F.	.977	54	103	151	6	23
Wiggins, S.D.	.962	157	391	410	32	95
Woods, Chi.	1.000	3	1	1	0	0
Wotus, Pitt.	1.000	7	5	15	0	1
Youngblood, S.F.	.944	5	6	11	1	1
Zuvella, Atl.	1.000	6	7	12	0	3

SECOND BASEMEN WITH TWO OR MORE CLUBS

Player—Club	Pct.	G.	PO.	A.	E.	DP.
Lawless, Cin.	1.000	23	34	35	0	5
Lawless, Mtl.	1.000	9	9	12	0	2
Oberkfell, St.L.	1.000	2	1	1	0	0
Oberkfell, Atl.	1.000	4	3	5	0	0
Ramsey, St.L.	1.000	7	3	12	0	1
Ramsey, Mtl.	.952	12	10	10	1	3

THIRD BASEMEN

Leader—Club	Pct.	G.	PO.	A.	E.	DP.
CEY, Chi.	.967	144	97	230	11	22

(Listed Alphabetically)

Player—Club	Pct.	G.	PO.	A.	E.	DP.
Aguayo, Phila.	.909	14	1	19	2	1
Anderson, L.A.	.970	11	7	25	1	4
Bailor, L.A.	.962	17	6	19	1	1
Barnes, Cin.	1.000	11	6	15	0	0
Berra, Pitt.	.000	1	0	0	0	0
Bevacqua, S.D.	.933	10	4	10	1	2
Braun, St.L.	.000	1	0	0	0	0
Brooks, N.Y.	.929	129	79	211	22	22
Brown, S.F.	.900	23	3	40	7	3
Cey, Chi.	.967	144	97	230	11	22
Chapman, N.Y.	.800	3	1	3	1	1
Concepcion, Cin.	.944	54	28	74	6	3
Esasky, Cin.	.910	82	51	130	18	8
Flannery, S.D.	.947	14	6	12	1	2
Foley, Cin.	.000	1	0	0	0	0
Garcia, Phila.	1.000	23	6	15	0	4
Gardenhire, N.Y.	.867	7	2	11	2	0
Garner, Hou.	.979	82	71	163	5	16
Gonzalez, Pitt.	1.000	11	6	25	0	3
Guerrero, L.A.	.917	76	36	141	16	12
Hebner, Chi.	.963	14	2	24	1	2
Horner, Atl.	.965	32	21	61	3	6
Howe, St.L.	.979	45	23	70	2	6
Jeltz, Phila.	1.000	1	0	2	0	0
Johnson, Atl.	.939	81	44	171	14	14
Jones, N.Y.	.000	1	0	0	0	0
Knight, Hou.-N.Y.	.951	81	51	122	9	10
Krenchicki, Cin.	.967	62	25	91	4	5
Landestoy, L.A.	.833	11	2	8	2	1
Lawless, Cin.	.923	6	7	5	1	1
Lefebvre, Phila.	1.000	1	1	0	0	0
Lyons, St.L.	1.000	3	2	4	0	0
Madlock, Pitt.	.942	98	66	176	15	17
Maldonado, L.A.	.333	4	0	1	2	0
Mitchell, N.Y.	.833	5	1	4	1	2
Moreland, Chi.	1.000	8	5	4	0	1
Morrison, Pitt.	.938	61	32	119	10	8
Mullins, S.F.	.952	28	6	34	2	2
Nettles, S.D.	.936	119	93	201	20	14
Oberkfell, St.L.-Atl.	.966	91	60	167	8	15
O'Malley, S.F.	1.000	7	5	8	0	1
Owen, Chi.	1.000	6	2	2	0	0
Pendleton, St.L.	.943	66	59	155	13	10
Pittman, S.F.	.000	2	0	0	0	0
Ramirez, S.D.	.909	6	3	7	1	0
Ramsey, St.L.	.000	1	0	0	0	0
Reynolds, Hou.	1.000	1	0	1	0	0
Rivera, L.A.	.937	90	55	167	15	12
Rohn, Chi.	1.000	7	1	8	0	1
Rowdon, Cin.	1.000	1	1	0	1	0
Royster, Atl.	.943	17	14	19	2	0
Runge, Atl.	.500	3	0	1	1	0
Salazar, S.D.	.970	58	41	90	4	5
Schmidt, Phila.	.941	145	85	329	26	19
Schu, Phila.	.952	15	7	13	1	3
Shines, Mtl.	.000	1	0	0	0	0
Speier, Mtl.-St.L.	1.000	6	0	11	0	0
Thomas, Mtl.	1.000	4	1	3	0	0
Trillo, S.F.	1.000	4	3	7	0	0
Van Slyke, St.L.	.929	32	24	68	7	10
Veryzer, Chi.	.000	5	0	0	1	0
Wallach, Mtl.	.959	160	162	332	21	29
Walling, Hou.	.956	52	30	100	6	14
Wellman, S.F.	1.000	9	5	5	0	0
Wilson, Phila.	.818	4	6	3	2	0
Wockenfuss, Phila.	.000	2	0	0	0	0
Wohlford, Mtl.	1.000	2	0	1	0	1
Youngblood, S.F.	.887	117	87	195	36	11

THIRD BASEMEN WITH TWO OR MORE CLUBS

Player—Club	Pct.	G.	PO.	A.	E.	DP.
Knight, Hou.	.946	54	37	86	7	6
Knight, N.Y.	.962	27	14	36	2	4
Oberkfell, St.L.	.967	46	29	90	4	7
Oberkfell, Atl.	.964	45	31	77	4	8
Speier, Mtl.	1.000	4	0	9	0	0
Speier, St.L.	1.000	2	0	2	0	0

SHORTSTOPS

Leader—Club	Pct.	G.	PO.	A.	E.	DP.
O. SMITH, St.L.	.982	124	233	437	12	94

(Listed Alphabetically)

Player—Club	Pct.	G.	PO.	A.	E.	DP.
Aguayo, Phila.	.917	10	3	8	1	1
Anderson, L.A.	.965	111	169	334	18	63
Backman, N.Y.	1.000	8	5	12	0	1
Bailor, L.A.	1.000	16	15	51	0	10
Bannister, Hou.	.947	4	10	8	1	1
Belliard, Pitt.	.889	12	11	13	3	4
Berra, Pitt.	.955	135	186	449	30	65
Bowa, Chi.	.974	132	217	378	16	64
Brooks, N.Y.	.938	26	33	73	7	19
Concepcion, Cin.	.978	104	156	247	9	41

SHORTSTOPS—Continued

Player—Club	Pct.	G.	PO.	A.	E.	DP.
DeJesus, Phila.	.951	141	166	400	29	57
Doran, Hou.	.944	13	13	21	2	7
Flannery, S.D.	.973	14	13	23	1	6
Flynn, Mtl.	.956	34	41	68	5	19
Foley, Cin.	.965	83	104	197	11	31
Garcia, Phila.	.965	30	17	38	2	2
Gardenhire, N.Y.	.947	49	78	100	10	15
Gonzales, Mtl.	.957	27	17	28	2	5
Gonzalez, Pitt.	.956	10	15	28	2	7
Gonzalez, St.L.	.955	5	7	14	1	4
Howe, St.L.	1.000	5	0	4	0	0
Jeltz, Phila.	.992	27	37	91	1	8
Jones, N.Y.	.833	6	0	5	1	1
LeMaster, S.F.	.964	129	222	391	23	70
Little, Mtl.	1.000	2	0	2	0	0
Lyons, St.L.	1.000	11	4	12	0	3
Morrison, Pitt.	1.000	2	2	3	0	0
Mullins, S.F.	.969	28	31	63	3	12
Oberkfell, St.L.	.000	1	0	0	0	0
Oester, Cin.	.000	1	0	0	0	0
Oquendo, N.Y.	.972	67	95	152	7	33
Owen, Chi.	.969	35	37	86	4	19
Pankovits, Hou.	1.000	4	2	2	0	0
Pena, Hou.	.956	21	26	39	3	5
Pittman, S.F.	.900	6	2	7	1	0
Ramirez, S.D.	.971	33	29	38	2	11
Ramirez, Atl.	.959	145	251	443	30	94
Ramsey, St.L.-Mtl.	.978	33	31	57	2	15

Player—Club	Pct.	G.	PO.	A.	E.	DP.
Reynolds, Hou.	.965	143	212	472	25	91
Rohn, Chi.	1.000	5	1	3	0	0
Rowdon, Cin.	1.000	1	2	4	0	1
Royster, Atl.	.957	16	20	47	3	7
Runge, Atl.	1.000	7	7	18	0	3
Russell, L.A.	.965	65	81	165	9	29
Salazar, Mtl.	.960	80	88	155	10	35
Salazar, S.D.	1.000	4	3	5	0	0
Santana, N.Y.	.970	50	92	104	6	34
Schmidt, Phila.	.000	1	0	0	0	0
O. Smith, St.L.	.982	124	233	437	12	94
Speier, Mtl.-St.L.	.980	47	56	141	4	29
Templeton, S.D.	.960	146	225	407	26	79
Thomas, Mtl.	.963	62	73	111	7	27
Thon, Hou.	1.000	5	8	13	0	1
Veryzer, Chi.	.966	36	37	48	3	10
Wallach, Mtl.	.000	1	0	0	0	0
Wellman, S.F.	.967	34	43	102	5	14
Wotus, Pitt.	.976	17	23	57	2	11
Zuvella, Atl.	1.000	6	6	9	0	3

SHORTSTOPS WITH TWO OR MORE CLUBS

Player—Club	Pct.	G.	PO.	A.	E.	DP.
Ramsey, St.L.	1.000	7	5	6	0	3
Ramsey, Mtl.	.975	26	26	51	2	12
Speier, Mtl.	.960	13	7	17	1	4
Speier, St.L.	.983	34	49	124	3	25

OUTFIELDERS

Leader—Club	Pct.	G.	PO.	A.	E.	DP.
LACY, Pitt.	.996	127	268	15	1	4

(Listed Alphabetically)

Player—Club	Pct.	G.	PO.	A.	E.	DP.
Amelung, L.A.*	1.000	23	31	0	0	0
Baker, S.F.	.974	62	112	1	3	0
Bannister, Hou.	1.000	1	1	0	0	0
Barnes, Cin.	1.000	3	1	0	0	0
Bass, Hou.	.975	81	149	4	4	2
Beane, N.Y.	1.000	5	2	0	0	0
Bevacqua, S.D.	1.000	3	3	0	0	0
Bosley, Chi.*	.976	33	39	2	1	0
Braun, St.L.	1.000	19	10	1	0	0
Brenly, S.F.	1.000	3	1	0	0	0
Brewer, L.A.	1.000	10	9	0	0	0
Brown, S.D.	.971	53	100	2	3	0
Buckner, Chi.*	1.000	2	5	1	0	0
Cedeno, Cin.	.980	77	140	7	3	0
Christensen, N.Y.	.500	5	1	0	1	0
Clark, S.F.	.990	54	94	3	1	0
Corcoran, Phila.*	1.000	17	20	0	0	0
Cotto, Chi.	.984	88	117	3	2	1
Cruz, Hou.*	.976	160	310	11	8	1
C. Davis, S.F.	.971	123	292	9	9	2
Davis, Cin.	.992	51	125	4	1	2
Dawson, Mtl.	.975	134	297	11	8	0
Deer, S.F.	.905	9	19	0	2	0
Dernier, Chi.	.986	140	355	5	5	1
Dilone, Mtl.	.987	41	76	1	1	0
Distefano, Pitt.*	.946	20	33	2	2	1
Foster, N.Y.	.976	141	278	6	7	1
Francona, Mtl.*	1.000	6	4	1	0	0
Frobel, Pitt.	.956	112	188	9	9	3
Fuentes, Mtl.	1.000	1	4	0	0	0
Gladden, S.F.	.988	85	232	8	3	1
Gonzalez, Pitt.	.833	3	5	0	1	0
Green, St.L.	1.000	14	15	1	0	1
G. Gross, Phila.*	.986	48	67	2	1	0
Guerrero, L.A.	1.000	58	106	4	0	0
Gwynn, S.D.*	.989	156	345	11	4	4
Hall, Atl.	.932	66	64	4	5	1
Hall, Chi.*	.961	46	69	5	3	2
Harper, Pitt.	.981	37	48	3	1	0
Harper, Atl.	1.000	29	60	3	0	0
Hatcher, Chi.	1.000	4	2	1	0	0
Hayes, Phila.	.988	148	341	2	4	1
Hebner, Chi.	1.000	3	2	0	0	0

Player—Club	Pct.	G.	PO.	A.	E.	DP.
Heep, N.Y.*	.967	48	86	1	3	1
Hendrick, St.L.	.990	116	188	9	2	1
Householder, Cin.-St.L.	1.000	18	9	1	0	0
Iorg, St.L.	1.000	5	5	1	0	0
Rn. Johnson, Mtl.	.000	1	0	0	0	0
Ry. Johnson, Mtl.*	.938	10	15	0	1	0
Johnstone, Chi.	1.000	15	12	0	0	0
Jorgensen, Atl.*	1.000	4	3	0	0	0
Komminsk, Atl.	.993	80	135	2	1	0
Lacy, Pitt.	.996	127	268	15	1	4
Landestoy, L.A.	1.000	5	5	0	0	0
Landreaux, L.A.	.986	129	212	3	3	2
Landrum, St.L.	.979	88	93	1	2	0
Lefebvre, Phila.	.966	47	82	4	3	1
Leonard, S.F.	.970	131	247	14	8	4
Lezcano, Phila.	.981	87	151	3	3	0
Linares, Atl.	.958	13	21	2	1	0
Lopes, Chi.	1.000	9	6	0	0	0
Maddox, Phila.	1.000	69	160	3	0	1
Maldonado, L.A.	.955	102	124	4	6	0
Marshall, L.A.	.981	118	200	9	4	1
Martin, N.Y.	1.000	30	40	2	0	1
Martinez, S.D.	.976	142	312	15	8	4
Matthews, Chi.	.955	145	224	7	11	0
Matuszek, Phila.	.500	1	1	0	1	0
Mazzilli, Pitt.	.989	74	92	2	1	0
McGee, St.L.	.985	141	374	10	6	4
McReynolds, S.D.	.991	143	422	10	4	1
Miller, S.D.	1.000	8	5	2	0	0
Miller, L.A.	1.000	5	3	0	0	0
Milner, Cin.*	.983	108	285	8	5	4
Monday, L.A.*	1.000	2	2	0	0	0
Moreland, Chi.	.976	103	154	6	4	0
Mumphrey, Hou.	.988	137	317	5	4	2
Murphy, Atl.	.987	160	369	10	5	1
Oliver, Phila.*	1.000	5	4	1	0	0
Orsulak, Pitt.*	1.000	25	41	1	0	0
Otis, Pitt.	.964	32	49	5	2	0
Pankovits, Hou.	1.000	3	3	0	0	0
Parker, Cin.	.974	151	296	6	8	1
Perry, Atl.	.927	53	74	2	6	0
Puhl, Hou.	.986	126	213	6	3	4
Rabb, S.F.	1.000	8	12	0	0	0
Raines, Mtl.	.988	160	420	8	5	1
Redus, Cin.	.967	114	200	6	7	3
Reynolds, L.A.	.973	63	104	4	3	1
Richards, S.F.*	.940	26	46	1	3	0

OUTFIELDERS—Continued

Player—Club	Pct.	G.	PO.	A.	E.	DP.
Robinson, Pitt.	1.000	1	2	0	0	0
Roenicke, S.D.*	1.000	10	10	0	0	0
Rose, Mtl.	.964	28	51	2	2	0
Royster, Atl.	1.000	11	14	1	0	1
Russell, Phila.	1.000	29	50	1	0	0
Russell, L.A.	1.000	18	31	1	0	0
Salas, St.L.	1.000	3	2	0	0	0
Salazar, S.D.	.957	24	43	2	2	0
Sanchez, S.F.	.952	11	18	2	1	0
T. Scott, Hou.-Mtl.	1.000	23	30	1	0	0
L. Smith, St.L.	.948	140	184	18	11	0
Stenhouse, Mtl.	.986	48	67	4	1	2
Stone, Phila.	.916	46	75	1	7	0
Strawberry, N.Y.*	.980	146	276	11	6	3
Stubbs, L.A.*	.957	20	22	0	1	0
Thomas, Mtl.	1.000	48	28	0	0	0
Thompson, Atl.	.956	25	37	6	2	1
Thompson, S.F.*	.875	6	7	0	1	0
Tolman, Hou.	1.000	3	4	0	0	0
Vail, L.A.	.000	1	0	0	0	0
Van Slyke, St.L.	1.000	81	88	5	0	0
Venable, Mtl.	1.000	27	33	0	0	0
Walker, Cin.*	.950	68	110	3	6	0
Walling, Hou.	1.000	6	3	0	0	0
Washington, Atl.*	.967	107	170	4	6	0
Whitfield, L.A.	.988	58	76	4	1	0
Wilson, Phila.	.968	109	147	4	5	0
Wilson, N.Y.	.990	146	396	8	4	6
Winningham, N.Y.	1.000	10	7	0	0	0
Wohlford, Mtl.	.989	59	85	3	1	1
Woods, Chi.	1.000	62	53	2	0	1
Wynne, Pitt.*	.990	154	373	4	4	1
Youngblood, S.F.	1.000	11	9	0	0	0

OUTFIELDERS WITH TWO OR MORE CLUBS

Player—Club	Pct.	G.	PO.	A.	E.	DP.
Householder, Cin.	1.000	10	6	1	0	0
Householder, St.L.	1.000	8	3	0	0	0
T. Scott, Hou.	1.000	6	8	0	0	0
Scott, Mtl.	1.000	17	22	1	0	0

CATCHERS

Leader—Club	Pct.	G.	PO.	A.	E.	DP.	PB.
FITZGERALD, N.Y.	.995	107	715	47	4	6	7

(Listed Alphabetically)

Player—Club	Pct.	G.	PO.	A.	E.	DP.	PB.
Ashby, Hou.	.986	63	303	42	5	3	15
Bailey, Hou.	.983	108	629	56	12	4	17
Benedict, Atl.	.991	95	504	37	5	2	2
Bilardello, Cin.	.992	68	323	34	3	3	7
Bochy, S.D.	.988	36	147	12	2	2	0
Brenly, S.F.	.986	127	635	69	10	4	11
Brummer, St.L.	.973	26	101	9	3	0	1
Butera, Mtl.	1.000	2	9	0	0	0	0
Carter, Mtl.	.993	143	772	65	6	6	7
Davis, Chi.	.984	146	811	89	15	9	10
Diaz, Phila.	.992	23	114	9	1	1	2
Fimple, L.A.	.983	12	54	4	1	0	1
Fitzgerald, N.Y.	.995	107	715	47	4	6	7
Gibbons, N.Y.	.983	9	54	5	1	0	0
Gomez, S.F.	.951	14	69	8	4	1	1
Gulden, Cin.	.975	100	485	53	14	8	10
Gwosdz, S.D.	.963	6	25	1	1	0	2
Harper, Pitt.	1.000	2	9	0	0	0	0
Hassey, Chi.	1.000	6	30	1	0	0	0
Hodges, N.Y.	.979	35	165	20	4	2	4
Kennedy, S.D.	.982	147	708	54	14	6	10
Knicely, Cin.	1.000	1	2	0	0	0	0
Lake, Chi.	.955	24	72	13	4	0	0
Lavalliere, Phila.	1.000	6	20	2	0	0	0
May, Pitt.	.993	26	135	15	1	2	0
Moreland, Chi.	1.000	3	4	0	0	0	0
Nicosia, S.F.	.985	41	190	11	3	1	6
Nieto, St.L.	.994	32	135	18	1	0	2
Ortiz, N.Y.	.980	32	136	13	3	3	3
Pena, Pitt.	.991	146	895	95	9	15	6
Porter, St.L.	.984	122	620	58	11	6	11
Rabb, S.F.	.895	6	16	1	2	0	0
Ramos, Mtl.	.982	31	138	22	3	1	1
Reyes, L.A.	1.000	2	5	0	0	0	1
Russell, Phila.	1.000	2	1	0	0	0	0
Salas, St.L.	1.000	4	11	2	0	0	0
Scioscia, L.A.	.985	112	701	64	12	8	4
Sinatro, Atl.	1.000	2	4	0	0	0	1
Spilman, Hou.	1.000	8	13	3	0	0	1
Stearns, N.Y.	1.000	4	20	1	0	1	0
Trevino, Cin.-Atl.	.989	83	403	61	5	5	5
Van Gorder, Cin.	1.000	36	194	11	0	1	1
Virgil, Phila.	.992	137	722	58	6	6	6
Wieghaus, Hou.	1.000	6	30	3	0	0	5
Wockenfuss, Phila.	.943	21	92	7	6	1	2
Yeager, L.A.	.994	65	317	30	2	1	5

CATCHERS WITH TWO OR MORE CLUBS

Player—Club	Pct.	G.	PO.	A.	E.	DP.	PB.
Trevino, Cin.	1.000	4	4	1	0	0	0
Trevino, Atl.	.989	79	399	60	5	5	5

PITCHERS

Leader—Club	Pct.	G.	PO.	A.	E.	DP.
THURMOND, S.D.*	1.000	32	11	38	0	3

(Listed Alphabetically)

Player—Club	Pct.	G.	PO.	A.	E.	DP.
Allen, St.L.	1.000	57	5	22	0	0
Altamirano, Chi.	1.000	5	0	4	0	0
Andersen, Phila.	.840	64	5	16	4	1
Andujar, St.L.	.958	36	15	54	3	2
Bargar, Mtl.	.750	3	1	2	1	0
Barker, Atl.	.951	21	5	34	2	2
Bedrosian, Atl.	.900	40	1	8	1	0
Berenyi, Cin.-N.Y.	1.000	32	12	17	0	1
Bielecki, Pitt.	1.000	4	0	1	0	0
Booker, S.D.	.941	32	9	7	1	1
Bordi, Chi.	.875	31	4	10	2	0
Breining, Mtl.	.000	4	0	0	0	0
Brizzolara, Atl.	1.000	10	4	3	0	0
Browning, Cin.*	1.000	3	1	3	0	0
Brusstar, Chi.	1.000	41	8	7	0	0
Bystrom, Phila.	1.000	11	4	6	0	0
Calhoun, Hou.*	1.000	9	1	1	0	0
Calvert, S.F.	1.000	10	2	8	0	0
Camp, Atl.	.973	31	12	24	1	0
Campbell, Phila.	1.000	57	6	5	0	0
Candelaria, Pitt.*	1.000	33	3	21	0	1
Carlton, Phila.*	1.000	33	7	22	0	0
Carman, Phila.*	.000	11	0	0	0	0
Cato, Cin.	1.000	8	2	3	0	1
Chiffer, S.D.	1.000	15	0	2	0	0
Citarella, St.L.	1.000	10	0	6	0	0
Cornell, S.F.	1.000	23	0	4	0	1
Cox, St.L.	.974	29	11	27	1	4
Darling, N.Y.	.948	33	17	38	3	3
M. Davis, S.F.*	.885	46	1	22	3	1
Dawley, Hou.	.944	60	6	11	1	0
Dayley, Atl.-St.L.*	1.000	7	1	4	0	0
Dedmon, Atl.	.923	54	2	22	2	1
DeLeon, Pitt.	.917	30	6	16	2	1
DeLeon, S.D.	.889	32	4	4	1	1
Denny, Phila.	.982	22	20	36	1	2
Diaz, L.A.*	1.000	37	2	2	0	0
DiPino, Hou.*	1.000	57	3	12	0	0
Dravecky, S.D.*	.960	50	5	19	1	1
Eckersley, Chi.	.915	24	16	27	4	1
Falcone, Atl.*	.944	35	0	17	1	0
Fernandez, N.Y.*	1.000	15	0	6	0	0

PITCHERS—Continued

Player—Club	Pct.	G.	PO.	A.	E.	DP.
Fireovid, Phila.	1.000	6	3	1	0	1
Forsch, St.L.	1.000	16	8	8	0	0
Forster, Atl.*	1.000	25	2	4	0	1
Franco, Cin.*	1.000	54	5	15	0	0
Frazier, Chi.	.833	37	4	6	2	0
Gaff, N.Y.	.958	47	11	12	1	0
Garber, Atl.	1.000	62	6	19	0	1
Gardner, N.Y.*	1.000	21	1	3	0	0
Garrelts, S.F.	1.000	21	2	4	0	0
Gooden, N.Y.	.956	31	21	22	2	0
Gorman, N.Y.*	1.000	36	2	9	0	0
Gossage, S.D.	1.000	62	5	8	0	0
Grant, S.F.	.923	11	6	6	1	0
Grapenthin, Mtl.	1.000	13	2	4	0	0
Green, Pitt.*	1.000	4	0	1	0	0
K. Gross, Phila.	.939	44	9	22	2	3
Guante, Pitt.	1.000	27	2	3	0	0
Gullickson, Mtl.	.892	32	14	19	4	2
Hagen, St.L.	.500	4	0	1	1	0
Hammaker, S.F.*	1.000	6	0	6	0	0
Harris, Mtl.-S.D.	.909	34	3	7	1	0
Hassler, St.L.*	1.000	3	0	1	0	0
Hawkins, S.D.	.929	36	10	16	2	1
Hershiser, L.A.	.900	45	17	28	5	2
Hesketh, Mtl.*	.889	11	2	6	1	1
Holland, Phila.*	1.000	68	1	8	0	0
Honeycutt, L.A.*	.945	29	10	42	3	2
Hooton, L.A.	1.000	54	6	15	0	1
Horton, St.L.*	.930	37	5	35	3	3
Howell, L.A.	1.000	32	6	6	0	0
Hudson, Phila.	.923	30	4	20	2	1
Hume, Cin.	1.000	54	14	17	0	1
James, Mtl.	.750	62	5	7	4	0
Johnson, Chi.	1.000	4	0	3	0	0
Kepshire, St.L.	.824	17	4	10	3	0
Kern, Phila.	1.000	8	0	2	0	0
Knepper, Hou.*	.951	35	7	32	2	2
Koosman, Phila.*	.915	36	9	34	4	1
Krawczyk, Pitt.	.000	4	0	0	0	0
Krukow, S.F.	.970	35	12	20	1	3
Lacey, S.F.*	1.000	34	1	10	0	0
LaCoss, Hou.	.935	39	9	20	2	2
Lahti, St.L.	.950	63	4	15	1	1
LaPoint, St.L.*	.962	33	2	23	1	4
Laskey, S.F.	1.000	35	12	23	0	0
Lavelle, S.F.*	1.000	77	1	13	0	0
Lea, Mtl.	.981	30	19	33	1	1
Leary, N.Y.	.875	20	3	4	1	0
Lefferts, S.D.*	.938	62	5	10	1	2
Lerch, S.F.*	1.000	37	5	12	0	1
Lesley, Cin.	.833	16	1	4	1	0
Lollar, S.D.*	1.000	31	1	22	0	1
Lucas, Mtl.*	1.000	55	2	15	0	1
Lynch, N.Y.	.957	40	9	13	1	0
Madden, Hou.*	1.000	17	0	2	0	0
Mahler, Atl.	.969	38	20	42	2	5
McGaffigan, Mtl.-Cin.	.900	30	3	6	1	1
McGraw, Phila.*	.889	25	2	6	1	0
McMurtry, Atl.	.983	37	10	48	1	2
McWilliams, Pitt.*	1.000	34	15	32	0	4
Meridith, Chi.*	1.000	3	1	0	0	0
Minton, S.F.	.951	74	8	31	2	1
Monge, S.D.*	1.000	13	1	1	0	0
Moore, Atl.	.929	47	3	10	1	0
Niedenfuer, L.A.	.857	33	1	5	1	0
Niekro, Hou.	.967	38	19	39	2	5
Noles, Chi.	1.000	21	1	4	0	1
Orosco, N.Y.*	.929	60	2	11	1	1
Owchinko, Cin.*	1.000	49	4	11	0	0
Ownbey, St.L.	1.000	4	1	1	0	0
Palmer, Mtl.	.971	20	20	13	1	1
Pastore, Cin.	.957	24	6	16	1	2
Patterson, Chi.	1.000	3	1	1	0	0
Payne, Atl.	1.000	3	0	1	0	0
Pena, L.A.	.905	28	17	21	4	1
Perez, Atl.	.983	30	19	40	1	1
Power, Cin.	.957	78	6	16	1	3
Price, Cin.*	1.000	30	4	14	0	0
Puleo, Cin.	1.000	5	0	1	0	0
Pulido, Pitt.*	.000	1	0	0	0	0
Rainey, Chi.	1.000	17	10	15	0	0
Rawley, Phila.*	.952	18	8	12	1	1
Reardon, Mtl.	.875	68	2	5	1	0
Reuschel, Chi.	.963	19	6	20	1	1
Reuss, L.A.*	.952	30	4	16	1	0
Rhoden, Pitt.	.967	33	14	44	2	2
Riley, S.F.*	1.000	5	1	4	0	0
Robinson, Pitt.	1.000	51	8	18	0	0
Robinson, S.F.	.974	34	14	24	1	1
Robinson, Cin.	1.000	12	1	7	0	0
Rodas, L.A.*	1.000	3	1	0	0	0
Rogers, Mtl.	.933	31	17	25	3	5
Ross, Hou.	.000	2	0	0	0	0
Rucker, St.L.*	.737	50	4	10	5	1
Ruhle, Hou.	.917	40	4	18	2	1
Russell, Cin.	.953	33	7	34	2	4
Ruthven, Chi.	1.000	23	8	19	0	1
Ryan, Hou.	.900	30	7	11	2	0
St. Claire, Mtl.	1.000	4	0	1	0	0
Sambito, Hou.*	1.000	32	1	3	0	0
Sanderson, Chi.	.972	24	11	24	1	0
Schatzeder, Mtl.*	.773	36	9	8	5	0
Scherrer, Cin.*	.923	36	1	11	1	0
Schiraldi, N.Y.	1.000	5	0	3	0	1
Schulze, Chi.	1.000	1	1	0	0	0
M. Scott, Hou.	.971	31	10	23	1	1
Scurry, Pitt.*	.900	43	0	9	1	0
Show, S.D.	.955	32	14	28	2	2
Sisk, N.Y.	.947	50	5	13	1	1
Smith, Mtl.	.930	28	25	28	4	3
Smith, Hou.	.933	53	5	9	1	1
Smith, Chi.	1.000	69	6	13	0	2
Smith, Cin.	1.000	8	1	0	0	0
Smith, Atl.*	.833	3	2	3	1	1
Solano, Hou.	.800	31	5	3	2	0
Soto, Cin.	.919	33	12	22	3	1
Stoddard, Chi.	.923	58	4	8	1	0
Stuper, St.L.	.944	15	5	12	1	0
Sutcliffe, Chi.	.973	20	12	24	1	0
Sutter, St.L.	1.000	71	14	19	0	2
Swan, N.Y.	1.000	10	1	2	0	0
Tekulve, Pitt.	1.000	72	6	25	0	3
Terrell, N.Y.	.960	33	16	32	2	5
Thurmond, S.D.*	1.000	32	11	38	0	3
Tibbs, Cin.	.941	14	6	10	1	1
Tidrow, N.Y.	1.000	11	3	3	0	0
Toliver, Cin.	1.000	3	0	1	0	0
Torrez, N.Y.	.889	9	2	6	1	2
Trout, Chi.*	.938	32	13	48	4	5
Tudor, Pitt.*	1.000	32	11	31	0	0
Tunnell, Pitt.	.957	26	8	14	1	1
Valenzuela, L.A.*	.972	34	21	48	2	4
Von Ohlen, St.L.*	1.000	27	2	10	0	2
Walk, Pitt.	.000	2	0	0	0	0
Wehrmeister, Phila.	1.000	7	1	3	0	1
Welch, L.A.	.960	31	20	28	2	5
White, L.A.	.667	7	1	1	1	0
Whitson, S.D.	1.000	31	11	35	0	3
Williams, S.F.	.907	61	4	35	4	2
Willis, Cin.	1.000	7	0	3	0	0
Winn, Pitt.	1.000	9	1	3	0	1
Zachry, L.A.	.909	58	4	16	2	2
Zaske, Pitt.	1.000	3	0	2	0	0

PITCHERS WITH TWO OR MORE CLUBS

Player—Club	Pct.	G.	PO.	A.	E.	DP.
Berenyi, Cin.	1.000	13	1	8	0	0
Berenyi, N.Y.	1.000	19	11	9	0	1
Dayley, Atl.	1.000	4	1	4	0	0
Dayley, St.L.	.000	3	0	0	0	0
Harris, Mtl.	1.000	15	1	3	0	0
Harris, S.D.	.857	19	2	4	1	0
Martin, S.F.	1.000	12	1	7	0	0
Martin, Phila.	1.000	9	2	7	0	1
McGaffigan, Mtl.	1.000	21	3	5	0	1
McGaffigan, Cin.	.500	9	0	1	1	0

OFFICIAL NATIONAL LEAGUE PITCHING AVERAGES

CLUB PITCHING

Club	ERA.	G.	CG.	ShO.	Sv.	IP.	H.	BFP.	R.	ER.	HR.	SH.	SF.	HB.	Tot. BB.	Int. BB.	SO.	WP.	Bk.
Pittsburgh	3.11	162	27	13	34	1470.0	1344	6095	567	508	102	66	46	11	502	48	995	43	16
Los Angeles	3.17	162	39	16	27	1460.2	1381	6134	600	514	76	62	35	18	499	81	1033	41	11
Montreal	3.31	161	19	10	48	1431.0	1333	5956	585	526	114	56	46	21	474	54	861	40	13
Houston	3.32	162	24	18	29	1449.1	1350	6064	630	534	91	55	50	17	502	58	950	45	11
San Diego	3.48	162	13	17	44	1460.1	1327	6162	634	565	122	84	44	22	563	28	812	44	13
Atlanta	3.57	162	17	7	49	1447.0	1401	6127	655	574	122	81	46	18	525	60	859	37	14
St. Louis	3.58	162	19	12	51	1449.0	1427	6071	645	577	94	66	41	25	494	68	808	50	13
New York	3.60	162	12	15	50	1442.2	1371	6141	676	577	104	55	48	27	573	43	1028	41	20
Philadelphia	3.62	162	11	8	35	1458.1	1416	6179	690	586	101	69	45	17	448	65	904	41	27
Chicago	3.75	161	19	6	50	1434.0	1458	6053	658	598	99	67	57	22	442	63	879	40	10
Cincinnati	4.16	162	25	9	25	1461.1	1445	6298	747	675	128	75	48	17	578	57	946	33	7
San Francisco	4.39	162	11	7	38	1461.0	1589	6428	807	713	125	73	64	34	549	83	854	58	21
Totals	3.59	971	234	130	480	17424.2	16842	73708	7894	6947	1278	809	570	249	6149	707	10929	513	183

NOTE: Total earned runs for four clubs do not agree with composite total of respective club's pitchers due to provisions of Scoring Rule Section 10.18 (i). The following differences are to be noted: Cincinnati pitchers add to 676 earned runs, Houston pitchers add to 536; Los Angeles pitchers add to 515, New York pitchers add to 582.

PITCHERS' RECORDS

(Top Fifteen Qualifiers for Earned-Run Leadership—162 or More Innings)

*Throws lefthanded

Pitcher and Club	W.	L.	Pct.	ERA.	G.	GS.	CG.	ShO.	GF.	Sv.	IP.	H.	BFP.	R.	ER.	HR.	SH.	SF.	HB.	Tot. BB.	Int. BB.	SO.	WP.	Bk.
Pena, Alejandro, Los Angeles	12	6	.667	2.48	28	28	8	4	0	0	199.1	186	813	67	55	7	6	2	2	46	7	135	5	3
Gooden, Dwight, New York	17	9	.654	2.60	31	31	7	3	0	0	218.0	161	879	72	63	7	3	2	1	73	2	276	5	7
Hershiser, Orel, Los Angeles	11	8	.579	2.66	45	20	8	4	10	0	189.2	160	771	65	56	9	2	4	4	50	8	150	8	1
Rhoden, Richard, Pittsburgh	14	9	.609	2.72	33	33	9	3	0	0	238.1	216	961	81	72	13	6	6	1	62	0	136	10	4
Candelaria, John, Pittsburgh*	11	11	.522	2.72	33	28	6	3	1	2	185.1	179	751	69	56	19	10	1	6	34	3	133	1	1
Honeycutt, Frederick, Los Angeles*	10	9	.526	2.84	29	28	3	1	0	0	183.2	180	762	72	58	11	6	5	2	51	3	133	6	2
Lea, Charles, Montreal	15	10	.600	2.89	30	30	8	2	0	0	224.1	198	918	82	72	19	9	5	2	68	11	75	4	0
McWilliams, Larry, Pittsburgh*	15	11	.522	2.93	34	32	7	2	1	1	227.1	226	957	86	74	17	12	10	2	78	7	149	3	3
Thurmond, Mark, San Diego*	14	8	.636	2.97	32	29	4	1	2	1	178.2	174	750	70	59	18	11	6	0	55	3	57	2	2
Valenzuela, Fernando, Los Angeles*	12	17	.414	3.03	34	34	12	2	0	2	261.0	218	1078	109	88	14	11	7	3	106	4	240	11	3
Ryan, L. Nolan, Houston	12	11	.522	3.04	30	30	5	2	0	0	183.2	143	760	78	62	12	4	8	4	69	2	197	6	1
Niekro, Joseph, Houston	16	12	.571	3.04	38	38	6	1	1	0	248.1	223	1027	84	84	16	1	8	3	89	7	127	12	3
Mahler, Richard, Atlanta	13	10	.565	3.12	38	29	9	1	3	0	222.0	209	918	86	77	13	13	8	3	62	4	106	4	1
Knepper, Robert, Houston*	15	10	.600	3.20	35	34	7	4	1	0	233.2	223	954	93	83	26	7	4	1	55	5	140	3	1
Whitson, Eddie, San Diego	14	8	.636	3.24	31	31	1	0	0	0	189.0	181	773	72	68	16	10	7	3	42	1	103	3	1

DEPARTMENTAL LEADERS: W—Andujar, 20; L—Russell, 18; Pct.—Sutcliffe, .941; G—Power, 78; GS—Niekro, 38; CG—Soto, 13; ShO.—Andujar, Hershiser, Pena, 4; GF—Sutter, 63; Sv.—Sutter, 45; IP—Andujar, 261.1; H—Krukow, 234; BFP—Valenzuela, 1,078; R—Krukow, 117; ER—M. Davis, 104; HR—Gullickson, 27; SH—Show, 17; SF—M. Scott, 12; HB—Andujar, Cox, J. Robinson, 7; Tot.BB.—Valenzuela, 106; Int. BB.—Minton, 20; SO—Gooden, 276; WP—LaPoint, 15; Bk—Carlton, Gooden, 7.

(All Pitchers Listed Alphabetically)

Pitcher and Club	W.	L.	Pct.	ERA.	G.	GS.	CG.	ShO.	GF.	Sv.	IP.	H.	BFP.	R.	ER.	HR.	SH.	SF.	HB.	Tot. BB.	Int. BB.	SO.	WP.	Bk.
Allen, Neil, St. Louis	9	6	.600	3.55	57	1	0	0	18	3	119.0	105	495	54	47	6	4	2	0	49	9	66	6	0
Altamirano, Porfirio, Chicago	0	1	.000	4.76	5	0	0	0	2	0	11.1	8	43	6	6	5	0	1	0	6	0	7	1	0
Andersen, Larry, Philadelphia	3	7	.300	2.38	64	0	0	0	25	4	90.2	85	376	32	24	5	4	1	0	25	6	54	2	0
Andujar, Joaquin, St. Louis	20	14	.588	3.34	36	36	12	4	0	0	261.1	218	1052	104	97	20	12	9	7	70	13	147	6	4
Bargar, Gregory, Montreal	0	2	.000	7.88	3	0	0	0	0	0	8.0	8	36	7	7	1	1	2	0	7	2	8	3	0
Barker, Leonard, Atlanta	7	8	.467	3.85	21	20	1	0	1	0	126.1	120	528	59	54	10	10	5	2	38	5	95	1	1
Bedrosian, Stephen, Atlanta	9	6	.600	2.37	40	4	0	0	12	11	83.2	65	345	23	22	5	10	1	0	33	4	81	11	0
Berenyi, Bruce, Cin.-N.Y.	12	13	.480	4.45	32	30	2	1	1	0	166.0	163	737	93	82	6	12	3	1	95	5	134	0	0
Bielecki, Michael, Pittsburgh	0	1	.000	0.00	1	1	0	0	0	0	4.1	4	17	0	0	0	0	0	0	0	0	1	0	0
Booker, Gregory, San Diego	0	2	.000	3.30	32	7	0	0	10	0	57.1	67	262	27	21	11	6	2	0	27	4	28	6	0
Bordi, Richard, Chicago	1	1	.500	3.46	31	0	0	0	12	4	83.1	78	347	37	32	11	12	3	0	20	0	41	0	0
Breining, Fred, Montreal	0	0	.000	1.35	4	0	0	0	2	0	6.2	4	27	1	1	0	0	0	0	5	1	5	0	0
Brizzolara, Anthony, Atlanta	1	2	.333	5.28	3	3	0	0	0	0	29.0	33	132	22	17	7	0	4	0	13	0	17	2	1
Browning, Thomas, Cincinnati*	1	0	1.000	1.54	3	3	0	0	0	0	23.1	27	95	4	4	4	9	0	0	5	1	14	0	0
Brusstar, Warren, Chicago	0	1	.000	3.11	41	0	0	0	16	3	63.2	57	260	23	22	0	10	0	0	21	7	36	2	0
Bystrom, Martin, Philadelphia	4	4	.500	5.08	11	11	0	0	0	0	56.2	66	258	36	32	4	2	3	0	22	2	36	1	4
Calhoun, Jeffrey, Houston*	0	1	.000	1.17	9	0	0	0	2	0	15.1	11	54	3	2	5	0	0	0	2	1	11	1	0
Calvert, Mark, San Francisco	1	2	.333	5.06	10	5	0	0	1	0	32.0	40	146	18	18	0	1	2	0	9	3	5	0	0
Camp, Rick, Atlanta	8	6	.571	3.27	57	21	1	0	8	1	148.2	134	621	59	54	11	0	2	3	63	13	69	5	2
Campbell, William, Philadelphia	6	5	.545	3.43	33	0	0	0	15	4	81.1	68	351	43	31	2	9	0	0	35	3	52	3	1
Candelaria, John, Pittsburgh*	12	11	.522	2.72	33	28	3	1	4	2	185.1	179	751	69	56	19	10	6	6	34	7	133	11	7
Carlton, Steven, Philadelphia*	13	7	.650	3.58	33	33	1	2	0	1	229.0	214	964	91	91	14	7	0	0	79	3	163	1	7
Carman, Donald, Philadelphia*	0	1	.000	5.40	9	0	0	0	9	0	13.1	14	61	9	8	2	0	0	0	6	4	16	0	0
Cato, J. Keefe, Cincinnati	0	1	.000	8.04	8	0	0	0	6	0	15.2	22	72	14	14	5	0	2	0	14	0	12	1	0
Chiffer, Floyd, San Diego	0	3	.000	7.71	15	0	0	0	6	1	28.0	42	139	24	24	1	0	2	3	16	2	20	0	0
Citarella, Ralph, St. Louis	1	0	1.000	3.63	10	2	0	0	2	0	22.1	20	95	9	9	2	2	0	1	7	2	15	3	0
Cornell, Jeffery, San Francisco	0	3	.000	6.10	23	0	0	0	5	0	38.1	51	181	30	26	0	10	5	7	22	2	19	1	0
Cox, Danny, St. Louis	3	9	.250	4.03	29	27	1	1	0	0	156.1	171	668	81	70	4	7	6	5	54	6	70	3	3
Darling, Ronald, New York	12	9	.571	3.81	33	33	2	0	0	0	205.2	179	884	97	87	5	7	6	5	104	2	136	7	1
Davis, Mark, San Francisco*	5	17	.227	5.36	46	27	2	0	6	0	174.2	201	766	113	104	6	10	10	5	54	12	124	8	4
Dawley, William, Houston	11	4	.733	1.93	60	0	0	0	27	5	98.0	82	402	24	21	4	6	0	0	35	12	47	2	4
Dayley, Kenneth, Atl.-St.L.*	0	5	.000	7.99	7	6	0	0	1	0	23.2	44	124	28	21	9	0	2	2	11	1	10	0	1
Dedmon, Jeffrey, Atlanta	4	3	.571	3.78	54	0	0	0	19	4	81.0	86	354	39	34	5	7	2	2	35	5	51	3	0
DeLeon, Jose, Pittsburgh	7	13	.350	3.74	28	28	3	2	0	0	192.1	147	795	86	80	17	7	2	2	92	2	153	1	0
DeLeon, Luis, San Diego	2	2	.500	5.48	32	0	0	0	10	5	42.2	44	191	26	26	6	6	2	1	12	6	44	6	1
Denny, John, Philadelphia	7	7	.500	2.45	22	22	1	2	0	0	154.1	122	612	53	42	11	11	3	1	29	2	94	1	0
Diaz, Carlos, Los Angeles*	1	0	1.000	5.49	37	0	0	0	17	0	41.0	47	191	26	25	4	6	5	3	24	5	36	3	2
DiPino, Frank, Houston*	4	9	.308	3.35	57	0	0	0	44	14	75.1	74	329	32	28	3	8	6	4	36	11	65	1	0
Dravecky, David, San Diego*	9	8	.529	2.93	50	14	2	0	17	1	156.2	125	631	59	51	11	8	6	2	51	0	71	3	2
Eckersley, Dennis, Chicago	10	8	.556	3.03	24	24	2	0	0	0	160.1	152	662	59	54	11	6	3	3	36	7	81	3	2
Falcone, Peter, Atlanta*	5	7	.417	4.13	35	16	2	1	6	0	120.0	115	523	61	55	15	8	5	0	57	3	55	4	0
Fernandez, C. Sid, New York*	6	5	.500	3.50	15	15	2	0	0	0	90.0	74	371	40	35	8	3	2	0	34	0	62	1	0
Fireovid, Stephen, Philadelphia	0	0	.000	1.59	6	0	0	0	5	0	5.2	4	20	1	1	0	0	0	0	0	0	3	0	0
Forster, Terry, Atlanta*	2	5	.286	6.02	16	0	0	0	14	0	52.1	64	233	38	35	6	4	1	0	19	3	21	5	0
Franco, John, Cincinnati*	6	2	.750	2.61	54	0	0	0	30	4	79.1	74	335	28	23	3	8	4	1	36	8	55	2	3
Frazier, George, Chicago	6	3	.667	4.10	37	0	0	0	17	3	63.2	53	273	29	29	3	11	2	2	26	11	58	4	2
Gaff, Brent, New York	3	2	.600	3.63	47	0	0	0	18	8	84.1	77	358	39	34	4	3	7	1	36	9	42	5	5
Garber, H. Eugene, Atlanta	3	6	.333	3.06	62	0	0	0	42	11	106.0	103	443	45	36	7	4	2	2	24	9	55	1	1

Pitcher and Club	W.	L.	Pct.	ERA.	G.	GS.	CG.	ShO.	GF.	Sv.	IP.	H.	BFP.	R.	ER.	HR.	SH.	SF.	HB.	Tot. BB.	Int. BB.	SO.	WP.	Bk.
Gardner, Wesley, New York	1	1	.500	6.39	21	0	0	0	12	0	25.1	34	116	19	18	6	5	1	0	34	2	19	1	0
Garrelts, Scott, San Francisco	2	3	.400	5.65	21	3	0	0	5	0	43.0	45	206	33	27	6	1	2	1	34	1	32	3	0
Gooden, Dwight, New York	17	9	.654	2.60	31	31	7	3	0	0	218.0	161	879	72	63	7	3	2	2	73	3	276	3	7
Gorman, Thomas, New York*	6	0	1.000	2.97	36	0	0	0	12	0	57.2	51	230	20	19	7	4	1	1	13	4	40	2	0
Gossage, Richard, San Diego	10	6	.625	2.90	62	0	0	0	51	25	102.1	75	412	34	33	6	2	3	1	36	0	84	2	2
Grant, Mark, San Francisco	1	4	.200	6.37	11	10	2	0	1	0	53.2	56	231	40	38	6	1	1	1	19	0	32	2	0
Grapenthin, Richard, Montreal	0	2	.000	3.52	13	1	0	0	1	0	23.0	19	92	9	9	3	3	0	1	7	0	9	0	0
Green, Christopher, Pittsburgh°	8	5	.615	6.00	4	0	0	0	0	0	3.0	5	14	2	2	0	0	3	0	1	0	3	0	0
Gross, Kevin, Philadelphia	8	5	.615	4.12	44	14	2	0	0	0	129.0	140	566	66	59	8	9	3	5	44	4	84	4	0
Guante, Cecilio, Pittsburgh	2	3	.400	2.61	27	0	0	0	9	2	41.1	32	166	12	12	3	2	2	1	16	7	30	0	4
Gullickson, William, Montreal	12	9	.571	3.61	32	32	8	0	0	0	226.2	230	919	100	91	27	8	4	5	37	1	100	0	1
Hagen, Kevin, St. Louis	1	0	1.000	2.45	4	1	0	0	1	0	7.1	9	31	2	2	0	0	2	0	1	1	1	5	0
Hammaker, C. Atlee, San Francisco*	2	2	.500	2.18	6	6	0	0	0	0	33.0	32	139	10	8	2	3	0	4	9	2	24	0	0
Harris, Greg, Mtl.-S.D.	1	0	1.000	2.48	34	6	0	0	14	2	54.1	38	226	18	15	3	2	3	0	25	1	45	3	0
Hassler, Andrew, St. Louis*	0	1	.000	11.57	3	0	0	0	0	0	2.1	1	13	3	3	3	0	0	0	2	0	1	0	2
Hawkins, M. Andrew, San Diego	8	8	.500	4.68	36	22	2	0	9	0	146.0	143	650	90	76	13	10	4	2	72	2	77	1	0
Hershiser, Orel, Los Angeles	11	8	.579	2.66	45	20	8	4	1	2	189.2	160	771	65	56	9	5	3	0	50	3	150	8	0
Hesketh, Joseph, Montreal*	2	2	.500	1.80	11	5	0	0	0	0	45.0	38	182	12	11	9	1	3	1	15	6	32	1	2
Holland, Alfred, Philadelphia*	5	10	.333	3.39	68	0	0	0	61	29	98.1	82	404	38	37	14	6	5	5	30	3	61	1	1
Honeycutt, Frederick, Los Angeles*	10	9	.526	2.84	29	28	1	2	0	0	183.2	180	762	72	58	15	6	4	3	51	6	75	1	3
Hooton, Burt, Los Angeles	3	6	.333	3.44	54	6	2	1	2	0	110.0	109	463	43	42	14	6	2	6	43	4	62	2	3
Horton, Ricky, St. Louis*	9	4	.692	3.44	37	18	0	0	7	4	125.2	140	537	53	48	7	4	3	2	39	6	76	5	2
Howell, Kenneth, Los Angeles	5	5	.500	3.33	32	4	0	0	19	6	51.1	51	207	21	19	12	1	4	6	52	2	54	0	6
Hudson, Charles, Philadelphia	9	11	.450	5.64	30	30	5	2	0	0	173.2	181	748	101	78	14	6	8	2	52	4	94	1	0
Hume, Thomas, Cincinnati	4	6	.400	4.04	54	0	0	0	23	3	113.1	92	518	83	71	7	11	6	4	41	9	59	4	4
James, Robert, Montreal	6	6	.500	3.66	62	0	0	0	33	10	96.0	100	430	47	39	0	8	3	1	45	7	91	0	0
Johnson, William, Chicago	6	5	.545	1.69	17	0	0	0	2	0	5.1	4	19	3	2	0	1	0	0	1	1	3	5	2
Kepshire, Kurt, St. Louis	6	5	.545	3.30	8	16	2	2	0	0	109.0	100	453	47	40	7	5	4	5	44	4	71	2	0
Kern, James, Philadelphia	0	1	.000	10.13	35	0	0	0	8	1	13.1	20	70	16	15	3	1	1	1	10	1	8	2	0
Knepper, Robert, Houston*	15	10	.600	3.20	36	34	11	3	1	0	233.2	223	954	93	83	26	11	7	5	55	5	140	6	0
Koosman, Jerry, Philadelphia*	14	15	.483	3.25	35	34	3	1	0	0	224.0	232	950	95	81	8	13	6	2	60	5	137	3	2
Krawczyk, Raymond, Pittsburgh	0	3	.000	3.38	4	0	0	0	2	0	5.1	7	25	9	2	0	0	1	0	4	1	4	9	0
Krukow, Michael, San Francisco	11	12	.478	4.56	35	33	3	1	0	0	199.1	234	903	117	101	22	5	7	5	78	5	141	0	3
Lacey, Robert, San Francisco*	1	5	.167	3.88	34	0	0	0	14	3	51.0	55	216	22	22	5	2	3	2	13	4	26	15	1
LaCoss, Michael, Houston	4	7	.364	4.02	39	18	2	1	6	0	132.0	132	565	64	59	9	5	2	5	55	5	86	0	1
Lahti, Jeffrey, St. Louis	5	2	.714	3.72	63	0	0	0	29	8	84.2	69	353	36	35	6	3	3	0	34	12	45	6	3
LaPoint, David, St. Louis*	12	10	.545	3.96	33	33	2	1	0	0	193.0	205	827	94	85	20	8	8	3	77	6	130	2	1
Laskey, William, San Francisco	5	14	.263	4.33	35	34	1	0	0	0	207.2	222	883	112	100	19	8	8	6	50	6	71	9	0
Lavelle, Gary, San Francisco*	5	5	.500	2.76	77	0	0	0	42	12	101.0	92	426	34	31	3	1	10	1	42	14	43	6	3
Lea, Charles, Montreal	15	10	.600	2.89	30	30	9	0	0	0	224.1	198	918	82	72	18	6	4	0	68	3	123	6	1
Leary, Timothy, New York	3	3	.500	4.02	20	7	0	0	6	0	53.2	61	237	28	24	5	1	6	3	18	3	29	6	0
Lefferts, Craig, San Diego*	3	4	.429	2.13	62	0	0	0	13	10	105.2	88	420	29	25	4	4	3	1	24	1	56	0	0
Lerch, Randy, San Francisco*	5	3	.625	4.23	37	4	0	0	3	2	72.1	80	326	36	34	14	3	7	3	36	2	48	2	3
Lesley, Bradley, Cincinnati	1	0	1.000	5.12	16	0	0	0	6	0	19.1	17	87	11	11	1	0	1	0	14	0	7	1	0
Lollar, W. Timothy, San Diego*	11	13	.458	3.91	31	31	3	2	0	0	195.2	168	836	89	85	14	8	4	5	105	5	131	3	3
Lucas, Gary, Montreal*	9	8	.529	2.72	55	0	0	0	22	8	53.0	54	225	20	16	13	1	2	4	20	5	42	2	2
Lynch, Edward, New York	9	8	.529	4.50	40	13	9	1	2	0	124.0	169	556	77	62	13	1	5	0	24	5	62	1	2
Madden, Michael, Houston*	2	3	.400	5.53	17	7	0	0	1	0	40.2	46	193	25	25	4	13	8	3	35	3	29	0	0
Mahler, Richard, Atlanta	13	10	.565	3.12	38	29	9	1	4	0	222.0	209	918	86	77	20	13	8	3	62	7	106	3	1
Martin, D. Renie, S.F.-Philadelphia	1	3	.250	4.15	21	0	0	0	4	0	39.0	46	189	25	18	4	4	0	0	28	4	13	2	0

Pitcher and Club	W.	L.	Pct.	ERA.	G.	GS.	CG.	ShO.	GF.	Sv.	IP.	H.	BFP.	R.	ER.	HR.	SH.	SF.	HB.	Tot. BB.	Int. BB.	SO.	WP.	Bk.
McGaffigan, Andrew, Mtl.-Cincinnati	3	6	.333	3.52	30	6	0	0	10	1	69.0	60	282	28	27	4	2	1	0	23	2	57	1	2
McGraw, Frank, Philadelphia*	3	0	1.000	3.79	25	0	0	0	11	0	38.0	36	160	17	16	1	1	2	0	10	4	26	1	1
McMurtry, J. Craig, Atlanta	9	17	.346	4.32	37	30	0	0	1	0	183.1	184	811	100	88	16	12	9	0	102	4	99	4	3
McWilliams, Larry, Pittsburgh*	12	11	.522	2.93	34	32	7	2	0	0	227.1	226	957	86	74	18	12	6	2	78	7	149	3	3
Meridith, Ronald, Chicago*	0	0	.000	3.38	3	1	0	0	2	0	5.1	6	25	5	2	1	0	0	0	2	1	4	1	0
Minton, Gregory, San Francisco	4	9	.308	3.76	74	0	0	0	43	19	124.1	130	556	60	52	6	6	6	3	57	20	48	4	0
Monge, Isidro, San Diego*	2	1	.667	4.80	13	0	0	0	4	0	15.0	17	78	10	8	3	0	2	0	17	3	7	1	0
Moore, Donnie, Atlanta	4	5	.444	2.94	47	0	0	0	29	16	64.1	63	271	27	21	3	6	1	1	18	6	47	1	1
Niedenfuer, Thomas, Los Angeles	2	5	.286	2.47	33	0	0	0	21	11	47.1	39	203	14	13	3	3	0	1	23	7	45	1	0
Niekro, Joseph, Houston	16	12	.571	3.04	38	38	6	1	0	0	248.1	223	1027	104	84	16	9	8	4	89	4	127	12	1
Noles, Dickie, Chicago	2	2	.500	5.15	21	4	0	0	6	0	50.2	60	216	29	29	4	5	3	2	16	6	14	1	1
Orosco, Jesse, New York*	10	6	.625	2.59	60	0	0	0	52	31	87.0	58	355	29	25	7	5	2	0	34	9	85	3	0
Owchinko, Robert, Cincinnati*	3	5	.375	4.12	49	4	0	0	9	0	94.0	91	407	47	43	10	7	2	3	39	6	60	0	0
Ownbey, Richard, St. Louis	0	3	.000	4.74	20	4	0	0	0	0	19.0	23	88	13	10	1	5	1	0	8	0	11	1	0
Palmer, David, Montreal	7	3	.700	3.84	20	19	1	1	0	0	105.1	101	444	45	45	5	5	2	3	44	4	66	5	2
Pastore, Frank, Cincinnati	3	8	.273	6.50	24	16	1	0	0	0	98.1	110	437	74	71	10	5	5	3	40	3	53	4	0
Patterson, Reginald, Chicago	0	0	.000	10.50	3	1	0	0	1	0	6.0	10	30	7	7	1	0	1	0	2	0	5	1	0
Payne, Michael, Atlanta	0	0	.000	6.35	3	1	0	0	0	0	5.2	7	25	4	4	0	0	0	0	3	0	6	1	1
Pena, Alejandro, Los Angeles	12	6	.667	2.48	28	28	4	4	0	0	199.1	186	813	67	55	5	5	4	3	46	7	135	5	5
Perez, Pascual, Atlanta	14	8	.636	3.74	30	30	3	1	0	0	211.2	208	864	96	88	7	6	8	0	51	5	145	4	0
Power, Ted, Cincinnati	9	7	.563	2.82	78	0	0	0	42	11	108.2	93	456	37	34	7	9	5	0	46	8	81	3	0
Price, Joseph, Cincinnati	7	13	.350	4.19	30	30	3	1	0	0	171.2	176	748	91	80	19	5	8	2	61	5	129	3	0
Puleo, Charles, Cincinnati	1	2	.333	5.73	18	0	0	0	0	0	22.0	27	107	15	14	2	0	1	0	15	2	6	0	0
Pulido, Alfonso, Pittsburgh*	0	0	.000	9.00	5	0	0	0	0	0	2.0	3	10	3	2	0	0	0	0	1	0	2	0	0
Rainey, Charles, Chicago	5	7	.417	4.28	17	16	0	0	1	0	88.1	102	399	55	42	4	6	2	1	38	7	45	3	0
Rawley, Shane, Philadelphia*	10	6	.625	3.81	18	18	3	0	0	0	120.1	117	491	51	51	13	3	5	2	27	7	58	4	0
Reardon, Jeffrey, Montreal	7	7	.500	2.90	68	0	0	0	58	23	70.1	70	363	31	28	5	2	2	0	37	7	79	4	4
Reuschel, Ricky, Chicago	5	5	.500	5.17	19	14	0	0	2	0	92.1	123	405	57	53	7	9	2	3	23	7	43	2	0
Reuss, Jerry, Los Angeles*	5	7	.417	3.82	30	15	2	1	0	0	99.0	102	428	51	42	13	3	9	1	31	3	44	4	0
Rhoden, Richard, Pittsburgh	14	9	.609	2.72	33	33	3	0	0	0	238.1	216	961	81	72	13	6	4	1	62	4	136	10	4
Riley, George, San Francisco*	0	0	.000	3.99	12	4	0	0	1	0	29.1	39	134	14	13	6	4	1	0	7	0	12	1	0
Robinson, Don, Pittsburgh	5	6	.455	3.02	31	5	1	0	28	10	122.0	99	500	45	41	12	9	4	1	49	4	110	5	0
Robinson, Jeffrey, San Francisco	7	15	.318	4.56	33	33	3	0	0	0	171.2	195	749	99	87	15	5	9	2	52	4	102	7	2
Robinson, Ronald, Cincinnati	1	2	.333	2.72	12	5	0	0	7	0	39.2	35	166	18	12	3	11	1	0	13	3	24	0	2
Rodas, Richard, Los Angeles*	0	0	.000	5.40	3	0	0	0	1	0	3.2	5	21	3	3	0	0	0	0	3	0	1	0	0
Rogers, Stephen, Montreal	6	15	.286	4.31	31	28	4	1	0	0	169.1	171	732	93	81	12	6	5	2	78	5	64	1	0
Ross, Mark, Houston	0	0	.000	0.00	2	0	0	0	0	0	2.1	1	8	0	0	0	0	0	0	0	0	0	0	0
Rucker, David, St. Louis*	3	0	1.000	2.10	50	0	0	0	15	0	73.0	62	304	23	17	5	5	2	1	34	2	38	1	0
Ruhle, Vernon, Houston	1	9	.100	4.58	40	6	2	0	11	0	90.1	112	405	58	46	15	8	8	3	29	7	60	1	3
Russell, Jeffrey, Cincinnati	6	18	.250	4.26	33	30	0	0	1	0	181.2	186	787	97	86	14	3	3	4	65	8	101	3	3
Ruthven, Richard, Chicago	6	10	.375	5.04	23	22	2	0	0	0	126.2	154	562	75	75	12	7	6	4	41	2	55	1	1
Ryan, L. Nolan, Houston	12	11	.522	3.04	30	30	5	2	0	0	183.2	143	760	78	62	12	4	4	4	69	1	197	6	3
St. Claire, Randy, Montreal	0	0	.000	4.50	4	0	0	0	0	0	8.0	11	38	4	4	0	1	1	0	2	0	2	0	0
Sambito, Joseph, Houston*	0	0	.000	3.02	32	0	0	0	14	9	47.2	39	191	16	16	5	3	3	0	16	3	26	3	0
Sanderson, Scott, Chicago	8	5	.615	3.14	24	24	0	0	0	0	140.2	140	571	54	49	9	6	4	2	24	1	76	3	2
Schatzeder, Daniel, Montreal*	7	7	.500	2.71	36	14	3	1	6	0	136.0	112	547	44	41	5	8	8	1	36	4	89	3	1
Scherrer, William, Cincinnati*	1	1	.500	4.99	36	0	0	0	12	6	52.1	64	232	31	29	6	4	3	3	15	3	35	3	0
Schiraldi, Calvin, New York	1	1	.500	5.71	5	5	0	0	1	0	17.1	20	80	13	11	3	1	1	0	10	0	16	0	0
Schulze, Donald, Chicago	0	2	.000	12.00	1	1	0	0	0	0	3.0	8	16	4	4	0	0	0	1	1	0	2	0	0
Scott, Michael, Houston	5	11	.313	4.68	31	29	0	0	1	0	154.0	179	675	96	80	7	8	11	3	43	4	83	2	2

Pitcher and Club	W.	L.	Pct.	ERA.	G.	GS.	CG.	ShO.	GF.	Sv.	IP.	H.	BFP.	R.	ER.	HR.	SH.	SF.	HB.	Tot. BB.	Int. BB.	SO.	WP.	Bk.
Scurry, Rodney, Pittsburgh*	5	6	.455	2.53	43	0	0	0	25	4	46.1	28	186	14	13	8	4	4	0	22	3	48	7	0
Show, Eric, San Diego	15	9	.625	3.40	32	32	0	1	0	0	206.2	175	862	88	78	18	17	4	0	88	3	104	6	2
Sisk, Douglas, New York	1	3	.250	2.09	50	0	0	0	31	15	77.2	57	329	24	18	1	7	2	3	54	5	32	1	0
Smith, Bryn, Montreal	12	13	.480	3.32	28	28	3	2	0	0	179.0	178	751	72	66	15	7	1	2	51	4	101	2	2
Smith, David, Houston	5	4	.556	2.21	53	0	0	0	24	5	77.1	60	304	22	19	5	5	1	3	20	3	45	1	1
Smith, Lee, Chicago	9	7	.563	3.65	69	0	0	0	59	33	101.0	98	428	42	41	6	2	5	0	35	7	86	6	0
Smith, Michael, Cincinnati	1	0	1.000	5.23	8	0	0	0	5	0	10.1	12	47	6	6	1	0	0	0	5	0	7	0	0
Smith, Zane, Atlanta*	1	0	1.000	2.25	3	3	0	0	0	0	20.0	16	87	7	5	1	0	0	0	13	2	16	1	0
Solano, Julio, Houston	1	3	.250	1.95	8	0	0	0	0	0	50.2	31	197	13	11	3	3	1	0	18	1	33	3	1
Soto, Mario, Cincinnati	18	7	.720	3.53	33	33	13	0	0	0	237.1	181	971	102	93	26	3	0	5	87	6	185	3	0
Stoddard, Timothy, Chicago	10	6	.625	3.82	58	0	0	0	26	7	92.0	77	398	41	39	9	8	6	1	57	11	87	3	1
Stuper, John, St. Louis	3	5	.375	5.28	15	12	0	0	2	0	61.1	73	272	39	36	4	9	3	2	20	0	19	0	0
Sutcliffe, Richard, Chicago	16	1	.941	2.69	20	20	7	3	0	0	150.1	123	602	53	45	9	1	4	1	39	2	155	3	2
Sutter, H. Bruce, St. Louis	5	7	.417	1.54	71	0	0	0	63	45	122.2	109	477	26	21	5	4	4	0	23	4	77	2	0
Swan, Craig, New York	1	0	1.000	8.20	10	0	0	0	5	0	18.2	18	81	17	17	5	0	2	0	7	0	10	2	0
Tekulve, Kenton, Pittsburgh	3	9	.250	2.66	72	0	0	0	51	13	88.0	86	370	30	26	4	6	2	4	33	12	36	2	2
Terrell, C. Walter, New York	11	12	.478	3.52	33	33	3	1	0	0	215.0	232	926	99	84	16	11	8	1	80	1	114	6	0
Thurmond, Mark, San Diego*	14	8	.636	2.97	32	29	1	1	0	0	178.2	174	750	79	59	12	11	5	2	55	3	57	1	2
Tibbs, Jay, Cincinnati	6	2	.750	2.86	14	14	3	1	0	0	100.2	87	403	34	32	4	5	0	0	33	0	40	0	0
Tidrow, Richard, New York	0	0	.000	9.19	11	0	0	0	5	1	15.2	25	78	19	16	5	0	1	0	7	0	8	1	0
Toliver, Freddie, Cincinnati	0	0	.000	0.90	3	1	0	0	0	0	10.0	7	42	2	1	0	2	0	0	7	0	4	0	0
Torrez, Michael, New York	1	5	.167	5.02	9	8	0	0	1	0	37.2	55	175	25	21	3	2	4	2	18	0	16	2	2
Trout, Steven, Chicago*	13	7	.650	3.41	32	31	6	2	0	0	190.0	205	797	80	72	11	13	6	0	59	7	81	2	2
Tudor, John, Pittsburgh*	12	11	.522	3.27	32	32	6	1	0	0	212.0	200	881	81	77	19	10	7	3	56	7	117	7	1
Tunnell, B. Lee, Pittsburgh	1	7	.125	5.27	26	6	0	0	5	3	68.1	81	317	44	40	6	3	1	2	40	6	51	1	1
Valenzuela, Fernando, Los Angeles*	12	17	.414	3.03	34	34	12	2	0	0	261.0	218	1078	109	88	14	11	7	0	106	6	240	11	1
Von Ohlen, David, St. Louis*	1	0	1.000	3.12	27	0	0	0	12	1	34.2	39	141	13	12	3	0	0	0	8	3	19	1	1
Walk, Robert, Pittsburgh	1	1	.500	2.61	2	2	0	0	0	0	10.1	8	44	5	3	1	1	0	0	4	1	10	0	0
Wehrmeister, David, Philadelphia	0	0	.000	7.20	7	2	0	0	1	0	15.0	18	71	12	12	1	0	2	1	7	1	13	1	0
Welch, Robert, Los Angeles	13	13	.500	3.78	31	31	4	0	0	0	178.2	191	771	86	75	11	10	2	0	58	7	126	4	1
White, Larry, Los Angeles	1	0	1.000	3.00	7	0	0	0	4	0	12.0	9	50	5	4	2	0	2	0	6	2	10	1	0
Whitson, Eddie, San Diego	14	8	.636	3.24	31	31	2	0	0	0	189.0	181	773	72	68	16	9	7	3	42	6	103	3	2
Williams, Frank, San Francisco	9	4	.692	3.55	61	0	0	0	15	3	106.1	88	454	49	42	2	3	3	0	51	6	91	3	1
Willis, Carl, Cincinnati	1	0	1.000	3.72	9	0	0	0	1	0	9.2	8	39	4	4	1	3	0	0	2	0	3	0	0
Winn, James, Pittsburgh	0	1	.000	3.86	9	0	0	0	2	0	18.2	19	81	8	8	3	3	0	0	9	1	11	0	0
Zachry, Patrick, Los Angeles	5	6	.455	3.81	58	0	0	0	23	2	82.2	84	376	38	35	3	3	5	5	51	13	55	2	0
Zaske, L. Jeffrey, Pittsburgh*	0	0	.000	0.00	2	0	0	0	2	0	5.0	4	20	0	0	0	0	0	0	2	0	2	0	0

NOTE—Following pitchers combined to pitch shutout games: Atlanta (4)—McMurtry and Bedrosian 2, Barker and Forster, Barker and Moore; Chicago (3)—Bordi and Smith, Rainey and Smith, Sanderson and Bordi; Cincinnati (2)—Hume, Owchinko and Power, Robinson, Franco and Power; Houston (6)—LaCoss and Smith 2, Knepper and DiPino, Madden and Ruhle, Niekro and DiPino, Ryan and Smith; Los Angeles (3)—Hershiser, Howell and Reuss, Welch and Niedenfuer, Welch and Zachry; Montreal (5)—Hesketh and Reardon, Lea and Reardon, Rogers and James, Schatzeder and James, Smith and James; New York (9)—Berenyi and Orosco 2, Berenyi and Gorman, Berenyi and Sisk, Darling and Orosco, Darling and Sisk, Gooden and Orosco, Lynch and Sisk, Terrell and Orosco; Philadelphia (4)—Bystrom and Holland, Carlton and Campbell, K. Gross and Holland, Rawley and Holland; Pittsburgh (5)—Candelaria and Robinson 2, McWilliams and Tekulve, Rhoden and Scurry, Tudor, Bielecki, Tekulve, Candelaria and Robinson; St. Louis (3)—Andujar, Allen and Sutter, Forsch, Lahti and Sutter, Kepshire and Sutter; San Diego (10)—Thurmond and Gossage 2, Show and Gossage 3, Show and Gossage 2, Dravecky, DeLeon and Gossage, Lollar and Lefferts, Show, Gossage and Hawkins, Whitson and Dravecky, Whitson and Gossage; San Francisco (4)—Robinson, Laskey and Minton, Robinson, Lerch and Williams, Robinson and Lavelle, Robinson, Lerch and Williams, Robinson and Minton.

PITCHERS WITH TWO OR MORE CLUBS
(Alphabetically Arranged With Pitcher's First Club on Top)

Pitcher and Club	W.	L.	Pct.	ERA.	G.	GS.	CG.	ShO.	GF.	Sv.	IP.	H.	BFP.	R.	ER.	HR.	SH.	SF.	HB.	Tot. BB.	Int. BB.	SO.	WP.	Bk.
Berenyi, Cincinnati	3	7	.300	6.00	13	11	0	0	1	0	51.0	63	251	35	34	0	2	1	0	42	2	53	4	0
Berenyi, New York	9	6	.600	3.76	19	19	0	0	0	0	115.0	100	486	58	48	6	10	2	1	53	2	81	7	0
Dayley, Atlanta	0	3	.000	5.30	4	4	0	0	0	0	18.2	28	92	18	11	5	3	0	1	6	1	10	0	0
Dayley, St. Louis	0	2	.000	18.00	3	2	0	0	1	0	5.0	16	32	10	10	1	1	0	0	5	0	0	0	0
Harris, Montreal	2	1	.667	2.04	15	0	0	0	4	2	17.2	10	68	4	4	0	1	0	2	7	1	15	0	0
Harris, San Diego	1	1	.500	2.70	19	1	0	0	10	1	36.2	28	158	14	11	3	1	3	2	18	0	30	3	0
Martin, San Francisco	1	1	.500	3.86	12	0	0	0	3	0	23.1	29	112	13	10	2	3	0	0	16	4	8	1	0
Martin, Philadelphia	0	2	.000	4.60	9	0	0	0	1	0	15.2	17	77	12	8	2	2	0	0	12	4	5	1	0
McGaffigan, Montreal	3	4	.429	2.54	21	3	0	0	8	1	46.0	37	184	14	13	2	0	1	0	15	2	39	1	2
McGaffigan, Cincinnati	0	2	.000	5.48	9	3	0	0	2	0	23.0	23	98	14	14	2	2	0	0	8	0	18	0	0

1984 N.L. Pitching Against Each Club

ATLANTA—80-82

Pitcher	Chi. W—L	Cin. W—L	Hou. W—L	L.A. W—L	Mtl. W—L	N.Y. W—L	Phil. W—L	Pitt. W—L	St.L. W—L	S.D. W—L	S.F W—L	Totals W—L
Barker	0—1	2—0	0—2	0—2	1—0	1—0	1—1	0—0	1—1	0—1	1—0	7— 8
Bedrosian	0—0	1—1	0—1	1—1	1—1	1—0	0—0	2—0	0—0	2—2	1—0	9— 6
Brizzolara	0—0	0—0	0—0	0—1	0—0	0—0	0—0	0—0	1—0	0—0	0—1	1— 2
Camp	0—1	1—0	1—1	0—1	0—1	0—0	2—0	1—0	0—1	1—0	2—1	8— 6
Dayley	0—0	0—1	0—0	0—0	0—1	0—1	0—1	0—0	0—0	0—0	0—0	0— 3
Dedmon	0—0	0—0	1—0	1—1	1—0	0—1	0—0	1—1	0—0	0—0	0—0	4— 3
Falcone	0—1	1—0	2—1	0—1	0—1	0—0	1—0	0—1	1—0	0—2	0—0	5— 7
Forster	0—0	1—0	0—0	0—0	0—0	0—0	0—0	1—0	0—0	0—0	0—0	2— 0
Garber	0—1	0—1	1—0	1—0	0—1	0—0	0—0	1—0	0—1	0—0	0—2	3— 6
Mahler	1—1	3—0	2—0	1—0	0—1	0—2	0—2	1—1	1—0	1—2	3—1	13—10
McMurtry	0—2	2—1	1—0	1—2	2—0	1—2	1—2	0—0	0—3	0—3	1—2	9—17
Moore	1—0	0—0	1—1	0—1	0—0	1—1	0—0	0—0	0—0	0—1	1—1	4— 5
Payne	0—0	0—0	0—0	0—0	0—0	0—0	0—0	0—1	0—0	0—0	0—0	0— 1
Perez	1—2	2—1	2—0	1—2	0—1	0—1	2—0	1—0	1—1	3—0	1—0	14— 8
Smith	0—0	0—0	1—0	0—0	0—0	0—0	0—0	0—0	0—0	0—0	0—0	1— 0
Totals	3—9	13—5	12—6	6—12	5—7	4—8	7—5	8—4	5—7	7—11	10—8	80—82

CHICAGO—96-65

Pitcher	Atl. W—L	Cin,. W—L	Hou. W—L	L.A. W—L	Mtl. W—L	N.Y. W—L	Phil. W—L	Pitt. W—L	St.L. W—L	S.D. W—L	S.F. W—L	Totals W—L
Bordi	1—0	0—0	1—0	0—0	0—0	0—0	0—1	1—0	1—1	0—0	1—0	5— 2
Brusstar	0—1	0—0	0—0	0—0	0—0	0—0	0—0	0—0	0—0	1—0	0—0	1— 1
Eckersley	0—0	1—1	1—1	2—0	2—1	0—0	2—1	0—3	2—0	0—0	0—1	10— 8
Frazier	0—0	1—0	0—1	1—0	1—1	0—1	1—0	0—0	1—0	0—0	1—0	6— 3
Noles	0—0	1—1	1—0	0—0	0—0	0—0	0—0	0—1	0—0	0—0	0—0	2— 2
Patterson	0—0	0—0	0—0	0—0	0—0	0—0	0—0	0—1	0—0	0—0	0—0	0— 1
Rainey	1—0	0—0	0—0	0—1	1—0	0—0	0—2	0—3	1—1	0—0	2—0	5— 7
Reuschel	1—0	0—0	1—1	0—0	1—1	0—0	1—1	0—0	0—0	0—1	0—1	5— 5
Ruthven	1—0	1—2	2—0	1—0	0—0	2—3	0—0	1—0	0—1	0—2	1—0	6—10
Sanderson	0—1	2—0	0—0	1—2	0—0	2—0	1—0	1—0	2—1	0—0	1—0	8— 5
Smith	1—1	0—0	0—0	0—0	1—1	2—1	1—2	0—1	1—0	2—1	1—0	9— 7
Stoddard	0—0	0—0	1—0	1—0	2—2	1—0	1—2	2—1	1—1	0—0	1—0	10— 6
Sutcliffe	1—0	2—0	0—0	1—1	2—0	3—0	1—0	2—0	1—0	2—0	1—0	16— 1
Trout	3—0	1—1	1—0	1—1	0—1	2—1	1—0	1—0	2—0	1—2	0—1	13— 7
Totals	9—3	7—5	6—6	7—5	10—7	12—6	9—9	8—10	13—5	6—6	9—3	96—65

No Decisions—Altamirano, Johnson, Meridith, Schulze.

CINCINNATI—70-92

Pitcher	Atl. W—L	Chi. W—L	Hou. W—L	L.A. W—L	Mtl. W—L	N.Y. W—L	Phil. W—L	Pitt. W—L	St.L. W—L	S.D. W—L	S.F. W—L	Totals W—L
Berenyi	0—1	1—0	0—1	0—0	0—1	0—1	0—1	0—0	0—1	1—0	1—1	3— 7
Browning	0—0	0—0	0—0	1—0	0—0	0—0	0—0	0—0	0—0	0—0	0—0	1— 0
Cato	0—0	0—0	0—0	0—0	0—0	0—1	0—0	0—0	0—0	0—0	0—0	0— 1
Franco	1—0	0—0	2—0	1—2	0—0	0—0	1—0	0—0	1—0	0—0	0—0	6— 2
Hume	0—2	1—0	0—1	0—3	1—0	0—1	0—2	0—0	1—1	0—3	1—0	4—13
Lesley	0—0	0—0	0—0	0—0	0—0	0—0	0—0	0—0	0—0	0—0	0—1	0— 1
McGaffigan	0—0	0—1	0—1	0—0	0—0	0—0	0—0	0—0	0—0	0—0	0—0	0— 2
Owchinko	0—2	0—0	1—0	0—0	0—0	0—0	0—0	1—0	0—1	0—1	1—1	3— 5
Pastore	0—2	0—2	0—1	1—0	1—0	0—0	0—1	0—0	0—0	0—0	0—2	3— 8
Power	1—2	0—0	0—2	1—1	0—0	0—1	1—0	2—0	0—0	1—1	2—0	9— 7
Price	0—0	0—0	0—2	2—0	1—1	0—1	0—2	0—3	1—1	1—3	2—0	7—13
Puleo	0—0	0—0	0—0	0—0	0—0	0—0	1—0	0—0	0—0	0—1	0—0	1— 2
Robinson	0—0	0—1	0—0	0—1	0—0	0—0	0—0	1—0	0—0	0—0	0—0	1— 2
Russell	0—3	0—3	0—1	1—2	2—1	0—1	0—1	1—1	1—1	1—2	0—2	6—18
Scherrer	0—0	1—0	0—0	0—0	0—1	0—0	0—0	0—0	0—0	0—0	0—0	1— 1
Smith	0—0	0—0	0—0	0—0	0—0	0—0	1—0	0—0	0—0	0—0	0—0	1— 0
Soto	2—0	2—0	3—1	0—2	1—1	3—1	0—0	1—0	1—2	2—0	3—0	18— 7
Tibbs	1—0	0—0	1—0	0—0	1—0	0—0	0—0	1—1	0—1	0—0	2—0	6— 2
Willis	0—1	0—0	0—0	0—0	0—0	0—0	0—0	0—0	0—0	0—0	0—0	0— 1
Totals	5—13	5—7	8—10	7—11	7—5	3—9	5—7	7—5	4—8	7—11	12—6	70—92

No Decisions—Toliver.

HOUSTON—80-82

Pitcher	Atl. W—L	Chi. W—L	Cin. W—L	L.A. W—L	Mtl. W—L	N.Y. W—L	Phil. W—L	Pitt. W—L	St.L. W—L	S.D. W—L	S.F. W—L	Totals W—L
Calhoun	0—0	0—0	0—1	0—0	0—0	0—0	0—0	0—0	0—0	0—0	0—0	0— 1
Dawley	1—0	1—1	1—1	2—0	0—0	1—0	1—1	1—0	1—0	1—0	1—1	11— 4
DiPino	0—2	0—1	1—1	0—1	1—0	1—0	1—0	0—2	0—1	0—1	0—0	4— 9
Knepper	0—1	1—1	3—0	2—2	1—0	1—2	1—1	0—1	3—0	0—1	3—1	15—10
LaCoss	1—0	0—0	1—0	0—1	2—0	0—0	1—0	1—0	0—0	0—3	1—1	7— 5
Madden	0—1	1—0	0—0	1—1	0—0	0—0	0—0	0—0	0—0	0—1	0—0	2— 3
Niekro	2—1	0—0	2—3	2—1	2—2	0—1	1—1	1—1	1—1	3—1	2—0	16—12

	Atl.	Chi.	Cin.	L.A.	Mtl.	N.Y.	Phil.	Pitt.	St.L.	S.D.	S.F.	Totals
Ross	0—0	0—0	0—0	0—0	0—0	0—0	0—0	0—0	1—0	0—0	0—0	1— 0
Ruhle	0—2	0—0	0—0	0—1	0—1	1—0	0—0	0—1	0—0	0—0	2—1	1— 9
Ryan	0—1	2—0	1—0	1—2	1—1	1—2	0—2	2—0	1—2	1—1	2—0	12—11
M. Scott	1—1	0—2	1—0	1—0	0—1	0—3	1—0	0—1	0—0	0—1	1—2	5—11
Smith	1—1	0—1	0—1	0—0	0—0	0—0	0—0	1—0	1—0	1—1	1—0	5— 4
Solano	0—2	1—0	0—1	0—0	0—0	0—0	0—0	0—0	0—0	0—0	0—0	1— 3
Totals	6—12	6—6	10—8	9—9	7—5	4—8	6—6	6—6	8—4	6—12	12—6	80—82

No Decisions—Sambito.

LOS ANGELES—79-83

Pitcher	Atl. W—L	Chi. W—L	Cin. W—L	Hou. W—L	Mtl. W—L	N.Y. W—L	Phil. W—L	Pitt. W—L	St.L. W—L	S.D. W—L	S.F. W—L	Totals W—L
Diaz	0—0	0—0	0—0	0—0	0—0	0—0	0—0	0—0	0—0	1—0	0—0	1— 0
Hershiser	1—2	2—0	2—1	1—1	0—2	0—1	0—0	1—1	2—0	0—0	2—0	11— 8
Honeycutt	0—2	1—0	0—0	2—0	1—1	1—2	1—0	0—1	1—1	2—1	1—1	10— 9
Hooton	1—1	0—1	1—0	0—1	0—0	0—0	0—1	0—0	0—0	1—0	0—2	3— 6
Howell	1—0	0—1	2—1	0—0	0—1	0—0	0—1	0—1	1—0	1—0	0—0	5— 5
Niedenfuer	0—0	0—1	0—0	0—0	0—1	0—1	0—0	1—0	0—0	0—0	1—2	2— 5
Pena	2—0	0—1	1—2	1—0	1—0	0—1	0—0	2—1	1—0	2—1	2—0	12— 6
Reuss	0—0	1—0	1—1	2—1	0—0	0—0	0—2	0—1	1—0	0—2	0—0	5— 7
Valenzuela	3—0	0—2	0—2	1—2	3—0	0—3	1—1	0—2	0—2	3—1	1—2	12—17
Welch	4—0	1—1	2—0	1—3	0—1	2—0	1—3	0—1	0—2	0—2	2—0	13—13
White	0—1	0—0	0—0	0—0	0—0	0—0	0—0	0—0	0—0	0—0	0—0	0— 1
Zachry	0—0	0—0	2—0	1—1	1—0	0—1	0—1	0—0	0—1	0—1	1—1	5— 6
Totals	12—6	5—7	11—7	9—9	6—6	3—9	3—9	4—8	6—6	10—8	10—8	79—83

No Decisions—Rodas.

MONTREAL—78-83

Pitcher	Atl. W—L	Chi. W—L	Cin. W—L	Hou. W—L	L.A. W—L	N.Y. W—L	Phil. W—L	Pitt. W—L	St.L. W—L	S.D. W—L	S.F. W—L	Totals W—L
Bargar	0—0	0—0	0—0	0—0	0—0	0—0	0—0	0—1	0—0	0—0	0—0	0— 1
Grapenthin	0—0	0—1	0—0	0—0	0—0	0—0	0—0	1—0	0—0	0—0	0—1	1— 2
Gullickson	0—2	1—0	1—2	1—1	2—1	2—0	2—0	0—1	1—2	0—0	2—0	12— 9
Harris	0—0	0—0	0—0	0—0	0—0	1—0	0—0	0—0	0—0	0—0	0—0	0— 1
Hesketh	0—0	0—0	0—0	0—0	0—0	1—1	0—1	0—0	1—0	0—0	0—0	2— 2
James	0—1	2—0	0—1	0—1	1—0	0—1	1—1	2—1	0—0	0—0	0—0	6— 6
Lea	1—2	1—3	2—0	1—0	0—1	1—1	1—1	2—2	1—0	2—0	3—0	15—10
Lucas	0—0	0—1	0—0	0—1	0—0	0—0	0—1	0—0	0—0	0—0	0—0	0— 3
McGaffigan	1—0	0—0	0—0	0—0	1—0	0—1	0—0	0—0	0—0	0—2	0—1	3— 4
Palmer	2—0	1—0	0—0	1—0	0—0	0—1	1—0	0—1	2—1	0—0	0—0	7— 3
Reardon	0—0	1—0	0—0	0—0	0—0	0—1	2—1	1—1	1—1	1—2	1—1	7— 7
Rogers	0—0	0—1	0—2	1—2	0—1	0—1	1—1	0—3	2—3	2—0	0—1	6—15
Schatzeder	1—0	1—1	0—0	1—0	1—1	1—2	0—1	1—0	0—1	0—1	1—0	7— 7
Smith	2—0	0—3	2—2	0—2	1—2	2—1	2—1	0—0	2—1	1—0	0—1	12—13
Totals	7—5	7—10	5—7	5—7	6—6	7—11	11—7	7—11	9—9	7—5	7—5	78—83

No Decisions—Breining, St. Claire.

NEW YORK—90-72

Pitcher	Atl. W—L	Chi. W—L	Cin. W—L	Hou. W—L	L.A. W—L	Mtl. W—L	Phil. W—L	Pitt. W—L	St.L. W—L	S.D. W—L	S.F. W—L	Totals W—L
Berenyi	1—1	1—1	1—1	1—0	1—0	1—0	0—0	1—1	0—1	1—0	1—1	9— 6
Darling	2—0	1—2	2—0	1—0	0—0	1—2	2—2	2—1	1—1	0—0	0—1	12— 9
Fernandez	0—0	0—1	1—0	1—0	1—0	1—0	1—0	0—1	1—2	0—0	0—0	6— 6
Gaff	0—0	0—0	0—0	0—0	0—0	0—0	0—0	0—0	1—0	1—1	1—1	3— 2
Gardner	0—0	0—1	0—0	0—0	0—0	0—0	0—0	1—0	0—0	0—0	0—0	1— 1
Gooden	0—1	3—2	1—0	2—1	3—0	1—1	0—2	3—0	1—1	2—1	1—0	17— 9
Gorman	0—0	0—0	1—0	0—0	0—0	1—0	1—0	2—0	0—0	1—0	0—0	6— 0
Leary	1—0	0—1	0—1	1—0	0—0	0—0	0—0	0—1	0—0	0—0	0—0	3— 3
Lynch	0—1	1—1	0—0	0—1	1—0	2—1	2—1	1—0	2—1	0—2	0—0	9— 8
Orosco	1—0	0—0	2—0	0—1	1—0	2—0	2—0	0—0	0—3	1—0	1—2	10— 6
Schiraldi	0—0	0—0	0—0	0—0	0—0	0—1	0—0	0—1	0—0	0—0	0—0	0— 2
Sisk	0—0	0—1	0—0	0—1	0—0	0—0	1—1	0—0	0—0	0—0	0—0	1— 3
Swan	1—0	0—0	0—0	0—0	0—0	0—0	0—0	0—0	0—0	0—0	0—0	1— 0
Terrell	2—1	0—2	1—0	2—0	1—1	1—2	1—1	2—1	1—1	0—0	0—3	11—12
Torrez	0—0	0—0	0—1	0—0	0—2	1—0	0—0	0—1	0—1	0—0	0—0	1— 5
Totals	8—4	6—12	9—3	8—4	9—3	11—7	10—8	12—6	7—11	6—6	4—8	90—72

No Decisions—Tidrow.

PHILADELPHIA—81-81

Pitcher	Atl. W—L	Chi. W—L	Cin. W—L	Hou. W—L	L.A. W—L	Mtl. W—L	N.Y. W—L	Pitt. W—L	St.L. W—L	S.D. W—L	S.F. W—L	Totals W—L
Andersen	0—0	0—0	0—1	0—0	0—0	2—0	0—3	0—1	0—2	0—0	1—0	3— 7
Bystrom	0—1	1—1	0—0	0—0	0—0	0—0	1—0	0—1	0—1	1—0	1—0	4— 4
Campbell	0—0	0—0	0—0	1—0	1—0	0—1	1—1	0—1	2—2	1—0	0—0	6— 5
Carlton	2—0	1—1	1—1	2—0	1—2	2—2	1—1	2—0	1—0	0—0	0—0	13— 7
Carman	0—0	0—0	0—0	0—1	0—0	0—0	0—0	0—0	0—0	0—0	0—0	0— 1

	Atl.	Chi.	Cin.	Hou.	L.A.	Mtl.	N.Y.	Pitt.	St.L.	S.D.	S.F.	Totals
Denny	0—2	0—0		1—0	0—1	0—2	1—0	0—1	1—0	2—1	2—0	7— 7
K. Gross	0—2	1—1	1—0	0—1	1—0	2—0	1—0	1—0	0—1	0—0	1—0	7— 5
Holland	0—0	2—1	0—1	0—1	1—0	0—0	0—2	0—0	0—2	1—1	1—2	8— 5
Hudson	1—1	3—2	1—1	0—2	1—0	0—0	1—1	1—1	0—1	0—1	1—1	9—11
Kern	0—0	0—0	0—0	0—0	0—0	0—0	0—0	0—1	0—0	0—0	0—0	0— 1
Koosman	2—0	1—1	2—1	1—1	3—0	0—3	1—2	2—3	1—1	1—2	0—1	14—15
Martin	0—0	0—1	0—0	0—0	0—0	0—1	0—0	0—0	0—0	0—0	0—0	0— 2
McGraw	0—0	0—0	0—0	0—0	0—0	0—0	0—0	1—0	1—0	0—0	0—0	2— 0
Rawley	0—1	0—1	2—0	1—0	1—0	1—2	1—0	0—2	2—0	1—0	1—0	10— 6
Totals	5—7	9—9	7—5	6—6	9—3	7—11	8—10	7—11	8—10	7—5	8—4	81—81

No Decisions—Fireovid, Wehrmeister.

PITTSBURGH—75-87

Pitcher	Atl.	Chi.	Cin.	Hou.	L.A.	Mtl.	N.Y.	Phil.	St.L.	S.D.	S.F.	Totals
	W—L	W—L	W—L	W—L	W—L	W—L	W—L	W—L	W—L	W—L	W—L	W—L
Candelaria	0—2	0—1	3—0	1—2	2—0	0—0	0—1	2—2	1—3	2—0	1—0	12—11
DeLeon	0—0	4—0	0—2	1—2	0—1	1—1	0—2	0—0	0—4	0—1	1—0	7—13
Guante	0—1	0—0	0—0	1—0	0—0	0—0	0—0	1—0	0—0	0—0	0—2	2— 3
McWilliams	2—0	1—3	1—0	0—0	1—1	2—1	2—1	2—1	1—2	0—1	0—1	12—11
Rhoden	0—1	3—0	1—0	1—0	1—0	2—2	2—1	1—0	0—2	1—2	2—1	14— 9
Robinson	1—0	0—0	0—2	1—0	0—0	0—0	0—1	1—2	1—0	0—0	0—1	5— 6
Scurry	0—0	0—1	0—1	0—0	0—0	2—0	0—2	2—0	0—0	0—2	1—0	5— 6
Tekulve	0—3	1—1	0—1	0—1	1—1	1—1	0—0	0—0	0—1	0—0	0—0	3— 9
Tudor	1—1	1—1	0—1	1—1	2—1	2—0	1—1	2—3	1—0	0—1	1—1	12—11
Tunnell	0—0	0—1	0—0	0—0	0—0	0—0	1—1	0—2	0—1	0—2	0—0	1— 7
Walk	0—0	0—0	0—0	0—0	1—0	0—0	0—0	0—0	0—0	0—0	0—0	1— 1
Winn	0—0	0—0	0—0	0—0	0—0	0—0	0—0	0—0	0—0	1—0	0—0	1— 0
Totals	4—8	10—8	5—7	6—6	8—4	11—7	6—12	11—7	4—14	4—8	6—6	75—87

No Decisions—Bielecki, Green, Krawczyk, Pulido, Zaske.

ST. LOUIS—84-78

Pitcher	Atl.	Chi.	Cin.	Hou.	L.A.	Mtl.	N.Y.	Phil.	Pitt.	S.D.	S.F.	Totals
	W—L	W—L	W—L	W—L	W—L	W—L	W—L	W—L	W—L	W—L	W—L	W—L
Allen	1—1	0—0	1—0	1—0	1—1	0—1	1—2	1—0	1—0	1—0	1—1	9— 6
Andujar	3—0	2—2	2—0	0—1	0—1	3—2	3—1	1—2	3—1	2—2	1—2	20—14
Citarella	0—0	0—0	0—0	0—0	0—0	0—1	0—0	0—0	0—0	0—0	0—0	0— 1
Cox	0—3	0—2	0—0	0—0	2—1	1—1	1—2	1—1	4—0	0—0	0—1	9—11
Dayley	0—0	0—0	0—0	0—0	0—0	0—1	0—0	0—0	0—1	0—0	0—0	0— 2
Forsch	0—0	0—0	0—0	1—0	0—0	0—2	1—0	1—0	0—0	0—1	0—0	2— 5
Hagen	0—0	0—0	0—0	0—0	0—0	1—0	0—0	0—0	0—0	0—0	0—0	1— 0
Hassler	0—0	0—0	0—0	0—0	0—0	0—0	0—0	0—0	1—0	0—0	0—0	1— 0
Horton	1—0	0—1	1—0	2—1	0—0	0—0	1—0	2—0	0—2	1—0	1—0	9— 4
Kepshire	0—0	1—0	0—1	1—1	1—0	0—0	1—1	0—1	0—0	0—1	1—0	6— 5
Lahti	0—0	2—0	1—0	0—0	0—1	0—0	1—0	0—1	0—0	0—0	0—0	4— 2
LaPoint	1—1	0—2	1—1	0—2	1—1	2—0	2—0	1—1	3—0	1—1	0—1	12—10
Ownbey	0—0	0—1	0—0	0—0	0—1	0—0	0—0	0—0	0—0	0—1	0—0	0— 3
Rucker	0—0	0—1	0—0	0—1	0—0	0—0	0—0	1—1	1—0	0—0	0—0	2— 3
Stuper	0—0	0—2	2—0	0—0	0—0	0—0	1—1	0—0	0—0	0—1	0—0	3— 5
Sutter	1—0	0—2	0—2	0—1	1—0	0—0	0—0	2—1	1—1	0—0	0—0	5— 7
Von Ohlen	0—0	0—0	0—0	0—0	0—0	0—0	0—0	0—0	0—0	0—0	1—0	1— 0
Totals	7—5	5—13	8—4	4—8	6—6	9—9	11—7	10—8	14—4	5—7	5—7	84—78

SAN DIEGO—92-70

Pitcher	Atl.	Chi.	Cin.	Hou.	L.A.	Mtl.	N.Y.	Phil.	Pitt.	St.L.	S.F.	Totals
	W—L	W—L	W—L	W—L	W—L	W—L	W—L	W—L	W—L	W—L	W—L	W—L
Booker	1—1	0—0	0—0	0—0	0—0	0—0	0—0	0—0	0—0	0—0	0—0	1— 1
Chiffer	0—0	0—0	1—0	0—0	0—0	0—0	0—0	0—0	0—0	0—0	0—0	1— 0
DeLeon	0—1	0—0	0—0	0—0	0—0	0—0	0—0	0—0	1—0	0—1	1—0	2— 2
Dravecky	1—1	2—0	2—0	0—0	1—3	1—1	0—1	0—1	1—1	1—0	0—0	9— 8
Gossage	0—1	0—0	3—2	2—1	0—0	2—0	1—0	1—0	1—1	0—1	1—0	10— 6
Harris	0—0	0—0	0—1	0—0	0—0	1—0	0—0	0—0	0—0	0—0	1—0	2— 1
Hawkins	1—0	0—0	0—0	2—1	1—1	0—0	0—2	0—3	1—0	1—0	2—2	8— 9
Lefferts	1—0	0—1	1—0	0—1	0—0	0—1	1—0	1—1	0—0	0—0	0—1	3— 4
Lollar	0—0	0—0	1—2	3—1	1—2	0—1	1—0	1—1	0—1	1—3	3—2	11—13
Monge	1—0	1—1	0—0	0—0	0—0	0—0	0—0	0—0	0—0	0—0	0—0	2— 1
Show	2—0	2—1	0—2	2—1	0—1	1—2	2—1	1—0	1—0	1—1	3—0	15— 9
Thurmond	2—2	1—2	2—0	1—0	3—0	0—2	1—0	1—1	1—1	2—0	0—0	14— 8
Whitson	2—1	0—1	1—0	2—1	1—3	0—1	2—0	1—1	2—0	1—0	2—0	14— 8
Totals	11—7	6—6	11—7	12—6	8—10	5—7	6—6	5—7	8—4	7—5	13—5	92—70

SAN FRANCISCO—66-96

Pitcher	Atl.	Chi.	Cin.	Hou.	L.A.	Mtl.	N.Y.	Phil.	Pitt.	St.L.	S.D.	Totals
	W—L	W—L	W—L	W—L	W—L	W—L	W—L	W—L	W—L	W—L	W—L	W—L
Calvert	1—1	0—0	0—0	0—1	1—0	0—1	0—0	0—1	0—0	0—0	0—0	2— 4
Cornell	0—1	0—0	0—0	0—0	1—0	0—0	0—0	0—0	0—1	0—0	0—1	1— 3
M. Davis	1—2	0—4	0—0	0—1	0—2	0—1	2—2	1—1	0—1	0—2	1—1	5—17
Garretts	0—0	0—0	0—0	0—1	1—0	1—0	0—0	0—0	0—0	0—0	0—2	2— 3

Pittsburgh's Jose DeLeon had all kinds of trouble with the Cardinals last season, losing all four decisions, but beat the division's best club, the Cubs, four times.

	Atl.	Chi.	Cin.	Hou.	L.A.	Mtl.	N.Y.	Phil.	Pitt.	St.L.	S.D.	Totals
Grant	1—0	0—0	0—2	0—1	0—0	0—1	0—0	0—0	0—0	0—0	0—0	1— 4
Hammaker	0—0	0—0	0—0	0—0	0—0	0—0	0—0	1—0	1—0	0—0	0—0	2— 0
Krukow	1—2	2—1	1—1	1—1	0—1	1—0	1—2	0—1	1—1	2—0	1—2	11—12
Lacey	0—0	0—0	0—0	0—0	0—0	0—1	0—0	1—0	0—0	0—1	0—1	1— 3
Laskey	2—1	0—1	0—1	1—3	2—2	0—2	0—0	1—0	0—1	2—1	1—2	9—14
Lavelle	1—1	0—0	0—1	0—0	1—1	0—0	1—0	0—0	2—0	0—0	0—1	5— 4
Lerch	0—0	0—0	1—2	1—1	1—0	0—0	2—0	0—0	0—0	0—0	0—0	5— 3
Martin	0—0	0—0	1—0	0—0	0—0	0—0	0—0	0—1	0—0	0—0	0—0	1— 1
Minton	1—1	0—3	2—2	0—0	0—1	1—1	0—0	0—1	0—0	0—0	0—0	4— 9
Riley	0—0	0—0	0—0	0—0	1—0	0—0	0—0	0—0	0—0	0—0	0—0	1— 0
Robinson	0—1	1—0	1—2	1—3	0—1	1—0	0—0	0—2	1—2	2—1	0—3	7—15
Williams	0—0	0—0	0—1	2—0	0—2	1—0	2—0	0—1	1—0	1—0	2—0	9— 4
Totals	8—10	3—9	6—12	6—12	8—10	5—7	8—4	4—8	6—6	7—5	5—13	66—96

1984 CHAMPIONSHIP SERIES

Including

American League Review

American League Box Scores

American League Composite Box Score

National League Review

National League Box Scores

National League Composite Box Score

Detroit's Milt Wilcox made the most of his moment in the sun, shutting out the Royals on three hits over eight innings in the Tigers' pennant-clinching victory.

Tigers Sweep Royals Aside

By LARRY WIGGE

When Milt Wilcox was a fuzzy-cheeked 20-year-old rookie with the Cincinnati Reds in 1970, he didn't often see eye to eye with Sparky Anderson, a rookie manager with the Reds that season. But in the intervening 14 years, the two have come closer together in their way of thinking.

"He did so much talking, I was never sure whether he knew what he was talking about," Wilcox said of his first impressions of Anderson, who went on to lead the Reds to five National League West titles and four visits to the World Series before being fired after the 1978 season. He was hired by the Detroit Tigers the next season.

"Now I know he handles his players well," Wilcox said. "He gets everyone into the game and makes everyone feel a part of the team."

The future didn't materialize quite as nicely for Wilcox as it did for Anderson following their days with the Reds. Wilcox was traded to Cleveland in December of 1971, then hurt his arm the next season. He was traded again in 1975, this time to the Chicago Cubs, and a year later he was sold to the Tigers. His fortune improved at that point, and he has won at least 11 games in seven of his eight seasons in Detroit since then. He fashioned his best record ever at 17-8 in 1984 and helped the Tigers win the American League East title.

Prior to starting Game 3 of the A.L. Championship Series against the Kansas City Royals, Wilcox said one of his first big thrills in baseball was when Anderson brought him in to pitch in the third game of the 1970 N.L. Championship Series. He hurled three shutout innings and was credited with a 3-2 victory over the Pittsburgh Pirates that clinched the pennant for the Reds.

On October 5, 1984, 14 years to the day after he had been summoned from the bullpen to help wrap up the Reds' title, Anderson again showed confidence in Wilcox, sending him to the mound against the Royals with a chance to clinch the A.L. pennant for the Tigers. When the results were in, Wilcox had become the first pitcher to record clinching victories in the Championship Series in each league.

Wilcox was the beneficiary of a single run that night in Detroit. Designated hitter Barbaro Garbey opened the second inning with a single up the middle. Center fielder Chet Lemon forced Garbey at sec-

Tigers' relief ace Willie Hernandez celebrates after recording the final out in Detroit's pennant-clinching victory.

Kansas City's Willie Wilson shows his frustration after being called out on a close play at first in Game 3 of the A.L. Championship Series.

ond, but Lemon went to third on an ensuing single by Darrell Evans. Third baseman Marty Castillo then hit a two-hopper to Kansas City shortstop Onix Concepcion, who flipped to Frank White for the force on Evans at second. White's relay to first, however, was an instant late, and Castillo was safe as Lemon scored. That was to be the only run surrendered by Kansas City lefthander Charlie Leibrandt, who allowed the Tigers just three hits while starting and finishing for the Royals.

But Wilcox made that one run look monumental. He struck out eight batters, walked two and allowed only a single by third baseman George Brett in the fourth and another by catcher Don Slaught in the eighth. There were two outs in the eighth when first baseman Evans made a diving stop of center fielder Willie Wilson's hard-

hit grounder in the hole, scrambled to his feet and narrowly beat a sliding Wilson at first.

Wilcox, who completed none of his 33 starts during the regular season, gave way to Willie Hernandez at the start of the ninth. The lefthander preserved the 1-0 decision that gave the Tigers a three-game sweep over the Royals.

Before the playoffs, Detroit had become the fourth team in major league history to be in first place from the start of its season to the end of the year, joining the 1923 New York Giants, 1927 New York Yankees and 1955 Brooklyn Dodgers in that category. The Tigers started the season at a 35-5 pace and finished with 104 regular-season victories.

The Tigers proved they were no fluke right from the start against the Royals. In the first inning of the opener in Kansas City, they exploded for two runs, the 62nd time in 1984 they had scored in the first inning. This time, second baseman Lou Whitaker stroked a leadoff single to right and shortstop Alan Trammell followed with a run-scoring triple over the head of left fielder Darryl Motley. Trammell scored one out later on a sacrifice fly by catcher Lance Parrish.

The Royals put in a serious bid to erase Detroit's 2-0 lead in their half of the third inning when George Brett sent a hard smash to right field with the bases loaded and two out, but Kirk Gibson made a diving catch to snuff out the threat.

"It was a great play by Gibson," Anderson said. "The ball was hooking and sinking, and he stayed with it. A year ago Brett would have been running for a while."

Brett, too, thought he had provided a key hit. "When I saw him start to dive, I said to myself, 'Oh, man. Beautiful. That's three runs and I'm on third.' When I saw him start to dive I thought he was crazy. It turned out I was crazy."

The Tigers slowly started to pull away as left fielder Larry Herndon hit a leadoff homer off loser Bud Black in the fourth inning. Trammell opened the fifth with a home run off Black and two innings later delivered a run-scoring single off reliever Mark Huismann to make the score 5-0. Evans and Castillo drove in one run each in the eighth before Parrish pounded out the Tigers' third homer (all leadoff shots) of the game in the ninth.

Kansas City's only run came in the seventh when designated hitter Jorge Orta smashed a leadoff triple and came home on a grounder by Motley. The Royals managed only five hits off winner Jack

Morris and none off Hernandez, who worked the final two innings to wrap up Detroit's 8-1 victory.

In Game 2 of the playoffs, the Tigers were to win the eighth of eight games between the two clubs at Royals Stadium in '84, but not without a struggle.

In yet another first-inning explosion, the Tigers scored two runs. Whitaker opened the game by reaching first base on an error by Concepcion at short. One out later, Gibson and Parrish smacked back-to-back run-scoring doubles. Gibson made it 3-0 in the third when he slugged a home run over the center-field wall.

The Royals got to starter Dan Petry for a run in the fourth on a walk to right fielder Pat Sheridan, a single by Brett and a fielder's-choice grounder by Orta. Then they turned to their bench. Dane Iorg drove in a run with a two-out pinch-hit single in the seventh. Lynn Jones, batting for Sheridan, greeted Hernandez with another pinch single to open the eighth. After Brett struck out, Hal McRae ripped a pinch double into the left-field corner, scoring Jones and tying the game, 3-3.

Entering the ninth, Kansas City Manager Dick Howser removed starter Bret Saberhagen, a 20-year-old rookie. Saberhagen had gotten off to a shaky start and was behind, 3-0, after three innings, but he yielded only a pair of singles in the next five innings to keep the Royals in the game.

After Hernandez was touched for the tying run in the eighth, the game came down to a duel of relievers: Kansas City's Dan Quisenberry vs. Detroit's Aurelio Lopez.

Parrish singled sharply off the glove of third baseman Greg Pryor to open the winning uprising for the Tigers in the 11th. Evans sacrificed, but both runners were safe when catcher Slaught fumbled the ball. After left fielder Ruppert Jones failed in his bunt attempt and forced Parrish at third, designated hitter Johnny Grubb belted a high sinker from Quisenberry into right-center, scoring Evans and Jones and giving the Tigers a 5-3 margin.

Lopez was not overpowering, but he was tough when he had to be for the Tigers. He escaped from a 10th-inning jam by getting first baseman Steve Balboni to fly to center with two men on and two out, and he retired Lynn Jones on a fly to right with two on in the 11th to earn the victory and give Detroit a 2-0 edge in the playoffs.

After squeaking by the Royals with one run in Game 3, the Tigers captured their first A.L. pennant since 1968. Gibson, who blunted a rally with his diving catch in

Game 1 and was 5 for 12 with a homer in the three games, was named the Most Valuable Player of the playoffs. But the Tigers' entire pitching staff, which held the Royals to a combined .170 batting average, shared in the credit.

Kansas City's leadoff hitter, Wilson, was 2 for 13. Balboni, who led the club in runs batted in during the regular season, was 1 for 11 with no RBIs. Brett, who also failed to drive in a run in the series, was 3 for 13. White was 1 for 11, while Concepcion and Sheridan, key Kansas City hitters down the stretch, were a combined 0 for 13. The Royals never led in any game, were outscored, 14-4, were outhomered, 4-0, and had only two extra-base hits. Defensively, the Royals committed seven errors in the three games.

Howser, now winless in nine postseason games as a manager, shook his head and said: "We weren't in the first game, but our pitching was good enough to win the last two, which is what makes it frustrating. We definitely didn't swing the bats real good, but you have to credit their pitching. I've said all along that improved pitching is what sets this Detroit team apart from others of recent years."

GAME OF TUESDAY, OCTOBER 2, AT KANSAS CITY (N)

Detroit	AB.	R.	H.	RBI.	PO.	A.
Whitaker, 2b	5	2	1	0	0	1
Brookens, 2b	0	0	0	0	0	0
Trammell, ss	3	2	3	3	1	5
Baker, ss	0	0	0	0	0	0
Gibson, rf	5	0	2	0	3	0
Parrish, c	4	1	1	2	6	0
Herndon, lf	3	1	1	1	3	0
R. Jones, ph-lf	1	0	0	0	2	0
Kuntz, ph-lf	1	0	0	0	0	0
Garbey, dh	5	1	2	0	0	0
Lemon, cf	5	0	0	0	2	0
Evans, 1b	4	0	2	1	8	1
Bergman, pr-1b	0	1	0	0	1	0
Castillo, 3b	4	0	2	1	0	1
Morris, p	0	0	0	0	1	1
Hernandez, p	0	0	0	0	0	0
Totals	40	8	14	8	27	9

Kansas City	AB.	R.	H.	RBI.	PO.	A.
Wilson, cf	4	0	1	0	4	0
Sheridan, rf	2	0	0	0	3	0
L. Jones, ph-rf	1	0	0	0	1	0
Brett, 3b	4	0	0	0	2	1
Orta, dh	4	1	1	0	0	0
Motley, lf	4	0	0	1	4	0
Balboni, 1b	4	0	0	0	6	1
White, 2b	3	0	1	0	1	2
Slaught, c	3	0	2	0	5	0
Concepcion, ss	3	0	0	0	0	2
Black, p	0	0	0	0	1	1
Huismann, p	0	0	0	0	0	0
M. Jones, p	0	0	0	0	0	0
Totals	32	1	5	1	27	7

Detroit	2 0 0	1 1 0	1 2 1—8
Kansas City	0 0 0	0 0 0	1 0 0—1

Detroit	IP.	H.	R.	ER.	BB.	SO.
Morris (Winner)	7	5	1	1	4	4
Hernandez	2	0	0	0	0	2

Kansas City	IP.	H.	R.	ER.	BB.	SO.
Saberhagen	8	6	3	2	1	5
Quisenberry (Loser)	3	2	2	1	1	1

Game-winning RBI—Grubb.

Error—Concepcion, Saberhagen, Brookens, Slaught. Left on bases—Detroit 7, Kansas City 11. Two-base hits—Gibson, Parrish, McRae, Grubb. Home run—Gibson. Stolen base—Bergman. Caught stealing—Wilson. Sacrifice hits—Grubb, Evans. Umpires—Deegan, Bible, Christal, Jones, Denny and Nothnagel. Time—3:37. Attendance—42,019.

Kansas City	IP.	H.	R.	ER.	BB.	SO.
Black (Loser)	5	7	4	4	1	3
Huismann	2⅔	6	3	2	1	2
M. Jones	1⅓	1	1	1	0	0

Game-winning RBI—Trammell.

Error—Sheridan. Double play—Kansas City 1. Left on bases—Detroit 8, Kansas City 5. Two-base hit—Trammell. Three-base hits—Trammell, Orta. Home runs—Herndon, Trammell, Parrish. Sacrifice fly—Parrish. Wild pitch—Huismann. Umpires—Deegan, Bible, Christal, Zirbel, Jordan and O'Dell. Time—2:42. Attendance—41,973.

GAME OF WEDNESDAY, OCTOBER 3, AT KANSAS CITY (N)

Detroit	AB.	R.	H.	RBI.	PO.	A.
Whitaker, 2b	5	1	1	0	5	5
Trammell, ss	5	0	1	0	0	2
Gibson, rf	4	2	2	2	3	0
Parrish, c	5	0	2	1	7	2
Evans, 3b-1b	4	1	0	0	7	1
R. Jones, lf	4	1	0	0	3	0
Grubb, dh	4	0	1	2	0	0
Lemon, cf	5	0	0	0	4	0
Bergman, 1b	1	0	1	0	4	0
Brookens, 3b	2	0	0	0	0	2
Garbey, ph	1	0	0	0	0	0
Castillo, 3b	1	0	0	0	0	0
Petry, p	0	0	0	0	0	0
Hernandez, p	0	0	0	0	0	0
Lopez, p	0	0	0	0	0	0
Totals	41	5	8	5	33	12

Kansas City	AB.	R.	H.	RBI.	PO.	A.
Wilson, cf	5	0	1	0	4	0
Sheridan, rf	2	1	0	0	6	0
L. Jones, ph-rf	3	1	1	0	1	0
Brett, 3b	5	0	2	0	0	2
Pryor, pr-3b	0	0	0	0	1	0
Orta, dh	3	0	0	1	0	0
McRae, ph	1	0	1	1	0	0
Wathan, pr-dh	1	0	0	0	0	0
Motley, lf	4	0	2	0	4	0
Balboni, 1b	5	0	1	0	7	1
White, 2b	5	1	0	0	1	0
Slaught, c	5	0	1	0	6	0
Concepcion, ss	2	0	0	0	0	2
Iorg, ph	1	0	1	1	0	0
Biancalana, pr-ss	1	0	0	0	1	2
Washington, ph	1	0	0	0	0	0
Saberhagen, p	0	0	0	0	1	1
Quisenberry, p	0	0	0	0	1	1
Totals	44	3	10	3	33	9

Detroit	2 0 1	0 0 0	0 0 0	0	2—5
Kansas City	0 0 0	1 0 0	1 1 0	0	0—3

Detroit	IP.	H.	R.	ER.	BB.	SO.
Petry	7	4	2	2	1	4
Hernandez	1	2	1	1	1	1
Lopez (Winner)	3	4	0	0	1	2

GAME OF FRIDAY, OCTOBER 5, AT DETROIT (N)

Kansas City	AB.	R.	H.	RBI.	PO.	A.
Wilson, cf	4	0	0	0	2	0
Sheridan, rf	2	0	0	0	0	0
L. Jones, ph	1	0	0	0	0	0
Brett, 3b	4	0	1	0	0	4
Orta, dh	3	0	0	0	0	0
McRae, ph	1	0	1	0	0	0
Washington, pr	0	0	0	0	0	0
Motley, lf	4	0	0	0	3	0
Balboni, 1b	2	0	0	0	7	1
White, 2b	3	0	0	0	5	1
Slaught, c	3	0	1	0	6	0
Concepcion, ss	2	0	0	0	0	2
Iorg, ph	1	0	0	0	0	0
Biancalana, ss	0	0	0	0	0	0
Leibrandt, p	0	0	0	0	1	2
Totals	30	0	3	0	24	10

Detroit	AB.	R.	H.	RBI.	PO.	A.
Whitaker, 2b	4	0	0	0	0	0
Trammell, ss	3	0	0	0	0	1
Gibson, rf	3	0	1	0	1	0
Parrish, c	3	0	0	0	8	0
Herndon, lf	2	0	0	0	3	0
Garbey, dh	3	0	1	0	0	0
Lemon, cf	3	1	0	0	3	0
Evans, 1b	2	0	1	0	7	2
Castillo, 3b	3	0	0	1	3	3
Wilcox, p	0	0	0	0	2	0
Hernandez, p	0	0	0	0	0	0
Totals	26	1	3	1	27	6

Kansas City	000	000	0 0 0—0
Detroit	010	000	0 0 x—1

Kansas City	IP.	H.	R.	ER.	BB.	SO.
Leibrandt (Loser)	8	3	1	1	4	6

Detroit	IP.	H.	R.	ER.	BB.	SO.
Wilcox (Winner)	8	2	0	0	2	8
Hernandez (Save)	1	0	0	0	0	0

Game-winning RBI—Castillo.

Errors—Slaught 2, Balboni. Double play—Kansas City 1. Left on bases—Kansas City 5, Detroit 5. Stolen bases—Castillo, Gibson, Evans. Umpires—Deegan, Bible, Christal, Cossey, Runchey and Zivic. Time—2:39. Attendance—52,168.

DETROIT TIGERS' BATTING AND FIELDING AVERAGES

Player—Position	G.	AB.	R.	H.	TB.	2B.	3B.	HR.	RBI.	B.A.	PO.	A.	E.	F.A.
Bergman, pr-1b	2	1	1	1	1	0	0	0	0	1.000	5	0	0	1.000
Gibson, rf	3	12	2	5	9	1	0	1	2	.417	7	0	0	1.000
Trammell, ss	3	11	2	4	9	0	1	1	3	.364	1	8	0	1.000
Garbey, dh-ph	3	9	1	3	3	0	0	0	0	.333	0	0	0	.000
Evans, 1b-3b	3	10	1	3	4	1	0	0	1	.300	22	4	0	1.000
Parrish, c	3	12	1	3	7	1	0	1	3	.250	21	2	0	1.000
Castillo, 3b	3	8	0	2	2	0	0	0	2	.250	3	4	0	1.000
Grubb, dh	1	4	0	1	2	1	0	0	2	.250	0	0	0	.000
Herndon, lf	2	5	1	1	4	0	0	1	1	.200	6	0	0	1.000

Player—Position	G.	AB.	R.	H.	TB.	2B.	3B.	HR.	RBI.	B.A.	PO.	A.	E.	F.A.
Whitaker, 2b	3	14	3	2	2	0	0	0	0	.143	5	6	0	1.000
Hernandez, p	3	0	0	0	0	0	0	0	0	.000	0	0	0	.000
Baker, ss	1	0	0	0	0	0	0	0	0	.000	0	0	0	.000
Lopez, p	1	0	0	0	0	0	0	0	0	.000	0	0	0	.000
Morris, p	1	0	0	0	0	0	0	0	0	.000	1	1	0	1.000
Petry, p	1	0	0	0	0	0	0	0	0	.000	0	0	0	.000
Wilcox, p	1	0	0	0	0	0	0	0	0	.000	2	0	0	1.000
Kuntz, ph-lf	1	1	0	0	0	0	0	0	0	.000	0	0	0	.000
Brookens, 2b-3b	2	2	0	0	0	0	0	0	0	.000	0	2	1	.667
R. Jones, ph-lf	2	5	1	0	0	0	0	0	0	.000	5	0	0	1.000
Lemon, cf	3	13	1	0	0	0	0	0	0	.000	9	0	0	1.000
Totals	3	107	14	25	43	4	1	4	14	.234	87	27	1	.991

KANSAS CITY ROYALS' BATTING AND FIELDING AVERAGES

Player—Position	G.	AB.	R.	H.	TB.	2B.	3B.	HR.	RBI.	B.A.	PO.	A.	E.	F.A.
McRae, ph	2	2	0	2	3	1	0	0	1	1.000	0	0	0	.000
Iorg, ph	2	2	0	1	1	0	0	0	1	.500	0	0	0	.000
Slaught, c	3	11	0	4	4	0	0	0	0	.364	17	0	3	.850
Brett, 3b	3	13	0	3	3	0	0	0	0	.231	2	7	0	1.000
L. Jones, ph-rf	3	5	1	1	1	0	0	0	0	.200	2	0	0	1.000
Motley, lf	3	12	0	2	2	0	0	0	1	.167	11	0	0	1.000
Wilson, cf	3	13	0	2	2	0	0	0	0	.154	10	0	0	1.000
Orta, dh	3	10	1	1	3	0	1	0	1	.100	0	0	0	.000
Balboni, 1b	3	11	0	1	1	0	0	0	0	.091	20	3	1	.958
White, 2b	3	11	1	1	1	0	0	0	0	.091	7	3	0	1.000
Black, p	1	0	0	0	0	0	0	0	0	.000	1	1	0	1.000
Huismann, p	1	0	0	0	0	0	0	0	0	.000	0	0	0	.000
M. Jones, p	1	0	0	0	0	0	0	0	0	.000	0	0	0	.000
Leibrandt, p	1	0	0	0	0	0	0	0	0	.000	1	2	0	1.000
Pryor, pr-3b	1	0	0	0	0	0	0	0	0	.000	1	0	0	1.000
Quisenberry, p	1	0	0	0	0	0	0	0	0	.000	1	1	0	1.000
Saberhagen, p	1	0	0	0	0	0	0	0	0	.000	1	1	1	.667
Biancalana, pr-ss	2	1	0	0	0	0	0	0	0	.000	1	2	0	1.000
Washington, ph-pr	2	1	0	0	0	0	0	0	0	.000	0	0	0	.000
Wathan, pr-dh	1	1	0	0	0	0	0	0	0	.000	0	0	0	.000
Sheridan, rf	3	6	1	0	0	0	0	0	0	.000	9	0	1	.900
Concepcion, ss	3	7	0	0	0	0	0	0	0	.000	0	6	1	.857
Totals	3	106	4	18	21	1	1	0	4	.170	84	26	7	.940

DETROIT TIGERS' PITCHING RECORDS

Pitcher	G.	GS.	CG.	IP.	H.	R.	ER.	BB.	SO.	HB.	WP.	W.	L.	Pct.	ERA.
Wilcox	1	1	0	8	2	0	0	2	8	0	1	1	0	1.000	0.00
Lopez	1	0	0	3	4	0	0	1	2	0	0	1	0	1.000	0.00
Morris	1	1	0	7	5	1	1	4	0	0	1	1	0	1.000	1.29
Hernandez	3	0	0	4	3	1	1	1	3	0	0	0	0	.000	2.25
Petry	1	1	0	7	4	2	2	1	4	0	0	0	0	.000	2.57
Totals	3	3	0	29	18	4	4	6	21	0	0	3	0	1.000	1.24

Shutout—Wilcox-Hernandez (combined). Save—Hernandez.

KANSAS CITY ROYALS' PITCHING RECORDS

Pitcher	G.	GS.	CG.	IP.	H.	R.	ER.	BB.	SO.	HB.	WP.	W.	L.	Pct.	ERA.
Leibrandt	1	1	1	8	3	1	1	4	6	0	0	0	1	.000	1.13
Saberhagen	1	1	0	8	6	3	2	1	5	0	0	0	0	.000	2.25
Quisenberry	1	0	0	3	2	2	1	1	0	0	0	0	1	.000	3.00
Huismann	1	0	0	2⅔	6	3	2	1	2	0	1	0	0	.000	6.75
M. Jones	1	0	0	1⅓	1	1	1	0	0	0	0	0	0	.000	6.75
Black	1	1	0	5	7	4	4	1	3	0	0	0	1	.000	7.20
Totals	3	3	1	28	25	14	11	8	17	0	1	0	3	.000	3.54

No shutouts or saves.

COMPOSITE SCORE BY INNINGS

Detroit	4	1	1	1	1	0	1	2	1	0	2	— 14
Kansas City	0	0	0	1	0	0	2	1	0	0	0	— 4

Game-winning RBIs—Trammell, Grubb, Castillo.
Sacrifice hits—Grubb, Evans.
Sacrifice fly—Parrish.
Stolen bases—Bergman, Castillo, Gibson, Evans.
Caught stealing—Wilson.
Double plays—Concepcion, White and Balboni; Brett, White and Balboni.
Left on bases—Detroit 8, 7, 5—20; Kansas City 5, 11, 5—21.
Hit by pitcher—None.
Passed balls—None.
Balks—None.
Time of games—First game, 2:42; second game, 3:37; third game, 2:39.
Attendance—First game, 41,973; second game, 42,019; third game, 52,168.
Umpires—Deegan, Bible, Christal (all three games); Zirbel, Jordan, O'Dell (first game); Jones, Denny, Nothnagel (second game); Cossey, Runchey, Zivic (third game).
Official scorers—Del Black, Kansas City official scorer; Ed Browalski, Polish News (Detroit).

Chicago ace Rick Sutcliffe won Game 1 and was sailing along in Game 5 until the Padres struck in the sixth and seventh innings for six runs.

Padres Come Back to Life

By LARRY WIGGE

All of America, it seemed, was behind them. Two victories in two games—the first by a 13-0 score, the second a 4-2 margin—also were behind them. Needing just one more win, the Chicago Cubs appeared to be on their way to ending their 39-year World Series famine.

But a funny thing happened to the Cubs en route to the Fall Classic. The San Diego Padres, given up for dead after losing the first two games in Chicago, came back to life, won the next three games and became the first team ever to recover from a 2-0 deficit and win the National League Championship Series. Such a comeback had been achieved only once before, by the Milwaukee Brewers against the California Angels in the 1982 American League playoffs.

The beginning of the 1984 N.L. playoffs was almost as stunning as its improbable conclusion.

Numerous Championship Series batting records were broken or tied as the Cubs thrashed the Padres in the opener. They banged out 16 hits, including five home runs, and scored 13 runs, all N.L. playoff records. That cushion made it easy on starter Rick Sutcliffe, who allowed only two hits—a bunt single by first baseman Steve Garvey and a bloop single by shortstop Garry Templeton—while striking out eight and walking five over seven innings.

The outcome never really was in doubt. After the Padres went down in order in the top of the first, center fielder Bob Dernier, aided by a 20-mph wind, belted Eric Show's second pitch of the game into the left-field bleachers, making him the first player in an N.L. playoff game to hit a first-inning leadoff home run. After second baseman Ryne Sandberg struck out, left fielder Gary Matthews slugged another homer to left.

It got worse for San Diego.

Sutcliffe added insult to injury when he led off the third with a tremendous home run that cleared the right-field bleachers and landed outside Wrigley Field on Sheffield Avenue. The Cubs added two more runs in that inning on a run-scoring single by first baseman Leon Durham and a sacrifice fly by right fielder Keith Moreland.

Moreland also provided the Cubs with the play of the game defensively, snaring a sinking liner by left fielder Carmelo Martinez with the bases loaded and two out in the fourth.

"Moreland's play turned what could

Series MVP Steve Garvey jumps for joy as teammates Rich Gossage (54) and Terry Kennedy hug after San Diego's pennant-clinching victory.

have been a close game into a runaway," said Sutcliffe, the winning pitcher.

The Cubs poured it on after that, exploding off Greg Harris, who had taken over for Show. They had six runs in the fifth, half of which came on Matthews' second homer of the game. Third baseman Ron Cey supplied the coup de grace with a solo shot in the two-run sixth.

Every player in the Cubs' starting lineup had at least one hit and one run batted in. Matthews' two home runs extended his streak of Championship Series homers to four (a major league record), having hit one in each of the last three games of the 1983 playoffs when he led the Philadelphia Phillies to the league pennant.

The Cubs showed a different side of their attack in Game 2, using speed and daring to defeat the Padres. Dernier and Sandberg were the architects of the 4-2 victory.

Dernier opened Chicago's half of the first with a single off Mark Thurmond and then caught the Padres napping on the next play, Sandberg's hit-and-run groundout to third baseman Luis Salazar. Dernier raced all the way to third on the play, beating a weak throw by Garvey. Dernier then scored on Matthews' grounder to short. It was the fifth straight Championship Series game in which Matthews had driven in a run, another record.

In the third, Moreland singled and scored on Cey's double to left-center as Templeton's relay throw to the plate skipped away from Padres catcher Terry Kennedy. Cey took third on the play and scored on catcher Jody Davis' sacrifice fly, giving Chicago a 3-0 lead.

After San Diego scored its first run of the series on a double by right fielder Tony Gwynn and a sacrifice fly by center fielder Kevin McReynolds in the fourth, the Cubs put the final nail in the Padres' coffin in their half of the inning. Starting pitcher Steve Trout hit a one-out single and was forced at second by Dernier, who promptly stole second and then scored on a double by Sandberg. That double knocked out Thurmond, who took the loss.

Trout yielded only a run-scoring single by Garvey in the sixth after that. The lefthander went 8⅓ innings to gain the victory, allowing just five hits while walking three and striking out two. Lee Smith relieved Trout and recorded the final two outs for the save.

When the Cubs took a 1-0 lead in the second inning of Game 3 on a double by Moreland and an RBI single by Cey, they appeared to be on the verge of a three-game sweep. But the Padres were to have none of that script.

Kennedy and McReynolds opened the Padres' fifth with singles, and one out later, Templeton came to the plate for the biggest hit of his career, a two-run double to the wall in left-center. That gave the Padres a 2-1 edge, their first lead of the series. Templeton scored the third run of the inning on a single by second baseman Alan Wiggins.

One inning later, third baseman Graig Nettles singled in Gwynn, who had led off with a single, and knocked out Cubs starter (and loser) Dennis Eckersley. Kennedy greeted reliever George Frazier with a single, setting the stage for a three-run homer by McReynolds.

That 7-1 lead was in the capable hands of starter Ed Whitson, a righthander who in 1984 went from a below-.500 pitcher to

a 14-game winner thanks to his palmball, a pitch he developed when a cut on his index finger required him to hold the ball differently. With his palmball and his outstanding fastball, Whitson allowed only five hits before being relieved in the ninth by Goose Gossage, who struck out two of the three batters he faced and preserved the win.

Game 4 was, by far, the most competitive and dramatic of the playoffs. It also was a showcase for San Diego's Garvey.

Garvey had four hits and five RBIs in Game 4, including a run-scoring double that capped a two-run third, marking the first time the Padres had scored first in the series. Garvey's hit followed a single and stolen base by Templeton, a single by Wiggins and a sacrifice fly by Gwynn.

But the Cubs came right back to take the lead with three runs in the fourth. Matthews led off with a walk, and two outs later, Davis and Durham—the latter breaking out of a 1-for-14 postseason slump—banged out back-to-back homers off Padres starter Tim Lollar.

That put the ball right back into Garvey's court. After Tim Flannery stroked a pinch-hit single to open the fifth and advanced to third on a bunt and a groundout, Garvey singled up the middle off Cubs starter Scott Sanderson to tie the score at 3-3. In the seventh, pinch-hitter Bobby Brown walked with one out and stole second before reliever Tim Stoddard was ordered to walk Gwynn and pitch to Garvey. The first baseman responded with a single to left, scoring Brown with the go-ahead run. Gwynn then scored on a passed ball to make it 5-3.

The seesaw battle continued, however, when the Cubs came to bat against Gossage in the eighth. Sandberg reached first on an infield hit and stole second as Matthews struck out. Moreland singled for one run, and one out later, Davis doubled off the center-field wall to even the score, 5-5.

It looked ominous for the Padres in the ninth when the Cubs loaded the bases with two out. Dernier doubled, Matthews was walked intentionally and Henry Cotto, who had entered the game as a pinch runner for Moreland in the eighth, was hit by a Craig Lefferts delivery. But Lefferts retired Cey on a weak grounder to second to thwart the rally.

Garvey had saved his best act of the day for the bottom of the ninth. After Wiggins struck out to open the inning, Gwynn singled, bringing Garvey to the plate. Smith, Chicago's ace reliever, challenged Garvey with a fastball, which the veteran crushed into the bleachers in right-center, making a winner of Lefferts and a loser of Smith.

"As soon the ball went toward the fence, everything froze in time," Garvey said. "It was as if all sound stopped."

It was Garvey's first homer since August 15, and his five RBIs gave him 20 during his 21-game Championship Series career. (He added one more RBI in Game 5.) Reggie Jackson had held the major league record with 18 playoff RBIs.

The Padres had met the challenge of evening the series at two games each. But in the decisive fifth game, they still had to beat the Cy Young Award winner Sutcliffe, who finished the season with 15 straight victories (including Game 1 of the playoffs). The righthander had a 0.37 earned-run average in three of those games against San Diego.

The Padres managed just two weak infield hits in the first five innings against Sutcliffe, one by Kennedy in the second and one by Templeton in the fifth. Meanwhile, Durham had belted a two-run homer in the first inning and Davis had contributed a leadoff blast in the second for a 3-0 Chicago lead.

Two batters later, the San Diego bullpen took control. Righthander Andy Hawkins replaced Show with one out in the second and Dave Dravecky, Lefferts and Gossage followed to total 7⅔ innings of shutout relief.

The Padres began to whittle at Chicago's lead in the sixth. Wiggins laid down a bunt for a single. Gwynn followed with a single to left. Garvey then walked to load the bases. Nettles got Wiggins home with a sacrifice fly to center as Gwynn advanced to third. Kennedy then lined a Sutcliffe pitch to left, where Matthews made a diving catch. Gwynn tagged up and scored to make the score 3-2.

Sutcliffe was back in trouble in the seventh after he walked Martinez, the first batter of the inning, on four straight pitches. Templeton sacrificed Martinez to second, and pinch-hitter Flannery followed with a sharp grounder to Durham at first. The ball went between Durham's legs for an error, and Martinez scored to tie the game, 3-3.

The Cubs' only luck in that inning was bad luck. The next batter, Wiggins, punched a check-swing single into short left field. Gwynn then delivered the key blow, a smash at Sandberg that took a bad hop and rocketed over the second baseman's shoulder and into right-center for a double, scoring Flannery and Wiggins. Gwynn took third on the throw home and scored on Garvey's single, giving San Diego its final 6-3 edge.

"I knew we would find a way, but I also knew we'd have to scrap against Sutcliffe," Gwynn said. "He put his pitches where he wanted to for five innings—low, inside, on the corners. I knew he was getting tired in the seventh, though, when he threw me a high fastball."

The victory was the culmination of a dream for the Padres, an expansion team in 1969 that never had finished better than fourth in the N.L. West before 1984.

Though the Cubs failed in their bid to go to the World Series for the first time since 1945, they had a terrific season, only to fall one game short. "We had them by the throat," Cubs General Manager Dallas Green said, "and let them get away."

GAME OF TUESDAY, OCTOBER 2, AT CHICAGO

San Diego	AB.	R.	H.	RBI.	PO.	A.
Wiggins, 2b	5	0	0	0	2	3
Gwynn, rf	4	0	0	0	1	0
Garvey, 1b	4	0	2	0	6	0
Nettles, 3b	4	0	1	0	1	1
Kennedy, c	3	0	0	0	6	0
McReynolds, cf	2	0	0	0	3	0
Martinez, lf	3	0	1	0	1	0
Templeton, ss	3	0	2	0	4	1
Show, p	1	0	0	0	0	0
Flannery, ph	0	0	0	0	0	0
Harris, p	0	0	0	0	0	0
Brown, ph	1	0	0	0	0	0
Booker, p	0	0	0	0	0	0
Summers, ph	1	0	0	0	0	0
Totals	31	0	6	0	24	5

Chicago	AB.	R.	H.	RBI.	PO.	A.
Dernier, cf	3	3	2	1	6	0
Sandberg, 2b	4	2	2	1	2	3
Matthews, lf	4	2	2	4	0	0
Cotto, lf	1	0	1	0	0	0
Durham, 1b	5	0	1	1	4	0
Moreland, rf	3	1	1	1	0	0
Woods, ph-rf	1	0	0	0	1	0
Cey, 3b	3	2	1	1	0	0
Veryzer, 3b	0	0	0	0	0	0
Davis, c	4	1	2	1	8	0
Lake, c	1	0	1	0	0	0
Bowa, ss	4	1	1	1	5	2
Sutcliffe, p	4	1	2	1	0	0
Brusstar, p	1	0	0	0	0	0
Totals	38	13	16	12	27	5

San Diego	000	000	000—	0
Chicago	203	062	00x—	13

San Diego	IP.	H.	R.	ER.	BB.	SO.
Show (Loser)	4	5	5	5	2	2
Harris	2	9	8	7	3	2
Booker	2	2	0	0	1	2

Chicago	IP.	H.	R.	ER.	BB.	SO.
Sutcliffe (Winner)	7	2	0	0	5	8
Brusstar	2	4	0	0	0	0

Game-winning RBI—Dernier.

Error—Templeton. Double play—San Diego 1, Chicago 2. Left on bases—San Diego 10, Chicago 8. Two-base hits—Dernier, Davis, Lake. Home runs —Dernier, Matthews 2, Sutcliffe, Cey. Sacrifice

fly—Moreland. Hit by pitcher—By Sutcliffe
(Flannery). Umpires—Cavanaugh, Schlickenmeyer, Pomponi and Maher. Time—2:49. Attendance—36,282.

GAME OF WEDNESDAY, OCTOBER 3, AT CHICAGO

San Diego	AB.	R.	H.	RBI.	PO.	A.
Wiggins, 2b	3	1	1	0	3	1
Gwynn, rf	4	1	1	0	4	0
Garvey, 1b	4	0	1	1	9	2
McReynolds, cf	2	0	0	1	2	0
Martinez, lf	4	0	1	0	2	0
Kennedy, c	4	0	0	0	1	1
Salazar, 3b	3	0	0	0	1	3
Templeton, ss	2	0	0	0	1	3
Thurmond, p	1	0	1	0	0	1
Hawkins, p	0	0	0	0	0	0
Ramirez, ph	1	0	0	0	0	0
Dravecky, p	0	0	0	0	1	1
Bevacqua, ph	1	0	0	0	0	0
Lefferts, p	0	0	0	0	0	0
Totals	29	2	5	2	24	12

Chicago	AB.	R.	H.	RBI.	PO.	A.
Dernier, cf	3	2	1	0	0	0
Sandberg, 2b	4	0	2	1	2	5
Matthews, lf	3	0	0	1	3	0
Cotto, lf	0	0	0	0	2	0
Moreland, rf	4	1	2	0	2	0
Smith, p	0	0	0	0	0	0
Cey, 3b	3	1	1	0	0	2
Davis, c	3	0	0	1	3	0
Durham, 1b	4	0	0	0	14	0
Bowa, ss	3	0	1	0	1	7
Trout, p	2	0	1	0	0	1
Lopes, lf	0	0	0	0	0	0
Totals	29	4	8	4	27	15

San Diego .... 000　101　000—2
Chicago.................................. 102　100　00x—4

San Diego	IP.	H.	R.	ER.	BB.	SO.
Thurmond (Loser)	2⅔	7	4	4	2	1
Hawkins	1⅓	0	0	0	1	0
Dravecky	2	1	0	0	0	1
Lefferts	1	0	0	0	0	0

Chicago	IP.	H.	R.	ER.	BB.	SO.
Trout (Winner)	8⅓	5	2	2	3	2
Smith (Save)	⅔	0	0	0	0	1

Game-winning RBI—Matthews.
Error—Trout. Double plays—Chicago 2. Left on
bases—San Diego 4, Chicago 6. Two-base hits—
Moreland, Cey, Gwynn, Sandberg. Stolen base—
Dernier. Caught stealing—Sandberg. Sacrifice hit
—Trout. Sacrifice flies—Davis, McReynolds. Um-
pires—Schlickenmeyer, Pomponi, Maher and Ca-
vanaugh. Time—2:18. Attendance—36,282.

GAME OF THURSDAY, OCTOBER 4, AT SAN DIEGO (N)

Chicago	AB.	R.	H.	RBI.	PO.	A.
Dernier, cf	3	0	0	0	3	1
Sandberg, 2b	4	0	1	0	4	5
Matthews, lf	3	0	1	0	2	0
Durham, 1b	4	0	0	0	11	2
Moreland, rf	4	1	1	0	0	0
Cey, 3b	4	0	1	1	0	1
Davis, c	3	0	1	0	2	2
Bowa, ss	3	0	0	0	1	2
Eckersley, p	2	0	0	0	0	0
Frazier, p	0	0	0	0	0	0

Chicago	AB.	R.	H.	RBI.	PO.	A.
Bosley, ph	1	0	0	0	0	0
Stoddard, p	0	0	0	0	1	0
Totals	31	1	5	1	24	13

San Diego	AB.	R.	H.	RBI.	PO.	A.
Wiggins, 2b	4	0	2	1	0	4
Gwynn, rf	4	1	3	0	0	0
Garvey, 1b	4	0	0	0	8	0
Nettles, 3b	4	1	1	1	0	2
Kennedy, c	4	2	2	0	8	1
McReynolds, cf	3	2	2	3	3	0
Martinez, lf	3	0	0	0	0	0
Templeton, ss	3	1	1	2	7	2
Whitson, p	3	0	0	0	1	0
Gossage, p	0	0	0	0	0	0
Totals	32	7	11	7	27	9

Chicago.............................. 010　000　000—1
San Diego .... 000　034　00x—7

Chicago	IP.	H.	R.	ER.	BB.	SO.
Eckersley (Loser)	5⅓	9	5	5	0	0
Frazier	1⅔	2	2	2	0	1
Stoddard	1	0	0	0	0	2

San Diego	IP.	H.	R.	ER.	BB.	SO.
Whitson (Winner)	8	5	1	1	2	6
Gossage	1	0	0	0	0	2

Game-winning RBI—Templeton.
Errors—None. Double plays—Chicago 1, San
Diego 1. Left on bases—Chicago 5, San Diego 1.
Two-base hits—Gwynn, Moreland, Templeton,
Sandberg. Home run—McReynolds. Stolen base—
Sandberg. Caught stealing—Wiggins. Umpires—
Bovey, Campagna, Fisher and Stewart. Time—
2:19. Attendance—58,346.

GAME OF SATURDAY, OCTOBER 6, AT SAN DIEGO (N)

Chicago	AB.	R.	H.	RBI.	PO.	A.
Dernier, cf	4	0	1	0	0	0
Sandberg, 2b	3	1	1	0	3	2
Matthews, lf	3	1	0	0	3	0
Moreland, rf	4	0	1	1	4	0
Cotto, pr-rf	0	1	0	0	0	0
Cey, 3b	5	0	0	0	1	1
Davis, c	4	1	3	3	4	0
Durham, 1b	3	1	1	1	10	0
Bowa, ss	3	0	1	0	0	4
Hebner, ph	1	0	0	0	0	0
Smith, p	0	0	0	0	0	0
Sanderson, p	2	0	0	0	0	1
Brusstar, p	0	0	0	0	0	0
Lopes, ph	1	0	0	0	0	0
Stoddard, p	0	0	0	0	0	1
Veryzer, ss	1	0	0	0	0	0
Totals	34	5	8	5	25	10

San Diego	AB.	R.	H.	RBI.	PO.	A.
Wiggins, 2b	4	1	1	0	1	1
Gwynn, rf	3	2	1	1	2	0
Garvey, 1b	5	1	4	5	8	0
Nettles, 3b	3	0	0	0	3	3
Kennedy, c	4	0	1	0	7	0
McReynolds, cf	3	0	1	0	2	0
Salazar, ph-cf	1	0	0	0	0	0
Martinez, lf	4	0	1	0	0	0
Templeton, ss	4	1	1	0	4	3
Lollar, p	1	0	0	0	0	0
Hawkins, p	0	0	0	0	0	1
Flannery, ph	1	1	1	0	0	0
Dravecky, p	0	0	0	0	0	0

San Diego	AB.	R.	H.	RBI.	PO.	A.
Brown, ph	0	1	0	0	0	0
Gossage, p	0	0	0	0	0	0
Summers, ph	1	0	0	0	0	0
Lefferts, p	0	0	0	0	0	0
Totals	34	7	11	6	27	8

Chicago	AB.	R.	H.	RBI.	PO.	A.
Trout, p	0	0	0	0	0	0
Hebner, ph	0	0	0	0	0	0
Brusstar, p	0	0	0	0	0	1
Totals	30	3	5	3	24	6

Chicago .... 000 300 020—5
San Diego .... 002 010 202—7
One out when winning run scored.

Chicago	IP.	H.	R.	ER.	BB.	SO.
Sanderson	4⅔	6	3	3	1	2
Brusstar	1⅓	1	0	0	0	0
Stoddard	1	1	2	1	2	0
Smith (Loser)	1⅓	3	2	2	0	2

San Diego	IP.	H.	R.	ER.	BB.	SO.
Lollar	4⅓	3	3	3	4	3
Hawkins	⅔	0	0	0	0	0
Dravecky	2	1	0	0	0	1
Gossage	1	3	2	2	1	1
Lefferts (Winner)	1	1	0	0	1	0

Game-winning RBI—Garvey.

Error—Sandberg. Double plays—Chicago 1, San Diego 1. Left on bases—Chicago 9, San Diego 7. Two-base hits—Bowa, Garvey, Dernier, Davis. Home runs—Davis, Durham, Garvey. Stolen bases—Templeton, Dernier, Brown, Sandberg. Sacrifice hit—Wiggins. Sacrifice fly—Gwynn. Hit by pitch—By Lefferts (Cotto). Passed ball—Davis. Umpires—Bovey, Campagna, Fisher and Stewart. Time—3:13. Attendance—58,354.

GAME OF SUNDAY, OCTOBER 7, AT SAN DIEGO

Chicago	AB.	R.	H.	RBI.	PO.	A.
Dernier, cf	4	0	0	0	3	0
Sandberg, 2b	4	0	1	0	2	3
Matthews, lf	2	1	0	0	2	0
Durham, 1b	4	1	1	2	8	0
Moreland, lf	3	0	1	0	2	0
Cey, 3b	4	0	0	0	0	2
Davis, c	4	1	1	1	6	0
Bowa, ss	2	0	0	0	1	0
Bosley, ph	1	0	0	0	0	0
Veryzer, ss	0	0	0	0	0	0
Sutcliffe, p	2	0	1	0	0	0

San Diego	AB.	R.	H.	RBI.	PO.	A.
Wiggins, 2b	3	2	2	0	5	2
Gwynn, rf	4	2	2	2	2	0
Garvey, 1b	3	0	1	1	4	1
Nettles, 3b	3	0	0	1	1	2
Kennedy, c	3	0	1	1	6	2
Brown, cf	3	0	0	0	3	0
Salazar, cf	1	0	1	0	0	0
Martinez, lf	3	1	0	0	3	0
Templeton, ss	3	0	1	0	3	2
Show, p	0	0	0	0	0	0
Hawkins, p	0	0	0	0	0	0
Ramirez, ph	1	0	0	0	0	0
Dravecky, p	0	0	0	0	0	0
Bevacqua, ph	1	0	0	0	0	0
Lefferts, p	0	0	0	0	0	0
Flannery, ph	1	1	0	0	0	0
Gossage, p	0	0	0	0	0	0
Totals	29	6	8	5	27	9

Chicago .... 210 000 000—3
San Diego .... 000 002 40x—6

Chicago	IP.	H.	R.	ER.	BB.	SO.
Sutcliffe (Loser)	6⅓	7	6	5	3	2
Trout	⅔	0	0	0	0	1
Brusstar	1	1	0	0	0	1

San Diego	IP.	H.	R.	ER.	BB.	SO.
Show	1⅓	3	3	3	2	0
Hawkins	1⅔	0	0	0	1	1
Dravecky	2	0	0	0	0	2
Lefferts (Winner)	2	0	0	0	0	1
Gossage (Save)	2	2	0	0	0	2

Game-winning RBI—Gwynn.

Error—Durham. Double play—San Diego 1. Left on bases—Chicago 4, San Diego 5. Two-base hit—Gwynn. Three-base hit—Salazar. Home runs—Durham, Davis. Stolen bases—Matthews, Sandberg. Caught stealing—Dernier, Matthews, Salazar. Sacrifice hit—Templeton. Sacrifice fly—Nettles, Kennedy. Hit by pitch—by Gossage (Hebner). Umpires—Kibler, Runge, McSherry and Harvey. Time—2:41. Attendance—58,359.

SAN DIEGO PADRES' BATTING AND FIELDING AVERAGES

Player—Position	G.	AB.	R.	H.	TB.	2B.	3B.	HR.	RBI.	B.A.	PO.	A.	E.	F.A.
Thurmond, p	1	1	0	1	1	0	0	0	0	1.000	0	1	0	1.000
Flannery, ph	3	2	2	1	1	0	0	0	0	.500	0	0	0	.000
Garvey, 1b	5	20	1	8	12	1	0	1	7	.400	35	3	0	1.000
Gwynn, rf	5	19	6	7	10	3	0	0	3	.368	9	0	0	1.000
Templeton, ss	5	15	2	5	6	1	0	0	2	.333	19	11	1	.968
Wiggins, 2b	5	19	4	6	6	0	0	0	1	.316	11	11	0	1.000
McReynolds, cf	4	10	2	3	6	0	0	1	4	.300	10	0	0	1.000
Kennedy, c	5	18	2	4	4	0	0	0	1	.222	28	4	0	1.000
Salazar, 3b-ph-cf	3	5	0	1	3	0	1	0	0	.200	1	3	0	1.000
Martinez, lf	5	17	1	3	3	0	0	0	0	.176	6	0	0	1.000
Nettles, 3b	4	14	1	2	2	0	0	0	2	.143	5	8	0	1.000
Dravecky, p	3	0	0	0	0	0	0	0	0	.000	1	1	0	1.000
Gossage, p	3	0	0	0	0	0	0	0	0	.000	0	0	0	.000
Hawkins, p	3	0	0	0	0	0	0	0	0	.000	0	1	0	1.000
Lefferts, p	3	0	0	0	0	0	0	0	0	.000	0	0	0	.000
Booker, p	1	0	0	0	0	0	0	0	0	.000	0	0	0	.000
Harris, p	1	0	0	0	0	0	0	0	0	.000	0	0	0	.000
Show, p	2	1	0	0	0	0	0	0	0	.000	0	0	0	.000
Lollar, p	1	1	0	0	0	0	0	0	0	.000	0	0	0	.000
Bevacqua, ph	2	2	0	0	0	0	0	0	0	.000	0	0	0	.000
Ramirez, ph	2	2	0	0	0	0	0	0	0	.000	0	0	0	.000
Summers, ph	2	2	0	0	0	0	0	0	0	.000	0	0	0	.000
Whitson, p	1	3	0	0	0	0	0	0	0	.000	1	0	0	1.000
Brown, ph-cf	3	4	1	0	0	0	0	0	0	.000	3	0	0	1.000
Totals	5	155	22	41	54	5	1	2	20	.265	129	43	1	.994

CHICAGO CUBS' BATTING AND FIELDING AVERAGES

Player—Position	G.	AB.	R.	H.	TB.	2B.	3B.	HR.	RBI.	B.A.	PO.	A.	E.	F.A.
Cotto, lf-pr-rf	3	1	1	1	1	0	0	0	0	1.000	2	0	0	1.000
Lake, c	1	1	0	1	2	1	0	0	0	1.000	0	0	0	.000
Sutcliffe, p	2	6	1	3	6	0	0	1	1	.500	0	0	0	.000
Trout, p	2	2	0	1	1	0	0	0	0	.500	0	1	1	.500
Davis, c	5	18	3	7	15	2	0	2	6	.389	23	2	0	1.000
Sandberg, 2b	5	19	3	7	9	2	0	0	2	.368	13	18	1	.969
Moreland, rf	5	18	3	6	8	2	0	0	2	.333	9	0	0	1.000
Dernier, cf	5	17	5	4	9	2	0	1	1	.235	12	1	0	1.000
Bowa, ss	5	15	1	3	4	1	0	0	1	.200	8	15	0	1.000
Matthews, lf	5	15	4	3	9	0	0	2	5	.200	10	0	0	1.000
Cey, 3b	5	19	3	3	7	1	0	1	3	.158	1	6	0	1.000
Durham, 1b	5	20	2	3	9	0	0	2	4	.150	47	3	1	.980
Smith, p	2	0	0	0	0	0	0	0	0	.000	0	0	0	.000
Stoddard, p	2	0	0	0	0	0	0	0	0	.000	1	1	0	1.000
Frazier, p	1	0	0	0	0	0	0	0	0	.000	0	0	0	.000
Brusstar, p	3	1	0	0	0	0	0	0	0	.000	0	1	0	1.000
Veryzer, 3b-ss	3	1	0	0	0	0	0	0	0	.000	0	0	0	.000
Hebner, ph	2	1	0	0	0	0	0	0	0	.000	0	0	0	.000
Lopes, rf-ph	2	1	0	0	0	0	0	0	0	.000	1	0	0	1.000
Woods, ph-rf	1	1	0	0	0	0	0	0	0	.000	0	0	0	.000
Bosley, ph	2	2	0	0	0	0	0	0	0	.000	0	0	0	.000
Eckersley, p	1	2	0	0	0	0	0	0	0	.000	0	0	0	.000
Sanderson, p	1	2	0	0	0	0	0	0	0	.000	0	1	0	1.000
Totals	5	162	26	42	80	11	0	9	25	.259	127	49	3	.983

SAN DIEGO PADRES' PITCHING RECORDS

Pitcher	G.	GS.	CG.	IP.	H.	R.	ER.	BB.	SO.	HB.	WP.	W.	L.	Pct.	ERA.
Dravecky	3	0	0	6	2	0	0	0	5	0	0	0	0	.000	0.00
Lefferts	3	0	0	4	1	0	0	1	1	1	0	2	0	1.000	0.00
Hawkins	3	0	0	3⅔	0	0	0	2	1	0	0	0	0	.000	0.00
Booker	1	0	0	2	2	0	0	1	2	0	0	0	0	.000	0.00
Whitson	1	1	0	8	5	1	1	2	6	0	0	1	0	1.000	1.13
Gossage	3	0	0	4	5	2	2	1	5	1	0	0	0	.000	4.50
Lollar	1	1	0	4⅓	3	3	3	4	3	0	0	0	0	.000	6.23
Thurmond	1	1	0	3⅔	7	4	4	2	1	0	0	0	1	.000	9.82
Show	2	2	0	5⅓	8	8	8	4	2	0	0	0	1	.000	13.50
Harris	1	0	0	2	9	8	7	3	2	0	0	0	0	.000	31.50
Totals	5	5	0	43	42	26	25	20	28	2	0	3	2	.600	5.23

No shutouts. Save—Gossage.

CHICAGO CUBS' PITCHING RECORDS

Pitcher	G.	GS.	CG.	IP.	H.	R.	ER.	BB.	SO.	HB.	WP.	W.	L.	Pct.	ERA.
Brusstar	3	0	0	4⅓	6	0	0	1	0	0	0	0	0	.000	0.00
Trout	2	1	0	9	5	2	2	3	3	0	0	1	0	1.000	2.00
Sutcliffe	2	2	0	13⅓	9	6	5	8	10	1	0	1	1	.500	3.38
Stoddard	2	0	0	2	1	2	1	2	2	0	0	0	0	.000	4.50
Sanderson	1	1	0	4⅔	6	3	3	1	2	0	0	0	0	.000	5.79
Eckersley	1	1	0	5⅓	9	5	5	0	0	0	0	0	1	.000	8.44
Smith	2	0	0	2	3	2	2	0	3	0	0	0	1	.000	9.00
Frazier	1	0	0	1⅔	2	2	2	0	1	0	0	0	0	.000	10.80
Totals	5	5	0	42⅓	41	22	20	14	22	1	0	2	3	.400	4.25

No shutouts. Save—Smith.

COMPOSITE SCORE BY INNINGS

San Diego	0	0	2	1	4	7	6	0	2 — 22
Chicago	5	2	5	4	6	2	0	2	0 — 26

Game-winning RBIs—Dernier, Matthews, Templeton, Garvey, Gwynn.

Sacrifice hits—Trout, Wiggins, Templeton.

Sacrifice flies—Moreland, Davis, McReynolds, Gwynn, Nettles, Kennedy.

Stolen bases—Sandberg 3, Dernier 2, Templeton, Brown, Matthews.

Caught stealing—Sandberg, Wiggins, Dernier, Matthews, Salazar.

Double plays—Sandberg, Bowa and Durham 3; Bowa, Sandberg and Durham 3; Templeton and Garvey; Wiggins, Templeton and Garvey; Hawkins, Templeton and Garvey; Kennedy, Templeton, Garvey and Wiggins.

Left on bases—San Diego 10, 4, 1, 7, 5—27; Chicago 8, 6, 5, 9, 4—32.

Hit by pitcher—By Sutcliffe (Flannery); by Lefferts (Cotto), by Gossage (Hebner).

Passed ball—Davis.

Balks—None.

Time of games—First game, 2:49; second game, 2:18; third game, 2:19; fourth game, 3:13; fifth game, 2:41.

Attendance—First game, 36,282; second game, 36,282; third game, 58,346; fourth game, 58,354; fifth game, 58,359.

Umpires—Cavanaugh, Schlickenmeyer, Pomponi, Maher (first and second games); Bovy, Campagna, Fisher, Stewart (third and fourth games); Kibler, Runge, McSherry, Harvey (fifth game).

Official scorers—John Cunningham, San Diego official scorer; Jay Dunn, Trentonian (N.J.); Randy Minkoff, United Press International (Chicago); Dave Nightingale, The Sporting News.

1984 WORLD SERIES

Including

Review of 1984 Series

Official Play-by-Play, Each Game

Official Composite Box Score

World Series Tables—Attendance, Money, Results

World Series MVP Alan Trammell watches his second homer of
Game 4 sail out of Tiger Stadium.

Tigers Complete Dream Season

By LARRY WIGGE

The record will show that the only people shortstop Alan Trammell really stranded during the course of the 1984 World Series were his wife and kids, his cousins from Indiana and a houseful of other relatives and friends.

Put a man on base in front of Trammell and he'd bring him home every time, or so it seemed. It was the most successful script that the Detroit Tigers had going for them—along with some stalwart pitching by Jack Morris—as they conquered the San Diego Padres in five games to win their first Series title since 1968.

Trammell, in fact, followed his cue to perfection in the first inning of the first game of the Series, when he singled home Lou Whitaker. It happened again in the second inning of Game 3, when Trammell doubled home Whitaker. The Tigers beat the Padres both times. But the real highlight for Trammell came in Game 4 when he went 3 for 4 with four RBIs on a pair of two-run homers, boosting his batting average to .563, as the Tigers took control of the Series, three games to one.

You might say it was one of those Mr. October sort of performances.

In the locker room after Detroit's 4-2 victory in Game 4, however, Trammell was fretting over whether his wife and kids would be just as thrilled about his feats as his many fans.

"We had 19 friends over to our house, and in a rush to get to the stadium early, I drove the family car," Trammell explained, shaking his head. "I was really shocked when I discovered that I also had the keys to the van, which my wife, Barbara, planned to drive to the game. Boy, was she steamed when I talked to her before the game. I don't even know if she made it to the game."

Though Trammell was held hitless in four at-bats in Game 5, he already had built enough support to be selected the Most Valuable Player of the Series. And, in the greatest bit of irony, he was presented the keys to a new car as the prize.

Trammell's single in the first inning of Game 1, following a double by Whitaker, gave the Tigers the first run of the Series. But the lead was short-lived as first baseman Steve Garvey and third baseman Graig Nettles each singled in the Padres' half of the first and catcher Terry Kennedy brought them both home with a ringing double into the right-field corner.

Tigers ace Jack Morris (center) is greeted by catcher Lance Parrish and Dave Bergman after stopping San Diego in the opener of the 1984 World Series.

San Diego clung to its 2-1 cushion until the fifth. With two outs, Detroit catcher Lance Parrish doubled past the third-base bag and came home ahead of Larry Herndon, who belted starter Mark Thurmond's 3-1 delivery into the right-field stands. Herndon, who had an unspectacular year while platooning in left field, was the first of several unlikely heroes in the 81st World Series.

Morris, who pitched a no-hitter during the season and raced to a 10-1 record by May 28 only to struggle in the second half and finish at 19-11, was a little shaky in the first six innings. He worked out of a two-on, two-out jam in the third and then put himself into a full-blown pickle in the sixth when he permitted leadoff singles by Nettles and Kennedy.

"It got so loud," Morris said of the San Diego crowd, "that it was almost like silence."

At that point Morris, who had been known to bear down in the later innings, decided enough was enough. He struck out center fielder Bobby Brown, who failed in a bunting assignment, left fielder Carmelo Martinez and shortstop Garry Templeton in succession, blunting the threat. And except for a leadoff double in the seventh by designated hitter Kurt Bevacqua, who stumbled rounding second and was thrown out trying to stretch the hit into a triple, Morris was in command the rest of the game.

The Detroit righthander struck out nine batters in going the route. Morris was so dominant, in fact, that he became the first starter ever to complete a game in the World Series for Tigers Manager Sparky Anderson, also known as Captain Hook for his frequent use of relief pitchers. In 23 previous Series games when Anderson was the skipper of the 1970, '72, '75 and '76 Cincinnati Reds, none of his pitchers had gone the distance.

The Tigers struck quickly again in Game 2, scoring three times in the first inning and knocking San Diego starter Ed Whitson from the mound. Whitaker, Trammell and right fielder Kirk Gibson started the proceedings with singles on Whitson's first three pitches of the game for one run. Parrish produced a second tally with a sacrifice fly and Darrell Evans made it 3-0 with another run-scoring single.

But Detroit starter Dan Petry didn't have the same magic that Morris did in Game 1, and he became the Tigers' only losing pitcher in postseason action.

The Padres cut the lead to 3-1 in their half of the first on Nettles' sacrifice fly. They added another run in the fourth on a fielder's-choice grounder by Brown, who was trying to fill the shoes of San Diego's regular center fielder, Kevin McReynolds, the victim of a broken wrist in the National League Championship Series against the Chicago Cubs.

Then, clinging to a 3-2 lead with one out in the fifth, Petry walked Nettles and gave up an infield single to Kennedy, whose one-hop grounder took a bad bounce off the chest of second baseman Whitaker and allowed both runners to reach base safely. Coming to the plate was Bevacqua, whose baserunning blunder

the night before had squelched a potential San Diego rally.

Dirty Kurt atoned for that goof by blasting Petry's 0-1 pitch into the left-field bleachers for a three-run homer and a 5-3 Padres lead.

"I knew I wasn't going to be thrown out at third on that one," said Bevacqua, a .200 hitter with only one homer and nine runs batted in during the regular season. The 37-year-old veteran celebrated by turning a pirouette when the ball left the park, pumping his fist skyward and then blowing kisses at the fans as he headed for home plate.

"Everyone has peaks and valleys in his life," Bevacqua said. "I sure as hell didn't stumble on purpose in the first game. And I don't think I stumbled because I was running too quick. It was just one of those things. I've stumbled going down the sidewalk before."

Righthander Andy Hawkins shared the spotlight with Bevacqua, coming into the game in the first inning to get the final out and then hurling five more innings of brilliant relief in which he permitted only one baserunner—and that runner was erased on a double play. Craig Lefferts added three more shutout innings to preserve a 5-3 victory for Hawkins and put the Padres on even terms in the Series.

To say that the Tigers walked to an easy 5-2 victory in Game 3 would be true. To say that they supplied their answer to Bevacqua in third baseman Marty Castillo, who hit a two-run homer in the second inning, also would be true. Castillo became the Classic's third improbable star in three nights.

With one out in the second, center fielder Chet Lemon hit a single to right and advanced to second on a wild pitch by Padres starter Tim Lollar. Castillo, who batted only .234 with four homers during the regular season, then sent Lollar's 1-2 pitch into the second deck in left field. Before the inning was over, Trammell had doubled in a third tally and Lollar had walked two more batters, giving him four walks in 1⅔ innings of work before he was replaced by Greg Booker. Booker promptly walked Herndon to force in another run and put Detroit on top, 4-0, after two innings.

After Garvey's fielder's-choice grounder got the Padres on the scoreboard in the top of the third, the Tigers responded quickly to regain their four-run margin. Booker walked the bases loaded and then watched as his replacement, Greg Harris, hit Gibson in the foot to force in yet another easy run.

Righthander Milt Wilcox, the eventual winner, worked six innings for the Tigers before giving way to lefty Bill Scherrer, who immediately got in trouble in the seventh. Scherrer served up a one-out infield single to right fielder Tony Gwynn and a smash by Garvey that fell for a double when left fielder Herndon failed to make a shoestring catch. After Nettles lofted a fly to center that scored Gwynn, Anderson called to his bullpen for his ace reliever, Willie Hernandez.

When the count on Kennedy went to three balls and two strikes, center fielder Lemon, figuring Kennedy would not be swinging for the fences, came in a few steps. But the muscular catcher drove the ball on a line to deep center, where Tiger Stadium's fence is a distant 440 feet from home plate.

"As soon as Kennedy hit it," Lemon said of his back-to-the-infield, twisting-and-turning catch, "I just put my head down and started running. When I got there, I looked to my right, and it wasn't there. I turned back to my left, and there it was. The rest is history."

Hernandez had no trouble after that, retiring six of the last seven batters he faced, and the lefty recorded the save, while the victory went to Wilcox.

And let us not forget about the walks. San Diego pitchers ended up with 11, tying a Series record for walks in one game. And the Tigers, who managed only three hits after the second inning, stranded 14 runners to tie another Series mark, while the 24-man left-on-base total for both clubs became a Series record.

The Trammell-Morris show came front and center in Game 4. Whitaker reached first when second baseman Alan Wiggins' throw pulled Garvey off first base for an error in the Tigers' half of the first inning and then Trammell slammed an Eric Show delivery high into the left-field bleachers for a 2-0 Detroit lead.

After Kennedy responded with a homer for San Diego to halve the Detroit lead in the second, Whitaker again set the stage for Trammell by singling to right. On a 1-1 pitch, Trammell deposited another Show serving into the second deck in left field for a 4-1 cushion.

The rest was up to Morris, whose split-fingered fastball continued to baffle San Diego hitters. The Padres were able to muster only four hits through eight innings before they finally reached Morris for another run. In the ninth, Garvey lined a double into the left-field corner with one out, advanced to third on a groundout by Nettles and scored on a wild pitch. But

Morris retired Kennedy on a line drive to right fielder Gibson to end the game and thus became the first pitcher since Mike Torrez of the 1977 New York Yankees to pitch two complete games in the same Series.

By this time, San Diego Manager Dick Williams would have given almost anything to get a stellar performance from his starters, who had been charged with all three losses thus far but were not responsible for the club's lone victory. Through the first four games, the Padres' starting staff had worked only 10 innings, yielding the preposterous totals of 20 hits and 14 runs (13 earned) for an 11.70 earned-run average. In stark comparison, San Diego relievers had limited the Tigers to one run and nine hits in 24 innings for a brilliant 0.38 ERA entering Game 5.

But the worst was yet to come for Williams, who chose Thurmond as his starter in Game 5. For the eighth consecutive time in postseason play in '84, the Tigers broke out on top, this time knocking out Thurmond after he had retired only one batter.

Whitaker started the assault with a single. Trammell then forced Whitaker at second, but Gibson followed with a tremendous homer into the upper deck in right-center. Consecutive singles by Parrish, Herndon and Lemon produced the inning's third run and spelled the end for Thurmond.

Though the Padres rallied to tie the contest on a run-scoring single by Garvey in the third and a sacrifice fly by Brown and a two-out single by Wiggins in the fourth (knocking out starter Petry), this day belonged to Gibson.

The former All-America wide receiver at Michigan State University singled off Nettles' glove to open the Tigers' half of the fifth and alertly advanced to second by tagging up on Parrish's long fly to left. After walking Herndon, Hawkins was replaced by Lefferts, who gave Lemon a free pass to load the bases. Rusty Kuntz, who struck out in the second game in his only other Series appearance, came up as a pinch-hitter and sent a short fly to right field.

Right fielder Gwynn lost sight of the ball as it went high into the clouds, and second baseman Wiggins had to race to the outfield to make the grab with his back to the infield. Wiggins made a weak, off-balance throw to the plate and the swift Gibson tagged up and scored to give the Tigers a 4-3 lead.

"I was going to go no matter who caught the ball," Gibson said later. "Gwynn probably could have had a good shot at getting me. I was just glad to see Mr. Wiggins catch the ball."

San Diego's late-inning relief ace, Goose Gossage, was brought into the game with one out in the seventh to face Parrish. The catcher promptly laced one of Gossage's 90-mph fastballs into the left-field seats for a 5-3 Detroit lead.

After Bevacqua narrowed the margin to 5-4 with his second homer of the Series in the eighth, the Tigers geared up for one last explosion.

Castillo drew a walk from Gossage to open the eighth. Whitaker followed with a sacrifice bunt, but both Whitaker and Castillo were safe when Templeton was not on the bag to take Nettles' throw to second for an attempted force out. Trammell then laid down another sacrifice bunt to advance the runners to second and third. An intentional pass appeared to be in order as Gibson was up next, and Anderson held four fingers in the air, signalling to Gibson that he would be walked. Gibson, who recalled that Gossage struck him out in his first major league at-bat in 1979, thought otherwise, however, and held up 10 fingers to Anderson, indicating that he would bet his manager $10 that Gossage would pitch to him—and that he would cash in.

Gossage remembered that encounter in 1979, too, and persuaded Williams to let him pitch to Gibson. Permission was granted.

One pitch later, Gibson sent a Gossage delivery deep into the upper deck in right field for his second home run of the day, an 8-4 Tiger lead—plus a $10 payoff on his wager.

"Sparky hasn't paid me yet," Gibson said afterward, "but believe me, he will. It's pocket change, but I'll take it."

Said Anderson: "He'll get his $10. I could pay him the $10 one-thousand times over and it would be worth it."

The pitchers who sewed up the clinching victory for Detroit were, quite appropriately, Hernandez and his bullpen partner, Aurelio Lopez. Lopez pitched 2⅓ innings of perfect relief to earn the victory, while Hernandez, the American League Cy Young Award winner and Most Valuable Player in '84, earned the save after working two innings.

Anderson was pleased to win the Series, though he said the Tigers, who started the season by winning 35 of their first 40 games and led the A.L. East from start to finish, already had proved that they were the best team in baseball during the regular season. He also was honored that the

triumph made him the first manager ever to win a world championship in each league.

"When we weren't running on all cylinders, like it was in the first four games, we still had enough to get by," Anderson said. "The good teams win when not everything goes their way. The best teams can overcome things. And since we were the best team all year, this is the way it should end."

Game 1

**At San Diego
October 9**

Detroit (A.L.)	AB.	R.	H.	PO.	A.	E.
Whitaker, 2b	4	1	1	3	3	0
Trammell, ss	5	0	2	0	2	0
Gibson, rf	4	0	0	1	1	0
Parrish, c	3	1	2	9	1	0
Herndon, lf	3	1	2	1	0	0
Garbey, dh	4	0	0	0	0	0
Lemon, cf	4	0	1	2	0	0
Evans, 1b	3	0	0	4	1	0
cBergman, 1b	0	0	0	3	0	0
Castillo, 3b	2	0	0	1	0	0
bGrubb	0	0	0	0	0	0
dBrookens, 3b	1	0	0	0	2	0
Morris, p	0	0	0	3	0	0
Totals	33	3	8	27	10	0

San Diego (N.L.)	AB.	R.	H.	PO.	A.	E.
Wiggins, 2b	4	0	1	1	2	0
Gwynn, rf	2	0	1	3	0	0
Garvey, 1b	4	1	1	9	2	0
Nettles, 3b	2	1	2	3	1	0
aSalazar, 3b	1	0	0	0	0	0
Kennedy, c	4	0	2	3	0	0
Brown, cf	4	0	0	3	0	0
Martinez, lf	4	0	0	3	0	1
Templeton, ss	4	0	0	2	2	0
Bevacqua, dh	3	0	1	0	0	0
Thurmond, p	0	0	0	0	2	0
Hawkins, p	0	0	0	0	1	0
Dravecky, p	0	0	0	0	0	0
Totals	32	2	8	27	10	1

Detroit	1 0 0	0 2 0	0 0 0—3
San Diego	2 0 0	0 0 0	0 0 0—2

Detroit	IP.	H.	R.	ER.	BB.	SO.
Morris (W)	9	8	2	2	3	9

San Diego	IP.	H.	R.	ER.	BB.	SO.
Thurmond (L)	5	7	3	3	3	2
Hawkins	2⅔	1	0	0	3	0
Dravecky	1⅓	0	0	0	0	1

Bases on balls—Off Morris 3 (Gwynn 2, Nettles), off Thurmond 3 (Parrish, Castillo, Gibson), off Hawkins 3 (Whitaker, Herndon, Evans).

Strikeouts—By Morris 9 (Wiggins, Garvey, Kennedy, Brown 2, Martinez, 2, Templeton 2), by Thurmond 2 (Gibson, Garbey), by Dravecky 1 (Whitaker).

Game-winning RBI—Herndon.

aRan for Nettles in sixth. bAnnounced as pinch-hitter for Castillo in eighth. cRan for Evans in eighth. dFlied out for Grubb in eighth. Runs batted in—Trammell, Herndon 2, Kennedy 2. Two-base hits—Whitaker, Kennedy, Parrish, Bevacqua. Home run—Herndon. Stolen bases—Trammell, Gwynn. Caught stealing—Trammell, Gibson, Gwynn. Double plays—Whitaker and Evans; Garvey unassisted. Left on bases—Detroit 9, San Diego 6. Umpires—Harvey (N.L.) plate,

Barnett (A.L.) first, Froemming (N.L.) second, Garcia (A.L.) third, Runge (N.L.) left, Reilly (A.L.) right. Time—3:18. Attendance—57,908.

FIRST INNING

Detroit—Whitaker smashed a double over the head of San Diego center fielder Brown. Trammell lined a single to left, scoring Whitaker. Trammell was picked off first and thrown out trying to steal second, Thurmond to Garvey to Templeton. Gibson flied to Martinez. Parrish was credited with an infield single when he beat a long throw to first by Nettles, who fielded the smash deep behind the third-base bag. Herndon also was credited with an infield single when Nettles fielded his high chopper and couldn't make a throw. Garbey forced Parrish at third base, Nettles unassisted. One run, four hits, no errors, two left.

San Diego—Wiggins struck out. Gwynn flied to Gibson. Garvey lined a single to right. Nettles looped a single to left, Garvey stopping at second. Kennedy ripped a double into the right-field corner, Garvey and Nettles scoring and Kennedy going to third on the throw to the plate. Brown bounced out, Evans to Morris covering first. Two runs, three hits, no errors, one left.

SECOND INNING

Detroit—Nettles speared Lemon's one-hop smash and threw to Garvey for the out. Wiggins made a diving backhand stop of Evans' grounder and threw to Garvey for the out. Castillo flied to Brown. No runs, no hits, no errors, none left.

San Diego—Trammell fielded Martinez's grounder deep in the hole and threw to Evans at first for the out. Templeton struck out. Bevacqua flied to Herndon, who made a good running catch in left-center. No runs, no hits, no errors, none left.

THIRD INNING

Detroit—Whitaker flied to Martinez. Trammell singled to left. Trammell stole second as Gibson struck out. Parrish walked on four pitches. Herndon forced Trammell at third, Nettles unassisted. No runs, one hit, no errors, two left.

San Diego—Wiggins singled up the middle, his smash deflecting off Morris to Trammell, who had no play. After two pitchouts put Morris in a hole on the count, Gwynn walked. Garvey grounded into a double play, Whitaker taking his one-hopper, tagging Gwynn and then relaying to Evans at first. Wiggins advanced to third on the play. Nettles walked. Kennedy flied to Lemon. No runs, one hit, no errors, two left.

FOURTH INNING

Detroit—Garbey grounded out to Garvey unassisted. Martinez caught up to Lemon's liner and then missed a shoestring catch for a two-base error. Evans grounded out to Wiggins, Lemon advancing to third. Castillo walked. Whitaker flied to Brown. No runs, no hits, one error, two left.

San Diego—Brown, attempting to bunt his way on base, popped to Morris, who hustled to his left to make the catch. Martinez struck out. Templeton grounded to Trammell, who threw him out from behind second base. No runs, no hits, no errors, none left.

FIFTH INNING

Detroit—Trammell flied to Gwynn. Gibson walked. Gibson was picked off and thrown out attempting to steal, Thurmond to Garvey to Templeton. Parrish doubled past the third-base bag and down the left-field line. Herndon belted a 3-1 pitch into the right-field bleachers, scoring Parrish ahead of him and giving the Tigers a 3-2 lead. Garbey struck out. Two runs, two hits, no errors, none left.

Terry Kennedy's bad-hop single off the chest of Tigers second baseman Lou Whitaker set the stage for Kurt Bevacqua's game-winning homer in Game 2.

San Diego—Bevacqua flied to Lemon. Wiggins lined to Whitaker. Gwynn singled to center. Gwynn stole second. Garvey grounded out to Whitaker. No runs, one hit, no errors, one left.

SIXTH INNING

Detroit—Hawkins came in to pitch for San Diego. Lemon singled to left. Evans hit a liner to Garvey, who made leaping catch and then stepped on first to double up Lemon. Castillo popped to Nettles. No runs, one hit, no errors, none left.

San Diego—Nettles singled to center. Kennedy also lined a single to center, Nettles stopping at second. Salazar went in to run for Nettles. After failing on two bunt attempts, Brown struck out. Martinez also struck out. Templeton made it three straight when Morris fanned him. No runs, two hits, no errors, two left.

SEVENTH INNING

Detroit—Salazar remained in the game and played third base. Whitaker walked. Trammell flied to Gwynn. Gibson popped to Garvey. Parrish flied to Martinez. No runs, no hits, no errors, one left.

San Diego—Bevacqua ripped a double into the right-field corner, but he was out at third trying to stretch the hit into a triple, Gibson to Whitaker to Castillo. Wiggins attempted a drag bunt, but Morris made a fine play to his left and tagged Wiggins for the out. Gwynn walked. Gwynn was caught stealing, Parrish to Whitaker. No runs, one hit, no errors, none left.

EIGHTH INNING

Detroit—Herndon walked. Garbey grounded out off Hawkins' glove to Templeton to Garvey, with Herndon advancing to second on the play. Lemon flied to Brown, Herndon holding at second. Evans was walked intentionally. Grubb was announced as a pinch-hitter for Castillo. When Dravecky came in to pitch for San Diego, Bergman went in to run for Evans and Brookens batted for Grubb. Brookens flied to Gwynn. No runs, no hits, no errors, two left.

San Diego—Bergman remained in the game and played first base, while Brookens took over at third. Garvey struck out. Salazar grounded out to Brookens. Kennedy struck out. No runs, no hits, no errors, none left.

NINTH INNING

Detroit—Whitaker struck out. Trammell lined to Wiggins. Gibson grounded out to Templeton. No runs, no hits, no errors, none left.

San Diego—Brown struck out. Martinez grounded out to Brookens. Templeton grounded out to Bergman unassisted. No runs, no hits, no errors, none left.

Game 2

**At San Diego
October 10**

Detroit (A.L.)	AB.	R.	H.	PO.	A.	E.
Whitaker, 2b	4	1	1	2	1	0
Trammell, ss	4	1	2	3	2	1
Gibson, rf	4	1	2	1	0	2
Parrish, c	3	0	0	3	2	0
Evans, 3b-1b	4	0	1	4	1	0
Jones, lf	2	0	0	2	0	0
aHerndon, lf	2	0	0	0	0	0
Grubb, dh	2	0	1	0	0	0
bKuntz	1	0	0	0	0	0
Lemon, cf	3	0	0	5	0	0
Bergman, 1b	2	0	0	4	1	0
cBrookens, 3b	1	0	0	0	1	0
Petry, p	0	0	0	0	1	0
Lopez, p	0	0	0	0	0	0
Scherrer, p	0	0	0	0	1	0
Bair, p	0	0	0	0	0	0
Hernandez, p	0	0	0	0	0	0
Totals	32	3	7	24	10	3

San Diego (N.L.)	AB.	R.	H.	PO.	A.	E.
Wiggins, 2b	5	1	3	2	1	0
Gwynn, rf	3	0	1	2	1	0
Garvey, 1b	3	0	0	7	0	0
Nettles, 3b	1	1	0	1	4	0
Kennedy, c	4	1	1	9	0	0
Bevacqua, dh	4	2	3	0	0	0
Martinez, rf	3	0	0	1	0	0
Templeton, ss	4	0	3	4	0	0
Brown, cf	3	0	0	0	0	0
Salazar, cf	1	0	0	1	0	0
Whitson, p	0	0	0	0	0	0
Hawkins, p	0	0	0	0	0	0
Lefferts, p	0	0	0	0	0	0
Totals	31	5	11	27	6	0

Detroit	3 0 0	0 0 0	0 0 0	—3
San Diego	1 0 0	1 3 0	0 0 *	—5

Detroit	IP.	H.	R.	ER.	BB.	SO.
Petry (L)	4⅓	8	5	5	3	2
Lopez	⅔	1	0	0	1	0
Scherrer	1⅓	2	0	0	0	0
Bair	⅔	0	0	0	0	1
Hernandez	1	0	0	0	0	0

San Diego	IP.	H.	R.	ER.	BB.	SO.
Whitson	⅔	5	3	3	0	0
Hawkins (W)	5⅓	1	0	0	0	3
Lefferts (S)	3	1	0	0	0	5

Bases on balls—Off Petry 3 (Gwynn, Nettles 2), off Lopez 1 (Martinez).

Strikeouts—By Petry 2 (Brown, Martinez), by Bair 1 (Martinez), by Hawkins 3 (Trammell 2, Whitaker), by Lefferts 5 (Kuntz, Brookens, Gibson, Parrish, Evans).

Game-winning RBI—Bevacqua.

aFlied out for Jones in seventh. bStruck out for Grubb in seventh. cStruck out for Bergman in eighth. Runs batted in—Gibson, Parrish, Evans, Nettles, Bevacqua 3, Brown. Home run—Bevacqua. Stolen base—Gibson. Caught stealing—Wiggins, Gwynn, Bevacqua. Sacrifice hit—Garvey. Sacrifice flies—Parrish, Nettles. Balk—Petry. Double plays—Gwynn and Garvey; Parrish and Whitaker. Left on bases—Detroit 3, San Diego 8. Umpires—Barnett (A.L.) plate, Froemming (N.L.) first, Garcia (A.L.) second, Runge (N.L.) third, Reilly (A.L.) left, Harvey (N.L.) right. Time—2:44. Attendance—57,911.

FIRST INNING

Detroit—Whitaker lined a single to left. With Whitaker running on the pitch, Trammell also singled to left, Whitaker advancing to third on the play. Gibson smashed a single to right-center, Whitaker scoring and Trammell going to third. Gibson stole second. Parrish fouled out to Martinez deep in the left-field bullpen area, Trammell scoring after the catch and Gibson advancing to third. Evans looped a single to left over the outstretched glove of Templeton, scoring Gibson. Jones popped to Templeton. With Evans running on the pitch, Grubb singled through the shortstop hole and into left field, Evans advancing to third on the play. Hawkins replaced Whitson on the mound for San Diego. Nettles fielded Lemon's hard smash on one hop and threw to Garvey at first for the out. Three runs, five hits, no errors, two left.

San Diego—Wiggins executed a perfect drag bunt past the pitcher. Gwynn walked. Garvey sacrificed, Petry to Bergman, with Wiggins advancing to third and Gwynn to second. Nettles flied out to Jones, Wiggins scoring after the catch and Gwynn advancing to third on Jones' throw to the plate. Kennedy fouled out to Evans. One run, one hit, no errors, one left.

SECOND INNING

Detroit—Bergman flied to Gwynn on the warning track in right-center. Whitaker grounded out, Garvey unassisted. Trammell struck out. No runs, no hits, no errors, none left.

San Diego—Bevacqua grounded out to Evans. Martinez flied to Lemon. Templeton smashed a single up the middle. Petry committed a balk, Templeton advancing to second. Brown was called out on strikes. No runs, one hit, no errors, one left.

THIRD INNING

Detroit—Gibson grounded out to Wiggins. Parrish lined to Templeton. Evans popped to Nettles. No runs, no hits, no errors, none left.

San Diego—Wiggins hit a soft fly into short left for a single. Wiggins was caught stealing, Parrish to Trammell. Gwynn grounded out to Whitaker. Trammell booted Garvey's grounder for an error. Nettles walked. Kennedy forced Nettles at second, Trammell unassisted. No runs, one hit, one error, two left.

FOURTH INNING

Detroit—Jones popped to Templeton. Nettles fielded Grubb's high chopper and threw to Garvey at first for the out. Lemon also grounded out to Nettles. No runs, no hits, no errors, none left.

San Diego—Bevacqua singled to left. Martinez was called out on strikes. Templeton singled to right, Bevacqua advancing to third. Brown forced Templeton at second, Trammell to Whitaker, with Bevacqua scoring on the play. Wiggins lined a single to right, Brown stopping at second. Gwynn lined hard to Gibson in deep right-center. One run, three hits, no errors, two left.

FIFTH INNING

Detroit—Templeton ranged to short left to snare Bergman's fly ball. Whitaker struck out. Trammell also struck out. No runs, no hits, no errors, none left.

San Diego—Garvey flied deep to Lemon. Nettles walked. Kennedy received credit for an infield hit when his one-hop smash took a bad bounce off the chest of Whitaker, Nettles advancing to second. Bevacqua drilled an 0-1 pitch into the left-field bleachers for a home run, Nettles and Kennedy scoring ahead of him, to give the Padres a 5-3 lead. Lopez replaced Petry on the mound for Detroit. Martinez walked. Templeton singled sharply to right, Martinez advancing to third with Templeton moving to second when Gibson bobbled the ball for an error. Brown popped to Evans. Wiggins lined to Lemon, who closed quickly to make the grab in short center. Three runs, three hits, one error, two left.

SIXTH INNING

Detroit—Salazar took over in center field for San Diego. Parrish blooped a single to left. Parrish popped to Wiggins. With Gibson running on the pitch, Evans lined to Gwynn, who threw to Garvey to double up Gibson. No runs, one hit, no errors, none left.

San Diego—Scherrer came in to pitch for Detroit. Gwynn laid down a perfect drag bunt, beating Whitaker's throw to Scherrer covering first. Garvey flied to Jones. Gwynn was picked off and caught attempting to steal second, Scherrer to Bergman to Trammell. Nettles flied to Lemon. No runs, one hit, no errors, none left.

SEVENTH INNING

Detroit—Lefferts replaced Hawkins on the mound for San Diego. Herndon batted for Jones and flied to Salazar. Kuntz, batting for Grubb, struck out. Lemon grounded out to Nettles. No runs, no hits, no errors, none left.

San Diego—Herndon remained in the game and played left field for Detroit. Gibson misplayed Kennedy's foul fly near the Tigers' bullpen for an error. Kennedy grounded out, Bergman unassisted. Bevacqua lined a single to left. Bair replaced Scherrer on the mound for Detroit. On a third strike to Martinez, Bevacqua was caught stealing for a double play, Parrish to Whitaker. No runs, one hit, one error, none left.

EIGHTH INNING

Detroit—Brookens batted for Bergman and struck out. Whitaker fouled out to Kennedy. Trammell lined a single to left. Gibson struck out. No runs, one hit, no errors, one left.

San Diego—Hernandez came in to pitch for Detroit, with Brookens taking over at third base and Evans moving to first. Templeton flied to Lemon, who made a good running catch in short center. Salazar grounded out to Brookens. Trammell ranged far to his left to field Wiggins' one-hopper and threw to Evans at first for the out. No runs, no hits, no errors, none left.

NINTH INNING

Detroit—Parrish was called out on strikes. Evans also struck out. Herndon fouled out to Wiggins. No runs, no hits, no errors, none left.

Game 3

At Detroit
October 12

San Diego (N.L.)	AB.	R.	H.	PO.	A.	E.
Wiggins, 2b	5	1	2	4	1	0
Gwynn, rf	5	1	2	2	0	0
Garvey, 1b	5	0	1	7	0	0
Nettles, 3b	2	0	0	0	2	0
Kennedy, c	3	0	0	5	0	0
Bevacqua, dh	4	0	1	0	0	0
Martinez, lf	4	0	1	0	0	0
Templeton, ss	4	0	2	1	3	0
Brown, cf	3	0	0	5	0	0
aSalazar	1	0	1	0	0	0
Lollar, p	0	0	0	0	0	0
Booker, p	0	0	0	0	1	0
Harris, p	0	0	0	0	0	0
Totals	36	2	10	24	7	0

Detroit (A.L.)	AB.	R.	H.	PO.	A.	E.
Whitaker, 2b	3	1	0	3	4	0
Trammell, ss	3	1	2	3	1	0
Gibson, rf	2	0	0	1	0	0
Parrish, c	3	0	1	6	0	0
Herndon, lf	4	0	1	1	0	0
Garbey, dh	5	0	0	0	0	0
Lemon, cf	5	1	2	4	0	0
Evans, 1b	2	1	0	3	1	0
Bergman, 1b	0	0	0	3	0	0
Castillo, 3b	4	1	1	2	2	0
Wilcox, p	0	0	0	1	1	0
Scherrer, p	0	0	0	0	0	0
Hernandez, p	0	0	0	0	0	0
Totals	31	5	7	27	9	0

San Diego .... 0 0 1 0 0 0 1 0 0—2
Detroit .... 0 4 1 0 0 0 0 0 *—5

San Diego	IP.	H.	R.	ER.	BB.	SO.
Lollar (L)	1⅔	4	4	4	4	0
Booker	1	0	1	1	4	0
Harris	5⅓	3	0	0	3	5

Detroit	IP.	H.	R.	ER.	BB.	SO.
Wilcox (W)	6	7	1	1	2	4
Scherrer	⅔	2	1	1	0	0
Hernandez (S)	2⅓	1	0	0	0	0

Bases on balls—Off Lollar 4 (Trammell, Parrish, Whitaker, Gibson), off Booker 4 (Herndon, Evans, Whitaker, Trammell), off Harris 3 (Evans, Gibson, Parrish), off Wilcox 2 (Nettles, Kennedy).

Strikeouts—By Harris 5 (Lemon, Whitaker 2, Garbey, Evans), by Wilcox 4 (Garvey, Martinez 2, Gwynn).

Game-winning RBI—Castillo.

aSingled for Brown in ninth. Runs batted in—Garvey, Nettles, Trammell, Gibson, Herndon, Castillo 2. Two-base hits—Wiggins, Trammell, Garvey. Home run—Castillo. Stolen base—Gibson. Sacrifice fly—Nettles. Hit by pitcher—By Harris (Gibson). Wild pitch—Lollar. Left on bases—San Diego 10, Detroit 14. Umpires—Froemming (N.L.) plate, Garcia (A.L.) first, Runge (N.L.) second, Reilly (A.L.) third, Harvey (N.L.) left, Barnett (A.L.) right. Time—3:11. Attendance—51,970.

FIRST INNING

San Diego—Wiggins slapped a double just inside the third-base line. Gwynn grounded sharply back to the mound, where Wilcox faked Wiggins back to second before throwing to Evans at first for the out. Garvey struck out. Nettles walked. Kennedy grounded out to Whitaker. No runs, one hit, no errors, two left.

Detroit—Whitaker flied to Gwynn in short right field. Trammell walked. Wiggins charged Gibson's high chopper and threw to Garvey at first for the out, Trammell advancing to second. Parrish walked. Herndon flied to Brown in deep center field. No runs, no hits, no errors, two left.

SECOND INNING

San Diego—Bevacqua lined hard to Whitaker. Martinez struck out. Whitaker ranged far to his left to knock down Templeton's grounder but had no play. Brown lined sharply to Gibson. No runs, one hit, no errors, one left.

Detroit—Garbey grounded out to Templeton. Lemon smashed a single to right. Lemon advanced to second on Lollar's wild pitch. Evans flied deep to Brown in center field, Lemon advancing to third after the catch. Castillo drilled a 1-2 pitch into the upper deck in left field, Lemon scoring ahead of him to give the Tigers a 2-0 lead. Whitaker walked on a 3-2 pitch. Trammell smashed a double into the left-field corner, Whitaker scoring ahead of Templeton's relay throw. Gibson walked. Nettles dived to his left to knock down Parrish's grounder but had no play; Parrish was credited with a single to load the bases. Booker replaced Lollar on the mound for San Diego. Booker walked Herndon, allowing Trammell to score. Garbey flied to Brown. Four runs, four hits, no errors, three left.

THIRD INNING

San Diego—Wiggins looped a single to center. With Wiggins running on the pitch, Gwynn singled to right-center, Wiggins advancing to third. Whitaker fielded Garvey's chopper and threw to Trammell at second to force Gwynn, but the relay to first was too late to double up Garvey, Wiggins scoring on the play. Nettles fouled out to Parrish near the screen. Kennedy grounded out to Whitaker. One run, two hits, no errors, one left.

Detroit—Lemon grounded out to Nettles. Evans walked. Booker came off the mound to field Castillo's tapper in front of the plate and threw to Garvey at first for the out, Evans advancing to second on the play. Whitaker walked. Trammell also walked, loading the bases. Harris replaced Booker on the mound for San Diego. Gibson was hit on the foot by a Harris delivery, allowing Evans to score. Parrish lined hard to Brown in left-center field. One run, no hits, no errors, three left.

FOURTH INNING

San Diego—Bevacqua grounded a single to center past a diving Whitaker. Martinez was called out on strikes. Castillo made a barehanded pickup of Templeton's nubber down the third-base line but had no play; Templeton was credited with a single and Bevacqua stopped at second. Brown's grounder bounced off Castillo's chest, but the third baseman recovered in time to scramble to third base and force Bevacqua. Wiggins forced Brown at second, Whitaker unassisted. No runs, two hits, no errors, two left.

Detroit—Herndon singled off Nettles' glove. Garvey forced Herndon at second, Templeton to Wiggins. Lemon struck out. Evans walked, Garvey advancing to second. Castillo flied to Brown. No runs, one hit, no errors, two left.

FIFTH INNING

San Diego—Gwynn struck out. Evans backhanded Garvey's grounded in the hole and threw to Wilcox covering first for the out. Nettles fouled out to Castillo. No runs, no hits, no errors, none left.

Detroit—Whitaker was called out on strikes. Wiggins ran into short right-center and made a leaping catch of Trammell's soft liner. Gibson walked. Gibson stole second. Parrish walked. Herndon popped to Templeton in short center. No runs, no hits, no errors, two left.

SIXTH INNING

San Diego—Kennedy walked. Bevacqua fouled out to Parrish near the screen. Castillo made a diving stab of Martinez's grounder but had no play; Martinez was credited with a single and Kennedy stopped at second. Templeton lined hard to Lemon in center. Brown lined hard to Herndon in left. No runs, one hit, no errors, two left.

Detroit—Garbey was called out on strikes. Lemon grounded to Templeton but beat the throw to Garvey with a head-first dive for a single. Evans struck out. Castillo popped to Wiggins. No runs, one hit, no errors, one left.

SEVENTH INNING

San Diego—Scherrer came in to pitch and Bergman went to first base for Detroit. Wiggins grounded out to Castillo. Gwynn singled off Scherrer's glove, Whitaker fielding the ball but unable to make a play. Garvey was credited with a double when Herndon tried to make a backhanded, shoestring grab near the left-field line, Gwynn advancing to third. Nettles flied to Lemon, Gwynn scoring after the catch and Garvey advancing to third just ahead of Lemon's throw. Hernandez replaced Scherrer on the mound for Detroit. Lemon had to race back to make a spinning, twisting grab of Kennedy's hard liner to center. One run, two hits, no errors, one left.

Detroit—Whitaker was called out on strikes. Trammell bunted down the third-base line for a single, beating Nettles' throw to Garvey at first. Garvey fielded Gibson's grounder and stepped on first for one out, but his throw to second, trying to double up Trammell, was too high and too late. Parrish popped to Wiggins. No runs, one hit, no errors, one left.

EIGHTH INNING

San Diego—On a check swing, Bevacqua bounced out, Castillo to Bergman. Martinez grounded out to Trammell. Templeton popped to Whitaker. No runs, no hits, no errors, none left.

Detroit—Herndon grounded out to Templeton. Garbey grounded out to Nettles. Lemon flied to Gwynn. No runs, no hits, no errors, none left.

NINTH INNING

San Diego—Salazar batted for Brown and lined a single to right. Wiggins popped to Trammell. Whitaker made a backhanded stab of Gwynn's high hopper up the middle and tossed to Trammell at second to force Salazar. Garvey flied out to Lemon. No runs, one hit, no errors, one left.

Game 4

**At Detroit
October 13**

San Diego (N.L.)	AB.	R.	H.	PO.	A.	E.
Wiggins, 2b	3	0	0	2	2	1
dSummers	1	0	0	0	0	0
Roenicke, lf	0	0	0	0	0	0
Gwynn, rf	4	0	1	1	0	1
Garvey, 1b	4	1	1	8	0	0
Nettles, 3b	4	0	0	1	4	0
Kennedy, c	4	1	1	8	1	0
Bevacqua, dh	3	0	1	0	0	0
Martinez, lf	2	0	0	1	0	0
cFlannery, 2b	1	0	1	1	0	0
Templeton, ss	3	0	0	0	3	0
Brown, cf	3	0	0	2	0	0
Show, p	0	0	0	0	0	0
Dravecky, p	0	0	0	0	0	0
Lefferts, p	0	0	0	0	0	0
Gossage, p	0	0	0	0	0	0
Totals	32	2	5	24	10	2

Kurt Bevacqua gets a warm greeting at home plate after hitting a three-run homer in Game 2 to provide the margin in San Diego's only Series victory.

Detroit (A.L.)	AB.	R.	H.	PO.	A.	E.
Whitaker, 2b	4	2	2	3	7	0
Trammell, ss	4	2	3	2	1	0
Gibson, rf	4	0	1	1	0	0
Parrish, c	4	0	0	4	0	0
Evans, 3b	2	0	0	1	1	0
Brookens, 3b	1	0	0	0	0	0
Grubb, dh	1	0	0	0	0	0
aGarbey, dh	2	0	0	0	0	0
Jones, lf	1	0	0	1	0	0
bHerndon, lf	2	0	1	0	0	0
Lemon, cf	2	0	0	2	0	0
Bergman, 1b	3	0	0	11	2	0
Morris, p	0	0	0	2	1	0
Totals	30	4	7	27	12	0

San Diego .... 0 1 0   0 0 0   0 0 1—2
Detroit .... 2 0 2   0 0 0   0 0 *—4

San Diego	IP.	H.	R.	ER.	BB.	SO.
Show (L)	2⅔	4	4	3	1	2
Dravecky	3⅓	3	0	0	1	4
Lefferts	1	0	0	0	0	0
Gossage	1	0	0	0	0	0

Detroit	IP.	H.	R.	ER.	BB.	SO.
Morris (W)	9	5	2	2	0	4

Bases on balls—Off Show 1 (Evans), off Dravecky 1 (Lemon).

Strikeouts—By Show 2 (Jones, Lemon), by Dravecky 4 (Herndon, Bergman, Gibson, Evans), by Morris 4 (Martinez, Templeton, Bevacqua, Summers).

Game-winning RBI—Trammell.

aHit into forceout for Jones in fourth. bStruck out for Martinez in eighth. cSingled for Martinez in eighth. dStruck out for Wiggins in eighth. Runs batted in—Kennedy, Trammell 4. Two-base hits—Bevacqua, Whitaker, Garvey. Home runs—Trammell 2, Kennedy. Stolen bases—Gibson, Lemon. Caught stealing—Lemon. Wild pitches—Morris 2. Double plays—Kennedy and Nettles; Templeton, Wiggins and Garvey. Left on bases—San Diego 3, Detroit 4. Umpires—Garcia (A.L.) plate, Runge (N.L.) first, Reilly (A.L.) second, Harvey (N.L.) third, Barnett (A.L.) left, Froemming (N.L.) right. Time—2:20. Attendance—52,130.

FIRST INNING

San Diego—Morris fielded Wiggins' bunt in front of the plate and threw to Bergman at first for the out. Gwynn grounded out to Whitaker. Whitaker ranged to his right to field Garvey's chopper over the mound and threw to Bergman for the out. No runs, no hits, no errors, none left.

Detroit—Whitaker reached first base safely when Wiggins fielded his chopper over the mound and pulled Garvey off first with a wide throw for an error. Trammell belted a 2-0 pitch into the left-field bleachers for a home run, scoring Whitaker ahead of him and giving the Tigers a 2-0 lead. Gibson flied to Brown. Nettles backed up to take Parrish's high bouncer and made a long throw to Garvey at first for the out. Evans fouled out to Kennedy. Two runs, one hit, one error, none left.

SECOND INNING

San Diego—Nettles became the third straight San Diego batter to ground out to Whitaker. Kennedy drilled an 0-1 pitch into the right-field upper-deck bleachers to cut Detroit's lead to 2-1. Bevacqua grounded a double past third baseman Evans into the left-field corner. Martinez was called out on strikes. Templeton grounded out to Whitaker. One run, two hits, no errors, one left.

Detroit—Garvey dived to stab Grubb's smash down the first-base line and raced to the bag to make the play unassisted. Jones struck out. Lemon also struck out. No runs, no hits, no errors, none left.

THIRD INNING

San Diego—Brown bounced to Bergman, who threw to Morris covering first for the out. Wiggins fouled out to Evans. Gwynn lined a single to right. Trammell fielded Garvey's bouncer and threw to Whitaker at second to force Gwynn for the out. No runs, one hit, no errors, one left.

Detroit—Bergman bounced out to Wiggins. Whitaker lined a single to right and went to second when Gwynn misplayed the ball for an error. Trammell smashed a 1-1 pitch into the upper deck in left field for his second home run of the game, scoring Whitaker ahead of him and giving the Tigers a 4-1 lead. Gibson singled sharply up the middle. Parrish fouled out to Garvey. Gibson stole second. Evans walked. Dravecky replaced Show on the mound for San Diego. Garbey batted for Grubb and forced Evans at second, Nettles to Wiggins. Two runs, three hits, one error, two left.

FOURTH INNING

San Diego—Nettles popped to Whitaker. Kennedy flied to Jones. Bevacqua fouled out to Bergman. No runs, no hits, no errors, none left.

Detroit—Herndon, batting for Jones, struck out. Lemon walked. Lemon stole second. With Lemon running with the pitch, Bergman struck out and Lemon was thrown out stealing third for a double play, Kennedy to Nettles. No runs, no hits, no errors, none left.

FIFTH INNING

San Diego—Herndon remained in the game and went to left field for Detroit. Martinez bounced out to Evans. Templeton struck out. Brown popped to Trammell. No runs, no hits, no errors, none left.

Detroit—Whitaker doubled into the left-field corner. Trammell lined a single to left, Whitaker stopping at third. Gibson struck out. Nettles fielded Parrish's broken-bat bouncer and threw to Kennedy to retire Whitaker at the plate, with Trammell going to second and Parrish reaching first. Evans struck out. No runs, two hits, no errors, two left.

SIXTH INNING

San Diego—Bergman went far into the hole for Wiggins' grounder and threw to Morris covering first for the out. Gwynn bounced to Whitaker. Garvey popped to Trammell. No runs, no hits, no errors, none left.

Detroit—Garbey flied to Gwynn. Herndon looped a single to right-center. Lemon's one-hopper to short was turned into a double play, Templeton to Wiggins to Garvey. No runs, one hit, no errors, none left.

SEVENTH INNING

San Diego—Nettles bounced out, Bergman unassisted. Kennedy flied to Lemon. Bevacqua was called out on strikes. No runs, no hits, no errors, none left.

Detroit—Lefferts came in to pitch for San Diego. Bergman flied to Brown. Whitaker grounded out to Templeton. Trammell, making a bid to become only the third player to hit three homers in a World Series game, flied deep to Martinez. No runs, no hits, no errors, none left.

EIGHTH INNING

San Diego—Brookens came into the game at third base for Detroit. Flannery batted for Martinez and blooped a single to center. Templeton flied to Lemon. Brown popped to Whitaker in short right field. With Summers at the plate, batting for Wiggins, Morris made a wild pitch, sending Flannery to second. Summers struck out. No runs, one hit, no errors, one left.

Detroit—Flannery remained in the game and played second base. Gossage came in to pitch and Roenicke went in to play left field for San Diego. Gibson popped to Flannery in short center. Parrish bounced out to Nettles. Brookens grounded out to Templeton. No runs, no hits, no errors, none left.

NINTH INNING

San Diego—Gwynn bounced out to Whitaker. Garvey drilled a double off the left-field fence. Nettles bounced out to Whitaker, Garvey advanc-

ing to third. With Kennedy at the plate, Garvey scored on Morris' second wild pitch of the game. Kennedy lined hard to Gibson. One run, one hit, no errors, none left.

Game 5

At Detroit
October 14

San Diego (N.L.)	AB.	R.	H.	PO.	A.	E.
Wiggins, 2b	5	0	2	4	0	1
Gwynn, rf	5	0	0	4	0	0
Garvey, 1b	4	0	1	3	1	0
Nettles, 3b	3	0	1	2	1	0
Kennedy, c	4	0	0	5	1	0
Bevacqua, dh	3	2	1	0	0	0
Martinez, lf	4	0	2	2	0	0
dSalazar, cf	0	0	0	0	0	0
Templeton, ss	4	1	1	1	3	0
Brown, cf-lf	2	1	1	3	0	0
eBochy	1	0	1	0	0	0
fRoenicke	0	0	0	0	0	0
Thurmond, p	0	0	0	0	0	0
Hawkins, p	0	0	0	0	0	0
Lefferts, p	0	0	0	0	0	0
Gossage, p	0	0	0	0	1	0
Totals	35	4	10	24	7	1

Detroit (A.L.)	AB.	R.	H.	PO.	A.	E.
Whitaker, 2b	3	1	1	4	3	0
Trammell, ss	4	1	0	0	3	0
Gibson, rf	4	3	3	1	0	0
Parrish, c	5	2	2	8	0	1
Herndon, lf	4	0	1	4	0	0
Lemon, cf	3	0	2	2	0	0
Garbey, dh	1	0	0	0	0	0
aGrubb	0	0	0	0	0	0
bKuntz	0	0	0	0	0	0
cJohnson	1	0	0	0	0	0
Evans, 1b	4	0	0	6	1	0
Bergman, 1b	0	0	0	1	1	0
Castillo, 3b	3	1	2	0	1	0
Petry, p	0	0	0	1	0	0
Scherrer, p	0	0	0	0	1	0
Lopez, p	0	0	0	0	0	0
Hernandez, p	0	0	0	0	1	0
Totals	32	8	11	27	11	1

San Diego	0	0	1		2	0	0		1	0—4
Detroit	3	0	0		0	1	0		1	3 *—8

San Diego	IP.	H.	R.	ER.	BB.	SO.
Thurmond	⅓	5	3	3	0	0
Hawkins (L)	4	2	1	1	3	1
Lefferts	2	1	0	0	1	2
Gossage	1⅔	3	4	4	1	2

Detroit	IP.	H.	R.	ER.	BB.	SO.
Petry	3⅔	6	3	3	2	2
Scherrer	1	1	0	0	0	0
Lopez (W)	2⅓	0	0	0	0	4
Hernandez (S)	2	3	1	1	0	0

Bases on balls—Off Hawkins 3 (Gibson, Whitaker, Herndon), off Lefferts 1 (Lemon), off Gossage 1 (Castillo), off Petry 2 (Nettles, Bevacqua).

Strikeouts—By Hawkins 1 (Castillo), by Lefferts 2 (Evans, Gibson), by Gossage 2 (Parrish, Herndon), by Petry 2 (Gwynn, Martinez), by Lopez 4 (Bevacqua, Martinez, Brown, Wiggins).

Game-winning RBI—Kuntz.

aHit by pitch for Garbey in fourth. bHit sacrifice fly for Grubb in fifth. cReached first base on error for Kuntz in seventh. dRan for Martinez in eighth. eSingled for Brown in ninth. fRan for Bochy in ninth. Runs batted in—Wiggins, Garvey, Bevacqua, Brown, Gibson 5, Parrish, Lemon, Kuntz. Two-base hit—Templeton. Home runs—Gibson 2, Parrish, Bevacqua. Stolen bases—Wiggins, Parrish, Lemon. Caught stealing—Herndon,

Detroit right fielder Kirk Gibson celebrates after hitting the first of his two Game 5 homers, a two-run first-inning blast.

Salazar. Sacrifice hits—Whitaker, Trammell. Sacrifice flies—Brown, Kuntz. Hit by pitcher—By Hawkins (Grubb). Wild pitch—Hawkins. Double play—Garvey and Templeton. Left on bases—San Diego 7, Detroit 9. Umpires—Runge (N.L.) plate, Reilly (A.L.) first, Harvey (N.L.) second, Barnett (A.L.) third, Froemming (N.L.) left, Garcia (A.L.) right. Time—2:55. Attendance—51,901.

FIRST INNING

San Diego—Wiggins lined a single up the middle. With Wiggins running with the pitch, Gwynn struck out, but Wiggins stole second and went to third when Parrish's throw went into center field for an error. Whitaker charged Garvey's bouncer and threw to Parrish to retire a sliding Wiggins at the plate, Garvey reaching first. Nettles grounded out to Whitaker. No runs, one hit, one error, one left.

Detroit—Whitaker lined a single to right. Templeton came in two steps to field Trammell's chopper and threw to Wiggins at second to barely beat Whitaker on a forceout. Gibson clouted Thurmond's first pitch for a tremendous home run into the upper deck in right-center field, Trammell scoring ahead of him to give the Tigers a 2-0 lead. Parrish lined a single to left. Parrish stole second. Herndon blooped a single to center, Parrish stopping at third. Lemon smashed a single through the hole and into left field, Parrish scoring and Herndon advancing to second. Hawkins came in to replace Thurmond on the mound for San Diego. With Garbey at the plate, Herndon was thrown out trying to steal third, Kennedy to Nettles, with Lemon advancing to second on the play. Lemon went to third on Hawkins' wild pitch. Garbey popped to Wiggins. Three runs, five hits, no errors, one left.

SECOND INNING

San Diego—Kennedy bounced to Evans, who threw to Petry covering first for the out. Bevacqua lined hard to Herndon. Martinez lined a single to left. Templeton grounded out, Evans unassisted. No runs, one hit, no errors, one left.

Detroit—Evans flied to Gwynn near the warning track in right field. Castillo was called out on strikes. Whitaker flied to Brown in short center field. No runs, no hits, no errors, none left.

THIRD INNING

San Diego—Trammell fielded Brown's high chopper behind second base, but Brown beat the throw to first for a single. Wiggins bounced out to Whitaker, Brown advancing to second. Gwynn grounded out to Trammell, Brown advancing to third. Trammell knocked down Garvey's smash to deep short but had no play; Garvey was credited with a single and Brown scored on the play. Nettles walked, Garvey advancing to second. Kennedy bounced to Trammell, who threw to Whitaker at second to force Nettles. One run, two hits, no errors, two left.

Detroit—Trammell flied out to right-center, Gwynn making the catch after some confusion between Gwynn and center fielder Brown. Gibson walked. Parrish flied to Martinez. Templeton fielded Herndon's chopper in the hole and made a strong throw to Garvey at first for the out. No runs, no hits, no errors, one left.

FOURTH INNING

San Diego—Bevacqua walked. Martinez struck out. Templeton was credited with a double when his hit to left-center was fielded by Herndon, who fell down, Templeton going to second and Bevac-

The explosive Tigers made short work of the Padres' starters throughout the Series. Ed Whitson (above) lasted only two-thirds of an inning in Game 2.

qua advancing to third. Brown lined hard to Lemon, Bevacqua scoring after the catch. Wiggins looped a single to center, Templeton scoring and Wiggins taking second on Lemon's throw to the plate. Scherrer replaced Petry on the mound for Detroit. Gwynn flied to Gibson on the warning track in deep right-center. Two runs, two hits, no errors, one left.

Detroit—Lemon lined hard to Nettles. Grubb, batting for Garbey, was hit on the elbow by Hawkins' delivery. Evans flied to Gwynn. Castillo lined a single to right, Grubb stopping at second. Hawkins walked Whitaker on four pitches, loading the bases. Trammell jumped on the first pitch and flied to Brown. No runs, one hit, no errors, three left.

FIFTH INNING

San Diego—Garvey flied to Lemon. Nettles blooped a single to center. Scherrer fielded Kennedy's tapper back to the mound and threw to Evans at first for the out, Nettles advancing to second on the play. Lopez replaced Scherrer on the mound for Detroit. Bevacqua struck out. No runs, one hit, no errors, one left.

Detroit—Gibson smashed a single off Nettles' glove and into short left field. Martinez caught Parrish's towering fly just in front of the left-field fence, Gibson tagging up and advancing to second after the catch. Herndon walked. Lefferts replaced Hawkins on the mound for San Diego. Lemon walked, loading the bases. Kuntz, batting for Grubb, was credited with a sacrifice fly when Wiggins caught his pop in short right field—after Gwynn appeared to lose the ball in the lights—and Gibson tagged up and beat Wiggins' off-balance throw to the plate. Evans was called out on strikes. One run, one hit, no errors, two left.

SIXTH INNING

San Diego—Martinez was called out on strikes. Herndon made a fine running grab of Templeton's liner in left-center. Brown was called out on strikes. No runs, no hits, no errors, none left.

Detroit—Castillo was credited with an infield hit when he beat Templeton's throw from deep in the hole. Garvey fielded Whitaker's high chopper, stepped on the bag for one out and threw to Templeton, who tagged a sliding Castillo at second for a double play. Templeton fielded Trammell's liner off Nettles' glove and made a strong throw to Garvey at first for the out. No runs, one hit, no errors, none left.

SEVENTH INNING

San Diego—Wiggins was called out on strikes. Gwynn flied to Herndon. Garvey bounced out to Castillo. No runs, no hits, no errors, none left.

Detroit—Gibson was called out on strikes. Gossage came in to pitch for San Diego. Parrish lined an 0-1 pitch into the bleachers in left field for a home run, giving the Tigers a 5-3 lead. Herndon flied to Gwynn, who made a leaping catch in front of the right-field fence. Lemon smashed a single to center. With Johnson at the plate, batting for Kuntz, Lemon stole second. Wiggins fielded Johnson's grounder but fumbled the ball for an error, Lemon advancing to third. Evans flied to Brown. One run, two hits, one error, two left.

EIGHTH INNING

San Diego—Hernandez came in to pitch and Bergman took over at first for Detroit. Nettles popped to Whitaker in short right-center. Kennedy lined to Whitaker, who made a leaping catch. Bevacqua belted an 0-1 pitch into the upper deck in left field for a home run, cutting the Detroit lead to 5-4. Martinez lined a single to left. Salazar went in to run for Martinez. Salazar was picked off and caught stealing from Hernandez to Bergman to Whitaker. One run, two hits, no errors, none left.

Detroit—Salazar remained in the game and played center field for San Diego, with Brown moving to left. Castillo walked. Whitaker laid down a sacrifice bunt, and when Templeton was not on the bag to take Nettles' throw to second, both runners were safe. Trammell laid down another sacrifice bunt, Gossage to Wiggins covering first, with Castillo advancing to third and Whitaker to second. Gibson cracked his second tremendous homer into the upper deck in right field on a 1-0 pitch, Castillo and Whitaker scoring ahead of him to give the Tigers an 8-4 lead. Parrish struck out. Herndon also struck out. Three runs, one hit, no errors, none left.

NINTH INNING

San Diego—Templeton grounded out to Trammell. Bochy, batting for Brown, singled to left. Roenicke ran for Bochy. Wiggins fouled out to Parrish near the screen. Gwynn flied to Herndon, who made a running catch near the left-field line. No runs, one hit, no errors, one left.

DETROIT TIGERS' BATTING AND FIELDING AVERAGES

Player—Position	G.	AB.	R.	H.	TB.	2B.	3B.	HR.	RBI.	BB.	IBB.	SO.	B.A.	PO.	A.	E.	F.A.
Trammell, ss	5	20	5	9	16	1	0	2	6	2	0	2	.450	8	9	1	.944
Gibson, rf	5	18	4	6	12	0	0	2	7	4	0	4	.333	5	1	2	.750
Herndon, lf-ph	5	15	1	5	8	0	0	1	3	3	0	2	.333	6	0	0	1.000
Castillo, 3b	3	9	2	3	6	0	0	1	2	2	0	1	.333	3	3	0	1.000
Grubb, ph-dh	4	3	0	1	1	0	0	0	0	0	0	0	.333	0	0	0	.000
Lemon, cf	5	17	1	5	5	0	0	0	1	2	0	2	.294	15	0	0	1.000
Parrish, c	5	18	3	5	9	1	0	1	2	3	0	2	.278	30	3	1	.971
Whitaker, 2b	5	18	6	5	7	2	0	0	0	4	0	4	.278	15	18	0	1.000
Evans, 1b-3b	5	15	1	1	1	0	0	0	1	4	1	4	.067	18	5	0	1.000
Bair, p	1	0	0	0	0	0	0	0	0	0	0	0	.000	0	0	0	.000
Hernandez, p	3	0	0	0	0	0	0	0	0	0	0	0	.000	0	1	0	1.000
Lopez, p	2	0	0	0	0	0	0	0	0	0	0	0	.000	0	0	0	.000
Morris, p	2	0	0	0	0	0	0	0	0	0	0	0	.000	5	1	0	1.000
Petry, p	2	0	0	0	0	0	0	0	0	0	0	0	.000	1	1	0	1.000
Scherrer, p	3	0	0	0	0	0	0	0	0	0	0	0	.000	0	2	0	1.000
Wilcox, p	1	0	0	0	0	0	0	0	0	0	0	0	.000	1	1	0	1.000
Johnson, ph	1	1	0	0	0	0	0	0	0	0	0	0	.000	0	0	0	.000
Kuntz, ph	2	1	0	0	0	0	0	0	1	0	0	1	.000	0	0	0	.000
Brookens, ph-3b	3	3	0	0	0	0	0	0	0	0	0	1	.000	0	3	0	1.000
Jones, lf	2	3	0	0	0	0	0	0	0	0	0	1	.000	3	0	0	1.000
Bergman, pr-1b	5	5	0	0	0	0	0	0	0	0	0	1	.000	22	4	0	1.000
Garbey, dh-ph	4	12	0	0	0	0	0	0	0	0	0	2	.000	0	0	0	.000
Totals	5	158	23	40	65	4	0	7	23	24	1	27	.253	132	52	4	.979

Bergman—Ran for Evans in eighth inning of first game.

Brookens—Flied out for Grubb in eighth inning of first game; struck out for Bergman in eighth inning of second game.

Garbey—Hit into forceout for Grubb in third inning of fourth game.

Grubb—Announced as pinch-hitter for Castillo in eighth inning of first game; hit by pitcher for Garbey in fourth inning of fifth game.

Herndon—Flied out for Jones in seventh inning of second game; struck out for Jones in fourth inning of fourth game.

Kuntz—Struck out for Grubb in seventh inning of second game; hit sacrifice fly for Grubb in fifth inning of fifth game.

Johnson—Reached first base on error for Kuntz in seventh inning of fifth game.

SAN DIEGO PADRES' BATTING AND FIELDING AVERAGES

Player—Position	G.	AB.	R.	H.	TB.	2B.	3B.	HR.	RBI.	BB.	IBB.	SO.	B.A.	PO.	A.	E.	F.A.
Bochy, ph	1	1	0	1	1	0	0	0	0	0	0	0	1.000	0	0	0	.000
Flannery, ph-2b	1	1	0	1	1	0	0	0	0	0	0	0	1.000	1	0	0	1.000
Bevacqua, dh	5	17	4	7	15	2	0	2	4	1	0	2	.412	0	0	0	.000
Wiggins, 2b	5	22	2	8	9	1	0	0	1	0	0	2	.364	13	6	2	.905
Salazar, pr-3b-cf-ph	4	3	0	1	1	0	0	0	0	0	0	0	.333	1	0	0	1.000
Templeton, ss	5	19	1	6	7	1	0	0	0	0	0	3	.316	8	11	0	1.000
Gwynn, rf	5	19	1	5	5	0	0	0	3	0	2	.263	12	1	1	.929
Nettles, 3b	5	12	2	3	3	0	0	0	2	5	0	0	.250	7	12	0	1.000
Kennedy, c	5	19	2	4	8	1	0	1	3	1	0	1	.211	30	2	0	1.000
Garvey, 1b	5	20	2	4	6	2	0	0	2	0	0	2	.200	34	3	0	1.000
Martinez, lf	5	17	0	3	3	0	0	0	0	1	0	9	.176	7	0	1	.875
Brown, cf-lf	5	15	1	1	1	0	0	0	2	0	0	4	.067	13	0	0	1.000
Booker, p	1	0	0	0	0	0	0	0	0	0	0	0	.000	0	1	0	1.000
Dravecky, p	2	0	0	0	0	0	0	0	0	0	0	0	.000	0	0	0	.000
Gossage, p	2	0	0	0	0	0	0	0	0	0	0	0	.000	0	1	0	1.000
Harris, p	1	0	0	0	0	0	0	0	0	0	0	0	.000	0	0	0	.000
Hawkins, p	3	0	0	0	0	0	0	0	0	0	0	0	.000	0	1	0	1.000
Lefferts, p	3	0	0	0	0	0	0	0	0	0	0	0	.000	0	0	0	.000
Lollar, p	1	0	0	0	0	0	0	0	0	0	0	0	.000	0	0	0	.000
Roenicke, lf-pr	2	0	0	0	0	0	0	0	0	0	0	0	.000	0	0	0	.000
Show, p	1	0	0	0	0	0	0	0	0	0	0	0	.000	0	0	0	.000
Thurmond, p	2	0	0	0	0	0	0	0	0	0	0	0	.000	0	2	0	1.000
Whitson, p	1	0	0	0	0	0	0	0	0	0	0	0	.000	0	0	0	.000
Summers, ph	1	1	0	0	0	0	0	0	0	0	0	1	0.000	0	0	0	.000
Totals	5	166	15	44	60	7	0	3	14	11	0	26	.265	126	40	4	.976

Bochy—Singled for Brown in ninth inning of fifth game.

Flannery—Singled for Martinez in eighth inning of fourth game.

Roenicke—Ran for Bochy in ninth inning of fifth game.

Salazar—Ran for Nettles in sixth inning of first game; singled for Brown in ninth inning of third game; ran for Martinez in eighth inning of fifth game.

Summers—Struck out for Wiggins in eighth inning of fourth game.

DETROIT TIGERS' PITCHING RECORDS

Pitcher	G.	GS.	CG.	IP.	H.	R.	ER.	HR.	BB.	IBB.	SO.	HB.	WP.	W.	L.	Pct.	ERA.
Lopez	2	0	0	3	1	0	0	0	1	0	4	0	0	1	0	1.000	0.00
Bair	1	0	0	⅔	0	0	0	0	0	0	1	0	0	0	0	.000	0.00
Wilcox	1	1	0	6	7	1	1	0	2	0	4	0	0	1	0	1.000	1.50
Hernandez	3	0	0	5⅓	4	1	1	1	0	0	0	0	0	0	0	.000	1.69
Morris	2	2	2	18	13	4	4	1	3	0	13	0	2	2	0	1.000	2.00
Scherrer	3	0	0	3	5	1	1	0	0	0	0	0	0	0	0	.000	3.00
Petry	2	2	0	8	14	8	8	1	5	0	4	0	0	0	1	.000	9.00
Totals	5	5	2	44	44	15	15	3	11	0	26	0	2	4	1	.800	3.07

No shutouts. Saves—Hernandez 2.

SAN DIEGO PADRES' PITCHING RECORDS

Pitcher	G.	GS.	CG.	IP.	H.	R.	ER.	HR.	BB.	IBB.	SO.	HB.	WP.	W.	L.	Pct.	ERA.
Lefferts	3	0	0	6	2	0	0	0	1	0	7	0	0	0	0	.000	0.00
Harris	1	0	0	5⅓	3	0	0	0	3	0	5	1	0	0	0	.000	0.00
Dravecky	2	0	0	4⅔	3	0	0	0	1	0	5	0	0	0	0	.000	0.00
Hawkins	3	0	0	12	4	1	1	0	6	1	4	1	1	1	1	.500	0.75
Booker	1	0	0	1	0	1	1	0	4	0	0	0	0	0	0	.000	9.00
Thurmond	2	2	0	5⅓	12	6	6	2	3	0	2	0	0	0	1	.000	10.13
Show	1	1	0	2⅔	4	4	3	2	1	0	2	0	0	0	1	.000	10.13
Gossage	2	0	0	2⅔	3	4	4	2	1	0	2	0	0	0	0	.000	13.50
Lollar	1	1	0	1⅔	4	4	4	1	4	0	0	0	1	0	1	.000	21.60
Whitson	1	1	0	⅔	5	3	3	0	0	0	0	0	0	0	0	.000	40.50
Totals	5	5	0	42	40	23	22	7	24	1	27	2	2	1	4	.200	4.71

No shutouts. Save—Lefferts.

COMPOSITE SCORE BY INNINGS

Detroit	9	4	3	0	3	0	1	3	0	— 23
San Diego	3	1	2	3	3	0	1	1	1	— 15

Game-winning RBI—Castillo, Herndon, Kuntz, Trammell, Bevacqua.

Sacrifice hits—Trammell, Whitaker, Garvey.

Sacrifice flies—Kuntz, Parrish, Nettles 2, Brown.

Stolen bases—Gibson 3, Lemon 2, Parrish, Trammell, Gwynn, Wiggins.

Caught stealing—Gibson, Herndon, Lemon, Trammell, Gwynn 2, Bevacqua, Salazar, Wiggins.

Double plays—Whitaker and Evans; Parrish and Whitaker; Garvey unassisted; Gwynn and Garvey; Kennedy and Nettles; Templeton, Wiggins and Garvey; Garvey and Templeton.

Passed balls—None.

Hit by pitcher—By Harris (Gibson), by Hawkins (Grubb).

Balk—Petry.

Bases on balls—Off Petry 5 (Nettles 3, Bevacqua, Gwynn), off Morris 3 (Gwynn 2, Nettles), off Wilcox 2 (Kennedy, Nettles), off Lopez 1 (Martinez), off Hawkins 6 (Herndon 2, Whitaker 2, Evans, Gibson), off Booker 4 (Evans, Herndon, Trammell, Whitaker), off Lollar (Gibson, Parrish, Trammell, Whitaker), off Harris 3 (Evans, Gibson, Parrish), off Thurmond 3 (Castillo, Gibson, Parrish), off Dravecky 1 (Lemon), off Gossage 1 (Castillo), off Lefferts 1 (Lemon), off Show 1 (Evans).

Strikeouts—By Morris 13 (Martinez 3, Templeton 3, Brown 2, Bevacqua, Garvey, Kennedy, Summers, Wiggins), by Lopez 4 (Bevacqua, Brown, Martinez, Wiggins), by Petry 4 (Martinez 2, Brown, Gwynn), by Wilcox 4 (Martinez 2, Garvey, Gwynn), by Bair 1 (Martinez), by Lefferts 7 (Evans 2, Gibson 2, Brookens, Kuntz, Parrish), by Dravecky 5 (Bergman, Evans, Gibson, Herndon, Whitaker), by Harris 5 (Whitaker 2, Evans, Garbey, Lemon), by Hawkins 4 (Trammell 2, Castillo, Whitaker), by Gossage 2 (Herndon, Parrish), by Show 2 (Jones, Lemon), by Thurmond 2 (Garbey, Gibson).

Left on bases—Detroit 39—9, 3, 14, 4, 9; San Diego 34—6, 8, 10, 3, 7.

Time of games—First game, 3:18; second game, 2:44; third game, 3:11; fourth game, 2:20; fifth game, 2:55.

Attendance—First game, 57,908; second game, 57,911; third game, 51,970; fourth game, 52,130; fifth game, 51,901.

Umpires—Harvey (N.L.), Barnett (A.L.), Froemming (N.L.), Garcia (A.L.), Runge (N.L.), Reilly (A.L.).

Official scorers—Jim Henneman, Baltimore Evening Sun; Ed Browalski, Polish News (Detroit); Bill Weurding, San Diego Tribune.

1984 ALL-STAR GAME

Including

Review of 1984 Game

Official Box Score

Official Play-by-Play

Results of Previous Games

One of the key plays of the 1984 All-Star Game occurred in the first inning when the N.L.'s Steve Garvey crashed into A.L. catcher Lance Parrish to jar the ball loose and score the game's first run.

All-Star Pitchers Dominate

By DAVE SLOAN

It was a near-perfect script.

There he was, 81-year-old Carl Hubbell, the famed "Meal Ticket" of the old New York Giants, throwing out the first ball for the 55th All-Star Game at Candlestick Park, home of the San Francisco Giants.

Why Carl Hubbell? Because exactly 50 years ago to the day, Hubbell had struck out five consecutive future Hall of Famers in succession during the 1934 Classic. It was the stuff from which legends are built.

As if to honor the oldest living member of baseball's Hall of Fame, American and National league pitchers combined for a record number of strikeouts, including six in a row by the Dodgers' Fernando Valenzuela and Mets rookie Dwight Gooden. National League pitchers recorded 11 strikeouts while their A.L. counterparts responded with 10 for a record All-Star Game total of 21.

Between whiffs, N.L. hitters managed enough hits to sneak away with a 3-1 victory, avenging an embarrassing 13-3 loss in 1983 that snapped the N.L.'s 11-game winning streak. The victory lifted the N.L.'s advantage in the series history to 35-19-1.

Most of the scoring was provided by the long ball.

After the N.L. had pushed across a first-inning run on Dale Murphy's single, Kansas City's George Brett connected off Montreal starter Charlie Lea to tie the game. The N.L.'s margin of victory was provided on home runs by Montreal's Gary Carter and Atlanta's Murphy. Carter's homer, which gave the N.L. a lead it never relinquished, was his third in All-Star Game competition and earned him his second Most Valuable Player award.

The biggest highlight of the 1984 Classic began in the fourth inning with Valenzuela in relief of Lea. He made short work of three A.L. sluggers, setting down New York's Dave Winfield, California's Reggie Jackson and Brett on strikes. The 19-year-old Gooden, not to be outdone, took over in the fifth and overpowered Detroit's Lance Parrish and Chet Lemon and Seattle rookie Alvin Davis. The six straight strikeouts broke Hubbell's All-Star record.

The testimonials on Gooden flowed after the game.

"Overpowering," said Winfield.

"A kid with his stuff and composure comes about once every 50 years," said

In the fourth and fifth innings, the Dodgers' Fernando Valenzuela (above) and Mets' rookie Dwight Gooden combined to strike out a record six straight batters.

San Diego reliever Goose Gossage, who finished the game and earned a save. "He's the best-looking kid I've ever seen. It's amazing how mature he is."

Valenzuela and Gooden became the fifth and sixth pitchers in All-Star history to strike out the side in order. Oakland reliever Bill Caudill joined them when he struck out the only three National Leaguers he faced in the seventh inning.

The American League's failure to capitalize on two early scoring opportunities seemed to give the Nationals momentum. In the first inning, Detroit's Lou Whitaker, the A.L. leadoff man, doubled down the right-field line on the second pitch of the game. But Lea struck out California's Rod Carew and retired both Baltimore's Cal Ripken and Winfield on grounders to third.

The Nationals didn't waste their scoring chance in the bottom of the inning. With two out, San Diego's Steve Garvey singled to right and reached second base when Jackson, a designated hitter who hadn't played the outfield since August of the previous year, booted the ball for an error. Murphy, the next batter, lined a single to left.

Winfield, the A.L. left fielder, picked up the ball cleanly and made a strong, one-hop throw to the plate. But Parrish, the American League catcher, failed to come up with the ball as Garvey bowled him over to score the game's first run.

"I got a pretty good piece of him," Garvey said. "When he is blocking the plate without the ball, there is only one thing to do—go right through him. I wanted to set the tone of the game early by being aggressive."

"If I had hung onto the ball, he would have been out," Parrish said. "I thought I had it in my mitt and he jarred it loose."

That lead didn't last long. In the top of the second, Brett belted a 2-0 pitch over the center-field wall. It was Brett's seventh hit in 20 All-Star at-bats and his first home run.

The Nationals struck back quickly in the bottom of the second when Carter sent Dave Stieb's first pitch over the left-field fence. Stieb, Toronto's hard-throwing righthander, was making his second consecutive start in the All-Star Game. It marked the first time in the history of the Classic that both starting pitchers played for teams outside the United States.

The game's pivotal play came in the American League third inning. Cleveland's Andre Thornton pinch-hit for Stieb and singled to center off Valenzuela. Whitaker then singled to right, putting runners on first and third with none out.

But Carew, who had struck out in the first with Whitaker on second, hit a chopper down the first-base line. Garvey fielded the ball, stepped on the bag and threw home to nail a sliding Thornton. Carter caught the ball a few feet up the line while blocking the plate to complete the double play.

"That was a great play for a first baseman," said American League Manager Joe Altobelli. Valenzuela then retired Ripken on a groundout to third baseman Mike Schmidt.

Only two American Leaguers reached base after the third inning. Eddie Murray hit a pop double in the sixth and Winfield lined a two-out double in the ninth. But Gossage, a familiar face to the American Leaguers after six big seasons with the Yankees, got Oakland's Rickey Henderson to take a called third strike to end the game.

AMERICANS	AB.	R.	H.	RBI.	PO.	A.
Whitaker (Tigers), 2b..	3	0	2	0	0	5
Garcia (Blue Jays), 2b	1	0	0	0	1	0
Carew (Angels), 1b	2	0	0	0	5	0
Murray (Orioles), 1b....	2	0	1	0	3	0
Ripken (Orioles), ss......	3	0	0	0	0	0
Griffin (Blue Jays), ss .	0	0	0	0	0	1
gMattingly (Yankees).	1	0	0	0	0	0
Winfield (Yanks), lf-rf	4	0	1	0	2	1
Re. J'kson (Angels), rf.	2	0	0	0	0	0
Henderson (A's), lf-cf ..	2	0	0	0	0	0
Brett (Royals), 3b	3	1	1	1	3	0
Caudill (A's), p	0	0	0	0	0	0
W. Her'dez (Tigers), p .	0	0	0	0	0	0
Parrish (Tigers), c	2	0	0	0	3	1
Sundberg (Brewers), c	1	0	0	0	6	0
Lemon (Tigers), cf	2	0	1	0	0	0
fRice (Red Sox), lf	1	0	0	0	1	0
Stieb (Blue Jays), p	0	0	0	0	0	0
bThornton (Indians)	1	0	1	0	0	0
Morris (Tigers), p	0	0	0	0	0	1
dA. Davis (Mariners) ..	1	0	0	0	0	0
Dotson (White Sox), p..	0	0	0	0	0	0
Bell (Rangers), 3b	1	0	0	0	0	1
Totals	32	1	7	1	24	10

NATIONALS	AB.	R.	H.	RBI.	PO.	A.
Gwynn (Padres), lf	3	0	1	0	0	0
Raines (Expos), lf	1	0	0	0	4	0
Sandberg (Cubs), 2b	4	0	1	0	0	0
Garvey (Padres), 1b....	3	1	1	0	5	1
K. Hern'dez (Mets), 1b	1	0	0	0	1	0
Murphy (Braves), cf.....	3	1	2	1	0	0
Schmidt (Phillies), 3b..	3	0	0	0	0	4
Wallach (Expos), 3b	1	0	0	0	0	0
Strawberry (Mets), rf .	2	0	1	0	0	0
Wash'ton (Braves), rf..	2	0	1	0	1	0
Carter (Expos), c	2	1	1	1	9	0
J. Davis (Cubs), c	1	0	0	0	1	0
Gossage (Padres), p	0	0	0	0	0	0
O. Smith (Cards), ss	3	0	0	0	3	0
Lea (Padres), p	0	0	0	0	0	1
aC. Davis (Giants)	1	0	0	0	0	0
Valenz'la (Dodgers), p.	0	0	0	0	0	0
cMumphrey (Astros) ...	1	0	0	0	0	0
Gooden (Mets), p	0	0	0	0	1	0
eBrenly (Giants)	1	0	0	0	0	0
Soto (Reds), p	0	0	0	0	0	0
Pena (Pirates), c	0	0	0	0	2	0
Totals	32	3	8	2	27	6

Americans................................ 0 1 0 0 0 0 0 0 0—1
Nationals................................ 1 1 0 0 0 0 0 1 x—3

AMERICANS	IP.	H.	R.	ER.	BB.	SO.
Stieb (Blue Jays)	2	3	2	1	0	2
Morris (Tigers)	2	2	0	0	1	2
Dotson (White Sox)	2	2	0	0	1	2
Caudill (A's)	1	0	0	0	0	3
W. Hern'dez (Tigers) .	1	1	1	1	0	1

NATIONALS	IP.	H.	R.	ER.	BB.	SO.
Lea (Expos)	2	3	1	1	0	2
Valenzuela (Dodgers)	2	2	0	0	0	3
Gooden (Mets)	2	1	0	0	0	3
Soto (Reds)	2	0	0	0	0	1
Gossage (Padres)	1	1	0	0	0	2

Winning Pitcher—Lea. Losing pitcher—Stieb.
Save—Gossage.

Game-winning RBI—Carter.

aLined out for Lea in second. bSingled for Stieb in third. cStruck out for Valenzuela in fourth. dStruck out for Morris in fifth. eStruck out for Gooden in sixth. fStruck out for Lemon in eighth. gFlied out for Griffin in ninth. Errors—Jackson, Parrish. Double play—Garvey and Carter. Left on bases—American 4, National 7. Two-base hits—Whitaker, Murray, Washington, Winfield. Home runs—Brett, Carter, Murphy. Stolen bases—Sandberg, Strawberry, Gwynn, O. Smith. Bases on balls—Off Morris 1 (Murphy), off Dotson 1 (Carter). Strikeouts—By Stieb 2 (Schmidt, Strawberry), by Morris 2 (Gwynn, Mumphrey), by Dotson 2 (Schmidt, Brenly), by Caudill 3 (Raines, Sandberg, K. Hernandez), by W. Hernandez 1 (Washington), by Lea 2 (Carew, Parrish), by Valenzuela 3 (Winfield, Jackson, Brett), by Gooden 3 (Parrish, Lemon, A. Davis), by Soto 1 (Rice), by Gossage 2 (Murray, Henderson). Umpires—Weyer (N.L.) plate, Clark (A.L.) first base, Rennert (N.L.) second base, Merrill (A.L.) third base, Brocklander (N.L.) left field, Roe (A.L.) right field. T—2:29. Attendance—57,756. Official scorers—Jim Henneman, Baltimore Evening Sun, Bob Stevens (retired writer from San Francisco Chronicle) and Nick Peters, Oakland Tribune.

Players listed on roster but not used: A.L.—Armas, Boddicker, Engle, Niekro, Quisenberry; N.L.—Holland, Marshall, Orosco, Ramirez, Samuel, Sutter.

FIRST INNING

Americans—Whitaker blooped a double just inside the right-field foul line. Carew was called out on strikes. Ripken grounded out to Schmidt, Whitaker holding second. Winfield also grounded out to Schmidt. No runs, one hit, no errors, one left.

Nationals—Gwynn grounded out to Whitaker. Sandberg also grounded out to Whitaker. Garvey lined a single to right and went to second when Jackson misplayed the ball for an error. Murphy singled sharply through the left side of the infield and Garvey scored when catcher Parrish dropped Winfield's strong throw from left field for an error. Murphy advanced to second on the throw. Schmidt struck out, but had to be thrown out at first when Parrish failed to handle the third strike cleanly. One run, two hits, two errors, one left.

SECOND INNING

Americans—Jackson popped out to Smith. Brett belted a 2-0 pitch over the center-field fence for his first All-Star Game home run. Parrish struck out. Lemon looped a single into right-center field. Lemon was picked off, Lea to Garvey. One run, two hits, no errors, none left.

Nationals—Strawberry was called out on strikes. Carter clubbed Stieb's first pitch over the left-field fence for his third All-Star Game homer, giving the N.L. a 2-1 lead. Smith grounded out to Whitaker. Chili Davis batted for Lea and lined out to Brett. One run, one hit, none left.

THIRD INNING

Americans—Valenzuela came in to pitch for the Nationals. Thornton batted for Stieb and singled to center. Whitaker rapped a single through the right side of the infield, Thornton beating a strong throw by Strawberry to third. Carew hit a high chopper to Garvey, who stepped on first for one out and threw to Carter in time to nail a sliding Thornton, thus completing a double play. Whitaker advanced to second on the play. Ripken grounded to Schmidt, who ranged far to his left before throwing to Garvey for the final out of the inning. No runs, two hits, no errors, one left.

Nationals—Morris came in to pitch for the Americans. Gwynn struck out. Sandberg hit a high chopper off home plate and was credited with an infield hit when he beat Carew's tag attempt at first base. Sandberg stole second. Garvey flied to Winfield just in front of the warning track in left field, Sandberg holding second. Murphy walked. Schmidt grounded out, Morris to Carew. No runs, one hit, no errors, two left.

FOURTH INNING

Americans—Winfield struck out. Jackson struck out. Brett was called out on strikes. No runs, no hits, no errors, none left.

Nationals—Murray went in to play first base, Henderson went to left and Winfield moved to right field for the Americans. Strawberry lined a single to right. Carter popped out to Brett. Smith also popped out to Brett, who reached into an auxiliary photographer's box to make the catch. Strawberry stole second. Mumphrey batted for Valenzuela and struck out. No runs, one hit, no errors, one left.

FIFTH INNING

Americans—Gooden entered the game to pitch for the Nationals and Washington went in to right field. Parrish struck out. Lemon struck out. Alvin Davis batted for Morris and struck out. The six consecutive strikeouts for N.L. hurlers broke the All-Star Game record set by the Giants' Carl Hubbell in 1934. No runs, no hits, no errors, none left.

Nationals—Dotson came in to pitch for the Americans and Sundberg took over as catcher. Gwynn lined a single to left. Gwynn stole second. Sandberg grounded to Whitaker, Gwynn taking third on the play. Garvey also grounded to Whitaker, Gwynn holding. Murphy flied to Winfield. No runs, one hit, no errors, one left.

SIXTH INNING

Americans—Raines took over in left field for the Nationals while Keith Hernandez went in to play first base. Whitaker was retired by Gooden unassisted when the Mets' pitcher fielded a chopper to the left of the mound and raced to first base to make the play himself. Murray was credited with a wind-blown double when his fly ball to short left-center field deflected off the glove of shortstop Smith, who was trying to make an over-the-shoulder catch. Ripken grounded to Schmidt, Murray holding second. Winfield flied to Raines. No runs, one hit, no errors, one left.

Nationals—Garcia entered the game at second base and Griffin took over at shortstop for the Americans. Schmidt struck out. Washington doubled down the left-field line. Carter walked. Smith grounded to Griffin, who threw to Garcia to force Carter, Washington advancing to third on the play. With Brenly at the plate, batting for Gooden, Smith stole second. Brenly struck out. No runs, one hit, no errors, two left.

SEVENTH INNING

Americans—Wallach took over at third, Jody Davis at catcher and Soto at pitcher for the Nationals. Henderson flied to Washington. Brett flied to Raines. Sundberg flied to Raines. No runs, no hits, no errors, none left.

Nationals—Caudill came in to pitch and Bell went to third base for the Americans. Raines struck out. Sandberg struck out. Keith Hernandez struck out. It was the third time in the game that a pitcher had struck out the side in order. No runs, no hits, no errors, none left.

EIGHTH INNING

Americans—Rice batted for Lemon and struck out. Bell popped out to Smith. Garcia fouled out to Smith. No runs, no hits, no errors, none left.

Nationals—Willie Hernandez came in to pitch, Rice went to left field and Henderson moved to center for the Americans. Murphy slammed a 2-2 pitch over the left-field fence for his first All-Star Game home run, giving the N.L. a 3-1 lead. Wallach bounced to Bell. Washington struck out. Jody Davis flied to Rice. One run, one hit, no errors, none left.

NINTH INNING

Americans—Gossage came in to pitch for the Nationals and Pena was the new catcher. Murray struck out. Mattingly batted for Griffin and flied to Raines. Winfield doubled into the left-field corner. Henderson was called out on strikes, breaking the record of 20 strikeouts by both clubs in the 1968 All-Star Game. No runs, one hit, no errors, one left.

RESULTS OF PREVIOUS GAMES

1933—At Comiskey Park, Chicago, July 6. Americans 4, Nationals 2. Managers—Connie Mack, John McGraw. Winning pitcher—Lefty Gomez. Losing pitcher—Bill Hallahan. Attendance—47,595.

1934—At Polo Grounds, New York, July 10. Americans 9, Nationals 7. Managers—Joe Cronin, Bill Terry. Winning pitcher—Mel Harder. Losing pitcher—Van Mungo. Attendance—48,363.

1935—At Municipal Stadium, Cleveland, July 8. Americans 4, Nationals 1. Managers—Mickey Cochrane, Frankie Frisch. Winning pitcher—Lefty Gomez. Losing pitcher—Bill Walker. Attendance—69,831.

1936—At Braves Field, Boston, July 7. Nationals 4, Americans 3. Managers—Charlie Grimm, Joe McCarthy. Winning pitcher—Dizzy Dean. Losing pitcher—Lefty Gomez. Attendance—25,556.

1937—At Griffith Stadium, Washington, July 7. Americans 8, Nationals 3. Managers—Joe McCarthy, Bill Terry. Winning pitcher—Lefty Gomez. Losing pitcher—Dizzy Dean. Attendance—31,391.

1938—At Crosley Field, Cincinnati, July 6. Nationals 4, Americans 1. Managers—Billy Terry, Joe McCarthy. Winning pitcher—Johnny Vander Meer. Losing pitcher—Lefty Gomez. Attendance—27,067.

1939—At Yankee Stadium, New York, July 11. Americans 3, Nationals 1. Managers—Joe McCarthy, Gabby Hartnett. Winning pitcher—Tommy Bridges. Losing pitcher—Bill Lee. Attendance—62,892.

1940—At Sportsman's Park, St. Louis—July 9. Nationals 4, Americans 0. Managers—Bill McKechnie, Joe Cronin. Winning pitcher—Paul Derringer. Losing pitcher—Red Ruffing. Attendance—32,373.

1941—At Briggs Stadium, Detroit, July 8. Americans 7, Nationals 5. Managers—Del Baker, Bill McKechnie. Winning pitcher—Ed Smith. Losing pitcher—Claude Passeau. Attendance—54,674.

1942—At Polo Grounds, New York, July 6. Americans 3, Nationals 1. Managers—Joe Cronin, Leo Durocher. Winning pitcher—Spud Chandler. Losing pitcher—Mort Cooper. Attendance—34,178.

1943—At Shibe Park, Philadelphia, July 13 (night). Americans 5, Nationals 3. Managers—Joe McCarthy, Billy Southworth. Winning pitcher—Dutch Leonard. Losing pitcher—Mort Cooper. Attendance—31,938.

1944—At Forbes Field, Pittsburgh, July 11 (night). Nationals 7, Americans 1. Managers—Billy Southworth, Joe McCarthy. Winning pitcher—Ken Raffensberger. Losing pitcher—Tex Hughson. Attendance—29,589.

1945—No game played.

1946—At Fenway Park, Boston, July 9. Americans 12, Nationals 0. Managers—Steve O'Neill, Charlie Grimm. Winning pitcher—Bob Feller. Losing pitcher—Claude Passeau. Attendance—34,906.

1947—At Wrigley Field, Chicago, July 8. Americans 2, Nationals 1. Managers—Joe Cronin, Eddie Dyer. Winning pitcher—Frank Shea. Losing pitcher—Johnny Sain. Attendance—41,123.

1948—At Sportsman's Park, St. Louis, July 13. Americans 5, Nationals 2. Managers—Bucky Harris, Leo Durocher. Winning pitcher—Vic Raschi. Losing pitcher—Johnny Schmitz. Attendance—34,009.

1949—At Ebbets Field, Brooklyn, July 12. Americans 11, Nationals 7. Managers—Lou Boudreau, Billy Southworth. Winning pitcher—Virgil Trucks. Losing pitcher—Don Newcombe. Attendance—32,577.

1950—At Comiskey Park, Chicago, July 11. Nationals 4, Americans 3 (14 innings). Managers—Burt Shotton, Casey Stengel. Winning pitcher—Ewell Blackwell. Losing pitcher—Ted Gray. Attendance—46,127.

1951—At Briggs Stadium, Detroit, July 10. Nationals 8, Americans 3. Managers—Eddie Sawyer, Casey Stengel. Winning pitcher—Sal Maglie. Losing pitcher—Ed Lopat. Attendance—52,075.

1952—At Shibe Park, Philadelphia, July 8. Nationals 3, Americans 2 (five innings—rain). Managers—Leo Durocher, Casey Stengel. Winning pitcher—Bob Rush. Losing pitcher—Bob Lemon. Attendance—32,785.

1953—At Crosley Field, Cincinnati, July 14. Nationals 5, Americans 1. Managers—Chuck Dressen, Casey Stengel. Winning pitcher—Warren Spahn. Losing pitcher—Allie Reynolds. Attendance—30,846.

1954—At Municipal Stadium, Cleveland, July 13. Americans 11, Nationals 9. Managers—Casey Stengel, Walter Alston. Winning pitcher—Dean Stone. Losing pitcher—Gene Conley. Attendance—68,751.

1955—At Milwaukee County Stadium, Milwaukee, July 12. Nationals 6, Americans 5 (12 innings). Managers—Leo Durocher, Al Lopez. Winning pitcher—Gene Conley. Losing pitcher—Frank Sullivan. Attendance—45,643.

1956—At Griffith Stadium, Washington, July 10. Nationals 7, Americans 3. Managers—Walter Alston, Casey Stengel. Winning pitcher—Bob

Montreal's Gary Carter clubbed the first pitch from Toronto hurler Dave Stieb over the left-field fence in the second inning to give the N.L. a lead it never relinquished and received congratulations at the plate afterward.

Friend. Losing pitcher—Billy Pierce. Attendance—28,843.

1957—At Busch Stadium, St. Louis, July 9. Americans 6, Nationals 5. Managers—Casey Stengel, Walter Alston. Winning pitcher—Jim Bunning. Losing pitcher—Curt Simmons. Attendance—30,693.

1958—At Memorial Stadium, Baltimore, July 8. Americans 4, Nationals 3. Managers—Casey Stengel, Fred Haney. Winning pitcher—Early Wynn. Losing pitcher—Bob Friend. Attendance—48,829.

1959 (first game)—At Forbes Field, Pittsburgh, July 7. Nationals 5, Americans 4. Managers—Fred Haney, Casey Stengel. Winning pitcher—Johnny Antonelli. Losing pitcher—Whitey Ford. Attendance—35,277.

1959 (second game)—At Memorial Coliseum, Los Angeles, August 3. Americans 5, Nationals 3. Managers—Casey Stengel, Fred Haney. Winning pitcher—Jerry Walker. Losing pitcher—Don Drysdale. Attendance—55,105.

1960 (first game)—At Municipal Stadium, Kansas City, July 11. Nationals 5, Americans 3. Managers—Walter Alston, Al Lopez. Winning pitcher—Bob Friend. Losing pitcher—Bill Monbouquette. Attendance—30,619.

1960 (second game)—At Yankee Stadium, New York, July 13. Nationals 6, Americans 0. Managers—Walter Alston, Al Lopez. Winning pitcher—Vernon Law. Losing pitcher—Whitey Ford. Attendance—38,362.

1961 (first game)—At Candlestick Park, San Francisco, July 11. Nationals 5, Americans 4 (10 innings). Managers—Danny Murtaugh, Paul Richards. Winning pitcher—Stu Miller. Losing pitcher—Hoyt Wilhelm. Attendance—44,115.

1961 (second game)—At Fenway Park, Boston, July 13. Americans 1, Nationals 1 (nine-inning tie, stopped by rain). Managers—Paul Richards, Danny Murtaugh. Attendance—31,851.

1962 (first game)—At District of Columbia Stadium, Washington, July 10. Nationals 3, Americans 1. Managers—Fred Hutchinson, Ralph Houk. Winning pitcher—Juan Marichal. Losing pitcher—Camilo Pascual. Attendance—45,480.

1962 (second game)—At Wrigley Field, Chicago, July 30. Americans 9, Nationals 4. Managers—Ralph Houk, Fred Hutchinson. Winning pitcher—Ray Herbert. Losing pitcher—Art Mahaffey. Attendance—38,359.

1963—At Municipal Stadium, Cleveland, July 9. Nationals 5, Americans 3. Managers—Alvin Dark, Ralph Houk. Winning pitcher—Larry Jackson. Losing pitcher—Jim Bunning. Attendance—44,160.

1964—At Shea Stadium, New York, July 7. Nationals 7, Americans 4. Managers—Walter Alston, Al Lopez. Winning pitcher—Juan Marichal. Losing pitcher—Dick Radatz. Attendance—50,850.

1965—At Metropolitan Stadium, Bloomington (Minnesota), July 13. Nationals 6, Americans 5. Managers—Gene Mauch, Al Lopez. Winning pitcher—Sandy Koufax. Losing pitcher—Sam McDowell. Attendance—46,706.

1966—At Busch Memorial Stadium, St. Louis, July 12. Nationals 2, Americans 1 (10 innings). Managers—Walter Alston, Sam Mele. Winning pitcher—Gaylord Perry. Losing pitcher—Pete Richert. Attendance—49,936.

1967—At Anaheim Stadium, Anaheim (California), July 11. Nationals 2, Americans 1 (15 innings). Managers—Walter Alston, Hank Bauer. Winning pitcher—Don Drysdale. Losing pitcher—Jim Hunter. Attendance—46,309.

1968—At Astrodome, Houston, July 9 (night). Nationals 1, Americans 0. Managers—Red Schoendienst, Dick Williams. Winning pitcher—

Don Drysdale. Losing pitcher—Luis Tiant. Attendance—48,321.

1969—At Robert F. Kennedy Memorial Stadium, Washington, July 23. Nationals 9, Americans 3. Managers—Red Schoendienst, Mayo Smith. Winning pitcher—Steve Carlton. Losing pitcher—Mel Stottlemyre. Attendance—45,259.

1970—At Riverfront Stadium, Cincinnati, July 14 (night). Nationals 5, Americans 4 (12 innings). Managers—Gil Hodges, Earl Weaver. Winning pitcher—Claude Osteen. Losing pitcher—Clyde Wright. Attendance—51,838.

1971—At Tiger Stadium, Detroit, July 13 (night). Americans 6, Nationals 4. Managers—Earl Weaver, George (Sparky) Anderson. Winning pitcher—Vida Blue. Losing pitcher—Dock Ellis. Attendance—53,559.

1972—At Atlanta Stadium, Atlanta, July 25 (night). Nationals 4, Americans 3 (10 innings). Managers—Danny Murtaugh, Earl Weaver. Winning pitcher—Tug McGraw. Losing pitcher—Dave McNally. Attendance—53,107.

1973—At Royals Stadium, Kansas City, July 24 (night). Nationals 7, Americans 1. Managers—George (Sparky) Anderson, Dick Williams. Winning pitcher—Rick Wise. Losing pitcher—Bert Blyleven. Attendance—40,849.

1974—At Three Rivers Stadium, Pittsburgh, July 23 (night). Nationals 7, Americans 2. Managers—Yogi Berra, Dick Williams. Winning pitcher—Ken Brett. Losing pitcher—Luis Tiant. Attendance—50,706.

1975—At Milwaukee County Stadium, Milwaukee, July 15 (night). Nationals 6, Americans 3. Managers—Walter Alston, Alvin Dark. Winning pitcher—Jon Matlack. Losing pitcher—Jim Hunter. Attendance—51,480.

1976—At Veterans Stadium, Philadelphia, July 13 (night). Nationals 7, Americans 1. Managers—George (Sparky) Anderson, Darrell Johnson. Winning pitcher—Randy Jones. Losing pitcher—Mark Fidrych. Attendance—63,974.

1977—At Yankee Stadium, New York, July 19 (night). Nationals 7, Americans 5. Managers—Alfred (Billy) Martin, George (Sparky) Anderson. Winning pitcher—Don Sutton. Losing pitcher—Jim Palmer. Attendance—56,683.

1978—At San Diego Stadium, San Diego, July 11 (night). Nationals 7, Americans 3. Managers—Alfred (Billy) Martin, Thomas Lasorda. Winning pitcher—Bruce Sutter. Losing pitcher—Rich Gossage. Attendance—51,549.

1979—At Kingdome, Seattle, July 17. Nationals 7, Americans 6. Managers—Chuck Tanner, Bob Lemon. Winning pitcher—Bruce Sutter. Losing pitcher—Jim Kern. Attendance—58,905.

1980—At Dodger Stadium, Los Angeles, July 8. Nationals 4, Americans 2. Managers—Chuck Tanner, Earl Weaver. Winning pitcher—Jerry Reuss. Losing pitcher—Tommy John. Attendance—56,088.

1981—At Municipal Stadium, Cleveland, August 9 (night). Nationals 5, Americans 4. Managers—Dallas Green, Jim Frey. Winning pitcher—Vida Blue. Losing pitcher—Rollie Fingers. Attendance—72,086.

1982—At Olympic Stadium, Montreal, July 13 (night). Nationals 4, Americans 1. Managers—Tommy Lasorda, Alfred (Billy) Martin. Winning pitcher—Steve Rogers. Losing pitcher—Dennis Eckersley. Attendance—59,057.

1983—At Comiskey Park, Chicago, July 6 (night). Americans 13, Nationals 3. Managers—Harvey Kuenn, Dorrel (Whitey) Herzog. Winning pitcher—Dave Stieb. Losing pitcher—Mario Soto. Attendance—43,801.

BATTING, PITCHING FEATURES

Including

Low-Hit Pitching Performances

Top Strikeout Performances

Baseball's Top Firemen

Pitchers Winning 1-0 Games

Multi-Home Run Performances

Batters Hitting Grand Slams

Top One-Game Hitting Performances

Baseball's Top Pinch-Hitters

Top Performances in Debuts

Homers by Parks

Award Winners

Hall of Fame Electees

Hall of Famers List, Years Selected

California's Mike Witt gets a big hug from catcher Bob Boone after shutting out Texas in the 13th nine-inning perfect game in major league history.

Witt, Palmer Are Perfect

By DAVE SLOAN

When California Angels righthander Mike Witt took the mound on September 30 for the season finale against the Rangers in Arlington, Tex., his motivation was simple. All he wanted to do was pitch a good game, help the Angels finish their disappointing season with a .500 record and take some of the sting out of a late-season collapse that had cost them a chance at the American League West Division title.

He accomplished all three of those objectives and threw in a bonus. In so doing, the 6-foot-7 Witt made it perfectly clear that he is a force to be reckoned with for years to come.

Witt faced 27 Ranger hitters and retired all 27, becoming only the 13th pitcher in major league history to accomplish the feat. Witt threw just 94 pitches and allowed only four Texas hitters to get the ball out of the infield. The nine-inning perfect game was the first in the major leagues since Cleveland's Len Barker shut down Toronto in 1981.

"I was awestruck," said Witt, who struck out 10 in the Angels' 1-0 victory. "Getting 27 outs is incredible. All you're trying to do is get outs. All I know is it's hard as heck to get."

It also was hard as heck for Rangers hitters to get their bats on Witt's pitches. Their only hard-hit ball was Larry Parrish's eighth-inning drive that was caught on the warning track by Mike Brown. Only Ranger second baseman Wayne Tolleson came close to reaching base. Witt fell behind Tolleson 3-0 in the seventh inning but came back to retire him on a 3-2 grounder.

The victory, Witt's 15th, was his second memorable performance of the season. On July 23, Witt struck out 16 Mariners in a 7-1 victory over Seattle.

"I knew I was throwing it (a perfect game) in the fourth inning," Witt said. "I didn't know whether I could do it until the seventh inning. I was real nervous walking out there in the ninth inning, but after I threw the first pitch for a strike, I fell back into it."

Witt's gem was the first no-hitter in the history of Arlington Stadium and the first by a California pitcher since Nolan Ryan's 1-0 victory over Baltimore on June 1, 1975.

But, ironically, it wasn't the first perfect game or first no-hitter of the '84 campaign. Jack Morris of the Detroit Tigers and David Palmer of the Montreal Expos each threw no-hitters during the first 20 days of the regular season. Palmer's was a five-inning, rain-shortened perfect game.

Morris' no-hitter came on April 7 in a nationally-televised game against the White Sox in Comiskey Park. It was only the Tigers' fourth game of the year, the White Sox' third, and Morris' second start.

The no-hitter was the first thrown by a Detroit pitcher since Jim Bunning turned the trick against Boston on July 20, 1958. No major-league team had gone as long as the Tigers without a no-hitter.

The forkball, or split-fingered fastball, proved to be Chicago's undoing. Morris, who had learned the pitch just one year earlier, threw it flawlessly and had the defending American League West Division champions flailing helplessly all afternoon.

"He threw about 35 to 40 percent fork-

Witt's Perfect Game

California	AB.	R.	H.	RBI.	E.
Wilfong, 2b	4	0	0	0	0
Sconiers, 1b	4	0	0	0	0
Grich, 1b	0	0	0	0	0
Lynn, cf-rf	3	0	2	0	0
DeCinces, 3b	4	1	2	0	0
Downing, lf	4	0	0	0	0
Thomas, lf	0	0	0	0	0
Re. Jackson, dh	4	0	0	1	0
Brown, rf	3	0	3	0	0
Pettis, pr-cf	0	0	0	0	0
Boone, c	3	0	0	0	0
Schofield, ss	2	0	0	0	0
Totals	31	1	7	1	0

Texas	AB.	R.	H.	RBI.	E.
Rivers, dh	3	0	0	0	0
Tolleson, 2b	3	0	0	0	0
Ward, lf	3	0	0	0	0
Parrish, 3b	3	0	0	0	0
O'Brien, 1b	3	0	0	0	0
G. Wright, cf	3	0	0	0	0
Dunbar, rf	3	0	0	0	0
Scott, c	2	0	0	0	0
B. Jones, ph	1	0	0	0	0
Wilkerson, ss	2	0	0	0	0
Foley, ph	1	0	0	0	0
Totals	27	0	0	0	0

California .... 000 000 100—1
Texas .... 000 000 000—0

California	IP.	H.	R.	ER.	BB.	SO.
WITT (W. 15-11)	9	0	0	0	0	10

Texas	IP.	H.	R.	ER.	BB.	SO.
Hough (L. 16-14)	9	7	1	0	3	3

Game-winning RBI—Reggie Jackson.
DP—Texas 2. LOB—California 6, Texas 0. 2B—Brown. 3B—Brown. WP—Hough. PB—Scott. T—1:49. A—8,375.

Detroit catcher Lance Parrish greets Jack Morris after the righthander's April no-hitter against Chicago.

Morris' No-Hitter

Detroit	AB.	R.	H.	RBI.	E.
Whitaker, 2b	4	0	1	1	0
Trammell, ss	4	0	1	0	0
Garbey, 1b	3	0	0	0	0
Bergman, 1b	1	0	0	0	0
Parrish, c	3	1	0	0	0
Herndon, lf	4	0	0	0	0
Allen, dh	3	0	0	0	0
Grubb, ph	1	0	0	0	0
Lemon, cf	4	2	2	2	0
Gibson, rf	1	1	1	1	0
Brookens, 3b	2	0	0	0	0
Totals	30	4	5	4	0

Chicago	AB.	R.	H.	RBI.	E.
R. Law, cf	3	0	0	0	0
Dybzinski, ss	0	0	0	0	0
Fisk, c	3	0	0	0	0
Baines, rf	3	0	0	0	0
Luzinski, dh	2	0	0	0	0
Stegman, pr	0	0	0	0	0
Kittle, lf	4	0	0	0	0
Paciorek, 1b	3	0	0	0	0
V. Law, 3b	1	0	0	0	0
Walker, ph	1	0	0	0	0
Hulett, 3b	0	0	0	0	0
Fletcher, ss	2	0	0	0	0
Hairston, ph-cf	1	0	0	0	0
Cruz, 2b	3	0	0	0	0
Totals	26	0	0	0	0

Detroit	0 2 0	0 2 0	0 0 0—4
Chicago	0 0 0	0 0 0	0 0 0—0

Detroit	IP.	H.	R.	ER.	BB.	SO.
MORRIS (W. 2-0)	9	0	0	0	6	8

Chicago	IP.	H.	R.	ER.	BB.	SO.
Bannister (L. 0-1)	6	4	4	4	2	3
Brennan	2	1	0	0	1	3
Barojas	1	0	0	0	0	1

Game-winning RBI—Lemon.
DP—Detroit 1, Chicago 1. LOB—Detroit 3, Chicago 5. 2B—Lemon, Gibson. HR—Lemon (1). SB —R. Law, Trammell. SH—Brookens. T—2:44. A—24,616.

balls," said Tigers catcher Lance Parrish. "He could have told the Sox it was coming and they still wouldn't have hit it."

Morris' gem was the second thrown against the Sox in their last seven regular-season games (Oakland's Mike Warren no-hit Chicago on September 29, 1983, after the Sox had clinched the A.L. West Division title).

"I don't see a no-hitter for my whole career," lamented Chicago catcher Carlton Fisk, a 13-year veteran, "and now I'm on the wrong end of two in one week."

Morris struck out eight and walked six in the 4-0 Detroit victory, the first nationally-televised no-hitter since Nolan Ryan of Houston defeated Los Angeles on September 26, 1981, for his record-setting fifth career no-hitter. The turning point probably came in the White Sox fourth inning when Morris walked the bases loaded but escaped damage when he got designated hitter Greg Luzinski to ground into a double play.

"I can't ever remember going past the fifth inning without giving up a hit," Morris said. "Once I got past the fifth, I started to think about it."

Two plays late in the game by Tigers' first baseman Dave Bergman saved the day. Bergman, who was sent into the game in the seventh inning by Manager Sparky Anderson as a defensive replacement for rookie Barbaro Garbey, leaped high to grab a hard liner by Tom Paciorek in that inning. It probably was the hardest hit ball by the White Sox all day. Then, in the Chicago eighth, Bergman went to his knees to stop a shot down the line by Jerry Hairston.

"You go out and dive for balls when a guy has a no-hitter," Bergman said. "You

Palmer's Perfect Game

SECOND GAME

Montreal	AB.	R.	H.	RBI.	E.
Dilone, lf	3	0	1	0	0
Little, 2b	3	1	1	0	0
Raines, cf	3	1	0	0	0
Wallach, 3b	2	2	1	1	0
Francona, 1b	3	0	2	2	0
Wohlford, rf	2	0	1	0	0
Ramos, c	1	0	0	1	0
Speier, ss	2	0	0	0	0
Palmer, p	2	0	0	0	0
Totals	21	4	6	4	0

St. Louis	AB.	R.	H.	RBI.	E.
L. Smith, lf	2	0	0	0	0
Van Slyke, 3b	2	0	0	0	0
Green, 1b	0	0	0	0	0
Iorg, 1b	2	0	0	0	0
Hendrick, rf	2	0	0	0	1
McGee, cf	2	0	0	0	0
Herr, 2b	1	0	0	0	0
Ramsey, 2b	1	0	0	0	0
O. Smith, ss	1	0	0	0	0
Brummer, c	1	0	0	0	0
Forsch, p	1	0	0	0	0
Totals	15	0	0	0	1

Montreal .... 3 0 1 0 0 0—4
St. Louis .... 0 0 0 0 0 —0
*Stopped by rain with Montreal batting in top of sixth inning.

Montreal	IP.	H.	R.	ER.	BB.	SO.
PALMER (W. 2-0)	5	0	0	0	0	2

St. Louis	IP.	H.	R.	ER.	BB.	SO.
Forsch (L. 0-2)	5*	6	4	2	2	1

Game-winning RBI—Francona.
DP—None. LOB—Montreal 5, St. Louis 0. 2B—Dilone. HR—Wallach (4). SF—Ramos. T—1:25. A—13,207.

Montreal's David Palmer made the record books by pitching a rain-shortened perfect game against St. Louis on April 21.

do more than you are capable of doing."

A no-hitter was the last thing on Palmer's mind when he took the mound April 21 for a game against the Cardinals in St. Louis. He was just happy to be pitching at all.

Plagued by a bad elbow on his pitching arm that required two operations, Palmer missed the entire 1983 season. But in just his second start of 1984, Palmer found perfection—with a little help from Mother Nature.

It was the fourth perfect game in big-league history to go less than nine innings. But for Palmer, who had spent better than one-third of his major league career on the disabled list, a perfect game is a perfect game—regardless of the innings pitched. Besides, he didn't have to sit around in the dugout and keep thinking about it.

"I started thinking about it about five minutes before they called the game," Palmer said. "It's a five-inning perfect game, but it still goes down as a perfect

game. I'll take it. I've had games where I've thrown just as well, but the ball would find a way through."

Of the 15 outs Palmer registered, 11 were ground balls, two were strikeouts, one was a fly ball and one was a line drive. Andy Van Slyke's fourth-inning liner, which was caught by second baseman Bryan Little, was the only ball hit hard off Palmer.

The 4-0 victory was the first shortened perfect game in the majors since Minnesota's Dean Chance stopped Boston, 2-0, on August 6, 1967, in another five-inning game. It also was the first perfect game ever thrown against a St. Louis Cardinals team.

But the historical aspects of his feat were probably lost on Palmer, who had fewer innings pitched in the big leagues than days spent on the disabled list entering the '84 season.

"I'm just happy I'm here pitching," he said.

Soto Loses Close Encounter

By DAVE SLOAN

As Cincinnati ace righthander Mario Soto entered the ninth inning of a May 12 game against St. Louis, he was so nervous that he "couldn't even see the fans."

That's because he was three outs away from his first career no-hitter while trying to protect an uncomfortable 1-0 Reds lead. Soto made quick work of Ozzie Smith on a grounder and Lonnie Smith on a pop to second baseman Ron Oester. All that stood between Soto and immortality was George Hendrick, who was hitting .220 and mired in a deep slump.

Soto quickly got two strikes on Hendrick and the Cardinals cleanup hitter meekly fouled off two more pitches. Soto's next pitch, a fastball, spun Hendrick around and sent him reeling out of the box. Ball two, another fastball, also was close.

Soto tried to put the finishing touch on his masterpiece with a 2-2 changeup. But Hendrick, a sleeping giant properly aroused by the preceding two pitches, was ready for it and put a 415-foot monkey wrench into Soto's best-laid plans. The game was tied.

That the Reds scored the winning run in the bottom of the ninth was only minor consolation to Soto, whose one-hitter ranked as the most dramatic low-hit game (one- and two-hitters) of the 1984 season. Detroit's Jack Morris already had pitched a 1984 no-hitter and Montreal's David Palmer and California's Mike Witt later would pitch perfect games (Palmer's shortened to five innings because of rain).

Every major-league club was involved in at least one of the 45 low-hit games pitched in 1984, but Cincinnati and Los Angeles pitchers seemed to take particular delight in stopping each other during a three-game series in late July at Dodger Stadium.

On July 27, in the series opener, Reds righthander Joe Price blanked the Dodgers, 4-0, on a two-hitter. A first-inning double by Mike Marshall and a third-inning single by Candy Maldonado were the only Dodger hits.

The next afternoon, Los Angeles rebounded to win, 1-0, as righthander Bob Welch allowed the Reds only two hits—singles by Gary Redus in the first and ninth innings.

On July 29, Orel Hershiser of the Dodgers pitched the third straight two-hitter of the series, winning 1-0. Singles by Nick Esasky in the eighth and Redus in the ninth were the only hits off the L.A. righthander.

Not surprisingly, the Reds (eight) and the Dodgers (seven) were involved in more low-hit games than any other clubs. In fact, the Dodgers were held to just one hit in their next game after the Cincinnati series—a 12-0 thrashing by Dave Dravecky and the San Diego Padres.

Hershiser and Bert Blyleven of the Cleveland Indians were the only hurlers to throw three low-hit games. In addition to his two-hitter against Cincinnati on July 29, Hershiser also pitched two-hitters against Chicago on July 14 and St. Louis on July 19. In his only other start during that span, Hershiser allowed just five hits in eight and one-third innings against Atlanta on July 24, but was tagged with a 4-2 loss.

Blyleven, a 19-game winner for the sixth-place Indians, pitched a one-hit gem against Texas on July 13. The only hit was a fourth-inning single by Larry Parrish.

Blyleven also threw a pair of two-hitters. The first came in a 5-0 victory against Seattle on June 24 and the other came in a 7-1 win against California on September 12.

A complete list of one- and two-hit games for 1984 follows:

AMERICAN LEAGUE
One-Hit Games

May 2—Hoyt, Chicago vs. New York, 3-0—Mattingly, single in seventh.

June 23—Conroy (eight innings) and Caudill (one inning), Oakland vs. Texas, 5-1—Bannister, homer in fifth.

July 13—Blyleven, Cleveland vs. Texas, 5-0—Parrish, single in fourth.

Aug. 5—Fontenot (five and two-thirds innings), Armstrong (two and one-third innings) and Niekro (one inning), New York vs. Cleveland, 4-0—Jacoby, single in sixth.

Aug. 13—Boddicker, Baltimore vs. Toronto, 2-1—Mulliniks, double in third.

Two-Hit Games

April 29—Petry (eight innings) and Hernandez (one inning), Detroit vs. Cleveland, 6-1—Vukovich, double in eighth; Franco, double in ninth.

May 1—John (eight innings) and Sanchez (one inning), California vs. Oakland, 4-1—Lopes, single in seventh; Henderson, single in eighth.

May 6—Hurst, Boston vs. Chicago, 3-1—V. Law, homer in eighth; Fletcher, single in eighth.

May 23—Rasmussen (eight innings) and Righetti (one inning), New York vs. Seattle, 3-0—D. Henderson, double in fifth and double in seventh.

June 16—Leal, Toronto vs. Boston, 7-0—Miller, single in second; Rice, double in seventh.

San Diego lefty Dave Dravecky pitched one of the N.L.'s six one-hit games, shutting out the Dodgers on July 30.

June 24—Blyleven, Cleveland vs. Seattle, 5-0—Presley, double in fifth; Perconte, single in eighth.

June 28—Flanagan (eight innings), Stewart (one-third inning) and T. Martinez (two-thirds inning), Baltimore vs. Chicago, 2-0—Paciorek, single in first; Dybzinski, single in eighth.

July 3—Gott, Toronto vs. California, 4-0—Carew, single in fourth; Re. Jackson, single in fifth.

July 16—Jones (eight innings) and Quisenberry (one inning), Kansas City vs. Cleveland, 3-1—Butler, single in fourth; Vukovich, single in ninth.

July 17—Langston (eight innings) and Stanton (one inning), Seattle vs. Milwaukee, 3-1—Gantner, double in sixth; Cooper, single in sixth.

July 28—Burris, Oakland vs. Seattle, 1-2—Davis, double in first; D. Henderson, homer in fifth.

Aug. 22—Darwin (seven and one-third innings) and Schmidt (one and two-thirds innings), Texas vs. Chicago, 3-1—Baines, single in third; Walker, single in third.

Aug. 29—Boyd, Boston vs. Minnesota, 4-0—Puckett, single in fourth; Teufel, single in sixth.

Aug. 29—Langston, Seattle vs. Detroit, 5-1—Trammell, single in first; Kuntz, single in second.

Sept. 2—Alexander, Toronto vs. Minnesota, 6-0—Brunansky, single in second; Putnam, double in seventh.

Sept. 12—Blyleven, Cleveland vs. California, 7-1

—Carew, single in sixth; Downing, homer in seventh.

Sept. 15—Gibson, Milwaukee vs. Baltimore, 7-0—Bumbry, single in first and single in sixth.

Sept. 23—Morris (six innings), Scherrer (one inning) and Hernandez (two innings), Detroit vs. New York, 4-1—Moreno, single in third; Gamble, single in fourth.

NATIONAL LEAGUE
One-Hit Games

April 27—Honeycutt, Los Angeles vs. San Diego, 1-0—Salazar, single in fourth.

May 12—Soto, Cincinnati vs. St. Louis, 2-1—Hendrick, homer in ninth.

June 14—Barker (seven innings) and Moore (two innings), Atlanta vs. Cincinnati, 3-0—Milner, single in fourth.

July 30—Dravecky, San Diego vs. Los Angeles, 12-0—Russell, double in seventh.

Aug. 24—DeLeon, Pittsburgh vs. Cincinnati, 0-2—Parker, single in seventh.

Sept. 7—Gooden, New York vs. Chicago, 10-0—Moreland, single in fifth.

Two-Hit Game

April 28—Sanderson, Chicago vs. Pittsburgh, 7-1—Ray, double in first and single in fourth.

May 5—Williams, San Francisco (five innings) vs. St. Louis, 7-0—Herr, single in third; Oberkfell, single in fourth.

May 10—Pastore, Cincinnati vs. Montreal, 2-1—Little, single in fourth; Raines, single in seventh.

May 30—Trout (seven and two-thirds innings) and Smith (one and one-third innings), Chicago vs. Atlanta, 6-2—Hall, single in eighth; Ramirez, single in eighth.

June 19—Show, San Diego vs. Houston, 2-0—Mumphrey, single in second; Cabell, single in seventh.

June 29—Horton, St. Louis vs. San Diego, 5-0—McReynolds, double in eighth; Wiggins, single in ninth.

July 2—Rawley (seven innings) and Holland (two innings), Philadelphia vs. Cincinnati, 4-0—Parker, single in fifth; Esasky, single in fifth.

July 14—Berenyi (seven innings) and Gorman (two innings), New York vs. Atlanta, 7-0—Chambliss, single in second; Washington, single in sixth.

July 14—Hershiser, Los Angeles vs. Chicago, 8-0—Johnstone, single in first; Dernier, single in third.

July 19—Hershiser, Los Angeles vs. St. Louis, 10-0—L. Smith, single in first; Pendleton, double in second.

July 27—Price, Cincinnati vs. Los Angeles, 4-0—Marshall, double in first; Maldonado, single in third.

July 28—Welch, Los Angeles vs. Cincinnati, 1-0—Redus, single in first and single in ninth.

July 29—Lollar, San Diego vs. Houston, 9-0—Ashby, single in third; Cabell, single in fourth.

July 29—Hershiser, Los Angeles vs. Cincinnati, 1-0—Esasky, single in eighth; Redus, single in ninth.

Aug. 9—Rhoden, Pittsburgh vs. New York, 11-0—Santana, double in third; Wilson, double in fourth.

Sept. 24—Sutcliffe, Chicago vs. Pittsburgh, 4-1—Orsulak, triple in fourth and single in sixth.

Gooden Has a Striking Season

By RON SMITH

When New York Mets rookie sensation Dwight Gooden committed a run-scoring, eighth-inning balk against the Philadelphia Phillies on September 17, it cost his team a game. It also was costly to Gooden for personal reasons.

Not only did the balk end Gooden's seven-game winning streak, but it also cost him a shot at the record books. The youngster already had compiled 16 strikeouts in eight innings and was within striking distance of the major league record (19 strikeouts in a nine-inning game, held by Steve Carlton, Tom Seaver and Nolan Ryan). But the Mets, suddenly down 2-1, were retired quietly in the ninth inning and the Phillies were not required to bat.

High-strikeout performances were not uncommon for the hard-throwing right-hander with the rookie arm and the veteran poise. In fact, that September 17 performance was his second straight 16-strikeout effort and capped a stretch of five starts in which Gooden averaged 13 strikeouts per game.

Gooden struck out 10 or more batters 15 times, led the major leagues with 276 strikeouts en route to a rookie strikeout record and set National League records for two- and three-game strikeout totals. His 2.60 earned-run average was second in the N.L. and he finished with a non-rookie-like record of 17-9.

Gooden, whose ratio of 11.39 strikeouts per nine innings set a rookie record, easily outdistanced all competitors in double-figure strikeout performances. Los Angeles ace Fernando Valenzuela reached double figures seven times to finish second while Chicago Cubs ace Rick Sutcliffe made it five times. And both joined Gooden in the 15-strikeout club.

Valenzuela struck out 15 Phillies May 23 in the Dodgers' 1-0 victory. Sutcliffe also victimized the Phillies, striking out 15 in eight innings of a September game in which he failed to gain a decision.

Two American Leaguers had 15-plus strikeout games in 1984.

California's Mike Witt, who later would strike out 10 Texas batters in a season-ending perfect game, made short work of the Seattle Mariners on July 23 when he struck out 16 en route to a five-hit, 7-1 victory.

Boston rookie Roger Clemens enjoyed his day in the sun August 21 when he set down 15 Royals on strikes in an 11-1 Red Sox victory.

The six 15-plus strikeout performances were in stark contrast to 1983, when no pitcher reached the milestone.

A rookie also led the American League in strikeouts. Seattle lefthander Mark Langston finished with 204 and led the way with four 10-plus strikeout performances. Toronto's Dave Stieb, Witt and Clemons all made it three times.

Houston veteran Nolan Ryan reached the 10-strikeout plateau four times in 1984 to extend his major league record for such performances to 155.

Following is a list of all pitchers who achieved 10 strikeouts in a game in 1984, with the number of times the feat was accomplished:

AMERICAN LEAGUE: Baltimore—None. Boston (5)—Clemons 3, Boyd, Ojeda. California (3)—Witt 3. Chicago (3)—Bannister 2, Dotson. Cleveland (1)—Blyleven. Detroit (4)—Petry 2, Berenguer, Morris. Kansas City—None. Milwaukee—None. Minnesota (1)—Viola. New York (4)—Guidry 2, Cowley, Rasmussen. Oakland—None. Seattle (8)—Langston 4, Beattie 2, Moore 2. Texas—None. Toronto (4)—Stieb 3, Leal.

NATIONAL LEAGUE—Atlanta (2)—Barker, McMurtry. Chicago (5)—Sutcliffe 5. Cincinnati (5)—Soto 3, Price, Russell. Houston (4)—Ryan 4. Los Angeles (8)—Valenzuela 7, Hershiser. Montreal (1)—Schatzeder. New York (17)—Gooden 15, Berenyi, Darling. Philadelphia (5)—Carlton 3, Denny, Gross. Pittsburgh (7)—Candelaria 2, DeLeon 2, McWilliams, Rhoden, Tunnell. St. Louis—None. San Diego (3)—Lollar 2, Whitson. San Francisco (1)—Krukow.

1984 Games With 15 or More Strikeouts

Date	Pitcher—Club—Opp.	Place	IP	H	R	ER	BB	SO	Result
May 23—Valenzuela, L.A. vs. Phila.		Phila.	9	3	0	0	6	15	W 1-0
July 23—Witt, California vs. Seattle		Calif.	9	5	1	1	2	16	W 7-1
Aug. 21—Clemens, Boston vs. Kan. City		Boston	9	7	1	1	0	15	W 11-1
Sept. 3—Sutcliffe, Cubs vs. Phila.		Phila.	8	3	3	3	1	15	ND 4-3
Sept. 12—Gooden, Mets vs. Pittsburgh		New York	9	5	0	0	0	16	W 2-0
Sept. 17—Gooden, Mets vs. Phila.		Phila.	8	7	2	1	0	16	L 1-2

Sutter Matches Save Record

By LARRY WIGGE

When Kansas City relief ace Dan Quisenberry compiled the amazing total of 45 saves in 1983, he thoroughly annihilated John Hiller's major league record of 38 that had stood since 1973. It figured that nobody would threaten Quisenberry's total for years to come.

So much for the law of averages.

The ink barely was dry on Quisenberry's entry in the baseball record books when St. Louis ace Bruce Sutter put together his best major league season. Sutter set a National League record and tied Quisenberry's major league mark with 45 saves for the Cardinals in 1984. Sutter's timing was impeccable. He entered his name in the free-agent sweepstakes after the season with ideas of becoming one of the highest paid players in baseball.

Ironically, Quisenberry was not far away from matching his own save record. He finished the '84 season with 44 and was one of the major reasons behind the Royals' surprising victory in the American League West Division title chase.

For their efforts, Sutter and Quisenberry won The Sporting News Fireman of the Year award for the fourth time in their careers. Sutter did it in the National League by recording 50 points (45 saves and five relief wins), while Quisenberry matched that point total with 44 saves and six wins in the A.L.

Sutter captured his first Fireman award in 1979 when he was with the Chicago Cubs. He won again in 1981 and '82 in St. Louis. Quisenberry has won four times in the last five years, missing only in the strike-shortened 1981 season. The only

AMERICAN LEAGUE

Pitcher—Club	Saves	Relief Wins	Tot. Pts.	Pitcher—Club	Saves	Relief Wins	Tot. Pts.
Quisenberry, Kansas City	44	6	50	Burgmeier, Oakland	2	3	5
Caudill, Oakland	36	9	45	Easterly, Cleveland	2	3	5
Hernandez, Detroit	32	9	41	Filson, Minnesota	1	4	5
Davis, Minnesota	29	7	36	Jeffcoat, Cleveland	1	4	5
Righetti, New York	31	5	36	Mirabella, Seattle	3	2	5
Stanley, Boston	22	9	31	Saberhagen, Kansas City	1	4	5
Camacho, Cleveland	23	5	28	Waits, Milwaukee	3	2	5
Fingers, Milwaukee	23	1	24	Acker, Toronto	1	3	4
Lopez, Detroit	14	10	24	Armstrong, New York	1	3	4
T. Martinez, Baltimore	17	4	21	Burns, Chicago	3	1	4
Sanchez, California	11	9	20	Christiansen, New York	2	2	4
Stewart, Baltimore	13	7	20	Frazier, Cleveland	1	3	4
Schmidt, Texas	12	6	18	Geisel, Seattle	3	1	4
Jackson, Toronto	10	7	17	Gott, Toronto	2	2	4
Clear, Boston	8	8	16	O. Jones, Seattle	2	2	4
Howell, New York	7	8	15	Kison, California	2	2	4
Key, Toronto	10	4	14	Rijo, New York	2	2	4
Lamp, Toronto	9	5	14	R. Thomas, Seattle	1	3	4
Waddell, Cleveland	6	7	13	Gleaton, Chicago	2	1	3
Aase, California	8	4	12	Henke, Texas	2	1	3
Reed, Chicago	12	0	12	Kaufman, California	1	2	3
Stanton, Seattle	8	4	12	Mason, Texas	0	3	3
Beckwith, Kansas City	2	8	10	Nelson, Chicago	1	2	3
Tellmann, Milwaukee	4	6	10	Roberge, Chicago	0	3	3
Vande Berg, Seattle	7	3	10	Spillner, Cleve.-Chicago	2	1	3
Agosto, Chicago	7	2	9	Whitehouse, Minnesota	1	2	3
Atherton, Oakland	2	7	9	Barojas, Chicago-Seattle	2	0	2
Bair, Detroit	4	5	9	Farr, Cleveland	1	1	2
Lysander, Minnesota	5	4	9	Johnson, Boston	1	1	2
Nunez, Seattle	7	2	9	McLaughlin, Toronto-Texas	0	2	2
Beard, Seattle	5	3	8	Noles, Texas	0	2	2
Corbett, California	4	4	8	Pashnick, Minnesota	0	2	2
Searage, Milwaukee	6	2	8	Rainey, Oakland	1	1	2
Ladd, Milwaukee	3	4	7	Sorensen, Oakland	1	1	2
Crawford, Boston	1	5	6	Stoddard, Seattle	0	2	2
Huismann, Kansas City	3	3	6	Swaggerty, Baltimore	0	2	2
Jones, Chicago	5	1	6	Underwood, Baltimore	1	1	2
Tobik, Texas	5	1	6	Walters, Minnesota	2	0	2

One save—Bettendorf, Oakland; Codiroli, Oakland; Davis, Baltimore; Lazorko, Milwaukee; Mason, Detroit; McClure, Milwaukee; Musselman, Toronto.

One relief win—Abbott, Detroit; Aponte, Cleveland; Best, Seattle; Brown, Baltimore; Brown, New York, Burris, Oakland; Castillo, Minnesota; Clark, Toronto; Cowley, New York; Curtis, California; Fontenot, New York; Gale, Boston; Gura, Kansas City; Jackson, Kansas City; Kern, Milwaukee; Langston, Seattle; Leiper, Oakland; D. Martinez, Baltimore; McCatty, Oakland; Monge, Detroit; Murray, New York; Scherrer, Detroit; Seaver, Chicago; Shirley, New York; Slaton, California; Snell, Baltimore; Splittorff, Kansas City; Udjur, Cleveland; Williams, Minnesota; Wills, Kansas City.

other relief pitcher to capture four Fireman awards since The Sporting News began honoring the top relief pitchers in 1960 is Rollie Fingers.

Chicago's Lee Smith finished second in the N.L. to Sutter's 50 points. Smith had 33 saves and nine wins for 42 points while New York's Jesse Orosco was third with 41. San Diego's Rich Gossage (35 points) and Philadelphia's Al Holland (34 points) rounded out the top five. Smith and Holland shared the National League honor in 1983.

In the A.L., Oakland's Bill Caudill had 36 saves and nine wins for 45 points, four more than Detroit's Willie Hernandez, who captured both the A.L. Cy Young and Most Valuable Player awards. Minnesota's Ron Davis and New York's Dave Righetti tied for fourth with 36 points apiece. Boston's Bob Stanley also broke the 30-point mark with 22 saves and nine victories.

Following is a complete list of major league players who recorded saves and relief wins in 1984:

Bruce Sutter made his final season in St. Louis memorable.

NATIONAL LEAGUE

Pitcher—Club	Saves	Relief Wins	Tot. Pts.	Pitcher—Club	Saves	Relief Wins	Tot. Pts.
Sutter, St. Louis	45	5	50	Zachry, Los Angeles	2	5	7
Smith, Chicago	33	9	42	Bordi, Chicago	4	2	6
Orosco, New York	31	10	41	Gorman, New York	0	6	6
Gossage, San Diego	25	10	35	Hume, Cincinnati	3	3	6
Holland, Philadelphia	29	5	34	Lerch, San Francisco	2	4	6
Reardon, Montreal	23	7	30	K. Gross, Philadelphia	1	4	5
Minton, San Francisco	19	4	23	Lahti, St. Louis	1	4	5
Moore, Atlanta	16	4	20	Brusstar, Chicago	3	1	4
Power, Cincinnati	11	9	20	Gaff, New York	1	3	4
DiPino, Houston	14	4	18	Guante, Pittsburgh	2	2	4
Bedrosian, Atlanta	11	6	17	Harris, Montreal-San Diego	3	1	4
Lavelle, San Francisco	12	5	17	Hershiser, Los Angeles	2	2	4
Stoddard, Chicago	7	10	17	LaCoss, Houston	3	1	4
Dawley, Houston	5	11	16	Owchinko, Cincinnati	2	2	4
James, Montreal	10	6	16	M. Davis, San Francisco	0	3	3
Sisk, New York	15	1	16	Falcone, Atlanta	2	1	3
Tekulve, Pittsburgh	13	3	16	Grapenthin, Montreal	2	1	3
Robinson, Pittsburgh	10	5	15	Leary, New York	0	3	3
Garber, Atlanta	11	3	14	McGaffigan, Mont.-Cincinnati	1	2	3
Lefferts, San Diego	10	3	13	Candelaria, Pittsburgh	2	0	2
Niedenfuer, Los Angeles	11	2	13	DeLeon, San Diego	0	2	2
Allen, St. Louis	3	9	12	Diaz, Los Angeles	1	1	2
Dravecky, San Diego	8	4	12	Gardner, New York	1	1	2
Howell, Los Angeles	6	5	11	Garrelts, San Francisco	0	2	2
Williams, San Francisco	3	8	11	Hawkins, San Diego	0	2	2
Franco, Cincinnati	4	6	10	Horton, St. Louis	1	1	2
Smith, Houston	5	5	10	Lesley, Cincinnati	2	0	2
Frazier, Chicago	3	6	9	McGraw, Philadelphia	0	2	2
Scurry, Pittsburgh	4	5	9	Monge, San Diego	0	2	2
Dedmon, Atlanta	4	4	8	Noles, Chicago	0	2	2
Lucas, Montreal	8	0	8	Rucker, St. Louis	0	2	2
Andersen, Philadelphia	4	3	7	Ruhle, Houston	2	0	2
Campbell, Philadelphia	1	6	7	Schatzeder, Montreal	1	1	2
Forster, Atlanta	5	2	7	Scherrer, Cincinnati	1	1	2
Hooton, Los Angeles	4	3	7	Von Ohlen, St. Louis	1	1	2
Lynch, New York	2	5	7	Winn, Pittsburgh	1	1	2

One save—Cato, Cincinnati; Grant, San Francisco; Hesketh, Montreal; Krukow, San Francisco; McWilliams, Pittsburgh; Reuss, Los Angeles; Tunnell, Pittsburgh; Willis, Cincinnati.

One relief win—Berenyi, Cincinnati-New York; Booker, San Diego; Camp, Atlanta; Chiffer, San Diego; Cornell, San Francisco; Cox, St. Louis; DeLeon, Pittsburgh; Forsch, St. Louis; Hagen, St. Louis; Hassler, St. Louis; Lacey, San Francisco; Laskey, San Francisco; Madden, Houston; Martin, San Francisco; Palmer, Montreal; Pastore, Cincinnati; Reuschel, Chicago; Ross, Houston; Smith, Cincinnati; Solano, Houston; Swan, New York.

Dodgers Win Seven 1-0 Games

By DAVE SLOAN

Forty-one games during the 1984 major league season ended in a 1-0 score, but California righthander Mike Witt saved the best for last.

On the final day of the season, Witt became only the 13th pitcher in baseball history to throw a perfect game. Witt's victory over Charlie Hough and the Texas Rangers was the first nine-inning perfect game in three seasons and the first by a 1-0 score since the Dodgers' Sandy Koufax carved his masterpiece against the Chicago Cubs on September 9, 1965.

Every club was involved in at least one 1-0 contest, with Los Angeles leading the way with 10. The Dodgers won seven of those games, with three pitchers, Rick Honeycutt, Fernando Valenzuela and Orel Hershiser, winning two games each. Two of the Dodgers' 1-0 wins came on consecutive days against the Cincinnati Reds. On July 28, Bob Welch got the decision over Tom Hume and Hershiser came back the following day to beat Mario Soto.

The Reds led the majors in 1-0 games lost with five. Soto lost twice, including the season's first 1-0 decision on April 13 against Houston.

Nolan Ryan of the Astros and Dan Schatzeder of the Montreal Expos joined Honeycutt, Valenzuela and Hershiser as the only pitchers to win two 1-0 games. The Astros won five 1-0 games, second in the majors to the Dodgers' seven.

Larry McWilliams of the Pittsburgh Pirates and Jim Beattie of the Seattle Mariners joined Soto as the only pitchers to lose two 1-0 games. One of Beattie's 1-0 losses came in the 10th inning of a July 25 game in Anaheim against the Angels, the first of only two 1-0 games that went extra innings. Gary Pettis singled home Juan Beniquez from second base with the winning run after Beattie had blanked the Angels on four hits through nine and two-thirds innings.

Schatzeder was more fortunate in his 1-0 extra-inning game. On August 9 against the Cubs in Montreal, Schatzeder shut down the eventual National League East Division champs on just four hits through 10 innings. He got the victory when Andre Dawson singled home Tim Raines, who had singled and stolen second and third, with the game's only run.

Five of the 1-0 games were decided by home runs. Honeycutt, Hershiser, Bob Ojeda of Boston, Ron Darling of the Mets and Mark Langston of Seattle were the beneficiaries of the longball. On July 1 at Boston, Langston shut out the Red Sox on three hits before Dave Henderson belted a homer off rookie Al Nipper in the top of the ninth inning, the only 1-0 contest decided by a homer in the final inning.

The complete list of 1-0 games, including the winning and losing pitchers and the inning in which the run was scored, follows:

AMERICAN LEAGUE (16)

Date	Winner	Loser	Inning
APRIL—			
21	—*Tanana, Tex.	*Fontenot, N.Y.	6
27	—*Alexander, Tor.	*Gubicza, K.C.	1
MAY—			
3	— Ojeda, Bos.	Morris, Detroit	8
4	—*Porter, Mil.	Niekro, N.Y.	8
19	—*Gott, Tor.	Seaver, Chi.	3
23	— Black, K.C.	Burns, Chi.	1
JUNE—			
29	—*Haas, Mil.	Romanick, Cal.	8
JULY—			
1	— Langston, Sea.	Nipper, Bos.	9
25	—*Sanchez, Cal.	Beattie, Sea.	10
25	—*Young, Oak.	*Schrom, Minn.	9
AUGUST—			
18	— Boddicker, Balt.	*Witt, Cal.	1
SEPTEMBER—			
5	—*Berenguer, Det.	Flanagan, Balt.	1
10	—*Burris, Oak.	*Dotson, Chi.	3
15	— Smithson, Minn.	Darwin, Tex.	3
26	— Blyleven, Clev.	Beattie, Sea.	4
30	— Witt, Cal.	Hough, Tex.	7

NATIONAL LEAGUE (25)

Date	Winner	Loser	Inning
APRIL—			
13	—*Niekro, Hou.	*Soto, Cin.	7
15	—*Rucker, St.L.	*McWilliams, Pitts.	1
17	— Honeycutt, L.A.	*Niekro, Hou.	3
27	— Honeycutt, L.A.	Lollar, S.D.	2
30	— Valenzuela, L.A.	*Laskey, S.F.	2
MAY—			
13	—*Madden, Hou.	Reuschel, Chi.	4
16	— Ryan, Hou.	*Candelaria, Pitts.	6
18	—*Bystrom, Phil.	*Krukow, S.F.	7
23	— Valenzuela, L.A.	*Carlton, Phil.	5
29	—*Knepper, Hou.	*LaPoint, St.L.	6
JUNE—			
3	— LaPoint, St.L.	*Torrez, N.Y.	4
15	—*Schatzeder, Mont.	*DeLeon, Pitts.	2
17	—*Ryan, Hou.	*Welch, L.A.	5
JULY—			
5	— Hudson, Phil.	Mahler, Atl.	2
6†	— Darling, N.Y.	*Russell, Cin.	6
7	—*Dravecky, S.D.	*McWilliams, Pitts.	3
28	— Welch, L.A.	*Hume, Cin.	6
28‡	—*Show, S.D.	*Ryan, Hou.	3
29	— Hershiser, L.A.	Soto, Cin.	3
31	—*Thurmond, S.D.	*Honeycutt, L.A.	4
AUGUST—			
6	—*Gossage, S.D.	Price, Cin.	9
9	— Schatzeder, Mont.	*Frazier, Chi.	10
9	—*Hershiser, L.A.	*Camp, Atl.	4
SEPTEMBER—			
7	—*Franco, Cin.	*Howell, L.A.	9
19	— Cox, St.L.	*Rogers, Mont.	6

*Did not pitch complete game.
†First game of doubleheader.
‡Second game of doubleheader.

Kingman Gets 5th 3-HR Game

By DAVE SLOAN

After being released by the New York Mets in late January, 35-year-old Dave Kingman was not exactly a hot commodity among major league teams. But the Oakland A's, needing another bat in their lineup, signed the temperamental slugger shortly before the 1984 season began and Kingman rewarded them with a 35-homer, 118-RBI performance.

During his ninth game in the Oakland lineup on April 16, Kingman exploded for three home runs, one a grand slam, and drove home eight runs in a 9-6 victory at Seattle. Kingman connected for a grand slam in the first inning and a two-run homer in the third against Matt Young before hitting another two-run blast off Ed Vande Berg in the fifth. The three consecutive home runs tied Kingman with Hall of Famer Johnny Mize as the only big leaguers to hit three consecutive home runs in a game in both leagues. Kingman hit three homers in one game four times in the National League while Mize holds the major league mark with six three-homer games.

After hitting his three homers, Kingman struck out on three pitches in the seventh inning and popped to the shortstop in the ninth, ending his quest to become the 11th player in history to hit four homers in a single game.

The only other player to enjoy a three-homer game in 1984 was Chicago White Sox outfielder Harold Baines, whose blasts came September 17 in a 7-3 victory at Minnesota. Baines' first- and fifth-inning homers were solo drives while his seventh-inning blast was a two-run shot.

Although three-homer games were at a minimum, multi-homer games were not. There were 141 multi-homer performances (two or more homers in one game), with American League batsmen registering twice as many as their National League counterparts (94 to 47).

The Red Sox and White Sox led the major leagues with 12 multi-homer performances each. Three White Sox players, Baines, Ron Kittle and Greg Walker, each did it three times. The Phillies led the National League with nine multi-homer games.

Pittsburgh's Jason Thompson had just two multi-homer games last season, but they both came on the same day. In the first game of a June 26 doubleheader at Chicago's Wrigley Field, Thompson belted solo homers in the third and sixth inning as the Pirates crushed the Cubs, 9-0. In the nightcap, Thompson again homered twice though the Cubs eventually prevailed in a wild 9-8 game. Doug Frobel also hit a pair of homers for the Pirates in the nightcap.

Houston's Mark Bailey was the only batter to connect from both sides of the plate in the same game. In a September 16 contest against San Diego that the Astros eventually won, 10-9, Bailey stroked a second-inning homer from the right side against Padres lefthander Mark Thurmond. Batting lefthanded against righthander Luis DeLeon, Bailey smacked his second homer in the sixth.

Following is a list of players who had multi-homer games in '84 and the number of times they did it:

AMERICAN LEAGUE: Baltimore (6)—Ripken 3, Dempsey, Gross, Young. Boston (12)—Evans 3, Armas 2, Gedman 2, Rice 2, Boggs, Buckner, Easler. California (10)—Lynn 3, Brown 2, Downing 2, Beniquez, DeCinces, Re. Jackson. Chicago (12)—Baines 3, Kittle 3, Walker 3, Fisk, V. Law, Stegman. Cleveland (8)—Carter 3, Thornton 3, Vukovich, Willard. Detroit (5)—Gibson 2, Grubb, Lemon, Parrish. Kansas City (6)—Balboni 3, Motley 2, White. Milwaukee (6)—Schroeder 2, Yount 2, Loman, Sundberg. Minnesota (4)—Hrbek 2, Brunansky, Teufel. New York (2)—Baylor 2, Oakland (6)—Kingman 3, Murphy 3. Seattle (4)—Phelps 3, Presley, Presley. Texas (5)—Parrish 2, Ward 2, O'Brien. Toronto (8)—Barfield 2, Johnson 2, Aikens, Garcia, Martinez, Upshaw.

NATIONAL LEAGUE: Atlanta (4)—Murphy 2, Komminsk, Washington. Chicago (8)—Durham 2, Moreland 2, Sandberg 2, Cey, Davis. Cincinnati (2)—Cedeno, Davis. Houston (4)—Bailey 2, Cruz, Mumphrey. Los Angeles (2)—Guerrero, Marshall. Montreal (3)—Dawson, Driessen, Wohlford. New York (2)—Strawberry 2. Philadelphia (9)—Schmidt 3, Hayes 2, Lezcano 2, Virgil, Wockenfuss. Pittsburgh (5)—Thompson 2, Frobel, Madlock, Pena. St. Louis (1)—Green. San Diego (2)—Nettles 2. San Francisco (5)—Brenly 2, C. Davis, Clark.

A recap of the three-homer games:

Date	Player—Club—Opp.	Place	AB.	R.	H.	2B.	3B.	HR.	RBI.	Result
Apr. 16	Kingman, A's vs. Mariners	A	5	3	3	0	0	3	8	W 9-6
Sept. 17	Baines, White Sox vs. Twins	A	4	3	3	0	0	3	4	W 7-3

A.L. Batters Set Slam Record

By DAVE SLOAN

On July 4, 1983, Yankee lefty Dave Righetti silenced the bats of Jim Rice and his Boston Red Sox teammates by pitching a no-hit gem. On July 4, 1984, however, Red Sox's bats were anything but silent as they pounded out 14 hits in a 13-9 triumph over the Oakland A's. Rice led the assault with five hits in six at-bats, including the biggest hit of all—a game-winning grand-slam off A's reliever Gorman Heimueller in the bottom of the 10th inning.

Rice's blow was one of three 1984 final-inning grand slams that sent hometown fans home happy.

On July 18 at St. Louis, Cardinals catcher Darrell Porter drilled the first pitch offered by Giants reliever Bob Lacey over the right-field wall to give St. Louis an 8-4 victory in 11 innings. And on August 31 at Arlington, Tex., Rangers third baseman Buddy Bell capped a ninth-inning Texas rally with a two-out slam that gave the Rangers a 7-6 triumph over Milwaukee. Trailing 6-1 entering their half of the ninth, the Rangers pushed six runs across against Brewers relievers Jack Lazorko, Rick Waits and Pete Ladd.

Ladd was one of eight pitchers who allowed two grand slams. The others were Seattle's Dave Beard, Oakland's Chris Codiroli, California's Curt Kaufman and Mike Witt and Detroit's Jack Morris in the American League and San Francisco's Scott Garrelts and Montreal's Bob James in the National.

The top grand-slam hitter in 1984 was Oakland's Dave Kingman, The Sporting News A.L. Comeback Player of the Year who belted three in his first season with the A's. One of Kingman's slams came on April 16 against Seattle, a game in which he also hit two other homers and drove in eight runs.

The only team to hit two slams in the same game was Boston. Bill Buckner connected in the first inning and Tony Armas blasted his slam in the second, off Detroit's Morris in an August 7 game. It marked the 33rd time in major league history that one club hit two slams in the same game.

Seven players hit two grand slams in 1984. Wayne Gross, Eddie Murray and Ken Singleton of the Orioles, Buckner of the Red Sox, Alvin Davis of the Mariners, Greg Luzinski of the White Sox and Pittsburgh's Tony Pena connected twice. Luzinski's blows were delivered in consecutive games, June 8-9, against the

Oakland's Dave Kingman led the majors with three grand slams last season.

Minnesota Twins.

For the third straight season, Baltimore led all major league teams with eight grand slams. The National League team leader was Pittsburgh with five. Every major league club hit at least one grand slam and every pitching staff, except Philadelphia's and Pittsburgh's surrendered at least one.

Phillies lefthander Steve Carlton and Cardinals' righthander Joaquin Andujar were the only pitchers to hit grand slams in '84.

There were 77 grand slams last season, a record 51 coming off the bats of American League hitters. The 26 slams by National League hitters was a dozen fewer than in 1983.

The complete list of grand slams, with the inning in which each was hit in parentheses, follows:

AMERICAN LEAGUE (51)

APRIL—

15 —Downing, California vs. Codiroli, Oakland	(2)
16 —Kingman, Oakland vs. Young, Seattle	(1)
16 —Hrbek, Minnesota vs. Curtis, California	(6)
20 —Moseby, Toronto vs. Witt, California	(6)
28 —Pettis, California vs. Beard, Seattle	(7)
28 —Cruz, Chicago vs. Ojeda, Boston	(6)

Chicago White Sox slugger Greg Luzinski clubbed grand slams off Minnesota pitching on consecutive days, June 8-9.

MAY—
8	—Trammell, Detroit vs. Quisenberry, K.C.	(7)
11	—Parrish, Texas vs. Bannister, Chicago	(1)
18	—Thornton, Cleveland vs. Ladd, Milwaukee	(7)
19	—Sheridan, Kansas City vs. Hough, Texas	(4)
25	—Kingman, Oakland vs. Brown, New York	(8)
27	—Gross, Baltimore vs. Witt, California	(4)
28	—Re. Jackson, California vs. Rasmussen, N.Y.	(4)

JUNE—
8	—Luzinski, Chicago vs. Viola, Minnesota	(1)
9	—Luzinski, Chicago vs. Walters, Minnesota	(7)
17	—Roenicke, Baltimore vs. Rasmussen, New York	(8)
19	—Murray, Baltimore vs. Stanley, Boston	(8)
20	—Kingman, Oakland vs. Gubicza, Kansas City	(1)
23	—Davis, Seattle vs. Smith, Cleveland	(2)
23	—Hargrove, Cleveland vs. Nunez, Seattle	(4)

JULY—
1	—Castillo, Cleveland vs. McLaughlin, Texas	(4)
4	—Rice, Boston vs. Heimueller, Oakland	(10)
5	—Evans, Boston vs. Kison, California	(5)
7*	—Murray, Baltimore vs. Gura, Kansas City	(7)
16	—Winfield, New York vs. Noles, Texas	(1)
20	—Davis, Seattle vs. Jackson, Toronto	(9)
21	—Buckner, Boston vs. Kaufman, California	(6)
28	—Bush, Minnesota vs. Slaton, California	(5)

AUGUST—
3	—White, Kansas City vs. Wilcox, Detroit	(4)
7*	—Buckner, Boston vs. Morris, Detroit	(1)
7*	—Armas, Boston vs. Morris, Detroit	(2)
9	—Baines, Chicago vs. Rasmussen, N.Y.	(6)
12	—Carter, Cleveland vs. Guidry, N.Y.	(6)
16	—Slaught, Kansas City vs. Mason, Texas	(6)
21	—Parrish, Detroit vs. Sorensen, Oakland	(1)
26	—Lemon, Detroit vs. Kaufman, California	(3)
31	—Bell, Texas vs. Ladd, Milwaukee	(9)
31	—Presley, Seattle vs. Flanagan, Baltimore	(5)

SEPTEMBER—
1	—Singleton, Baltimore vs. Vande Berg, Seattle	(7)
2	—Franco, Cleveland vs. Johnson, Boston	(8)
3	—Young, Kansas City vs. Lopez, Detroit	(8)
14	—Butler, Cleveland vs. Codiroli, Oakland	(2)
15	—Yount, Milwaukee vs. Stewart, Baltimore	(6)
17	—Whitaker, Detroit vs. Lazorko, Milwaukee	(6)
17	—Gross, Baltimore vs. Niekro, New York	(5)

18	—Pagliarulo, N.Y. vs. D. Martinez, Baltimore	(2)
20	—Singleton, Baltimore vs. Nipper, Boston	(3)
21	—Brett, Kansas City vs. Leiper, Oakland	(7)
24†	—Motley, Kansas City vs. LaCorte, California	(6)
25	—Johnson, Detroit vs. Gibson, Milwaukee	(1)
25	—Tabler, Cleveland vs. Beard, Seattle	(5)

NATIONAL LEAGUE (26)

APRIL—
5	—Frobel, Pittsburgh vs. Hawkins, San Diego	(3)
10	—Esasky, Cincinnati vs. James, Montreal	(6)
10	—Summers, San Diego vs. Forsch, St. Louis	(5)
17	—Carter, Montreal vs. Darling, New York	(4)

MAY—
8	—Cey, Chicago vs. Garrelts, San Francisco	(3)
15	—Andujar, St. Louis vs. Dedmon, Atlanta	(8)
16	—Carlton, Philadelphia vs. Valenzuela, Los Ang.	(4)
18	—Pena, Pittsburgh vs. Garber, Atlanta	(8)

JUNE—
6	—Brenly, San Francisco vs. Falcone, Atlanta	(3)
13	—Marshall, Los Angeles vs. Garrelts, San Fran.	(3)
19	—Komminsk, Atlanta vs. Cornell, San Francisco..	(3)
21	—Yeager, Los Angeles vs. Owchinko, Cincinnati...	(7)
27	—C. Davis, San Francisco vs. Puleo, Cin.	(5)

JULY—
18	—Porter, St. Louis vs. Lacey, San Francisco	(11)
24	—Distefano, Pittsburgh vs. James, Montreal	(11)
29	—Templeton, San Diego vs. LaCoss, Houston	(6)

AUGUST—
5	—Moreland, Chicago vs. Grapenthin, Montreal	(3)
5	—Leonard, San Francisco vs. Moore, Atlanta	(9)
8	—Berra, Pittsburgh vs. Lahti, St. Louis	(6)
9	—Parker, Cincinnati vs. Lollar, San Diego	(2)
22	—Cruz, Houston vs. Ruthven, Chicago	(2)
26	—Chapman, New York vs. M. Davis, San Fran.	(6)
31	—L. Smith, St. Louis vs. Ryan, Houston	(1)

SEPTEMBER—
6	—Reynolds, Houston vs. Laskey, San Francisco	(1)
14	—Davis, Chicago vs. Gaff, New York	(6)
19	—Pena, Pittsburgh vs. Bordi, Chicago	(6)

*First game of doubleheader.
†Second game of doubleheader.

Raines Led Multi-Hit Parade

By RON SMITH

As the Chicago Cubs prepared to bat in the bottom of the sixth inning of a June 23 game at Wrigley Field, it was apparent that this day belonged to the St. Louis Cardinals and center fielder Willie McGee. McGee already had driven in five runs with a single, triple and home run and the Cardinals were coasting with a 9-3 lead.

Their only real concern was whether McGee could complete his first major league cycle with the necessary double. The answer turned out to be yes, but that accomplishment was shoved unceremoniously into the background.

The spotlight instead focused on Chicago second baseman Ryne Sandberg, who finished the day with five hits, two home runs and seven RBIs. Sandberg almost singlehandedly kept the Cubs in the game. In both the ninth and 10th innings, Cardinals relief ace Bruce Sutter had the lead and was one out from victory. Both times he was burned by Sandberg homers. A run in the bottom of the 11th finally ended the marathon and gave the Cubs an amazing come-from-behind 12-11 victory.

The dueling bats of McGee and Sandberg were but a small part of a crazy season. Sandberg's five-hit barrage was one of 23 such performances in 1984 and McGee's cycle was the third of four after a three-year-famine. When Baltimore shortstop Cal Ripken hit for the cycle on May 6 against Texas, he became the first major leaguer to accomplish the feat since Milwaukee's Charlie Moore did it on October 1, 1980. Others who hit for the cycle in 1984 were White Sox catcher Carlton Fisk and Boston's Dwight Evans.

It was only fitting that Don Mattingly and Dave Winfield, the Yankee clippers who battled to the last day of the season for the A.L. batting title, should lead the five-hit parade. Both reached the plateau three times.

Winfield, in fact, collected five hits in a June 3 game against Toronto, did it again two days later against Boston and capped a big month with a five-hit outburst against Detroit on June 25.

Mattingly, not to be outdone, collected five hits June 2 against the Blue Jays, came back again on June 12 against the Red Sox and capped his five-hit performances with an August 25 outburst against Seattle.

One National Leaguer made the list more than once. Chicago's Bob Dernier burned the Atlanta Braves for five hits on

The Chicago Cubs' Bob Dernier had two five-hit games against Atlanta in the same week.

May 24 and added insult to injury on May 30 when the Cubs and Braves hooked up again.

Mattingly and Winfield might have been the undisputed leaders in five-hit games, but they had to settle for second place on the multi-hit (four or more in one game) list. Chicago White Sox outfielder Harold Baines led the way with eight four-hit performances, while Mattingly, Winfield and Boston's Wade Boggs shared second place with seven apiece.

Minnesota rookie outfielder Kirby Puckett recorded his first four-hit performance on May 8 and it came in his first major league game. All four hits were singles.

Chicago's Tom Paciorek made the five-hit list, but he had a big advantage. Paciorek finished the May 8 game against Milwaukee with five hits in nine at-bats. The 25-inning marathon, won by the White Sox, 7-6, lasted eight hours and six minutes, the longest game in terms of time in major league history.

The longest hitting streaks of the season were recorded by Mets third baseman Hubie Brooks and Oakland third baseman Carney Lansford. Brooks' 24-game streak started on May 1 and ended exactly one month later on June 1. Lansford started his 24-game surge on July 27 and came up empty on August 22.

Twenty-six players compiled hitting streaks of 15 or more games in '84, with three of them performing the feat twice. Yankee Dave Winfield had streaks of 20 and 17 games, Detroit's Alan Trammell had streaks of 20 and 18 and the Chicago Cubs' Ryne Sandberg had streaks of 18 and 15.

Streaks of 15 or more games also were recorded by these major leaguers in 1984: 22 games—Eddie Murray, Orioles; 21 games—Ron Oester, Reds; 20 games— Mike Easler, Red Sox; 19 games—Tony Armas, Red Sox; 18 games—Chili Davis, Giants; Dwight Evans, Red Sox; Tony Pena, Pirates; Willie Wilson, Royals; 17 games—Henry Cotto, Cubs; Steve Garvey, Padres; 16 games—Julio Franco, Indians; Gary Gaetti, Twins; Butch Wynegar, Yankees; Marvell Wynne, Pirates; 15 games—Tom Brunansky, Twins; Jody Davis, Cubs; Bill Doran, Astros; Dan Gladden, Giants; Rudy Law, White Sox; Juan Samuel, Phillies; Mookie Wilson, Mets.

The complete list of players with four or more hits in one game follows:

AMERICAN LEAGUE: Baltimore (10)—Bumbry 2, Murray 2, Rayford 2, Ripken 2, Dauer, Shelby. Boston (20)— Boggs 7, Buckner 3, Easler 3, Rice 3, Armas 2, Barrett, Evans. California (12) —Beniquez 4, Lynn 4, Boone, Carew, Grich, Re. Jackson. Chicago (14)—Baines 8, Fisk, Kittle, R. Law, Luzinski, Paciorek, Walker. Cleveland (12)—Franco 3, Bernazard 2, Tabler 2, Thornton 2, Butler, Hall, Jacoby. Detroit (14)—Lemon 3, Whitaker 3, Evans 2, Trammell 2, Baker, Bergman, Gibson, Jones. Kansas City (10)—Concepcion 2, Motley 2, Slaught 2, Wilson 2, McRae, Orta. Milwaukee (9)— James 3, Gantner 2, Yount 2, Cooper, Lozado. Minnesota (17)—Hatcher 5, Puckett 3, Hrbek 2, Laudner 2, Teufel 2, Brunansky, Bush, David. New York (20)— Mattingly 7, Winfield 7, Harrah 2, Griffey, Kemp, Meacham, Randolph. Oakland (5) —Lansford 2, Henderson, Hill, Murphy. Seattle (8)—Bradley 3, Cowens 2, Kearney, Owen, Perconte. Texas (12)—O'Brien 3, Ward 3, Bell 2, Bannister, Sample, Scott, Wright. Toronto (11)—Barfield 3, C. Johnson 2, Collins, Fernandez, Garcia, Griffin, Iorg, Upshaw.

NATIONAL LEAGUE: Atlanta (11)— Ramirez 3, Murphy 2, Thompson 2, Benedict, Horner, Perry, Washington. Chicago (13)—Sandberg 4, Dernier 3, Matthews 2, Moreland 2, Cotto, Davis. Cincinnati (8)— Concepcion 2, Parker 2, Cedeno, Driessen, Foley, Oester. Houston (9)—Cruz 2, Doran 2, Walling 2, Garner, Puhl, Reynolds. Los Angeles (6)—Guerrero 5, Marshall. Montreal (6)—Raines 4, Gonzalez, Thomas. New York (9)—Foster 2, Hernandez 2, Brooks, Knight, Santana, Strawberry, Wilson. Philadelphia (19)—Stone 5, Hayes 3, Lefebvre 2, Maddox 2, Corcoran, DeJesus, Garcia, Gross, Samuel, Virgil, Wilson. Pittsburgh (14)—Lacy 4, Ray 3, Madlock 2, Morrison 2, Wynne 2, Berra. St. Louis (9)—Herr 2, McGee 2, Pendleton 2, Hendrick, L. Smith, Van Slyke. San Diego (8) —McReynolds 3, Gwynn, Martinez, Nettles, Salazar, Templeton. San Francisco (9)—C. Davis 3, Leonard 2, Brenly, LeMaster, Oliver, Richards.

The records of all players with five hits in a game follow:

Date	Player—Club—Opp.	Place	AB	R	H	2B	3B	HR	RBI	Result
April 22	Marshall, Dodgers vs. Padres	H	6	3	5	1	0	2	6	W 15-7
May 8	Paciorek, White Sox vs. Brewers (25 inn.)	H	9	1	5	0	0	0	3	W 7-6
May 24*	Dernier, Cubs vs. Braves	H	5	2	5	0	0	0	1	W 10-7
May 29	Beniquez, Angels vs. Yankees	H	5	2	5	0	0	0	0	W 6-5
May 30	Dernier, Cubs vs. Braves	A	5	3	5	0	0	0	1	W 6-2
June 2	Mattingly, Yankees vs. Blue Jays (10 inn.)	A	6	1	5	0	0	0	1	L 8-9
June 3	Winfield, Yankees vs. Blue Jays	A	6	3	5	0	0	0	2	W 15-2
June 5	Winfield, Yankees vs. Red Sox	H	5	1	5	1	0	0	1	L 4-5
June 12	Mattingly, Yankees vs. Red Sox	A	5	3	5	0	0	0	2	L 8-9
June 12	Guerrero, Dodgers vs. Giants	H	5	3	5	1	0	1	1	W 8-7
June 23	Sandberg, Cubs vs. Cardinals (11 innings)	H	6	2	5	0	0	2	7	W 12-11
June 25	Winfield, Yankees vs. Tigers	H	5	1	5	1	0	0	4	W 7-3
July 4	Rice, Red Sox vs. A's (10 innings)	H	6	3	5	0	0	1	6	W 13-9
July 6†	Doran, Astros vs. Expos	H	5	1	5	0	0	0	0	L 5-7
July 15	Madlock, Pirates vs. Giants	H	5	2	5	1	0	0	2	W 9-3
July 24	Ray, Pirates vs. Expos (11 innings)	A	6	2	5	0	0	0	0	W 12-5
Aug. 7	Leonard, Giants vs. Astros	A	5	1	5	0	0	0	3	W 9-2
Aug. 18	Murphy, Braves vs. Cardinals	A	5	4	5	3	0	0	0	W 8-3
Aug. 25	Mattingly, Yankees vs. Mariners	A	6	2	5	1	0	0	2	W 14-1
Sept. 5	McGee, Cardinals vs. Phillies	H	5	2	5	0	1	0	1	W 6-5
Sept. 5	McReynolds, Padres vs. Reds	H	5	2	5	0	0	0	1	W 15-11
Sept. 8	Thornton, Indians vs. A's	H	5	0	5	0	0	0	2	L 5-9
Sept. 21	Buckner, Red Sox vs. Orioles	A	5	1	5	0	0	0	3	W 8-0

*First game of doubleheader.
†Second game of doubleheader.

Cliff Johnson of Toronto set a big-league record with his 19th career pinch homer in 1984.

Perry, Sconiers Led in Pinch

By DAVE SLOAN

Gerald Perry of the Atlanta Braves was No. 2, so he tried harder.

In 1983, Perry finished second to Pittsburgh's Mike Easler in National League pinch-hitting. But in 1984, while Easler played regularly for the Boston Red Sox after an off-season trade, Perry collected eight pinch-hits in 16 at-bats to lead all N.L. pinch-hitters. Perry's .500 pinch-hitting average was second only to California's Daryl Sconiers, who collected six hits in the minimum 10 at-bats for a .600 average.

Though Easler did not have the opportunity to exhibit his pinch-hitting prowess in Boston (he had led the National League in pinch-hitting in both 1982 and '83 with the Pirates), his brother-in-law kept up family tradition by setting a major league record.

Cliff Johnson, a veteran first baseman-designated hitter with the Toronto Blue Jays, blasted his 19th career pinch homer off Baltimore's Tippy Martinez on August 5. That blow eclipsed the old mark of 18 held by Jerry Lynch, who played with the Pirates and Reds in the 1950s and '60s.

There were 89 pinch homers hit in the majors last season, four more than in 1983, when N.L. batters clubbed a record 55. Philadelphia's Len Matuszek and Detroit's John Grubb led the way with three apiece. Matuszek's Phillies led all clubs with 10 pinch homers while Grubb's Tigers, the eventual world champs, led baseball with a .312 team pinch-hitting average.

The Los Angeles Dodgers nailed Houston pitching for pinch homers on three consecutive days (June 1-3). Candy Maldonado, Steve Yeager and Rafael Landestoy did the honors.

Four players blasted pinch-hit grand slam homers in 1984. They were San Diego's Champ Summers (on April 10), Los Angeles' Yeager (on June 21), San Francisco's Chili Davis (on June 27) and Baltimore's Ken Singleton (on September 1).

Following is a list of all pinch-hitters with at least 10 at-bats in 1984:

NATIONAL LEAGUE PINCH-HITTING
(Compiled by Elias Sports Bureau)

Club Pinch-Hitting

Club	AB.	H.	HR.	RBI.	Pct.	Club	AB.	H.	HR.	RBI.	Pct.
Houston	243	65	2	33	.267	Montreal	248	56	1	22	.226
New York	238	61	2	25	.256	San Diego	183	40	4	33	.219
Atlanta	196	49	1	38	.250	Pittsburgh	165	35	3	18	.212
St. Louis	210	52	2	43	.248	San Francisco	264	55	2	42	.208
Philadelphia	288	68	10	58	.236	Cincinnati	253	47	4	18	.186
Chicago	219	51	5	31	.233	Los Angeles	294	54	6	38	.184
						Totals	2801	633	42	399	.226

Individual Pinch-Hitting
(10 or More At-Bats)

Player-Club	AB.	H.	HR.	RBI.	Pct.	Player-Club	AB.	H.	HR.	RBI.	Pct.
Perry, Atlanta	16	8	0	4	.500	Wockenfuss, Phila.	27	6	0	5	.222
Matuszek, Phila.	24	10	3	10	.417	Heep, New York	38	8	0	0	.211
C. Davis, S. Fran.	15	6	1	9	.400	Richards, San Fran.	48	10	0	0	.208
Knight, Hou.-N.Y.	10	4	0	0	.400	Watson, Atlanta	29	6	0	7	.207
Komminsk, Atlanta.	10	4	1	2	.400	Wohlford, Montreal	39	8	0	3	.205
Nicosia, San Fran.	10	4	0	4	.400	Krenchicki, Cin.	36	7	0	1	.194
Landrum, St. Louis..	23	9	2	12	.391	Summers, S. Diego...	36	7	1	10	.194
Foley, Cincinnati	13	5	1	1	.385	Stenhouse, Montreal	26	5	0	2	.192
Hall, Atlanta	13	5	0	0	.385	Kuiper, San Fran.	47	9	0	8	.191
Mumphrey, Hous.	13	5	0	2	.385	Mazzilli, Pitts.	32	6	1	4	.188
Reynolds, Los Ang.	13	5	0	5	.385	Aguayo, Phila.	16	3	1	1	.188
Brown, San Diego	24	9	0	10	.375	Landreaux, L.A.	16	3	0	2	.188
Van Slyke, St. Louis	11	4	0	3	.364	Speier, Mon.-St.L.	16	3	0	0	.188
Chapman, N.Y.	14	5	0	1	.357	Stubbs, Los Ang.	22	4	0	1	.182
Page, Pittsburgh	12	4	0	0	.333	Harper, Pitts.	11	2	1	2	.182
Hebner, Chicago	26	8	1	4	.308	Porter, St. Louis	11	2	0	1	.182
Venable, Montreal	13	4	1	3	.308	Frobel, Pitts.	17	3	0	1	.176
W. Johnson, Mont.	10	3	0	2	.300	Monday, Los Ang.	17	3	1	4	.176
Redus, Cincinnati	10	3	0	1	.300	Flannery, S. Diego	40	7	0	0	.175
Bass, Houston	44	13	0	6	.295	Chambliss, Atlanta..	24	4	0	6	.167
Cabell, Houston	17	5	1	4	.294	Landestoy, Los Ang.	18	3	1	1	.167
Maldonado, L.A.	31	9	2	5	.290	May, Pittsburgh	18	3	0	1	.167
Perez, Cincinnati	38	11	1	8	.289	Harper, Atlanta	12	2	0	2	.167
Howe, St. Louis	21	6	0	2	.286	Hayes, Philadelphia	12	2	2	3	.167
Salazar, San Diego	14	4	0	0	.286	Washington, Atl.	12	2	0	3	.167
Walker, Cincinnati..	14	4	1	1	.286	Thompson, S.F.	31	5	0	5	.161
Braun, St. Louis	60	17	0	12	.283	Morales, Los Ang.	19	3	0	0	.158
G. Gross, Phila.	46	13	0	9	.283	Rohn, Chicago	13	2	1	2	.154
Whitfield, Los Ang.	29	8	0	5	.276	Gulden, Cincinnati	20	3	0	2	.150
Staub, New York	66	18	1	18	.273	Cedeno, Cincinnati	14	2	1	2	.143
Backman, N.Y.	11	3	0	0	.273	Distefano, Pitts.	14	2	1	3	.143
Corcoran, Phila.	37	10	0	10	.270	Milner, Cincinnati	14	2	0	0	.143
Walling, Houston	26	7	0	6	.269	Moreland, Chicago...	15	2	0	4	.133
Richardt, Houston	15	4	0	2	.267	Martin, New York	24	3	0	0	.125
Jorgensen, Atl.-St.L.	38	10	0	8	.263	Wilson, Phila.	19	2	0	2	.105
Scott, Hou.-Mont.	38	10	0	3	.263	Householder, Ci.-SL.	10	1	0	0	.100
Bosley, Chicago	23	6	1	5	.261	Ortiz, New York	10	1	0	0	.100
Rose, Mont.-Cin.	27	7	0	5	.259	Spilman, Houston	10	1	0	0	.100
Johnstone, Chi.	39	10	0	2	.256	Tolman, Houston	10	1	0	0	.100
Garner, Houston	24	6	0	3	.250	Amelung, Los Ang.	11	1	0	0	.091
Hodges, New York	24	6	1	4	.250	Bream, Los Ang.	11	1	0	3	.091
Linares, Atlanta	20	5	0	8	.250	Concepcion, Cin.	13	1	0	0	.077
Oliver, S.F.-Phil.	16	4	0	2	.250	Melendez, Phila.	13	1	0	0	.077
Buckner, Chicago	12	3	0	0	.250	Morrison, Pitts.	13	1	0	1	.077
Dilone, Montreal	37	9	0	3	.243	Vail, Los Angeles	13	1	0	2	.077
Yeager, Los Ang.	17	4	2	7	.235	Rabb, San Fran.	28	2	0	0	.071
Baker, San Fran.	30	7	1	10	.233	Brewer, Los Ang.	14	1	0	0	.071
Bevacqua, S. Diego..	30	7	1	7	.233	Royster, Atlanta	15	1	0	0	.067
Cotto, Chicago	13	3	0	1	.231	Barnes, Cincinnati	16	1	0	0	.063
Johnson, Atlanta	13	3	0	1	.231	Driessen, Cin.-Mont.	17	1	0	2	.059
Nettles, S. Diego	13	3	1	5	.231	Esasky, Cincinnati..	12	0	0	0	.000
Woods, Chicago	31	7	0	3	.226	Thomas, Montreal	12	0	0	0	.000
Pankovits, Houston.	40	9	1	8	.225	Maddox, Phila.	14	0	0	1	.000
Lezcano, Phila.	27	6	1	5	.222						

AMERICAN LEAGUE PINCH-HITTING
(Compiled by Sports Information Center)

Club Pinch-Hitting

Club	AB.	H.	HR.	RBI.	Pct.	Club	AB.	H.	HR.	RBI.	Pct.
Detroit	186	58	6	42	.312	New York	104	25	2	17	.240
Toronto	215	61	6	39	.284	Minnesota	122	27	1	15	.221
California	129	35	3	17	.271	Texas	156	34	2	27	.218
Boston	106	28	3	24	.264	Seattle	124	27	1	19	.218
Kansas City	118	31	2	20	.263	Milwaukee	89	18	0	11	.202
Chicago	209	54	9	29	.258	Oakland	156	28	3	17	.179
Baltimore	215	55	8	40	.256	Cleveland	142	25	1	21	.176
						Totals	2071	506	47	338	.244

Individual Pinch-Hitting
(10 or More At-Bats)

Player-Club	AB.	H.	HR.	RBI.	Pct.	Player-Club	AB.	H.	HR.	RBI.	Pct.
Sconiers, Calif.	10	6	1	3	.600	Foley, Texas	28	7	0	6	.250
R. Law, Chicago	11	5	1	2	.455	Nichols, Boston	20	5	1	8	.250
Collins, Toronto	14	6	0	2	.429	Meyer, Oakland	16	4	0	0	.250
Iorg, Kansas City	12	5	1	4	.417	Narron, Calif.	29	7	2	6	.241
Kuntz, Detroit	12	5	0	0	.417	McRae, Kansas City	21	5	0	2	.238
Barfield, Toronto	20	8	1	5	.400	Roenicke, Balt.	21	5	0	2	.238
Bush, Minnesota	20	8	1	7	.400	Lowenstein, Balt.	26	6	0	3	.231
Jones, Detroit	15	6	1	4	.400	Roberts, Kan. City	13	3	0	1	.231
Paciorek, Chicago	18	7	1	2	.389	Bannister, Texas	14	3	0	2	.214
Grubb, Detroit	22	8	3	6	.364	Brown, Calif.	14	3	0	2	.214
Leach, Toronto	22	8	0	4	.364	Jones, Texas	24	5	1	7	.208
Bochte, Oakland	11	4	1	4	.364	Aikens, Toronto	15	3	1	3	.200
Christmas, Chicago	11	4	1	4	.364	Almon, Oakland	15	3	1	2	.200
Sample, Texas	11	4	0	2	.364	Baylor, New York	10	2	0	1	.200
Cruz, Baltimore	14	5	1	2	.357	Dunbar, Texas	10	2	0	1	.200
Milbourne, Seattle	23	8	0	1	.348	Sanchez, K.C.-Balt.	10	2	0	3	.200
Mulliniks, Toronto	18	6	0	2	.333	Walker, Chicago	16	3	0	1	.188
Gedman, Boston	15	5	2	5	.333	Hancock, Oakland	33	6	0	5	.182
Carew, California	12	4	0	1	.333	Bando, Cleveland	11	2	1	4	.182
Shelby, Baltimore	12	4	1	1	.333	Harrah, New York	11	2	0	3	.182
Johnson, Toronto	34	11	1	8	.324	James, Milwaukee	17	3	0	1	.176
Garbey, Detroit	25	8	0	9	.320	Castillo, Cleve.	18	3	0	4	.167
Whitt, Toronto	16	5	1	4	.313	Evans, Detroit	18	3	0	2	.167
Ayala, Baltimore	29	9	2	9	.310	Bumbry, Baltimore	12	2	0	2	.167
Gross, Baltimore	13	4	0	2	.308	Morgan, Oakland	12	2	0	2	.167
Kittle, Chicago	13	4	2	7	.308	Washington, Minn.	12	2	0	0	.167
Orta, Kansas City	13	4	0	3	.308	Iorg, Toronto	25	4	0	1	.160
Hairston, Chicago	59	18	2	5	.305	Putnam, Sea.-Minn.	25	4	0	2	.160
Beniquez, Calif.	10	3	0	1	.300	Stein, Texas	13	2	0	2	.154
Hall, Cleveland	10	3	0	2	.300	Vukovich, Cleve.	13	2	0	0	.154
Oglivie, Milw.	10	3	0	4	.300	Perkins, Cleveland	41	6	0	4	.146
Herndon, Detroit	24	7	1	6	.292	Squires, Chicago	22	3	0	1	.136
Brown, Minnesota	35	10	0	4	.286	David, Minnesota	15	2	0	0	.133
Bergman, Detroit	21	6	1	5	.286	Phelps, Seattle	15	2	1	2	.133
Smalley, N.Y.-Chi.	21	6	1	5	.286	Howell, Milwaukee	16	2	0	2	.125
Griffey, New York	18	5	0	2	.278	Burroughs, Oakland	33	4	1	3	.121
Wilfong, Calif.	18	5	0	2	.278	Singleton, Balt.	17	2	1	5	.118
Luzinski, Chicago	11	3	1	2	.273	Heath, Oakland	10	1	0	0	.100
Manning, Milw.	11	3	0	0	.273	Fisk, Chicago	11	1	1	1	.091
S. Henderson, Sea.	15	4	0	4	.267	Gibson, Detroit	11	1	0	1	.091
Nolan, Baltimore	15	4	1	3	.267	Hargrove, Cleve.	12	1	0	2	.083
Miller, Boston	53	14	0	8	.264	Willard, Cleveland	12	1	0	1	.083
Dwyer, Baltimore	27	7	1	5	.259	Gamble, New York	13	1	1	3	.077
Rivers, Texas	31	8	1	5	.258	Martinez, Toronto	18	1	0	2	.056

PINCH-HOMERS FOR 1984

NATIONAL LEAGUE: Atlanta (1)—Kominsk. Chicago (5)—Bosley, Davis, Hassey, Hebner, Rohn. Cincinnati (4)—Cedeno, Foley, Perez, Walker. Houston (2)—Cabell, Pankovits. Los Angeles (6)—Maldonado 2, Yeager 2, Landestoy, Monday. Montreal (1)—Venable. New York (2)—Hodges, Staub. Philadelphia (10)—Matuszek 3, Hayes 2, Aguayo, Lezcano, Russell, Schmidt, Virgil. Pittsburgh (3)—Distefano, Harper, Mazzilli. St. Louis (2)—Landrum 2. San Diego (4)—Bevacqua, McReynolds, Nettles, Summers. San Francisco (2)—Baker, C. Davis.

AMERICAN LEAGUE: Baltimore (8)—Ayala 2, Cruz, Dwyer, Nolan, Shelby, Singleton, Young. Boston (3)—Gedman 2, Nichols. California (3)—Narron 2, Sconiers. Chicago (9)—Hairston 2, Kittle 2, Christmas, Fisk, R. Law, Luzinski, Paciorek. Cleveland (1)—Bando. Detroit (6)—Grubb 3, Bergman, Herndon, Jones. Kansas City (2)—Biancalana, Iorg. Milwaukee (0). Minnesota (1)—Bush. New York (2)—Gamble, Smalley. Oakland (3)—Almon, Bochte, Burroughs. Seattle (1)—Phelps. Texas (2)—Jones, Rivers. Toronto (6)—Aikens, Barfield, Bell, Gruber, Johnson, Whitt.

Gooden, Davis Ace Debuts

By DAVE SLOAN

How well a player performs in his major league debut is not necessarily a good barometer for how his rookie season will unfold. Many players have made poor debuts and gone on to big rookie campaigns. Conversely, some players have started out with a bang only to suffer through unspectacular first years.

Baseball's top 1984 rookies, New York's Dwight Gooden in the National League and Seattle's Alvin Davis in the American, proved they were ready for the bigtime in their opening games.

Gooden, a fireballing 19-year-old right-hander who struck out 300 batters in 191 innings at Class A Lynchburg (Carolina) in 1983, started his major league career with a 3-2 win at Houston on April 7. Gooden went five innings, gave up three hits and one run and struck out five. It was a solid, if not spectacular, debut that set the stage for things to come. Gooden kept up his amazing one-strikeout-per-inning ratio for the entire '84 season, finishing the year with a major league-leading 276 strikeouts in 218 innings pitched. His 17-9 record in 31 starting assignments helped make the Mets a contender in the N.L. Eastern Division for the first time in more than a decade.

Davis' Mariners didn't fare nearly so well during the '84 season, but the rookie first baseman wasn't to blame. Davis finished the year with 27 homers, 116 RBIs and a .284 batting average. He, too, gave an indication of what was to come by slugging a three-run, game-winning homer off Boston's Dennis Eckersley in his first game on April 11. The Arizona State product cracked another home run in his second game two nights later.

Two Minnesota Twins outfielders enjoyed memorable debuts. Kirby Puckett, selected third in the country in the 1982 free-agent draft, opened with a 4-for-5 performance May 8 against the California Angels. No slouch defensively, either, Puckett went on to lead American League outfielders with 16 assists.

Andre David, who toiled in the Minnesota farm system the previous four seasons, got a shot at big-league ball on June 29 at Detroit against the eventual world champions. In the second inning with a man on base, David slugged a homer off Jack Morris in his first big-league at-bat. That blow helped the Twins defeat the Tigers, 5-3, in the first game of a twi-night doubleheader and hand Morris, baseball's

Seattle's Alvin Davis slugged a game-winning homer in his major-league debut.

hottest pitcher at the time, only his fourth defeat in 16 decisions.

Davis and David were the only 1984 players to homer in their first games.

Of the 131 players who broke into the majors last season, 59 were pitchers. Nine won their debut game, with St. Louis' Kurt Kepshire and Cincinnati's Tom Browning coming up with the best performances. Each pitcher went 8⅓ innings, gave up one earned run and recorded a 5-1 victory. Kepshire's effort came on July 4 in the second game on a doubleheader against San Francisco while Browning's first win came on September 9 against Los Angeles. Kepshire gave up eight hits, Browning 11.

Two pitchers had debuts they would just as soon forget. Atlanta's Mike Payne was touched for six hits and four earned runs in just 2⅔ innings on August 22 against Pittsburgh. Cleveland's Jose Roman gave up four hits and five earned runs in 3⅓ innings against California on September 5. Both starters finished their debuts with an 0-1 record and 13.50 ERA.

An alphabetical list of the players who made their debuts in '84 follows:

Minnesota's Kirby Puckett singled four times in his May 8 debut against California.

Player	Pos.	Club	Date and Place of Birth	Debut
Amelung, Edward Allen	OF	Los Angeles	4-13-59—Fullerton, Calif.	7-28
Bailey, John Mark	C	Houston	11- 4-61—Springfield, Mo.	4-27
Baker, Douglas Lee	SS	Detroit	4- 3-61—Fullerton, Calif.	7- 2
Barkley, Jeffrey Carver	P	Cleveland	11-21-59—Hickory, N.C.	9-16
Beane, William Lamar	PH-OF	New York N.L.	3-29-62—Orlando, Fla.	9-13
Bettendorf, Jeffrey Allen	P	Oakland	12-10-61—Lompoc, Calif.	4- 8
Bielecki, Michael Joseph	P	Pittsburgh	7-31-59—Baltimore, Md.	9-14
Boston, Daryl Lamont	OF	Chicago A.L.	1- 4-63—Cincinnati, O.	5-13
Bradley, Scott William	C	New York A.L.	3-22-60—Essex Falls, N.J.	9- 9
Brewer, Anthony Bruce	PH-OF	Los Angeles	11-25-57—Coushatta, La.	8- 1
Brown, John Christopher	3B	San Francisco	8-15-61—Jackson, Miss.	9- 3
Brown, Mark Anthony	P	Baltimore	7-13-59—Bellows Falls, Vt.	8- 9
Browning, Thomas Leo	P	Cincinnati	4-28-60—Casper, Wyo.	9- 9
Buckley, Kevin John	PH	Texas	1-16-59—Quincy, Mass.	9- 4
Calderon, Ivan	OF	Seattle	3-19-62—Fajardo, P.R.	8-10
Calhoun, Jeffrey Wilton	P	Houston	4-11-58—LaGrange, Ga.	9- 2
Christensen, John L.	PH-OF	New York N.L.	9- 5-60—Downey, Calif.	9-13
Christiansen, Clay C.	P	New York A.L.	6-28-58—Wichita, Kan.	5-10
Clemens, William Roger	P	Boston	8- 4-62—Dayton, O.	5-15
Cliburn, Stewart Walker	P	California	12-19-56—Jackson, Miss.	9-17
Comstock, Keith Martin	P	Minnesota	12-23-55—San Francisco, Calif.	4- 3
Cornell, Jeffery Ray	P	San Francisco	2-10-57—Kansas City, Mo.	6- 2
Cotto, Henry	OF	Chicago N.L.	1- 5-61—New York, N.Y.	4- 5
David, Andre Anter	OF	Minnesota	5-18-58—Hollywood, Calif.	6-29
Davis, Alvin Glenn	1B	Seattle	9- 9-60—Riverside, Calif.	4-11
Davis, Eric Keith	PH	Cincinnati	5-29-62—Los Angeles, Calif.	5-19
Davis, Glenn Earl	1B	Houston	3-28-61—Jacksonville, Fla.	9- 2
Deer, Robert George	PH	San Francisco	9-29-60—Orange, Calif.	9- 4
Deshaies, James Joseph	P	New York A.L.	6-23-60—Massena, N.Y.	8- 7
Distefano, Benito James	OF	Pittsburgh	1-23-62—Brooklyn, N.Y.	5-18
Dixon, Kenneth John	P	Baltimore	10-17-60—Monroe, Va.	9-22
Earl, William Scott	PR-2B	Detroit	9-18-60—Seymour, Ind.	9-10
Fallon, Robert Joseph	P	Chicago A.L.	2-18-60—New York, N.Y.	4-26
Farr, Steven Michael	P	Cleveland	12-12-56—Cheverly, Md.	5-16
Franco, John Anthony	P	Cincinnati	9-17-60—Brooklyn, N.Y.	4-24
Garbey, Barbaro	PH-1B	Detroit	12- 4-56—Santiago, Cuba	4- 3
Gardner, Wesley Brian	P	New York N.L.	4-29-61—Benton, Ark.	7-29
Gibbons, John Michael	C	New York N.L.	6- 8-62—Great Falls, Mont.	4-11
Gomez, Randall Scott	C	San Francisco	2- 4-58—San Mateo, Calif.	8-21
Gonzales, Rene Adrian	SS	Montreal	9-23-61—Austin, Tex.	7-27
Gonzalez, Denio Mariano	3B	Pittsburgh	7-22-63—S. Grande Boya, D.R.	8- 6
Gonzalez, Jose Alta	SS	St. Louis	1-21-59—San Cristobal, D.R.	9-13
Gooden, Dwight Eugene	P	New York N.L.	11-16-64—Tampa, Fla.	4- 7
Grant, Mark Andrew	P	San Francisco	10-24-63—Aurora, Ill.	4-27
Green, Christopher DeWayne	P	Pittsburgh	9- 5-61—Los Angeles, Calif.	4-17
Gruber, Kelly Wayne	3B	Toronto	2-26-62—Bellaire, Tex.	4-20
Gubicza, Mark Steven	P	Kansas City	8-14-62—Philadelphia, Pa.	4- 6
Guetterman, Arthur Lee	P	Seattle	11-22-58—Chattanooga, Tenn.	9-12
Hart, Michael Lawrence	OF	Minnesota	2-17-58—Milwaukee, Wis.	5- 8
Hatcher, William Augustus	PH	Chicago N.L.	10- 4-60—Williams, Ariz.	9-10
Henry, Dwayne Allen	P	Texas	2-16-62—Elkton, Md.	9- 7

Player	Pos.	Club	Date and Place of Birth	Debut
Hernandez, Tobias, Rafael	PR-C	Toronto	11-30-58—Barquismento, Venez.	6-22
Hesketh, Joseph Thomas	P	Montreal	2-15-59—Lackawanna, N.Y.	8- 7
Hodge, Ed Oliver	P	Minnesota	4-19-58—Bellflower, Calif.	5- 1
Horton, Ricky Neal	P	St. Louis	7-30-59—Poughkeepsie, N.Y.	4- 7
Howell, Kenneth	P	Los Angeles	11-28-60—Detroit, Mich.	6-25
Hudler, Rex Allen	PR-2B	New York A.L.	9- 2-60—Tempe, Ariz.	9- 9
Javier, Stanley Julian	OF	New York A.L.	1- 9-65—S.F. Macoris, D.R.	4-15
Jones, Ross A.	PH	New York N.L.	1-14-60—Miami, Fla.	4- 2
Kepshire, Kurt David	P	St. Louis	7- 3-59—Bridgeport, Conn.	7- 4
Key, James Edward	P	Toronto	4-22-61—Huntsville, Ala.	4- 6
Keifer, Steven George	SS	Oakland	10-18-60—Chicago, Ill.	9- 3
Krawczyk, Raymond Allen	P	Pittsburgh	10- 9-59—Pittsburgh, Pa.	6-29
Kunkel, Jeffrey William	SS	Texas	3-25-63—West Palm Beach, Fla.	7-23
Langston, Mark Edward	P	Seattle	8-20-60—San Diego, Calif.	4- 7
Lavalliere, Michael E.	C	Philadelphia	8-18-60—Charlotte, N.C.	9- 9
Lazorko, Jack Thomas	P	Milwaukee	3-30-56—Hoboken, N.J.	6- 4
Leeper, David Dale	PH	Kansas City	10-30-59—Santa Ana, Calif.	9-10
Leiper, David Paul	P	Oakland	6-18-62—Whittier, Calif.	9- 2
Loman, Douglas Edward	OF	Milwaukee	5- 5-58—Bakersfield, Calif.	9- 3
Lowry, Dwight	C	Detroit	10-23-57—Robeson County, N.C.	4- 3
Lozado, William	PH-SS	Milwaukee	5-12-59—Brooklyn, N.Y.	7-16
Mason, Roger LeRoy	P	Detroit	9-18-58—Bellaire, Mich.	9- 4
Mata, Victor Jose	OF	New York A.L.	6-17-61—Santiago, D.R.	7-22
Meier, David Keith	PH	Minnesota	8- 8-59—Helena, Mont.	4- 3
Melendez, Francisco Javier	PH	Philadelphia	1-25-64—Rio Piedras, P.R.	8-26
Meridith, Ronald Knox	P	Chicago N.L.	11-26-55—San Pedro, Calif.	9-16
Miller, Darrell Keith	PR-OF	California	2-26-59—Washington, D.C.	8-14
Miller, Lemmie Earl	OF	Los Angeles	6- 2-60—Dallas, Tex.	5-22
Mitchell, Charles Ross	P	Boston	6-24-62—Dickson, Tenn.	8- 9
Mitchell, Kevin Darrell	PH	New York N.L.	1-13-62—San Diego, Calif.	9- 4
Moronko, Jeffrey Robert	3B	Cleveland	8-17-59—Houston, Tex.	9- 1
Nieto, Thomas Andrew	C	St. Louis	10-27-60—Downey, Calif.	5-10
Noboa, Milciades Arturo	2B	Cleveland	11-10-64—Santo Domingo, D.R.	8-22
O'Neal, Randall Jeffrey	P	Detroit	8-30-60—Ashland, Ky.	9-12
Pagliarulo, Michael Timothy	3B	New York A.L.	3-15-60—Medford, Mass.	7- 7
Pankovits, James Franklin	PH	Houston	8- 6-55—Pennington Gap, Va.	5-27
Payne, Michael Earl	P	Atlanta	11-15-61—Woonsocket, R.I.	8-22
Pendleton, Terry Lee	3B	St. Louis	7-16-60—Los Angeles, Calif.	7-18
Presley, James Arthur	3B	Seattle	10-23-61—Pensacola, Fla.	6-24
Puckett, Kirby	OF	Minnesota	3-14-61—Chicago, Ill.	5- 8
Reed, Jeffrey Scott	C	Minnesota	11-12-62—Joliet, Ill.	4- 5
Rijo, Jose Antonio	P	New York A.L.	5-13-65—San Cristobal, D.R.	4- 5
Robinson, Jeffrey Daniel	P	San Francisco	12-13-60—Santa Ana, Calif.	4- 7
Robinson, Ronald Dean	P	Cincinnati	3-24-62—Exeter, Calif.	8-14
Rodriguez, Victor M.	PR	Baltimore	7-14-61—New York, N.Y.	9- 5
Roman, Jose	P	Cleveland	5-21-63—Santo Domingo, D.R.	9- 5
Romanick, Ronald James	P	California	11- 6-60—Burley, Ida.	4- 5
Romero, Ramon	P	Cleveland	1-22-59—S.P. de Macoris, D.R.	9-18
Rowdon, Wade Lee	PR	Cincinnati	9- 7-60—Riverhead, N.Y.	9- 8
Russell, John William	OF	Philadelphia	1- 5-61—Oklahoma City, Okla.	6-22
Saberhagen, Bret William	P	Kansas City	4-13-64—Chicago Heights, Ill.	4- 4
St. Claire, Randy Anthony	P	Montreal	8-23-60—Glens Falls, N.Y.	9-11
Salas, Mark Bruce	PH	St. Louis	3- 8-61—Montebello, Calif.	6-19
Schiraldi, Calvin Drew	P	New York N.L.	6-16-62—Houston, Tex.	9- 1
Schu, Richard Spencer	3B	Philadelphia	1-26-62—Philadelphia, Pa.	9- 1
Scranton, James Dean	SS	Kansas City	4- 5-60—Torrance, Calif.	9- 5
Sheets, Larry Kent	OF	Baltimore	12- 6-59—Staunton, Va.	9-18
Shepherd, Ronald Wayne	PR	Toronto	10-27-60—Longview, Tex.	9- 5
Simmons, Nelson Bernard	OF	Detroit	6-27-63—Washington, D.C.	9- 4
Smith, David Wayne	P	California	8-30-57—Tomball, Tex.	9-18
Smith, Leroy Purdy	P	Cleveland	9- 6-61—Mt. Vernon, N.Y.	6-23
Smith, Michael Anthony	P	Cincinnati	2-23-61—Jackson, Miss.	4- 6
Smith, Patrick Keith	SS	New York A.L.	10-20-61—Los Angeles, Calif.	4-12
Smith, Zane William	P	Atlanta	12-28-60—Madison, Wis.	9-10
Snell, Nathaniel	P	Baltimore	9- 2-55—Orangeburg, S.C.	9-20
Stubbs, Franklin Lee	1B	Los Angeles	10-21-60—Laurinburg, N.C.	4-28
Tartabull, Danilo	PR	Seattle	10-30-62—San Juan, P.R.	9- 7
Tettleton, Mickey Lee	C	Oakland	9-16-60—Oklahoma City, Okla.	6-30
Thompson, Milton B.	PH-OF	Atlanta	1- 5-59—Washington, D.C.	9- 4
Tibbs, Jay Lindsey	P	Cincinnati	1- 4-62—Birmingham, Ala.	7-15
Toliver, Freddie Lee	P	Cincinnati	2- 3-61—Natchez, Miss.	9-15
Traber, James Joseph	DH	Baltimore	12-26-61—Columbus, O.	9-21
Valle, David	C	Seattle	10-30-60—Bayside, N.Y.	9- 7
Waddell, Thomas David	P	Cleveland	9-17-58—Dundee, Scotland	4-15
Wardle, Curtis Ray	P	Minnesota	11-16-60—Downey, Calif.	8-30
Willard, Gerald Duane	C	Cleveland	3-14-60—Oxnard, Calif.	4-11
Williams, Frank Lee	P	San Francisco	2-13-58—Seattle, Wash.	4- 5
Willis, Carl Blake	P	Detroit	12-28-60—Danville, Va.	6- 9
Winningham, Herman S.	OF	New York N.L.	12- 1-61—Orangeburg, S.C.	9- 1
Zaske, Lloyd Jeffrey	P	Pittsburgh	10- 6-60—Seattle, Wash.	7-21

Homers by Parks for 1984

National League

	At Atl.	At Chi.	At Cin.	At Hou.	At L.A.	At Mont.	At N.Y.	At Phil.	At Pitt.	At St.L.	At S.D.	At S.F.	Totals 1984	1983
Atlanta...............	53	3	11	10	5	2	2	3	2	4	9	7	111	130
Chicago.............	5	86	8	1	2	2	4	9	4	2	3	10	136	140
Cincinnati..........	10	2	58	3	1	6	6	3	1	2	9	5	106	107
Houston	11	7	9	18	3	5	3	5	4	4	1	9	79	97
Los Angeles........	12	4	6	0	49	5	5	2	4	0	9	6	102	146
Montreal............	7	8	3	3	2	45	5	3	2	5	6	7	96	102
New York..........	6	5	4	3	2	6	56	7	4	7	2	5	107	112
Philadelphia	2	12	8	4	5	5	4	79	9	4	11	4	147	125
Pittsburgh.........	4	15	4	1	1	5	3	4	48	8	2	3	98	121
St. Louis............	1	3	7	0	5	7	5	3	8	29	3	4	75	83
San Diego	6	4	7	4	7	5	3	3	3	4	60	3	109	93
San Francisco....	8	7	6	0	7	8	7	3	3	2	6	55	112	142
1984 Totals	125	156	131	47	89	101	103	124	92	71	121	118	1278	....
1983 Totals	137	140	116	54	123	96	116	122	123	96	135	140	....	1398

AT ATLANTA (125): Atlanta (53)—Murphy 18, Washington 12, Chambliss 6, Hubbard 3, Komminsk 3, Perry 3, Benedict 2, Johnson, Linares, Oberkfell, Ramirez, Trevino, Watson. Chicago (5)—Cey 2, Bosley, Durham, Sandberg. Cincinnati (10)—Walker 2, Concepcion, Driessen, Esasky, Foley, Gulden, Krenchicki, Lawless, Parker. Houston (11)—Bailey 2, Cruz 2, Reynolds 2, Bass, Cabell, Mumphrey, Puhl, Walling. Los Angeles (12)—Brock 4, Guerrero 2, Landreaux, Maldonado, Marshall, Reynolds, Scioscia, Stubbs. Montreal (7)—Wallach 3, Raines 2, Dawson, Palmer. New York (6)—Strawberry 2, Brooks, Foster, Hernandez, Hodges. Philadelphia (2)—Schmidt 2. Pittsburgh (4)—Berra, Frobel, Pena, Thompson. St. Louis (1)—L. Smith. San Diego (6)—Nettles 3, Bochy, McReynolds, Miller. San Francisco (8)—Brenly 4, C. Davis 2, LeMaster, Leonard.

AT CHICAGO (156): Atlanta (3)—Horner, Hubbard, Komminsk. Chicago (86)—Durham 19, Davis 13, Moreland 13, Cey 12, Sandberg 11, Matthews 8, Hall 3, Dernier 2, Woods 2, Hassey, Hebner, Lake. Cincinnati (2)—Milner, Oester. Houston (7)—Cruz 2, Mumphrey 2, Cabell, Doran, Garner. Los Angeles (4)—Marshall 2, Rivera, Stubbs. Montreal (8)—Dawson 3, Wallach 3, Carter, Roy Johnson. New York (5)—Foster 2, Brooks, Hernandez, Strawberry. Philadelphia (12)—Hayes 3, Corcoran 2, Samuel 2, Virgil 2, Lefebvre, Matuszek, Schmidt. Pittsburgh (15)—Thompson 5, Frobel 2, Madlock 2, Morrison 2, Lacy, Mazzilli, Pena, Ray. St. Louis (3)—Brummer, Green, McGee. San Diego (4)—Brown, Garvey, Martinez, McReynolds. San Francisco (7)—Brenly 2, Clark 2, C. Davis, Trillo, Youngblood.

AT CINCINNATI (131): Atlanta (11)—Hubbard 2, Murphy 2, Washington 2, Benedict, Chambliss, Johnson, Komminsk, Thompson. Chicago (8)—Cey 3, Davis 2, Durham 2, Bosley. Cincinnati (58)—Parker 10, Walker 6, Cedeno 5, Esasky 5, Milner 5, Redus 4, Concepcion 3, Davis 3, Driessen 3, Bilardello 2, Foley 2, Gulden 2, Krenchicki 2, Oester 2, Perez 2, Barnes, Soto. Houston (9)—Puhl 3, Ashby 2, Cruz, Knight, Mumphrey, Pankovits. Los Angeles (6)—Marshall 2, Brock, Guerrero, Landreaux, Yeager. Montreal (3)—Carter, Dawson, Wallach. New York (4)—Strawberry 4. Philadelphia (4)—Schmidt 3, Lezcano 2, Lefebvre, Maddox, Matuszek. Pittsburgh (4)—Pena 2, Lacy, Morrison. St. Louis (7)—Hendrick 2, Jorgensen, McGee, Nieto, Pendleton, Porter. San Diego (7)—Brown, Garvey, Kennedy, Martinez, McReynolds, Nettles, Show. San Francisco (6)—C. Davis 2, Baker, Brenly, Clark, Leonard.

AT HOUSTON (47): Atlanta (10)—Murphy 6, Chambliss, Johnson, Washington, Watson. Chicago (1)—Davis. Cincinnati (3)—Cedeno 2, Esasky. Houston (18)—Bailey 7, Cabell 2, Doran 2, Puhl 2, Bass, Davis, Garner, Knight, Mumphrey. Los Angeles—None. Montreal (3)—Carter 2, Dawson. New York (3)—Foster, Hernandez, Strawberry. Philadelphia (4)—Schmidt 2, Corcoran, Virgil. Pittsburgh (1)—Robinson. St. Louis—None. San Diego (4)—Bochy, Garvey, Gwynn, McReynolds. San Francisco—None.

AT LOS ANGELES (89): Atlanta (5)—Murphy 2, Chambliss, Johnson, Perry. Chicago (2)—Dernier, Sandberg. Cincinnati (1)—Parker. Houston (3)—Cruz 2, Ashby. Los Angeles (49)—Marshall 11, Brock 8, Guerrero 7, Landreaux 4, Stubbs 4, Whitfield 4, Anderson 2, Brewer, Landestoy, Maldonado, Reynolds, Rivera, Sax, Valenzuela, Yeager. Montreal (2)—Carter 2. New York (2)—Foster 2. Philadelphia (5)—Aguayo 2, Carlton, Matuszek, Schmidt. Pittsburgh (1)—Thompson. St. Louis (5)—Porter 2, Hendrick, McGee, Van Slyke. San Diego (7)—Kennedy 2, McReynolds 2, Martinez, Nettles, Ramirez. San Francisco (7)—Leonard 2, Clark, Deer, LeMaster, Rabb, Youngblood.

AT MONTREAL (101): Atlanta (2)—Murphy, Royster. Chicago (2)—Cey, Matthews. Cincinnati (6)—Driessen 2, Esasky, Parker, Redus, Walker. Houston (5)—Ashby, Cabell, Cruz, Puhl, Reynolds. Los Angeles (5)—Landreaux 2, Scioscia, Stubbs, Valenzuela. Montreal (45)—Carter 14, Dawson 6, Stenhouse 4, Wallach 4, Wohlford 3, Raines 2, Ramos 2, Dilone, Francona. New York (6)—Strawberry 3, Foster 2, Wilson. Philadelphia (5)—Schmidt 3, Samuel 2. Pittsburgh (5)—Distefano 2, Pena 2, Thompson. St. Louis (7)—Green 2, Porter 2, Andujar, Howe, L. Smith. San Diego (5)—Nettles 2, Bochy, McReynolds, Salazar. San Francisco (8)—C. Davis 4, Brenly 3, Youngblood.

AT NEW YORK (103): Atlanta (2)—Johnson, Trevino. Chicago (4)—Matthews 2, Davis, Sandberg. Cincinnati (6)—Davis, Driessen, Foley, Krenchicki, Parker, Walker. Houston (3)—Cruz, Mumphrey, Spilman. Los Angeles (5)—Anderson, Guerrero, Maldonado, Scioscia, Stubbs. Montreal (5)—Carter 2, Dawson, Raines, Wallach. New York (56)—Brooks 12, Foster 11, Hernandez 10, Strawberry 8, Wilson 7, Fitzgerald 2, Chapman, Gardenhire, Heep, Knight, Santana, Staub. Philadelphia (4)—Hayes, Samuel, Schmidt, Virgil. Pittsburgh (3)—Frobel, Harper, Lacy. St. Louis (5)—Green, Hendrick, Herr, Landrum, Speier. San Diego (3)—Kennedy, Martinez, McReynolds. San Francisco (7)—Brenly 4, Clark 2, Leonard.

AT PHILADELPHIA (124): Atlanta (3)—Murphy 2, Washington. Chicago (9)—Cey 3, Sandberg 2, Davis, Durham, Matthews, Moreland. Cincinnati (3)—Cedeno 2, Davis. Houston (5)—Mumphrey 2,

Puhl, Reynolds, Walling. **Los Angeles** (2)—Landreaux, Yeager. **Montreal** (3)—Carter, Raines, Wallach. **New York** (7)—Strawberry 2, Chapman, Foster, Hernandez, Leary, Wilson. **Philadelphia** (79)—Schmidt 16, Hayes 10, Virgil 10, Lezcano 9, Samuel 8, Matuszek 5, Wilson 5, Wockenfuss 5, Maddox 3, Corcoran 2, Aguayo, Diaz, Lefebvre, Russell, Schu, Stone. **Pittsburgh** (4)—Distefano, Lacy, Madlock, Morrison. **St. Louis** (3)—Green, Hendrick, McGee. **San Diego** (3)—Kennedy, Martinez, Nettles. **San Francisco** (3)—C. Davis 2, Leonard.

AT PITTSBURGH (92): Atlanta (2)—Hall, Murphy. **Chicago** (4)—Cey, Hassey, Lake, Sandberg. **Cincinnati** (1)—Gulden. **Houston** (4)—Cabell, Doran, Garner, Knepper. **Los Angeles** (4)—Landreaux, Maldonado, Marshall, Monday. **Montreal** (2)—Carter, Wohlford. **New York** (4)—Chapman, Foster, Martin, Strawberry. **Philadelphia** (9)—Lezcano 2, Schmidt, Hayes, Jeltz, Maddox, Virgil, Wilson. **Pittsburgh** (48)—Berra 7, Pena 7, Frobel 6, Lacy 6, Morrison 6, Thompson 6, Mazzilli 3, Ray 3, Candelaria, Harper, Madlock, May. **St. Louis** (8)—Green 3, Hendrick 2, Van Slyke 2, Herr. **San Diego** (3)—Gwynn, Salazar, Show. **San Francisco** (3)—C. Davis, Rabb, Youngblood.

AT ST. LOUIS (71): Atlanta (4)—Hubbard 2, Komminsk, Trevino. **Chicago** (2)—Hebner, Matthews. **Cincinnati** (2)—Esasky, Redus. **Houston** (4)—Cabell, Pena, Spilman, Walling. **Los Angeles**—None. **Montreal** (5)—Carter, Dawson, Driessen, Wallach, Wohlford. **New York** (7)—Strawberry 4, Brooks 2, Hernandez. **Philadelphia** (4)—Hayes, Russell, Schu, Wockenfuss. **Pittsburgh** (8)—Lacy 2, Ray 2, Thompson 2, Berra, Frobel. **St. Louis** (29)—Green 5, Porter 4, L. Smith 3, Van Slyke 3, Hendrick 2, Landrum 2, McGee 2, Nieto 2, Speier 2, Andujar, Herr, Howe, O. Smith. **San Diego** (4)—Kennedy, Martinez, McReynolds, Nettles. **San Francisco** (2)—Clark, Leonard.

AT SAN DIEGO (121): Atlanta (9)—Horner 2, Hubbard 2, Komminsk, Murphy, Perry, Ramirez, Thompson, Washington. **Chicago** (3)—Hall, Moreland, Sandberg. **Cincinnati** (2)—Davis 2, Parker 2, Cedeno, Esasky, Foley, Krenchicki, Redus. **Houston** (1)—Puhl. **Los Angeles** (9)—Guerrero 4, Marshall 2, Scioscia, Valenzuela, Yeager. **Montreal** (6)—Carter 2, Dawson 2, Raines, Wallach. **New York** (2)—Foster, Martin. **Philadelphia** (11)—Schmidt 4, Matuszek 3, Virgil 2, Lezcano, Samuel. **Pittsburgh** (2)—Frobel, Thompson. **St. Louis** (3)—Herr, Porter, L. Smith. **San Diego** (60)—Nettles 11, McReynolds 10, Kennedy 8, Martinez 6, Garvey 5, Gwynn 3, Lollar 3, Wiggins 3, Flannery 2, Templeton 2, Bevacqua, Brown, Ramirez, Roenicke, Salazar, Show, Summers. **San Francisco** (6)—C. Davis 2, Brown, LeMaster, Leonard, Rabb.

AT SAN FRANCISCO (118): Atlanta (7)—Murphy 3, Perry 2, Benedict, Komminsk. **Chicago (10)**—Cey 3, Davis, Matthews, Moreland, Owen, Rohn, Sandberg, Woods. **Cincinnati** (5)—Davis 3, Krenchicki, Milner. **Houston** (9)—Cruz 3, Reynolds 2, Cabell, Davis, Garner, Mumphrey. **Los Angeles** (6)—Marshall 2, Brock, Guerrero, Maldonado, Scioscia. **Montreal** (7)—Wallach 3, Venable 2, Dawson, Raines. **New York** (5)—Foster 2, Backman, Martin, Wilson. **Philadelphia** (4)—Matuszek, Samuel, Schmidt, Virgil. **Pittsburgh** (3)—Pena 2, Morrison. **St. Louis** (4)—Green 2, Porter, Van Slyke. **San Diego** (3)—Bochy, Martinez, McReynolds. **San Francisco** (55)—Leonard 13, C. Davis 7, Brenly 6, Youngblood 6, Clark 4, Gladden 4, Trillo 3, Baker 2, Deer 2, Mullins 2, Nicosia 2, Wellman 2, LeMaster, Thompson.

American League

	At Balt.	At Bos.	At Cal.	At Chi.	At Clev.	At Det.	At K.C.	At Mil.	At Min.	At N.Y.	At Oak.	At Sea.	At Tex.	At Tor.	Totals 1984	1983
Baltimore	82	3	7	6	7	5	7	7	5	8	4	9	6	4	160	168
Boston	4	100	7	9	10	5	5	6	3	4	4	6	6	12	181	142
California	3	9	79	7	3	9	0	5	2	4	11	5	3	10	150	154
Chicago	5	1	1	103	5	4	6	7	12	6	5	6	5	6	172	157
Cleveland	1	4	5	5	65	4	3	9	6	1	7	6	4	3	123	86
Detroit	4	12	11	7	9	85	8	7	9	7	6	6	8	8	187	156
Kansas City	6	3	9	1	7	5	48	5	8	1	5	3	11	5	117	109
Milwaukee	5	5	4	8	3	5	4	42	5	2	3	2	4	4	96	132
Minnesota	1	3	6	3	3	6	1	5	63	4	4	11	3	1	114	141
New York	6	6	8	2	5	2	4	1	7	62	7	7	5	8	130	153
Oakland	6	9	9	9	6	7	7	5	5	2	77	7	3	6	158	121
Seattle	3	8	4	8	3	2	6	4	5	3	5	68	5	5	129	111
Texas	7	3	6	6	5	2	4	4	6	7	3	6	55	6	120	106
Toronto	8	10	6	6	7	13	4	3	4	0	8	8	7	59	143	167
1984 Totals	141	176	162	180	138	154	107	110	140	111	149	150	125	137	1980	
1983 Totals	145	141	153	148	119	170	116	121	147	122	114	144	78	185		1903

AT BALTIMORE (141): Baltimore (82)—Murray 18, Ripken 16, Gross 12, Young 9, Roenicke 7, Dempsey 6, Rayford 4, Lowenstein 2, Shelby 2, Singleton 2, Ayala, Dauer, Dwyer, Sakata. **Boston** (4)—Armas 3, Rice. **California** (3)—DeCinces, Downing, Grich. **Chicago** (5)—Baines, Cruz, Fisk, Hill, Luzinski. **Cleveland** (1)—Jacoby. **Detroit** (4)—Evans, Gibson, Herndon, Johnson. **Kansas City** (6)—Balboni 2, Brett, Sheridan, Slaught, Washington. **Milwaukee** (5)—Cooper, Gantner, Howell, Manning, Sundberg. **Minnesota** (1)—Hrbek. **New York** (6)—Baylor 3, Dayett, Kemp, Smalley. **Oakland** (6)—Lansford 2, Bochte, Henderson, Lopes, Morgan. **Seattle** (3)—Cowens 2, D. Henderson. **Texas** (7)—Parrish 2, Hostetler, Kunkel, O'Brien, Ward, Yost. **Toronto** (8)—Upshaw 2, Aikens, Barfield, Bell, Griffin, Johnson, Martinez.

AT BOSTON (176): Baltimore (3)—Murray, Ripken, Sheets. **Boston** (100)—Armas 21, Rice 17, Easler 16, Gedman 16, Evans 15, Buckner 6, Boggs 5, Gutierrez 2, Barrett, Nichols. **California** (9)—DeCinces 2, Grich 2, Re. Jackson 2, Beniquez, Downing, Narron. **Chicago** (1)—V. Law. **Cleveland** (4)—Thornton 2, Willard 2. **Detroit (12)**—Parrish 5, Johnson 2, Brookens, Gibson, Herndon, Lemon, Trammell. **Kansas City** (3)—Motley 2, Brett. **Milwaukee** (5)—Cooper 2, Clark, Lozado, Yount. **Minnesota** (3)—Brunansky, Hrbek, Laudner. **New York** (6)—Baylor 3, Mattingly, Randolph, Winfield. **Oakland** (9)—Kingman 5, Almon, Burroughs, Davis, Murphy. **Seattle** (8)—Cowens 2, Davis 2, D. Henderson 2, Bonnell, Presley. **Texas** (3)—O'Brien 2, Sample. **Toronto (10)**—Bell 2, Johnson 2, Martinez 2, Barfield, Gruber, Upshaw, Whitt.

AT CALIFORNIA (162): Baltimore (7)—Murray 2, Bumbry, Dempsey, Gross, Lowenstein, Ripken. **Boston (7)**—Armas 2, Evans 2, Buckner, Easler, Rice. **California (79)**—Lynn 16, Re. Jackson 15, DeCinces 10, Downing 9, Grich 9, Beniquez 5, Sconiers 4, Brown 3, Carew 3, Wilfong 3, Boone, Pettis. **Chicago (1)**—Kittle. **Cleveland (5)**—Thornton 2, Bando, Carter, Vukovich. **Detroit (11)**—Castillo 2, Gibson 2, Lemon 2, Parrish 2, Evans, Jones, Trammell. **Kansas City (9)**—Balboni 4, Biancalana, Iorg, Orta, Sheridan, Slaught. **Milwaukee (4)**—Yount 2, Schroeder, Simmons. **Minnesota (6)**—Brunansky 4, Gaetti, Laudner. **New York (8)**—Mattingly 3, Baylor, Pagliarulo, Smalley, Winfield, Wynegar. **Oakland (9)**—Murphy 3, Davis 2, Heath, Henderson, Lansford, Phillips. **Seattle (4)**—Bonnell 2, Davis 2. **Texas (6)**—Ward 4, Parrish, Wright. **Toronto (6)**—Johnson 2, Moseby 2, Upshaw 2.

AT CHICAGO (180): Baltimore (6)—Murray 2, Ripken 2, Gross, Young. **Boston (9)**—Gedman 3, Armas 2, Boggs, Buckner, Easler, Rice. **California (7)**—Lynn 3, Schofield 2, Grich, Pettis. **Chicago (103)**—Kittle 17, Baines, 16, Walker 16, Fisk 11, V. Law 11, Luzinski 9, Hill 4, R. Law 4, Smalley 4, Hairston 3, Fletcher 2, Paciorek 2, Stegman 2, Cruz, Dybzinski. **Cleveland (5)**—Thornton 2, Bando, Fischlin, Franco. **Detroit (7)**—Evans, Gibson, Grubb, Johnson, Jones, Lemon, Parrish. **Kansas City (1)**—Motley. **Milwaukee (8)**—Oglivie 2, Cooper, Howell, Schroeder, Simmons, Sundberg, Yount. **Minnesota (3)**—Brunansky, Bush, Hrbek. **New York (2)**—Mattingly 2. **Oakland (9)**—Bochte 2, Morgan 2, Murphy 2, Davis, Lansford, Phillips. **Seattle (8)**—D. Henderson 2, Phelps 2, Chambers, Davis, S. Henderson, Tartabull. **Texas (6)**—Parrish 3, Foley, Ward, Wright. **Toronto (6)**—Whitt 2, Bell, Johnson, Moseby, Upshaw.

AT CLEVELAND (138): Baltimore (7)—Gross 2, Young 2, Ayala, Ripken, Sakata. **Boston (10)**—Evans 4, Gedman 2, Rice 2, Buckner, Easler. **California (3)**—Brown, Downing, Lynn. **Chicago (5)**—Kittle 3, Fisk 2. **Cleveland (65)**—Thornton 19, Carter 9, Castillo 7, Bando 5, Tabler 5, Willard 5, Hall 4, Vukovich 4, Jacoby 2, Bernazard, Butler, Franco, Hargrove, Quirk. **Detroit (9)**—Gibson 2, Bergman, Evans, Grubb, Johnson, Lemon, Parrish, Whitaker. **Kansas City (7)**—Balboni 4, Brett, McRae, White. **Milwaukee (3)**—Schroeder 2, Yount. **Minnesota (3)**—Laudner, Teufel, Washington. **New York (5)**—Baylor 2, Mattingly, Pagliarulo, Winfield. **Oakland (6)**—Almon, Bochte, Hill, Kingman, Lansford, Murphy. **Seattle (3)**—Bonnell, Davis, Phelps. **Texas (5)**—Bell 2, O'Brien 2, Jones. **Toronto (7)**—Moseby 3, Bell 2, Barfield, Garcia.

AT DETROIT (154): Baltimore (5)—Dempsey, Gross, Lowenstein, Singleton, Young. **Boston (5)**—Evans 3, Gedman, Rice. **California (9)**—DeCinces 3, Boone, Downing, Grich, Re. Jackson, Lynn, Wilfong. **Chicago (4)**—Hairston 2, Kittle 2, **Cleveland (4)**—Vukovich 2, Tabler, Thornton. **Detroit (85)**—Parrish 13, Lemon 12, Gibson 11, Whitaker 8, Trammell 7, Evans 6, Bergman 4, Brookens 4, Johnson 4, Herndon 3, Castillo 2, Garbey 2, Grubb, Kuntz, Lowry. **Kansas City (5)**—White 3, Orta, Sheridan. **Milwaukee (5)**—Gantner, Howell, Oglivie, Sundberg, Yount. **Minnesota (6)**—Brunansky 2, Hrbek 2, David, Laudner. **New York (2)**—Mattingly, Winfield. **Oakland (7)**—Murphy 3, Davis, Heath, Henderson, Kingman. **Seattle (2)**—Cowens, Owen. **Texas (2)**—Jones, O'Brien. **Toronto (13)**—Aikens 3, Bell 3, Whitt 3, Upshaw 2, Griffin, Moseby.

AT KANSAS CITY (107): Baltimore (7)—Ayala, Cruz, Dempsey, Gross, Ripken, Shelby, Young. **Boston (5)**—Armas 2, Barrett, Buckner, Evans. **California**—None. **Chicago (6)**—Fisk 2, Baines, Cruz, Kittle, Walker. **Cleveland (3)**—Castillo, Hall, Jacoby. **Detroit (8)**—Gibson 2, Jones 2, Evans, Herndon, Parrish, Trammell. **Kansas City (48)**—Balboni 10, Brett 6, White 6, Motley 5, Pryor 4, Iorg 3, Orta 3, Sheridan 3, McRae 2, Concepcion, Davis, Jones, Slaught, Wathan, Wilson. **Milwaukee (4)**—Yount 2, Manning, Schroeder. **Minnesota (1)**—Brunansky. **New York (4)**—Cerone, Dayett, Kemp, Winfield. **Oakland (7)**—Murphy 3, Henderson 2, Kingman, Lopes. **Seattle (6)**—Presley 2, Cowens, Davis, D. Henderson, S. Henderson. **Texas (4)**—Ward 2, Kunkel, O'Brien. **Toronto (4)**—Bell 2, Upshaw 2.

AT MILWAUKEE (110): Baltimore (7)—Murray 2, Gross, Lowenstein, Roenicke, Shelby, Young. **Boston (6)**—Armas 4, Easler, Rice. **California (5)**—Downing 2, Re. Jackson, Narron, Schofield. **Chicago (7)**—Walker 3, Fisk, R. Law, V. Law, Luzinski. **Cleveland (9)**—Carter 3, Thornton 3, Bando, Bernazard, Hall. **Detroit (7)**—Parrish 2, Evans, Johnson, Jones, Lemon, Whitaker. **Kansas City (5)**—Motley 2, White 2, Sheridan. **Milwaukee (42)**—Yount 8, Oglivie 7, Schroeder 7, Brouhard 5, Sundberg 4, Cooper 3, Ready 3, Clark, James, Manning, Moore, Romero. **Minnesota (5)**—Hrbek 2, Brunansky, Gaetti, Teufel. **New York (1)**—Moreno. **Oakland (5)**—Murphy 2, Heath, Henderson, Lansford. **Seattle (4)**—Davis 2, Nahorodny, Phelps. **Texas (4)**—Ward 2, Parrish, Wright. **Toronto (3)**—Aikens 2, Johnson.

AT MINNESOTA (140): Baltimore (5)—Gross 2, Cruz, Ford, Lowenstein. **Boston (3)**—Allenson, Buckner, Rice. **California (2)**—Re. Jackson, Schofield. **Chicago (12)**—Baines 5, Kittle 2, Walker 2, Christmas, Fisk, R. Law. **Cleveland (6)**—Thornton 2, Willard 2, Butler, Vukovich. **Detroit (9)**—Evans 2, Bergman, Garbey, Gibson, Grubb, Parrish, Trammell, Whitaker. **Kansas City (8)**—Brett 3, Motley 2, Balboni, White, Wilson. **Milwaukee (5)**—Gantner, Manning, Oglivie, Schroeder, Simmons. **Minnesota (63)**—Hrbek 15, Brunansky 14, Teufel 9, Bush 8, Engle 4, Hatcher 4, Laudner 3, Gaetti 2, Washington 2, Brown, Faedo. **New York (7)**—Baylor 3, Gamble 3, Smalley. **Oakland (5)**—Murphy 2, Heath, Kingman, Lansford. **Seattle (5)**—Cowens, Davis, S. Henderson, Kearney, Nelson. **Texas (6)**—Bannister, Bell, Sample, Scott, Ward, Wilkerson. **Toronto (4)**—Aikens, Bell, Mulliniks, Whitt.

AT NEW YORK (111): Baltimore (8)—Bumbry 2, Dempsey, Dwyer, Gross, Ripken, Roenicke, Young. **Boston (4)**—Rice 2, Armas, Easler. **California (4)**—Grich 2, DeCinces, Wilfong. **Chicago (6)**—Baines 3, Fisk, Luzinski, Walker. **Cleveland (1)**—Castillo. **Detroit (7)**—Parrish 3, Garbey, Herndon, Lowry, Whitaker. **Kansas City (1)**—Davis. **Milwaukee (2)**—Cooper, Oglivie. **Minnesota (4)**—Brunansky 2, Hrbek 2, New York (62)—Mattingly 12, Baylor 10, Winfield 9, Gamble 5, Griffey 5, Pagliarulo 4, Smalley 4, Wynegar 3, Dayett 2, Kemp 2, Moreno 2, Mata, Meacham, Piniella, Randolph. **Oakland (2)**—Henderson, Kingman. **Seattle (3)**—Phelps 2, Calderon. **Texas (7)**—Parrish 2, Bell, Dunbar, Rivers, Scott, Yost. **Toronto**—None.

AT OAKLAND (149): Baltimore (4)—Dauer, Dempsey, Murray, Singleton. **Boston (4)**—Armas 4. **California (11)**—Downing 3, Beniquez 2, Re. Jackson 2, Boone, Lynn, Narron, Wilfong. **Chicago (5)**—Kittle 3, V. Law, Paciorek. **Cleveland (7)**—Bando, Butler, Franco, Hall, Tabler, Thornton, Vukovich. **Detroit (6)**—Garbey, Gibson, Jones, Lemon, Parrish, Trammell. **Kansas City (5)**—Balboni, Brett, Orta, Sheridan, White. **Milwaukee (3)**—Manning, Moore, Simmons. **Minnesota (4)**—Brunansky, Bush, Gaetti, Laudner. **New York (7)**—Baylor, Gamble, Griffey, Meacham, Pagliarulo, Winfield, Wynegar. **Oakland (77)**—Kingman 19, Murphy 12, Heath 8, Henderson 7, Lansford 7, Lopes 6, Almon 5, Davis 4, Essian 2, Morgan 2, Phillips 2, Bochte, Burroughs, Tettleton. **Seattle (5)**—S. Henderson 2, Phelps 2,

Davis. **Texas** (3)—O'Brien 2, Bannister. **Toronto** (8)—Johnson 2, Barfield, Bell, Garcia, Mulliniks, Upshaw, Whitt.

AT SEATTLE (150): Baltimore (9)—Ripken 3, Singleton 2, Cruz, Lowenstein, Murray, Shelby. **Boston** (6)—Easler 3, Armas, Evans, Gedman. **California** (5)—DeCinces 2, Downing 2, Re. Jackson. **Chicago** (6)—Baines 2, Fisk, Kittle, V. Law, Paciorek. **Cleveland** (6)—Bando 2, Castillo, Hargrove, Tabler, Thornton. **Detroit** (6)—Gibson 2, Trammell 2, Kuntz, Lemon. **Kansas City** (3)—Orta 2, Balboni. **Milwaukee** (2)—Brouhard, Manning. **Minnesota** (11)—Teufel 3, Brunansky 2, Hrbek 2, Laudner 2, Bush, Hatcher. **New York** (7)—Baylor 3, Cerone, Griffey, Mattingly, Winfield. **Oakland** (7)—Kingman 3, Murphy 2, Hill, Morgan. **Seattle** (68)—Davis 15, Phelps 13, D. Henderson 8, Cowens 7, Kearney 6, Presley 5, Bonnell 4, S. Henderson 4, Owen 2, Milbourne, Putnam, Tartabull, Valle. **Texas** (6)—Bell, Jones, Parrish, Sample, Scott, Ward. **Toronto** (8)—Johnson 2, Aikens, Fernandez, Garcia, Moseby, Upshaw, Whitt.

AT TEXAS (125): Baltimore (6)—Murray 2, Ayala, Ripken, Roenicke, Shelby. **Boston** (6)—Evans 2, Allenson, Armas, Barrett, Rice. **California** (3)—Brown, Downing, Re. Jackson. **Chicago** (5)—Kittle 2, V. Law 2, Walker. **Cleveland** (4)—Jacoby 2, Bando, Tabler. **Detroit** (8)—Parrish 3, Johnson 2, Evans, Gibson, Grubb. **Kansas City** (11)—Balboni 4, Motley 2, White 2, Biancalana, Orta, Slaught. **Milwaukee** (4)—Cooper, Howell, Manning, Schroeder. **Minnesota** (3)—Brunansky 2, Hrbek. **New York** (5)—Kemp 2, Winfield 2, Baylor. **Oakland** (3)—Henderson, Lopes, Murphy. **Seattle** (5)—Phelps 2, Davis, S. Henderson, Presley. **Texas** (55)—Parrish 11, O'Brien 7, Ward 7, Bell 6, Wright 6, Foley 4, Yost 4, Rivers 3, Hostetler 2, Sample 2, Dunbar, Jones, Kunkel. **Toronto** (7)—Johnson 2, Bell, Fernandez, Griffin, Upshaw, Whitt.

AT TORONTO (137): Baltimore (4)—Lowenstein, Nolan, Sakata, Young. **Boston** (12)—Evans 4, Easler 3, Armas 2, Gedman, Jurak, Newman. **California** (10)—Brown 2, Downing 2, Grich 2, DeCinces, Re. Jackson, Lynn, Picciolo. **Chicago** (6)—Cruz 2, Baines, Fisk, Fletcher, Luzinski. **Cleveland** (3)—Jacoby, Tabler, Willard. **Detroit** (8)—Grubb 3, Gibson 2, Bergman, Evans, Parrish. **Kansas City** (5)—Balboni, Iorg, Motley, Wathan, White. **Milwaukee** (4)—Cooper 2, Loman 2. **Minnesota** (1)—Brunansky. **New York** (8)—Mattingly 2, Gamble, Harrah, Kemp, Moreno, Winfield, Wynegar. **Oakland** (6)—Kingman 3, Heath, Henderson, Murphy. **Seattle** (5)—Cowens, Phelps, Presley, Putnam, Thomas. **Texas** (6)—O'Brien 2, Ward 2, Foley, Parrish. **Toronto** (59)—Bell 12, Barfield 10, Moseby 10, Upshaw 6, Whitt 5, Aikens 3, Johnson 3, Collins 2, Garcia 2, Martinez 2, Fernandez, Griffin, Iorg, Mulliniks.

The Sporting News AWARDS

THE SPORTING NEWS MVP AWARDS

AMERICAN LEAGUE

Year	Player	Club	Points
1929	Al Simmons, Philadelphia, of		40
1930	Joseph Cronin, Washington, ss		52
1931	H. Louis Gehrig, New York, 1b		40
1932	James Foxx, Philadelphia, 1b		46
1933	James Foxx, Philadelphia, 1b		49
1934	H. Louis Gehrig, New York, 1b		51
1935	Henry Greenberg, Detroit, 1b		64
1936	H. Louis Gehrig, New York, 1b		55
1937	Charles Gehringer, Detroit, 2b		78
1938	James Foxx, Boston, 1b		304
1939	Joseph DiMaggio, New York, of		280
1940	Henry Greenberg, Detroit, of		292
1941	Joseph DiMaggio, New York, of		291
1942	Joseph Gordon, New York, 2b		270
1943	Spurgeon Chandler, New York, p		246
1944	Robert Doerr, Boston, 2b		
1945	Edward J. Mayo, Detroit, 2b		

NATIONAL LEAGUE

Player	Club	Points
No selection		
William Terry, New York, 1b		47
Charles Klein, Philadelphia, of		40
Charles Klein, Philadelphia, of		46
Carl Hubbell, New York, p		64
Jerome Dean, St. Louis, p		57
J. Floyd Vaughan, Pittsburgh, ss		42
Carl Hubbell, New York, p		61
Joseph Medwick, St. Louis, of		70
Ernest Lombardi, Cincinnati, c		229
William Walters, Cincinnati, p		303
Frank McCormick, Cincinnati, 1b		274
Adolph Camilli, Brooklyn, 1b		300
Morton Cooper, St. Louis, p		263
Stanley Musial, St. Louis, of		267
Martin Marion, St. Louis, ss		
Thomas Holmes, Boston, of		

THE SPORTING NEWS PLAYER, PITCHER OF YEAR

AMERICAN LEAGUE

1948—Louis Boudreau, Cleveland, ss
    Robert Lemon, Cleveland, p
1949—Theodore Williams, Boston, of
    Ellis Kinder, Boston, p
1950—Philip Rizzuto, New York, ss
    Robert Lemon, Cleveland, p
1951—Ferris Fain, Philadelphia, 1b
    Robert Feller, Cleveland, p
1952—Luscious Easter, Cleveland, 1b
    Robert Shantz, Philadelphia, p
1953—Albert Rosen, Cleveland, 3b
    Erv (Bob) Porterfield, Washington, p
1954—Roberto Avila, Cleveland, 2b
    Robert Lemon, Cleveland, p
1955—Albert Kaline, Detroit, of
    Edward Ford, New York, p
1956—Mickey Mantle, New York, of
    W. William Pierce, Chicago, p
1957—Theodore Williams, Boston, of
    W. William Pierce, Chicago, p
1958—Jack Jensen, Boston, of
    Robert Turley, New York, p
1959—J. Nelson Fox, Chicago, 2b
    Early Wynn, Chicago, p
1960—Roger Maris, New York, of
    Charles Estrada, Baltimore, p
1961—Roger Maris, New York, of
    Edward Ford, New York, p
1962—Mickey Mantle, New York, of
    Richard Donovan, Cleveland, p
1963—Albert Kaline, Detroit, of
    Edward Ford, New York, p
1964—Brooks Robinson, Baltimore, 3b
    Dean Chance, Los Angeles, p
1965—Pedro (Tony) Oliva, Minnesota, of
    James Grant, Minnesota, p
1966—Frank Robinson, Baltimore, of
    James Kaat, Minnesota, p
1967—Carl Yastrzemski, Boston, of
    Jim Lonborg, Boston, p
1968—Ken Harrelson, Boston, of
    Denny McLain, Detroit, p
1969—Harmon Killebrew, Minnesota, 1b-3b
    Denny McLain, Detroit, p
1970—Harmon Killebrew, Minnesota, 3b
    Sam McDowell, Cleveland, p
1971—Pedro (Tony) Oliva, Minnesota, of
    Vida Blue, Oakland, p
1972—Richie Allen, Chicago, 1b
    Wilbur Wood, Chicago, p

NATIONAL LEAGUE

1948—Stanley Musial, St. Louis, of-1b
    John Sain, Boston, p
1949—Enos Slaughter, St. Louis, of
    Howard Pollet, St. Louis, p
1950—Ralph Kiner, Pittsburgh, of
    C. James Konstanty, Philadelphia, p
1951—Stanley Musial, St. Louis, of
    Elwin Roe, Brooklyn, p
1952—Henry Sauer, Chicago, of
    Robin Roberts, Philadelphia, p
1953—Roy Campanella, Brooklyn, c
    Warren Spahn, Milwaukee, p
1954—Willie Mays, New York, of
    John Antonelli, New York, p
1955—Edwin Snider, Brooklyn, of
    Robin Roberts, Philadelphia, p
1956—Henry Aaron, Milwaukee, of
    Donald Newcombe, Brooklyn, p
1957—Stanley Musial, St. Louis, 1b
    Warren Spahn, Milwaukee, p
1958—Ernest Banks, Chicago, ss
    Warren Spahn, Milwaukee, p
1959—Ernest Banks, Chicago, ss
    Samuel Jones, San Francisco, p
1960—Richard Groat, Pittsburgh, ss
    Vernon Law, Pittsburgh, p
1961—Frank Robinson, Cincinnati, of
    Warren Spahn, Milwaukee, p
1962—Maurice Wills, Los Angeles, ss
    Donald Drysdale, Los Angeles, p
1963—Henry Aaron, Milwaukee, of
    Sanford Koufax, Los Angeles, p
1964—Kenton Boyer, St. Louis, 3b
    Sanford Koufax, Los Angeles, p
1965—Willie Mays, San Francisco, of
    Sanford Koufax, Los Angeles, p
1966—Roberto Clemente, Pittsburgh, of
    Sanford Koufax, Los Angeles, p
1967—Orlando Cepeda, St. Louis, 1b
    Mike McCormick, San Francisco, p
1968—Pete Rose, Cincinnati, of
    Bob Gibson, St. Louis, p
1969—Willie McCovey, San Francisco, 1b
    Tom Seaver, New York, p
1970—Johnny Bench, Cincinnati, c
    Bob Gibson, St. Louis, p
1971—Joe Torre, St. Louis, 3b
    Ferguson Jenkins, Chicago, p
1972—Billy Williams, Chicago, of
    Steve Carlton, Philadelphia, p

PLAYER, PITCHER OF YEAR—Continued

AMERICAN LEAGUE	NATIONAL LEAGUE
1973—Reggie Jackson, Oakland, of	1973—Bobby Bonds, San Francisco, of
Jim Palmer, Baltimore, p	Ron Bryant, San Francisco, p
1974—Jeff Burroughs, Texas, of	1974—Lou Brock, St. Louis, of
Jim Hunter, Oakland, p	Mike Marshall, Los Angeles, p
1975—Fred Lynn, Boston, of	1975—Joe Morgan, Cincinnati, 2b
Jim Palmer, Baltimore, p	Tom Seaver, New York, p
1976—Thurman Munson, New York, c	1976—George Foster, Cincinnati, of
Jim Palmer, Baltimore, p	Randy Jones, San Diego, p
1977—Rod Carew, Minnesota, 1b	1977—George Foster, Cincinnati, of
Nolan Ryan, California, p	Steve Carlton, Philadelphia, p
1978—Jim Rice, Boston, of	1978—Dave Parker, Pittsburgh, of
Ron Guidry, New York, p	Vida Blue, San Francisco, p
1979—Don Baylor, California, of	1979—Keith Hernandez, St. Louis, 1b
Mike Flanagan, Baltimore, p	Joe Niekro, Houston, p
1980—George Brett, Kansas City, 3b	1980—Mike Schmidt, Philadelphia, 3b
Steve Stone, Baltimore, p	Steve Carlton, Philadelphia, p
1981—Tony Armas, Oakland, of	1981—Andre Dawson, Montreal, of
Jack Morris, Detroit, p	Fernando Valenzuela, Los Angeles, p
1982—Robin Yount, Milwaukee, ss	1982—Dale Murphy, Atlanta, of
Dave Stieb, Toronto, p	Steve Carlton, Philadelphia, p
1983—Cal Ripken, Baltimore, ss	1983—Dale Murphy, Atlanta, of
LaMarr Hoyt, Chicago, p	John Denny, Philadelphia, p
1984—Don Mattingly, New York, 1b	1984—Ryne Sandberg, Chicago, 2b
Willie Hernandez, Detroit, p	Rick Sutcliffe, Chicago, p

FIREMAN (Relief Pitcher) OF THE YEAR

Year Player Club	Player Club
1960—Mike Fornieles, Boston	Lindy McDaniel, St. Louis
1961—Luis Arroyo, New York	Stu Miller, San Francisco
1962—Dick Radatz, Boston	Roy Face, Pittsburgh
1963—Stu Miller, Baltimore	Lindy McDaniel, Chicago
1964—Dick Radatz, Boston	Al McBean, Pittsburgh
1965—Eddie Fisher, Chicago	Ted Abernathy, Chicago
1966—Jack Aker, Kansas City	Phil Regan, Los Angeles
1967—Minnie Rojas, California	Ted Abernathy, Cincinnati
1968—Wilbur Wood, Chicago	Phil Regan, L.A.-Chicago
1969—Ron Perranoski, Minnesota	Wayne Granger, Cincinnati
1970—Ron Perranoski, Minnesota	Wayne Granger, Cincinnati
1971—Ken Sanders, Milwaukee	Dave Giusti, Pittsburgh
1972—Sparky Lyle, New York	Clay Carroll, Cincinnati
1973—John Hiller, Detroit	Mike Marshall, Montreal
1974—Terry Forster, Chicago	Mike Marshall, Los Angeles
1975—Rich Gossage, Chicago	Al Hrabosky, St. Louis
1976—Bill Campbell, Minnesota	Rawly Eastwick, Cincinnati
1977—Bill Campbell, Boston	Rollie Fingers, San Diego
1978—Rich Gossage, New York	Rollie Fingers, San Diego
1979—Mike Marshall, Minnesota	Bruce Sutter, Chicago
Jim Kern, Texas	
1980—Dan Quisenberry, Kansas City	Rollie Fingers, San Diego
	Tom Hume, Cincinnati
1981—Rollie Fingers, Milwaukee	Bruce Sutter, St. Louis
1982—Dan Quisenberry, Kansas City	Bruce Sutter, St. Louis
1983—Dan Quisenberry, Kansas City	Al Holland, Philadelphia
	Lee Smith, Chicago
1984—Dan Quisenberry, Kansas City	Bruce Sutter, St. Louis

THE SPORTING NEWS ROOKIE AWARDS

1946—Combined selection—Delmer Ennis, Philadelphia, N. L., of
1947—Combined selection—Jack Robinson, Brooklyn, 1b
1948—Combined selection—Richie Ashburn, Philadelphia, N. L., of

AMERICAN LEAGUE	NATIONAL LEAGUE
Year Player Club	Player Club
1949—Roy Sievers, St. Louis, of	Donald Newcombe, Brooklyn, p
1950—Combined selection—Edward Ford, New York, A. L., p	
1951—Orestes Minoso, Chicago, of	Willie Mays, New York, of
1952—Clinton Courtney, St. Louis, c	Joseph Black, Brooklyn, p
1953—Harvey Kuenn, Detroit, ss	James Gilliam, Brooklyn, 2b
1954—Robert Grim, New York, p	Wallace Moon, St. Louis, of
1955—Herbert Score, Cleveland, p	William Virdon, St. Louis, of
1956—Luis Aparicio, Chicago, ss	Frank Robinson, Cincinnati, of
1957—Anthony Kubek, New York, inf-of	Edward Bouchee, Philadelphia, 1b
(No pitcher named)	Jack Sanford, Philadelphia, p
1958—Albert Pearson, Washington, of	Orlando Cepeda, San Francisco, 1b
Ryne Duren, New York, p	Carlton Willey, Milwaukee, p
1959—W. Robert Allison, Washington, of	Willie McCovey, San Francisco, 1b
1960—Ronald Hansen, Baltimore, ss	Frank Howard, Los Angeles, of

THE SPORTING NEWS ROOKIE AWARDS—Continued

AMERICAN LEAGUE

Year	Player	Club
1961	Richard Howser, Kansas City, ss	
	Donald Schwall, Boston, p	
1962	Thomas Tresh, New York, of-ss	
1963	Peter Ward, Chicago, 3b	
	Gary Peters, Chicago, p	
1964	Pedro (Tony) Oliva, Minnesota, of	
	Wallace Bunker, Baltimore, p	
1965	Curtis Blefary, Baltimore, of	
	Marcelino Lopez, California, p	
1966	Tommie Agee, Chicago, of	
	James Nash, Kansas City, p	
1967	Rod Carew, Minnesota, 2b	
	Tom Phoebus, Baltimore, p	
1968	Del Unser, Washington, of	
	Stan Bahnsen, New York, p	
1969	Carlos May, Chicago, of	
	Mike Nagy, Boston, p	
1970	Roy Foster, Cleveland, of	
	Bert Blyleven, Minnesota, p	
1971	Chris Chambliss, Cleveland, 1b	
	Bill Parsons, Milwaukee, p	
1972	Carlton Fisk, Boston, c	
	Dick Tidrow, Cleveland, p	
1973	Al Bumbry, Baltimore, of	
	Steve Busby, Kansas City, p	
1974	Mike Hargrove, Texas, 1b	
	Frank Tanana, California, p	
1975	Fred Lynn, Boston, of	
	Dennis Eckersley, Cleveland, p	
1976	Butch Wynegar, Minnesota, c	
	Mark Fidrych, Detroit, p	
1977	Mitchell Page, Oakland, of	
	Dave Rozema, Detroit, p	
1978	Paul Molitor, Milwaukee, 2b	
	Rich Gale, Kansas City, p	
1979	Pat Putnam, Texas, 1b	
	Mark Clear, California, p	
1980	Joe Charboneau, Cleveland, of	
	Britt Burns, Chicago, p	
1981	Rich Gedman, Boston, c	
	Dave Righetti, New York, p	
1982	Cal Ripken, Baltimore, ss-3b	
	Ed Vande Berg, Seattle, p	
1983	Ron Kittle, Chicago, of	
	Mike Boddicker, Baltimore, p	
1984	Alvin Davis, Seattle, 1b	
	Mark Langston, Seattle, p	

NATIONAL LEAGUE

Player	Club
Billy Williams, Chicago, of	
Kenneth Hunt, Cincinnati, p	
Kenneth Hubbs, Chicago, 2b	
Peter Rose, Cincinnati, 2b	
Raymond Culp, Philadelphia, p	
Richard Allen, Philadelphia, 3b	
William McCool, Cincinnati, p	
Joseph Morgan, Houston, 2b	
Frank Linzy, San Francisco, p	
Tommy Helms, Cincinnati, 3b	
Donald Sutton, Los Angeles, p	
Lee May, Cincinnati, 1b	
Dick Hughes, St. Louis, p	
Johnny Bench, Cincinnati, c	
Jerry Koosman, New York, p	
Coco Laboy, Montreal, 3b	
Tom Griffin, Houston, p	
Bernie Carbo, Cincinnati, of	
Carl Morton, Montreal, p	
Earl Williams, Atlanta, c	
Reggie Cleveland, St. Louis, p	
Dave Rader, San Francisco, c	
Jon Matlack, New York, p	
Gary Matthews, San Francisco, of	
Steve Rogers, Montreal, p	
Greg Gross, Houston, of	
John D'Acquisto, San Francisco, p	
Gary Carter, Montreal, of-c	
John Montefusco, San Francisco, p	
Larry Herndon, San Francisco, of	
Butch Metzger, San Diego, p	
Andre Dawson, Montreal, of	
Bob Owchinko, San Diego, p	
Bob Horner, Atlanta, 3b	
Don Robinson, Pittsburgh, p	
Jeff Leonard, Houston, of	
Rick Sutcliffe, Los Angeles, p	
Lonnie Smith, Philadelphia, of	
Bill Gullickson, Montreal, p	
Tim Raines, Montreal, of	
Fernando Valenzuela, Los Angeles, p	
Johnny Ray, Pittsburgh, 2b	
Steve Bedrosian, Atlanta, p	
Darryl Strawberry, New York, of	
Craig McMurtry, Atlanta, p	
Juan Samuel, Philadelphia, 2b	
Dwight Gooden, New York, p	

MAJOR LEAGUE EXECUTIVE

Year	Executive	Club
1936	Branch Rickey, St. Louis NL	
1937	Edward Barrow, New York AL	
1938	Warren Giles, Cincinnati NL	
1939	Larry MacPhail, Brooklyn NL	
1940	W. O. Briggs, Sr., Detroit AL	
1941	Edward Barrow, New York AL	
1942	Branch Rickey, St. Louis NL	
1943	Clark Griffith, Washington AL	
1944	Wm. O. DeWitt, St. Louis AL	
1945	Philip K. Wrigley, Chicago NL	
1946	Thomas A. Yawkey, Boston AL	
1947	Branch Rickey, Brooklyn NL	
1948	Bill Veeck, Cleveland AL	
1949	Robt. Carpenter, Phila'phia NL	
1950	George Weiss, New York AL	
1951	George Weiss, New York AL	
1952	George Weiss, New York AL	
1953	Louis Perini, Milwaukee NL	
1954	Horace Stoneham, N. York NL	
1955	Walter O'Malley, Brooklyn NL	
1956	Gabe Paul, Cincinnati NL	
1957	Frank Lane, St. Louis NL	
1958	Joe L. Brown, Pittsburgh NL	
1959	E. J. (Buzzie) Bavasi, L.A. NL	
1960	George Weiss, New York AL	

Year	Executive	Club
1961	Dan Topping, New York AL	
1962	Fred Haney, Los Angeles AL	
1963	Vaughan (Bing) Devine, St.L.NL	
1964	Vaughan (Bing) Devine, St.L.NL	
1965	Calvin Griffith, Minnesota AL	
1966	Lee MacPhail, Commissioner's Office	
1967	Dick O'Connell, Boston AL	
1968	James Campbell, Detroit AL	
1969	John Murphy, New York NL	
1970	Harry Dalton, Baltimore AL	
1971	Cedric Tallis, Kansas City AL	
1972	Roland Hemond, Chicago AL	
1973	Bob Howsam, Cincinnati NL	
1974	Gabe Paul, New York AL	
1975	Dick O'Connell, Boston AL	
1976	Joe Burke, Kansas City AL	
1977	Bill Veeck, Chicago AL	
1978	Spec Richardson, San Fran. NL	
1979	Hank Peters, Baltimore AL	
1980	Tal Smith, Houston NL	
1981	John McHale, Montreal NL	
1982	Harry Dalton, Milwaukee AL	
1983	Hank Peters, Baltimore AL	
1984	Dallas Green, Chicago NL	

MAJOR LEAGUE MANAGER

Year	Manager	Club
1936—Joe McCarthy, New York AL		
1937—Bill McKechnie, Boston NL		
1938—Joe McCarthy, New York AL		
1939—Leo Durocher, Brooklyn NL		
1940—Bill McKechnie, Cincinnati NL		
1941—Billy Southworth, St. Louis NL		
1942—Billy Southworth, St. Louis NL		
1943—Joe McCarthy, New York AL		
1944—Luke Sewell, St. Louis AL		
1945—Ossie Bluege, Washington AL		
1946—Eddie Dyer, St. Louis NL		
1947—Bucky Harris, New York AL		
1948—Bill Meyer, Pittsburgh NL		
1949—Casey Stengel, New York AL		
1950—Red Rolfe, Detroit AL		
1951—Leo Durocher, New York NL		
1952—Eddie Stanky, St. Louis NL		
1953—Casey Stengel, New York AL		
1954—Leo Durocher, New York NL		
1955—Walter Alston, Brooklyn NL		
1956—Birdie Tebbetts, Cincinnati NL		
1957—Fred Hutchinson, St. Louis NL		
1958—Casey Stengel, New York AL		
1959—Walter Alston, Los Angeles NL		
1960—Danny Murtaugh, Pitts. NL		

Year	Manager	Club
1961—Ralph Houk, New York AL		
1962—Bill Rigney, Los Angeles AL		
1963—Walter Alston, Los Angeles NL		
1964—Johnny Keane, St. Louis NL		
1965—Sam Mele, Minnesota AL		
1966—Hank Bauer, Baltimore AL		
1967—Dick Williams, Boston AL		
1968—Mayo Smith, Detroit AL		
1969—Gil Hodges, New York NL		
1970—Danny Murtaugh, Pittsb'gh NL		
1971—Charlie Fox, San Francisco NL		
1972—Chuck Tanner, Chicago AL		
1973—Gene Mauch, Montreal NL		
1974—Bill Virdon, New York AL		
1975—Darrell Johnson, Boston AL		
1976—Danny Ozark, Philadelphia NL		
1977—Earl Weaver, Baltimore AL		
1978—George Bamberger, Milw'kee AL		
1979—Earl Weaver, Baltimore AL		
1980—Bill Virdon, Houston NL		
1981—Billy Martin, Oakland AL		
1982—Whitey Herzog, St. Louis NL		
1983—Tony LaRussa, Chicago AL		
1984—Jim Frey, Chicago NL		

MAJOR LEAGUE PLAYER

Year	Player	Club
1936—Carl Hubbell, New York NL		
1937—Johnny Allen, Cleveland AL		
1938—Johnny Vander Meer, Cinn. NL		
1939—Joe DiMaggio, New York AL		
1940—Bob Feller, Cleveland AL		
1941—Ted Williams, Boston AL		
1942—Ted Williams, Boston AL		
1943—Spud Chandler, New York AL		
1944—Marty Marion, St. Louis NL		
1945—Hal Newhouser, Detroit AL		
1946—Stan Musial, St. Louis NL		
1947—Ted Williams, Boston AL		
1948—Lou Boudreau, Cleveland AL		
1949—Ted Williams, Boston AL		
1950—Phil Rizzuto, New York AL		
1951—Stan Musial, St. Louis NL		
1952—Robin Roberts, Philadelphia NL		
1953—Al Rosen, Cleveland AL		
1954—Willie Mays, New York NL		
1955—Duke Snider, Brooklyn NL		
1956—Mickey Mantle, New York AL		
1957—Ted Williams, Boston AL		
1958—Bob Turley, New York AL		
1959—Early Wynn, Chicago AL		
1960—Bill Mazeroski, Pittsburgh NL		

Year	Player	Club
1961—Roger Maris, New York AL		
1962—Maury Wills, Los Angeles NL		
Don Drysdale, Los Angeles NL		
1963—Sandy Koufax, Los Angeles NL		
1964—Ken Boyer, St. Louis NL		
1965—Sandy Koufax, Los Angeles NL		
1966—Frank Robinson, Baltimore AL		
1967—Carl Yastrzemski, Boston AL		
1968—Denny McLain, Detroit AL		
1969—Willie McCovey, San Fran. NL		
1970—Johnny Bench, Cin. NL		
1971—Joe Torre, St. Louis NL		
1972—Billy Williams, Chicago NL		
1973—Reggie Jackson, Oakland AL		
1974—Lou Brock, St. Louis NL		
1975—Joe Morgan, Cincinnati NL		
1976—Joe Morgan, Cincinnati NL		
1977—Rod Carew, Minnesota AL		
1978—Ron Guidry, New York AL		
1979—Willie Stargell, Pittsburgh NL		
1980—George Brett, Kansas City AL		
1981—Fernando Valenzuela, Los Angeles NL		
1982—Robin Yount, Milwaukee AL		
1983—Cal Ripken, Baltimore AL		
1984—Ryne Sandberg, Chicago NL		

MINOR LEAGUE EXECUTIVE (HIGHER CLASSIFICATIONS)
(Restricted to Class AAA Starting in 1963)

Year	Executive	Club
1936—Earl Mann, Atlanta, Southern		
1937—Robt. LaMotte, Savannah, Sally		
1938—Louis McKenna, St. Paul, A.A.		
1939—Bruce Dudley, Louisville, A.A.		
1940—Roy Hamey, Kansas City, A.A.		
1941—Emil Sick, Seattle, PCL		
1942—Bill Veeck, Milwaukee, A.A.		
1943—Clar. Rowland, Los Angeles, PCL		
1944—William Mulligan, Seattle, PCL		
1945—Bruce Dudley, Louisville, A.A.		
1946—Earl Mann, Atlanta, Southern		
1947—Wm. Purnhage, Waterloo, I.I.I.		
1948—Ed. Glennon, Bir'ham, Southern		
1949—Ted Sullivan, Indianapolis, A.A.		
1950—Cl. (Brick) Laws, Oakland, PCL		
1951—Robert Howsam, Denver, West.		
1952—Jack Cooke, Toronto, Int.		
1953—Richard Burnett, Dallas, Texas		
1954—Edward Stumpf, Indpls., A.A.		
1955—Dewey Soriano, Seattle, PCL		

Year	Executive	Club
1956—Robert Howsam, Denver, A.A.		
1957—John Stiglmeier, Buffalo, Int.		
1958—Ed. Glennon, Bir'ham, Southern		
1959—Ed. Leishman, Salt Lake, PCL		
1960—Ray Winder, Little Rock, Sou.		
1961—Elten Schiller, Omaha, A.A.		
1962—Geo. Sisler, Jr., Rochester, Int.		
1963—Lewis Matlin, Hawaii, PCL		
1964—Ed. Leishman, San Diego, PCL		
1965—Harold Cooper, Columbus, Int.		
1966—John Quinn, Jr., Hawaii, PCL		
1967—Hillman Lyons, Richmond, Int.		
1968—Gabe Paul, Jr., Tulsa, PCL		
1969—Bill Gardner, Louisville, Int.		
1970—Dick King, Wichita, A.A.		
1971—Carl Steinfeldt, Jr., Roch'ter, Int.		
1972—Don Labbruzzo, Evansville, A.A.		
1973—Merle Miller, Tucson, PCL		
1974—John Carbray, Sacramento, PCL		
1975—Stan Naccarato, Tacoma, PCL		

MINOR LEAGUE EXECUTIVE (HIGHER CLASSIFICATIONS)—Continued

Year	Manager	Club
1976	Art Teece, Salt Lake City, PCL	
1977	George Sisler, Jr., Col'bus, Int.	
1978	Willie Sanchez, Albu'que, PCL	
1979	George Sisler, Jr., Col'bus, Int.	
1980	Jim Burris, Denver, A.A.	
1981	Pat McKernan, Albuquerque, PCL	
1982	A. Ray Smith, Louisville, A.A.	
1983	A. Ray Smith, Louisville, A.A.	
1984	Mike Tamburro, Pawtucket, Int.	

MINOR LEAGUE EXECUTIVE (LOWER CLASSIFICATIONS)
(Separate Awards for Class AA and Class A Started in 1963)

Year	Executive	Club
1950	H. Cooper, Hutch'son, West. A.	
1951	O. W. (Bill) Hayes, T'ple, B.S.	
1952	Hillman Lyons, Danville, MOV	
1953	Carl Roth, Peoria, III	
1954	James Meaghan, Cedar R., III	
1955	John Petrakis, Dubuque, MOV	
1956	Marvin Milkes, Fresno, Calif.	
1957	Richard Wagner, L'coln, West.	
1958	Gerald Waring, Macon, Sally	
1959	Clay Dennis, Des Moines, III	
1960	Hubert Kittle, Yakima, Northw.	
1961	David Steele, Fresno, California	
1962	John Quinn, Jr., S. Jose, Calif.	
1963	Hugh Finnerty, Tulsa, Texas	
	Ben Jewell, M. Valley, Pioneer	
1964	Glynn West, Birmingham, Sou.	
	Jas. Bayens, Rock Hill, W. Car.	
1965	Dick Butler, Dallas-Ft.W., Tex.	
	Ken. Blackman, Quad C., Midw.	
1966	Tom Fleming, Evansville, South.	
	Cappy Harada, Lodi, California	
1967	Robt. Quinn, Reading, East.	
	Pat Williams, Spar'burg, W. C.	
1968	Phil Howser, Charlotte, South.	
	Merle Miller, Burlington, Midw.	
1969	Charlie Blaney, Albuq., Texas	
	Bill Gorman, Visalia, Calif.	
1970	Carl Sawatski, Arkansas, Texas	
	Bob Williams, Bakersfield, Calif.	
1971	Miles Wolff, Savannah, Dixie A.	
	Ed Holtz, Appleton, Midwest	
1972	John Begzos, S. Antonio, Texas	
	Bob Piccinini, Modesto, Calif.	
1973	Dick Kravitz, Jacksonville, Sou.	
	Fritz Colschen, Clinton, Midw.	
1974	Jim Paul, El Paso, Texas	
	Bing Russell, Portland, N'west	
1975	Jim Paul, El Paso, Texas	
	Cordy Jensen, Eugene, N'west	
1976	Woodrow Reid, Chat'ooga, Sou.	
	Don Buchheister, Ced. Rap., Mid.	
1977	Jim Paul, El Paso, Texas	
	Harry Pells, Quad Cities, Midw.	
1978	Larry Schmittou, Nashville, Sou.	
	Dave Hersh, Appleton, Midwest	
1979	Bill Rigney Jr., Midland, Tex.	
	Tom Romenesko, G'sboro, W.C.	
1980	Frances Crockett, C'lotte, Sou.	
	Tom Romenesko, G'sboro, W.C.	
1981	Allie Prescott, Memphis, Southern	
	Dan Overstreet, Hagerstown, Caro.	
1982	Art Clarkson, Birmingham, Sou.	
	Bob Carruesco, Stockton, Calif.	
1983	Edward Kenney, New Britain, East.	
	Terry Reynolds, Vero Beach, Fla. St.	
1984	Bruce Baldwin, Greenville, Sou.	
	Dave Tarrolly, Beloit, Midwest	

MINOR LEAGUE MANAGER

Year	Manager	Club
1936	Al Sothoron, Milwaukee, A.A.	
1937	Jake Flowers, Salis'y, East. Sh.	
1938	Paul Richards, Atlanta, South.	
1939	Bill Meyer, Kansas City, A.A.	
1940	Larry Gilbert, Nashville, South.	
1941	Burt Shotton, Columbus, A.A.	
1942	Eddie Dyer, Columbus, A.A.	
1943	Nick Cullop, Columbus, A.A.	
1944	Al Thomas, Baltimore, Int.	
1945	Lefty O'Doul, San Fran., PCL	
1946	Clay Hopper, Montreal, Int.	
1947	Nick Cullop, Milwaukee, A.A.	
1948	Casey Stengel, Oakland, PCL	
1949	Fred Haney, Hollywood, PCL	
1950	Rollie Hemsley, Columbus, A.A.	
1951	Charlie Grimm, Milw., A.A.	
1952	Luke Appling, Memphis, South.	
1953	Bobby Bragan, Hollywood, PCL	
1954	Kerby Farrell, Indpls., A.A.	
1955	Bill Rigney, Minneapolis, A.A.	
1956	Kerby Farrell, Indpls., A.A.	
1957	Ben Geraghty, Wichita, A.A.	
1958	Cal Ermer, Birmingham, South.	
1959	Pete Reiser, Victoria, Texas	
1960	Mel McGaha, Toronto, Int.	
1961	Kerby Farrell, Buffalo, Int.	
1962	Ben Geraghty, Jackson'le, Int.	
1963	Rollie Hemsley, Indpls., Int.	
1964	Harry Walker, Jacks'vle., Int.	
1965	Grady Hatton, Okla. City, PCL	
1966	Bob Lemon, Seattle, PCL	
1967	Bob Skinner, San Diego, PCL	
1968	Jack Tighe, Toledo, Int.	
1969	Clyde McCullough, Tide., Int.	
1970	Tom Lasorda, Spokane, PCL	
1971	Del Rice, Salt Lake City, PCL	
1972	Hank Bauer, Tidewater, Int.	
1973	Joe Morgan, Charleston, Int.	
1974	Joe Altobelli, Rochester, Int.	
1975	Joe Frazier, Tidewater, Int.	
1976	Vern Rapp, Denver, A.A.	
1977	Tommy Thompson, Arkan., Tex.	
1978	Les Moss, Evansville, A.A.	
1979	Vern Benson, Syracuse, Int.	
1980	Hal Lanier, Springfield, A.A.	
1981	Del Crandall, Albuquerque, PCL	
1982	George Scherger, Indianapolis, A.A.	
1983	Bill Dancy, Reading, East.	
1984	Bob Rodgers, Indianapolis, A.A.	

MINOR LEAGUE PLAYER

Year	Player	Club
1936	Jn. Vander Meer, Durham, Pied.	
1937	Charlie Keller, Newark, Int.	
1938	Fred Hutchinson, Seattle, PCL	
1939	Lou Novikoff, Tulsa-Los A'les.	
1940	Phil Rizzuto, Kansas City, A.A.	
1941	John Lindell, Newark, Int.	
1942	Dick Barrett, Seattle, PCL	
1943	Chet Covington, Scranton, East.	

MINOR LEAGUE PLAYER—Continued

Year	Executive	Club
1944	Rip Collins, Albany, Eastern
1945	Gil Coan, Chattanooga, South.
1946	Sibby Sisti, Indianapolis, A.A.
1947	Hank Sauer, Syracuse, Int.
1948	Gene Woodling, S. F., PCL
1949	Orie Arntzen, Albany, Eastern
1950	Frank Saucier, San Ant'o, Tex.
1951	Gene Conley, Hartford, Eastern
1952	Bill Skowron, Kans. City, A.A.
1953	Gene Conley, Toledo, A.A.
1954	Herb Score, Indianapolis, A.A.
1955	John Murff, Dallas, Texas
1956	Steve Bilko, Los Angeles, PCL
1957	Norm Siebern, Denver, A.A.
1958	Jim O'Toole, Nashville, South.
1959	Frank Howard, Victoria-Spok.
1960	Willie Davis, Spokane, PCL
1961	Howie Koplitz, Bir'ham, South.
1962	Bob Bailey, Columbus, Int.
1963	Don Buford, Indianapolis, Int.
1964	Mel Stottlemyre, Richm'd., Int.

Year	Executive	Club
1965	Joe Foy, Toronto, International
1966	Mike Epstein, Rochester, Int.
1967	Johnny Bench, Buffalo, Int.
1968	Merv Rettenmund, Roch'ter, Int.
1969	Danny Walton, Okla. City, A.A.
1970	Don Baylor, Rochester, Int.
1971	Bobby Grich, Rochester, Int.
1972	Tom Paciorek, Albuq'que, PCL
1973	Steve Ontiveros, Phoenix, PCL
1974	Jim Rice, Pawtucket, Int.
1975	Hector Cruz, Tulsa, A.A.
1976	Pat Putnam, Asheville, W. Car.
1977	Ken Landreaux, S.L.C., PCL-El Paso, Tex.
1978	Champ Summers, Indi'polis, A.A.
1979	Mark Bomback, Vancouver, PCL
1980	Tim Raines, Denver, A.A.
1981	Mike Marshall, Albuquerque, PCL
1982	Ron Kittle, Edmonton, PCL
1983	Kevin McReynolds, Las Vegas, PCL
1984	Alan Knicely, Wichita, A.A.

Baseball Writers' Association Awards
Most Valuable Player Citations

CHALMERS AWARD

	AMERICAN LEAGUE			NATIONAL LEAGUE	
Year	Player Club	Points		Player Club	Points
1911	Tyrus Cobb, Detroit, of	64		Frank Schulte, Chicago, of	29
1912	Tristram Speaker, Boston, of	59		Lawrence Doyle, New York, 2b	48
1913	Walter Johnson, Washington, p	54		Jacob Daubert, Brooklyn, 1b	50
1914	Edward Collins, Philadelphia, 2b	63		John Evers, Boston, 2b	50

LEAGUE AWARDS

	AMERICAN LEAGUE			NATIONAL LEAGUE	
Year	Player Club	Points		Player Club	Points
1922	George Sisler, St. Louis, 1b	59		No selection	
1923	George Ruth, New York, of	64		No selection	
1924	Walter Johnson, Washington, p	55		Arthur Vance, Brooklyn, p	74
1925	Roger Peckinpaugh, Washington, ss	45		Rogers Hornsby, St. Louis, 2b	73
1926	George Burns, Cleveland, 1b	63		Robert O'Farrell, St. Louis, c	79
1927	H. Louis Gehrig, New York, 1b	56		Paul Waner, Pittsburgh, of	72
1928	Gordon Cochrane, Philadelphia, c	53		James Bottomley, St. Louis, 1b	76
1929	No selection			Rogers Hornsby, Chicago, 2b	60

BASEBALL WRITERS' ASSOCIATION MVP AWARDS

	AMERICAN LEAGUE			NATIONAL LEAGUE	
Year	Player Club	Points		Player Club	Points
1931	Robert Grove, Philadelphia, p	78		Frank Frisch, St. Louis, 2b	65
1932	James Foxx, Philadelphia, 1b	75		Charles Klein, Philadelphia, of	78
1933	James Foxx, Philadelphia, 1b	74		Carl Hubbell, New York, p	77
1934	Gordon Cochrane, Detroit, c	67		Jerome Dean, St. Louis, p	78
1935	Henry Greenberg, Detroit, 1b	*80		Charles Hartnett, Chicago, c	75
1936	H. Louis Gehrig, New York, 1b	73		Carl Hubbell, New York, p	60
1937	Charles Gehringer, Detroit, 2b	78		Joseph Medwick, St. Louis, of	70
1938	James Foxx, Boston, 1b	305		Ernest Lombardi, Cincinnati, c	229
1939	Joseph DiMaggio, New York, of	280		William Walters, Cincinnati, p	303
1940	Henry Greenberg, Detroit, of	292		Frank McCormick, Cincinnati, 1b	274
1941	Joseph DiMaggio, New York, of	291		Adolph Camilli, Brooklyn, 1b	300
1942	Joseph Gordon, New York, 2b	270		Morton Cooper, St. Louis, p	263
1943	Spurgeon Chandler, New York, p	246		Stanley Musial, St. Louis, of	267
1944	Harold Newhouser, Detroit, p	236		Martin Marion, St. Louis, ss	190
1945	Harold Newhouser, Detroit, p	236		Philip Cavarretta, Chicago, 1b	279
1946	Theodore Williams, Boston, of	224		Stanley Musial, St. Louis, 1b	319
1947	Joseph DiMaggio, New York, of	202		Robert Elliott, Boston, 3b	205
1948	Louis Boudreau, Cleveland, ss	324		Stanley Musial, St. Louis, of	303
1949	Theodore Williams, Boston, of	272		Jack Robinson, Brooklyn, 2b	264
1950	Philip Rizzuto, New York, ss	284		C. James Konstanty, Philadelphia, p	286
1951	Lawrence Berra, New York, c	184		Roy Campanella, Brooklyn, c	243
1952	Robert Shantz, Philadelphia, p	280		Henry Sauer, Chicago, of	226
1953	Albert Rosen, Cleveland, 3b	*336		Roy Campanella, Brooklyn, c	297
1954	Lawrence Berra, New York, c	230		Willie Mays, New York, of	283

BASEBALL WRITERS' ASSOCIATION MVP AWARDS—Cont.

	AMERICAN LEAGUE				NATIONAL LEAGUE		
Year	Player	Club	Points		Player	Club	Points
1955	Lawrence Berra, New York, c		218		Roy Campanella, Brooklyn, c		226
1956	Mickey Mantle, New York, of		*336		Donald Newcombe, Brooklyn, p		223
1957	Mickey Mantle, New York, of		233		Henry Aaron, Milwaukee, of		239
1958	Jack Jensen, Boston, of		233		Ernest Banks, Chicago, ss		283
1959	J. Nelson Fox, Chicago, 2b		295		Ernest Banks, Chicago, ss		232½
1960	Roger Maris, New York, of		225		Richard Groat, Pittsburgh, ss		276
1961	Roger Maris, New York, of		202		Frank Robinson, Cincinnati, of		219
1962	Mickey Mantle, New York, of		234		Maurice Wills, Los Angeles, ss		209
1963	Elston Howard, New York, c		248		Sanford Koufax, Los Angeles, p		237
1964	Brooks Robinson, Baltimore, 3b		269		Kenton Boyer, St. Louis, 3b		243
1965	Zoilo Versalles, Minnesota, ss		275		Willie Mays, San Francisco, of		224
1966	Frank Robinson, Baltimore, of		*280		Roberto Clemente, Pittsburgh, of		218
1967	Carl Yastrzemski, Boston, of		275		Orlando Cepeda, St. Louis, 1b		*280
1968	Dennis McLain, Detroit, p		*280		Robert Gibson, St. Louis, p		242
1969	Harmon Killebrew, Minnesota, 1-3b		294		Willie McCovey, San Francisco, 1b		265
1970	John (Boog) Powell, Baltimore, 1b		234		Johnny Bench, Cincinnati, c		326
1971	Vida Blue, Oakland, p		268		Joseph Torre, St. Louis, 3b		318
1972	Richie Allen, Chicago, 1b		321		Johnny Bench, Cincinnati, c		263
1973	Reggie Jackson, Oakland, of		*336		Pete Rose, Cincinnati, of		274
1974	Jeff Burroughs, Texas, of		248		Steve Garvey, Los Angeles, 1b		270
1975	Fred Lynn, Boston, of		326		Joe Morgan, Cincinnati, 2b		321½
1976	Thurman Munson, New York, c		304		Joe Morgan, Cincinnati, 2b		311
1977	Rod Carew, Minnesota, 1b		273		George Foster, Cincinnati, of		291
1978	Jim Rice, Boston, of		352		Dave Parker, Pittsburgh, of		320
1979	Don Baylor, California, of		347		Willie Stargell, Pittsburgh, 1b		216
					Keith Hernandez, St. Louis, 1b		216
1980	George Brett, Kansas City, 3b		335		Mike Schmidt, Philadelphia, 3b		*336
1981	Rollie Fingers, Milwaukee, p		319		Mike Schmidt, Philadelphia, 3b		321
1982	Robin Yount, Milwaukee, ss		385		Dale Murphy, Atlanta, of		283
1983	Cal Ripken, Baltimore, ss		322		Dale Murphy, Atlanta, of		318
1984	Willie Hernandez, Detroit, p		306		Ryne Sandberg, Chicago, 2b		326

*Unanimous selection.

BASEBALL WRITERS' ASSOCIATION ROOKIE AWARDS

1947—Combined selection—Jack Robinson, Brooklyn, 1b.
1948—Combined selection—Alvin Dark, Boston, N. L., ss.

	AMERICAN LEAGUE				NATIONAL LEAGUE		
Year	Player	Club	Votes		Player	Club	Votes
1949	Roy Sievers, St. Louis, of		10		Donald Newcombe, Brooklyn, p		21
1950	Walter Dropo, Boston, 1b		15		Samuel Jethroe, Boston, of		11
1951	Gilbert McDougald, New York, 3b		13		Willie Mays, New York, of		18
1952	Harry Byrd, Philadelphia, p		9		Joseph Black, Brooklyn, p		19
1953	Harvey Kuenn, Detroit, ss		23		James Gilliam, Brooklyn, 2b		11
1954	Robert Grim, New York, p		15		Wallace Moon, St. Louis, of		17
1955	Herbert Score, Cleveland, p		18		William Virdon, St. Louis, of		15
1956	Luis Aparicio, Chicago, ss		22		Frank Robinson, Cincinnati, of		*24
1957	Anthony Kubek, New York, inf-of		23		John Sanford, Philadelphia, p		16
1958	Albert Pearson, Washington, of		14		Orlando Cepeda, San Francisco, 1b		*†21
1959	W. Robert Allison, Washington, of		18		Willie McCovey, San Francisco, 1b		*24
1960	Ronald Hansen, Baltimore, ss		22		Frank Howard, Los Angeles, of		12
1961	Donald Schwall, Boston, p		7		Billy Williams, Chicago, of		10
1962	Thomas Tresh, New York, of-ss		13		Kenneth Hubbs, Chicago, 2b		19
1963	Gary Peters, Chicago, p		10		Peter Rose, Cincinnati, 2b		17
1964	Pedro (Tony) Oliva, Minnesota, of		19		Richard Allen, Philadelphia, 3b		18
1965	Curtis Blefary, Baltimore, of		12		James Lefebvre, Los Angeles, 2b		13
1966	Tommie Agee, Chicago, of		16		Tommy Helms, Cincinnati, 3b		12
1967	Rod Carew, Minnesota, 2b		19		Tom Seaver, New York, p		11
1968	Stan Bahnsen, New York, p		17		Johnny Bench, Cincinnati, c		10½
1969	Lou Piniella, Kansas City, of		9		Ted Sizemore, Los Angeles, 2b		14
1970	Thurman Munson, New York, c		23		Carl Morton, Montreal, p		11
1971	Chris Chambliss, Cleveland, 1b		11		Earl Williams, Atlanta, c		18
1972	Carlton Fisk, Boston, c		*24		Jon Matlack, New York, p		19
1973	Al Bumbry, Baltimore, of		13½		Gary Matthews, San Francisco, of		11
1974	Mike Hargrove, Texas, 1b		16½		Bake McBride, St. Louis, of		16
1975	Fred Lynn, Boston, of		23		John Montefusco, San Francisco, p		12
1976	Mark Fidrych, Detroit, p		22		Butch Metzger, San Diego, p		11
					Pat Zachry, Cincinnati, p		11
1977	Eddie Murray, Baltimore, dh-1b		12½		Andre Dawson, Montreal, of		10
1978	Lou Whitaker, Detroit, 2b		21		Bob Horner, Atlanta, 3b		12½
1979	John Castino, Minnesota, 3b		7		Rick Sutcliffe, Los Angeles, p		20
	Alfredo Griffin, Toronto, ss		7				
1980	Joe Charboneau, Cleveland, of		103		Steve Howe, Los Angeles, p		80
1981	Dave Righetti, New York, p		127		Fernando Valenzuela, Los Angeles, p		107
1982	Cal Ripken, Baltimore, ss-3b		132		Steve Sax, Los Angeles, 2b		63
1983	Ron Kittle, Chicago, of		104		Darryl Strawberry, New York, of		109
1984	Alvin Davis, Seattle, 1b		134		Dwight Gooden, New York, p		118

*Unanimous selection. †Three writers did not vote.

After being acquired in an early-season trade from Cleveland, the Cubs' Rick Sutcliffe won 16 of 17 decisions to capture the N.L. Cy Young Award.

CY YOUNG MEMORIAL AWARD

Year	Pitcher Club	Votes
1956—Donald Newcombe, Brooklyn		10
1957—Warren Spahn, Milwaukee		15
1958—Robert Turley, New York, A.L.		5
1959—Early Wynn, Chicago, A.L.		13
1960—Vernon Law, Pittsburgh		8
1961—Edward Ford, New York, A.L.		9
1962—Don Drysdale, Los Angeles, N.L.		14
1963—Sanford Koufax, Los Angeles, N.L.		*20
1964—Dean Chance, Los Angeles, A.L.		17
1965—Sanford Koufax, Los Angeles, N.L.		*20
1966—Sanford Koufax, Los Angeles, N.L.		*20
1967—A. L.—Jim Lonborg, Boston		18
N. L.—M. McCormick, San Francisco		18
1968—A. L.—Dennis McLain, Detroit		*20
N. L.—Bob Gibson, St. Louis		*20
1969—A. L.—Dennis McLain, Detroit		10
Mike Cuellar, Baltimore		10
N. L.—Tom Seaver, New York		23
1970—A. L.—Jim Perry, Minnesota		†55
N. L.—Bob Gibson, St. Louis		†118
1971—A. L.—Vida Blue, Oakland		†98
N. L.—Fergy Jenkins, Chicago		†97
1972—A. L.—Gaylord Perry, Cleveland		†64
N. L.—Steve Carlton, Philadelphia		*†120

Year	Pitcher Club	Votes
1973—A. L.—Jim Palmer, Baltimore		†88
N. L.—Tom Seaver, New York		†71
1974—A. L.—Jim Hunter, Oakland		†90
N. L.—Mike Marshall, Los Angeles		†96
1975—A. L.—Jim Palmer, Baltimore		†98
N. L.—Tom Seaver, New York		†98
1976—A. L.—Jim Palmer, Baltimore		†108
N. L.—Randy Jones, San Diego		†96
1977—A. L.—Sparky Lyle, New York		†56½
N. L.—Steve Carlton, Philadelphia		*†104
1978—A. L.—Ron Guidry, New York		*†140
N. L.—Gaylord Perry, San Diego		‡116
1979—A. L.—Mike Flanagan, Baltimore		†136
N. L.—Bruce Sutter, Chicago		†72
1980—A. L.—Steve Stone, Baltimore		100
N. L.—Steve Carlton, Philadelphia		118
1981—A. L.—Rollie Fingers, Milwaukee		126
N. L.—Fernando Valenzuela, Los Ang.		70
1982—A. L.—Pete Vuckovich, Milwaukee		87
N. L.—Steve Carlton, Philadelphia		112
1983—A. L.—LaMarr Hoyt, Chicago		116
N. L.—John Denny, Philadelphia		103
1984—A. L.—Willie Hernandez, Detroit		88
N. L.—Rick Sutcliffe, Chicago		120

*Unanimous selection. †Point system used.

Brock, Wilhelm Enter Hall

By LARRY WIGGE

Lou Brock didn't even need a leadoff before stealing his way into the Baseball Hall of Fame. But Hoyt Wilhelm had to wait until the final innings before getting a call from the Baseball Writers' Association of America.

Fittingly, in a day and age of specialization, Brock, the ultimate base stealer with his career-high 938 stolen bases, and Wilhelm, the dean of relief pitchers who appeared in more games (1,070) than any hurler in history, were elected by comfortable margins.

Wilhelm, who failed to gain election to the Hall of Fame in 1983 when he finished 13 votes short of the required 75 percent of votes cast, was named on 331 of the 395 ballots. His election ended an eight-year wait. Brock received 315 votes and became only the 15th player to win election during his first year of eligibility.

Nellie Fox, a splendid second baseman who starred for the White Sox in the 1950s, finished third in the balloting with 295 votes, just two short of the required 75 percent. It was the closest a player ever had come to election without making it since the shrine opened its doors in 1936. And, unfortunately for the late second sacker, it was his 15th and final year of eligibility. Fox's name can be given consideration by the Veterans Committee, but only after a three-year waiting period.

Billy Williams was next in the voting with 252, while other players given lofty consideration included Jim Bunning (214 votes) and Jim (Catfish) Hunter (212 votes).

Wilhelm, who hit a home run in his first major league at-bat and then never hit another one in his 21-year career, made his name by baffling hitters with his dancing knuckleball. Though his career won-lost record of 143-122 might not seem that impressive, he compiled a brilliant 2.52 career earned-run average, including six years of having an ERA of less than 2.00. Five of those sub-2.00 ERAs came in consecutive years (1964 through 1968) when Wilhelm was with the White Sox.

He won the 1952 National League ERA crown in his rookie season with the New York Giants with a 2.43 mark. Wilhelm's 2.19 ERA with Baltimore in 1959 was the best in the American League and he tied his career high with 15 victories that season.

After spending five seasons with the Giants, he had a brief whirl with the Cardinals and Indians, pitched four-plus seasons with the Orioles, six years with the White Sox and made short stops with the Angels, Braves and Cubs before putting the finishing touches to his career with the Dodgers in 1972.

Though he was best known as a late-inning stopper, Wilhelm did start 52 games in his career, but none before 1958. Ironically, it was as a starter that Wilhelm enjoyed his most memorable game, a 1-0 no-hitter against the New York Yankees on September 20, 1958. Oddly, it was the only game the ageless knuckleballer won for the Orioles that season.

He was a prototype master of the trick pitch. The oversized mitt that catchers use today was first tested by Baltimore's Paul Richards in 1960. Its purpose was for handling Wilhelm's dancing deliveries.

Brock was an unheralded young outfielder with the Chicago Cubs from 1961 until the trading deadline of June 15, 1964, when he was traded with pitchers Paul Toth and Jack Spring to St. Louis for pitchers Ernie Broglio and Bobby Shantz and outfielder Doug Clemens. Brock was one of the major reasons that the Cardinals won the National League pennant and World Series that season, the first Series title for St. Louis since 1946.

Brock compiled eight .300 seasons from 1964 through 1979 and helped the Cardinals to two more World Series appearances, including another championship in 1967. Brock's career .391 Series batting average stands as the best for players who competed in at least 20 games and his seven steals in 1967 and '68 also is a record.

In addition to being the all-time leading base stealer and holding the record for 12 consecutive 50-steal seasons from 1965 through 1976, Brock is one of only 15 players to collect 3,000 career hits. He finished his career with 3,023 and a lifetime average of .293.

Brock was named National League and Major League Player of the Year by The Sporting News in 1974 when he stole 118 bases to break Maury Wills' record of 104 set in 1962. Brock's record later was broken by Oakland's Rickey Henderson, who swiped 130 bases in 1982.

In 1967, Brock became the first player in history to steal 50 bases and hit 20 or more home runs in the same season (52 steals and 21 homers). He led the N.L. in stolen bases eight times, had 200-hit seasons four times, led the N.L. in runs scored with 126 in 1971 and tied for the lead with 113 in

1967.

In 1978, Brock seemed to be on his last legs, slumping to a .221 average. But, not wanting to retire on a bad note, he rebounded with a .304 season and was named Comeback Player of the Year by The Sporting News. It was a memorable swan song.

The addition of Wilhelm and Brock—coming after the Veterans Committee's election of Rick Ferrell and Pee Wee Reese in March of 1984—brought the Hall of Fame membership to 191.

The complete 1985 Hall of Fame voting totals follow:

Wilhelm, 331; Brock, 315; Fox, 295; Williams, 252; Bunning, 214; Hunter, 212; Roger Maris, 128; Harvey Kuenn, 125; Orlando Cepeda, 114; Tony Oliva, 114; Maury Wills, 93; Bill Mazeroski, 87; Lew Burdette, 82; Mickey Lolich, 78; Ken Boyer, 68; Elroy Face, 62; Elston Howard, 54; Ron Santo, 53; Joe Torre, 44; Don Larsen, 32; Thurman Munson, 32; Dick Allen, 28; Curt Flood, 28; Vada Pinson, 19; Wilbur Wood, 16; Harvey Haddix, 15; Dave McNally, 7; Ken Holtzman, 4; Ron Fairly, 3; Jim Lonborg, 3; Andy Messersmith, 3; Don Kessinger, 2; Denny McLain, 2; Jesus Alou, 1; Rico Carty, 1; Dock Ellis, 1. Failing to receive votes were Clay Carroll, Ed Kranepool, George Scott, Bobby Tolan and Roy White.

Following is a complete list of those enshrined in the Hall of Fame prior to 1984 with the vote by which each enrollee was elected:

1936—Tyrus Cobb (222), John (Honus) Wagner (215), George (Babe) Ruth (215), Christy Mathewson (205), Walter Johnson (189), named by Baseball Writers' Association of America. Total ballots cast, 226.

1937—Napoleon Lajoie (168), Tristram Speaker (165), Denton (Cy) Young (153), named by the BBWAA. Total ballots cast, 201. George Wright, Morgan G. Bulkeley, Byron Bancroft Johnson, John J. McGraw, Cornelius McGillicuddy (Connie Mack), named by Centennial Commission.

1938—Grover C. Alexander (212), named by BBWAA. Total ballots, 262. Henry Chadwick, Alexander J. Cartwright, named by Centennial Commission.

1939—George Sisler (235), Edward Collins (213), William Keeler (207), Louis Gehrig, named by BBWAA (Gehrig by special election after retirement from game was announced). Total ballots cast, 274. Albert G. Spalding, Adrian C. Anson, Charles A. Comiskey, William (Buck) Ewing, Charles Radbourn, William A. (Candy) Cummings, named by committee of old-time players and writers.

1942—Rogers Hornsby (182), named by BBWAA. Total ballots cast, 233.

Lou Brock steals one of his 118 bases during the 1974 season.

1944—Judge Kenesaw M. Landis, named by committee on old-timers.

1945—Hugh Duffy, Jimmy Collins, Hugh Jennings, Ed Delahanty, Fred Clarke, Mike Kelly, Wilbert Robinson, Jim O'Rourke, Dennis (Dan) Brouthers and Roger Bresnahan, named by committee on old-timers.

1946—Jesse Burkett, Frank Chance, Jack Chesbro, Johnny Evers, Clark Griffith, Tom McCarthy, Joe McGinnity, Eddie Plank, Joe Tinker, Rube Waddell and Ed Walsh, named by committee on old-timers.

1947—Carl Hubbell (140), Frank Frisch (136), Gordon (Mickey) Cochrane (128) and Robert (Lefty) Grove (123), named by BBWAA. Total ballots, 161.

1948—Herbert J. Pennock (94) and Harold (Pie) Traynor (93), named by BBWAA. Total ballots cast, 121.

1949—Charles Gehringer (159), named by BBWAA in runoff election. Total ballots cast, 187. Charles (Kid) Nichols and Mordecai (Three-Finger) Brown, named by committee on old timers.

1951—Mel Ott (197) and Jimmie Foxx (179), named by BBWAA. Total ballots cast, 226.

1952—Harry Heilmann (203) and Paul Waner (195), named by BBWAA. Total ballots cast, 234.

1953—Jerome (Dizzy) Dean (209) and Al Simmons (199), named by BBWAA. Total ballots cast, 264. Charles Albert (Chief) Bender, Roderick (Bobby) Wallace, William Klem, Tom Connolly, Edward G. Barrow and William Henry (Harry)

Wright, named by the new Committee on Veterans.

1954—Walter (Rabbit) Maranville (209), William Dickey (202) and William Terry (195), named by BBWAA. Total ballots cast, 252.

1955—Joe DiMaggio (223), Ted Lyons (217), Arthur (Dazzy) Vance (205) and Charles (Gabby) Hartnett (195), named by BBWAA. Total ballots cast, 251. J. Franklin (Home Run) Baker and Ray Schalk, named by Committee on Veterans.

1956—Hank Greenberg (164) and Joe Cronin (152), named by BBWAA. Total ballots cast, 193.

1957—Joseph V. McCarthy and Sam Crawford, named by Committee on Veterans.

1959—Zachariah (Zack) Wheat, named by Committee on Veterans.

1961—Max Carey and William Hamilton, named by Committee on Veterans.

1962—Bob Feller (150) and Jackie Robinson (124), named by BBWAA. Total ballots cast, 160. Bill McKechnie and Edd Roush, named by Committee on Veterans.

1963—Eppa Rixey, Edgar (Sam) Rice, Elmer Flick and John Clarkson, named by Committee on Veterans.

1964—Luke Appling (189), named by BBWAA in runoff election. Total ballots cast, 225. Urban (Red) Faber, Burleigh Grimes, Tim Keefe, Heinie Manush, Miller Huggins and John Montgomery Ward, named by Committee on Veterans.

1965—James (Pud) Galvin, named by Committee on Veterans.

1966—Ted Williams (282), named by BBWAA. Total ballots cast, 302. Casey Stengel, named by Committee on Veterans.

1967—Charles (Red) Ruffing (266), named by BBWAA in runoff election. Total ballots cast, 306. Branch Rickey and Lloyd Waner, named by Committee on Veterans.

1968—Joseph (Ducky) Medwick (240), named by BBWAA. Total ballots cast, 283. Leon (Goose) Goslin and Hazen (Kiki) Cuyler, named by Committee on Veterans.

1969—Stan (The Man) Musial (317) and Roy Campanella (270), named by BBWAA. Total ballots cast, 340. Stan Coveleski and Waite Hoyt, named by Committee on Veterans.

1970—Lou Boudreau (232), named by BBWAA. Total ballots cast, 300. Earle Combs, Jesse Haines and Ford Frick, named by Committee on Veterans.

1971—Chick Hafey, Rube Marquard, Joe Kelley, Dave Bancroft, Harry Hooper, Jake Beckley and George Weiss, named by Committee on Veterans. Satchel Paige, named by Special Committee on Negro Leagues.

1972—Sandy Koufax (344), Yogi Berra (339) and Early Wynn (301), named by BBWAA. Total ballots cast, 396. Lefty Gomez, Will Harridge and Ross Youngs, named by Committee on Veterans. Josh Gibson and Walter (Buck) Leonard, named by Special Committee on Negro Leagues.

1973—Warren Spahn (316), named by BBWAA. Total ballots cast, 380. Roberto Clemente (393), in special election by BBWAA in which 424 ballots were cast. Billy Evans, George Kelly and Mickey Welch, named by Committee on Veterans. Monte Irvin, named by Special Committee on Negro Leagues.

1974—Mickey Mantle (322) and Whitey Ford (284), named by BBWAA. Total ballots cast, 365. Jim Bottomley, Sam Thompson and Jocko Conlan, named by Committee on Veterans. James (Cool Papa) Bell, named by Special Committee on Negro Leagues.

1975—Ralph Kiner (273), named by BBWAA. Total ballots cast, 362. Earl Averill, Bucky Harris and Billy Herman, named by Committee on Veterans. William (Judy) Johnson, named by Special Committee on Negro Leagues.

1976—Robin Roberts (337) and Bob Lemon (305), named by BBWAA. Total ballots cast, 388. Roger Connor, Cal Hubbard and Fred Lindstrom, named by Committee on Veterans. Oscar Charleston, named by Special Committee on Negro Leagues.

1977—Ernie Banks (321), named by BBWAA. Total ballots cast, 383. Joe Sewell, Al Lopez and Amos Rusie, named by Committee on Veterans. Martin Dihigo and John Henry Lloyd, named by Special Committee on Negro Leagues.

1978—Eddie Mathews (301), named by BBWAA. Total ballots cast, 379. Larry MacPhail and Addie Joss, named by Committee on Veterans.

1979—Willie Mays (409), named by BBWAA. Total ballots cast, 432. Hack Wilson and Warren Giles, named by Committee on Veterans.

1980—Al Kaline (340) and Duke Snider (333), named by BBWAA. Total ballots cast, 385. Chuck Klein and Tom Yawkey, named by Committee on Veterans.

1981—Bob Gibson (337), named by BBWAA. Total ballots cast, 401. Johnny Mize and Rube Foster, named by Committee on Veterans.

1982—Henry Aaron (406) and Frank Robinson (370), named by BBWAA. Total ballots cast, 415. Albert B. (Happy) Chandler and Travis Jackson, named by Committee on Veterans.

1983—Brooks Robinson (344) and Juan Marichal (313), named by BBWAA. Total ballots cast, 374. George Kell and Walter Alston, named by Committee on Veterans.

1984—Luis Aparicio (341), Harmon Killebrew (335) and Don Drysdale (316), named by BBWAA. Total ballots cast, 403. Rick Ferrell and Pee Wee Reese, named by Committee on Veterans.

New York baseball fans hope to have plenty to cheer about in 1985 as both the Mets and Yankees acquired All-Star performers in off-season trades. Gary Carter (left) will join the Mets while Rickey Henderson is now a Yankee.

BASEBALL RE-ENTRY DRAFT

MINOR LEAGUE DRAFT

MAJOR LEAGUE TRANSACTIONS

NECROLOGY

Only time will tell whether reliever Bruce Sutter, shown above with Braves Owner Ted Turner, can pitch as well as an Atlanta Brave as he did against them (left) as a member of the St. Louis Cardinals last season.

Will Sutter's Brave New World Make Atlanta a Contender?

By LARRY WIGGE

Where would the Detroit Tigers have been without relief ace Willie Hernandez in 1984? Would the Chicago Cubs have ended 39 years of frustration without pitchers Rick Sutcliffe and Dennis Eckersley? Could the Kansas City Royals have won the American League West title without the development of young hurlers like Bret Saberhagen and Mark Gubicza? And what would the San Diego Padres have done without Goose Gossage?

That baseball sage who pronounced many years ago that pitching is 75 percent of the game may have been a little off, but a quick look at last season's divisional champions reveals improved pitching as the key to success.

That sage probably never envisioned anything like baseball's re-entry draft, but he would have to agree that the phenomenon has become an influential tool in the building of champions. The Padres' signing of free agent Gossage away from the New York Yankees would be a prime example. So would the Tigers' signing of free-agent slugger Darrell Evans, who had enjoyed a productive 1983 season with the San Francisco Giants.

Just the threat of free agency can affect pennant races. The Cubs, for example, probably never would have been able to lure Cy Young winner Sutcliffe away from the Cleveland Indians or Eckersley from the Boston Red Sox if the players had not played out their option and announced plans to enter the 1984 re-entry draft.

The draft itself is merely a formality. The real drama unfolds slowly over the ensuing weeks as baseball executives wheel and deal in an attempt to plug their teams' holes. The 1984 draft and ensuing bidding wars certainly fit that description.

The top plums were St. Louis relief ace Bruce Sutter and Sutcliffe. Other prizes included two more members of the Cubs' starting rotation, Eckersley and Steve Trout, outfielders Fred Lynn of the Angels and Lee Lacy of the Pirates and designated hitters Andre Thornton of the Indians, Dave Kingman of the A's and Toronto's Cliff Johnson.

Sutter, who had won N.L. Fireman of the Year honors in three of the four seasons he spent with the Cardinals, became baseball's highest-paid pitcher when he agreed to terms with the Atlanta Braves on December 7. Terms of Sutter's contract included a base annual salary of $750,000 for six years. Another $5.5 million would be paid by the Braves to an insurance company so that beginning in 1991, Sutter would receive deferred payments of $1.3 million per year for 30 years. The terms of agreement were guaranteed and the contract included a no-trade provision.

The signing of Sutter, who tied a major league record last season with 45 saves, came after weeks of meetings with the Braves, Orioles Angels, Rangers, Blue Jays and Cardinals. In the end, Sutter had to decide between the Cardinals and the guaranteed bonanza being offered by the Braves. The Cardinals had offered a handsome $1.4 million-a-year, five-year deal with an annuity that would have paid him $240,000 annually for 17 years beginning in 1990 and then $100,000 a year for 10 years beginning in 2007.

"I had four great years in St. Louis and I hate to leave there, but I'd be a fool not to take the money," Sutter said. "I'm a product of the system. I don't make the rules, but I'm going to live by the rules."

Less than a week after the ink had dried on Sutter's pact, Sutcliffe cashed in, re-signing with the Cubs for a $9.5 million deal for five years. It was also the final link for Chicago General Manager Dallas Green to retain his starting rotation, having previously re-signed Eckersley and Trout. Other serious bidders in the Sutcliffe sweepstakes were San Diego, Atlanta and Kansas City.

Fifty-six free agents had their names entered in the re-entry draft on November 8. Sutter, Sutcliffe, Thornton, Lynn and Johnson were listed as Type-A free agents, meaning they ranked in the top 20 percent statistically among all other players at their position over the last two seasons. Compensation for a team losing such a player is a draft choice plus a player from the compensation pool. The only Type-B player in the draft was Seattle outfielder Steve Henderson. He was ranked between the top 20 and 30 percent of all the outfielders in 1983 and '84. Two draft choices is the compensation for losing a Type-B player.

The Baltimore Orioles were the busiest buyers in the '84 re-entry market, signing their limit of three—Lynn, Lacy and former Angels reliever Don Aase. San Diego righthander Ed Whitson bolted to the Yankees for a lucrative pact. Johnson left Toronto for a new deal with the Texas Rangers, who also signed former Dodgers' hurler Burt Hooton and Detroit righthander Dave Rozema. The Padres dipped into the pool for infielder-outfielder Jerry Royster of the Braves and Cubs reliever Tim Stoddard. Houston pitcher Vern Ruhle opted for a new contract in Cleveland.

Among the notables that stayed with their clubs after participating in the draft were Thornton of the Indians, Kingman of the A's, outfielder Johnny Grubb of the Tigers and infielder Greg Pryor of the Royals.

Following is a team-by-team listing of which players each team chose the negotiation rights to in baseball's re-entry draft November 8:

AMERICAN LEAGUE

Baltimore (12): Don Aase, Dennis Eckersley, Cliff Johnson, Lee Lacy, Sixto Lezcano, Fred Lynn, Rick Sutcliffe, Bruce Sutter, Andre Thornton, Steve Trout, Ed Whitson, Rob Wilfong.

Boston (3): Don Aase, Lee Lacy, Greg Pryor.

California (7): Al Bumbry, John Grubb, Burt Hooton, Lee Lacy, Rick Sutcliffe, Bruce Sutter, Steve Trout. The Angels also retained the negotiating rights to Don Aase, Fred Lynn and Rob Wilfong.

Chicago (10): Don Aase, Dennis Eckersley, Rollie Fingers, Oscar Gamble, John Grubb, Burt Hooton, Cliff Johnson, Lee Lacy, Sixto Lezcano, Fred Lynn.

Cleveland (3): Dave Rozema, Tim Stoddard, Steve Trout. The Indians also retained the negotiating rights to Andre Thornton.

Detroit: None. The Tigers did retain the negotiating rights to Ruppert Jones.

Kansas City (3): John Grubb, Rick Sutcliffe, Andre Thornton. The Royals also retained the negotiating rights to Greg Pryor.

Milwaukee (4): Lee Lacy, Andre Thornton, Steve Trout, Ed Whitson.

Minnesota (1): Andre Thornton.

New York (13): Don Aase, Bobby Castillo, Lee Lacy, Sixto Lezcano, Fred Lynn, Steve Nicosia, Greg Pryor, Rick Sutcliffe, Bruce Sutter, Andre Thornton, Steve Trout, Ed Whitson, Rob Wilfong. The Yankees chose not to retain the negotiating rights to Oscar Gamble.

Oakland (9): Don Aase, Al Bumbry, Bobby Castillo, Dennis Eckersley, Burt Hooton, Ruppert Jones, Sixto Lezcano, Tug McGraw, Ed Whitson.

Seattle (8): Don Aase, Bobby Castillo, Burt Hooton, Ruppert Jones, Lee Lacy, Tim Stoddard, Steve Trout, Ed Whitson.

Texas (16): Don Aase, Dennis Eckersley, Burt Hooton, Cliff Johnson, Ruppert Jones, Lee Lacy, Sixto Lezcano, Fred Lynn, Steve Nicosia, Tim Stoddard, Rick Sutcliffe, Bruce Sutter, Andre Thornton, Steve Trout, Ed Whitson, Rob Wilfong.

Toronto (11): Don Aase, Gary Allenson, Rollie Fingers, Oscar Gamble, Lee Lacy, Steve Nicosia, Dave Rozema, Tim Stoddard, Bruce Sutter, Andre Thornton, Steve Trout.

NATIONAL LEAGUE

Atlanta (4): Rick Sutcliffe, Bruce Sutter, Steve Trout, Ed Whitson.

Chicago: None. The Cubs did retain the negotiating rights to Dennis Eckersley, Tim Stoddard, Rick Sutcliffe and Steve Trout.

Cincinnati (3): Greg Pryor, John Stearns, Steve Trout.

Houston (1): Sixto Lezcano.

Los Angeles (8): Don Aase, Bobby Castillo, Miguel Dilone, John Grubb, Lee Lacy, Tim Stoddard, Steve Trout, Jim Wohlford. The Dodgers chose not to retain the negotiating rights to Burt Hooton.

Montreal (12): Don Aase, Bill Almon, Ruppert Jones, Bruce Kison, Lee Lacy, Steve Nicosia, Jerry Royster, John Stearns, Tim Stoddard, Steve Trout, Ed Whitson, Rob Wilfong.

New York: None.

Philadelphia (4): Don Aase, Steve Trout, Ed Whitson, Rob Wilfong. The Phillies chose not to retain the negotiating rights to Sixto Lezcano.

Pittsburgh (16): Don Aase, Bobby Castillo, Dennis Eckersley, Rollie Fingers, Oscar Gamble, Ruppert Jones, Dave Kingman, Sixto Lezcano, Greg Luzinsi, Steve Nicosia, Greg Pryor, John Stearns, Tim Stoddard, Steve Trout, Ed Whitson, Rob Wilfong. The Pirates also retained the negotiating rights to Lee Lacy.

St. Louis (5): Don Aase, Lee Lacy, Rick Sutcliffe, Steve Trout, Ed Whitson. The Cardinals also retained the negotiating rights to Bruce Sutter.

San Diego (6): Lee Lacy, Fred Lynn, Jerry Royster, Tim Stoddard, Rick Sutcliffe, Steve Trout. The Padres also retained the negotiating rights to Ed Whitson.

San Francisco (6): Oscar Gamble, John Grubb, Lee Lacy, Tim Stoddard, Steve Trout, Rob Wilfong. The Giants also retained the negotiating rights to Steve Nicosia.

A look at the most popular players among the 56 players in the draft, with the number of times each was selected in parentheses:

Steve Trout (17), Lee Lacy (14), Don Aase (13), Ed Whitson (11), Tim Stoddard (9), Rick Sutcliffe (8), Sixto Lezcano, Andre Thornton and Rob Wilfong (7 times each), Bruce Sutter (6), Bobby Castillo, Dennis Eckersley, John Grubb, Burt Hooton, Ruppert Jones, Fred Lynn and Steve Nicosia (5 each), Oscar Gamble and Greg Pryor (4 each).

The following players, each chosen by fewer than four clubs, have the right to negotiate with every team: Rollie Fingers, Cliff Johnson and John Stearns (3 each), Al Bumbry, Jerry Royster and Dave Rozema (2 each), Gary Allenson, Bill Almon, Miguel Dilone, Dave Kingman, Bruce Kison, Greg Luzinski, Tug McGraw, Jim Wohlford (1 each). Players who were not selected at all in the draft were: Jerry Augustine, Benny Ayala, John Curtis, Rich Gale, Steve Henderson, Jim Kern, Mike LaCoss, Randy Lerch, Milt May, Rudy May, Dan Meyer, Bob Owchinko, Tony Perez, Pat Putnam, Rick Reuschel, Gene Richards, Vern Ruhle, Ken Singleton, Chris Speier, Champ Summers, Craig Swan, Derrel Thomas and Mark Wagner.

Mets Lose 4 Players in Draft

By LARRY WIGGE

New York Mets General Manager Frank Cashen could have felt flattered. His major league counterparts thought so much of some of the Mets' prospects that four of the 13 players taken in the 1984 major league draft were selected from his organization. But Cashen lost the four players so fast, and at bargain-basement prices, that he felt like he had just been fleeced.

The draft, which opened the activity at baseball's 83rd annual winter meetings in Houston December 3, normally doesn't turn too many heads because available players normally are not good enough to be protected on the 40-man rosters of the parent clubs. But, Cashen, for one, noticed. And the $25,000 he got for each of the players he lost hardly seemed enough payment for all the time and effort he felt the Mets had spent developing those players.

With clubs drafting in inverse order of their 1984 records and alternating by leagues, the San Francisco Giants made the first $25,000 selection, tabbing veteran catcher Doug Gwosdz from the Padres' organization. The 24-year-old Gwosdz, who had previously played in 62 games while in San Diego over the past three seasons, batted .228 with six homers and 27 RBIs at Las Vegas of the Pacific Coast League in 1984 in addition to compiling a .250 average in seven games with the Padres.

Milwaukee, choosing second, took Mets' farmhand Brian Giles. Giles, who had been the starting second baseman for the Mets in 1983, batted .242 at Tidewater (International League) in '84. After the Reds passed, the Padres lost their second player, lefthanded pitcher Mitchell Williams.

Junior Ortiz, another Mets' farmhand, was taken next by the Pirates. Ortiz had previously had brief whirls in the majors with the Mets and Pirates. Later, the Phillies opted for lefthander Ed Olwine and the Blue Jays selected outfielder Louis Thornton, the third and fourth players chosen from the Mets' system.

Draft choices in order of selection:

FIRST ROUND

Giants —Catcher Doug Gwosdz from Las Vegas (Pacific Coast) of the Padres' organization.

Brewers —Infielder Brian Giles from Tidewater (International) of the Mets' organization.

Rangers —Lefthanded pitcher Mitchell Williams from Las Vegas (Pacific Coast) of the Padres' organization.

Pirates —Catcher Junior Ortiz from Tidewater (International) of the Mets' organization.

White Sox —Righthander Bill Landrum from Wichita (American Association) of the Reds' organization.

Mariners —Righthanded pitcher Mike Morgan from Syracuse (International) of the Blue Jays' organization.

Twins —Catcher Mark Salas from Louisville (American Association) of the Cardinals' organization.

Phillies —Lefthanded pitcher Ed Olwine from Tidewater (International) of the Mets' organization.

Cardinals —Infielder Willie Lozado from Vancouver (Pacific Coast) of the Brewers' organization.

Red Sox —Righthanded pitcher Mike Trujillo from Phoenix (Pacific Coast) of the Giants' organization.

Blue Jays —Infielder Manny Lee from Tucson (Pacific Coast) of the Astros' organization.

Tigers —Outfielder James Weaver from Toledo (International) of the Twins' organization.

SECOND ROUND

Blue Jays—Outfielder Louis Thornton Jr. from Tidewater (International) of the Mets' organization.

Major League Attendance for 1984

NATIONAL LEAGUE

	Home	Away
Atlanta	1,724,892	1,635,302
Chicago	2,104,219	1,998,933
Cincinnati	1,275,887	1,686,328
Houston	1,229,862	1,526,616
Los Angeles	3,134,824	1,933,463
Montreal	1,606,531	1,695,962
New York	1,842,695	1,767,982
Philadelphia	2,062,693	1,839,010
Pittsburgh	773,500	1,765,114
St. Louis	2,037,448	1,597,594
San Diego	1,983,904	1,730,411
San Francisco	1,001,545	1,601,285
Total	20,778,000	20,778,000

AMERICAN LEAGUE

	Home	Away
Baltimore	2,045,784	1,759,964
Boston	1,661,618	1,742,097
California	2,402,997	1,723,267
Chicago	2,136,988	1,803,928
Cleveland	734,079	1,538,069
Detroit	2,704,794	2,160,289
Kansas City	1,810,018	1,582,510
Milwaukee	1,608,509	1,832,360
Minnesota	1,598,692	1,549,501
New York	1,821,815	1,941,023
Oakland	1,353,281	1,565,597
Seattle	870,372	1,491,641
Texas	1,102,471	1,561,739
Toronto	2,110,009	1,709,172
Total	23,961,427	23,961,427

Dealer Green Rebuilt Cubs

By DAVE SLOAN

There are three ways to build a pennant contender—the farm system, trades and free agents. Financially, building from within makes the most sense. But there comes a time when holes need to be plugged and gaps filled. The price for being a contender can be high.

The Detroit Tigers, San Diego Padres and Chicago Cubs, all division title winners in 1984, were baseball's three winningest teams. Although each had a nucleus of home-grown talent on its roster, it's doubtful that any of the three would have won its division without making trades or signing free agents.

The Tigers, for example, had a strong home-grown core featuring Lou Whitaker, Alan Trammell, Lance Parrish, Kirk Gibson, Jack Morris and Dan Petry. But the Tigers didn't become a dominating team until they acquired Willie Hernandez in a spring-training trade with the Phillies. Used primarily as the second reliever behind Bruce Sutter during his days with the Cubs and behind Al Holland with Philadelphia, Hernandez exploded with a terrific 1984 campaign as the Tigers' No. 1 man out of the bullpen. Hernandez posted 32 saves, a 9-3 record and a 1.92 earned-run average as Detroit rolled to 104 regular-season victories and its first World Series title in 16 years. Hernandez's value to the Tigers was so obvious that he won both the American League Most Valuable Player and Cy Young awards for 1984.

First baseman Dave Bergman (7 homers, 44 runs batted in, .273 average), acquired from the Phils along with Hernandez in that March 24 trade for Glenn Wilson and John Wockenfuss, and free agents Darrell Evans and Ruppert Jones also contributed heavily to the Tigers' cause. Bergman often was used by Manager Sparky Anderson as a late-inning defensive specialist while Evans (16 homers, 63 RBIs) and Jones (12 homers, 37 RBIs, .284 average) supplied power.

The Padres, who won their first National League pennant before losing to the Tigers in the World Series, also made some key moves before the '84 season.

The biggest came on January 6 when they signed former Yankee relief ace Rich Gossage, a free agent, to a multiyear contract worth more than $6 million. Gossage gave his new team some much-needed relief, recording 10 victories, 25 saves and a 2.90 ERA.

Ex-Yankee veterans Rich Gossage (above) and Graig Nettles were key ingredients to San Diego's first N.L. pennant in 1984.

The Padres followed that act by acquiring 39-year-old third baseman Graig Nettles on March 30 from the Yanks for pitcher Dennis Rasmussen and a player to be named. Not only did Nettles belt 20 homers and drive in 65 runs, but he, along with Gossage and Steve Garvey, a free agent who had signed with San Diego the previous winter, provided the clubhouse leadership and playoff experience needed by a young Padres team.

The most dramatic 1984 turnaround was recorded by the Chicago Cubs. The Cubs won the N.L. East Division title, the franchise's first championship in 39 years, and came within one game of reaching the World Series. Lovable and laughable for so many years, the Cubs' turnaround can be traced directly to the many deals pulled off by General Manager Dallas Green.

Shortly before the season, Green traded relief pitcher Bill Campbell and catcher Mike Diaz to the Phillies for outfielders Gary Matthews and Bob Dernier and pitcher Porfi Altamirano. Dernier, batting leadoff, and Matthews, batting third, became regulars in Manager Jim Frey's lineup. And with The Sporting News Major League Player of the Year Ryne Sandberg batting second, the Cubs had one of baseball's best 1-2-3 batting punches.

The day before the Matthews-Dernier deal, Green had traded two minor leaguers to the A's for pitcher Tim Stoddard. Stoddard responded with a 10-6 record and seven saves.

The parade continued when, on May 25, Green sent one of the Cubs' most popular players, first baseman Bill Buckner, to the Red Sox for pitcher Dennis Eckersley and a minor leaguer. Eckersley pitched well and won 10 games for the Cubs.

Dealer Green, however, saved his best for last.

On June 13, he traded promising outfielders Mel Hall and Joe Carter and two minor-league pitchers to the Indians for pitchers Rick Sutcliffe and George Frazier and catcher Ron Hassey. Frazier and Hassey performed well, but Sutcliffe was the difference. Off to a mediocre 4-5 start with a poor Cleveland team, Sutcliffe won 16 games for Chicago, including 14 in a row, against only one loss. The Cubs, 34-25 and in first place at the time of the trade, were 62-40 with Sutcliffe as their ace and took control in the N.L. East. A former Rookie of the Year in 1979 with the Dodgers, Sutcliffe won the National League Cy Young Award and Green followed that up by being named TSN's Executive of the Year.

Pete Rose not only returned to play for the club he started with 22 seasons earlier, he now manages it.

Aside from those deals directly affecting pennant races, other player moves drew headlines in 1984.

Pete Rose, in hot pursuit of Ty Cobb's all-time hits record, signed on as a free agent with the Expos on January 20. He collected his 4,000th career hit on April 13, but before his first season north of the border was complete, he moved again. On August 16, Montreal dealt the future Hall of Famer back to the club with which Rose began his career and enjoyed his greatest success—the Cincinnati Reds. Rose, who also assumed the managerial chores from Vern Rapp, batted .365 in 26 games and guided the club to a 19-22 record and fifth-place finish in the N.L. West Division.

Tom Seaver, a star pitcher for the New York Mets during their glory years, ended up in a Chicago White Sox uniform because of a blunder by Mets General Manager Frank Cashen. Cashen, the man responsible for submitting his club's protected list for baseball's annual player compensation pool draft, left Seaver's name off the list. So when the White Sox lost free-agent pitcher Dennis Lamp to Toronto, they replaced him on January 20 with the 39-year-old Seaver, a 273-game winner in 17 big-league seasons. The

White Sox made a good choice. Seaver posted 15 wins in his first American League season.

Another compensation controversy arose February 8 involving a pitcher of less prominence, but great potential. When Oakland hurler Tom Underwood signed as a free agent with Baltimore in February, the A's grabbed young Yankee prospect Tim Belcher as compensation.

Belcher, a 6-foot-3, 210-pound, hard-throwing righthander, was chosen first overall by the Minnesota Twins in the June, 1983 free-agent draft. Unsigned by Minnesota, Belcher was grabbed first overall by the Yankees in the secondary phase (for unsigned players) of the January, 1984 draft. The consensus among many scouts is that someday Belcher will be an outstanding big-league pitcher.

When the A's chose Belcher, the Yankees cried foul, claiming that Belcher shouldn't have been eligible for the draft because he wasn't a member of the Yankees—and therefore subject to protection—until after the protected lists had to be submitted. Since those lists are frozen, the Yanks had no way to protect Belcher after he was signed, just six days before the A's selected him. But Commissioner Bowie Kuhn, while acknowledging that the system has flaws, nonetheless awarded Belcher to the A's.

Two veterans, Phil Niekro and Dave Kingman, showed their former clubs that they weren't at the end of the line. Niekro, cut loose by the Atlanta Braves after 25 years in the Braves' organization, signed on as a free agent with the Yankees on January 6. Niekro responded with a 16-8 record and 3.09 ERA as the Yankees No. 1 pitcher and was named to the American League All-Star team.

Kingman, released by the Mets after the '83 season, hooked on with the A's just before the start of the season. He responded with 35 home runs and 118 RBIs and was named American League Comeback Player of the Year.

There was no shortage of trades after the season as clubs began preparing for 1985:

• On December 5, the A's sent five-time A.L. base-stealing king Rickey Henderson and a minor leaguer to the Yankees for five players, including highly touted pitching prospects Jose Rijo and Jay Howell. Some scouts put the 19-year-old Rijo in the same class with Mets sensation Dwight Gooden.

• The Padres acquired 1983 A.L. Cy Young Award winner LaMarr Hoyt from the White Sox on December 6 in an effort to shore up a starting rotation that was dismantled by Detroit in the World Series. Hoyt, who was acquired along with pitchers Kevin Kristan and Todd Simmons, slumped from a 24-10 record in '83 to 13-18 last season. The White Sox received starting pitcher Tim Lollar, third baseman Luis Salazar, shortstop Ozzie Guillen and pitcher Bill Long.

• On December 8, the Blue Jays picked up reliever Bill Caudill from Oakland for shortstop Alfredo Griffin, outfielder Dave Collins and cash.

• On December 10, the Mets acquired seven-time All-Star catcher Gary Carter from the Expos for four players, including third baseman Hubie Brooks and catcher Mike Fitzgerald.

• On December 20, the Yankees traded outfielder Steve Kemp, infielder Tim Foli and $800,000 to the Pirates for shortstop Dale Berra, a .222 hitter last season, pitcher Alfonso Pulido and minor-league outfielder Jay Buhner. Yankee Manager Yogi Berra will team with son Dale to form the first father-son, manager-player combination since former Philadelphia A's Manager Connie Mack managed his son.

Several big-name players either retired or were released in 1984. Pitchers Jim Kaat, Jim Palmer, Ferguson Jenkins, J.R. Richard and Paul Splittorff called it quits after successful careers.

Outfielders Lou Piniella, Rick Monday and Amos Otis were among the players who cut off long-time associations with their teams. Piniella and Monday retired while Otis signed with Pittsburgh after a 14-year career with Kansas City.

Following is a list of all player transactions for the 1984 calendar year:

January 5—Cubs signed infielder Richie Hebner, a re-entry free agent formerly with the Pirates.

January 6—Yankees signed pitcher Phil Niekro, a free agent.

January 6—Padres signed pitcher Rich Gossage, a re-entry free agent formerly with the Yankees.

January 8—White Sox re-signed second baseman Julio Cruz, a re-entry free agent.

January 10—Blue Jays signed pitcher Dennis Lamp, a re-entry free agent formerly with the White Sox.

January 13—Dodgers signed outfielder Terry Whitfield, a free agent.

January 16—Brewers re-signed catcher Ted Simmons, a re-entry free agent.

January 17—Expos signed outfielder Miguel Dilone, a re-entry free agent formerly with the Pirates.

January 17—Brewers released infielder Don Money.

January 17—Indians re-signed pitcher Jamie

Easterly, a re-entry free agent.

January 19—Indians signed pitcher Steve Comer, a free agent, and assigned him to Maine.

January 20—Expos signed first baseman-outfielder Pete Rose, a free agent.

January 20—White Sox selected Mets pitcher Tom Seaver as compensation for the loss of Type A free-agent pitcher Dennis Lamp, who signed with the Blue Jays.

January 23—Indians traded pitcher Tom Brennan to the White Sox for a player to be named; White Sox assigned Brennan to Denver.

January 23—A's signed pitcher Lary Sorensen, a re-entry free agent formerly with the Indians.

January 23—Orioles re-signed outfielder Dan Ford, a re-entry free agent.

January 26—Mariners re-signed outfielder Steve Henderson, a re-entry free agent.

January 27—Mets signed pitcher Dick Tidrow, a re-entry free agent formerly with the White Sox.

January 30—White Sox released third baseman Lorenzo Gray.

January 30—Mets released first baseman-outfielder Dave Kingman.

January 31—Cardinals signed outfielder Vic Harris, a free agent, and assigned him to Louisville.

February 1—Pirates signed outfielder Joe Charboneau, a free agent, and assigned him to Hawaii.

February 2—Expos signed infielder-outfielder Derrel Thomas, a re-entry free agent formerly with the Dodgers.

February 5—Indians traded third baseman Toby Harrah and a player to be named to the Yankees for pitcher George Frazier, outfielder Otis Nixon and a player to be named; to complete the transaction, the Yankees sent pitcher Guy Elston, who was on their Columbus, O., roster, to the Indians for pitcher Rick Browne, who was on the Waterloo roster.

February 6—Angels signed infielder Rob Picciolo, a re-entry free agent formerly with the A's.

February 7—Orioles signed pitcher Tommy Underwood, a re-entry free agent formerly with the A's.

February 8—Rangers signed pitcher Jim Bibby, a re-entry free agent formerly with the Pirates.

February 8—A's selected pitcher Tim Belcher from Yankees organization as compensation for the loss of Type A free-agent pitcher Tommy Underwood, who signed with the Orioles.

February 10—Indians signed third baseman Lorenzo Gray, a free agent, and assigned him to Maine.

February 14—Yankees traded infielder Larry Milbourne to Mariners for pitchers Scott Nielsen and Eric Parent; Yankees assigned Nielsen and Parent to Nashville.

February 15—Phillies acquired pitcher Jerry Koosman from White Sox, completing December 5 deal in which Phillies traded pitcher Ron Reed to White Sox for cash or a player to be named.

February 17—Astros re-signed pitcher J.R. Richard, a re-entry free agent, and assigned him to Tucson.

February 17—A's released pitcher Scott Dye.

February 20—Red Sox signed pitcher Rich Gale, a free agent, and assigned him to Pawtucket.

February 20—Astros signed infielder Enos Cabell, a re-entry free agent formerly with the Tigers.

February 21—Dodgers outfielder Dusty Baker became a free agent after rejecting a waiver claim by the Giants.

February 22—Mets released outfielder Mark Bradley.

February 24—Expos traded catcher Tom Wieghaus to Astros for a player to be named; Expos acquired catcher George Bjorkman on March 26 and assigned him to Indianapolis.

February 27—Expos traded first baseman Al Oliver to Giants for pitcher Fred Breining and a player to be named; because of an injury to Breining, Expos acquired outfielder Max Venable and pitcher Andy McGaffigan on March 31. Venable was assigned to Indianapolis.

March 1—White Sox released pitcher Jim Kern.

March 10—Rangers released catcher Bobby Johnson.

March 13—Blue Jays traded pitcher Don Cooper to Yankees for outfielder Derwin McNealy; Yankees assigned Cooper to Columbus, O., and Blue Jays assigned McNealy to Syracuse.

March 17—Mets signed outfielder Jerry Martin, a re-entry free agent formerly with the Royals.

March 19—Cubs released pitcher Ferguson Jenkins.

March 21—White Sox released infielder Kelly Paris.

March 21—Cardinals signed infielder Art Howe, a re-entry free agent formerly with the Astros.

March 23—Cubs released pitcher Mike Chris.

March 23—Mariners released infielder Manny Castillo, outfielder Ron Roenicke and catcher Rick Sweet.

March 24—Phillies traded outfielder Alejandro Sanchez to Giants for first baseman Dave Bergman; Giants assigned Sanchez to Phoenix.

March 24—Phillies traded first baseman Dave Bergman and pitcher Willie Hernandez to Tigers for outfielder Glenn Wilson and catcher-first baseman John Wockenfuss.

March 24—Red Sox traded pitcher Luis Aponte to Indians for pitchers Mike Poindexter and Paul Perry; Red Sox assigned Poindexter and Perry to Winter Haven.

March 24—Tigers released infielder-outfielder Rick Leach and infielder Jim Smith.

March 24—Braves reclaimed catcher Terry Cormack from Blue Jays, who had selected him from Richmond in the 1983 major league draft.

March 25—Astros purchased outfielder-infielder Alan Bannister from Indians.

March 25—Orioles traded outfielder Tito Landrum to Cardinals for pitcher Jose Brito and cash; Orioles assigned Brito to Rochester.

March 25—Royals released pitchers Don Hood and Roger Erickson.

March 26—Padres released second baseman Juan Bonilla.

March 26—Padres released second baseman Juan Bonilla.

March 26—Cardinals released catcher Jamie Quirk.

March 26—Braves released pitcher Bob Walk.

March 26—Tigers released pitcher Jerry Ujdur.

March 26—A's traded pitcher Tim Stoddard to Cubs for pitcher Stan Kyles and a player to be named; A's acquired outfielder Stan Boderick on March 31. Kyles was assigned to Tacoma, Boderick to Madison.

March 26—White Sox released pitchers Randy Martz, Steve Mura and Kevin Hickey.

March 26—Expos released outfielder Mike Vail.

March 26—A's released pitcher Ed Farmer.

March 26—Rangers released pitcher Pat Underwood.

March 27—Astros released pitcher J. R. Richard.

March 27—Phillies traded outfielders Bob Dernier and Gary Matthews and pitcher Porfi Altamirano to Cubs for pitcher Bill Campbell and catcher Mike Diaz; Phillies assigned Diaz, who was on Iowa roster, to Portland.

March 28—Giants signed outfielder Gene Richards, a re-entry free agent formerly with the Padres.

March 28—Cubs released pitcher Mike Proly.

March 28—Pirates signed infielder Kelly Paris, a free agent, and assigned him to Hawaii.

March 29—A's signed first baseman-outfielder Dave Kingman, a free agent, and released outfielder Mitchell Page.

March 29—Mets reclaimed pitcher Jay Tibbs from Phillies, who had selected him from Tidewater in the 1983 major league draft.

March 30—Orioles purchased third baseman-catcher Floyd Rayford from Cardinals and assigned him to Rochester.

March 30—Yankees traded third baseman Graig Nettles to Padres for pitcher Dennis Rasmussen and a player to be named. Yankees assigned Rasmussen to Columbus, O.; acquired pitcher Darin Cloninger, who was on Miami roster, on April 26 and assigned him to Fort Lauderdale.

March 31—Indians purchased catcher Juan Espino from Yankees and assigned him to Maine.

March 31—Royals traded pitcher Derek Botelho and catcher Don Werner to Cubs for pitcher Alan Hargesheimer and a player to be named.

March 31—Pirates released catcher-first baseman Gene Tenace.

April 1—Indians released pitcher Juan Eichelberger.

April 1—Royals traded pitcher Tom Edens to Mets for infielder Tucker Ashford; Mets assigned Edens, who was on Fort Myers roster, to Columbia.

April 1—Giants signed outfielder Dusty Baker, a free agent, and released pitcher Jim Barr.

April 1—Mariners released catcher Bill Nahorodny.

April 1—Angels released pitcher Andy Hassler.

April 2—Rangers released shortstop Bucky Dent.

April 2—Orioles signed pitcher Pat Underwood, a free agent, and assigned him to Rochester.

April 2—White Sox signed pitcher Kevin Hickey (whom they had released March 26) and assigned him to Glens Falls.

April 3—Pirates signed pitcher Bob Walk, a free agent, and assigned him to Hawaii.

April 3—Blue Jays signed first baseman-outfielder Rick Leach and infielder Manny Castillo, both free agents, and assigned them to Syracuse.

April 5—Cardinals' Louisville affiliate purchased outfielder-first baseman Gary Rajsich from Mets.

April 9—Cubs traded pitcher Terry Leach to Braves for pitcher Ron Meridith. Cubs assigned Meridith to Iowa, and Braves assigned Leach to Richmond.

April 10—Red Sox released pitcher David Schoppee.

April 18—Tigers signed outfielder Ruppert Jones, a free agent, and assigned him to Evansville.

April 24—Braves released catcher Biff Pocoroba.

April 24—Reds traded catcher Alex Trevino to Braves for a player to be named; deal was settled in July with cash, reportedly about $50,000.

May 1—Blue Jays signed pitcher Mike Proly, a free agent, and assigned him to Syracuse.

May 2—Cardinals signed pitcher Andy Hassler, a free agent, and assigned him to Arkansas.

May 8—Indians' Maine affiliate purchased catcher Geno Petralli from Blue Jays.

May 8—Mets released pitcher Dick Tidrow.

May 9—Royals purchased outfielder Dane Iorg from Cardinals.

May 9—Mets released pitcher Craig Swan.

May 9—A's traded pitcher Jeff Bettendorf to Mets for a player to be named; Mets assigned Bettendorf to Jackson.

May 13—Blue Jays released pitcher Joey McLaughlin.

May 16—Orioles purchased catcher Orlando Sanchez from Royals and assigned him to Rochester.

May 17—Orioles released pitcher Jim Palmer.

May 19—Orioles purchased infielder Tucker Ashford from Royals and assigned him to Rochester.

May 23—Angels signed pitcher Craig Swan, a free agent.

May 23—White Sox signed catcher Jamie Quirk, a free agent, and assigned him to Denver.

May 24—Cardinals purchased first baseman-outfielder Gary Rajsich from Louisville.

May 25—Rangers traded second baseman Mike Richardt to Astros for infielder-outfielder Alan Bannister; Astros assigned Richardt to Tucson.

May 25—Cubs traded first baseman-outfielder Bill Buckner to Red Sox for pitcher Dennis Eckersley and outfielder Mike Brumley; Cubs assigned Brumley, who was on New Britain roster, to Midland.

June 1—Rangers released pitcher Jim Bibby.

June 3—Phillies signed pitcher Jim Kern, a free agent.

June 7—Dodgers released catcher Jose Morales.

June 7—Yankees signed shortstop Bucky Dent, a free agent, and assigned him to Columbus, O.

June 9—Cardinals signed pitcher Jim Bibby, a free agent, and assigned him to Louisville.

June 10—Tigers purchased pitcher Sid Monge from Padres.

June 10—Dodgers signed outfielder Mike Vail, a free agent.

June 13—Indians traded catcher Ron Hassey and pitchers Rick Sutcliffe and George Frazier to Cubs for outfielders Mel Hall and Joe Carter and pitchers Don Schulze and Darryl Banks. Indians assigned Schulze, who was on Iowa roster, to Maine, and Banks, who was on Midland roster, to Buffalo. Carter, who was on Iowa roster, remained with the Indians.

June 15—Cardinals traded third baseman Ken Oberkfell to Braves for first baseman Mike Jorgensen and pitcher Ken Dayley, who was on Richmond roster.

June 15—Reds traded pitcher Bruce Berenyi to Mets for third baseman Eddie Williams and pitchers Jay Tibbs and Matt Bullinger. Reds assigned Williams, who was on Columbia roster, to Tampa; Tibbs, who was on Tidewater roster, to Wichita, and Bullinger, who was on Jackson roster, to Wichita.

June 17—Yankees announced the retirement of outfielder Lou Piniella.

June 21—Indians traded pitcher Dan Spillner to White Sox for a player to be named; Indians acquired pitcher Jim Siwy on June 26 and assigned him to Maine.

June 22—Dodgers released outfielder Rick Monday.

June 22—Mets released pitcher Mike Torrez.

June 27—White Sox traded pitcher Salome Barojas to Mariners for pitchers Gene Nelson and Jerry Don Gleaton, who were on Salt Lake City roster; White Sox assigned Gleaton to Denver.

June 29—Astros released outfielder Tony Scott.

June 29—Expos signed outfielder Tony Scott, a free agent.

June 30—Yankees traded pitcher Shane Rawley to Phillies for pitcher Marty Bystrom and outfielder Keith Hughes; Yankees assigned Hughes, who was on Reading roster, to Nashville.

July 1—Royals announced the retirement of pitcher Paul Splittorff.

July 1—Cardinals traded infielder Mike Ramsey to Expos for shortstop Chris Speier and cash.

July 2—Cubs traded pitcher Dickie Noles to Rangers for players to be named; Cubs acquired pitcher Tim Henry and infielder Jorge Gomez on December 11. Henry and Gomez, who were on Tulsa roster, were assigned to Pittsfield.

July 3—A's signed pitcher Mike Torrez, a free agent, and assigned him to Tacoma.

July 9—Yankees released shortstop Bucky Dent, who was on Columbus, O., roster.

July 15—Cubs traded pitcher Chuck Rainey to A's for a player to be named; Cubs acquired infielder-outfielder Davey Lopes on August 31.

July 18—Yankees traded infielder Roy Smalley to White Sox for two players to be named; Yankees acquired pitchers Kevin Hickey and Doug Drabek on August 13. Hickey, who was on Denver roster, was assigned to Columbus, O., and Drabek, who was on Glens Falls roster, was assigned to Nashville.

July 20—Expos traded pitcher Greg Harris to Padres for infielder Al Newman, who remained on Beaumont roster.

July 26—Reds traded first baseman Dan Driessen to Expos for pitchers Andy McGaffigan and Jim Jefferson; Reds assigned Jefferson, who was on Jacksonville roster, to Vermont.

July 27—Phillies released pitcher Jim Kern.

August 2—Angels released infielder Ron Jackson.

August 6—Pirates released outfielder Amos Otis.

August 8—A's released pitcher Mike Torrez.

August 14—Tigers released pitcher Glenn Abbott.

August 14—Orioles signed infielder Ron Jackson, a free agent, and assigned him to Rochester.

August 16—Royals signed shortstop Bucky Dent, a free agent.

August 16—Expos traded first baseman-outfielder Pete Rose to Reds for infielder Tom Lawless. Rose, in addition to continuing his playing career, replaced Vern Rapp as the Reds' manager. Lawless was assigned to Indianapolis.

August 19—Cardinals traded shortstop Chris Speier to Twins for cash and a player to be named; Cardinals acquired pitcher Jay Pettibone on October 2, who was on Orlando roster, and assigned him to Arkansas.

August 20—Giants traded first baseman Al Oliver and a player to be named to Phillies for

pitchers Kelly Downs and George Riley, who were on Portland roster; Phillies acquired pitcher Renie Martin, who was on Phoenix roster, on August 30.

August 27—Reds traded pitcher Bill Scherrer to Tigers for cash and a player to be named; Reds acquired pitcher Carl Willis on September 1.

August 28—Astros traded infielder Ray Knight to Mets for three players to be named; Astros acquired outfielder Gerald Young and infielder Manny Lee, who were on Columbia roster, on August 31, and pitcher Mitch Cook, who was on Lynchburg roster, on September 10.

August 29—Mariners traded first baseman Pat Putnam to Twins for a player to be named; Mariners acquired infielder Carson Carroll, who was on Visalia roster, and assigned him to Salt Lake City.

August 31—Giants traded infielder Tom O'Malley, who was on Phoenix roster, to White Sox for two players to be named; Giants acquired pitcher Mike Trujillo and first baseman Pat Adams on September 7. Trujillo and Adams, who were on Glens Falls roster, was assigned to Phoenix.

September 1—Royals traded pitcher James Miner to Astros for catcher Luis Pujols, who was on Tucson roster; Miner, who was on Memphis roster, was assigned to Columbus, Ga.

September 4—Royals released outfielder Mark Ryal.

September 6—Expos traded infielder-outfielder Derrel Thomas to Angels for cash and a player to be named.

September 9—Cubs released outfielder Jay Johnstone.

September 9—Reds traded outfielder Paul Householder to Cardinals for pitcher John Stuper.

September 24—Indians purchased catcher Jamie Quirk from White Sox.

September 30—Mets released outfielder Jerry Martin.

October 1—Braves announced the retirement of pitcher Pete Falcone.

October 1—Expos released outfielder Tony Scott.

October 1—Brewers released infielder Roy Howell.

October 2—Orioles released pitcher Tommy Underwood.

October 2—Cardinals traded outfielders Paul Householder and Jim Adduci to Brewers for shortstop Ron Koenigsfeld and pitchers Jim Koontz and Rich Buonantony. Adduci, who was on Louisville roster, was assigned to Vancouver. Buonantony, who was on Stockton roster, and Koontz and Koenigsfeld, who were on Vancouver roster, were assigned to Louisville.

October 10—Royals released outfielder Leon Roberts and shortstop Bucky Dent.

October 10—Dodgers released infielder Rafael Landestoy.

October 15—Indians released first baseman Broderick Perkins, pitcher Steve Comer and catcher Jamie Quirk.

October 16—A's released pitcher Lary Sorensen.

October 17—Twins released pitcher Al Williams.

October 19—A's released pitcher Jeff Jones.

October 19—White Sox released pitcher Guy Hoffman and outfielder Casey Parsons.

October 19—Royals released catcher Luis Pujols.

October 22—A's released outfielder Garry Hancock.

October 29—Rangers released pitcher Joey McLaughlin.

October 31—Reds traded pitcher Keefe Cato to Padres for pitcher Darren Burroughs.

October 31—Mets released catcher Ron Hodges.

November 1—Padres released outfielder Ed Miller.

November 5—Mariners released catcher Bill Nahorodny.

November 5—Yankees released pitcher Matt Keough.

November 5—Giants released infielders Joe Pittman and Guy Sularz.

November 6—Twins released pitcher Keith Comstock.

November 7—Angels released outfielder Ellis Valentine.

November 7—Expos traded pitcher Chris Welsh to Rangers for first baseman Dave Hostetler. Hostetler was assigned to Indianapolis, Welsh to Oklahoma City.

November 9—Cardinals released pitcher Dave Von Ohlen.

November 9—Red Sox purchased pitcher Ed Glynn from Mets.

November 9—Phillies released pitchers Renie Martin and Steve Fireovid.

November 12—Brewers purchased pitcher Brad Lesley from Reds and assigned him to Vancouver.

November 13—Braves released outfielder Rufino Linares.

November 26—Rangers released catcher Marvis Foley.

November 27—Cubs re-signed pitcher Dennis Eckersley, a re-entry free agent.

December 2—Cubs conditionally purchased catcher Jamie Nelson from Brewers.

December 4—Yankees traded pitcher Ray Fontenot and outfielder Brian Dayett to Cubs for outfielder Henry Cotto, catcher Ron Hassey and pitchers Rich Bordi and Porfi Altamirano; Yankees assigned Cotto and Altamirano to Columbus, O.

December 4—Indians re-signed designated hitter Andre Thornton, a re-entry free agent.

December 4—Tigers signed catcher Marvis Foley, a free agent, and assigned him to Nashville.

December 5—Rangers signed designated hitter Cliff Johnson, a re-entry free agent formerly with the Blue Jays.

December 5—Indians released pitcher Luis Aponte.

December 5—A's traded outfielder Rickey Henderson, pitcher Bert Bradley and cash to Yankees for outfielder Stan Javier and pitchers Jay Howell, Jose Rijo, Eric Plunk and Tim Birtsas; Yankees assigned Bradley to Columbus, O.

December 5—Yankees traded catcher Rick Cerone to Braves for pitcher Brian Fisher; Yankees assigned Fisher to Columbus, O.

December 6—Padres traded pitchers Tim Lollar and Bill Long, third baseman Luis Salazar and shortstop Ozzie Guillen to White Sox for pitchers LaMarr Hoyt, Kevin Kristan and Todd Simmons. Padres assigned Simmons to Reno and Kristan to Beaumont; White Sox assigned Long to Buffalo.

December 7—Cubs re-signed pitcher Steve Trout, a re-entry free agent.

December 7—Expos traded infielder Bryan Little to White Sox for pitcher Bert Roberge; White Sox assigned Little to Buffalo.

December 7—White Sox traded infielder Vance Law to Expos for pitcher Bob James.

December 7—Orioles signed outfielder Lee Lacy, a re-entry free agent formerly with the Pirates.

December 7—Braves signed pitcher Bruce Sutter, a re-entry free agent formerly with the Cardinals.

December 7—Twins traded catcher Ray Smith to Padres for pitcher Floyd Chiffer. Twins assigned Chiffer, who was on Las Vegas roster, to Toledo; Padres assigned Smith to Las Vegas.

December 7—Tigers traded third baseman Howard Johnson to Mets for pitcher Walt Terrell.

December 7—Brewers traded pitcher Don Sutton to A's for pitchers Ray Burris and Eric Barry and a player to be named; Brewers assigned Barry to Vancouver.

December 8—A's traded pitcher Bill Caudill to Blue Jays for shortstop Alfredo Griffin, oufielder Dave Collins and cash.

December 10—Orioles released pitcher John Pacella and catcher Orlando Sanchez.

December 10—White Sox released catcher Steve Christmas.

December 10—Expos traded catcher Gary Carter to Mets for infielder Hubie Brooks, catcher Mike Fitzgerald, outfielder Herm Winningham and pitcher Floyd Youmans.

December 11—Orioles signed outfielder Fred Lynn, a re-entry free agent formerly with the Angels.

December 12—Pirates traded pitcher John Tudor and outfielder-catcher Brian Harper to Cardinals for outfielder George Hendrick and catcher Steve Barnard; Pirates assigned Barnard, who was on Erie roster, to Macon.

December 13—Cubs signed pitcher Lary Sorensen, a free agent.

December 13—Orioles signed pitcher Don Aase, a re-entry free agent formerly with the Angels.

December 14—Cubs re-signed pitcher Rick Sutcliffe, a re-entry free agent.

December 17—Orioles released first baseman Ron Jackson.

December 19—A's re-signed designated hitter Dave Kingman, a re-entry free agent.

December 19—Rangers signed catcher Luis Pujols, a free agent; Pujols was assigned to Oklahoma City.

December 20—Yankees traded outfielder Steve Kemp, infielder Tim Foli and $800,000 to Pirates for shortstop Dale Berra, pitcher Alfonso Pulido and outfielder Jay Buhner; Yankees assigned Buhner to Albany.

December 20—Royals re-signed infielder Greg Pryor, a re-entry free agent.

December 20—Rangers signed pitcher Burt Hooton, a re-entry free agent formerly with the Dodgers.

December 22—Blue Jays purchased designated hitter Jeff Burroughs from A's.

December 22—Indians signed pitcher Vern Ruhle, a re-entry free agent formerly with the Astros; Ruhle was assigned to Maine.

December 23—Tigers re-signed designated hitter-outfielder John Grubb, a re-entry free agent.

December 24—A's re-signed first baseman Bruce Bochte, a free agent.

December 27—Yankees signed pitcher Ed Whitson, a re-entry free agent formerly with the Padres.

December 28—Rangers signed pitcher Dave Rozema, re-entry free agent formerly with the Tigers.

5 Hall of Famers Died in '84

By CARL CLARK

Five members of the Hall of Fame, who together played on or managed 10 world championship teams, died in 1984. Baseball mourned the loss of Joe Cronin, the American League's Most Valuable Player in 1930 and president of the circuit from 1959 to 1973; Stan Coveleski and Waite Hoyt, the pitching stars of the 1920 and 1921 World Series; George (High Pockets) Kelly, whose timely hitting and sure first baseman's mitt helped John McGraw's New York Giants win four successive pennants, and Walter Alston, taciturn leader of the Brooklyn and Los Angeles Dodgers.

Few could have foreseen in 1928 the heights to which Cronin would rise. Joe was a nondescript American Association infielder that summer, one who already had been rejected by the Pittsburgh Pirates. When Clark Griffith, owner of the Washington Senators, learned that one of his scouts, Joe Engel, had bought Cronin's contract, he was furious.

"You paid $7,500 for a minor league shortstop who was hitting only .245? Are you crazy?" Griffith screamed.

"Griff was boiling mad, but he finally cooled off and I got to stay with the Washington club," Cronin recalled.

Cronin hit only .242 for the Senators in 1928, but an off-season conditioning program increased his strength and put some pop in his bat. The San Francisco native raised his average to .281 the next season and socked eight home runs, eight more than he had hit in '28.

And that was just the beginning. In 1930, Cronin batted .346, hit 13 homers, scored 127 runs and drove in 126. He was named the American League's Most Valuable Player.

When Griffith needed someone to succeed Walter Johnson as field boss in 1933, he chose Cronin, then 26. The Boy Manager guided the Senators to the A.L. championship in his first season.

Then, however, the bubble burst. Though Joe hit .318 in the World Series, Washington bowed to Bill Terry's Giants in five games and followed up by winning 33 fewer games in 1934 while tumbling to seventh place. When Tom Yawkey, owner of the Boston Red Sox, offered Griffith $250,000 and shortstop Lyn Lary for Cronin, Griffith accepted, even though Joe was now his son-in-law—having married his niece and adopted daughter, Mildred Robertson—and had batted in more than

Joe Cronin's career with the Washington Senators began in 1928.

100 runs in each of the previous four seasons.

As playing manager of the Red Sox for the next 10 seasons, Cronin knocked in 90 or more runs six times and scored 90 or more five times. Boston won no pennants, but finished runner-up to the New York Yankees four times.

Cronin established an A.L. record in 1943 with five pinch homers, four with two men on base. Connie Mack lauded him as the league's toughest clutch hitter, but Joe dismissed the praise. "I couldn't possibly hit as many game-winning homers as I have if the pitchers weren't throwing right down my alley," he said. "It's not any extraordinary ability on my part but extraordinary dumbness on the pitchers' part that's responsible for my success."

Cronin retired as a player after suffering a fractured leg in the first series of the 1945 campaign. He finished his career with a .301 batting average, 170 home runs, 1,423 runs batted in, a .468 slugging percentage and 2,285 hits in 2,124 games.

In 1946, Cronin's first season as solely a manager, the Red Sox flattened everyone in their path and entered the World Series with a 104-50 record. But a world championship again eluded Cronin, as St. Louis captured Game 7 on Enos Slaughter's fabled dash.

Yawkey promoted Cronin to general manager after the 1947 season, and he served in that capacity until he became president of the American League in 1959. During Cronin's 14 years in office, the league expanded from eight clubs to 12 and adopted divisional playoffs and the designated hitter.

Cronin was inducted into the Hall of Fame as a player in 1956. He was 77 when he died at his home in Osterville, Mass., a small town on Cape Cod, on September 7.

While Cronin was the Boy Manager, Waite Hoyt was Schoolboy, a professional pitcher at 16 and a 19-year-old when he joined the Giants for one game in 1918.

John McGraw was to regret overlooking the youngster from Brooklyn, because in 1921, Hoyt, in his first year with the Yankees after two with the Red Sox, nearly extinguished Little Napoleon's club in the World Series. Hoyt pitched three complete games without allowing an earned run. Nevertheless, he was the loser in the final game. The Giants won, 1-0, pushing across a run in the first inning with two walks and an error on shortstop Roger Peckinpaugh.

Hoyt won 19 games in each of his first two seasons with the Yankees, and 62 in the four succeeding seasons. He posted records of 22-7 and 23-7 in the Yanks' world championship seasons of 1927 and 1928, and won two games in the '28 Series, his sixth as a Yankee.

The Yankees traded Hoyt to Detroit on May 30, 1930, and he subsequently pitched for the Tigers, Philadelphia Athletics, Brooklyn, the Giants and Pittsburgh. He won 237 games and pitched 3,762 innings in 21 major league seasons. He worked 83⅔ innings in seven World Series (he appeared in the 1931 Series with the A's), compiling a 6-4 record and a 1.83 earnedrun average. He pitched for seven pennant winners and three world champions.

At the conclusion of his mound career (his last year was with Brooklyn in 1938), Hoyt became one of the first former players to take up broadcasting. Eloquent and urbane, he was an immediate hit as the voice of the Cincinnati Reds. His listeners welcomed rain delays, for that was when he would reminisce about the escapades of Babe Ruth and the other original Bronx Bombers.

Hoyt was forever proud to have been a Yankee. "I can imagine any rookie player just joining the Yanks and, on entering the Stadium, being indelibly impressed—

marked for life," he said. "It would be only human for him to look about in astonishment and say to himself, 'I never want to leave here. This is the home of big doings. I want to be a part of it. I've got to hustle to stay.' "

Hoyt retired as a broadcaster in 1965 and was named to the Hall of Fame by the Veterans Committee four years later. He died of a heart attack August 25 in Cincinnati. He was 84.

Stan Coveleski was a model of economy in the 1920 World Series, using 72, 78 and 82 pitches in five-hit victories for the Cleveland Indians, who defeated Brooklyn, five games to two.

Coveleski, a product of Shamokin, Pa., had won 24 games for the Indians that year, fashioning a 2.49 ERA and striking out a league-leading 133 batters.

Such a season was typical for Coveleski, one of the last legitimate spitballers. He won 15 games for the Indians in his first full season in the majors, 1916, and then strung together seasons of 19, 22, 24, 24 and 23 victories. He had earned-run averages of 1.81 in 1917 and 1.82 in 1918.

Stan, younger brother of the late Harry Coveleski, three times a 20-game winner for Detroit, saw nothing wrong with the spitball. "There was an art to throwing a good spitter," he said. "One thing you need was a jawful of slippery elm. You didn't use much of it, but plain sweat was no substitute for slippery elm. Elm would make the ball as slippery as ice. It would react like a knuckleball and wouldn't spin. I could throw it much faster than pitchers can the knuckler. And I could control its break."

Though his 2.76 ERA was the American League's best in 1923, Coveleski endured his first losing season, finishing 13-14. When he followed that with a 15-16 season, the Indians traded him to Washington. He rebounded in 1925 with a 20-5 record and regained the ERA crown with a 2.84 mark. The Senators won the pennant, but Coveleski was unable to duplicate his previous postseason magnificence. He lost the second and fifth games of the Series, and Pittsburgh won the championship.

Coveleski won 14 games for the Senators in 1926, then was released in June of 1927. He won five of six decisions with the Yankees in 1928, his last year in the majors, but lost an opportunity to appear in a third World Series when he was released before the end of the season with a 5.74 ERA.

Coveleski, who won 215 games in the big leagues, entered the Hall of Fame with Hoyt in 1969 by vote of the Veterans Com-

George "High Pockets" Kelly was the Giants' first baseman during the club's glory years of the early '20s.

mittee. He died at South Bend, Ind., on March 20. He was 93.

George Kelly, nicknamed High Pockets because of his 6-foot, 3½-inch frame, drove in more than 100 runs in each of the Giants' four consecutive championship seasons from 1921 through 1924, reaching a career high with 136 in 1924.

He was the first player to hit three home runs in a game twice, accomplishing the second leg of that feat on the same day (June 14, 1924) that he drove in all of the Giants' runs in an 8-6 victory over Cincinnati. Only Bob Johnson of the 1938 Philadelphia Athletics ever delivered as many runs as his club's lone RBI man.

Kelly clouted seven homers in six games in 1924, a National League record he shares with Walker Cooper and Willie Mays. He led the league in home runs with 23 in 1921.

The Giants traded Kelly to Cincinnati for outfielder Edd Roush, also a member of the Hall of Fame, after the 1926 season. He spent three full seasons with the Reds, split the 1930 campaign between Cincinnati and the Chicago Cubs, then played out the string with Brooklyn in 1932.

Kelly, who holds the National League single-season records for most putouts and most chances accepted by a first baseman, finished his career with a .297 bat-

ting average, 148 home runs and 1,019 RBIs. He hit .248 in 26 World Series games with the Giants, world champions in 1921 and 1922.

Kelly, like Cronin a San Franciscan, was inserted into the Cooperstown pantheon in 1973 by vote of the Veterans Committee. He died October 13 at Burlingame, Calif. He was 88.

Walter Alston managed the Dodgers to seven National League championships and four World Series titles, and ranks fifth on the all-time victory list behind Connie Mack, John McGraw, Bucky Harris and Joe McCarthy. But he was never offered more than a one-year contract. Said Charlie Dressen, Alston's predecessor, who quit when the Dodgers would not meet his demand for a three-year pact, "The Dodgers never plan to fire Alston. They prefer to torment him."

Alston held up well. He piloted the Dodgers for 23 years. Only Mack and McGraw managed one team for a longer period.

Brooklyn, which had won pennants under Dressen in 1952 and 1953, finished second in Alston's shakedown season, but won its first and only world championship in 1955, finally knocking off the Yankees in seven games.

The Yanks dethroned the Dodgers the next fall, but in 1959, the Dodgers' second season in Los Angeles, Alston's men again reigned supreme after beating the Chicago White Sox.

Alston won his fourth National League title in 1963, and who awaited the Dodgers in the World Series but their old nemesis. Los Angeles swept the Yankees, limiting them to four runs and 22 hits in four games. Sandy Koufax struck out 23 in his two starts, Don Drysdale pitched a three-hitter and Johnny Podres, who had blanked the Yankees in the deciding game of the '55 Series, hooked up with Ron Perranoski for a 4-1 victory in Game 2.

Alston bagged his fourth world championship in 1965 and National League crowns in 1966 and 1974. He retired after the 1976 season with a record of 2,042-1,615 (.558).

Alston, who played in only one game in the major leagues, with the St. Louis Cardinals in 1936, was inducted into the Hall of Fame in 1983. He died October 1 at Oxford, O., home of his alma mater, Miami University. He was 72.

Among the other baseball personalities who died in 1984 were Ray Kroc, owner of the San Diego Padres since 1974; Billy Goodman, American League batting champion in 1950; Glenn Wright, an out-

Shown here during his rookie season as manager of Brooklyn in 1954, Walter Alston was unique for having signed 23 consecutive one-year contracts during his long and successful career as manager of the Dodgers.

standing shortstop for Pittsburgh and Brooklyn in the 1920s and '30s; Virgil (Spud) Davis, one of the National League's leading hitters in the '30s as a catcher for the Phillies and Cardinals; Joe Kuhel, longtime first baseman for the Washington Senators and Chicago White Sox; catchers Jim Hegan and Gus Mancuso, whose defensive skills were unparalleled; Charlie Robertson, who pitched a perfect game as a White Sox rookie in 1922; Ed Short, White Sox general manager in the 1960s; White Sox coaches Loren Babe and Charlie Lau; former National League umpires Beans Reardon and Babe Pinelli; and Lynn McGlothen, former Red Sox and Cardinals pitcher who was killed in a fire at Dubach, La.

An alphabetical list of baseball deaths in 1984 follows:

Tommie Lee Aaron, 45, an Atlanta Braves coach since 1979, of leukemia, at Atlanta on August 16; batted .229 and hit 13 home runs in seven seasons as a first baseman and outfielder for the Braves, both in Milwaukee and Atlanta; managed Braves farm clubs at Savannah and Richmond before becoming an Atlanta coach; younger brother of all-time home run leader Henry Aaron.

Walter Emmons (Smokey) Alston, 72, inducted into the Hall of Fame in 1983 in recognition of his seven National League championships and four World Series titles as manager of the Brooklyn and Los Angeles Dodgers, at Oxford, O., October 1; managed in the minors for 13 years before the Dodgers tapped him to succeed Charlie Dressen after the 1953 season; Brooklyn, which had won pennants in 1952 and '53, finished second in Alston's maiden season, but won the world championship the following season, defeating the Yankees in seven games—the Dodgers were the first club to win a seven-game World Series after losing the first two games; Alston's troops marched to the Series again in 1956, but, after winning the first two games, succumbed to the Yankees in seven games; the Dodgers and Yankees did not meet again in the Series until 1963, when the Dodgers, now in Los Angeles, swept the Yankees in four games; Alston's Los Angeles clubs also won world championships in 1959 and 1965 and N.L. flags in 1966 and 1974; Alston retired after the 1976 season with a major league managerial record of 2,042-1,615 (.558); he ranks fifth on the all-time victory list behind Connie Mack, John McGraw, Bucky Harris and Joe McCarthy; his major league playing career consisted of one game with the St. Louis Cardinals in 1936—he struck out in his only plate appearance and made an error as a first baseman.

Herbert E. Armstrong, 91, longtime business manager of the Baltimore Orioles, at Baltimore on July 28; since his retirement in 1972, he had been a club consultant and president of the Oriole Foundation, created in 1965 to provide financial aid and encouragement to Baltimore youngsters via sports and scholarship programs.

Loren Rolland Babe, 56, former third baseman for the New York Yankees and Philadelphia Athletics who had worked in the Chicago White Sox' organization since the mid-1970s, of lung cancer, at Omaha, Neb., February 14; batted .223 in 120 games for the Yankees and A's in 1952 and 1953; following his retirement as a player in 1959 he managed in the minors until he joined the Yankees as a coach in 1967; scouted for the Yankees from 1968 through 1974, with a year out in 1971 to manage their Triple-A club at Syracuse; managed White Sox farm clubs at Denver and Des Moines before becoming a special assignments scout in 1977; when it was determined in April 1983 that Babe was suffering from cancer, batting coach Charley Lau voluntarily gave up his spot with the White Sox so that Babe could spend enough time with the club to qualify for pension benefits; ironically, a month later, cancer was diagnosed in Lau's colon—he succumbed to the disease less than five weeks after Babe's death.

Joe Barletta, 60, scout for the Los Angeles Dodgers from 1960 through 1973, at Hazleton, Pa., June 27.

Foster Edwin (Babe) Blackburn, 89, a right-hander who pitched briefly for Kansas City in the Federal League in 1915 and the Chicago White Sox in 1921, at New Port Richey, Fla., March 9.

Wallace O. (Wally) Bock, 72, trainer for the Cleveland Indians from 1948 through 1970, at Richmond, Va., January 23.

Kerry Dru Burchett, 29, a pitcher in the St. Louis Cardinals' organization from 1978 through 1982, from complications of heart disease, at Little Rock, Ark., October 8.

Arthur Edward (Art) Butler, 96, an infielder for the Boston Nationals in 1911, Pittsburgh in 1912 and 1913 and the St. Louis Cardinals from 1914 to 1916, at Fall River, Mass., October 7; Butler, born Arthur Bouthillier, led the National League in pinch hits in 1916, collecting 13 in 54 at-bats; one of his pinch hits that season broke up a no-hitter by Grover Cleveland Alexander with two out in the ninth; batted .241 in 454 games.

Harry Caplan, 84, onetime scout for the Houston Colt .45s, at Phoenix on July 5.

Dorsey L. (Dixie) Carroll, 90, an outfielder who appeared in 15 games for the Boston Braves in 1919, at Jacksonville, Fla.

Paul W. (Nick) Carter, 90, a righthanded pitcher with Cleveland and the Chicago Cubs from 1914-20, at Lake Park, Ga., September 11; he compiled a lifetime big-league record of 20-27.

John W. (Moose) Clabaugh, 83, an outfielder who batted .071 in 11 games with Brooklyn in 1926, July 11.

Stanley Anthony Coveleski (born Stanislaus Kowalewski), 93, Hall of Fame pitcher who won 215 games in the majors and three games for Cleveland in the 1920 World Series, at South Bend, Ind., March 20; pitched briefly for the Philadelphia Athletics in 1912, but returned to the majors in a big way with Cleveland in 1916, just about the time older brother, Harry, was leaving the scene (Harry's 81 victories in the majors included three consecutive 20-win seasons for Detroit); Stan, one of the last great legal spitballers, won 15 games for the Indians in 1916, then won 19 or more in each of the next five seasons, with a high of 24 in 1919 and 1920; in 1920, he led the American League in strikeouts and pitched the Tribe to its first world championship; he hurled three complete-game victories over Brooklyn in the Series, winning by 3-1, 5-1 and 3-0 scores; after losing seasons in 1923 and '24, he was traded to Washington, where he rebounded with a 20-5 record in 1925, leading the A.L. in winning percentage (.800) and earned-run average (2.84); he lost two games to Pittsburgh in the World Series that fall, and the Pirates won the championship in seven games; he spent two more seasons with the Senators, winning 14 games in 1926, then appearing in

just five contests in 1927 before he was released; he won five of six decisions with the New York Yankees in 1928, his last year in the majors; he was elected to the Hall of Fame in 1969.

Plateau Rex (Red) Cox, 89, a pitcher who appeared in three games for Detroit in 1920, at Roanoke, Va., October 15.

Joseph Edward (Joe) Cronin, 77, Hall of Fame shortstop, pennant-winning manager and president of the American League between 1959 and 1973, at Osterville, Mass., September 7; played for Pittsburgh in 1926 and 1927, Washington from 1928 through 1934 and the Boston Red Sox from 1935 through 1945; selected Most Valuable Player in the American League in 1930, when he batted .346, hit 13 home runs, scored 127 runs and drove in 126; he batted in more than 100 runs for the Senators in each of the next four years, collecting an average of 61 extra-base hits per season; in 1933, the first of his 15 seasons as a manager, Washington won the A.L. pennant, finishing seven games ahead of the Yankees; the Senators fell to seventh place the following season, 34 games out, and Clark Griffith, owner of the club and Cronin's father-in-law, startled the baseball world by selling Joe's contract to the Red Sox for a record $250,000 and shortstop Lyn Lary; during the Red Sox portion of his career, Cronin knocked in 90 or more runs six times and scored 90 or more five times; established A.L. record with five home runs as a pinch-hitter in 1943; retired as a player after suffering a fractured leg in the first series of 1945—his career marks included a .301 batting average, 170 home runs, 1,423 runs batted in, a .468 slugging percentage and 2,285 hits in 2,124 games; he managed for two more seasons— the Red Sox won the pennant in 1946 but lost the World Series to St. Louis in seven games—then moved up to general manager, in which capacity he served until he became league president in 1959; he was voted into the Hall of Fame as a player in 1956.

Bruce Lee Cunningham, 78, a pitcher for the Boston Braves from 1929 through 1932, at Hayward, Calif., March 8; posted a 13-24 record in 104 appearances, most of them as a reliever; later worked for the Cleveland Indians and the Chicago Cubs.

George Oliver Darrow, 78, a lefthander who had a 2-6 record in 17 appearances for the Philadelphia Phillies in 1934, in March.

Isaac Marion (Ike) Davis, 88, a shortstop for Washington in 1919 and the Chicago White Sox in 1924 and 1925, at Tucson on April 2; as a regular for the White Sox in '25, Davis batted .240 in 146 games, but drew 71 walks, stole 19 bases and scored 105 runs.

Virgil Lawrence (Spud) Davis, 79, a catcher who compiled a .308 batting average over 16 seasons in the majors, at Birmingham, Ala., August 14; broke into the big leagues with the St. Louis Cardinals in 1928 and was traded that season to the Philadelphia Phillies, for whom he became a leading hitter, batting .342, .313, .326, .336 and .349 in successive seasons between 1929 and 1933; he was traded back to the Cardinals in 1934 and batted .300 in 107 games—in the World Series that year, won by St. Louis in seven games, Davis went to bat twice as a pinch-hitter and singled both times, driving in one run; stayed with the Cardinals through 1936 and later played with Cincinnati, the Phillies and Pittsburgh; served as manager of the Pirates for three games in 1946.

Leo M. Dixon, 87, a catcher for the St. Louis Browns and Cincinnati from 1925-29, at Chicago, April 11; he batted .206 in 159 major league games.

John Enzmann, 94, a pitcher for Brooklyn in 1914, Cleveland in 1918 and 1919 and the Philadelphia Phillies in 1920, at Riverhead, N.Y., March 14; in 20 starts and 47 relief appearances, he compiled a 10-12 record and a 2.84 earned-run average.

Aubrey L. Epps, 72, a catcher in one game for Pittsburgh in 1935; he went 3-for-4 in his one major league contest.

Walter Edward French, 83, an outfielder for the Philadelphia Athletics for six seasons in the 1920s and a member of the Pro Football Hall of Fame, at Mountain Home, Ark., May 13; batted .370 in 67 games for the Athletics in 1925 and had a career average of .303 in 398 games; a gridiron standout at West Point and a member of Walter Camp's 1920-21 All-America team, the 5-7, 160-pounder was a star halfback for the Pottsville (Pa.) Maroons, professional champions in 1925; he also played for the Frankfort Yellowjackets and was inducted into the Canton shrine in 1949; his appearance as a pinch-hitter in the 1929 World Series makes him one of the few athletes to play in both a professional football championship game and a World Series.

John L. (Jackie) Gallagher, 82, an outfielder who singled in his lone big-league at-bat for Cleveland in 1923, at Providence, R.I., in September.

Debs Garms, 76, an outfielder-third baseman for four big-league clubs, at Glen Rose, Tex., December 16; Garms, a .293 lifetime hitter, played for the St. Louis Browns, Boston Braves, Pittsburgh and St. Louis Cardinals in a 12-year career spanning 1932-45; in 1940, his first year for the Pirates, he led the National League in batting with a .355 mark although he played in only 103 games and had 358 at-bats (in those years players needed to play only 100 games to qualify for the hitting title).

Ival Richard Goodman, 76, an outfielder for Cincinnati from 1935 to 1942 and the Chicago Cubs in 1943 and 1944, at Cincinnati on November 25; a slightly built lefthanded hitter who played right field almost exclusively, he had a .281 average and 95 homers in 1,107 games; hit .292 with 30 homers and 92 RBIs in 1938; appeared in the 1939 and 1940 World Series for the Reds, batting .295 in 11 games; scouted for the Cubs in the 1950s.

William Dale (Billy) Goodman, 58, American League batting champion in 1950 and a .300 hitter over 16 seasons in the majors, of cancer, at Sarasota, Fla., October 1; broke in with the Boston Red Sox as an outfielder-shortstop in late 1947, but was converted to first base the next season by Manager Joe McCarthy; over the next nine seasons, Goodman played at every infield position and in the outfield—he batted over .300 in five of those years (.354 in '50) and never finished below .293; traded to Baltimore in June 1957, he batted .308 in 73 games for the Orioles that season; he was one of six players involved in a Baltimore-Chicago White Sox swap in December 1957 and filled a utility role with the Sox for the next four seasons, finally ending his big-league career with Houston in 1962; he was a playing manager and scout in the minor leagues for Houston from 1963 to 1965, scouted for the Red Sox in 1966, was an instructor in the Kansas City system in 1967 and then joined the Atlanta organization, serving as a coach and manager in the Braves' farm system.

Howard Paul (Howie) Gorman, 70, an outfielder who played in 14 games for the Philadelphia Phillies in 1937 and 1938, at Harrisburg, Pa., April 29.

Nicholas Edward (Nick) Goulish, 66, an outfielder who played in 14 games for the Philadelphia Phillies in 1944 and 1945, at Youngstown, O., May 15.

Odbert H. (Bert) Hamric, 56, a pinch-hitter in 10 games with Brooklyn and Baltimore in the '50s, at Springboro, O., August 8; he singled once in eight at-bats with the Orioles in 1958 after failing to hit in his lone at-bat with the Dodgers in 1955.

Raymond James (Cowboy) Harrell, 71, pitcher for five National League teams between 1935 and 1945, at Alexandria, La., January 28; worked for St. Louis in 1935-37-38, Chicago and Philadelphia in 1939, Pittsburgh in 1940 and New York in 1945; finished with a 9-20 record in 119 games, all but 31 of them as a reliever.

James Edward (Jim) Hegan, 63, a catcher whose defensive skills won him a berth on the American League All-Star Game squad five times between 1947 and 1952, at Swampscott, Mass., June 17; those same skills enabled Hegan, whose career batting average was .228, to play in the majors for 17 seasons, the first 14 of them with Cleveland (1941-42, 1946-57); he never batted over .249, but his handling of such pitchers as Bob Feller, Bob Lemon, Early Wynn and Mike Garcia was instrumental in Cleveland's 1948 world championship and 1954 A.L. championship; caught three no-hitters while with the Indians—Don Black's in 1947, Lemon's in 1948 and Feller's in 1951 (Rapid Robert's third); led A.L. catchers in putouts in 1947-48-49 and in assists in 1948-49-50; traded to Detroit after 1957 season, he appeared in 45 games for the Tigers, then finished his career in the National League, making brief stops at Philadelphia, San Francisco and Chicago; coached for the New York Yankees from August 1960 through 1973, for Detroit from 1974 through 1978 and again for the Yankees the next two seasons; his son Mike, a first baseman, played for several A.L. clubs in the 1960s and '70s, including the Yankees in 1973.

Henry Hartz (Hank) Helf, 71, a catcher who once caught a baseball dropped from the top of the 52-story Terminal Tower in Cleveland, at Austin, Tex., October 27; appeared in seven games for the Indians in 1938 and 1940 and was the backup catcher for the St. Louis Browns in 1946; finished his major league career with a .184 average in 78 games; his epic catch was part of a publicity stunt sponsored by the Cleveland Chamber of Commerce.

Waite Charles Hoyt, 84, Hall of Fame pitcher who won 237 games in the majors, most of them with the New York Yankees in the 1920s, of a heart attack, at Cincinnati on August 25; appeared in one game for John McGraw's New York Giants in 1918 and pitched two seasons for the Boston Red Sox before joining the Yankees in a trade following the 1920 season; he won 19 games in each of his first two seasons with the Yanks and 62 in the four succeeding seasons; posted records of 22-7 and 23-7 in the Yankees' world championship seasons of 1927 and 1928; the Yankees traded him to Detroit on May 30, 1930, and he subsequently pitched for the Tigers, Philadelphia Athletics, Brooklyn, the Giants and Pittsburgh; his last strong season was 1934, when he was 15-6 for the Pirates; in addition to 237 wins and 182 losses, his career totals include 675 games, 3,762 innings pitched and 1,206 strikeouts; his earned-run average for 21 major league seasons was 3.59; pitched in seven World Series and compiled a 6-4 record in 12 appearances—in the 1921 Series, won by the Giants, he pitched three complete games without allowing an earned run, but was a 1-0 loser in the eighth and final game; at the conclusion of his playing career, with Brooklyn in 1938, Hoyt turned to the broadcast booth and for 25 years was the voice of the Cincinnati Reds; he was named to the Hall of Fame in 1969.

A 237-game winner in his major-league career, Waite Hoyt was the star pitcher of the New York Yankees' championship teams of the late '20s and later a broadcaster for 25 years with the Cincinnati Reds.

Chester Lawrence (Chet) Kehn, 62, a pitcher who appeared in three games for Brooklyn in 1942, at San Diego on April 5.

George Lange (High Pockets) Kelly, 88, a Hall of Fame first baseman who helped the New York Giants win four successive pennants in the early 1920s, at Burlingame, Calif., October 13; tied for the National League lead in runs batted in (94) in 1920, his fifth season wih the Giants, but his first as a regular (he also played a few games with Pittsburgh in 1917); drove in more than 100 runs in each of the Giants' four consecutive championship seasons from 1921 through 1924 (he tied for the N.L. RBI title with a career-high 136 in '24) and batted better than .300 in six successive seasons beginning in '21; led the National League with 23 homers in 1921; hit .248 in 26 World Series games with the Giants, who won the World championship in '21 and '22; the Giants traded him to Cincinnati for outfielder Edd Roush (also a member of the Hall of Fame) following the 1926 season; after 3½ seasons with the Reds, Kelly played briefly with the Chicago Cubs in 1930 and Brooklyn in 1932; compiled a career batting average of .297, hit 148 home runs and drove in 1,019 runs; coached for Cincinnati and the Boston Braves in the 1930s and '40s; he was elected to the Hall of Fame by the Veterans Committee in 1973.

Paul Kerr, 85, president of the Hall of Fame from 1961 through 1977 and associated with the Cooperstown shrine in various capacities since 1939, at Delray Beach, Fla., April 8; he also was a longtime member of the Hall's Committee on Veterans, and was instrumental in revising the process by which the group selects old-timers for enshrinement.

Leo Patrick Kiely, 54, a pitcher for the Boston Red Sox for six seasons in the 1950s and for the Kansas City Athletics in 1960, of cancer, at Glen Ridge, N.J., January 18; primarily a reliever, he posted a 26-27 career record, with a 3.37 earned-run average; had a 5-2 ledger and 12 saves in 1958; he was the Pacific Coast League's premier reliever in 1957, winning 21 games for the San Francisco Seals.

Ray A. Kroc, 81, owner of the San Diego Padres since 1974, of heart failure, at San Diego on January 14, less than 10 months before the Padres won their first National League championship; a high school dropout whose business acumen built the McDonald's hamburger operation into the nation's largest fast-food chain, Kroc bought the Padres from C. Arnholt Smith for about $11 million; the Padres finished above .500 only once during Kroc's tenure, although he invested in expensive free agents such as Rollie Fingers, Gene Tenace and Oscar Gamble; Commissioner Kuhn fined Kroc $100,000 in 1979 for tampering after Kroc said he would pursue Joe Morgan and Graig Nettles if they became free agents; shortly thereafter, he turned over the operation of the Padres to his son-in-law, Ballard Smith Jr., current president of the club.

Joseph Anthony (Joe) Kuhel, 77, longtime first baseman for the Washington Senators and Chicago White Sox and manager of the Senators in 1948 and 1949, at Kansas City on February 26; broke into the majors with Washington in 1930 and was a standout for the Senators until he was traded to the White Sox after the 1937 season for Zeke Bonura; after six seasons with Chicago, he was sold to Washington; he returned to Chicago in 1946 and wound up his career there the next year; batted .277 in 2,105 games; hit 27 homers in 1940, which at the time tied the White Sox' one-season record; tied a league record with three triples in a game in 1937; managed the Kansas City Blues, the New York Yankees' top farm team, in 1950 and 1951.

Charles Richard (Charley) Lau, 50, a major league catcher for 11 seasons who found greater renown as a batting coach, at Key Colony Beach, Fla., March 18, following a year-long battle with cancer of the colon; tutored Kansas City hitters from 1971 through 1978, New York Yankees hitters from 1979 through 1981 and Chicago White Sox hitters in 1982 and 1983; wrote two books on hitting; ironically, his highest average in the majors (he played for Detroit, the Milwaukee and Atlanta Braves, Baltimore and the Kansas City A's in a career that began in 1956 and ended in 1967) was .295, for Baltimore in 1965; his career average for 527 games was .255; voluntarily gave up his position on the White Sox' staff in May 1983 so that Loren Babe, a Chicago scout who was suffering from lung cancer, could join the Sox as a coach and qualify for his major league pension— Babe died February 14, less than five weeks before Lau.

Eugene F. (Gene) Layden, 90, an outfielder who batted .286 in three games with the New York Yankees in 1915, at Pittsburgh, December 12.

Gene Leahy, 87, a scout for the Chicago Cubs and Milwaukee Braves in the 1950s, at Rushville, Neb., February 11; brother of late Notre Dame football coach Frank Leahy.

William Joseph (Bill) Lee, 88, an outfielder who batted .186 in 25 games with the St. Louis Browns in 1915 and 1916, at West Hazelton, Pa., January 6.

Lyle Kenneth Luttrell, 54, a shortstop who hit .192 in 57 games with Washington in 1956 and 1957, of a heart attack, at Chattanooga, Tenn., July 11.

August Rodney (Gus) Mancuso, 78, a highly regarded handler of pitchers during his long career as a National League catcher, at Houston on October 26; spent 14 seasons with either St. Louis or New York and one season each with Chicago, Brooklyn and Philadelphia; in 1930, his second season in the majors, he sparked the Cardinals to the pennant when, filling in for injured Jimmy Wilson, he batted .366 and drove in 59 runs in 76 games; traded to New York following the 1932 season, he became captain of the Giants and Carl Hubbell's favorite receiver; New York won the world championship in 1933 and N.L. titles in 1936 and 1937; a .265 career hitter whose best mark was .301 in 1936, Mancuso appeared in five World Series in all, batting .173 in 18 games; after concluding his playing career in 1945 with the Phillies, he managed in the minors at Tulsa and San Antonio, coached for Cincinnati in 1950 and teamed with Harry Caray to broadcast Cardinals games from 1951 through 1953; his younger brother, Frank, caught for the St. Louis Browns and Washington Senators in the 1940s.

John Alfred Marcum, 76, a righthander who compiled a 65-63 record with four American League clubs between 1933 and 1939, at Louisville, Ky., September 10; his 17-12 record in 1935, his third and final season with Philadelphia, was the best of his career; he pitched for Boston from 1936 through 1938 and for Chicago and St. Louis in 1939.

Harry Duquesne (Duke) Markell, 60, a righthander who split two decisions in five appearances with the St. Louis Browns in 1951, of a heart attack, at Fort Lauderdale, Fla., June 14; Markell, born Harry Makowsky in Paris in 1923, pitched three no-hitters in the minor leagues, two of them in the International League.

Nicholas Charles (Ben) Marmo, 69, a scout for the Philadelphia Phillies from 1950 through 1982 and for Montreal from 1983 until his death, at Little Falls, N.Y., April 9.

Gonzalo Marquez, 38, an infielder for Oakland and the Chicago Cubs, killed in an auto accident at Venezuela, December 19; the accident occurred on a return trip to Caracas after Marquez, a player-coach for the Caracas Lions, was returning from a Venezuelan Winter League game in Valencia; in three major league seasons (1972-74) he compiled only a .235 batting average, but batted .600 in five at-bats in the 1972 World Series as he collected three straight pinch-hits for the A's.

Joseph Anton (Joe) Marty, 71, an outfielder for the Chicago Cubs and Philadelphia Phillies in the late 1930s and early '40s, at Sacramento, Calif., October 4; as a Cub, he collected six hits in 12 at-bats in the 1938 World Series, which the Yankees won in four games; batted .261 in 538 major league games.

William Herbert (Buckshot) May, 84, a righthander who pitched one inning for Pittsburgh in 1924, at Bakersfield, Calif., March 15.

Lynn Everratt McGlothen, 34, a major league pitcher from 1972 to 1982, killed in a fire, at Dubach, La., August 14; began his professional career with the Boston organization, reaching the majors with the Red Sox in 1972, but it was after being traded to St. Louis that he enjoyed his greatest success; he won 44 games for the Cardinals from 1974 through 1976; he was traded to San Francisco after the '76 season and subsequently pitched for the Giants, both Chicago clubs and the New York Yankees; compiled a career record of 86-93 and once, as a Cardinal in '75, struck out the side on nine pitches.

Charles R. (Bud) Meister, 77, traveling secretary for the Philadelphia Phillies from 1959 until his retirement in 1970, at Cumberland, Md., March 16.

Bill Messman, 66, longtime Midwest scouting supervisor for the Minnesota Twins, of cancer, at St. Louis on May 18.

Hal Middlesworth, 74, former public relations director for the Detroit Tigers, of cancer, at Detroit on April 24; joined the Tigers late in 1960 after a 25-year career in the sports department of the Detroit Free Press; retired after the 1979 season.

Bob Neal, 67, radio announcer for the Cleveland Indians in the 1950s, at Cleveland on January 3.

Oliverio (Baby) Ortiz, 64, a pitcher for two games with Washington in 1944, at Camaguey, Cuba, March 27; Ortiz, the losing hurler in both games he pitched for the Nats, was the younger brother of outfielder Roberto Ortiz, who played for the Senators and Philadelphia A's in the 1940s.

Theodore R. (Ted) Page, 81, a member of the Negro Baseball Hall of Fame and an outfielder in the old Negro leagues, was found dead at his home in Pittsburgh, December 1, the victim of a robbery and fatal beating; league records credited him with a .335 lifetime batting average in a 12-year career that ended in 1935; he appeared in seven different clubs, including the Homestead Grays and Pittsburgh Crawfords.

Chris G. Pelekoudas, a National League umpire who spent 28 years in the profession after an unsuccessful tryout as a player, at Sunnyvale, Calif., November 30; he gave up as a player after being rejected by the St. Louis Cardinals in a 1934 tryout camp; Pelekoudas began umpiring while serving as a Special Services officer during World War II and then attended a professional umpires' school; after spending more than a decade umpiring in the minors, he advanced to the N.L. in 1960, where he stayed until his retirement in 1975.

Jesse W. Pike, 67, an outfielder who batted .171 in 16 games for the New York Giants in 1946, at San Diego, March 28.

Ralph Arthur (Babe) Pinelli, 89, a major league infielder for eight seasons and a National League umpire from 1935 through 1956, at Daly City, Calif., October 22; primarily a third baseman, Pinelli, born Rinaldo Angelo Paolinelli, played for the Chicago White Sox in 1918, Detroit in 1920 and Cincinnati from 1922 through 1927; though twice a .300 hitter for the Reds, he lacked power, hitting only five home runs in his career, which he finished with a .276 batting average in 774 games; umpired in four All-Star Games (1937-41-50-56) and six World Series (1939-41-47-48-52-56); he was behind the plate for three no-hitters, including Don Larsen's perfect game in the 1956 World Series, the final time Pinelli called balls and strikes.

James William (Jimmy) Pofahl, 67, an infielder who batted .220 in 225 games with Washington from 1940 through 1942, at Owatonna, Minn., September 14.

Hugh Reid Poland, 71, a catcher for four National League teams during the 1940s and a scout for the New York and San Francisco Giants since 1955, at Guthrie, Ky., March 30; batted .185 in 83 games with Boston, New York, Philadelphia and Cincinnati.

John E. (Beans) Reardon, 86, who for 24 years was one of the most respected and colorful umpires in the National League, at Long Beach, Calif., July 31; worked in the senior circuit from 1926 through 1949; umpired in five World Series (1930-34-39-43-49) and three All-Star Games (1936-40-48).

Howard D. (Howie) Reed, 47, righthanded reliever for five major league clubs in 10 seasons, at Corpus Christi, Tex., December 7; his big-league career spanned from 1958-71 and included stops in Kansas City, Los Angeles, California, Houston and Montreal; Reed's major league career mark was only 26-29, but he enjoyed considerable success in the minors, where he won 19 games for Oklahoma City in 1967 and pitched a no-hitter for the same club the next year; he appeared in two World Series games for the Dodgers in 1965, but had no record.

Earl Percy Reid, 70, a righthander who won one game in two relief appearances for the Boston Braves in 1946, at Cullman, Ala., May 11.

Stephan Allen Reish, 24, a righthander who had a 10-11 record with the Kansas City Royals' Southern League club in Memphis in 1984, killed October 3 near his hometown of Union City, Ind., when the automobile he was driving crossed the center line on a county road and struck a tractor trailer head-on; pitched in the Toronto organization from 1981 to 1983; he was a member of the Indiana University basketball team that won the 1979 National Invitation Tournament.

Robert John (Bobby) Rhawn, an infielder who batted .237 in 90 games in the late 1940s with the New York Giants, Pittsburgh and the Chicago White Sox, at Danville, Pa., June 9.

Elmer Ray Riddle, 69, a righthander who had two brilliant seasons for Cincinnati in the 1940s, at Columbus, Ga., May 14; led the National League in winning percentage (.826, 19-4) and earned-run average (2.24) in 1941 and in victories (21, against 11 losses) in 1943; in his six other seasons with the Reds, he had a 12-19 record; finished his career with Pittsburgh in 1948 and 1949, posting records of 12-10 and 1-8; his career record was 65-52, and his ERA was 3.40; scouted for Kansas City for several years; brother of Johnny Riddle, a catcher who played sparingly for several major league clubs, including the Reds and Pirates.

John Duncan Rigney, 69, a righthanded pitcher for the Chicago White Sox from 1937 through 1942 and, after three years in the Navy, in 1946 and 1947, at Lombard, Ill., October 21; his best season was 1939, when he finished with a 15-8 record and a 3.70 earned-run average; compiled a career mark of 63-64; in 1941 he married Dorothy Comiskey, treasurer of the White Sox and granddaughter of franchise founder Charles Comiskey; became director of the Sox' minor league operations late in 1947 and a vice-president in 1956; held the latter position until the White Sox were sold to Bill Veeck in 1959.

James N. (Jim) Roberts, 88, a righthander who had an 0-3 record in 12 games with Brooklyn in 1924 and 1925, at Columbus, Miss., June 24.

Charles Culbertson (Charlie) Robertson, 87, a righthander who pitched a perfect game as a Chicago White Sox rookie in 1922 but finished his eight seasons in the majors with a 49-80 record, at Fort Worth, Tex., August 23; making his second start of the season—and only his third in the majors—he threw the fifth perfect game in major league history April 30, 1922, blanking Detroit, 2-0; he finished the '22 season with a 14-15 record, the closest he ever came to a winning campaign in the majors; he had a 39-56 record with the White Sox over a five-year period, then was 1-2 with the St. Louis Browns in 1926 and 9-22 with the Boston Braves in 1927 and 1928.

Tony Rosenkranz, 62, Northeast scouting supervisor for Montreal, Cincinnati, Oakland and the Milwaukee Brewers, at Northvale, N.J.

Joseph W. (Joe) Rue, 86, an American League umpire from 1938 through 1947, at Laguna Hills, Calif., December 1; Rue spent 12 years umpiring in Triple-A baseball before reaching the big leagues; he worked in two major league All-Star Games and one World Series.

Guido L. Rugo, 86, a part owner of the Boston Braves from 1944 to 1951, at Boston on November 18.

Roger Savard, 64, manager of season-ticket sales for the Montreal Expos, at Dorval, a suburb of Montreal, on January 10; he had been with the franchise since its inception and had held positions in promotions and public relations.

Frank Joseph (Skeeter) Scalzi, 71, an infielder who batted .333 in 11 games with the New York Giants in 1939, at Pittsburgh on August 25.

Alexander (Al) Schacht, 91, a pitcher for the Washington Senators from 1919 to 1921 who earned recognition as a comic pantomimist of baseball, at Waterbury, Conn., July 14; after his brief mound career, which encompassed 53 games in the majors (14 wins, 10 losses), Schacht coached for the Senators until 1934; he began performing his act in major league parks in 1921; before his retirement in 1968, he entertained at 25 World Series and 18 All-Star Games and made numerous trips overseas to entertain American troops; he worked for 10 years with Nick Altrock, once a fellow Senators coach, but the two never got along well and broke up their act.

William D. (Bill) Shores, 79, a righthanded pitcher who appeared in 96 major league games in six seasons spanning 1928-36, at Purcell, Okla., February 19; he compiled a 26-15 record for the Philadelphia Athletics, New York Giants and Chicago White sox, including 11-6 and 12-4 marks for the world-champion A's in 1929 and '30.

Ed Short, 64, who spent 10 years as general manager of the Chicago White Sox before he was fired at the end of the 1970 season, at Skokie, Ill., July 14; he was sports director at WJJD, the radio station that carried White Sox games, when Sox G.M. Frank Lane offered him a job as the club's public relations director in 1950; he later became the team's traveling secretary and was appointed general manager in 1961; his slickest move as White Sox G.M. was the acquisition of pitcher

Tommy John, catcher John Romano and outfielder Tommie Agee from Cleveland for outfielder Rocky Colavito and catcher Camilo Carreon.

Elmer John Smith, 91, who as a member of the Cleveland Indians hit the first grand slam in World Series history, at Columbia, Ky., August 3; an outfielder who played with Cleveland, Washington, the Boston Red Sox, New York Yankees and Cincinnati during a 10-year major league career, Smith smacked his bases-loaded homer off Brooklyn's Burleigh Grimes in the fifth game of the 1920 Series—the Indians won the game, 8-1, and the Series, five games to two; batted .316 and drove in 103 runs for the 1920 champions; compiled a career average of .276, with 70 homers and 540 RBIs in 1,012 games.

Karl Benjamin Spooner, 52, lefthanded pitcher who burst onto the major league stage with two spectacular shutouts for Brooklyn in 1954 and then disappeared almost as quickly, victim of a serious arm problem, at Vero Beach, Fla., April 10; promoted by the Dodgers after an outstanding season at Fort Worth, where his 21 victories and 262 strikeouts had led the Texas League, he blanked New York and Pittsburgh in his only two starts in '54, striking out 27; he had an 8-6 record and a 3.65 earned-run average for the Dodgers in 1955, but was plagued by a sore arm; he relieved in the second game of the World Series that year and started the sixth game, in which he was the loser, lasting just one-third of an inning—he never threw another pitch in the majors.

Charles Morris (Charley) Suche, 68, a lefthanded pitcher who appeared in one game for Cleveland in 1938 and later was a scout for the Boston Red Sox, at San Antonio on February 11.

Dan Taylor, 82, oldest member of the Baseball Writers' Association of America, at Mayfield Heights, O., July 28; a 50-year member of the BBWAA, he held card No. 2.

Robert G. (Bob) Trocolor Sr., 67, a scout for the New York Yankees since 1979, at Franklin Lakes, N.J., July 27; previously scouted for the New York Giants and played in the National Football League in the 1940s with the New York Giants and the Brooklyn Tigers.

William Felix (Bill) Trotter, 76, a righthander who compiled a 22-34 record with the St. Louis Browns, Washington Senators and St. Louis Cardinals between 1937 and 1944, at Arlington, Mass., August 26.

Cleon Walfoort, 73, a retired sportswriter who covered the Braves for the Milwaukee Journal, at Milwaukee on February 28 as the result of burns suffered in a fire January 30 at the home where he boarded in Waukesha, Wis.

Nathan M. (Nate) Wallack, 71, public relations director for the Cleveland Indians from 1953 through 1964, at Beachwood, O., January 16; joined the Indians as promotions director in 1949; he was the Cleveland Browns' first publicity man, in 1946, and rejoined the NFL team in '64.

Harold W. (Doc) Wendler, 82, former trainer for the Brooklyn and Los Angeles Dodgers, at Baton Rouge, La., August 25.

Forrest Glenn Wright, 83, standout shortstop for Pittsburgh from 1924 through 1928 and for Brooklyn from 1929 through 1933, at Olathe, Kan., April 7; he had four 100-RBI seasons, including 126 in 1930, when he batted .321 and swatted 22 homers; compiled a career average of .294 in 1,119 games; played in the 1925 and 1927 World Series with the Pirates and in the former year was named shortstop of The Sporting News' Major League All-Star Team; made an unassisted triple play in '25 on a line drive hit by Jim Bottomley of St. Louis; played briefly for the Chicago White Sox as a second baseman in 1935.

LEAGUE AND CLUB
INFORMATION

Including

Major League Directory

National League Directory

National League Team Directories

American League Directory

American League Team Directories

Major League Players Association Directory

Major League Farm Systems

Minor League Presidents

Directory of Organized Baseball

MAJOR LEAGUES

COMMISSIONER—Peter V. Ueberroth
SECRETARY-TREASURER & GENERAL COUNSEL—Alexander H. Hadden
HEADQUARTERS—350 Park Avenue
New York, N. Y. 10022
Telephone—371-7800 (area code 212)
Teletype—710-581-4279

EXECUTIVE COUNCIL—Peter V. Ueberroth, Commissioner; Robert W. Brown, President of American League; Charles S. Feeney, President of National League; Roy Eisenhardt, Peter Hardy, Jerry Reinsdorf and Edward Bennett Williams, representatives of American League, and Charles Bronfman, Nelson Doubleday, Peter F. O'Malley and Ballard F. Smith, Jr., representatives of National League.

ADMINISTRATOR—William A. Murray
DIRECTOR OF BROADCASTING—Bryan L. Burns
DIRECTOR OF INFORMATION—Robert A. Wirz
DIRECTOR OF SECURITY—Horace J. (Harry) Gibbs
CONTROLLER—Donald C. Marr, Jr.
ASSISTANTS TO ADMINISTRATIVE OFFICER—
George E. Pfister, Miguel A. Rodriguez
(Winter League Baseball Coordinators)
ASSISTANT COUNSEL—Edwin M. Durso
ASSOCIATE DIRECTOR OF INFORMATION, MEDIA—Charles B. Adams
ASSISTANT DIRECTOR OF INFORMATION—Richard Cerrone
MANAGER OF BROADCAST OPERATIONS—David Alworth
OFFICE MANAGER—Mary Ann Burns
BOOKKEEPER—Rita Datz

NATIONAL ASSOCIATION REPRESENTATIVES—John Johnson, President of the National Association, and members of National Association Executive Committee.

NATIONAL ASSOCIATION
OF PROFESSIONAL BASEBALL LEAGUES

PRESIDENT-TREASURER—John H. Johnson
ADMINISTRATOR—Sal Artiaga
VICE-PRESIDENT—Jimmy Bragan
LEGAL COUNSEL—Charles J. Crist, Jr.
DIRECTOR OF PROMOTIONS—Bob Sparks
HEADQUARTERS—201 Bayshore Dr. S.E., P. O. Box A
St. Petersburg, Fla. 33731
Telephone—822-6937 (area code 813)
Teletype—810-863-0361

EXECUTIVE COMMITTEE—Jimmy Bragan, Chairman, President of the Southern League; Bill Cutler, President of the Pacific Coast League, Bill Walters, President of the Midwest League.

National League

Organized 1876

CHARLES S. FEENEY
President and Treasurer

JOHN J. McHALE
Vice-President

PHYLLIS B. COLLINS
Secretary

BLAKE CULLEN
Administrator and Public Relations Director

KATY FEENEY
Assistant Public Relations Director

LOUIS H. KREMS
Business Manager

JOSEPHINE TROY
Administrative Assistant

Headquarters—350 Park Avenue, New York, N. Y. 10022

Telephone—371-7300 (area code 212)

UMPIRES—Fred Brocklander, Jerry Crawford, Jerry Dale, Robert Davidson, Gerry Davis, Robert Engel, Bruce Froemming, Eric Gregg, Lanny Harris, H. Douglas Harvey, John Kibler, Randy Marsh, John McSherry, Ed Montague, Dave Pallone, Frank Pulli, Jim Quick, Lawrence (Dutch) Rennert, Steve Rippley, Paul Runge, Dick Stello, Terry Tata, Harry Wendelstedt, Joe West, Lee Weyer, Charles Williams, William G. Williams.

OFFICIAL STATISTICIANS—Elias Sports Bureau, Inc., 500 5th Ave., Suite 2114, New York, N. Y. 10036. Telephone (212) 869-1530.

Players cannot be transferred from one major league club to another after June 15 to the close of the championship season except through regular waiver channels.

WAIVER PRICE, $20,000. Interleague waivers, $20,000, except for selected players and draft-excluded players.

ATLANTA BRAVES

Chairman of the Board—William C. Bartholomay

President—R.E. (Ted) Turner, III
Executive Vice-President—Allison Thornwell, Jr.
Vice-President and General Manager—John W. Mullen
Vice-President and Business Manager—Charles S. Sanders
Vice-President, Player Development—Henry L. Aaron
Assistant Vice-President, Scouting—Paul L. Snyder, Jr.
Assistant Scouting Director—Rod Gilbreath
Director of Broadcasting—Ernie Johnson
Manager of Broadcast Sales and Administration—Wayne Long
Ticket Distribution Manager—Ed Newman
Director of Public Relations, Promotions—Wayne Minshew
Director of Publications and Publicity Manager—Bob Korch
Director of Stadium Operations and Security—Joe Shirley
Director of Matrix Operations—Bob Larson
Assistant Controller—Martin Mathews
Traveling Secretary and Equipment Manager—Bill Acree
Director of Ticket Sales—Andre DeLorenzo
Manager—Eddie Haas
Club Physician—Dr. David T. Watson
Executive Offices—P.O. Box 4064, Atlanta, Ga. 30302
Telephone—522-7630 (area code 404)

SCOUTS—Mike Arbuckle, Sam Berry, Forrest (Smoky) Burgess, Stu Cann, Joe Caputo, Harold Cronin, Tony DeMacio, Lou Fitzgerald, Pedro Gonzalez, John Groth, Al Harper, Gene Hassell, Herb Hippauf, Ray Holton, Jim Johnson, Burney R. (Dickey) Martin, Rance Pless, Bob Scruggs, Bill Serena, Charles Smith, Tony Stiel, Bob Turzilli, Bob Wadsworth, Wesley Westrum, William R. Wight, Don Williams, H.F. (Red) Wooten.

PARK LOCATION—Atlanta-Fulton County Stadium, on Capitol Avenue at the junction of Interstate Highways 20, 75 and 85.

Seating capacity—53,046.

FIELD DIMENSIONS—Home plate to left field at foul line, 330 feet; to center field, 402 feet; to right field at foul line, 330 feet.

CHICAGO CUBS

Chairman of the Board—Andrew J. McKenna
President and General Manager—Dallas Green
Director of Minor Leagues and Scouting—Gordon Goldsberry
Vice President, Planning and Special Projects—Mark McGuire
Vice President, Marketing—Jeff Odenwald
Vice President, Special Assignments—Jack Brickhouse
Chief Financial Officer—Leo M. Breen
Special Baseball Consultant to Exec. V. P. and G. M.—Charlie Fox
Special Assistant to Exec. V. P. and V. P., Business Operations—E.R. Saltwell
Assistant to the Exec. V. P. and Traveling Secretary—John Cox
Director of Scouting—A.B. "Vedie" Himsl
Chief Accounting Officer—Joseph A. Kirchen
Secretary—Stanley J. Gradowski, Jr.
Director, Public Relations and Publications—Bob Ibach
Director, Ticket Sales—Frank Maloney
Director, Stadium Operations—Tom Cooper
Director, Ticket Services—Lamar Vernon
Director, Promotions and Sales—John McDonough
Director, Community Services—Mary Beth Hughes
Associate Director, Minor Leagues—William Harford
Assistant Director, Publications and Statistics—Ned Colletti
Assistant Director, Stadium Operations/Facilities—Lubie Veal
Manager—Jim Frey
Executive Offices—Wrigley Field, N. Clark and Addison Streets, Chicago, Ill. 60613
Telephone—281-5050 (area code 312)

SCOUTS—(Major League)—Charlie Fox, Scott Reid. (Supervisors)—Brandon Davis, Frank DeMoss, Gene Handley, Gary Nickels. (Regular)—Billy Blitzer, William Capps, Billy Champion, Kenn Cunningham, Tom Davis, Edward DiRamio, Walt Dixon, Nino Espinosa, John Hennessy, Ron Hollingsworth, Roy Johnson, John "Spider" Jorgensen, Doug Laumann, Doug Mapson, Julio Navarro, John "Buck" O'Neil, Andrew Pienovi, Evo Pusich, Joaquin Velilla, H.D. Wilson, Earl Winn, Harold Younghans, James Zerilla.

PARK LOCATION—Wrigley Field, Addison Street, N. Clark Street, Waveland Avenue and Sheffield Avenue.

Seating capacity—37,272.

FIELD DIMENSIONS—Home plate to left field at foul line, 355 feet; to center field, 400 feet; to right field at foul line, 353 feet.

CINCINNATI REDS

General Partner—Marge Schott

President and Chief Executive Officer—Robert L. Howsam, Sr.
General Manager—Bill Bergesch
Vice-President, Marketing—Robert L. Howsam, Jr.
Vice-President, Player Personnel—Sheldon Bender
Vice-President, Controller—D.L. Porco
Vice-President, Publicity—Jim Ferguson
Chief Administrative Assistant—Joyce Pfarr
Business Manager—Doug Bureman
Director, Scouting—Larry Doughty
Director, Minor League Clubs—Greg Riddoch
Director, Stadium Operations—Doug Duennes
Director, Promotions—Greg McCollam
Director, Ticket Department—Bill Stewart
Director, Season Tickets—Janet Wendel
Director, Group Sales—Tony Harris
Director, Broadcasting—Jim Winters
Director of Speakers Bureau—Gordy Coleman
Traveling Secretary—Steve Cobb
Assistant Scout—Jim Stewart
Assistant, Player Development and Scouting—Brian Granger
Assistant Publicity Director—Jon Braude
Assistant Controller—Chris Krabbe
Assistant Ticket Director—John O'Brien
Chairman Emeritus—Louis Nippert
Manager—Pete Rose
Executive Offices—100 Riverfront Stadium, Cincinnati, O. 45202
Telephone—421-4510 (area code 513)

SCOUTS—Larry Barton, Jr., Gene Bennett, Cameron Bonifay, Dave Calaway, Bill Clark, Martin Daily, Roger Ferguson, Edwin Howsam, Jeff McKay, Sam Mejias, Julian Mock, Chet Montgomery, Robert Myer, Ed Roebuck, Tom Severtson, Neil Summers, Fred Uhlman, Mickey White, George Zuraw.

PARK LOCATION—Riverfront Stadium, downtown Cincinnati, bounded by Second Street to Ohio River and from Walnut Street to Broadway.

Seating capacity—52,392.

FIELD DIMENSIONS—Home plate to left field at foul line, 330 feet; to center field, 404 feet; to right field at foul line, 330 feet.

HOUSTON ASTROS

Board of Directors—Dr. John J. McMullen, Chairman. Owners—Dr. John J. McMullen, Mrs. R.E. (Bob) Smith, Mrs. Thomas E. (Mimi) Dompier, James A. Elkins, Jr., Alfred C. Glassell, Jr., Bob Marco, Don Sanders, Jack T. Trotter, H.L. Brown and Jacqueline, Peter, Catherine and John, Jr. McMullen.

President and General Manager—Albert L. Rosen
Vice-President, Baseball Operations—Bob Kennedy
Special Assistant to the President and General Manager —Donald Davidson
Traveling Secretary—John Davis
Director of Minor League Operations—William J. Wood
Director of Scouting—Dan O'Brien, Jr.
Assistant, Minor League Operations and Scouting—Grady Mack
Director of Public Relations—Mike Ryan
Asst. Director of Public Relations—Rick Rivers
Director of Broadcasting—Art Elliott
Director of Promotions—Karen Williams
Scoreboard Operations—Paul Darst
Broadcast and Promotions Sales—Hugh Pickett, Art Bradshaw
Director of Group and Season Ticket Sales—Evan Burian
Manager, Season Ticket Sales—M.M. (Buddy) Hancken
Manager, Group Sales—Donna deGruyter
Administrative Asst., Major League Operations—Sandra Zimmerman
Secretary, Public Relations—Beverly Rains
Club Physician—Dr. William Bryan
Public Address Announcer—J. Fred Duckett
Manager—Bob Lillis
Executive Offices—Astrodome, P.O. Box 288
Houston, Tex. 77001
Telephone—799-9500 (area code 713)
HOUSTON SPORTS ASSOCIATION, INC.
President and Chief Operating Officer—Robert G. Harter
Executive Vice-President—Neal Gunn
Vice-President, Operations—W. Gary Keller
Senior Vice-President, Marketing and Sales—Mike Storen
Executive Vice-President, Astrodome-Astrohall Stadium Corporation—Jimmie Fore
Director, Special Projects—Jim Weidler
Director, Service and Administration—Bill Boyd
Treasurer—A. Eugene Stoffel
Controller—Adam C. Richards
Ticket Manager—Charles T. Wall

SCOUTS—Clary Anderson, Stan Benjamin, Jack Bloomfield, Joe Campise, Walter Cress, C.V. Davis, Doug Deutsch, Ben Galante, Carl Greene, Bill Hallauer, Bob Hartsfield, Red Hayworth, Bob Kennedy, Jr., David Lakey, Gordon Lakey, Julio Linares, Grady Mack, Walter Matthews, William Melendez, Domingo Mercedes, Carlos Muro, Hal Newhouser, Dan O'Brien, Jr., Tony Pacheco, Pedro Prado, Adriano Rodriguez, Lynwood Stallings, Reggie Waller, Paul Weaver, Harrison Wickel.

PARK LOCATION—Astrodome, Kirby and Interstate Loop 610

Seating capacity—45,000.

FIELD DIMENSIONS—Home plate to left field at foul line, 330 feet; to center field, 400 feet; to right field at foul line, 330 feet.

LOS ANGELES DODGERS

Board of Directors—Peter O'Malley, President; Harry M. Bardt;
Roland Seidler, Jr., Vice-President and Treasurer;
Mrs. Roland (Terry) Seidler, Secretary

President—Peter O'Malley
Executive Vice-President—Fred Claire
Vice-President, Player Personnel—Al Campanis
Vice-President, Minor League Operations—William P. Schweppe
Vice-President, Marketing—Merritt Willey
Controller and Assistant Treasurer—Ken Hasemann
Assistant Secretary—Irene Tanji
Resident Council—Santiago Fernandez
Director, Advertising, Novelties and Souvenirs—Jim Campbell
Director, Dodgertown—Charles Blaney
Director, Stadium Operations—Bob Smith
Director, Ticket Department—Walter Nash
Director, Stadium Club and Transportation—Bob Schenz
Director, Dodger Network—David Van de Walker
Director, Scouting—Ben Wade
Director, Publicity—Steve Brener
Director, Publications—Toby Zwikel
Director, Community Relations—Don Newcombe
Community Relations—Roy Campanella, Lou Johnson
Director, Ticket Marketing and Promotions—Barry Stockhamer
Director, Community Services and Special Events—Bill Shumard
Assistant to the President—Ike Ikuhara
Traveling Secretary—Billy DeLury
Auditor—Michael Strange
Manager—Tom Lasorda
Club Physicians—Dr. Frank Jobe, Dr. Robert Woods
Executive Offices—Dodger Stadium, 1000 Elysian Park Avenue,
Los Angeles, Calif. 90012
Telephone—224-1500 (area code 213)

SCOUTS—Eleodoro Arias, Rafael Avila, Boyd Bartley, Bob Bishop, Gib Bodet,
Mike Brito, Marco Cobos, Bob Darwin, Paul Duval, Eddie Fajardo, Sergio Ferrer,
Jim Garland, Rafael Gonzalez, Dick Hanlon, Dennis Haren, Gail Henley, Elvio Ji-
menez, Tony John, Tim Johnson, Hank Jones, John Keenan, Ron King, Steve Lembo,
Ed Liberatore, Carl Lowenstine, Dale McReynolds, Bob Miske, Tommy Mixon, John
O'Neil, Regie Otero, Bill Pleis, Phil Pote, Glen Van Proyen, Tomas Silverio, Jerry
Stephenson, Dick Teed, Corito Varona, Guy Wellman.

PARK LOCATION—Dodger Stadium, 1000 Elysian Park Avenue.

Seating capacity—56,000.

FIELD DIMENSIONS—Home plate to left field at foul line, 330 feet; to center
field, 395 feet; to right field at foul line, 330 feet.

MONTREAL EXPOS

Board of Directors—Charles R. Bronfman, Lorne C. Webster,
John J. McHale, Sydney Maislin, Hugh Hallward, E. Leo Kolber,
Melvin W. Griffin, Louis R. Desmarais,
Arnold Ludwick, Honorary Treasurer

Chairman of the Board—Charles R. Bronfman
President and Chief Executive Officer—John J. McHale
Vice-President, Player Development, Scouting—Jim Fanning
Vice-President and General Manager—Murray Cook
Vice-President, Baseball Operations—Bill Stoneman
Director of Minor League Operations—Bob Gebhard
Director, Team Travel—Peter Durso
Group Vice-President—Pierre Gauvreau
Vice-President, Business Operations—Gerry Trudeau
Vice-President, Marketing & Public Affairs—Rene Guimond
Publicists—Monique Giroux, Richard Griffin
Field Coordinator, Player Development—Pat Daugherty
Coordinator, Spring Training—Kevin McHale
Manager—Buck Rodgers
Club Physician—Dr. Robert Brodrick
Mailing Address—P. O. Box 500, Station M, Montreal, Quebec,
Canada H1V 3P2
Telephone—253-3434 (area code 514)

SCOUTS—(Special assignment)—Eddie Lyons, Carroll (Whitey) Lockman, Ed Lopat; (Supervisors)—Danny Menendez, Bob Fontaine, Jr.; (Regular)—Bill Adair, Jesus Alou, Kelvin Bowles, Terry Boyle, Harry Bright, Lloyd Christopher, Cliff Ditto, Joe Frisina, Mercer Harris, Tom Hinkle, Bob Johnson, Dick Lemay, Roy McMillan, Walter Millies, John (Red) Murff, Herb Newberry, Bob Oldis, Ron Piche, Harry Pritikin, Earl Rapp, Bob Rogers.

PARK LOCATION—Olympic Stadium, 4545 Pierre de Coubertin, Montreal, Quebec, Canada H1V 3N7.

Seating capacity—59,149.

FIELD DIMENSIONS—Home plate to left field at foul line, 325 feet; to center field, 404 feet; to right field at foul line, 325 feet.

NEW YORK METS

Chairman of the Board—Nelson Doubleday

Directors—Nelson Doubleday, Fred Wilpon, Walter E. Freese
John W. O'Donnell, John T. Sargent, Gerard Toner
President & Chief Executive Officer—Fred Wilpon
Exec. Vice-President, G.M. & Chief Operating Officer—J. Frank Cashen
Vice-President, Operations—Bob Mandt
Vice-President, Baseball Administration—Alan E. Harazin
Vice-President, Finance and Administration—Harold W. O'Shaughnessy
Special Asst. to the G.M. & Team Travel Director—Arthur Richman
Vice-President, Marketing—Michael Aronin
Vice-President, Special Projects—John Doht
Assistant V.P. and Director of Player Personnel—Joseph McIlvaine
Ticket Manager—Bill Ianniciello
Director of Minor League Operations—Stephen Schryver
Director of Public Relations—Jay Horwitz
Director of Promotions—Tim Hamilton
Stadium Manager—John McCarthy
Manager—Dave Johnson
Club Physician—Dr. James C. Parkes II
Team Trainer—Steve Garland
Executive Offices—William A. Shea Stadium, Roosevelt
Avenue and 126th Street, Flushing, N.Y. 11368
Telephone—507-6387 (area code 718)

SCOUTS—Carmen Fusco, Roland Johnson, Dean Jongewaard, Buddy Kerr, Dave Madison, Joe Mason, Harry Minor, Robert Minor, Danny Monzon, Julian Morgan, Roy Partee, Carlos Pascual, Junior Roman, Terry Ryan, Bob Scheffing, Marvin Scott, Jim Terrell, Eddy Toledo, Bob Wellman, Len Zanke, Jack Zduriencik.

PARK LOCATION—William A. Shea Stadium, Roosevelt Avenue and 126th Street, Flushing, N. Y. 11368.

Seating capacity—55,300.

FIELD DIMENSIONS—Home plate to left field at foul line, 338 feet; to center field, 410 feet; to right field at foul line, 338 feet.

PHILADELPHIA PHILLIES

President—Bill Giles

Partners—The Taft Baseball Co., John Drew Betz Associates, Tri-Play Associates, Fitz Eugene Dixon Jr., Mrs. Rochelle Levy
Assistant to President—Paul Owens
Executive Vice-President—David Montgomery
Vice-President, Finance—Jerry Clothier
Vice-President, Baseball Administration—Tony Siegle
Vice-President, Public Relations—Larry Shenk
Secretary and Counsel—William Y. Webb
Financial Consultant—Robert D. Hedberg
Vice-President, Player Development and Scouting—Jim Baumer
Player Personnel Advisor—Hugh Alexander
Director of Promotions—Frank Sullivan
Director of Advertising—Tom Hudson
Traveling Secretary—Eddie Ferenz
Director of Sales and Ticket Operations—Richard Deats
Director of Scouting—Jack Pastore
Director of Community Relations and Broadcaster—Chris Wheeler
Director of Marketing—Dennis Lehman
Director of Stadium Operations—Mike DiMuzio
Director of Office Services—Pat Cassidy
Director of Management Information—Jeff Eisenberg
Director of Financial Analysis and Planning—Mike Kent
Director of Group Sales—Bettyanne Joyce
Director of Season Ticket Sales—Dennis Mannion
Ticket Manager—Ray Krise
Assistant Director of Promotions—Chris Legault
Assistant Director of Marketing—Jo-Anne Levy
Assistant Director of Public Relations—Vince Nauss
Executive Secretary to Minor Leagues—Bill Gargano
Club Physician—Dr. Phillip Marone
Club Trainer—Jeff Cooper
Strength and Flexibility Instructor—Gus Hoefling
Manager—John Felske
Executive Offices—Philadelphia Veterans Stadium
Mailing Address—P.O. Box 7575, Philadelphia, Pa. 19101
Telephone—463-6000 (area code 215)

SCOUTS—(Special assignment)—Hugh Alexander and Ray Shore. (Regular)—Oliver Bidwell, Edward Bockman, Carlos Cervo, George Farson, Tom Ferguson, Doug Gassaway, Charles Gault, Bill Harper, Gary Jordan, Dick Lawlor, Anthony Lucadello, Fred Mazuca, Luis Peraza, Bob Reasonover, Larry Reasonover, Joe Reilly, Jay Robertson, Tony Roig, Andy Seminick, Rudy Terrasas, Randy Waddill, Don Williams.

PARK LOCATION—Philadelphia Veterans Stadium, Broad Street and Pattison Avenue.

Seating capacity—66,744.

FIELD DIMENSIONS—Home plate to left field at foul line, 330 feet; to center field, 408 feet; to right field at foul line, 330 feet.

PITTSBURGH PIRATES

President—Daniel M. Galbreath

Chairman of the Board—John W. Galbreath
Directors—Daniel M. Galbreath, James W. Phillips,
Deane F. Johnson, Martin Payson
Executive Vice-President—Harding Peterson
Vice-President Administration—Joseph M. O'Toole
Vice-President Public Relations and Marketing—Jack Schrom
Treasurer/Assistant Secretary—Douglas G. McCormick
Secretary—James W. Phillips
Assistant to Vice-President for Marketing—Steve Greenberg
Director of Publicity—Edward A. Wade
Assistant Directors of Publicity—Sally O'Leary, Greg Johnson
Director of Scouting—Elmer Gray
Minor League Director—Branch B. Rickey
Assistant Minor League Director—Tom Kayser
Assistant Director of Scouting—Jon Neiderer
Traveling Secretary—Charles Muse
Radio and TV Coordinator—Greg Brown
Director of Promotions—Kathy Saba
Asst. Dir. of Promotions and Community Relations Dir.—Patty Paytas
Assistant to the Treasurer—Kenneth C. Curcio
Ticket Manager—Richard C. Holland
Director of Season and Group Sales—Steve Greenberg
Manager—Chuck Tanner
Club Physicians—Drs. Joseph Coroso, Jack Failla
Team Trainer—Tony Bartirome, Kent Biggerstaff
Equipment Manager—John Hallahan
Executive Offices—Three Rivers Stadium, 600 Stadium Circle, Pittsburgh, PA 15212
Telephone—323-5000 (area code 412)

SCOUTS—(Scouting Supervisors)—Gene Baker, Jack Bowen, Bart Braun, Joe L. Brown, Bill Bryk, Joe Consoli, Pablo Cruz, Larry D'Amato, George Detore, Angel Figueroa, Jerry Gardner, Pete Gebrian, Fred Goodman, Howie Haak, Carlton Keller, Jim Maxwell, Lenny Yochim. (Associate Scouts)—Jose Luna, Boyd Odom, Steve Oleschuk, Mark Tanner, Bob Whalen.

PARK LOCATION—Three Rivers Stadium, 600 Stadium Circle.

Seating capacity—58,429.

FIELD DIMENSIONS—Home plate to left field at foul line, 335 feet; to center field, 400 feet; to right field at foul line, 335 feet.

ST. LOUIS CARDINALS

Chairman of the Board, President and Chief Executive Officer—
August A. Busch, Jr.

Executive Vice-President, Chief Operating Officer—Fred L. Kuhlmann
Vice-Presidents—August A. Busch, III, Margaret S. Busch
Senior Vice-President—Stan Musial
Vice-President, Administration—Gary Blase
Secretary and Treasurer—John L. Hayward
Assistant Secretary—Richard Schwartz
Controller—John McMinn
Board of Directors—Adolphus A. Busch, IV, August A. Busch, Jr.,
August A. Busch, III, Margaret S. Busch, Frederic E. Giersch, Jr., Louis B. Hager,
John Hayward, Ben Kerner, Fred L. Kuhlmann, J.W. McAfee, Stanley F. Musial,
W.R. Persons, Walter C. Reisinger, Louis B. Susman
Manager—Whitey Herzog
Administrative Assistant to G.M.—Judy Lovelace
Director of Marketing—Marty Hendin
Administrative Asst. to Director of Marketing—Nancy McElroy
Director of Player Development—Lee Thomas
Director of Scouting—Fred McAlister
Director of Minor League Operations—Paul Fauks
Director of Public Relations—Jim Toomey
Assistant Director of Public Relations—Kip Ingle
Director of Promotions—Dan Farrell
Director of Sales—Joe Cunningham
Director of Season Ticket Sales—Sue Ann McClaren
Asst. Director of Season Ticket Sales—Dave Edmonds
Director of Tickets and Stadium Operations—Mike Bertani
Assistant Director of Tickets—Josephine Arnold
Assistant Director of Stadium Operations—Bruce Schulze
Traveling Secretary—C.J. Cherre
Club Physician—Dr. Stan London
Executive Offices—Busch Stadium, 250 Stadium Plaza,
St. Louis, Mo. 63102
Telephone—421-3060 (area code 314)

SCOUTS—(Chief Scout)—Mo Mozzali. (Special Assignment)—Joe Frazier, Rich Hacker. (Supervisors)—Jim Belz, Vern Benson, Willie Calvino, Lazardo Del Orbe, Steve Flores, Jim Johnston, Hank Kelly, Marty Keough, Marty Maier, Tom McCormack, Mike Roberts, Hal Smith, Charles (Tim) Thompson. (Regular)—James Brown, Roberto Diaz, Cecil Espy, Manuel Guerra, Ray King, Thornton Lee, Juan Melo, Virgil Melvin, Albert Osorio, Bob Parks, Medaro Perez, Joe Popek, Bart Shelly, Kenneth Thomas.

PARK LOCATION—Busch Stadium, Broadway, Walnut Street, Stadium Plaza and Spruce Street.

Seating capacity—50,100.

FIELD DIMENSIONS—Home plate to left field at foul line, 330 feet; to center field, 414 feet; to right field at foul line, 330 feet.

SAN DIEGO PADRES

Board of Directors—Joan Kroc, Ballard F. Smith, Jr., Anthony J. Zulfer, Jr.

President and Treasurer—Ballard F. Smith, Jr.
Senior Vice-President, Business Operations—Elten F. Schiller
Vice-President, Baseball Operations—Jack McKeon
Administrative Assistant—Rhoda Polley
Vice-President, Administration—Dick Freeman
Accounting Dept. Supervisor—Bob Wells
Major League Scout, Special Assignments—Dick Hager
Administrator, Minor Leagues and Scouting—Tom Romenesko
Director of Media Relations—Bill Beck
Assistant Director of Media Relations—Mike Swanson
Administrative Assistant—Mil Chipp
Media Relations Assistant—Be Barnes
Asst. Dir. Community Relations/Publications—Jim Geschke
Director of Broadcasting—Jerry Coleman
Director of Group Sales—Tom Mulcahy
Director of Marketing—Andy Strasberg
Director of Business Development—Fred Whitacre
Director of Ticket Sales—Dave Gilmore
Traveling Secretary—John Mattei
Manager—Dick Williams
Club Physician—Scripps Clinic
Executive Offices—P. O. Box 2000, San Diego, Calif. 92120
Telephone—283-7294 (area code 619)

SCOUTS—Richard Arche, Dave Bartosch, Ken Bracey, Jose Casino, Billy Castell, Ray Coley, Manny Crespo, David Freeland, Denny Galehouse, Jose Gonzalez, Dick Hager, Donald Hennelly, Earl Jones, John Kosciak, Jim Marshall, Abe Martinez, Bill McKeon, Luis Rosa, Ernie Sierra, Brad Sloan, Vince Valecce, Bob Warner, Hank Zacharias.

PARK LOCATION—San Diego Jack Murphy Stadium, 9949 Friars Road.

Seating capacity—58,671.

FIELD DIMENSIONS—Home plate to left field at foul line, 330 feet; to center field, 405 feet; to right field at foul line, 330 feet.

SAN FRANCISCO GIANTS

President—Robert A. Lurie

Executive Vice-President, Baseball Operations—Thomas F. Haller
Executive Vice-President, Administration—Corey Busch
Vice-President, Business Operations—Patrick J. Gallagher
Asst. Vice-President, Baseball Operations/Minor Leagues—Ralph E. Nelson, Jr.
Director of Player Personnel and Scouting—Bob Fontaine
Field Director of Player Development—Jim Lefebvre
Minor League Consultant—Jack Schwarz
Director of Publicity—Duffy Jennings
Director of Community and Public Relations—Stu Smith
Director of Marketing—Dale Kaetzel
Director of Stadium Operations—Don Foreman
Ticket Manager—Arthur Schulze
Accounting Manager—Jeannie Adamo
Director of Sales—Bob Gaillard
Traveling Secretary—Dirk Smith
Speakers Bureau—Joe Orengo
Community Representatives—Mike Sadek, Willie McCovey
Director of Graphics and Photography—Dennis Desprois
Manager—Jim Davenport
Executive Offices—Candlestick Park, San Francisco, Calif. 94124
Telephone—468-3700 (area code 415)

SCOUTS—Edward A. Barberis, Harry Craft, Dutch Deutsch, Jack DiGrace, Nino Escalera, Jim Fairey, Jack French, Robert Folkins, Maurice D. Fisher, George M. Genovese, Grady Hatton, Carl Hubbell, Herman Hannah, Al Heist, Richard Klaus, Harvey Koepf, Andy Korenek, Jim Lyke, Marty Miller, Frank Ontiveros, Danny Ozark, Jack Paepke, Bill Parese, Ken (Squeaky) Parker, Mike Sadek, Hank Sauer, Marvin Stendel, John Shafer, Bill Teed, Gene Thompson, Mike Toomey, Jack Uhey, John Van Ornum, Joe Winstead, Tom Zimmer.

PARK LOCATION—Candlestick Point, Bayshore Freeway.

Seating capacity—58,000.

FIELD DIMENSIONS—Home plate to left field at foul line, 335 feet; to center field, 400 feet; to right field at foul line, 330 feet.

American League

Organized 1900

ROBERT W. BROWN, M.D.
President

JOHN E. FETZER, GENE AUTRY
Vice-Presidents

ROBERT O. FISHEL
Executive Vice President

DONALD C. MARR, Jr.
Controller

RICHARD BUTLER
Supervisor of Umpires

ROBERT F. HOLBROOK
Special Assistant

STEPHANIE VARDAVAS
Manager, Waivers & Player Records Department

PHYLLIS MERHIGE
Director of Public Relations

TESS BASTA, DAVID GLAZIER, CAROLYN COEN
Administrators

Headquarters—350 Park Avenue, New York, N. Y. 10022

Telephone—371-7600 (area code 212)

ASSISTANT SUPERVISORS OF UMPIRES—William Haller, Henry Soar, Larry Napp.

UMPIRES—Lawrence Barnett, Nicholas Bremigan, Joseph Brinkman, Alan Clark, Drew Coble, Terrance Cooney, Derryl Cousins, Donald Denkinger, James Evans, Dale Ford, Richard Garcia, Ted Hendry, John Hirschbeck, Mark Johnson, Kenneth Kaiser, Greg Kosc, William Kunkel, Tim McClelland, Larry McCoy, James McKean, Durwood Merrill, Dan Morrison, Jerome Neudecker, Stephen Palermo, David Phillips, Rick Reed, Michael Reilly, John (Rocky) Roe, John Shulock, Martin Springstead, Vic Voltaggio, Tim Welke.

OFFICIAL STATISTICIANS—Sports Information Center, 1776 Heritage Drive, No. Quincy, Mass. 02171. Telephone—(617) 328-4674.

Players cannot be transferred from one major league to another after June 15 to close of the championship season except through regular waiver channels.

WAIVER PRICE, $20,000. Interleague waivers, $20,000, except for selected players and draft-excluded players.

BALTIMORE ORIOLES

Chairman of the Board and President—Edward Bennett Williams

Executive Vice-President, General Manager—Henry J. Peters
Vice-President, Secretary, General Counsel—Lawrence Lucchino
Vice-President, Stadium Operations—Jack Dunn, III
Vice-President, Finance—Joseph P. Hamper, Jr.
Directors—Edward Bennett Williams, Joseph P. DiMaggio, Jack Dunn, III,
Jay Emmett, Robert J. Flanagan, Gerald T. Gabrys, Charles H. Hoffberger,
Jerold C. Hoffberger, Zanvyl Krieger, Lawrence Lucchino, Henry J. Peters,
Peter P. Weidenbruch, Jr.
Special Assistant to the General Manager—James J. Russo
Director of Business Affairs—Robert R. Aylward
Director of Public Relations—Robert W. Brown
Director, Player Development and Scouting—Thomas A. Giordano
Traveling Secretary—Philip E. Itzoe
Executive Director of Sales—Louis I. Michaelson
Director of Corporate Marketing—Drew M. Sheinman
Community Relations Manager—Julia A. Wagner
Sales Manager—Daniel J. O'Dowd
Ticket Office Manager—Timothy Geraghty
Assistant Director, Player Development and Scouting—John J. McCall
Assistant Public Relations Director—Richard L. Vaughn
Assistant Ticket Manager—Joseph B. Codd
Special Projects Coordinator—Kenneth E. Nigro
Baltimore Sales Representative—Martin J. Smith
Manager—Joseph S. Altobelli
Club Physician—Dr. Leonard Wallenstein
Executive Offices—Memorial Stadium, Baltimore, Md. 21218
Telephone—243-9800 (area code 301)

SCOUTS—(Major League)—Jim Russo, John Stokoe, Bill Werle. (Regular)—
Juan Amador, Jack Baker, Joe Bowman, Dan Cressman, Ray Crone, Ed Crosby, Joe
DeLucca, Jose Garcia, Jim Gilbert, John Hagemann, Jesus Halibi, Len Johnston, Bill
Lawlor, George Lauzerique, Minnie Mendoza, Lamar North, Jim Pamlanye, Jack
Sanford, Al Zarilla, Jerry Zimmerman.

PARK LOCATION—Memorial Stadium, 33rd Street, Ellerslie Avenue, 36th
Street and Ednor Road.

Seating capacity—53,198.

FIELD DIMENSIONS—Home plate to left field at foul line, 309 feet; to center
field, 405 feet; to right field at foul line, 309 feet.

BOSTON RED SOX

President—Jean R. Yawkey

Chief Executive Officer/Chief Operating Officer—Haywood C. Sullivan
General Partner, Administration—Edward G. LeRoux, Jr.
Vice-President, General Manager—James L. Gorman
Chief Financial Officer/Treasurer—Robert C. Furbush
V. P., Player Development Director—Edward F. Kenney
Minor League Administrative Assistant—Edward Kenney, Jr.
Scouting Director—Edward M. Kasko
Public Relations and Publicity Director—Richard L. Bresciani
Traveling Secretary—John J. Rogers
Broadcasting Director—James P. Healey
Executive Assistant—Joseph F. McDermott
Controller—John J. Reilly
Ticket Director—Arthur J. Moscato
Consultants—Theodore S. Williams, Carl Yastrzemski
Superintendent, Grounds & Maintenance—Joseph Mooney
Manager—John McNamara
Club Physician—Dr. Arthur M. Pappas
Executive Offices—24 Yawkey Way, Boston, Mass. 02215
Telephone—267-9440 (area code 617)

SCOUTS—Rafael Batista, Milton Bolling, Ray Boone, Wayne Britton, George Digby, Howard (Danny) Doyle, Bill Enos, Larry Flynn, Earl Johnson, Charles Koney, Wilfrid (Lefty) Lefebvre, Don Lenhardt, Tommy McDonald, Felix Maldonado, Frank Malzone, Sam Mele, Willie Paffen, Peter Randall, Philip Rossi, Edward Scott, Matt Sczesny, Joe Stephenson, Larry Thomas, Charlie Wagner.

PARK LOCATION—Fenway Park, Yawkey Way, Lansdowne Street and Ipswich Street.

Seating capacity—33,583.

FIELD DIMENSIONS—Home plate to left field at foul line, 315 feet; to center field, 420 feet; to right field at foul line, 302 feet; average right-field distance, 382 feet.

CALIFORNIA ANGELS

President and Chairman of the Board—Gene Autry

Executive Vice-President and General Manager—Mike Port
Vice-President—Jackie Autry
Vice-President/Secretary-Treasurer—Michael Schreter
Vice-Chairman—Arthur E. Patterson
Vice-President, Marketing—John W. Hays
Vice-President, Finance and Administration—James Wilson
Director Public Relations and Promotions—Tom Seeberg
Director of Accounting—Jim Kaczmarek
Director Scouting & Player Development—Larry Himes
Director of Minor League Operations—Bill Bavasi
Director Ticket Development—Carl Gordon
Director Group Sales—Lynn Kirchmann Biggs
Director Stadium Operations—Jean (Corky) Lippert
Traveling Secretary—Frank Sims
Assistant Director Public Relations—Tim Mead, John Sevano
Assistant Ticket Director—Bob Terzes
Stadium Operations—Kevin Uhlich
Film Coordinator and Special Statistics—George Goodale
Medical Director—Dr. Robert K. Kerlan
Orthopedist—Dr. Lewis Yocum
Trainers—Rick Smith, Ned Bergert
Manager—Gene Mauch
Executive Offices—Anaheim Stadium, 2000 State College Blvd.,
Anaheim, Calif. 92806
Telephone—937-6700 (area code 714) or 625-1123 (area code 213)

SCOUTS—Edmundo Borrome, Joe Carpenter, Alex Cosmidis, Pompeyo Davillo, Preston Douglas, Jesse Flores, Bob Gardner, Al Goldis, Steve Gruwell, Bruce Hines, Rick Ingalls, Nick Kamzic, Kevin Malone, Eusebio Perez, Vic Power, Philip Rizzo, Cookie Rojas, Rich Schlenker, Lou Snipp, Mark Snipp, Hank Weaver, Mark Weidemaier.

PARK LOCATION—Anaheim Stadium, 2000 State College Blvd.

Seating capacity—65,158.

FIELD DIMENSIONS—Home plate to left field at foul line, 333 feet; to center field, 404 feet; to right field at foul line, 333 feet.

CHICAGO WHITE SOX

Chairman, Board of Directors—Jerry M. Reinsdorf

President—Eddie M. Einhorn
Executive Vice-President, General Manager—Roland A. Hemond
Executive Vice-President—Howard C. Pizer
Vice-President, Marketing—Michael D. McClure
Vice-President, Broadcasting and Special Projects—Laureen Ong Fadil
Vice-President, Baseball Administration—Jack Gould
Assistant General Manager—David Dombrowski
Director of Player Development—Bob Winkles
Assistant to Vice-President, Marketing—Stephen M. Schanwald
Director of Public Relations and Promotions—Paul H. Jensen
Sales Manager—Millie Johnson
Director, Season Sales—Jeff Overton
Director of Broadcast Sales—Edwin M. Doody
Controller—Timothy L. Buzard
Traveling Secretary—Glen Rosenbaum
Ticket Manager—Robert K. Devoy
Director, Group Sales and Park Entertainment—M. Scott Smith
Assistant Director of Public Relations—Tim Clodjeaux
Director of Latin American Baseball Operations—Angel Vasquez
Administrative Assistants, Baseball Operations—Daniel Evans, Brian Boles
General Counsel—Allan B. Muchin
Trainer—Herman Schneider
Assistant Trainer—Brandt McFarlin
Team Physicians—Drs. Richard D. Corzatt, James B. Boscardin, Hugo Cuadros
Manager—Tony LaRussa
Equipment/Club House Mgr., White Sox—Willie Thompson
Equipment/Club House Mgr., Visitors—John MacNamara, Jr.
Director of Park Operations—David M. Schaffer
Groundskeepers—Gene and Roger Bossard
P.A. Announcer—Wayne Mesmer
Organist—Nancy Faust
Executive Offices—Comiskey Park, Dan Ryan at 35th Street, Chicago, Ill. 60616
Telephone—924-1000 (area code 312)

SCOUTS—(Advance)—Bart Johnson. (Special Assignment)—Jerry Krause, Fred Shaffer. (Supervisor)—Walt Widmayer. (Regular)—Juan Bernhardt, James Busby, Bobby Gardner, Jr., Bill Gayton, Eric Gluck, Joseph Ingalls, Leo Labossiere, Carlos Lareto, Dario Lodigiani, Terry Logan, Larry Monroe, Rich Morales, Thomas Roberts, Cucho Rodriguez, Mark Servais, Duane Shaffer, Fred Shaffer, George Sobek, Lynn Squires, Kenneth Stauffer, Walt Widmeyer, Stan Zielinski.

PARK LOCATION—Comiskey Park, Dan Ryan at 35th Street, Chicago, Ill. 60616.

Seating capacity—44,432.

FIELD DIMENSIONS—Home plate to left field at foul line, 341 feet; to center field, 401 feet; to right field at foul line, 341 feet.

CLEVELAND INDIANS

President and Chief Executive Officer—Gabe Paul

Chairman of the Board—Patrick J. O'Neill
Directors—Dudley S. Blossom, III, Alva T. Bonda, G.E. DiGeronimo, Michael J. Fetchko, Bernard S. Goldfarb, Walter Laich, Patrick J. O'Neill, Gabriel H. Paul, Arnold R. Pinkney, Robert E. Quinn, Phillip D. Seghi, Maurice L. Stonehill
Vice-President and General Manager—Phillip D. Seghi
Vice-President, Player Development and Scouting—Bob Quinn
Secretary and Club Legal Counsel—Edward C. Crouch
Manager—Pat Corrales
Traveling Secretary—Mike Seghi
Director of Public Relations—Bob DiBiasio
Assistant Director of Public Relations—Rick Minch
Director of Sales and Marketing—Tom Pulchinski
Director of Stadium Operations—Dan Zerbey
Ticket Director—Jerry Waring
Controller—Jason Rosenthal
Special Assistant to the General Manager—Dan Carnevale
Special Assignment Representative—Birdie Tebbetts
Broadcasting Director—Pete Spudich
Minor League Administrator—Joe Pavia
Asst. Farm Director—Phil Thomas
Trainer—Jim Warfield
Assistant Strength and Conditioning Coach—Paul Spicuzza
Club Physicians—Drs. William Wilder, William Bohl
Club Dentist—Dr. Marvin Schermer
Equipment Manager—Cy Buynak
Executive Offices—Cleveland Stadium, Cleveland, Ohio 44114
Telephone—861-1200 (area code 216)

SCOUTS—Hector Acevedo, Eddie Bane, Dan Carnevale, Jack Cassini, Tom Chandler, Tom Couston, Red Gaskill, Leon Hamilton, Luis Issac, Bobby Malkmus, Bill Meyer, Jim Miller, Dave Roberts, Woody Smith, Dale Sutherland, Gary Sutherland, Birdie Tebbetts, Jack Vallely.

PARK LOCATION—Cleveland Stadium, Boudreau Blvd.

Seating capacity—74,208.

FIELD DIMENSIONS—Home plate to left field at foul line, 320 feet; to center field, 400 feet; to right field at foul line, 320 feet.

DETROIT TIGERS

Chairman of the Board—John E. Fetzer

Vice-Chairman and Owner—Thomas S. Monaghan
President & Chief Executive Officer—James A. Campbell
Executive Vice-President & Chief Operating Officer—William E. Haase
Vice-President & General Manager—William R. Lajoie
Vice-President/Finance—Alexander C. Callam
Director of Public Relations—Dan Ewald
Director of Radio & TV—Neal Fenkell
Director of Stadium Operations—Ralph E. Snyder
Director of Player Development—Frank Franchi
Administrator of Player Development—Dave Miller
Director of Ticket Sales—Jerry Bucholtz
Director of Concession Operations (Bismarck Corp.)—Bob Sherman
Executive Secretary/Baseball—Alice Sloane
Executive Secretary/Operations—Hazel McLane
Traveling Secretary—Bill Brown
Executive Consultant—Rick Ferrell
Special Assignment Scout—Walter A. Evers
Scouting Coordinator—George Bradley
Box Office Treasurer—William H. Willis
Assistant Director of Public Relations—Bob Miller
Assistant Director of Public Relations/Special Events/Scoreboard—Lew Matlin
Assistant Director of Public Relations/Community Relations—Vince Desmond
Group Sales Coordinator—Irwin Cohen
Assistant Director of Stadium Operations/Grounds Maintenance—Frank Feneck
Assistant Director of Stadium Operations/Grounds Maintenance—Ed Goward
Manager—Sparky Anderson
Club Physician—Clarence S. Livingood M.D.
Orthopedic Consultant—David Collon M.D.
Executive Offices—Tiger Stadium, Detroit, Mich. 48216
Telephone—962-4000 (area code 313)

SCOUTS—Rick Arnold, John Barkley, Ray Bellino, Wayne Blackburn, Joe Henderson, Roger Jongewaard, Joe Lewis, Orlando Pena, Jax Robertson, Paul Robinson, Bill Schudlich, Jack Tighe, Marti Wolever.

PARK LOCATION—Tiger Stadium, Michigan Avenue, Cochrane Avenue, Kaline Drive and Trumbull Avenue.

Seating capacity—52,806.

FIELD DIMENSIONS—Home plate to left field at foul line, 340 feet; to center field, 440 feet; to right field at foul line, 325 feet.

KANSAS CITY ROYALS

Board of Directors
Joe Burke, William Deramus, III, Avron Fogelman, Charles Hughes,
Ewing Kauffman, Mrs. Ewing Kauffman, Earl Smith

Chairman of the Board—Ewing Kauffman
Vice Chairman of the Board—Avron Fogelman
President—Joe Burke
Executive Vice-President and General Manager—John Schuerholz
Executive Vice-President, Administration—Spencer (Herk) Robinson
Vice-President, Controller—Dale Rohr
Vice-President and Legal Counsel—Phil Koury
Special Assistant to General Manager—Joe Klein
Director of Public Relations—Dean Vogelaar
Director of Marketing and Broadcasting—Dennis Cryder
Traveling Secretary/Lancer Coordinator—Will Rudd
Assistant Director of Public Relations—Jeffrey Coy
Director of Player Development—Dick Balderson
Director of Scouting—Art Stewart
Assistant Director of Scouting and Player Development—Dean Taylor
Administrative Assistant of Scouting & Player Development—Rick Matthews
Assistant Director of Marketing—Scott Pederson
Director of Ticket Operations—Stacy Sherrow
Director of Season Ticket Sales—Joe Grigoli
Director of Group Sales—Chris Muehlbach
Director of Event Personnel—Jay Hinrichs
Stadium Engineer—George Humphrey
Stadium Maintenance Coordinator—Bob Frank
Data Processing Manager—Loretta Krazberg
Accountants—Tom Pfannenstiel, Ken Willeke
Manager—Dick Howser
Equipment Manager—Al Zych
Groundskeeper—George Toma
Team Physician—Dr. Paul Meyer
Trainers—Mickey Cobb, Paul McGannon
Executive Offices—Royals Stadium, Harry S Truman Sports Complex
Mailing Address—P. O. Box 1969, Kansas City, Mo. 64141
Telephone—921-2200 (area code 816)

SCOUTS—Carl Blando, Al Diez, Tom Ferrick, Rosey Gilhousen, Ken Gonzales, Ron Hopkins, Joe Klein, Al Kubski, Tony Levato, Chuck McMichael, Brian Murphy, George Noga, Jerry Stephens, Roy Tanner, Jerry Terrell, Red Whitsett.

PARK LOCATION—Royals Stadium, Harry S Truman Sports Complex.

Seating capacity—40,625.

FIELD DIMENSIONS—Home plate to left field at foul line, 330 feet; to center field, 410 feet; to right field at foul line, 330 feet.

MILWAUKEE BREWERS

President, Chief Executive Officer—Allan H. (Bud) Selig

Executive Vice-President, General Manager—Harry Dalton
Vice-President, Marketing—Richard Hackett
Vice-President, Broadcast Operations—William Haig
Vice-President, Finance—Richard Hoffmann
Vice-President, Stadium Operations—Gabe Paul, Jr.
Assistant General Manager—Walter Shannon
Special Assistants to the General Manager—Dee Fondy, Sal Bando
Traveling Secretary—Jimmy Bank
Director of Player Procurement—Ray Poitevint
Coordinator of Player Development—Bob Humphreys
Coordinator of Minor League Operations—Bruce Manno
Administrative Assistant for Scouting and Player Development—Dan Duquette
Director of Publicity—Tom Skibosh
Assistant Director of Stadium Operations and Advertising—Jack Hutchinson
Ticket Sales Director—Tim Trovato
Director of the Speakers Bureau—John Counsell
Assistant Director of Publicity—Mario Ziino
Ticket Office Manager—John Barnes
Director of Ticket Office Computer Operations—Alice Boettcher
Director of Special Events—Mark Paget
Manager—George Bamberger
Club Physician—Dr. Paul Jacobs
Trainer—John Adam
Superintendent of Grounds and Maintenance—Harry Gill
Assistant Groundskeeper—Gary Vandenberg
Equipment Manager—Bob Sullivan
P.A. Announcer—Bob Betts
Organist—Frank Charles
Executive Offices—Milwaukee Brewers Baseball Club
Milwaukee County Stadium, Milwaukee, Wis. 53214
Telephone—933-4114 (area code 414)

SCOUTS—Scouting supervisors: Julio Blanco-Herrera, Nelson Burbrink, Felix Delgado, Tom Gamboa, Roland LeBlanc, Walter Youse. Regular scouts: Fred Beene, Tom Bourque, Ken Califano, Bill Castro, Lou Cohenour, Gerry Craft, Dick Ehrig, Charles Fitzgerald, Dave Garcia, Hy Gomberg, Jack Hubbard, Gene Kerns, Frank Kolarek, Don Kohler, Meno Larreal, Cal McLish, Billy Moffitt, Johnny Neun, Ken Richardson, Lee Sigman, Earl Silverthorn, Harry Smith, Milt Sobel, Sam Suplizio, Paul Tretiak.

PARK LOCATION—Milwaukee County Stadium, S. 46th St. off Bluemound Rd.

Seating capacity—53,192.

FIELD DIMENSIONS—Home plate to left field at foul line, 315 feet; to center field, 402 feet; to right field at foul line, 315 feet.

MINNESOTA TWINS

Owner—Carl R. Pohlad

Chairman of the Board—Calvin R. Griffith
President—Howard T. Fox, Jr.
Board of Directors—Carl R. Pohlad, James Pohlad, Calvin R. Griffith, Howard T.
Fox, Jr., H. Gabriel Murphy, Paul Christen, Don Benson
Vice-President—Bruce G. Haynes
Vice-President, Farm Director—George Brophy
Vice-President—William S. Robertson
Vice-President—James K. Robertson
Vice-President—Don Schiel
Assistant Farm Director—Jim Rantz
Controller—Jack Alexander
Director of Public Relations—Tom Mee
Traveling Secretary—Mike Robertson
Manager—Billy Gardner
Club Physicians—Dr. Leonard J. Michienzi and Dr. Harvey O'Phelan
Executive Offices—Hubert H. Humphrey Metrodome, 501 Chicago Ave. South,
Minneapolis, Minn. 55415
Telephone—375-1366 (area code 612)

SCOUTS—Floyd Baker, Vern Borning, Ellsworth Brown, Buck Chamberlin, Spud
Chandler, Ellis Clary, Edward Dunn, Jesse Flores, Jr., Jesse Flores, Sr., Angelo
Giuliani, Lee Irwin, Hank Izquierdo, Vern McKee, Bobby Morgan, Marvin Olson,
Spencer (Red) Robbins, Herb Stein, Harry Warner.

PARK LOCATION—Hubert H. Humphrey Metrodome, 501 Chicago Ave. South.

Seating capacity—55,122.

FIELD DIMENSIONS—Home plate to left field at foul line, 343 feet; to center
field, 408 feet; to right field at foul line, 327 feet.

NEW YORK YANKEES

Principal Owner—George M. Steinbrenner, III

Limited Partners—Harold M. Bowman, Lester Crown, Michael Friedman,
Marvin Goldklang, Barry Halper, Harvey Leighton, Daniel McCarthy,
Harry Nederlander, Robert Nederlander, William Rose, Edward Rosenthal,
Jack Satter, Joan Z. Steinbrenner, Charlotte Witkind, Richard Witkind
President—Eugene J. McHale
Vice-President/General Manager—Clyde King
Manager—Yogi Berra
Administrative Vice-President and Treasurer—M. David Weidler
Vice-President, Baseball Administration—Woody Woodward
Vice-President—Ed Weaver
Vice-President/General Counsel—Mel Southard, Jr.
Director of Player Development—Bobby Hofman
Assistant General Manager—Roy White
Director of Scouting—Doug Melvin
Traveling Secretary—Bill Kane
Director of Marketing—Richard Kraft
Director of Media Relations—Joseph V. Safety
Director of Publications—David Szen
Assistant Baseball Administration Director—Pete Jameson
Assistant Media Relations Director—Lou D'Ermilio
Director, Television and Radio Relations—Kim Gallas
Message Board Operations Director—Betsy Leesman
Speakers Bureau—Bob Pelegrino
Stadium Manager—Patrick Kelly
Executive Director of Ticket Operations—Frank Swaine
Ticket Director—Michael Rendine
Director, Customer Services and Asst. Stadium Manager—Jim Naples
Assistant Scouting Director—Roy Krasik
Assistant Player Development Director—John Dato
Director of Group Sales—Jim Aldridge
Director of Accounting—Warren Atkinson
Stadium Superintendent—Jimmy Esposito
Club Physician—Dr. John J. Bonamo
P.A. Announcer—Bob Sheppard
Executive Offices—Yankee Stadium, Bronx, N.Y. 10451
Telephone—293-4300 (area code 212)
Ticket Information—293-6000 (area code 212)

SCOUTS—Luis Arroyo, Hank Bauer, Joe Begani, Vince Capece, Jim Cartwright, Howard Cassady, Brian Collins, David Cook, Al Cuccinello, Joe DiCarlo, Henry Dotterer, Fred Ferreira, Whitey Ford, Orrin Freeman, Jack Gillis, Ray Goodman, Tom Greenwade, Dick Groch, Jim Gruzdis, Gary Hughes, John Kennedy, Bob Lemon, Don Lindeberg, Bill Livesey, Jim Marshall, Jim Naples, Sr., Ramon Naranjo, Don Nichols, Bob Nieman, Frank O'Rourke, Greg Orr, Meade Palmer, Roberto Rivera, Eddie Robinson, Brian Sabean, Stan Saleski, Russ Sehon, Robert Shaw, Charlie Silvera, George Silvey, Mike Snyder, Tommy Thompson, Luis Tiant, Dick Tidrow, Ron Walters, Dick Wilson.

PARK LOCATION—Yankee Stadium, E. 161st St. and River Ave., Bronx, N.Y. 10451.

Seating capacity—57,545.

FIELD DIMENSIONS—Home plate to left field at foul line, 312 feet; to center field, 417 feet; to right field at foul line, 310 feet.

OAKLAND A's

President—Roy Eisenhardt

Executive Vice-President—Walter J. Haas
Vice-President of Baseball Operations—Sandy Alderson
Vice-President, Business Operations—Andy Dolich
Vice-President, Finance—Kathleen McCracken
Assistant to the President, Baseball Matters—Bill Rigney
Director of Scouting—Dick Bogard
Director of Player Development—Karl Kuehl
Director of Baseball Administration—Walt Jocketty
Director of Latin American Scouting—Juan Marichal
Director of Medical Services—Hirsch Handmaker
Director of Press Relations and Team Travel—Mickey Morabito
Director of Telecommunications—David Rubinstein
Director of Sales—Ray Fosse
Director of Ticket Operations—Raymond B. Krise Jr.
Director of Special Projects—Earl Robinson
Director of Stadium Operations—Jorge Costa
Director of Publications—Art Worthington
Media Manager—Kathy Jacobson
Managing Editor, Publications—David Azevedo
Executive Assistant—Sharon Jones
Business Operations Coordinator/Promotions Director—Sharon Kelly
Ticket Manager—Bettina Flores
Director of Broadcast Operations—Bill King
Director of Ticket Sales—Steve Page
Assistant Director of Press Relations-Statistician—Jay Alves
Manager—Jackie Moore
Trainer—Barry Weinberg, Larry Davis
Equipment Manager—Frank Ciensczyk
Visiting Clubhouse Manager—Steve Vucinich
Marketing Representatives—Tom Cordova, Clarence Jackson, Doris Messina
Executive Offices—Oakland-Alameda County Coliseum, Oakland, Calif. 94621
Telephone—638-4900 (area code 415)

SCOUTS—Mark Conkin, Albert Elliott, Jr., Grady Fuson, Juan Marichal, Mel Nelson, Camilo Pascual, Ed Stevens, Mike Wallace, Gary Wiencek, Del Wilber.

PARK LOCATION—Oakland-Alameda County Coliseum, Nimitz Freeway and Hegenberger Road.

Seating capacity—50,255.

FIELD DIMENSIONS—Home plate to left field at foul line, 330 feet; to center field, 397 feet; to right field at foul line, 330 feet.

SEATTLE MARINERS

Owner & Chairman of the Board—George L. Argyros

President—Charles G. Armstrong
Vice President, Baseball Operations & General Manager—Hal Keller
Assistant G.M. and Special Assignments—Bob Harrison
Vice President, Sales and Marketing—Bill Knudsen
Vice President, Finance—Brian Beggs
Director of Marketing Services—Randy Adamack
Director of Sales—Roger King
Director of Publicity—Bob Porter
Director of Team Travel—Lee Pelekoudas
Director of Stadium Operations—Jeff Klein
Director of Player Development—Jeff Scott
Director of Ticket Services—Doug Hopkins
Assistant Director of Player Development, Instruction—Bill Haywood
Assistant Director of Player Development, Administration—Gary Pellant
Assistant Director of Publicity—Craig Detwiler
Assistant Director of Ticket Services—Mark Mitchell
Manager of Sales and Promotion—Larry Sindall
Manager of Communications and Youth Marketing—Randy Stearnes
Controller/Office Manager—Denise Podosek
Manager—Chuck Cottier
Club Physician—Dr. Larry Pedegana
Club Dentist—Dr. Richard Leshgold
Head Groundskeeper—Wilbur Loo
P.A. Announcer—Gary Spinnell
Executive Offices—P.O. Box 4100
100 South King Street, Suite 300, Seattle, Washington 98104
Telephone—628-3555 (area code 206)

SCOUTS—David Blume, John Cole, Bob Harrison, Steve Hill, Bill Kearns, Coco Laboy, Jeff Malinoff, Tom Mooney, Whitey Piurek, Mike Roberts, Bill Tracy, Rip Tutor, Ray Vince, Steve Vrablik, Luke Wrenn, Bob Zuk.

PARK LOCATION—Kingdome, 201 South King Street, Seattle, Washington.

Seating capacity—59,438.

FIELD DIMENSIONS—Home plate to left field at foul line, 316 feet; to center field, 410 feet; to right field at foul line, 316 feet.

TEXAS RANGERS

Chairman of the Board, Chief Executive Officer—Eddie Chiles

President, Chief Operating Officer—Mike Stone
Vice President, General Manager—Tom Grieve
Vice President, Marketing and Administration—Larry Schmittou
Vice President, Finance and Treasurer—Charles F. Wangner
Assistant G.M., Player Personnel and Scouting—Sandy Johnson
Assistant General Manager—Wayne Krivsky
Director of Player Development—Marty Scott
Special Assistant, Baseball Operations—Paul Richards
Director of Media Relations—John Blake
Assistant Director of Media Relations—Jim Small
Director of Public Relations and Speakers' Bureau—Bobby Bragan
Director, Sales, Broadcasting and Producer, Diamond Vision—Chuck Morgan
Director of Promotions and Diamond Vision—Dave Fendrick
Director of Ticket Sales and Management—Mary Ann Bosher
Director of Season Ticket Sales—Jay Miller
Stadium Manager—Mat Stolley
Medical Director—Dr. B.J. Mycoskie
Sabremetrician—Craig Wright
Traveling Secretary—Dan Schimek
Controller—John McMichael
Manager—Doug Rader
Field Superintendent—Jim Anglea
Field and Grounds Consultant—John Oliveria
Home Clubhouse and Equipment Manager—Joe Macko
Visiting Clubhouse Manager—Mike Wallace
Executive Offices—1200 Copeland Road, Arlington, Tex. 76011
Arlington Stadium—1500 Copeland Road, P.O. Box 1111, Arlington, Tex. 76010
Telephone—273-5222 (area code 817)

SCOUTS—Lee Anthony, Joseph Branzell, Jackie Brathwaite, Paddy Cottrell, Bill Earnhart, Dick Gernert, Orlando Gomez, Andy Hancock, Jack Hayes, Sid Hudson, Joseph Lewis, Joseph Marchese, Jerry Marik, Jim McLaughlin, Omar Miania, Cotton Nix, Rick Schroeder, Herman Welsh, John Young.

PARK LOCATION—Arlington Stadium, 1500 Copeland Road, Arlington, Tex.

Seating capacity—43,508.

FIELD DIMENSIONS—Home plate to left field at foul line, 330 feet; to center field, 400 feet; to right field at foul line, 330 feet.

TORONTO BLUE JAYS

Vice-Chairman, Chief Executive Officer—N. E. Hardy

Board of Directors—John Craig Eaton, L. G. Greenwood, N. E. Hardy,
R. Howard Webster, P. N. T. Widdrington
Chairman of the Board—R. Howard Webster
Executive Vice-President, Business—Paul Beeston
Executive Vice-President, Baseball—Pat Gillick
Vice-Presidents, Baseball—Bobby Mattick, Al LaMacchia
Vice-President, Finance—Bob Nicholson
Director, Public Relations—Howard Starkman
Director, Operations—Ken Erskine
Director, Ticket Operations—George Holm
Director of Marketing—Paul Markle
Director, Team Travel—Ken Carson
Director, Group Sales—Maureen Haffey
Director, Canadian Scouting—Bob Prentice
Assistant Director, Public Relations—Gary Oswald
Administrator, Player Personnel—Gord Ash
Assistant Director, Ticket Operations—Len Frejlich
Director, Security—Fred Wootton
Equipment Manager—Jeff Ross
Coordinator, Promotions & Group Services—John MacLachlan
Supervisor, Grounds—Dave Hamilton
Manager—Bobby Cox
Team Physician—Dr. Ron Taylor
Executive Offices—Exhibition Stadium, Exhibition Place,
Toronto, Ontario
Mailing Address—Box 7777, Adelaide St. P. O., Toronto, Ont. M5C 2K7
Telephone—595-0077 (area code 416)

SCOUTS—Christopher Bourjos, Ellis Dungan, Robert Engle (Eastern Regional
Scouting Director), Joe Ford, Epy Guerrero, Jim Hughes, Al LaMacchia (Senior
Scouting Supervisor), Duane Larson (off-season), Larry Maxie, Ben McLure, Steve
Minor, Wayne Morgan (Western Regional Scouting Director), Paul Ricciarini,
Gerald Sobeck, Don Welke, Bob Wilber, Tim Wilken, Dave Yoakum.

PARK LOCATION—Exhibition Stadium on the grounds of Exhibition Place. En-
trances to Exhibition Place via Lakeshore Boulevard, Queen Elizabeth Way High-
way and Dufferin and Bathurst Streets.

Seating capacity—43,737.

FIELD DIMENSIONS—Home plate to left field at foul line, 330 feet; to center
field, 400 feet; to right field at foul line, 330 feet.

RYNE SANDBERG
• CHICAGO CUBS •
MAJOR LEAGUE
PLAYER OF THE YEAR

DALLAS GREEN
• CHICAGO CUBS •
MAJOR LEAGUE EXECUTIVE

JIM FREY
• CHICAGO CUBS •
MAJOR LEAGUE MANAGER

ALAN KNICELY
• WICHITA •
MINOR LEAGUE PLAYER

The Sporting News

No. 1

MEN

of

1984

BUCK RODGERS
• INDIANAPOLIS •
MINOR LEAGUE MANAGER

MIKE TAMBURRO
• PAWTUCKET •
MINOR LEAGUE EXECUTIVE
IN CLASS AAA

BRUCE BALDWIN
• GREENVILLE •
MINOR LEAGUE EXECUTIVE
IN CLASS AA

DAVE TARROLLY
• BELOIT •
MINOR LEAGUE EXECUTIVE
IN CLASS A

Major League Players Association

805 Third Avenue
New York, N.Y. 10022
Telephone— (212) 826-0808

Acting Executive Director &
General Counsel—Donald Fehr
Special Assistant—Mark Belanger
Associate General Counsel—Eugene Orza
Counsel—Arthur Schack
Staff—Joyce Reiss, Bonnie White and Pilar Whitney

EXECUTIVE BOARD

Don Baylor—American League Representative
Buck Martinez—Alternate American League Representative
Kent Tekulve—National League Representative
Keith Moreland—Alternate National League Representative
Ted Simmons—Pension Committee
Jim Beattie—Pension Committee Alternate
Steve Rogers—Pension Committee
Rick Honeycutt—Pension Committee Alternate
Plus all remaining player representatives

NATIONAL LEAGUE PLAYER REPRESENTATIVES

Bruce Benedict—Atlanta Braves
Keith Moreland—Chicago Cubs
Joe Price—Cincinnati Reds
Bob Knepper—Houston Astros
Mike Scioscia—Los Angeles Dodgers
Steve Rogers—Montreal Expos
Keith Hernandez—New York Mets
Von Hayes—Philadelphia Phillies
Kent Tekulve—Pittsburgh Pirates
Tommy Herr—St. Louis Cardinals
Terry Kennedy—San Diego Padres
Gary Lavelle—San Francisco Giants

AMERICAN LEAGUE PLAYER REPRESENTATIVES

Scott McGregor—Baltimore Orioles
Rick Miller—Boston Red Sox
Ron Romanick—California Angels
Marc Hill—Chicago White Sox
Mike Hargrove—Cleveland Indians
Darrell Evans—Detroit Tigers
Dan Quisenberry—Kansas City Royals
Paul Molitor—Milwaukee Brewers
Dave Engle—Minnesota Twins
Dave Winfield—New York Yankees
Tom Burgmeier—Oakland A's
Jim Beattie—Seattle Mariners
Billy Sample—Texas Rangers
Buck Martinez—Toronto Blue Jays

Major League Farm Systems for '85

AMERICAN LEAGUE

BALTIMORE (6): AAA—Rochester. AA—Charlotte. A—Hagerstown, Newark, Daytona Beach (co-op). Rookie—Bluefield.

BOSTON (5): AAA—Pawtucket. AA—New Britain, Conn. A—Elmira, Greensboro, Winter Haven.

CALIFORNIA (5): AAA—Edmonton. AA—Midland. A—Davenport, Redwood, Salem.

CHICAGO (5): AAA—Buffalo. AA—Glens Falls. A—Appleton, Niagara Falls. Rookie—Sarasota.

CLEVELAND (4): AAA—Old Orchard Beach, Me. AA—Waterbury. A—Batavia, Waterloo.

DETROIT (4): AAA—Nashville. AA—Birmingham. A—Lakeland. Rookie—Bristol, Va.

KANSAS CITY (5): AAA—Omaha. AA—Memphis. A—Eugene, Fort Myers. Rookie—Sarasota.

MILWAUKEE (5): AAA—Vancouver. AA—El Paso. A—Beloit, Stockton. Rookie—Helena.

MINNESOTA (5): AAA—Toledo. AA—Orlando. A—Kenosha, Visalia. Rookie—Elizabethton.

NEW YORK (5): AAA—Columbus, O. AA—Albany-Colonie, N.Y. A—Fort Lauderdale, Oneonta. Rookie—Sarasota.

OAKLAND (6): AAA—Tacoma. AA—Huntsville. A—Medford, Modesto, Madison. Rookie—Pocatello.

SEATTLE (5): AAA—Calgary. AA—Chattanooga. A—Bellingham, Wausau, Salinas.

TEXAS (6): AAA—Oklahoma City. AA—Tulsa. A—Burlington, Salem, Daytona Beach (co-op). Rookie—Sarasota.

TORONTO (6): AAA—Syracuse. AA—Knoxville. A—Florence, Kinston. Rookie—Bradenton, Medicine Hat.

NATIONAL LEAGUE

ATLANTA (6): AAA—Richmond. AA—Greenville. A—Anderson, Durham. Rookie—Bradenton, Pulaski.

CHICAGO (5): AAA—Iowa. AA—Pittsfield. A—Geneva, Peoria, Winston-Salem.

CINCINNATI (6): AAA—Denver. AA—Burlington, Vt. A—Cedar Rapids, Tampa. Rookie—Billings, Sarasota.

HOUSTON (6): AAA—Tucson. AA—Columbus, Ga. A—Asheville, Auburn, Osceola, Fla. Rookie—Sarasota.

LOS ANGELES (6): AAA—Albuquerque. AA—San Antonio. A—Bakersfield, Vero Beach. Rookie—Great Falls, Bradenton.

MONTREAL (4): AAA—Indianapolis. AA—Jacksonville. A—Jamestown, West Palm Beach.

NEW YORK (6): AAA—Tidewater. AA—Jackson. A—Columbia, S.C., Little Falls, Lynchburg. Rookie—Kingsport.

PHILADELPHIA (6): AAA—Portland. AA—Reading. A—Clearwater, Bend, Peninsula, Spartanburg.

PITTSBURGH (6): AAA—Hawaii. AA—Nashua. A—Prince William, Macon, Watertown. Rookie—Bradenton.

ST. LOUIS (7): AAA—Louisville. AA—Arkansas. A—Erie, St. Petersburg, Savannah, Springfield. Rookie—Johnson City.

SAN DIEGO (5): AAA—Las Vegas. AA—Beaumont. A—Charleston, S.C., Reno, Spokane.

SAN FRANCISCO (5): AAA—Phoenix. AA—Shreveport. A—Clinton, Fresno, Everett.

Minor League Presidents for '85

CLASS AAA

American Association—Joe Ryan, P. O. Box 382, Wichita, Kan. 67201

International League—Harold Cooper, Box 608, Grove City, Ohio 43123

Mexican League—Pedro Treto Cisneros, Angel Pola No. 16, Col. del Periodista, Mexico 10, D. F., Mexico

Pacific Coast League—Bill Cutler, 2101 E. Broadway Rd., Tempe, Ariz. 85282

CLASS AA

Eastern League—Charles Eshbach, Box 716, Plainville, Conn. 06062

Southern League—Jimmy Bragan, 235 Main St., Suite 200, Trussville, Ala. 35173

Texas League—Carl Sawatski, 1501 N. University, Suite 412, Little Rock, Ark. 72207

CLASS A

California League—Joe Gagliardi, 1060 Willow, San Jose, Calif. 95125

Carolina League—John Hopkins, 4241 United Street, Greensboro, N.C. 27407

Florida State League—George MacDonald, Jr., P. O. Box 414, Lakeland, Fla. 33802

Midwest League—William K. Walters, P. O. Box 444, Burlington, Ia. 52601

New York-Pennsylvania League—Leo A. Pinckney, 168 E. Jenesee St., Auburn, N. Y. 13021.

Northwest League—To Be Announced

South Atlantic League—John H. Moss, P. O. Box 49, Kings Mountain, N. C. 28086

ROOKIE CLASSIFICATION

Appalachian League—Bill Halstead, 157 Carson Lane, Bristol, Va. 24201

Gulf Coast League—Thomas J. Saffell, 11 Sunset Drive, Suite 905, Sarasota, Fla. 33577

Pioneer League—Ralph C. Nelles, P. O. Box 1144, Billings, Mont. 59103

OFFICIAL MINOR LEAGUE AVERAGES

Including

Official Averages of All Class AAA, Class AA, Class A and Rookie Leagues

National Association President John Johnson.

American Association

CLASS AAA

**Leading Batter
TOMMY DUNBAR
Oklahoma City**

**League President
JOE RYAN**

**Leading Pitcher
CHRIS WELSH
Indianapolis**

CHAMPIONSHIP WINNERS IN PREVIOUS YEARS

1902—Indianapolis	.683	
1903—St. Paul	.657	
1904—St. Paul	.646	
1905—Columbus	.658	
1906—Columbus	.615	
1907—Columbus	.584	
1908—Indianapolis	.601	
1909—Louisville	.554	
1910—Minneapolis	.637	
1911—Minneapolis	.600	
1912—Minneapolis	.636	
1913—Milwaukee	.599	
1914—Milwaukee	.590	
1915—Minneapolis	.597	
1916—Louisville	.605	
1917—Indianapolis	.588	
1918—Kansas City	.589	
1919—St. Paul	.610	
1920—St. Paul	.701	
1921—Louisville	.583	
1922—St. Paul	.641	
1923—Kansas City	.675	
1924—St. Paul	.578	
1925—Louisville	.635	
1926—Louisville	.629	
1927—Toledo	.601	
1928—Indianapolis	.593	
1929—Kansas City	.665	
1930—Louisville	.608	
1931—St. Paul	.623	
1932—Minneapolis	.595	
1933—Columbus*	.604	
Minneapolis	.562	
1934—Minneapolis	.570	
Columbus*	.556	
1935—Minneapolis	.591	
1936—Milwaukee†	.584	
1937—Columbus†	.584	
1938—St. Paul	.596	
Kansas City (2nd)‡	.556	

1939—Kansas City	.695	
Louisville (4th)‡	.490	
1940—Kansas City	.625	
Louisville (4th)‡	.500	
1941—Columbus†	.621	
1942—Kansas City	.549	
Columbus (3rd)‡	.532	
1943—Milwaukee	.596	
Columbus (3rd)‡	.532	
1944—Milwaukee	.667	
Louisville (3rd)‡	.574	
1945—Milwaukee	.604	
Louisville (3rd)‡	.545	
1946—Louisville†	601	
1947—Kansas City	.608	
Milwaukee (3rd)‡	.513	
1948—Indianapolis	.649	
St. Paul (3rd)‡	.558	
1949—St. Paul	.608	
Indianapolis (2nd)‡	.604	
1950—Minneapolis	.584	
Columbus (3rd)‡	.549	
1951—Milwaukee†	.623	
1952—Milwaukee	.656	
Kansas City (2nd)‡	.578	
1953—Toledo	.584	
Kansas City (2nd)‡	.571	
1954—Indianapolis	.625	
Louisville (2nd)‡	.556	
1955—Minneapolis†	.597	
1956—Indianapolis†	.597	
1957—Wichita	.604	
Denver (2nd)‡	.584	
1958—Charleston	.589	
Minneapolis (3rd)‡	.536	
1959—Louisville§	.599	
Omaha§	.516	
Minneapolis (2nd)‡	.586	
1960—Denver	.571	
Louisville (2nd)‡	.556	

1961—Indianapolis	.573	
Louisville (2nd)‡	.533	
1962—Indianapolis	.605	
Louisville (4th)‡	.486	
1963-1968—Did not operate.		
1969—Omaha	.607	
1970—Omaha*	.529	
Denver	.504	
1971—Indianapolis	.604	
Denver*	.521	
1972—Wichita	.621	
Evansville*	.593	
1973—Iowa	.610	
Tulsa*	.504	
1974—Indianapolis	.578	
Tulsa*	.567	
1975—Evansville*	.566	
Denver	.596	
1976—Denver*	.632	
Omaha	.574	
1977—Omaha	.563	
Denver*	.522	
1978—Indianapolis	.578	
Omaha*	.489	
1979—Evansville*	.574	
Oklahoma City	.533	
1980—Denver	.676	
Springfield*	.551	
1981—Omaha	.581	
Denver*	.559	
1982—Indianapolis*	.551	
Omaha	.518	
1983—Louisville	.578	
Denver‡	.545	

*Won playoff (East vs. West). †Won championship and four-team playoff. ‡Won four-team playoff. §Respective Eastern and Western division winners.

STANDING OF CLUBS AT CLOSE OF SEASON, SEPTEMBER 4

Club	Ind.	Iowa	Den.	Lou.	Wich.	Evan.	O.C.	Oma.	W.	L.	T.	Pct.	G.B.
Indianapolis (Expos)	....	12	15	7	15	14	16	12	91	63	0	.591	....
Iowa (Cubs)	10	....	11	12	8	10	15	14	80	74	0	.519	11
Denver (White Sox)	7	11	....	13	12	14	10	12	79	75	0	.513	12
Louisville (Cardinals)	15	10	9	....	14	10	8	13	79	76	0	.510	12½
Wichita (Reds)	7	14	10	9	....	11	15	12	78	77	0	.503	13½
Evansville (Tigers)	8	12	8	12	11	....	11	10	72	82	0	.468	19
Oklahoma City (Rangers)	6	7	12	14	7	11	....	13	70	84	0	.455	21
Omaha (Royals)	10	8	10	9	10	12	9	....	68	86	0	.442	23

Louisville defeated Wichita in a one-game playoff for fourth place.

Iowa club represented Des Moines, Iowa.

Major league affiliations in parentheses.

Playoffs—Louisville defeated Indianapolis four games to two; Denver defeated Iowa four games to one, and Louisville defeated Denver four games to one to win league championship.

Regular Season Attendance—Denver, 366,262; Evansville, 100,326; Indianapolis, 223,262; Iowa, 275,163; Louisville, 846,878; Oklahoma City, 243,423; Omaha, 149,369; Wichita, 137,018. Total 2,341,701. Playoff attendance, 39,088.

Managers—Denver, Vernon Law and Adrian Garrett; Evansville, Gordy Mackenzie; Indianapolis, Bob Rodgers; Iowa, Jim Napier; Louisville, Jim Fregosi; Oklahoma City, Tom Burgess and Rusty Gerhardt; Omaha, Gene Lamont; Wichita, Gene Dusan.

All-Star Team—1B—Alan Knicely, Wichita; 2B—Scotty Earl, Evansville; 3B—Jose Castro, Denver; SS—Jose Gonzales, Louisville; OF—Daryl Boston, Denver; Vince Coleman, Louisville; Tommy Dunbar, Oklahoma City; C—Kevin Buckley, Oklahoma City and Russ Stephans, Omaha; DH—Gary Rajsich, Louisville; RHP—Dick Grapenthin, Indianapolis; LHP—Joe Hesketh, Indianapolis; Most Valuable Player—Alan Knicely, Wichita; Pitcher of the Year—Joe Hesketh, Wichita; Manager of the Year—Bob Rodgers, Indianapolis.

(Compiled by Howe News Bureau, Boston, Mass.)

CLUB BATTING

Club	Pct.	G.	AB.	R.	OR.	H.	TB.	2B.	3B.	HR.	RBI.	GW.	SH.	SF.	HP.	BB.	Int. BB.	SO.	SB.	CS.	LOB.
Wichita	.274	155	5045	786	715	1383	2153	243	52	141	718	70	40	53	32	549	28	769	209	89	1010
Denver	.274	155	5015	756	782	1374	2112	241	70	119	690	71	29	69	19	603	23	761	119	82	1051
Louisville	.267	155	5033	697	652	1345	2016	273	46	102	647	69	53	45	35	515	27	818	180	96	1026
Indianapolis	.266	154	4894	697	630	1303	1902	225	28	106	633	88	67	34	28	529	31	719	150	78	987
Oklahoma City	.264	154	4962	673	742	1311	1985	244	41	116	626	66	58	46	27	629	33	901	127	57	1116
Iowa	.263	154	4879	724	724	1285	2135	245	43	173	700	73	43	42	29	596	36	946	195	82	1020
Evansville	.261	154	4892	649	715	1275	2005	262	45	126	608	67	53	40	27	482	26	1015	105	71	998
Omaha	.252	154	4791	605	652	1208	1812	213	50	97	571	66	56	39	25	457	24	792	97	60	939

INDIVIDUAL BATTING

(Leading Qualifiers for Batting Championship—416 or More Plate Appearances)

*Bats lefthanded.   †Switch-hitter.

Player and Club	Pct.	G.	AB.	R.	H.	TB.	2B.	3B.	HR.	RBI.	GW.	SH.	SF.	HP.	BB.	Int. BB.	SO.	SB.	CS.
Dunbar, Thomas, Oklahoma City*	.337	105	368	69	124	191	21	5	12	61	3	3	6	0	55	6	54	11	8
Knicely, Alan, Wichita	.333	152	570	94	190	326	29	4	33	126	9	0	11	5	54	6	102	2	4
Castro, Jose, Denver	.316	129	433	70	137	213	32	4	12	67	8	1	1	0	57	1	45	7	2
Boston, Daryl, Denver*	.312	127	471	94	147	251	21	19	15	82	5	1	11	2	65	1	82	40	17
Simmons, Nelson, Wichita†	.307	142	501	79	154	271	41	5	22	83	9	1	6	0	53	0	106	0	4
Johnson, Ronald, Indianapolis	.303	109	376	50	114	168	24	0	10	53	7	0	2	2	44	3	56	1	2
Harris, John, Evansville*	.303	122	360	48	109	158	21	2	8	50	5	4	5	1	50	2	60	2	1
Roof, Eugene, Louisville†	.302	134	496	67	150	222	38	8	6	64	8	12	7	4	47	3	74	17	8
Adduci, James, Louisville*	.289	113	412	62	119	192	25	6	12	58	8	0	2	3	38	2	85	1	5
Bogener, Terry, Wichita*	.288	135	423	63	122	170	19	7	5	47	6	3	5	8	64	3	52	12	11
Rajsich, Gary, Louisville*	.286	117	416	71	119	239	29	2	29	95	9	0	6	2	49	9	82	1	1

Departmental Leaders: G—Earl, Laga, 153; AB—Coleman, 608; R—Coleman, 97; H—Knicely, 190; TB—Knicely, 326; 2B—Simmons, 41; 3B—Boston, 19; HR—Hicks, 37; RBI—Knicely, 126; GWRBI—Fuentes, 13; SH—Scranton, 17; SF—Boston, Knicely, 11; HP—Hatcher, 9; BB—Earl, Gilbert, 77; IBB—Rajsich, 9; SO—Buckley, 171; SB—Coleman, 101; CS—Coleman, 36.

(All Players—Listed Alphabetically)

Player and Club	Pct.	G.	AB.	R.	H.	TB.	2B.	3B.	HR.	RBI.	GW.	SH.	SF.	HP.	BB.	Int. BB.	SO.	SB.	CS.
Abrego, Johnny, Iowa	.000	5	2	0	0	0	0	0	0	0	0	0	0	0	0	0	1	0	0
Adduci, James, Louisville*	.289	113	412	62	119	192	25	6	12	58	8	0	2	3	38	2	85	1	5
Allen, Roderick, Evansville	.282	74	234	24	66	91	14	4	1	25	4	3	0	2	21	2	51	4	3
Altamirano, Porfirio, Iowa	.333	49	3	1	1	4	0	1	2	0	0	0	0	0	0	0	1	0	0
Anderson, James, Oklahoma City	.214	36	117	10	25	34	6	0	1	9	1	0	3	0	15	1	21	0	0
Augustine, Gerald, 4 Lou.–17 Iowa*	.000	21	2	0	0	0	0	0	0	0	0	0	0	0	0	0	0	0	0
Ayer, Jonathan, Louisville	.254	110	342	41	87	139	21	5	7	55	6	4	2	0	20	1	68	2	3
Babitt, Mack, Indianapolis	.230	55	122	22	28	37	7	1	0	13	1	6	1	0	22	0	21	9	3
Baker, Douglas, Evansville†	.259	77	243	34	63	110	21	1	8	30	2	4	2	2	45	0	58	6	4
Baker, Kenneth, Indianapolis*	.143	2	7	0	1	1	0	0	0	0	0	0	0	0	0	0	1	0	0
Baker, Ricky, Iowa†	.190	54	121	13	23	29	2	2	0	8	2	2	1	1	10	0	21	9	4
Baker, Steven, Louisville	.000	28	1	0	0	0	0	0	0	2	1	1	0	0	0	0	1	0	0
Bargar, Gregory, Indianapolis	.056	31	18	0	1	1	0	0	0	1	0	1	0	0	3	0	12	0	0
Barnes, William, Wichita	.328	92	360	59	118	191	23	4	14	67	6	1	5	1	26	3	30	24	5
Barranca, German, Oklahoma City	.279	62	179	28	50	74	7	4	3	26	6	1	6	0	20	1	22	9	0
Benton, Alfred, Evansville	.280	109	350	38	98	136	20	0	6	41	3	4	0	2	8	3	45	10	9
Biancalana, Roland, Omaha†	.260	58	204	33	53	103	11	9	7	25	1	2	1	2	24	0	52	5	6
Bilardello, Dann, Wichita	.240	49	167	21	40	64	9	0	5	17	2	0	2	1	22	0	29	2	1
Bjorkman, George, Indianapolis	.260	91	235	25	61	100	21	0	6	27	1	1	0	2	29	2	64	3	3
Bogener, Terry, Wichita*	.288	135	423	63	122	170	19	7	5	47	6	3	5	8	64	3	52	12	11
Booker, Roderick, Louisville*	.254	63	185	19	47	52	3	1	0	14	0	9	0	0	22	0	13	3	7
Bosley, Thaddis, Iowa*	.358	51	162	23	58	94	16	1	6	43	7	0	2	2	28	0	24	11	3
Boston, Daryl, Denver*	.312	127	471	94	147	251	21	19	15	82	5	1	11	2	65	1	82	40	17
Botelho, Derek, Iowa	.118	28	17	2	2	4	0	1	0	0	0	3	0	0	2	0	5	0	0
Brewer, Michael, Omaha	.203	104	330	46	67	118	10	4	11	41	8	3	1	3	52	2	97	19	4
Brooks, Fred, Iowa	.261	129	398	58	104	167	17	2	14	43	3	4	1	1	61	1	56	14	7
Brower, Robert, Oklahoma City	.224	35	107	18	24	33	2	2	1	8	1	5	0	0	27	0	22	14	3
Brown, Jeffrey, Denver	.000	1	1	0	0	0	0	0	0	0	0	0	0	0	0	0	1	0	0

Player and Club	Pct.	G.	AB.	R.	H.	TB.	2B.	3B.	HR.	RBI.	GW.	SH.	SF.	HP.	BB.	Int. BB.	SO.	SB.	CS.
Brown, Jeffrey M., Omaha	.364	3	11	1	4	5	1	0	0	5	0	0	1	0	0	0	2	0	0
Browning, Thomas, Wichita°	.080	31	25	0	2	3	1	0	0	4	0	1	0	0	1	0	10	0	0
Brummer, Glenn, Louisville	.208	16	53	3	11	16	2	0	1	4	2	0	0	2	4	1	5	0	0
Brunenkant, S. Barry, Oklahoma City	.248	49	157	14	39	62	8	0	5	16	2	2	2	0	22	0	13	1	1
Buchanan, Robert, Wichita°	.000	39	4	0	0	0	0	0	0	0	0	0	0	0	0	0	0	0	0
Buckley, Kevin, Oklahoma City	.261	139	499	72	130	237	32	3	23	92	10	1	3	2	56	5	171	0	2
Buechele, Steven, Oklahoma City	.264	131	447	48	118	170	25	3	7	59	7	7	5	4	36	3	71	7	2
Burke, Timothy, Indianapolis	.125	37	16	0	2	2	0	0	0	0	0	2	1	0	0	0	5	0	0
Butera, Salvatore, Indianapolis	.269	111	283	36	76	108	11	0	7	41	3	2	2	0	52	1	32	1	1
Canady, Chuckie, Oklahoma City	.265	86	317	48	84	135	16	4	9	60	6	4	3	3	51	3	59	5	6
Capra, Nick, Oklahoma City	.256	123	442	68	113	139	18	1	2	21	3	12	1	0	76	1	67	47	18
Carter, Joseph, Iowa	.310	61	248	45	77	145	12	7	14	67	7	0	2	3	20	5	31	11	6
Castro, Jose, Denver	.316	129	433	70	137	213	32	4	12	67	8	1	1	0	57	1	45	7	2
Cates, Timothy, Indianapolis	.000	21	5	0	0	0	0	0	0	0	0	0	0	0	0	0	4	0	0
Cato, J. Keefe, Wichita	.250	37	8	4	2	4	0	1	0	1	0	1	0	1	0	0	4	0	0
Chavez, Pedro, Evansville	.269	88	334	47	90	119	18	4	1	27	1	6	4	3	23	0	39	6	6
Christmas, Stephen, Denver°	.278	74	198	24	55	82	9	3	4	29	3	2	5	0	28	0	11	1	1
Citarella, Ralph, Louisville	.182	16	11	1	2	2	0	0	0	0	0	2	0	0	0	0	2	0	0
Clements, David, Louisville	.278	44	162	22	45	65	8	3	2	18	0	1	2	0	8	0	28	0	1
Coleman, Vincent, Louisville	.257	152	608	97	156	203	21	7	4	48	5	2	1	5	55	1	112	101	36
Cotto, Henry, Iowa	.200	8	30	3	6	8	2	0	0	0	0	0	0	1	2	0	3	1	2
Davis, Eric, Wichita	.314	52	194	42	61	122	9	5	14	34	4	1	1	2	25	1	55	27	10
Davis, Wallace, Omaha	.325	83	314	45	102	148	15	5	7	43	7	2	1	1	24	4	56	9	7
De Sa, Joseph, Denver°	.282	141	511	73	144	220	32	7	10	81	11	4	9	4	58	6	47	2	3
Dilks, Darren, Indianapolis°	.143	16	7	0	1	2	1	0	0	0	0	1	0	0	0	0	2	0	0
Dunbar, Thomas, Oklahoma City°	.337	105	368	69	124	191	21	5	12	61	3	3	6	0	55	6	54	11	8
Dunston, Shawon, Iowa	.233	61	210	25	49	83	11	1	7	27	7	2	1	0			40	9	3
Earl, W. Scott, Evansville	.251	153	534	82	134	204	21	8	11	51	7	8	4	7	77	1	120	41	20
Earley, William, Iowa	.143	54	7	1	1	1	0	0	0	0	0	0	0	0	2	0	4	0	0
Eaton, Craig, Indianapolis	.000	19	3	0	0	0	0	0	0	0	0	0	0	0	0	0	3	0	0
Faedo, Leonardo, 22 Evns.-53 OkC	.259	75	278	24	72	86	11	0	1	24	4	2	5	0	18	0	18	2	0
Filer, Thomas, Iowa	.222	26	9	1	2	2	0	0	0	0	0	1	0	0	1	0	2	0	0
Ford, Curtis, Louisville°	.263	13	38	5	10	12	2	0	0	1	0	1	0	0	4	1	9	5	1
Foussianes, George, Evansville	.214	21	56	12	12	18	3	0	1	4	1	1	0	1	13	1	10	0	2
Fuentes, Michael, Indianapolis	.251	148	522	88	131	227	22	4	22	80	13	0	2	6	62	1	133	12	6
Garcia, A. Leonardo, Wichita°	.283	117	336	47	95	128	12	6	3	39	4	4	3	1	22	2	44	19	4
Gates, Michael, Indianapolis°	.297	99	340	58	101	121	14	0	2	28	4	6	0	1	37	3	35	11	7
Geren, Robert, Louisville	.175	15	40	3	7	8	1	0	0	3	0	0	0	0	5	0	8	0	0
Gil, Carlos, Iowa	.000	25	1	0	0	0	0	0	0	0	0	0	0	0	0	0	0	0	0
Gilbert, Mark, Wichita†	.280	137	486	84	136	186	18	7	6	46	5	4	1	4	77	3	86	55	18
Glynn, Eugene, Indianapolis	.212	56	104	9	22	26	4	0	0	8	1	5	0	0	13	0	14	0	4
Gonzales, Rene, Indianapolis	.234	114	359	41	84	106	12	2	2	32	5	10	4	2	20	0	33	10	4
Gonzalez, Jose, Louisville†	.279	145	484	68	135	168	20	2	3	46	8	6	9	1	26	1	52	11	5
Grant, Thomas, Iowa°	.260	135	423	51	110	146	15	0	7	58	5	5	5	1	69	6	68	8	11
Grapenthin, Richard, Indianapolis	.000	53	3	0	0	0	0	0	0	0	0	0	0	0	0	0	1	0	0
Gulliver, Glenn, Louisville	.236	55	144	17	34	47	7	0	2	17	2	1	1	2	43	1	21	1	2
Hagen, Kevin, Louisville	.000	29	7	0	0	0	0	0	0	0	0	1	0	1	0	0	2	0	0
Hammond, Steven, Omaha°	.239	127	402	45	96	146	22	2	8	44	4	4	3	4	44	4	52	2	3
Harris, Greg, Indianapolis	.000	15	4	0	0	0	0	0	0	0	0	0	0	0	0	0	2	0	0
Harris, John, Evansville°	.303	122	360	48	109	158	21	2	8	50	5	4	5	1	50	2	60	2	1
Harris, Victor, Louisville†	.231	75	221	31	51	78	12	0	5	29	3	4	3	2	30	2	34	0	3
Hatcher, William, Iowa	.276	150	595	96	164	254	27	18	9	59	4	1	3	9	51	4	54	56	18
Hayes, William, Iowa	.221	118	366	52	81	156	25	1	16	49	1	4	2	3	38	2	95	1	1
Heidenreich, Curtis, Wichita	.000	37	5	0	0	0	0	0	0	0	0	0	0	0	0	0	2	0	0
Hesketh, Joseph, Indianapolis°	.100	22	10	1	1	2	1	0	0	0	0	1	0	0	0	0	5	0	0
Hicks, Joseph, Iowa	.266	136	451	87	120	259	20	4	37	90	9	1	3	3	52	2	155	11	6
Hostetler, David, Oklahoma City	.304	64	227	28	69	115	9	2	11	43	5	0	1	4	28	1	64	0	1
Householder, Paul, Wichita†	.248	118	408	64	101	183	14	7	18	64	2	0	2	0	59	6	73	27	11
Hulett, Timothy, Denver	.263	139	475	72	125	217	32	6	16	80	8	3	9	0	67	3	88	3	4
Hyman, Donald, Iowa	.000	1	3	0	0	0	0	0	0	0	0	0	0	0	0	0	1	0	0
Jirschele, Michael, Oklahoma City	.227	92	299	28	68	92	11	2	3	18	1	8	1	1	30	0	68	8	4
Johnson, Ronald, Indianapolis	.303	109	376	50	114	168	24	0	10	53	7	0	2	2	44	3	56	1	2
Johnson, Rondin, Omaha†	.252	131	488	60	123	152	18	4	1	49	9	8	6	2	38	1	60	16	9
Johnson, Roy, Indianapolis°	.270	107	356	48	96	148	17	4	9	49	9	1	5	1	41	5	48	22	7
Johnson, Wallace, Indianapolis†	.283	97	357	50	101	126	12	2	3	38	6	7	2	2	23	3	15	27	7
Johnson, William, Iowa	.000	44	7	0	0	0	0	0	0	0	0	2	0	0	0	0	1	0	0
Jones, Lynn, Omaha	.254	17	63	8	16	25	6	0	1	3	0	0	1	0	8	0	9	0	2
Jones, Ruppert, Evansville°	.313	48	160	30	50	92	9	3	9	45	5	0	2	1	27	1	33	8	3
Kable, David, Louisville°	.240	23	50	6	12	24	3	0	3	14	0	0	0	0	10	1	11	1	0
Karkovice, Ronald, Denver	.221	31	86	7	19	26	1	0	2	10	2	1	3	1	8	0	25	1	0
Kepshire, Kurt, Louisville°	.333	16	6	0	2	2	0	0	0	1	0	1	0	0	0	0	2	0	0
Kinnunen, Michael, Indianapolis°	.000	16	1	0	0	0	0	0	0	0	0	1	0	0	0	0	1	0	0
Kneuer, Frank, Oklahoma City	.000	2	2	1	0	0	0	0	0	0	0	0	0	0	0	0	1	0	0
Knicely, Alan, Wichita	.333	152	570	94	190	326	29	4	33	126	9	0	11	5	54	6	102	2	4
Krenchicki, Wayne, Wichita°	.281	18	64	14	18	31	7	0	2	5	0	0	0	0	6	1	6	1	0
Kuntz, Russell, Evansville	.185	10	27	4	5	5	0	0	0	2	0	0	0	2	7	2	7	0	1
Laga, Michael, Evansville°	.265	153	569	86	151	289	30	9	30	94	7	0	5	3	38	6	130	1	1
Landrum, T. William, Wichita	.143	47	7	0	1	1	0	0	0	0	0	0	0	0	0	0	4	0	0
Lawless, Thomas 31 Wich-19 Ind.	.272	50	173	36	47	74	5	5	4	23	3	1	0	0	11	0	35	13	2
Leeper, David, Omaha°	.257	149	534	67	137	233	26	11	16	79	9	1	7	2	37	3	81	1	2
Leibrandt, Charles, Omaha	.000	10	1	0	0	0	0	0	0	0	0	0	0	0	0	0	0	0	0
Lesley, Bradley, Wichita	.000	27	2	0	0	0	0	0	0	0	0	0	0	0	0	0	1	0	0
Little, R. Bryan, Indianapolis†	.292	35	106	15	31	35	2	1	0	5	1	5	0	0	12	0	8	3	5
Lombarski, Thomas, Iowa°	.269	114	316	57	85	151	19	1	15	47	2	0	3	1	54	5	49	24	3
Lopez, Juan, Evansville	.233	61	159	20	37	60	6	1	5	18	3	7	0	0	9	1	35	0	0
Loucks, Scott, Indianapolis	.203	54	138	19	28	43	5	2	2	20	4	2	1	0	13	0	42	4	3
Lowery, Edward, Omaha	.000	2	3	1	0	0	0	0	0	0	0	0	0	0	0	0	0	0	0
Lowry, Dwight, Evansville°	.220	61	177	23	39	61	5	1	5	28	3	2	1	1	18	3	51	2	0
Lozado, William, Denver	.276	86	275	48	76	119	14	1	9	38	3	1	5	0	44	0	51	5	10
Lyons, William, Louisville	.278	60	205	38	57	86	17	3	2	28	4	1	3	6	45	1	30	22	6
Mackanin, Peter, Iowa	.248	105	326	43	81	122	17	0	8	44	5	5	3	1	31	1	79	4	1
Mahler, Michael, Louisville†	.000	26	4	0	0	0	0	0	0	0	0	0	1	0	0	1	0	0	0

Player and Club	Pct.	G.	AB.	R.	H.	TB.	2B.	3B.	HR.	RBI.	GW.	SH.	SF.	HP.	BB.	Int. BB.	SO.	SB.	CS.
Manuel, Jerry, Denver	.293	109	335	43	98	130	14	3	4	40	5	8	5	0	37	4	32	7	6
McBride, Arnold, Oklahoma City°	.296	32	108	13	32	49	5	3	2	12	1	0	0	4	0	12	1	2
McClendon, Lloyd, Wichita	.296	48	152	28	45	78	13	1	6	28	3	0	1	0	21	0	33	2	0
Mejia, Oscar, Oklahoma City	.279	13	43	7	12	15	1	1	0	4	1	0	0	4	0	1	0	1
Melvin, Robert, Evansville	.248	44	141	12	35	48	13	0	0	11	1	1	0	0	3	0	32	0	1
Meridith, Ronald, Iowa°	.571	49	7	3	4	4	0	0	0	0	0	0	0	0	0	0	1	0	0
Mesa, Ivan, Denver	.067	11	15	0	1	2	1	0	0	1	0	0	0	0	3	0	3	0	0
Miley, David, Wichita°	.244	78	205	24	50	71	6	0	5	26	4	1	2	1	28	0	20	0	3
Mills, J. Bradley, Indianapolis°	.315	66	197	34	62	82	9	1	3	34	2	3	1	2	35	3	10	0	1
Morales, Jose, Indianapolis	.188	31	80	6	15	24	3	0	2	8	1	0	0	1	4	0	14	0	0
Morris, John, Omaha°	.270	148	492	77	133	210	24	4	15	60	8	3	3	4	65	2	96	18	5
Murphy, Daniel, Oklahoma City°	.236	61	203	25	48	71	10	2	3	23	1	5	2	2	29	3	23	2	0
Mustad, Eric, Indianapolis	.500	25	2	1	1	1	0	0	0	0	0	0	0	0	1	0	0	0	0
Nail, Charlie, Wichita	.105	31	19	3	2	2	0	0	0	0	0	3	0	0	0	0	6	0	0
Neuzil, Jeffrey, Omaha	.000	3	11	0	0	0	0	0	0	0	0	0	0	0	0	0	2	0	0
Newman, Albert, Indianapolis†	.301	37	123	13	37	40	3	0	0	11	4	3	0	0	6	0	9	11	5
Nieto, Thomas, Louisville	.277	77	253	23	70	105	12	1	7	34	5	2	2	8	14	0	41	0	1
Owen, Dave, Iowa†	.228	43	136	18	31	41	5	1	1	9	0	2	0	0	27	2	33	11	3
Parsons, Casey, Denver°	.265	141	513	58	136	200	24	8	8	52	3	2	2	1	49	1	70	12	13
Pastore, Frank, Wichita	.000	2	2	0	0	0	0	0	0	0	0	0	0	0	0	0	0	0	0
Pastornicky, Clifford, Omaha	.248	95	318	29	79	106	13	1	4	37	3	1	3	1	13	1	43	3	6
Patterson, Reginald, Iowa	.227	32	22	1	5	5	0	0	0	2	1	5	0	0	1	0	8	0	0
Pendleton, Terry, Louisville†	.297	91	330	52	98	143	23	5	4	44	3	1	3	0	24	1	51	6	7
Perlman, Jonathan, Iowa°	.077	24	13	2	1	2	1	0	0	0	0	1	0	0	1	0	6	0	0
Pettini, Joseph, Louisville	.223	32	112	13	25	31	3	0	1	10	0	0	1	0	15	0	15	3	4
Poldberg, Brian, Omaha	.219	73	201	17	44	50	4	1	0	17	0	5	0	0	23	0	31	1	2
Pryce, Kenneth, Iowa	.000	34	11	0	0	0	0	0	0	0	0	0	0	0	1	0	4	0	0
Puleo, Charles, Wichita	.231	19	13	0	3	3	0	0	0	0	0	1	0	0	0	0	6	0	0
Quirk, James, Denver°	.209	70	201	23	42	60	6	3	2	24	3	0	2	1	21	1	39	0	1
Rajsich, Gary, Louisville°	.286	117	416	71	119	239	29	2	29	95	9	0	6	2	49	9	82	1	1
Rhodes, Michael, Louisville°	.000	11	1	1	0	0	0	0	0	0	0	0	0	0	2	0	1	0	0
Richardt, Michael, Oklahoma City	.308	17	65	14	20	30	7	0	1	5	0	1	0	1	5	0	8	2	1
Rincones, Hector, Wichita	.262	116	324	42	85	105	15	1	1	34	2	1	4	2	18	1	26	9	5
Robinson, Ronald, Wichita	.167	25	24	1	4	5	1	0	0	0	0	0	0	0	0	0	4	0	0
Robles, Ruben, Evansville	.179	49	151	10	27	38	6	1	1	15	3	0	0	0	14	1	47	5	0
Rohn, Daniel, Iowa°	.268	109	370	74	99	147	22	1	8	46	4	2	5	1	67	4	65	14	10
Rollin, Rondal, Evansville	.261	55	199	29	52	102	5	0	15	34	4	0	2	0	15	1	70	1	2
Roof, Eugene, 2 Ind.-132 Lou.†	.302	134	496	67	150	222	38	8	6	64	8	12	7	4	47	3	74	17	8
Rowdon, Wade, Wichita	.251	144	479	78	120	206	30	4	16	72	10	4	6	5	41	1	95	9	9
Rubel, Michael, Oklahoma City	.207	116	382	41	79	135	13	2	13	49	3	1	2	4	65	3	105	1	0
Ruiz, Benny, Evansville†	.180	55	150	20	27	31	4	0	0	7	2	7	0	0	13	0	30	3	2
Runnells, Thomas, Wichita†	.247	125	438	67	108	153	21	3	6	61	9	10	4	0	51	1	37	8	6
Ryal, Mark, Omaha°	.237	131	435	56	103	162	18	1	13	64	4	2	6	1	44	3	71	5	3
Salas, Mark, Louisville°	.244	95	316	28	77	137	20	2	12	48	4	1	3	0	20	1	43	2	1
Salazar, Argenis, Indianapolis	.276	50	156	11	43	56	8	1	1	14	4	2	0	2	4	0	30	6	4
Sattler, William, Indianapolis	.000	58	2	0	0	0	0	0	0	0	0	0	0	0	0	0	0	0	0
Scherrer, William, Wichita°	.000	10	1	0	0	0	0	0	0	0	0	0	0	0	0	0	0	0	0
Schuler, David, Indianapolis	.000	42	2	0	0	0	0	0	0	0	0	0	0	0	0	0	1	0	0
Schulze, Donald, Iowa	.125	13	8	1	1	4	0	0	1	1	1	0	0	0	0	0	3	0	0
Scott, Donald, Oklahoma City†	.327	46	168	25	55	82	14	2	3	25	2	3	2	0	12	1	20	0	1
Scranton, James, Omaha†	.251	136	430	47	108	143	16	5	3	37	6	17	3	2	17	0	59	8	5
Seilheimer, Ricky, Denver°	.216	38	102	14	22	26	1	0	1	6	0	0	1	1	16	0	16	0	0
Sexton, Jimmy, Louisville	.217	9	23	4	5	5	0	0	0	4	0	0	0	0	2	0	3	1	2
Shines, Anthony, Indianapolis†	.282	131	443	73	125	207	26	1	18	80	9	1	4	4	42	6	41	2	6
Simmons, Nelson, Evansville†	.307	142	501	79	154	271	41	5	22	83	9	1	6	0	53	0	106	0	4
Skinner, Joel, Denver	.284	42	141	27	40	76	6	0	10	27	3	1	4	1	13	1	31	1	0
Sodders, Michael, Denver	.221	40	140	20	31	51	9	1	3	22	2	0	0	17	1	32	0	0
Stegman, David, Denver	.286	34	105	17	30	48	10	1	2	9	1	1	0	2	30	0	24	7	1
Stenhouse, Michael, Indianapolis°	.333	27	93	22	31	63	4	2	8	27	5	0	3	0	16	0	15	1	2
Stephans, Russell, Omaha	.290	109	334	54	97	151	21	3	9	48	4	3	1	4	50	2	61	7	3
Stockstill, David, Oklahoma City°	.282	102	358	66	101	173	20	2	16	55	9	2	2	1	67	5	24	1	3
Stoll, Richard, Indianapolis	.000	11	4	1	0	0	0	0	0	0	0	0	0	0	0	0	0	0	0
Strutton, Michael, Omaha	.000	2	2	0	0	0	0	0	0	0	0	0	0	0	0	0	1	0	0
Terry, Scott, Wichita	.000	2	2	1	0	0	0	0	0	0	0	1	0	0	1	0	2	0	0
Thomas, Reginald, Evansville°	.221	41	113	6	25	35	4	0	2	14	2	0	4	0	5	0	31	3	0
Tillman, Kerry, Denver	.306	75	255	43	78	117	6	3	9	43	5	0	2	3	21	1	49	9	5
Toliver, Freddie, Wichita	.105	37	19	3	2	2	0	0	0	0	2	0	0	0	0	0	10	0	0
Tovar, Raul, Evansville	.259	42	135	17	35	47	8	2	0	12	3	0	2	1	11	0	20	0	4
Tracy, James, Iowa°	.312	62	189	27	59	83	12	0	4	27	4	0	4	0	26	1	38	1	0
Van Gorder, David, Wichita	.263	67	205	26	54	82	14	1	4	36	4	0	6	1	23	1	17	2	0
Venable, William, Indianapolis°	.248	99	330	57	82	128	13	3	9	47	5	4	5	1	41	4	42	22	3
Von Ohlen, David, Louisville°	.000	22	2	0	0	0	0	0	0	0	0	0	0	0	0	0	0	0	0
Welsh, Christopher, Indianapolis°	.214	29	14	1	3	7	1	0	1	3	0	3	1	0	3	0	3	0	0
Werner, Donald, Iowa	.283	131	427	64	121	224	22	3	25	77	11	3	7	2	48	3	98	10	4
Werth, Dennis, Louisville	.239	46	117	26	28	44	8	1	2	10	1	2	0	1	30	1	26	3	3
Wherry, Clifton, Oklahoma City	.250	75	232	26	58	69	7	2	0	14	1	2	2	3	17	0	56	17	4
Wilborn, Thaddeus, Denver†	.258	122	449	80	116	151	13	8	2	32	6	3	6	1	40	1	61	24	17
Wilkerson, Martin, Omaha°	.211	70	218	19	46	60	8	2	0	19	2	4	1	0	18	2	19	3	3
Williams, Dallas, Evansville°	.190	54	189	18	36	54	10	4	0	10	1	1	3	1	18	1	25	12	7
Wright, George, Oklahoma City†	.333	8	30	7	10	17	2	1	1	8	0	0	1	2	0	5	0	0	
Wright, J. Richard, Oklahoma City°	.429	33	7	0	3	4	1	0	0	1	0	0	0	2	0	2	0	0	
Yobs, David, Denver°	.249	93	309	43	77	123	10	3	10	47	3	1	4	2	29	2	54	0	2
Younger, Stanley, Evansville°	.189	12	37	3	7	8	0	1	0	6	1	1	0	0	5	0	11	0	1

The following pitchers, listed alphabetically by club, with games in parentheses, had no plate appearances, primarily through use of designated hitters:

DENVER—Arroyo, Fernando (5); Barojas, Salome (3); Biercevicz, Gregory (18); Brennan, Thomas (35); Burns, Britt (1); Fallon, Robert (19); Gleaton, Jerry Don (12); Hickey, Kevin (16); Hoffman, Guy (35); Johnson, Charles (32); Jones, Alfornia (24); Niemann, Randy (32); Renz, Kevin (3); Roberge, Bertrand (26); Rothschild, Lawrence (33); Siwy, James (15); Speck, Clifford (29); Trujillo, Michael (8).

EVANSVILLE—Abbott, Glenn (5); Bailey, Howard (13); Conner, Jeffrey (32); Dacko, Mark (15); Erickson, Roger (19); Gumpert, David (56); Heinkel, Donald (30); Larkin, Patrick (17); Martin, John (29); Mason, Roger (25); Monteleone, Richard (11); Moreno, Angel (20); Morogiello, Daniel (23); O'Neal, Randall (25); Willis, Carl (40).

INDIANAPOLIS—St. Claire, Randy (13).

IOWA—Banks, Darryl (3); Kaufman, Ronald (3).

LOUISVILLE—Augustine, Gerald (4); Bibby, James (2); Clark, Terry (18); Cox, Daniel (6); Dayley, Kenneth (13); Hassler, Andrew (38); Johnson, Jerry (2); Keener, Jeffrey (53); Miller, Dyar (6); Morlock, Allen (3); Ownbey, Richard (17); Perry, Patrick (21); Pimentel, Rafael (2); Shade, Michael (2); Stuper, John (2); Thurberg, Thomas (17).

OKLAHOMA CITY—Boggs, Thomas (11); Clark, Robert (20); Cook, Glen (27); Cruz, Victor (37); Fossas, Anthony (29); Griffin, Michael (31); Henke, Thomas (39); Lachowicz, Allen (21); Larson, Daniel (17); McLaughlin, Joey (3); Mengwasser, Bradley (11); Musselman, Ronald (13); Shimp, Tommy Joe (12); Tobik, David (14); Zwolensky, Mitchell (33).

OMAHA—Alvarez, Evelio (28); Creel, Keith (27); Ferreira, Anthony (40); Hargesheimer, Alan (11); Huismann, Mark (15); Jackson, Danny (16); Jones, Michael (11); Keeton, Rickey (27); Martinez, Arthur (16); Parrott, Michael (33); Reyes, Jose (21); Shaw, Theodore (19); St. Clair, Daniel (29); Strode, Lester (12); Wills, Frank (15); Yuhas, Vincent (3).

WICHITA—Franco, John (6); Smith, Michael (12); Tibbs, Jay (4); Wise, Brett (5).

GRAND SLAM HOME RUNS—Buckley, Hostetler, Rajsich, Salas, Yobs, 2 each; Adduci, Ayer, Buechele, Boston, Castro, Christmas, De Sa, Earl, Fuentes, J. Harris, V. Harris, Hicks, Rond. Johnson, R. Jones, Knicely, Laga, Loucks, Shines, Stenhouse, Stockstill, 1 each.

AWARDED FIRST BASE ON CATCHER'S INTERFERENCE—Scranton 5 (Benton, Bilardello, Bjorkman, Butera, Nieto); Roof 3 (Hammond, Lowry, Scott); J. Harris 2 (Brummer, Buckley); Leeper 2 (Buckley, Butera); Ayer (Brunenkant); Hicks (Lowry); Householder (Salas).

CLUB FIELDING

Club	Pct.	G.	PO.	A.	E.	DP.	PB.	Club	Pct.	G.	PO.	A.	E.	DP.	PB.
Wichita	.978	155	3924	1543	124	134	11	Denver	.969	154	3938	1706	182	170	18
Indianapolis	.977	154	3905	1709	132	147	16	Evansville	.969	154	3832	1752	176	180	6
Louisville	.976	155	3967	1651	140	144	11	Iowa	.969	154	3841	1662	175	123	6
Oklahoma City	.976	154	3903	1553	133	135	20	Omaha	.969	154	3806	1549	170	93	8

Triple Plays—Denver, Evansville.

INDIVIDUAL FIELDING

*Throws lefthanded.

FIRST BASEMEN

Player and Club	Pct.	G.	PO.	A.	E.	DP.	Player and Club	Pct.	G.	PO.	A.	E.	DP.
Adduci, Louisville*	.978	20	165	10	4	16	Leeper, Omaha*	1.000	2	13	0	0	0
Ayer, Louisville	.990	13	91	7	1	8	Lombarski, Iowa	.990	24	184	17	2	16
Barnes, Wichita	1.000	10	59	3	0	8	McClendon, Wichita	.986	14	130	15	2	16
Benton, Evansville	.980	7	46	4	1	2	Melvin, Evansville	1.000	2	13	0	0	0
Bjorkman, Indianapolis	.979	8	42	4	1	5	Morales, Indianapolis	1.000	1	6	0	0	0
Bogener, Wichita*	.991	17	103	10	1	9	Murphy, Oklahoma City*	.969	4	28	3	1	2
Brown, Denver	1.000	1	4	1	0	1	Poldberg, Omaha	1.000	7	59	2	0	3
Buckley, Oklahoma City	1.000	6	41	3	0	7	Quirk, Denver	1.000	3	24	4	0	3
Castro, Denver	1.000	2	5	0	0	0	Rajsich, Wichita*	.992	113	965	93	8	94
Christmas, Denver	.978	20	128	6	3	20	Rubel, Oklahoma City	.989	104	837	96	10	70
Davis, Omaha	.964	10	72	9	3	5	Ryal, Omaha*	.979	70	591	47	14	39
DE SA, Denver*	.993	139	1157	119	9	131	Shines, Indianapolis	.993	90	667	73	5	61
Hammond, Omaha	.989	61	495	42	6	32	Stenhouse, Indianapolis	.985	16	113	16	2	14
Harris, Evansville*	.991	41	302	34	3	40	Stephans, Omaha	.947	2	16	2	1	0
Hicks, Iowa	.986	132	1123	101	17	89	Stockstill, Oklahoma City	1.000	3	15	1	0	1
Hostetler, Oklahoma City	.983	43	305	35	6	35	Tovar, Evansville	1.000	1	2	0	0	0
Ron Johnson, Indianapolis	.993	34	259	22	2	26	Tracy, Iowa*	1.000	7	49	2	0	3
W. Johnson, Indianapolis	.986	37	269	20	4	25	Van Gorder, Wichita	.900	2	7	2	1	0
Kable, Louisville*	1.000	2	8	0	0	0	Werner, Louisville	1.000	5	27	2	0	2
Knicely, Wichita	.983	123	957	88	18	86	Werth, Louisville	.993	17	137	9	1	13
Laga, Evansville*	.987	111	1008	92	14	112	Wilkerson, Omaha	.985	9	65	2	1	2

Triple Play—De Sa.

SECOND BASEMEN

Player and Club	Pct.	G.	PO.	A.	E.	DP.	Player and Club	Pct.	G.	PO.	A.	E.	DP.
Anderson, Oklahoma City	1.000	3	7	6	0	0	Johnson, Omaha	.971	123	219	342	17	51
Babitt, Indianapolis	.957	9	20	24	2	6	W. Johnson, Indianapolis	.947	4	7	11	1	2
Barnes, Wichita	1.000	1	1	1	0	0	Krenchicki, Wichita	.963	15	35	42	3	10
Barranca, Oklahoma City	.959	24	45	73	5	17	Lawless, 12 Wich.-7 Ind	.963	19	30	47	3	8
Benton, Evansville	1.000	1	0	1	0	0	Little, Indianapolis	.972	26	42	61	3	10
Biancalana, Omaha	.984	30	45	78	2	11	Lyons, Louisville	.983	60	101	185	5	39
Booker, Louisville	.979	37	71	114	4	27	Mackanin, Iowa	1.000	4	1	4	0	0
Brooks, Iowa	.964	117	216	381	22	60	Manuel, Denver	.951	27	57	79	7	20
Buechele, Oklahoma City	.978	105	207	291	11	61	Mills, Indianapolis	1.000	1	0	3	0	0
Capra, Oklahoma City	1.000	1	1	1	0	0	Neuzil, Denver	.929	2	4	9	1	1
Castro, Denver	.946	15	42	45	5	12	Newman, Indianapolis	.987	17	27	48	1	8
Chavez, Evansville	.958	12	18	51	3	9	Owen, Iowa	1.000	2	1	3	0	0
Clements, Louisville	1.000	1	1	1	0	0	Pendleton, Louisville	.889	4	3	5	1	2
Earl, Evansville	.971	137	277	423	21	105	Pettini, Louisville	.961	32	48	75	5	14
Faedo, Evansville	1.000	1	1	0	0	1	Richardt, Oklahoma City	.986	17	29	42	1	5
Ford, Louisville	1.000	1	0	2	0	0	Rincones, Wichita	.992	32	51	77	1	11
Gates, Indianapolis	.966	92	163	260	15	58	Rohn, Iowa	.978	46	81	143	5	25
Glynn, Indianapolis	.959	27	35	59	4	16	Ruiz, Evansville	.970	6	12	20	1	4
Gonzales, Indianapolis	1.000	2	2	1	0	1	RUNNELLS, Wichita	.993	105	213	340	4	60
Gulliver, Louisville	.972	24	44	59	3	12	Stegman, Denver	.625	1	0	5	3	0
Harris, Louisville	.952	6	7	13	1	5	Strutton, Omaha	1.000	2	2	3	0	1
Hulett, Denver	.966	118	247	321	20	86	Wilborn, Denver	1.000	1	2	1	0	0
Jirschele, Oklahoma City	.974	8	14	23	1	3	Wilkerson, Omaha	1.000	1	2	2	0	1

Triple Plays—Earl, Hulett.

THIRD BASEMEN

Player and Club	Pct.	G.	PO.	A.	E.	DP.	Player and Club	Pct.	G.	PO.	A.	E.	DP.
Anderson, Oklahoma City	1.000	27	26	46	0	3	Bjorkman, Indianapolis	.857	4	0	6	1	0
Barnes, Wichita	.936	76	73	117	13	11	Booker, Louisville	.935	12	5	24	2	3
Barranca, Oklahoma City	1.000	1	1	3	0	0	Buechele, Oklahoma City	.918	27	29	38	6	0
Benton, Evansville	1.000	7	1	4	0	1	Castro, Denver	.943	93	74	193	16	19
Biancalana, Omaha	1.000	13	13	16	0	1	Chavez, Evansville	.977	18	13	30	1	4

THIRD BASEMEN—Continued

Player and Club	Pct.	G.	PO.	A.	E.	DP.
Clements, Louisville	.945	43	28	75	6	4
Earl, Evansville	.922	17	16	43	5	3
Faedo, 20 Evan.-9 OkC	.932	29	19	50	5	6
Foussianes, Evansville	.846	21	12	21	6	4
Gates, Indianapolis	1.000	4	4	6	0	0
Glynn, Indianapolis	.895	15	4	13	2	1
Gonzales, Indianapolis	.963	16	5	21	1	3
Gulliver, Louisville	.964	11	3	24	1	2
Hammond, Omaha	.977	21	13	29	1	2
Hulett, Denver	.901	25	19	45	7	7
Jirschele, Oklahoma City	.957	62	66	89	7	11
Knicely, Wichita	1.000	3	2	3	0	0
Krenchicki, Wichita	1.000	2	3	2	0	1
Lawless, 19 Wich.-14 Ind	.987	33	22	54	1	4
Lombarski, Iowa	.962	74	57	118	7	10
Lopez, Evansville	.915	53	43	75	11	7
Lyons, Louisville	.667	1	1	1	1	0
Mackanin, Iowa	.931	90	57	131	14	4
McClendon, Wichita	.955	21	12	30	2	3
Mills, Indianapolis	.901	64	29	99	14	9
Neuzil, Omaha	1.000	1	1	0	0	0
Newman, Indianapolis	.964	14	8	19	1	2
Pastornicki, Omaha	.910	76	46	126	17	6
Pendleton, Louisville	.964	86	88	152	9	18
Quirk, Denver	.919	20	12	45	5	4
Rincones, Wichita	1.000	5	4	4	0	0
Rohn, Iowa	.800	4	1	3	1	0
Rowdon, Wichita	.919	52	37	65	9	11
Ruiz, Evansville	.972	33	25	45	2	2
Runnells, Wichita	.938	9	8	7	1	1
Salazar, Indianapolis	.909	5	0	10	1	1
Sexton, Louisville	1.000	6	3	9	0	1
Shines, Indianapolis	.892	43	29	62	11	8
Sodders, Denver	.841	29	14	39	10	4
Stegman, Denver	1.000	1	0	2	0	0
Stockstill, Okla. City	.924	34	19	42	5	3
Wilkerson, Omaha	.894	52	28	82	13	3

SHORTSTOPS

Player and Club	Pct.	G.	PO.	A.	E.	DP.
Anderson, Oklahoma City	1.000	1	2	1	0	0
Babitt, Indianapolis	1.000	3	0	2	0	0
Baker, Evansville	.963	77	152	270	16	71
Barranca, Oklahoma City	.956	9	18	25	2	5
Biancalana, Omaha	1.000	15	20	34	0	3
Booker, Louisville	.964	14	24	29	2	9
Brooks, Iowa	1.000	1	0	1	0	0
Chavez, Evansville	.958	58	104	173	12	44
Dunston, Iowa	.907	60	90	165	26	30
Earl, Evansville	1.000	3	3	6	0	1
Faedo, 2 Evan.-46 Okla. City	.982	48	62	104	3	22
Glynn, Indianapolis	1.000	11	8	23	0	1
Gonzales, Indianapolis	.976	100	154	327	12	78
GONZALEZ, Louisville	.956	144	233	455	32	96
Hulett, Denver	.889	3	3	5	1	0
Jirschele, Oklahoma City	.945	22	36	50	5	8
Lawless, Indianapolis	1.000	1	1	2	0	0
Little, Indianapolis	1.000	10	15	23	0	5
Lopez, Evansville	.800	1	1	3	1	1
Lozado, Denver	.948	85	155	248	22	66
Mackanin, Iowa	.882	8	1	14	2	3
Manuel, Denver	.965	66	116	183	11	48
Mejia, Oklahoma City	1.000	13	34	33	0	11
Mesa, Denver	1.000	9	5	20	0	3
Newman, Indianapolis	1.000	4	8	11	0	2
Owen, Iowa	.960	39	62	108	7	20
Rincones, Wichita	.969	74	99	147	8	36
Rohn, Iowa	.956	55	86	152	11	32
Rowdon, Wichita	.951	99	138	230	19	48
Ruiz, Evansville	.947	15	31	41	4	13
Runnells, Wichita	1.000	3	2	3	0	0
Salazar, Indianapolis	.988	42	54	107	2	22
Scranton, Omaha	.948	136	197	373	31	57
Wherry, Oklahoma City	.963	71	138	201	13	44
Wilkerson, Omaha	1.000	5	7	12	0	0

OUTFIELDERS

Player and Club	Pct.	G.	PO.	A.	E.	DP.
Adduci, Louisville*	.989	61	87	3	1	0
Allen, Evansville	.991	60	106	5	1	2
Ayer, Louisville	1.000	81	115	10	0	1
Babitt, Indianapolis	.947	41	54	0	3	0
K. Baker, Indianapolis*	1.000	2	4	0	0	0
R. Baker, Iowa	.974	45	71	3	2	0
Barnes, Wichita	1.000	10	10	1	0	0
Barranca, Oklahoma City	1.000	11	15	2	0	0
Benton, Evansville	.800	13	10	2	3	0
Bogener, Wichita*	.978	101	176	5	4	0
Bosley, Iowa*	.946	27	31	4	2	1
Boston, Denver*	.970	126	311	11	10	4
Brewer, Omaha	.949	102	181	6	10	0
Brower, Oklahoma City	.974	35	69	7	2	1
Buckley, Oklahoma City	.951	20	35	4	2	2
Canady, Oklahoma City	.955	78	165	5	8	0
Capra, Oklahoma City	.988	120	329	10	4	2
Carter, Iowa	.987	60	142	6	2	1
Castro, Denver	1.000	2	2	0	0	0
Coleman, Louisville	.974	151	357	14	10	2
Cotto, Iowa	1.000	8	12	3	0	1
E. Davis, Iowa	.958	50	110	5	5	3
W. Davis, Omaha	.966	40	81	4	3	1
De Sa, Denver*	1.000	3	8	0	0	0
Dunbar, Oklahoma City*	.980	104	184	10	4	1
Ford, Louisville	1.000	11	13	0	0	0
Fuentes, Indianapolis	.988	146	227	10	3	2
Garcia, Wichita*	.982	100	147	13	3	0
Gilbert, Wichita	.977	124	234	19	6	4
Glynn, Indianapolis	1.000	3	2	0	0	0
Grant, Iowa	.976	127	199	8	5	1
Hammond, Omaha	1.000	5	8	1	0	0
J. Harris, Evansville*	1.000	5	2	0	0	0
V. Harris, Evansville	.954	42	62	0	3	0
Hatcher, Iowa	.978	148	303	15	7	4
Householder, Wichita	.982	108	209	9	4	2
Roy Johnson, Indianapolis*	.976	101	160	3	4	2
W. Johnson, Indianapolis	1.000	52	74	8	0	3
L. Jones, Omaha	1.000	16	38	0	0	0
R. Jones, Evansville*	.961	48	97	1	4	0
Kuntz, Evansville	1.000	10	18	0	0	0
Leeper, Omaha*	.971	110	194	6	6	1
Lombarski, Iowa	.800	2	3	1	1	0
Loucks, Indianapolis	.989	51	83	3	1	1
Manuel, Denver	1.000	6	11	0	0	0
MORRIS, Omaha*	.989	143	359	7	4	1
Murphy, Oklahoma City*	1.000	38	65	1	0	1
Newman, Indianapolis	1.000	5	6	1	0	0
Owen, Iowa	1.000	2	2	0	0	0
Parsons, Denver	.973	124	206	8	6	2
Quirk, Denver	.889	8	16	0	2	0
Robles, Evansville	.992	48	123	4	1	1
Rohn, Iowa	1.000	1	1	0	0	0
Rollin, Evansville	.922	32	43	4	4	1
Roof, 1 Ind.-128 Lou.*	.987	129	226	6	3	0
Rothschild, Denver	1.000	1	1	0	0	0
Runnells, Wichita	1.000	6	6	0	0	0
Ryal, Omaha*	.980	50	89	9	2	4
Salas, Louisville	.857	9	5	1	1	1
Sexton, Louisville	.750	1	3	0	1	0
Simmons, Evansville	.976	139	232	10	6	3
Sodders, Denver	.923	7	12	0	1	0
Stegman, Denver	.984	30	60	1	1	0
Stenhouse, Indianapolis	.882	15	15	0	2	0
Stockstill, Oklahoma City	.991	63	102	6	1	3
Thomas, Evansville*	.919	34	51	6	5	1
Tillman, Denver	.961	67	114	8	5	3
Tovar, Evansville	.963	42	78	1	3	0
Tracy, Iowa*	1.000	13	13	0	0	0
Venable, Indianapolis	.979	93	183	4	4	0
Werner, Iowa	1.000	53	64	7	0	2
Wilborn, Denver	.969	106	184	4	6	0
Williams, Evansville*	.929	53	91	1	7	0
Younger, Evansville*	1.000	2	1	0	0	0

Triple Plays—Robles, Wilborn.

CATCHERS

Player and Club	Pct.	G.	PO.	A.	E.	DP.	PB.
Anderson, Oklahoma City	1.000	3	14	2	0	1	0
Benton, Evansville	.956	73	323	49	17	7	5
Bilardello, Wichita	.991	45	290	31	3	2	4
Bjorkman, Indianapolis	.990	74	361	35	4	2	7
Brummer, Louisville	.965	16	133	4	5	1	0
Brunenkant, Oklahoma City	.970	44	241	17	8	2	6
Buckley, Oklahoma City	.973	75	382	47	12	5	12
BUTERA, Indianapolis	.9907	101	588	54	6	8	7

CATCHERS

Player and Club	Pct.	G.	PO.	A.	E.	DP.	PB.	Player and Club	Pct.	G.	PO.	A.	E.	DP.	PB.
Christmas, Denver	1.000	25	120	16	0	0	1	Nieto, Louisville	.984	75	446	43	8	4	5
Geren, Louisville	.989	13	80	6	1	2	3	Poldberg, Omaha	.986	65	324	39	5	6	5
Hammond, Omaha	.958	13	41	5	2	0	1	Quirk, Denver	.978	39	160	18	4	5	7
Hayes, Iowa	.979	111	589	58	14	9	4	Salas, Louisville	.979	48	255	27	6	4	2
Hyman, Iowa	1.000	1	5	1	0	0	0	Scott, Oklahoma City	.985	38	222	46	4	2	2
Karkovice, Denver	.983	31	149	28	3	0	4	Seilheimer, Denver	.980	38	180	19	4	4	3
Kneuer, Oklahoma City	1.000	2	3	1	0	0	0	Shines, Indianapolis	1.000	10	39	6	0	0	2
Knicely, Wichita	1.000	4	8	1	0	0	0	Skinner, Denver	.982	42	255	24	5	3	3
Lowry, Evansville	.979	57	240	45	6	7	0	Stephans, Omaha	.9906	89	484	47	5	3	2
McClendon, Wichita	1.000	1	1	0	0	0	0	Van Gorder, Wichita	.992	58	343	24	3	1	4
Melvin, Evansville	.996	40	201	21	1	4	1	Werner, Iowa	.986	52	261	13	4	0	2
Miley, Wichita	.990	63	335	44	4	4	3	Werth, Louisville	1.000	12	55	2	0	0	1

Triple Plays—Lowry, Skinner

PITCHERS

Player and Club	Pct.	G.	PO.	A.	E.	DP.	Player and Club	Pct.	G.	PO.	A.	E.	DP.
Abbott, Evansville	.917	5	2	9	1	0	Lachowicz, Oklahoma City	.962	21	18	7	1	0
Abrego, Iowa	.750	5	1	5	2	0	Landrum, Wichita	.931	47	12	15	2	0
Altamirano, Iowa	.813	49	5	8	3	0	Larkin, Evansville*	.900	17	1	8	1	0
Alvarez, Omaha	1.000	28	12	23	0	0	Larson, Oklahoma City	.885	17	10	13	3	1
Arroyo, Denver	1.000	5	1	5	0	0	Leibrandt, Omaha*	1.000	9	4	10	0	0
Augustine, 4 Lou.-17 Iowa*	1.000	21	5	7	0	0	Lesley, Wichita	1.000	27	1	2	0	0
Bailey, Evansville*	.870	13	8	12	3	0	Mahler, Louisville*	.941	26	9	23	2	4
Baker, Louisville	1.000	28	14	17	0	2	Martin, Evansville	1.000	29	3	9	0	2
Bargar, Indianapolis	1.000	31	20	21	0	2	Martinez, Omaha	1.000	16	1	3	0	0
Barojas, Denver	1.000	3	1	2	0	1	Mason, Evansville	1.000	25	10	17	0	1
Biercevicz, Denver	.958	18	10	13	1	1	McLaughlin, Oklahoma City	1.000	3	2	1	0	0
Bogener, Wichita*	1.000	1	0	1	0	0	Mengwasser, Oklahoma City	1.000	11	4	6	0	1
Boggs, Oklahoma City	.950	11	11	8	1	0	Meridith, Iowa*	1.000	49	7	14	0	1
Botelho, Iowa	.889	28	10	22	4	2	Miller, Louisville	.500	6	1	0	1	0
Brennan, Denver	1.000	35	8	22	0	2	Monteleone, Evansville	.846	11	3	8	2	2
Browning, Wichita*	.938	30	9	21	2	1	Moreno, Evansville*	1.000	20	2	9	0	1
Buchanan, Wichita*	1.000	39	2	8	0	1	Morlock, Louisville	1.000	3	1	0	0	0
Burke, Indianapolis	.940	35	27	20	3	3	Morogiello, Evansville*	1.000	23	1	6	0	0
Burns, Denver*	1.000	1	0	2	0	1	Musselman, Oklahoma City	1.000	13	3	7	0	0
Cates, Indianapolis	.750	21	3	6	3	0	Mustad, Indianapolis	.938	25	5	10	1	1
Cato, Wichita	1.000	37	9	16	0	3	Nail, Wichita	.926	31	12	13	2	0
Citarella, Louisville	1.000	16	5	9	0	1	Niemann, Denver*	.970	32	8	24	1	2
R. Clark, Oklahoma City*	1.000	20	10	20	0	2	O'NEAL, Evansville	1.000	25	21	29	0	2
T. Clark, Louisville	1.000	18	3	4	0	1	Ownbey, Louisville	.813	17	2	11	3	2
Conner, Evansville*	.949	32	9	28	2	1	Parrott, Omaha	.938	33	11	34	3	1
Cook, Oklahoma City	.966	27	17	11	1	0	Pastore, Wichita	1.000	2	0	1	0	0
Cox, Louisville	.917	6	6	5	1	0	Patterson, Iowa	.918	32	16	29	4	3
Creel, Omaha	.944	27	19	32	3	0	Perlman, Iowa*	.909	24	17	23	4	0
Cruz, Oklahoma City	.857	37	0	6	1	0	Perry, Louisville*	1.000	21	3	4	0	0
Dacko, Evansville	1.000	15	5	8	0	0	Pimentel, Louisville	1.000	2	0	1	0	1
Dayley, Louisville*	1.000	13	4	18	0	0	Pryce, Iowa	.885	34	8	15	3	1
Dilks, Indianapolis*	1.000	16	3	10	0	0	Puleo, Oklahoma City	1.000	19	12	13	0	2
Earley, Iowa*	.963	54	10	16	1	1	Renz, Denver	1.000	3	0	1	0	0
Eaton, Indianapolis	1.000	19	2	1	0	1	Reyes, Omaha	.857	21	7	5	2	0
Erickson, Evansville	1.000	19	7	14	0	0	Rhodes, Louisville*	1.000	11	0	3	0	1
Fallon, Denver*	.828	19	5	19	5	0	Roberge, Denver	1.000	26	3	9	0	0
Ferreira, Omaha*	.950	40	6	13	1	2	Robinson, Denver	.970	25	9	23	1	1
Filer, Iowa	.971	26	10	23	1	0	Rothschild, Denver	1.000	31	13	18	0	2
Fossas, Oklahoma City*	1.000	29	10	20	0	1	Sattler, Indianapolis	.923	58	7	17	2	0
Franco, Wichita*	1.000	6	0	2	0	1	Scherrer, Wichita*	1.000	10	1	1	0	0
Gil, Iowa	.889	24	3	5	1	0	Schuler, Indianapolis*	1.000	42	4	2	0	0
Gleaton, Denver*	.600	12	0	3	2	0	Schulze, Iowa	1.000	13	9	14	0	1
Grapenthin, Indianapolis	.967	53	13	16	1	1	Sebra, Oklahoma City	1.000	9	2	4	0	0
Griffin, Oklahoma City	.880	31	6	16	3	2	Shaw, Omaha	.909	19	10	10	2	2
Gumpert, Evansville	.935	56	8	21	2	1	Shimp, Oklahoma City	.857	12	2	4	1	1
Hagen, Louisville	.947	29	28	43	4	7	Siwy, Denver	.955	15	4	17	1	2
Hargesheimer, Omaha	1.000	11	0	4	0	0	Smith, Wichita	1.000	12	1	0	0	0
Harris, Indianapolis	1.000	14	3	8	0	0	Speck, Denver	.917	29	12	21	3	2
Hassler, Louisville*	1.000	38	4	7	0	0	St. Clair, Omaha	.800	29	2	6	2	0
Heidenreich, Wichita	.960	37	11	13	1	0	St. Claire, Indianapolis	1.000	13	1	1	0	0
Heinkel, Evansville	.971	30	28	38	2	6	Stoll, Indianapolis	.957	9	8	14	1	0
Henke, Oklahoma City	1.000	39	3	11	0	0	Strode, Omaha*	1.000	12	1	9	0	0
Hesketh, Indianapolis*	.886	22	6	25	4	1	Stuper, Louisville	.667	2	1	1	1	0
Hickey, Denver*	1.000	16	0	8	0	0	Terry, Wichita	1.000	2	0	3	0	0
Hoffman, Denver*	.920	35	5	18	2	3	Thurberg, Louisville	1.000	17	1	4	0	0
Huismann, Omaha	.857	15	2	4	1	1	Tibbs, Wichita	1.000	4	1	4	0	1
Jackson, Omaha*	.821	16	5	18	5	0	Tobik, Oklahoma City	1.000	14	2	3	0	1
C. Johnson, Denver	1.000	32	15	15	0	2	Toliver, Wichita	.939	32	9	22	2	2
J. Johnson, Louisville	1.000	2	3	2	0	1	Trujillo, Denver	.900	8	4	5	1	0
W. Johnson, Iowa	1.000	44	8	21	0	3	Von Ohlen, Louisville*	.929	22	8	5	1	0
A. Jones, Denver	1.000	24	0	7	0	1	Welsh, Indianapolis*	.981	29	12	39	1	4
M. Jones, Omaha*	.857	11	3	9	2	0	Willis, Evansville	1.000	40	9	11	0	0
Kaufman, Iowa	1.000	3	1	0	0	0	Wills, Omaha	.875	15	7	21	4	2
Keener, Louisville	.950	53	4	15	1	1	Wise, Wichita	1.000	5	1	1	0	1
Keeton, Omaha	.941	25	4	12	1	0	Wright, Oklahoma City*	1.000	31	5	15	0	3
Kepshire, Louisville	.958	16	6	17	1	1	Yuhas, Omaha	1.000	3	1	1	0	0
Kinnunen, Indianapolis*	1.000	3	3	7	0	0	Zwolensky, Oklahoma City	1.000	32	12	24	0	3

The following players had no accepted recorded chances at the positions indicated; therefore, are not listed in the fielding averages for those particular positions: Anderson, of, p; Banks, p; Bibby, p; J. Brown (Den.), 2b; Buckley, p; Castro, ss; Christmas, of; Earley, 1b; V. Harris, 1b; Kuntz, 3b; Little, 3b; Lombarski, ss; Lopez, 2b, p; Lowery, 3b; Mesa, 3b; Parsons, 1b, p; Pastornicky, 1b; Quirk, p; Rincones, of; Sexton, 2b; Shade, p; Shines, p; Werner, 3b; Zwolensky, of.

CLUB PITCHING

Club	ERA.	G.	CG.	ShO.	Sv.	IP.	H.	R.	ER.	HR.	HB.	BB.	Int. BB.	SO.	WP.	Bk.
Indianapolis	3.86	154	15	11	52	1301.2	1221	630	558	106	28	560	27	934	69	22
Louisville	3.89	155	41	8	34	1322.1	1236	652	571	117	30	580	40	934	58	23
Omaha	4.02	154	43	14	20	1268.2	1192	652	567	121	26	545	38	771	38	16
Evansville	4.24	154	33	10	27	1277.1	1405	715	602	122	16	511	30	702	38	26
Iowa	4.37	154	24	9	39	1280.1	1343	724	622	129	24	509	34	805	39	20
Wichita	4.46	155	31	9	29	1308.0	1304	715	648	153	26	586	20	906	44	18
Oklahoma City	4.65	154	18	8	27	1301.0	1413	742	672	113	38	515	25	833	72	18
Denver	4.73	154	33	9	34	1312.2	1370	782	690	119	34	554	14	836	71	14

PITCHERS' RECORDS
(Leading Qualifiers for Earned-Run Average Leadership — 123 or More Innings)

*Throws lefthanded.

Pitcher—Club	W.	L.	Pct.	ERA.	G.	GS.	CG.	GF.	ShO.	Sv.	IP.	H.	R.	ER.	HR.	HB.	BB.	Int. BB.	SO.	WP.
Welsh, Indianapolis*	13	4	.765	3.01	29	26	1	0	0	0	167.2	165	63	56	8	7	80	0	87	9
Hesketh, Indianapolis*	12	3	.800	3.05	22	22	5	0	1	0	147.2	120	60	50	8	3	54	2	135	10
Landrum, Wichita	7	4	.636	3.45	47	9	2	16	0	2	130.1	120	58	50	1	1	52	1	120	4
Hagen, Louisville	10	9	.526	3.46	29	26	6	2	2	0	176.2	174	88	68	13	6	57	2	77	5
Burke, Indianapolis	11	8	.579	3.49	35	27	1	4	0	2	180.2	192	81	70	15	4	61	5	108	10
O'Neal, Evansville	9	10	.474	3.57	25	25	8	0	1	0	166.1	152	82	66	12	0	59	2	110	4
Perlman, Iowa	11	6	.647	3.79	24	24	4	0	1	0	147.1	131	69	62	10	5	51	1	61	3
Mason, Evansville	9	7	.563	3.80	25	25	6	0	2	0	151.2	175	78	64	10	1	64	1	88	6
Parrott, Omaha	5	8	.385	3.81	33	19	7	8	2	2	151.1	141	69	64	13	3	53	4	103	2
Botelho, Iowa	10	11	.476	3.81	28	28	7	0	0	0	177.1	179	89	75	20	7	65	2	136	5
Browning, Wichita*	12	10	.545	3.95	30	28	8	1	1	0	189.1	169	88	83	24	6	73	1	160	2

Departmental Leaders: G—Sattler, 58; W—Patterson, 14; L—Creel, 15; Pct.—Citarella, .818; GS—Bargar, Niemann, Patterson, 29; CG—Baker, Creel, Jackson, 10; GF—Grapenthin, 39; ShO—Creel, Heinkel, Jackson, Leibrandt, 3; Sv.—Grapenthin, 18; IP—Niemann, 190.1; H—Niemann, 235; R—Niemann, 136; ER—Niemann, 124; HR—Browning, Cook, 24; HB—Cook, 8; BB—Toliver, 116; IBB—Hassler, 8; SO—Browning, 160; WP—Lachowicz, Mahler, 15.

(All Pitchers—Listed Alphabetically)

Pitcher—Club	W.	L.	Pct.	ERA.	G.	GS.	CG.	GF.	ShO.	Sv.	IP.	H.	R.	ER.	HR.	HB.	BB.	Int. BB.	SO.	WP.
Abbott, Evansville	0	4	.000	3.94	5	5	0	0	0	0	29.2	30	14	13	2	0	8	0	8	0
Abrego, Iowa	1	1	.500	5.06	5	0	0	0	0	0	26.2	28	16	15	4	0	9	0	17	0
Altamirano, Iowa	4	4	.500	3.03	49	0	0	33	0	17	59.1	56	26	20	4	1	23	4	35	1
Alvarez, Omaha	5	2	.714	4.44	28	2	0	11	0	1	99.1	113	59	49	13	1	28	3	38	3
Anderson, Oklahoma City	0	0	.000	0.00	1	0	0	1	0	0	2.2	0	0	0	0	1	0	0	0	0
Arroyo, Denver	4	1	.800	4.40	5	5	0	0	0	0	30.2	30	16	15	5	0	8	0	11	1
Augustine, 4 Lou.-17 Iowa*	2	6	.250	5.65	21	5	0	4	0	2	51.0	47	38	32	5	0	23	1	34	2
Bailey, Evansville*	0	8	.000	6.47	13	10	0	0	0	0	55.2	75	53	40	5	3	29	1	26	6
Baker, Louisville	10	9	.526	4.35	28	25	10	1	0	0	171.2	186	91	83	17	4	52	1	86	3
Banks, Iowa	0	1	.000	19.29	3	0	0	1	0	0	2.1	5	6	5	0	0	4	0	0	0
Bargar, Indianapolis	9	8	.529	4.64	31	29	3	0	0	0	180.1	156	101	93	18	2	83	2	121	8
Barojas, Denver	1	0	1.000	1.00	3	0	0	3	0	2	9.0	6	1	1	0	0	5	1	3	0
Bibby, Louisville	0	0	.000	0.00	2	0	0	1	0	0	5.0	2	0	0	0	0	6	0	3	2
Biercevicz, Denver	7	5	.583	4.02	18	16	4	0	1	0	112.0	113	51	50	10	2	36	0	58	5
Bogener, Wichita*	0	0	.000	31.50	1	0	0	1	0	0	2.0	7	7	7	3	0	0	0	1	0
Boggs, Oklahoma City	5	4	.556	5.40	11	11	1	0	1	0	55.0	67	38	33	2	1	24	0	30	6
Botelho, Iowa	10	11	.476	3.81	28	28	7	0	0	0	177.1	179	89	75	20	7	65	2	136	5
Brennan, Denver	9	5	.643	3.25	35	7	3	20	0	7	105.1	86	42	38	12	5	32	1	51	5
Browning, Wichita*	12	10	.545	3.95	30	28	8	1	1	0	189.1	169	88	83	24	6	73	1	160	2
Buchanan, Wichita*	1	2	.333	7.03	39	0	0	31	0	11	58.2	51	21	20	4	0	28	2	35	1
Buckley, Oklahoma City	0	0	.000	12.00	1	0	0	1	0	0	6.0	10	8	8	3	1	3	0	3	1
Burke, Indianapolis	11	8	.579	3.49	35	27	1	4	0	2	180.2	192	81	70	15	4	61	5	108	10
Burns, Denver*	1	0	1.000	4.50	1	1	0	0	0	0	6.0	6	3	3	1	1	3	0	5	1
Cates, Indianapolis	6	6	.500	4.76	21	16	3	0	2	0	92.2	70	50	49	15	0	56	1	90	4
Cato, Wichita	8	9	.471	4.19	37	8	4	13	1	3	103.0	103	52	48	15	1	27	2	71	4
Citarella, Louisville	9	2	.818	3.91	16	14	4	1	0	1	89.2	91	43	39	7	3	30	0	38	2
R. Clark, Oklahoma City*	4	10	.286	6.42	20	20	1	0	0	0	104.2	142	79	70	6	2	42	1	49	2
T. Clark, Louisville	1	3	.250	4.72	18	1	0	9	0	1	34.1	41	19	18	5	1	12	2	24	2
Conner, Evansville*	6	11	.353	4.28	32	16	2	4	1	0	128.1	150	76	61	16	0	43	2	84	4
Cook, Oklahoma City	9	8	.529	4.85	27	27	2	0	0	0	167.0	159	92	90	24	8	57	0	124	4
Cox, Louisville	4	1	.800	2.13	6	6	4	0	0	0	42.1	34	16	10	3	0	7	0	34	0
Creel, Omaha	9	15	.375	4.34	27	27	10	0	3	0	168.0	169	99	81	16	4	58	3	98	4
Cruz, Oklahoma City	6	4	.600	4.99	37	0	0	32	0	5	52.1	50	32	29	7	4	30	7	52	4
Dacko, Evansville	3	7	.300	5.71	15	14	4	0	0	0	82.0	98	60	52	8	3	38	0	49	1
Dayley, Louisville*	4	6	.400	3.27	13	13	3	0	0	0	96.1	86	42	35	6	2	22	1	79	3
Dilks, Indianapolis*	1	4	.200	6.08	16	5	0	3	0	0	40.0	40	32	27	1	2	20	1	27	5
Earley, Iowa*	6	6	.500	3.77	54	3	1	30	0	6	86.0	93	44	36	9	2	34	4	61	2
Eaton, Indianapolis	3	3	.500	6.53	19	1	0	11	0	2	30.1	46	32	22	4	0	11	0	16	0
Erickson, Evansville	7	4	.636	3.24	19	14	2	3	0	0	108.1	109	48	39	15	1	23	1	54	1
Fallon, Evansville*	5	8	.385	3.75	19	17	3	0	0	0	115.1	101	63	48	8	3	58	1	101	11
Ferreira, Omaha*	7	10	.412	4.57	40	15	1	16	0	4	114.1	128	65	58	8	3	52	5	69	3
Filer, Iowa	9	7	.563	4.89	26	20	4	1	1	0	123.1	149	86	67	17	0	48	3	80	5
Fossas, Oklahoma City*	5	9	.357	4.31	29	15	3	5	0	0	121.0	143	65	58	12	2	34	1	74	3
Franco, Wichita*	1	0	1.000	5.79	6	0	0	3	0	0	9.1	8	6	6	1	0	4	0	11	0
Gil, Iowa	0	3	.000	9.07	24	4	1	9	0	1	45.2	68	50	46	14	0	23	1	18	3
Gleaton, Denver*	1	1	.500	1.80	12	0	0	8	0	3	20.0	20	5	4	0	1	4	0	10	0
Grapenthin, Indianapolis	6	7	.462	3.07	53	0	0	39	0	18	91.0	81	38	31	4	2	33	7	44	5
Griffin, Oklahoma City	8	5	.615	4.46	31	10	0	13	0	1	113.0	138	67	56	14	2	41	1	69	5
Gumpert, Evansville	7	4	.636	4.95	56	0	0	35	0	7	87.1	105	51	48	10	1	40	6	48	4
Hagen, Louisville	10	9	.526	3.46	29	26	6	2	2	0	176.2	174	88	68	13	6	57	2	77	5
Hargesheimer, Omaha	1	2	.333	3.07	11	0	0	9	0	2	14.2	13	7	5	1	0	9	0	9	2
Harris, Indianapolis	4	4	.500	4.43	14	6	0	4	0	1	44.2	44	27	22	7	3	29	0	45	3
Hassler, Louisville*	7	4	.636	2.11	38	1	0	25	0	10	64.0	47	19	15	3	1	24	8	51	4
Heidenreich, Wichita	1	10	.091	5.94	37	8	0	14	0	5	94.0	111	70	62	18	4	41	2	46	1
Heinkel, Evansville	11	13	.458	3.99	30	26	7	2	3	0	178.1	205	101	79	15	5	58	7	75	6
Henke, Oklahoma City	6	2	.750	2.64	39	0	0	34	0	7	64.2	59	21	19	1	1	25	6	65	5
Hesketh, Indianapolis*	12	3	.800	3.05	22	22	5	0	1	0	147.2	120	60	50	8	3	54	2	135	10
Hickey, Denver*	2	2	.500	6.27	16	7	0	2	0	1	47.1	61	39	33	6	0	23	2	20	2
Hoffman, Denver*	4	8	.333	4.74	35	13	3	12	1	3	112.0	124	71	59	6	2	40	2	76	6
Huismann, Omaha	2	0	1.000	0.00	15	0	0	14	0	3	19.0	11	0	0	0	0	5	2	18	1
Jackson, Omaha*	5	8	.385	3.67	16	16	10	0	3	0	110.1	91	50	45	8	1	45	3	82	3

Pitcher—Club	W.	L.	Pct.	ERA.	G.	GS.	CG.	GF.	ShO.	Sv.	IP.	H.	R.	ER.	HR.	HB.	BB.	Int. BB.	SO.	WP.
C. Johnson, Denver	4	5	.444	4.83	32	2	0	14	0	1	78.1	85	48	42	7	3	35	1	33	1
J. Johnson, Louisville	0	1	.000	9.72	2	2	0	0	0	0	8.1	9	9	9	3	0	7	0	6	0
W. Johnson, Iowa	5	9	.357	4.85	44	5	0	18	0	2	89.0	100	54	48	8	0	51	7	46	7
A. Jones, Denver	2	3	.400	4.71	24	0	0	21	0	7	28.2	26	16	15	0	0	20	2	20	1
M. Jones, Omaha*	4	5	.444	3.44	11	11	5	0	1	0	73.1	65	39	28	8	3	27	0	38	3
Kaufman, Iowa	1	0	1.000	8.31	3	0	0	0	0	0	8.2	11	8	8	2	0	5	0	6	1
Keener, Louisville	3	5	.375	3.47	53	1	0	31	0	10	83.0	78	36	32	10	3	42	4	54	3
Keeton, Omaha	4	4	.500	4.11	25	5	0	7	0	2	65.2	61	32	30	6	2	18	6	28	0
Kepshire, Louisville	7	5	.583	4.60	16	16	3	0	0	0	107.2	87	56	55	13	1	63	5	85	3
Kinnunen, Indianapolis*	3	1	.750	4.62	16	4	0	4	0	0	37.0	35	20	19	3	0	19	0	32	4
Lachowicz, Oklahoma City	2	11	.154	4.18	21	19	2	1	0	0	116.1	115	64	54	7	3	58	1	60	15
Landrum, Wichita	7	4	.636	3.45	47	9	2	16	0	2	130.1	120	58	50	8	1	52	1	120	4
Larkin, Evansville*	1	0	1.000	4.95	17	0	0	8	0	0	36.1	40	23	20	3	0	24	1	26	2
Larson, Oklahoma City	6	9	.400	5.62	17	17	4	0	0	0	105.2	119	68	66	9	2	31	2	58	5
Leibrandt, Omaha*	7	1	.875	1.24	9	9	4	0	3	0	72.2	51	14	10	4	3	16	2	38	0
Lesley, Wichita	3	3	.500	3.25	27	0	0	20	0	6	36.0	26	21	13	4	0	29	0	33	3
Lopez, Evansville	0	0	.000	36.00	1	0	0	1	0	0	1.0	4	4	4	0	0	1	0	0	0
Mahler, Louisville*	8	12	.400	4.28	26	26	5	0	1	0	153.1	149	83	73	12	3	88	2	142	15
Martin, Evansville*	5	3	.625	6.06	29	3	0	11	0	3	49.0	57	36	33	8	1	31	2	32	0
Martinez, Omaha	4	3	.571	3.47	16	0	0	15	0	4	23.1	19	10	9	1	0	14	0	18	2
Mason, Evansville	9	7	.563	3.80	25	25	6	0	2	0	151.2	175	78	64	10	1	64	1	88	6
McLaughlin, Oklahoma City	1	1	.500	2.25	3	1	0	1	0	0	8.0	5	2	2	0	0	5	1	3	0
Mengwasser, Oklahoma City	1	3	.250	6.61	11	0	0	4	0	1	32.2	48	30	24	4	0	18	0	16	1
Meridith, Iowa*	7	3	.700	3.17	49	5	0	24	0	8	93.2	88	33	33	7	0	33	4	78	2
Miller, Louisville	1	0	1.000	4.91	6	0	0	5	0	0	11.0	12	6	6	0	0	5	1	5	0
Monteleone, Evansville	5	3	.625	4.50	11	11	2	0	0	0	64.0	64	33	32	7	0	36	0	42	0
Moreno, Evansville*	2	3	.400	3.59	20	4	2	9	0	1	47.2	44	21	19	4	1	30	2	27	1
Morlock, Louisville	2	4	.333	6.10	3	2	1	1	0	0	10.1	15	9	7	1	0	6	1	3	0
Morogiello, Evansville*	2	2	.500	2.30	23	0	0	16	0	1	31.1	38	9	8	2	0	7	3	6	0
Musselman, Oklahoma City	2	2	.333	4.05	13	0	0	5	0	2	26.2	29	13	12	0	2	8	0	18	1
Mustad, Indianapolis	3	5	.375	6.72	25	9	0	7	0	0	64.1	75	49	48	6	3	47	1	53	3
Nail, Wichita	9	11	.450	4.55	31	28	4	1	1	0	176.0	199	100	89	20	5	48	4	91	7
Niemann, Denver*	10	12	.455	5.86	32	29	9	1	1	0	190.1	235	136	124	14	4	86	0	110	12
O'Neal, Evansville	9	10	.474	3.57	25	25	8	0	1	0	166.1	152	82	66	12	0	59	2	110	4
Ownbey, Louisville	6	6	.500	4.02	17	17	4	0	2	0	96.1	75	52	43	10	4	61	0	111	3
Parrott, Omaha	5	8	.385	3.81	33	19	7	8	2	2	151.1	141	69	64	13	3	53	4	103	2
Parsons, Denver	0	0	.000	54.00	1	0	0	1	0	0	1.0	7	6	6	1	0	0	0	0	0
Pastore, Wichita	0	1	.000	2.77	2	2	0	0	0	0	13.0	6	4	4	2	1	8	0	12	0
Patterson, Iowa	14	7	.667	4.33	32	29	5	1	1	1	178.2	185	105	86	18	2	65	1	116	7
Perlman, Iowa	11	6	.647	3.79	24	24	4	0	1	0	147.1	131	69	62	10	5	51	1	61	3
Perry, Louisville*	4	3	.571	2.22	21	0	0	9	0	2	44.2	35	12	11	4	0	21	4	43	5
Pimentel, Louisville	0	1	.000	7.84	2	1	1	0	0	0	10.1	12	9	9	1	1	10	0	6	0
Pryce, Iowa	5	6	.455	4.34	34	13	1	10	0	2	120.1	133	68	58	9	5	51	5	76	1
Puleo, Wichita	8	9	.471	5.35	19	19	2	0	2	0	104.1	117	71	62	14	1	59	1	59	10
Quirk, Denver	0	0	.000	13.50	2	0	0	2	0	0	2.0	6	3	3	0	0	0	0	0	0
Renz, Denver	0	0	.000	15.19	3	0	0	2	0	0	5.1	11	9	9	2	0	3	0	2	2
Reyes, Omaha	1	4	.200	4.75	21	3	0	15	0	1	41.2	40	27	22	2	1	17	0	19	6
Rhodes, Louisville*	1	0	1.000	3.86	11	0	0	3	0	1	16.1	19	7	7	2	1	9	2	10	2
Roberge, Denver	5	1	.833	1.95	26	0	0	22	0	8	37.0	27	8	8	4	1	10	2	36	2
Robinson, Wichita	9	6	.600	4.61	25	24	3	0	2	0	150.1	168	86	77	11	4	60	1	98	1
Rothschild, Denver	6	3	.667	4.02	31	9	1	10	1	2	109.2	109	58	49	12	4	51	0	71	10
Sattler, Indianapolis	7	7	.500	3.67	58	0	0	34	0	15	95.2	92	41	39	8	2	36	6	87	4
Scherrer, Wichita*	2	3	.400	3.24	10	0	0	8	0	1	16.2	16	6	6	1	0	11	0	14	1
Schuler, Indianapolis*	8	0	1.000	3.06	42	0	0	19	0	6	47.0	48	16	16	5	0	7	0	42	0
Schulze, Iowa	5	5	.500	4.33	13	13	1	0	0	0	79.0	79	40	38	3	2	29	1	44	0
Sebra, Oklahoma City	4	4	.500	3.38	9	9	2	0	1	0	53.1	37	23	20	2	1	25	0	38	6
Shade, Louisville	0	1	.000	10.13	2	0	0	2	0	0	2.2	5	4	3	0	0	3	0	3	1
Shaw, Omaha	3	10	.231	8.63	19	18	1	1	0	0	73.0	81	75	70	14	3	77	1	40	3
Shimp, Oklahoma City	2	2	.500	6.84	12	9	0	2	0	0	52.2	72	44	40	10	2	29	2	32	3
Shines, Indianapolis	0	0	.000	0.00	1	0	0	0	0	0	1.0	1	1	0	0	0	1	0	1	0
Siwy, Denver	4	5	.444	5.25	15	14	3	1	1	0	96.0	93	63	56	9	4	47	0	72	2
Smith, Wichita	3	2	.600	4.00	12	0	0	10	0	1	18.0	17	8	8	2	0	13	4	20	2
Speck, Denver	12	11	.522	5.20	29	28	6	1	0	0	176.2	186	117	102	16	3	73	2	148	9
St. Clair, Omaha	2	2	.500	3.92	29	0	0	14	0	1	64.1	57	28	28	8	1	29	3	35	1
St. Claire, Indianapolis	1	1	.500	1.02	13	0	0	13	0	8	17.2	15	2	2	0	0	6	1	17	1
Stoll, Indianapolis	4	2	.667	1.97	9	9	2	0	0	0	64.0	41	17	14	4	0	18	1	29	3
Strode, Omaha*	1	7	.125	4.26	12	12	2	0	0	0	76.0	61	38	36	9	1	41	6	65	3
Stuper, Louisville	0	0	.000	4.63	2	2	0	0	0	0	11.2	10	6	6	0	0	7	0	8	1
Terry, Wichita	0	0	.000	5.79	2	2	0	0	0	0	9.1	13	6	6	1	0	7	1	6	1
Thurber, Louisville	3	1	.750	6.11	17	1	0	9	0	1	35.1	30	26	24	5	0	25	1	41	1
Tibbs, Wichita	3	0	1.000	3.58	4	4	2	0	1	0	27.2	22	13	11	3	1	8	0	14	1
Tobik, Oklahoma City	1	1	.500	3.06	14	0	0	8	0	3	32.1	34	12	11	1	0	9	0	30	3
Toliver, Wichita	11	6	.647	4.83	32	23	6	4	0	0	164.0	142	90	88	19	2	116	1	113	5
Trujillo, Denver	2	5	.286	7.80	8	6	1	1	1	0	30.0	38	27	26	6	1	20	0	9	1
Von Ohlen, Louisville*	1	3	.250	2.28	22	1	0	13	0	8	43.1	30	11	11	1	0	18	6	22	3
Welsh, Indianapolis*	13	4	.765	3.01	29	26	1	0	0	0	167.2	165	63	56	8	7	80	0	87	9
Willis, Evansville	5	3	.625	3.73	40	1	0	32	0	16	60.1	59	26	25	5	0	20	2	27	3
Wills, Omaha	7	4	.636	2.81	15	15	2	0	1	0	89.2	75	32	28	9	0	49	0	69	2
Wise, Wichita	0	1	.000	12.00	5	0	0	2	0	0	6.0	9	8	8	3	0	4	0	6	0
Wright, Oklahoma City*	2	1	.667	2.40	31	0	0	21	0	7	48.2	37	14	13	2	1	24	2	38	3
Yuhas, Omaha	1	1	.500	3.00	3	2	1	0	0	0	12.0	16	8	4	1	0	6	0	4	0
Zwolensky, Oklahoma City	7	8	.467	4.36	32	16	3	8	2	1	138.1	149	70	67	4	5	52	1	74	5

BALKS—Heidenreich, O'Neal, Pryce, 6 each; Sattler, 5; C. Johnson, Mahler, Ownbey, Welsh, Zwolensky, 4 each; Botelho, R. Clark, Conner, Erickson, Ferreira, Hesketh, Keeton, Tolliver, Willis, 3 each; Abbott, Augustine, Bargar, Biercevicz, Burke, Citarella, Cruz, Dacko, Filer, Griffin, Hagen, Kepshire, Landrum, Meridith, Moreno, Morlock, Mustad, Nail, Niemann, Parrott, Perlman, Puleo, Reyes, Speck, St. Clair, Stoll, 2 each; Altamirano, Arroyo, Baker, Bibby, Boggs, Brennan, Cates, Cook, Cox, Dayley, Earley, Grapenthin, Gumpert, Heinkel, Henke, Huismann, M. Jones, Keener, Lachowicz, Martin, Martinez, Mason, Monteleone, Musselman, Patterson, Robinson, Rothschild, Scherrer, Sebra, Shimp, Smith, Strode, Stuper, Thurberg, Trujillo, 1 each.

COMBINATION SHUTOUTS—Speck-Roberge, Fallon-Barojas, Brennan-Hickey, Denver; Heinkel-Martin, Erickson-Moreno, O'Neal-Gumpert, Evansville; Hesketh-Sattler, Welsh-Sattler-Schuler, Burke-Grapenthin-Sattler, Bargar-Schuler, Kinnunen-Sattler, Cates-Sattler-Schuler, Burke-St. Clair, Stoll-Schuler, Indianapolis; Botelho-Earley, Meridith-Gil, Patterson-Augustine, Pryce-Altamirano, Johnson-Earley, Meridith-Altamirano, Iowa; Ownbey-Baker, Dayley-Keener-Hassler, Dayley-Keener, Louisville; Cook-Mengwasser, Boggs-Henke-Wright, Lachowicz-Tobik, Fossas-Tobik, Oklahoma City; Wills-Parrott, Omaha; Browning-Heidenreich, Wichita.

NO-HIT GAMES—Browning, Wichita, defeated Iowa, 2-0 (seven innings), July 31; Patterson, Iowa, defeated Omaha, 2-0, August 21.

International League

CLASS AAA

Leading Batter
SCOTT BRADLEY
Columbus

League President
HAROLD COOPER

Leading Pitcher
JIM DESHAIES
Columbus

CHAMPIONSHIP WINNERS IN PREVIOUS YEARS

1884—Trenton .520	1928—Rochester .549	1957—Toronto .575
1885—Syracuse .584	1929—Rochester .613	Buffalo (2nd)† .571
1886—Utica .646	1930—Rochester .629	1958—Montreal‡ .588
1887—Toronto .644	1931—Rochester .601	1959—Buffalo .582
1888—Syracuse .723	1932—Newark .649	Havana (3rd)† .523
1889—Detroit .649	1933—Newark .622	1960—Toronto‡ .649
1890—Detroit .617	Buffalo (4th)† .494	1961—Columbus .597
1891—Buffalo (reg. season) .727	1934—Newark .608	Buffalo (3rd)† .559
Buffalo (supplem'l) .680	Toronto (3rd)† .559	1962—Jacksonville .610
1892—Providence .615	1935—Montreal .597	Atlanta (3rd)† .539
Binghamton* .667	Syracuse (2nd)† .565	1963—Syracuse x .533
1893—Erie .606	1936—Buffalo‡ .610	Indianapolis‡ .562
1894—Providence .696	1937—Newark‡ .717	1964—Jacksonville .589
1895—Springfield .687	1938—Newark‡ .684	Rochester (4th)† .532
1896—Providence .602	1939—Jersey City .582	1965—Columbus .582
1897—Syracuse .632	Rochester (2nd)† .556	Toronto (3rd)† .556
1898—Montreal .586	1940—Rochester .611	1966—Rochester .565
1899—Rochester .624	Newark (2nd)† .594	Toronto (2nd-tied)† .558
1900—Providence .616	1941—Newark .649	1967—Richmond .574
1901—Rochester .642	Montreal (2nd)† .584	Toledo (3rd)† .525
1902—Toronto .669	1942—Newark .601	1968—Toledo .565
1903—Jersey City .642	Syracuse (3rd)† .513	Jacksonville (4th)† .514
1904—Buffalo .657	1943—Toronto .625	1969—Tidewater .563
1905—Providence .638	Syracuse (3rd)† .536	Syracuse (3rd)† .536
1906—Buffalo .607	1944—Baltimore‡ .553	1970—Syracuse‡ .600
1907—Toronto .619	1945—Montreal .621	1971—Rochester‡ .614
1908—Baltimore .593	Newark (2nd)† .582	1972—Louisville .563
1909—Rochester .596	1946—Montreal‡ .649	Tidewater (3rd)† .545
1910—Rochester .601	1947—Jersey City .610	1973—Charleston .586
1911—Rochester .645	Syracuse (3rd)† .575	Pawtucket y† .534
1912—Toronto .595	1948—Montreal‡ .614	1974—Memphis .613
1913—Newark .625	1949—Buffalo .584	Rochester x‡ .611
1914—Providence .617	Montreal (3rd)† .545	1975—Tidewater‡ .610
1915—Buffalo .632	1950—Rochester .609	1976—Rochester .638
1916—Buffalo .586	Baltimore (3rd)† .556	Syracuse (2nd)† .590
1917—Toronto .604	1951—Montreal‡ .617	1977—Pawtucket .571
1918—Toronto .693	1952—Montreal .629	Charleston (2nd)† .557
1919—Baltimore .671	Rochester (3rd)† .619	1978—Charleston .607
1920—Baltimore .719	1953—Rochester .630	Richmond (4th)† .511
1921—Baltimore .717	Montreal (2nd)† .586	1979—Columbus‡ .612
1922—Baltimore .689	1954—Toronto .630	1980—Columbus‡ .593
1923—Baltimore .677	Syracuse (4th)§ .510	1981—Columbus‡ .633
1924—Baltimore .709	1955—Montreal .617	1982—Tidewater (3rd)† .540
1925—Baltimore .633	Rochester (4th)† .497	Rochester .514
1926—Toronto .657	1956—Toronto .566	1983—Richmond .576
1927—Buffalo .667	Rochester (2nd)† .553	Tidewater† .511

*Won split-season playoff. †Won four-team playoff. ‡Won championship and four-team playoff. §Defeated Havana in game to decide fourth place, then won four-team playoff. xLeague was divided into Northern, Southern divisions. yLeague divided into American, National divisions. (NOTE—Known as Eastern League in 1884, New York State League in 1885, International League in 1886-87, International Association in 1888, International League in 1889-90, Eastern Association in 1891, and Eastern League from 1892 until 1912.)

STANDING OF CLUBS AT CLOSE OF SEASON, SEPTEMBER 3

Club	Col.	Me.	Tol.	Paw.	Tide.	Rich.	Syr.	Roch.	W.	L.	T.	Pct.	G.B.
Columbus (Yankees)	....	11	11	10	11	9	14	16	82	57	0	.590	....
Maine (Indians)	8	....	9	9	9	11	16	15	77	59	0	.566	3½
Toledo (Twins)	9	8	....	11	10	11	12	13	74	63	0	.540	7
Pawtucket (Red Sox)	10	11	9	....	11	10	13	11	75	65	0	.536	7½
Tidewater (Mets)	9	11	10	9	....	11	10	11	71	69	0	.507	11½
Richmond (Braves)	11	9	9	10	9	....	8	10	66	73	0	.475	16
Syracuse (Blue Jays)	6	4	8	7	10	11	....	12	58	81	0	.417	24
Rochester (Orioles)	4	5	7	9	9	10	8	....	52	88	0	.371	30½

Major league affiliations in parentheses.

Maine club represented Old Orchard Beach, Maine.

Tidewater club represented Norfolk and Portsmouth, Virginia.

PLAYOFFS—Pawtucket defeated Columbus, three games to one; Maine defeated Toledo, three games to none; Pawtucket defeated Maine, three games to two to win Governor's Cup.

REGULAR SEASON ATTENDANCE—Columbus, 520,478; Maine, 183,289; Pawtucket, 198,786; Richmond, 165,513; Rochester, 191,607; Syracuse, 141,499; Tidewater, 132,260; Toledo, 182,247. Total—1,715,679. Playoffs, 23,937. All-Star Game at Rochester, 2,378.

MANAGERS—Columbus, Carl Merrill; Maine, Doc Edwards; Pawtucket, Tony Torchia; Richmond, Eddie Haas (to July 20) and Bobby Dews; Rochester, Frank Verdi; Syracuse, Jim Beauchamp; Tidewater, Bob Schaefer; Toledo, Cal Ermer.

ALL-STAR TEAM—1B—Dan Briggs, Columbus; 2B—Rex Hudler, Columbus; 3B—Steve Lyons, Pawtucket; SS—Paul Zuvella, Richmond; OF—Milt Thompson, Richmond; Mitch Webster, Syracuse; John Christensen, Tidewater; C—Scott Bradley, Columbus; DH—Jerry Keller, Syracuse; Starting Pitcher—Brad Havens, Toledo; Relief Pitcher—Wes Gardner, Tidewater; Most Valuable Player—Scott Bradley, Columbus; Most Valuable Pitcher—Brad Havens, Toledo; Manager-of-the-Year—Tony Torchia, Pawtucket.

(Compiled by Howe News Bureau, Boston, Mass.)

CLUB BATTING

Club	Pct.	G.	AB.	R.	OR.	H.	TB.	2B.	3B.	HR.	RBI.	GW.	SH.	SF.	HP.	BB.	Int. BB.	SO.	SB.	CS.	LOB.
Columbus	.266	139	4615	657	554	1228	1859	219	41	110	592	76	46	45	20	454	27	765	51	39	967
Richmond	.265	139	4525	629	632	1199	1721	168	33	96	582	65	27	30	25	558	27	737	154	78	1005
Rochester	.259	140	4499	570	702	1163	1759	222	28	106	529	49	40	56	13	425	22	722	19	17	939
Tidewater	.257	140	4483	581	547	1151	1623	175	15	89	524	64	27	41	24	492	27	847	129	58	943
Maine	.257	136	4348	645	575	1119	1616	164	18	99	584	68	50	46	27	561	22	757	140	62	921
Pawtucket	.253	140	4473	706	637	1130	1745	183	21	130	649	71	33	40	18	711	33	852	143	77	981
Syracuse	.252	139	4473	554	730	1128	1705	181	30	112	525	54	51	42	18	453	12	780	63	32	930
Toledo	.252	137	4364	539	504	1098	1581	177	33	80	489	64	89	28	20	548	35	711	121	59	983

INDIVIDUAL BATTING

(Leading Qualifiers for Batting Championship—378 or More Plate Appearances)

°Bats lefthanded.   †Switch-hitter.

Player and Club	Pct.	G.	AB.	R.	H.	TB.	2B.	3B.	HR.	RBI.	GW.	SH.	SF.	HP.	BB.	Int. BB.	SO.	SB.	CS.
Bradley, Scott, Columbus°	.335	138	538	84	180	233	31	2	6	84	14	5	6	2	33	7	31	1	2
Tarver, LaSchelle, Tidewater°	.326	108	368	63	120	135	13	1	0	26	2	0	3	1	46	3	57	36	18
Christensen, John, Tidewater	.316	129	421	57	133	190	12	0	15	71	13	1	8	2	58	2	70	2	5
Zuvella, Paul, Richmond	.303	127	462	77	140	188	18	6	6	55	6	4	3	8	58	3	39	14	6
Sheets, Larry, Rochester°	.302	134	431	76	130	203	26	4	13	67	6	0	3	1	54	4	73	0	0
Webster, Mitchell, Syracuse†	.300	95	360	60	108	149	22	5	3	25	2	9	0	0	51	4	36	16	4
Hudler, Rex, Columbus	.292	114	394	49	115	146	26	1	1	35	4	2	1	3	16	1	61	11	7
Thompson, Milton, Richmond°°	.288	134	503	91	145	174	11	3	4	40	6	2	2	3	83	3	86	47	17
Wilson, Michael, Toledo	.287	132	460	70	132	158	13	5	1	46	10	16	3	4	94	1	45	48	29
Briggs, Daniel, Columbus°	.285	134	474	70	135	221	33	4	15	71	8	2	2	3	37	2	93	3	1

Departmental Leaders: G—Bradley, 138; AB—Bradley, 538; R—M. Thompson, Walker, 91; H—Bradley, 180; TB—L. Hernandez, 237; 2B—Briggs, 33; 3B—Meacham, Rodriguez, Zuvella, 6; HR—Keller, 28; RBI—Bradley, J. Wilson, 84; GWRBI—Bradley, Keller, 14; SH—Espinoza, M. Wilson, 16; SF—Rosado, 12; HP—Zuvella, 8; BB—M. Wilson, 94; IBB—Walker, 9; SO—J. Wilson, 113; SB—M. Wilson, 48; CS—M. Wilson, 29.

(All Players—Listed Alphabetically)

Player and Club	Pct.	G.	AB.	R.	H.	TB.	2B.	3B.	HR.	RBI.	GW.	SH.	SF.	HP.	BB.	Int. BB.	SO.	SB.	CS.
Anderson, Richard, Tidewater	.286	26	7	0	2	4	0	1	0	1	0	0	0	0	0	0	1	0	0
Ashford, Thomas, Rochester	.247	105	384	55	95	140	20	2	7	40	4	5	3	0	40	1	32	1	1
Baker, David, Toledo°	.226	131	442	54	100	160	20	2	12	47	5	6	1	0	64	5	104	0	2
Bando, Christopher, Maine†	.261	29	92	18	24	35	2	0	3	13	1	1	0	0	23	1	16	0	0
Barrett, Thomas, Columbus†	.381	5	21	3	8	9	1	0	0	0	0	0	0	0	2	0	3	0	1
Bettendorf, Jeffrey, Tidewater	.000	17	3	0	0	0	0	0	0	0	0	0	0	0	0	0	1	0	0
Bittiger, Jeffrey, Tidewater	.600	24	5	1	3	3	0	0	0	0	0	1	0	0	1	0	0	0	0
Blocker, Terry, Tidewater°	.220	115	386	45	85	106	10	1	3	31	3	1	2	1	28	7	60	12	3
Bonner, Robert, Rochester	.277	111	390	49	108	134	21	1	1	26	3	6	6	2	12	2	27	4	2
Bradford, Larry, Richmond	.333	35	3	0	1	1	0	0	0	0	0	0	0	0	0	0	1	0	0
Bradley, Scott, Columbus°	.335	138	538	84	180	233	31	2	6	84	14	5	6	2	33	7	31	1	2
Briggs, Daniel, Columbus°	.285	134	474	70	135	221	33	4	15	71	8	2	2	3	37	2	93	3	1
Brizzolara, Anthony, Richmond	.000	18	4	1	0	0	0	0	0	0	0	0	0	0	0	0	2	0	0
Broersma, Eric, Tidewater	.000	43	3	0	0	0	0	0	0	0	0	0	0	0	0	0	1	0	0
Burgess, Gus, Pawtucket°	.272	132	445	80	121	176	16	3	11	65	4	2	2	1	62	6	73	17	11
Bustabad, Juan, Pawtucket°	.126	41	103	10	13	17	4	0	0	5	0	2	0	0	8	0	16	1	3
Calise, Michael, Rochester	.235	104	315	41	74	138	11	1	17	45	4	0	5	0	55	2	110	0	0
Castillo, Manuel, Syracuse†	.257	91	292	26	75	104	14	3	3	36	5	2	7	0	17	0	23	1	2
Cerone, Richard, Columbus	.200	8	25	2	5	7	2	0	0	1	0	0	0	0	3	0	0	0	0
Chapman, Kelvin, Tidewater	.275	12	40	4	11	15	2	1	0	6	1	0	0	1	9	0	8	2	0
Christensen, John, Tidewater	.316	129	421	57	133	190	12	0	15	71	13	1	8	2	58	2	70	2	5
Clay, David, Richmond	.000	9	1	0	0	0	0	0	0	0	0	0	0	0	0	0	0	0	0
Comstock, Keith, Toledo†	.000	24	1	0	0	0	0	0	0	0	0	0	0	0	1	0	0	0	0
Craig, Rodney, Maine†	.267	122	416	71	111	169	16	0	14	63	10	7	4	2	66	6	56	21	13
Culmer, Wilfred, Maine	.200	16	40	12	8	17	0	0	3	9	0	0	1	2	11	0	12	0	2
Dalena, Peter, Columbus°	.111	10	27	1	3	3	0	0	0	0	0	0	0	0	3	0	8	0	0
David, Andre, Toledo°	.294	61	194	30	57	94	14	1	7	24	4	2	2	3	23	1	20	8	1
Davis, Michael, Pawtucket	.252	68	202	21	51	73	6	2	4	26	2	0	2	0	17	2	22	0	1
Dayett, Brian, Columbus	.301	45	166	26	50	77	8	2	5	24	4	0	0	1	21	1	16	1	4
Dayley, Kenneth, Richmond°	.000	9	6	0	0	0	0	0	0	0	0	0	0	0	1	0	3	0	0

Player and Club	Pct.	G.	AB.	R.	H.	TB.	2B.	3B.	HR.	RBI.	GW.	SH.	SF.	HP.	BB.	Int. BB.	SO.	SB.	CS.
DeLeon, Luis, Maine†	.103	28	68	8	7	9	2	0	0	6	1	0	2	0	3	0	20	0	1
Dent, Russell, Columbus	.250	17	60	4	15	19	1	0	1	5	2	2	2	1	0	6	0	0	
Dodson, Patrick, Pawtucket°	.257	114	292	51	75	140	17	0	16	51	10	0	1	3	82	3	75	2	1
Dugas, Shanie, Maine°	.253	115	372	68	94	156	13	2	15	49	4	4	0	0	51	3	103	5	1
Espino, Juan, Maine	.251	97	327	38	82	111	6	1	7	41	5	4	5	4	36	0	64	0	0
Espinoza, Alvaro, Toledo	.233	104	344	22	80	102	12	5	0	30	5	16	2	3	3	0	49	3	1
Evans, Barry, Maine	.329	53	164	15	54	67	8	1	1	21	4	3	3	2	13	1	18	0	1
Falcone, David, Rochester°	.213	61	169	20	36	59	6	1	5	15	0	1	1	0	26	4	45	0	0
Fernandez, C. Sidney, Tidewater°	.286	17	7	0	2	2	0	0	0	1	0	0	0	0	0	0	3	0	0
Fernandez, O. Antonio, Syracuse†	.255	26	94	12	24	25	1	0	0	6	0	1	1	0	13	0	9	1	3
Fisher, Brian, Richmond	.125	29	8	0	1	1	0	0	0	0	0	2	0	0	0	0	6	0	0
Flores, Gilberto, Tidewater	.246	43	126	14	31	39	5	0	1	12	2	3	0	0	20	0	18	3	4
Gagne, Gregory, Toledo	.280	70	236	31	66	104	7	2	9	27	0	2	1	1	34	2	52	2	3
Galasso, Robert, Richmond°	.000	31	2	0	0	0	0	0	0	0	0	0	0	0	0	0	2	0	0
Gallagher, David, Maine	.247	116	380	49	94	141	19	5	6	49	1	10	9	3	49	0	42	4	1
Gardner, Wesley, Tidewater	.000	40	1	0	0	0	0	0	0	0	0	0	0	0	0	0	0	0	0
Gates, Michael, Rochester°	.206	21	63	4	13	15	2	0	0	1	0	0	0	1	6	0	13	0	1
Gibbons, John, Tidewater	.256	65	211	31	54	83	9	1	6	27	2	0	2	0	20	1	50	1	1
Giles, Brian, Tidewater	.242	118	384	59	93	137	24	1	6	37	2	4	2	6	56	3	74	19	6
Gonzalez, Julian, Rochester°	.000	19	1	0	0	0	0	0	0	0	0	0	0	0	0	0	1	0	0
Gorman, Thomas, Tidewater°	.000	3	1	0	0	0	0	0	0	0	0	0	0	0	0	0	0	0	0
Graham, Lee, Pawtucket°	.244	97	340	43	83	98	10	1	1	30	3	2	1	0	29	0	36	15	9
Granger, L. Randle, Rochester†	.222	26	81	10	18	22	4	0	0	1	0	1	0	0	6	0	27	4	1
Gray, Lorenzo, Maine	.253	126	455	71	115	180	13	2	16	71	11	3	6	4	62	0	65	9	2
Gruber, Kelly, Syracuse	.269	97	342	53	92	171	12	2	21	55	5	0	1	7	23	0	67	12	2
Gulliver, Glenn, Rochester°	.216	63	185	35	40	61	12	0	3	13	2	1	2	1	44	3	16	1	0
Harper, Terry, Richmond	.324	59	216	41	70	109	3	3	10	38	6	0	1	3	34	2	33	2	4
Hart, Michael L., Toledo°	.271	92	329	37	89	135	11	4	9	48	4	5	3	0	41	8	43	6	1
Hayes, Thomas, Maine	.251	96	335	33	84	116	11	0	7	50	3	1	3	2	31	1	60	0	6
Heath, Kelly, Columbus	.249	108	350	72	87	138	17	5	8	38	2	6	3	0	33	1	57	12	2
Hernandez, Leonardo, Rochester	.275	136	512	66	141	237	25	4	21	83	9	1	5	0	21	2	73	3	2
Hernandez, Tobias, Syracuse	.188	60	165	18	31	39	6	1	0	11	0	8	1	1	7	0	29	1	0
Hobson, Clell, Columbus	.251	116	382	49	96	155	18	1	13	56	7	3	7	1	48	3	63	0	1
Holman, Q. Dale, Syracuse°	.261	106	387	45	101	156	23	4	8	60	6	5	5	0	42	2	78	0	3
Holman, R. Scott, Tidewater	.000	26	5	1	0	0	0	0	0	0	0	0	0	0	2	0	3	0	1
Hudler, Rex, Columbus	.292	114	394	49	115	146	26	1	1	35	4	2	1	3	16	1	61	11	7
Hundhammer, Paul, Pawtucket	.270	123	393	61	106	146	17	1	7	60	7	8	6	4	65	0	53	14	8
Hurdle, Clinton, Tidewater°	.243	128	412	60	100	180	15	1	21	64	11	1	3	0	79	6	107	0	1
Infante, Alexis, Syracuse	.222	72	225	27	50	58	6	1	0	7	0	5	1	1	14	0	33	7	3
Jackson, Ronnie, Rochester	.194	13	31	5	6	7	1	0	0	1	0	1	0	1	4	0	5	0	0
Javier, Stanley, Columbus†	.222	32	99	12	22	27	3	1	0	7	0	1	2	0	12	1	26	1	1
Johnson, Anthony, Syracuse	.263	23	76	10	20	21	1	0	0	6	0	1	1	0	7	0	16	5	3
Johnson, Bobby, Columbus	.154	5	13	1	2	5	0	0	1	4	1	0	0	0	1	1	8	0	0
Johnson, Joseph, Richmond	.000	4	1	0	0	0	0	0	0	0	0	0	0	0	1	0	1	0	0
Johnson, Randall, Toledo°	.222	24	63	7	14	18	4	0	0	6	0	1	0	0	6	1	15	0	0
Johnston, Christopher, Syracuse	.263	6	19	1	5	5	0	0	0	3	0	0	0	0	4	0	8	0	0
Jones, Craig, Richmond	.000	27	3	0	0	0	0	0	0	0	0	0	0	0	1	0	1	0	0
Jones, Ricky, Rochester	.224	38	107	13	24	46	4	0	6	16	1	1	2	1	6	0	24	0	0
Jones, Ross, Tidewater	.221	95	290	35	64	93	14	0	5	40	4	4	5	1	48	1	73	6	3
Keller, Charles, Syracuse	.249	124	438	70	109	203	10	0	28	82	14	1	5	3	55	3	94	0	0
Komminsk, Brad, Richmond	.257	42	144	23	37	69	11	3	5	28	3	0	2	0	31	1	20	8	2
LaFrancois, Roger, Richmond°	.184	50	152	9	28	37	6	0	1	9	2	0	0	1	9	0	23	0	1
Latham, William, Tidewater°	.200	21	10	0	2	2	0	0	0	0	0	1	0	0	1	0	4	0	0
Leach, Richard, Syracuse°	.304	23	79	16	24	43	6	2	3	8	1	0	1	0	13	0	8	0	0
Leach, Terry, 12 Rich.-31 Tide.	.000	43	2	0	0	0	0	0	0	0	0	0	0	0	0	0	0	0	0
Leary, Timothy, Tidewater	.333	11	6	1	2	4	2	0	0	1	0	0	0	0	0	0	2	0	0
Lickert, John, Pawtucket	.294	88	204	39	60	88	10	0	6	44	6	3	4	1	67	0	29	0	1
Linares, Rufino, Richmond	.296	57	216	26	64	96	13	5	3	39	4	0	2	0	13	2	21	3	2
Lindsey, William, Columbus	.136	8	22	2	3	8	0	1	1	1	0	0	0	0	0	0	1	0	0
Lisi, Riccardo, Richmond	.220	75	227	27	50	63	7	3	0	18	1	5	2	1	20	0	42	3	5
Lomastro, Gerardo, Toledo	.204	15	54	3	11	13	2	0	0	3	0	1	0	0	3	1	12	0	0
Lombardozzi, Stephen, Toledo	.249	119	385	57	96	140	15	1	9	31	3	7	1	2	37	0	57	3	0
Lyons, Stephen, Pawtucket°	.268	131	444	80	119	195	21	2	17	62	5	3	6	1	66	3	71	35	14
Maler, James, Tidewater	.208	32	106	7	22	31	3	0	2	10	0	0	1	1	8	1	17	0	1
Malpeso, David, Pawtucket	.277	100	329	37	91	132	10	2	9	53	7	0	2	1	32	3	71	1	0
Manrique, Fred, Syracuse	.282	129	517	63	146	189	15	5	6	45	7	6	3	2	29	0	61	14	7
Martin, Jerry, Tidewater	.250	6	24	4	6	11	2	0	1	5	0	0	1	0	1	0	6	0	0
Martz, Randy, Richmond°	.000	36	1	0	0	0	0	0	0	0	0	0	0	0	0	0	0	0	0
Mata, Victor, Columbus	.277	87	314	42	87	140	13	5	10	49	7	6	5	2	25	1	59	4	3
McGriff, Frederick, Syracuse°	.235	70	238	28	56	107	10	1	13	28	2	1	1	0	26	0	89	0	1
Meacham, Robert, Columbus†	.283	46	187	35	53	84	13	6	2	13	2	3	0	0	19	1	35	6	5
Mitchell, Charles, Pawtucket	.000	37	1	0	0	0	0	0	0	0	0	0	0	0	0	0	1	0	0
Mitchell, Kevin, Tidewater	.243	120	432	51	105	162	21	3	10	54	7	2	9	3	25	0	89	1	2
Mitchell, Robert, Toledo°	.272	85	276	47	75	102	19	4	0	26	4	6	1	0	64	6	37	10	5
Moore, Alvin, Columbus	.303	31	89	7	27	42	3	0	4	21	2	1	0	0	8	0	13	0	1
Mulligan, Robert, Toledo°	.000	22	2	0	0	0	0	0	0	0	0	0	0	0	0	0	2	0	0
Nandin, Robert, Syracuse†	.231	9	13	4	3	3	0	0	0	2	0	0	0	0	4	0	0	1	0
Nixon, Otis, Maine†	.277	72	253	42	70	77	5	1	0	22	2	6	2	0	44	0	45	39	10
O'Berry, P. Michael, Columbus	.225	70	187	17	42	60	4	1	4	26	3	4	6	1	20	0	36	1	0
Oquendo, Ismael, Rochester°	.230	29	87	11	20	32	2	2	2	11	0	0	2	0	5	0	19	0	0
Oquendo, Jose, Tidewater	.159	38	113	8	18	22	1	0	1	8	0	1	0	1	5	0	14	8	0
Owen, Lawrence, Richmond	.242	94	314	33	76	110	13	0	7	45	5	6	3	0	32	2	44	2	0
Pagel, Karl, Maine°	.229	35	109	21	25	49	6	0	6	20	1	0	1	0	33	2	33	2	1
Pagliarulo, Michael, Columbus†	.212	58	146	24	31	59	5	1	7	25	2	3	0	18	0	30	0	0	
Patterson, Michael, Columbus°	.252	100	301	44	76	122	14	4	8	34	5	1	2	1	42	2	60	6	5
Pautt, Juan, Pawtucket	.083	16	36	2	3	4	1	0	0	3	3	1	0	0	1	0	7	0	0
Payne, Michael, Richmond	.000	26	3	0	0	0	0	0	0	0	0	0	0	0	0	0	2	0	0
Petralli, Eugene, Maine†	.217	23	83	9	18	21	3	0	0	5	1	0	0	0	13	2	10	0	2
Poole, Mark, Syracuse	.308	10	39	5	12	15	3	0	0	3	0	0	0	0	1	0	6	0	0
Puckett, Kirby, Toledo	.263	21	80	9	21	26	2	0	1	5	0	2	1	0	4	0	14	8	2
Quinones, Luis, Maine†	.268	131	473	71	127	184	27	3	8	60	7	1	5	1	39	3	73	5	6
Ransom, Jeffrey, Rochester†	.185	23	65	5	12	22	4	0	2	8	1	0	0	1	4	0	19	0	0

Player and Club	Pct.	G.	AB.	R.	H.	TB.	2B.	3B.	HR.	RBI.	GW.	SH.	SF.	HP.	BB.	Int. BB.	SO.	SB.	CS.
Rayford, Floyd, Rochester	.056	7	18	1	1	4	0	0	1	1	0	0	0	0	3	0	1	0	0
Reed, Jeffrey, Toledo°	.266	94	301	30	80	111	16	3	3	35	6	4	1	2	37	3	35	1	3
Reiter, Gary, Richmond°	.500	41	2	0	1	1	0	0	0	0	0	0	0	0	0	0	1	0	0
Reynolds, Michael, Richmond°	.231	52	134	12	31	49	5	2	3	15	2	1	0	0	15	1	16	0	2
Reynolds, Ronn, Tidewater	.261	90	280	35	73	117	11	0	11	46	8	1	5	2	17	1	55	0	2
Rhomberg, Kevin, Maine	.236	49	157	27	37	48	8	0	1	16	0	1	1	2	36	0	20	9	6
Robertson, Andre, Columbus	.239	69	226	30	54	82	8	1	6	19	2	1	5	2	8	1	42	1	4
Rodriguez, Victor, Rochester	.274	132	478	54	131	183	22	6	6	46	3	7	4	3	32	0	53	0	1
Romine, Kevin, Pawtucket	.253	113	336	62	85	133	10	1	12	72	12	1	5	0	83	4	66	13	7
Rooney, Patrick, Columbus	.193	77	187	26	36	66	2	2	8	25	2	4	0	1	15	1	39	3	1
Rosado, Luis, Rochester	.291	85	258	18	75	101	11	0	5	48	3	4	12	0	14	0	27	0	1
Ruiz, Manuel, Richmond	.077	5	13	0	1	1	0	0	0	0	0	1	0	0	1	0	3	0	1
Runge, Paul, Richmond	.239	91	301	44	72	111	9	3	8	41	6	2	3	2	55	2	57	9	4
Saavedra, Edwin, Maine	.300	3	10	2	3	3	0	0	0	2	1	0	0	0	1	0	2	0	0
Sanchez, Orlando, Rochester°	.305	74	223	23	68	100	17	3	3	34	4	3	3	1	15	2	33	0	0
Santana, Rafael, Tidewater	.278	77	255	34	71	80	6	0	1	23	3	2	0	0	11	0	19	10	2
Schaefer, Jeffrey, Rochester	.264	31	91	10	24	31	5	1	0	3	0	3	0	0	9	0	20	0	0
Schiraldi, Calvin, Tidewater	.000	4	3	0	0	0	0	0	0	0	0	0	0	0	0	0	1	0	0
Schmidt, August, Syracuse	.201	46	144	14	29	35	4	1	0	8	0	2	1	0	16	0	25	0	1
Schmitz, Daniel, Toledo°	.197	63	157	18	31	35	4	0	0	13	0	5	3	0	23	1	16	1	0
Sheets, Larry, Rochester°	.302	134	431	76	130	203	26	4	13	67	6	0	3	1	54	4	73	0	0
Shepherd, Ronald, Syracuse	.220	113	363	37	80	138	16	3	12	50	2	1	3	2	41	0	99	6	3
Shields, Stephen, Richmond	.000	39	5	0	0	0	0	0	0	0	0	0	0	0	0	0	1	0	0
Simunic, Douglas, Maine	.600	1	5	1	3	4	1	0	0	0	0	0	0	0	0	0	1	0	0
Smith, Kenneth, Richmond°	.272	136	453	72	123	175	17	4	9	59	9	0	2	4	92	5	99	32	11
Smith, Raymond, Toledo	.231	80	247	24	57	76	10	3	1	26	4	4	2	2	8	2	19	1	1
Smith, Zane, Richmond°	.286	19	7	0	2	2	0	0	0	0	0	0	0	0	0	0	2	0	0
Sorce, Samuel, Toledo	.125	16	24	1	3	3	0	0	0	0	2	0	0	0	1	0	7	0	0
Sosa, Miguel, Richmond	.295	64	258	34	76	132	11	0	15	41	3	1	2	1	7	0	50	3	2
Stearns, John, Tidewater	.250	10	28	4	7	9	0	1	0	1	0	0	1	0	5	0	7	2	1
Stefero, John, Rochester°	.067	5	15	0	1	1	0	0	0	1	0	0	1	0	3	0	8	0	0
Stenhouse, David, Syracuse	.235	89	247	16	58	78	8	0	4	27	4	6	3	0	29	0	42	0	0
Sullivan, Marc, Pawtucket	.204	116	383	54	78	139	14	1	15	63	4	6	4	5	47	0	105	1	1
Tarver, LaSchelle, Tidewater°	.326	108	368	63	120	135	13	1	0	26	2	0	3	1	46	3	57	36	18
Taylor, Dwight, Maine°	.271	108	406	64	110	142	16	2	4	50	7	8	4	3	41	3	53	46	16
Thompson, Milton, Richmond°	.288	134	503	91	145	174	11	3	4	40	6	2	2	3	83	3	86	47	17
Thompson, Timothy, Syracuse°	.232	54	177	16	41	60	8	1	3	22	2	3	0	2	25	3	32	0	0
Tillman, Kerry, Tidewater	.219	44	151	17	33	49	5	1	3	13	1	3	0	2	4	0	27	4	3
Tutt, Johnny, Rochester	.305	27	95	11	29	35	3	0	1	9	2	1	1	0	9	0	11	1	4
Ullger, Scott, Toledo	.258	113	357	50	92	143	16	1	11	58	11	4	5	3	58	2	84	1	2
Valdez, Julio, Pawtucket†	.254	55	118	15	30	55	7	0	6	21	0	2	2	0	9	0	28	1	2
Valle, John, Rochester	.190	68	205	21	39	71	9	1	7	28	2	4	4	0	28	1	39	0	0
Vargas, Leonel, Richmond	.260	121	458	58	119	172	21	1	10	62	6	1	3	0	19	1	66	18	11
Walker, Cleotha, Pawtucket†	.263	130	499	91	131	221	26	5	18	51	6	4	4	0	80	9	88	42	17
Weaver, James, Toledo°	.230	111	409	49	94	161	12	5	15	64	8	6	2	0	47	2	99	29	9
Webster, Mitchell, Syracuse†	.300	95	360	60	108	149	22	5	3	25	2	9	0	0	51	4	36	16	4
Whisenton, Larry, Richmond°	.266	98	293	48	78	114	12	0	8	42	3	1	2	0	55	4	56	13	4
Whittemore, Reginald, Pawtucket	.241	107	348	60	84	128	14	3	8	43	4	0	1	2	63	3	111	1	2
Williams, Dallas, Rochester°	.242	67	223	25	54	73	11	1	2	17	2	0	2	1	20	0	27	5	3
Wilson, James, Maine	.261	133	490	56	128	194	19	1	15	84	11	1	3	4	37	1	113	0	0
Wilson, Michael, Toledo	.287	132	460	70	132	158	13	5	1	46	10	16	3	4	94	1	45	48	29
Wilson, Phillip, Maine	.196	17	46	2	9	9	0	0	0	3	1	1	0	0	3	0	11	0	0
Winningham, Herman, Tidewater°	.281	115	406	50	114	149	20	3	3	47	5	2	1	1	48	2	81	23	5
Winters, Matthew, Columbus°	.248	130	407	57	101	156	17	4	10	54	9	3	1	2	90	4	80	1	1
Woods, Alvis, Syracuse°	.248	85	258	33	64	106	16	1	8	41	4	1	5	2	36	0	25	0	0
Young, Michael, Rochester†	.333	20	72	17	24	44	6	1	4	15	3	1	0	0	9	1	19	0	1
Zuvella, Paul, Richmond	.303	127	462	77	140	188	18	6	6	55	6	4	3	8	58	3	39	14	6

The following pitchers, listed alphabetically by club, with games in parentheses, had no plate appearances, primarily through use of designated hitters:

COLUMBUS—Brown, Curtis (32); Cappuzzello, George (23); Christiansen, Clay (22); Cooper, Donald (41); Cowley, Joseph (17); Deshaies, James (18); Faulk, Kelly (19); Fowler, Don (8); Hickey, Kevin (5); Johnson, Jerry (2); Montefusco, John (3); Murray, Dale (8); Nielson, Scott (11); Patterson, Scott (11); Rasmussen, Dennis (6); Rasmussen, James (4); Rijo, Jose (11); Scott, Kelly (25); Silva, Mark (42).

MAINE—Anderson, Karl (40); Aponte, Luis (10); Baller, Jay (15); Barkley, Jeffrey (51); Barnes, Richard (29); Comer, Steven (7); Elston, Guy (26); Farr, Steven (6); Farrell, John (5); Fuson, Robin (6); Glynn, Edward (22); MacWhorter, Keith (3); Marsden, Steven (4); Reed, Jerry (27); Romero, Ramon (27); Schulze, Donald (2); Siwy, James (7); Smith, Leroy (12); Ujdur, Gerald (26).

PAWTUCKET—Boyd, Dennis (5); Brown, Michael (12); Burtt, Dennis (26); Clemens, Roger (7); Crawford, Steven (7); Dale, Charles (6); Denman, Brian (16); Dorsey, James (41); Fuson, Robin (13); Gale, Richard (15); Gnacinski, Paul (30); Herron, Anthony (36); Kane, Kevin (15); Mecerod, George (17); Moloney, William (1); Rochford, Michael (31).

RICHMOND—Boris, Paul (7); Dedmon, Jeffrey (6); Leach, Terry (12).

ROCHESTER—Arnold, Tony (14); Barr, James (10); Brito, Jose (22); Brown, Mark (44); Carlucci, Richard (39); Concepcion, Carlos (6); Dooner, Glenn (13); Heise, Larry (1); Hoover, John (5); Kucharski, Joseph (25); Martin, John (18); Morogiello, Daniel (25); Oliveras, Francisco (12); Pacella, John (22); Ramirez, Allan (18); Snell, Nathaniel (6); Swaggerty, William (12); Underwood, Patrick (3); Welchel, Donald (9); Werly, James (11); Willsher, Christopher (4).

SYRACUSE—Baker, James (35); Bomback, Mark (21); Cerutti, John (29); Clark, Bryan (6); Clarke, Stanley (29); Eichhorn, Mark (36); Gillam, Donald (24); Harper, Devallon (20); Lukish, Thomas (15); McLaughlin, Colin (5); Morgan, Michael (34); Musselman, Ronald (26); Proly, Michael (13); Rodgers, Timothy (15); Shanks, William (1); Shipanoff, David (5); Taylor, Johnny (2); Walsh, David (9); Williams, Matthew (32).

TIDEWATER—Gaff, Brent (4); Glynn, Edward (23); Huffman, Phillip (17); Olwine, Edward (50); Pickett, Richard (12); Tibbs, Jay (8).

TOLEDO—Field, Gregory (28); Havens, Bradley (25); Hodge, Eddie (3); Klawitter, Thomas (26); Lysander, Richard (28); O'Connor, Jack (48); Pashnick, Larry (12); Pettibone, Harry (11); Walters, Michael (2); Whitehouse, Leonard (4); Williams, Alberto (3); Yett, Richard (26).

GRAND SLAM HOME RUNS—Burgess, 3; Gibbons, Hundhammer, 2 each; Bando, Briggs, Gray, Gruber, L. Hernandez, Hobson, Ro. Jones, Keller, Lickert, Malpeso, J. Martin, Pagel, M. Reynolds, Rooney, Runge, R. Smith, Stenhouse, Valdez, J. Wilson, Zuvella, 1 each.

AWARDED FIRST BASE ON CATCHER'S INTERFERENCE—Lombardozzi 7 (Owen 2, Bando, Cerone, Espino, T. Hernandez, Stenhouse); I. Oquendo (Lindsey); Quinones (Bradley); Webster (Espino).

CLUB FIELDING

Club	Pct.	G.	PO.	A.	E.	DP.	PB.
Tidewater	.978	140	3544	1539	117	144	14
Columbus	.973	139	3601	1548	144	157	15
Richmond	.973	139	3514	1470	138	143	9
Toledo	.973	137	3549	1411	136	128	14
Maine	.972	136	3479	1335	138	115	21
Rochester	.970	140	3487	1460	155	152	16
Pawtucket	.966	140	3600	1505	182	117	16
Syracuse	.966	139	3522	1489	175	143	28

*Throws lefthanded.

INDIVIDUAL FIELDING
FIRST BASEMEN

Player and Club	Pct.	G.	PO.	A.	E.	DP.
Ashford, Rochester	.978	20	159	15	4	24
Baker, Toledo	.997	35	284	16	1	29
Bando, Maine	.984	9	57	4	1	5
BRIGGS, Columbus*	.993	117	939	84	7	108
Calise, Rochester	.984	31	241	13	4	19
Castillo, Syracuse	.990	12	90	5	1	8
Christensen, Tidewater	1.000	2	7	1	0	0
Culmer, Maine	1.000	4	27	3	0	1
Dalena, Columbus	1.000	4	35	0	0	4
David, Toledo*	.962	7	48	2	2	7
Dodson, Pawtucket*	.988	86	667	48	9	55
Evans, Maine	1.000	2	11	1	0	0
Falcone, Rochester	.989	56	428	31	5	40
Gray, Maine	1.000	10	44	3	0	2
Hernandez, Rochester	.987	10	66	9	1	8
Hobson, Columbus	.989	24	159	13	2	20
Hurdle, Tidewater	.992	98	895	47	8	88
Jackson, Rochester	1.000	4	24	3	0	2
Johnson, Toledo*	1.000	13	76	4	0	8
Jones, Tidewater	1.000	7	64	7	0	5
Keller, Syracuse	.984	8	58	2	1	9
Leach, Syracuse*	.980	6	47	3	1	7
Lisi, Richmond	1.000	3	15	2	0	2
Maler, Tidewater	.985	31	244	16	4	31
McGriff, Syracuse*	.996	70	644	45	3	57
Mitchell, Tidewater	.964	7	49	5	2	7
Oquendo, Rochester*	.986	25	199	18	3	29
Petralli, Maine	.846	2	11	0	2	1
Reynolds, Tidewater	.800	1	4	0	1	0
Rhomberg, Maine	.985	33	248	19	4	26
Rosado, Rochester	1.000	7	33	7	0	4
Runge, Richmond	1.000	2	4	0	0	0
Santana, Tidewater	1.000	2	8	0	0	1
K. Smith, Richmond	.989	136	1159	56	13	121
R. Smith, Toledo	.950	4	16	3	1	2
Stearns, Tidewater	1.000	2	15	3	0	2
Sullivan, Pawtucket	1.000	10	26	2	0	1
Thompson, Syracuse*	.985	48	424	25	7	54
Ullger, Toledo	.994	91	722	54	5	68
Valle, Rochester	1.000	3	25	0	0	4
Whittemore, Pawtucket	.987	72	544	46	8	49
Wilson, Maine	.988	86	715	53	9	71
Winters, Columbus	.986	22	124	12	2	17

SECOND BASEMEN

Player and Club	Pct.	G.	PO.	A.	E.	DP.
Bonner, Rochester	.960	5	9	15	1	3
Castillo, Syracuse	.976	24	35	46	2	10
Chapman, Tidewater	.964	12	17	37	2	6
DeLeon, Maine	.967	13	26	32	2	2
DUGAS, Maine	.986	102	206	271	7	68
Evans, Maine	.992	29	44	74	1	18
Flores, Tidewater	.889	2	3	5	1	0
Gagne, Toledo	.980	14	18	31	1	8
Gates, Rochester	1.000	3	5	13	0	2
Giles, Tidewater	.973	105	223	315	15	75
Gulliver, Rochester	.875	2	3	4	1	0
Heath, Columbus	.971	37	63	72	4	17
Hudler, Columbus	.975	113	266	348	16	95
Hundhammer, Pawtucket	.966	78	130	182	11	41
Jones, Tidewater	.989	20	34	52	1	16
Lisi, Richmond	.945	20	42	62	6	9
Lombardozzi, Toledo	.976	100	207	249	11	61
Manrique, Syracuse	.961	121	225	364	24	81
Nandin, Syracuse	.958	4	9	14	1	5
Quinones, Maine	1.000	1	4	2	0	1
Reynolds, Richmond	.927	9	21	17	3	7
Rhomberg, Maine	.857	1	1	5	1	0
Robertson, Columbus	1.000	1	4	2	0	1
Rodriguez, Rochester	.980	128	272	403	14	91
Ruiz, Richmond	.917	5	5	6	1	0
Runge, Richmond	.973	49	120	166	8	51
Santana, Tidewater	1.000	6	15	16	0	6
Schaefer, Rochester	1.000	5	9	12	0	4
Schmitz, Toledo	.980	25	42	58	2	15
Sorce, Toledo	.889	2	4	4	1	1
Sosa, Richmond	.980	58	131	169	6	39
Ullger, Toledo	.974	10	18	19	1	6
Walker, Pawtucket	.961	89	160	231	16	44

THIRD BASEMEN

Player and Club	Pct.	G.	PO.	A.	E.	DP.
Ashford, Rochester	.915	83	53	129	17	10
Baker, Toledo	.945	83	42	165	12	16
Barrett, Columbus	1.000	2	2	3	0	2
Bonner, Rochester	1.000	6	7	14	0	1
Bradley, Columbus	.909	6	1	9	1	0
Calise, Rochester	.692	7	2	7	4	0
Castillo, Syracuse	.931	50	37	98	10	13
Davis, Pawtucket	.935	38	35	66	7	10
DeLeon, Maine	.889	5	1	7	1	1
Dugas, Maine	.917	11	5	17	2	0
Evans, Maine	.975	19	6	33	1	1
Gagne, Toledo	.889	41	26	102	16	5
Giles, Tidewater	1.000	1	4	2	0	0
GRAY, Maine	.957	112	85	184	12	23
Gruber, Syracuse	.924	81	54	154	17	11
Gulliver, Rochester	.887	27	23	32	7	2
Hayes, Richmond	.910	82	66	136	20	16
Heath, Columbus	.831	34	27	27	11	4
L. Hernandez, Rochester	.931	15	6	21	2	1
Hobson, Columbus	.940	67	48	108	10	11
Hundhammer, Pawtucket	.875	1	2	5	1	1
Hurdle, Tidewater	1.000	7	2	4	0	0
Ri. Jones, Tidewater	1.000	1	1	3	0	1
Ro. Jones, Tidewater	1.000	21	8	29	0	1
Lyons, Pawtucket	.925	112	98	209	25	19
Manrique, Syracuse	1.000	1	0	2	0	1
Mitchell, Tidewater	.933	109	65	215	20	19
Moore, Columbus	.667	1	0	2	1	0
O'Berry, Columbus	.000	1	0	0	1	0
Pagliarulo, Columbus	.902	55	26	93	13	14
Reynolds, Richmond	.970	32	15	50	2	7
Robertson, Columbus	.941	5	3	13	1	5
Runge, Richmond	.978	32	23	66	23	7
Santana, Tidewater	.935	10	8	21	2	4
Schaefer, Rochester	.970	10	10	22	1	6
Schmidt, Syracuse	.938	10	11	19	2	0
Schmitz, Toledo	1.000	17	10	22	0	4
Sorce, Toledo	.714	4	1	4	2	0
Stearns, Tidewater	1.000	2	2	2	0	0
Tillman, Tidewater	.857	2	2	4	1	0
Ullger, Toledo	1.000	2	1	1	0	0
Walker, Pawtucket	.923	6	4	8	1	0

SHORTSTOPS

Player and Club	Pct.	G.	PO.	A.	E.	DP.
Bonner, Rochester	.955	86	144	239	18	60
Bustabad, Pawtucket	.927	39	40	75	9	13
Castillo, Syracuse	1.000	1	1	4	0	0
Davis, Pawtucket	.921	23	21	49	6	10
DeLeon, Maine	1.000	7	3	11	0	1
Dent, Columbus	.961	14	23	50	3	10
Dugas, Maine	1.000	2	6	9	0	1
Espinoza, Toledo	.959	104	157	293	19	64
Fernandez, Syracuse	.959	26	46	72	5	23
Gagne, Toledo	.942	16	14	35	3	7
Gates, Rochester	.949	18	26	48	4	8
Giles, Tidewater	.980	11	21	27	1	3
Gulliver, Rochester	.889	5	3	5	1	0
Heath, Columbus	.916	19	35	52	8	8
Hundhammer, Pawtucket	.926	63	78	161	19	26
Infante, Syracuse	.938	72	88	229	21	43
Ri. Jones, Rochester	.935	29	27	60	6	13
Ro. Jones, Tidewater	.957	42	57	122	8	28
Lisi, Richmond	1.000	3	6	5	0	2
Lombardozzi, Toledo	.968	21	30	61	3	10
Lyons, Pawtucket	.750	1	3	0	1	0
Manrique, Syracuse	.886	15	8	23	4	5

SHORTSTOPS—Continued

Player and Club	Pct.	G.	PO.	A.	E.	DP.
Meacham, Columbus	.935	46	67	133	14	28
Oquendo, Tidewater	.988	37	54	111	2	24
Pagliarulo, Columbus	1.000	2	1	2	0	1
Quinones, Maine	.926	130	209	328	43	73
Reynolds, Richmond	.800	2	1	3	1	0
Robertson, Columbus	.965	64	102	205	11	41
Runge, Richmond	.889	10	16	32	6	10
Santana, Tidewater	.958	62	76	195	12	44
Schaefer, Rochester	.987	16	25	50	1	10
Schmidt, Syracuse	.937	36	46	102	10	25
Schmitz, Toledo	.913	9	6	15	2	2
Stearns, Tidewater	1.000	1	4	1	0	0
Valdez, Pawtucket	.926	50	55	108	13	21
ZUVELLA, Richmond	.975	127	219	409	16	85

OUTFIELDERS

Player and Club	Pct.	G.	PO.	A.	E.	DP.
Baker, Toledo	1.000	1	2	0	0	0
Blocker, Tidewater*	.973	105	215	2	6	0
Bonner, Rochester	1.000	15	26	2	0	1
Bradley, Columbus	.974	64	107	4	3	1
Briggs, Columbus*	.909	15	17	3	2	1
Burgess, Pawtucket*	.968	132	234	10	8	0
CHRISTENSEN, Tidewater	.994	118	170	6	1	2
Craig, Maine	.989	115	251	14	3	1
Culmer, Maine	.750	3	3	0	1	0
David, Toledo*	.976	26	39	2	1	0
Dayett, Columbus	.979	44	91	1	2	1
Dodson, Pawtucket*	1.000	10	14	0	0	0
Flores, Tidewater	1.000	14	15	0	0	0
Gallagher, Maine	.986	84	208	7	3	3
Graham, Pawtucket*	.976	93	204	3	5	1
Granger, Rochester	.963	23	51	1	2	0
Gray, Maine	1.000	12	25	1	0	0
Gruber, Syracuse	.960	16	22	2	1	1
Harper, Richmond	.969	55	118	7	4	1
Hart, Toledo*	.985	90	193	6	3	1
Heath, Columbus	1.000	10	13	0	0	0
Hernandez, Rochester	.940	112	176	12	12	4
Holman, Syracuse	.959	106	180	5	8	0
Jackson, Rochester	1.000	4	10	0	0	0
Javier, Columbus	.976	32	77	4	2	1
A. Johnson, Syracuse	.938	20	28	2	2	0
R. Johnson, Toledo*	1.000	1	1	0	0	0
Jones, Tidewater	1.000	14	14	1	0	0
Komminsk, Richmond	.959	37	66	4	3	1
Leach, Syracuse*	.960	17	23	1	1	1
Lickert, Pawtucket	1.000	29	25	5	0	2
Linares, Richmond	.960	15	24	0	1	0
Lisi, Richmond	.973	41	68	3	2	2
Lomastro, Toledo	1.000	1	7	0	0	0
Lyons, Pawtucket	1.000	25	40	2	0	0
Malpeso, Pawtucket	.950	13	19	0	1	0
Martin, Tidewater	1.000	6	3	0	0	0
Mata, Columbus	.986	87	200	6	3	1
R. Mitchell, Toledo*	.989	84	186	2	2	0
Moore, Columbus	1.000	5	1	0	0	0
Nixon, Maine	.995	70	206	7	1	1
Pagel, Maine	1.000	7	7	0	0	0
Patterson, Columbus	.989	91	168	7	2	2
Pautt, Pawtucket	.882	16	14	1	2	0
Petralli, Maine	.846	5	10	1	2	0
Puckett, Toledo	.923	21	35	1	3	0
Quinones, Maine	1.000	3	4	0	0	0
Ransom, Rochester	1.000	1	1	0	0	0
Rhomberg, Maine	.905	11	18	1	2	1
Romine, Pawtucket	.977	109	202	12	5	0
Rooney, Columbus	1.000	69	77	3	0	1
Sanchez, Rochester	.917	7	10	1	1	0
Schmidt, Syracuse	1.000	1	1	0	0	0
Schmitz, Toledo	1.000	1	3	0	0	0
Sheets, Rochester	.991	129	201	19	2	5
Shepherd, Syracuse	.961	110	241	7	10	1
Tarver, Tidewater*	1.000	53	97	0	0	0
Taylor, Maine*	.988	107	234	9	3	1
Thompson, Richmond	.968	132	317	13	11	1
Tillman, Tidewater	.983	37	54	4	1	1
Tutt, Rochester	.979	25	47	0	1	0
Ullger, Toledo	1.000	5	5	0	0	0
Valle, Rochester	.972	62	98	5	3	1
Vargas, Richmond	.948	83	124	3	7	1
Walker, Pawtucket	.953	58	59	2	3	0
Weaver, Toledo*	.921	71	114	3	10	2
Webster, Syracuse*	.972	95	239	7	7	1
Whisenton, Richmond*	.983	66	113	6	2	1
Williams, Rochester*	.971	54	128	8	4	2
M. Wilson, Toledo	.966	121	247	12	9	1
P. Wilson, Maine	1.000	1	2	0	0	0
Winningham, Tidewater	.983	112	228	8	4	1
Winters, Columbus	.988	64	82	2	1	1
Woods, Syracuse*	.984	60	119	4	2	0
Young, Rochester	.929	19	39	0	3	0

CATCHERS

Player and Club	Pct.	G.	PO.	A.	E.	DP.	PB
Baker, Toledo	1.000	1	3	0	0	0	0
Bando, Maine	.957	16	81	8	4	1	1
Bradley, Columbus	.986	73	324	37	5	5	6
Cerone, Columbus	.979	8	42	5	1	0	0
DeLeon, Maine	1.000	1	1	1	0	0	0
Espino, Maine	.978	83	432	47	11	4	13
Falcone, Rochester	1.000	1	2	0	0	1	0
Gibbons, Tidewater	.982	41	199	20	4	1	3
Hernandez, Syracuse	.981	58	278	29	6	4	7
Hurdle, Tidewater	.993	21	139	9	1	0	7
Johnson, Columbus	1.000	1	1	0	0	0	0
LaFrancois, Richmond	.992	48	234	22	2	4	5
Lickert, Pawtucket	.992	46	233	29	2	2	2
Lindsey, Columbus	.897	8	30	5	4	0	0
Malpeso, Pawtucket	1.000	7	33	0	0	0	2
O'Berry, Columbus	.980	69	356	44	8	5	9
Owen, Richmond	.978	93	572	62	14	8	4
Petralli, Maine	.982	17	101	10	2	3	0
Poole, Syracuse	1.000	10	44	8	0	0	3
Ransom, Rochester	.990	20	86	10	1	1	3
Rayford, Rochester	.968	5	25	5	1	1	1
REED, Toledo	.992	83	546	43	5	2	10
Reynolds, Tidewater	.988	83	453	25	6	3	3
Rhomberg, Maine	1.000	3	21	1	0	0	4
Rosado, Rochester	.987	72	414	50	6	9	7
Sanchez, Rochester	.972	48	284	24	9	7	5
Simunic, Maine	1.000	1	7	0	0	0	0
Smith, Columbus	.995	62	379	38	2	4	4
Sorce, Toledo	1.000	2	5	1	0	0	0
Stearns, Tidewater	.929	3	11	2	1	1	1
Stefero, Rochester	.905	5	18	1	2	0	0
Stenhouse, Syracuse	.984	86	442	42	8	3	18
Sullivan, Pawtucket	.986	98	574	57	9	5	12
Wilson, Maine	.980	17	84	13	2	0	3

PITCHERS

Player and Club	Pct.	G.	PO.	A.	E.	DP.
K. Anderson, Maine	.950	40	9	10	1	0
R. Anderson, Tidewater	.978	26	6	38	1	4
Aponte, Maine	1.000	10	0	1	0	0
Arnold, Rochester	.955	14	6	15	1	1
Baker, Syracuse	.889	35	5	11	2	1
Baller, Maine	.897	15	9	17	3	1
Barkley, Maine	1.000	51	5	4	0	0
Barnes, Maine*	.933	29	1	13	1	0
Barr, Rochester	.929	10	7	6	1	1
Bettendorf, Tidewater	.947	17	1	17	1	1
Bittiger, Tidewater	.976	24	15	26	1	1
Bomback, Syracuse	.833	21	6	4	2	1
Boris, Richmond	1.000	7	0	1	0	0
Boyd, Pawtucket	1.000	5	2	3	0	0
Bradford, Richmond*	1.000	35	2	5	0	0
Briggs, Columbus*	1.000	5	0	2	0	0
Brito, Rochester	.667	22	0	4	2	1
Brizzolara, Richmond	1.000	18	3	12	0	0
Broersma, Toledo	1.000	20	1	8	0	1
C. Brown, Columbus	.955	32	7	14	1	1
Ma. Brown, Rochester	.950	44	3	16	1	2
Mi. Brown, Pawtucket	.947	12	9	9	1	1
Burtt, Pawtucket	.867	26	12	27	6	3
Cappuzzello, Columbus*	.944	23	7	10	1	0
Carlucci, Rochester	.870	39	8	12	3	2
Cerutti, Syracuse*	1.000	29	7	17	0	0
Christiansen, Columbus	1.000	22	6	20	0	2
Clark, Syracuse*	1.000	6	0	8	0	1
Clarke, Syracuse*	.833	29	0	5	1	0
Clay, Richmond	1.000	9	0	3	0	0
Clemens, Pawtucket	.833	7	2	8	2	0
Comer, Maine	.917	7	5	6	1	1

PITCHERS—Continued

Player and Club	Pct.	G.	PO.	A.	E.	DP.	Player and Club	Pct.	G.	PO.	A.	E.	DP.
Comstock, Toledo*	.903	23	8	20	3	2	McLaughlin, Syracuse	1.000	5	1	1	0	0
Concepcion, Rochester	1.000	6	0	2	0	1	Mecerod, Pawtucket	.958	17	6	17	1	1
Cooper, Columbus	.964	41	6	21	1	2	Mitchell, Pawtucket	.931	37	9	18	2	1
Cowley, Columbus	1.000	17	8	24	0	2	Montefusco, Columbus	1.000	3	1	3	0	0
Crawford, Pawtucket	1.000	7	2	9	0	0	Morgan, Syracuse	.932	34	17	24	3	3
Dale, Pawtucket	1.000	6	1	3	0	0	Morogiello, Rochester*	1.000	25	4	8	0	1
Dayley, Richmond*	1.000	9	0	6	0	0	Mulligan, Toledo*	.938	21	4	11	1	5
Dedmon, Richmond	1.000	6	1	2	0	0	Murray, Columbus	1.000	8	1	1	0	0
Denman, Pawtucket	.913	16	6	15	2	1	Musselman, Syracuse	.889	26	3	5	1	1
Deshaies, Columbus*	.955	18	7	14	1	0	Nielson, Columbus	.950	11	6	13	1	2
Dooner, Rochester	.750	13	2	1	1	0	O'Connor, Toledo*	1.000	48	1	10	0	0
Dorsey, Pawtucket	.857	41	3	9	2	1	Oliveras, Rochester	1.000	12	1	2	0	0
Eichhorn, Syracuse	.931	36	10	17	2	0	Olwine, Tidewater*	.923	50	10	14	2	1
Elston, Maine	.909	26	4	6	1	0	Pacella, Rochester	.900	22	7	11	2	0
Farr, Maine	1.000	6	5	9	0	0	Pashnick, Toledo	.944	12	7	10	1	0
Farrell, Maine	.875	5	1	6	1	0	Patterson, Columbus	1.000	11	1	2	0	0
Faulk, Columbus	1.000	19	10	14	0	0	Payne, Richmond	.966	26	7	21	1	1
Fernandez, Tidewater*	.889	17	3	5	1	2	Pettibone, Toledo	.810	11	4	13	4	0
Field, Toledo	1.000	28	5	11	0	1	Pickett, Tidewater*	.857	12	1	5	1	1
Fisher, Richmond	.951	29	5	34	2	3	Proly, Syracuse	.857	13	2	4	1	0
Fowler, Columbus	.900	8	2	7	1	0	Ramirez, Rochester	1.000	18	9	14	0	0
Fuson, 6 Maine-13 Paw	.900	19	9	18	3	0	D. Rasmussen, Columbus*	1.000	6	2	8	0	1
Gaff, Tidewater	1.000	4	0	9	0	2	J. Rasmussen, Columbus	1.000	4	2	1	0	0
Galasso, Richmond	.900	30	1	8	1	0	Reed, Maine	.980	27	17	31	1	2
Gale, Pawtucket	.923	15	4	8	1	0	Reiter, Richmond*	1.000	41	0	5	0	0
Gardner, Tidewater	1.000	40	2	10	0	0	Rijo, Columbus	1.000	11	5	9	0	0
Gillam, Syracuse*	.929	24	3	10	1	0	Rochford, Pawtucket*	.935	31	9	20	2	0
Glynn, 22 Maine-23 Tide.*	1.000	45	0	5	0	1	Rodgers, Syracuse	.929	15	3	10	1	0
Gnacinski, Pawtucket	1.000	30	8	20	0	1	Romero, Maine*	1.000	27	0	12	0	1
Gonzalez, Rochester*	1.000	19	2	8	0	0	Schiraldi, Tidewater	1.000	4	2	3	0	0
Gorman, Tidewater*	1.000	3	0	4	0	0	Schulze, Maine	1.000	2	0	3	0	0
Harper, Syracuse	.826	20	8	11	4	0	Scott, Columbus	1.000	25	10	27	0	4
Havens, Toledo*	.889	25	3	13	2	0	Shanks, Syracuse	1.000	1	0	1	0	0
Herron, Pawtucket*	1.000	36	5	12	0	1	Shields, Richmond	.875	39	2	12	2	0
Hickey, Columbus*	1.000	5	1	2	0	0	Shipanoff, Syracuse	.333	5	1	0	2	0
Hodge, Toledo*	.900	3	2	7	1	0	Silva, Columbus	1.000	42	6	7	0	3
Holman, Tidewater	.974	25	9	28	1	2	Siwy, Maine	1.000	7	0	3	0	0
Hoover, Rochester	1.000	5	1	2	0	0	L. Smith, Maine	.833	12	2	8	2	1
Huffman, Tidewater	.750	17	2	1	1	0	Z. Smith, Richmond*	1.000	19	5	30	0	1
Je. Johnson, Columbus	1.000	2	2	0	0	1	Snell, Rochester	1.000	6	0	2	0	0
Jo. Johnson, Richmond	1.000	4	0	4	0	0	Swaggerty, Rochester	.905	11	6	13	2	0
Jones, Richmond	.955	27	5	16	1	2	Taylor, Syracuse	.500	2	0	1	1	0
Kane, Pawtucket	.800	15	2	2	1	0	Tibbs, Tidewater	.857	8	3	9	2	1
Klawitter, Toledo*	.864	26	9	29	6	2	Ujdur, Syracuse	.875	26	12	23	5	0
Kucharski, Rochester	1.000	25	7	13	0	2	Underwood, Rochester*	1.000	3	1	2	0	0
Latham, Tidewater*	.917	21	3	19	2	0	Walsh, Syracuse*	1.000	9	3	9	0	1
Leach, 12 Rich.-31 Tide	.969	43	5	26	1	1	Walters, Toledo	1.000	2	1	0	0	0
Leary, Tidewater	1.000	10	5	8	0	0	Welchel, Rochester	.900	9	5	4	1	2
Lickert, Pawtucket	1.000	3	1	1	0	0	Werly, Rochester	1.000	11	2	8	0	1
Lukish, Syracuse	1.000	15	1	5	0	1	Whitehouse, Toledo*	1.000	4	1	0	0	0
Lysander, Toledo*	1.000	28	5	10	0	0	A. Williams, Toledo	.667	3	0	2	1	0
MacWhorter, Maine	1.000	3	0	1	0	0	M. WILLIAMS, Syracuse	1.000	32	14	33	0	2
Marsden, Maine	1.000	4	1	0	0	0	Willsher, Rochester	1.000	4	0	1	0	0
Martin, Rochester*	1.000	18	0	5	0	1	Yett, Toledo	1.000	26	11	21	0	1
Martz, Richmond	1.000	36	2	11	0	0							

The following players do not have any recorded accepted chances at the positions indicated; therefore, are not listed in the fielding averages for those particular positions: Ashford, ss, p; Bonner, p; Broersma, of; Davis, 2b, of; Falcone, of; T. Hernandez, 3b; Hurdle, of; Keller, 3b; Heise, p; Leary, of; Malpeso, 1b; K. Mitchell, of; Moloney, p; Nandin, 3b; Rooney, 1b; Rosado, 3b; Sanchez, 1b; Sorce, p; M. Wilson, 3b.

CLUB PITCHING

Club	ERA.	G.	CG.	ShO.	Sv.	IP.	H.	R.	ER.	HR.	HB.	BB.	Int. BB.	SO.	WP.	Bk.
Toledo	3.32	137	40	10	29	1183.0	1070	504	437	110	19	453	11	910	48	17
Tidewater	3.44	140	23	13	37	1181.1	1039	547	452	96	20	511	26	778	44	4
Columbus	3.52	139	31	11	34	1200.1	1095	554	470	91	25	517	27	716	46	11
Maine	3.80	136	26	12	34	1159.2	1107	575	490	103	17	529	22	689	42	10
Pawtucket	3.92	140	27	8	35	1200.0	1212	637	523	126	29	495	34	787	52	7
Richmond	4.11	139	20	10	27	1171.1	1218	632	535	87	17	586	23	771	60	9
Syracuse	4.57	139	23	7	25	1174.0	1227	730	596	103	19	549	31	747	66	11
Rochester	4.72	140	20	6	24	1162.1	1248	702	609	106	19	562	31	773	62	4

PITCHERS' RECORDS
(Leading Qualifiers for Earned-Run Average Leadership — 112 or More Innings)

*Throws lefthanded.

Pitcher—Club	W.	L.	Pct.	ERA.	G.	GS.	CG.	GF.	ShO.	Sv.	IP.	H.	R.	ER.	HR.	HB.	BB.	Int. BB.	SO.	WP.
Deshaies, Columbus*	10	5	.667	2.39	18	18	9	0	4	0	135.2	99	45	36	9	1	62	4	117	3
Havens, Toledo*	11	10	.524	2.61	25	25	12	0	1	0	169.0	142	56	49	14	3	70	0	169	10
Comstock, Toledo*	12	6	.667	2.79	23	23	6	0	0	0	164.1	132	58	51	13	0	56	0	154	5
Faulk, Columbus	11	1	.917	2.82	19	17	2	1	0	0	118.0	93	38	37	3	8	48	1	51	4
Latham, Tidewater*	11	3	.786	3.06	21	19	5	1	2	0	132.1	119	49	45	10	3	42	0	57	1
Pacella, Rochester	6	3	.667	3.11	22	17	2	4	0	1	113.0	92	45	39	6	1	48	1	120	11
Yett, Toledo	12	9	.571	3.25	26	26	9	0	2	0	174.2	159	71	63	14	6	66	2	129	6
Payne, Richmond	10	10	.500	3.28	26	25	4	0	2	0	145.1	155	68	53	5	0	89	1	80	4
M. Williams, Syracuse	9	12	.429	3.34	32	24	3	8	0	0	178.0	172	81	66	12	0	63	7	118	8
R. Anderson, Tidewater	6	9	.400	3.38	26	17	3	5	1	3	130.1	118	59	49	9	1	48	3	93	3

Departmental Leaders: G—Barkley, 51; W—Ujdur, 14; L—Cerutti, Holman, Kucharski, 13; Pct.—Faulk, .917; GS—Fisher, 29; CG—Havens, 12; GF—Gardner, 37; ShO—Deshaies, Morgan, 4; Sv.—Gardner, 20; IP—Morgan, 185.2; H—Reed, 193; R—Fisher, Morgan, 101; ER—Fisher, 87; HR—Kucharski, 22; HB—Faulk, 8; BB—Fisher, Morgan, 100; IBB—M. Williams, 7; SO—Havens, 169; WP—Jones, 20.

(All Pitchers—Listed Alphabetically)

Pitcher—Club	W.	L.	Pct.	ERA.	G.	GS.	CG.	GF.	ShO.	Sv.	IP.	H.	R.	ER.	HR.	HB.	BB.	Int. BB.	SO.	WP.
K. Anderson, Maine	7	11	.389	4.80	40	12	2	15	0	7	99.1	106	58	53	10	0	51	2	44	3
R. Anderson, Tidewater	6	9	.400	3.38	26	17	3	5	1	3	130.1	118	59	49	9	1	48	3	93	3
Aponte, Maine	1	1	.500	3.07	10	0	0	9	0	2	14.2	13	5	5	1	0	8	2	9	2
Arnold, Rochester	5	6	.455	4.53	14	14	4	0	2	0	91.1	92	50	46	12	1	24	1	55	0
Ashford, Rochester	0	0	.000	27.00	1	0	0	1	0	0	1.0	4	3	3	1	0	1	0	1	1
Baker, Syracuse	5	4	.556	4.13	35	4	0	14	0	3	72.0	83	46	33	6	1	37	3	38	7
Baller, Maine	9	4	.692	5.38	15	13	3	1	1	0	83.2	82	57	50	15	3	48	2	52	5
Barkley, Maine°	5	6	.455	2.85	51	0	0	34	0	11	85.1	62	32	27	3	2	44	4	76	3
Barnes, Maine°	4	4	.500	4.02	29	8	0	9	0	2	87.1	85	48	39	9	0	55	2	41	2
Barr, Rochester	1	4	.200	5.71	10	5	0	2	0	0	34.2	50	23	22	1	2	11	1	20	0
Bettendorf, Tidewater	4	8	.333	5.70	17	12	3	1	0	0	71.0	76	48	45	11	3	34	2	38	7
Bittiger, Tidewater	8	8	.500	3.88	24	23	3	0	3	0	134.2	124	72	58	14	2	53	1	70	5
Bomback, Syracuse	3	6	.333	3.56	21	8	0	6	0	0	68.1	66	42	27	7	0	21	2	31	1
Bonner, Rochester	0	0	.000	15.75	3	0	0	2	0	0	4.0	6	7	7	2	0	3	0	4	0
Boris, Richmond	0	0	.000	3.95	7	0	0	3	0	1	13.2	18	7	6	1	0	6	0	9	0
Boyd, Pawtucket	3	1	.750	2.89	5	3	2	1	0	0	37.1	30	12	12	2	1	12	0	45	0
Bradford, Richmond°	3	1	.750	2.53	35	0	0	14	0	1	57.0	58	18	16	2	1	20	2	35	0
Briggs, Columbus°	0	0	.000	5.40	5	0	0	5	0	0	8.1	9	5	5	0	0	6	0	4	3
Brito, Rochester	3	5	.375	4.04	22	4	0	7	0	1	64.2	50	33	29	7	2	49	2	58	3
Brizzolara, Richmond	7	7	.500	3.23	18	18	5	0	3	0	111.1	110	53	40	8	1	38	0	76	4
Broersma, Toledo	3	4	.429	3.95	42	0	0	16	0	5	66.0	56	30	29	8	1	32	3	78	5
C. Brown, Columbus	4	4	.500	2.36	32	0	0	23	0	5	72.1	58	28	19	4	1	18	5	26	2
Ma. Brown, Rochester	4	4	.500	3.74	44	0	0	34	0	8	77.0	85	39	32	1	2	41	5	50	4
Mi. Brown, Pawtucket	6	3	.667	3.40	12	12	3	0	0	0	87.1	90	44	33	7	5	27	3	54	2
Burtt, Pawtucket	6	8	.429	4.93	26	25	5	0	0	0	131.1	151	89	72	8	2	67	3	70	10
Cappuzzello, Columbus°	4	5	.444	3.57	23	7	1	9	0	2	68.0	71	33	27	9	0	26	1	37	2
Carlucci, Rochester	4	6	.400	3.70	39	4	1	23	0	7	92.1	88	50	38	7	2	26	2	56	2
Cerutti, Syracuse°	7	13	.350	4.44	29	22	6	3	0	0	148.0	152	89	73	20	2	52	3	114	5
Christiansen, Columbus	6	3	.667	3.10	22	13	4	4	0	2	107.1	109	44	37	7	0	39	4	56	4
Clark, Syracuse°	3	1	.750	3.44	6	6	0	0	0	0	34.0	32	16	13	3	1	26	0	26	2
Clarke, Syracuse°	2	3	.400	4.13	29	5	0	16	0	8	56.2	40	32	26	6	4	46	0	55	1
Clay, Richmond	0	3	.000	4.50	9	0	0	2	0	1	14.0	19	9	7	1	0	8	1	7	1
Clemens, Pawtucket	2	3	.400	1.93	7	6	3	1	1	0	46.2	39	12	10	3	0	14	0	50	0
Comer, Maine	2	1	.667	3.33	7	7	1	0	0	0	46.0	55	26	17	2	3	14	0	24	1
Comstock, Toledo°	12	6	.667	2.79	23	23	6	0	0	0	164.1	132	58	51	13	0	56	0	154	5
Concepcion, Rochester	0	0	.000	12.96	6	0	0	5	0	0	8.1	16	12	12	0	2	10	0	4	6
Cooper, Columbus	8	6	.571	3.17	41	3	0	25	0	9	88.0	81	42	31	8	1	31	3	62	2
Cowley, Columbus	10	3	.769	3.66	17	15	6	1	2	0	113.0	100	59	46	10	6	50	2	96	1
Crawford, Pawtucket	2	1	.667	1.96	7	0	0	5	0	2	18.1	11	10	4	2	0	9	3	8	0
Dale, Pawtucket	0	1	.000	1.38	6	0	0	5	0	1	13.0	12	3	2	1	0	3	1	2	0
Dayley, Richmond°	5	1	.833	4.04	9	9	2	0	0	0	62.1	66	31	28	6	0	24	0	45	4
Dedmon, Richmond	1	2	.333	8.10	6	0	0	5	0	0	10.0	11	10	9	0	0	13	2	10	1
Denman, Pawtucket	3	5	.375	8.32	16	15	1	1	0	0	70.1	98	73	65	16	4	32	1	22	2
Deshaies, Columbus°	10	5	.667	2.39	18	18	9	0	4	0	135.2	99	45	36	9	1	62	4	117	3
Dooner, Rochester	0	0	.000	1.24	13	0	0	9	0	4	29.0	26	11	4	0	0	8	2	12	1
Dorsey, Pawtucket	6	4	.600	2.91	41	0	0	29	0	13	105.1	87	41	34	8	2	49	5	83	7
Eichhorn, Syracuse	5	9	.357	5.97	36	18	3	7	1	0	117.2	147	92	78	13	4	51	0	54	8
Elston, Maine	3	8	.273	3.69	26	10	1	7	0	1	92.2	87	43	38	10	0	50	0	63	2
Farr, Maine	4	0	1.000	2.60	6	6	2	0	1	0	45.0	37	14	13	3	0	8	0	40	0
Farrell, Maine	2	1	.667	3.76	5	5	0	0	0	0	26.1	20	11	11	2	1	20	2	12	1
Faulk, Columbus	11	1	.917	2.82	19	17	2	1	0	0	118.0	93	38	37	3	8	48	1	51	4
Fernandez, Tidewater°	6	5	.545	2.56	17	17	3	0	0	0	105.2	69	39	30	2	3	63	1	123	8
Field, Toledo	1	5	.167	4.78	28	2	1	12	0	0	52.2	59	31	28	7	2	24	2	29	6
Fisher, Richmond	9	11	.450	4.28	29	29	4	0	1	0	183.0	188	101	87	9	2	100	1	122	12
Fowler, Columbus	2	2	.500	5.18	8	8	0	0	0	0	40.0	42	25	23	5	3	18	0	11	1
Fuson, 6 Maine-13 Paw	10	5	.667	3.98	19	17	2	1	1	0	110.2	110	56	49	15	1	44	2	84	2
Gaff, Tidewater	3	1	.750	4.26	4	4	0	0	0	0	25.1	28	16	12	2	1	5	0	13	0
Galasso, Richmond	4	6	.400	3.20	30	2	0	16	0	2	70.1	57	31	25	2	3	51	5	70	0
Gale, Pawtucket	9	5	.643	2.79	15	15	6	0	2	0	96.2	80	40	30	8	1	42	1	83	2
Gardner, Tidewater	1	2	.333	1.61	40	0	0	37	0	20	56.0	40	11	10	2	0	19	3	36	1
Gillam, Syracuse°	0	4	.000	6.13	24	4	0	10	0	2	39.2	52	31	27	2	0	18	5	23	3
Glynn, 22 Maine-23 Tide.°	2	4	.333	2.62	45	0	0	33	0	14	55.0	38	17	16	3	0	30	5	76	6
Gnacinski, Pawtucket	6	5	.545	4.23	30	11	1	12	1	1	123.1	120	65	58	13	5	55	3	60	7
Gonzalez, Rochester°	2	7	.222	6.05	19	10	0	8	0	0	58.0	77	44	39	7	0	34	0	38	4
Gorman, Tidewater°	1	2	.333	3.00	3	3	0	0	0	0	18.0	17	8	6	2	0	4	0	13	0
Harper, Syracuse	5	4	.556	6.14	20	9	0	3	0	0	70.1	76	58	48	9	2	40	1	44	7
Havens, Toledo°	11	10	.524	2.61	25	25	12	0	1	0	169.0	142	56	49	14	3	70	0	169	10
Heise, Rochester°	0	0	.000	20.25	1	0	0	0	0	0	1.1	2	3	3	0	0	3	0	1	0
Herron, Pawtucket°	1	3	.250	2.85	36	1	0	11	0	2	72.2	81	29	23	4	0	36	5	53	5
Hickey, Columbus°	1	1	.500	8.68	5	1	0	0	0	0	9.1	14	10	9	1	0	8	0	3	1
Hodge, Toledo°	2	0	1.000	2.01	3	3	1	0	0	0	22.1	15	5	5	2	1	5	1	16	0
Holman, Tidewater	7	13	.350	4.18	25	22	2	0	1	0	135.2	129	79	63	16	3	70	3	62	6
Hoover, Rochester	2	3	.400	5.21	5	4	1	1	1	0	19.0	19	14	11	1	0	11	0	13	1
Huffman, Tidewater	0	2	.000	6.00	17	2	0	6	0	0	45.0	51	32	30	6	1	16	0	42	1
Je. Johnson, Columbus	0	1	.000	11.05	2	1	0	0	0	0	7.1	8	9	9	2	0	7	1	2	0
Jo. Johnson, Richmond	0	2	.000	5.75	4	3	0	0	0	0	20.1	27	18	13	2	0	4	0	11	1
Jones, Richmond	4	12	.250	4.42	27	22	1	3	0	1	126.1	123	68	62	13	2	80	0	68	20
Kane, Pawtucket	2	1	.667	1.83	15	1	1	9	1	1	34.1	28	11	7	2	1	14	4	25	3
Klawitter, Toledo°	10	6	.625	3.59	26	26	5	0	3	0	168.0	167	80	67	20	1	60	0	91	3
Kucharski, Rochester	7	13	.350	4.99	25	25	2	0	1	0	148.0	159	94	82	22	2	62	5	106	3
Latham, Tidewater°	11	3	.786	3.06	21	19	5	1	2	0	132.1	119	49	45	10	3	42	0	57	1
Leach, 12 Rich.-31 Tide.	11	4	.733	3.03	43	0	0	26	0	1	95.0	98	42	32	4	3	30	5	59	0
Leary, Tidewater	4	4	.500	4.05	10	10	0	0	0	0	53.1	47	26	24	4	3	42	0	27	4
Lickert, Pawtucket	0	0	.000	3.00	3	0	0	3	0	0	3.0	2	1	1	0	0	2	0	0	0
Lukish, Syracuse	1	4	.200	6.32	15	1	0	8	0	2	31.1	46	23	22	0	1	10	2	23	1
Lysander, Toledo	3	2	.600	3.41	28	0	0	23	0	9	37.0	22	14	14	2	1	11	1	23	4
MacWhorter, Maine	0	0	.000	8.31	3	0	0	2	0	1	4.1	4	4	4	1	0	4	0	2	1
Marsden, Maine	0	0	.000	1.08	4	0	0	1	0	0	8.1	6	1	1	0	0	1	0	4	1
Martin, Rochester°	2	2	.500	5.18	18	3	0	6	0	0	41.2	51	26	24	5	1	23	1	22	2
Martz, Richmond	3	5	.375	4.33	36	1	0	24	0	9	62.1	69	36	30	6	2	24	3	28	2

Pitcher—Club	W.	L.	Pct.	ERA.	G.	GS.	CG.	GF.	ShO.	Sv.	IP.	H.	R.	ER.	HR.	HB.	BB.	Int. BB.	SO.	WP.
McLaughlin, Syracuse	2	1	.667	3.65	5	3	1	1	0	0	24.2	16	11	10	1	0	17	0	21	3
Mecerod, Pawtucket	5	6	.455	5.81	17	16	2	0	1	0	79.0	91	57	51	13	3	29	2	49	7
Mitchell, Pawtucket	10	4	.714	2.11	37	0	0	33	0	15	59.2	48	20	14	7	0	14	0	43	2
Moloney, Pawtucket°	0	0	.000	0.00	1	0	0	0	0	0	0.0	0	0	0	0	0	1	0	0	0
Montefusco, Columbus	1	0	1.000	0.69	3	3	0	0	0	0	13.0	6	1	1	1	1	0	0	7	1
Morgan, Syracuse	13	11	.542	4.07	34	28	10	4	4	1	185.2	167	101	84	11	2	100	3	105	11
Morogiello, Rochester°	0	1	.000	3.42	25	1	0	10	0	3	68.1	82	31	26	3	0	26	2	27	0
Mulligan, Toledo°	6	6	.500	4.52	21	10	2	5	0	0	81.2	87	47	41	6	2	29	0	33	2
Murray, Columbus	0	3	.000	5.94	8	0	0	5	0	2	16.2	18	12	11	1	0	7	0	13	2
Musselman, Syracuse	1	2	.333	2.90	26	0	0	19	0	8	31.0	27	10	10	2	1	12	3	19	2
Nielson, Columbus	5	4	.556	3.97	11	10	1	1	0	0	56.2	59	27	25	4	0	23	0	21	2
O'Connor, Toledo°	9	5	.643	2.04	48	0	0	32	0	14	92.2	62	28	21	7	0	41	2	96	4
Oliveras, Rochester	1	3	.250	7.97	12	7	2	4	0	0	40.2	58	37	36	6	1	19	1	39	2
Olwine, Tidewater°	4	2	.667	2.38	50	0	0	27	0	5	68.0	47	26	18	5	0	25	6	50	2
Pacella, Rochester	6	3	.667	3.11	22	17	2	4	0	1	113.0	92	45	39	6	1	48	1	120	11
Pashnick, Toledo	4	4	.500	4.21	12	9	2	1	0	0	68.1	78	37	32	8	0	29	0	47	2
Patterson, Columbus	1	3	.250	6.50	11	4	0	4	0	0	36.0	47	26	26	6	0	15	1	18	1
Payne, Maine	10	10	.500	3.28	26	25	4	0	2	0	145.1	155	68	53	5	0	89	1	80	4
Pettibone, Toledo	1	6	.143	4.95	11	10	2	0	0	0	60.0	63	38	33	8	1	22	0	31	1
Pickett, Tidewater°	0	1	.000	6.23	12	0	0	6	0	1	21.2	19	16	15	3	0	13	0	7	1
Proly, Syracuse	0	3	.000	8.31	13	0	0	7	0	0	21.2	35	24	20	3	0	8	2	15	1
Ramirez, Rochester	4	10	.286	4.36	18	17	2	0	0	0	95.0	94	46	46	8	2	50	1	64	3
D. Rasmussen, Columbus°	4	1	.800	3.09	6	6	3	0	1	0	43.2	24	15	15	1	0	27	0	30	8
J. Rasmussen, Columbus	1	0	1.000	4.91	4	1	0	1	0	0	14.2	16	8	8	2	0	7	0	10	1
Reed, Maine	12	6	.667	3.61	27	27	7	0	2	0	179.1	193	86	72	16	1	57	1	77	2
Reiter, Richmond°	3	3	.500	5.55	41	0	0	25	0	7	47.0	54	35	29	6	0	22	3	35	1
Rijo, Columbus	3	3	.500	4.41	11	11	0	0	0	0	65.1	67	35	32	7	1	40	0	47	4
Rochford, Pawtucket°	8	10	.444	4.90	31	22	2	3	0	0	141.1	156	88	77	20	6	59	1	73	3
Rodgers, Syracuse	0	3	.000	4.53	15	3	0	3	0	1	51.2	62	35	26	5	1	13	0	31	1
Romero, Maine°	1	1	.500	2.56	27	1	0	13	0	1	59.2	47	18	17	3	0	38	5	50	5
Schiraldi, Tidewater	3	1	.750	1.15	4	4	3	0	1	0	31.1	18	6	4	0	0	10	0	24	0
Schulze, Maine	1	1	.500	8.68	2	2	0	0	0	0	9.1	14	12	9	3	1	3	0	7	0
Scott, Columbus	8	9	.471	3.99	25	21	5	1	2	0	119.2	123	70	53	9	2	42	1	46	1
Shanks, Syracuse	1	0	1.000	0.00	1	0	0	1	0	0	4.0	3	0	0	0	0	0	0	5	0
Shields, Richmond	9	4	.692	4.75	39	11	1	17	0	4	110.0	122	69	58	12	2	39	3	101	3
Shipanoff, Syracuse	0	0	.000	12.96	5	0	0	2	0	0	8.1	9	15	12	0	0	18	0	8	1
Silva, Columbus	3	3	.500	2.67	42	0	0	28	0	14	67.1	51	22	20	2	1	42	4	59	3
Siwy, Maine	1	0	1.000	2.04	7	3	0	3	0	2	17.2	11	7	4	1	0	12	0	13	0
L. Smith, Maine	5	4	.556	4.35	12	12	2	0	0	0	80.2	77	47	39	9	2	29	0	48	6
Z. Smith, Richmond°	7	4	.636	4.15	19	19	3	0	0	0	123.2	113	62	57	11	3	65	1	68	7
Snell, Rochester	0	2	.000	4.82	6	0	0	2	0	0	9.1	13	6	5	0	0	7	2	6	2
Sorce, Toledo	0	0	.000	0.00	3	0	0	3	0	0	2.2	3	3	0	0	0	2	0	3	0
Swaggerty, Rochester	6	2	.750	2.66	11	10	4	0	2	0	64.1	53	25	19	3	0	30	1	22	5
Taylor, Syracuse	0	0	.000	3.86	2	0	0	1	0	0	2.1	2	1	1	0	0	2	0	2	0
Tibbs, Tidewater	3	5	.375	5.23	8	7	1	0	1	0	41.1	44	27	24	5	0	23	0	27	2
Ujdur, Maine	14	8	.636	3.69	26	26	7	0	3	0	166.0	171	82	68	11	4	60	0	77	4
Underwood, Rochester°	0	2	.000	9.00	3	0	0	1	0	0	4.0	10	9	4	0	0	3	1	1	1
Walsh, Syracuse°	1	1	.500	6.59	9	4	0	3	0	0	28.2	40	23	21	3	0	15	0	15	4
Walters, Toledo	0	0	.000	4.50	2	0	0	1	0	0	4.0	4	2	2	0	1	0	0	3	0
Welchel, Rochester	4	5	.444	4.42	9	9	2	0	0	0	53.0	53	29	26	1	0	32	1	29	6
Werly, Rochester	1	6	.143	9.80	11	9	0	0	0	0	37.2	54	50	41	8	1	31	0	21	5
Whitehouse, Toledo°	0	0	.000	0.00	4	0	0	4	0	1	4.1	5	0	0	0	0	0	0	3	0
A. Williams, Toledo	0	0	.000	1.76	3	3	0	0	0	0	15.1	16	4	3	1	0	5	0	5	0
M. Williams, Syracuse	9	12	.429	3.34	32	24	3	8	0	0	178.0	172	81	66	12	0	63	7	118	8
Willsher, Rochester	0	4	.000	20.25	4	1	0	1	0	0	6.2	14	15	15	1	0	12	2	4	0
Yett, Toledo	12	9	.571	3.25	26	26	9	0	2	0	174.2	159	71	63	14	6	66	2	129	6

BALKS—Rochford, 5; Cerutti, Comstock, Klawitter, 4 each; Broersma, Fisher, 3 each; K. Anderson, Barnes, Cooper, Farr, Field, Havens, Nielson, Schiraldi, Shields, Ujdur, 2 each; R. Anderson, Arnold, Barkley, Bettendorf, Mi. Brown, Cappuzzello, Christiansen, Clark, Clarke, Dayley, Dedmon, Deshaies, Faulk, Gnacinski, Harper, Lukish, Marsden, Mulligan, Musselman, Pacella, Ramirez, Reiter, Rijo, Scott, Shipanoff, Silva, Z. Smith, Walsh, Werly, Yett, 1 each.

COMBINATION SHUTOUTS—Scott-Christiansen, Deshaies-Murray-Cooper-Brown-Silva, Columbus; Reed-MacWhorter, Smith-Barkley, Fuson-Barkley, Anderson-Romero-Barkley, Maine; Clemens-Gnacinski, Fuson-Dorsey, Pawtucket; Shields-Galasso-Reiter, Fisher-Martz, Z. Smith-Martz, Richmond; Morgan-Clarke, Williams-Rodgers, Syracuse; Bittiger-Gardner, Anderson-Gardner, Fernandez-Olwine, Leary-Olwine, Tidewater; Yett-Whitehouse, Havens-Lysander, Comstock-Broersma-Field, Pashnick-O'Connor, Toledo.

NO-HIT GAME—None.

Mexican League

CLASS AAA

CHAMPIONSHIP WINNERS IN PREVIOUS YEARS

1955—Mexico City Tigers* .... .539	1967—Jalisco .... .607	1976—Mexico City Reds x .... .543
1956—Mexico City Reds .... .692	1968—Mexico City Reds .... .586	Union Laguna .... .547
1957—Yucatan .... .567	1969—Reynosa .... .591	1977—Mexico City Reds .... .623
Mex. C. Reds (2nd)† .... .550	1970—Aguila§ .... .580	Nuevo Laredo x .... .507
1958—Nuevo Laredo .... .625	Mexico City Reds .... .607	1978—Aguascalientes x .... .589
1959—Poza Rica .... .575	1971—Jalisco§ .... .558	Union Laguna .... .523
Mex. C. Reds (3rd)† .... .507	Saltillo .... .593	1979—Saltillo .... .704
1960—Mexico City Tigers .... .538	1972—Saltillo .... .636	Puebla x .... .628
1961—Veracruz .... .575	Cordoba§ .... .541	1980—No champion y
1962—Monterrey .... .592	1973—Saltillo .... .656	1981—Mexico City Reds .... .615
1963—Puebla .... .606	Mexico City Reds x .... .590	Reynosa .... .492
1964—Mexico City Reds .... .586	1974—Jalisco .... .627	1982—Ciudad Juarez x................. .570
1965—Mexico City Tigers .... .590	Mexico City Reds x .... .551	Mexico City Tigers .... .508
1966—Mexico City Tigers‡ .... .614	1975—Tampico x .... .541	1983—Campeche z .... .614
Mexico City Reds .... .571	Cordoba .... .649	Ciudad Juarez...................... .535

*Defeated Nuevo Laredo, two games to none, in playoff for pennant. †Won four-team playoff. ‡Won split-season playoff. §League divided into Northern, Southern divisions; won two-team playoff. xLeague divided into Northern, Southern zones; sub-divided into Eastern, Western divisions, won eight-team playoff. yA players strike on July 1 forced the cancellation of the regular season and playoff schedule. zLeague divided into Northern, Southern zones; four clubs from each zone qualified for postseason play. Campeche defeated Ciudad Juarez, four games to three, in final series for championship.

STANDING OF CLUBS AT CLOSE OF SEASON

NORTHERN ZONE

Club	Ags.	N.L.	C.J.	Sal.	Tam.	Mon.	Leo.	Mva.	M.R.	M.T.	Tol.	Yuc.	Cor.	Ver.	Tab.	Cam.	W.	L.	T.	Pct.	G.B.
Aguascalientes	...	10	7	8	7	6	6	9	0	0	1	1	3	3	2	2	65	52	1	.556	....
Nuevo Laredo	2	...	6	8	7	7	8	10	3	3	1	1	1	2	3	2	64	53	2	.547	1
Ciudad Juarez	5	6	...	8	3	7	7	5	0	1	3	3	0	3	2	4	57	55	3	.509	5½
Saltillo	4	4	6	...	7	9	6	6	2	2	2	2	2	1	2	3	58	58	0	.500	6½
Tampico	4	5	8	5	...	5	6	9	2	1	1	0	2	2	2	2	54	56	1	.491	7½
Monterrey	6	5	5	3	9	...	6	9	1	1	1	2	2	1	3	2	56	60	1	.483	8½
Leon	8	3	3	6	6	6	...	7	2	1	2	2	1	1	3	3	53	61	2	.465	10½
Monclova	3	4	7	6	2	3	5	...	0	1	1	2	1	2	2	0	39	76	1	.339	25

SOUTHERN ZONE

Club	Ags.	N.L.	C.J.	Sal.	Tam.	Mon.	Leo.	Mva.	M.R.	M.T.	Tol.	Yuc.	Cor.	Ver.	Tab.	Cam.	W.	L.	T.	Pct.	G.B.
Mexico City Reds...........	4	1	4	3	2	1	3	2	4	...	6	8	6	6	10	8	75	41	0	.647	....
Mexico City Tigers	4	1	2	2	3	2	2	3	8	...	7	6	7	7	5	7	66	44	3	.600	6
Toluca	3	3	1	2	3	3	2	3	4	4	...	6	8	7	8	10	67	49	1	.578	8
Yucatan	3	3	1	2	2	2	2	6	6	6	...	6	7	8	9	6	65	51	0	.560	10
Cordoba	1	3	3	2	2	2	3	2	6	5	6	6	...	6	8	5	60	52	2	.536	13
Veracruz	1	2	1	3	2	3	2	2	5	5	5	6	...	9	7	5	55	62	1	.470	20½
Tabasco	2	1	1	0	2	1	3	2	2	4	3	4	1	5	...	8	39	68	3	.364	31½
Campeche	2	2	0	1	0	1	1	3	3	4	2	5	6	4	3	...	37	72	3	.339	34½

Playoffs—Ciudad Juarez defeated Aguascalientes, four games to three, in the North Zone finals. Yucatan defeated the Mexico City Tigers, four games to three, in the South Zone finals. Yucatan defeated Ciudad Juarez, four games to two, in the final series to capture the league championship.

Regular-Season Attendance—Aguascalientes, 251,135; Campeche, 116,660; Ciudad Juarez, 140,642; Cordoba, 159,135; Leon, 119,734; Mexico City Reds, 211,084; Mexico City Tigers, 232,664; Monclova, 95,409; Monterrey, 136,005; Nuevo Laredo, 160,030; Saltillo, 222,764; Tabasco, 90,055; Tampico, 305,297; Toluca, 56,839; Veracruz, 157,758; Yucatan, 515,440. Total, 2,970,651.

Managers—Aguascalientes, Francisco Rodriguez; Campeche, David Garcia, Jose Dolores Juarez; Ciudad Juarez, Jose Guerrero; Cordoba, Roberto Castellon; Leon, Marcelo Juarez, Benjamin Valenzuela; Mexico City Reds, Benjamin Reyes; Mexico City Tigers, Fernando Remes; Monclova, Mario Mendoza, Servando Gonzalez, Vinicio Garcia; Monterrey, Mario Pelaez; Nuevo Laredo, Jorge Calvo; Saltillo, Moises Camecho, Juan Navarrete; Tabasco, Alberto Joachin, Domingo Cruz; Tampico, Gregorio Luque; Toluca, Francisco Estrada, Max Oliveras; Veracruz, Luis Garcia, George Scott, Cesas Gutierrez; Yucatan, Carlos Paz.

All-Star Team—North Zone: 1B—Jack Pierce, Leon; Leonardo Clayton, Saltillo. 2B—Eddie Cervantes, Aguascalientes; Antonio Briones, Ciudad Juarez. 3B—Enrique Aguilar, Aguascalientes; Alejandro Ortiz, Nuevo Laredo. SS—Guadalupe Valle, Ciudad Juarez; Ali Uzcanga, Monterrey. OF—Alejandro Lizarraga, Ciudad Juarez; Jay Petters, Monclova; Andres Mora, Nuevo Laredo; Alvin Moore, Leon; Henry Cruz; Saltillo; Bobby Smith, Ciudad Juarez. C—Clemente Rosas, Aguascalientes; Alfredo Torres, Tampico. P—Martin Rivas, Tampico; Jesus Moreno, Nuevo Laredo; Florentino Duarte, Monterrey; Abraham Rivera, Ciudad Juarez; Miguel Solis, Saltillo; Diego Segui, Leon; Luis Villanueva, Aguascalientes; Hector Lopez, Aguascalientes; Arturo Gonzalez, Monterrey. Manager—Jose (Zacatillo) Guerrero, Ciudad Juarez. South Zone: 1B—Guillermo Rodriguez, Toluca; Gary Gray, Mexico City Reds. 2B—Leobardo Guerrero, Tabasco; Jose J. Rodriguez, Mexico City Tigers. 3B—Nelson Barrera, Mexico City Reds; Aurelio Rodriguez, Mexico City Tigers. SS—Manuel Morales, Mexico City Tigers; Fernando Elizondo, Veracruz. OF—Matias Carrillo, Mexico City Tigers; Juan Monasterio, Mexico City Reds; Paul Herring, Tabasco; Don Cossey, Campeche; Arturo Rosales, Cordoba; Albino Diaz, Toluca. C—Antonio Castillo, Mexico City Tigers; Miguel Hernandez, Cordoba. P—Luis Fernando Mendez, Mexico City Reds; Antonio Pulido, Mexico City Reds; Jaime Orozco, Toluca; Ramon Arano, Veracruz; Salvador Colorado, Cordoba; Pilar Rodriguez, Yucatan; German Jimenez, Toluca; Jesus Rios, Mexico City Tigers; Cecilio Ruiz, Mexico City Tigers. Manager—Francisco (Paquin) Estrada, Toluca.

(Compiled by Ana Luisa T, League Statistician, Mexico, D.F.)

CLUB BATTING

Club	Pct.	G.	AB.	R.	OR.	H.	TB.	2B.	3B.	HR.	RBI.	GW.	SH.	SF.	HP.	BB.	Int. BB.	SO.	SB.	CS.	LOB.
Mexico City Reds	.323	116	4091	727	591	1322	1920	186	44	108	663	66	40	31	403	37	465	62	45	877
Mexico City Tigers	.313	113	3934	691	579	1232	1760	206	44	78	632	60	63	50	23	508	55	506	77	51	945
Leon	.313	113	3962	707	783	1240	1864	151	28	139	638	40	57	38	28	379	30	434	63	42	802
Ciudad Juarez	.313	115	3996	675	643	1249	1758	204	31	81	590	50	61	39	19	425	44	433	76	52	854
Aguascalientes	.312	118	4141	798	718	1290	1949	207	28	132	725	53	36	37	42	540	33	551	43	43	926
Toluca	.306	117	4054	720	636	1240	1835	226	36	99	673	60	41	44	41	425	42	537	120	78	849
Tampico	.299	111	3697	634	639	1105	1730	166	36	129	578	48	33	34	30	381	33	613	49	33	737
Cordoba	.295	114	3818	569	500	1127	1531	159	34	59	492	49	62	32	45	437	48	530	97	69	878
Monclova	.295	116	3951	601	816	1166	1691	180	24	99	559	33	32	35	20	454	22	533	73	41	916
Nuevo Laredo	.294	119	4099	630	574	1207	1810	201	21	120	560	58	68	29	31	384	33	531	58	54	847
Saltillo	.291	116	3959	729	676	1154	1767	175	33	124	661	50	58	30	42	599	37	553	73	67	937
Monterrey	.290	117	3882	544	568	1126	1605	163	29	86	499	49	51	29	36	331	20	647	64	47	789
Tabasco	.281	110	3649	425	554	1026	1309	142	15	37	389	34	68	24	17	300	37	388	47	60	796
Veracruz	.280	118	3842	560	563	1075	1496	148	18	79	494	43	53	28	34	446	25	558	78	52	848
Yucatan	.279	116	3791	550	543	1056	1511	167	27	78	499	55	61	35	38	454	48	462	80	69	845
Campeche	.274	112	3645	479	656	1000	1376	153	14	64	414	26	70	28	31	384	30	532	26	54	812

INDIVIDUAL BATTING

(Leading Qualifiers for Batting Championship—319 or More Plate Appearances)

*Bats lefthanded.   †Switch-hitter.

Player and Club	Pct.	G.	AB.	R.	H.	TB.	2B.	3B.	HR.	RBI.	GW.	SH.	SF.	HP.	BB.	Int. BB.	SO.	SB.	CS.
Collins, James, MC Reds-Cordoba*	.412	109	403	81	166	227	35	4	6	59	6	4	5	4	62	15	39	12	10
Bryant, Derek, Tampico	.389	100	355	98	138	286	19	3	41	99	6	0	5	5	73	10	50	6	5
Mora, Andres, Nuevo Laredo	.383	113	426	86	163	297	36	1	32	95	13	0	3	3	62	16	34	9	5
Munoz, Eduardo, Veracruz	.383	110	413	77	158	214	22	2	10	68	7	2	6	2	44	0	30	5	10
Gray, Gary, Mexico City Reds	.379	105	409	93	155	249	19	6	21	108	10	0	8	8	47	6	48	6	5
Lora, Ramon, Toluca	.377	110	414	82	156	259	28	6	21	127	16	0	10	5	53	14	52	16	7
Greene, Altar, Saltillo*	.377	116	385	100	145	266	28	3	29	107	11	1	5	6	133	11	54	10	13
Monreal, Luis, Mexico City Reds*	.366	111	446	88	163	199	26	5	0	43	4	5	1	43	3	33	2	9	
Pierce, Jack, Leon	.364	115	437	98	159	228	22	1	35	117	9	1	4	5	53	5	46	1	1
Cotes, Eugenio, Cordoba*	.364	85	319	62	116	191	19	7	14	62	9	2	2	2	47	4	39	16	10
Torres, Alfredo, Tampico	.362	110	412	69	149	251	23	2	25	101	10	1	7	5	37	7	78	9	2
Rodriguez, Rodolfo, Aguascalientes*	.359	107	410	85	147	173	24	1	0	33	3	1	5	0	93	4	26	1	2
Cosey, Donald Ray, Tabasco	.356	112	441	65	157	233	20	1	18	82	3	1	3	2	28	15	50	1	8

Departmental Leaders: G—Ale. Ortiz, 118; AB—Ri. Herrera, 481; R—Monasterio, J. Rivera, 105; H—Monasterio, 167; TB—Mora, 297; 2B—Mora, 36; 3B—Olivares, 10; HR—Bryant, 41; RBI—Lora, 127; GWRBI—Lora, 16; SH—M. Hernandez, 17; SF—Lora, 10; HP—Evans, 16; BB—Greene, 133; IBB—Mora, M. Carrillo, 16; SO—D. Edwards, 97; SB—M. Carrillo, 30; CS—Adams, 16.

(All Players—Listed Alphabetically)

Player and Club	Pct.	G.	AB.	R.	H.	TB.	2B.	3B.	HR.	RBI.	GW.	SH.	SF.	HP.	BB.	Int. BB.	SO.	SB.	CS.
Aceves, Alfredo, Yucatan	.237	39	97	17	23	46	5	0	6	15	0	1	1	0	19	1	24	2	1
Acosta, Marcos, Tabasco	.160	13	25	0	4	5	1	0	0	1	0	0	0	0	3	0	8	0	0
Adams, Calvin, Monclova	.353	114	468	92	165	214	31	3	4	48	5	2	2	4	60	0	47	17	16
Aguilar, Enrique, Aguascalientes	.309	112	460	95	142	246	19	2	27	115	10	2	4	9	41	2	40	17	6
Alexander, Matthew, 29 Vera.-9 Tol.	.265	38	147	25	39	61	6	5	2	25	0	0	1	22	0	21	16	5	
Alicea, Miguel, Ciudad Juarez	.000	1	1	0	0	0	0	0	0	0	0	0	0	0	0	0	1	0	
Alvarado, Natanael, 5 CJ-50 Cam	.250	55	212	37	53	75	6	2	4	15	1	6	3	6	20	0	35	2	7
Alvarez, Jorge, Tabasco	.196	48	102	4	20	26	2	2	0	10	1	1	0	4	0	28	2	0	
Alvarez, J. Carlos, Monterrey	.274	90	299	37	82	101	10	0	3	34	5	2	4	0	23	0	52	2	4
Alvarez, Orlando, Cordoba*	.267	24	86	9	23	34	2	0	3	15	2	0	1	0	5	1	16	0	0
Andrade, Reynaldo, Leon	.318	99	340	59	108	143	21	4	2	33	1	1	3	1	50	2	40	4	4
Aranda, Severo, Campeche	.250	8	20	0	5	5	0	0	0	2	0	1	1	0	2	0	3	0	0
Arzate, Martin, Nuevo Laredo	.287	109	349	60	100	121	12	3	1	23	1	7	2	1	32	1	40	5	3
Avila, Ruben, Tampico	.325	69	206	31	67	97	10	1	6	42	4	2	1	3	21	1	47	2	1
Ayala, Javier, Leon	.250	25	32	8	8	9	1	0	0	2	0	0	0	3	0	7	0	0	
Baca, Manuel, Leon	.315	89	257	42	81	96	8	2	1	31	3	2	0	3	9	1	42	2	3
Barrera, J. Antonio, Nuevo Laredo	.274	89	226	25	62	74	6	3	0	19	1	13	1	1	17	0	33	1	6
Barrera, Nelson, Mexico City Reds	.354	114	449	71	159	263	21	7	23	101	12	2	3	3	77	7	63	9	7
Batista, Rafael, Cordoba*	.176	11	34	5	6	8	2	0	0	4	0	0	0	2	10	2	7	0	0
Bazan, Pedro, Yucatan*	.309	83	291	36	90	112	20	1	0	28	3	8	3	4	45	12	29	4	2
Bellacetin, Jose Juan, MC Tigers*	.318	107	399	78	127	180	27	4	6	51	5	14	4	4	102	8	28	7	6
Benitez, Jose Luis, 11 Yuc-7 Cam	.200	18	38	5	11	14	3	0	0	4	0	0	0	5	1	5	0	2	
Benitez, Julio, 15 Sal-16 Tam-7 Tab	.283	38	92	9	26	34	3	1	1	10	0	3	1	0	5	1	9	0	2
Blanco, Geronimo, Veracruz	.221	32	86	9	19	32	4	0	3	9	0	3	1	0	5	0	11	1	2
Blanks, Larvell, Campeche*	.320	109	391	76	125	178	23	3	8	52	4	4	1	63	6	38	7	3	
Blassit, Ike, 35 Sal-10 Tam*	.308	45	159	27	49	80	6	2	7	30	3	0	1	2	19	2	29	0	5
Bobadilla, Manuel, 3 Cor-81 Monc	.272	84	335	38	91	115	15	0	3	31	2	2	1	25	0	42	2	1	
Bojorquez, Jose, Nueva Laredo	.275	96	302	32	83	125	18	0	8	41	6	4	3	4	29	0	38	1	6
Bravo, Luis, Tabasco	.281	77	260	49	73	105	14	0	6	27	4	3	1	7	26	4	23	7	8
Briones, Antonio, Ciudad Juarez	.284	115	398	80	113	127	12	1	0	27	3	10	2	3	58	2	31	23	14
Brown, Mike, Monterrey	.000	1	3	0	0	0	0	0	0	0	0	0	0	0	0	0	2	0	0
Bruno, Joseph, Monterrey*	.337	28	92	14	31	48	6	1	3	15	1	3	1	0	17	0	14	3	0
Bryant, Derek, Tampico	.389	100	355	98	138	286	19	3	41	99	6	0	5	5	73	10	50	6	5
Buenrostro, Jose Luis, Yucatan	.000	17	5	1	0	0	0	0	0	0	1	0	1	0	1	0	4	0	0
Burke, Norberto, Saltillo	.235	102	311	60	73	106	9	3	6	41	2	3	3	5	74	0	55	4	7
Caballero, Juan, Monterrey	.311	97	350	50	109	170	18	5	11	64	5	3	2	2	25	1	88	2	5
Cabrera, Jorge, 3 Cor-26 Monc	.278	29	79	8	22	29	4	0	1	6	0	0	0	2	0	7	0	1	
Cage, Wayne, Veracruz*	.324	76	253	48	82	158	16	0	20	59	5	0	2	0	44	8	63	1	2
Calderon, Francisco, Campeche	.121	50	33	3	4	5	1	0	0	3	0	0	0	1	4	0	9	0	1
Camacho, Adulfo, Mex. City Tigers	.268	61	142	26	38	49	6	1	1	15	2	5	0	1	14	0	22	1	0
Canedo, Donald, 18 Aguas.-89 Monc	.297	107	390	71	116	164	16	4	8	63	2	9	4	0	70	2	63	6	5
Cano, F. Javier, Saltillo	.259	77	259	36	67	84	6	4	1	29	3	5	0	0	31	1	43	5	7
Carrillo, Francisco, Aguascalientes	.200	47	75	15	15	16	1	0	0	5	1	0	0	0	3	0	13	3	1
Carrillo, Matias, MC Tigers*	.348	113	442	100	154	240	32	6	14	76	6	6	5	2	74	16	82	30	9
Castaneda, Antonio, Toluca	.252	60	159	29	40	63	5	3	4	25	3	2	2	1	20	0	46	5	0
Castelan, Miguel Angel, Toluca*	.259	93	336	56	87	129	17	5	5	42	3	2	1	1	40	7	63	16	13
Castillo, Antonio, Mex. City Tigers	.327	113	459	62	150	215	20	3	13	97	9	4	5	3	44	8	56	2	6
Castillo, Raul, Cordoba	.293	30	47	3	12	16	2	1	0	3	0	1	1	4	0	8	1	0	
Castro, Antonio, Mex. City Tigers*	.338	105	370	56	125	199	22	5	14	73	7	8	6	0	44	8	34	2	4

Player and Club	Pct.	G.	AB.	R.	H.	TB.	2B.	3B.	HR.	RBI.	GW.	SH.	SF.	HP.	BB.	Int. BB.	SO.	SB.	CS.
Castro, Jose Antonio, Veracruz	.273	45	150	15	41	45	1	0	1	9	1	6	0	0	12	0	23	2	2
Cazarin, Manuel, Veracruz	.278	9	18	3	5	7	2	0	0	0	0	1	0	0	4	0	5	0	1
Cerda, Benjamin, Tabasco	.252	39	103	9	26	44	9	0	3	12	0	4	1	0	7	3	10	0	1
Cervantes, Eduardo, Aguascalientes	.303	82	353	62	107	138	14	1	5	32	1	4	1	1	42	1	44	2	3
Chaidez, Jose Antonio, Tabasco	.148	26	61	6	9	9	0	0	0	1	0	2	0	0	2	0	4	0	2
Chavarria, Miguel Angel, Saltillo	.231	5	13	1	3	3	0	0	0	0	0	1	0	0	2	0	2	1	0
Chavarria, Roberto, Nuevo Laredo	.211	60	71	15	15	23	5	0	1	7	0	0	1	2	6	0	11	0	0
Chavez, Guadalupe, Saltillo*	.249	87	285	36	71	77	3	0	1	28	2	6	3	1	29	1	29	1	1
Chavez, Jose Santos, N. Laredo*	.259	103	324	55	84	135	18	3	9	38	3	9	2	3	32	3	56	3	4
Chavez, Juan de Dios, Monclova	.227	72	229	27	52	76	11	2	3	23	1	2	4	2	29	0	40	0	2
Chavez, Luis, Mexico City Reds	.250	6	16	3	4	4	0	0	0	1	0	0	0	0	3	1	3	1	0
Chavez, Ricardo, Campeche	.213	109	282	37	60	65	3	1	0	10	0	8	0	1	23	0	44	3	3
Collins, James, 45 MC Reds-64 Cor*.	.412	109	403	81	166	227	35	4	6	59	6	4	5	4	62	15	39	12	10
Contreras, Juan Carlos, Tampico	.235	86	230	35	54	70	8	4	0	15	1	6	2	0	29	0	34	3	2
Contreras, Roberto, Tampico	.000	1	1	0	0	0	0	0	0	0	0	0	0	0	0	0	1	0	0
Cordova, Ignacio, Campeche	.279	24	61	6	17	22	2	0	1	8	2	0	0	0	8	0	17	0	2
Cosey, Donald Ray, Campeche*	.356	112	441	65	157	233	20	1	18	82	3	1	3	2	28	15	50	1	8
Cotes, Eugenio, Cordoba*	.364	85	319	62	116	191	19	7	14	62	9	2	2	2	47	4	39	16	10
Covarrubias, Hector, Campeche	.204	21	54	1	11	12	1	0	0	0	0	0	0	1	2	0	8	0	1
Cruz, Domingo, Tabasco	.189	36	95	9	18	21	3	0	0	9	0	0	2	1	6	0	9	0	0
Cruz, Fernando, Nuevo Laredo	.244	67	123	13	30	39	3	0	2	19	3	2	1	1	12	0	21	0	3
Cruz, Henry, Saltillo*	.324	85	330	76	107	197	13	1	25	78	8	0	3	5	55	7	31	2	3
Cruz, Javier, Mexico City Tigers	.200	13	10	2	2	5	0	0	1	1	0	0	0	0	1	0	3	0	0
Cruz, Luis Alfonso, Tampico	.251	103	355	58	89	168	16	3	19	66	3	4	3	2	21	2	77	3	3
Daut, Manuel, Monterrey	.278	37	126	17	35	51	7	0	3	13	1	2	1	2	5	0	31	0	0
Davila, Luis Alberto, Saltillo	.233	16	43	5	10	11	1	0	0	2	0	0	0	1	1	0	9	0	0
DeFreites, Arturo, Yucatan	.295	103	393	69	116	214	22	2	24	87	10	1	8	1	33	3	57	5	5
DeLeon, Silverio, Monclova	.188	10	32	3	6	10	1	0	1	5	0	0	0	0	1	0	7	1	0
De Los Santos, Carlos, Cordoba	.294	86	289	35	85	90	5	0	0	31	2	9	1	10	20	0	36	4	5
Diaz, Albino, Toluca	.350	107	417	82	146	200	25	4	7	67	7	10	2	3	48	0	39	7	9
Diaz, Gustavo, Tabasco	.304	21	56	5	17	18	1	0	0	3	1	2	1	0	4	0	6	1	1
Diaz, Jesus, Leon	.236	31	55	13	13	17	1	0	1	9	1	1	0	0	5	0	8	1	2
Diaz, Larry, Mexico City Reds	.200	7	20	3	4	6	2	0	0	1	0	0	0	0	0	0	4	0	0
Diaz, Ricardo, 36 Reds-37 Tam.	.312	73	250	38	78	118	11	7	5	32	5	2	2	3	21	1	52	3	1
Douglas, Frederick, Monterrey	.071	5	14	0	1	1	0	0	0	0	0	0	0	0	1	0	6	0	0
Dyes, Andy, Monterrey	.299	59	221	45	66	124	5	1	17	52	3	0	0	2	32	6	66	0	2
Edwards, Dave, Monterrey	.253	114	396	57	100	159	27	1	10	46	6	2	1	6	56	4	97	4	4
Edwards, Mike, Monterrey	.351	113	436	68	153	199	18	8	4	63	8	8	4	1	33	1	35	11	7
Elizondo, Fernando, Veracruz	.250	112	388	52	97	115	15	0	1	36	5	11	2	3	35	1	40	0	6
Enriquez, Graciano, Monclova	.245	49	155	25	38	45	1	0	2	13	0	1	1	1	7	0	17	2	2
Espino, Hector, 1 Monc.-23 Mont.	.220	20	50	3	11	14	0	0	1	8	0	0	2	0	6	3	5	0	1
Espinosa, R. Ernesto, Veracruz	.094	24	32	3	3	3	0	0	0	1	0	0	0	0	5	0	6	0	0
Estrada, Fco., 50 Toluca-36 Leon	.246	86	284	33	70	82	12	0	0	23	1	3	2	2	24	4	9	2	3
Evans, John, 34 Tol-67 Aguas*	.317	101	328	83	104	185	17	2	20	65	3	0	1	16	85	7	54	1	8
Everett, Oscar, Monterrey	.000	2	6	0	0	0	0	0	0	0	0	0	0	0	0	0	1	0	0
Felix, Victor, 25 Yuc-74 Cam	.256	99	328	37	84	107	10	2	3	29	2	12	1	1	49	1	56	2	7
Fernandez, Daniel, Cordoba*	.254	76	260	46	66	79	6	2	1	25	2	7	1	2	39	4	35	18	7
Figueroa, Leobardo, 42 Yuc-34 Tam	.261	76	276	50	72	94	5	1	5	29	3	5	1	7	33	0	22	9	4
Firoba, Dan, Saltillo	.315	91	330	54	104	148	20	6	4	50	4	9	0	3	27	2	44	0	3
Flores, Mario, Yucatan	.262	21	61	4	16	16	0	0	0	6	0	2	0	1	3	0	16	0	0
Frias, Jesus, Cordoba	.167	9	30	3	5	5	0	0	0	1	0	1	0	1	3	0	4	1	0
Fucci, Dominic, Yucatan*	.250	33	100	14	25	35	5	1	1	9	3	0	1	0	23	2	21	1	2
Gage, Ralph, Tabasco*	.344	94	331	50	114	149	18	1	5	53	4	0	2	0	57	11	42	7	7
Gamundi, Timoteo, 49 Cam-49 Yuc	.289	98	357	41	103	137	16	6	2	37	3	16	2	4	36	1	48	5	11
Garboza, Toribio, Aguascalientes	.259	15	54	9	14	20	3	0	1	7	0	2	0	0	5	3	13	1	0
Garcia, Cornelio, Yucatan*	.225	24	71	11	16	23	4	0	1	6	0	0	1	1	9	0	22	1	3
Garcia, Jose Luis, Monclova*	.000	1	3	0	0	0	0	0	0	0	0	0	0	0	0	0	3	0	0
Garcia, Sabino, Campeche	.167	6	12	1	2	2	0	0	0	0	0	0	0	0	3	0	3	1	0
Garza, Adolfo, 30 Tam-67 Tab*	.302	97	331	39	100	145	17	2	8	51	3	5	2	4	44	14	47	2	6
Garza, Carlos, Mexico City Tigers*	.290	90	252	47	73	106	4	1	9	46	2	2	4	0	38	6	38	5	3
Garza, Gerardo, Saltillo	.000	2	1	0	0	0	0	0	0	0	0	0	0	0	0	0	0	0	0
Garzon, Felix, Cordoba	.292	114	418	72	122	196	26	3	14	70	7	2	3	3	61	4	81	2	2
Gomez, Alejandro, Nuevo Laredo	.285	103	302	50	86	121	22	2	3	33	5	10	2	0	17	1	36	8	2
Gomez, Graciano, 49 Monc-40 Leon	.279	89	294	42	82	116	10	3	6	36	2	8	5	3	15	0	30	6	3
Gomez, Marcos, Tabasco	.129	9	31	2	4	5	1	0	0	0	0	0	0	0	2	0	4	0	1
Gonzalez, Arturo, Monclova	.196	31	97	9	19	27	5	0	1	6	0	1	1	0	7	0	25	0	2
Gonzalez, Danny, Toluca	.302	52	189	26	57	92	6	1	9	40	4	0	3	0	14	5	16	1	0
Gonzalez, Fernando, 32 Cor-11 Mont	.283	43	159	14	45	55	7	0	1	23	2	1	5	0	20	1	15	4	7
Gonzalez, Jesus, Toluca	.279	100	383	51	107	133	21	1	1	38	4	4	0	4	28	0	34	3	5
Gonzalez, Julio Cesar, Cordoba	.197	18	66	10	13	14	1	0	0	4	0	0	1	1	7	0	9	0	0
Gonzalez, Noe, Monterrey	.248	82	210	25	52	62	5	1	1	13	1	4	0	3	23	0	28	0	2
Gray, Gary, Mexico City Reds	.379	105	409	93	155	249	19	6	21	108	10	0	8	8	47	6	48	6	5
Greene, Altar, Saltillo*	.377	116	385	100	145	266	28	3	29	107	11	1	5	6	133	11	54	10	13
Guerra, Ricardo, Yucatan	.289	107	370	49	107	179	18	3	16	67	5	4	5	2	54	5	29	4	3
Guerrero, Leobardo, 87 Tab-26 Ags.	.304	113	467	72	142	174	18	4	2	42	9	7	3	3	31	2	30	5	7
Gutierrez, Jose Luis, Yucatan	.000	1	1	0	0	0	0	0	0	0	0	0	0	0	0	0	1	0	0
Gutierrez, Miguel, MC Reds	.231	13	26	5	6	7	1	0	0	1	1	0	0	0	3	0	7	1	0
Guzman, Andres, Tabasco	.243	97	334	30	81	109	14	1	4	35	4	7	3	2	19	1	32	1	0
Guzman, Marco Antonio, Campeche	.288	87	278	33	80	129	17	1	10	54	7	2	4	4	32	3	33	1	5
Heras, Roberto, Ciudad Juarez	.328	94	323	44	106	155	20	1	9	42	5	9	2	1	13	1	54	2	5
Hernandez, Javier, Leon	.302	83	252	37	76	95	7	3	2	22	3	4	1	0	32	1	31	1	2
Hernandez, Jorge Luis, Toluca	.309	30	81	19	25	29	4	0	0	9	0	0	0	5	8	0	7	0	0
Hernandez, Miguel, Cordoba	.253	112	367	48	93	105	10	1	0	37	3	17	2	5	45	0	41	7	3
Hernandez, Pedro, Toluca*	.384	53	219	49	84	114	12	3	4	41	2	1	2	1	15	2	30	10	3
Hernandez, Rodolfo, Yucatan	.302	64	215	31	65	104	10	1	9	44	8	1	3	3	27	3	33	1	1
Hernandez, Victor, Monclova	.083	3	12	0	1	1	0	0	0	1	0	0	0	0	0	0	4	0	0
Herrera, Rene, 9 Cor-41 MC Reds	.297	50	128	18	38	50	6	3	0	12	0	3	1	0	14	0	26	3	2
Herrera, Ricardo, Leon	.324	113	481	80	156	196	22	9	0	46	4	7	2	2	42	5	35	23	11
Herring, Paul, Tabasco	.333	109	433	68	144	223	24	5	15	69	6	5	0	0	33	5	39	6	7
Isales, Orlando, Aguascalientes	.325	104	379	76	123	164	14	3	7	65	8	3	5	3	70	4	61	8	9
Jimenez, Leopoldo, Campeche	.237	74	198	19	47	60	7	0	2	20	0	5	0	1	18	3	37	1	1
Johnson, Randy, Veracruz	.267	89	285	43	76	119	14	1	9	43	4	3	5	4	53	7	34	2	2

Player and Club	Pct.	G.	AB.	R.	H.	TB.	2B.	3B.	HR.	RBI.	GW.	SH.	SF.	HP.	BB.	Int. BB.	SO.	SB.	CS.
Juarez, Marcelo, Leon	.000	1	1	0	0	0	0	0	0	0	0	0	0	0	0	0	0	0	0
Lara, Francisco, Veracruz	.250	18	52	8	13	14	1	0	0	2	1	1	0	0	3	0	5	3	0
Leal, Guadalupe, 41 Yuc-45 Monc°	.291	86	292	45	85	131	14	4	8	34	1	2	0	1	31	2	57	1	1
Lee, Terry, Ciudad Juarez	.351	110	407	75	143	234	27	5	18	92	11	1	4	2	66	14	57	0	3
Leon, Juan Carlos, Yucatan	.083	6	12	1	1	1	0	0	0	0	0	0	0	0	0	0	2	0	0
Leonard, Bernard, Tabasco	.265	31	102	13	27	33	3	0	1	9	1	1	1	0	16	2	20	3	3
Limon, Arturo, Tabasco	.274	82	215	23	59	67	4	2	0	23	0	7	1	0	12	0	7	3	8
Limon, Salvador, Leon	.231	27	52	8	12	18	3	0	1	10	0	2	4	0	2	0	12	0	2
Lizarraga, Alejandro, Ciudad Juarez	.353	106	442	72	156	198	22	1	6	83	3	16	7	2	13	0	7	5	3
Llanes, Ramon Ernesto, Aguas	1.000	2	1	1	1	1	0	0	0	0	0	0	0	0	0	0	0	0	0
Lopez, Alfonso, Mex. City Tigers	.292	53	106	13	31	36	5	0	0	14	1	2	2	0	5	0	9	0	3
Lopez, Carlos, Monterrey	.325	99	372	58	121	194	15	2	18	63	4	0	5	5	33	3	46	29	8
Lopez, Fernando, Saltillo	.000	6	3	1	0	0	0	0	0	0	0	0	0	0	0	0	1	0	0
Lopez, Jaime, Ciudad Juarez°	.325	91	342	31	111	153	19	1	7	60	2	1	5	0	18	8	11	1	1
Lopez, Victor Manuel, Monclova	.310	55	210	29	65	83	7	1	3	23	1	2	0	0	16	1	17	1	0
Lora, Ramon, Toluca	.377	110	414	82	156	259	28	6	21	127	16	0	10	5	53	14	52	16	7
Luna, Jose Luis, Monclova	.259	53	166	23	43	58	3	0	4	22	1	0	1	1	14	0	24	0	0
Marquez, Francisco, Campeche	.143	11	21	1	3	3	0	0	0	3	0	0	1	3	0	4	0	1	
Martinez, Antonio, Tampico	.239	34	46	9	11	16	2	0	1	4	0	0	1	1	7	0	12	3	2
Martinez, Francisco, Cordoba	.264	113	420	44	111	121	10	0	0	37	3	8	4	2	27	1	52	4	7
Martinez, Oscar, Cordoba	.249	76	245	32	61	86	11	1	4	34	4	4	4	2	24	3	40	4	2
Martinez, Raul, Leon	.233	27	60	8	14	18	1	0	1	8	2	0	2	1	2	0	8	0	0
Martinez, Teodoro, Tabasco	.276	47	185	17	51	60	4	1	1	24	3	5	3	1	6	1	22	5	3
Maza, Celerino, Ciudad Juarez	.306	26	85	5	26	27	1	0	0	5	1	2	0	4	0	12	1	1	
Mendez, Roberto, Mex. City Tigers	.143	5	7	2	1	1	0	0	0	0	0	0	0	1	2	0	1	1	0
Mendoza, Luis Alonso, Monclova	.311	71	235	28	73	98	7	3	4	34	3	3	2	0	33	2	20	1	2
Mendoza, Mario, 19 Monc-77 Aguas	.325	96	369	61	120	157	23	4	2	51	3	6	3	2	25	1	34	1	2
Mendoza, Porfirio, Toluca	.281	100	299	55	84	105	18	0	1	44	8	12	7	5	34	0	43	4	7
Mendoza, Saul, Campeche	.296	98	335	51	99	145	23	1	7	46	2	9	5	0	58	1	32	1	2
Molina, Jose Maria, Campeche	.157	45	115	9	18	31	4	0	3	16	1	0	1	2	10	0	26	0	1
Monasterio, Juan, Mex. City Reds	.351	112	476	105	167	270	24	5	23	94	8	3	2	4	26	3	25	4	5
Monreal, Luis, Mexico City Reds°	.366	111	446	88	163	199	26	5	0	43	4	6	5	1	43	3	33	2	9
Monroy, Victor Hugo, Saltillo	.261	43	111	17	29	48	7	0	4	15	1	2	1	1	13	0	19	1	1
Montano, Nicolas, Ciudad Juarez	.222	5	9	0	2	2	0	0	0	2	0	0	0	0	0	0	3	0	0
Montiel, J. Cesar 19 Tab-60 Leon	.248	79	222	29	55	62	5	1	0	12	2	11	0	1	17	0	14	2	5
Moore, Alvin, Leon	.349	100	347	73	121	239	4	3	36	92	5	1	4	1	50	8	28	5	1
Moore, Stephen, 25 Vera-34 Cor°	.313	59	217	32	68	76	6	1	0	9	2	3	0	1	26	0	28	12	14
Mora, Andres, Nuevo Laredo	.383	113	426	86	163	297	36	1	32	95	13	0	3	62	16	34	9	5	
Morales, Carlos, Tabasco	.248	59	165	12	41	54	7	0	2	24	1	0	2	3	23	1	32	0	1
Morales, Manuel, Mex. City Tigers	.336	111	473	85	159	195	22	7	0	69	8	11	5	1	52	2	36	14	8
Moran, Jorge, Mexico City Reds	.171	33	76	5	13	22	3	0	2	6	0	1	1	0	5	0	25	0	1
Munoz, Eduardo, Veracruz	.383	110	413	77	158	214	22	2	10	68	7	2	6	2	44	0	30	5	10
Munoz, Jose Luis, Yucatan	.212	30	52	11	11	16	3	1	0	4	0	3	0	0	12	0	11	0	1
Navarrete, Juan, Saltillo°	.296	115	469	78	139	163	17	2	1	51	4	15	4	5	51	5	21	26	12
Navarro, Ruben, Monterrey	.216	64	153	11	33	43	2	4	0	15	2	2	0	3	11	0	43	2	2
Negron, Miguel Angel, N. Laredo°	.333	2	6	0	2	3	1	0	0	0	0	0	0	0	1	0	0	0	0
Novelo, Jaime, Tabasco	.231	7	13	3	3	4	1	0	0	1	0	0	0	0	3	0	3	0	0
Ochoa, Porfirio, Nuevo Laredo	.333	2	3	0	1	1	0	0	0	0	0	0	0	0	0	0	0	0	0
Olivares, Oswaldo, 37 Cor-45 Reds°	.349	82	304	78	106	160	16	10	6	46	5	2	4	2	53	11	23	20	4
Ortiz, Alejandro, Nuevo Laredo	.326	118	426	97	139	251	17	1	31	86	7	5	1	6	73	3	69	17	9
Ortiz, Alfredo, Veracruz°	.000	2	1	0	0	0	0	0	0	0	0	0	0	0	1	0	1	0	0
Ortiz, Jose Manuel, Monterrey	.257	65	183	16	47	56	9	0	0	14	3	5	5	5	7	0	26	2	0
Ortiz, Rigoberto, Toluca	.167	4	6	0	1	1	0	0	0	0	0	0	0	1	1	0	1	0	0
Pacheco, Claudio, Campeche	.245	85	257	28	63	77	8	0	2	23	2	6	4	5	13	0	44	0	0
Pacho, Juan Jose, Mex. City Reds	.306	51	180	24	55	61	4	1	0	10	1	2	0	1	9	0	16	2	3
Paredes, Jesus 20 Yuc-57 Leon	.289	77	280	37	81	110	8	3	5	29	2	4	2	1	18	1	40	5	5
Peralta, Amado, Mex. City Tigers	.302	75	189	33	57	77	9	1	3	25	3	3	0	3	29	1	38	1	3
Peraza, Jose, Yucatan	.250	4	4	0	1	1	0	0	0	3	0	0	0	1	0	0	5	0	0
Perez, Alfredo, Tabasco	.154	13	26	2	4	5	1	0	0	3	0	0	1	0	5	0	0	0	
Perez, Jose Luis, Aguascalientes°	.318	113	453	79	144	238	29	4	19	96	4	4	8	3	39	4	46	3	4
Perez, Julian, Tampico°	.450	34	131	28	59	94	12	1	7	30	6	0	0	1	7	1	7	3	2
Peters, Jay, Monclova°	.289	116	398	94	115	225	19	2	29	99	5	1	5	4	106	12	96	27	3
Pierce, Jack, Leon°	.364	115	437	86	159	288	22	1	35	117	9	1	4	5	53	5	46	1	1
Ponce, Hector, Toluca	.174	31	46	5	8	12	4	0	0	5	0	0	4	0	4	0	11	1	1
Quinonez, Ventura, Monterrey	.000	3	0	0	0	0	0	0	0	0	0	0	0	0	0	0	0	0	0
Quintero, Guadalupe, Veracruz	.233	94	266	21	62	82	4	2	4	34	3	11	5	2	25	0	37	2	4
Quintero, Victor, Saltillo	.286	97	343	51	98	135	18	2	5	43	2	4	1	4	23	1	36	4	2
Quiroz, Jose Julian, Nuevo Laredo°	.300	106	360	47	108	148	22	3	4	38	3	10	2	3	36	2	49	1	2
Ramirez, Manuel, Monclova	.349	106	398	56	139	194	26	4	7	72	5	2	6	5	38	2	19	11	2
Raygoza, Martin, Leon	.000	1	0	0	0	0	0	0	0	0	0	0	0	0	0	0	0	0	0
Raymundo, Oscar, Yucatan	.000	5	3	0	0	0	0	0	0	0	0	0	0	0	0	0	1	0	0
Rendon, Josue, Saltillo	.285	99	355	62	101	183	22	3	18	85	4	5	4	3	40	6	60	1	0
Reyes, A. Gustavo, 4 Tam-27 Tab	.233	31	43	6	10	11	1	0	0	3	0	2	0	0	5	0	5	0	1
Reyes, Enrique, Nuevo Laredo	.258	106	329	29	85	107	10	0	4	30	4	6	4	2	23	0	63	2	3
Reyes, Gerardo, Mexico City Tigers	.242	15	33	6	8	9	1	0	0	2	0	1	0	0	2	0	7	0	0
Reyes, Juan, Aguascalientes°	.312	84	253	40	79	135	13	2	13	48	1	1	1	0	20	7	38	0	3
Rios, Carlos, Monterrey	.295	114	471	63	139	184	22	4	5	46	4	11	1	1	15	0	42	6	6
Rivera, Angel, Mexico City Tigers	.222	3	9	1	2	3	1	0	0	0	0	0	0	0	0	0	5	0	0
Rivera, Carlos, Campeche	.279	87	319	44	89	127	17	0	7	42	3	9	2	2	25	2	49	3	3
Rivera, Eduardo, Ciudad Juarez	.225	44	129	19	29	41	6	0	2	13	2	8	2	2	8	0	7	0	1
Rivera, Jesus, Aguascalientes	.326	106	400	105	132	256	29	4	29	108	10	2	1	6	70	4	87	5	4
Rivero, Gener, Yucatan	.257	81	222	33	57	61	4	0	0	22	1	10	1	2	44	0	11	3	8
Robles, Sergio, Mexico City Reds	.237	102	338	35	80	92	12	0	0	33	4	3	0	0	18	0	32	1	0
Rodriguez, Arturo, Leon	.000	2	0	0	0	0	0	0	0	0	0	0	0	0	0	0	0	0	0
Rodriguez, Aurelio, MC Tigers	.318	44	154	34	49	80	8	4	5	21	3	0	4	1	28	5	23	2	0
Rodriguez, C. Leonardo, Saltillo†	.270	115	455	95	123	205	18	5	18	86	6	7	3	2	88	0	89	15	12
Rodriguez, Francisco, Aguascalientes	.000	7	19	1	0	0	0	0	0	0	0	1	0	0	1	0	4	0	0
Rodriguez, Genaro, Ciudad Juarez	.275	78	262	35	72	113	11	3	8	42	4	1	2	0	15	1	39	4	1
Rodriguez, Guillermo, Toluca	.295	114	451	68	133	247	24	3	28	93	3	3	8	3	21	0	83	2	6
Rodriguez, Jaime, Mexico City Tigers	.275	83	276	40	76	105	14	3	3	42	5	4	8	2	30	0	20	3	5
Rodriguez, Jose J., MC Tigers	.309	107	402	69	124	177	25	5	6	60	8	5	2	3	31	0	60	7	2
Rodriguez, Juan Fco., Leon	.316	104	395	88	125	159	15	2	5	48	2	12	4	5	45	0	23	13	5
Rodriguez, Rodolfo, Aguascalientes°..	.359	107	410	85	147	173	24	1	0	33	3	1	5	0	93	4	26	1	2

Player and Club	Pct.	G.	AB.	R.	H.	TB.	2B.	3B.	HR.	RBI.	GW.	SH.	SF.	HP.	BB.	Int. BB.	SO.	SB.	CS.
Rojas, Omar, Mexico City Tigers	.263	64	205	37	54	80	9	4	3	28	2	2	2	2	12	1	43	2	2
Rojo, Diaz, Gonzalo, Cordoba	.333	3	9	2	3	4	1	0	0	3	0	0	0	1	0	4	0	0	
Rosales, Arturo, Cordoba	.347	113	427	63	148	220	24	6	12	67	7	4	4	9	33	6	49	18	5
Rosas, Clemente, Aguascalientes	.345	94	348	57	120	173	19	2	10	73	3	2	3	1	20	1	58	1	0
Rubio, Arturo, Tabasco	.290	96	310	37	90	107	15	1	0	20	2	10	3	4	16	4	19	9	6
Ruiz, Demetrio, Mexico City Reds	.160	33	81	8	13	16	1	1	0	10	0	0	0	1	4	0	6	1	0
Ruiz, Porfirio, 61 Leon-19 Tol	.312	80	237	35	74	106	10	2	6	28	1	4	4	4	22	0	23	1	1
Saenz, Ricardo, Toluca	.294	101	361	58	106	161	22	3	9	54	1	0	4	3	32	4	38	24	8
Saiz, Herminio, Ciudad Juarez	.264	103	299	46	79	108	9	4	4	35	4	7	1	3	46	1	53	7	8
Salazar, Ronaldo, Veracruz	.253	113	400	58	101	149	18	0	10	53	5	6	2	2	46	1	62	7	5
Salinas, Luis, Mexico City Reds	.243	22	37	4	9	17	2	0	2	10	0	0	0	1	4	1	17	0	0
Samaniego, Manuel, Campeche	.000	1	0	1	0	0	0	0	0	0	0	0	0	0	1	0	0	0	0
Sanchez, Andres, Mexico City Reds	.333	4	3	0	1	1	0	0	0	1	0	0	0	0	0	0	1	0	0
Sanchez, Armando, MC Reds°	.285	88	340	51	97	116	11	4	0	39	4	3	6	1	45	6	17	4	0
Sanchez, Gerardo, Nuevo Laredo	.294	106	402	61	118	164	11	4	9	45	3	1	3	3	20	3	37	11	8
Santana, Blas, Yucatan	.290	116	466	67	135	173	19	5	3	54	10	3	2	3	30	6	46	16	10
Santos, Edgardo, Toluca°	.381	21	84	12	32	50	8	2	2	17	3	0	3	1	5	0	10	3	2
Santos, Eduardo, Saltillo	.313	24	99	23	31	53	6	2	4	15	1	0	0	2	12	1	31	2	1
Santos, Ernesto, Veracruz	.000	1	1	0	0	0	0	0	0	0	0	0	0	0	0	0	0	0	0
Sarabia, Antonio, Veracruz	.275	101	320	50	88	120	14	6	2	31	2	2	0	8	41	4	70	16	3
Sauceda, Victor, Ciudad Juarez	.280	57	211	25	59	81	13	0	3	28	0	1	1	2	11	1	33	3	0
Scott, George, Veracruz	.305	86	302	47	92	149	12	0	15	51	3	0	1	3	43	2	51	4	4
Scott, Rodney, Toluca°	.309	62	233	57	72	102	18	3	2	24	5	2	0	0	47	1	26	23	6
Serna, Joel, Veracruz	.277	112	415	61	115	136	8	2	3	35	3	4	3	3	49	2	63	9	5
Serratos, Miguel, Cordoba	.253	64	178	25	45	66	6	3	3	22	3	0	1	3	14	1	43	0	4
Smith, Robert, Ciudad Juarez°	.353	100	365	97	129	222	25	7	18	65	4	0	4	2	87	14	40	17	10
Sommers, Jesus, Leon	.327	109	425	95	139	240	18	1	27	101	2	2	8	1	41	3	63	4	1
Sosa, Arturo, Tampico	.269	46	93	17	25	35	5	1	1	6	1	2	2	0	8	0	17	0	1
Sotelo, Emilio, 37 Leon-24 Tam	.255	61	192	24	49	67	9	0	3	27	1	0	1	1	21	2	33	2	2
Soto, Carlos, Nuevo Laredo	.324	102	395	59	128	196	20	0	16	83	7	1	4	2	24	4	43	0	3
Soto, Gregorio, 21 Vera-41 Cam	.202	62	173	14	35	39	4	0	0	7	0	2	0	2	14	0	28	3	3
Stone, Steven, Nuevo Laredo	.600	4	5	1	3	5	0	1	0	3	2	0	0	0	0	0	0	0	0
Suarez, Miguel, 50 Tab-46 Vera°	.332	96	370	59	123	140	14	0	1	36	2	7	0	7	26	0	26	4	5
Tapia, Noe, Tabasco	.000	2	1	0	0	0	0	0	0	0	0	0	0	0	0	0	0	0	0
Thompson, Steve, Tabasco	.200	3	5	0	1	1	0	0	0	0	0	0	0	0	0	0	1	0	0
Torres, Alfredo, Tampico	.362	110	412	69	149	251	23	2	25	101	10	1	7	5	37	7	78	9	2
Torres, Nemesio, Veracruz	.273	68	154	19	42	47	5	0	0	24	4	3	1	1	7	0	23	0	0
Torres, Rafael, Aguascalientes	.213	52	136	18	29	36	4	0	1	14	3	6	2	1	16	0	31	1	0
Torres, Raymundo, 42 Reds-45 Yuc	.266	87	297	51	79	125	6	5	10	52	7	2	7	3	40	5	47	3	4
Uresti, Guadalupe, Leon	.000	1	2	0	0	0	0	0	0	0	0	0	0	0	0	0	2	0	0
Uribe, Fernando, Tampico	.222	78	225	29	50	56	2	2	0	13	0	3	1	1	18	0	50	1	3
Uzcanga, Ali, Monterrey	.295	115	468	78	138	187	18	2	9	47	5	9	2	6	39	1	59	3	6
Valdez, Baltazar, Monclova	.294	106	381	46	112	191	18	2	19	65	5	2	3	1	29	3	58	1	2
Valenzuela, Horacio, Leon	.279	82	240	30	67	119	11	1	13	49	2	1	1	2	20	3	32	3	2
Valle, Guadalupe, Ciudad Juarez	.325	108	431	100	140	191	31	4	4	66	8	2	6	1	56	0	55	4	2
Vargas, Antonio, Mexico City Tigers	.333	3	6	0	2	3	1	0	0	0	0	0	0	0	0	0	1	0	0
Vega, Abelardo, Mexico City Reds	.290	37	107	11	31	35	4	0	0	11	0	1	1	0	12	0	21	1	1
Vega, Jesus, Mexico City Reds	.332	91	343	72	114	210	16	1	26	86	6	0	3	5	50	3	46	8	4
Vega, Ramon, Aguascalientes	.122	31	98	7	12	19	1	0	2	10	1	2	3	2	5	0	17	0	0
Velarde, Roman, Veracruz	.045	18	22	0	1	1	0	0	0	0	0	0	0	0	1	0	11	0	1
Velez, Otoniel, Aguascalientes	.350	8	20	9	7	11	0	1	0	1	2	1	1	0	1	13	0	6	0	1
Villa, Victor, 9 Veracruz-16 Tol	.300	25	40	9	12	14	0	1	0	7	0	4	0	0	3	0	3	0	1
Villaescusa, Fernando, Yucatan°	.301	113	425	64	128	157	15	4	2	34	4	8	2	4	42	5	25	22	10
Villagomez, David, Tampico	.289	110	401	60	116	161	17	2	8	69	7	5	6	2	34	1	55	4	2
Villela, Carlos, Tampico	.263	104	419	73	110	164	14	8	8	37	4	6	3	0	18	1	66	5	4
Yepez, Francisco, Campeche	.171	12	35	2	6	6	0	0	0	1	0	0	0	0	6	0	4	0	0
Zambrano, Rosario, Ciudad Juarez°	.295	85	275	41	81	101	8	3	2	29	3	2	2	1	27	2	29	9	3

The following pitchers, listed alphabetically by club, with games in parentheses, had no plate appearances, primarily through use of designated hitters:

AGUASCALIENTES—Becerra, Jose (14); Canedo, Guillermo (2); Castillejos, Jose M. (28); Cordova, Ernesto (16); Delgadillo, Gustavo (2); Guzman, Ramon (12); Lopez, Hector (39); Low, Gabriel (24); Martinez, Gabriel (17); Matus, Nelson (6); Munoz, Miguel (9); Ogawa, Kuni (25); Pina, Horacio (1); Sandoval, Frank (3); Santiago, John (1); Santoya, Jesus (11); Vazquez, Jesse (36); Villanueva, Luis (25).

CAMPECHE—Acosta, Cecilio (26); Baruch, Matias (28); Brown, Mike (2); Divison, J. Cesar (23); Franco, Francisco (3); Gonzalez, Roberto (26); Hernandez, F. Angel (6); Hernandez, R. Angel (37); Madrigal, Jose (28); Posadas, Rafael (7); Purata, Julio (7); Rios, Rogelio (11); Rivera, Jose Antonio (7); Rodriguez, Ramon (29); Rondon, Gilberto (12); Saldivar, Arturo (2); Valdez, Humberto (10); Valdez, Rodolfo (30); Vazquez, Rafael (9).

CIUDAD JUAREZ—Alicea, Miguel (33); Dominguez, Manuel (12); Feola, Larry (34); Garcia, Rafael (28); Gutierrez, Porfirio (7); Jaime, G. Ismael (26); Medina, Ramiro (1); Montano, Nicolas (24); Montenegro, Francisco (15); Ochoa, Domingo (7); Quinonez, Rene (15); Rivera, Abraham (27); Serna, Ramon (19); Torres, Antonio (9).

CORDOBA—Beltran, Jorge (4); Blanco, Arturo (1); Castaneda, Aurelio (1); Colorado, Salvador (23); Delfin, Justino (12); Diaz, Cesar (26); Gaxiola, Fernando (16); Miranda, Francisco (10); Pimentel, Rafael (16); Quijada, Armando (8); Quintero, Frank (1); Rivera, Oscar (25); Serafin, Hector (38); Solis, Ricardo (28); Torres, Martin (12); Velazquez, Agustin (14); Vila Martinez, Jesus (3).

LEON—Abarca, David (9); Beltran, Jorge (18); Corona, Benjamin (3); Garcia, Enrique (7); Garcia, Rogelio (14); Guzman, P. Gelacio (5); Jefferson, Jesse (19); Jimenez, Raymundo (8); Madrigal, Hector (2); Miranda, Francisco (7); Moncada, Mario (8); Moore, Alvin (1); Osuna, Roberto (1); Pena, Jose (8); Peralta, Alvaro (8); Ramirez, Jose Edgardo (7); Raygoza, Martin (38); Rios, Hector (5); Rodriguez, Arturo (38); Segui, Diego (24); Uresti, Guadalupe (24); Valenzuela, Guillermo (5); Valle, Urbano (11); Villegas, David (1).

MEXICO CITY REDS—Armas, Isidro (27); Carranza, Javier (18); Chavez, Luis (9); Garcia, F. Rene Javier (5); Ibarra, Carlos (15); Leal, Bernabe (8); Leon, Maximino (11); Mendez, Luis Fernando (26); Morales, Isidro (2); Ortiz, Alfredo (12); Osuna, Ricardo (3); Pulido, Antonio (47); Rios, Rogelio (6); Rodriguez, Mario A. (24); Romo, Vicente (22); Sanchez, Pablo (39); Velazquez, Agustin (2); Veliz, A. Francisco (11).

MEXICO CITY TIGERS—Aguilar, J. Miguel (19); Alvarado, Jose (4); Buitimea, Martin (12); Cartagena, Ruben (2); Cota, Francisco (28); Dimas, Rodolfo (38); Garcia, Jorge Luis (11); Guzman, Ramon (10); Ledon, Juan Carlos (2); Montano, Francisco (40); Palafox, Juan (9); Retes, Lorenzo (14); Rios, Jesus (32); Romero, Emigdio (7); Ruiz, Cecilio (35); Salas, Ernesto (11); Vargas, Antonio (1); Velazquez, Ildefonso (31); Villegas, Ramon (14).

MONCLOVA—Cutty, Francis (29); Escarrega, Ernesto (14); Garcia, Enrique (10); Garcia, Jose Luis (31); Guzman, Jose (27); Ibarra, Carlos (20); Jimenez, Raymundo (20); McCoy, Kevin (9); Molina, Hilton (6); Mundo, Jesus (22); Ontiveros, Francisco (31); Osuna, Roberto (12); Rivas, Lorenzo (29); Ruiz, Pablo (15); Sanchez, Abelardo (5); Sanchez, Salvador (5).

MONTERREY—Antunez, Martin (21); Brown, Mike (10); Brunet, George (14); Duarte, Florentino (26); Ellis, Duane (3); Garza, Adrian (12); Gaxiola, Fernando (9); Gonzalez, M. Arturo (28); Gonzalez, Isidro (1); Heredia, Hector (39); Mariscal, Tomas (11); Martinez, Freddie (22); Miranda, Julio Cesar (8); Mundo, Jesus (9); Murillo, Felipe (1); Ochoa, Domingo (12); Rodriguez, Ramiro (7); Trevino, Noel (20).

NUEVO LAREDO—Buice, Dewayne (14); Castillo, Luis T. (26); Edwards, Allen (6); Enriquez, Martin (10); Lester, Joseph (6); McLaughlin, Byron (8); Moreno, Jesus (28); Navarro, Adolfo (20); Ochoa, Domingo (7); Ochoa, Porfirio (45); Quiroz, Jose Julian (9); Rincon, Juan (25); Sanchez, Felipe (19); Silva, Eduardo (1); Smith, Billy (29); Stone, Steven (45); Stottlemyre, Jeff (4); Viscarra, Faustino (2); Wax, Gary (4); Widales, Oscar (3).

SALTILLO—Brunet, George (7); Castaneda, Mario A. (11); Cecena, Jose Isabel (24); Gallo, Raymond (23); Lopez, Fernando (1); McCoy, Kevin (9); Morales, Isidro (12); Moya, Ramon (36); Parroth, Steve (8); Pollorena, Antonio (16); Rodriguez, Eulogio (3); Rendon, Josue (1); Solis, Miguel (26); Tapia, Ramiro (3); Urrea, Leonel (36); Valenzuela, Jairo (29); Vidana, Alejandro (31); Viesca, Rodrigo (13).

TABASCO—Aguilar, J. Miguel (10); Belman, Andres (21); Delfin, Juan M. (1); Diaz, Anibal (8); Franco, David (11); Gage, Ralph (1); Garcia, Jorge Luis (18); Huerta, Luis E. (18); Matus, Nelson (21); Nunez, Jorge (8); Ochoa, Julio (33); Palacios, Raul (16); Pollorena, Oscar (25); Rogers, Charles (21); Rojo Mendez, Gonzalo (20); Salas, Ernesto (1); Sandoval, Frank (2); Velazquez, Luis A. (17); Villegas, Ramon (6); Yucupicio, Jesus (16).

TAMPICO—Beltran, Eleazar (6); Blanco, Jaime (4); Chavez, Guadalupe (43); Contreras, Roberto (12); Cota, Martin (3); Cruz, Luis Alfonso (1); DeLeon, Ricardo (4); Gutierrez, Porfirio (13); Luna, Jose M. (21); MacDonald, Marck (6); Morales, Isidro (6); Palafox, Juan (15); Perez, Americo (34); Purata, Julio (21); Rios, Miguel (15); Rivas, Martin (46); Sosa, Carlos (27); Tinajero, Juan (18); Valenzuela, Humberto (9).

TOLUCA—Alcala, Santos (5); Calderon, Jose R. (7); Divison, J. Cesar (23); Dominguez, Heminio (29); Hernandez, Pedro (1); Jimenez, German (25); Jimenez, Isaac (24); Ontiveros, Juan (3); Orozco, Jaime (33); Perez, Cipriano (25); Quijano, Enrique (13); Soto, Alvaro (38); Urias, Reyes (28).

VERACRUZ—Arano, Ramon (22); Contreras, Patricio (9); Delfin, Juan M. (1); Figueroa, Miguel (4); Franco, David (11); Franco, Francisco (5); Garcia, Enrique (3); Garcia, Jorge Luis (13); Gurman, Gelacio (7); Inzunza, Sergio (13); Lara, Hugo (2); Lozano, Jose (2); Lugo, Manuel (35); Morales, Mario (29); Nunez, Mario (7); Ortiz, Alfredo (13); Palacios, Vicente (24); Ramirez, Jose Edgardo (21); Salas, Roberto (12); Santos, Ernesto (3); Silva, Eduardo (34); Valdez, Humberto (13); Vazquez, Rafael (7); Velarde, Roman (1); Zamudio, Aurelio (3).

YUCATAN—Angulo, Kenneth (21); Arceo, Luis (1); Arroyo, Freddie (11); Escarrega, Ernesto (11); Espinosa, Javier (5); Guzman, Sergio (1); Hernandez, Jesus (8); Leal, Guadalupe (2); Menendez, Rolando (23); Moreno, Cesar (24); Navarette, Jorge (1); Ochoa, Domingo (5); Peralta, Alvaro (6); Rodriguez, Pilar (35); Rondon, Gilberto (13); Salas, Roberto (7); Salcido, Ray (6); Salinas, Guadalupe (20); Sauceda, Ramiro (25); Uribe, Juan Carlos (9); Villalobos, Ernesto (10); Villarreal, Ricardo (16).

GRAND SLAM HOME RUNS—Mora, 4; Avila, L. Cruz, Gray, Ale. Ortiz, 2 each; Aguilar, Bojorquez, Caballero, Cage, M. Carrillo, H. Cruz, DeFreites, Dyes, D. Edwards, Evans, Fernandez, A. Garza, Garzon, D. Gonzalez, J. Lopez, V. Lopez, Lora, S. Mendoza, Molina, A. Perez, Peters, Quiroz, Rendon, J. Rivera, Gu. Rodriguez, Rosales, Sommers, Ray. Torres, Valdez, 1 each.

AWARDED FIRST BASE ON CATCHER'S INTERFERENCE—Navarette 2 (J.L. Benitez, R. Vega); F. Martinez (G. Quintero); G. Quintero (Robles); Au. Rodriguez (Robles); Serna (Rojas); A. Torres (L.A. Mendoza).

CLUB FIELDING

Club	Pct.	G.	PO.	A.	E.	DP.	PB.	Club	Pct.	G.	PO.	A.	E.	DP.	PB.
Yucatan	.975	116	3015	1357	111	108	7	Saltillo	.970	116	3017	1375	138	129	11
Ciudad Juarez	.974	115	3024	1319	118	101	20	Mexico City Reds	.969	116	3056	1330	138	122	3
Veracruz	.972	118	2962	1449	127	102	15	Monterrey	.969	117	3003	1205	133	104	25
Cordoba	.972	114	2967	1291	128	121	6	Leon	.968	116	2940	1287	141	123	18
Toluca	.972	117	3071	1486	133	132	19	Monclova	.968	116	2943	1357	133	123	15
Mexico City Tigers	.971	113	2986	1293	127	119	10	Tampico	.967	111	2822	1187	136	110	16
Campeche	.970	112	2819	1268	125	95	15	Aguascalientes	.967	118	3053	1350	151	118	13
Nuevo Laredo	.970	119	3103	1392	139	113	8	Tabasco	.963	110	2790	1250	157	90	18

Triple Plays—Mexico City Reds, Nuevo Laredo, Toluca.

INDIVIDUAL FIELDING

*Throws lefthanded

FIRST BASEMEN

Player and Club	Pct.	G.	PO.	A.	E.	DP.	Player and Club	Pct.	G.	PO.	A.	E.	DP.
Reyes, Aguascalientes	1.000	36	308	15	0	26	Cosey, Campeche*	.991	106	974	57	9	83
Villagomez, Tampico	1.000	24	193	8	0	21	Gu. Rodriguez, Toluca	.991	54	509	44	5	58
A. Lopez, Mexico City Tigers	1.000	37	147	11	0	18	Morales, Tabasco	.991	36	307	22	3	24
Santos, Saltillo	1.000	14	134	9	0	16	Perez, Aguascalientes*	.991	46	409	25	4	41
R. Hernandez, Yucatan	1.000	10	66	5	0	7	A. Sosa, Tampico	.991	31	207	10	2	11
Navarro, Monterrey	1.000	11	61	5	0	8	Garboza, Aguascalientes	.991	11	101	6	1	10
Johnson, Veracruz	.998	50	461	3	1	28	Evans, 20 Tol.-31 Aguas*	.990	51	468	35	5	49
J. LOPEZ, Ciudad Juarez*	.996	88	785	48	3	76	Garza, 11 Tam-43 Tabasco*	.990	55	457	37	5	39
Aceves, Yucatan	.996	33	251	20	1	28	Ge. Rodriguez, Ciudad Juarez.	.988	29	240	12	3	20
Garza, Mexico City Tigers*	.996	98	429	26	2	50	Caballero, Monterrey	.988	89	773	58	10	73
Avila, Tampico	.996	26	218	8	1	14	Castillo, Mexico City Tigers	.988	46	371	24	5	38
Ramirez, Monclova	.996	23	214	9	1	23	DeFreites, Yucatan	.986	31	276	14	4	17
Gray, Mexico City Reds	.995	99	928	41	5	93	Garcia, Yucatan	.986	17	133	6	2	19
J. Vega, Mexico City Reds	.995	18	167	14	1	19	Pierce, Leon	.985	105	953	54	15	106
Cage, Veracruz*	.994	59	512	30	3	54	C.L. Rodriguez, Saltillo*	.985	90	821	51	13	98
C. Soto, Nuevo Laredo	.994	76	645	32	4	63	Valdez, Monclova	.985	79	672	54	11	74
Bojorquez, Nuevo Laredo	.994	33	290	22	2	20	Ortiz, Monterrey	.982	14	103	5	2	10
Fucci, Yucatan	.994	31	286	21	2	23	Quiroz, Nuevo Laredo*	.981	22	155	4	3	13
Garzon, Cordoba	.993	112	1056	59	8	107	Torres, Tampico	.981	36	299	16	6	37
Gage, Tabasco*	.992	26	226	12	2	16	Scott, Veracruz	.978	12	128	3	3	11
H. Cruz, Saltillo*	.992	12	113	5	1	12	V. Lopez, Monclova	.975	16	155	4	4	20
Lora, Toluca	.991	49	441	23	4	45							

(Fewer Than Ten Games)

Player and Club	Pct.	G.	PO.	A.	E.	DP.	Player and Club	Pct.	G.	PO.	A.	E.	DP.
Sommers, Leon	1.000	9	74	6	0	11	Ja. Rodriguez, MC Tigers	1.000	1	7	0	0	0
Guerra, Yucatan	1.000	8	67	2	0	5	Gomez, Monclova	1.000	1	4	0	0	0
Saenz, Toluca	1.000	4	27	3	0	2	N. Gonzalez, Monterrey	1.000	1	4	0	0	2
Acosta, Tabasco	1.000	4	23	3	0	2	Leal, Monclova	1.000	2	3	0	0	0
F. Gonzalez, Cordoba	1.000	3	26	0	0	2	DeLeon, Monclova	1.000	1	2	1	0	1
Lee, Ciudad Juarez	1.000	4	24	0	0	1	Isales, Aguascalientes	1.000	1	1	1	0	0
G. Soto, Campeche	1.000	3	18	1	0	0	Espino, Monterrey	.986	8	69	2	1	4
H. Valenzuela, Leon	1.000	3	18	0	0	1	Cerda, Tabasco	.978	5	41	4	1	2
Guzman, Campeche	1.000	1	12	2	0	0	Cordova, Campeche	.976	3	41	4	1	4
F. Cruz, Nuevo Laredo	1.000	3	11	2	0	1	Rivera, Mexico City Tigers	.952	3	16	4	1	1
Enriquez, Monclova	1.000	1	13	0	0	0	Salinas, Mexico City Reds	.947	5	18	0	1	2
Navarrete, Saltillo	1.000	1	9	1	0	0	Heras, Ciudad Juarez	.943	6	32	1	2	1
Castro, Mexico City Tigers*	1.000	2	5	2	0	1	Peralta, Mexico City Tigers	.933	4	14	0	1	1
F. Rodriguez, Aguascalientes	1.000	1	6	1	0	0	Alvarez, Tabasco	.917	4	11	0	1	3
Firoba, Saltillo	1.000	1	7	0	0	0							

Triple Plays—Gray, Gu. Rodriguez, C. Soto.

SECOND BASEMEN

Player and Club	Pct.	G.	PO.	A.	E.	DP.	Player and Club	Pct.	G.	PO.	A.	E.	DP.
R. Torres, Aguascalientes	1.000	15	20	27	0	11	Cervantes, Aguascalientes	.970	82	230	253	15	70
J.L. Hernandez, Toluca	.992	24	53	79	1	20	Scott, Toluca	.970	35	97	95	6	29
J. Gonzalez, Toluca	.986	69	212	214	6	53	Villela, Tampico	.969	104	275	290	18	60
CHAVEZ, Campeche	.985	110	258	316	9	66	Chavez, Monclova	.968	69	180	213	13	52
Serna, Veracruz	.984	112	256	342	10	71	Guerrero, 78 Tab-25 Aguas	.966	103	295	306	21	58
Villaescusa, Yucatan	.982	98	253	242	9	62	G. Sanchez, Nuevo Laredo	.963	73	177	190	14	47
Ju. Rodriguez, Leon	.981	104	279	333	12	84	Rios, Monterrey	.963	108	298	295	23	75
Bobadilla, Monclova	.980	11	28	22	1	7	Munoz, Yucatan	.958	23	38	54	4	6
Navarrete, Saltillo	.979	115	326	323	14	95	G. Diaz, Tabasco	.949	21	37	57	5	7
Briones, Ciudad Juarez	.978	115	295	364	15	83	Cabrera, 1 Cord.-21 Monclova	.949	21	47	44	5	5
F. Martinez, Cordoba	.976	113	286	331	15	92	A. Vega, Mexico City Reds	.938	16	40	36	5	9
A. Gonzalez, Monclova	.975	23	51	64	3	18	Chavarria, Nuevo Laredo	.915	24	34	41	7	10
Barrera, Nuevo Laredo	.973	59	121	133	7	29	Limon, Tabasco	.902	15	15	22	4	5
Jo. Rodriguez, Mex. City Tigers	.972	107	320	281	17	72	Calderon, Campeche	.860	29	27	22	8	7
Ar. Sanchez, Mexico City Reds	.972	86	241	279	15	86							

Triple Play—Ar. Sanchez.

(Fewer Than Ten Games)

Player and Club	Pct.	G.	PO.	A.	E.	DP.	Player and Club	Pct.	G.	PO.	A.	E.	DP.
J.C. Contreras, Tampico	1.000	9	28	24	0	10	Herrera, Leon	.982	6	30	25	1	8
Pacho, Mexico City Reds	1.000	9	20	21	0	5	R. Hernandez, Yucatan	.980	8	22	26	1	4
Barrera, Mexico City Reds	1.000	9	13	16	0	4	N. Torres, Veracruz	.977	9	19	24	1	9
Leon, Yucatan	1.000	3	3	11	0	2	T. Martinez, Tabasco	.976	8	20	21	1	4
Ortiz, Monterrey	1.000	3	2	10	0	0	Limon, Leon	.956	8	24	19	2	5
Quintero, Saltillo	1.000	2	3	8	0	3	Isales, Aguascalientes	.947	3	7	11	1	2
R. Diaz, Mexico City Reds	1.000	3	6	5	0	3	Mendez, Mexico City Tigers	.944	3	10	7	1	0
Bojorquez, Nuevo Laredo	1.000	2	3	3	0	0	M. Edwards, Monterrey	.929	9	18	21	3	1
Castillo, Cordoba	1.000	1	2	2	0	2	Camacho, Mexico City Tigers	.923	5	14	10	2	1
Jimenez, Campeche	1.000	1	0	5	0	0	Yepez, Campeche	.889	6	8	8	2	1
Herrera, Mexico City Reds	1.000	1	2	2	0	0	Sommers, Leon	.882	3	9	6	2	3
Velarde, Veracruz	1.000	1	2	1	0	1	O. Martinez, Cordoba	.800	3	9	3	3	1
J. Perez, Tampico	1.000	1	1	1	0	0							
J. Gonzalez, Cordoba	1.000	1	1	0	0	0							

THIRD BASEMEN

Player and Club	Pct.	G.	PO.	A.	E.	DP.	Player and Club	Pct.	G.	PO.	A.	E.	DP.
Santana, Yucatan	.976	116	116	296	10	23	Salazar, Veracruz	.927	87	88	166	20	22
Au. Rodriguez, MC Tigers	.972	22	22	48	2	5	Cruz, Tampico	.926	30	28	60	7	5
Saiz, Ciudad Juarez	.963	92	62	149	8	13	Ramirez, Monclova	.925	50	41	107	12	12
Ortiz, Nuevo Laredo	.961	118	129	244	15	18	Mondoza, Campeche	.923	11	9	15	2	1
Barrera, Mexico City Reds	.957	103	100	209	14	29	Bobadilla, 3 Cor-66 Monclova	.923	69	58	109	14	16
N. Torres, Veracruz	.953	32	29	71	5	3	F. Gonzalez, 28 Cor-3 Mont	.922	31	25	70	8	7
N. Gonzalez, Monterrey	.949	78	68	101	9	14	Peralta, Mexico City Tigers	.921	68	42	92	12	6
O. Martinez, Cordoba	.946	35	28	60	5	4	Castro, Tabasco	.920	28	31	50	7	4
Montiel, 3 Tabasco-44 Leon	.941	47	33	95	8	19	Sommers, Leon	.912	66	46	109	15	11
Castaneda, Toluca	.940	22	15	48	4	7	Lee, Ciudad Juarez	.909	37	24	66	9	4
Aguilar, Aguascalientes	.940	93	77	172	16	16	Serratos, Cordoba	.906	37	32	83	12	5
C. Rivera, Campeche	.939	77	76	170	16	22	Cerda, Tabasco	.905	13	6	13	2	0
Chaidez, Tabasco	.938	25	18	43	4	3	J.C. Gonzalez, Cordoba	.904	17	14	33	5	2
T. Martinez, Tabasco	.937	40	45	73	8	6	Limon, Leon	.900	13	11	16	3	1
Burke, Saltillo	.933	92	82	170	18	13	Diaz, Tampico	.898	28	18	35	6	7
Ortiz, Monterrey	.933	36	22	48	5	3	Quintero, Saltillo	.894	29	21	38	7	3
Camacho, Mexico City Tigers	.933	45	37	74	8	7	J. Gonzalez, Toluca	.875	18	10	25	5	2
R. Torres, Aguascalientes	.932	26	16	39	4	3	Jimenez, Campeche	.868	20	9	24	5	1
J.C. Contreras, Tampico	.929	32	31	48	6	2	J. Vega, Mexico City Reds	.833	14	9	16	5	1
J. Perez, Tampico	.928	21	31	59	7	4	Limon, Tabasco	.794	11	7	22	5	2
Saenz, Toluca	.927	87	62	168	18	15							

Triple Play—Saenz.

(Fewer Than Ten Games)

Player and Club	Pct.	G.	PO.	A.	E.	DP.	Player and Club	Pct.	G.	PO.	A.	E.	DP.
Yepez, Campeche	1.000	3	2	9	0	1	Chavez, Campeche	1.000	1	0	2	0	0
Baca, Leon	1.000	3	3	6	0	1	Garboza, Aguascalientes	1.000	1	0	2	0	0
Monroy, Saltillo	1.000	3	2	6	0	1	Munoz, Yucatan	1.000	1	0	1	0	0
Calderon, Campeche	1.000	3	4	4	0	0	Chavarria, Nuevo Laredo	1.000	1	0	1	0	0
F. Rodriguez, Aguascalientes	1.000	2	0	5	0	0	Pacho, Mexico City Reds	.833	2	1	4	1	1
Bojorquez, Nuevo Laredo	1.000	2	1	4	0	1	Rios, Monterrey	.800	6	3	5	2	0
Valenzuela, Mexico City Tigers	1.000	5	0	4	0	1	M. Edwards, Monterrey	.800	8	2	10	3	0
Guerrero, Tabasco	1.000	2	2	2	0	0	Cazarin, Veracruz	.800	7	6	6	3	1
Velarde, Veracruz	1.000	2	2	2	0	0	A. Vega, Mexico City Reds	.750	8	3	3	2	0
Monasterio, Mexico City Reds	1.000	1	2	1	0	0	A. Gonzalez, Monclova	.750	3	1	2	1	0
Moran, Mexico City Reds	1.000	4	1	1	0	0	DeFreites, Yucatan	.667	1	1	1	1	0
Perez, Tabasco	1.000	2	2	0	0	0	Maza, Ciudad Juarez	.500	2	0	1	1	0
Isales, Aguascalientes	1.000	2	0	2	0	1	Mendez, Mexico City Tigers	.000	2	0	0	1	0
Jo. Rodriguez, MC Tigers	1.000	2	0	2	0	0							

SHORTSTOPS

Player and Club	Pct.	G.	PO.	A.	E.	DP.	Player and Club	Pct.	G.	PO.	A.	E.	DP.
J.C. Contreras, Tampico	.974	45	58	129	5	18	A. Limon, Tabasco	.959	50	99	109	9	17
CHAVEZ, Saltillo	.971	81	130	301	13	63	Uzcanga, Monterrey	.952	115	198	353	28	76
Rivero, Yucatan	.968	81	133	260	13	43	O. Martinez, Cordoba	.950	14	18	39	3	10
De Los Santos, Cordoba	.968	86	157	296	15	63	Flores, Yucatan	.950	22	42	71	6	16
Castro, Tabasco	.966	21	33	52	3	9	M. Mendoza, 19 Monc-77 Ags	.948	96	159	347	28	64
Barrera, Mexico City Reds	.965	11	21	34	2	9	P. Mendoza, Toluca	.946	93	147	344	28	69
Elizondo, Veracruz	.964	111	205	432	24	60	Gomez, Nuevo Laredo	.945	102	158	302	27	63
Blanks, Campeche	.963	105	171	349	22	57	Canedo, 18 Aguas-89 Monc	.943	107	193	367	34	78
Valle, Ciudad Juarez	.962	104	204	374	23	73	Herrera, 8 Cor-39 MC Reds	.942	47	54	142	12	22
Pacho, Mexico City Reds	.961	44	87	135	9	21	Scott, Toluca	.942	37	61	85	9	17
Morales, Mex. City Tigers	.959	111	236	389	27	70	Herrera, Leon	.942	105	186	348	33	76

SHORTSTOPS—Continued

Player and Club	Pct.	G.	PO.	A.	E.	DP.	Player and Club	Pct.	G.	PO.	A.	E.	DP.
Quintero, Saltillo	.938	51	80	164	16	39	A.G. Reyes, Tabasco	.920	23	28	41	6	8
Villaescusa, Yucatan	.938	19	33	42	5	8	Barrera, Nuevo Laredo	.919	33	68	114	16	21
Aguilar, Aguascalientes	.935	23	50	79	9	11	Saiz, Ciudad Juarez	.917	12	25	41	6	8
Montiel, 17 Tabasco-12 Leon	.927	29	42	85	10	13	R. Diaz, Mexico City Reds	.910	29	52	100	15	24
Torres, Veracruz	.927	12	8	30	3	5	Guerrero, 11 Tab-1 Aguas	.881	12	11	41	7	6
Uribe, Tampico	.927	73	112	204	25	37							

Triple Plays—Gomez, An. Sanchez.

(Fewer Than Ten Games)

Player and Club	Pct.	G.	PO.	A.	E.	DP.	Player and Club	Pct.	G.	PO.	A.	E.	DP.
Castaneda, Toluca	1.000	2	4	6	0	0	Bobadilla, Monclova	.963	9	6	20	1	3
Thompson, Tabasco	1.000	2	4	0	2	A. Gonzalez, Monclova	.958	5	9	14	1	0
S. Limon, Leon	1.000	1	0	6	0	0	Frias, Cordoba	.925	9	9	28	3	4
Chavarria, Nuevo Laredo	1.000	4	2	2	0	0	An. Sanchez, Mex. City Reds	.909	3	4	6	1	1
Serratos, Cordoba	1.000	1	2	1	0	0	Cruz, Tampico	.909	2	3	7	1	2
Leon, Yucatan	1.000	4	1	1	0	1	Rios, Monterrey	.889	2	3	5	1	1
J.L. Hernandez, Toluca	1.000	1	1	1	0	0	Yepez, Campeche	.882	3	4	11	2	0
J. Perez, Tampico	1.000	1	1	1	0	0	Camacho, Mexico City Tigers	.867	4	4	9	2	3
Ge. Rodriguez, Ciudad Juarez	1.000	1	0	2	0	0	Novelo, Tabasco	.857	5	6	12	3	2
R. Hernandez, Yucatan	1.000	1	0	1	0	0	L. Diaz, Mexico City Reds	.810	4	5	12	4	6
C. Rivera, Campeche	.967	6	7	22	1	2	Je. Gonzalez, Toluca	.750	2	0	6	2	0

OUTFIELDERS

Player and Club	Pct.	G.	PO.	A.	E.	DP.	Player and Club	Pct.	G.	PO.	A.	E.	DP.
Alexander, 27 Vera-8 Tol	1.000	35	62	4	0	1	Gamundi, 49 Cam-49 Yuc	.963	98	169	11	7	0
Enriquez, Monclova	1.000	31	41	3	0	0	M. Edwards, Monterrey	.962	86	161	16	8	3
D. Gonzalez, Toluca	1.000	19	28	4	0	0	Serratos, Cordoba	.962	15	22	3	1	1
F. Lara, Veracruz	1.000	13	23	1	0	0	Carrillo, Mex. City Tigers°	.961	112	281	13	12	2
Moran, Mexico City Reds	1.000	14	18	0	0	0	Monasterio, Mex. City Reds	.961	110	237	7	10	0
Reyes, Mexico City Tigers	1.000	10	11	1	0	0	Rivera, Aguascalientes	.960	90	206	11	9	1
Ayala, Leon	1.000	11	7	1	0	0	Sauceda, Ciudad Juarez	.960	45	67	5	3	1
R. Rodriguez, Aguascalientes°	.994	107	172	4	1	0	Perez, Aguascalientes°	.960	49	113	6	5	0
Guerra, Yucatan	.992	67	121	6	1	1	Martinez, Tampico	.958	19	22	1	1	1
Moore, Leon	.992	79	118	5	1	1	Ja. Rodriguez, MC Tigers	.958	14	21	2	1	1
Torres, 39 MC Reds-44 Yuc	.990	83	189	13	2	1	Cotes, Cordoba°	.957	81	102	9	5	1
Diaz, Toluca	.990	107	176	18	2	0	G. Gomez, 49 Monc-38 Leon	.957	87	146	9	7	1
Lizarraga, Ciudad Juarez	.989	105	169	10	2	1	Herring, Tabasco°	.956	109	252	11	12	3
Castelan, Toluca°	.987	72	149	6	2	0	Adamas, Monclova°	.956	115	179	17	9	1
Andrade, Tampico	.986	68	130	9	2	1	Alvarado, 3 Jua-50 Cam	.955	53	100	7	5	1
Paredes, 11 Yucatan-55 Leon	.986	66	134	2	2	0	H. Valenzuela, Leon	.953	33	37	4	2	1
Leal, 30 Yucatan-43 Monclova	.983	73	157	19	3	2	Collins, 19 MC Reds-21 Cor°	.953	40	61	0	3	0
Mora, Nuevo Laredo	.982	109	203	12	4	2	G. Sanchez, Nuevo Laredo	.950	25	37	1	2	0
Leonard, Tabasco°	.981	28	50	3	1	1	Blanco, Veracruz	.950	21	33	5	2	0
Castro, Mex. City Tigers°	.980	104	186	8	4	1	Bruno, Monterrey	.949	23	37	1	0	0
Cano, Saltillo	.978	74	167	12	4	1	Chavez, Nuevo Laredo°	.948	96	136	11	8	3
Navarro, Monterrey	.977	31	37	5	1	0	Baca, Leon	.947	79	153	9	9	1
Bellacetin, MC Tigers°	.977	105	155	12	4	1	Carrillo, Aguascalientes	.947	19	35	1	2	1
Smith, Ciudad Juarez°	.976	92	193	7	5	1	Rubio, Tabasco	.947	86	165	14	10	2
Arzate, Nuevo Laredo	.976	105	143	17	4	3	DeFreites, Tabasco	.946	54	131	9	8	1
Fernandez, Cordoba°	.976	67	155	5	4	0	Blassit, 28 Sal-10 Tam°	.946	38	66	4	4	0
Monreal, Mex. City Reds°	.975	111	220	18	6	1	Hernandez, Leon	.943	68	98	1	6	0
Jimenez, Campeche	.974	24	35	2	1	2	Bryant, Tampico	.942	54	78	3	5	0
Maza, Ciudad Juarez	.974	23	35	2	1	0	Olivares, 34 Cor-43 MC Reds°	.941	77	123	5	8	1
Zambrano, Ciudad Juarez°	.970	74	126	4	4	0	Moore, 25 Vera-34 Cor°	.940	59	120	6	8	0
Munoz, Veracruz°	.970	108	214	13	7	1	Peters, Monclova°	.938	115	237	7	16	3
Santos, Toluca	.970	21	30	2	1	0	Suarez, 36 Tab-39 Vera°	.938	75	127	10	9	1
P. Hernandez, Toluca	.970	16	31	1	1	0	Isales, Aguascalientes	.938	102	279	21	20	7
Felix, 22 Yuc-71 Cam	.969	93	176	13	6	3	Quiroz, Nuevo Laredo°	.937	65	84	5	6	0
Rosales, Cordoba	.969	101	207	10	7	3	L.A. Cruz, Tampico	.936	74	153	9	11	1
Soto, 14 Aguas-39 Campeche	.969	53	90	3	3	0	Gu. Rodriguez, Toluca	.936	59	79	9	6	0
Castaneda, Toluca	.969	23	29	2	1	0	Sotelo, 37 Leon-23 Tampico	.935	60	93	7	7	1
Gage, Tabasco°	.968	66	116	6	4	1	Johnson, Veracruz°	.930	41	88	2	3	0
Figueroa, 39 Yuc-32 Tam	.968	71	148	4	5	0	Ponce, Toluca	.917	23	21	1	2	0
Davila, Saltillo	.968	14	28	2	1	0	Quintero, Saltillo	.913	14	21	0	2	0
Rendon, Saltillo	.967	93	196	8	7	0	Covarrubias, Campeche	.911	19	37	4	4	0
Sarabia, Veracruz	.967	70	139	6	5	0	C.L. Rodriguez, Saltillo°	.898	26	41	3	5	0
Lopez, Monterrey	.966	66	109	6	4	0	Lora, Toluca	.889	13	13	3	2	0
Bravo, Yucatan	.966	55	103	11	4	3	Gutierrez, Mexico City Reds	.875	13	13	1	2	0
Villagomez, Tampico	.966	82	139	3	5	0	Ge. Rodriguez, Ciudad Juarez°	.850	18	15	2	3	0
Greene, Saltillo	.965	101	213	8	8	2	Espinosa, Veracruz°	.833	11	5	0	1	0
D. Edwards, Monterrey	.965	115	296	7	11	1	Dyes, Monterrey	.800	17	15	1	4	0
Pacheco, Campeche	.965	75	127	9	5	4							

Triple Play—Mora.

(Fewer Than Ten Games)

Player and Club	Pct.	G.	PO.	A.	E.	DP.	Player and Club	Pct.	G.	PO.	A.	E.	DP.
Caballero, Monterrey	1.000	6	11	1	0	0	Calderon, Campeche	1.000	3	1	1	0	0
Aranadas, Campeche	1.000	6	10	0	0	0	J. Cruz, Mexico City Tigers	1.000	3	1	0	0	0
D. Cruz, Tabasco	1.000	3	10	0	0	0	F. Cruz, Nuevo Laredo	1.000	2	1	0	0	0
F. Gonzalez, Monterrey	1.000	6	8	0	0	0	An. Sanchez, Mexico City Reds	1.000	2	1	0	0	0
Ruiz, Mexico City Reds	1.000	2	7	1	0	0	Scott, Toluca	.917	6	9	2	1	1
Garcia, Campeche	1.000	5	5	2	0	0	M. Gomez, Tabasco	.900	5	8	1	1	0
Monroy, Saltillo	1.000	5	7	0	0	0	Guzman, Campeche	.889	5	8	0	1	0
Chavarria, Saltillo	1.000	4	6	0	0	0	J. Vega, Mexico City Reds	.957	8	12	0	2	0
Everett, Monterrey	1.000	2	4	1	0	0	Cordova, Campeche	.929	9	13	0	1	0
Buenrostro, Yucatan	1.000	5	3	0	0	0	Salazar, Veracruz	.813	7	13	0	3	0
Douglas, Monterrey	1.000	2	3	0	0	0							

CATCHERS

Player and Club	Pct.	G.	PO.	A.	E.	DP.	PB.
Diaz, Leon	1.000	24	83	17	0	1	6
Soto, Nuevo Laredo	1.000	18	78	7	0	1	3
Castillo, Cordoba	1.000	22	34	3	0	0	0
Luna, Monclova	.996	49	210	46	1	5	6
ALVAREZ, Monterrey	.994	89	468	61	3	5	10
Reyes, Nuevo Laredo	.993	107	496	68	4	12	4
L.A. Mendoza, Monclova	.993	71	358	40	3	7	9
E. Rivera, Ciudad Juarez	.992	39	224	28	2	0	3
Ruiz, Mexico City Reds	.991	29	103	8	1	2	0
Daut, Monterrey	.991	35	181	30	2	2	15
Robles, Mexico City Reds	.990	102	437	55	5	2	2
Monroy, Saltillo	.989	22	81	9	1	1	1
Martinez, Leon	.987	24	64	14	1	0	6
Molina, Campeche	.986	41	130	14	2	2	3
Castillo, Mexico City Tigers	.985	65	335	55	6	10	4
A. Guzman, Tabasco	.984	97	407	95	8	5	16
Ruiz, 58 Leon-19 Toluca	.984	77	327	48	6	5	6
Quintero, Veracruz	.983	91	387	69	8	4	8
Hernandez, Cordoba	.982	111	572	61	11	1	6
Estrada, 49 Toluca-36 Leon	.980	85	385	54	9	5	6
Cruz, Nuevo Laredo	.979	29	81	13	2	0	1
Rosas, Aguascalientes	.978	93	384	60	10	10	8
Firoba, Saltillo	.978	88	382	61	10	2	9
Avila, Tampico	.976	41	182	25	5	3	4
Torres, Tampico	.975	74	341	53	10	2	12
Bazan, Yucatan	.975	82	397	63	12	5	1
Lora, Toluca	.974	54	266	29	8	5	9
Heras, Ciudad Juarez	.973	83	460	50	14	7	17
M.A. Guzman, Campeche	.973	73	344	48	11	3	12
Rojas, Mexico City Tigers	.968	61	287	45	11	5	6
Benitez, 11 Yuc-5 Cam	.962	16	65	10	3	2	1
Guerra, Yucatan	.956	28	110	21	6	6	5
Villa, 7 Vera-9 Tol	.955	16	57	6	3	2	3
Alvarez, Tabasco	.947	18	64	8	4	1	1
Vega, Aguascalientes	.944	31	85	16	6	3	5
Sarabia, Veracruz	.942	31	110	21	8	2	4
Benitez, 16 S.-7 Tam-6 Tab.	.924	29	85	24	9	2	2

(Fewer Than Ten Games)

Player and Club	Pct.	G.	PO.	A.	E.	DP.	PB.
DeLeon, Monclova	1.000	2	16	2	0	0	0
Ortiz, Toluca	1.000	3	14	0	0	0	2
Raymundo, Yucatan	1.000	4	6	1	0	0	0
Barrera, Mexico City Reds	1.000	2	1	1	0	0	0
Moran, Mexico City Reds	1.000	1	2	2	0	0	1
Marquez, Campeche	.963	6	22	4	1	1	0
Castaneda, Toluca	.875	5	6	1	1	0	2
Rojo, Cordoba	.667	1	2	0	1	0	0

PITCHERS

Player and Club	Pct.	G.	PO.	A.	E.	DP.
MATUS, 21 Tab-6 Aguas	1.000	21	11	59	0	3
Purata, 7 Cam-21 Tam	1.000	28	4	39	0	4
G. Martinez, Aguascalientes	1.000	17	7	31	0	4
R. Solis, Cordoba	1.000	28	5	32	0	3
P. Ochoa, Nuevo Laredo	1.000	45	7	28	0	4
Silva, 1 N. Laredo-34 Vera	1.000	35	2	28	0	1
M. Rivas, Tampico	1.000	46	7	20	0	2
Rogers, Tabasco	1.000	21	8	19	0	1
Vidana, Saltillo	1.000	31	7	18	0	2
Armas, Mexico City Reds	1.000	27	3	22	0	2
Rincon, Nuevo Laredo	1.000	25	9	16	0	0
C. Sosa, Tampico	1.000	27	3	21	0	0
Gutierrez 7 C. Juarez-13 Tam	1.000	20	7	17	0	3
Palacios, Veracruz	1.000	24	2	21	0	1
Arroyo, Yucatan	1.000	11	7	16	0	1
Montano, Mexico City Tigers	1.000	40	3	19	0	0
Divison, 23 Tol-23 Cam	1.000	46	4	16	0	2
R.A. Hernandez, Campeche	1.000	37	8	12	0	1
H. Rios, Leon	1.000	25	10	10	0	0
Antunez, Monterrey*	1.000	21	7	13	0	0
N. Montano, Ciudad Juarez	1.000	34	2	17	0	0
H. Valdez, 13 Vera-10 Cam	1.000	23	2	17	0	2
D. Franco, 11 Tab-11 Vera	1.000	22	2	17	0	1
E. Garcia, 3 Ver-7 Ln-10 Monc	1.000	20	4	15	0	1
Cecena, Saltillo	1.000	24	4	14	0	0
R. Rios, 6 MC Reds-11 Cam	1.000	17	4	13	0	0
Raygoza, Leon	1.000	38	3	12	0	0
Moya, Saltillo	1.000	36	2	13	0	1
A. Perez, Tampico	1.000	34	3	12	0	0
Luna, Tampico	1.000	21	3	12	0	0
Jaime, Ciudad Juarez	1.000	26	2	12	0	0
Rondon, 13 Yuc-12 Cam	1.000	25	3	11	0	0
Menendez, Yucatan	1.000	23	3	11	0	0
Cota, Mexico City Tigers	1.000	28	1	12	0	0
J. Ochoa, Tabasco	1.000	33	2	10	0	0
Heredia, Monterrey	1.000	39	3	8	0	0
C. Moreno, Yucatan	1.000	24	1	10	0	0
Rojo, Tabasco	1.000	20	2	9	0	0
Dimas, Mexico City Tigers	1.000	38	2	8	0	0
Urias, Toluca	1.000	28	2	8	0	0
D.Ochoa, 7 C.J.-12 Mont-5 Yuc	1.000	24	1	9	0	0
Ruiz, Monclova*	1.000	15	2	8	0	0
Urrea, Saltillo	1.000	36	1	8	0	2
Baruch, Campeche	1.000	28	1	8	0	0
Buice, Nuevo Laredo	1.000	14	4	5	0	1
Serafin, Cordoba	1.000	38	1	7	0	0
Ramo. Rodriguez, Campeche	1.000	29	1	7	0	0
M. Torres, Cordoba	1.000	12	0	8	0	1
P. Rodriguez, Yucatan	1.000	35	2	5	0	0
Rivas, Monclova	1.000	29	1	6	0	0
Castillejos, Aguascalientes	1.000	28	3	4	0	0
Ramirez, 7 Leon-21 Veracruz	1.000	28	2	5	0	0
R. Guzman, 10 Tigers-12 Aguas	1.000	22	2	5	0	0
Trevino, Monterrey	1.000	20	3	4	0	0
Becerra, Aguascalientes	1.000	14	2	5	0	0
Buitimea, Mexico City Tigers	1.000	12	0	7	0	0
Pimentel, Cordoba	1.000	16	1	6	0	0
Palacios, Tabasco	1.000	16	2	5	0	2
R. Gonzalez, Campeche	1.000	26	1	5	0	0
I. Jimenez, Toluca	1.000	24	0	6	0	1
F. Sanchez, Nuevo Laredo	1.000	19	2	4	0	0
Villarreal, Yucatan	1.000	16	2	4	0	0
Osuna, 1 Leon-12 Monclova	1.000	13	1	5	0	0
Salas, 1 Tab-11 MC Tigers	1.000	12	2	4	0	0
Navarro, Nuevo Laredo	1.000	20	1	4	0	0
Yucupicio, Tabasco	1.000	16	1	4	0	0
M. Rios, Tampico	1.000	15	1	4	0	1
R. Garcia, Leon	1.000	14	3	2	0	0
Brown, 10 Mont-2 Cam	1.000	12	0	5	0	0
Palafox, 9 Tigers-15 Tam	1.000	24	0	4	0	0
Miranda, 10 Cordoba-7 Leon	1.000	17	0	4	0	0
Nunez, 8 Tabasco-7 Veracruz	1.000	15	0	4	0	0
Montenegro, Ciudad Juarez	1.000	15	0	4	0	0
Beltran, 18 Leon-4 Cordoba	1.000	22	0	3	0	0
Morales, 2 Reds-12 Sal-6 Tam	1.000	20	1	2	0	0
Retes, Mexico City Tigers	1.000	14	0	3	0	0
Inzunza, Veracruz	1.000	13	0	3	0	0
Garza, Monterrey	1.000	12	0	3	0	0
Castaneda, Saltillo*	1.000	11	0	3	0	1
Quijano, Toluca	1.000	13	2	0	0	0
Tinajero, Tampico	1.000	18	0	1	0	0
Delfin, Cordoba	1.000	12	0	1	0	0
R. Contreras, Tampico	1.000	12	0	1	0	0
Mata, Monterrey	.985	28	16	49	1	4
M. Solis, Saltillo	.982	26	9	47	1	3
Colorado, Cordoba	.980	23	9	39	1	2
Ra. Garcia, Ciudad Juarez	.980	28	8	40	1	2
G. Jimenez, Toluca*	.979	25	6	41	1	3
R. Valdez, Campeche	.978	30	7	38	1	5
Dominguez, Toluca*	.978	29	7	38	1	1
Mundo, 9 Mont-22 Monc	.976	31	6	40	1	5
Ruiz, Mexico City Tigers*	.976	35	8	33	1	2
J. Rios, Mexico City Tigers	.973	32	9	27	1	1
Low, Aguascalientes	.972	24	13	22	1	2
Salinas, Yucatan	.972	20	6	29	1	2
Ortiz, 12 MC Reds-13 Vera*	.971	25	5	28	1	2
Soto, Toluca	.970	38	7	25	1	2
Villegas, 14 Tigers-6 Tab	.963	20	6	20	1	2
Ontiveros, Monclova	.962	31	8	17	1	3
Ogawa, Aguascalientes	.962	25	8	17	1	0
M. Rodriguez, Mexico City Reds	.962	24	3	22	1	2
Morales, Veracruz	.962	29	7	18	1	0
Orozco, Toluca	.959	33	16	54	3	7
Vazquez, 9 Cam-7 Vera	.958	16	3	20	1	1
Jefferson, Leon	.955	19	6	15	1	1
A. Rivera, Ciudad Juarez	.953	27	9	32	2	5
Ibarra, 20 Monc-15 MC Reds	.952	35	5	15	1	0
Garcia, 11 Ver-9 Tab-11 Tig	.950	31	3	16	1	0
Villanueva, Aguascalientes*	.949	25	4	33	2	3
Huerta, Yucatan	.947	18	3	15	1	1
Romo, Mexico City Reds	.944	22	3	31	2	1
Acosta, Campeche	.944	26	4	13	1	0
C. Diaz, Cordoba	.943	26	4	29	2	2
Arano, Veracruz	.941	22	0	32	2	0
Gallo, Saltillo	.941	23	1	15	1	1
Madrigal, Campeche	.939	28	10	21	2	0
Castillo, Nuevo Laredo	.939	26	5	26	2	1
Salas, 12 Veracruz-7 Yucatan	.938	19	3	12	1	2

PITCHERS—Continued

Player and Club	Pct.	G.	PO.	A.	E.	DP.
Pollorena, Saltillo	.938	16	6	9	1	0
Cordova, Aguascalientes	.933	16	1	13	1	0
Cutty, Monclova	.930	29	10	30	3	2
Mendez, Mexico City Reds	.929	26	5	21	2	0
Rivera, Cordoba	.923	25	14	22	3	1
Duarte, Monterrey	.927	26	8	30	3	0
Gaxiola, 9 Mont-16 Cordoba	.920	25	8	20	3	0
Smith, Nuevo Laredo	.919	29	4	30	3	1
J. Valenzuela, Saltillo	.919	29	10	24	3	1
I. Velazquez, Mexico City Tigers	.919	31	6	28	3	2
Lopez, Aguascalientes	.917	39	8	14	2	2
F. Martinez, Monterrey	.917	22	5	17	2	1
Brunet, 7 Sal-14 Mont°	.917	21	2	21	1	2
Stone, Nuevo Laredo	.917	45	4	7	1	0
Sauceda, Yucatan	.917	25	3	8	1	0
Belman, Tabasco	.917	21	4	7	1	2
Carranza, Mexico City Reds°	.917	18	4	7	1	1
Chavez, Tampico	.913	43	6	36	4	3
Jimenez, 20 Monclova-8 Leon	.909	28	9	21	3	2
Segui, Leon	.909	24	3	17	2	1
Pulido, Mexico City Reds	.909	47	2	8	1	0
J. Vazquez, Aguascalientes	.905	36	3	16	2	1
Angulo, Yucatan°	.905	21	2	17	2	0
Escarrega, 14 Monc-11 Yuc	.900	25	7	34	2	4
A. Rodriguez, Leon	.900	38	1	8	1	1

Player and Club	Pct.	G.	PO.	A.	E.	DP.
Leon, Mexico City Reds	.900	11	2	7	1	0
J. Moreno, Nuevo Laredo	.898	28	11	33	5	2
Lugo, Veracruz	.889	35	5	19	3	1
McCoy, 9 Monclova-9 Saltillo	.882	18	3	12	2	1
Villalobos, Yucatan	.882	10	1	14	2	0
Perez, Toluca°	.875	25	6	22	4	3
P. Sanchez, Mexico City Reds	.875	39	3	11	2	1
Alicea, Ciudad Juarez	.875	33	5	9	2	0
Guzman, Monclova	.864	27	0	19	3	1
Uresti, Leon	.864	24	5	14	3	1
Pollorena, Tabasco	.862	25	10	15	4	2
Quinonez, Ciudad Juarez	.857	15	3	9	2	0
Feola, Ciudad Juarez°	.846	34	2	9	2	0
J.L. Garcia, Monclova°	.846	31	4	7	2	0
Serna, Ciudad Juarez	.833	19	4	4	2	0
A. Velazquez, 2 Reds-14 Cor	.833	16	1	4	1	0
L. Velazquez, Tabasco	.824	17	1	13	3	0
Aguilar, 19 Tigers-10 Tam	.800	29	1	3	1	0
Dominguez, Ciudad Juarez	.750	12	0	3	1	0
Peralta, 8 Leon-6 Yucatan	.667	14	1	7	4	0
Valle, Leon	.667	11	0	2	1	0
Veliz, Mexico City Reds	.667	11	0	2	1	0
Enriquez, Nuevo Laredo	.500	10	0	1	1	0
Mariscal, Monterrey	.333	11	0	1	2	0

(Fewer Than Ten Games)

Player and Club	Pct.	G.	PO.	A.	E.	DP.
Chavez, Mexico City Reds	1.000	9	2	6	0	0
Beltran, Tampico	1.000	6	2	4	0	1
H. Valenzuela, Tampico	1.000	9	1	4	0	0
Moncada, Leon	1.000	8	3	2	0	0
Lester, Nuevo Laredo	1.000	6	2	3	0	0
Alcala, Leon	1.000	5	1	4	0	0
Miranda, Monterrey	1.000	8	1	3	0	0
Re. Garcia, Mexico City Reds	1.000	5	0	4	0	0
Zamudio, Veracruz	1.000	3	1	3	0	0
Munoz, Aguascalientes	1.000	9	0	3	0	0
J. Hernandez, Yucatan	1.000	8	1	2	0	0
Pena, Leon	1.000	8	0	3	0	1
McLaughlin, Nuevo Laredo	1.000	8	0	3	0	0
Molina, Monclova	1.000	6	2	1	0	0
Wax, Nuevo Laredo	1.000	4	2	1	0	1
Osuna, Mexico City Reds	1.000	3	0	3	0	0
Abarca, Leon	1.000	9	0	2	0	0
Contreras, Veracruz	1.000	9	0	2	0	0
A. Diaz, Tabasco	1.000	8	1	1	0	0
J. Rivera, Campeche	1.000	7	0	2	0	0
G. Guzman, Veracruz	1.000	7	1	1	0	0

Player and Club	Pct.	G.	PO.	A.	E.	DP.
R.A. Hernandez, Campeche	1.000	6	1	1	0	0
G. Valenzuela, Leon	1.000	5	0	3	0	1
P.G. Guzman, Leon	1.000	5	0	2	0	1
Uribe, Yucatan	1.000	9	0	1	0	0
Quiroz, Nuevo Laredo°	1.000	8	0	1	0	0
F. Franco, 3 Cam-5 Vera	1.000	8	0	1	0	0
A. Sanchez, Monclova	1.000	5	1	0	0	0
Duane, Monterrey	1.000	3	1	0	0	0
Ledon, Mexico City Tigers	1.000	2	0	1	0	0
Saldivar, Campeche	1.000	2	0	1	0	0
I. Gonzalez, Monterrey	1.000	1	1	0	0	0
Parroth, Saltillo	.900	8	2	7	1	1
McDonald, Tampico	.857	6	0	6	1	0
Quijada, Cordoba	.833	8	3	2	1	0
Salcido, Monclova	.833	6	1	4	1	1
Romero, Mexico City Tigers	.800	7	0	4	1	0
Torres, Ciudad Juarez	.750	9	1	2	1	0
DeLeon, Tampico	.750	4	0	3	1	0
S. Sanchez, Monclova	.750	5	1	2	1	0
Allen, Nuevo Laredo	.500	6	0	1	1	0
Stottlemyre, Nuevo Laredo	.000	4	0	1	1	0

CLUB PITCHING

Club	ERA.	G.	CG.	ShO.	Sv.	IP.	H.	R.	ER.	HR.	HB.	BB.	Int. BB.	SO.	WP.	Bk.
Cordoba	3.84	114	43	8	16	989.0	1085	500	422	66	22	367	29	542	53	1
Monterrey	4.26	117	41	7	17	1001.0	1113	568	474	76	21	424	31	581	41	2
Yucatan	4.26	118	47	17	16	1005.0	1118	543	476	79	30	380	15	525	61	6
Tabasco	4.31	110	30	6	8	930.0	1007	554	445	50	40	441	76	445	34	4
Nuevo Laredo	4.32	119	19	6	20	1034.1	1050	574	497	100	38	467	31	614	39	3
Mexico City Reds	4.38	116	26	7	29	1018.2	1139	591	496	64	38	418	24	498	62	0
Veracruz	4.40	118	31	7	21	987.1	1069	563	483	88	33	457	68	479	60	7
Mexico City Tigers	4.50	113	20	9	21	995.1	1145	579	498	81	33	434	32	559	55	2
Toluca	4.82	117	41	9	17	1023.2	1267	636	548	76	39	403	43	544	43	1
Ciudad Juarez	4.91	115	37	7	17	1008.0	1197	643	550	95	30	450	26	641	50	6
Tampico	5.33	111	12	3	18	940.2	1084	639	557	126	46	493	40	497	75	3
Saltillo	5.34	116	29	3	11	1005.2	1223	676	597	131	34	446	41	446	46	2
Aguascalientes	5.42	118	32	4	13	1017.2	1314	718	613	117	19	343	35	426	29	1
Campeche	5.44	112	14	2	13	939.2	1203	676	568	89	24	365	20	428	44	3
Leon	5.94	116	24	1	13	980.0	1268	783	647	134	26	467	39	527	58	3
Monclova	6.47	116	31	0	9	981.0	1333	816	705	141	35	495	24	521	45	0

PITCHERS' RECORDS

(Leading Qualifiers for Earned-Run Average Leadership—94 or More Innings)

°Throws lefthanded.

Pitcher—Club	W.	L.	Pct.	ERA.	G.	GS.	CG.	GF.	ShO.	Sv.	IP.	H.	R.	ER.	HR.	HB.	BB.	Int. BB.	SO.	WP.
Colorado, Cordoba	17	6	.739	2.20	23	23	16	0	1	0	196.2	187	53	48	7	1	26	3	85	2
M. Rivas, Tampico	9	7	.563	2.40	46	4	3	42	1	15	131.0	117	42	35	12	7	32	7	91	0
Angulo, Yucatan	14	4	.778	2.65	21	19	11	2	6	0	136.0	117	51	40	7	3	71	0	162	10
J. Moreno, Nuevo Laredo	12	8	.600	2.90	28	25	11	3	2	0	176.2	156	69	57	14	6	69	5	74	2
Duarte, Monterrey	15	7	.682	2.98	26	25	13	1	2	0	187.0	199	73	62	11	7	53	7	78	3
Matus, Tabasco-Aguas	10	10	.500	3.22	27	25	10	2	1	0	170.1	169	81	61	7	8	69	11	64	5
M.A. Gonzalez, Monterrey	13	12	.520	3.29	28	26	13	2	3	1	197.0	203	87	72	11	5	58	7	121	9
Salinas, Cordoba	12	5	.706	3.29	20	20	9	0	2	0	153.0	155	62	56	11	4	39	1	66	7
R.A. Hernandez, Campeche	4	4	.500	3.31	37	1	0	36	0	4	103.1	110	50	38	14	2	17	1	52	1
J. Rios, Mexico City Tigers	17	17	.500	3.33	32	31	16	1	5	0	221.2	194	92	82	13	9	86	3	194	10
P. Ochoa, Nuevo Laredo	4	4	.500	3.43	45	0	1	45	0	7	99.2	106	40	38	8	5	33	8	37	0

Departmental Leaders: G—Pulido, 47; W—Colorado, Mendez, Orozco, J. Rios, M. Solis, 17; L—Ibarra, 14; Pct.—M. Solis, .810; GS—J. Rios, 31; CG—Orozco, 19; GF—Pulido, 47; ShO—Angulo, 6; Sv.—Pulido, 23; IP—Orozco, 238; H—Orozco, 265; R—Orozco, 126; ER—Orozco, 111; HR—M. Solis, 26; HB—F. Ontiveros, A. Rivera, 11; BB—J. Rios, 86; IBB—Arano, 12; SO—J. Rios, 194; WP—O. Rivera, 16.

(All Pitchers—Listed Alphabetically)

Pitcher—Club	W.	L.	Pct.	ERA.	G.	GS.	CG.	GF.	ShO.	Sv.	IP.	H.	R.	ER.	HR.	HB.	BB.	Int. BB.	SO.	WP.
Abarca, Leon	0	2	.000	6.98	9	0	0	4	0	0	29.2	41	24	23	6	0	13	0	10	5
Acosta, Campeche	5	13	.278	5.94	26	24	2	2	1	0	125.2	166	91	83	11	3	42	2	36	0
Aguilar, 19 MC Tigers-10 Tab ...	2	2	.500	4.42	29	0	0	29	0	1	20.2	25	14	9	1	1	17	3	13	1
Alcala, Toluca	0	0	.000	6.60	5	3	0	2	0	0	15.0	18	15	11	1	2	20	4	4	1
Alicea, Ciudad Juarez	3	4	.429	1.88	33	0	0	33	0	11	62.2	54	22	13	0	2	26	5	48	5
Alvarado, Mexico City Tigers	0	1	.000	8.59	4	2	0	2	0	0	7.1	12	8	7	1	0	4	0	6	0
Angulo, Yucatan	14	4	.778	2.65	21	19	11	2	6	0	136.0	117	51	40	7	3	71	0	162	10
Antunez, Monterrey	4	7	.364	4.15	21	14	4	7	0	1	89.0	108	47	41	9	0	32	0	63	4
Arano, Veracruz	11	9	.550	3.45	22	22	6	0	0	0	143.1	161	64	55	17	1	45	12	47	3
Arceo, Yucatan	0	0	.000	0.00	1	0	0	1	0	0	1.2	0	0	0	0	0	1	0	0	0
Armas, Mexico City Reds	8	3	.727	5.29	27	12	2	15	0	1	100.1	118	68	59	8	9	51	3	43	5
Arroyo, Yucatan	8	3	.727	1.55	11	11	10	0	3	0	87.1	64	20	15	3	1	7	0	29	1
Baruch, Campeche	1	2	.333	3.34	28	1	1	27	0	0	67.1	80	32	25	4	1	19	0	29	5
Becerra, Aguascalientes	1	1	.500	5.86	14	0	0	14	0	0	27.2	49	22	18	4	0	8	1	4	1
Belman, Tabasco	2	4	.333	5.84	21	9	1	12	0	0	69.1	83	51	45	2	6	38	10	33	2
E. Beltran, Tampico	3	0	1.000	1.82	6	5	0	1	0	0	24.2	15	5	5	0	0	11	0	8	3
J. Beltran, 18 Leon-4 Cordoba ..	1	4	.200	7.63	22	6	0	16	0	0	63.2	92	65	54	12	6	34	4	27	5
A. Blanco, Cordoba	0	0	.000	13.50	1	0	0	1	0	0	.2	0	1	1	0	0	1	0	0	0
J. Blanco, Tampico	0	0	.000	2.35	4	0	0	4	0	0	7.2	9	2	2	0	1	5	1	1	0
Brown, 10 Mont-2 Cam	1	1	.500	7.53	12	10	0	2	0	1	43.0	52	36	36	4	3	29	0	35	6
Brunet, 7 Salt-14 Mont°	6	9	.400	4.66	21	19	5	2	2	1	121.2	147	79	63	11	1	50	0	65	7
Buice, Nuevo Laredo	4	1	.800	2.25	14	2	0	12	0	3	40.0	26	12	10	1	0	17	1	35	3
Buitimea, Mexico City Tigers	2	0	1.000	5.57	12	2	0	10	0	0	32.1	44	21	20	5	1	11	0	20	3
Calderon, Toluca	0	1	.000	5.93	7	1	0	6	0	0	13.2	9	10	9	0	0	12	1	9	1
G. Canedo, Aguascalientes	0	0	.000	5.40	2	0	0	2	0	0	3.1	4	2	2	0	0	1	1	1	0
Carranza, Mexico City Reds°	2	4	.333	6.20	18	5	0	13	0	1	49.1	67	42	34	6	2	24	5	21	5
Cartagena, Mexico City Tigers...	0	0	.000	16.20	2	0	0	2	0	0	3.1	9	6	6	0	0	4	0	2	0
A. Castaneda, Cordoba	0	0	.000	......	1	0	0	1	0	0	0.0	0	0	0	0	0	0	0	0	0
M. Castaneda, Saltillo	2	0	1.000	3.04	11	2	0	9	0	0	26.2	16	9	9	1	0	19	1	14	2
Castillejos, Aguascalientes	7	3	.700	6.95	28	2	0	26	0	0	77.2	131	67	60	11	1	16	2	21	1
Castillo, Nuevo Laredo	6	6	.500	4.46	26	15	1	11	0	0	121.0	138	64	60	12	5	45	4	74	8
Cecena, Saltillo	1	4	.200	5.97	24	13	0	11	0	0	78.1	92	61	52	7	6	58	2	61	3
G. Chavez, Tampico	13	10	.650	4.43	43	21	3	22	0	3	180.2	200	100	89	25	7	85	10	92	7
L. Chavez, Mexico City Reds	4	1	.800	4.17	9	7	1	2	0	0	41.0	49	20	19	1	0	18	1	6	1
COLORADO, Cordoba	17	6	.739	2.20	23	23	16	0	1	0	196.2	187	53	48	7	1	26	3	85	2
P. Contreras, Veracruz	0	1	.000	3.52	9	4	1	5	0	0	23.0	18	11	9	0	0	21	1	7	1
R. Contreras, Tampico	0	2	.000	7.94	12	3	0	9	0	0	28.1	42	30	25	8	1	29	0	8	10
Cordova, Aguascalientes	4	6	.400	5.42	16	15	1	1	0	0	78.0	105	60	47	8	0	32	6	29	2
Corona, Leon	0	0	.000	6.75	3	0	0	3	0	0	6.2	7	10	5	3	0	3	0	0	1
F. Cota, Mexico City Tigers	6	0	1.000	4.95	28	0	0	28	0	2	60.0	72	33	33	4	1	18	2	27	3
M. Cota, Tampico	0	0	.000	11.57	3	0	0	3	0	0	4.2	7	6	6	2	0	6	0	0	0
Cruz, Tampico	0	0	.000	9.00	1	0	0	1	0	0	1.0	3	1	1	0	0	1	0	1	0
Cutty, Monclova	8	11	.421	4.55	29	23	10	6	0	1	162.1	173	100	82	18	8	19	5	103	3
DeLeon, Tampico	0	0	.000	3.86	4	2	0	2	0	0	13.0	14	7	6	2	1	6	1	6	0
J.M. Delfin, 1 Ver-1 Tab	0	0	.000	27.00	2	0	0	2	0	0	1.1	2	5	4	0	1	2	0	0	0
J. Delfin, Cordoba	0	0	.000	4.41	12	0	0	12	0	1	16.1	21	14	8	0	1	5	0	5	0
Delgadillo, Aguascalientes	0	0	.000	6.00	2	0	0	2	0	0	6.0	8	5	4	1	0	0	0	2	1
A. Diaz, Tabasco	0	0	.000	6.24	8	0	0	8	0	0	13.0	16	11	9	3	0	6	0	5	0
C. Diaz, Cordoba	8	11	.421	4.21	26	21	7	5	2	1	141.0	189	81	66	10	4	47	4	74	8
Dimas, Mexico City Tigers	7	6	.539	4.50	38	0	0	38	0	6	58.0	61	30	29	4	3	27	6	18	8
Divison, 23 Tol-23 Cam	6	7	.462	5.65	46	0	0	46	0	11	65.1	88	50	41	7	7	26	3	34	3
H. Dominguez, Toluca°	11	12	.478	4.55	29	28	9	1	1	0	186.0	223	117	94	16	6	63	4	98	10
M. Dominguez, C. Juarez	0	2	.000	10.66	12	1	0	11	0	0	25.1	43	35	30	5	1	17	1	11	1
Duarte, Monterrey	15	7	.682	2.98	26	25	13	1	2	0	187.0	199	73	62	11	7	53	7	78	3
Edwards, Nuevo Laredo	0	1	.000	11.40	6	4	0	2	0	0	15.0	23	21	19	3	0	13	0	10	3
Ellis, Monterrey	0	1	.000	22.50	3	1	0	0	0	0	2.0	4	5	5	0	0	3	0	2	0
Enriquez, Nuevo Laredo	0	3	.000	11.32	10	1	0	5	0	0	20.2	36	28	26	1	1	24	0	16	3
Escarrega, 14 Monc-11 Yuc	9	13	.409	4.94	25	25	10	0	1	0	176.2	243	110	97	15	4	37	5	88	1
Espinosa, Yucatan	0	0	.000	4.50	5	0	0	5	0	0	8.0	12	6	4	0	1	1	0	3	1
Feola, Ciudad Juarez°	3	6	.333	4.54	34	1	1	33	1	3	69.1	65	39	35	5	0	50	4	42	6
Figueroa, Veracruz	0	1	.000	9.53	4	0	0	4	0	0	5.2	6	6	6	2	5	0	1	0	0
D. Franco, 11 Tab-11 Ver	3	11	.214	5.81	22	16	3	6	1	0	93.0	111	65	60	12	3	38	7	34	1
F. Franco, 3 Cam-5 Ver	0	3	.000	8.68	3	3	0	0	0	0	5.2	12	19	18	2	0	8	1	3	3
Gage, Tabasco	0	0	.000	0.00	1	0	0	1	0	0	1.0	0	0	0	0	0	2	0	0	0
Gallo, Saltillo	4	5	.444	4.07	23	0	0	23	0	5	40.2	48	28	22	4	0	28	2	20	2
E. Garcia, 3 Ver-7 Leon-10 Mva	3	12	.200	6.08	20	17	3	3	0	0	100.2	130	79	68	18	1	36	1	39	3
Jor. Garcia, 11 Ver-9 Tb-10 Ti	4	5	.444	6.78	31	6	1	25	1	2	71.2	83	56	54	10	3	39	7	46	8
Jos. Garcia, Monclova°	2	4	.333	6.75	31	2	0	29	0	1	40.0	51	36	30	7	1	18	1	25	4
Ra. Garcia, Ciudad Juarez	16	9	.640	3.96	28	28	16	0	2	0	225.0	244	121	99	18	4	72	0	184	11
Re. Garcia, Mexico City Reds	2	0	1.000	3.27	5	2	0	3	0	0	11.0	11	4	4	1	0	3	0	2	0
Ro. Garcia, Leon	1	3	.250	7.52	14	1	0	13	0	0	26.1	42	23	22	6	1	19	3	14	7
Garza, Monterrey	1	2	.333	5.68	12	2	0	10	0	0	19.0	22	14	12	2	1	20	1	10	3
Gaxiola, 9 Mont-16 Cor	8	10	.444	3.63	25	22	5	3	0	1	146.1	165	77	59	15	5	50	5	86	5
I. Gonzalez, Monterrey	0	0	.000	0.00	1	0	0	1	0	0	2.0	1	0	0	0	0	3	0	0	0
M.A. Gonzalez, Monterrey	13	12	.520	3.29	28	26	13	2	3	1	197.0	203	87	72	11	5	58	7	121	9
R. Gonzalez, Campeche	1	4	.200	9.39	26	1	0	25	0	0	46.0	74	57	48	9	3	32	2	28	7
Gutierrez, 7 C. Juarez-13 Tam ..	7	7	.500	6.15	20	1	0	3	0	0	90.2	115	67	62	12	5	57	7	41	6
G. Guzman, Veracruz	0	3	.000	6.38	7	4	1	3	0	0	18.1	28	18	13	0	0	12	1	10	1
J. Guzman, Monclova	4	6	.400	7.13	27	8	1	19	0	1	65.2	96	59	52	5	0	38	1	42	6
P.G. Guzman, Leon	0	0	.000	15.42	5	0	0	5	0	0	4.2	12	8	8	1	0	4	3	1	4
R. Guzman, 10 Tigers-12 Aguas	3	2	.600	7.12	22	0	0	22	0	1	36.2	55	34	29	7	0	17	1	11	4
S. Guzman, Yucatan	0	0	.000	......	1	0	0	1	0	0	2.0	0	0	0	0	0	2	0	0	0
Heredia, Monterrey	3	7	.300	4.18	39	0	0	39	0	13	66.2	56	37	31	5	1	31	7	41	2
F.A. Hernandez, Campeche	1	3	.250	7.18	6	6	0	0	0	0	26.1	38	23	21	1	1	8	1	7	0
J. Hernandez, Yucatan	1	0	1.000	4.66	8	0	0	8	0	0	19.1	26	12	10	5	1	7	0	7	1
P. Hernandez, Toluca	0	0	.000	0.00	1	0	0	1	0	0	2.0	0	0	0	0	0	0	0	1	0
R.A. Hernandez, Campeche	4	4	.500	3.31	37	1	0	36	0	4	103.1	110	50	38	14	2	17	1	52	1
Huerta, Tabasco	3	8	.273	3.35	18	9	3	9	0	0	80.2	86	40	30	5	4	39	6	47	4
Ibarra, 20 Monc-15 MC Reds	7	14	.333	7.00	35	16	4	19	0	1	118.1	159	121	92	16	5	62	4	61	8
Inzunza, Veracruz	2	0	1.000	5.88	13	2	0	11	0	0	26.0	25	17	17	3	1	18	1	11	2

Pitcher—Club	W.	L.	Pct.	ERA.	G.	GS.	CG.	GF.	ShO.	Sv.	IP.	H.	R.	ER.	HR.	HB.	BB.	Int. BB.	SO.	WP.
Jaime, Ciudad Juarez	2	3	.400	6.50	26	0	0	26	0	0	44.1	78	36	32	7	1	11	1	18	2
Jefferson, Leon	11	4	.733	3.56	19	17	7	2	1	0	124.0	144	64	49	7	1	44	2	82	3
G. Jimenez, Toluca*	11	6	.647	4.57	25	25	7	0	3	0	167.1	227	90	85	12	7	75	3	98	4
I. Jimenez, Toluca	0	3	.000	6.54	24	0	0	24	0	0	31.2	38	30	23	3	4	36	0	19	5
R. Jimenez, 20 Monc-8 Leon	4	6	.400	5.86	28	8	1	20	0	0	87.2	121	69	57	14	2	36	1	35	0
H. Lara, Veracruz	0	0	.000	13.50	2	0	0	2	0	0	1.1	6	4	2	0	1	0	0	2	0
B. Leal, Mexico City Reds	0	0	.000	3.68	8	0	0	8	0	0	14.2	13	7	6	2	0	9	0	9	1
G. Leal, Yucatan	0	0	.000	7.71	2	0	0	2	0	0	2.1	2	2	2	0	0	1	1	1	1
Ledon, Mexico City Tigers	1	0	1.000	0.00	2	0	0	2	0	0	1.0	0	0	0	0	1	3	0	0	0
Leon, Mexico City Reds	5	1	.833	2.41	11	9	2	2	0	2	59.2	51	21	16	1	0	8	0	17	1
Lester, Nuevo Laredo	1	2	.333	6.29	6	4	0	2	0	0	24.1	29	20	17	3	0	14	0	16	1
F. Lopez, Saltillo	0	0	.000	13.50	1	0	0	1	0	0	.2	1	2	1	0	0	2	0	0	0
H. Lopez, Aguascalientes	4	4	.500	4.65	39	0	0	39	0	6	69.2	85	42	36	7	3	31	8	44	1
Low, Aguascalientes	7	6	.539	5.21	24	18	4	6	0	0	126.0	150	82	73	14	1	59	7	70	3
Lozano, Veracruz	0	0	.000	2.45	2	0	0	2	0	0	7.1	8	2	2	0	0	2	0	2	0
Lugo, Veracruz	4	1	.800	5.15	35	0	0	35	0	2	73.1	83	50	42	3	4	38	9	39	11
Luna, Tampico	1	6	.143	7.09	21	11	0	10	0	0	53.1	67	48	42	7	2	28	2	20	4
MacDonald, Tampico	2	2	.500	6.84	6	3	0	3	0	0	25.0	34	26	19	5	4	12	1	10	5
H. Madrigal, Leon	0	0	.000	21.60	2	0	0	2	0	0	1.2	7	9	4	1	0	5	0	1	0
J. Madrigal, Campeche	5	9	.357	5.05	28	19	5	9	0	2	137.1	165	89	77	15	2	47	1	75	8
Mariscal, Monterrey	1	0	1.000	5.23	11	0	0	11	0	0	10.1	15	8	6	1	0	6	1	6	0
F. Martinez, Monterrey	10	7	.588	3.97	22	19	8	3	0	0	152.0	160	76	67	12	1	75	3	124	3
G. Martinez, Aguascalientes	7	6	.539	4.29	17	17	7	0	0	0	107.0	115	67	51	8	1	36	3	31	3
Matus, 21 Tab-6 Aguas	10	10	.500	3.22	27	25	10	2	1	0	170.1	169	81	61	7	8	69	11	64	5
McCoy, 9 Monc-9 Sal	5	8	.385	6.43	18	15	3	3	0	2	77.0	90	66	55	8	2	60	3	39	5
McLaughlin, Nuevo Laredo	2	1	.667	5.16	8	6	0	2	0	1	36.2	26	23	21	4	3	22	0	40	3
Medina, Ciudad Juarez	0	0	.000	0.00	1	0	0	1	0	0	1.0	1	1	0	0	0	0	0	0	0
Mendez, Mexico City Reds	17	5	.772	3.61	26	25	10	1	3	0	184.1	181	85	74	13	4	52	0	94	5
Menendez, Yucatan	7	10	.412	5.73	23	18	5	5	1	0	108.1	128	74	69	16	1	43	2	24	5
F. Miranda, 10 Cor-7 Leon	2	1	.667	7.32	17	0	0	17	0	2	35.2	46	30	29	3	4	21	1	20	6
J. Miranda, Monterrey	0	0	.000	4.61	8	0	0	8	0	0	27.1	24	14	14	3	0	13	0	3	1
Molina, Monclova	0	0	.000	13.50	6	0	0	6	0	0	5.1	14	8	8	2	1	4	0	6	0
Moncada, Leon	1	1	.500	7.36	8	1	0	7	0	0	22.0	25	20	18	5	0	11	1	8	0
F. Montano, MC Tigers	2	5	.286	5.18	40	6	0	34	0	9	80.0	109	51	46	4	1	44	8	40	3
N. Montano, Ciudad Juarez	5	5	.500	5.37	24	14	1	10	0	0	104.0	131	64	62	13	3	42	6	37	4
Montenegro, Ciudad Juarez	0	0	.000	5.04	15	0	0	15	0	0	30.1	38	21	17	2	1	12	0	5	1
Moore, Leon	0	0	.000	0.00	1	0	0	1	0	0	1.1	1	0	0	0	0	2	0	2	0
Morales, 2 MCR-12 Sal-6 Tam..	0	0	.000	8.35	20	1	0	19	0	0	18.1	23	18	17	2	1	19	2	13	4
Morales, Veracruz	7	4	.636	3.78	29	5	0	24	0	2	87.1	104	48	41	10	1	23	4	21	3
C. Moreno, Yucatan	2	1	.667	6.00	24	1	0	23	0	0	57.0	68	40	38	6	4	30	0	38	9
J. Moreno, Nuevo Laredo	12	8	.600	2.90	28	25	11	3	2	0	176.2	156	69	57	14	6	69	5	74	2
Moya, Saltillo	4	2	.667	5.30	36	0	0	36	0	1	69.2	86	44	41	5	1	32	4	32	4
Mundo, 9 Mont-22 Monc	5	11	.313	7.39	31	19	3	12	0	2	126.2	181	118	104	18	3	75	1	47	7
Munoz, Aguascalientes	1	0	1.000	7.94	9	0	0	9	0	0	22.2	37	23	20	9	0	2	0	5	1
Murillo, Monterrey	0	0	.000	0.00	1	0	0	1	0	0	1.2	1	0	0	0	0	0	0	1	0
Navarrete, Yucatan	0	0	.000	0.00	1	0	0	1	0	0	1.0	0	0	0	0	0	0	0	1	0
Navarro, Nuevo Laredo	1	2	.333	6.92	20	3	0	17	0	0	40.1	51	38	31	5	2	31	2	46	3
J. Nunez, Tabasco	0	0	.000	8.22	8	0	0	8	0	0	15.1	28	15	14	3	1	7	2	10	0
M. Nunez, Veracruz	0	2	.000	11.42	7	4	0	3	0	0	17.1	29	24	22	4	0	15	0	16	2
D. Ochoa, 7 C.J.-12 Mont-5 Yuc	2	3	.400	6.32	24	1	0	23	0	1	47.0	79	44	33	5	6	22	3	21	5
J. Ochoa, Tabasco	3	5	.375	2.09	33	0	0	33	0	5	64.2	55	24	15	1	1	21	6	19	2
P. Ochoa, Nuevo Laredo	4	4	.500	3.43	45	0	1	45	0	7	99.2	106	40	38	8	5	33	8	37	0
Ogawa, Aguascalientes	10	11	.476	5.84	25	25	9	0	0	0	140.1	183	109	91	13	7	39	2	74	3
F. Ontiveros, Monclova	0	4	.000	6.39	31	5	0	26	0	0	93.0	150	74	66	17	11	27	6	35	2
J. Ontiveros, Toluca	0	0	.000	14.54	3	0	0	3	0	0	4.1	12	9	7	2	0	1	0	3	0
Orozco, Toluca	17	9	.654	4.20	33	28	19	5	1	3	238.0	265	126	111	19	4	53	10	150	3
Ortiz, 12 Reds-13 Veracruz*	10	7	.588	3.70	25	19	5	6	1	2	138.2	176	72	57	7	3	20	4	54	5
Ri. Osuna, Mexico City Reds	0	0	.000	37.80	3	0	0	3	0	0	1.2	7	7	7	0	1	3	0	2	1
Ro. Osuna, 1 Leon-12 Monc	1	1	.500	4.05	13	0	0	13	0	1	33.1	32	17	15	1	1	17	0	25	2
R. Palacios, Tabasco	3	3	.500	7.34	16	2	0	14	0	1	30.2	32	27	25	3	0	19	2	9	1
V. Palacios, Veracruz	7	8	.468	3.52	24	20	7	4	1	4	128.0	117	64	50	11	2	79	6	120	13
Palafox, 9 Tigers-15 Tam	2	3	.400	5.33	24	2	0	22	0	0	49.0	66	37	29	5	2	31	1	22	2
Parroth, Saltillo	2	4	.333	5.68	8	6	1	2	0	0	38.0	52	33	24	6	3	24	1	23	3
Pena, Leon	2	4	.333	5.89	8	7	0	1	0	0	36.2	45	27	24	6	3	11	0	13	1
Peralta, 8 Leon-6 Yucatan	0	4	.000	12.36	14	6	0	8	0	0	27.2	50	45	38	5	0	23	0	16	4
A. Perez, Tampico	3	3	.500	8.19	34	3	0	31	0	0	51.2	64	50	47	6	4	30	1	29	9
C. Perez, Toluca*	12	6	.667	4.82	25	23	4	2	1	0	142.0	194	88	76	5	6	51	2	51	6
Pimentel, Cordoba	2	2	.500	4.45	16	2	1	14	0	1	30.1	29	17	15	2	1	20	1	22	3
Pina, Aguascalientes	0	0	.000	....	1	0	0	1	0	0	0.0	2	3	3	1	0	1	0	0	0
A. Pollorena, Saltillo	5	5	.500	6.70	16	16	2	0	0	0	90.0	128	70	67	19	3	18	2	23	3
O. Pollorena, Tabasco	5	5	.500	4.01	25	18	4	7	2	0	114.1	114	70	51	8	4	75	4	46	6
Posadas, Campeche	0	1	.000	18.69	7	0	0	7	0	0	4.1	17	9	9	0	0	1	0	4	2
Pulido, Mexico City Reds	4	2	.667	2.22	47	0	0	47	0	23	65.0	62	26	16	1	1	20	2	47	4
Purata, 7 Cam-21 Tam	10	6	.625	4.04	28	16	5	12	0	0	133.2	123	72	60	13	6	60	4	96	11
Quijada, Cordoba	1	0	1.000	4.62	8	1	0	7	0	0	25.1	30	14	13	1	1	6	0	9	4
Quijano, Toluca	1	1	.500	9.53	13	1	0	12	0	0	28.1	43	32	30	3	0	15	3	5	4
Quinonez, Ciudad Juarez	5	5	.500	7.57	15	14	2	1	0	1	60.2	77	59	51	4	2	55	0	45	3
Quintero, Cordoba	0	0	.000	0.00	1	0	0	1	0	0	0.0	1	0	0	0	0	2	0	0	0
Quiroz, Nuevo Laredo*	1	0	1.000	3.86	9	0	9	9	0	1	4.2	5	2	2	1	0	4	0	4	0
Ramirez, 7 Leon-21 Veracruz*	3	2	.600	5.94	28	2	0	26	0	0	33.1	42	22	22	5	0	27	3	16	1
Raygoza, Leon	3	3	.500	5.57	38	2	0	36	0	2	93.2	125	72	58	17	3	38	3	49	2
Rendon, Saltillo	0	0	.000	18.00	1	0	0	1	0	0	3.0	6	6	6	0	0	4	0	1	0
Retes, Mexico City Tigers	0	2	.000	6.10	14	0	0	13	0	0	20.2	19	16	14	1	0	16	1	13	1
Rincon, Nuevo Laredo	8	11	.421	4.47	25	23	2	2	1	1	149.0	152	86	74	21	5	64	3	78	3
H. Rios, Leon	8	11	.421	5.15	25	24	3	1	0	0	153.2	182	114	88	14	2	66	9	70	2
J. Rios, Mexico City Tigers	17	6	.739	3.33	32	31	16	1	5	0	221.2	194	92	82	13	9	86	3	194	10
M. Rios, Tampico	0	0	.000	6.84	15	1	0	14	0	0	25.0	40	22	19	3	3	13	0	10	4
R. Rios, 6 MC Reds-11 Cam	1	1	.500	5.84	17	10	1	7	0	0	61.2	85	48	40	2	5	25	1	20	1
L. Rivas, Monclova	1	3	.250	7.35	29	1	0	28	0	2	53.0	89	54	47	10	2	21	0	19	4
M. Rivas, Tampico	9	7	.563	2.40	46	4	3	42	1	15	131.0	117	42	35	12	7	32	7	91	0
A. Rivera, Ciudad Juarez	13	9	.591	4.17	27	27	11	0	1	0	196.0	219	112	91	16	11	80	6	131	14
J. Rivera, Campeche	1	0	1.000	4.50	7	0	0	7	0	0	12.0	13	7	6	3	0	8	0	4	0

Pitcher—Club	W.	L.	Pct.	ERA.	G.	GS.	CG.	GF.	ShO.	Sv.	IP.	H.	R.	ER.	HR.	HB.	BB.	Int. BB.	SO.	WP.
O. Rivera, Cordoba	8	9	.471	4.40	25	23	5	2	2	0	147.1	147	77	72	9	4	85	7	94	16
A. Rodriguez, Leon	5	3	.625	4.84	38	1	1	37	0	9	61.1	73	42	33	6	2	35	5	37	8
E. Rodriguez, Saltillo	0	0	.000	9.45	3	0	0	3	0	0	6.2	12	7	7	2	0	2	0	2	0
M. Rodriguez, MC Reds	6	9	.400	4.90	24	18	4	6	0	1	125.0	143	70	68	8	6	59	3	54	6
P. Rodriguez, Yucatan	3	4	.429	3.32	35	0	0	35	0	15	59.2	67	24	22	2	1	19	5	26	1
Rami. Rodriguez, Monterrey	0	0	.000	1.86	7	0	0	7	0	0	9.2	4	2	2	0	0	8	0	6	0
Ramo. Rodriguez, Campeche	1	3	.250	3.58	29	0	0	29	0	1	65.1	75	29	26	6	1	23	3	40	5
Rogers, Tabasco	7	13	.350	4.58	21	19	6	2	1	1	120.0	147	72	61	11	7	27	3	48	2
Rojo Mendez, Tabasco	1	2	.333	2.62	20	4	2	16	0	1	65.1	54	26	19	3	2	20	4	46	1
Romero, Mexico City Tigers	1	0	1.000	1.50	7	0	0	7	0	0	18.0	17	5	3	0	2	10	1	7	0
Romo, Mexico City Reds	10	6	.625	3.46	22	22	7	0	2	0	140.2	143	70	54	8	5	40	0	110	13
Rondon, 13 Yuc-12 Cam	7	12	.368	4.90	25	23	3	2	0	0	126.2	172	87	69	7	4	53	2	65	5
C. Ruiz, Mex. City Tigers*	15	6	.714	3.58	35	30	3	5	1	0	191.0	226	92	76	13	6	78	4	91	6
P. Ruiz, Monclova*	5	4	.556	6.01	15	11	4	4	0	0	79.1	89	56	53	10	0	76	3	56	4
E. Salas, 1 Tab-11 Tigers	2	0	1.000	7.43	12	0	0	12	0	0	26.2	36	26	22	3	0	14	0	10	1
R. Salas, 12 Ver-7 Yuc	4	5	.444	7.09	19	12	3	7	1	0	66.0	98	55	52	9	2	35	4	28	6
Salcido, Yucatan	0	0	.000	10.13	6	0	0	6	0	0	13.1	25	17	15	3	1	4	0	4	1
Saldivar, Campeche	0	1	.000	43.20	2	2	0	0	0	0	1.2	6	9	8	0	0	5	0	0	0
Salinas, Yucatan	12	5	.706	3.29	20	20	9	0	2	0	153.0	155	62	56	11	4	39	1	66	7
A. Sanchez, Monclova	0	0	.000	10.93	5	1	0	4	0	0	14.0	26	18	17	3	1	7	0	8	1
F. Sanchez, Nuevo Laredo	1	2	.333	6.19	19	3	0	16	0	0	36.1	46	31	25	4	3	18	0	18	2
P. Sanchez, Mex. City Reds	8	1	.889	4.30	39	0	0	39	0	0	88.0	83	46	42	8	2	62	7	49	10
S. Sanchez, Monclova	0	2	.000	10.95	5	3	0	2	0	0	12.1	17	17	15	5	0	11	1	6	0
Sandoval, 3 Aguas-2 Tab	0	1	.000	4.82	5	0	0	5	0	0	9.1	10	7	5	1	1	3	3	1	1
Santiago, Aguascalientes	0	1	.000	21.60	1	1	0	0	0	0	1.2	6	4	4	0	0	0	0	0	0
Santos, Veracruz	0	0	.000	10.12	3	0	0	3	0	0	2.2	2	5	3	0	0	6	1	1	2
Santoya, Aguascalientes	0	1	.000	6.92	11	0	0	11	0	0	13.0	21	16	10	1	0	7	3	4	2
Sauceda, Yucatan	1	1	.500	6.69	25	0	0	25	0	1	39.0	58	32	29	2	2	17	1	22	4
Segui, Leon	10	9	.526	5.55	24	23	7	1	0	0	133.0	173	103	82	12	1	58	2	79	8
Serafin, Cordoba	7	1	.875	2.80	38	0	0	38	0	3	54.2	49	23	17	6	1	28	4	27	3
Serna, Ciudad Juarez	5	6	.455	5.36	19	16	4	3	1	1	100.2	128	67	60	10	0	38	1	71	1
Silva, 1 N. Laredo-34 Veracruz	4	3	.571	2.13	35	0	0	35	0	10	71.2	61	22	17	1	3	32	9	44	1
M. Solis, Saltillo	17	4	.810	3.75	26	26	16	0	1	0	201.2	221	95	84	26	5	49	3	75	4
R. Solis, Cordoba	9	12	.429	4.18	28	23	9	5	1	1	157.1	179	88	73	9	0	47	3	105	4
C. Sosa, Tampico	6	11	.353	6.88	27	24	1	3	0	0	125.2	164	106	96	17	1	79	9	55	10
Soto, Toluca	11	7	.611	3.86	38	8	2	30	1	6	112.0	128	57	48	4	7	33	8	66	5
Smith, Nuevo Laredo	11	7	.611	4.14	29	21	4	8	1	0	143.2	156	80	66	11	2	55	8	65	6
Stone, Nuevo Laredo	9	3	.750	3.12	45	1	0	44	0	7	83.2	54	33	29	11	3	43	3	78	1
Stottlemyre, Nuevo Laredo	3	0	1.000	5.71	4	3	0	1	0	0	17.1	21	13	11	0	0	8	0	9	0
Tapia, Saltillo	0	0	.000	30.38	3	0	0	3	0	0	2.2	8	9	9	0	0	3	1	1	1
Tinajero, Tampico	1	0	1.000	6.41	18	0	0	18	0	0	26.2	32	23	19	5	2	19	0	9	1
A. Torres, Ciudad Juarez	1	2	.333	5.22	9	7	1	2	0	0	39.2	49	25	23	5	0	22	0	29	1
M. Torres, Cordoba	1	3	.250	6.81	12	5	0	7	0	1	35.2	45	31	27	4	0	19	1	26	1
Trevino, Monterrey	1	2	.333	7.63	20	0	0	20	0	0	46.0	65	50	39	3	0	27	3	15	4
Uresti, Leon	4	6	.400	7.00	24	12	4	12	0	0	90.0	113	74	70	12	2	55	3	63	10
Urias, Toluca	1	1	.500	5.61	28	0	0	28	0	3	51.1	66	37	32	6	3	32	8	21	3
Uribe, Yucatan	1	1	.500	8.34	9	5	0	4	0	0	18.1	23	17	17	3	2	22	0	5	5
Urrea, Saltillo	5	8	.385	4.75	36	1	0	35	0	4	55.0	70	34	29	9	2	35	9	21	0
H. Valdez, 13 Ver-10 Cam	2	7	.222	5.66	23	13	1	10	0	0	97.0	108	68	61	7	9	47	6	30	5
R. Valdez, Campeche	9	12	.429	5.21	30	26	5	4	1	0	145.0	170	93	84	19	2	76	1	73	11
G. Valenzuela, Leon	2	2	.500	5.96	5	4	1	1	0	0	25.2	30	20	17	4	0	14	2	11	1
H. Valenzuela, Tampico	1	2	.335	10.92	9	7	0	2	0	0	29.2	46	39	36	12	1	23	0	20	2
J. Valenzuela, Saltillo	10	9	.526	5.70	29	28	6	1	1	1	172.0	222	121	109	25	8	58	6	58	5
Valle, Leon	1	0	1.000	8.53	11	0	0	11	0	0	12.2	23	13	12	2	2	3	0	6	3
Vargas, Mexico City Tigers	0	0	.000	0.00	1	0	0	1	0	0	1.0	2	0	0	0	0	2	0	1	0
J. Vazquez, Aguascalientes	5	7	.417	5.73	36	10	1	26	0	6	110.0	150	81	70	9	1	40	1	33	1
R. Vazquez, 9 Cam-7 Ver	4	8	.333	4.37	16	14	4	2	1	0	70.0	80	40	34	10	3	25	6	29	1
Velarde, Veracruz	0	0	.000	27.00	1	0	0	1	0	0	1.1	2	4	4	1	0	2	0	0	0
A. Velazquez, 2 Reds-14 Cor	0	1	.000	3.74	16	0	0	16	0	1	33.2	41	23	14	6	1	18	1	13	4
I. Velazquez, M. City Tigers	6	10	.375	5.56	31	27	1	4	0	1	147.1	193	118	91	13	6	69	4	63	10
L. Velazquez, Tabasco	4	6	.400	3.79	17	15	4	2	1	0	92.2	87	47	39	2	0	60	7	68	6
Veliz, Mexico City Reds	2	0	1.000	6.04	11	1	0	10	0	0	22.1	28	18	15	0	2	34	0	7	6
Vidana, Saltillo	3	9	.250	5.04	31	8	1	23	0	0	80.1	100	53	45	9	4	37	4	40	5
Viesca, Saltillo	1	1	.500	9.67	13	1	0	12	0	0	27.0	43	35	29	8	1	16	0	22	4
Vila Martinez, Cordoba	0	0	.000	0.00	3	0	0	3	0	1	2.0	0	0	0	0	0	2	0	2	0
Villalobos, Yucatan	4	4	.500	4.83	10	10	2	0	0	0	69.0	81	43	37	5	4	22	1	18	3
Villanueva, Aguascalientes*	12	5	.706	4.61	25	24	8	0	2	0	162.0	186	91	83	23	2	47	1	92	7
Villarreal, Yucatan	0	6	.000	6.56	16	4	0	12	0	0	35.2	38	30	26	3	0	23	1	24	2
D. Villegas, Leon	0	0	.000	54.00	1	0	0	1	0	0	0.2	3	4	4	0	2	0	0	0	1
R. Villegas, 14 Tigers-6 Tab	6	6	.500	4.64	20	19	2	1	0	0	106.2	129	61	55	12	2	25	3	47	4
Viscarra, Nuevo Laredo	1	0	1.000	0.00	2	0	0	2	0	0	2.1	1	0	0	1	0	1	0	1	0
Wax, Nuevo Laredo	0	2	.000	3.86	4	3	0	1	0	0	14.0	11	9	6	0	2	4	0	8	1
Widales, Nuevo Laredo	0	0	.000	2.57	3	1	0	2	0	0	7.0	8	2	2	1	0	2	0	3	0
Yucupicio, Tabasco	1	0	1.000	8.31	16	0	0	16	0	0	17.1	23	21	16	1	0	19	4	13	1
Zamudio, Veracruz	0	0	.000	2.77	3	0	0	3	0	0	13.0	14	4	4	1	0	10	1	8	1

BALKS—M. Morales, 5; Baruch, Ra. Garcia, O. Pollorena, M. Rivas, 2 each; Belman, C. Diaz, Dimas, Enriquez, Garza, Gaxiola, R. Guzman, S. Guzman, Jaime, I. Jimenez, Lozano, F. Miranda, N. Montano, I. Morales, C. Moreno, J. Moreno, Ogawa, Palafox, Rojo Mendez, Rondon, A. Rivera, Salinas, Sauceda, Serna, Uresti, Urrea, H. Valdez, R. Valdez, G. Valenzuela, Villalobos, Widales, 1 each.

COMBINATION SHUTOUTS—Ogawa-Lopez, Vazquez-Castillejos, Aguascalientes; A. Rivera-Dominguez, Torres-Alicea, Ciudad Juarez; Colorado-Delfin, Cordoba; Leon-P. Sanchez, Garcia-Pulido, Mexico City Reds; Ruiz-Dimas 2, Villegas-Dimas, Mexcio City Tigers; M.A. Gonzalez-Heredia, Monterrey; Moreno-Ochoa, Widales-Rincon-Stone, Nuevo Laredo; Velazquez-Aguilar-Palacios-Yucupicio-Ochoa, Tabasco; Beltran-Rivas 2, Tampico; Perez-Orozco, Dominguez-Soto, Toluca; Ramirez-Guzman-Morales, Arano-Lugo-Ortiz, Veracruz; Rondon-Rodriguez, Salinas-Rodriguez, Escarrega-Rodriguez, Yucatan.

PERFECT GAME—J. Velazquez, Saltillo, defeated Cordoba, 5-0 (seven innings), June 10.

NO-HIT GAME—J. Rios, Mexico City Tigers, defeated Cordoba, 2-0, May 12.

Pacific Coast League

CLASS AAA

**Leading Batter
TONY BREWER
Albuquerque**

**League President
BILL CUTLER**

**Leading Pitcher
BOB WALK
Hawaii**

CHAMPIONSHIP WINNERS IN PREVIOUS YEARS

1903—Los Angeles .630	1934—Los Angeles z .786	1964—Arkansas .609
1904—Tacoma .589	Los Angeles z .689	San Diego a .576
Tacoma§ .571	1935—Los Angeles .648	1965—Oklahoma City a .628
Los Angeles§ .571	San Francisco° .608	Portland .547
1905—Tacoma .583	1936—Portland‡ .549	1966—Seattle a .561
Los Angeles° .604	1937—Sacramento .573	Tulsa .578
1906—Portland .657	San Diego (3rd)† .545	1967—San Diego a .574
1907—Los Angeles .608	1938—Los Angeles .590	Spokane .541
1908—Los Angeles .585	Sacramento (3rd)† .537	1968—Tulsa a .642
1909—San Francisco .623	1939—Seattle .589	Spokane .586
1910—Portland .567	Sacramento (4th)† .500	1969—Tacoma a .589
1911—Portland .589	1940—Seattle‡ .629	Eugene .603
1912—Oakland .591	1941—Seattle‡ .598	1970—Spokane a .644
1913—Portland .559	1942—Sacramento .590	Hawaii .671
1914—Portland .574	Seattle (3rd)† .539	1971—Salt Lake City .534
1915—San Francisco .570	1943—Los Angeles .710	Tacoma .545
1916—Los Angeles .601	S. Francisco (2nd)† .574	1972—Albuquerque .622
1917—San Francisco .561	1944—Los Angeles .586	Eugene .534
1918—Vernon .569	S. Francisco (3rd)† .509	1973—Tucson .583
Los Angeles (2nd) x .548	1945—Portland .622	Spokane a .563
1919—Los Angeles .613	S. Francisco (4th)† .525	1974—Spokane a .549
1920—Vernon .556	1946—San Francisco° .628	Albuqerque .535
1921—Los Angeles .574	1947—Los Angeles†† .567	1975—Salt Lake City .556
1922—San Francisco .638	1948—Oakland‡ .606	Hawaii a .611
1923—San Francisco .617	1949—Hollywood‡ .583	1976—Salt Lake City .625
1924—Seattle .545	1950—Oakland .590	Hawaii a .531
1925—San Francisco .643	1951—Seattle‡ .593	1977—Phoenix a .579
1926—Los Angeles .599	1952—Hollywood .606	Hawaii .541
1927—Oakland .615	1953—Hollywood .589	1978—Tacoma b .584
1928—San Francisco° .630	1954—San Diego y .604	Albuquerque b .557
Sacramento§§ .626	1955—Seattle .552	1979—Albuquerque .581
San Francisco§§ .626	1956—Los Angeles .637	Salt Lake City c .541
1929—Mission .643	1957—San Francisco .601	1980—Albuquerque° .578
Hollywood° .592	1958—Phoenix .578	Hawaii .539
1930—Los Angeles .576	1959—Salt Lake City .552	1981—Albuquerque° .712
Hollywood° .650	1960—Spokane .601	Tacoma .561
1931—Hollywood .626	1961—Tacoma .630	1982—Albuquerque° .594
San Francisco° .608	1962—San Diego .604	Spokane .545
1932—Portland .587	1963—Spokane .620	1983—Albuquerque .594
1933—Los Angeles .610	Oklahoma City a .632	Portland° .528

°Won split-season playoff. †Won four-team playoff. ‡Won pennant and four-team playoff. §Tied for second-half title with Tacoma winning playoff. §§Tied for second-half title, with Sacramento winning playoff. ††Ended regular season in tie with San Francisco and won one-game playoff for pennant, then won four-club playoff. xWon playoff from first-place Vernon and awarded championship. yDefeated Hollywood in one-game playoff for pennant. zWon both halves, no playoff. aLeague was divided into Northern, Southern divisions in 1963, 1969-70-71, and Eastern, Western divisions in 1964 through 1968 and 1972 through 1977, won two-team playoff. bLeague divided into Eastern and Western divisions, Tacoma and Albuquerque declared co-champions following cancellation of four-team playoff due to continuing rain and wet grounds. cWon second-half title and defeated Hawaii in four-team playoff.

STANDING OF CLUBS AT CLOSE OF FIRST HALF, JUNE 17

NORTHERN DIVISION

Club	W.	L.	T.	Pct.	G.B.
Edmonton (Angels)	35	35	0	.500	......
Salt Lake City (Mariners)	33	37	0	.471	2
Vancouver (Brewers)	32	40	0	.444	4
Portland (Phillies)	29	40	0	.420	5½
Tacoma (A's)	29	41	0	.414	6

SOUTHERN DIVISION

Club	W.	L.	T.	Pct.	G.B.
Las Vegas (Padres)	42	28	0	.600	......
Hawaii (Pirates)	42	29	0	.591	½
Tucson (Astros)	38	32	0	.543	4
Phoenix (Giants)	37	35	0	.514	6
Albuquerque (Dodgers)	36	36	0	.500	7

STANDING OF CLUBS AT CLOSE OF SECOND HALF, AUGUST 30

NORTHERN DIVISION

Club	W.	L.	T.	Pct.	G.B.
Salt Lake City (Mariners)	41	29	0	.586	......
Tacoma (A's)	40	30	0	.571	1
Vancouver (Brewers)	39	31	0	.557	2
Edmonton (Angels)	34	38	0	.472	8
Portland (Phillies)	33	38	0	.465	8½

SOUTHERN DIVISION

Club	W.	L.	T.	Pct.	G.B.
Hawaii (Pirates)	45	24	1	.652	......
Phoenix (Giants)	32	39	1	.451	14
Tucson (Astros)	31	39	0	.443	14½
Las Vegas (Padres)	29	37	0	.439	14½
Albuquerque (Dodgers)	26	45	0	.366	20

COMPOSITE STANDING OF CLUBS AT CLOSE OF SEASON, AUGUST 30

NORTHERN DIVISION

Club	SLC.	Van.	Tac.	Edm.	Port.	Haw.	LV.	Tuc.	Phx.	Alb.	W.	L.	T.	Pct.	G.B.
Salt Lake City (Mariners)	....	11	8	9	7	8	7	8	9	7	74	66	0	.529	......
Vancouver (Brewers)	5	....	9	10	11	4	5	10	8	9	71	71	0	.500	4
Tacoma (A's)	7	7	....	8	10	6	5	7	8	11	69	71	0	.493	5
Edmonton (Angels)	7	6	8	....	6	6	8	9	10	9	69	73	0	.486	6
Portland (Phillies)	7	5	6	10	....	6	8	3	8	9	62	78	0	.443	12

SOUTHERN DIVISION

Club	SLC.	Van.	Tac.	Edm.	Port.	Haw.	LV.	Tuc.	Phx.	Alb.	W.	L.	T.	Pct.	G.B.
Hawaii (Pirates)	8	12	10	10	9	....	10	9	11	8	87	53	1	.621	......
Las Vegas (Padres)	9	9	8	8	8	3	....	8	10	8	71	65	0	.522	14
Tucson (Astros)	7	6	9	5	12	7	8	....	5	10	69	71	0	.493	18
Phoenix (Giants)	7	8	8	6	8	5	6	11	....	10	69	74	1	.483	19½
Albuquerque (Dodgers)	9	7	5	7	7	8	8	6	5	....	62	81	0	.434	26½

Hawaii club represented Honolulu, Hawaii.

Major league affiliations in parentheses.

Playoffs—Hawaii defeated Las Vegas, three games to none; Edmonton defeated Salt Lake City, three games to two, and Edmonton defeated Hawaii, two games to none, to win league championship.

Regular-Season Attendance—Albuquerque, 244,229; Edmonton, 228,102; Hawaii, 144,232; Las Vegas, 320,157; Phoenix, 163,843; Portland, 184,143; Salt Lake City, 167,803; Tacoma, 203,821; Tucson, 124,232; Vancouver, 147,599.

Managers—Albuquerque, Terry Collins; Edmonton, Moose Stubing; Hawaii, Tommy Sandt; Las Vegas, Bob Cluck; Phoenix, Jack Mull; Portland, Lee Elia; Salt Lake City, Bobby Floyd; Tacoma, Ed Nottle; Tucson, Matt Galante; Vancouver, Tony Muser.

All-Star Team: 1B—Sid Bream, Albuquerque; 2B—Harold Reynolds, Salt Lake City; 3B—Rick Schu, Portland; SS—Ozzie Guillen, Las Vegas; OF—Alejandro Sanchez, Phoenix; Doug Loman, Vancouver; Tony Brewer, Albuquerque; C—Jamie Nelson, Vancouver; DH—Rick Lancellotti, Las Vegas; RHP—Mike Bielecki, Hawaii; LHP—Alfonso Pulido, Hawaii; Manager—Tommy Sandt, Hawaii; Most Valuable Player—Alejandro Sanchez, Phoenix.

(Compiled by William J. Weiss, League Statistician, San Mateo, Calif.)

CLUB BATTING

Club	Pct.	G.	AB.	R.	OR.	H.	TB.	2B.	3B.	HR.	RBI.	GW.	SH.	SF.	HP.	BB.	Int. BB.	SO.	SB.	CS.	LOB.
Albuquerque	.298	143	4939	823	923	1474	2219	275	46	126	751	56	54	54	26	546	37	641	81	47	1069
Salt Lake City	.296	140	4806	822	790	1421	2149	239	66	119	749	70	46	55	28	538	36	772	162	79	1002
Edmonton	.289	142	4802	828	820	1386	2079	252	75	97	745	61	38	49	28	567	30	715	95	47	1036
Phoenix	.284	144	4830	750	777	1371	2024	225	52	108	670	63	60	47	30	558	40	794	161	89	1040
Las Vegas	.278	136	4635	769	742	1290	2041	229	51	140	717	67	45	41	30	554	38	724	101	49	1008
Tacoma	.275	140	4649	670	686	1279	1864	218	32	101	615	65	66	46	27	503	23	748	154	68	1010
Portland	.273	140	4793	685	751	1309	2029	236	89	102	639	57	37	42	37	522	31	831	70	34	1049
Tucson	.265	140	4604	640	633	1221	1797	229	64	73	594	64	61	47	26	513	29	793	84	55	1016
Vancouver	.264	142	4606	608	597	1214	1717	203	45	70	562	65	50	55	35	522	53	700	56	33	1057
Hawaii	.262	141	4534	626	502	1190	1819	239	54	94	575	83	57	47	28	502	46	623	155	57	961

INDIVIDUAL BATTING

(Leading Qualifiers for Batting Championship—389 or More Plate Appearances)

*Bats lefthanded. †Switch-hitter.

Player and Club	Pct.	G.	AB.	R.	H.	TB.	2B.	3B.	HR.	RBI.	GW.	SH.	SF.	HP.	BB.	Int. BB.	SO.	SB.	CS.
Brewer, Anthony, Albuquerque	.357	104	420	88	150	247	32	4	19	83	3	0	5	3	29	1	35	6	2
Amelung, Edward, Albuquerque*	.351	107	433	89	152	240	35	4	15	63	4	6	3	0	18	3	30	10	2
O'Malley, Thomas, Phoenix*	.346	105	387	44	134	173	20	2	5	72	6	1	6	4	61	4	31	5	2
Bream, Sidney, Albuquerque*	.343	114	429	82	147	240	25	4	20	90	7	1	8	1	67	7	62	2	2
Clark, Christopher, Edmonton†	.335	131	481	104	161	271	37	8	19	104	15	2	6	2	89	4	86	2	5
Kruk, John, Las Vegas*	.326	115	340	56	111	181	25	6	11	57	7	2	4	1	45	4	37	2	6
Loman, Douglas, Vancouver*	.324	142	524	79	170	276	34	9	18	102	17	0	9	7	57	13	50	4	4
Sanchez, Alejandro, Phoenix	.318	135	532	98	169	294	29	9	26	108	13	0	2	5	22	5	108	34	15
Melendez, Francisco, Portland*	.312	128	506	63	158	219	36	8	3	65	6	1	5	1	43	6	50	1	2
Miller, Lemmie, Albuquerque	.311	124	514	90	160	212	27	8	3	39	2	2	6	2	55	1	60	27	17

Departmental Leaders: G—Loman, 142; AB—H. Reynolds, 558; R—Clark, 104; H—Loman, 170; TB—Sanchez, 294; 2B—Clark, 37; 3B—Schu, Stone, 14; HR—Deer, 31; RBI—Lancellotti, 131; GWRBI—Lancellotti, 19; SH—Davidsmeier, 14; SF—Ponce, 12; HP—Lancellotti, 11; BB—Ge. Davis, 103; IBB—Loman, 13; SO—Deer, 175; SB—T. Davis, 53; CS—L. Miller, H. Reynolds, 17.

(All Players—Listed Alphabetically)

Player and Club	Pct.	G.	AB.	R.	H.	TB.	2B.	3B.	HR.	RBI.	GW.	SH.	SF.	HP.	BB.	Int. BB.	SO.	SB.	CS.
Adams, Ricky, Edmonton	.286	105	370	67	106	166	24	9	6	48	4	3	2	4	39	1	60	20	4
Aguayo, Luis, Portland	.538	3	13	3	7	11	1	0	1	2	0	0	0	0	0	0	3	1	0
Allen, James, Salt Lake City	.288	124	472	69	136	185	23	4	6	67	9	6	3	6	45	4	67	4	6
Allen, Robert, Albuquerque	.218	68	174	14	38	48	4	0	2	15	2	2	0	0	20	1	31	2	0

Player and Club	Pct.	G.	AB.	R.	H.	TB.	2B.	3B.	HR.	RBI.	GW.	SH.	SF.	HP.	BB.	Int. BB.	SO.	SB.	CS.
Alvarez, Jose, Tucson	.417	33	12	1	5	5	0	0	0	1	0	1	0	0	1	0	3	0	0
Amelung, Edward, Albuquerque°	.351	107	433	89	152	240	35	4	15	63	4	6	3	0	18	3	30	10	2
Anderson, Michael, Van. 7-Tuc. 12°	.250	19	16	1	4	4	0	0	0	3	0	1	0	0	0	0	4	0	0
Arnold, Ronald, Tacoma	.212	13	33	9	7	9	2	0	0	6	0	0	2	0	8	1	8	0	1
Bathe, Robert, Tacoma	.303	34	109	23	33	51	7	1	3	23	4	3	3	1	31	2	20	1	0
Bathe, William, Tacoma	.257	84	245	27	63	86	12	1	3	42	3	3	6	3	19	0	39	3	0
Bennett, James, Tacoma°	.056	8	18	1	1	2	1	0	0	0	0	0	0	0	1	0	7	0	0
Bernard, Dwight, Tucson	.000	41	7	1	0	0	0	0	0	0	0	0	0	0	0	1	4	0	0
Bielecki, Michael, Hawaii	.135	28	37	0	5	6	1	0	0	2	0	4	0	0	0	0	11	0	0
Blobaum, Jeffrey, Phoenix†	.222	44	18	0	4	4	0	0	0	2	1	7	0	0	1	0	1	0	0
Bochy, Bruce, Las Vegas	.264	34	121	18	32	60	7	0	7	22	2	0	2	0	17	0	13	0	0
Bockus, Randy, Phoenix°	.222	9	9	1	2	2	0	0	0	0	0	2	0	0	1	0	1	0	0
Bonine, Eddie, Tucson	.222	33	36	3	8	8	0	0	0	1	0	0	0	0	3	0	14	0	0
Booker, Gregory, Las Vegas	.143	9	7	0	1	1	0	0	0	0	0	0	0	0	0	0	2	0	0
Borbon, Ernesto, Albuquerque	.143	58	7	3	1	1	0	0	0	0	0	0	0	0	0	0	1	0	0
Bradley, Bert, Tacoma†	.000	50	1	1	0	0	0	0	0	0	0	0	0	0	0	0	0	0	0
Brantley, Michael, Salt Lake City	.235	4	17	2	4	4	0	0	0	1	0	1	0	0	2	0	1	0	0
Bream, Sidney, Albuquerque	.343	114	429	82	147	240	25	4	20	90	7	1	8	1	67	7	62	2	2
Brewer, Anthony, Albuquerque	.357	104	420	88	150	247	32	4	19	83	3	0	5	3	29	1	35	6	2
Brock, Gregory, Albuquerque°	.312	24	93	19	29	54	7	0	6	15	1	0	0	0	14	4	9	2	1
Brown, Christopher, Phoenix	.283	84	283	41	80	130	13	5	9	64	11	1	5	4	30	1	52	5	4
Brown, Lawrence, Las Vegas	.250	43	4	0	1	2	1	0	0	1	0	0	0	0	0	0	1	0	0
Brown, Michael, Edmonton	.343	26	102	22	35	64	9	4	4	24	1	0	0	0	14	2	10	2	1
Brown, Renard, Salt Lake City	.309	25	81	9	25	28	3	0	0	8	2	0	1	0	6	0	4	7	2
Bullock, Eric, Tucson°	.276	60	185	22	51	64	6	2	1	16	2	2	0	1	20	1	18	7	4
Bundy, Lorenzo, Hawaii°	.300	9	30	4	9	17	4	2	0	3	1	0	0	0	2	0	4	0	0
Burroughs, Darren, Las Vegas	.100	48	10	1	1	4	0	0	1	3	0	0	0	0	0	0	3	0	0
Bystrom, Martin, Portland	.000	5	4	0	0	0	0	0	0	0	0	0	0	0	0	0	4	0	0
Calderon, Ivan, Salt Lake City	.365	66	255	61	93	130	7	9	4	45	3	1	3	1	21	1	32	18	6
Calhoun, Jeffrey, Tucson°	.000	14	1	0	0	0	0	0	0	0	0	0	0	0	0	0	0	0	0
Calvert, Mark, Phoenix	.083	21	12	0	1	1	0	0	0	0	0	4	0	0	0	0	2	0	0
Carman, Donald, Portland°	.167	39	6	1	1	2	1	0	0	0	0	0	0	0	0	0	0	0	0
Castillo, Juan, Vancouver†	.333	8	30	6	10	10	0	0	0	2	0	1	0	1	6	0	3	1	1
Chambers, Albert, Salt Lake City°	.291	100	340	69	99	171	21	6	13	73	7	1	4	1	62	8	70	19	4
Charboneau, Joseph, Hawaii	.224	15	49	4	11	15	4	0	0	3	0	1	0	0	3	0	5	0	0
Chiffer, Floyd, Las Vegas	.000	36	3	0	0	0	0	0	0	0	0	0	0	0	0	0	1	0	0
Clark, Christopher, Edmonton†	.335	131	481	104	161	271	37	8	19	104	15	2	6	2	89	4	86	2	5
Clements, Wesley, Tucson	.244	38	131	19	32	57	7	3	4	18	1	0	0	2	18	1	39	0	0
Cliburn, Stanley, Hawaii	.243	89	292	37	71	120	19	0	10	48	7	1	5	1	33	2	44	0	0
Cole, Rodger, Portland	.125	20	16	1	2	2	0	0	0	0	0	0	3	1	1	0	6	0	0
Coleman, Rickey, Las Vegas	.571	3	7	2	4	10	3	0	0	2	0	0	0	0	0	0	0	0	0
Coles, Darnell, Salt Lake City	.318	69	242	57	77	147	22	3	14	68	7	6	6	2	48	2	41	7	2
Collins, Terry, Albuquerque°	.167	3	6	1	1	1	0	0	0	0	0	0	0	0	0	0	1	0	0
Connally, Fritzie, Las Vegas	.310	124	429	71	133	206	25	0	16	76	5	2	4	2	69	4	47	3	1
Cornell, Jeffery, Phoenix°	.000	35	9	1	0	0	0	0	0	0	0	0	0	0	3	0	9	0	0
Couchee, Michael, Las Vegas	.000	37	2	0	0	0	0	0	0	0	0	0	0	0	0	0	1	0	0
Crone, William, Salt Lake City	.239	17	46	7	11	14	3	0	0	5	1	1	0	0	10	0	7	0	1
Cypret, Gregory, Tucson	.248	108	314	32	78	91	8	1	1	35	3	2	3	2	32	2	41	0	3
Darkis, William, Portland	.265	89	223	25	59	94	9	4	6	29	2	0	3	1	16	0	67	0	0
Daulton, Darren, Portland°	.298	80	252	45	75	123	19	4	7	38	4	3	1	0	57	3	49	3	3
Davidsmeier, Daniel, Vancouver	.277	118	440	61	122	163	20	3	5	52	7	14	5	7	24	2	47	0	0
Davis, Alvin, Salt Lake City°	.667	1	3	2	2	2	0	0	0	0	1	0	0	0	0	1	0	0	0
Davis, Gerald, Las Vegas	.302	129	450	98	136	200	23	7	9	64	8	0	6	6	103	3	72	35	11
Davis, Glenn, Tucson	.297	131	471	66	140	230	28	7	16	94	10	1	9	5	49	3	88	3	2
Davis, Trench, Hawaii°	.259	141	553	79	143	185	23	8	1	39	6	5	8	3	53	6	55	53	13
Davisson, Jay, Portland	.107	25	28	1	3	3	0	0	0	0	0	3	0	0	1	0	14	0	0
Debus, Jon, Albuquerque	.267	77	165	21	44	56	3	0	3	26	3	0	5	0	23	1	25	1	1
Decker, Martin, Las Vegas	.176	47	17	4	3	3	0	0	0	0	0	1	0	0	2	0	5	0	0
Deer, Robert, Phoenix	.227	133	449	88	102	218	21	1	31	69	6	2	2	2	96	4	175	9	3
DeLeon, Luis, Las Vegas	.333	6	3	0	1	1	0	0	0	0	0	0	0	0	0	0	2	0	0
DeSimone, Gerald, Las Vegas†	.272	74	195	36	53	74	9	0	4	18	1	12	0	0	28	1	36	8	4
Diaz, Carlos, Albuquerque	.500	20	4	1	2	4	2	0	0	0	0	0	0	0	0	0	1	0	0
Diaz, Michael, Portland	.270	105	341	52	92	151	15	1	14	46	4	1	3	0	32	1	65	2	1
Distefano, Benito, Hawaii°	.304	66	240	40	73	120	13	8	6	33	9	0	1	5	24	6	14	2	1
Dowell, Kenneth, Portland	.207	50	145	15	30	35	3	1	0	8	0	0	1	0	28	0	24	4	2
Downs, Kelly, Portland	.097	30	31	1	3	3	0	0	0	1	0	0	0	0	0	0	11	0	0
Duncan, John, Salt Lake City	.333	9	24	8	8	11	3	0	0	0	0	0	0	0	2	0	5	0	0
Edwards, Marshall, Vancouver°	.243	93	342	35	83	99	7	3	1	18	1	2	1	1	14	3	33	5	7
Felt, Richard, Albuquerque	.125	10	8	1	1	1	0	0	0	0	0	1	0	0	0	0	4	0	0
Fimple, John, Albuquerque	.249	107	334	39	83	137	15	3	11	60	4	1	6	1	35	6	72	0	0
Fireovid, Stephen, Portland†	.389	46	18	2	7	9	0	1	0	2	0	0	0	0	2	0	3	0	0
Foley, Rickey, Tucson	.000	5	0	0	0	0	0	0	0	0	0	1	0	0	0	0	0	0	0
Followell, Vernon, Tucson†	.286	46	182	32	52	76	3	9	1	25	2	3	1	0	24	1	27	0	3
Fowlkes, Alan, Phoenix	.294	18	17	3	5	6	1	0	0	6	0	0	0	0	0	0	1	0	0
Gallego, Michael, Phoenix	.243	101	288	29	70	80	8	1	0	18	1	7	2	0	27	0	39	7	5
Garcia, Steven, Las Vegas°	.222	5	9	1	2	2	0	0	0	1	0	0	0	0	0	0	5	0	0
Garrelts, Scott, Phoenix	.263	21	19	4	5	12	2	1	1	5	1	0	1	0	2	0	5	0	0
Gaynor, Richard, Portland	.444	53	9	3	4	9	2	0	1	3	0	1	0	0	0	0	3	0	0
Geisel, David, Salt Lake City°	.000	28	6	0	0	0	0	0	0	0	0	2	0	0	1	0	2	0	0
Gerber, Craig, Edmonton°	.230	114	365	55	84	119	18	7	1	40	1	3	3	1	33	2	29	5	3
Gladden, Daniel, Phoenix†	.397	59	234	70	93	127	11	7	3	27	0	0	1	0	45	2	23	32	11
Gleaton, Jerry Don, Salt Lake City°	.000	30	1	0	0	0	0	0	0	0	0	0	0	0	0	0	0	0	0
Gomez, Randall, Phoenix	.274	99	307	41	84	107	11	3	2	40	1	6	6	0	40	4	24	0	2
Gonzalez, Denio, Hawaii	.300	113	380	61	114	195	22	7	15	67	9	7	3	4	49	3	89	40	10
Goodwin, Danny, Tacoma°	.296	119	429	59	127	211	20	2	20	82	9	0	8	4	54	5	99	5	7
Grant, Mark, Phoenix	.059	17	17	0	1	1	0	0	0	0	0	0	5	0	1	0	7	0	0
Gray, Gary, Vancouver	.196	14	46	3	9	9	0	0	0	8	0	0	0	0	2	0	8	0	0
Green, Christopher, Hawaii°	1.000	13	1	1	1	2	1	0	0	0	0	0	0	0	0	0	0	0	0
Guillen, Oswaldo, Las Vegas†	.296	122	463	81	137	190	26	6	5	53	3	7	2	3	13	6	40	9	5
Gwosdz, Douglas, Las Vegas	.228	61	197	20	45	73	10	6	2	27	1	2	1	1	20	0	47	1	0
Hamm, Timothy, Las Vegas	.000	16	12	1	0	0	0	0	0	0	0	0	1	0	0	0	5	0	0
Hammaker, Atlee, Phoenix†	.000	2	1	0	0	0	0	0	0	0	0	0	0	0	0	0	0	0	0

Player and Club	Pct.	G.	AB.	R.	H.	TB.	2B.	3B.	HR.	RBI.	GW.	SH.	SF.	HP.	BB.	Int. BB.	SO.	SB.	CS.
Hamric, Russell, Portland	.205	45	127	14	26	40	6	4	0	18	1	2	0	1	8	1	11	0	2
Hancock, Garry, Tacoma°	.262	12	42	5	11	22	0	1	3	10	0	2	0	0	5	1	5	0	0
Harrison, Ronald, Tacoma°	.270	55	222	36	60	80	10	2	2	24	2	8	1	0	7	0	27	5	1
Hayward, Raymond, Las Vegas°	.214	31	28	5	6	6	0	0	0	2	1	1	0	0	1	0	3	0	0
Hernandez, Manuel, Tucson	.115	29	26	3	3	4	1	0	0	0	0	3	0	0	1	0	14	0	0
Herz, Steven, Hawaii	.236	101	331	43	78	118	12	2	8	39	4	3	3	2	33	4	38	1	0
Hill, Donald, Tacoma†	.326	42	141	28	46	70	12	3	2	24	4	1	2	1	18	0	15	7	2
Hinshaw, George, Las Vegas	.269	121	420	57	113	173	16	4	12	53	3	0	2	0	33	2	81	17	10
Holton, Brian, Albuquerque	.000	12	0	0	0	0	0	0	0	0	0	1	0	0	0	0	0	0	0
Hotchkiss, John, Tacoma	.227	34	110	8	25	29	4	0	0	11	1	1	0	1	12	1	28	1	0
Howard, Michael, Hawaii†	.217	58	129	11	28	42	9	1	1	15	3	3	1	0	17	3	14	8	0
Howell, Kenneth, Albuquerque	.200	18	25	4	5	6	1	0	0	2	1	1	0	1	1	0	8	0	0
Hudgens, David, Tacoma°	.217	44	129	14	28	40	9	0	1	14	3	0	0	2	25	1	36	1	1
Huppert, David, Vancouver	.167	60	150	17	25	28	3	0	0	7	1	5	1	0	25	0	46	1	0
Jeltz, Steven, Portland†	.220	134	436	68	96	130	10	9	2	46	8	5	2	5	79	1	96	9	4
Jones, Christopher, Tucson°	.305	120	452	78	138	205	29	10	6	49	6	3	3	1	51	0	53	29	11
Jones, Glenn, Phoenix	.143	3	7	1	1	1	0	0	0	0	0	0	0	0	0	0	3	0	0
Keedy, Patrick, Edmonton	.259	100	348	64	90	169	20	4	17	53	5	2	1	2	51	1	102	9	3
Kiefer, Steven, Tacoma	.268	125	455	63	122	194	18	3	16	54	3	5	1	3	22	0	113	19	5
Kingman, Brian, Phoenix	.000	30	7	0	0	0	0	0	0	0	0	0	0	0	0	0	4	0	0
Knudson, Mark, Tucson	.118	13	17	1	2	2	0	0	0	2	0	0	1	0	1	0	7	0	0
Koenigsfeld, Ronald, Vancouver	.257	104	338	38	87	127	14	1	8	33	9	8	3	0	35	1	72	3	3
Krauss, Timothy, Edmonton°	.290	115	442	64	128	170	21	3	5	49	4	6	8	3	31	4	43	6	2
Krawczyk, Raymond, Hawaii	.167	43	6	0	1	2	1	0	0	3	0	3	0	0	0	0	4	0	0
Kromy, Ted, Portland	.000	23	8	1	0	0	0	0	0	0	0	0	0	0	0	1	6	0	0
Kruk, John, Las Vegas°	.326	115	340	56	111	181	25	6	11	57	7	2	4	1	45	4	37	2	6
Kutcher, Randy, Phoenix	.277	103	336	37	93	122	17	3	2	31	5	5	1	1	16	0	49	16	16
Lacey, Robert, Phoenix	.000	24	4	0	0	0	0	0	0	0	0	1	0	0	0	0	2	0	0
Lancellotti, Richard, Las Vegas°	.287	133	522	88	150	278	29	6	29	131	19	0	6	11	40	10	67	2	1
Landestoy, Rafael, Albuquerque†	.313	66	256	41	80	102	10	6	0	34	5	10	3	0	27	0	15	5	7
Lansford, Joseph, Las Vegas	.267	131	464	82	124	222	22	8	20	80	5	0	9	1	60	4	91	1	2
Lavalliere, Michael, Portland°	.311	37	122	20	38	65	6	3	5	21	3	1	1	1	15	1	11	0	0
Legg, Gregory, Portland	.241	50	141	17	34	45	8	0	1	15	2	0	2	3	14	1	13	0	1
Leopold, James, Las Vegas	.000	2	3	0	0	0	0	0	0	0	0	0	0	0	0	0	1	0	0
Lezcano, Carlos, Tacoma	.219	25	73	8	16	24	3	1	1	8	1	1	0	0	8	0	19	1	1
Liddle, Steven, Edmonton	.262	92	301	40	79	116	11	4	6	51	4	5	6	1	44	3	53	0	0
Loman, Douglas, Vancouver°	.324	142	524	79	170	276	34	9	18	102	17	0	9	7	57	13	50	4	4
Long, Robert, Salt Lake City	.200	52	5	0	1	1	0	0	0	0	0	0	0	0	0	0	2	0	0
Loucks, Scott, Tucson	.248	28	109	17	27	32	1	2	0	3	0	4	1	0	14	1	24	8	5
Lubratich, Steven, Edmonton	.305	127	498	95	152	216	27	5	9	85	9	3	8	5	38	0	34	4	5
Madden, Michael, Tucson°	.000	12	14	1	0	0	0	0	0	0	0	0	2	0	0	0	8	0	0
Maddux, Michael, Portland	.250	8	4	0	1	2	1	0	0	0	0	0	0	0	1	0	1	0	0
Maler, James, Portland	.235	37	98	16	23	47	4	1	6	18	2	0	0	4	10	0	14	0	0
Malkin, John, Hawaii	.284	79	218	34	62	118	17	0	13	36	4	2	3	5	33	1	57	0	0
Martin, Renie, Phoenix	.063	33	16	1	1	1	0	0	0	0	0	0	0	0	0	0	6	0	0
Martin, Michael, Las Vegas°	.258	71	209	28	54	82	10	0	6	35	2	2	2	0	25	2	35	1	1
Mathis, Ronald, Tucson	.400	12	10	2	4	4	0	0	0	2	0	0	0	1	0	1	0	0	0
McHenry, Vance, Haw. 15-SLC 27	.305	42	95	19	29	42	6	2	1	17	1	5	1	0	10	0	12	5	2
McLaughlin, Michael, Phoenix	.211	25	19	1	4	4	0	0	0	1	0	1	0	0	3	0	12	0	0
Melendez, Francisco, Portland°	.312	128	506	63	158	219	36	8	3	65	6	1	5	1	43	6	50	1	2
Mercado, Orlando, Salt Lake City	.358	29	109	18	39	70	9	2	6	22	2	0	0	0	6	1	20	0	0
Meyer, Daniel, Tacoma°	.293	124	457	63	134	178	19	2	7	57	7	4	7	0	26	1	40	18	2
Miller, Darrell, Edmonton	.326	92	328	65	107	180	19	9	12	67	7	3	4	2	34	1	52	2	4
Miller, Lemmie, Albuquerque	.311	124	514	90	160	212	27	8	3	39	2	6	2	5	55	1	60	27	17
Mills, Bradley, Tucson°	.220	51	164	14	36	43	7	0	0	13	1	4	0	0	25	2	13	0	1
Minetto, Craig, Tucson°	.200	45	5	0	1	1	0	0	0	0	0	0	2	0	0	0	1	0	0
Miscik, Robert, Hawaii	.276	131	442	66	122	157	19	2	4	44	7	1	4	4	73	5	29	9	6
Mitchell, Robert, Portland°	.260	117	362	52	94	120	12	7	0	30	0	4	6	3	26	2	35	3	4
Mohorcic, Dale, Hawaii	.000	9	8	0	0	0	0	0	0	0	0	0	0	0	0	0	2	0	0
Money, Kyle, Portland	.286	10	7	1	2	2	0	0	0	0	0	0	0	0	0	0	1	0	0
Montalvo, Rafael, Albuquerque	.400	45	5	0	2	2	0	0	0	1	0	0	0	0	0	0	14	0	0
Moore, Kelvin, Vancouver	.221	58	199	26	44	63	4	0	5	28	4	2	0	1	23	2	58	0	0
Moore, Robert, Phoenix	.333	6	3	0	1	1	0	0	0	0	0	0	0	0	0	0	0	0	0
Moses, John, Salt Lake City†	.275	70	276	45	76	97	11	5	0	27	1	10	4	2	24	0	38	21	9
Mura, Stephen, Portland	.222	48	9	1	2	2	0	0	0	0	0	2	0	0	0	0	2	0	0
Murray, Richard, Phoenix	.287	121	404	43	116	163	17	6	6	65	5	0	3	0	27	2	66	5	5
Nahorodny, William, Salt Lake City	.273	57	183	22	50	70	14	0	2	28	0	1	3	2	8	0	26	1	0
Nandin, Robert, Tucson†	.163	16	43	4	7	7	0	0	0	4	0	0	1	0	6	0	6	0	0
Nanni, Tito, Salt Lake City°	.273	135	466	72	127	182	23	7	6	59	2	0	4	0	53	8	104	18	7
Nelson, James, Vancouver	.276	107	330	36	91	118	15	0	4	36	0	3	1	0	60	3	33	4	4
Nelson, Ricky, Salt Lake City°	.294	75	310	54	91	143	11	4	11	42	4	4	2	0	19	3	44	11	6
Nelson, Eugene, Salt Lake City	.167	20	6	0	1	1	0	0	0	0	0	1	0	0	0	0	4	0	0
Norman, Nelson, Hawaii†	.287	73	209	29	60	70	8	1	0	18	2	0	2	0	37	4	14	0	3
O'Brien, Charles, Tacoma	.226	69	195	33	44	82	11	0	9	22	3	8	0	6	28	0	31	0	1
O'Malley, Thomas, Phoenix°	.346	105	387	44	134	173	20	2	5	72	6	1	6	4	61	4	31	5	2
Oroz, Felix, Las Vegas°	.065	36	31	2	2	2	0	0	0	2	0	8	0	0	0	0	14	0	0
Orsulak, Joseph, Portland	.284	98	388	51	110	162	19	12	3	53	7	3	3	2	29	5	38	14	12
Ott, Edward, Edmonton°	.319	14	47	6	15	18	3	0	0	7	1	0	0	0	4	0	3	0	0
Ouellette, Philip, Phoenix†	.263	70	171	32	45	82	8	4	7	29	4	0	2	2	41	6	31	1	1
Paciorek, James, Vancouver	.279	68	251	27	70	98	12	5	2	38	2	2	2	4	22	2	45	2	2
Page, Mitchell, Hawaii°	.258	53	151	30	39	77	7	2	9	32	8	1	2	0	29	5	36	9	2
Pankovits, James, Tucson	.332	49	187	41	62	101	12	3	7	39	8	1	2	3	31	1	25	11	4
Paris, Kelly, Hawaii	.250	127	460	65	115	177	26	3	10	58	3	2	8	0	34	1	57	14	8
Patterson, Robert, Las Vegas	.263	60	19	0	5	6	1	0	0	0	0	3	0	0	0	0	5	0	0
Pena, Adalberto, Tucson	.260	89	281	34	73	104	10	3	5	35	4	7	5	2	32	5	41	4	4
Perry, Stephen, Albuquerque°	.000	41	5	0	0	0	0	0	0	0	0	1	0	0	1	0	2	0	0
Peters, Richard, Tacoma†	.327	74	260	38	85	112	10	4	3	30	4	4	2	2	32	0	31	6	9
Pettini, Joseph, Phoenix	.298	72	235	37	70	90	11	3	1	16	1	4	1	2	26	0	19	10	8
Peyton, Eric, Vancouver°	.258	127	431	49	111	145	23	1	3	47	4	9	5	5	37	7	65	15	5
Phelps, Kenneth, Salt Lake City°	.311	12	45	7	14	26	3	0	3	13	2	0	1	1	7	1	10	0	1
Pittman, Joseph, Phoenix	.286	95	357	69	102	127	14	1	3	28	3	4	4	2	36	2	35	16	10
Ponce, Carlos, Vancouver	.246	112	414	50	102	153	20	5	7	55	5	0	12	2	30	1	65	4	0

Player and Club	Pct.	G.	AB.	R.	H.	TB.	2B.	3B.	HR.	RBI.	GW.	SH.	SF.	HP.	BB.	Int. BB.	SO.	SB.	CS.
Powell, Hosken, Vancouver*	.213	57	183	22	39	53	6	1	2	14	1	1	3	0	19	2	24	1	0
Presley, James, Salt Lake City	.317	69	265	43	84	144	13	4	13	56	7	0	6	1	15	1	46	1	1
Pujols, Luis, Tucson	.277	110	375	39	104	160	22	2	10	58	3	2	3	2	22	1	79	0	1
Pulido, Alfonso, Hawaii*	.265	28	34	2	9	10	1	0	0	2	1	5	0	0	2	0	10	0	0
Pyznarski, Timothy, Tacoma	.260	31	96	12	25	42	5	0	4	15	2	0	0	0	8	0	36	2	3
Randall, James, Edmonton†	.284	119	426	61	121	185	17	7	11	71	2	2	1	1	66	6	69	2	4
Rasmussen, Eric, Tucson	.061	28	33	1	2	3	1	0	0	1	0	6	0	0	2	0	13	0	1
Ray, Larry, Tucson 53–Portland 63...	.258	116	356	53	92	161	21	6	12	63	7	1	5	1	44	6	65	2	0
Ready, Randy, Vancouver	.325	43	151	48	49	73	7	4	3	18	3	2	0	5	43	2	21	10	4
Reid, Jessie, Phoenix*	.231	36	121	13	28	36	5	0	1	9	0	1	1	0	10	1	27	11	0
Rennicke, Dean, Albuquerque	.067	30	30	1	2	2	0	0	0	0	0	2	0	0	4	0	11	0	0
Renteria, Richard, Hawaii	.247	19	77	8	19	24	3	1	0	11	3	1	0	0	6	0	7	1	0
Reynolds, Harold, Salt Lake City†	.296	135	558	94	165	208	22	6	3	54	4	9	3	3	73	2	72	37	17
Reynolds, Robert, Albuquerque†	.347	47	199	38	69	96	10	4	3	30	0	1	1	6	22	1	22	13	2
Richardt, Michael, Tucson	.295	38	122	24	36	58	9	2	3	20	3	2	3	0	17	1	16	2	0
Riles, Earnest, Vancouver	.267	123	424	59	113	155	19	7	3	54	5	1	8	1	67	8	67	1	2
Riley, George, Portland*	.105	36	19	2	2	2	0	0	0	0	0	0	0	0	1	0	4	0	0
Rincon, Andrew, Hawaii	.233	20	30	0	7	9	2	0	0	5	0	2	0	0	0	0	7	0	0
Rivera, German, Albuquerque	.315	51	181	30	57	87	12	3	4	39	3	0	2	0	16	0	13	3	0
Robinson, Bruce, Tacoma*	.244	37	78	8	19	26	2	1	1	10	3	1	1	1	7	0	7	0	0
Robles, Ruben, Tucson	.291	43	127	24	37	52	6	3	1	11	0	0	2	4	7	0	30	4	7
Rodas, Richard, Albuquerque*	.375	10	8	1	3	4	1	0	0	1	0	0	0	0	1	0	0	0	0
Rodriguez, Edwin, Las Vegas	.235	105	341	45	80	124	10	8	6	38	4	4	1	4	27	1	58	10	3
Roenicke, Ronald, Las Vegas†	.310	90	290	65	90	134	14	3	8	45	6	0	2	1	67	1	32	12	4
Rollin, Rondal, Tucson	.204	42	108	10	22	34	5	2	1	13	2	0	1	0	6	0	36	1	1
Romano, Thomas, Tacoma	.280	133	503	81	141	228	28	7	15	75	8	7	5	1	39	2	63	37	7
Romero, Albert, Edmonton	.307	64	228	36	70	102	13	2	5	43	3	1	3	5	20	0	37	1	0
Ross, Mark, Tucson	.000	57	8	0	0	0	0	0	0	0	0	0	0	0	1	0	4	0	0
Russell, John, Portland	.289	93	350	75	101	190	22	5	19	77	8	0	3	6	44	0	91	1	0
Salava, Randy, Portland*	.287	110	394	46	113	179	15	9	11	69	7	1	5	1	50	3	69	5	0
Sanchez, Alejandro, Phoenix	.318	135	532	98	169	294	29	9	26	108	13	0	2	5	22	5	108	34	15
Sandt, Thomas, Hawaii	.500	1	2	0	1	1	0	0	0	0	0	0	0	0	0	0	0	0	0
Sax, David, Albuquerque	.259	106	294	54	76	122	14	1	10	41	2	1	1	1	68	4	46	0	3
Schu, Richard, Portland	.301	140	552	70	166	265	35	14	12	82	7	1	8	3	43	3	83	7	4
Schultz, Greg, Albuquerque	.321	107	336	48	108	161	32	0	7	54	5	3	5	6	27	1	27	2	4
Schuster, Mark, Phoenix*	.261	96	249	37	65	98	13	1	6	31	2	3	5	0	42	5	39	2	2
See, Laurence, Albuquerque	.290	58	217	32	63	100	11	1	8	44	3	1	3	3	23	0	40	1	1
Semall, Paul, Hawaii	.208	26	24	3	5	5	0	0	0	2	0	5	0	0	2	0	4	0	0
Semprini, John, Salt Lake City	.000	34	1	0	0	0	0	0	0	0	0	0	0	0	0	0	1	0	0
Senteney, Steven, Hawaii	.000	13	3	0	0	0	0	0	0	0	0	0	0	0	0	0	0	0	0
Sheehy, Mark, Albuquerque*	.111	9	9	5	1	1	0	0	0	0	0	0	0	0	1	0	0	0	0
Simpson, Joe, Edmonton*	.276	135	496	73	137	178	19	8	2	73	3	3	5	0	58	3	76	16	7
Skube, Robert, Vancouver*	.267	61	210	32	56	104	13	4	9	40	5	0	1	0	35	7	43	0	3
Smith, Don, Albuquerque	.222	61	9	2	2	3	1	0	0	0	0	1	0	0	0	0	1	0	0
Solano, Julio, Tucson	.000	17	10	1	0	0	0	0	0	1	0	2	0	0	3	0	5	0	0
Sonberg, Erik, Albuquerque	.167	28	24	2	4	4	0	0	0	4	0	2	0	0	3	0	14	0	0
Stephenson, Phillip, Tacoma*	.302	124	398	70	120	177	25	1	10	69	6	6	3	0	85	9	54	15	4
Stone, Jeffrey, Portland*	.307	82	355	59	109	173	15	14	7	34	1	2	0	6	24	3	50	33	11
Stubbs, Franklin, Albuquerque*	.324	29	108	26	35	68	5	5	6	24	0	4	3	1	12	3	23	3	0
Sularz, Guy, Phoenix	.283	114	400	60	113	163	25	5	5	56	3	10	8	6	38	1	28	5	6
Tartabull, Danilo, Salt Lake City	.304	116	418	69	127	206	22	9	13	73	11	1	7	1	57	3	69	11	13
Taveras, Alejandro, Albuquerque	.265	114	392	61	104	142	20	3	4	61	6	4	5	1	66	3	43	1	5
Thomas, Franklin, Vancouver	.231	48	143	20	33	43	6	2	0	9	1	3	2	0	22	0	20	3	1
Thomas, James, Tucson†	.244	16	45	9	11	14	3	0	0	3	0	1	0	0	7	1	5	1	1
Tingley, Ronald, Salt Lake City	.500	3	2	1	1	4	0	0	1	1	0	0	0	0	1	0	1	0	0
Tolman, Timothy, Tucson	.292	102	363	63	106	174	27	7	9	54	9	1	6	2	53	1	37	1	0
Tomlin, David, Hawaii*	.143	23	7	0	1	1	0	0	0	0	0	2	0	0	1	0	3	0	0
Tracy, James, Tucson*	.244	52	156	22	38	59	12	3	1	21	3	1	2	0	31	2	39	2	1
Vail, Michael, Albuquerque	.264	25	91	12	24	39	6	0	3	10	0	1	0	1	8	0	17	1	0
Valentine, Ellis, Edmonton	.000	2	3	0	0	0	0	0	0	0	0	0	0	0	1	0	2	0	0
Valle, David, Salt Lake City	.278	86	284	54	79	130	13	1	12	54	5	0	3	3	45	2	36	0	1
Vanderbush, Walter, Las Vegas*	.250	38	8	5	2	2	0	0	0	0	0	0	0	0	2	0	1	0	0
Vargas, Hediberto, Hawaii	.293	43	147	24	43	82	10	1	9	30	4	1	2	1	13	1	40	0	1
Vavra, Joseph, Albuquerque*	.227	11	44	5	10	10	0	0	0	3	0	1	0	0	3	0	3	0	1
Vega, Jesus, Albuquerque	.177	22	62	7	11	19	2	0	2	8	0	2	1	1	4	0	9	0	0
Vega, Luis, Salt Lake City	.000	1	3	0	0	0	0	0	0	0	0	0	0	0	1	0	0	0	0
Violette, John, Phoenix	.074	30	27	2	2	2	0	0	0	0	0	1	0	0	2	0	14	0	0
Voigt, Paul, Albuquerque	.130	33	23	1	3	3	0	0	0	2	0	1	0	0	3	0	6	0	0
Wagner, Mark, Tacoma	.343	11	35	7	12	16	4	0	0	4	0	0	0	0	8	0	9	1	1
Walk, Robert, Hawaii	.091	18	22	0	2	3	1	0	0	3	1	2	0	0	0	0	6	0	0
Walker, Glen, Salt Lake City	.271	90	314	42	85	139	13	4	11	49	3	0	3	1	27	0	67	0	2
Waller, Tyrone, Tucson	.244	107	308	44	75	104	17	3	2	39	0	4	2	0	21	3	50	10	4
Ward, Colin, Phoenix*	.167	46	18	0	3	3	0	0	0	0	0	1	0	0	2	0	6	0	0
Wehrmeister, David, Portland	.111	28	18	0	2	3	1	0	0	0	0	5	0	0	0	0	4	0	0
Wellman, Brad, Phoenix	.296	43	159	26	47	57	8	1	0	11	1	0	1	2	13	2	11	11	2
West, Reginald, Edmonton*	.271	94	377	74	102	125	13	5	0	29	2	5	2	2	45	3	60	26	9
Wheeler, Timothy, Hawaii	.000	6	9	0	0	0	0	0	0	0	0	0	0	0	0	0	6	0	0
White, Larry, Albuquerque†	.233	41	30	4	7	7	0	0	0	0	0	3	0	0	0	0	6	0	0
Wieghaus, Thomas, Tucson	.281	33	96	6	27	34	7	0	0	6	2	0	0	0	6	2	7	0	0
Williams, Jaime, Tucson	.161	14	31	3	5	7	2	0	0	4	0	2	0	0	6	2	11	0	1
Winn, James, Hawaii	.167	21	6	0	1	1	0	0	0	0	0	0	0	0	1	0	1	0	0
Wojna, Edward, Las Vegas	.125	29	32	2	4	5	1	0	0	3	0	2	0	0	1	0	21	0	0
Woodard, Michael, Tacoma*	.274	95	325	47	89	104	8	2	1	17	1	7	1	3	32	0	20	24	11
Wotus, Ronald, Hawaii	.254	61	224	32	57	95	15	4	5	23	3	0	1	2	23	0	20	4	1
Zaske, Jeffrey, Hawaii	.000	37	2	0	0	0	0	0	0	0	0	0	0	0	0	0	1	0	0

The following pitchers, listed alphabetically by club, with games in parentheses, had no plate appearances, primarily through use of designated hitters:

ALBUQUERQUE—Alexander, Roberto (4); Martin, Steven (4); Wallace, David (4).

EDMONTON—Angulo, Kenneth (1); Brown, Steven (23); Browning, Michael (32); Cliburn, Stewart (45); Corbett, Douglas (2); Curtis, John (9); Finch, Steven (21); Kain, Martin (40); Kibbe, Jay (29); LaCorte, Frank (7); McCaskill, Kirk (24); Mooneyham, William (16); Moreno, Angel (16); Smith, David (50); Steirer, Ricky (22).

HAWAII—Lamonde, Lawrence (3); Pippin, Craig (6).

PHOENIX—Farr, James (3); Segelke, Herman (7).

PORTLAND—Calderon, Jose (8); Ghelfi, Anthony (1).

SALT LAKE CITY—Allard, Brian (17); Babcock, Robert (21); Beard, David (2); Best, Karl (46); Cuellar, Robert (6); Lewis, James (30); Murray, Jed (5); Newman, Randall (3); Nunez, Edwin (18); Snyder, Brian (27); Stoddard, Robert (9); Thomas, Roy (7); Whitmer, Joseph (12); Young, Matthew (6).

TACOMA—Codiroli, Christopher (9); de los Santos, Ramon (46); Farmer, Edward (21); Ford, David (29); Heimueller, Gorman (24); Hensley, Charles (11); Hudson, Robert (38); Jones, Jeffrey (9); Kaiser, Jeffrey (14); Krueger, William (5); Langford, Rick (3); Leiper, David (28); McDonald, Russell (34); Myers, Edward (13); Ontiveros, Steven (2); Rodriguez, Ricardo (6); Torrez, Michael (3); Warren, Michael (11); Young, Curtis (14).

TUCSON—Heathcock, Jeffrey (4); Kerfeld, Charles (1); Sambito, Joseph (8).

VANCOUVER—Alicea, Miguel (1); Augustine, Gerald (13); Beene, Andrew (16); Boone, Daniel (27); Burns, Daniel (28); Candiotti, Thomas (15); Duquette, Bryan (7); Eichelberger, Juan (25); Gibson, Robert (14); Hartzell, Paul (10); Hensley, Charles (3); Higuera, Teodoro (8); Jones, Douglas (3); Koontz, James (43); Lazorko, Jack (28); Lesley, Bradley (5); Moffitt, Randall (1); Roberts, Scott (26); Searage, Raymond (33); Stuper, John (10); Wegman, William (6).

GRAND SLAM HOME RUNS—Lubratich 2; Adams, R. Allen, Amelung, W. Bathe, Bochy, Bream, Brewer, Clark, Cliburn, Coles, Deer, Loman, Malkin, Murray, Peters, Randall, Salava, Sax, Sularz, Tolman, Walker, 1 each.

AWARDED FIRST BASE ON CATCHER'S INTERFERENCE—Wellman 5 (Cliburn, Debus, Gwosdz, Miller, Nahorodny); Krauss 3 (Fimple, Martin, Sax); W. Bathe 2 (Fimple, Nelson); Charboneau 2 (Liddle 2); Paris 2 (Diaz, Gomez); Davidsmeier (Miller); T. Davis (Liddle); Gonzalez (Ouellette); C. Jones (Martin); Murray (Daulton); Nanni (Ouellette); Romano (Gomez).

CLUB FIELDING

Club	Pct.	G.	PO.	A.	E.	DP.	PB.	Club	Pct.	G.	PO.	A.	E.	DP.	PB.
Tucson	.974	140	3604	1534	139	120	12	Vancouver	.971	142	3597	1394	150	108	10
Hawaii	.973	141	3644	1467	143	121	4	Edmonton	.970	142	3632	1684	164	142	10
Las Vegas	.972	136	3535	1484	143	119	13	Salt Lake City	.968	140	3658	1517	169	141	13
Tacoma	.972	140	3611	1541	149	127	12	Phoenix	.966	144	3738	1550	185	139	13
Portland	.971	140	3684	1478	155	113	11	Albuquerque	.962	143	3697	1708	216	151	34

Triple Play—Salt Lake City.

INDIVIDUAL FIELDING

⁕Throws lefthanded.

FIRST BASEMEN

Player and Club	Pct.	G.	PO.	A.	E.	DP.	Player and Club	Pct.	G.	PO.	A.	E.	DP.
Allen, Salt Lake City	.989	110	969	72	12	92	Miller, Edmonton	1.000	2	3	0	0	0
W. Bathe, Tacoma	1.000	1	3	0	0	1	Moore, Vancouver⁕	.988	37	295	26	4	25
Bream, Albuquerque⁕	.986	113	1071	112	17	106	Murray, Phoenix	.975	69	549	43	15	48
Brock, Albuquerque	.979	17	124	18	3	15	Nahorodny, Salt Lake City	1.000	1	7	1	0	2
Bundy, Hawaii⁕	.963	6	50	2	2	7	Nanni, Salt Lake City	.984	28	234	16	4	24
Clark, Edmonton⁕	1.000	2	13	0	0	4	Norman, Hawaii	1.000	1	4	0	0	0
Clements, Tucson	.985	20	179	16	3	15	O'Malley, Phoenix	.984	22	181	7	3	15
Cliburn, Hawaii	.984	16	113	14	2	8	Ott, Edmonton	.974	8	71	3	2	3
Connally, Las Vegas	.993	29	253	23	2	16	Page, Hawaii	.976	23	187	14	5	16
Cypret, Tucson	1.000	2	15	0	0	0	Phelps, Salt Lake City⁕	1.000	4	25	5	0	5
A. Davis, Salt Lake City	1.000	1	2	0	0	0	Ponce, Vancouver	.982	66	567	31	11	53
Gl. Davis, Tucson	.979	105	894	91	21	85	Pujols, Tucson	1.000	1	3	0	0	0
Diaz, Portland	.952	3	20	0	1	1	Randall, Edmonton⁕	.972	100	887	95	28	92
Distefano, Hawaii⁕	1.000	36	282	22	0	29	Roenicke, Las Vegas⁕	1.000	1	6	1	0	0
Goodwin, Tacoma	.996	60	477	40	2	44	Russell, Portland	.981	7	45	6	1	4
Howard, Hawaii	1.000	1	10	0	0	1	Sax, Albuquerque	.982	14	106	4	2	11
Hudgens, Tacoma⁕	.964	3	26	1	1	3	Schultz, Albuquerque	1.000	3	7	3	0	4
Keedy, Edmonton	1.000	1	8	2	0	2	Schuster, Phoenix⁕	.988	70	550	43	7	56
Lancellotti, Las Vegas⁕	.976	32	227	14	6	23	See, Albuquerque	1.000	1	8	1	0	1
Lansford, Las Vegas	.996	87	698	46	3	65	Skube, Vancouver⁕	.992	43	355	21	3	24
Lubratich, Edmonton	.989	38	352	24	4	30	Stephenson, Tacoma⁕	.984	38	272	32	5	28
Maler, Portland	1.000	10	90	9	0	5	Stubbs, Albuquerque	.933	2	12	2	1	1
Malkin, Hawaii	.982	50	409	26	8	31	Tolman, Tucson⁕	1.000	22	153	10	0	9
Martin, Las Vegas	.939	5	30	1	2	1	Tracy, Tucson⁕	1.000	1	3	0	0	0
MELENDEZ, Portland⁕	.991	126	1085	85	11	94	Vargas, Hawaii	.990	17	98	5	1	8
Mercado, Salt Lake City	1.000	2	16	0	0	4	Wotus, Hawaii	.984	8	55	5	1	6
Meyer, Tacoma	.989	47	402	28	5	42							

Triple Play—Allen.

SECOND BASEMEN

Player and Club	Pct.	G.	PO.	A.	E.	DP.	Player and Club	Pct.	G.	PO.	A.	E.	DP.
Adams, Edmonton	.975	8	15	24	1	1	Miscik, Hawaii	.977	27	60	66	3	17
Allen, Albuquerque	.978	12	16	28	1	6	Mitchell, Portland	.974	60	102	157	7	25
Castillo, Vancouver	.971	8	16	18	1	4	Nandin, Tucson	.957	11	21	24	2	2
Collins, Albuquerque	1.000	1	0	1	0	0	Norman, Hawaii	.968	49	90	121	7	24
Crone, Salt Lake City	1.000	1	2	2	0	0	Pankovits, Tucson	.972	49	103	176	8	35
Cypret, Tucson	.976	44	94	110	5	23	Paris, Hawaii	1.000	7	15	19	0	4
Davidsmeier, Vancouver	1.000	2	0	2	0	0	Peters, Tacoma	1.000	1	1	2	0	0
Debus, Albuquerque	.667	1	0	2	1	0	Pettini, Phoenix	1.000	6	9	12	0	2
DeSimone, Las Vegas	.984	33	41	81	2	14	Pittman, Phoenix	.958	71	124	261	17	33
Gallego, Tacoma	.983	54	115	119	4	22	Ready, Vancouver	.972	34	70	102	5	19
Garcia, Las Vegas	1.000	4	4	4	0	1	Renteria, Hawaii	.971	11	22	45	2	8
Gerber, Edmonton	.941	8	13	19	2	5	REYNOLDS, Salt Lake City	.967	135	326	396	25	104
Gonzalez, Hawaii	1.000	2	3	5	0	1	Richardt, Tucson	.987	29	69	84	2	18
Guillen, Las Vegas	1.000	3	2	2	0	1	Rodriguez, Las Vegas	.971	87	181	216	12	50
Hamric, Portland	.970	40	60	99	5	13	Schultz, Albuquerque	.970	42	86	139	7	34
Hill, Tacoma	.989	17	45	43	1	13	Sheehy, Albuquerque	.833	2	3	2	1	1
Hinshaw, Las Vegas	.952	36	57	81	7	21	Sularz, Phoenix	.968	33	59	92	5	27
Jeltz, Portland	.967	30	70	78	5	19	Taveras, Albuquerque	.942	21	45	53	6	15
Koenigsfeld, Vancouver	.974	71	148	192	9	36	F. Thomas, Vancouver	.952	35	78	79	8	14
Krauss, Edmonton	.966	114	252	380	22	83	J. Thomas, Tucson	.971	14	18	48	2	7
Kutcher, Phoenix	1.000	1	4	4	0	3	Vail, Albuquerque	.889	6	6	10	2	2
Landestoy, Albuquerque	.966	65	183	211	14	50	Vavra, Albuquerque	.944	9	19	32	3	4
Legg, Portland	.979	39	53	88	3	13	Wagner, Tacoma	1.000	7	7	23	0	1
Lubratich, Edmonton	.989	17	43	43	1	17	Wellman, Phoenix	.973	42	91	123	6	22
McHenry, Haw.-Salt Lake City	.915	10	18	25	4	2	Woodard, Tacoma	.985	80	164	229	6	48
							Wotus, Hawaii	.973	44	94	122	6	23

Triple Play—Reynolds.

THIRD BASEMEN

Player and Club	Pct.	G.	PO.	A.	E.	DP.
Adams, Edmonton	.967	26	16	43	2	6
Allen, Salt Lake City	.923	5	7	5	1	2
R. Bathe, Tacoma	.950	33	23	73	5	7
W. Bathe, Tacoma	1.000	4	1	3	0	0
Brock, Albuquerque	.789	9	10	20	8	3
Brown, Phoenix	.905	74	43	119	17	10
Coles, Salt Lake City	.929	67	45	164	16	9
CONNALLY, Las Vegas	.959	101	87	174	11	21
Crone, Salt Lake City	1.000	4	8	4	0	0
Cypret, Tucson	.966	40	24	60	3	6
Davidsmeier, Vancouver	.933	116	102	218	23	15
Debus, Albuquerque	.909	8	4	16	2	2
Duncan, Salt Lake City	1.000	1	1	1	0	0
Gallego, Tacoma	.951	19	17	41	3	6
Gonzalez, Hawaii	.960	37	22	73	4	3
Hinshaw, Las Vegas	.896	46	35	103	16	5
Hotchkiss, Tacoma	.904	34	19	75	10	5
Howard, Hawaii	1.000	2	1	7	0	0
Jeltz, Portland	1.000	2	3	4	0	0
Keedy, Edmonton	.906	50	37	107	15	14
Kiefer, Tacoma	.953	25	14	47	3	6
Koenigsfeld, Vancouver	.815	10	7	15	5	1
Kutcher, Phoenix	.800	11	3	13	4	2
Lubratich, Edmonton	.940	74	53	134	12	10
McHenry, Salt Lake City	1.000	2	0	1	0	0
Meyer, Tacoma	.935	32	15	57	5	8
Mills, Tucson	.978	51	30	102	3	12
Miscik, Hawaii	.952	102	99	201	15	29
Murray, Phoenix	.875	3	5	2	1	0
Nelson, Vancouver	1.000	4	0	2	0	0
Norman, Hawaii	.923	4	4	8	1	1
O'Malley, Phoenix	.935	65	46	127	12	11
Presley, Salt Lake City	.941	66	53	140	12	14
Pyznarski, Tacoma	.917	8	5	17	2	0
Ready, Vancouver	.964	9	4	23	1	2
Rivera, Albuquerque	.948	33	21	70	5	8
Sax, Albuquerque	1.000	2	0	4	0	0
Schu, Portland	.931	139	109	254	27	20
Schultz, Albuquerque	.916	38	27	82	10	8
See, Albuquerque	.903	53	33	116	16	6
Sularz, Phoenix	1.000	14	4	22	0	4
Taveras, Albuquerque	.905	7	5	14	2	0
Thomas, Vancouver	.857	13	3	9	2	2
Tolman, Tucson	.789	5	4	11	4	3
Wagner, Tacoma	.750	1	0	3	1	0
Waller, Tucson	.869	60	29	84	17	7

SHORTSTOPS

Player and Club	Pct.	G.	PO.	A.	E.	DP.
Adams, Edmonton	.941	43	61	129	12	31
Aguayo, Portland	.929	3	6	7	1	2
J. Allen, Salt Lake City	.930	11	10	30	3	6
R. Allen, Albuquerque	.966	45	59	140	7	23
R. Bathe, Tacoma	1.000	2	1	0	0	0
Collins, Albuquerque	1.000	1	5	2	0	1
Crone, Salt Lake City	.925	9	13	24	3	6
DeSimone, Las Vegas	.928	17	21	43	5	5
Dowell, Portland	.944	45	72	146	13	24
Followell, Tucson	.969	46	81	135	7	25
Gallego, Tacoma	.946	27	35	71	6	12
GERBER, Edmonton	.976	105	173	320	12	60
Guillen, Las Vegas	.969	114	170	362	17	62
Hamric, Portland	1.000	1	2	4	0	0
Hill, Tacoma	.962	22	26	49	3	11
Jeltz, Portland	.950	91	169	264	23	53
Keedy, Edmonton	.964	5	14	13	1	2
Kiefer, Tacoma	.929	105	175	281	35	53
Koenigsfeld, Vancouver	.950	25	35	61	5	17
Kutcher, Phoenix	.966	20	28	58	3	9
Landestoy, Albuquerque	1.000	2	6	0	0	0
Legg, Portland	1.000	8	8	7	0	1
McHenry, Hawaii-SLC	.954	17	19	43	3	15
Mills, Tucson	1.000	1	0	2	0	0
Nandin, Tucson	1.000	5	10	14	0	3
Norman, Hawaii	1.000	17	23	45	0	18
Paris, Hawaii	.938	117	188	294	32	52
Pena, Tucson	.967	89	152	254	14	55
Pettini, Phoenix	.964	59	109	162	10	41
Pittman, Portland	.951	20	31	47	4	8
Riles, Vancouver	.967	122	190	316	17	57
Rivera, Albuquerque	.898	18	32	47	9	17
Rodriguez, Las Vegas	.964	16	24	30	2	7
Sularz, Phoenix	.945	54	100	159	15	27
Tartabull, Salt Lake City	.955	111	181	333	24	68
Taveras, Albuquerque	.928	88	152	263	32	62
Vavra, Albuquerque	.800	2	0	4	1	0
Wagner, Tacoma	1.000	3	4	5	0	0
Wotus, Hawaii	1.000	8	16	21	0	5

Triple Play—Tartabull.

OUTFIELDERS

Player and Club	Pct.	G.	PO.	A.	E.	DP.
Adams, Edmonton	.971	29	64	4	2	1
Amelung, Albuquerque*	.987	100	216	8	3	2
Arnold, Tacoma	1.000	13	17	0	0	0
Bennett, Tacoma*	1.000	4	6	0	0	0
Brantley, Salt Lake City	1.000	4	8	0	0	0
Brewer, Albuquerque	.994	96	160	7	1	0
M. Brown, Edmonton	1.000	26	50	5	0	0
R. Brown, Salt Lake City	.981	22	50	1	1	0
Bullock, Tucson*	.951	47	96	2	5	0
Calderon, Salt Lake City	.946	62	132	9	8	3
Chambers, Salt Lake City*	.963	23	25	1	1	0
Charboneau, Hawaii	1.000	13	27	0	0	0
Clark, Edmonton*	.931	16	25	2	2	0
Clements, Tucson	1.000	1	1	0	0	0
Coleman, Las Vegas	1.000	1	3	0	0	0
Darkis, Portland	1.000	35	42	3	0	0
Ge. Davis, Las Vegas	.955	123	240	17	12	2
Gl. Davis, Tucson	.969	20	28	3	1	1
T. Davis, Hawaii*	.962	141	311	18	13	3
Debus, Albuquerque	1.000	5	7	1	0	0
Deer, Phoenix	.968	131	251	19	9	3
Diaz, Tacoma	.964	33	52	1	2	0
Distefano, Hawaii*	1.000	32	52	8	0	1
EDWARDS, Vancouver*	.995	87	205	9	1	1
Gladden, Phoenix	.985	59	130	4	2	1
Gonzalez, Hawaii	.990	74	96	6	1	1
Goodwin, Tacoma	.972	21	34	1	1	0
Hancock, Tacoma*	1.000	10	16	2	0	0
Harrison, Tacoma	.972	50	135	5	4	2
Hinshaw, Las Vegas	.988	45	72	9	1	1
Howard, Hawaii	.968	43	58	3	2	2
Hudgens, Tacoma*	.979	25	46	1	1	0
Jeltz, Portland	1.000	11	28	3	0	2
C. Jones, Tucson*	.993	113	262	6	2	2
G. Jones, Phoenix	1.000	2	4	0	0	0
Keedy, Edmonton	.969	42	60	2	2	0
Kruk, Las Vegas*	.990	89	183	7	2	4
Kutcher, Phoenix	.973	64	137	5	4	0
Lancellotti, Las Vegas*	.953	72	113	9	6	2
Lansford, Las Vegas	.967	43	57	2	2	0
Lezcano, Tacoma	.955	24	41	1	2	1
Loman, Vancouver*	.989	122	267	15	3	3
Long, Salt Lake City	1.000	2	2	0	0	0
Loucks, Tucson	.971	28	62	6	2	1
Maler, Portland	1.000	4	6	0	0	0
Melendez, Portland*	1.000	3	5	0	0	0
Mercado, Salt Lake City	1.000	2	1	1	0	0
Meyer, Tacoma	.889	5	8	0	1	0
D. Miller, Edmonton	1.000	44	78	3	0	0
L. Miller, Albuquerque	.954	118	189	18	10	2
Mitchell, Portland	.953	31	58	3	3	1
Moses, Salt Lake City*	.994	68	161	8	1	1
Murray, Phoenix	.972	16	33	2	1	1
Nahorodny, Salt Lake City	.500	5	1	0	1	0
Nanni, Salt Lake City*	.971	112	190	11	6	1
R. Nelson, Salt Lake City	.986	72	141	3	2	1
Orsulak, Hawaii*	.992	98	258	6	2	0
Paciorek, Vancouver	.978	67	133	3	3	0
Page, Hawaii	1.000	11	12	0	0	0
Peters, Tucson	.984	71	185	2	3	1
Peyton, Vancouver*	.985	121	249	6	4	1
Powell, Vancouver*	.949	26	34	3	2	0
Pyznarski, Tacoma	1.000	2	1	0	0	0
Randall, Edmonton*	.833	6	5	0	1	0
Ray, Tucson-Portland	.984	93	183	6	3	1
Reid, Phoenix*	.986	35	70	0	1	0
Reynolds, Albuquerque	.947	47	104	4	6	1
Robinson, Tacoma	1.000	4	1	0	0	0
Robles, Tucson	.959	41	67	3	3	0
Roenicke, Las Vegas*	.994	65	155	6	1	0
Rollin, Tucson	.947	17	18	0	1	0
Romano, Tacoma	.969	127	298	10	10	1
Romero, Edmonton	.982	49	106	5	2	0
Russell, Phoenix	.973	85	134	11	4	1
Salava, Portland	.981	107	255	9	5	2
Sanchez, Phoenix	.956	134	249	10	12	2
Sax, Albuquerque	.923	22	34	2	3	0
Schultz, Albuquerque	.750	4	3	0	1	0
Simpson, Edmonton*	.972	135	328	16	10	1
Skube, Vancouver*	1.000	8	16	1	0	1

OUTFIELDERS—Continued

Player and Club	Pct.	G.	PO.	A.	E.	DP.	Player and Club	Pct.	G.	PO.	A.	E.	DP.
Stephenson, Tacoma°	.975	76	146	8	4	1	Vail, Albuquerque	1.000	18	35	2	0	1
Stone, Portland	.944	81	194	7	12	4	Vargas, Hawaii	.947	29	34	2	2	0
Stubbs, Albuquerque°	.963	23	24	2	1	0	Vega, Albuquerque	.958	14	23	0	1	0
Sularz, Phoenix	.966	15	26	2	1	1	Walker, Salt Lake City	.956	75	123	8	6	0
Thomas, Vancouver	1.000	1	2	0	0	0	Waller, Tucson	.940	36	44	3	3	0
Tolman, Tucson	.942	79	142	4	9	2	West, Edmonton	.969	93	180	9	6	3
Tracy, Tucson°	.970	41	64	0	2	0	Woodard, Tacoma	1.000	13	27	0	0	0

CATCHERS

Player and Club	Pct.	G.	PO.	A.	E.	DP.	PB.	Player and Club	Pct.	G.	PO.	A.	E.	DP.	PB.
W. Bathe, Tacoma	.983	69	377	26	7	2	9	Mercado, Salt Lake City	.988	26	152	17	2	1	3
Bochy, Las Vegas	.990	31	189	17	2	1	4	Miller, Edmonton	.982	47	189	24	4	1	3
Cliburn, Hawaii	.978	45	254	17	6	0	0	Nahorodny, Salt Lake City	.979	40	218	19	5	1	1
Daulton, Portland	.983	64	322	26	6	4	3	Nelson, Vancouver	.986	95	518	58	8	5	6
Debus, Albuquerque	.919	29	114	11	11	2	12	O'Brien, Tacoma	1.000	62	260	39	0	5	3
Diaz, Portland	.966	52	301	15	11	0	5	Ouellette, Phoenix	.990	60	265	25	3	4	6
Duncan, Salt Lake City	1.000	2	8	0	0	0	0	PUJOLS, Tacoma	.991	106	575	69	6	6	11
Fimple, Albuquerque	.985	91	481	45	8	3	16	Robinson, Tacoma	.967	24	82	6	3	1	0
Gomez, Phoenix	.976	97	558	56	15	8	7	Romero, Edmonton	1.000	7	24	5	0	0	0
Gwosdz, Las Vegas	.985	59	300	32	5	5	7	Russell, Portland	1.000	2	3	1	0	0	0
Herz, Hawaii	.985	96	600	65	10	10	4	Sax, Albuquerque	.967	38	157	17	6	0	6
Huppert, Vancouver	.975	59	288	29	8	2	4	Tingley, Salt Lake City	1.000	2	3	0	0	0	0
Kutcher, Phoenix	1.000	1	5	0	0	0	0	Valle, Salt Lake City	.987	78	433	34	6	4	8
Lavalliere, Portland	.995	33	186	16	1	3	3	Vega, Salt Lake City	.833	1	5	0	1	0	0
Liddle, Edmonton	.974	91	387	62	12	5	7	Wieghaus, Tucson	.988	31	141	21	2	0	1
Malkin, Hawaii	.857	3	5	1	1	1	0	Williams, Tucson	1.000	13	57	9	0	0	0
Martin, Las Vegas	.970	58	305	14	10	3	2								

PITCHERS

Player and Club	Pct.	G.	PO.	A.	E.	DP.	Player and Club	Pct.	G.	PO.	A.	E.	DP.
Alexander, Albuquerque	1.000	4	1	2	0	0	Hamm, Las Vegas	.966	16	8	14	1	3
Allard, Salt Lake City	.842	17	7	9	3	0	Hammaker, Phoenix°	1.000	2	1	3	0	0
Alvarez, Tucson	.952	33	7	13	1	2	Hartzell, Vancouver	.700	10	4	3	3	0
Anderson, Vancouver-Tucson°	.875	19	6	15	3	3	Hayward, Las Vegas°	.833	26	7	28	7	1
Angulo, Edmonton°	1.000	2	1	0	0	0	Heathcock, Tucson	1.000	4	3	1	0	0
Augustine, Vancouver°	.929	13	3	10	1	1	Heimueller, Tacoma°	1.000	24	10	31	0	4
Babcock, Salt Lake City	.733	21	5	6	4	1	Hensley, Tacoma-Vancouver°	1.000	14	4	9	0	1
Beard, Salt Lake City	1.000	2	1	2	0	0	Hernandez, Tucson	.909	28	13	17	3	3
Beene, Vancouver	.917	16	4	18	2	1	Higuera, Vancouver°	.889	8	2	6	1	1
Bernard, Tucson	.969	41	7	24	1	0	Holton, Albuquerque	1.000	12	4	4	0	0
Best, Salt Lake City	.946	46	2	9	2	0	Howell, Albuquerque	1.000	18	10	13	0	0
Bielecki, Hawaii	.975	28	16	23	1	2	Hudson, Tacoma	.900	38	1	8	1	1
Blobaum, Phoenix	.950	43	12	26	2	2	D. Jones, Vancouver	1.000	3	0	3	0	0
Bockus, Phoenix	1.000	8	0	2	0	0	J. Jones, Tacoma	1.000	9	8	6	0	0
Bonine, Tucson	.969	33	11	20	1	0	Kain, Edmonton	1.000	40	10	24	0	0
Booker, Las Vegas	1.000	9	4	10	0	1	Kaiser, Tacoma°	.826	14	5	14	4	1
Boone, Vancouver°	1.000	27	1	9	0	0	Kerfeld, Tucson	1.000	1	0	1	0	0
Borbon, Albuquerque	.933	54	3	11	1	1	Kibbe, Edmonton	.972	29	13	22	1	1
Bradley, Tacoma	.900	49	5	13	2	1	Kingman, Phoenix	.929	30	3	10	1	2
L. Brown, Las Vegas	1.000	43	6	12	0	1	Knudson, Tucson	1.000	13	8	9	0	0
M. Brown, Edmonton	1.000	23	17	23	0	0	Koontz, Vancouver	.900	43	2	7	1	1
Browning, Edmonton	.935	32	9	20	2	2	Krawczyk, Hawaii	1.000	43	3	8	0	1
Burns, Vancouver	.857	28	1	5	1	0	Kromy, Portland	1.000	23	4	5	0	0
Burroughs, Las Vegas°	.933	48	3	11	1	1	Krueger, Tacoma°	1.000	5	3	6	0	2
Bystrom, Portland	1.000	5	1	2	0	0	Lacey, Phoenix°	1.000	24	0	7	0	0
Calderon, Portland°	1.000	8	0	2	0	0	LaCorte, Edmonton	1.000	7	0	1	0	0
Calhoun, Tucson°	1.000	14	5	2	0	1	Lamonde, Hawaii	.750	3	3	0	1	0
Calvert, Phoenix	.857	21	10	14	4	1	Langford, Tacoma	1.000	3	3	2	0	1
Candiotti, Vancouver	.958	15	5	18	1	0	Lazorko, Vancouver	1.000	28	3	6	0	0
Carman, Portland°	1.000	39	3	10	0	0	Leiper, Tacoma°	1.000	28	1	7	0	1
Chiffer, Las Vegas	1.000	36	5	6	0	0	Leopold, Las Vegas	1.000	2	0	3	0	0
Cliburn, Edmonton	.957	45	6	16	1	1	Lesley, Vancouver	.000	5	0	0	1	0
Codiroli, Tacoma	.846	9	5	6	2	0	Lewis, Salt Lake City	1.000	30	17	43	0	4
Cole, Portland	.964	17	9	18	1	0	Long, Salt Lake City	.941	50	9	7	1	0
Corbett, Edmonton	1.000	2	1	0	0	0	Madden, Tucson°	.929	11	3	10	1	0
Cornell, Phoenix	.750	35	2	4	2	0	Maddux, Portland	1.000	8	9	10	0	0
Couchee, Las Vegas	1.000	37	2	11	0	1	R. Martin, Phoenix	1.000	32	9	9	0	0
Cuellar, Salt Lake City	.500	6	0	1	1	1	S. Martin, Albuquerque	.667	4	1	1	1	0
Davisson, Portland	.977	25	15	28	1	3	Mathis, Tucson	.905	12	8	11	2	0
Decker, Las Vegas	.957	47	9	13	1	1	McCaskill, Edmonton	.977	24	14	28	1	2
DeLeon, Las Vegas	1.000	6	0	1	0	0	McDonald, Tacoma	.909	34	10	20	3	3
de los Santos, Tacoma°	1.000	46	1	8	0	1	McLaughlin, Phoenix	.968	25	7	23	1	0
Diaz, Albuquerque	1.000	20	3	12	0	0	Minetto, Tucson°	1.000	45	5	10	0	1
Downs, Portland	.900	30	7	11	2	0	Mohorcic, Hawaii	1.000	9	2	11	0	1
Duquette, Vancouver°	1.000	7	1	3	0	1	Money, Portland	1.000	10	4	7	0	0
Eichelberger, Vancouver	.788	25	9	17	7	0	Montalvo, Albuquerque	1.000	45	5	8	0	1
Farmer, Tacoma	.857	21	1	5	1	1	Mooneyham, Edmonton	.882	16	2	13	2	0
Farr, Phoenix	1.000	3	3	2	0	0	Moore, Phoenix	1.000	6	1	1	0	0
Felt, Phoenix°	.800	10	1	3	1	0	Moreno, Edmonton°	1.000	16	6	7	0	0
Finch, Edmonton	1.000	21	14	22	0	0	Mura, Portland	1.000	48	0	11	0	0
Fireovid, Portland	.938	46	13	17	2	2	Murray, Salt Lake City	1.000	5	3	5	0	0
Foley, Tucson	1.000	5	1	2	0	0	Myers, Tacoma	.929	13	3	10	1	1
Ford, Tacoma	.967	29	9	20	1	1	W. E. Nelson, Salt Lake City	.762	17	2	14	5	1
Fowlkes, Phoenix	.923	16	3	9	1	0	Newman, Salt Lake City°	1.000	3	1	1	0	0
Garrelts, Phoenix	.727	21	1	7	3	0	Nunez, Salt Lake City	1.000	18	0	2	0	0
Gaynor, Portland	.889	53	5	11	2	3	Ontiveros, Tacoma	1.000	2	1	4	0	1
Geisel, Salt Lake City°	1.000	26	1	5	0	1	Oroz, Las Vegas°	.974	35	12	25	1	1
Gibson, Vancouver	1.000	14	5	7	0	0	Patterson, Las Vegas°	1.000	60	3	20	0	1
Gleaton, Salt Lake City°	.875	29	0	7	1	0	Perry, Albuquerque	.727	41	4	12	6	1
Grant, Phoenix	.933	17	7	7	1	0	Pippin, Hawaii	1.000	6	1	0	0	0
Green, Hawaii	1.000	13	0	4	0	1	Pulido, Hawaii°	.962	28	11	40	2	2

PITCHERS—Continued

Player and Club	Pct.	G.	PO.	A.	E.	DP.
Rasmussen, Tucson	1.000	28	16	24	0	2
Rennicke, Albuquerque	1.000	30	11	37	0	4
Riley, Portland*	.929	36	8	18	2	1
Rincon, Hawaii	.960	20	9	15	1	3
Roberts, Vancouver	.842	26	4	12	3	0
Rodas, Albuquerque*	1.000	10	2	18	0	0
Ross, Tucson	1.000	57	9	17	0	2
Sambito, Tucson*	1.000	8	0	1	0	0
Searage, Vancouver*	.880	33	7	15	3	1
Segelke, Phoenix	.500	7	1	0	1	0
Semall, Hawaii	.906	26	8	21	3	0
Semprini, Salt Lake City	.923	34	6	6	1	1
Senteney, Hawaii	.857	13	3	3	1	0
Da. Smith, Edmonton	.870	50	8	12	3	1
Do. Smith, Albuquerque	1.000	59	8	8	0	2
Snyder, Salt Lake City*	.886	27	9	22	4	1
Solano, Tucson	.917	17	3	8	1	0
Sonberg, Albuquerque*	.917	28	6	16	2	1
Steirer, Edmonton	1.000	22	11	20	0	0
Stoddard, Salt Lake City	.923	9	6	6	1	1
Stuper, Vancouver	1.000	10	2	6	0	1

Player and Club	Pct.	G.	PO.	A.	E.	DP.
Thomas, Salt Lake City	1.000	7	1	1	0	0
Tomlin, Hawaii*	.938	22	2	13	1	0
Torrez, Tacoma	1.000	3	0	5	0	0
Vanderbush, Las Vegas	.933	34	7	7	1	1
Violette, Phoenix	.962	30	3	22	1	0
Voigt, Albuquerque	1.000	33	22	25	0	6
Walk, Hawaii	.925	18	10	27	3	2
Wallace, Albuquerque	1.000	4	2	1	0	0
Ward, Phoenix*	.935	46	10	19	2	2
Warren, Tacoma	.875	11	1	6	1	0
Wegman, Vancouver	1.000	6	1	3	0	0
Wehrmeister, Portland	.941	28	1	15	1	1
Wheeler, Hawaii	1.000	6	0	9	0	0
White, Albuquerque	.923	37	22	26	4	0
Whitmer, Salt Lake City	1.000	12	10	13	0	0
Winn, Hawaii	1.000	21	6	12	0	1
Wojna, Las Vegas	.946	29	10	25	2	1
C. Young, Tacoma*	.960	14	5	19	1	0
M. Young, Salt Lake City*	.875	6	0	7	1	0
Zaske, Hawaii	.947	37	4	14	1	2

The following players do not have any recorded accepted chances at the positions indicated; therefore, are not listed in the fielding averages for those particular positions: Alicea, p; R. Allen, p; Curtis, p; Davidsmeier, ss; DeSimone, 3b; Duncan, 1b; Gerber, of; Ghelfi, p; Howard, p; Lansford, 3b; Moffitt, p; Nahorodny, p; O'Brien, of; Ouellette, p; Pyznarski, 1b; E. Rodriguez, 3b, p; R. Rodriguez, p; Simpson, p; Waller, p; Wieghaus, p; Woodard, ss.

CLUB PITCHING

Club	ERA.	G.	CG.	ShO.	Sv.	IP.	H.	R.	ER.	HR.	HB.	BB.	Int. BB.	SO.	WP.	Bk.
Hawaii	3.16	141	43	14	29	1214.2	1112	502	427	68	19	508	25	813	45	13
Vancouver	3.90	142	22	11	27	1199.0	1178	597	520	82	25	518	29	768	41	11
Tucson	4.15	140	15	10	31	1201.1	1260	633	554	66	20	471	46	731	52	7
Tacoma	4.33	140	17	2	29	1203.2	1280	686	579	110	36	473	35	683	40	9
Phoenix	4.61	144	13	3	31	1246.0	1390	777	638	104	26	583	25	771	69	9
Portland	4.66	140	18	7	18	1228.0	1284	751	636	119	24	523	58	753	56	9
Las Vegas	4.99	136	12	3	27	1178.1	1290	742	653	121	28	542	46	759	65	17
Edmonton	5.19	142	13	1	34	1210.2	1471	820	698	121	30	502	25	547	52	8
Salt Lake City	5.19	140	22	6	31	1219.1	1384	790	703	115	53	601	29	789	56	12
Albuquerque	5.59	143	10	2	30	1232.1	1506	923	765	124	34	604	45	727	74	12

PITCHERS' RECORDS
(Leading Qualifiers for Earned-Run Average Leadership — 115 or More Innings)

*Throws lefthanded.

Pitcher—Club	W.	L.	Pct.	ERA.	G.	GS.	CG.	GF.	ShO.	Sv.	IP.	H.	R.	ER.	HR.	HB.	BB.	Int. BB.	SO.	WP.
Walk, Hawaii	9	5	.643	2.26	18	18	5	0	3	0	127.1	100	39	32	3	2	42	0	85	2
Pulido, Hawaii*	18	6	.750	2.54	28	28	16	0	4	0	216.0	190	73	61	16	4	46	0	123	2
Riley, Portland*	11	7	.611	2.97	36	20	5	12	2	4	163.2	127	65	54	16	1	52	3	138	4
Bielecki, Hawaii	19	3	.864	2.97	28	28	9	0	2	0	187.2	162	70	62	11	2	88	2	162	4
Blobaum, Phoenix	7	6	.538	3.17	43	18	1	17	0	2	145.0	163	74	51	10	6	42	1	86	1
McDonald, Tacoma	7	4	.636	3.25	34	7	1	11	0	4	116.1	125	51	42	11	1	25	3	67	5
Patterson, Las Vegas*	8	9	.471	3.27	60	7	1	41	0	13	143.1	129	63	52	12	1	37	7	97	3
Roberts, Vancouver	8	6	.571	3.58	26	26	3	0	0	0	151.0	156	72	60	11	2	74	3	89	3
Davisson, Portland	7	10	.412	3.58	25	25	4	0	1	0	161.0	154	78	64	13	1	49	3	43	2
Steirer, Edmonton	12	4	.750	3.71	22	22	2	0	1	0	133.1	154	70	55	12	7	35	0	61	3

Departmental Leaders: G—Patterson, 60; W—Bielecki, 19; L—Rennicke, 18; Pct.—Bielecki, .864; GS—Lewis, 30; CG—Pulido, 16; GF—Ross, 45; ShO—Pulido, 4; Sv.—Ross, 20; IP—Pulido, 216.0; H—Lewis, 249; R—Kibbe, 152; ER—Kibbe, 123; HR—Kibbe, 25; HB—Semprini, 12; BB—White, 89; IBB—Gaynor, 15; SO—Bielecki, 162; WP—Hayward, Wojna, 10.

(All Pitchers—Listed Alphabetically)

Pitcher—Club	W.	L.	Pct.	ERA.	G.	GS.	CG.	GF.	ShO.	Sv.	IP.	H.	R.	ER.	HR.	HB.	BB.	Int. BB.	SO.	WP.
Alexander, Albuquerque	0	0	.000	1.17	4	0	0	3	0	0	7.2	9	2	1	0	0	1	0	0	0
Alicea, Vancouver	0	0	.000	0.00	1	0	0	0	0	0	0.1	0	0	0	0	0	0	0	0	0
Allard, Salt Lake City	3	9	.250	6.95	17	17	0	0	0	0	88.0	116	76	68	10	5	50	1	34	3
Allen, Albuquerque	0	0	.000	3.00	3	0	0	3	0	0	3.0	3	1	1	0	0	2	0	0	0
Alvarez, Tucson	4	3	.571	5.38	33	2	0	12	0	1	87.0	91	56	52	9	2	48	3	69	8
Anderson, Van. 7-Tucson 12*	6	6	.500	4.49	19	18	1	1	1	0	100.1	113	59	50	6	0	53	0	48	8
Angulo, Edmonton*	1	0	1.000	0.00	2	0	0	1	0	0	3.2	1	0	0	0	1	2	0	1	0
Augustine, Vancouver*	3	8	.273	4.55	13	11	1	2	0	1	65.1	70	37	33	5	1	26	1	32	0
Babcock, Salt Lake City	2	3	.400	5.44	21	2	0	12	0	0	49.2	66	35	30	4	1	34	4	19	1
Beard, Salt Lake City	0	1	.000	5.79	2	2	0	0	0	0	9.1	13	7	6	2	0	1	0	0	0
Beene, Vancouver	6	6	.500	4.12	16	16	1	0	1	0	87.1	80	41	40	2	3	41	1	68	6
Bernard, Tucson	6	3	.667	4.57	41	0	0	24	0	2	65.0	63	39	33	3	2	35	4	33	2
Best, Salt Lake City	6	5	.545	5.21	46	0	0	26	0	8	76.0	69	52	44	7	2	55	5	77	5
Bielecki, Hawaii	19	3	.864	2.97	28	28	9	0	2	0	187.2	162	70	62	11	2	88	2	162	4
Blobaum, Phoenix	7	6	.538	3.17	43	18	1	17	0	2	145.0	163	74	51	10	6	42	1	86	1
Bockus, Phoenix	0	4	.000	7.18	8	8	0	0	0	0	36.1	60	39	29	6	1	28	1	23	0
Bonine, Tucson	9	10	.474	4.90	33	18	1	5	0	1	143.1	194	85	78	8	4	41	10	93	1
Booker, Las Vegas	4	3	.571	5.50	9	9	2	0	0	0	55.2	66	39	34	4	0	24	2	23	3
Boone, Vancouver*	4	4	.500	4.74	27	0	0	17	0	3	57.0	63	35	30	5	1	25	5	22	0
Borbon, Albuquerque*	4	6	.400	7.30	54	1	0	28	0	5	81.1	111	72	66	10	4	44	4	45	9
Bradley, Tacoma	10	2	.833	4.28	49	11	1	22	0	4	122.0	148	63	58	8	4	34	1	48	4
L. Brown, Las Vegas	1	2	.333	5.38	45	2	0	10	0	1	75.1	87	52	45	12	1	41	5	54	2
S. Brown, Las Vegas	6	10	.375	6.26	23	22	5	0	0	0	143.2	184	111	100	15	2	55	0	43	3
Browning, Edmonton	6	6	.500	5.99	32	9	1	15	0	3	100.2	134	73	67	9	2	40	0	45	2
Burns, Vancouver	6	3	.667	3.12	28	0	0	22	0	3	60.2	65	27	21	5	3	26	4	42	0
Burroughs, Las Vegas*	3	4	.429	5.22	48	6	1	7	0	3	79.1	82	53	46	6	2	51	4	61	4
Bystrom, Portland	0	2	.000	5.56	5	5	0	0	0	0	22.2	26	17	14	1	0	9	1	10	0

Pitcher—Club	W.	L.	Pct.	ERA.	G.	GS.	CG.	GF.	ShO.	Sv.	IP.	H.	R.	ER.	HR.	HB.	BB.	Int. BB.	SO.	WP.
Calderon, Portland*	0	0	.000	15.88	8	0	0	1	0	0	5.2	14	10	10	0	0	10	1	2	1
Calhoun, Tucson*	1	1	.500	1.66	14	0	0	11	0	2	21.2	16	4	4	0	0	12	3	20	1
Calvert, Phoenix	6	6	.500	5.75	21	19	1	0	0	0	108.0	138	87	69	4	1	47	1	32	7
Candiotti, Vancouver	8	4	.667	2.89	15	15	4	0	0	0	96.2	96	36	31	4	2	22	0	53	3
Carman, Portland*	3	3	.500	5.34	39	2	0	24	0	3	55.2	66	36	33	8	3	22	6	53	3
Chiffer, Las Vegas	5	4	.556	4.91	36	0	0	25	0	5	55.0	59	31	30	5	1	27	3	50	3
Cliburn, Edmonton	7	7	.500	2.88	45	0	0	37	0	12	75.0	71	30	24	6	1	28	5	48	2
Codiroli, Tacoma	2	1	.667	3.79	9	9	0	0	0	0	57.0	49	35	24	4	2	30	2	52	2
Cole, Portland	3	5	.375	5.33	17	17	0	0	0	0	96.1	110	66	57	10	1	41	2	46	3
Corbett, Edmonton	1	0	1.000	0.00	2	0	0	1	0	0	4.2	2	0	0	0	0	0	0	5	1
Cornell, Phoenix	5	5	.500	3.45	35	1	0	29	0	11	62.2	72	29	24	1	0	37	7	38	8
Couchee, Las Vegas	5	2	.714	4.45	37	0	0	18	0	2	58.2	74	36	29	7	0	12	5	35	3
Cuellar, Salt Lake City	0	1	.000	6.30	6	0	0	4	0	0	10.0	17	7	7	0	0	6	1	6	0
Curtis, Edmonton*	0	0	.000	7.20	9	0	0	4	0	0	5.0	7	4	4	1	0	3	1	6	1
Davisson, Portland	7	10	.412	3.58	25	25	4	0	1	0	161.0	154	78	64	13	1	49	3	43	2
Decker, Portland	9	8	.529	4.42	47	12	1	15	0	3	114.0	112	68	56	11	4	60	6	94	5
DeLeon, Las Vegas	1	1	.500	4.79	6	4	0	0	0	0	20.2	24	11	11	2	1	5	0	11	0
de los Santos, Tacoma*	3	2	.600	3.15	46	0	0	20	0	3	40.0	30	17	14	1	1	28	5	43	2
Diaz, Albuquerque*	1	2	.333	4.47	20	0	0	8	0	3	46.1	48	30	23	6	3	20	2	35	0
Downs, Portland	7	12	.368	5.30	30	25	5	2	0	0	163.0	166	106	96	12	4	65	3	104	7
Duquette, Vancouver*	0	0	.000	3.18	7	0	0	6	0	2	11.1	12	4	4	0	1	7	0	9	0
Eichelberger, Vancouver	8	11	.421	4.96	25	22	6	0	1	0	139.2	136	84	77	9	3	75	1	91	7
Farmer, Tacoma	3	4	.429	6.04	21	0	0	15	0	2	28.1	27	28	19	5	0	22	4	29	1
Farr, Phoenix	1	0	1.000	4.15	3	3	0	0	0	0	13.0	20	7	6	0	0	1	0	3	0
Felt, Albuquerque*	2	3	.400	6.75	10	7	0	1	0	0	37.1	57	42	28	3	3	22	0	20	8
Finch, Edmonton	5	7	.417	4.46	21	15	0	3	0	0	105.0	122	61	52	8	3	34	4	34	5
Fireovid, Portland	5	9	.357	4.35	46	8	1	12	0	1	111.2	133	71	54	7	2	44	5	45	7
Foley, Tucson	1	1	.500	4.63	5	1	0	0	0	0	11.2	10	6	6	0	0	10	1	7	2
Ford, Tacoma	7	8	.467	4.39	29	20	0	3	0	0	137.1	142	75	67	13	2	42	3	60	6
Fowlkes, Phoenix	4	4	.500	3.76	16	11	1	3	0	0	79.0	83	41	33	9	0	17	1	52	2
Garrelts, Phoenix	5	7	.417	5.90	21	19	2	0	1	0	97.2	97	75	64	8	2	82	2	69	9
Gaynor, Portland	4	7	.364	6.09	53	2	0	25	0	3	78.1	105	67	53	10	1	57	15	44	7
Geisel, Salt Lake City*	4	2	.667	4.88	26	7	0	11	0	4	72.0	81	41	39	4	2	40	2	52	0
Ghelfi, Portland	0	0	.000	0.00	1	1	0	0	0	0	1.0	0	0	0	0	0	0	0	0	0
Gibson, Vancouver	3	4	.429	4.54	14	11	3	1	1	0	73.1	50	40	37	8	2	39	0	75	6
Gleaton, Salt Lake City*	4	1	.800	5.80	29	2	0	13	0	2	49.2	62	39	32	6	2	17	0	39	1
Grant, Phoenix	5	7	.417	3.96	17	17	4	0	1	0	111.1	102	64	49	7	1	61	2	78	8
Green, Hawaii*	2	2	.500	5.94	13	0	0	11	0	3	16.2	15	15	11	2	1	8	0	18	3
Hamm, Las Vegas	4	5	.444	6.44	16	13	1	0	0	0	65.2	98	57	47	6	0	19	2	22	2
Hammaker, Phoenix*	0	1	.000	4.50	2	2	0	0	0	0	8.0	14	7	4	0	0	2	0	5	0
Hartzell, Vancouver	5	1	.833	2.91	10	7	1	1	0	1	46.1	54	20	15	1	2	5	0	14	0
Hayward, Las Vegas*	9	6	.600	4.87	26	24	1	0	1	0	129.1	129	78	70	11	6	79	2	91	16
Heathcock, Tucson	1	1	.500	4.32	4	4	0	0	0	0	16.2	12	8	8	1	0	6	0	8	0
Heimueller, Tacoma*	4	7	.364	4.34	24	13	1	6	0	0	103.2	119	51	50	7	5	51	3	45	4
Hensley, Tac. 11-Vancouver 3*	0	4	.000	6.63	14	5	0	3	0	0	38.0	58	36	28	5	0	16	1	24	1
Hernandez, Tucson	6	9	.400	4.91	28	26	1	2	0	0	146.2	153	96	80	8	3	65	1	107	12
Higuera, Vancouver*	1	4	.200	4.73	8	6	0	2	0	0	40.0	49	26	21	3	0	14	0	29	0
Holton, Albuquerque	0	0	.000	5.63	12	2	0	1	0	0	32.0	39	23	20	5	1	9	0	15	1
Howard, Hawaii	0	0	.000	18.00	1	0	0	0	0	0	1.0	2	2	2	1	0	0	0	0	0
Howell, Albuquerque	8	2	.800	4.60	18	9	3	7	0	2	72.1	79	48	37	10	0	37	1	58	7
Hudson, Tacoma	5	7	.417	6.55	38	1	0	22	0	4	55.0	63	43	40	5	4	25	3	34	1
D. Jones, Vancouver	1	0	1.000	10.13	3	0	0	0	0	0	8.0	9	9	9	3	1	3	0	2	2
J. Jones, Tacoma	3	5	.375	2.93	9	9	3	0	0	0	61.1	47	26	20	4	2	25	3	47	1
Kain, Edmonton	6	6	.500	4.33	40	4	0	22	0	5	116.1	148	67	56	11	1	30	8	49	2
Kaiser, Tacoma*	4	7	.364	4.58	14	12	0	1	0	1	74.2	81	52	38	4	1	28	1	38	1
Kerfeld, Tucson	0	1	.000	9.82	1	1	0	0	0	0	3.2	6	4	4	0	0	1	0	3	0
Kibbe, Edmonton	7	12	.368	6.18	29	29	3	0	0	0	179.0	233	152	123	25	6	85	2	66	13
Kingman, Phoenix	5	5	.500	6.37	30	6	1	12	0	1	82.0	97	65	58	10	3	43	1	52	8
Knudson, Tucson	4	6	.400	3.64	13	13	1	0	0	0	84.0	93	41	34	6	1	20	3	42	1
Koontz, Vancouver	7	4	.636	2.91	43	1	0	25	0	7	92.2	81	39	30	7	0	30	4	71	1
Krawczyk, Hawaii	4	5	.444	2.13	43	0	0	32	0	15	72.0	57	21	17	3	3	36	4	77	3
Kromy, Portland	4	0	.000	4.48	23	1	0	7	0	2	60.1	63	37	30	6	3	35	7	32	5
Krueger, Tacoma*	2	2	.500	3.69	5	5	2	0	0	0	31.2	29	17	13	3	0	21	1	20	0
Lacey, Phoenix*	5	3	.625	5.80	24	3	0	13	0	3	49.2	65	36	32	11	1	19	2	29	1
LaCorte, Edmonton	0	1	.000	11.17	7	0	0	0	0	0	9.2	16	16	12	1	1	5	0	7	2
Lamonde, Hawaii	0	1	.000	6.75	3	3	0	0	0	0	10.2	18	8	8	2	0	10	0	4	1
Langford, Tacoma	2	2	.000	6.00	3	3	0	0	0	0	15.0	22	11	10	1	0	2	0	3	0
Lazorko, Vancouver	2	3	.400	3.76	28	1	1	21	0	6	52.2	43	24	22	6	1	15	4	35	3
Leiper, Tacoma*	2	3	.400	3.03	28	0	0	20	0	11	32.2	33	11	11	4	0	14	1	13	2
Leopold, Las Vegas	0	1	.000	7.45	2	2	0	0	0	0	9.2	12	9	8	1	0	3	0	3	0
Lesley, Vancouver	0	0	.000	0.00	5	0	0	4	0	2	7.2	3	1	0	0	1	0	0	6	0
Lewis, Salt Lake City	15	9	.625	4.43	30	30	10	0	0	0	207.0	249	117	102	13	6	79	3	122	8
Long, Salt Lake City	6	3	.667	5.16	50	0	0	22	0	10	90.2	93	53	52	15	4	37	2	73	4
Madden, Tucson*	4	3	.571	4.30	11	11	2	0	1	0	60.2	60	29	29	2	0	30	0	38	4
Maddux, Portland	2	4	.333	5.84	8	8	1	0	0	0	44.2	58	32	29	5	1	17	2	22	2
R. Martin, Phoenix	4	1	.833	2.32	32	1	0	22	0	9	62.0	47	17	16	2	0	34	3	37	3
S. Martin, Albuquerque	0	1	.000	6.14	4	0	0	4	0	1	7.1	10	9	5	0	0	3	0	4	1
Mathis, Tucson	5	2	.714	3.34	12	12	1	0	1	0	67.1	62	26	25	3	0	12	0	47	1
McCaskill, Edmonton	7	11	.389	5.73	24	22	2	0	0	0	143.0	162	104	91	19	1	74	1	75	1
McDonald, Tacoma	7	4	.636	3.25	34	7	1	11	0	4	116.1	125	51	42	11	1	25	3	67	5
McLaughlin, Phoenix	6	7	.462	3.69	25	12	0	5	0	0	102.1	118	49	42	8	4	30	1	60	4
Minetto, Tucson*	5	5	.500	4.47	45	0	0	17	0	5	58.1	58	30	29	3	0	40	5	40	6
Moffitt, Vancouver	0	0	.000	0.00	1	0	0	0	0	0	0.0	1	0	0	0	0	2	0	0	0
Mohorcic, Hawaii	1	3	.250	3.92	9	9	2	0	0	0	57.1	67	29	25	1	0	17	0	21	2
Money, Portland	4	3	.571	5.36	10	8	2	1	0	0	50.1	47	31	30	5	2	21	0	34	1
Montalvo, Albuquerque	3	3	.500	4.41	45	0	0	31	0	12	63.1	73	42	31	5	1	40	10	46	4
Mooneyham, Edmonton	5	3	.625	5.94	16	14	0	1	0	0	72.2	99	55	48	5	2	46	0	40	8
Moore, Phoenix	1	2	.333	6.28	6	0	0	2	0	0	14.1	16	10	10	4	0	10	1	8	0
Moreno, Edmonton*	0	3	.000	6.89	16	5	0	3	0	1	47.0	56	40	36	5	2	34	1	29	3
Mura, Portland	9	4	.692	5.00	48	3	0	30	0	4	99.0	94	57	55	12	2	53	7	82	7
Murray, Salt Lake City	1	1	.500	6.94	5	5	0	0	0	0	23.1	31	18	18	3	0	15	0	11	2
Myers, Tacoma	5	4	.556	4.01	13	13	4	0	1	0	92.0	95	45	41	11	5	32	2	42	3

Pitcher—Club	W.	L.	Pct.	ERA.	G.	GS.	CG.	GF.	ShO.	Sv.	IP.	H.	R.	ER.	HR.	HB.	BB.	Int. BB.	SO.	WP.
Nahorodny, Salt Lake City	0	0	.000	0.00	1	0	0	1	0	0	1.0	0	0	0	0	0	2	0	0	0
Nelson, Salt Lake City	6	8	.429	5.63	17	17	6	0	1	0	112.0	138	75	70	15	5	54	3	89	11
Newman, Salt Lake City°	0	2	.000	5.52	3	2	0	0	0	0	14.2	16	11	9	0	0	8	0	8	0
Nunez, Salt Lake City	3	2	.600	3.58	18	0	0	13	0	3	27.2	24	12	11	2	1	12	1	26	0
Ontiveros, Tacoma	1	1	.500	7.94	2	2	0	0	0	0	11.1	18	11	10	3	1	5	0	6	0
Oroz, Las Vegas°	6	8	.429	5.19	35	21	2	2	0	0	138.2	162	92	80	19	2	45	2	57	3
Ouellette, Phoenix	0	1	.000	2.35	3	0	0	3	0	0	7.2	6	2	2	0	0	3	0	2	0
Patterson, Las Vegas°	8	9	.471	3.27	60	7	1	41	0	13	143.1	129	63	52	12	1	37	7	97	3
Perry, Albuquerque	3	8	.273	5.50	41	6	0	10	0	0	90.0	124	71	55	1	3	55	5	60	8
Pippin, Hawaii	1	2	.333	4.11	6	0	0	4	0	0	15.1	10	7	7	1	1	7	2	12	1
Pulido, Hawaii°	18	6	.750	2.54	28	28	16	0	4	0	216.0	190	73	61	16	4	46	0	123	2
Rasmussen, Tucson	10	12	.455	4.31	28	28	7	0	1	0	185.2	204	97	89	11	3	56	7	100	2
Rennicke, Albuquerque	7	18	.280	5.37	30	27	2	1	0	0	154.1	196	119	92	14	1	59	5	68	10
Riley, Portland°	11	7	.611	2.97	36	20	5	12	2	4	163.2	127	65	54	16	1	52	3	138	4
Rincon, Hawaii	7	6	.538	4.29	20	19	4	0	2	0	128.0	135	65	61	7	1	55	2	54	1
Roberts, Vancouver	8	6	.571	3.58	26	26	3	0	0	0	151.0	156	72	60	11	2	74	3	89	3
Rodas, Albuquerque°	5	2	.714	2.56	10	9	2	0	0	0	59.2	56	23	17	3	2	15	1	55	1
Rodriguez, Tacoma	0	1	.000	8.82	6	3	0	1	0	0	16.1	21	17	16	2	3	7	2	9	0
Ross, Tucson	5	6	.455	2.93	57	0	0	45	0	20	92.0	88	35	30	5	2	24	8	32	1
Sambito, Tucson°	0	0	.000	2.25	8	0	0	4	0	0	8.0	5	2	2	1	1	4	0	5	1
Searage, Vancouver	6	3	.667	3.07	33	5	0	16	0	1	76.1	62	29	26	6	1	44	4	59	6
Segelke, Phoenix	1	0	1.000	10.13	7	0	0	1	0	0	10.2	15	13	12	1	0	12	0	5	5
Semall, Hawaii	10	10	.500	3.83	26	26	5	0	1	0	157.1	155	83	67	10	1	75	2	85	4
Semprini, Salt Lake City	1	1	.500	4.92	34	0	0	13	0	2	60.1	53	40	33	6	12	45	4	38	10
Senteney, Hawaii	3	1	.750	1.46	13	2	0	7	0	1	37.0	29	7	6	1	1	14	3	28	0
Simpson, Edmonton°	0	0	.000	21.00	3	0	0	3	0	0	3.0	11	7	7	0	0	1	0	1	0
Da. Smith, Edmonton	6	3	.667	3.13	50	0	0	39	0	13	69.0	71	30	24	4	1	30	3	37	6
Do. Smith, Albuquerque	7	5	.583	5.77	59	3	0	22	0	5	115.1	142	82	74	13	1	39	9	82	3
Snyder, Salt Lake City°	8	9	.471	6.25	27	26	1	0	1	0	129.2	155	105	90	14	3	80	0	83	4
Solano, Tucson	3	5	.375	2.57	17	13	0	2	0	0	80.2	74	41	23	2	2	37	1	55	4
Sonberg, Albuquerque°°	5	13	.278	7.34	28	27	1	0	0	0	133.2	169	121	109	19	3	79	2	75	7
Steirer, Edmonton	12	4	.750	3.71	22	22	2	0	1	0	133.1	154	70	55	12	7	35	0	61	3
Stoddard, Salt Lake City	4	4	.500	4.91	9	9	3	0	1	0	58.2	47	34	32	7	1	20	0	29	2
Stuper, Vancouver	2	3	.400	3.86	10	10	2	0	0	0	63.0	58	28	27	3	0	26	0	30	3
Thomas, Salt Lake City	0	0	.000	3.93	7	0	0	3	0	2	18.1	15	10	8	0	1	12	1	13	0
Tomlin, Hawaii°	3	2	.600	2.66	22	2	0	10	0	3	50.2	45	17	15	2	2	21	0	43	4
Torrez, Tacoma	1	1	.500	7.88	3	3	0	0	0	0	16.0	28	16	14	1	0	12	0	2	0
Vanderbush, Las Vegas	2	4	.333	5.74	34	8	0	6	0	0	73.2	74	54	47	10	3	58	2	66	5
Violette, Phoenix	6	7	.462	4.30	30	12	1	5	0	1	129.2	134	77	62	14	2	44	2	97	7
Voigt, Albuquerque	9	6	.600	4.83	33	26	2	5	0	1	164.0	183	100	88	12	8	87	5	66	13
Walk, Hawaii	9	5	.643	2.26	18	18	5	0	3	0	127.1	100	39	32	3	2	42	0	85	2
Wallace, Albuquerque	1	0	1.000	17.36	4	0	0	4	0	0	4.2	10	10	9	0	0	4	1	4	0
Waller, Tucson	0	0	.000	0.00	2	0	0	2	0	0	2.0	1	0	0	0	0	3	0	1	1
Ward, Phoenix°	7	8	.467	5.26	46	12	2	19	0	4	126.2	143	85	74	9	4	71	0	95	6
Warren, Tacoma	4	3	.571	4.95	11	11	0	0	0	0	67.1	67	45	37	11	4	33	0	44	7
Wegman, Vancouver	0	3	.000	1.95	6	3	0	2	0	1	27.2	30	11	6	0	1	8	0	16	0
Wehrmeister, Portland	7	8	.467	5.73	28	15	0	8	0	1	114.2	120	79	73	12	3	49	3	98	7
Wheeler, Hawaii	2	2	.500	3.58	6	6	1	0	0	0	32.2	32	19	13	2	0	21	0	13	3
White, Albuquerque	7	12	.368	6.09	37	26	0	5	0	1	159.2	196	128	108	22	4	89	1	94	2
Whitmer, Salt Lake City	5	5	.500	5.08	12	12	2	0	0	0	79.2	106	49	45	7	5	14	2	33	2
Wieghaus, Tucson	0	0	.000	0.00	1	0	0	1	0	0	1.0	1	0	0	0	0	0	0	0	0
Winn, Hawaii	6	1	.857	3.43	21	0	0	6	0	0	44.2	44	19	17	1	0	28	4	28	5
Wojna, Las Vegas	14	8	.636	5.08	29	28	3	0	0	0	159.1	182	99	90	15	7	81	5	95	16
C. Young, Tacoma°	6	4	.600	3.78	14	14	5	0	1	0	95.1	88	45	40	8	1	28	1	61	5
M. Young, Salt Lake City°	6	0	1.000	1.51	6	6	0	0	0	0	41.2	32	9	7	0	2	20	0	37	4
Zaske, Hawaii	2	4	.333	3.58	37	0	0	28	0	7	60.1	51	28	24	4	1	40	6	60	11

BALKS—Hernandez, Oroz, 5 each; de los Santos, Hayward, Roberts, White, Wojna, 4 each; Bielecki, Blobaum, Davisson, Walk, 3 each; Booker, Borbon, Downs, Finch, Heimueller, Higuera, McCaskill, Pulido, Rodas, Semprini, Snyder, Sonberg, Ward, Whitmer, Winn, 2 each; Alvarez, Anderson, Best, Boone, S. Brown, Burroughs, Candiotti, Cliburn, Cole, Diaz, Eichelberger, Ford, Fowlkes, Gleaton, Hamm, Hensley, Howell, Kaiser, Kibbe, Krawczyk, Lesley, Lewis, Long, R. Martin, Money, Moreno, Mura, Murray, Nelson, Segelke, Violette, Wegman, Wehrmeister, Wheeler, Zaske, 1 each.

COMBINATION SHUTOUTS—Rodas-Alexander, White-Smith-Borbon, Albuquerque; Tomlin-Krawczyk, Semall-Krawczyk, Hawaii; Decker-Vanderbush, Oroz-Chiffer, Las Vegas; Blobaum-Martin, Phoenix; Davisson-Fireovid, Davisson-Gaynor, Riley-Fireovid, Wehrmeister-Riley, Portland; Lewis-Best, Snyder-Best, Stoddard-Long, Salt Lake City; Rasmussen-Ross 2, Foley-Bernard, Heathcock-Minetto, Mathis-Bernard, Mathis-Minetto-Ross, Tucson; Augustine-Boone, Beene-Boone, Beene-Koontz, Higuera-Koontz, Roberts-Hartzell, Roberts-Lazorko, Searage-Koontz, Stuper-Burns, Vancouver.

NO-HIT GAMES—Eichelberger, Vancouver, defeated Portland, 2-0 (seven innings, second game), May 26; Rincon, Hawaii, defeated Tacoma, 3-0, June 12.

Eastern League

CLASS AA

Leading Batter
THAD REECE
Albany

League President
CHARLES ESHBACH

Leading Pitcher
SCOTT TERRY
Vermont

CHAMPIONSHIP WINNERS IN PREVIOUS YEARS

Year	Team	Avg
1923	Williamsport	.661
1924	Williamsport	.654
1925	York§	.583
	Williamsport§	.583
1926	Scranton	.627
1927	Harrisburg	.630
1928	Harrisburg	.603
1929	Binghamton	.597
1930	Wilkes-Barre	.572
1931	Harrisburg	.597
1932	Wilkes-Barre	.561
1933	Binghamton	.690
1934	Binghamton	.694
	Williamsport°	.603
1935	Scranton	.657
	Binghamton°	.580
1936	Scranton°	.609
	Elmira	.629
1937	Elmira†	.622
1938	Binghamton	.622
	Elmira (3rd)‡	.522
1939	Scranton†	.571
1940	Scranton	.568
	Binghamton (2nd)‡	.554
1941	Wilkes-Barre	.630
	Elmira (3rd)‡	.514
1942	Albany	.600
	Scranton (2nd)‡	.593
1943	Scranton	.630
	Elmira (2nd)‡	.568
1944	Hartford	.723
	Binghamton (4th)‡	.474
1945	Utica	.615
	Albany (3rd)‡	.564

Year	Team	Avg
1946	Scranton†	.691
1947	Utica†	.652
1948	Scranton†	.636
1949	Albany	.664
	Binghamton (4th)‡	.500
1950	Wilkes-Barre‡	.652
1951	Wilkes-Barre	.612
	Scranton (2nd)†	.562
1952	Albany	.603
	Binghamton (2nd)‡	.562
1953	Reading	.682
	Binghamton (2nd)‡	.636
1954	Wilkes-Barre	.576
	Albany (3rd)‡	.540
1955	Reading	.613
	Allentown (2nd)‡	.565
1956	Schenectady†	.609
1957	Binghamton	.607
	Reading (3rd)‡	.529
1958	Lancaster x	.568
	Binghamton (6th)‡	.493
1959	Springfield†	.607
1960	Williamsport y	.551
	Springfield (3rd)y	.496
1961	Springfield	.612
1962	Williamsport	.593
	Elmira (2nd)‡	.514
1963	Charleston	.593
1964	Elmira	.586
1965	Pittsfield	.607
1966	Elmira	.633
1967	Binghamton z	.586
	Elmira	.532

Year	Team	Avg
1968	Pittsfield	.604
	Reading (2nd)‡	.579
1969	York	.640
1970	Waterbury a	.560
	Reading a	.553
1971	Three Rivers	.569
	Elmira b	.561
1972	West Haven b	.600
	Three Rivers	.559
1973	Reading b	.551
	Pittsfield	.551
1974	Thetford Mines (2nd)c	.536
	Pittsfield (2nd)	.496
1975	Reading	.613
	Bristol°	.587
1976	Three Rivers	.601
	West Haven d	.576
1977	West Haven e	.623
	Three Rivers	.551
1978	Reading	.642
	Bristol°	.580
1979	West Haven f	.597
1980	Holyoke°	.561
	Waterbury	.540
1981	Glens Falls	.615
	Bristol°	.577
1982	West Haven°	.614
	Lynn	.590
1983	Lynn	.554
	New Britain‡	.518

°Won split-season playoff. †Won championship and four-team playoff. ‡Won four-team playoff. §Tied for pennant, York winning playoff. xLeague was divided into Northern, Southern divisions and played a split season; Lancaster over-all season leader. yPlayoff finals canceled after one game because of rain with Williamsport and Springfield declared playoff co-champions. zLeague was divided into Eastern, Western divisions; Binghamton won playoff. aTied for pennant, Waterbury winning playoff. bLeague was divided into American, National divisions; won playoff. cLeague was divided into American and National divisions; won four-team playoff. dLeague was divided into Northern, Southern divisions, won playoff. eLeague was divided into New England and Canadian-American divisions; won playoff. fWon both halves of split season (no playoffs). (NOTE—Known as New York-Pennsylvania League prior to 1938.)

STANDING OF CLUBS AT CLOSE OF SEASON, SEPTEMBER 1

Club	Alb.	G.F.	Wat.	Vrt.	Buff.	N.B.	Nash.	Read.	W.	L.	T.	Pct.	G.B.
Albany (Athletics)	....	7	11	12	11	13	16	11	81	57	1	.587	......
Glens Falls (White Sox)	12	....	6	9	11	12	11	14	75	63	1	.543	6
Waterbury (Angels)	9	14	....	11	9	11	13	9	76	64	0	.543	6
Vermont (Reds)	8	11	9	....	12	10	10	15	75	65	0	.536	7
Buffalo (Indians)	8	9	11	8	....	12	12	12	72	67	0	.518	9½
New Britain (Red Sox)	7	8	9	10	8	....	12	10	64	76	0	.457	18
Nashua (Pirates)	4	9	7	10	8	8	....	12	58	82	0	.414	24
Reading (Phillies)	9	5	11	5	8	10	8	....	56	83	0	.403	25½

Vermont club represented Burlington, Vermont.

Major league affiliations in parentheses.

PLAYOFFS—Vermont defeated Albany, three games to none; Waterbury defeated Glens Falls, three games to one; Vermont defeated Waterbury, three games to two, to win league championship.

REGULAR-SEASON ATTENDANCE—Albany, 199,534; Buffalo, 223,443; Glens Falls, 103,225; Nashua, 126,263; New Britain, 79,949; Reading, 67,333; Vermont, 121,102; Waterbury, 36,323. Total—957,172. Playoffs—12,528. All-Star Game at Albany, N.Y., 6,753.

MANAGERS—Albany, Keith Lieppman; Buffalo, Jack Aker; Glens Falls, John Boles; Nashua, Bill Scripture; New Britain, Rac Slider; Reading, Bill Dancy; Vermont, Jack Lind; Waterbury, Winston Llenas.

ALL-STAR TEAM—1B—Pat Adams, Glens Falls; 2B—Norm Carrasco, Waterbury; 3B—Rick Stromer, Waterbury; SS—Jeff Moronko, Buffalo; OF—Kal Daniels, Vermont; Don Carter, Buffalo; John Cangelosi, Glens Falls; C—Mickey Tettleton, Albany; DH—Wally Joyner, Waterbury; RHP—Scott Terry, Vermont; LHP—Dave Lochner, Vermont; Relief Pitcher—Chuck Dale, New Britain; Most Valuable Player—Pat Adams, Glens Falls; Manager-of-the-Year—Keith Lieppman, Albany.

(Compiled by Howe News Bureau, Boston, Mass.)

CLUB BATTING

Club	Pct.	G.	AB.	R.	OR.	H.	TB.	2B.	3B.	HR.	RBI.	GW.	SH.	SF.	HP.	BB.	Int. BB.	SO.	SB.	CS.	LOB.
Buffalo	.273	139	4519	694	687	1232	1719	186	29	81	605	64	52	46	42	522	13	725	142	80	995
Albany	.267	139	4453	654	516	1190	1599	188	40	47	567	68	52	45	21	598	35	685	99	51	1056
Reading	.258	139	4365	565	658	1126	1567	168	45	61	498	48	53	53	504	20	656	119	81	946
Waterbury	.255	140	4487	629	631	1146	1577	173	33	64	536	72	65	46	39	561	38	632	79	64	985
Glens Falls	.254	139	4386	643	581	1114	1635	186	34	89	579	67	32	48	35	542	29	789	168	46	967
New Britain	.250	140	4476	515	583	1104	1537	191	40	54	469	56	66	36	24	477	23	760	91	30	1004
Nashua	.249	140	4519	557	640	1126	1525	203	35	42	491	52	32	41	27	444	30	800	152	79	907
Vermont	.243	140	4408	580	541	1071	1575	179	26	91	522	69	35	46	25	527	26	803	155	63	935

INDIVIDUAL BATTING

(Leading Qualifiers for Batting Championship—378 or More Plate Appearances)

*Bats lefthanded. †Switch-hitter.

Player and Club	Pct.	G.	AB.	R.	H.	TB.	2B.	3B.	HR.	RBI.	GW.	SH.	SF.	HP.	BB.	Int. BB.	SO.	SB.	CS.
Reece, Thad, Albany*	.331	120	420	70	139	175	22	4	2	46	5	8	4	1	45	2	27	15	6
Joyner, Wallace, Waterbury*	.317	134	467	81	148	222	24	7	12	72	12	5	8	1	67	8	60	0	5
Nattile, Samuel, New Britain*	.315	119	429	51	135	203	34	2	10	78	9	0	3	2	38	5	68	0	3
Moronko, Jeffrey, Buffalo	.314	131	468	84	147	224	30	4	13	95	10	3	7	7	60	2	87	7	12
Daniels, Kalvoski, Vermont*	.313	122	415	81	130	218	29	4	17	62	9	0	1	2	73	5	59	43	11
Eppard, James, Albany*	.312	118	417	58	130	156	14	6	0	51	7	5	4	2	71	2	40	7	7
Glass, Timothy, Buffalo	.306	107	360	58	110	186	13	3	19	68	2	3	4	1	37	1	85	1	2
Carter, Don, Buffalo*	.302	132	493	86	149	162	13	0	0	28	5	11	0	5	58	1	63	72	15
Hobbs, Rodney, Albany	.300	129	423	82	127	186	16	8	9	74	9	4	1	3	79	1	78	22	13
Moses, Stephen, Albany*	.300	125	437	59	131	148	11	3	0	31	2	6	2	0	50	1	30	15	13
Cangelosi, John, Glens Falls*	.287	138	464	91	133	155	17	1	1	38	1	7	3	4	101	2	66	65	16

Departmental Leaders: G—Madril, 139; AB—Ford, 523; R—Madril, 95; H—Carter, 149; TB—Adams, 234; 2B—Nattile, 34; 3B—James, 12; HR—Adams, 24; RBI—Adams, 102; GWRBI—Adams, 17; SH—Noboa, 17; SF—Cecchetti, 9; HP—Madril, 15; BB—Cangelosi, 101; IBB—Adams, Joyner, Stromer, Tettleton, 8; SO—Adams, 106; SB—Carter, 72; CS—Madril, 19.

(All Players—Listed Alphabetically)

Player and Club	Pct.	G.	AB.	R.	H.	TB.	2B.	3B.	HR.	RBI.	GW.	SH.	SF.	HP.	BB.	Int. BB.	SO.	SB.	CS.
Ackley, John, New Britain	.196	88	285	36	56	88	13	2	5	20	1	3	2	1	31	0	74	1	0
Adams, Patrick, Glens Falls	.283	137	467	78	132	234	28	1	24	102	17	2	5	10	65	8	106	1	1
Allanson, Andrew, Buffalo	.252	39	111	12	28	32	4	0	0	11	0	1	0	0	15	0	18	0	5
Aponte, Edwin, Buffalo	.268	83	287	45	77	101	15	0	3	25	4	3	0	2	23	1	18	0	4
Arnold, Jerry, Reading*	.143	49	7	1	1	2	1	0	0	0	0	0	0	0	1	0	1	0	0
Arnold, Ronald, Albany	.239	102	301	46	72	92	12	1	2	35	4	7	2	3	41	1	45	9	3
Ashman, Michael, Albany*	.274	97	314	34	86	110	12	0	4	35	4	4	2	0	44	6	35	2	1
Aulenback, James, Nashua	.400	10	15	1	6	10	1	0	1	4	0	1	0	0	2	0	2	1	0
Bailes, Scott, Nashua*	.000	54	3	0	0	0	0	0	0	0	0	0	0	0	0	0	3	0	0
Bathe, Robert, Albany	.234	89	295	39	69	105	17	2	5	41	2	0	5	2	38	1	42	3	2
Beal, Anthony, New Britain	.260	99	323	41	84	121	13	6	4	28	2	7	1	4	47	1	93	14	7
Bennett, James, Albany*	.220	82	287	28	63	94	13	0	6	35	3	0	1	2	26	5	75	3	1
Benzinger, Todd, New Britain†	.258	110	391	49	101	166	25	5	10	60	8	3	2	1	33	4	89	0	1
Bernstine, Nehames, Buffalo†	.286	126	479	88	137	195	16	9	8	52	4	1	3	5	64	1	69	23	11
Bohnet, John, Buffalo*	.000	28	2	0	0	0	0	0	0	0	0	0	0	0	0	0	2	0	0
Bonilla, Roberto, Nashua†	.264	136	484	74	128	190	19	5	11	71	7	1	7	3	49	7	89	15	7
Brown, Samuel, Nashua	.173	25	81	5	14	19	3	1	0	7	2	0	1	2	2	0	19	4	2
Brumley, A. Michael, New Britain†	.231	34	121	14	28	38	6	2	0	9	3	2	1	0	18	0	33	3	0
Bullinger, D. Matthews, Vermont*	.000	21	3	0	0	0	0	0	0	0	0	0	0	0	0	0	0	0	0
Bulls, David, Reading	.143	19	7	0	1	1	0	0	0	2	0	1	0	0	3	0	4	0	0
Bundy, Lorenzo, Nashua*	.255	103	357	54	91	131	20	1	6	38	3	1	7	5	51	2	64	6	0
Bustabad, Juan, New Britain*	.265	67	230	28	61	73	4	4	0	10	1	7	2	0	21	0	17	15	5
Cangelosi, John, Glens Falls*	.287	138	464	91	133	155	17	1	1	38	1	7	3	4	101	2	66	65	16
Carrasco, Norman, Waterbury	.285	134	516	78	147	203	23	3	9	64	11	10	4	3	40	3	71	19	7
Carter, Don, Buffalo*	.302	132	493	86	149	162	13	0	0	28	5	11	0	5	58	1	63	72	15
Cecchetti, George, Buffalo*	.236	128	390	52	92	136	16	2	8	62	10	0	9	8	56	4	57	3	4
Childress, Rodney, Reading	.400	62	5	1	2	2	0	0	0	0	0	1	0	0	0	0	2	0	0
Christenson, Kim, Nashua	.275	16	40	3	11	14	3	0	0	4	0	0	0	0	3	0	7	1	0
Ciampa, Michael, New Britain*	.243	62	235	24	57	66	9	0	0	15	2	5	1	0	30	0	20	7	3
Cipolloni, Joseph, Reading	.201	95	283	30	57	82	10	0	5	31	4	3	6	1	30	2	55	4	1
Clack, Marvin, Nashua†	.253	108	332	43	84	94	8	1	0	21	1	3	0	1	46	3	56	27	5
Clark, David, Buffalo*	.179	17	56	12	10	20	1	0	3	10	1	0	2	1	9	0	13	1	1

Player and Club	Pct.	G.	AB.	R.	H.	TB.	2B.	3B.	HR.	RBI.	GW.	SH.	SF.	HP.	BB.	Int. BB.	SO.	SB.	CS.
Clements, Patrick, Waterbury	.000	43	2	0	0	0	0	0	0	0	0	0	0	0	0	0	2	0	0
Cole, William, Reading	.200	10	5	0	1	1	0	0	0	0	0	0	0	0	0	0	0	0	0
Coughlon, Kevin, Albany	.226	26	84	12	19	25	3	0	1	4	0	2	1	1	10	0	11	0	0
Cox, Jeffrey, Vermont	.263	38	118	19	31	33	2	0	0	15	1	2	3	1	18	0	17	1	0
Cruz, Juan, Albany	.000	3	1	0	0	0	0	0	0	0	0	0	0	0	0	0	0	0	0
Culmer, Wilfred, Buffalo	.256	56	172	19	44	65	13	1	2	26	2	1	1	5	16	0	43	2	2
Daniels, Kalvoski, Vermont*	.313	122	415	81	130	218	29	4	17	62	9	0	1	2	73	5	59	43	11
Davis, Stanley, Glens Falls*	.203	35	133	16	27	37	5	1	1	19	1	0	2	0	9	1	26	2	0
DeLaRosa, Nelson, Nashua*	.169	73	225	16	38	50	10	1	0	22	1	1	1	1	17	0	55	5	9
DeLeon, Luis, Buffalo†	.212	25	66	9	14	16	2	0	0	2	0	1	0	0	4	0	16	0	0
Dempsey, Mark, Glens Falls	.000	26	4	0	0	0	0	0	0	0	0	0	0	0	0	0	0	0	0
Diaz, Baudilio, Reading	.429	3	7	2	3	6	0	0	1	3	0	0	0	2	0	0	0	0	0
Dodd, Thomas, Glens Falls	.259	135	448	72	116	194	19	4	17	75	13	0	8	4	50	2	99	6	1
Eppard, James, Albany*	.312	118	417	58	130	156	14	6	0	51	7	5	4	2	71	2	40	7	7
Evans, Anthony, Vermont	.207	117	334	45	69	104	11	3	6	40	4	5	4	2	49	2	72	6	7
Ferguson, Billy, Reading	.000	18	3	1	0	0	0	0	0	1	0	2	0	1	3	0	2	0	0
Fischer, Todd, Albany	.000	31	3	1	0	0	0	0	0	0	0	0	0	0	0	0	1	0	0
Ford, Kenneth, Nashua	.283	135	523	68	148	201	25	5	6	71	9	0	6	2	30	3	79	20	10
Franklin, Glen, Vermont*	.302	102	324	49	98	132	9	5	5	43	4	1	5	1	42	3	26	17	2
Fryer, Paul, Nashua	.285	111	375	39	107	132	15	5	0	39	4	3	3	1	18	4	56	3	4
Garrett, Eric, Albany	.239	26	71	9	17	20	1	1	0	11	2	4	1	1	7	0	15	0	1
Gentile, Gene, Albany*	.197	37	117	15	23	30	3	2	0	11	1	0	1	0	15	0	16	1	1
Ghelfi, Anthony, Reading	.500	4	2	0	1	1	0	0	0	0	0	0	0	0	0	0	0	0	0
Glass, Timothy, Buffalo	.306	107	360	58	110	186	13	3	19	68	2	3	4	1	37	1	85	1	2
Goldthorn, Burk, Nashua*	.211	101	251	22	53	68	12	0	1	32	2	2	3	4	56	3	36	4	8
Gonzales, Arturo, Reading	.000	7	6	0	0	0	0	0	0	0	0	0	0	0	0	0	0	0	0
Gonzalez, Fernando, Nashua	.100	23	10	1	1	1	0	0	0	0	0	0	0	0	0	0	6	0	0
Graham, J. Brian, Albany	.246	89	285	49	70	88	9	3	1	30	7	6	1	1	32	1	42	4	3
Griffin, Frankie, Reading*	.000	38	5	0	0	0	0	0	0	0	0	1	0	0	0	0	3	0	0
Grimm, Peter, Vermont	.100	27	10	1	1	1	0	0	0	0	1	0	2	0	0	3	0	5	0	0
Guzman, Ruben, Vermont	.263	120	410	53	108	161	13	5	10	56	7	1	3	3	41	3	80	34	10
Hall, Jeffrey, New Britain	.204	100	319	16	65	92	8	2	5	37	6	0	5	0	16	2	59	0	0
Hallas, Robert, Albany	.667	19	3	0	2	2	0	0	0	0	0	0	0	0	1	0	1	0	0
Hamric, Russell, Reading	.303	48	175	29	53	77	5	2	5	24	1	2	2	2	21	1	12	10	6
Harper, Therron, Vermont	.278	104	317	31	88	118	13	4	3	50	7	3	5	4	40	7	31	0	3
Hartsock, Brian, Waterbury*	.300	35	110	11	33	42	5	2	0	8	0	1	1	0	11	0	12	0	3
Heath, David, Waterbury	.185	121	426	35	79	118	12	0	9	41	10	0	6	2	20	0	99	0	2
Hobbs, Rodney, Albany	.300	129	423	82	127	186	16	8	9	74	9	4	1	3	79	1	78	22	13
Hopkins, Mark, Buffalo	.143	3	7	0	1	1	0	0	0	0	1	0	0	1	0	0	0	0	0
Hoppie, Bryan, Reading†	.301	48	146	13	44	54	7	0	1	13	2	3	2	1	10	1	9	6	5
Hudgens, David, Albany*	.290	30	100	16	29	50	8	2	3	12	0	0	2	1	10	2	24	0	1
Hughes, Keith, Reading*	.261	70	230	35	60	83	7	5	2	20	1	0	2	0	31	2	43	1	0
Ibarra, Miguel, Reading	.196	66	168	12	33	41	4	2	0	17	2	2	3	3	17	1	35	1	7
Jackson, Kenneth, Reading	.240	72	225	31	54	70	9	2	1	19	3	4	0	7	36	2	49	10	7
James, D. Christopher, Reading	.256	128	457	66	117	184	19	12	8	57	10	3	4	3	40	1	74	19	5
Jelks, Gregory, Reading	.225	92	329	35	74	107	13	1	6	42	1	4	5	2	33	2	64	5	5
Johnson, David, Nashua	.143	17	7	1	1	1	0	0	0	0	1	0	2	0	0	0	4	0	0
Joyner, Wallace, Waterbury*	.317	134	467	81	148	222	24	7	12	72	12	5	8	1	67	8	60	0	5
Karkovice, Ronald, Glens Falls	.215	88	260	37	56	106	9	1	13	39	5	1	0	1	25	1	102	3	1
Key, Gregory, Waterbury	.235	112	388	68	91	124	11	5	4	44	5	10	4	4	56	2	65	26	6
Khalifa, Sam, Nashua	.238	91	344	39	82	105	12	4	1	36	3	3	3	1	34	0	42	6	3
Knight, Timothy, Reading*	.296	54	216	33	64	87	10	2	3	19	2	3	1	0	28	1	31	12	11
Knox, Michael, Vermont	.182	29	22	1	4	5	1	0	0	1	0	3	0	0	1	0	6	0	0
Lamar, Daniel, Vermont	.163	46	141	13	23	39	4	0	4	20	5	0	1	2	14	0	32	0	0
Lamonde, Lawrence, Nashua	.000	4	2	1	0	0	0	0	0	0	0	1	0	0	0	0	0	0	0
Lavalliere, Michael, Reading*	.252	55	147	19	37	61	6	0	6	22	2	3	2	1	36	3	15	0	1
LeBoeuf, Alan, Reading*	.283	110	361	61	102	158	19	5	9	56	7	1	7	3	37	2	36	5	3
Ledbetter, Jeffrey, New Britain*	.214	115	374	36	80	135	11	4	12	44	4	4	0	2	43	3	68	0	0
Lee, Terry, Vermont	.242	134	422	56	102	149	10	2	11	47	9	2	4	3	44	1	94	2	4
Lefebvre, Joseph, Reading*	.333	6	12	5	4	5	1	0	0	0	0	0	0	1	2	0	3	0	0
Legg, Gregory, Reading	.241	64	224	16	54	73	11	1	2	27	4	4	2	3	19	0	19	2	2
Little, Ronald, Vermont*	.262	122	355	37	93	106	11	1	0	34	4	1	5	0	30	5	69	5	5
Lochner, David, Vermont*	.063	27	16	0	1	1	0	0	0	0	1	0	0	0	1	0	2	0	0
Maddux, Michael, Reading	.143	22	7	0	1	1	0	0	0	0	0	0	0	0	0	0	3	0	0
Madril, Michael, Waterbury†	.262	139	504	95	132	167	17	9	0	43	4	12	3	15	68	2	73	23	19
Maitland, Michael, Nashua*	.375	19	8	3	3	4	1	0	0	2	0	0	1	0	1	0	2	0	0
Mangual, Jose, Waterbury	.197	81	239	34	47	69	7	0	5	31	2	2	5	3	59	2	58	1	3
Manzanillo, Ravelo, Nashua*	.143	23	14	1	2	2	0	0	0	0	0	0	0	0	0	0	4	0	0
Marcheskie, Lee, Nashua	.250	45	8	1	2	2	0	0	0	0	0	0	0	0	0	0	5	0	0
McClendon, Lloyd, Vermont	.277	60	202	36	56	93	16	0	7	27	5	0	1	2	28	0	28	2	2
McCullock, Alec, Buffalo	.000	24	0	0	0	0	0	0	0	0	0	0	0	0	0	0	1	0	0
McGehee, C. Connor, Nashua*	.216	37	125	23	27	40	6	2	1	6	1	1	2	0	18	1	21	7	3
McHenry, Vance, Reading	.244	24	90	17	22	31	4	1	1	6	1	1	0	0	12	0	14	2	1
Meier, Scott, Glens Falls	.000	4	12	1	0	0	0	0	0	0	0	0	0	0	0	0	4	0	0
Mesa, Ivan, Glens Falls	.243	33	74	12	18	23	3	1	0	4	1	1	1	0	6	0	6	3	1
Mesh, Michael, New Britain	.240	118	400	78	96	128	11	6	3	31	4	9	5	5	67	3	76	39	3
Miller-Jones, Gary, New Britain†	.268	124	400	42	107	130	18	1	1	31	4	11	2	2	32	1	52	1	1
Mohorcic, Dale, Nashua	.000	28	5	0	0	0	0	0	0	0	0	0	0	0	0	0	4	0	0
Moronko, Jeffrey, Buffalo	.314	131	468	84	147	224	30	4	13	95	10	3	7	7	60	2	87	7	12
Morse, Michael, Glens Falls	.069	31	58	7	4	6	2	0	0	1	0	0	0	0	8	0	11	0	0
Moses, Stephen, Reading*	.300	125	437	59	131	148	11	3	0	31	2	6	2	0	50	1	30	15	13
Murphy, Michael, Buffalo	.000	9	1	0	0	0	0	0	0	0	0	0	0	0	0	0	0	0	0
Murphy, Robert, Vermont*	.500	45	4	0	2	2	0	0	0	0	0	0	1	0	0	0	2	0	0
Nattile, Samuel, New Britain*	.315	119	429	51	135	203	34	2	10	78	9	0	3	2	38	5	68	0	3
Nix, David, Glens Falls*	.255	134	462	58	118	179	26	6	9	62	6	1	1	1	39	5	61	6	0
Noboa, Milciades, Buffalo	.253	117	383	55	97	126	18	4	1	45	1	17	3	2	31	0	28	12	7
Olander, James, Reading	.262	117	362	44	95	135	12	2	8	47	3	1	5	2	29	0	62	10	10
Oliva, David, New Britain	.265	30	117	6	31	37	4	0	0	11	1	1	1	2	11	1	21	5	4
Oliver, H. Scott, Waterbury	.000	35	2	0	0	0	0	0	0	0	0	0	0	0	0	0	2	0	0
Olson, James, Reading	.222	22	8	0	2	2	0	0	0	0	0	0	1	0	1	0	3	0	0
O'Neill, Paul, Vermont*	.265	134	475	70	126	215	31	5	16	76	13	0	2	2	52	6	72	29	11
Opie, James, Nashua	.254	133	468	49	119	170	28	1	7	56	9	1	3	3	42	0	102	22	10

Player and Club	Pct.	G.	AB.	R.	H.	TB.	2B.	3B.	HR.	RBI.	GW.	SH.	SF.	HP.	BB.	Int. BB.	SO.	SB.	CS.
Pacho, Juan, Glens Falls	.231	36	91	10	21	23	2	0	0	7	0	5	1	1	5	0	14	0	0
Pippin, Craig, Nashua	.167	16	6	2	1	1	0	0	0	1	0	1	0	0	3	0	0	0	0
Polidor, Gustavo, Waterbury	.223	119	394	42	88	104	11	1	1	32	2	10	1	1	25	1	32	3	7
Porte, Carlos, Vermont	.198	42	126	12	25	36	5	0	2	12	1	4	0	1	8	0	16	4	2
Pratt, Crestwell, Vermont	.172	39	99	13	17	29	3	0	3	11	0	0	3	0	7	0	39	0	1
Pryor, Depew, Vermont	.194	100	288	30	56	84	13	0	5	29	3	1	5	1	49	0	84	2	3
Quinones, Rene, Buffalo†	.278	84	306	32	85	115	13	1	5	43	5	2	2	1	18	1	35	1	3
Reece, Thad, Albany°	.331	120	420	70	139	175	22	4	2	46	5	8	4	1	45	2	27	15	6
Reed, Curtis, Glens Falls°	.290	30	93	8	27	35	8	0	0	12	2	2	0	0	5	1	8	0	0
Renteria, Rich, Nashua	.273	113	443	63	121	160	22	7	1	34	3	3	2	1	39	2	43	21	15
Rice, A. Cepedia, Nashua	.231	27	26	3	6	12	0	0	2	5	1	0	0	0	1	0	12	0	0
Riley, Thomas, Vermont	.196	52	163	16	32	34	2	0	0	7	0	3	0	0	19	0	18	0	0
Rincon, Andrew, Nashua	.250	6	4	0	1	1	0	0	0	0	0	0	0	0	1	0	1	0	0
Robles, Gregory, Albany°	.244	26	82	8	20	21	1	0	0	5	0	1	0	1	13	0	9	0	1
Rodriguez, D. Ruben, Nashua	.219	87	242	26	53	80	13	1	4	32	4	5	2	3	14	5	63	7	2
Rodriguez, Eduardo, Waterbury	.195	64	154	20	30	42	6	0	2	4	0	3	0	1	16	0	27	0	2
Rollins, Rip, Reading	.182	26	11	0	2	2	0	0	0	0	0	0	0	0	0	0	7	0	0
Romero, E. Albert, Waterbury	.301	39	133	17	40	54	5	0	3	21	3	2	2	1	11	0	13	2	3
Romero, Ramon, Glens Falls†	.236	92	258	28	61	73	7	1	1	25	2	4	3	0	49	0	49	2	0
Saavedra, Edwin, Buffalo	.284	91	299	53	85	127	17	2	7	44	6	5	3	2	30	0	33	8	5
Sabo, Christopher, Vermont	.213	125	441	44	94	130	19	1	5	38	2	2	4	4	44	1	62	10	5
Sauveur, Richard, Nashua°	.200	10	5	1	1	1	0	0	0	0	0	0	0	0	2	0	0	0	0
Scott, Timothy, Vermont	.125	29	8	1	1	1	0	0	0	0	0	0	1	0	1	0	4	0	0
Sedar, Edward, Glens Falls	.259	134	409	64	106	148	16	7	4	52	4	4	2	6	77	1	77	23	8
Seibert, B. Gibson, Reading	.247	129	425	64	105	149	16	8	4	51	3	3	7	1	70	1	77	19	5
Seiler, David, Reading°	.333	12	3	0	1	1	0	0	0	0	0	0	0	0	0	0	2	0	0
Seilheimer, Ricky, Glens Falls°	.227	17	44	6	10	11	1	0	0	3	0	1	0	1	5	1	13	0	0
Senteney, Steve, Nashua	.000	25	2	0	0	0	0	0	0	0	0	0	0	0	0	0	1	0	0
Sheaffer, Danny, New Britain	.241	93	303	33	73	86	10	0	1	27	4	1	6	0	29	2	31	2	2
Simunic, Douglas, Buffalo	.241	29	87	12	21	31	1	0	3	18	1	0	2	1	11	1	17	2	0
Smajstrla, Craig, Glens Falls†	.264	133	497	78	131	173	18	6	4	41	5	4	2	2	49	4	49	36	11
Smith, David A., Waterbury	.000	36	1	0	0	0	0	0	0	0	0	0	0	0	0	0	1	0	0
Smith, Michael, Vermont	.000	35	1	0	0	0	0	0	0	0	0	1	0	0	0	0	1	0	0
Sodders, Michael, Glens Falls	.257	87	303	42	78	121	22	0	7	52	3	0	8	2	26	2	28	5	0
Stalp, R. Joseph, Vermont	.100	24	10	2	1	1	0	0	0	0	2	1	3	0	1	0	5	0	0
Steinbach, Eugene, Buffalo	.111	22	45	1	5	6	1	0	0	3	0	0	1	0	7	0	19	1	0
Stephens, Darryl, Waterbury°	.273	122	381	47	104	147	21	2	6	56	5	2	2	2	50	5	39	2	2
Stromer, Richard, Waterbury	.263	138	453	70	119	167	18	0	10	69	10	5	5	2	98	8	47	3	2
Surhoff, Richard, Reading	.250	62	4	1	1	1	0	0	0	0	0	1	0	0	0	0	3	0	0
Susce, Steven, Nashua	.091	20	11	0	1	1	0	0	0	0	0	0	0	0	2	0	4	0	0
Tejada, Wilfredo, Reading	.333	28	72	7	24	31	7	0	0	15	1	1	3	2	5	0	8	0	0
Terry, Scott, Vermont	.059	20	17	2	1	1	0	0	0	0	0	0	0	0	2	0	10	0	0
Tettleton, Mickey, Albany†	.231	86	281	32	65	98	18	0	5	47	3	0	6	0	52	8	52	2	2
Thoma, Raymond, Albany	.240	131	417	56	100	131	14	4	3	53	5	7	6	4	29	1	82	5	5
Tolentino, Jose, Albany°	.284	71	257	32	73	103	13	1	5	43	7	2	3	0	16	0	35	2	1
Trujillo, Louie, Vermont	.000	19	3	0	0	0	0	0	0	0	0	0	0	0	0	0	2	0	0
Valdez, Julio, New Britain†	.267	56	187	24	50	72	11	4	1	29	1	4	2	2	14	1	25	3	0
Valera, Alcadio, Buffalo†	.200	4	5	1	1	1	0	0	0	0	0	0	0	0	2	0	0	0	0
Walck, Craig, New Britain	.265	93	302	37	80	102	14	1	2	39	6	9	3	4	46	0	34	1	1
Warner, Harold, Reading°	.125	22	16	0	2	2	0	0	0	0	0	1	0	0	4	0	0	0	0
Washington, Randy, Buffalo	.282	120	379	66	107	152	12	3	9	63	11	3	6	2	71	1	89	9	8
Wheeler, Timothy, Nashua	.231	23	13	1	3	4	1	0	0	2	0	0	0	0	3	0	3	1	0
Wilder, David, Albany	.261	70	199	47	52	77	10	6	1	25	5	3	3	0	58	4	50	13	3
Williams, Kenneth, Glens Falls	.246	97	309	35	76	117	7	5	8	47	7	1	4	4	21	1	70	16	7
Wilson, Phillip E., Buffalo	.225	24	71	7	16	17	1	0	0	6	2	0	2	0	8	0	19	0	1
Wise, Brett, Vermont	.000	20	1	0	0	0	0	0	0	0	0	2	0	0	0	0	0	0	0
Woodard, Michael, Albany°	.354	23	96	19	34	36	2	0	0	9	4	0	1	0	12	1	5	11	0
Wooster, Robert, Buffalo	.115	28	52	2	6	6	0	0	0	3	0	1	0	0	3	0	12	0	0

The following pitchers, listed alphabetically by club, with games in parentheses, had no plate appearances, primarily through use of designated hitters.

ALBANY—Bauer, Mark (17); Belcher, Timothy (10); Dozier, Thomas (44); Hudson, Robert (4); Kaiser, Jeffrey (7); Kendrick, Peter (43); Kobernus, Jeffrey (4); Kyles, Stanley (26); Lambert, Timothy (27); McDonald, Russell (6); Myers, Edward (12); Rodriguez, Ricardo (10); Straker, Lester (28); Strichek, James (8); Zmudosky, Thomas (33).

BUFFALO—Baller, Jay (14); Banks, Darryl (8); Doyle, Richard (25); Fuson, Robin (7); Marsden, Steven (43); Miglio, John (14); Myles, Rick (8); Ortiz, Andrew (29); Pierorazio, Wesley (10); Roche, Stephen (9); Roman, Jose (27); Romero, Ramon (11); Santarelli, Calvin (6); Szymczak, David (12); Thompson, Richard (51).

GLENS FALLS—Davis, Joel (4); DeVincenzo, Richard (25); Drabek, Douglas (19); Geiger, Burwell (47); Hardy, John (32); Hickey, Kevin (3); Kristan, Kevin (57); Layton, Thomas (26); McKeon, Joel (45); Moncrief, Homer (12); Palacios, Vicente (5); Ruzek, Donald (13); Stranski, Scott (33); Tanzi, Michael (6); Trujillo, Michael (20).

NASHUA—Guante, Cecilio (1); Little, Jeffrey (10).

NEW BRITAIN—Birrell, Robert (22); Bolton, Thomas (33); Cappadona, Anthony (4); Dale, Charles (36); Davis, Charles (22); Denman, Brian (13); Ellsworth, Steven (3); Gering, Scott (38); Johnson, Mitchell (26); Kane, Kevin (12); McCarthy, Thomas (38); Mecerod, George (8); Schmid, Michael (38); Woodward, Robert (28).

READING—Kromy, Ted (8).

VERMONT—Buchanan, Robert (14); Jefferson, James (7); Konderla, Michael (15); Lind, Jackson (1); Montgomery, Jeff (22).

WATERBURY—Bastian, Robert (29); Bryden, Thomas (25); Buckle, Larry (22); Groh, Donald (9); Kammeyer, Timothy (22); Lugo, Rafael (24); Mack, Tony (25); Price, Kevin (19); Pruneda, Armando (14).

GRAND SLAM HOME RUNS—Ashman, Bathe, Benzinger, Bonilla, Bundy, Cipolloni, Daniels, Guzman, Hobbs, Jelks, Joyner, Lee, Mangual, Opie, D.R. Rodriguez, Stromer, Tolentino, Williams, 1 each.

AWARDED FIRST BASE ON CATCHER'S INTERFERENCE—Bundy 7 (Ashman 2, Dodd, Harper, Heath, Ibarra, Steinbach); Adams 4 (Lamar 2, Harper, Ibarra); Mesh 3 (Tettleton 2, Harper); Ashman 2 (Ackley, D.R. Rodriguez); Oliva 2 (Ashman, Harper); Cecchetti (Cipolloni); S. Davis (Cipolloni); R. Little (Harper); Moronko (Dodd).

CLUB FIELDING

Club	Pct.	G.	PO.	A.	E.	DP.	PB.	Club	Pct.	G.	PO.	A.	E.	DP.	PB.
New Britain	.972	140	3486	1527	145	129	25	Glens Falls	.965	139	3457	1463	178	97	27
Albany	.969	139	3502	1533	162	133	32	Nashua	.963	140	3574	1475	192	123	14
Buffalo	.966	139	3496	1379	172	115	36	Vermont	.961	140	3548	1511	208	113	19
Waterbury	.966	140	3594	1384	176	128	18	Reading	.955	139	3455	1501	233	131	16

Triple Play—Vermont.

INDIVIDUAL FIELDING

*Throws lefthanded.

FIRST BASEMEN

Player and Club	Pct.	G.	PO.	A.	E.	DP.	Player and Club	Pct.	G.	PO.	A.	E.	DP.
Adams, Glens Falls	.992	137	1097	131	10	87	Lamar, Vermont	1.000	5	31	4	0	1
Benzinger, New Britain	.982	43	348	24	7	29	LeBoeuf, Reading	.987	79	609	71	9	65
Bonilla, Nashua	1.000	2	4	0	0	1	Ledbetter, New Britain*	1.000	5	45	3	0	5
Brown, Nashua	1.000	1	7	2	0	0	Lee, Vermont	.987	134	1105	85	16	93
Bundy, Nashua	.988	101	896	58	12	76	McClendon, Vermont	.957	4	21	1	1	3
Cecchetti, Buffalo*	.984	113	834	66	15	72	NATTILE, New Britain	.996	97	832	67	4	79
Culmer, Buffalo	.983	35	227	11	4	19	Olander, Reading	1.000	1	7	0	0	0
Davis, Glens Falls	1.000	1	1	0	0	0	Pratt, Vermont	.974	13	108	6	3	9
DeLaRosa, Nashua*	.967	27	218	20	8	16	Quinones, Buffalo	1.000	2	11	2	0	1
Dodd, Glens Falls	1.000	4	29	2	0	0	Rice, Nashua	1.000	1	3	0	0	0
Eppard, Albany*	.998	58	443	31	1	38	Robles, Albany*	.992	24	219	16	2	22
Fryer, Nashua	.975	16	108	9	3	14	Stephens, Waterbury*	.977	11	79	7	2	2
Goldthorn, Nashua	1.000	1	1	0	0	1	Stromer, Waterbury	.935	5	26	3	2	1
Hamric, Reading	1.000	1	8	0	0	0	Tettleton, Albany	1.000	1	5	0	0	0
Harper, Waterbury	.988	28	223	14	3	25	Tolentino, Albany*	.992	70	602	52	5	57
Hughes, Reading*	1.000	2	8	0	0	0	Washington, Buffalo	1.000	1	0	0	0	0
Ibarra, Reading	.973	23	134	10	4	14	Wheeler, Nashua	1.000	1	1	0	0	0
Jelks, Reading	.990	46	383	32	4	40	Wooster, Buffalo	.988	13	79	6	1	9
Joyner, Waterbury*	.992	108	868	84	8	74							

Triple Play—Lee.

SECOND BASEMEN

Player and Club	Pct.	G.	PO.	A.	E.	DP.	Player and Club	Pct.	G.	PO.	A.	E.	DP.
Bundy, Nashua	1.000	2	1	0	0	0	Noboa, Buffalo	.967	116	228	305	18	62
Bustabad, New Britain	.967	14	28	31	2	10	Porte, Vermont	.955	40	87	106	9	22
Carrasco, Waterbury	.975	134	286	346	16	79	Quinones, Buffalo	.950	27	38	58	5	6
Clack, Nashua	.973	28	67	76	4	22	Reece, Albany	.993	36	67	70	1	17
Cox, Vermont	.955	35	59	90	7	20	Renteria, Nashua	.976	112	208	283	12	56
Franklin, Vermont	.936	27	52	79	9	11	Riley, Vermont	.969	42	82	135	7	20
Graham, Albany	.974	85	191	218	11	64	Rodriguez, Waterbury	.968	6	10	20	1	2
Hamric, Reading	.958	10	22	24	2	5	Sabo, Vermont	.870	10	16	24	6	5
Hoppie, Reading	.906	9	16	13	3	5	Smajstrla, Glens Falls	.959	78	158	192	15	35
Jackson, Reading	.960	62	131	178	13	38	Stromer, Waterbury	1.000	1	2	6	0	1
Lavalliere, Reading	1.000	4	12	12	0	4	Thoma, Albany	1.000	3	3	10	0	1
Legg, Reading	.953	57	108	156	13	33	Valdez, New Britain	1.000	5	12	13	0	1
Mesa, Glens Falls	1.000	3	2	4	0	0	Walck, New Britain	1.000	2	6	11	0	2
MILLER-JONES, New Britain	.988	123	236	365	7	79	Woodard, Albany	.957	23	62	72	6	21
Nix, Glens Falls	.971	63	120	148	8	29	Wooster, Buffalo	.857	4	4	2	1	0

Triple Play—Franklin.

THIRD BASEMEN

Player and Club	Pct.	G.	PO.	A.	E.	DP.	Player and Club	Pct.	G.	PO.	A.	E.	DP.
Aponte, Buffalo	.935	78	65	138	14	11	Morse, Glens Falls	.556	5	1	4	4	2
Ashman, Albany	.930	20	12	41	4	6	Nattile, New Britain	.750	5	1	5	2	0
Bathe, Albany	.921	83	63	147	18	17	Nix, Glens Falls	.935	57	39	106	10	10
Bustabad, New Britain	1.000	4	2	6	0	1	Opie, Nashua	.833	2	0	5	1	1
Christenson, Nashua	1.000	8	1	13	0	3	Pacho, Glens Falls	1.000	9	6	10	0	0
Clack, Nashua	.931	56	49	112	12	11	Quinones, Buffalo	.964	11	10	17	1	3
DeLeon, Buffalo	1.000	1	1	3	0	0	Reece, Albany	.945	38	38	82	7	12
Franklin, Vermont	.910	35	26	55	8	8	Riley, Vermont	1.000	2	2	5	0	0
Fryer, Nashua	.915	86	67	171	22	15	Rodriguez, Waterbury	.895	11	3	14	2	1
Garrett, Albany	.500	2	0	1	1	0	Romero, Waterbury	1.000	1	1	0	0	0
Heath, Waterbury	1.000	1	1	1	0	0	SABO, Vermont	.943	116	64	186	15	9
Hoppie, Reading	.905	8	6	13	2	2	Seilheimer, Glens Falls	1.000	4	2	4	0	1
James, Reading	.888	123	100	209	39	21	Sodders, Glens Falls	.911	73	63	112	17	8
Lavalliere, Reading	.920	10	5	18	2	0	Stromer, Waterbury	.920	134	130	239	32	33
LeBoeuf, Reading	1.000	5	3	5	0	0	Tettleton, Albany	1.000	1	1	0	0	0
Legg, Reading	1.000	1	0	2	0	0	Thoma, Albany	.818	2	0	9	2	1
McClendon, Vermont	1.000	2	0	1	0	1	Valdez, New Britain	.878	46	31	77	15	10
Mesa, Glens Falls	.909	3	4	6	1	0	Walck, New Britain	.969	91	63	186	8	17
Moronko, Buffalo	.955	49	52	98	7	3	Wooster, Buffalo	1.000	6	2	10	0	0

SHORTSTOPS

Player and Club	Pct.	G.	PO.	A.	E.	DP.	Player and Club	Pct.	G.	PO.	A.	E.	DP.
Ashman, Albany	1.000	2	2	3	0	0	Moronko, Buffalo	.931	84	140	235	28	55
Brumley, New Britain	.667	1	1	1	1	1	Morse, Glens Falls	.942	24	23	42	4	4
Bustabad, New Britain	.954	40	66	119	9	20	Nix, Glens Falls	.000	2	0	0	1	0
Cox, Vermont	.500	1	0	1	1	0	Opie, Nashua	.946	22	26	62	5	6
Cruz, Albany	1.000	3	0	2	0	1	Pacho, Glens Falls	.923	28	34	50	7	10
DeLeon, Buffalo	.925	21	26	48	6	6	POLIDOR, Waterbury	.951	118	200	322	27	57
Evans, Buffalo	.927	117	169	328	39	64	Quinones, Buffalo	.931	40	60	88	11	15
Franklin, Vermont	.913	24	29	65	9	11	Reece, Albany	.946	20	18	35	3	6
Fryer, Nashua	.923	4	3	9	1	4	Riley, Vermont	.951	10	15	24	2	3
Graham, Albany	.941	3	6	10	1	1	Rodriguez, Waterbury	.915	26	22	75	9	14
Hamric, Reading	.932	38	57	120	13	23	Romero, Glens Falls	.940	85	131	232	23	36
Hoppie, Reading	.958	7	9	14	1	3	Seibert, Buffalo	.884	86	158	254	54	51
Jackson, Reading	.976	9	15	25	1	7	Tettleton, Albany	1.000	1	1	0	0	0
Khalifa, Nashua	.946	91	151	266	24	58	Thoma, Albany	.936	125	165	379	37	65
Legg, Reading	.923	4	3	9	1	2	Valdez, New Britain	1.000	8	6	20	0	2
McHenry, Nashua	.908	24	28	31	6	9	Valera, Buffalo	1.000	3	5	6	0	2
Mesa, Glens Falls	.974	24	22	53	2	8	Walck, New Britain	.714	1	1	4	2	1
Mesh, New Britain	.942	97	151	288	27	52	Wooster, Buffalo	1.000	4	7	6	0	2

OUTFIELDERS

Player and Club	Pct.	G.	PO.	A.	E.	DP.
Ackley, New Britain	1.000	4	6	0	0	0
Aponte, Buffalo	1.000	1	1	0	0	0
ARNOLD, Albany	.9829	93	165	7	3	1
Ashman, Albany	.000	1	0	0	1	0
Aulenback, Nashua	1.000	4	8	0	0	0
Beal, New Britain	.967	92	194	13	7	1
Bennett, Albany*	1.000	6	12	0	0	0
Benzinger, New Britain	.946	71	117	5	7	1
Bernstine, Buffalo	.9826	109	219	7	4	1
Bonilla, Nashua	.955	131	308	8	15	2
Brown, Nashua	1.000	21	35	4	0	0
Brumley, New Britain	.938	34	70	5	5	0
Cangelosi, Glens Falls*	.967	137	310	11	11	3
Carter, Buffalo	.975	129	295	14	8	3
Cecchetti, Buffalo*	1.000	12	23	1	0	1
Christenson, Nashua	1.000	5	5	1	0	0
Ciampa, New Britain*	.984	59	115	6	2	0
Clack, Nashua	1.000	12	15	1	0	0
Clark, Buffalo	.962	15	23	2	1	0
Coughlin, Albany	.966	26	55	1	2	0
Daniels, Vermont	.967	81	143	2	5	0
DeLaRosa, Albany*	.924	39	59	2	5	2
Dodd, Glens Falls	.978	57	83	8	2	3
Eppard, Albany*	.975	60	108	10	3	0
Ford, Nashua	.938	83	162	5	11	0
Franklin, Vermont	1.000	5	5	0	0	0
Garrett, Albany	1.000	4	5	0	0	0
Gentile, Albany*	.947	30	68	4	4	1
Guzman, Vermont	.963	116	200	10	8	0
Hall, New Britain	.961	51	71	3	3	1
Hartsock, Waterbury	.895	14	14	3	2	0
Hobbs, Albany	.960	128	208	9	9	3
Hoppie, Reading	1.000	21	29	2	0	1
Hudgens, Albany*	.952	19	39	1	2	0
Hughes, Reading*	.928	67	109	7	9	1
James, Reading	1.000	3	4	0	0	0
Jelks, Reading	.948	32	55	0	3	0
Joyner, Waterbury*	.976	24	38	2	1	0
Key, Waterbury	.950	113	225	3	12	3
Knight, Reading*	.957	51	85	5	4	0
LeBoeuf, Reading	.875	2	6	1	1	0
Ledbetter, New Britain*	.968	61	87	5	3	2
Lefebvre, Reading	1.000	6	11	1	0	0
Little, Vermont*	.955	117	242	13	12	3
Madril, Waterbury	.969	138	360	11	12	5
Mangual, Waterbury	.962	29	25	0	1	0
McGehee, Nashua*	.973	35	72	1	2	0
Mesh, New Britain	.977	20	40	2	1	1
Moses, Reading*	.976	120	226	13	6	2
Nattile, New Britain	1.000	2	5	0	0	0
O'Neill, Vermont	.973	132	246	5	7	1
Olander, Reading	.966	103	248	10	9	3
Oliva, New Britain	.937	30	57	2	4	0
Opie, Nashua	.959	107	177	10	8	2
Reece, Albany	.966	19	27	1	1	0
Reed, Glens Falls	.947	24	33	3	2	0
Rice, Nashua	1.000	1	1	0	0	0
Romero, Waterbury	.958	38	64	4	3	1
Saavedra, Buffalo	1.000	56	87	8	0	1
Sedar, Glens Falls	.965	134	233	18	9	3
Seibert, Reading	.949	41	68	6	4	2
Sheaffer, New Britain	.929	14	11	2	1	0
Sodders, Glens Falls	.900	5	9	0	1	0
Stephens, Waterbury*	.963	88	125	4	5	0
Tettleton, Albany	1.000	3	3	0	0	0
Thoma, Albany	1.000	2	1	0	0	0
Warner, Reading*	1.000	2	4	0	0	0
Washington, Buffalo	.976	113	197	9	5	1
Wilder, Albany	.979	64	132	6	3	2
Williams, Glens Falls	.973	95	173	10	5	1

CATCHERS

Player and Club	Pct.	G.	PO.	A.	E.	DP.	PB.
Ackley, New Britain	.987	66	343	36	5	8	13
Allanson, Buffalo	.983	24	154	15	3	4	3
Ashman, Albany	.962	58	269	34	12	4	17
Aulenback, Nashua	1.000	2	3	1	0	0	2
Cipolloni, Reading	.980	90	440	61	10	4	9
Diaz, Reading	.938	3	11	4	1	0	1
Dodd, Glens Falls	.967	48	231	31	9	1	12
Garrett, Albany	.952	17	68	12	4	2	9
Glass, Buffalo	.971	69	368	27	12	2	11
Goldthorn, Nashua	.974	81	405	51	12	7	6
Hall, New Britain	.963	4	20	6	1	0	6
Harper, Waterbury	.973	49	303	19	9	4	10
Heath, Waterbury	.977	99	508	52	13	9	8
Hopkins, Buffalo	1.000	3	7	0	0	0	0
Ibarra, Reading	.951	13	67	11	4	1	2
Karkovice, Glens Falls	.979	87	442	68	11	4	9
Lamar, Vermont	.966	30	147	23	6	2	5
Lavalliere, Reading	1.000	19	96	15	0	3	1
McClendon, Vermont	.989	31	153	22	2	2	3
Meier, Glens Falls	.923	4	23	1	2	0	2
Pryor, Vermont	.977	91	468	53	12	5	11
D. R. Rodriguez, Nashua	.977	80	409	58	11	10	8
Romero, Glens Falls	1.000	8	42	5	0	0	2
Sedar, Glens Falls	1.000	1	3	0	0	0	1
Seilheimer, Glens Falls	1.000	10	33	3	0	0	1
Sheaffer, New Britain	.990	73	427	45	5	3	6
Simunic, Buffalo	.982	17	102	8	2	1	7
Steinbach, Buffalo	.958	19	62	6	3	1	5
Tejada, Reading	.935	23	107	22	9	3	3
TETTLETON, Albany	.993	70	358	42	3	6	6
Wilson, Buffalo	.992	23	104	16	1	1	10

PITCHERS

Player and Club	Pct.	G.	PO.	A.	E.	DP.
Arnold, Reading*	.929	49	11	28	3	0
Ashman, Albany	1.000	3	0	2	0	0
Bailes, Nashua*	.960	54	4	20	1	1
Baller, Buffalo	1.000	14	7	9	0	0
Banks, Buffalo	1.000	8	0	6	0	0
Bastian, Waterbury	.955	29	10	11	1	1
Bauer, Albany	1.000	17	4	15	0	1
Belcher, Albany	.900	10	5	4	1	1
Birrell, New Britain*	.824	22	2	12	3	0
Bohnet, Buffalo*	.885	26	5	18	3	3
Bolton, New Britain*	1.000	33	8	19	0	3
Bryden, Waterbury	.900	25	1	8	1	0
Buchanan, Vermont*	.571	14	1	3	3	0
Buckle, Waterbury	.800	22	5	11	4	2
Bullinger, Vermont*	.833	21	1	9	2	0
Bulls, Reading	.958	19	12	11	1	3
Childress, Reading	1.000	62	3	20	0	1
Clements, Waterbury*	.957	43	3	19	1	2
Cole, Reading	1.000	10	10	4	0	2
Dale, New Britain	1.000	36	3	9	0	1
C. Davis, New Britain	1.000	22	11	21	0	4
J. Davis, Glens Falls	.667	4	3	1	2	0
Dempsey, Glens Falls	1.000	25	9	15	0	1
Denman, New Britain	.933	13	3	11	1	2
DEVINCENZO, Glens Falls*	1.000	25	8	25	0	0
Doyle, Buffalo	.846	25	6	16	4	3
Dozier, Albany	.938	44	6	9	1	1
Drabek, Glens Falls	.955	19	10	11	1	0
Ellsworth, New Britain	.667	3	1	1	1	0
Ferguson, Reading	1.000	18	4	15	0	0
Fischer, Albany	.966	30	10	18	1	1
Fryer, Nashua	1.000	5	1	1	0	0
Fuson, Buffalo	.867	7	3	10	2	0
Geiger, Glens Falls	.957	47	10	12	1	0
Gering, New Britain	.842	38	7	9	3	0
Ghelfi, Reading	1.000	4	0	2	0	0
Gonzales, Reading	.900	7	3	6	1	1
Gonzalez, Nashua	.879	23	6	23	4	2
Griffin, Reading*	.920	38	11	12	2	2
Grimm, Vermont	.955	27	5	16	1	1
Groh, Waterbury*	.667	9	2	4	3	0
Hall, New Britain	1.000	5	1	0	0	0
Hallas, Albany	.893	19	5	20	3	0
Hardy, Glens Falls	.889	32	13	27	5	1
Hickey, Glens Falls*	1.000	3	1	0	0	0
Jefferson, Vermont	1.000	7	2	3	0	0
D. Johnson, Nashua	.950	12	5	14	1	2
M. Johnson, New Britain	.931	26	15	12	2	2
Kaiser, Albany*	1.000	7	4	11	0	0
Kammeyer, Waterbury	.969	22	14	17	1	1
Kane, New Britain	1.000	12	2	7	0	0
Kendrick, Albany*	.968	43	7	23	1	0
Knox, Vermont	.972	27	17	52	2	0
Konderla, Vermont	1.000	15	4	2	0	0
Kristan, Glens Falls	.926	57	4	21	2	5
Kromy, Reading	1.000	8	2	6	0	0
Kyles, Albany	.925	25	8	29	3	3
Lambert, Albany	.952	27	13	27	2	1
Lamonde, Nashua	.750	4	2	4	2	0
Layton, Glens Falls	.966	26	11	17	1	3
Lind, Vermont	1.000	1	0	3	0	0
Little, Nashua*	1.000	10	1	2	0	0

PITCHERS—Continued

Player and Club	Pct.	G.	PO.	A.	E.	DP.
Lochner, Vermont*	.917	23	7	15	2	2
Lugo, Waterbury	.925	24	16	21	3	4
Mack, Waterbury	.966	25	7	21	1	1
Maddux, Reading	.973	20	12	24	1	2
Maitland, Nashua*	1.000	19	5	6	0	1
Manzanillo, Nashua*	1.000	14	2	12	0	0
Marcheskie, Nashua	.935	45	9	20	2	3
Marsden, Buffalo	.957	43	9	13	1	1
McCarthy, New Britain	1.000	38	10	15	0	1
McCullock, Buffalo	.750	24	1	2	1	0
McDonald, Albany	1.000	6	1	0	0	0
McKeon, Glens Falls*	1.000	45	3	13	0	0
Mecerod, New Britain	1.000	8	5	6	0	0
Miglio, Buffalo*	1.000	14	1	2	0	0
Mohorcic, Nashua	1.000	28	9	21	0	2
Moncrief, Glens Falls	.667	12	2	6	4	0
Montgomery, Vermont	1.000	22	1	3	0	0
M. Murphy, Buffalo	.938	9	5	10	1	4
R. Murphy, Vermont*	.875	45	1	13	2	1
Myers, Albany	1.000	12	10	12	0	0
Myles, Buffalo*	1.000	8	0	2	0	0
Oliver, Waterbury	.880	35	8	14	3	1
Olson, Reading	1.000	22	9	7	0	0
Ortiz, Buffalo*	1.000	29	3	10	0	0
Palacios, Glens Falls	.667	5	3	1	2	0
Pierorazio, Buffalo*	1.000	10	0	8	0	0
Pippin, Nashua	1.000	16	4	18	0	0
Price, Waterbury	1.000	19	5	12	0	3
Pruneda, Waterbury	1.000	14	3	5	0	0
Rice, Nashua	1.000	20	3	5	0	0
Rincon, Nashua	1.000	6	1	7	0	1
Roche, Buffalo	.846	9	5	6	2	0
R. Rodriguez, Albany	.889	10	2	6	1	0
Rollins, Reading	.917	24	9	13	2	0
Roman, Buffalo	.955	27	9	12	1	0
Romero, Buffalo*	1.000	11	0	9	0	1
Ruzek, Glens Falls	.939	13	10	21	2	1
Santarelli, Buffalo	.700	6	4	3	3	0
Sauveur, Nashua*	1.000	10	4	19	0	0
Schmid, New Britain*	.950	38	8	30	2	2
Scott, Vermont	.870	29	8	12	3	2
Seiler, Reading*	.875	12	1	6	1	1
Senteney, Nashua	.917	25	3	8	1	0
D. Smith, Waterbury	1.000	36	7	16	0	1
M. Smith, Vermont	.571	35	1	3	3	0
Stalp, Vermont	.914	23	9	23	3	0
Straker, Albany	.913	28	6	15	2	1
Stranski, Glens Falls	.950	33	7	12	1	1
Strichek, Albany	1.000	8	0	4	0	0
Surhoff, Reading	1.000	62	4	14	0	0
Susce, Nashua	.938	20	9	21	2	0
Szymczak, Buffalo	.909	12	2	8	1	0
Tanzi, Glens Falls*	.800	6	2	2	1	1
Terry, Vermont	.970	20	14	18	1	2
Thompson, Buffalo	.900	51	4	23	3	3
L. Trujillo, Vermont	.875	19	5	2	1	0
M. Trujillo, Glens Falls	.951	20	14	25	2	2
Warner, Reading*	.933	19	4	10	1	0
Wheeler, Nashua	.821	21	8	15	5	0
Wise, Vermont	.929	20	2	11	1	2
Woodward, New Britain	.896	28	18	25	5	1
Zmudosky, Albany	.974	33	5	33	1	4

The following players do not have any recorded accepted chances at the positions indicated; therefore, are not listed in the fielding averages for those particular positions: Bustabad, of; Cappadona, p; S. Davis, of; Guante, p; Hudson, p; Ibarra, of; Kobernus, p; Lavalliere, p; McClendon, of; Mesa, p; Morse, 2b; Pacho, p; Polidor, p; Pratt, p; Pryor, p; E. Rodriguez, c, p; Steinbach, 3b; Stephens, p; Wilson, 1b.

CLUB PITCHING

Club	ERA.	G.	CG.	ShO.	Sv.	IP.	H.	R.	ER.	HR.	HB.	BB.	Int. BB.	SO.	WP.	Bk.
Vermont	3.13	140	28	19	39	1182.2	1089	541	411	50	17	479	24	735	58	13
Albany	3.28	139	23	11	38	1167.1	1104	516	426	58	25	485	30	658	59	8
Glens Falls	3.64	139	25	11	32	1152.1	1125	581	466	73	31	524	22	736	58	7
New Britain	3.73	140	20	5	35	1162.0	1134	583	482	45	40	436	14	743	46	12
Waterbury	3.87	140	37	13	22	1198.0	1164	631	515	67	40	526	22	756	57	7
Nashua	3.96	140	28	14	11	1191.1	1096	640	524	61	36	624	43	786	72	16
Reading	4.00	139	11	6	29	1151.2	1239	658	512	59	19	534	43	667	69	9
Buffalo	4.50	139	32	10	32	1165.1	1158	687	583	116	38	567	16	769	81	8

PITCHERS' RECORDS
(Leading Qualifiers for Earned-Run Average Leadership — 112 or More Innings)

*Throws lefthanded.

Pitcher—Club	W.	L.	Pct.	ERA.	G.	GS.	CG.	GF.	ShO.	Sv.	IP.	H.	R.	ER.	HR.	HB.	BB.	Int. BB.	SO.	WP.
Terry, Vermont	14	3	.824	1.50	20	20	9	0	6	0	144.0	110	31	24	1	1	43	0	100	5
Drabek, Glens Falls	12	5	.706	2.24	19	17	7	2	3	0	124.2	90	34	31	6	2	44	2	75	6
M. Trujillo, Glens Falls	13	3	.813	2.37	20	19	5	0	1	0	121.2	107	47	32	7	1	25	1	69	4
Bastian, Waterbury	11	8	.579	2.65	29	19	10	5	4	1	159.1	153	61	47	5	4	40	0	119	7
Stalp, Vermont	10	8	.556	2.69	23	23	3	0	2	0	133.2	124	66	40	3	2	54	1	50	11
Hallas, Albany	7	4	.636	2.78	19	18	3	0	0	0	120.0	114	43	37	7	4	35	3	53	3
Lugo, Waterbury	13	8	.619	2.79	24	24	9	0	1	0	164.1	135	63	51	5	0	68	0	117	7
M. Johnson, New Britain	11	10	.524	2.89	26	26	7	0	0	0	174.1	160	60	56	7	4	30	1	94	2
Knox, Vermont	13	8	.619	2.97	27	27	7	0	2	0	185.0	178	78	61	6	4	39	3	76	5
Mack, Waterbury	11	8	.579	3.26	25	25	6	0	4	0	171.1	155	67	62	9	6	74	4	83	2

Departmental Leaders: G—Childress, Surhoff, 62; W—Lambert, 17; L—Kammeyer, Maddux, Schmid, Woodward, 12; Pct.—Terry, .824; GS—Grimm, Knox, Lambert, Woodward, 27; CG—Bastian, 10; GF—Surhoff, 50; ShO—Terry, 6; Sv.—R. Murphy, Surhoff, 15; IP—Knox, 185.0; H—Knox, 178; R—Kammeyer, 102; ER—Kammeyer, 84; HR—Doyle, 19; HB—Woodward, 12; BB—DeVincenzo, 77; IBB—Childress, 13; SO—Bastian, 119; WP—Lambert, 17.

(All Pitchers—Listed Alphabetically)

Pitcher—Club	W.	L.	Pct.	ERA.	G.	GS.	CG.	GF.	ShO.	Sv.	IP.	H.	R.	ER.	HR.	HB.	BB.	Int. BB.	SO.	WP.
Arnold, Reading*	5	5	.500	3.03	49	7	1	8	0	0	107.0	110	49	36	1	2	44	5	68	5
Ashman, Albany	0	1	.000	4.26	3	0	0	3	0	0	6.1	5	3	3	1	0	2	1	1	0
Bailes, Albany*	6	8	.429	3.41	54	1	0	34	0	3	87.0	80	43	33	4	2	46	10	61	8
Baller, Buffalo	4	5	.444	4.54	14	13	4	1	2	0	79.1	73	50	40	6	7	48	0	74	6
Banks, Buffalo	1	3	.250	5.49	8	6	1	2	0	0	39.1	45	29	24	7	0	16	0	21	1
Bastian, Waterbury	11	8	.579	2.65	29	19	10	5	4	1	159.1	153	61	47	5	4	40	0	119	7
Bauer, Albany	7	2	.778	2.30	17	15	3	1	2	1	105.2	99	34	27	1	2	32	1	56	1
Belcher, Albany	3	4	.429	3.33	10	10	2	0	0	0	54.0	37	30	20	2	3	41	0	40	2
Birrell, New Britain*	3	10	.231	5.82	22	15	2	4	0	0	89.2	96	67	58	6	4	62	3	56	8
Bohnet, Buffalo*	5	4	.556	4.14	26	12	4	11	1	3	111.0	115	70	51	10	1	55	1	63	6
Bolton, New Britain*	4	5	.444	4.14	33	5	0	11	0	1	87.0	87	54	40	5	4	34	3	66	6
Bryden, Waterbury	2	3	.400	2.93	25	0	0	13	0	4	43.0	35	22	14	2	5	25	1	38	4
Buchanan, Vermont*	1	2	.333	2.18	14	0	0	12	0	6	20.2	14	8	5	0	0	14	1	18	1
Buckle, Waterbury	1	3	.250	5.85	22	10	0	5	0	0	80.0	85	67	52	3	4	57	2	56	14
Bullinger, Vermont*	1	2	.333	4.62	21	2	0	8	0	3	37.0	38	27	19	2	1	23	4	31	1
Bulls, Reading	5	8	.385	4.52	19	17	2	0	1	0	95.2	105	59	48	3	4	51	3	51	8
Cappadona, New Britain*	0	0	.000	0.00	2	0	0	3	0	2	3.1	2	0	0	0	0	2	0	1	0

Pitcher—Club	W.	L.	Pct.	ERA.	G.	GS.	CG.	GF.	ShO.	Sv.	IP.	H.	R.	ER.	HR.	HB.	BB.	Int. BB.	SO.	WP.
Childress, Reading	7	6	.538	2.96	62	0	0	40	0	11	103.1	107	38	34	4	3	40	13	50	4
Clements, Waterbury☆	4	2	.667	2.69	43	2	1	28	0	9	67.0	59	28	20	2	3	29	4	44	6
Cole, Reading	3	4	.429	1.98	10	10	0	0	0	0	63.2	64	26	14	1	0	21	2	38	1
Dale, New Britain	5	2	.714	2.15	36	0	0	30	0	12	58.2	49	18	14	1	0	12	0	45	0
C. Davis, New Britain	5	8	.385	4.54	22	19	2	0	0	0	111.0	114	63	56	7	2	56	0	56	4
J. Davis, Glens Falls	1	2	.333	7.71	4	4	0	0	0	0	11.2	12	13	10	1	0	14	0	9	1
Dempsey, Glens Falls	6	10	.375	4.42	25	21	3	2	1	1	126.1	128	69	62	14	3	41	0	100	5
Denman, New Britain	4	1	.800	2.51	13	10	0	2	0	2	61.0	63	21	17	3	4	10	0	39	0
DeVincenzo, Glens Falls☆	8	5	.615	3.97	25	24	1	0	0	0	127.0	124	71	56	10	1	77	1	98	6
Doyle, Buffalo	7	11	.389	5.66	25	21	4	1	1	1	119.1	125	86	75	19	5	56	1	67	6
Dozier, Albany	6	5	.545	2.92	44	5	1	26	0	8	89.1	74	37	29	3	2	34	3	57	5
Drabek, Glens Falls	12	5	.706	2.24	19	17	7	2	3	0	124.2	90	34	31	6	2	44	2	75	6
Ellsworth, New Britain	1	1	.500	2.95	3	3	0	0	0	0	21.1	18	8	7	2	0	5	0	12	0
Ferguson, Reading	3	8	.273	5.02	18	14	0	1	0	1	86.0	114	64	48	4	1	28	1	26	1
Fischer, Albany	2	9	.182	4.73	30	10	0	12	0	4	85.2	105	56	45	6	1	45	4	56	7
Fryer, Nashua	0	0	.000	5.63	5	0	0	4	0	0	8.0	6	5	5	0	1	7	0	5	1
Fuson, Buffalo	4	0	1.000	1.63	7	4	2	1	1	0	38.2	26	11	7	2	1	18	1	37	2
Geiger, Glens Falls	5	5	.500	3.16	47	2	1	27	1	9	79.2	80	32	28	3	5	54	5	44	8
Gering, New Britain	3	3	.500	2.67	38	4	0	18	0	3	91.0	84	37	27	3	3	32	0	63	3
Ghelfi, Reading	0	2	.000	9.45	4	4	0	0	0	0	13.1	13	14	14	1	1	19	0	12	2
Gonzales, Reading	3	3	.500	3.45	7	7	3	0	1	0	47.0	46	24	18	2	0	18	0	24	2
Gonzalez, Nashua	4	9	.308	3.65	23	19	5	2	3	0	128.1	129	67	52	9	2	49	5	74	1
Griffin, Reading☆	2	1	.667	1.60	38	1	0	17	0	2	78.2	53	30	14	6	2	36	2	80	4
Grimm, Vermont	10	11	.476	3.88	27	27	5	0	1	0	155.1	147	81	67	12	3	56	2	85	4
Groh, Waterbury☆	1	1	.500	10.69	9	1	0	6	0	1	16.0	21	19	19	4	0	16	2	18	2
Guante, Nashua	0	0	.000	3.00	1	1	0	0	0	0	3.0	5	1	1	0	0	0	0	2	0
Hall, New Britain	0	0	.000	7.11	5	0	0	5	0	0	6.1	7	5	5	1	0	3	0	3	0
Hallas, Albany	7	4	.636	2.78	19	18	3	0	0	0	120.0	114	43	37	7	4	35	3	53	3
Hardy, Glens Falls	7	8	.467	4.63	32	18	3	7	0	1	122.1	143	72	63	11	7	42	1	66	2
Hickey, Glens Falls☆	0	0	.000	5.40	3	0	0	1	0	0	1.2	5	1	1	1	0	0	0	1	0
Hudson, Albany	0	1	.000	2.45	4	0	0	4	0	2	3.2	5	1	1	0	0	0	0	3	0
Jefferson, Vermont	0	4	.000	7.31	7	4	0	3	0	0	28.1	44	25	23	1	0	12	1	22	1
D. Johnson, Nashua	1	8	.111	4.84	12	12	4	0	0	0	83.2	95	52	45	2	3	31	1	47	7
M. Johnson, New Britain	11	10	.524	2.89	26	26	7	0	0	0	174.1	160	60	56	7	4	30	1	94	2
Kaiser, Albany☆	5	1	.833	1.89	7	7	1	0	1	0	47.2	36	11	10	0	1	15	0	20	1
Kammeyer, Waterbury	7	12	.368	6.32	22	22	6	0	1	0	119.2	136	102	84	9	5	63	0	86	6
Kane, New Britain	2	4	.333	3.49	12	6	0	4	0	0	49.0	52	22	19	2	1	13	2	29	1
Kendrick, Albany☆	2	3	.400	2.85	43	1	0	26	0	10	75.2	63	29	24	8	1	39	5	47	3
Knox, Vermont	13	8	.619	2.97	27	27	7	0	2	0	185.0	178	78	61	6	4	39	3	76	5
Kobernus, Albany☆	0	0	.000	10.80	4	0	0	2	0	0	5.0	11	7	6	1	0	4	0	2	0
Konderla, Vermont	1	1	.500	4.87	15	0	0	4	1	0	20.1	19	12	11	2	0	19	1	19	3
Kristan, Glens Falls	6	5	.545	3.20	57	0	0	36	0	13	146.0	90	48	52	4	4	38	2	38	0
Kromy, Reading	1	0	1.000	1.33	8	0	0	2	0	0	20.1	13	5	3	0	0	11	1	13	0
Kyles, Albany	4	4	.500	3.50	25	9	0	14	0	6	64.1	58	28	25	4	1	30	0	29	6
Lambert, Albany	17	9	.654	3.71	27	27	5	0	1	0	179.1	169	84	74	10	0	74	2	97	17
Lamonde, Nashua	1	1	.500	6.89	4	3	0	1	0	0	15.2	18	18	12	1	0	15	1	11	2
Lavalliere, Reading	0	0	.000	18.00	1	0	0	1	0	0	1.0	3	2	2	0	0	1	0	1	0
Layton, Glens Falls	2	3	.400	3.42	26	4	1	8	1	2	68.1	70	35	26	3	0	32	2	24	4
Lind, Vermont	0	1	.000	2.25	1	1	0	0	0	0	4.0	8	8	1	0	0	3	0	2	0
Little, Nashua☆	2	0	1.000	1.54	10	0	0	6	0	1	11.2	7	4	2	0	0	7	0	9	0
Lochner, Vermont☆	10	7	.588	3.29	23	22	3	0	1	0	139.2	125	61	51	9	3	55	0	78	6
Lugo, Waterbury	13	8	.619	2.79	24	24	9	0	1	0	164.1	135	63	51	5	0	68	0	117	7
Mack, Waterbury	11	8	.579	3.26	25	25	6	0	4	0	171.1	155	67	62	9	6	74	4	83	2
Maddux, Reading	3	12	.200	5.04	20	19	4	2	0	0	116.0	143	82	65	10	2	49	2	77	12
Maitland, Nashua☆	3	8	.273	5.77	19	15	2	1	0	0	93.2	112	70	60	6	2	67	4	44	2
Manzanillo, Nashua☆	4	4	.500	4.24	14	13	2	0	1	0	74.1	56	40	35	6	1	62	1	50	6
Marcheskie, Nashua	7	7	.500	3.45	45	4	1	20	0	2	101.2	87	45	39	3	8	57	6	72	9
Marsden, Buffalo	4	3	.571	3.52	42	3	0	19	0	6	102.1	109	46	40	11	0	36	0	37	9
McCarthy, New Britain	8	5	.615	3.06	38	1	0	27	0	8	79.1	71	35	27	0	1	56	1	65	3
McCullock, Buffalo	3	3	.500	5.76	24	0	0	15	0	3	29.2	38	24	19	7	1	24	2	35	1
McDonald, Albany	1	0	1.000	1.13	6	0	0	5	0	2	8.0	7	3	1	1	0	0	0	8	1
McKeon, Glens Falls☆	2	3	.400	3.65	45	5	0	10	0	2	66.2	53	33	27	1	3	46	1	56	3
Mecerod, New Britain	3	3	.500	4.30	8	8	0	0	0	0	44.0	47	30	21	3	3	18	0	30	2
Mesa, Glens Falls	0	0	.000	0.00	1	0	0	1	0	0	1.0	2	1	0	0	0	0	0	0	0
Miglio, Buffalo☆	1	0	1.000	5.71	14	0	0	10	0	6	17.1	15	11	11	3	1	10	0	22	2
Mohorcic, Nashua	2	4	.333	4.39	28	4	0	15	0	4	65.2	59	38	32	3	2	25	3	41	6
Moncrief, Glens Falls	3	3	.500	7.50	12	1	1	5	0	0	30.0	32	27	25	3	1	19	4	18	4
Montgomery, Vermont	2	0	1.000	2.13	22	0	0	11	0	4	25.1	14	7	6	0	0	24	2	25	3
M. Murphy, Buffalo	2	4	.333	6.25	9	9	0	0	0	0	40.1	50	29	28	3	3	27	0	20	3
R. Murphy, Vermont☆	2	4	.333	2.71	45	1	0	25	0	15	69.2	57	23	21	0	1	35	3	69	7
Myers, Albany	8	2	.800	1.35	12	12	5	0	3	0	86.2	58	17	13	3	1	25	0	63	2
Myles, Buffalo☆	1	2	.333	11.57	8	0	0	2	0	0	11.2	12	16	15	2	3	16	0	7	0
Oliver, Waterbury	12	3	.800	2.14	35	2	0	16	0	1	105.0	85	33	25	3	1	35	7	47	2
Olson, Reading	6	10	.375	5.51	22	20	0	0	0	0	111.0	128	73	68	7	2	74	3	46	12
Ortiz, Buffalo☆	5	8	.385	5.11	29	17	3	7	1	1	111.0	109	70	63	12	3	52	3	84	10
Pacho, Glens Falls	0	0	.000	0.00	1	0	0	1	0	0	1.0	0	0	0	0	0	0	0	1	0
Palacios, Glens Falls	1	2	.333	2.49	5	0	0	2	0	0	25.1	23	12	7	0	0	11	0	10	1
Pierorazio, Buffalo☆	1	0	1.000	4.82	10	1	0	4	0	0	28.0	28	20	15	4	1	17	0	13	4
Pippin, Nashua	3	4	.429	2.10	16	9	2	4	0	0	68.2	52	30	16	2	4	31	3	52	8
Polidor, Waterbury	0	0	.000	0.00	1	0	0	1	0	0	1.0	0	0	0	0	0	0	0	0	0
Pratt, Vermont	0	0	.000	0.00	1	0	0	1	0	0	1.0	0	1	0	0	0	1	0	1	0
Price, Waterbury	6	6	.500	4.24	19	18	2	1	0	1	108.1	119	61	51	9	3	39	1	50	1
Pruneda, Waterbury	3	4	.429	6.67	14	10	1	1	1	0	59.1	79	57	44	10	1	40	0	37	2
Pryor, Vermont	0	0	.000	0.00	1	0	0	0	0	0	1.0	0	0	0	0	0	1	0	0	0
Rice, Nashua	5	3	.625	3.74	20	7	2	7	0	0	65.0	47	30	27	0	1	53	3	50	8
Rincon, Nashua	2	2	.500	2.05	6	6	1	0	0	0	44.0	32	11	10	2	1	17	0	38	2
Roche, Buffalo	4	3	.571	2.69	9	9	5	0	0	0	63.2	56	25	19	3	2	14	0	20	0
E. Rodriguez, Waterbury☆	0	0	.000	13.50	2	0	0	2	0	0	2.2	9	4	4	0	0	1	0	1	1
R. Rodriguez, Albany	5	1	.833	5.27	10	9	0	0	0	0	42.2	59	33	25	3	3	19	0	29	4
Rollins, Reading	4	7	.364	4.73	24	16	0	1	0	0	91.1	97	63	48	8	0	47	5	41	6
Roman, Buffalo	14	6	.700	3.88	27	24	6	1	3	0	143.2	130	69	62	8	9	63	1	105	10
Romero, Buffalo☆	3	4	.429	5.61	11	11	1	0	1	0	51.1	56	35	32	3	3	33	0	41	3

Pitcher—Club	W.	L.	Pct.	ERA.	G.	GS.	CG.	GF.	ShO.	Sv.	IP.	H.	R.	ER.	HR.	HB.	BB.	Int. BB.	SO.	WP.
Ruzek, Glens Falls	5	5	.500	4.31	13	12	3	0	0	0	79.1	84	46	38	4	3	41	0	41	5
Santarelli, Buffalo	3	1	.750	3.56	6	6	2	0	0	0	43.0	37	21	17	0	1	18	0	36	4
Sauveur, Nashua°	5	3	.625	2.93	10	10	2	0	2	0	70.2	54	27	23	4	3	34	1	48	2
Schmid, New Britain°	5	12	.294	4.80	38	12	6	16	0	7	120.0	117	76	64	4	2	38	1	84	8
Scott, Vermont°	6	8	.429	2.83	29	13	1	10	0	1	98.2	92	38	31	8	0	37	2	62	5
Seiler, Reading°	2	4	.333	6.42	12	6	0	5	0	0	33.2	48	33	24	4	0	17	0	9	4
Senteney, Nashua	1	3	.250	3.80	25	1	0	15	0	1	47.1	42	24	20	1	1	21	2	32	2
D. Smith, Waterbury	5	6	.455	3.55	36	7	2	24	0	5	99.0	88	43	39	6	8	36	1	60	3
M. Smith, Vermont	3	3	.500	3.35	35	0	0	23	0	6	51.0	51	28	19	2	0	20	3	49	4
Stalp, Vermont	10	8	.556	2.69	23	23	3	0	2	0	133.2	124	66	40	3	2	54	1	50	11
Stephens, Waterbury°	0	0	.000	13.50	2	0	0	2	0	0	2.0	5	4	3	0	0	2	0	0	0
Straker, Albany	6	5	.545	4.23	28	12	2	8	0	1	95.2	97	55	45	6	2	43	3	60	3
Stranski, Glens Falls	4	2	.667	2.50	33	3	0	12	0	3	72.0	61	26	20	4	1	27	3	70	7
Strichek, Albany	0	1	.000	8.53	8	1	0	1	0	0	12.2	24	12	12	0	1	5	0	11	0
Surhoff, Reading	7	6	.538	3.09	62	0	0	50	0	15	87.1	79	42	30	3	0	39	5	75	2
Susce, Nashua	9	7	.563	3.37	20	20	6	0	4	0	131.0	100	57	49	8	5	44	0	103	7
Szymczak, Buffalo	1	3	.250	7.55	12	1	0	5	0	2	31.0	38	27	26	8	0	17	1	6	2
Tanzi, Glens Falls°	0	2	.000	6.62	6	4	0	2	0	1	17.2	21	14	13	1	0	13	0	16	2
Terry, Vermont	14	3	.824	1.50	20	20	9	0	6	0	144.0	110	31	24	1	1	43	0	100	5
Thompson, Buffalo	9	7	.563	3.35	51	2	0	28	0	10	104.2	96	48	39	7	3	47	6	81	12
L. Trujillo, Vermont	0	3	.000	5.50	19	0	0	6	0	1	34.1	33	30	21	3	2	28	1	29	2
M. Trujillo, Glens Falls	13	3	.813	2.37	20	19	5	0	1	0	121.2	107	47	32	7	1	25	1	69	4
Warner, Reading°	5	7	.417	4.30	19	18	1	1	0	0	96.1	116	54	46	5	2	39	1	56	6
Wheeler, Nashua	3	11	.214	6.16	21	15	1	3	0	0	92.0	115	78	63	10	0	58	3	47	1
Wise, Vermont	2	1	.667	3.21	20	0	0	8	0	2	33.2	32	18	12	1	0	16	0	24	2
Woodward, New Britain	10	12	.455	3.96	28	27	3	0	0	0	166.0	167	87	73	1	12	65	3	100	9
Zmudosky, Albany	8	5	.615	3.07	33	3	1	14	0	4	85.0	83	33	29	2	3	42	8	26	4

BALKS—Sauveur, 4; M. Johnson, Lochner, M. Smith, Warner, 3 each; Bolton, Gonzales, Knox, Kristan, Marsden, Mecerod, Oliver, Price, Pruneda, Rice, Roman, Schmid, Susce, L. Trujillo, M. Trujillo, 2 each; Ashman, Bauer, Belcher, Buchanan, C. Davis, Dempsey, Denman, Dozier, Ferguson, Fischer, Fryer, Gonzalez, Hardy, D. Johnson, Kaiser, Kendrick, Kromy, Lambert, Lamonde, Lugo, Maitland, Manzanillo, Montgomery, Ortiz, Pierorazio, Pippin, Roche, Rollins, Seiler, Stranski, Szymczak, Terry, Wheeler, Woodward, 1 each.

COMBINATION SHUTOUTS—Myers-Kendrick-Dozier, Lambert-Kyles, Lambert-Zmudosky-Dozier, Lambert-Kendrick, Albany; Hardy-Stranski-McKeon-Kristan, Palacios-Stranski, Hardy-Stranski, Trujillo-McKeon-Kristan, Glens Falls; Rice-Bailes-Little, Rincon-Pippin, Rice-Senteney, Susce-Bailes, Nashua; Mecerod-Dale, Woodward-Schmid-Gering, Johnson-Schmid, McCarthy-Dale, Denman-Dale, New Britain; Ferguson-Childress-Surhoff, Maddux-Arnold-Surhoff, Bulls-Ferguson, Warner-Surhoff, Reading; Lochner-Murphy 2, Terry-Buchanan, Stalp-Bullinger, Stalp-Montgomery-Murphy, Lochner-Montgomery, Scott-Montgomery-Murphy, Vermont; Kammeyer-Oliver, Smith-Bryden, Waterbury.

NO-HIT GAMES—Myers, Albany, defeated Vermont, 2-0 (seven innings, first game), May 31; Susce, Nashua, defeated Waterbury, 4-0 (seven innings, first game), August 11.

Southern League

CLASS AA

**Leading Batter
DOC ESTES
Greenville**

**League President
JIMMY BRAGAN**

**Leading Pitcher
MARK WILLIAMS
Jacksonville**

CHAMPIONSHIP WINNERS IN PREVIOUS YEARS

1904—Macon	.598	
1905—Macon	.625	
1906—Savannah	.637	
1907—Charleston	.620	
1908—Jacksonville	.694	
1909—Chattanooga*	.738	
Augusta	.702	
1910—Columbus	.588	
1911—Columbus*	.681	
Columbia	.710	
1912—Jacksonville*	.679	
Columbus	.632	
1913—Savannah	.754	
Savannah	.593	
1914—Savannah*	.667	
Albany	.650	
1915—Macon	.588	
Columbus*	.686	
1916—Augusta*	.617	
Columbia	.631	
1917—Charleston	.741	
Columbia*	.667	
1918—Did not operate.		
1919—Columbia	.585	
1920—Columbia	.633	
1921—Columbia	.642	
1922—Charleston	.625	
1923—Charlotte*	.653	
Macon	.580	
1924—Augusta	.612	
1925—Spartanburg	.620	
1926—Greenville	.662	
1927—Greenville	.622	
1928—Asheville	.664	
1929—Asheville	.605	
Knoxville*	.634	
1930—Greenville*	.620	
Macon	.643	
1931-35—Did not operate.		

1936—Jacksonville	.652	
Columbus*	.650	
1937—Columbus	.572	
Savannah (3rd)†	.565	
1938—Savannah	.574	
Macon (2nd)†	.570	
1939—Columbus	.601	
Augusta (2nd)†	.597	
1940—Savannah	.627	
Columbus (2nd)†	.583	
1941—Macon	.643	
Columbia (2nd)†	.636	
1942—Charleston	.620	
Macon (2nd)†	.585	
1943-45—Did not operate.		
1946—Columbus	.568	
Augusta (4th)†	.547	
1947—Columbus	.575	
Savannah (2nd)†	.563	
1948—Charleston	.572	
Greenville (3rd)†	.549	
1949—Macon‡	.623	
1950—Macon‡	.588	
1951—Montgomery	.607	
1952—Columbus	.649	
Montgomery (3rd)†	.558	
1953—Jacksonville	.679	
Savannah (2nd)†	.571	
1954—Jacksonville	.593	
Savannah (2nd)†	.571	
1955—Columbia	.636	
Augusta (3rd)†	.543	
1956—Jacksonville‡	.621	
1957—Augusta	.636	
Charlotte (2nd)†	.562	
1958—Augusta	.550	
Macon (3rd)†	.500	
1959—Knoxville	.557	
Gastonia (4th)†	.504	

1960—Columbia	.597	
Savannah (3rd)†	.561	
1961—Asheville	.635	
1962—Savannah	.662	
Macon (3rd)†	.576	
1963—Augusta*	.661	
Lynchburg	.662	
1964—Lynchburg	.579	
1965—Columbus	.572	
1966—Mobile	.629	
1967—Birmingham	.604	
1968—Asheville	.614	
1969—Charlotte	.579	
1970—Columbus	.569	
1971—Did not operate as league—clubs were members of Dixie Association.		
1972—Asheville	.583	
Montgomery§	.561	
1973—Montgomery§	.580	
Jacksonville	.559	
1974—Jacksonville	.565	
Knoxville§	.533	
1975—Orlando	.587	
Montgomery§	.545	
1976—Montgomery x	.591	
Orlando	.540	
1977—Montgomery x	.628	
Jacksonville	.522	
1978—Knoxville x	.611	
Savannah	.500	
1979—Columbus x	.587	
Nashville x	.576	
1980—Memphis	.576	
Charlotte x	.500	
1981—Nashville	.566	
Orlando x	.556	
1982—Jacksonville	.576	
Nashville x	.535	
1983—Birmingham x	.628	
Jacksonville	.531	

*Won split-season playoff. †Won four-club playoff. ‡Won championship and four-club playoff. §League was divided into Eastern and Western divisions; won playoff. xLeague was divided into Eastern and Western divisions and played split season; won playoff.

STANDING OF CLUBS AT CLOSE OF FIRST HALF, JUNE 20

EASTERN DIVISION

Club	W.	L.	T.	Pct.	G.B.
Greenville (Braves)	38	33	0	.535	....
Jacksonville (Expos)	35	31	0	.530	½
Orlando (Twins)	34	35	0	.493	3
Columbus (Astros)	34	37	0	.479	4
Charlotte (Orioles)	29	43	0	.403	9½

WESTERN DIVISION

Club	W.	L.	T.	Pct.	G.B.
Knoxville (Blue Jays)	41	30	0	.577	....
Nashville (Yankees)	38	33	0	.535	3
Memphis (Royals)	37	33	0	.529	3½
Chattanooga (Mariners)	32	34	0	.485	6½
Birmingham (Tigers)	31	40	0	.437	10

STANDING OF CLUBS AT CLOSE OF SECOND HALF, SEPTEMBER 6

EASTERN DIVISION

Club	W.	L.	T.	Pct.	G.B.
Charlotte (Orioles)	46	29	0	.613	....
Orlando (Twins)	45	30	0	.600	1
Greenville (Braves)	42	28	0	.600	1½
Jacksonville (Expos)	41	38	0	.519	7
Columbus (Astros)	35	34	0	.507	8

WESTERN DIVISION

Club	W.	L.	T.	Pct.	G.B.
Nashville (Yankees)	36	40	0	.474	....
Birmingham (Tigers)	35	41	0	.461	1
Memphis (Royals)	34	42	0	.447	2
Chattanooga (Mariners)	31	47	0	.397	6
Knoxville (Blue Jays)	29	45	0	.392	6

Note: Charlotte defeated Orlando, 4-3, in one-game playoff for Eastern Division second-half title; Nashville defeated Birmingham, 3-2, in one-game playoff for Western Division second-half title.

COMPOSITE STANDING OF CLUBS AT CLOSE OF SEASON, SEPTEMBER 6

Club	Grn.	Orl.	Jax.	Char.	Nash.	Col.	Mem.	Knox.	Birm.	Chat.	W.	L.	T.	Pct.	G.B.
Greenville (Braves)	....	10	10	10	8	6	9	7	11	9	80	61	0	.567	....
Orlando (Twins)	6	....	11	12	11	6	9	7	8	9	79	65	0	.549	2½
Jacksonville (Expos)	6	7	....	9	9	8	9	10	9	9	76	69	0	.524	6
Charlotte (Orioles)	8	5	7	....	9	8	8	7	11	12	75	72	0	.510	8
Nashville (Yankees)	8	5	7	7	....	10	12	6	10	9	74	73	0	.503	9
Columbus (Astros)	6	8	8	8	6	....	8	12	6	7	69	71	0	.493	10½
Memphis (Royals)	7	7	7	8	6	8	....	10	11	7	71	75	0	.486	11½
Knoxville (Blue Jays)	8	9	6	9	10	6	6	....	8	8	70	75	0	.483	12
Birmingham (Tigers)	5	8	7	5	7	10	5	8	....	11	66	81	0	.449	17
Chattanooga (Mariners)	7	6	6	4	7	9	9	8	7	....	63	81	0	.438	18½

Major league affiliations in parentheses.

Playoffs—Charlotte defeated Greenville, three games to one; Knoxville defeated Nashville, three games to one; and Charlotte defeated Knoxville, three games to none, to win league championship.

Regular-Season Attendance—Birmingham, 175,958; Charlotte, 122,792; Chattanooga, 130,509; Columbus, 95,167; Greenville, 217,096; Jacksonville, 97,158; Knoxville, 100,576; Memphis, 208,851; Nashville, 372,701; Orlando, 72,258. Total, 1,593,066. Playoff attendance, 19,850. All-Star attendance, 3,179.

Managers—Birmingham, Roy Majtyka; Charlotte, Grady Little and John Hart; Chattanooga, Bill Plummer; Columbus, Bob Bailey and Jimmy Johnson; Greenville, Bobby Dews and Leo Mazzone; Jacksonville, Rick Renick; Knoxville, John McLaren; Memphis, Rick Mathews; Nashville, Jim Marshall; Orlando, Charlie Manuel.

All-Star Team—1B-Andres Galarraga, Jacksonville; 2B-Mike Sharperson, Knoxville; 3B-Bill Pecota, Memphis; SS-Keith Smith, Nashville; OF-Mickey Brantley, Chattanooga; Frank (Doc) Estes, Greenville; Ty Gainey, Columbus; Dan Pasqua, Nashville; C-Matt Sinatro, Greenville; DH-Stan Holmes, Orlando; RHP-Ken Dixon, Charlotte; LHP-Bryan Oelkers, Orlando. Most Valuable Player-Andres Galarraga, Jacksonville; Pitcher of the Year-Ken Dixon, Charlotte; Co-Managers of the Year-Charlie Manuel, Orlando, and Rick Renick, Jacksonville.

(Compiled by Howe News Bureau, Boston, Mass.)
CLUB BATTING

Club	Pct.	G.	AB.	R.	OR.	H.	TB.	2B.	3B.	HR.	RBI.	GW.	SH.	SF.	HP.	BB.	Int. BB.	SO.	SB.	CS.	LOB.
Birmingham	.271	147	4960	704	776	1342	1843	201	33	78	642	60	65	36	41	602	33	641	96	55	1153
Greenville	.268	141	4500	699	572	1208	1663	187	29	70	612	67	77	47	36	722	39	628	191	93	1089
Nashville	.263	147	4782	649	705	1259	1827	217	27	99	594	71	61	48	29	680	35	810	140	69	1156
Knoxville	.259	145	4744	605	605	1228	1703	180	41	71	523	57	34	41	22	481	37	842	104	73	989
Jacksonville	.258	145	4707	618	629	1213	1716	189	19	92	547	64	65	36	28	560	33	609	121	87	1026
Orlando	.256	144	4657	637	570	1192	1746	173	48	95	568	70	49	40	31	525	29	712	78	39	1016
Chattanooga	.255	144	4487	604	629	1142	1556	166	34	60	533	54	79	60	29	634	32	605	183	64	1061
Columbus	.247	140	4485	631	619	1109	1646	195	30	94	572	63	43	54	30	619	23	708	181	74	985
Charlotte	.244	147	4740	638	661	1156	1756	196	28	116	573	67	42	36	28	602	33	754	79	56	1016
Memphis	.232	146	4715	608	627	1096	1521	172	38	59	537	67	57	42	22	708	24	795	128	66	1114

INDIVIDUAL BATTING
(Leading Qualifiers for Batting Championship—394 or More Plate Appearances)

*Bats lefthanded.   †Switch-hitter.

Player and Club	Pct.	G.	AB.	R.	H.	TB.	2B.	3B.	HR.	RBI.	GW.	SH.	SF.	HP.	BB.	Int. BB.	SO.	SB.	CS.
Estes, Frank, Greenville*	.341	138	510	94	174	220	22	6	4	87	14	0	8	0	78	7	35	25	12
Brantley, Michael, Chattanooga	.316	131	472	73	149	221	21	9	11	76	8	12	10	0	52	3	44	23	7
Barrett, Thomas, Nashville†	.308	135	510	82	157	191	22	6	0	44	6	6	6	5	86	3	41	53	21
Cole, Michael, Greenville*	.305	137	502	105	153	182	11	6	2	38	6	7	2	7	110	0	60	85	30
Sharperson, Michael, Knoxville	.304	140	542	86	165	216	25	7	4	48	6	4	1	4	48	2	66	20	13
Hill, D. Clay, Chattanooga*	.303	104	330	55	100	126	11	3	3	34	3	13	2	1	72	5	39	7	3
Thompson, Tommy, Greenville*	.297	126	370	46	110	144	19	0	5	49	4	16	3	4	62	9	33	3	2
Dalena, Peter, Nashville*	.297	125	488	60	145	215	28	0	14	83	13	2	6	6	49	2	48	4	3
Kingery, Michael, Memphis*	.297	139	455	65	135	172	19	3	4	58	3	7	5	0	93	6	61	18	11
Galarraga, Andres, Jacksonville	.289	143	533	81	154	271	28	4	27	87	13	1	4	9	59	10	122	2	8
Lomastro, Gerardo, Orlando	.289	107	388	55	112	178	16	1	16	66	5	1	5	5	40	7	32	0	2
Trout, Jeffrey, Orlando†	.285	130	460	68	131	174	17	7	4	48	6	8	2	2	46	4	41	2	2
Davidson, J. Mark, Orlando	.284	114	348	55	99	134	11	6	4	37	5	0	4	3	52	1	57	15	4
Pittaro, Christopher, Birmingham†	.284	137	517	85	147	221	27	7	11	61	8	4	5	2	71	7	50	18	7
Bishop, James, Knoxville	.284	131	447	57	127	176	18	5	7	57	6	2	6	2	49	3	91	5	4

Departmental Leaders: G—Alfaro, 146; AB—M. Smith, 576; R—M. Cole, 105; H—Estes, 174; TB—Galarraga, 271; 2B—Curry, 32; 3B—Howe, 14; HR—Pasqua, 33; RBI—Holmes, 101; GWRBI—Pardo, 17; SH—P.K. Smith, 17; SF—Brantley, Strucher, 10; HP—Foussianes, Galarraga, Tovar, 9; BB—M. Cole, 110; IBB—Galarraga, 10; SO—Pasqua, 148; SB—Nixon, 102; CS—M. Cole, 30.

(All Players—Listed Alphabetically)

Player and Club	Pct.	G.	AB.	R.	H.	TB.	2B.	3B.	HR.	RBI.	GW.	SH.	SF.	HP.	BB.	Int. BB.	SO.	SB.	CS.
Acker, Larry, Columbus*	.182	28	11	1	2	2	0	0	0	1	0	1	0	0	2	0	1	0	0
Aitcheson, James, Knoxville*	.290	87	283	34	82	99	5	3	2	18	0	2	3	3	27	6	27	7	5

Player and Club	Pct.	G.	AB.	R.	H.	TB.	2B.	3B.	HR.	RBI.	GW.	SH.	SF.	HP.	BB.	Int. BB.	SO.	SB.	CS.
Alfaro, Jesus, Charlotte	.248	146	475	68	118	176	26	1	10	53	4	5	7	0	99	7	73	2	6
Arce, Lorenzo, Birmingham	.210	18	62	9	13	24	2	0	3	7	1	1	0	2	6	0	11	0	0
Ashmore, W. Mitchell, Memphis	.215	85	279	39	60	81	10	1	3	21	5	3	1	1	47	3	48	0	1
Auten, James, Charlotte	.207	35	116	10	24	36	3	0	3	15	1	0	2	1	5	0	17	1	1
Bailey, J. Mark, Columbus†	.283	17	53	5	15	22	3	2	0	9	0	1	0	0	11	1	12	0	0
Baker, Kenneth, Jacksonville°	.276	134	485	68	134	174	26	4	2	37	9	3	1	1	81	6	42	11	8
Bard, Paul, Charlotte	.226	40	93	11	21	38	5	0	4	17	2	0	0	1	10	0	29	0	0
Barrett, Thomas, Nashville†	.308	135	510	82	157	191	22	6	0	44	6	6	5	6	86	3	41	53	21
Barrett, Timothy, Jacksonville°	.000	2	2	0	0	0	0	0	0	0	0	0	0	0	0	0	1	0	0
Beauchamp, J. Kash, Knoxville	.400	3	10	3	4	7	0	0	1	3	1	0	0	0	1	0	2	1	0
Bell, Terence, Chattanooga	.143	2	7	1	1	1	0	0	0	0	0	0	0	0	1	0	1	0	0
Berti, Donald, Columbus	.161	13	31	3	5	6	1	0	0	1	0	1	0	0	9	0	3	0	0
Best, William, Memphis°	.269	98	305	50	82	118	18	0	6	48	2	8	5	1	83	2	50	10	4
Bishop, James, Knoxville	.284	131	447	57	127	176	18	5	7	57	6	2	6	2	49	3	91	5	4
Blaser, Mark, Nashville	.275	45	149	21	41	61	5	0	5	25	1	2	3	2	8	3	19	0	0
Bockhorn, Glen, Greenville	.242	124	359	61	87	136	16	0	11	61	8	3	6	2	69	3	52	0	2
Bormann, Michael, Greenville	.000	36	1	0	0	0	0	0	0	0	0	0	0	0	0	0	0	0	0
Brahs, Gary, Jacksonville°	.000	6	6	0	0	0	0	0	0	1	0	0	0	0	3	0	3	0	0
Brantley, Michael, Chattanooga	.316	131	472	73	149	221	21	9	11	76	8	12	10	0	52	3	44	23	7
Braun, Randall, Columbus°	.216	71	208	20	45	66	5	2	4	27	2	2	1	0	20	0	26	8	2
Brewer, Michael, Memphis	.225	35	129	17	29	39	4	0	2	23	3	0	2	1	23	0	29	10	2
Bullock, Eric, Columbus°	.291	71	265	47	77	105	15	2	3	41	5	1	4	1	36	4	23	41	7
Burke, Curtis, Columbus°	.169	26	71	10	12	21	0	0	3	6	0	0	0	1	8	0	22	0	1
Calhoun, Jeffrey, Columbus°	.000	37	2	0	0	0	0	0	0	0	0	0	0	0	0	0	0	0	0
Candaele, Casey, Jacksonville†	.273	132	532	68	145	178	23	2	2	53	3	5	6	1	30	1	35	26	18
Carl, Jeffrey, Jacksonville	.267	120	397	53	106	171	22	2	13	54	3	2	6	1	37	0	77	5	6
Carpenter, Glenn, Columbus	.202	35	94	15	19	28	3	0	2	14	2	0	2	1	15	0	18	1	0
Cates, Timothy, Jacksonville	.000	13	2	0	0	0	0	0	0	0	0	0	0	0	0	0	0	0	0
Chavez, Pedro, Birmingham	.237	60	228	26	54	65	8	0	1	25	4	7	0	1	19	0	22	8	5
Chmil, Stephen, Greenville	.261	77	184	18	48	50	2	0	0	16	1	8	0	3	20	2	28	6	6
Citari, Joseph, Memphis	.187	84	289	26	54	84	12	3	4	23	5	1	2	2	52	0	75	4	0
Clark, Henry, Columbus	.189	31	95	10	18	22	4	0	0	9	0	1	1	0	5	0	10	2	0
Clary, Martin, Greenville	.143	30	7	0	1	1	0	0	0	1	0	0	0	0	1	0	4	0	0
Clay, David, Greenville	.250	51	4	0	1	1	0	0	0	0	0	1	0	0	0	0	2	0	0
Clements, Wesley, Columbus	.234	84	290	41	68	135	13	0	18	66	8	0	7	3	44	5	76	2	2
Colbert, Richard, Columbus	.226	99	270	35	61	89	13	0	5	27	2	1	1	0	41	1	74	4	2
Cole, Michael, Greenville°	.305	137	502	105	153	182	11	6	2	38	6	7	2	7	110	0	60	85	30
Cole, Timothy, Greenville°	.500	31	2	0	1	1	0	0	0	0	0	0	0	0	0	0	0	0	0
Cormack, Terry, Greenville°	.107	11	28	4	3	4	1	0	0	1	1	0	1	0	5	1	11	0	0
Crabtree, Gary, Chattanooga	.343	9	35	5	12	17	1	2	0	3	0	0	0	0	4	0	3	0	0
Crist, Clark, Chattanooga	.222	2	9	1	2	3	1	0	0	4	0	1	0	0	0	0	0	0	0
Csefalvay, John, Nashville°	.246	112	370	42	91	141	22	2	8	40	5	0	4	1	56	6	58	5	3
Curry, Stephen, Greenville	.269	137	472	77	127	199	32	2	12	72	4	7	5	7	99	3	72	15	8
D'Onofrio, Gary, Columbus†	.189	40	74	11	14	16	2	0	0	7	1	0	0	1	11	0	7	0	2
Dalena, Peter, Nashville°	.297	125	488	60	145	215	28	0	14	83	13	2	6	6	49	2	48	4	3
Davidson, J. Mark, Orlando	.284	114	348	55	99	134	11	6	4	37	5	0	4	3	52	1	57	15	4
Delany, Dennis, Jacksonville	.258	72	198	13	51	63	6	0	2	27	2	4	2	0	25	2	30	1	0
Dempsey, Patrick, Nashville	.256	94	320	33	82	120	22	2	4	48	4	7	3	0	24	1	41	6	2
Destrade, Orestes, Nashville†	.240	35	121	15	29	53	6	0	6	12	2	0	1	0	15	0	36	0	1
Dewey, Duane, Nashville	.500	1	2	1	1	1	0	0	0	0	1	0	0	0	0	0	0	0	0
DeWillis, Jeffrey, Knoxville	.000	1	2	1	0	0	0	0	0	0	0	0	0	0	3	0	1	0	0
Diaz, Mario, Chattanooga	.208	108	322	23	67	79	7	1	1	19	1	13	5	0	21	0	18	6	5
Dopson, John, Jacksonville°	.077	26	13	1	1	2	1	0	0	0	0	0	2	0	0	0	4	0	0
Dumouchelle, Patrick, Charlotte	.219	105	315	35	69	104	11	0	8	28	2	2	2	0	34	1	37	7	4
Escobar, Jose, Knoxville	.235	96	340	40	80	104	13	4	1	45	6	2	4	2	14	0	56	6	2
Estepa, Ramon, Chattanooga	.260	112	366	53	95	121	14	3	2	45	6	5	3	2	54	1	63	2	3
Estes, Frank, Greenville°	.341	138	510	94	174	220	22	6	4	87	14	0	8	0	78	7	35	25	12
Eufemia, Frank, Orlando	.000	46	1	0	0	0	0	0	0	0	0	0	0	0	0	0	1	0	0
Falcone, David, Charlotte°	.259	69	224	25	58	87	15	1	4	33	8	3	3	2	32	3	41	2	2
Fielder, Cecil, Knoxville	.254	64	236	33	60	103	12	2	9	44	2	0	1		22	3	48	0	1
Fields, Bruce, Birmingham°	.300	93	307	49	92	121	11	3	4	38	5	10	4	1	31	1	34	11	12
Foley, Rickey, Columbus	.000	35	2	0	0	0	0	0	0	0	0	0	0	0	0	0	0	0	0
Followell, Vernon, Columbus†	.269	90	309	36	83	105	13	0	3	30	3	3	5	1	43	3	28	7	6
Foster, Kenneth, Orlando	.231	58	182	28	42	68	9	1	5	18	3	1	0	0	31	0	22	0	0
Foussianes, George, Birmingham	.262	116	393	56	103	150	18	1	9	54	3	0	3	9	77	0	70	6	4
Gainey, Telmanch, Columbus°	.276	133	467	85	129	200	28	2	13	78	11	2	5	4	59	2	83	39	12
Galarraga, Andres, Jacksonville	.289	143	533	81	154	271	28	4	27	87	13	1	4	9	59	10	122	2	8
Gallegos, Matthew, Nashville†	.203	33	79	18	16	17	1	0	0	5	2	0	0	0	25	0	10	11	3
Gerhart, H. Kenneth, Charlotte	.201	85	264	40	53	106	8	3	13	40	3	3	3	1	40	2	83	10	6
Gilbreath, Ronald, Jacksonville	.333	56	6	0	2	2	0	0	0	0	0	0	0	0	1	0	1	0	0
Gilcrease, Douglas, Memphis	.174	44	144	14	25	42	5	0	4	11	1	4	2	1	12	0	30	1	1
Glynn, Eugene, Jacksonville	.000	6	2	0	0	0	0	0	0	0	1	0	0	0	2	0	0	0	0
Gonzalez, Fernando, Nashville	.257	60	237	26	61	82	12	0	3	30	3	1	4	0	12	1	21	3	1
Granger, L. Randle, Charlotte†	.269	15	52	12	14	31	1	2	4	11	1	0	1	0	7	0	18	3	2
Griffin, Gregory, Knoxville	.176	40	102	14	18	27	3	0	2	4	2	1	1	2	24	3	25	1	3
Guerrero, Inocencio, Greenville	.268	132	444	78	119	180	23	4	10	80	8	0	3	3	62	2	88	4	2
Hanggie, Dan, Chattanooga†	.245	140	445	65	109	172	21	3	12	62	8	5	2	8	105	8	94	3	5
Hansen, Roger, Memphis	.217	93	327	32	71	90	10	0	3	31	9	2	1	0	39	1	41	4	2
Harsh, Nicholas, Columbus	.000	19	4	0	0	0	0	0	0	0	0	0	0	0	0	0	1	0	0
Hatcher, Harold, Memphis	.200	52	195	18	39	72	10	1	7	32	4	0	1	1	15	1	43	2	1
Hawkins, Johnny, Nashville†	.226	71	217	21	49	60	7	2	0	18	0	10	0	0	30	1	24	1	5
Hearron, Jeffrey, Knoxville	.250	81	240	30	60	90	9	0	7	28	5	1	1	2	47	2	36	1	2
Hegman, Robert, Memphis	.253	135	475	62	120	139	9	5	0	45	6	7	5	1	39	1	41	8	7
Hernandez, Juan M., Nashville	.143	4	7	0	1	1	0	0	0	0	0	0	0	0	0	0	0	0	0
Hertzler, Paul, Jacksonville°	.270	135	471	65	127	196	22	1	15	65	7	3	3	5	45	1	66	27	14
Hill, Anthony J., Chattanooga	.237	91	287	31	68	83	8	2	1	27	2	6	3	0	37	3	42	12	5
Hill, D. Clay, Chattanooga°	.303	104	330	55	100	126	11	3	3	34	3	13	2	1	72	5	39	7	3
Hocutt, Michael, Jacksonville°	.083	4	12	1	1	2	1	0	0	2	0	0	0	0	1	0	1	0	0
Hoeksema, David, Jacksonville	.270	145	552	74	149	210	21	2	12	71	6	2	4	6	37	3	74	6	1
Hogan, Michael, Columbus	.083	27	12	1	1	1	0	0	0	0	0	3	0	0	2	0	0	0	0
Holman, Q. Dale, Knoxville°	.244	23	78	9	19	21	2	0	0	5	1	0	2	0	16	2	14	2	0
Holmes, Stanley, Orlando	.280	142	507	71	142	246	25	2	25	101	16	0	4	3	61	3	113	1	0

| | | | | | | | | | | | | | | | | Int. | | | |
Player and Club	Pct.	G.	AB.	R.	H.	TB.	2B.	3B.	HR.	RBI.	GW.	SH.	SF.	HP.	BB.	BB.	SO.	SB.	CS.
Hotchkiss, John, Birmingham	.247	72	239	29	59	78	6	2	3	30	2	4	3	4	32	1	46	2	1
Howe, Gregory, Orlando	.255	139	466	83	119	205	22	14	12	61	3	6	4	5	77	0	82	32	11
Huber, Randolph, Jacksonville	.000	21	2	0	0	0	0	0	0	0	0	0	0	0	1	0	1	0	0
Hughes, Keith, Nashville*	.180	21	50	6	9	9	0	0	0	5	1	0	0	0	10	0	14	0	0
Infante, Alexis, Knoxville	.265	67	253	28	67	88	13	1	2	29	5	4	0	0	16	0	26	6	4
Ingle, Randy, Greenville	.187	32	75	5	14	16	2	0	0	8	1	5	1	0	5	1	12	0	0
Isherwood, Michael, Orlando	.223	99	287	32	64	80	8	1	2	23	2	8	4	1	32	0	34	0	2
Javier, Stanley, Nashville†	.290	76	262	40	76	122	17	4	7	38	4	1	1	1	39	1	57	17	5
Jefferson, James, Jacksonville	.000	8	2	0	0	0	0	0	0	0	0	0	0	0	0	0	1	0	0
Johnson, Bobby, Nashville	.214	5	14	0	3	3	0	0	0	2	0	0	0	0	2	0	5	0	0
Johnson, Joseph, Greenville	.182	24	11	0	2	2	0	0	0	2	0	1	0	0	4	0	2	0	0
Johnson, Wallace, Jacksonville†	.299	31	117	18	35	43	5	0	1	12	0	2	2	0	20	3	8	3	5
Johnston, Christopher, Knoxville	.245	106	359	38	88	133	17	2	8	36	4	0	2	5	35	1	84	2	2
Kasprzak, Michael, Columbus	.000	37	0	0	0	0	0	0	0	0	0	1	0	0	0	0	0	0	0
Kenaga, Jeffrey, Charlotte*	.238	52	143	13	34	53	9	2	2	10	2	1	1	0	20	3	20	2	0
Kerfeld, Charles, Columbus	.000	24	11	0	0	0	0	0	0	0	0	1	0	0	1	0	4	0	0
King, Kevin, Chattanooga†	.220	101	327	45	72	127	16	0	13	60	7	0	7	4	33	0	69	7	2
Kingery, Michael, Memphis*	.297	139	455	65	135	172	19	3	4	58	3	7	5	0	93	6	61	18	11
Kinnard, Kenneth, Knoxville	.244	130	422	54	103	135	9	7	3	37	5	3	1	0	51	2	130	18	8
Kinns, Glenn, Jacksonville	.000	11	1	0	0	0	0	0	0	0	0	0	0	0	0	0	0	0	0
Kinnunen, Michael, Jacksonville*	.000	38	0	0	0	0	0	0	0	0	0	1	0	0	1	0	0	0	0
Knight, Timothy, Nashville*	.289	82	263	39	76	104	13	3	3	34	0	2	2	2	48	4	42	5	4
Knudson, Mark, Columbus	.125	14	8	1	1	1	0	0	0	0	0	1	0	0	0	0	2	0	0
Leggatt, Richard, Greenville*	.000	18	1	0	0	0	0	0	0	0	0	0	0	0	0	0	1	0	0
Lezcano, Carlos, Birmingham	.222	22	72	13	16	23	4	0	1	12	1	0	1	0	13	0	14	1	0
Lindsey, William, Nashville	.189	13	37	3	7	10	1	1	0	4	1	1	2	0	6	2	3	0	1
Lockwood, Richard, Charlotte†	.167	6	12	2	2	3	1	0	0	1	0	1	0	0	0	0	3	0	0
Lomastro, Gerardo, Orlando	.289	107	388	55	112	178	16	1	16	66	5	1	5	5	40	7	32	0	2
Luzon, Robert, Greenville	.169	68	124	15	21	33	5	2	1	8	1	1	0	0	16	0	44	8	1
Madison, Charles, Birmingham†	.273	133	473	82	129	205	23	4	15	83	5	7	2	2	94	7	63	7	2
Mariano, Robert, Charlotte*	.212	117	321	33	68	80	6	3	0	24	2	3	1	1	40	2	52	2	1
McClure, David, Birmingham	.000	4	7	0	0	0	0	0	0	0	0	0	0	0	1	0	1	0	0
McGriff, Frederick, Knoxville*	.249	56	189	29	47	91	13	2	9	25	3	0	3	1	29	3	55	0	2
McKay, Troy, Jacksonville	.000	19	0	2	0	0	0	0	0	0	0	0	0	0	0	0	0	0	0
McNealy, Derwin, Knoxville*	.230	144	540	63	124	150	12	4	2	51	1	11	6	2	52	6	91	31	22
McNealy, Robert, Jacksonville*	.222	107	320	47	71	80	5	2	0	19	2	8	1	1	41	0	22	16	11
Meacham, Robert, Nashville†	.290	8	31	3	9	9	0	0	0	3	0	1	1	0	5	0	8	0	2
Meadows, Michael, Columbus*	.280	65	225	33	63	112	17	4	8	36	3	0	1	2	35	0	41	11	4
Melvin, Robert, Birmingham	.269	69	271	34	73	95	14	1	2	33	3	2	2	0	18	2	47	1	0
Miller, Michael, Memphis	.185	76	270	45	50	69	10	3	1	23	5	6	2	2	49	1	56	13	4
Mizerock, John, Columbus*	.238	61	181	19	43	62	7	0	4	23	1	1	0	2	32	0	19	0	2
Moore, William, Jacksonville	.214	6	14	0	3	3	0	0	0	1	0	1	0	1	3	0	2	0	1
Moreno, Armando, Jacksonville	.230	126	400	51	92	136	12	1	10	55	6	13	2	2	77	4	40	17	7
Moreno, Michael, Orlando	.263	131	433	51	114	158	16	5	6	51	4	7	2	1	38	1	67	5	5
Morhardt, Gregory, Orlando*	.233	77	262	30	61	89	11	1	5	32	7	0	4	2	10	3	22	0	2
Moses, John, Chattanooga†	.253	53	182	27	46	58	6	3	0	12	1	3	1	1	34	4	18	19	9
Nandin, Robert, Columbus†	.215	22	65	8	14	18	2	1	0	9	2	1	0	0	8	0	6	1	3
Neuzil, Jeffrey, Memphis	.233	75	219	32	51	66	4	4	1	26	4	8	2	1	19	0	20	2	2
Nicometi, Anthony, Jacksonville*	.000	14	2	0	0	0	0	0	0	0	0	0	0	0	0	0	1	0	0
Nixon, R. Donell, Chattanooga	.269	140	536	99	144	191	25	5	4	57	5	7	4	2	70	4	71	102	14
Norman, Gregory, Birmingham	.276	115	402	56	111	149	11	3	7	47	5	2	4	2	53	0	47	0	1
North, Roy, Greenville	.000	23	0	0	0	0	0	0	0	0	0	0	0	0	1	0	0	0	0
Oliver, Warren, Memphis	.200	2	5	0	1	1	0	0	0	0	0	0	0	0	0	0	2	0	0
Oquendo, Ismael, Charlotte*	.172	8	29	2	5	7	2	0	0	3	0	0	0	0	2	1	7	1	0
Palica, John, Orlando†	.237	48	139	18	33	45	3	0	3	19	2	0	2	0	20	2	27	0	0
Pardo, Alberto, Charlotte†	.265	138	483	72	128	194	23	2	13	81	17	4	2	1	73	5	76	2	1
Paris, Zacarias, Columbus	.000	24	2	1	0	0	0	0	0	0	0	0	0	0	0	0	2	0	0
Pasqua, Daniel, Nashville*	.243	136	460	78	112	231	14	3	33	91	12	0	3	3	95	7	148	5	2
Pastornicky, Clifford, Memphis	.259	29	108	10	28	43	5	2	2	20	1	0	4	0	9	0	16	0	0
Patterson, Scott, Nashville	.000	32	1	0	0	0	0	0	0	0	0	0	0	0	0	0	0	0	0
Pecota, William, Memphis	.241	145	543	84	131	181	19	2	9	50	3	7	3	3	99	2	72	43	15
Peterson, Erik, Nashville	.209	89	296	32	62	97	12	1	7	34	4	5	6	2	30	3	56	0	1
Pilla, Antonio, Orlando	.164	71	152	15	25	30	5	0	0	7	1	1	2	3	19	0	32	0	0
Pinkham, William, Birmingham	.212	16	52	5	11	18	4	0	1	5	1	1	0	0	7	0	5	0	0
Pirruccello, Mark, Memphis†	.113	19	62	7	7	14	2	1	1	5	1	0	0	0	11	1	17	0	0
Pittaro, Christopher, Birmingham†	.284	137	517	85	147	221	27	7	11	61	8	4	5	2	71	7	50	18	7
Poole, Mark, Knoxville	.287	78	247	31	71	88	11	0	2	25	3	0	4	1	15	1	19	2	1
Poole, Stine, Orlando	.224	88	281	30	63	101	14	3	6	33	5	2	1	2	20	1	59	0	1
Portugal, Mark, Orlando	.000	29	0	1	0	0	0	0	0	0	0	0	0	0	0	0	0	0	0
Purpura, Daniel, Charlotte	.179	32	78	5	14	17	1	1	0	8	0	0	1	0	14	0	16	2	0
Ralston, Robert, Orlando	.275	82	298	38	82	92	4	3	0	24	7	8	0	3	18	0	28	8	5
Ramler, Steven, Jacksonville	.263	10	19	4	5	8	0	0	1	3	0	1	0	0	3	0	3	0	0
Ransom, Jeffrey, Charlotte†	.221	47	149	23	33	46	3	2	2	19	1	1	0	1	15	0	24	1	0
Rasmussen, James, Nashville	.000	32	1	0	0	0	0	0	0	0	0	0	0	0	0	0	0	0	0
Reddish, Michael, Charlotte	.263	72	259	48	68	111	11	1	10	42	5	2	3	4	38	0	31	9	3
Reynolds, Jeffrey, Knoxville	.251	70	231	33	58	100	11	2	9	41	6	1	0	2	12	1	45	2	0
Rios, Carlos, Greenville	.255	110	345	48	88	103	11	2	0	32	5	13	6	1	66	0	36	11	6
Rizzo, Richard, Memphis	.206	87	287	39	59	82	8	3	3	28	1	2	3	1	40	0	49	9	8
Rood, Nelson, Columbus	.343	50	169	37	58	65	1	3	0	12	3	0	2	0	41	0	20	20	5
Rosario, Simon, Greenville	.167	5	6	0	1	1	0	0	0	1	0	0	0	0	1	0	1	0	0
Ruiz, August, Greenville*	.000	54	1	0	0	0	0	0	0	0	0	0	0	0	0	0	1	0	0
Ruiz, Manuel, Greenville	.215	45	93	19	20	29	4	1	1	21	1	1	1	1	22	0	9	2	3
Ryan, Michael, Orlando*	.214	48	145	12	31	46	4	1	3	16	3	0	1	0	11	2	41	1	0
Salcedo, Ronnie, Charlotte*	.233	129	473	66	110	169	24	1	11	49	7	6	3	4	62	5	41	4	8
Salery, Johnny, Orlando	.167	4	6	0	1	1	0	0	0	1	0	0	0	0	1	0	0	0	1
Santovenia, Nelson, Jacksonville	.216	90	255	27	55	79	9	0	5	29	7	4	2	0	43	2	30	0	3
Schaefer, Jeffrey, Charlotte	.235	99	383	47	90	110	8	0	4	31	2	6	3	6	23	1	45	8	3
Schmidt, August, Knoxville	.259	53	185	19	48	64	6	2	2	23	1	2	3	0	20	2	19	0	2
Scott, Richard, Nashville	.222	18	63	4	14	17	1	1	0	4	1	1	1	0	8	0	12	3	1
Serna, Paul, Chattanooga	.234	108	333	33	78	92	8	3	0	27	4	5	5	3	32	1	24	0	4
Sharperson, Michael, Knoxville	.304	140	542	86	165	216	25	7	4	48	6	4	1	1	48	2	66	20	13
Sherman, James, Columbus	.248	79	262	35	65	114	13	3	10	32	3	0	6	2	21	0	46	3	1

Player and Club	Pct.	G.	AB	R.	H.	TB.	2B.	3B.	HR.	RBI.	GW.	SH.	SF.	HP.	BB.	Int. BB.	SO.	SB.	CS.
Shouppe, Jamey, Columbus°	.000	38	1	0	0	0	0	0	0	0	0	1	0	0	0	0	1	0	0
Silverio, Virgilio, Birmingham°	.260	87	304	55	79	106	9	0	6	37	2	8	1	0	32	3	51	8	5
Simunic, Douglas, Chattanooga	.281	44	128	17	36	46	7	0	1	18	3	2	1	1	25	0	22	0	1
Sinatro, Matthew, Greenville	.227	101	352	36	80	113	16	1	5	49	3	5	4	2	36	1	43	8	5
Smith, Brick, Chattanooga	.249	100	334	36	83	111	13	0	5	35	1	1	6	2	42	2	35	1	4
Smith, Mark, Birmingham	.283	142	576	73	163	228	28	2	11	98	6	0	3	8	24	3	62	4	6
Smith, P. Keith, Nashville	.278	138	460	80	128	154	15	1	3	42	5	17	2	4	105	1	85	21	7
Smith, Zane, Greenville°	.000	9	3	1	0	0	0	0	0	0	0	2	0	0	0	0	1	0	0
Snider, Van, Memphis°	.246	132	488	52	120	182	23	9	7	62	7	2	3	6	51	6	132	3	6
Snyder, Benjamin, Columbus	.400	12	5	0	2	2	0	0	0	1	0	0	0	0	1	0	1	0	0
Sorce, Samuel, Orlando	.234	38	111	17	26	33	2	1	1	8	0	5	1	0	13	0	25	0	0
Soriano, Hilario, Knoxville	.125	7	16	1	2	3	1	0	0	1	0	0	0	0	0	0	3	0	0
Sosa, Miguel, Greenville	.294	53	187	30	55	96	6	1	11	31	2	0	3	4	4	1	28	7	5
Springer, Gary, Birmingham°	.277	90	267	26	74	86	8	2	0	37	5	10	2	0	41	1	19	7	4
St. Claire, Randy, Jacksonville	.000	48	1	0	0	0	0	0	0	0	0	0	0	0	0	0	0	0	0
Stefero, John, Charlotte°	.207	51	164	25	34	63	6	1	7	14	3	0	0	1	28	1	41	0	0
Stoll, Richard, Jacksonville	.100	19	10	2	1	1	0	0	0	0	0	0	0	0	1	0	4	0	0
Strasser, Richard, Columbus	.000	14	3	0	0	0	0	0	0	0	0	0	0	0	0	0	1	0	0
Strucher, Mark, Columbus	.238	115	353	47	84	148	20	4	12	53	6	2	10	2	47	1	69	3	2
Sutton, L. Ricardo, Knoxville	.227	8	22	1	5	8	0	0	1	3	0	1	0	0	0	0	4	2	1
Szajko, Daniel, Jacksonville	.259	30	81	10	21	21	0	0	0	5	1	2	0	1	7	0	8	1	0
Taylor, Jeffrey, Jacksonville°	.000	31	4	0	0	0	0	0	0	0	0	0	0	0	0	0	1	0	0
Thiessen, Timothy, Jacksonville	.226	78	248	32	56	72	8	1	2	22	3	9	1	1	38	1	20	6	5
Thomas, James, Columbus†	.251	111	394	48	99	123	12	3	2	38	4	9	5	3	45	5	34	10	8
Thomas, Reginald, Birmingham°	.228	29	92	11	21	30	4	1	1	10	1	0	1	0	6	0	24	1	1
Thomas, Thomas, Orlando°	.236	46	110	20	26	29	3	0	0	7	0	1	2	0	21	0	13	9	1
Thompson, Tommy, Greenville°	.297	126	370	46	110	144	19	0	5	49	4	16	3	4	62	9	33	3	2
Tiburcio, Fredrick, Greenville°	.251	130	391	61	98	146	16	4	8	51	8	4	4	2	61	9	62	17	11
Torres, Miguel, Jacksonville	.077	26	13	0	1	1	0	0	0	0	0	2	0	0	0	0	10	0	0
Tovar, Raul, Birmingham	.324	89	312	45	101	120	11	4	0	30	2	4	3	9	27	2	29	11	3
Traber, James, Charlotte°	.351	75	296	50	104	173	17	2	16	56	4	2	2	2	32	4	27	8	4
Treadway, W. Andre, Greenville	.125	27	8	0	1	1	0	0	0	1	0	1	0	0	0	0	4	0	0
Trout, Jeffrey, Orlando†	.285	130	460	68	131	174	17	7	4	48	6	8	2	2	46	4	41	2	2
Tutt, Johnny, Charlotte	.301	69	269	35	81	108	11	5	2	19	2	1	2	0	20	0	40	7	11
Walker, Anthony, Columbus†	.248	132	408	65	101	136	18	4	3	35	4	4	5	3	71	1	50	28	13
Walker, M. Glen, Chattanooga	.246	37	134	17	33	50	5	0	4	31	4	0	7	2	21	1	21	0	0
Ward, R. Duane, Greenville	.167	21	6	0	1	1	0	0	0	0	0	0	0	0	0	0	4	0	0
Weaver, James, Orlando°	.259	24	81	13	21	37	3	2	3	16	1	1	1	2	11	1	16	5	3
West, Matthew, Greenville†	.167	26	12	1	2	3	1	0	0	1	0	1	0	0	0	0	5	0	0
Whitmer, Daniel, Birmingham	.271	20	59	6	16	17	1	0	0	3	0	2	0	1	5	0	3	0	0
Wilkerson, Martin, Memphis°	.252	38	135	16	34	46	4	1	2	31	7	0	1	2	27	0	13	1	2
Williams, Jaime, Columbus	.214	45	140	17	30	47	5	0	4	17	3	3	1	2	11	0	24	1	2
Williams, Jeffrey, 53 Char-37 Knox°	.229	90	271	28	62	85	10	2	3	26	1	4	3	1	41	1	72	12	8
Williams, Mark, Jacksonville	.429	24	7	1	3	3	0	0	0	3	1	2	0	0	1	0	0	0	0
Wilson, Ricky, Chattanooga	.196	78	240	23	47	58	2	0	3	23	1	6	4	3	31	0	41	1	2
Worden, William, Nashville	.259	59	216	32	56	88	14	0	6	24	4	2	3	10	40	2	40	2	3
Younger, Stanley, Birmingham°	.245	93	327	44	80	107	12	3	3	32	6	3	2	0	45	6	43	11	4
Ziem, Stephen, Greenville	.500	8	2	0	1	1	0	0	0	0	0	0	0	0	0	0	0	0	0

The following pitchers, listed alphabetically by club, with games in parentheses, had no plate appearances, primarily through use of designated hitters:

BIRMINGHAM—Bailey, Howard (18); Cary, Charles (22); Cook, Kerry (22); Dacko, Mark (14); Duffy, John (7); Dunn, Allen (6); Garcia, Alejandro (14); Giordano, Michael (3); Gordon, Donald (27); Harvey, Randall (18); Henneman, Michael (29); Hinz, William (6); Jacob, Mark (4); James, Duane (10); Kelly, Bryan (28); Larkin, Patrick (22); Monteleone, Richard (19); Moya, Ernest (1); Pena, Ramon (40); Robinson, Jeffrey (20); Souza, Robert (5); Sprowl, Robert (5); Tabor, Scott (41).

CHARLOTTE—Arnold, Tony (16); Concepcion, Carlos (23); Cratch, Richard (5); Dixon, Kenneth (33); Gilbert, Jeffrey (42); Gonzalez, Julian (9); Habyan, John (13); Huffman, Phillip (11); Johnson, Jerry (14); Konopa, Robert (24); Krsnich, Nicholas (5); Ledbetter, David (4); Leiter, Kurt (5); Oliveras, Francisco (19); Pacella, John (12); Snell, Nathaniel (52); Summers, Jeffrey (30); Werly, James (3); Willsher, Christopher (27).

CHATTANOOGA—Adair, Richard (39); Bartley, Gregory (56); Evans, Michael (24); Grimsley, Ross (1); Guetterman, Lee (24); Hayes, Terry (14); Johnson, Michael (39); Luecken, Richard (26); McDonald, Jeffrey (27); Pedersen, Mark (18); Ramirez, Randolph (28); Rowe, Thomas (31); Semprini, John (7); Whitmer, Joseph (15).

COLUMBUS—Bombard, Richard (9); McCullock, Alec (2); Regalado, Uvaldo (7); Reilly, Edward (5).

GREENVILLE—Mortillaro, John (4).

JACKSONVILLE—Doerrer, Robert (1); Groves, Larry (5); Hess, James (2); Johnson, Gregory (2); Mustad, Eric (6).

KNOXVILLE—Alba, Gibson (45); Aquino, Luis (3); Blackmon, Thomas (10); Cullen, Michael (1); Davis, Steven (27); Esquer, Mercedes (11); Gallagher, Glenn (6); Gillam, Donald (29); Gordon, Donald (27); Harper, Devallon (10); McKnight, Jonathan (24); McLaughlin, Colin (27); Moore, Gregory (53); Rodgers, Timothy (17); Segura, Jose (12); Shipanoff, David (36); Taylor, Johnny (5); Walsh, David (23); Wells, David (8); Yearout, Michael (1).

MEMPHIS—Benedict, James (28); Bryant, John (14); Cone, David (29); Cook, Douglas (19); Martinez, Arthur (26); Miner, James (23); Olson, Michael (4); Radtke, John (11); Reish, Stephan (29); Reyes, Jose (14); Shaw, Theodore (6); Strode, Lester (13); Walberg, Mark (14); Wilder, William (47); Wyatt, Reginald (33); Yuhas, Vincent (6).

NASHVILLE—Baldwin, Johnny (49); Callahan, Benjamin (32); Cappuzzello, George (1); Deshaies, James (7); Drabek, Douglas (4); Faulk, Kelly (9); Ferguson, Mark (9); Fowler, Don (4); Graham, Randle (41); Keough, Matthew (7); King, Michael (28); Nielson, Scott (10); Shiflett, Mark (22); Silva, Mark (10); Tewksbury, Robert (26); Tomaselli, Charles (29); Wex, Gary (7); Woodworth, David (19).

ORLANDO—Cartwright, Mark (27); Gibson, Paul (27); Klump, Kenneth (22); Maack, Michael (23); McMahon, John (19); Oelkers, Bryan (29); Pettibone, Harry (12); Schrom, Kenneth (2); Wardle, Curtis (45).

GRAND SLAM HOME RUNS—Hertzler, Holmes, Kingery, 2 each; Bard, Best, Brewer, Citari, Clements, Davidson, Estes, Foussianes, Gainey, Hansen, Hatcher, Hoeksema, Lomastro, Madison, Ransom, Reddish, Sinatro, Strucher, Traber, 1 each.

AWARDED FIRST BASE ON CATCHER'S INTERFERENCE—Berti 2 (Madison 2); Burke (Hearron); Curry (Colbert); Hansen (Colbert); Hertzler (Hearron); McNealy (Hill); Oquendo (Wilson); Pardo (Wilson); Z. Smith (Colbert); Sosa (Colbert); Thiessen (Ashmore).

CLUB FIELDING

Club	Pct.	G.	PO.	A.	E.	DP.	PB.	Club	Pct.	G.	PO.	A.	E.	DP.	PB.
Jacksonville	.973	145	3766	1620	150	156	12	Charlotte	.968	147	3804	1496	178	141	20
Greenville	.971	141	3618	1556	156	118	22	Orlando	.968	144	3662	1439	169	133	16
Memphis	.970	146	3809	1497	163	144	24	Chattanooga	.966	144	3598	1700	185	175	27
Birmingham	.969	147	3826	1667	176	134	19	Columbus	.964	140	3626	1633	194	148	34
Knoxville	.969	145	3723	1627	173	140	24	Nashville	.958	147	3796	1628	240	145	10

Triple Plays—Memphis 3, Charlotte.

INDIVIDUAL FIELDING
FIRST BASEMEN

*Throws lefthanded.

Player and Club	Pct.	G.	PO.	A.	E.	DP.
Auten, Charlotte	.978	5	42	3	1	2
Bailey, Columbus	1.000	3	26	2	0	6
Bockhorn, Greenville	.988	70	512	48	7	39
Braun, Columbus	.984	24	163	16	3	14
Carpenter, Columbus*	.984	34	276	23	5	22
Chmil, Greenville	1.000	1	3	0	0	0
Citari, Memphis	.986	84	743	59	11	67
Clements, Columbus	.985	73	630	35	10	84
Csefalvay, Nashville*	1.000	11	75	5	0	6
Dalena, Nashville	.986	125	1162	79	17	109
Davidson, Orlando	1.000	3	28	1	0	3
Destrade, Nashville	1.000	1	10	0	0	1
Dumouchelle, Charlotte	1.000	5	16	2	0	1
Estepa, Chattanooga	1.000	17	128	16	0	15
Estes, Greenville*	.967	4	26	3	1	4
Falcone, Charlotte	.987	69	557	41	8	52
Fielder, Knoxville	.979	21	173	10	4	16
Foster, Orlando	.985	48	376	18	6	33
Foussianes, Birmingham	.996	28	258	14	1	26
Galarraga, Jacksonville	.989	142	1302	110	16	130
Guerrero, Greenville	.993	49	389	19	3	31
Hansen, Memphis	1.000	2	18	1	0	3
Hatcher, Memphis	.983	48	390	24	7	44
Hertzler, Jacksonville*	1.000	2	16	0	0	2
A. Hill, Chattanooga	1.000	2	11	1	0	2
C. Hill, Chattanooga	.990	31	289	21	3	39
Hocutt, Jacksonville	1.000	1	8	1	0	1
Holmes, Orlando	.974	4	37	0	1	3
Ingle, Greenville	1.000	1	2	1	0	0
Johnston, Knoxville	.990	51	480	26	5	41
Madison, Birmingham	.985	55	473	39	8	42
McGriff, Knoxville*	.981	56	481	45	10	50
Meadows, Columbus*	1.000	7	41	0	0	2
Melvin, Birmingham	1.000	3	26	3	0	4
Mizerock, Columbus	1.000	1	2	1	0	0
Morhardt, Orlando*	.989	50	349	13	4	36
Neuzil, Memphis	.985	8	63	2	1	7
Norman, Birmingham	.990	51	440	40	5	35
Palica, Orlando*	1.000	3	12	1	0	3
Pardo, Charlotte	1.000	1	8	0	0	1
Peterson, Nashville	.990	14	92	7	1	9
Pinkham, Birmingham	1.000	2	20	3	0	1
Poole, Orlando	.990	23	180	14	2	18
Reynolds, Knoxville	.973	21	166	17	5	18
Ryan, Orlando*	.983	31	225	10	4	24
Simunic, Chattanooga	.905	2	19	0	2	1
B. SMITH, Chattanooga	.993	97	877	77	7	103
M. Smith, Birmingham	.987	23	141	13	2	9
Sorce, Orlando	.962	3	24	1	1	1
Strucher, Columbus	1.000	18	116	7	0	9
Thompson, Greenville	.995	60	340	27	2	35
Traber, Charlotte*	.990	75	663	44	7	66
Wilkerson, Memphis	.981	7	50	3	1	8

Triple Plays—Citari, Hansen, Hatcher.

SECOND BASEMEN

Player and Club	Pct.	G.	PO.	A.	E.	DP.
Alfaro, Charlotte	.950	4	9	10	1	1
Barrett, Nashville	.958	132	325	365	30	89
Candaele, Jacksonville	.963	17	23	54	3	6
Colbert, Columbus	1.000	3	4	5	0	2
Cole, Greenville	1.000	1	3	2	0	0
Curry, Greenville	.974	108	217	314	14	58
D'Onofrio, Columbus	.943	15	33	33	4	9
Diaz, Chattanooga	1.000	2	5	5	0	1
Dumouchelle, Charlotte	.971	24	40	60	3	11
Escobar, Knoxville	.958	5	12	11	1	3
Gallegos, Nashville	1.000	1	2	1	0	1
Gilcrease, Memphis	.978	44	98	124	5	29
Gonzalez, Nashville	.973	17	25	46	2	7
Hanggie, Chattanooga	1.000	6	9	15	0	7
Hill, Chattanooga	.944	50	97	158	15	34
Ingle, Greenville	1.000	2	1	0	0	0
Madison, Birmingham	1.000	5	10	8	0	3
Miller, Memphis	.946	75	155	214	21	45
A. Moreno, Jacksonville	.960	125	255	375	26	79
M. Moreno, Orlando	.917	2	4	7	1	0
Morhardt, Orlando*	1.000	1	0	1	0	0
Nandin, Columbus	.943	21	46	54	6	9
Neuzil, Memphis	.991	24	48	60	1	16
Oliver, Memphis	1.000	2	6	4	0	4
Pilla, Orlando	.947	21	45	44	5	12
Pittaro, Birmingham	.968	135	254	414	22	90
Purpura, Charlotte	.963	32	58	71	5	16
Ralston, Orlando	.966	26	30	54	3	10
Reynolds, Knoxville	.923	6	5	7	1	2
SCHAEFER, Charlotte	.98245	98	245	259	9	64
Serna, Chattanooga	.98242	100	205	298	9	76
Sharperson, Knoxville	.973	140	331	423	21	103
Sosa, Greenville	.939	42	71	115	12	19
Springer, Birmingham	.964	13	20	34	2	9
Szajko, Jacksonville	1.000	6	11	27	0	9
Thomas, Columbus	.977	111	275	313	14	90
Trout, Orlando	.959	112	257	279	23	74
Walker, Chattanooga	1.000	2	7	8	0	2
Wilkerson, Memphis	1.000	4	9	11	0	4
Worden, Nashville	.929	3	5	8	1	0

Triple Plays—Gilcrease, Miller, Neuzil, Schaefer.

THIRD BASEMEN

Player and Club	Pct.	G.	PO.	A.	E.	DP.
Alfaro, Charlotte	.942	38	27	54	5	2
Arce, Birmingham	.854	16	10	31	7	2
Bishop, Knoxville	.911	118	92	214	30	15
Blaser, Nashville	.872	42	26	69	14	6
Brantley, Chattanooga	.250	1	0	1	3	0
Candaele, Jacksonville	1.000	2	2	3	0	2
Chmil, Greenville	.941	53	24	72	6	8
Clark, Columbus	.913	26	14	49	6	3
Colbert, Columbus	1.000	6	2	8	0	3
Crist, Chattanooga	.750	1	0	3	1	1
Curry, Greenville	.895	37	17	60	9	9
D'Onofrio, Columbus	.950	17	8	11	1	0
Davidson, Orlando	1.000	1	2	0	0	0
Dumouchelle, Charlotte	.899	56	42	101	16	5
Escobar, Knoxville	.909	6	1	9	1	2
Foussianes, Birmingham	.929	86	51	131	14	12
Gallegos, Nashville	.885	11	4	19	3	0
Gonzalez, Nashville	.806	9	3	22	6	2
Hanggie, Chattanooga	.922	138	107	281	33	32
Hawkins, Nashville	1.000	1	2	1	0	0
Hernandez, Nashville	.889	4	1	7	1	0
A. Hill, Chattanooga	.833	2	2	3	1	1
C. Hill, Chattanooga	1.000	2	0	1	0	0
Hoeksema, Jacksonville	.930	144	99	232	25	26
Holmes, Orlando	.873	55	32	105	20	10
Hotchkiss, Birmingham	.963	31	29	50	3	4
Ingle, Greenville	.727	4	2	6	3	0
Kenaga, Charlotte	.857	7	3	3	1	0
Lockwood, Charlotte	.889	5	1	7	1	0
Madison, Birmingham	.933	7	5	9	1	1
Mariano, Charlotte	.953	72	56	128	9	18
Melvin, Birmingham	1.000	1	0	2	0	0
Moreno, Orlando	1.000	4	6	5	0	0
Neuzil, Memphis	1.000	2	0	1	0	0
Nixon, Chattanooga	.667	7	1	1	1	0
Pastornicky, Memphis	1.000	1	2	1	0	0
PECOTA, Memphis	.942	143	142	267	25	28
Peterson, Nashville	.885	27	14	55	9	5
Pilla, Orlando	.948	39	13	42	3	4
Ralston, Orlando	.970	40	22	74	3	11
Reynolds, Knoxville	.964	11	8	19	1	2
Ruiz, Greenville	.935	30	12	46	4	5
Schmidt, Knoxville	.879	20	13	38	7	5
Scott, Nashville	.908	18	17	42	6	5
Serna, Chattanooga	.667	1	2	2	2	1
Sherman, Columbus	.882	58	42	107	20	7
Sorce, Orlando	.974	28	22	54	2	5
Springer, Birmingham	.957	21	15	30	2	4
Strucher, Columbus	.917	58	60	129	17	15
Thompson, Greenville	.963	53	32	73	4	5
Trout, Orlando	.905	9	8	11	2	1
Wilkerson, Memphis	.667	1	1	1	1	0
Worden, Nashville	.889	45	37	99	17	6

Triple Plays—Dumouchelle, Pecota.

SHORTSTOPS

Player and Club	Pct.	G.	PO.	A.	E.	DP.
Alfaro, Charlotte	.950	110	171	304	25	68
Candaele, Jacksonville	.960	69	104	211	13	50
Chavez, Birmingham	.958	59	128	167	13	32
Chmil, Greenville	.896	19	24	45	8	9
Crabtree, Chattanooga	.939	9	24	38	4	7
D'Onofrio, Columbus	1.000	2	2	1	0	0
Diaz, Chattanooga	.949	106	174	308	26	81
Escobar, Knoxville	.967	82	102	255	12	49
Followell, Columbus	.964	90	144	316	17	61
Gallegos, Nashville	1.000	2	2	3	0	1
Glynn, Jacksonville	1.000	1	1	0	0	0
HEGMAN, Memphis	.962	134	239	361	24	82
Hill, Chattanooga	.940	37	53	87	9	24
Hotchkiss, Birmingham	.948	37	83	116	11	23
Infante, Knoxville	.943	63	92	204	18	38
Ingle, Greenville	.942	23	28	53	5	10
Lockwood, Charlotte	1.000	1	0	1	0	0
Mariano, Charlotte	.943	47	47	103	9	20
Meacham, Nashville	.976	8	16	25	1	6
Moreno, Orlando	.936	119	158	339	34	64
Neuzil, Memphis	.962	14	17	34	2	5
Pilla, Orlando	.956	11	19	24	2	5
Pittaro, Birmingham	1.000	1	6	3	0	2
Ralston, Orlando	.904	22	21	64	9	12
Reynolds, Knoxville	.833	1	3	2	1	0
Rios, Greenville	.958	104	170	315	21	56
Rood, Columbus	.943	50	86	177	16	42
Ruiz, Greenville	.955	4	6	15	1	4
Schaefer, Charlotte	1.000	1	4	5	0	1
Schmidt, Knoxville	1.000	3	1	9	0	4
Serna, Chattanooga	1.000	3	5	10	0	6
Smith, Nashville	.936	138	238	440	46	97
Sorce, Orlando	1.000	1	1	3	0	1
Springer, Birmingham	.948	52	86	167	14	27
Szajko, Jacksonville	1.000	5	7	11	0	1
Thiessen, Jacksonville	.958	75	103	241	15	46

Triple Plays—Hegman 2.

OUTFIELDERS

Player and Club	Pct.	G.	PO.	A.	E.	DP.
Aitcheson, Knoxville	1.000	84	138	9	0	1
Auten, Charlotte	.962	28	50	1	2	1
Bailey, Columbus	1.000	2	2	0	0	0
Baker, Jacksonville*	1.000	78	141	7	0	1
Beauchamp, Knoxville	1.000	2	6	0	0	0
Berti, Columbus	1.000	1	1	0	0	0
Best, Memphis	.992	57	115	3	1	1
Bockhorn, Greenville	.769	15	10	0	3	0
Brantley, Chattanooga	.978	102	211	13	5	5
Braun, Columbus	.895	19	15	2	2	0
Brewer, Memphis	.950	35	73	3	4	1
Bullock, Columbus*	.971	69	133	3	4	0
Burke, Columbus	.939	20	45	1	3	0
Candaele, Jacksonville	.980	40	95	2	2	1
Carl, Jacksonville	.964	99	175	13	7	2
Clark, Columbus	1.000	4	2	0	0	0
Colbert, Columbus	1.000	15	19	0	0	0
Cole, Greenville	.983	135	268	17	5	1
Csefalvay, Nashville*	.945	81	114	6	7	1
Davidson, Orlando	.987	108	213	12	3	5
Destrade, Nashville	.941	26	46	2	3	0
Dumouchelle, Charlotte	.964	30	53	1	2	1
Escobar, Knoxville	.800	3	4	0	1	0
Estepa, Chattanooga	.965	77	131	6	5	0
Estes, Greenville*	.953	135	216	8	11	0
Fields, Birmingham	.978	87	169	8	4	2
Gainey, Columbus	.984	123	240	8	4	3
Gallegos, Nashville	.870	14	17	3	3	0
Gerhart, Charlotte	.979	78	183	5	4	3
Gonzalez, Nashville	.909	10	9	1	1	0
Granger, Charlotte	.917	12	21	1	2	0
Griffin, Knoxville	.982	37	50	5	1	1
Hertzler, Jacksonville*	.972	129	254	19	8	6
Hill, Chattanooga	1.000	9	7	1	0	0
Holman, Knoxville	1.000	8	7	0	0	0
Hotchkiss, Birmingham	1.000	4	7	0	0	0
Howe, Orlando	.982	137	372	5	7	2
Hughes, Nashville*	1.000	14	19	0	0	0
Javier, Nashville	.967	76	202	4	7	2
Johnston, Knoxville	1.000	2	2	0	0	0
Kenaga, Charlotte	.947	20	30	6	2	2
King, Charlotte	.940	37	60	3	4	0
Kingery, Memphis*	.981	136	291	18	6	5
Kinnard, Knoxville	.965	129	240	11	9	4
Knight, Nashville*	.943	80	159	5	10	2
Lezcano, Birmingham	1.000	22	48	3	0	0
Lomastro, Orlando	.990	91	187	11	2	3
Luzon, Greenville	.981	52	99	2	2	0
D. McNealy, Knoxville*	.977	144	366	9	9	1
R. McNealy, Jacksonville*	.959	93	201	8	9	3
Meadows, Columbus*	.975	60	109	6	3	0
Mizerock, Columbus	.667	6	4	0	2	0
Moore, Jacksonville*	1.000	5	7	0	0	0
Moreno, Orlando	1.000	9	7	0	0	0
Morhardt, Orlando*	.983	33	56	3	1	0
Moses, Chattanooga*	.982	51	107	4	2	0
Neuzil, Memphis	.968	16	28	2	1	0
Nixon, Chattanooga	.974	133	261	5	7	1
Oquendo, Charlotte*	1.000	4	4	0	0	0
Palica, Orlando*	.977	22	43	0	1	0
Pardo, Charlotte	1.000	4	4	0	0	0
Pasqua, Nashville*	.955	125	244	11	12	4
Peterson, Nashville	1.000	6	2	0	0	0
Ransom, Charlotte	1.000	11	18	2	0	1
Reddish, Charlotte	.994	69	160	2	1	0
Reynolds, Knoxville	.960	15	24	0	1	0
Rizzo, Memphis	.991	82	209	6	2	0
Rosario, Greenville	1.000	3	1	0	0	0
Ryan, Orlando*	.778	6	7	0	2	0
Salcedo, Charlotte	.980	120	233	11	5	1
Salery, Orlando	1.000	2	1	0	0	0
Schmidt, Knoxville	1.000	26	34	2	0	0
Sherman, Columbus	.875	11	7	0	1	0
Silverio, Birmingham*	.966	70	137	4	5	2
Smith, Birmingham	.970	126	214	13	7	4
SNIDER, Memphis	.988	128	319	24	4	5
Sorce, Orlando	1.000	2	3	0	0	0
Sutton, Knoxville	1.000	7	7	0	0	0
Szajko, Jacksonville	.971	13	33	0	1	0
R. Thomas, Birmingham*	.944	17	34	0	2	0
T. Thomas, Orlando	1.000	38	59	1	0	0
Tiburcio, Greenville	.977	126	293	6	7	0
Tovar, Birmingham	.969	86	212	7	7	1
Tutt, Charlotte	.977	61	118	9	3	2
A. Walker, Columbus	.974	129	281	15	8	2
G. Walker, Chattanooga	.975	36	71	6	2	2
Weaver, Orlando*	1.000	22	38	4	0	0
Ja. Williams, Columbus	1.000	2	1	0	0	0
Je. Williams, 37-Char-37 Nash*	.914	74	133	5	13	1
Worden, Nashville	1.000	4	2	0	0	0
Younger, Birmingham*	.965	64	132	5	5	1

Triple Play—Salcedo.

CATCHERS

Player and Club	Pct.	G.	PO.	A.	E.	DP.	PB.
Ashmore, Memphis	.972	67	317	33	10	3	15
Bailey, Columbus	1.000	11	55	9	0	1	10
Bard, Charlotte	.950	20	92	21	6	5	1
Bell, Chattanooga	.929	2	12	1	1	0	0
Berti, Columbus	.952	10	51	8	3	2	3
Bockhorn, Greenville	.988	31	156	14	2	0	5
Colbert, Columbus	.962	74	317	64	15	7	8
Cormack, Greenville	.957	3	16	6	1	2	2
Delany, Jacksonville	.979	70	343	39	8	9	3
Dempsey, Nashville	.980	75	348	50	8	6	4
Dewey, Nashville	1.000	1	4	0	0	0	1
DeWillis, Knoxville	1.000	1	2	2	0	0	1
Hansen, Memphis	.988	81	389	35	5	3	7
Hatcher, Memphis	1.000	4	14	6	0	0	2
Hawkins, Nashville	.970	70	381	38	13	5	4
Hearron, Knoxville	.969	78	387	45	14	3	12
Hill, Chattanooga	.961	55	191	31	9	4	11
Isherwood, Orlando	.987	99	462	54	7	0	12
Lindsey, Nashville	.973	11	63	9	2	1	2
Madison, Birmingham	.974	62	285	53	9	3	6
McClure, Birmingham	1.000	2	9	2	0	0	0
Melvin, Birmingham	.989	64	315	33	4	5	6
Mizerock, Columbus	.983	34	159	18	3	0	5
Pardo, Charlotte	.968	71	385	32	14	4	9
Pinkham, Birmingham	.932	9	38	3	3	1	6
Pirruccello, Memphis	.667	2	2	0	1	0	0
M. POOLE, Knoxville	.993	73	394	52	3	5	10
S. Poole, Orlando	.991	56	286	40	3	3	4
Ramler, Jacksonville	1.000	5	22	4	0	0	0
Ransom, Charlotte	.981	29	133	18	3	2	2
Santovenia, Jacksonville	.992	85	464	64	4	9	9
Simunic, Chattanooga	.989	20	83	6	1	0	4
Sinatro, Greenville	.987	94	466	64	7	5	12
Smith, Chattanooga	.750	1	4	2	2	0	0
Sorce, Orlando	1.000	1	4	0	0	0	0
Soriano, Knoxville	.960	6	21	3	1	0	1
Stefero, Charlotte	.987	38	195	30	3	2	8
Strucher, Columbus	1.000	3	3	1	0	0	1
Thompson, Nashville	.974	22	131	17	4	1	3
Whitmer, Birmingham	.981	18	91	14	2	1	1
Williams, Columbus	.977	31	150	23	4	1	7
Wilson, Chattanooga	.973	75	360	44	11	7	12

Triple Plays—Ashmore, Ransom.

PITCHERS

Player and Club	Pct.	G.	PO.	A.	E.	DP.
Acker, Columbus°	.917	28	11	33	4	1
Adair, Chattanooga°	.955	39	2	19	1	0
Alba, Knoxville°	.909	45	3	17	2	0
Aquino, Knoxville	1.000	3	0	1	0	0
Arnold, Charlotte	.962	16	7	18	1	0
Bailey, Birmingham	1.000	18	4	8	0	0
Baldwin, Nashville	.900	48	4	14	2	2
Barrett, Jacksonville	1.000	2	0	2	0	0
Bartley, Chattanooga	.933	56	8	20	2	2
Benedict, Memphis	1.000	28	6	15	0	0
Blackmon, Knoxville	.882	10	7	8	2	1
Bombard, Columbus	1.000	9	1	2	0	1
Bormann, Greenville	.952	36	9	11	1	1
Brahs, Jacksonville°	1.000	6	1	4	0	0
Bryant, Columbus	1.000	14	2	10	0	0
Calhoun, Columbus°	1.000	37	4	17	0	1
Callahan, Nashville	.870	32	6	14	3	2
Cappuzzello, Nashville°	1.000	1	1	0	0	0
Cartwright, Orlando	.960	27	8	16	1	1
CARY, Birmingham°	1.000	22	7	20	0	0
Cates, Jacksonville	.900	11	3	6	1	1
Clary, Greenville	.962	30	16	35	2	3
Clay, Greenville	.941	51	6	26	2	2
Cole, Greenville°	.923	31	2	10	1	0
Concepcion, Charlotte	1.000	23	1	5	0	0
Cone, Memphis	.786	29	7	15	6	4
D. Cook, Memphis	.871	19	6	21	4	1
K. Cook, Birmingham	.880	22	7	15	3	1
Dacko, Birmingham	.941	14	7	9	1	1
Davis, Knoxville°	1.000	27	3	17	0	1
Deshaies, Nashville°	1.000	7	1	6	0	0
Dixon, Charlotte	.892	31	10	23	4	2
Dopson, Jacksonville	.978	26	20	24	1	7
Drabek, Nashville	.714	4	2	3	2	1
Duffy, Birmingham°	.600	7	0	3	2	0
Dunn, Birmingham	1.000	6	3	0	0	0
Esquer, Knoxville°	1.000	10	0	5	0	0
Eufemia, Orlando	.923	46	3	9	1	1
Evans, Chattanooga°	1.000	24	1	4	0	0
Faulk, Nashville	.800	9	2	6	2	1
Ferguson, Nashville	1.000	9	3	9	0	0
Foley, Columbus	1.000	35	7	9	0	0
Fowler, Nashville	1.000	4	1	4	0	1
Gallagher, Knoxville	1.000	5	1	3	0	0
Garcia, Birmingham°	.900	14	1	8	1	0
Gibson, Orlando°	.944	27	3	14	1	1
Gilbert, Charlotte°	.923	42	6	6	1	0
Gilbreath, Jacksonville	.902	56	9	28	4	3
Gillam, Knoxville°	1.000	29	2	13	0	1
Giordano, Birmingham	1.000	3	1	0	0	0
Gonzalez, Charlotte°	.875	9	0	7	1	0
Gordon, 27 Bir-27 Knoxville°	.966	54	4	24	1	2
Graham, Nashville	1.000	41	1	3	0	0
Grimsley, Chattanooga°	1.000	1	0	1	0	0
Groves, Jacksonville	1.000	5	0	1	0	0
Guetterman, Chattanooga°	.967	24	15	44	2	9
Habyan, Charlotte	.667	13	2	4	3	0
Harper, Knoxville	1.000	10	7	3	0	1
Harsh, Columbus	.800	19	5	11	4	1
Harvey, Birmingham°	.900	18	3	6	1	0
Hayes, Chattanooga°	1.000	14	4	8	0	0
Henneman, Birmingham	.929	29	2	11	1	1
Hinz, Birmingham	1.000	6	0	1	0	0
Hogan, Columbus	.953	27	9	32	2	2
Huber, Jacksonville	.750	21	1	2	1	0
Huffman, Charlotte	.900	11	6	3	1	0
James, Birmingham	1.000	10	0	5	0	1
Jefferson, Jacksonville	1.000	8	1	2	0	0
Je. Johnson, Charlotte	.900	14	6	12	2	0
Jo. Johnson, Greenville	.962	24	9	16	1	1
M. Johnson, Chattanooga	.833	39	4	6	2	2
Kasprzak, Columbus	1.000	37	1	9	0	0
Kelly, Birmingham	.939	28	9	37	3	5
Keough, Nashville	1.000	7	2	5	0	0
Kerfeld, Columbus	.923	24	7	29	3	1
King, Nashville°	.929	28	2	11	1	1
Kinns, Jacksonville	1.000	11	5	0	0	0
KINNUNEN, Jacksonville°	1.000	38	9	18	0	3
Klump, Orlando	.944	22	6	11	1	4
Knudson, Columbus	.923	14	2	10	1	0
Konopa, Charlotte°	.842	24	3	13	3	0
Krsnich, Columbus	1.000	9	1	2	0	0
Larkin, Birmingham°	.900	22	2	7	1	0
Leggatt, Greenville	.818	18	3	6	2	1
Leiter, Charlotte	1.000	5	2	6	0	0
Luecken, Chattanooga	.978	26	8	37	1	6
Maack, Orlando°	.935	23	3	26	2	1
Martinez, Memphis	1.000	26	2	10	0	1
McDonald, Chattanooga	.919	27	11	23	3	2
McKay, Jacksonville	1.000	13	4	7	0	1
McKnight, Knoxville	.886	24	14	25	5	2
McLaughlin, Knoxville	1.000	27	4	3	0	0
McMahon, Orlando	.889	19	13	11	3	2
Miner, Memphis	.833	23	5	10	3	0
Monteleone, Birmingham	.882	19	9	21	4	1
Moore, Knoxville	1.000	53	8	18	0	3
Mortillaro, Greenville°	1.000	4	0	2	0	0
Mustad, Jacksonville	.900	6	6	3	1	1
Nicometi, Jacksonville°	1.000	14	1	6	0	0
Nielson, Nashville	1.000	10	8	14	0	1
North, Greenville	1.000	23	1	3	0	0
Oelkers, Orlando°	.957	29	2	20	1	1
Oliveras, Charlotte	.938	19	3	12	1	1
Olson, Memphis	1.000	4	0	4	0	0
Pacella, Charlotte	1.000	12	1	5	0	0
Paris, Columbus	.870	21	9	11	3	2
Patterson, Nashville	1.000	32	2	5	0	1
Pedersen, Chattanooga	1.000	18	3	5	0	0
Pena, Birmingham	.955	40	4	17	1	1
Pettibone, Orlando	.750	12	1	5	2	0
Portugal, Orlando	.907	27	11	28	4	1
Radtke, Memphis	1.000	11	5	7	0	1
Ramirez, Chattanooga	.944	28	10	24	2	2
Rasmussen, Nashville	1.000	31	0	7	0	1
Regalado, Columbus	.875	7	3	4	1	0
Reish, Memphis	.875	29	14	35	7	3
Reyes, Memphis	1.000	14	5	10	0	0
Robinson, Birmingham	.909	20	5	25	3	0
Rodgers, Knoxville	.929	15	9	4	1	0
Rowe, Chattanooga	.921	31	8	27	3	2
Ruiz, Greenville°	.963	54	8	18	1	2
Schrom, Columbus	1.000	2	0	1	0	0
Segura, Knoxville	1.000	12	6	11	0	1
Semprini, Chattanooga	1.000	7	2	5	0	1
Shaw, Memphis	.778	6	1	6	2	0
Shiflett, Nashville°	.974	22	8	29	1	1
Shipanoff, Knoxville	.857	36	6	18	4	0
Shouppe, Columbus°	1.000	37	1	10	0	1
Silva, Nashville	1.000	10	0	3	0	0
Smith, Greenville°	1.000	9	3	15	0	4
Snell, Charlotte	.960	52	8	16	1	2
Snyder, Columbus	.556	12	1	4	4	0
Souza, Birmingham	1.000	5	4	7	0	0
Springer, Birmingham	1.000	5	3	0	0	0
Sprowl, Birmingham°	1.000	5	0	1	0	0
St. Claire, Jacksonville	.950	48	3	16	1	2
Stoll, Jacksonville	.973	17	5	31	1	5
Strasser, Columbus	.889	14	1	7	1	1
Strode, Memphis°	.846	13	3	8	2	1
Summers, Charlotte	.919	30	15	19	3	2
Tabor, Birmingham	.955	41	9	33	2	1
Je. Taylor, Jacksonville°	1.000	31	0	8	0	0
Jo. Taylor, Knoxville	1.000	5	0	1	0	0
Tewksbury, Nashville	.976	26	6	35	1	1
Tomaselli, Nashville°	1.000	29	2	23	0	0
Torres, Jacksonville	.950	26	17	21	2	0
Treadway, Greenville	.962	27	7	18	1	1
Walberg, Memphis	.966	14	9	19	1	5
Walsh, Knoxville°	.938	23	3	27	2	2
Ward, Greenville	.962	21	8	17	1	1
Wardle, Orlando°	.778	45	3	4	2	0
Wells, Knoxville°	1.000	8	4	16	0	1
Werly, Charlotte	1.000	3	3	0	0	0
West, Chattanooga	.946	26	11	24	2	2
Wex, Nashville	1.000	7	1	4	0	0
Whitmer, Chattanooga	.882	15	9	21	4	1
Wilder, Memphis	.900	47	3	15	2	2
Williams, Jacksonville	.972	23	15	20	1	3
Willsher, Charlotte	.833	27	5	10	3	0
Woodworth, Nashville°	.800	19	2	6	2	0
Wyatt, Memphis	.929	33	2	11	1	0
Yuhas, Memphis	.714	6	1	4	2	0
Ziem, Greenville	1.000	8	0	7	0	0

The following players do not have any recorded accepted chances at the positions indicated; therefore, are not listed in the fielding averages for those particular positions: Baker, p; Blaser, of; Clements, of; Cratch, p; Csefalvay, p; Cullen, p; Curry, of; D'Onofrio, of; Foster, 3b; Foussianes, ss; Hess, p; Jacob, p; G. Johnson, p; Johnston, ss; Ledbetter, p; Lindsey, 1b; McCullock, p; Mizerock, 3b; Moya, p; Reilly, p; Reynolds, p; M. Ruiz, 2b; Schaefer, p; Yearout, p.

CLUB PITCHING

Club	ERA.	G.	CG.	ShO.	Sv.	IP.	H.	R.	ER.	HR.	HB.	BB.	Int. BB.	SO.	WP.	Bk.
Orlando	3.28	144	44	16	32	1220.2	1109	570	445	89	18	569	13	706	48	10
Knoxville	3.61	145	23	10	29	1241.0	1112	605	498	78	23	695	29	770	78	13
Greenville	3.69	141	31	10	30	1206.0	1169	572	495	71	31	570	28	727	65	14
Charlotte	3.72	147	39	11	28	1268.0	1191	661	524	92	27	615	39	771	70	9
Jacksonville	3.76	145	24	16	32	1255.1	1212	629	524	86	26	614	49	757	64	8
Columbus	3.78	140	32	7	25	1208.2	1211	619	507	84	37	532	47	709	73	5
Chattanooga	3.86	144	23	8	26	1199.1	1234	629	515	56	29	537	31	616	62	12
Memphis	3.93	146	43	9	20	1269.2	1189	627	555	94	39	618	20	657	74	11
Nashville	3.98	147	18	2	43	1265.1	1224	705	559	72	27	666	35	747	59	29
Birmingham	4.71	147	16	6	31	1275.1	1294	776	668	112	39	713	23	654	72	17

PITCHERS' RECORDS
(Leading Qualifiers for Earned-Run Average Leadership — 117 or More Innings)

*Throws lefthanded.

Pitcher—Club	W.	L.	Pct.	ERA.	G.	GS.	CG.	GF.	ShO.	Sv.	IP.	H.	R.	ER.	HR.	HB.	BB.	Int. BB.	SO.	WP.
Williams, Jacksonville	5	6	.455	2.49	23	14	2	3	0	1	119.1	107	46	33	9	1	49	4	67	9
Tewksbury, Nashville	11	9	.550	2.83	26	26	6	0	0	1	172.0	185	69	54	8	4	42	3	78	4
Dixon, Charlotte	16	8	.667	2.85	31	29	20	1	2	1	240.0	198	92	76	20	1	78	1	211	6
Portugal, Orlando	14	7	.667	2.98	27	27	10	0	3	0	196.0	171	80	65	16	3	113	2	110	9
Kerfeld, Columbus	14	9	.609	2.99	24	23	5	1	0	0	162.2	140	80	54	6	9	79	3	118	20
Tabor, Birmingham	10	4	.714	3.03	41	3	0	25	0	8	118.2	108	49	40	5	1	43	3	48	5
Summers, Charlotte	8	7	.533	3.12	30	21	5	2	2	0	144.1	127	69	50	6	4	70	4	57	6
Rowe, Chattanooga	3	9	.250	3.18	31	16	3	9	1	3	130.1	135	59	46	2	1	53	2	86	5
Clary, Greenville	14	9	.609	3.19	30	30	5	0	2	0	186.1	172	77	66	10	3	82	1	125	10
Walsh, Greenville*	5	8	.385	3.24	23	19	4	2	1	0	119.1	111	54	43	6	0	64	0	60	8

Departmental Leaders: G—Bartley, Gilbreath, 56; W—Dixon, Oelkers, 16; L—Luecken, 13; Pct.—Strode, .818; GS—Clary, 30; CG—Dixon, 20; GF—Snell, 48; ShO—Oelkers, 4; Sv.—Graham, Snell, Wardle, 17; IP—Dixon, 240.0; H—Acker, 213; R—Oelkers, 104; ER—Callahan, 88; HR—Dixon, Hogan, 20; HB—Kelly, 12; BB—Kelly, 145; IBB—St. Claire, 14; SO—Dixon, 211; WP—Cone, 27.

(All Pitchers—Listed Alphabetically)

Pitcher—Club	W.	L.	Pct.	ERA.	G.	GS.	CG.	GF.	ShO.	Sv.	IP.	H.	R.	ER.	HR.	HB.	BB.	Int. BB.	SO.	WP.
Acker, Columbus*	15	8	.652	3.54	28	28	8	0	1	0	198.1	213	90	78	17	5	48	2	81	7
Adair, Chattanooga*	4	6	.400	4.60	39	6	1	13	1	4	78.1	85	43	40	1	4	40	2	55	5
Alba, Knoxville*	11	9	.550	4.64	45	10	0	16	0	3	110.2	89	69	57	5	4	81	4	100	8
Aquino, Knoxville	0	0	.000	9.00	3	0	0	2	0	0	4.0	3	4	4	1	1	3	1	7	0
Arnold, Charlotte	7	5	.583	3.14	16	12	4	0	3	0	83.0	93	35	29	2	1	25	3	25	2
Bailey, Birmingham	2	2	.500	5.90	18	2	0	5	0	2	39.2	48	34	26	2	0	24	1	14	1
Baker, Jacksonville*	0	0		18.00	1	0	0	1	0	0	1.0	3	2	2	0	0	2	0	0	0
Baldwin, Nashville	5	4	.556	3.69	48	3	0	20	0	6	92.2	72	49	38	5	0	66	5	78	5
Barrett, Jacksonville	1	1	.500	2.19	2	2	1	0	1	0	12.1	11	3	3	0	0	7	1	12	0
Bartley, Chattanooga	4	7	.364	2.82	56	0	0	46	0	13	92.2	94	37	29	1	3	48	8	45	4
Benedict, Memphis	5	3	.625	2.54	28	0	0	23	0	5	60.1	54	17	17	3	0	25	7	37	2
Blackmon, Knoxville	3	5	.375	2.55	10	10	0	0	0	0	60.0	57	25	17	4	0	31	3	26	5
Bombard, Columbus	2	0	1.000	0.64	9	0	0	7	0	4	14.0	11	1	1	0	0	8	1	11	0
Bormann, Greenville	1	4	.200	3.41	36	1	0	18	0	3	60.2	57	26	23	6	2	24	2	18	2
Brahs, Birmingham*	2	2	.500	6.30	6	6	0	0	0	0	30.0	37	23	21	7	1	8	0	31	0
Bryant, Memphis	2	0	1.000	3.53	14	1	1	7	0	0	35.2	36	14	14	0	3	27	1	13	5
Calhoun, Columbus*	4	2	.667	2.83	37	1	0	28	0	8	63.2	52	21	20	3	0	26	1	51	3
Callahan, Nashville	7	10	.412	6.27	32	16	2	6	0	1	126.1	145	102	88	8	5	71	1	54	5
Cappuzzello, Nashville*	0	0	.000	9.64	1	1	0	0	0	0	4.2	9	6	5	0	2	6	0	3	2
Cartwright, Orlando	8	9	.471	3.45	27	18	3	7	0	0	138.1	148	67	53	7	2	52	3	60	1
Cary, Birmingham*	6	4	.600	4.82	22	20	1	1	0	0	108.1	118	61	58	10	1	46	1	62	9
Cates, Jacksonville	5	3	.625	2.45	11	10	2	0	1	0	69.2	50	25	19	9	2	32	1	55	2
Clary, Greenville	14	9	.609	3.19	30	30	5	0	2	0	186.1	172	77	66	10	3	82	1	125	10
Clay, Greenville	10	3	.769	1.80	51	0	0	40	0	16	100.0	87	26	20	4	1	39	10	44	4
Cole, Greenville*	5	5	.500	8.28	31	3	1	8	0	2	54.1	50	55	50	5	4	62	1	46	5
Concepcion, Charlotte	1	3	.250	4.38	23	0	0	17	0	5	24.2	20	17	12	1	1	32	7	15	1
Cone, Memphis	8	12	.400	4.28	29	29	9	0	1	0	178.2	162	103	85	9	5	114	1	110	27
D. Cook, Memphis	5	10	.333	4.21	19	19	5	0	0	0	124.0	108	61	58	11	3	83	1	79	4
K. Cook, Birmingham	8	9	.471	5.48	22	20	4	1	3	0	95.1	112	70	58	9	7	43	0	21	10
Cratch, Charlotte	0	1	.000	6.75	5	1	0	1	0	0	12.0	13	9	9	0	1	4	1	7	2
Csefalvay, Nashville*	0	0	.000	12.00	1	0	0	4	0	0	6.0	10	8	8	1	0	3	0	5	0
Cullen, Knoxville	0	0	.000	9.00	1	0	0	1	0	0	1.0	0	1	1	0	0	3	0	5	0
Dacko, Birmingham	5	8	.385	4.55	14	13	3	1	0	0	93.0	101	53	47	10	1	34	1	46	0
Davis, Knoxville*	9	6	.600	3.49	27	25	4	2	1	0	154.2	123	71	60	7	4	96	4	77	9
Deshaies, Nashville*	3	2	.600	2.80	7	7	1	0	0	0	45.0	33	20	14	3	1	29	1	42	1
Dixon, Charlotte	16	8	.667	2.85	31	29	20	1	2	1	240.0	198	92	76	20	1	78	1	211	6
Dopson, Jacksonville	10	8	.556	3.69	26	26	6	0	1	0	170.2	198	83	70	10	1	41	2	76	5
Drabek, Nashville	1	2	.333	2.32	4	4	2	0	0	0	31.0	30	11	8	1	0	10	0	22	2
Duffy, Birmingham*	0	0	.000	5.68	7	0	0	2	0	0	12.2	16	13	8	1	0	10	0	8	0
Dunn, Birmingham	0	2	.000	9.39	6	3	0	1	0	1	15.1	16	16	16	2	2	20	0	9	0
Esquer, Knoxville*	0	0	.000	3.06	10	0	0	3	0	1	17.2	16	9	6	1	1	10	2	9	0
Eufemia, Orlando	6	4	.600	2.88	45	0	0	38	0	12	75.0	74	30	24	7	1	23	3	42	4
Evans, Chattanooga*	0	1	.000	5.06	24	0	0	12	0	0	37.1	49	26	21	2	1	13	0	25	2
Faulk, Nashville	1	0	1.000	2.08	9	2	0	4	0	1	26.0	19	8	6	0	1	13	1	11	3
Ferguson, Nashville	3	1	.750	4.05	9	9	1	0	0	0	60.0	61	30	27	3	0	24	1	43	4
Foley, Columbus	4	7	.364	4.99	35	7	1	14	0	5	83.0	81	48	46	3	3	51	7	53	6
Fowler, Nashville	2	0	1.000	2.25	4	4	0	0	0	0	24.0	19	6	6	0	1	10	0	8	0
Gallagher, Knoxville	0	1	.000	11.32	5	1	0	2	0	0	10.1	20	13	13	3	0	3	0	5	0
Garcia, Birmingham*	0	5	.000	6.21	14	4	0	2	0	0	42.0	51	31	29	3	2	25	0	19	2
Gibson, Orlando*	7	7	.500	3.87	27	12	3	7	1	1	121.0	125	71	52	9	1	54	0	64	6
Gilbert, Charlotte*	3	4	.429	4.36	42	0	0	16	0	2	66.0	73	39	32	4	1	31	2	35	4
Gilbreath, Jacksonville	6	8	.429	3.94	56	0	0	21	0	3	118.2	113	60	52	6	4	68	12	60	11
Gillam, Knoxville*	1	0	1.000	1.96	29	0	0	16	0	11	46.0	34	13	10	1	0	18	1	24	2
Giordano, Birmingham	1	0	1.000	27.00	3	0	0	1	0	0	3.0	9	9	9	1	0	10	1	24	0
Gonzalez, Charlotte*	4	4	.500	6.26	9	9	1	0	1	0	46.0	44	39	32	3	1	47	1	32	3
Gordon, 27 Birm-27 Knox	6	4	.600	3.36	54	0	1	27	0	8	109.2	103	47	41	9	6	21	1	51	1

Pitcher—Club	W.	L.	Pct.	ERA.	G.	GS.	CG.	GF.	ShO.	Sv.	IP.	H.	R.	ER.	HR.	HB.	BB.	Int. BB.	SO.	WP.
Graham, Nashville	3	7	.300	2.16	41	0	0	29	0	17	66.2	64	29	16	3	0	18	5	38	1
Grimsley, Chattanooga*	1	0	1.000	0.00	1	0	0	1	0	0	2.0	2	0	0	0	0	0	0	1	0
Groves, Jacksonville	0	1	.000	4.50	5	1	0	1	0	0	14.0	19	10	7	1	1	9	0	9	1
Guetterman, Chattanooga*	11	7	.611	3.38	24	24	5	0	2	0	157.0	174	68	59	7	4	38	2	47	5
Habyan, Charlotte	4	7	.364	4.44	13	13	1	0	0	0	77.0	84	46	38	8	0	34	1	55	6
Harper, Knoxville	4	2	.667	2.68	10	8	0	1	0	0	40.1	36	14	12	4	0	27	1	31	1
Harsh, Columbus	3	9	.250	4.78	19	12	1	3	1	2	86.2	98	53	46	9	2	47	3	45	4
Harvey, Birmingham*	0	2	.000	5.59	18	0	0	5	0	0	29.0	33	20	18	5	0	14	3	18	1
Hayes, Chattanooga*	0	2	.000	5.84	14	0	0	4	0	1	24.2	27	19	16	1	1	18	0	11	1
Henneman, Birmingham	4	2	.667	2.43	29	1	0	16	0	6	59.1	48	22	16	1	2	33	2	39	3
Hess, Jacksonville	0	1	.000	22.50	2	0	0	2	0	0	2.0	5	5	5	1	0	3	1	2	0
Hinz, Birmingham	1	2	.333	4.30	6	5	0	1	0	0	23.0	19	15	11	3	1	31	1	5	1
Hogan, Columbus	9	9	.500	3.72	27	22	8	2	2	0	164.2	173	93	68	20	4	54	1	77	11
Huber, Jacksonville	2	2	.500	4.08	21	0	0	15	0	4	39.2	34	20	18	5	0	16	3	27	3
Huffman, Charlotte	6	1	.857	3.62	11	9	1	0	0	0	64.2	64	30	26	8	2	17	0	37	1
Jacob, Birmingham	1	2	.333	6.43	4	1	0	3	0	0	7.0	11	6	5	2	1	5	1	3	0
James, Birmingham	0	1	.000	6.46	10	4	0	3	0	1	23.2	21	21	17	1	1	26	0	17	7
Jefferson, Jacksonville	3	2	.600	5.09	8	8	1	0	0	0	40.2	43	26	23	3	0	25	1	29	2
G. Johnson, Jacksonville	0	0	.000	7.36	2	0	0	1	0	0	3.2	5	3	3	1	0	2	1	3	0
Je. Johnson, Charlotte	5	2	.714	2.03	14	9	3	5	0	1	80.0	54	27	18	5	1	28	0	45	2
Jo. Johnson, Greenville	8	10	.444	3.75	24	24	7	0	3	0	151.0	155	70	63	11	6	41	0	72	6
M. Johnson, Chattanooga	8	3	.727	3.62	39	7	1	25	0	5	69.2	58	33	28	1	2	56	3	43	6
Kasprzak, Columbus	2	2	.500	2.06	37	0	0	20	0	3	56.2	35	14	13	2	3	32	8	57	2
Kelly, Birmingham	7	10	.412	4.29	28	28	3	0	2	0	172.0	149	103	82	13	12	145	3	119	9
Keough, Nashville	2	4	.333	6.75	7	7	0	0	0	0	40.0	41	32	30	6	0	32	0	32	6
Kerfeld, Columbus	14	9	.609	2.99	24	23	5	1	0	0	162.2	140	80	54	6	9	79	3	118	20
King, Nashville*	3	6	.333	5.34	28	8	0	10	0	4	64.0	64	49	38	4	0	57	1	34	8
Kinns, Jacksonville	1	4	.200	8.83	11	7	0	2	0	0	35.2	50	39	35	5	3	24	0	16	4
Kinnunen, Jacksonville*	6	2	.750	3.72	38	1	0	15	0	4	75.0	61	33	31	3	2	56	4	42	4
Klump, Orlando	10	7	.588	4.29	22	18	5	2	1	0	107.0	109	70	51	9	2	82	1	44	2
Knudson, Columbus	4	5	.444	2.23	14	14	3	0	0	0	101.0	100	32	25	2	0	27	4	54	2
Konopa, Charlotte*	4	9	.308	4.29	24	18	2	1	1	0	109.0	104	62	52	10	5	67	1	53	7
Krsnich, Charlotte	0	0	.000	4.76	9	0	0	3	0	0	17.0	14	11	9	0	1	13	1	9	2
Larkin, Birmingham*	2	1	.667	5.76	22	0	0	13	0	0	29.2	35	21	19	3	0	24	0	16	1
Ledbetter, Charlotte	0	0	.000	39.00	4	0	0	0	0	0	3.0	14	13	13	0	1	5	0	0	1
Leggatt, Greenville	4	1	.800	1.66	18	2	1	7	0	0	48.2	48	15	9	3	1	17	1	32	3
Leiter, Charlotte	1	3	.250	6.75	5	5	0	0	0	0	18.2	29	21	14	2	2	11	0	8	3
Luecken, Chattanooga	11	13	.458	3.79	26	26	5	0	1	0	163.2	166	85	69	13	2	88	0	90	9
Maack, Orlando*	5	7	.417	3.38	23	16	6	3	2	1	114.1	88	54	43	9	2	61	1	88	4
Martinez, Memphis	6	2	.750	0.90	26	0	0	20	0	6	50.0	26	7	5	1	1	7	1	37	3
McCullock, Columbus	0	0	.000	0.00	2	0	0	1	0	0	3.0	1	0	0	0	0	3	0	6	0
McDonald, Chattanooga	8	12	.400	4.50	27	26	1	0	0	0	154.0	159	103	77	6	4	71	3	79	13
McKay, Jacksonville	3	5	.375	3.50	13	13	0	0	0	0	54.0	52	29	21	6	2	35	0	24	5
McKnight, Knoxville	11	8	.579	3.81	24	24	8	0	1	0	151.0	128	75	64	13	0	83	2	93	8
McLaughlin, Knoxville	1	5	.167	6.22	27	3	1	10	0	0	63.2	63	48	44	4	2	59	0	52	9
McMahon, Orlando	4	6	.400	3.41	19	14	1	1	0	0	100.1	81	44	38	6	2	55	1	52	10
Miner, Memphis	4	8	.333	4.86	23	9	2	4	0	0	83.1	88	52	45	13	4	48	0	44	5
Monteleone, Birmingham	7	8	.467	4.66	19	19	4	0	0	0	123.2	116	69	64	9	4	67	1	74	11
Moore, Knoxville	7	6	.538	2.31	53	0	0	39	0	6	70.0	71	28	18	2	1	42	4	43	5
Mortillaro, Greenville*	0	0	.000	5.40	4	0	0	3	0	0	5.0	5	3	3	0	0	4	0	4	0
Moya, Birmingham	0	0	.000	6.75	1	0	0	0	0	0	1.1	1	1	1	0	0	4	0	0	0
Mustad, Jacksonville	2	1	.667	2.92	6	4	1	2	1	1	24.2	22	8	8	1	2	12	0	17	2
Nicometi, Jacksonville*	1	0	1.000	5.00	14	0	0	5	0	3	18.0	17	10	10	1	0	14	3	9	0
Nielson, Nashville	6	3	.667	2.44	10	10	2	0	0	0	73.2	55	34	20	5	1	15	0	27	1
North, Greenville	1	1	.500	5.79	23	0	0	7	0	3	42.0	46	30	27	1	2	32	1	27	6
Oelkers, Charlotte*	16	11	.593	3.40	29	29	13	0	4	0	219.2	199	104	83	17	2	74	2	139	9
Oliveras, Charlotte	3	7	.300	4.20	19	6	0	4	0	0	75.0	68	45	35	8	4	39	2	52	9
Olson, Memphis	0	1	.000	4.91	4	2	0	2	0	1	14.2	15	8	8	1	2	6	0	7	2
Pacella, Charlotte	0	0	.000	4.28	12	1	0	2	0	1	27.1	27	21	13	1	0	28	3	21	3
Paris, Columbus	2	5	.286	4.32	21	10	1	8	0	0	73.0	65	43	35	3	4	47	2	45	6
Patterson, Nashville	5	4	.556	4.78	32	4	0	23	0	1	64.0	72	42	34	6	6	38	7	47	4
Pederson, Chattanooga	2	1	.667	3.26	18	2	0	8	0	0	47.0	47	18	17	5	1	15	2	13	1
Pena, Birmingham	3	8	.273	3.74	40	0	0	29	0	9	67.1	63	32	28	4	0	28	6	47	3
Pettibone, Orlando	3	6	.333	4.28	12	8	3	1	0	1	61.0	63	32	29	7	0	19	0	22	0
Portugal, Orlando	14	7	.667	2.98	27	27	10	0	3	0	196.0	171	80	65	16	3	113	2	110	9
Radtke, Memphis	3	2	.600	3.86	11	9	1	0	0	0	60.2	63	30	26	7	6	25	0	24	5
Ramirez, Chattanooga	4	12	.250	5.25	28	22	3	1	0	0	128.2	138	86	75	12	2	63	2	69	7
Rasmussen, Nashville	4	4	.500	3.01	31	5	0	11	0	4	80.2	58	33	27	1	3	36	2	84	2
Regalado, Columbus	0	3	.000	6.95	7	2	0	1	0	0	22.0	34	22	17	3	0	11	1	5	2
Reilly, Columbus	1	0	1.000	16.62	5	0	0	1	0	0	4.1	10	8	8	1	0	3	0	1	0
Reish, Memphis	10	11	.476	4.17	29	24	10	2	1	1	172.2	173	94	80	13	4	58	4	62	12
Reyes, Memphis	1	1	.500	3.28	14	0	0	7	0	3	46.2	46	20	17	2	3	12	0	21	3
Reynolds, Knoxville	0	0	.000	13.50	2	0	0	2	0	0	2.0	4	3	3	0	0	2	0	2	0
Robinson, Birmingham	6	6	.500	4.70	20	19	1	0	0	0	113.0	111	64	59	10	2	56	0	47	7
Rodgers, Knoxville	3	4	.429	3.82	15	8	1	3	0	0	61.1	66	34	26	7	2	20	0	33	9
Rowe, Chattanooga	3	9	.250	3.18	31	16	3	9	1	3	130.1	135	59	46	2	1	53	2	86	5
Ruiz, Greenville*	3	3	.500	3.10	54	0	0	19	0	4	69.2	78	26	24	1	2	48	5	57	4
Schaefer, Charlotte	0	0	.000	18.00	1	0	0	1	0	0	1.0	2	2	2	0	0	2	0	0	1
Schrom, Orlando	0	0	.000	2.70	2	2	0	0	0	0	10.0	10	8	3	1	1	6	0	10	2
Segura, Knoxville	4	6	.400	4.43	12	12	1	0	0	0	69.0	75	47	34	4	0	47	1	26	8
Semprini, Chattanooga	1	1	.500	1.98	7	0	0	2	0	0	13.2	11	3	3	1	1	6	1	6	0
Shaw, Memphis	1	2	.333	8.10	6	6	1	0	0	0	30.0	32	27	27	1	0	31	0	21	0
Shiflett, Nashville*	9	8	.529	3.94	22	20	3	1	0	0	123.1	110	68	54	7	0	80	2	60	3
Shipanoff, Knoxville	5	9	.357	3.58	36	15	1	10	1	2	130.2	108	60	52	11	3	68	4	108	3
Shouppe, Columbus*	3	0	1.000	4.98	37	0	0	19	0	0	56.0	63	36	31	3	2	43	10	41	4
Silva, Nashville	2	1	.667	6.38	10	0	0	4	0	1	18.1	20	14	13	2	0	13	3	7	3
Smith, Greenville*	7	0	1.000	1.65	9	9	3	0	1	0	60.0	47	13	11	0	1	23	0	35	1
Snell, Charlotte	9	4	.692	2.42	52	0	0	48	0	17	81.2	68	30	22	6	0	28	10	45	4
Snyder, Columbus	2	8	.200	5.43	12	10	3	0	0	0	54.2	66	41	33	3	5	29	2	16	3
Souza, Birmingham	0	3	.000	5.97	5	5	0	0	0	0	28.2	24	19	19	4	1	16	0	15	1
Springer, Birmingham*	0	0	.000	4.91	5	0	0	3	0	0	11.0	12	8	6	0	0	3	0	10	0
Sprowl, Birmingham*	0	0	.000	6.23	5	0	0	3	0	0	4.1	6	3	3	1	0	6	0	3	0

Pitcher—Club	W.	L.	Pct.	ERA.	G.	GS.	CG.	GF.	ShO.	Sv.	IP.	H.	R.	ER.	HR.	HB.	BB.	Int. BB.	SO.	WP.
St. Claire, Jacksonville	10	7	.588	2.88	48	0	0	40	0	15	75.0	64	35	24	4	2	29	14	56	2
Stoll, Jacksonville	10	5	.667	2.76	17	17	5	0	0	0	114.1	105	47	35	6	4	37	0	59	3
Strasser, Columbus	4	4	.500	4.43	14	11	2	1	0	0	65.0	69	37	32	9	0	24	2	48	3
Strode, Memphis*	9	2	.818	2.43	13	13	7	0	3	0	92.2	55	25	25	5	0	32	0	50	0
Summers, Charlotte	8	7	.533	3.12	30	21	5	2	2	0	144.1	127	69	50	6	4	70	4	57	6
Tabor, Birmingham	10	4	.714	3.03	41	3	0	25	0	8	118.2	108	49	40	5	1	43	3	48	5
Je. Taylor, Jacksonville*	3	4	.429	4.59	31	10	1	13	0	1	86.1	69	50	44	1	0	79	2	85	6
Jo. Taylor, Knoxville	0	0	.000	4.22	5	1	0	2	0	0	10.2	9	5	5	1	0	13	0	8	1
Tewksbury, Nashville	11	9	.550	2.83	26	26	6	0	0	0	172.0	185	69	54	8	4	42	3	78	4
Tomaselli, Nashville*	5	7	.417	5.07	29	20	1	4	1	1	110.0	124	81	62	8	2	89	1	49	5
Torres, Jacksonville	6	7	.462	3.58	26	26	5	0	3	0	150.2	147	72	60	7	1	66	0	78	5
Treadway, Greenville	11	8	.579	3.94	27	27	4	0	0	0	157.2	161	78	69	12	4	58	1	97	4
Walberg, Memphis*	5	7	.417	3.84	14	14	4	0	2	0	91.1	90	45	39	9	1	27	0	39	0
Walsh, Knoxville*	5	8	.385	3.24	23	19	4	2	1	0	119.1	111	54	43	6	0	64	0	60	8
Ward, Greenville	4	9	.308	4.99	21	20	4	0	0	0	104.2	108	71	58	9	2	57	0	54	8
Wardle, Orlando*	6	1	.857	0.69	45	0	0	41	0	17	78.0	41	10	6	1	2	30	0	75	1
Wells, Knoxville	3	2	.600	2.59	8	8	3	0	1	0	59.0	58	22	17	3	0	17	0	34	1
Werly, Charlotte	1	1	.500	4.67	3	3	0	0	0	0	17.1	20	9	9	2	0	11	0	13	0
West, Greenville	10	7	.588	4.47	26	25	6	1	1	0	145.0	143	81	72	9	3	75	2	102	11
Wex, Nashville	1	0	1.000	2.77	7	0	0	5	0	0	13.0	8	4	4	0	0	3	1	5	0
Whitmer, Chattanooga	6	7	.462	3.14	15	15	4	0	1	0	100.1	89	49	35	4	3	28	6	46	4
Wilder, Memphis	7	4	.636	3.67	47	0	0	32	0	2	90.2	96	38	37	7	5	30	4	26	1
Williams, Jacksonville	5	6	.455	2.49	23	14	2	3	0	1	119.1	107	46	33	9	1	49	4	67	9
Willsher, Charlotte	3	6	.333	3.70	27	11	2	7	0	1	80.1	75	44	33	6	1	45	2	51	7
Woodworth, Nashville*	1	1	.500	2.63	19	1	0	8	0	1	24.0	25	10	7	1	1	11	1	20	1
Wyatt, Memphis*	5	7	.417	5.21	33	14	1	6	0	0	103.2	112	71	60	9	1	80	1	60	5
Yearout, Knoxville*	0	0	.000	2.08	1	0	0	0	0	0	4.1	4	1	1	0	1	1	1	2	0
Yuhas, Memphis	0	3	.000	3.38	6	6	2	0	0	0	34.2	33	15	13	3	1	0	3	27	0
Ziem, Greenville	2	1	.667	0.00	8	0	0	7	0	2	21.0	12	1	0	0	0	9	4	14	1

BALKS—Shiflett, 11; Maack, 6; Clary, Cone, Ramirez, Shipanoff, Stoll, Tomaselli, 4 each; Cary, Deshaies, James, Ruiz, Walsh, 3 each; Alba, Arnold, Baldwin, Callahan, K. Cook, Garcia, Hogan, McDonald, Monteleone, Radtke, Treadway, West, 2 each; Acker, Adair, Aquino, Bailey, Bormann, Bryant, Cartwright, Cole, D. Cook, Dacko, Dixon, Drabek, Faulk, Ferguson, Foley, Gilbert, Gordon, Groves, Guetterman, Habyan, Hayes, Je. Johnson, Mi. Johnson, Kasprzak, King, Klump, Konopa, Krsnich, Larkin, McKay, McKnight, McLaughlin, McMahon, Patterson, Pedersen, Pettibone, Reish, Robinson, Rowe, Segura, Shaw, Summers, Tewksbury, Torres, Walberg, Ward, Williams, Woodworth, 1 each.

COMBINATION SHUTOUTS—Monteleone-Pena, Birmingham; Konopa-Concepcion, Werly-Snell, Charlotte; Whitmer-Bartley, Guetterman-Bartley, Chattanooga; Kerfeld-Foley, Paris-Foley-Shoupee, Harsh-Calhoun, Columbus; Treadway-Clay, Johnson-Ruiz-Leggatt, Clary-Ziem, Greenville; McKay-Gilbreath, Stoll-Graves-Cates-St. Claire, McKay-Taylor, Torres-St. Claire, Dopson-Kinnunen-St. Claire, Mustad-St. Claire, Jefferson-Gilbreath, Brahs-Huber, Williams-Nicometi, Jacksonville; McKnight-Moore, Harper-Moore-Gillam, Blackmon-Gillam-Moore, Shipan-off-Moore, Alba-Taylor-Moore, Knoxville; Cook-Miner, Reish-Benedict, Memphis; Shiflett-Baldwin-Woodworth-Patterson, Nashville; Oelkers-Eufemia, Klump-Eufemia, McMahon-Eufemia, Klump-Wardle, Portugal-Wardle, Orlando.

NO-HIT GAMES—Deshaies, Nashville, defeated Columbus, 5-1 (seven innings), May 4; Shipanoff-Esquer-Rodgers, Knoxville, lost to Charlotte, 1-0, August 28.

Texas League

CLASS AA

Leading Batter
JAMES STEELS
Beaumont

League President
CARL SAWATSKI

Leading Pitcher
TED HIGUERA
El Paso

CHAMPIONSHIP WINNERS IN PREVIOUS YEARS

1888—Dallas	.671	
1889—Houston	.551	
1890—Galveston	.705	
1892—Houston	.741	
Houston	.613	
1895—Dallas	.754	
Fort Worth°	.750	
1896—Fort Worth	.757	
Houston°	.679	
Galveston°	.548	
1897—San Antonio†	.657	
Galveston†	.717	
1898—League disbanded.		
1899—Galveston	.632	
Galveston	.762	
1900-01—Did not operate.		
1902—Corsicana	.866	
Corsicana	.682	
1903—Paris-Waco	.615	
Dallas°	.648	
1904—Corsicana°	.615	
Fort Worth	.800	
1905—Fort Worth	.545	
1906—Fort Worth	.677	
Cleburne x	.609	
1907—Austin	.629	
1908—San Antonio	.664	
1909—Houston	.601	
1910—Dallas†	.586	
Houston†	.586	
1911—Austin	.575	
1912—Houston	.626	
1913—Houston	.620	
1914—Houston†	.671	
Waco†	.671	
1915—Waco	.592	
1916—Waco	.587	
1917—Dallas	.600	
1918—Dallas	.584	
1919—Shreveport°	.677	
Fort Worth	.651	
1920—Fort Worth	.703	
Fort Worth	.750	
1921—Fort Worth	.691	
Fort Worth	.662	
1922—Fort Worth	.694	
Fort Worth	.711	
1923—Fort Worth	.632	
1924—Fort Worth	.689	
Fort Worth	.763	

1925—Fort Worth	.711	
Fort Worth y	.653	
1926—Dallas	.574	
1927—Wichita Falls	.654	
1928—Houston°	.679	
Wichita Falls	.731	
1929—Dallas°	.588	
Wichita Falls	.620	
1930—Wichita Falls	.697	
Fort Worth°	.632	
1931—Houston a	.625	
Houston	.734	
1932—Beaumont°	.640	
Dallas	.727	
1933—Houston	.623	
San Antonio (4th)§	.523	
1934—Galveston‡	.579	
1935—Oklahoma City‡	.590	
1936—Dallas	.604	
Tulsa (3rd)§	.519	
1937—Oklahoma City	.635	
Fort Worth (3rd)§	.535	
1938—Beaumont	.635	
1939—Houston	.606	
Fort Worth (4th)§	.540	
1940—Houston‡	.652	
1941—Houston	.673	
Dallas (4th)§	.519	
1942—Beaumont	.605	
Shreveport (2nd)§	.576	
1943-44-45—Did not operate.		
1946—Fort Worth	.656	
Dallas (2nd)§	.591	
1947—Houston‡	.623	
1948—Fort Worth‡	.601	
1949—Fort Worth	.649	
Tulsa (2nd)§	.584	
1950—Beaumont	.595	
San Antonio (4th)§	.513	
1951—Houston‡	.619	
1952—Dallas	.571	
Shreveport (3rd)§	.522	
1953—Dallas‡	.571	
1954—Shreveport	.559	
Houston (2nd)§	.553	
1955—Dallas	.581	
Shreveport (3rd)§	.540	
1956—Houston‡	.623	
1957—Dallas	.662	
Houston (2nd)§	.630	

1958—Fort Worth	.582	
Cor. Christi (3rd)§	.507	
1959—Victoria	.589	
Austin (2nd)§	.548	
1960—Rio Grande Valley	.590	
Tulsa (3rd)	.528	
1961—Amarillo	.643	
San Antonio (3rd)§	.532	
1962—El Paso	.571	
Tulsa (2nd)§	.550	
1963—San Antonio	.564	
Tulsa (3rd)§	.529	
1964—San Antonio‡	.607	
1965—Tulsa	.574	
Albuquerque b	.550	
1966—Arkansas	.579	
1967—Albuquerque	.557	
1968—Arkansas	.586	
El Paso b	.562	
1969—Amarillo	.593	
Memphis b	.504	
1970—Albuquerque a	.615	
Memphis	.507	
1971—Did not operate as league—clubs were members of Dixie Association.		
1972—Alexandria	.600	
El Paso b	.557	
1973—San Antonio	.590	
Memphis b	.558	
1974—Victoria b	.581	
El Paso	.555	
1975—Lafayette c	.558	
Midland c	.604	
1976—Amarillo b	.600	
Shreveport	.515	
1977—El Paso	.600	
Arkansas d	.485	
1978—El Paso d	.593	
Jackson	.567	
1979—Arkansas d	.571	
Midland	.563	
1980—Arkansas d	.596	
San Antonio	.544	
1981—San Antonio	.571	
Jackson d	.507	
1982—El Paso	.559	
Tulsa d	.515	
1983—Jackson	.507	
Beaumont d	.500	

°Won split-season playoff. †No playoff for title. ‡Finished first and won four-club playoff. §Won four-club playoff. xTitle to Cleburne by default. yTied with Dallas in second half and won playoff for championship. zFort Worth disbanded. aTied with Beaumont at end of first half and won title in best-of-five series played as part of second half schedule. bLeague divided into Eastern, Western divisions; won two-team playoff. cLeague divided into Eastern, Western divisions; declared co-champions when playoffs were not completed. dLeague divided into Eastern and Western divisions and played split-season; won playoffs. NOTE—Championship awarded to winner of four-team playoff, 1933-51; first-place team and playoff winner co-champions, 1952-64.

STANDING OF CLUBS AT CLOSE OF FIRST HALF, JUNE 19

EASTERN DIVISION

Club	W.	L.	T.	Pct.	G.B.
Jackson (Mets)	43	24	0	.642	......
Shreveport (Giants)	31	36	0	.463	12
Arkansas (Cardinals)	31	36	0	.463	12
Tulsa (Rangers)	29	37	0	.439	13½

WESTERN DIVISION

Club	W.	L.	T.	Pct.	G.B.
Beaumont (Padres)	44	24	0	.647	......
El Paso (Brewers)	37	30	0	.552	6½
San Antonio (Dodgers)	31	37	0	.456	13
Midland (Cubs)	23	45	0	.338	21

STANDING OF CLUBS AT CLOSE OF SECOND HALF, SEPTEMBER 1

EASTERN DIVISION

Club	W.	L.	T.	Pct.	G.B.
Jackson (Mets)	40	29	0	.580	......
Tulsa (Rangers)	33	36	0	.478	7
Arkansas (Cardinals)	31	38	0	.449	9
Shreveport (Giants)	28	41	0	.406	12

WESTERN DIVISION

Club	W.	L.	T.	Pct.	G.B.
Beaumont (Padres)	45	23	0	.662	......
El Paso (Brewers)	35	33	0	.515	10
San Antonio (Dodgers)	33	35	0	.485	12
Midland (Cubs)	29	39	0	.426	16

COMPOSITE STANDING OF CLUBS AT CLOSE OF SEASON, SEPTEMBER 1

Club	Beau.	Jax	ElP	S.A.	Tul.	Ark.	Shrev.	Mid.	W.	L.	T.	Pct.	G.B.
Beaumont (Padres)	....	5	20	19	6	10	7	22	89	47	0	.654	......
Jackson (Mets)	5	....	5	6	20	17	24	6	83	53	0	.610	6
El Paso (Brewers)	12	5	....	18	5	6	7	19	72	63	0	.533	16½
San Antonio (Dodgers)	13	4	14	....	4	5	4	20	64	72	0	.471	25
Tulsa (Rangers)	4	12	4	6	....	14	16	6	62	73	0	.459	26½
Arkansas (Cardinals)	0	15	4	5	18	....	14	6	62	74	0	.456	27
Shreveport (Giants)	3	8	3	6	16	18	....	5	59	77	0	.434	30
Midland (Cubs)	10	4	13	12	4	4	5	....	52	84	0	.382	37

Arkansas club represented Little Rock, Ark.

Major league affiliations in parentheses.

Playoffs—Jackson defeated Beaumont, four games to two, to win league championship.

Regular-Season Attendance—Arkansas, 212,029; Beaumont, 130,950; El Paso, 205,196; Jackson, 119,007; Midland, 101,312; San Antonio, 125,542; Shreveport, 42,384; Tulsa, 124,160. Total, 1,060,580. Playoff attendance, 16,959. All-Star Game attendance, 4,828.

Managers—Arkansas, Dave Bialas; Beaumont, Bobby Tolan; El Paso, Terry Bevington; Jackson, Sam Perlozzo; Midland, George Enright; San Antonio, Gary Larocque; Shreveport, Duane Espy; Tulsa, Orlando Gomez.

All-Star Team—1B-Pat Casey, Beaumont; 2B-Greg Tabor, Tulsa; 3B-Dale Sveum, El Paso; SS-Shawon Dunston, Midland; OF-Ralph Bryant, San Antonio; James Steels, Beaumont; Curt Ford, Arkansas; James Steels, Beaumont; C-Mark Parent, Beaumont and Gilberto Reyes, San Antonio; DH-Mark Gillaspie, Beaumont; Pitchers-Calvin Schiraldi, Jackson; Bill Long, Beaumont; Tim Meeks, San Antonio; Pete Kutsukos, Beaumont; Ted Higuera, El Paso; Most Valuable Player-James Steels, Beaumont; Pitcher of the Year-Calvin Schiraldi, Jackson; Manager of the Year-Sam Perlozzo, Jackson.

(Compiled by Howe News Bureau, Boston, Mass.)

CLUB BATTING

Club	Pct.	G.	AB.	R.	OR.	H.	TB.	2B.	3B.	HR.	RBI.	GW.	SH.	SF.	HP.	BB.	Int. BB.	SO.	SB.	CS.	LOB.
El Paso	.285	135	4559	738	674	1301	1842	231	35	80	657	69	35	49	20	620	19	628	136	79	1065
Midland	.268	136	4456	577	716	1193	1744	182	30	103	522	46	46	25	22	521	31	910	106	57	1033
Jackson	.265	136	4498	641	525	1191	1752	199	31	100	576	75	64	32	36	469	40	704	129	57	933
San Antonio	.264	136	4544	670	692	1198	1790	204	44	100	603	55	47	31	23	551	22	786	137	72	963
Beaumont	.262	136	4411	665	541	1157	1659	210	32	76	584	78	93	42	21	692	43	659	135	91	1046
Tulsa	.259	135	4280	571	586	1109	1637	200	32	88	502	60	38	36	36	472	13	774	153	75	921
Arkansas	.255	136	4463	545	642	1138	1584	180	28	70	484	57	58	40	26	463	33	777	104	47	977
Shreveport	.251	136	4343	552	583	1089	1633	200	37	90	503	53	42	36	18	540	18	837	92	56	949

INDIVIDUAL BATTING

(Leading Qualifiers for Batting Championship—367 or More Plate Appearances)

*Bats lefthanded.   †Switch-hitter.

Player and Club	Pct.	G.	AB.	R.	H.	TB.	2B.	3B.	HR.	RBI.	GW.	SH.	SF.	HP.	BB.	Int. BB.	SO.	SB.	CS.
Steels, James, Beaumont*	.340	127	474	90	161	243	26	10	12	81	12	5	2	1	48	3	45	35	17
Sveum, Dale, El Paso†	.329	131	523	92	172	256	41	8	9	84	9	1	6	0	43	1	72	6	3
Ford, Curtis, Arkansas*	.324	118	442	62	143	198	23	1	10	78	5	1	6	3	52	5	50	25	10
Casey, Patrick, Beaumont	.305	118	377	64	115	178	26	2	11	68	11	7	4	2	77	2	60	7	8
Jones, Jeffry, Midland	.304	113	391	60	119	203	20	2	20	82	6	0	6	5	65	3	95	12	4
Reyes, Gilberto, San Antonio	.303	120	433	55	131	181	16	2	10	78	8	2	5	2	29	2	50	1	4
Bryant, Ralph, San Antonio*	.300	115	434	71	130	252	21	4	31	86	7	1	4	5	39	4	113	5	3
Tabor, Gregory, Tulsa	.299	123	462	69	138	187	27	2	6	53	2	10	1	3	27	0	71	22	18
Ortiz, Javier, Tulsa	.298	94	325	42	97	148	21	3	8	53	5	4	4	5	47	2	67	4	5
Torve, Kelvin, Shreveport*	.297	114	316	59	94	173	21	5	16	62	9	0	6	2	43	3	42	2	0

Departmental Leaders: G—Espy, 133; AB—Espy, 535; R—Dykstra, 100; H—Sveum, 172; TB—Sveum, 256; 2B—Sveum, 41; 3B—Duncan, Pederson, 11; HR—R. Bryant, 31; RBI—Gillaspie, 87; GWRBI—Max, 16; SH—Wasinger, 16; SF—Felder, 9; HP—Nago, 10; BB—Gillaspie, 115; IBB—Gillaspie, 15; SO—Cochrane, 133; SB—Felder, 58; CS—Tabor, 18.

(All Players—Listed Alphabetically)

Player and Club	Pct.	G.	AB.	R.	H.	TB.	2B.	3B.	HR.	RBI.	GW.	SH.	SF.	HP.	BB.	Int. BB.	SO.	SB.	CS.
Adams, John, Arkansas	.045	19	22	3	1	1	0	0	0	2	0	1	1	0	2	0	9	0	0
Aguilera, Richard, Jackson	.267	11	15	0	4	5	1	0	0	2	0	1	0	0	1	0	2	0	0
Alvarez, Carmelo, San Antonio†	.213	93	272	38	58	71	9	2	0	10	0	6	1	3	33	4	50	13	6
Anderson, David Carl, San Antonio	.000	4	6	0	0	0	0	0	0	0	0	1	0	0	0	0	2	0	0
Anicich, Michael, Midland	.129	11	31	0	4	4	0	0	0	0	1	0	1	3	0	3	0	0	0
Asadoor, Randall, Tulsa	.249	124	425	65	106	182	22	3	16	53	7	2	4	3	74	4	119	17	9
Auten, James, Midland	.241	44	137	10	33	45	6	0	2	12	0	0	0	1	9	1	23	0	0
Baker, Ricky, Midland†	.302	61	202	32	61	72	5	3	0	12	0	3	1	0	32	0	19	13	12
Banks, Darryl, Midland	.545	10	11	1	6	7	1	0	0	3	0	0	0	1	0	0	2	0	0
Barba, Michael, Beaumont	.000	19	6	0	0	0	0	0	0	0	0	0	0	1	0	0	5	0	0
Bass, Barry, Tulsa	.188	39	16	2	3	3	0	0	0	3	0	0	0	0	2	0	3	0	1
Bates, Kevin, Shreveport*	.160	70	163	18	26	37	8	0	1	8	1	1	0	2	29	3	41	2	1
Beane, William, Jackson	.281	123	455	78	128	223	29	3	20	72	9	0	6	5	48	2	81	26	9
Bettendorf, Jeffrey, Jackson	.250	7	12	1	3	3	0	0	0	2	0	0	0	0	0	0	4	0	0

Player and Club	Pct.	G.	AB.	R.	H.	TB.	2B.	3B.	HR.	RBI.	GW.	SH.	SF.	HP.	BB.	Int. BB.	SO.	SB.	CS.
Biggus, Bengie, Shreveport	.000	8	2	0	0	0	0	0	0	0	0	0	0	0	0	0	2	0	0
Blackwell, Orlando, Shreveport†	.271	116	409	56	111	145	17	4	3	39	7	5	6	2	35	1	43	8	3
Bockus, Randy, Shreveport°	.136	18	22	0	3	3	0	0	0	0	0	4	0	0	4	0	6	1	0
Booker, Roderick, Arkansas°	.206	52	209	10	43	53	4	3	0	22	3	4	1	1	24	2	28	8	3
Boudreau, James, Midland°	.438	42	16	2	7	8	1	0	0	2	0	2	0	0	4	0	2	0	0
Brahms, Russell, Shreveport	.000	9	0	0	0	0	0	0	0	0	0	1	0	0	0	0	0	0	0
Brower, Robert, Tulsa	.285	96	344	69	98	151	14	9	7	30	4	3	1	3	59	1	56	54	12
Brumley, A. Michael, Midland†	.216	73	255	37	55	90	11	3	6	21	0	1	1	0	48	3	49	5	2
Brunenkant, S. Barry, Tulsa	.234	39	124	11	29	34	0	1	1	7	1	3	1	0	12	0	12	0	3
Bryant, R. Neil, Midland°	.250	6	4	0	1	1	0	0	0	0	0	0	0	0	1	0	1	0	0
Bryant, Ralph, San Antonio°	.300	115	434	71	130	252	21	4	31	86	7	1	4	5	39	4	113	5	3
Bullinger, D. Matthews, Jackson°	.000	22	2	0	0	0	0	0	0	0	0	1	0	0	0	0	1	0	0
Burns, Daniel, El Paso	.000	13	1	0	0	0	0	0	0	0	0	0	0	0	0	0	0	0	0
Capel, Michael, Midland	.200	16	10	0	2	2	0	0	0	0	0	1	0	0	1	0	1	0	0
Carpio, Jorge, Midland	.200	34	10	0	2	2	0	0	0	0	0	0	2	0	1	0	4	0	0
Carreon, Mark, Jackson	.280	119	435	64	122	145	14	3	1	43	3	7	5	5	38	1	24	12	8
Cartwright, Alan, El Paso°	.343	58	204	41	70	95	13	3	2	28	1	1	2	0	14	0	26	5	3
Casey, Patrick, Beaumont	.305	118	377	64	115	178	26	2	11	68	11	7	4	2	77	2	60	7	8
Castillo, Juan, El Paso	.288	119	448	78	129	176	21	7	4	59	4	4	4	3	30	0	60	15	13
Cataline, Daniel, San Antonio	.280	116	389	64	109	202	29	2	20	60	6	1	1	2	46	0	85	9	4
Charley, Tandy, Beaumont°	.381	13	21	4	8	8	0	0	0	3	0	1	0	0	0	0	6	0	0
Chestnut, Troy, Midland	.250	14	20	0	5	5	0	0	0	0	0	0	2	0	0	0	7	0	0
Cias, Darryl, Tulsa	.273	27	88	9	24	34	4	0	2	10	0	0	0	0	8	0	9	0	0
Clark, Robert, Tulsa°	.000	4	0	0	0	0	0	0	0	0	0	1	0	0	0	0	0	0	0
Clements, David, Arkansas	.305	77	259	43	79	126	15	1	10	39	5	3	0	2	24	0	35	3	2
Cochrane, David, Jackson†	.267	129	454	66	121	222	29	3	22	77	8	1	2	1	61	9	133	2	3
Cook, G. Timothy, Beaumont	.125	30	8	0	1	1	0	0	0	0	0	2	0	0	1	0	3	0	0
Cordova, Antonio, Midland	.231	80	199	21	46	56	7	0	1	20	4	1	1	1	7	1	36	0	0
Couchee, Michael, Beaumont	.200	15	5	0	1	1	0	0	0	0	0	1	0	0	0	0	1	0	0
Crews, Lawrence, Shreveport	.265	27	34	5	9	9	0	0	0	6	0	2	0	0	6	0	15	0	0
Cummings, Robert, Shreveport	.287	95	282	33	81	133	17	4	9	43	6	1	4	0	44	0	53	5	4
Cunningham, Michael, San Antonio	.000	18	9	0	0	0	0	0	0	0	0	0	0	0	0	0	5	1	0
Davis, Douglas, Tulsa	.207	10	29	3	6	6	0	0	0	4	0	0	0	0	0	0	6	0	0
Davis, Stanley, El Paso°	.266	67	248	38	66	123	12	3	13	46	7	0	4	0	29	1	41	6	3
Denby, Darryl, Jackson†	.258	83	248	36	64	105	9	4	8	40	2	2	2	1	11	0	51	4	3
Denton, David, Midland	.280	39	93	10	26	34	2	0	2	9	1	0	0	0	6	1	16	1	0
Dillard, Ronald, Tulsa	.159	29	82	5	13	17	2	1	0	9	2	2	1	0	8	0	14	5	1
Duncan, Mariano, San Antonio†	.253	125	502	80	127	169	14	11	2	44	3	4	2	5	41	0	110	41	13
Dunston, Shawon, Midland	.329	73	298	44	98	126	13	3	3	34	4	2	4	3	11	2	38	11	8
Dykstra, Leonard, Jackson°	.275	131	501	100	138	195	25	7	6	52	6	1	1	5	73	6	45	53	17
Espy, Cecil, San Antonio†	.273	133	535	99	146	205	19	8	6	60	4	5	7	1	54	5	75	48	16
Etchebarren, Raymond, Beaumont	.250	19	80	7	20	27	2	1	1	8	3	1	0	0	4	0	11	0	0
Felder, Michael, El Paso†	.290	122	496	98	144	194	19	2	9	72	3	2	9	1	63	2	57	58	16
Felt, Richard, San Antonio	.125	15	16	0	2	2	0	0	0	0	0	1	0	0	2	0	9	0	0
Felton, Terry, San Antonio	.000	7	4	0	0	0	0	0	0	0	0	0	0	0	0	0	2	0	0
Ford, Curtis, Arkansas°	.324	118	442	62	143	198	23	1	10	78	5	1	6	3	52	5	50	25	10
Fruge, Jeffrey, Midland	.250	6	4	0	1	1	0	0	0	0	0	0	0	0	0	0	10	0	0
Fultz, William, Jackson	.128	35	39	3	5	8	0	0	1	3	0	4	1	1	1	0	10	0	0
Gallo, Raymond, Shreveport	.000	12	1	0	0	0	0	0	0	0	0	0	0	0	0	0	0	0	0
Garcia, Steven, Beaumont°	.265	94	234	28	62	82	10	2	2	22	2	1	2	1	22	5	19	9	6
Gauntlett, G. Todd, San Antonio	.228	70	193	15	44	51	7	0	0	30	3	1	3	0	25	1	20	0	1
Gendron, Robert, Shreveport	.250	14	4	0	1	1	0	0	0	0	0	0	0	0	1	0	1	0	0
Geren, Robert, Arkansas	.247	86	292	39	72	129	12	0	15	40	6	3	1	3	34	1	69	1	0
Gergen, Robert, Tulsa	.279	105	344	45	96	134	12	1	8	44	4	1	5	5	30	0	62	1	4
Gillaspie, Mark, Beaumont†	.274	130	424	77	116	197	27	3	16	87	14	4	6	2	115	15	64	6	8
Gladden, Jeffery, Shreveport	.200	12	15	0	3	5	0	1	0	2	0	2	0	0	1	0	1	0	0
Gomez, Jorge, Tulsa	.232	122	426	52	99	185	26	3	18	78	13	0	7	2	52	1	90	3	1
Graham, Everett, Shreveport°	.260	40	154	24	40	64	7	4	3	9	1	1	0	0	17	0	24	4	2
Granillo, Carlos, San Antonio°	.158	45	19	0	3	4	1	0	0	1	0	0	0	0	4	0	4	0	0
Graves, Joseph, Jackson	.000	58	10	0	0	0	0	0	0	0	0	3	0	0	0	0	3	0	0
Gray, Gary, El Paso	.333	8	30	2	10	11	1	0	0	1	1	0	0	0	3	1	1	0	0
Guin, Gregory, Arkansas°	.264	112	318	33	84	113	17	3	2	32	1	2	4	4	29	3	36	4	1
Hamm, Timothy, Beaumont	.000	6	5	0	0	0	0	0	0	0	0	0	0	0	0	0	2	0	0
Hance, William, Tulsa°	.210	70	233	17	49	68	10	0	3	24	3	0	1	0	31	2	34	0	1
Harris, Michael, Arkansas	.269	92	320	36	86	96	6	2	0	23	5	7	1	0	25	2	57	10	6
Harry, Whitney, Tulsa	.222	121	405	52	90	138	18	3	8	33	5	1	4	7	42	0	128	6	6
Hearn, Edward, Jackson	.312	86	311	46	97	153	19	2	11	51	6	2	4	2	25	4	35	1	0
Helsom, Robert, Arkansas°	.248	108	306	31	76	111	19	2	4	32	7	1	3	2	32	2	57	0	0
Henderson, Joseph, Midland	.260	100	292	35	76	118	13	1	9	38	4	3	4	0	56	4	77	0	2
Henry, Dwayne, Tulsa	.000	33	1	0	0	0	0	0	0	0	0	0	0	0	0	0	0	0	0
Housey, Joseph, Midland	.083	30	24	1	2	2	0	0	0	0	0	2	0	0	0	0	5	0	0
Hrynko, Lawrence, Midland	.000	23	21	0	0	0	0	0	0	0	0	0	0	0	1	0	9	0	0
Huey, John, Midland	.000	18	2	0	0	0	0	0	0	0	0	0	0	0	0	0	2	0	0
Hunsinger, Alan, Arkansas	.053	9	19	2	1	1	0	0	0	0	0	0	0	0	4	0	4	0	0
Hunt, J. Randy, Arkansas	.222	27	90	7	20	26	6	0	0	4	1	0	0	0	8	1	16	4	0
Hyman, Donald, Midland	.246	103	313	37	77	109	15	1	5	39	2	3	1	2	43	2	74	2	0
Innis, Brian, San Antonio	.200	7	5	1	1	1	0	0	0	0	0	0	0	0	0	0	2	0	0
Innis, Jeffrey, Jackson	.250	42	4	0	1	1	0	0	0	0	0	1	0	0	0	0	2	0	0
Irvine, Edward, El Paso	.300	8	30	2	9	12	1	1	0	5	0	0	0	0	2	0	4	1	2
Jackson, Darrin, Midland	.270	132	496	63	134	201	18	2	15	54	9	6	2	2	49	2	103	13	8
Jackson, Reginald, Jackson	.000	28	9	0	0	0	0	0	0	0	0	2	0	0	1	0	3	0	0
Johnson, Jerry, Beaumont	.234	80	209	25	49	67	7	1	3	32	4	3	1	3	32	1	35	0	2
Johnson, Scott, Midland°	.286	21	7	1	2	2	0	0	0	0	0	0	0	0	1	0	2	0	0
Johnson, Steven, Beaumont†	.233	125	430	74	100	145	21	6	4	35	0	4	0	7	91	0	86	23	14
Johnson, Terrance, Tulsa°	.000	22	3	1	0	0	0	0	0	0	0	0	1	0	0	0	3	0	0
Johnston, Jody, San Antonio	.286	39	7	0	2	2	0	0	0	0	0	0	2	0	0	0	2	0	0
Jones, Glenn, Shreveport	.293	28	75	12	22	36	7	2	1	6	1	0	0	0	15	2	0	0	0
Jones, James, Beaumont	.000	15	18	0	0	0	0	0	0	0	0	0	0	0	0	0	6	0	0
Jones, Jeffry, Midland	.304	113	391	60	119	203	20	2	20	82	6	0	6	5	65	3	95	12	4
Jones, Keith, Tulsa†	.254	84	232	33	59	70	3	4	0	14	1	3	1	1	18	1	32	22	8
Jones, Michael, Shreveport°	.272	107	312	44	85	119	13	3	5	26	3	2	2	1	29	1	72	0	6
Kable, David, Arkansas°	.221	65	226	30	50	108	7	0	17	41	2	2	1	2	29	1	72	0	0

Player and Club	Pct.	G.	AB.	R.	H.	TB.	2B.	3B.	HR.	RBI.	GW.	SH.	SF.	HP.	BB.	Int. BB.	SO.	SB.	CS.
Kaufman, Ronald, Midland	.333	31	3	0	1	1	0	0	0	0	0	0	0	0	0	0	1	0	1
Kinzer, Matthew, Arkansas	.133	14	15	1	2	2	0	0	0	1	0	1	0	0	1	0	5	0	0
Klipstein, David, El Paso	.289	125	477	68	138	164	18	1	2	58	6	3	4	3	80	0	43	20	7
Kneuer, Frank, Tulsa	.176	17	51	2	9	14	2	0	1	4	0	1	1	0	3	0	1	0	0
Kolotka, Charles, Beaumont	.000	8	2	0	0	0	0	0	0	0	0	0	0	0	0	0	2	0	0
Kunkel, Jeffrey, Tulsa	.316	47	177	30	56	86	16	1	4	22	3	0	1	4	6	0	32	7	2
Kutsukos, Peter, Beaumont	.111	54	9	0	1	1	0	0	0	0	0	2	0	0	1	0	3	0	0
Lake, Steven, Midland	.160	9	25	2	4	4	0	0	0	1	0	0	0	1	0	0	5	0	0
Latham, William, Jackson°	.167	7	6	0	1	1	0	0	0	2	1	2	0	0	2	0	2	0	0
Leopold, James, Beaumont	.208	23	24	4	5	5	0	0	0	1	1	2	0	0	1	0	4	0	0
Lindeman, James, Arkansas	.190	40	137	14	26	36	4	3	0	13	2	2	1	1	10	0	34	3	1
Lockenmeyer, Mark, Jackson	.125	20	16	1	2	3	1	0	0	1	0	3	0	0	0	0	5	0	0
Long, William, Beaumont	.050	27	40	1	2	3	1	0	0	5	0	3	1	0	4	0	26	0	0
Lovelace, Vance, San Antonio°	.333	17	15	1	5	6	1	0	0	2	0	1	0	0	0	0	4	0	0
Lusted, Charles, Shreveport	.091	21	22	2	2	2	0	0	0	0	0	2	0	0	0	0	6	0	0
Martin, John, A., Arkansas	.000	11	2	0	0	0	0	0	0	0	0	1	0	0	0	0	1	0	0
Martin, Steven, San Antonio	.182	56	11	0	2	2	0	0	0	1	0	1	0	0	0	0	4	0	0
Martinez, Christian, Arkansas	.211	9	19	1	4	4	0	0	0	1	0	2	0	0	0	0	9	0	0
Mason, Martin, Arkansas	.000	42	3	0	0	0	0	0	0	0	0	0	0	0	2	0	2	0	0
Mattson, Kurt, Shreveport	.000	46	6	0	0	0	0	0	0	0	0	0	0	1	0	1	3	0	0
Max, William, Jacksonville	.254	107	339	41	86	130	9	1	11	58	16	0	3	2	39	2	77	3	2
McCulla, Henry, Arkansas	.234	51	145	18	34	46	9	0	1	12	0	1	2	0	14	0	30	0	0
McCullers, Lance, Beaumont†	.385	9	13	0	5	7	0	1	0	3	1	0	0	0	0	0	5	0	0
McDowell, Roger, Jackson	.000	3	0	0	0	0	0	0	0	0	0	1	0	0	0	0	0	0	0
McPhail, Marlin, Jackson	.281	30	89	18	25	32	4	0	1	7	1	0	0	0	9	1	13	1	0
Meeks, Timothy, San Antonio	.045	28	44	0	2	2	0	0	0	0	0	4	0	0	2	0	20	0	0
Mejia, Oscar, Tulsa	.295	98	339	40	100	129	18	1	3	37	5	6	3	2	26	0	19	2	1
Michael, Steven, El Paso°	.249	93	342	45	85	118	15	0	6	48	9	0	2	0	51	4	46	8	3
Milligan, Randy, Jackson	.275	62	193	32	53	85	5	0	9	34	3	0	2	4	53	4	39	15	7
Mills, R. Gotay, Arkansas	.247	95	316	61	78	99	11	2	2	26	3	1	3	3	39	2	52	28	11
Montalvo, Rafael, San Antonio	.000	20	0	0	0	0	0	0	0	0	0	1	0	0	0	0	0	0	0
Moore, Kelvin, El Paso	.286	59	217	31	62	105	10	0	11	31	4	1	1	0	29	1	54	1	1
Moore, Robert, Shreveport	.182	52	11	0	2	3	1	0	0	3	0	0	0	1	0	0	5	1	0
Morales, Joseph, El Paso†	.222	81	207	33	46	64	8	2	2	17	0	6	1	0	38	0	21	2	2
Morlock, Allen, Arkansas	.190	28	42	4	8	8	0	0	0	1	0	5	0	0	2	0	9	0	0
Morse, Randy, Shreveport	.059	13	17	2	1	2	1	0	0	0	0	1	0	0	3	0	10	0	0
Moscaret, Jeffrey, Midland†	.429	40	7	0	3	3	0	0	0	0	0	1	0	0	0	0	2	0	0
Murphy, Daniel, Tulsa°	.228	41	145	19	33	47	5	0	3	21	4	0	1	1	19	2	15	6	2
Murray, Steven, Beaumont	.190	87	200	27	38	67	7	2	6	16	1	1	1	2	40	3	60	3	4
Murtha, Brian, Shreveport°	.000	14	9	0	0	0	0	0	0	0	0	0	0	0	1	0	6	0	0
Myers, Randall, Jackson°	.000	5	9	1	0	0	0	0	0	0	0	2	0	0	1	0	3	0	0
Myles, Rick, Jackson°	.167	15	6	0	1	2	1	0	0	1	0	2	0	0	0	0	4	0	0
Nago, Garrett, El Paso	.263	104	323	41	85	124	19	1	6	48	5	3	5	10	64	0	34	2	8
Neufang, Gerald, Tulsa	.138	9	29	3	4	4	0	0	0	3	1	0	0	2	0	4	0	0	1
Newman, Albert, Beaumont†	.252	88	318	69	80	88	8	0	0	23	3	14	4	2	64	4	21	33	10
Newsom, Gary, San Antonio	.274	37	113	19	31	35	2	1	0	11	1	3	0	0	21	1	12	2	4
Noce, Paul, Midland	.288	109	364	49	105	143	16	5	4	29	2	2	0	3	26	5	84	12	4
Nokes, Matthew, Shreveport°	.289	97	308	32	89	145	19	2	11	61	7	0	2	0	30	0	34	0	2
Norman, Daniel, Midland	.284	129	444	66	126	223	30	2	21	76	5	1	1	2	67	4	96	2	6
O'Connor, Robert, Shreveport	.232	132	462	53	107	157	17	3	9	46	3	0	5	3	64	1	92	11	11
O'Keefe, Richard, Jackson°	.182	7	11	0	2	2	0	0	0	1	0	1	0	0	0	0	2	0	0
Olson, Gregory, Jackson	.235	74	234	27	55	64	9	0	0	22	3	5	2	1	30	5	16	1	1
Ortiz, Javier, Tulsa	.298	94	325	42	97	148	21	3	8	53	5	4	4	5	47	2	67	4	5
Paciorek, James, El Paso	.366	63	254	58	93	147	23	5	7	48	5	0	2	1	36	4	25	5	4
Parent, Mark, Beaumont	.287	111	380	52	109	160	24	3	7	60	7	4	7	1	38	5	39	1	4
Pederson, Stuart, San Antonio°	.288	131	476	78	137	217	25	11	11	86	11	0	5	3	77	4	62	7	6
Pedrique, Alfredo, Jackson	.285	109	362	47	103	131	15	5	1	35	3	9	1	6	37	2	32	3	2
Penigar, Charles, Shreveport†	.277	72	271	40	75	103	8	1	6	15	1	3	1	0	36	1	80	24	11
Perry, W. Patrick, Arkansas°	.000	25	4	0	0	0	0	0	0	0	0	1	0	0	0	0	0	0	0
Pickett, Richard, Jackson	.000	23	4	0	0	0	0	0	0	0	0	0	0	0	0	0	4	0	0
Pierce, Walter, Arkansas	.278	35	18	3	5	5	0	0	0	2	0	0	1	0	0	0	1	0	0
Piper, Brian, San Antonio	.067	30	15	0	1	1	0	0	0	0	0	3	0	0	2	0	8	0	0
Plante, Daniel, El Paso	.238	82	244	37	58	75	9	1	2	33	4	0	1	0	43	0	48	3	2
Porter, Jason, Beaumont	.400	6	10	1	4	4	0	0	0	1	0	0	0	0	0	0	1	0	0
Potestio, Douglas, Midland	.167	35	24	2	4	4	0	0	0	2	0	3	0	0	3	0	6	0	0
Powell, Dennis, San Antonio°	.200	25	35	3	7	8	1	0	0	2	0	6	0	0	7	0	4	0	0
Pryce, Kenneth, Midland	.000	1	2	1	0	0	0	0	0	2	1	0	0	1	0	0	1	0	0
Purpura, Daniel, El Paso	.272	46	151	18	41	47	3	0	1	26	5	2	3	0	24	0	21	0	4
Reid, Jessie, Shreveport°	.209	88	296	33	62	92	10	1	6	32	4	0	1	1	46	2	65	7	3
Reyes, Gilberto, San Antonio	.303	120	433	55	131	181	16	2	10	78	8	2	5	2	29	2	50	1	4
Reynolds, Larry, Arkansas†	.314	46	121	17	38	44	6	0	0	9	2	0	0	0	19	1	16	6	3
Rhodes, Michael, Arkansas°	.500	35	2	0	1	1	0	0	0	0	0	0	0	0	0	0	0	0	0
Richardson, Ronald, Midland	.000	7	6	1	0	0	0	0	0	0	0	1	0	0	0	0	1	0	0
Roman, Luis, Arkansas°	.000	1	2	0	0	0	0	0	0	0	0	0	0	0	0	0	0	0	0
Ronan, Kernan, Shreveport	.000	42	13	0	0	0	0	0	0	0	0	1	0	0	2	0	4	0	0
Ronk, Jeffrey, Beaumont	.252	112	357	44	90	116	17	0	3	47	3	7	4	3	44	2	34	1	8
Rosenhahn, David, Midland	.000	13	4	1	0	0	0	0	0	0	0	0	0	1	0	0	0	0	0
Rutledge, Jeff, Arkansas	.053	7	19	4	1	2	1	0	0	1	0	0	0	0	7	0	3	0	0
Samuel, Michael, El Paso	.186	65	161	21	30	31	1	0	0	12	2	11	0	1	31	0	30	3	3
Schefsky, Steven, Beaumont	.000	42	13	0	0	0	0	0	0	1	0	0	0	0	1	0	5	0	0
Schiraldi, Calvin, Jackson	.172	23	29	2	5	5	0	0	0	1	0	9	0	1	3	0	9	0	0
Schulte, Mark, Arkansas°	.226	32	93	13	21	25	2	1	0	6	2	1	0	0	10	2	7	1	0
Scudder, William, San Antonio°	.167	34	6	2	1	1	0	0	0	1	0	1	0	0	1	0	4	0	0
See, R. Laurence, San Antonio	.283	77	254	56	72	142	17	1	17	50	4	0	1	0	67	0	44	1	2
Shade, Michael, Arkansas	.000	27	7	0	0	0	0	0	0	0	0	1	0	1	0	0	4	0	0
Silkwood, Joe, Arkansas	.000	24	12	1	0	0	0	0	0	0	0	0	0	0	0	0	3	0	0
Skube, Robert, El Paso°	.312	56	202	35	63	102	17	2	6	41	4	1	5	1	31	5	46	1	5
Slezak, Robert, San Antonio	.000	17	3	1	0	0	0	0	0	0	0	1	0	1	1	0	2	0	0
Smith, Gregory, 31 San-2 Beau°	.145	33	69	5	10	12	2	0	0	5	0	0	0	0	17	0	18	3	0
Smith, Stephen, Shreveport†	.000	2	2	0	0	0	0	0	0	0	0	0	0	0	0	0	0	0	0
Snyder, Bryan, Shreveport	.260	111	369	44	96	144	20	2	8	52	3	0	4	2	44	3	74	0	5
Soff, Raymond, Midland	.000	10	8	0	0	0	0	0	0	0	0	0	0	0	0	0	2	0	0

Player and Club	Pct.	G.	AB.	R.	H.	TB.	2B.	3B.	HR.	RBI.	GW.	SH.	SF.	HP.	BB.	Int. BB.	SO.	SB.	CS.
Sowards, Van, Shreveport	.265	25	49	6	13	13	0	0	0	4	1	0	0	0	6	0	6	0	2
Springer, Steven, Jackson	.273	103	362	41	99	141	21	3	5	40	9	0	0	2	24	3	50	6	4
Stanicek, Stephen, Shreveport	.232	94	271	36	63	94	12	2	5	34	3	2	1	1	43	0	65	3	2
Steels, James, Beaumont°	.340	127	474	90	161	243	26	10	12	81	12	5	2	1	48	3	45	35	17
Stevenson, John, Shreveport	.243	124	423	55	103	152	22	3	7	51	2	3	4	2	38	1	72	4	4
Stryffeler, Daniel, Arkansas°	.288	123	385	53	111	157	19	6	5	35	7	4	6	2	36	3	67	7	7
Sveum, Dale, El Paso†	.329	131	523	92	172	256	41	8	9	84	9	1	6	0	43	1	72	6	3
Tabor, Gregory, Tulsa	.299	123	462	69	138	187	27	2	6	53	2	10	3	3	27	0	71	22	18
Tanner, Edwin, Arkansas†	.283	73	251	28	71	90	8	1	3	35	2	2	5	2	25	5	16	2	1
Teahan, James, Shreveport	.000	6	2	0	0	0	0	0	0	0	0	0	0	0	2	0	0	0	0
Thomas, Christopher, San Antonio†...	.263	17	19	1	5	6	1	0	0	0	0	1	0	0	3	0	3	0	0
Thomas, Deron, Arkansas†	.180	64	167	13	30	35	3	1	0	9	1	2	1	1	16	2	40	1	1
Thomas, Jimmy, Beaumont	.266	82	222	31	59	92	10	1	7	21	2	4	1	2	31	1	47	1	1
Thurberg, Thomas, Arkansas	.000	11	1	0	0	0	0	0	0	0	0	0	0	0	0	0	0	0	0
Tibbs, Jay, Jackson	.000	6	7	1	0	0	0	0	0	0	0	0	0	0	2	0	5	0	0
Torres, Jose, San Antonio	.000	8	2	1	0	0	0	0	0	0	0	0	0	0	0	0	0	0	0
Torve, Kelvin, Shreveport°	.297	114	316	59	94	173	21	5	16	62	9	0	6	2	43	3	42	2	0
Towers, Kevin, Beaumont	.140	28	43	3	6	6	0	0	0	4	0	5	1	0	1	0	9	0	0
Ubri, Fermin, Jackson	.236	86	296	34	70	90	8	0	4	27	2	3	0	0	10	1	34	2	1
Varsho, Gary, Midland°	.261	128	429	65	112	163	15	6	8	50	4	4	3	1	49	2	86	27	8
Vaughn, Dewayne, Jackson	.095	16	21	2	2	2	0	0	0	0	0	2	0	0	0	0	13	0	0
Vavra, Joseph, San Antonio°	.307	96	300	36	92	112	15	1	1	40	3	0	3	0	32	1	17	4	3
Veryzer, Thomas, Midland	.182	7	22	2	4	5	1	0	0	7	0	2	0	0	6	0	8	0	0
Vosberg, Edward, Beaumont°	.229	31	48	5	11	16	2	0	1	7	0	2	0	0	0	0	22	1	4
Walker, Johnny, San Antonio†	.229	62	175	23	40	53	11	1	0	19	4	1	2	0	17	0	29	0	0
Wallace, Timothy, Arkansas	.248	51	161	16	40	52	7	1	1	20	3	2	2	2	17	1	29	0	0
Walter, Gene, Beaumont°	.273	34	11	2	3	3	0	0	0	0	0	0	0	0	0	0	3	0	0
Wasinger, Mark, Beaumont	.285	106	362	54	103	132	20	0	3	48	8	16	4	2	62	2	46	15	7
White, William, San Antonio	.222	62	189	21	42	55	13	0	0	17	1	0	0	0	31	0	35	2	6
Wilhelmi, David, Shreveport	.043	29	23	0	1	1	0	0	0	2	1	10	0	0	2	0	10	0	0
Wood, Johnson, El Paso	.000	38	1	0	0	0	0	0	0	0	0	0	0	0	0	0	0	0	0
Woods, Tony, Midland	.281	73	242	26	68	100	7	2	7	29	4	2	0	0	24	1	44	8	2
Worrell, Todd, Arkansas	.150	21	20	1	3	4	1	0	0	0	0	3	0	0	2	0	11	0	0
Wrona, William, Beaumont	.169	26	83	7	14	16	2	0	0	11	0	3	1	0	5	0	8	1	2
Youmans, Floyd, Jackson	.211	16	19	0	4	4	0	0	0	5	1	2	0	0	5	0	10	1	0
Young, John, Arkansas°	.300	30	30	3	9	12	1	1	0	1	0	2	0	0	2	0	7	1	0
Young, Scott, Arkansas	.286	7	7	2	2	2	0	0	0	0	0	2	0	0	4	0	2	0	0

The following pitchers, listed alphabetically by club, with games in parentheses, had no plate appearances, primarily through use of designated hitters:

ARKANSAS—Boever, Joseph (8); Hassler, Andrew (9).

BEAUMONT—Mills, Michael (1).

EL PASO—Buonantony, Richard (8); Clutterbuck, Bryan (27); Crews, Timothy (8); Crim, Charles (55); Duquette, Bryan (48); Effrig, Mark (27); Hartzell, Paul (14); Higuera, Teodoro (19); Jones, Douglas (16); Kern, James (8); Martinez, Alfredo (7); Moloney, William (9); Plesac, Daniel (7); Schroeck, Robert (12); Villegas, Michael (30); Walker, Cameron (10); Wegman, William (10).

TULSA—Boggs, Thomas (3); Buckley, John (41); Fossas, Anthony (4); Guzman, Jose (25); Kordish, Steve (27); Leach, Martin (6); Meckes, Timothy (19); Sebra, Robert (17); Shimp, Tommy Joe (20); Smith, Daryl (7); Taylor, William (42); Winfield, Steven (13).

GRAND SLAM HOME RUNS—Hearn, 2; Asadoor, S. Davis, Denton, Felder, Gergen, Gomez, Harry, D. Jackson, Kunkel, Max, Norman, Ortiz, 1 each.

AWARDED FIRST BASE ON CATCHER'S INTERFERENCE—Casey 2 (Cummings, Reyes); Olson 2 (Geren, Nokes); S. Davis (Hyman); Guin (Reyes); Helsom (Harry); Leopold (Reyes); Sveum (Henderson); J. Thomas (Reyes); Torve (Harry).

CLUB FIELDING

Club	Pct.	G.	PO.	A.	E.	DP.	PB.	Club	Pct.	G.	PO.	A.	E.	DP.	PB.
Beaumont	.972	136	3613	1632	153	153	19	Tulsa	.966	135	3362	1535	171	153	20
Shreveport	.970	136	3452	1505	151	98	16	El Paso	.965	135	3499	1480	180	126	26
Jackson	.968	136	3570	1468	164	105	16	San Antonio	.962	136	3553	1523	200	147	38
Arkansas	.967	136	3514	1357	168	121	19	Midland	.960	136	3400	1479	202	136	14

INDIVIDUAL FIELDING
FIRST BASEMEN

°Throws lefthanded.

Player and Club	Pct.	G.	PO.	A.	E.	DP.	Player and Club	Pct.	G.	PO.	A.	E.	DP.
Anicich, Midland	.980	9	95	5	2	7	Kneuer, Tulsa	1.000	1	3	0	0	2
CASEY, Beaumont	.989	98	895	83	11	91	Max, Jackson	.986	60	518	31	8	49
Cataline, San Antonio	.980	56	466	35	10	54	McCulla, Arkansas	.857	1	12	0	2	0
Clements, Arkansas	.952	3	19	1	1	1	McPhail, Jackson	.969	8	52	10	2	4
D. Davis, Tulsa	1.000	1	3	0	0	0	Michael, El Paso°	.980	57	491	39	11	50
S. Davis, El Paso	1.000	2	9	0	0	1	Milligan, Jackson	.985	55	475	67	8	28
Gauntlett, San Antonio	1.000	10	63	6	0	5	Moore, El Paso°	.988	57	470	22	6	49
Geren, Arkansas	1.000	3	14	0	0	0	Murphy, Tulsa°	1.000	4	25	1	0	3
Gergen, Tulsa	.993	29	272	25	2	28	Norman, Midland	1.000	1	8	1	0	1
Gillaspie, Beaumont	.982	17	154	10	3	17	Parent, Beaumont	.900	25	179	20	2	18
Gray, El Paso	1.000	3	23	1	0	1	Plante, El Paso	1.000	1	4	0	0	0
Guin, Arkansas°	.995	75	526	49	3	41	Schulte, Arkansas	.969	15	117	7	4	11
Hance, Tulsa	1.000	1	1	1	0	0	See, San Antonio	.944	3	33	1	2	3
Harry, Tulsa	.982	108	961	58	19	102	Skube, El Paso°	.985	21	187	14	3	12
Hearn, Jackson	.989	19	176	8	2	13	Smith, 18 San-2 Beau°	.983	20	157	14	3	12
Helsom, Arkansas	1.000	3	14	0	0	2	Stanicek, Shreveport	.983	68	609	43	11	33
Henderson, Midland	.987	18	139	9	2	19	Steels, Beaumont°	1.000	2	13	1	0	0
Hunsinger, Arkansas	1.000	7	56	4	0	6	Thomas, Beaumont	.995	78	668	58	4	58
Johnson, Beaumont	1.000	7	35	4	0	4	Torve, Shreveport	.995	56	500	35	4	44
Jones, Midland	.988	112	930	74	12	89	Vavra, San Antonio	.993	56	500	35	4	44
Kable, Arkansas°	.991	48	400	26	4	39	White, San Antonio	.947	2	17	1	1	7

SECOND BASEMEN

Player and Club	Pct.	G.	PO.	A.	E.	DP.
Bates, Shreveport	.987	34	58	93	2	23
Blackwell, Shreveport	.961	111	250	274	21	47
Castillo, El Paso	.974	116	271	359	17	73
Denton, Midland	1.000	1	1	9	0	0
Dillard, Tulsa	.966	28	39	103	5	22
Duncan, San Antonio	.967	119	281	334	21	84
Espy, San Antonio	1.000	1	0	4	0	0
Etchebarren, Beaumont	.988	14	31	50	1	12
Ford, Arkansas	.959	25	50	67	5	11
Garcia, Beaumont	.964	26	52	55	4	19
Gomez, Tulsa	.957	9	13	31	2	7
Harris, Arkansas	.978	32	68	67	3	16
Johnson, Beaumont	.920	10	15	31	4	5
McPhail, Jackson	.970	7	11	21	1	1
Mejia, Tulsa	.988	14	34	47	1	11
Morales, El Paso	.965	24	47	62	4	13
Newsom, San Antonio	.956	9	16	27	2	5
Noce, Midland	.990	20	30	67	1	21
Pedrique, Jackson	.893	6	8	17	3	3
Purpura, El Paso	1.000	1	2	1	0	1
Reynolds, Arkansas	1.000	1	2	2	0	1
Ronk, Beaumont	.923	5	4	8	1	3
Samuel, El Paso	1.000	1	2	4	0	0
Springer, Jackson	.962	49	82	147	9	21
Tabor, Tulsa	.967	94	177	318	17	60
Tanner, Arkansas	.952	41	88	91	9	26
Thomas, Arkansas	.940	55	91	114	13	21
Ubri, Jackson	.976	77	145	259	10	47
Varsho, Midland	.955	115	286	335	29	73
Vavra, San Antonio	1.000	5	9	9	0	2
Veryzer, Midland	1.000	2	4	6	0	2
Walker, San Antonio	1.000	7	14	13	0	4
WASINGER, Beaumont	.977	94	199	322	12	66

THIRD BASEMEN

Player and Club	Pct.	G.	PO.	A.	E.	DP.
Asadoor, Tulsa	.908	122	70	208	28	19
Bates, Shreveport	.967	10	6	23	1	0
Clements, Arkansas	.932	68	44	106	11	5
Cochrane, Jackson	.893	99	66	151	26	11
Denton, Midland	.861	14	7	24	5	5
Etchebarren, Beaumont	.800	5	1	7	2	0
Ford, Arkansas	1.000	11	10	28	0	2
Garcia, Beaumont	.933	25	10	32	3	2
Gauntlett, San Antonio	.923	12	7	17	2	1
Gergen, Tulsa	.667	3	0	2	1	0
Gomez, Tulsa	.842	10	8	8	3	3
Henderson, Midland	.920	37	38	65	9	7
Hyman, Midland	1.000	3	0	1	0	0
Johnson, Beaumont	.966	31	26	58	3	5
Lindeman, Arkansas	.939	40	26	67	6	8
Max, Jackson	.959	28	28	66	4	5
Mejia, Tulsa	.857	4	4	2	1	0
Mills, Arkansas	.947	6	7	11	1	0
Morales, El Paso	1.000	6	3	7	0	0
Nago, El Paso	1.000	1	1	0	0	0
Newsom, San Antonio	1.000	3	0	1	0	0
Noce, Midland	.900	24	20	52	8	2
O'CONNOR, Shreveport	.960	131	102	283	16	21
Pedrique, Jackson	1.000	6	2	14	0	1
Reynolds, Arkansas	.833	3	0	5	1	0
Ronk, Beaumont	.952	82	64	155	11	20
Rutledge, Midland	.909	7	1	9	1	1
See, San Antonio	.887	73	52	136	24	15
Springer, Jackson	1.000	6	5	10	0	2
Sveum, El Paso	.925	131	111	259	30	19
Tanner, Arkansas	.857	4	1	5	1	1
Thomas, Beaumont	.931	10	6	21	2	2
Vavra, San Antonio	1.000	1	1	0	0	0
Veryzer, Midland	1.000	3	2	1	0	0
Wallace, Arkansas	.871	18	8	19	4	3
White, San Antonio	.969	54	40	117	5	19
Woods, Midland	.931	55	50	98	11	6

SHORTSTOPS

Player and Club	Pct.	G.	PO.	A.	E.	DP.
Alvarez, San Antonio	.912	82	155	239	38	48
Bates, Shreveport	.930	19	19	34	4	6
Blackwell, Shreveport	.900	5	2	7	1	0
Booker, Arkansas	.943	52	87	160	15	32
Castillo, El Paso	1.000	1	2	1	0	0
Clements, Arkansas	1.000	2	2	2	0	0
Cochrane, Jackson	.829	9	13	16	6	4
Denton, Midland	.854	13	10	31	7	3
Duncan, San Antonio	1.000	1	0	1	0	0
Dunston, Midland	.920	72	164	203	32	55
Etchebarren, Beaumont	1.000	1	1	0	0	0
Gergen, Tulsa	.941	7	5	11	1	1
Harris, Arkansas	.892	57	86	146	28	29
Johnson, Beaumont	.958	10	19	27	2	6
Kunkel, Tulsa	.913	37	64	103	16	30
Mejia, Tulsa	.950	72	128	231	19	55
Mills, Arkansas	1.000	4	2	4	0	0
Morales, El Paso	.936	49	58	103	11	26
Newman, Beaumont	.935	87	138	250	27	58
Newsom, San Antonio	.973	17	30	42	2	9
Noce, Midland	.924	52	85	145	19	31
PEDRIQUE, Jackson	.961	95	188	250	18	49
Purpura, Beaumont	.965	45	84	136	8	33
Reynolds, Arkansas	1.000	1	0	1	0	0
Ronk, Beaumont	.933	6	12	16	2	3
Samuel, El Paso	.893	60	67	150	26	24
Springer, Jackson	.911	37	55	88	14	17
Stevenson, Shreveport	.956	124	192	395	27	57
Sveum, El Paso	1.000	1	2	0	0	0
Tabor, Tulsa	.952	24	46	72	6	26
Tanner, Arkansas	.938	27	44	61	7	19
Veryzer, Midland	1.000	3	5	4	0	2
Walker, San Antonio	.922	41	57	109	14	25
Wasinger, Beaumont	.966	14	21	36	2	9
Wrona, Beaumont	.957	26	45	65	5	20

OUTFIELDERS

Player and Club	Pct.	G.	PO.	A.	E.	DP.
Auten, Midland	.923	21	23	1	2	0
Baker, Midland	.961	53	119	4	5	0
Bass, Tulsa	1.000	7	7	1	0	0
Beane, Jackson	.964	113	180	5	7	0
Brower, Tulsa	.986	94	209	10	3	1
Brumley, Midland	.964	70	128	4	5	1
Bryant, San Antonio	.944	101	191	11	12	2
Carreon, Jackson°	.974	104	146	1	4	0
Cartwright, El Paso°	.970	54	92	4	3	0
Casey, Beaumont	1.000	14	18	2	0	1
Cataline, San Antonio	.988	50	82	3	1	2
Cordova, Midland	.895	28	30	4	4	0
Davis, El Paso	1.000	9	10	0	0	0
Denby, Jackson	.977	62	120	10	3	2
Duncan, San Antonio	.667	2	2	0	1	0
DYKSTRA, Jackson°	.992	125	256	5	2	2
Espy, San Antonio	.986	131	348	12	5	4
Felder, El Paso	.982	121	321	13	6	4
Ford, Arkansas	.983	90	164	7	3	0
Gergen, Tulsa	.964	26	26	1	1	0
Gillaspie, Beaumont	.960	101	154	16	7	4
Gomez, Tulsa	.968	100	142	11	5	0
Graham, Shreveport°	.983	40	113	5	2	0
Guin, Arkansas°	.973	25	36	0	1	0
Helsom, Arkansas	.965	72	107	2	4	0
Irvine, El Paso	1.000	3	1	1	0	0
Jackson, Midland	.974	126	286	19	8	6
J. Johnson, Beaumont	1.000	4	3	1	0	0
St. Johnson, Beaumont	.972	122	238	7	7	3
G. Jones, Shreveport	.967	21	29	0	1	0
J. Jones, Midland	1.000	1	2	0	0	0
K. Jones, Tulsa	.943	66	107	8	7	1
M. Jones, Shreveport°	.953	85	114	9	6	2
Klipstein, El Paso	.978	122	213	12	5	2
Max, Jackson	1.000	3	6	2	0	1
McCulla, Arkansas	.926	17	25	0	2	0
McPhail, Jackson	1.000	3	2	0	0	0
Michael, Jackson	.982	25	53	3	1	1
Mills, Arkansas	.994	82	163	7	1	1
Murphy, Tulsa°	.965	38	52	3	2	0
Murray, Beaumont	.977	78	122	8	3	1
Nago, El Paso	1.000	2	1	0	0	0
Norman, Midland	.964	122	176	10	7	3
Ortiz, Tulsa	.941	85	115	13	8	5
Paciorek, El Paso	.955	62	100	5	5	0
Pederson, San Antonio°	.965	130	182	13	7	2
Penigar, Shreveport	.973	71	139	4	4	0
Reid, Shreveport°	.986	88	129	9	2	0
Reynolds, Arkansas	.983	32	55	4	1	2
Ronk, Beaumont	.960	18	19	5	1	0
Schulte, Arkansas	.944	10	14	3	1	2
Skube, El Paso°	1.000	16	14	1	0	0
Snyder, Shreveport°	.954	106	181	7	9	1
Sowards, Shreveport	1.000	17	14	0	0	0
Springer, Jackson	.667	3	2	0	1	0
Steels, Shreveport°	.975	124	182	13	5	1
Stryffeler, Arkansas	.975	109	184	12	5	6
Tabor, Tulsa	.900	8	18	0	2	0
Vavra, San Antonio	1.000	7	10	0	0	0
Walker, San Antonio	1.000	2	1	0	0	0
Wallace, Arkansas	1.000	11	10	0	0	0

CATCHERS

Player and Club	Pct.	G.	PO.	A.	E.	DP.	PB.
Brunenkant, Tulsa	.990	34	180	16	2	6	6
Cias, Tulsa	.994	27	143	18	1	2	5
Cordova, Midland	.983	10	48	10	1	0	1
Cummings, Shreveport	.981	71	340	31	7	1	10
Davis, Tulsa	1.000	1	1	0	0	0	0
Gauntlett, San Antonio	.990	33	172	23	2	3	7
Geren, Arkansas	.987	79	531	56	8	10	11
Hance, Tulsa	.987	48	272	27	4	4	3
Harry, Tulsa	.954	10	54	8	3	1	5
Hearn, Jackson	.992	64	437	46	4	4	9
Henderson, Midland	.975	31	128	26	4	4	6
Hunt, Arkansas	.974	23	143	8	4	2	2
Hyman, Midland	.987	95	459	66	7	6	6
Johnson, Beaumont	1.000	4	31	1	0	0	0
Kneuer, Tulsa	.990	15	87	16	1	3	1
Lake, Midland	1.000	9	46	7	0	0	1
McCulla, Arkansas	.966	26	132	10	5	4	6
Nago, El Paso	.975	90	526	62	15	4	17
Neufang, Tulsa	1.000	7	37	2	0	0	0
Nokes, Shreveport	.982	72	400	31	8	5	6
Olson, Jackson	.984	74	511	51	9	3	7
PARENT, Beaumont	.991	85	495	48	5	6	14
Plante, El Paso	.983	57	263	28	5	4	8
Porter, Beaumont	1.000	4	4	1	0	0	0
Reyes, San Antonio	.974	109	598	101	19	13	31
Thomas, Beaumont	.997	59	297	32	1	6	5
Vavra, San Antonio	1.000	1	1	0	0	0	0
Wallace, Arkansas	1.000	22	104	7	0	3	0

PITCHERS

Player and Club	Pct.	G.	PO.	A.	E.	DP.
Adams, Arkansas	.950	19	6	13	1	0
Aguilera, Jackson	1.000	11	4	12	0	0
Anderson, San Antonio	.667	4	1	1	1	0
Banks, Midland	1.000	10	9	6	0	1
Barba, Beaumont	1.000	19	2	2	0	1
Bass, Tulsa	.947	30	5	13	1	1
Bettendorf, Jackson	.875	7	2	5	1	0
Biggus, Shreveport	.889	8	3	5	1	0
Bockus, Shreveport	.938	18	4	26	2	1
Boever, Arkansas	1.000	8	2	0	0	0
Boggs, Tulsa	1.000	3	1	1	0	0
Boudreau, Midland*	.900	42	9	27	4	3
Brahms, Shreveport*	1.000	9	0	2	0	0
Bryant, Midland*	.818	6	0	9	2	1
Buckley, Tulsa	1.000	41	2	6	0	1
Bullinger, Jackson	.889	22	1	7	1	0
Buonantony, El Paso	.867	8	2	11	2	0
Burns, El Paso	.500	13	0	1	1	0
Capel, Midland	.938	16	7	8	1	2
Carpio, Midland	.933	34	1	13	1	1
Charley, Midland*	.950	13	4	15	1	0
Chestnut, Midland	.818	14	5	13	4	0
Clark, Tulsa*	1.000	4	1	6	0	1
Clutterbuck, El Paso	.933	27	17	25	3	3
Cook, Beaumont	.941	30	3	13	1	2
Couchee, Beaumont	1.000	15	3	5	0	0
L. Crews, Shreveport	.933	27	17	39	4	0
T. Crews, El Paso	1.000	8	1	10	0	0
Crim, El Paso	1.000	55	8	14	0	2
Cunningham, San Antonio	1.000	18	7	4	0	0
Duquette, El Paso*	.933	48	1	13	1	1
Effrig, El Paso	.857	27	4	8	2	0
Felt, San Antonio*	.864	15	2	17	3	0
Felton, San Antonio	1.000	7	0	1	0	0
Fossas, Tulsa*	1.000	4	0	1	0	0
Fruge, Midland	1.000	6	1	7	0	0
Fultz, Jackson	.962	32	11	40	2	4
Gallo, Shreveport*	1.000	12	2	0	0	0
Gendron, Shreveport	.889	14	4	4	1	0
Gladden, Shreveport	.867	12	10	16	4	0
Gomez, Tulsa	1.000	3	1	1	0	1
Granillo, San Antonio*	.880	45	6	16	3	2
Graves, Jackson	.900	58	6	19	3	1
Guin, Arkansas*	1.000	1	0	2	0	0
Guzman, Tulsa	.974	25	7	31	1	4
Hamm, Beaumont	.929	6	4	9	1	0
Hartzell, El Paso	1.000	14	0	3	0	0
Hassler, Arkansas*	1.000	9	1	3	0	0
Henry, Tulsa	.813	33	3	10	3	2
Higuera, El Paso*	.914	19	9	23	3	2
Housey, Midland	.957	30	10	12	1	0
Hrynko, Midland	.966	23	8	20	1	0
Huey, Midland	1.000	18	1	2	0	0
Hyman, Midland	1.000	1	0	1	0	0
B. Innis, San Antonio	.800	7	3	5	2	0
J. Innis, San Antonio	.929	42	4	9	1	1
Jackson, Jackson	.933	28	6	8	1	1
Sc. Johnson, Midland*	.867	20	3	10	2	1
T. Johnson, Tulsa*	.971	22	6	27	1	1
Johnston, San Antonio	1.000	39	1	6	0	0
D. Jones, El Paso	.880	16	7	15	3	2
J. Jones, Beaumont	1.000	13	8	21	0	1
Kaufman, Midland	.500	31	0	1	1	0
Kern, El Paso	.333	8	0	1	2	1
Kinzer, Arkansas	.955	14	6	15	1	2
Kolotka, Beaumont	1.000	8	1	3	0	0
Kordish, Tulsa	1.000	27	10	26	0	4
Kutsukos, Beaumont	.900	54	6	12	2	0
Latham, Jackson*	1.000	7	2	13	0	0
Leach, Tulsa	1.000	6	5	4	0	1
Leopold, Beaumont	.921	23	9	26	3	3
Lockenmeyer, Jackson	.905	20	8	11	2	2
Long, Beaumont	.909	25	11	29	4	2
Lovelace, San Antonio*	.895	16	2	15	2	0
Lusted, Shreveport	.861	21	13	18	5	4
J. Martin, Arkansas	1.000	11	1	6	0	0
S. Martin, San Antonio	.946	56	9	26	2	2
A. Martinez, El Paso	1.000	7	3	3	0	0
C. Martinez, Arkansas	.857	9	4	8	2	0
Mason, Arkansas	.917	42	4	18	2	3
Mattson, Shreveport	.929	46	6	7	1	0
McCullers, Beaumont	1.000	8	2	8	0	1
McDowell, Jackson	1.000	3	0	1	0	0
Meckes, Tulsa	1.000	19	1	12	0	2
Meeks, San Antonio	.909	28	16	24	4	1
Mills, Beaumont	1.000	1	0	1	0	0
Montalvo, San Antonio	.889	20	2	6	1	0
Moore, Shreveport	1.000	52	6	14	0	1
MORLOCK, Arkansas	1.000	28	13	30	0	0
Morse, Shreveport*	1.000	13	2	14	0	1
Moscaret, Midland*	1.000	40	4	14	0	0
Murtha, Shreveport*	.875	14	1	6	1	0
Myers, Jackson*	1.000	5	0	4	0	0
Myles, Jackson*	.923	15	3	9	1	0
O'Keefe, Jackson*	.909	7	2	8	1	0
Perry, Arkansas*	1.000	25	5	6	0	1
Pickett, Jackson*	.875	23	1	6	1	0
Pierce, Arkansas	1.000	34	8	12	0	0
Piper, San Antonio	.933	30	2	12	1	2
Plante, El Paso	1.000	2	0	1	0	0
Plesac, El Paso*	1.000	7	0	6	0	0
Potestio, Midland	.933	35	9	19	2	1
Powell, San Antonio*	.952	24	15	45	3	6
Pryce, Midland	.500	1	1	0	1	0
Rhodes, Arkansas*	1.000	35	0	10	0	0
Richardson, Midland	1.000	7	3	4	0	2
Roman, Arkansas*	1.000	9	0	2	0	0
Ronan, Shreveport	.941	42	8	24	2	0
Rosenhahn, Midland	1.000	13	3	5	0	0
Schefsky, Beaumont	.957	42	7	15	1	1
Schiraldi, Jackson	.906	23	12	17	3	0
Schroeck, El Paso*	1.000	12	1	5	0	0
Scudder, San Antonio	.941	34	3	13	1	2
Sebra, Tulsa	.950	17	5	14	1	1
Shade, Arkansas	1.000	27	1	5	0	2
Shimp, Tulsa	.947	19	2	16	1	1
Silkwood, Arkansas	1.000	24	4	10	0	1
Slezak, San Antonio	1.000	17	4	9	0	0
D. Smith, Tulsa	1.000	7	1	3	0	0
S. Smith, Shreveport	.500	2	0	1	1	0
Soff, Midland	1.000	10	2	3	0	1
Steels, Beaumont*	1.000	3	0	1	0	0
Taylor, Tulsa	.833	42	7	8	3	0
Teahan, Shreveport	.857	6	3	3	1	0
Thomas, San Antonio	.913	14	5	16	2	2
Thurberg, Arkansas	1.000	11	3	2	0	0
Tibbs, Jackson	1.000	6	3	4	0	1
Torres, San Antonio	.875	7	2	5	1	0
Towers, Beaumont	.870	26	14	33	7	0
Vaughn, Jackson	.920	16	10	13	2	0
Villegas, El Paso	.879	30	8	21	4	1
Vosberg, Beaumont*	.923	27	15	57	6	2
Walker, El Paso	1.000	10	4	7	0	0
Walter, Beaumont*	.941	34	7	9	1	0
Wegman, El Paso	.895	10	3	14	2	3
Wilhelmi, Shreveport	.933	29	8	20	2	1
Winfield, Tulsa	1.000	13	2	1	0	0
Wood, El Paso	.938	37	3	12	1	1
Worrell, Arkansas	.793	18	7	16	6	1
Youmans, Jackson	.800	16	9	7	4	0
J. Young, Arkansas*	.929	26	6	33	3	2
S. Young, Arkansas	1.000	7	3	5	0	1

The following players do not have any recorded accepted chances at the positions indicated; therefore, are not listed in the fielding averages for those particular positions: Asadoor, ss; Blackwell, of; Castillo, of; Espy, ss; Geren, 3b; Harry, of; Henderson, p; Sc. Johnson, of; St. Johnson, p; Kable, of; McCulla, p; Moloney, p; Pederson, p; Snyder, p; D. Thomas, of; Torve, ss; Vavra, p.

CLUB PITCHING

Club	ERA	G	CG	ShO	Sv	IP	H	R	ER	HR	HB	BB	Int. BB	SO	WP	Bk.
Jackson	3.31	136	20	17	33	1190.0	1090	525	438	69	21	516	32	901	49	12
Beaumont	3.46	136	21	17	43	1204.1	1130	541	463	67	24	603	30	771	61	8
Shreveport	3.75	136	16	9	21	1150.2	1201	583	479	102	32	392	19	688	58	7
Arkansas	3.97	136	24	7	29	1171.1	1153	642	517	74	25	577	38	869	74	8
Tulsa	3.99	135	19	13	26	1120.2	1078	586	497	87	24	533	28	735	60	9
El Paso	4.25	135	26	4	35	1166.1	1310	674	551	108	27	447	18	749	42	9
San Antonio	4.29	136	18	10	27	1184.1	1193	692	564	108	28	714	46	724	67	10
Midland	4.65	136	19	2	19	1133.1	1221	716	585	92	21	546	8	638	67	5

PITCHERS' RECORDS
(Leading Qualifiers for Earned-Run Average Leadership — 109 or More Innings)

*Throws lefthanded.

Pitcher—Club	W	L	Pct.	ERA	G	GS	CG	GF	ShO	Sv	IP	H	R	ER	HR	HB	BB	Int. BB	SO	WP
Higuera, El Paso*	8	7	.533	2.60	19	19	4	0	0	0	121.0	116	57	35	11	1	43	0	99	5
Bockus, Shreveport	8	5	.615	2.81	18	18	4	0	3	0	128.1	106	44	40	7	4	54	3	93	5
Schiraldi, Jackson	14	3	.824	2.88	23	22	5	0	1	0	156.1	118	58	50	10	3	69	1	131	4
Long, Beaumont	14	5	.737	2.93	25	24	4	1	2	0	159.2	149	56	52	8	1	67	1	114	5
Lusted, Shreveport	6	7	.462	2.96	21	21	2	0	1	0	124.2	125	49	41	8	3	38	0	93	5
Morlock, Arkansas	11	8	.579	3.01	28	24	9	3	3	0	173.2	144	72	58	15	5	59	4	124	3
Fultz, Jackson	10	6	.625	3.04	32	22	6	5	2	1	177.2	169	74	60	12	3	46	4	108	1
Leopold, Beaumont	8	2	.800	3.22	23	23	3	0	1	0	134.0	131	54	48	7	7	52	3	93	8
Potestio, Midland	6	10	.375	3.31	35	17	5	8	1	0	130.2	141	59	48	8	2	37	0	68	4
L. Crews, Shreveport	11	10	.524	3.32	27	27	6	0	1	0	178.2	173	76	66	11	4	50	0	87	4

Departmental Leaders: G—Graves, 58; W—Long, Meeks, Schiraldi, 14; L—Ronan, Vosberg, Wilhelmi, 11; Pct.—Schiraldi, .824; GS—Clutterbuck, L. Crews, Meeks, Vosberg, 27; CG—Morlock, 9; GF—Kutsukos, 41; ShO—Bockus, Meeks, Morlock, 3; Sv—Kutsukos, 20; IP—Meeks, 186.0; H—Clutterbuck, 198; R—Clutterbuck, 103; ER—Clutterbuck, 79; HR—Meeks, 19; HB—Leopold, 7; BB—J. Young, 122; IBB—Granillo, 9; SO—J. Young, 136; WP—J. Young, 16.

(All Pitchers—Listed Alphabetically)

Pitcher—Club	W	L	Pct.	ERA	G	GS	CG	GF	ShO	Sv	IP	H	R	ER	HR	HB	BB	Int. BB	SO	WP
Adams, Arkansas	6	5	.545	5.57	19	15	3	2	0	1	93.2	113	65	58	7	6	36	0	76	11
Aguilera, Jackson	4	4	.500	4.57	11	11	2	0	1	0	67.0	68	37	34	5	0	19	1	71	2
Anderson, San Antonio	1	3	.250	6.35	4	4	0	0	0	0	22.2	26	20	16	1	0	13	1	18	3
Banks, Midland	1	5	.167	4.91	10	10	1	0	0	0	51.1	53	32	28	4	1	29	0	26	1
Barba, Beaumont	4	1	.800	5.50	19	1	0	7	0	2	34.1	37	27	21	4	1	30	0	23	3
Bass, Tulsa	4	6	.400	3.31	30	9	1	10	0	0	100.2	112	52	37	6	3	51	2	64	5
Bettendorf, Jackson	5	0	1.000	2.20	7	7	1	0	0	0	45.0	38	13	11	2	2	19	0	26	1
Biggus, Shreveport	0	2	.000	6.30	8	3	0	2	0	1	20.0	23	17	14	5	1	8	0	8	1
Bockus, Shreveport	8	5	.615	2.81	18	18	4	0	3	0	128.1	106	44	40	7	4	54	3	93	5
Boever, Arkansas	0	1	.000	8.18	8	0	0	8	0	3	11.0	10	11	10	1	0	12	0	12	1
Boggs, Tulsa	1	1	.500	2.37	3	3	0	0	0	0	19.0	13	5	5	1	0	5	0	12	1
Boudreau, Midland*	7	8	.467	4.33	42	5	0	15	0	2	104.0	112	57	50	9	2	43	1	81	3
Brahms, Shreveport*	0	0	.000	3.27	9	0	0	4	0	0	11.0	13	4	4	0	0	1	0	6	0
Bryant, Midland*	1	3	.250	6.23	6	6	0	0	0	0	30.1	35	27	21	3	0	20	0	17	2
Buckley, Tulsa	5	7	.417	4.73	41	0	0	32	0	9	66.2	67	45	35	6	1	43	7	44	4
Bullinger, Jackson*	2	1	.667	2.81	22	0	0	11	0	1	25.2	25	12	8	3	0	12	3	18	1
Buonantony, El Paso	2	2	.500	9.44	8	8	0	0	0	0	34.1	46	39	36	7	2	31	1	17	3
Burns, El Paso	2	1	.667	1.04	13	0	0	13	0	8	17.1	10	4	2	1	0	14	0	14	0
Capel, El Paso	1	10	.091	6.31	16	11	0	3	0	0	61.1	69	53	43	7	1	37	0	20	11
Carpio, Midland	6	2	.750	4.54	34	1	0	9	0	2	67.1	77	53	34	5	1	51	1	54	5
Charley, Midland	3	4	.429	4.40	13	11	2	1	0	0	73.2	89	40	36	3	0	26	0	36	3
Chestnut, Midland	4	4	.500	4.46	14	14	2	0	0	0	82.2	71	48	41	9	2	39	0	59	4
Clark, Tulsa*	2	0	1.000	2.05	4	4	1	0	0	0	26.1	19	7	6	4	0	4	0	12	0
Clutterbuck, El Paso	10	9	.526	3.97	27	27	7	0	0	0	179.0	198	103	79	17	1	52	0	112	3
Cook, Beaumont	4	1	.800	4.24	30	0	0	13	0	4	70.0	55	35	33	4	1	52	2	55	4
Couchee, Beaumont	1	0	1.000	2.92	15	0	0	10	0	3	24.2	18	8	8	3	1	10	2	23	2
L. Crews, Shreveport	11	10	.524	3.32	27	27	6	0	1	0	178.2	173	76	66	11	4	50	0	87	4
T. Crews, El Paso	2	3	.400	6.75	8	8	1	0	0	0	36.0	56	32	27	1	1	10	0	22	0
Crim, El Paso	7	4	.636	1.50	55	0	0	33	0	17	90.0	77	20	15	4	2	25	4	69	2
Cunningham, San Antonio	2	5	.286	5.37	18	7	1	6	0	0	57.0	71	36	34	7	3	27	2	28	3
Duquette, El Paso*	4	4	.500	3.27	48	0	0	22	0	5	66.0	53	29	24	7	3	34	4	45	1
Effrig, El Paso	3	1	.750	4.03	27	0	0	5	0	0	51.1	62	28	23	4	0	33	1	32	4
Felt, San Antonio*	6	3	.667	3.89	15	10	2	1	1	0	74.0	73	53	32	7	2	41	0	38	4
Felton, San Antonio	0	1	.000	7.16	7	3	0	4	0	0	16.1	21	13	13	5	0	8	1	8	1
Fossas, Tulsa*	0	1	.000	4.50	4	0	0	4	0	2	10.0	12	5	5	0	0	3	0	7	0
Fruge, Midland	0	4	.000	10.80	6	6	0	0	0	0	26.2	45	37	32	3	2	16	1	12	2
Fultz, Jackson	10	6	.625	3.04	32	22	6	5	2	1	177.2	169	74	60	12	3	46	4	108	1
Gallo, Shreveport*	0	1	.000	6.16	12	0	0	6	0	0	19.0	31	13	13	1	0	7	0	9	1
Gendron, Shreveport	0	4	.000	6.93	14	3	0	3	0	0	37.2	53	31	29	7	1	18	0	23	3
Gladden, Shreveport	4	4	.500	3.46	12	12	0	0	1	0	75.1	85	41	29	11	1	20	0	44	1
Gomez, Tulsa	0	0	.000	3.68	3	0	0	3	0	0	7.1	8	3	3	1	0	6	0	4	1
Granillo, San Antonio*	3	10	.231	5.18	45	11	0	12	0	1	104.1	118	78	60	6	3	74	9	58	9
Graves, Jackson	9	9	.500	3.23	58	0	0	40	0	17	103.0	86	40	37	2	0	67	6	65	4
Guin, Arkansas*	0	0	.000	0.00	1	0	0	1	0	0	1.0	0	0	0	0	0	2	0	0	0
Guzman, Tulsa	7	9	.438	4.17	25	25	7	0	1	0	140.1	137	75	65	6	0	55	1	82	8
Hamm, Beaumont	1	0	1.000	3.51	6	2	1	2	1	1	25.2	23	12	10	0	2	12	0	14	2
Hartzell, El Paso	2	2	.500	1.37	14	1	1	12	0	1	19.2	17	3	3	1	0	4	1	11	1
Hassler, Arkansas*	1	1	.500	5.23	9	0	0	6	0	3	10.1	9	6	6	1	1	5	0	9	2
Henderson, Midland	1	0	1.000	0.00	1	0	0	0	0	0	0.2	1	0	0	0	0	0	0	1	2
Henry, Tulsa	5	8	.385	3.39	33	14	2	1	1	5	85.0	65	42	32	1	1	60	2	79	6
Higuera, El Paso*	8	7	.553	2.60	19	19	4	0	1	1	121.0	116	57	35	11	1	43	0	99	5
Housey, Midland	7	8	.467	4.88	30	18	2	7	0	3	121.2	131	74	66	7	3	39	0	60	7
Hrynko, Midland	3	8	.273	5.06	23	17	4	5	0	1	99.2	120	63	56	10	4	37	0	43	3
Huey, Midland	0	2	.000	3.10	18	0	0	15	0	2	20.1	12	12	7	2	1	15	2	13	2
Hyman, Midland	0	0	.000	0.00	1	0	0	1	0	0	1.0	0	0	0	0	0	0	0	0	0
B. Innis, San Antonio	1	0	1.000	6.29	7	5	0	0	0	0	24.1	32	23	17	2	0	40	0	9	3
J. Innis, Jackson	6	5	.545	4.25	42	0	0	27	0	8	59.1	65	34	28	3	0	40	8	63	6

Pitcher—Club	W.	L.	Pct.	ERA.	G.	GS.	CG.	GF.	ShO.	Sv.	IP.	H.	R.	ER.	HR.	HB.	BB.	Int. BB.	SO.	WP.
Jackson, Jackson	2	4	.333	3.46	28	0	0	14	0	0	54.2	51	27	21	6	1	19	3	65	4
Sc. Johnson, Midland°	2	3	.400	3.98	20	5	1	9	0	1	52.0	52	38	23	4	0	36	1	26	4
St. Johnson, Beaumont	0	0	.000	27.00	1	0	0	1	0	0	2.0	2	6	6	0	1	7	0	1	1
T. Johnson, Tulsa°	6	9	.400	4.53	22	20	1	1	0	0	115.1	102	70	58	10	4	72	0	59	6
Johnston, San Antonio	4	0	1.000	4.77	39	0	0	15	0	2	60.1	63	37	32	8	1	47	6	37	3
D. Jones, El Paso	6	8	.429	4.28	16	16	7	0	0	0	109.1	120	61	52	12	4	35	2	62	3
J. Jones, Beaumont	7	2	.778	2.10	13	13	0	0	0	0	85.2	63	28	20	5	0	39	0	49	4
Kaufman, Midland	5	5	.500	5.03	31	0	0	23	0	5	39.1	40	24	22	4	0	27	0	18	3
Kern, El Paso	2	0	1.000	6.00	8	1	0	2	0	1	15.0	19	10	10	0	1	8	0	13	3
Kinzer, Arkansas	5	6	.455	4.46	14	14	0	0	0	0	82.2	97	48	41	5	1	27	1	41	2
Kolotka, Beaumont	0	4	.000	10.13	8	0	0	5	0	0	10.2	18	13	12	1	0	7	1	2	0
Kordish, Tulsa	9	9	.500	3.97	27	26	3	1	1	0	165.1	166	83	73	17	2	53	3	85	5
Kutsukos, Beaumont	8	4	.667	2.50	54	0	0	41	0	20	79.1	79	28	22	3	0	29	4	30	2
Latham, Jackson°	2	2	.500	2.22	7	7	0	0	0	0	44.2	38	15	11	2	2	9	0	27	0
Leach, Tulsa	0	4	.000	3.62	6	6	1	0	0	0	37.1	39	17	15	5	2	15	2	10	0
Leopold, Beaumont	8	2	.800	3.22	23	23	3	0	1	0	134.0	131	54	48	7	7	52	3	93	8
Lockenmeyer, Jackson	5	2	.714	4.42	20	11	1	2	1	1	79.1	79	40	39	6	0	24	0	35	5
Long, Beaumont	14	5	.737	2.93	25	24	4	1	2	0	159.2	149	56	52	8	1	67	1	114	5
Lovelace, San Antonio°	3	7	.300	3.88	16	16	0	0	0	0	65.0	48	39	28	5	1	73	1	52	10
Lusted, Shreveport	6	7	.462	2.96	21	21	2	0	1	0	124.2	125	49	41	8	3	38	0	93	5
J. Martin, Arkansas	0	0	.000	6.20	11	1	0	2	0	1	24.2	28	19	17	3	0	17	4	18	2
S. Martin, San Antonio	4	8	.333	4.08	56	0	0	39	0	9	92.2	94	48	42	8	3	57	7	58	8
A. Martinez, El Paso	4	2	.667	4.58	7	6	1	0	0	0	39.1	46	25	20	5	0	14	1	18	0
C. Martinez, Arkansas	1	3	.250	4.40	9	9	1	0	0	0	61.1	58	32	30	4	1	27	2	49	6
Mason, Arkansas	4	7	.364	3.56	42	1	0	21	0	5	81.0	89	40	32	6	1	28	1	45	2
Mattson, Shreveport	6	7	.462	2.50	46	0	0	40	0	11	72.0	65	27	20	4	1	27	7	64	1
McCulla, Arkansas	0	0	.000	0.00	1	0	0	1	0	0	1.0	1	0	0	0	0	2	0	1	0
McCullers, Beaumont	4	1	.800	2.11	8	8	3	0	1	0	55.1	38	13	13	1	1	35	3	48	3
McDowell, Jackson	0	0	.000	3.68	3	2	0	0	0	0	7.1	9	3	3	0	0	1	0	8	0
Meckes, Tulsa	3	3	.500	3.96	19	1	0	8	0	0	38.2	36	18	17	3	2	22	4	23	3
Meeks, San Antonio	14	8	.636	3.48	28	27	8	0	3	0	186.0	175	77	72	19	1	63	4	125	3
Mills, Beaumont	1	0	1.000	0.00	1	1	0	0	0	0	5.0	1	0	0	0	0	0	0	3	0
Moloney, El Paso°	1	3	.250	10.59	9	1	0	2	0	0	17.0	33	20	20	3	0	6	0	12	3
Montalvo, San Antonio	0	1	.000	1.99	20	0	0	16	0	7	22.2	17	8	5	0	1	12	4	7	0
Moore, Shreveport	7	5	.583	3.06	52	0	0	38	0	7	85.1	85	36	29	6	1	24	1	69	9
Morlock, Arkansas	11	8	.579	3.01	28	24	9	3	3	0	173.2	144	72	58	15	5	59	4	124	3
Morse, Shreveport°	2	5	.286	4.62	13	13	1	0	0	0	74.0	76	43	38	8	2	15	0	45	1
Moscaret, Midland°	1	4	.200	4.76	40	2	0	17	0	2	68.0	66	39	36	7	1	44	2	56	6
Murtha, Shreveport°	4	3	.571	3.93	14	8	0	4	0	0	55.0	56	33	24	7	1	24	0	36	8
Myers, Jackson°	2	1	.667	2.06	5	5	1	0	0	0	35.0	29	14	8	2	0	16	1	35	2
Myles, Jackson°	2	3	.400	3.98	15	5	2	4	1	1	40.2	30	22	18	1	3	32	1	34	2
O'Keefe, Jackson°	2	0	1.000	4.89	7	7	1	0	1	0	35.0	43	25	19	2	1	20	0	20	4
Pederson, San Antonio°	0	0	.000	0.00	1	0	0	1	0	0	1.0	0	0	0	0	0	3	0	1	0
Perry, Arkansas°	4	2	.667	1.11	25	0	0	11	0	3	48.2	34	8	6	2	0	17	3	51	4
Pickett, Jackson°	5	0	1.000	2.27	23	0	0	13	0	4	31.2	35	9	8	1	2	10	3	19	2
Pierce, Arkansas	5	9	.357	4.53	34	10	0	12	0	2	101.1	112	61	51	5	1	43	4	48	7
Piper, San Antonio	6	6	.500	3.53	30	11	0	6	0	1	91.2	96	50	36	6	3	55	3	76	3
Plante, El Paso	0	0	.000	24.75	2	0	0	0	0	0	4.0	12	11	11	2	0	6	0	0	0
Plesac, El Paso°	2	2	.500	3.46	7	7	0	0	0	0	39.0	43	19	15	2	0	16	0	24	0
Potestio, Midland	6	10	.375	3.31	35	17	5	8	1	0	130.2	141	59	48	8	2	37	0	68	4
Powell, San Antonio°	9	8	.529	3.38	24	24	5	0	2	0	168.0	153	81	63	8	2	87	0	82	3
Pryce, Midland	1	0	1.000	3.18	1	1	0	0	0	0	5.2	7	2	2	0	0	1	0	3	0
Rhodes, Arkansas°	1	2	.333	4.39	35	0	0	14	0	6	41.0	39	26	20	2	1	16	1	30	6
Richardson, Midland	1	2	.333	6.23	7	7	1	0	0	0	30.1	39	30	21	3	1	23	0	15	1
Roman, Arkansas°	1	0	1.000	1.80	1	1	0	0	0	0	5.0	1	1	1	0	0	3	0	2	0
Ronan, Shreveport	6	11	.353	4.22	42	5	0	18	0	2	102.1	114	56	48	7	6	35	3	41	7
Rosenhahn, Midland	0	1	.000	4.26	13	0	0	2	0	1	25.1	26	16	12	3	0	14	0	13	3
Schefsky, Beaumont	9	5	.643	4.73	42	2	1	16	0	4	93.1	103	56	49	4	3	39	4	43	4
Schiraldi, Jackson	14	3	.824	2.88	23	22	5	0	1	0	156.1	118	58	50	10	3	69	1	131	4
Schroeck, El Paso°	1	0	1.000	2.36	12	1	0	6	0	1	26.2	25	7	7	2	1	11	0	15	0
Scudder, San Antonio	4	2	.667	3.88	34	0	0	14	0	6	60.1	60	32	26	4	3	30	2	27	4
Sebra, Tulsa	10	5	.667	3.41	17	17	2	0	1	0	100.1	86	45	38	11	3	41	0	90	3
Shade, Arkansas	2	4	.333	3.09	27	0	0	19	0	7	46.2	35	18	16	3	1	30	5	48	3
Shimp, Tulsa	3	6	.333	3.55	19	10	2	6	0	0	99.0	98	46	39	7	2	33	1	70	6
Silkwood, Arkansas	6	6	.500	4.02	24	10	2	4	1	0	85.0	89	44	38	6	3	44	4	58	3
Slezak, San Antonio	1	3	.250	7.82	17	4	0	1	0	1	38.0	42	36	33	8	0	36	1	34	0
D. Smith, Tulsa	0	1	.000	14.34	7	0	0	1	0	0	10.2	18	17	17	0	1	9	0	6	3
S. Smith, Shreveport	0	1	.000	5.06	2	1	0	0	0	0	5.1	7	4	3	0	0	2	0	2	0
Snyder, Shreveport°	0	0	.000	0.00	1	0	0	0	0	0	1.0	0	0	0	0	0	1	0	1	0
Soff, Midland	2	1	.667	1.52	10	5	1	1	0	0	41.1	36	12	7	1	0	12	0	17	1
Steels, Beaumont°	0	0	.000	7.71	3	0	0	3	0	0	4.2	3	4	4	1	0	10	0	2	0
Taylor, Tulsa	5	3	.625	3.83	42	2	0	28	0	7	80.0	65	38	34	8	2	51	6	80	7
Teahan, Shreveport	0	1	.000	4.08	6	2	0	2	0	0	17.2	19	12	8	3	1	5	0	5	0
Thomas, San Antonio	5	6	.455	4.52	14	14	0	0	0	0	81.2	85	45	41	10	1	37	4	47	6
Thurberg, Arkansas	1	0	1.000	3.09	11	0	0	4	0	0	11.2	7	7	4	0	1	7	0	9	0
Tibbs, Jackson	1	2	.333	3.13	6	6	0	0	0	0	37.1	28	15	13	2	0	19	0	31	0
Torres, San Antonio	1	1	.500	7.27	7	0	0	2	0	0	17.1	18	15	14	4	2	11	1	17	4
Towers, Beaumont	8	8	.500	4.15	26	26	3	0	1	0	160.1	161	89	74	11	2	106	4	100	7
Vaughn, Jackson	6	4	.600	2.24	16	16	1	0	0	0	104.1	104	40	26	7	2	20	1	58	5
Vavra, San Antonio	0	0	.000	0.00	1	0	0	0	0	0	1.0	1	0	0	0	0	2	0	0	0
Villegas, El Paso	8	5	.615	4.78	30	18	0	2	0	1	122.1	147	80	65	15	2	43	0	86	2
Vosberg, Beaumont°	13	11	.542	3.43	27	27	5	0	2	0	183.2	196	87	70	12	2	74	5	100	9
Walker, El Paso	1	4	.200	6.99	10	10	1	0	0	0	46.1	75	40	36	6	1	15	1	17	3
Walter, Beaumont°	7	3	.700	2.61	34	6	1	16	1	9	76.0	53	25	22	2	2	40	0	71	7
Wegman, El Paso	4	5	.444	2.67	10	10	4	0	0	0	64.0	62	25	19	5	3	15	0	42	1
Wilhelmi, Shreveport	5	11	.313	4.58	29	23	1	2	0	0	143.1	170	97	73	17	6	65	0	60	11
Winfield, Tulsa	2	1	.667	8.68	13	0	0	7	0	0	18.2	35	18	18	1	1	10	0	8	2
Wood, El Paso	3	1	.750	7.08	37	2	0	12	0	1	68.2	93	61	54	7	5	43	3	39	8
Worrell, Arkansas	3	10	.231	4.49	18	18	5	0	0	0	100.1	109	72	50	8	0	67	4	88	8
Youmans, Jackson	6	7	.462	4.60	16	15	0	0	0	0	86.0	75	47	44	3	2	74	0	87	6
J. Young, Arkansas°	9	7	.563	3.56	26	26	4	0	2	0	151.2	132	84	60	8	1	122	4	136	16
S. Young, Arkansas	2	3	.400	4.31	7	7	0	0	0	0	39.2	46	23	19	0	0	15	1	24	0

BALKS—Fultz, 6; Vosberg, 3; Bass, L. Crews, Effrig, Granillo, Higuera, Sc. Johnson, S. Martin, Moore, Morlock, Powell, Schiraldi, Sebra, Taylor, Walker, J. Young, 2 each; Adams, Banks, Chestnut, Clutterbuck, Cook, Cunningham, Gomez, Henry, J. Innis, Jackson, Johnston, Kordish, Leopold, Long, Lovelace, Lusted, A. Martinez, C. Martinez, McCullers, Meeks, Moloney, Myers, Richardson, Ronan, Silkwood, Walter, Wilhelmi, Worrell, Youmans, 1 each.

COMBINATION SHUTOUTS—Kinzer-Shade, Arkansas; Long-Couchee-Kutsukos, Jones-Couchee, Leopold-Cook, Leopold-Walter, Long-Kutsukos, Vosberg-Schefsky, McCullers-Walter, McCullers-Barba, Beaumont; Higuera-Effrig-Wood, Higuera-Crim, Plesac-Wood-Schroeck, Clutterbuck-Kern, El Paso; Tibbs-Graves, Schiraldi-Bullinger, Latham-Graves-Bullinger, Bettendorf-Graves, Schiraldi-Pickett, Youmans-Graves, Aguilera-Jackson-Lockenmeyer, Myers-Pickett, Vaughn-Pickett, McDowell-Youmans-Innis, Jackson; Soff-Carpio, Midland; Meeks-Slezak, Lovelace-Piper-Martin, Powell-Martin, Lovelace-Scudder, San Antonio; Bockus-Ronan, Wilhelmi-Moore, Lusted-Moore, Shreveport; Henry-Taylor-Buckley, Kordish-Winfield, Sebra-Buckley, Kordish-Taylor, Boggs-Winfield, Meckes-Taylor-Bass, Sebra-Buckley-Henry, Clark-Henry, Taylor-Buckley, Tulsa.

NO-HIT GAMES—Kordish, Tulsa, defeated Midland, 6-0 (seven innings, first game), May 29; Lovelace-Piper-Martin, San Antonio, defeated Beaumont, 1-0, June 19.

California League

CLASS A

CHAMPIONSHIP WINNERS IN PREVIOUS YEARS

1914—Fresno ... .571	1959—Bakersfield ... .592	1972—Modesto§ ... .547
1915—Modesto ... .857	Modesto§ ... .643	Bakersfield ... .629
1916-40—Did not operate.	1960—Reno ... .614	1973—Lodi§ ... .657
1941—Fresno ... .643	Reno ... .657	Bakersfield ... .571
S. Barbara (2nd)* ... .597	1961—Reno ... .743	1974—Fresno§ ... .607
1942—Santa Barbara† ... .642	Reno ... .643	San Jose ... .579
1943-44-45—Did not operate.	1962—San Jose§ ... .686	1975—Reno ... .614
1946—Stockton‡ ... .600	Reno ... .587	Reno ... .614
1947—Stockton‡ ... .679	1963—Modesto ... .589	1976—Salinas ... .650
1948—Fresno ... .607	Stockton§ ... .687	Reno§ ... .547
S. Barbara (3rd)* ... .529	1964—Fresno ... .638	1977—Salinas ... .564
1949—Bakersfield ... .612	Fresno ... .600	Lodi§ ... .579
San Jose (4th)* ... .543	1965—San Jose ... .586	1978—Visalia§ ... .698
1950—Ventura ... .607	Stockton§ ... .614	Lodi ... .607
Modesto (2nd)* ... .586	1966—Modesto ... .577	1979—San Jose§ ... .636
1951—Santa Barbara‡ ... .599	Modesto ... .671	Reno ... .525
1952—Fresno‡ ... .629	1967—San Jose§ ... .676	1980—Stockton§ ... .638
1953—San Jose‡ ... .664	Modesto ... .586	Visalia ... .507
1954—Modesto‡ ... .623	1968—San Jose ... .629	1981—Visalia ... .621
1955—Stockton ... .733	Fresno§ ... .623	Lodi§ ... .521
Fresno§ ... .718	1969—Stockton§ ... .600	1982—Modesto§ ... .671
1956—Fresno‡ ... .650	Visalia ... .614	Visalia ... .586
1957—Visalia x ... .622	1970—Bakersfield ... .667	1983—Visalia ... .621
Salinas (4th)* ... .504	Bakersfield ... .671	Redwood§ ... .529
1958—Fresno* ... .639	1971—Visalia§ ... .583	
Bakersfield ... .672	Fresno ... .500	

*Won four-club playoff. †League disbanded June 28. ‡Won championship and four-club playoff. §Won split-season playoff. xWon both halves of split-season.

STANDING OF CLUBS AT CLOSE OF FIRST HALF, JUNE 21

NORTHERN DIVISION

Club	W.	L.	T.	Pct.	G.B.
Modesto (A's)	44	25	0	.638	......
Redwood (Angels)	38	31	0	.551	6
Stockton (Brewers)	34	35	0	.493	10
Reno (Padres)	30	39	0	.435	14
Lodi (Cubs)	30	40	0	.429	14½

SOUTHERN DIVISION

Club	W.	L.	T.	Pct.	G.B.
Fresno (Giants)	43	27	0	.614	......
Visalia (Twins)	37	33	0	.529	6
Salinas (Mariners)	32	38	0	.457	11
San Jose (Independent)	32	38	0	.457	11
Bakersfield (Dodgers)	28	42	0	.400	15

STANDING OF CLUBS AT CLOSE OF SEASON, SEPTEMBER 2

NORTHERN DIVISION

Club	W.	L.	T.	Pct.	G.B.
Redwood (Angels)	53	17	0	.757	......
Modesto (A's)	39	31	0	.557	14
Reno (Padres)	35	35	0	.500	18
Stockton (Brewers)	30	40	0	.429	23
Lodi (Cubs)	28	42	0	.400	25

SOUTHERN DIVISION

Club	W.	L.	T.	Pct.	G.B.
Bakersfield (Dodgers)	40	30	0	.571	......
Fresno (Giants)	39	31	0	.557	1
Salinas (Mariners)	34	36	0	.486	6
Visalia (Twins)	29	41	0	.414	11
San Jose (Independent)	23	47	0	.329	17

COMPOSITE STANDING OF CLUBS AT CLOSE OF SEASON, SEPTEMBER 2

NORTHERN DIVISION

Club	Red.	Mod.	Reno	Sto.	Lodi	Fr.	Bak.	Sal.	Vis.	S.J.	W.	L.	T.	Pct.	G.B.
Redwood (Angels)	....	9	13	14	12	8	11	8	8	8	91	48	0	.655	......
Modesto (A's)	11	....	10	12	16	5	9	4	8	8	83	56	0	.597	8
Reno (Padres)	7	9	....	11	14	4	2	6	6	4	65	74	0	.468	26
Stockton (Brewers)	5	5	8	....	9	4	6	8	8	4	64	75	0	.460	27
Lodi (Cubs)	8	2	8	8	....	5	6	6	8	7	58	82	0	.414	33½

SOUTHERN DIVISION

Club	Red.	Mod.	Reno	Sto.	Lodi	Fr.	Bak.	Sal.	Vis.	S.J.	W.	L.	T.	Pct.	G.B.
Fresno (Giants)	4	7	8	8	7	....	12	9	11	16	82	58	0	.586	......
Bakersfield (Dodgers)	1	5	6	6	6	10	....	11	11	12	68	72	0	.486	14
Salinas (Mariners)	4	8	8	4	6	9	9	....	8	10	66	74	0	.471	16
Visalia (Twins)	4	4	6	4	4	9	9	12	....	14	66	74	0	.471	16
San Jose (Independent)	4	4	6	8	5	4	8	10	6	....	55	85	0	.393	27

Major league affiliations in parentheses.

Playoffs—Modesto defeated Redwood, two games to one; Bakersfield defeated Fresno, two games to one; and Modesto defeated Bakersfield, three games to one, to win league championship.

Regular-Season Attendance—Bakersfield, 102,053; Fresno, 86,711; Lodi, 45,027; Modesto, 70,356; Redwood, 60,282; Reno, 75,938; Salinas, 54,400; San Jose, 46,081; Stockton, 97,005; Visalia, 65,043. Playoffs, 16,163.

Managers—Bakersfield, Don LeJohn; Fresno, Wendell Kim; Lodi, Junior Kennedy; Modesto, George Mitterwald; Redwood, John Kotchman; Reno, Jim Skaalen; Salinas, Bob Harrison; San Jose, Al Gallagher; Stockton, Tim Nordbrook, Mike Pazik, Andy Etchebarren; Visalia, John Hilton.

All-Star Team: 1B—Mike Aldrete, Fresno; 2B—Ray Etchebarren, Reno; 3B—Steve Aragon, Visalia; SS—Keith Thrower, Modesto; OF—Rickey Coleman, Reno; Reggie Montgomery, Redwood; Rock Coyle, Modesto; C—Benito Santiago, Reno; DH—Glenn Braggs, Stockton; P—Bob Kipper, Redwood; Don Timberlake, Redwood; Johnny Abrego, Lodi; Manager—John Kotchman, Redwood; Most Valuable Player—Glenn Braggs, Stockton; Pitcher of the Year—Bob Kipper, Redwood.

(Compiled by William J. Weiss, League Statistician, San Mateo, Calif.)

CLUB BATTING

Club	Pct.	G.	AB.	R.	OR.	H.	TB.	2B.	3B.	HR.	RBI.	GW.	SH.	SF.	HP.	BB.	Int. BB.	SO.	SB.	CS.	LOB.
Reno	.281	139	4679	701	745	1316	1756	178	44	58	620	58	54	37	51	488	27	835	139	54	1070
Redwood	.267	139	4510	708	483	1205	1677	180	32	76	620	79	78	50	38	551	22	902	185	75	1017
Fresno	.265	140	4593	675	620	1215	1633	189	23	61	593	78	39	51	47	628	20	1019	177	73	1091
Modesto	.263	139	4505	662	541	1185	1665	199	34	71	574	70	68	43	46	565	24	945	220	101	1006
Salinas	.251	140	4582	607	586	1150	1574	174	47	52	531	60	38	52	45	635	22	786	188	112	1078
Stockton	.249	139	4607	646	742	1146	1508	155	42	41	557	53	55	46	35	649	24	903	151	69	1078
Bakersfield	.248	140	4581	659	644	1136	1552	208	26	52	579	58	56	44	47	538	25	834	124	56	995
Visalia	.246	140	4542	558	681	1118	1439	150	24	41	483	51	45	33	39	565	26	857	216	95	1054
Lodi	.240	140	4497	614	622	1080	1500	163	25	69	552	49	43	30	37	629	22	1070	136	70	1014
San Jose	.239	140	4567	521	687	1091	1398	136	30	37	463	50	40	29	31	620	17	1019	108	57	1107

INDIVIDUAL BATTING

(Leading Qualifiers for Batting Championship—378 or More Plate Appearances)

°Bats lefthanded.   †Switch-hitter.

Player and Club	Pct.	G.	AB.	R.	H.	TB.	2B.	3B.	HR.	RBI.	GW.	SH.	SF.	HP.	BB.	Int. BB.	SO.	SB.	CS.
Coleman, Rickey, Reno	.351	125	499	94	175	199	16	4	0	49	6	4	1	9	56	2	47	44	18
Aldrete, Michael, Fresno°	.339	136	457	89	155	225	28	3	12	72	14	1	4	1	109	5	77	14	5
Thrower, Keith, Modesto†	.324	119	435	81	141	171	12	6	2	48	7	11	3	2	57	6	52	89	38
Jones, Daniel, Reno	.309	110	356	54	110	147	15	8	2	38	1	5	1	7	37	0	58	7	3
Etchebarren, Raymond, Reno	.301	111	435	67	131	170	23	2	4	66	7	1	4	1	39	4	51	7	1
Cimo, Matthew, Fresno	.300	101	333	54	100	140	17	1	7	58	6	7	5	4	42	1	82	25	9
Coyle, Rock, Modesto	.296	124	439	72	130	185	33	5	4	42	3	8	3	10	44	0	57	21	14
Braggs, Glenn, Stockton	.296	108	399	76	118	196	29	2	15	86	13	0	8	6	66	4	87	9	1
McLemore, Mark, Redwood†	.295	134	482	102	142	156	8	3	0	45	5	11	3	1	106	1	75	59	15
Jones, Gary, Lodi°	.291	138	471	111	137	184	17	6	4	44	3	2	4	5	138	5	94	38	16

Departmental Leaders: G—S. Aragon, 140; AB—R. Hill, 556; R—Ga. Jones, 111; H—Coleman, 175; TB—Aldrete, 225; 2B—Coyle, 33; 3B—R. Brown, Carroll, 9; HR—Bonner, 20; RBI—Bonner, 92; GWRBI—Bonner, 19; SH—K. Davis, 18; SF—Colton, Francis, 9; HP—Gibbons, 12; BB—Ga. Jones, 138; IBB—Reibel, 10; SO—Kent, 220; SB—Thrower, 89; CS—Thrower, 38.

(All Players—Listed Alphabetically)

Player and Club	Pct.	G.	AB.	R.	H.	TB.	2B.	3B.	HR.	RBI.	GW.	SH.	SF.	HP.	BB.	Int. BB.	SO.	SB.	CS.
Abbott, Ricardo, Stockton	.220	62	182	21	40	50	10	0	0	19	4	3	2	0	28	0	54	0	0
Abrego, Johnny, Lodi	.063	23	16	0	1	1	0	0	0	0	0	0	2	0	0	0	5	0	0
Aldrete, Michael, Fresno°	.339	136	457	89	155	225	28	3	12	72	14	1	4	1	109	5	77	14	5
Allen, James, Lodi†	.259	102	294	45	76	96	14	0	2	33	2	5	4	1	53	1	64	3	2
Allen, David, Fresno	.191	29	94	12	18	26	3	1	1	12	1	1	2	1	6	0	20	1	3
Amaya, Benjamin, Salinas	.272	93	298	29	81	102	11	2	2	38	4	1	4	1	46	0	44	4	4
Antonelli, John, Stockton	.215	101	335	44	72	84	9	0	1	22	0	10	2	1	40	0	52	22	5
Aoyama, Michio, San Jose	.116	33	86	2	10	10	0	0	0	3	0	2	0	0	12	1	26	2	0
Aragon, Joey, Visalia	.192	65	203	22	39	45	6	0	0	12	0	2	1	0	18	2	34	3	3
Aragon, Steven, Visalia	.287	140	537	70	154	191	24	2	3	59	6	4	5	4	71	5	58	13	16
Baker, Mark, Lodi 21-Modesto 4	.000	25	2	0	0	0	0	0	0	0	0	0	0	0	0	0	0	0	0
Bargerhuff, Brian, Fresno	.000	58	5	1	0	0	0	0	0	0	0	0	0	0	1	0	3	0	0
Barling, Glenn, Fresno	.000	28	8	1	0	0	0	0	0	0	0	0	0	0	1	0	4	0	0
Barton, Gregory, San Jose	.203	59	182	21	37	47	5	1	1	13	2	0	1	3	31	1	41	1	0
Barton, Shawn, San Jose	.272	137	482	66	131	145	7	2	1	33	4	15	1	5	41	3	54	5	3
Bautista, Ramon, Fresno	.000	19	6	0	0	0	0	0	0	0	0	0	0	0	0	0	3	0	0
Beuerlein, John, Stockton	.208	76	221	29	46	51	3	1	0	19	1	4	1	1	34	0	64	4	1
Biko, Thomas, Reno°	.000	31	1	0	0	0	0	0	0	0	0	1	0	0	0	0	0	0	0
Black, Tracy, Visalia°	.206	17	34	2	7	7	0	0	0	2	0	1	0	0	8	1	9	1	0
Blevins, Bradley, Lodi	.000	59	6	0	0	0	0	0	0	0	0	2	0	0	0	0	1	0	0
Bogart, Fred, Salinas	.194	114	335	38	65	98	18	0	3	39	2	4	3	8	84	1	102	8	3
Bonner, Mark, Redwood	.273	133	469	85	128	211	21	1	20	92	19	1	6	1	68	1	119	1	1
Borowsky, Erez, Visalia	.248	108	347	38	86	125	13	1	8	55	9	2	5	3	58	0	46	5	7
Braddy, Leonard, Visalia°	.111	9	18	3	2	2	0	0	0	0	0	1	0	0	2	0	4	1	1
Bradley, Mark, San Jose	.242	40	128	18	31	39	3	1	1	16	1	0	2	0	41	1	32	5	3
Bradley, Paul, Modesto	.231	58	147	21	34	48	6	1	2	17	2	5	1	4	35	0	42	1	0
Brady, David, Redwood°	.222	11	36	4	8	12	1	0	1	5	0	0	1	0	0	0	11	0	0
Braggs, Glenn, Stockton	.296	108	399	76	118	196	29	2	15	86	13	0	8	6	66	4	87	9	1
Brahms, Russell, Fresno	.000	23	5	0	0	0	0	0	0	0	0	1	0	0	0	0	2	0	0
Briggs, Kenneth, Salinas	.169	40	118	10	20	27	2	1	1	11	0	0	1	1	13	0	35	7	2
Brock, Eric, Bakersfield°	.187	55	107	12	20	27	1	3	0	11	2	2	1	0	22	1	32	0	1
Brooks, Craig, San Jose°	.191	28	94	12	18	22	4	0	0	7	0	1	0	0	11	1	32	0	3
Brown, Jeffrey, Bakersfield	.272	78	272	57	74	117	11	1	10	48	8	1	0	9	53	1	49	4	2
Brown, Renard, Salinas	.285	110	407	64	116	153	13	9	2	58	6	1	2	8	60	1	51	29	10
Buss, Scott, Salinas	.237	45	131	17	31	40	6	0	1	6	2	3	0	2	24	0	33	7	5
Butcher, Matthew, Vis. 56-Sal. 25	.202	81	242	20	49	57	6	1	0	21	1	5	1	0	14	0	53	5	6
Calley, Robert, Visalia	.246	20	61	5	15	16	1	0	0	5	1	0	0	0	6	0	9	0	0
Calvert, Christopher, Visalia	.294	13	34	3	10	12	2	0	0	4	0	0	0	1	4	0	5	0	0
Cabrera, Antonio, Modesto	.274	25	95	14	26	29	3	0	0	13	1	4	1	0	7	0	14	5	2
Canseco, Jose, Modesto	.276	116	410	61	113	183	21	2	15	73	13	3	7	6	74	5	127	10	6
Capel, Michael, Lodi	.333	20	6	1	2	2	1	0	0	0	0	0	0	0	0	0	2	0	0
Carne, Gregory, Bakersfield°	.750	33	4	0	3	3	0	0	0	0	0	0	0	0	0	0	0	0	0
Carroll, Carson, Visalia	.286	134	482	67	138	183	15	9	4	64	10	7	3	5	68	1	90	35	19
Cartwright, Alan, Stockton°	.245	54	204	25	50	69	8	4	1	29	3	2	0	1	18	3	41	3	4
Champoux, Anthony, Modesto	.296	12	27	7	8	8	0	0	0	2	1	0	0	1	12	0	11	2	0
Chapman, Christopher, Bakersfield°	.252	109	361	52	91	146	17	1	12	64	7	3	7	6	60	2	69	0	1
Charley, Tandy, Lodi°	.200	14	5	2	1	1	0	0	0	0	1	0	0	0	0	0	0	0	0
Chestnut, Troy, Lodi	.333	12	9	1	3	3	0	0	0	2	0	1	0	0	0	0	2	0	0
Cimo, Matthew, Fresno	.300	101	333	54	100	140	17	1	7	58	6	7	5	4	42	1	82	25	9
Clawson, Kenneth, Reno	.223	67	211	22	47	53	3	0	1	16	1	1	2	2	19	0	49	1	3
Cobbs, Todd, Bakersfield	.000	21	5	0	0	0	0	0	0	0	0	1	0	0	0	0	2	0	0
Cockrell, Alan, Fresno	.215	61	214	20	46	55	6	0	1	32	7	0	2	5	28	0	66	0	1
Codinach, Rafael, Visalia°	.222	58	171	22	38	59	9	0	4	21	3	1	3	2	28	0	50	5	1
Coleman, Rickey, Reno	.351	125	499	94	175	199	16	4	0	49	6	4	1	9	56	2	47	44	18
Colton, Bradford, Salinas	.267	128	446	72	119	174	18	2	11	72	7	1	9	7	58	3	115	15	8
Conklin, Graham, Modesto	.258	129	492	49	127	173	15	5	7	61	7	3	5	5	30	2	95	5	10
Cordner, Steven, Lodi	.246	115	435	40	107	141	17	1	5	67	5	2	1	2	34	2	92	5	5
Coyle, Rock, Modesto	.296	124	439	72	130	185	33	5	4	42	3	8	3	10	44	0	57	21	14

Player and Club	Pct.	G.	AB.	R.	H.	TB.	2B.	3B.	HR.	RBI.	GW.	SH.	SF.	HP.	BB.	Int. BB.	SO.	SB.	CS.
Cruz, Juan, Modesto	.296	63	223	29	66	87	9	3	2	33	1	3	3	3	21	0	47	14	3
Cummings, Ronald, Modesto	.220	94	305	40	67	99	15	1	5	27	3	5	1	1	30	0	108	3	1
Damon, John, Lodi	.238	121	433	68	103	136	18	3	3	47	4	5	4	0	90	1	99	23	11
David, Brian, Salinas	.304	75	247	40	75	89	14	0	0	20	5	5	2	4	53	3	24	15	13
Davis, Kevin, Redwood	.238	131	420	37	100	123	10	5	1	47	9	18	3	2	30	1	112	16	14
Davis, Rodney, Bak. 61-S.J. 52°	.261	113	380	56	99	124	16	3	1	35	5	3	6	2	52	2	66	17	10
Dawson, Gary, Lodi	.213	98	338	36	72	106	10	3	6	34	4	2	0	3	13	0	77	4	6
Denton, David, Lodi	.261	61	180	20	47	56	9	0	0	20	3	2	2	5	24	1	42	6	2
Diaz, Edgar, Stockton	.258	123	419	58	108	123	1	7	0	35	0	11	1	0	46	1	54	8	6
Diaz, Lazaro, Visalia†	.147	29	95	4	14	16	2	0	0	8	1	4	0	0	7	0	29	1	1
Doerr, Jeffrey, San Jose	.250	11	36	6	9	11	0	1	0	1	0	1	0	0	9	0	14	0	0
Dorsett, Brian, Modesto	.264	99	375	39	99	142	19	0	8	52	8	0	7	2	23	1	93	0	1
Duffy, Thomas, Bakersfield	.333	12	3	0	1	2	1	0	0	0	0	1	0	0	0	0	0	0	0
Duncan, John, Salinas	.280	63	207	28	58	80	8	1	4	30	4	0	4	3	16	0	26	8	2
Eichhorn, David, Bakersfield†	.167	41	6	0	1	1	0	0	0	1	0	1	0	0	0	0	3	0	0
Empting, Michael, Lodi	.297	20	64	5	19	22	3	0	0	7	1	0	0	2	7	0	10	1	1
Engel, Steven, Lodi	.300	27	20	4	6	9	0	0	1	4	0	2	0	0	0	0	7	0	0
Erdahl, Jay, Salinas°	.223	126	421	62	94	157	17	8	10	55	6	4	3	5	60	4	78	9	6
Etchebarren, Raymond, Reno	.301	111	435	67	131	170	23	2	4	66	7	1	4	1	39	4	51	7	1
Everton, Sean, San Jose	.212	20	52	7	11	12	1	0	0	6	0	2	0	1	5	0	8	0	0
Farmar, Damon, Lodi†	.252	132	477	71	120	191	14	3	17	78	10	8	5	6	70	1	113	32	13
Ferraro, Robert, Lodi	.181	57	155	21	28	37	5	2	0	13	1	0	1	1	24	0	42	2	0
Ferraro, Vincent, Visalia	.105	18	38	5	4	4	0	0	0	2	0	1	2	2	0	0	12	1	1
Flores, Richard, Bakersfield°	.216	75	213	41	46	56	6	2	0	18	3	3	1	2	48	2	43	10	1
Francis, Thomas, Fresno°	.278	128	461	63	128	193	30	4	9	84	8	1	9	3	33	4	59	8	3
Freeman, Donald, Reno†	.295	73	190	31	56	74	7	4	1	21	3	3	0	2	25	3	51	5	4
Freeman, Lavel, Stockton°	.234	80	290	41	68	86	10	4	0	22	4	3	3	1	44	1	81	15	3
Fruge, Jeffrey, Lodi	.000	22	8	0	0	0	0	0	0	0	0	2	0	0	0	0	6	0	0
Garrett, Eric, Modesto	.185	10	27	4	5	6	1	0	0	2	0	1	0	0	4	0	7	0	1
Gatewood, Henry, Bakersfield	.163	53	147	9	24	29	5	0	0	9	1	6	2	2	19	3	21	1	1
Gentle, Michael, Bakersfield°	.000	10	1	0	0	0	0	0	0	0	0	0	0	0	0	0	0	0	0
Gibbons, John, Stockton°	.255	127	447	79	114	158	16	8	4	47	5	5	5	12	81	2	64	18	16
Gladden, Jeffrey, Fresno	.143	18	14	1	2	2	0	0	0	2	0	1	0	2	0	0	2	0	0
Gonzalez, Felipe, Fresno	.202	33	89	7	18	24	3	0	1	8	1	2	1	4	4	0	23	0	0
Gonzalez, Jose, Bakersfield	.221	129	484	86	107	168	26	1	11	59	9	5	3	4	58	2	126	49	15
Goto, Akemi, San Jose	.000	22	1	0	0	0	0	0	0	0	0	0	0	0	0	0	1	0	0
Grachen, Timothy, Lodi°	.250	22	16	2	4	4	0	0	0	0	0	2	0	0	1	0	5	0	0
Graham, Everett, Fresno°	.313	83	304	61	95	130	15	4	4	43	9	3	5	2	51	1	50	28	7
Graham, Brian, Modesto	.304	30	102	15	31	45	5	0	3	13	2	2	0	0	18	0	15	10	5
Grandstaff, Robert, Visalia	.261	62	199	23	52	80	9	2	5	27	1	1	0	3	29	0	53	5	1
Graupmann, Timothy, Visalia	.209	71	187	24	39	62	8	0	5	27	2	3	1	7	43	2	53	1	2
Guinn, Brian, Modesto†	.211	134	456	78	96	136	20	7	2	52	8	16	5	1	80	1	90	31	7
Gutierrez, Felipe, Bakersfield	.288	127	531	78	153	200	29	3	4	62	6	4	1	4	24	3	52	5	4
Hall, Andrew, Lodi°	.000	8	2	0	0	0	0	0	0	0	0	0	0	0	1	0	1	0	0
Hallgren, Tim, San Jose	.200	17	5	1	1	2	1	0	0	0	0	1	0	0	1	0	1	0	0
Hardgrave, Eric, Reno	.282	125	443	58	125	172	20	0	9	90	9	0	5	9	36	0	87	3	0
Hartsock, Brian, Redwood°	.287	71	254	36	73	97	11	5	1	37	7	2	6	0	24	2	37	17	3
Harvey, Steven, Lodi	.245	123	441	52	108	170	21	1	13	74	9	3	3	2	31	1	105	3	2
Heatherly, Stephen, Redwood	.236	59	123	15	29	33	4	0	0	9	4	0	0	1	16	0	24	0	2
Henderson, Wendell, Lodi	.262	26	84	10	22	27	3	1	0	20	2	0	1	1	13	0	12	0	0
Henning, Richard, Fresno	.091	31	11	0	1	2	1	0	0	2	0	1	1	0	0	0	2	0	0
Hill, Roger, Salinas°	.261	136	556	79	145	178	16	7	1	41	6	5	8	0	60	3	67	56	31
Hill, Timothy, Bakersfield	.170	70	194	20	33	58	13	0	4	26	1	2	0	1	7	0	51	1	1
Hoskins, Osbe, Reno	.281	97	352	58	99	114	12	0	1	44	3	5	3	1	46	0	41	23	7
Howell, Jack, Redwood°	.246	135	451	62	111	157	21	5	5	64	4	5	6	3	44	3	95	12	4
Hubbard, Henry, Reno	.181	31	105	11	19	21	2	0	0	3	1	1	0	0	7	0	20	6	1
Hubbard, Marlon, Reno	.571	44	7	1	4	4	0	0	0	1	0	0	0	0	0	0	2	0	0
Hudson, Lance, San Jose†	.177	27	96	9	17	20	3	0	0	11	0	2	2	0	5	0	18	9	2
Hummel, Dean, Fresno°	.333	27	15	2	5	7	2	0	0	1	0	0	0	0	0	0	1	0	0
Innis, Brian, Bakersfield	.000	16	11	1	0	0	0	0	0	0	0	0	0	0	0	0	5	0	0
Jackson, Larry, Stockton°	.272	52	162	25	44	66	8	4	2	30	4	1	0	2	24	1	20	9	5
Jacobson, Jeffrey, San Jose	.273	37	139	12	38	46	2	0	2	17	2	0	0	2	13	0	21	1	2
Jacoby, Donald, San Jose°	.184	38	136	4	25	30	5	0	0	9	0	0	0	1	8	0	30	0	0
James, Mark, Reno	.000	30	7	0	0	0	0	0	0	0	0	2	0	0	0	0	4	0	0
Jaremko, Thomas, Visalia	.155	25	71	7	11	11	0	0	0	2	0	1	0	0	6	0	13	0	1
Jimenez, Ramon, Redwood	.270	78	252	33	68	85	11	0	2	32	1	5	3	3	41	0	34	2	0
Johnson, Scott, Lodi°	.000	18	0	0	0	0	0	0	0	0	0	1	0	0	0	0	0	0	0
Johnson, Thomas, Lodi	.130	9	23	2	3	4	1	0	0	0	0	0	1	2	1	7	0	1
Jones, Daniel, Reno	.309	110	356	54	110	147	15	8	2	38	1	5	1	7	37	0	58	7	3
Jones, Gary, Lodi°	.291	138	471	111	137	184	17	6	6	44	3	2	4	5	138	5	94	38	16
Jones, Glenn, Fresno	.246	66	203	38	50	86	12	0	8	32	2	0	2	7	24	1	49	11	4
Kawamura, Kozuaki, San Jose	.000	21	1	0	0	0	0	0	0	0	0	0	0	0	0	0	1	0	0
Kent, Wesley, San Jose	.200	137	504	55	101	177	17	1	19	72	6	0	6	2	46	1	220	2	0
Kindred, Curtis, Visalia	.000	31	3	0	0	0	0	0	0	0	0	0	0	0	0	0	3	0	0
Kirby, Wayne, Bakersfield°	.274	23	84	14	23	26	3	0	0	10	0	2	1	0	4	0	5	8	3
Kobernus, Jeffrey, Mod. 5-Bak. 16†	.000	21	1	0	0	0	0	0	0	0	0	0	0	0	0	0	1	0	0
Kockenmeister, Ted, Reno	.000	46	2	1	0	0	0	0	0	0	0	1	0	0	1	0	1	0	0
Kopf, David, Lodi	.000	16	3	0	0	0	0	0	0	0	0	0	0	0	0	0	3	0	0
Kuhn, Todd, Fresno 10-San Jose 9	.000	19	5	0	0	0	0	0	0	0	0	0	0	0	0	0	5	0	0
Lane, Eric, Fresno	.260	95	327	40	85	115	13	1	5	49	5	0	3	2	41	0	78	2	1
Lane, Jerry, San Jose	.194	8	31	3	6	6	0	0	0	0	0	0	0	0	1	0	4	0	0
Lee, Derek, Bakersfield	.000	8	1	0	0	0	0	0	0	0	0	0	0	0	0	0	0	0	0
Loard, Billy, Fresno 18-San Jose 48	.179	66	184	18	33	46	7	0	2	21	2	3	3	4	45	0	50	0	1
Long, Donald, Fresno†	.243	106	337	44	82	105	8	3	3	30	5	1	2	4	50	1	105	2	3
Lora, Jose, Reno	.500	2	2	1	1	1	0	0	0	0	0	0	0	0	0	0	1	0	0
Loscalzo, Robert, Modesto°	.231	5	13	4	3	8	0	1	1	4	0	0	0	0	4	0	1	1	0
Mancuso, Paul, Visalia	.000	56	1	1	1	1	0	0	0	0	0	0	0	0	0	0	1	0	0
Marr, Alan, Fresno	.252	102	341	58	86	104	9	3	1	31	7	4	1	1	58	2	74	30	10
Marte, Alexis, Visalia°	.275	127	510	80	140	161	11	5	0	30	3	2	2	2	40	0	73	82	21
May, Scott, Bakersfield	.286	25	14	0	4	6	2	0	0	1	0	4	0	0	3	0	3	0	0
McCain, Michael, Salinas°	.256	89	328	41	84	115	22	3	1	25	5	0	2	0	50	0	51	2	4
McDougal, Julius, Lodi†	.186	62	220	15	41	46	5	0	0	11	0	2	0	1	8	1	57	7	1

Player and Club	Pct.	G.	AB.	R.	H.	TB.	2B.	3B.	HR.	RBI.	GW.	SH.	SF.	HP.	BB.	Int. BB.	SO.	SB.	CS.
McGwire, Mark, Modesto	.200	16	55	7	11	17	3	0	1	1	0	0	0	0	8	0	21	0	0
McLemore, Mark, Redwood†	.295	134	482	102	142	156	8	3	0	45	5	11	3	1	106	1	75	59	15
Miller, Edward, Reno†	.329	23	79	17	26	37	4	2	1	11	1	1	1	4	20	5	13	13	5
Miller, Scott, Lodi°	.238	41	122	14	29	41	8	2	0	18	2	0	2	0	20	2	23	1	1
Miller, Steven, Fresno°	.266	86	274	33	73	84	11	0	0	26	2	3	1	4	37	3	58	4	3
Mills, Michael, Reno	.056	28	18	3	1	1	0	0	0	1	0	2	0	0	5	0	13	0	0
Mills, Craig, Salinas	.270	12	37	6	10	10	0	0	0	2	1	0	0	1	3	0	6	0	0
Moncrief, Anthony, Modesto	.202	74	233	45	47	55	3	1	1	30	2	2	4	0	44	1	52	21	5
Montgomery, Reginald, Redwood	.291	120	447	81	130	202	28	1	14	79	13	4	8	5	21	2	56	10	4
Moran, Jorge, Bakersfield	.278	10	36	3	10	10	0	0	0	2	0	1	0	1	2	0	6	0	2
Moran, Mitchell, Bakersfield	.272	101	335	37	91	105	9	1	1	40	2	2	2	2	38	1	65	8	3
Mulholland, Terence, Fresno	.000	9	10	0	0	0	0	0	0	1	0	1	0	0	0	0	7	0	0
Murtha, Brian, Fresno°	.000	18	4	0	0	0	0	0	0	1	0	0	0	0	1	0	2	0	0
Myers, David, Salinas	.258	137	519	58	134	156	12	5	0	56	5	7	7	3	36	1	36	21	15
Naber, Robert, Fresno	.231	23	52	6	12	16	4	0	0	5	1	0	1	0	15	0	15	0	0
Narita, Yukihiro, San Jose°	.000	46	1	0	0	0	0	0	0	0	0	0	0	0	0	0	0	0	0
Nichols, Carl, S.J. 58-Redwood 63	.226	121	389	53	88	118	14	2	4	54	8	3	4	4	54	1	81	9	2
Nittoli, Michael, San Jose	.278	5	18	0	5	5	0	0	0	2	0	0	0	2	0	0	4	0	0
Noce, Paul, Reno	.429	9	35	8	15	19	2	1	0	4	0	1	0	0	4	0	8	3	1
Norman, Scott, Fresno	.250	28	12	3	3	3	0	0	0	0	0	4	0	0	1	0	5	0	0
Oakes, Todd, Fresno	.000	35	5	0	0	0	0	0	0	0	0	2	0	0	2	0	1	0	0
O'Brien, Charles, Modesto	.281	9	32	8	9	14	2	0	1	5	0	0	0	3	2	0	4	1	0
O'Dell, Jeffrey, San Jose	.239	81	280	36	67	91	10	4	2	31	7	0	2	4	41	0	91	10	5
Palma, Gerald, San Jose	.240	30	75	5	18	24	1	1	1	6	2	0	0	2	5	0	12	1	0
Parks, Jeffrey, Reno	.167	25	6	1	1	1	0	0	0	1	0	0	0	0	1	0	0	0	0
Parmenter, Gary, Lodi	.263	27	19	1	5	5	0	0	0	0	0	0	0	0	1	0	7	0	0
Penigar, Charles, Fresno†	.270	36	141	25	38	46	4	2	0	9	2	1	1	0	22	1	37	13	6
Perkins, Harold, Bak. 28-Sto. 36†	.232	64	220	35	51	69	6	6	0	24	1	2	3	1	32	3	41	13	3
Peterson, Allan, Redwood	.225	50	151	15	34	50	8	1	2	27	2	4	0	3	16	1	39	6	3
Phillips, James, Lodi	.000	13	0	0	0	0	0	0	0	0	0	0	0	0	0	0	0	0	0
Picart, Juan, Bakersfield	.316	26	79	13	25	28	3	0	0	7	1	0	0	2	1	1	11	0	0
Piper, Brian, Bakersfield	.000	8	0	0	0	0	0	0	0	0	0	1	0	0	0	0	0	0	0
Pitts, Daryl, San Jose°	.278	109	388	46	108	141	15	6	2	46	5	1	3	0	60	1	35	11	6
Pott, Lawrence, Reno	.261	100	329	45	86	140	13	4	11	59	10	4	2	3	32	1	66	1	0
Ray, Arthur, San Jose	.000	22	2	0	0	0	0	0	0	0	0	0	0	0	0	0	0	0	0
Raymer, Gregory, Reno	.167	27	18	1	3	5	2	0	0	3	1	1	0	0	2	0	11	0	0
Reibel, Douglas, Redwood°	.277	111	310	64	86	145	12	1	15	48	4	0	3	8	82	10	66	9	6
Rhinehart, Randy, San Jose	.167	13	36	0	6	6	0	0	0	2	1	1	0	0	5	0	12	1	1
Richie, Bennie, Visalia†	.226	110	340	38	77	87	10	0	0	27	3	3	3	6	52	4	81	8	3
Rivera, Luis, Bakersfield	.056	12	18	4	1	1	0	0	0	1	0	0	0	0	4	0	2	0	0
Rizzo, Michael, Redwood	.281	66	153	13	43	58	5	2	2	16	4	1	3	1	8	0	24	0	2
Roadcap, Steven, Lodi†	.152	64	171	25	26	37	3	1	2	15	0	2	0	3	48	4	33	0	0
Robidoux, William, Stockton°	.279	97	333	50	93	128	18	1	5	67	4	3	4	1	60	4	59	6	2
Robinson, Bruce, Modesto°	.151	21	53	5	8	14	0	0	2	5	0	0	0	3	1	0	11	0	0
Robles, Gregory, Modesto°	.260	56	200	21	52	59	7	0	0	26	5	0	2	2	27	0	31	1	0
Rodriguez, Rigo, Reno	.282	57	170	30	48	67	6	2	3	22	0	4	4	1	15	0	40	6	4
Roomes, Rolando, Lodi	.265	116	377	52	100	155	12	2	13	52	3	0	1	4	25	1	137	10	9
Rosenhahn, David, Lodi	.000	24	2	0	0	0	0	0	0	0	0	0	0	0	0	0	0	0	0
Roth, John, Modesto	.310	40	126	21	39	51	7	1	1	14	2	3	0	1	13	0	28	1	4
Rowen, Robert, Bakersfield°	.053	29	19	1	1	1	0	0	0	1	0	1	0	0	2	0	7	0	0
Rutledge, Jeffrey, Lodi	.261	18	46	8	12	14	2	0	0	8	0	0	1	2	5	0	12	0	0
Salery, Johnny, Visalia	.178	38	118	10	21	28	4	0	1	11	2	0	1	2	16	2	24	11	3
Santiago, Benito, Reno	.279	114	416	64	116	196	20	6	16	83	4	2	6	4	36	4	75	5	2
Sasser, Mack, Fresno°	.274	16	62	8	17	20	1	1	0	6	1	1	0	0	3	0	6	1	0
Saverino, Michael, Redwood	.000	6	4	1	0	0	0	0	0	0	0	1	0	1	2	0	1	0	0
Scheer, Ronald, Visalia†	.275	137	512	68	141	196	23	1	10	73	2	2	3	3	46	6	82	10	4
Schugel, Jeffrey, Visalia	.249	127	453	60	113	157	18	4	6	55	6	4	4	2	63	3	113	30	7
Scudder, William, Bakersfield°	.000	23	3	0	0	0	0	0	0	0	0	0	0	0	0	0	0	0	0
Serritella, John, Bakersfield°	.200	27	5	0	1	1	0	0	0	0	0	0	0	0	0	0	2	0	0
Sferrazza, Matthew, Stockton	.259	130	475	70	123	139	7	3	1	43	3	6	5	2	51	0	59	37	10
Shirahata, Katsuhiro, San Jose°	.229	98	297	25	68	86	10	1	2	29	3	2	2	3	36	1	57	6	3
Sierra, Ulises, Reno	.222	28	9	0	2	3	1	0	0	1	1	0	0	2	0	1	0	0	0
Smith, Curtis, Modesto°	.222	2	9	1	2	3	1	0	0	0	0	0	0	0	0	0	3	0	0
Smith, David, Salinas°	.238	127	408	51	97	170	13	6	16	71	8	1	7	3	62	6	79	5	4
Smith, Stephen, Fresno†	.000	11	13	0	0	0	0	0	0	0	0	1	0	0	0	0	8	0	0
Smith, Thomas, Redwood	.270	37	122	13	33	43	3	2	1	14	0	2	0	0	9	0	22	7	6
Sowards, Van, Fresno	.267	14	45	6	12	14	2	0	0	8	0	0	0	0	9	0	7	0	0
Stanek, Michael, Stockton	.246	67	236	30	58	75	8	3	0	26	5	1	5	2	27	0	56	0	3
Stewart, Charles, Lodi	.159	19	44	7	7	7	0	0	0	2	0	1	0	1	9	1	10	3	0
Strom, Phillip, San Jose	.266	66	214	21	57	77	11	0	3	35	3	0	3	3	41	3	51	2	0
Su'a, Murphy, Stockton	.184	31	76	12	14	26	4	1	2	15	1	0	1	1	9	0	25	1	0
Suarez, Brian, Lodi	.091	3	11	1	1	4	0	0	1	0	0	0	0	0	1	0	3	0	0
Szekely, Joseph, Bakersfield°	.275	110	353	54	97	141	26	3	4	61	6	3	8	1	49	5	83	4	2
Taft, Dennie, Fresno	1.000	7	1	0	1	1	0	0	0	0	0	0	0	0	0	0	0	0	0
Tarangelo, Joseph, Visalia	.200	36	110	10	22	25	1	1	0	8	1	3	0	0	6	0	30	1	0
Tejeda, Felix, Bakersfield†	.000	13	5	0	0	0	0	0	0	0	0	0	0	0	0	0	5	0	0
Thomas, Franklin, Stockton	.283	43	159	18	45	47	2	0	0	20	3	2	4	1	25	0	19	5	3
Thomas, Todd, Stockton	.277	92	314	40	87	94	7	0	0	29	1	2	2	1	36	0	53	17	11
Thomas, Troy, San Jose°	.284	122	436	64	124	155	18	5	1	44	5	2	1	1	60	1	80	24	11
Thompson, Robert, Fresno	.249	102	325	53	81	116	11	0	8	43	6	1	5	5	47	1	85	21	7
Thrower, Keith, Modesto†	.324	119	435	81	141	171	12	6	2	48	7	11	3	2	57	6	52	89	38
Tolentino, Jose, Modesto°	.283	66	251	40	71	132	17	4	14	54	5	0	5	5	29	7	34	4	4
Torres, Jose, Bakersfield	.167	25	12	1	2	2	0	0	0	1	0	1	0	0	1	0	10	0	0
Tunnell, Frank, Salinas	.037	14	27	3	1	1	0	0	0	0	2	0	0	2	1	0	11	1	1
Utecht, Timothy, Stockton	.243	117	403	32	98	136	14	3	6	52	2	2	3	49	5	95	3	5
Utley, James, Fresno	.000	7	2	1	0	0	0	0	0	0	0	0	0	0	1	0	1	0	0
VanBurkleo, Tyler, Stockton°	.163	47	129	14	21	29	5	0	1	12	1	3	0	0	22	0	48	2	2
Vanderburg, Michael, San Jose†	.259	44	158	18	41	49	2	3	0	16	2	1	1	2	19	0	22	11	5
Vega, Luis, Salinas	.200	12	15	2	3	4	1	0	0	0	0	1	0	0	7	0	6	0	0
Walker, Steven, Bakersfield	.000	20	4	0	0	0	0	0	0	0	0	0	0	0	2	0	2	0	0
Ward, James, Bakersfield	.215	57	172	30	37	44	3	2	0	15	0	1	2	2	48	0	35	5	4
Westmoreland, John, Reno°	.192	43	120	15	23	34	5	0	2	17	0	1	2	1	12	3	27	0	1
Wetzel, Thomas, Fresno	.250	18	52	4	13	13	0	0	0	5	0	1	2	1	11	0	12	0	0

Player and Club	Pct.	G.	AB.	R.	H.	TB.	2B.	3B.	HR.	RBI.	GW.	SH.	SF.	HP.	BB.	Int. BB.	SO.	SB.	CS.
White, Devon, Redwood†	.283	138	520	101	147	203	25	5	7	55	3	17	5	11	56	1	118	36	12
White, William, Bakersfield	.264	69	235	30	62	80	12	0	2	36	6	4	6	4	31	0	36	3	2
Wiggins, Kevin, Reno*	.287	101	331	50	95	124	9	7	2	38	2	6	3	1	32	5	75	8	1
Williams, Brian, Bakersfield*	.288	116	431	62	124	160	20	5	2	57	3	4	4	1	35	3	49	16	8
Williams, David, Visalia	.255	26	55	6	14	15	1	0	0	3	0	1	0	0	8	0	4	4	2
Williams, Edward, Bak. 56-S.J. 32	.269	88	294	36	79	99	10	2	2	30	2	4	0	6	23	0	50	5	7
Williams, Mitchell, Reno*	.250	26	16	4	4	4	0	0	0	0	0	3	0	0	1	0	8	0	0
Williamson, Mark, Reno	.222	56	9	0	2	2	0	0	0	1	0	0	0	0	0	0	1	0	0
Wilson, Randall, San Jose	.205	15	44	5	9	12	3	0	0	6	0	2	0	5	0	0	13	0	0
Wright, Paul, Redwood	.191	49	115	11	22	28	3	0	1	8	0	1	0	1	9	0	31	2	2
Wrona, William, Reno	.243	93	309	43	75	88	9	2	0	25	6	3	3	2	31	0	27	2	2
Yokubaitis, Dan, Fresno*	.000	54	5	0	0	0	0	0	0	0	0	0	0	0	0	0	1	0	0

The following pitchers, listed alphabetically by club, with games in parentheses, had no plate appearances, primarily through use of designated hitters:

BAKERSFIELD—Cunningham, Michael (1); Mayberry, Gregory (1).

LODI—Ayers, Jack (12); Ruthven, Richard (2); Sanderson, Scott (1); Thayer, Von (2).

MODESTO—Barry, Eric (27); Bauer, Mark (12); Cadaret, Gregory (26); deChavez, Oscar (25); Ferguson, Mark (7); Gorman, Michael (41); Harvey, Randall (12); Law, Joseph (29); Leiper, David (19); Rodriguez, Ricardo (2); Scherer, Douglas (27); Smith, Lawrence (20); Strichek, James (27); Zmudosky, Thomas (10).

REDWOOD—Aase, Donald (4); Bryden, Thomas (20); Delzer, Edwin (1); Gonzalez, Julian (52); Groh, Donald (35); Kemmerling, Byron (18); King, Joseph (28); Kipper, Robert (26); McKenzie, Douglas (28); Price, Bryan (7); Psaltis, Spiro (24); Rentschler, Thomas (17); Suehr, Scott (24); Timberlake, Donald (25); Wilburn, Fred (24).

RENO—Forbes, Terence (12).

SALINAS—Baldrick, Robert (27); Barnhouse, Scott (39); Bryant, James (33); Christ, Michael (12); Cooper, William (5); Ferguson, Michael (26); Hayes, Terry (28); Holland, Donald (11); Jarrett, Mark (20); Martin, Victor (28); Meister, Mickey (2); Moore, Richard (13); Newman, Randall (22); Pedersen, Mark (23); Raubolt, Arthur (7); Reinholtz, Jack (13); Taylor, Terry (17).

SAN JOSE—Blas, William (30); Heise, Larry (21); Ishii, Takeshi (21); Krsnich, Nicholas (15); Kudoh, Kimiysau (20); Kushihara, Yasuo (20); Roma, Daniel (13); Takayama, Ikuo (24); Wadley, Anthony (2); Wilson, Roger (15); Zamba, Michael (15).

STOCKTON—Aldrich, Jay (54); Antunez, Martin (10); Buonantony, Richard (20); Derksen, Robert (29); Diaz, Derek (43); Evans, Gary (8); Hartzell, Paul (5); McCoy, Kevin (3); Nieves, Juan (24); Norton, Douglas (38); Plesac, Daniel (16); Reece, Jeffrey (23); Walker, Cameron (14); Williams, Bruce (36); Winters, Mark (25).

VISALIA—Alfonzo, Osvaldo (31); Anderson, Allan (26); Dominguez, Jose (23); Gibson, Scott (24); Guerrero, Anthony (7); Hobaugh, Brian (29); Lindquist, Dan (14); Rojas, Jeffrey (17); Sheppard, Philip (9); Thompson, Timothy (27).

GRAND SLAM HOME RUNS—Roomes, 2; Bonner, Borowsky, Braggs, Cordner, Dorsett, Farmar, Francis, J. Gonzalez, E. Graham, Guinn, Grandstaff, Gutierrez, Jackson, E. Lane, Loard, Robidoux, Santiago, Scheer, Schugel, D. Smith, Strom, Tolentino, 1 each.

AWARDED FIRST BASE ON CATCHER'S INTERFERENCE—S. Aragon 5 (Amaya, Bradley, Duncan, Nichols, Santiago); G. Barton 2 (Amaya 2); Damon 2 (Nichols, Santiago); Utecht 2 (Bradley, Ferraro); Braggs (Bradley); Brooks (Amaya); Coleman (Calvert); David (Antonelli); Gibbons (Roadcap); F. Gonzalez (Szekely); Peterson (Lane); Wetzel (Dorsett); W. White (Gonzalez); E. Williams (Dorsett).

CLUB FIELDING

Club	Pct.	G.	PO.	A.	E.	DP.	PB.	Club	Pct.	G.	PO.	A.	E.	DP.	PB.
Redwood	.966	139	3568	1600	183	134	27	Visalia	.957	140	3601	1374	224	116	13
Salinas	.965	140	3658	1521	186	114	19	Stockton	.954	140	3656	1505	247	125	33
Fresno	.960	140	3629	1450	211	113	36	Lodi	.954	140	3592	1466	244	99	30
Modesto	.959	139	3585	1488	218	117	28	Reno	.954	139	3534	1568	247	146	32
Bakersfield	.958	140	3610	1661	230	156	22	San Jose	.952	140	3613	1371	250	112	49

Triple Plays—Salinas, San Jose.

INDIVIDUAL FIELDING

*Throws lefthanded.

FIRST BASEMEN

Player and Club	Pct.	G.	PO.	A.	E.	DP.	Player and Club	Pct.	G.	PO.	A.	E.	DP.
ALDRETE, Fresno	.994	136	1180	74	8	90	Kent, San Jose	.971	128	1013	41	31	79
Allen, Lodi	.991	37	296	36	3	29	Long, Fresno	1.000	2	14	1	0	2
Beuerlein, Stockton	.912	3	29	2	3	2	McGwire, Modesto	.991	14	107	6	1	9
Black, Visalia	.923	5	23	1	2	0	Pitts, San Jose*	1.000	1	3	0	0	0
Bonner, Redwood	.989	131	1242	76	14	111	Pott, Reno	.981	12	98	4	2	8
Brock, Bakersfield	.989	44	323	29	4	42	Reibel, Redwood*	.949	10	90	4	5	7
Butcher, Visalia	.833	1	8	2	2	4	Rivera, Bakersfield	1.000	1	2	1	0	0
Carroll, Visalia	.989	12	85	5	1	11	Robidoux, Stockton	.983	34	280	13	5	20
Chapman, Bakersfield	.989	96	875	48	10	83	Robinson, Modesto	1.000	2	15	0	0	2
Cimo, Fresno	1.000	9	46	4	0	6	Robles, Modesto*	.992	54	433	34	4	28
Codinach, Visalia	1.000	9	57	3	0	6	Rodriguez, Reno	1.000	4	15	0	0	0
Colton, Salinas	.991	49	402	20	4	25	Roth, Modesto	1.000	1	7	0	0	1
Conklin, Modesto	1.000	3	25	0	0	3	Sasser, Fresno	1.000	2	6	1	0	0
Cordner, Lodi	.989	103	901	76	11	57	Schugel, Visalia	.980	119	939	61	20	83
Dorsett, Modesto	1.000	2	17	3	0	3	Smith, Salinas*	.986	100	798	51	12	74
Duncan, Salinas	1.000	2	4	0	0	0	Strom, San Jose	.986	17	136	7	2	16
Everton, San Jose	1.000	3	3	0	0	0	Su'a, Stockton	.909	2	9	1	1	1
Francis, Fresno	1.000	3	5	0	0	0	Thomas, Stockton	.965	5	50	5	2	7
Garrett, Modesto	1.000	1	10	0	0	1	Tolentino, Modesto*	.992	66	566	54	5	52
Hardgrave, Reno	.978	114	982	62	24	106	Utecht, Stockton	.989	69	498	39	6	52
Henderson, Lodi	1.000	3	20	4	0	2	VanBurkleo, Stockton*	.988	41	301	16	4	27
Howell, Redwood	1.000	2	8	1	0	1	Westmoreland, Reno	.929	2	13	0	1	2
T. Johnson, Lodi	1.000	1	9	1	0	0	B. Williams, Bakersfield	.977	16	118	8	3	12
Jones, Reno	.987	21	136	12	2	14							

Triple Play—Colter.

SECOND BASEMEN

Player and Club	Pct.	G.	PO.	A.	E.	DP.	Player and Club	Pct.	G.	PO.	A.	E.	DP.
Abbott, Stockton	.964	31	67	94	6	21	Brock, Bakersfield	1.000	1	1	5	0	1
Aoyama, San Jose	1.000	2	1	2	0	0	Butcher, Salinas	.938	24	46	59	7	11
S. Aragon, Visalia	.958	21	31	60	4	10	Cabrera, Modesto	.966	25	41	73	4	15
Bogart, Salinas	.973	52	118	133	7	22	CARROLL, Visalia	.979	123	281	312	13	62

SECOND BASEMEN—Continued

Player and Club	Pct.	G.	PO.	A.	E.	DP.
Champoux, Modesto	1.000	1	1	1	0	0
Cruz, Modesto	.939	37	72	97	11	26
Damon, Lodi	.929	7	11	15	2	0
David, Salinas	.977	65	136	168	7	38
Denton, Lodi	.857	1	4	2	1	2
Etchebarren, Reno	.960	106	229	364	25	74
Everton, San Jose	1.000	1	0	1	0	0
Freeman, Reno	.961	38	71	126	8	31
Graham, Modesto	.981	30	61	92	3	12
Grandstaff, Reno	1.000	1	2	2	0	0
Guinn, Modesto	.952	47	95	121	11	23
Gutierrez, Bakersfield	.971	92	200	334	16	78
Heatherly, San Jose	.950	27	45	68	6	12
Hudson, San Jose	.886	15	29	49	10	12
Jacobson, San Jose	.988	36	65	102	2	20
Jacoby, San Jose	.901	19	38	53	10	11
Jones, Lodi	.945	134	290	385	39	67
Lane, San Jose	.857	2	2	4	1	0
Lora, Reno	1.000	1	0	1	0	0
Marr, Fresno	.932	14	33	36	5	7
McLemore, Redwood	.969	123	251	400	21	84
Miller, Fresno	1.000	2	1	4	0	0
Perkins, Bak.-Sto.	.955	44	90	141	11	32
Picart, Bakersfield	.933	16	29	55	6	9
Rhinehart, San Jose	1.000	2	3	1	0	0
Sferrazza, Stockton	.923	58	109	144	21	28
Shirahata, San Jose	.937	47	70	107	12	19
Stanek, Stockton	.906	19	31	46	8	11
Tarangelo, Visalia	1.000	1	1	1	0	0
F. Thomas, Stockton	.957	22	48	62	5	14
To. Thomas, Fresno	.974	47	77	108	5	24
Thompson, Fresno	.959	90	168	248	18	41
Thrower, Modesto	1.000	4	7	4	0	1
Tunnell, Salinas	.903	10	12	16	3	4
Ward, Bakersfield	.872	6	7	27	5	1
E. Williams, Bak.-S.J.	.942	36	58	89	9	10
Wrona, Reno	1.000	1	2	0	0	0

Triple Play—Jacobson.

THIRD BASEMEN

Player and Club	Pct.	G.	PO.	A.	E.	DP.
Abbott, Stockton	.864	13	4	15	3	0
Allen, Lodi	.910	37	18	53	7	5
J. Aragon, Visalia	1.000	1	0	1	0	0
S. Aragon, Visalia	.908	123	107	210	32	15
G. Barton, San Jose	.727	6	4	4	3	0
Bogart, Salinas	.867	47	33	91	19	5
Bradley, Modesto	1.000	2	1	3	0	0
Butcher, Visalia	.778	9	5	9	4	4
Calley, Visalia	.571	3	2	2	3	0
Champoux, Modesto	.826	9	3	16	4	3
Clawson, Reno	.940	24	13	34	3	3
Colton, Salinas	.875	5	3	4	1	0
Conklin, Modesto	.871	65	50	112	24	12
Damon, Lodi	.907	58	41	95	14	6
Denton, Lodi	.768	25	11	42	16	3
Doerr, San Jose	1.000	6	5	17	0	4
Everton, San Jose	.714	7	2	3	2	0
Freeman, Reno	.870	13	6	14	3	1
Garrett, Modesto	1.000	5	2	8	0	1
Grandstaff, Reno	.923	56	35	97	11	9
Gutierrez, Bakersfield	.949	15	10	27	2	4
Henderson, Lodi	.891	21	12	45	7	3
HOWELL, Redwood	.943	135	88	259	21	23
Hudson, San Jose	.600	5	3	0	2	0
Jones, Reno	1.000	8	4	16	0	1
Lane, San Jose	.857	2	2	4	1	0
Long, Fresno	.847	57	42	102	27	8
Marr, Fresno	.923	68	52	117	14	12
McCain, Salinas	.929	86	63	185	19	20
Miller, Fresno	.833	4	2	3	1	0
Mills, Salinas	.846	7	3	8	2	0
J. Moran, Bakersfield	.857	10	6	12	3	1
M. Moran, Bakersfield	.600	1	0	3	2	0
Noce, Reno	.913	9	9	12	2	0
Palma, San Jose	.908	28	15	44	6	7
Rivera, Bakersfield	.571	1	1	3	3	0
Rizzo, Redwood	.806	21	11	18	7	0
Robidoux, Stockton	.928	55	43	85	10	6
Rodriguez, Reno	.908	41	26	63	9	6
Rutledge, Lodi	.938	7	5	10	1	1
Sasser, Fresno	.818	6	4	14	4	3
Saverino, Redwood	1.000	2	0	2	0	0
Sferrazza, Stockton	.889	4	2	6	1	1
Stanek, Stockton	.941	46	28	84	7	10
Strom, San Jose	.815	14	8	14	5	3
Su'a, Stockton	1.000	1	1	2	0	0
Suarez, Lodi	1.000	1	1	1	0	0
Tarangelo, Visalia	.941	6	5	11	1	2
F. Thomas, Stockton	.926	12	3	22	2	3
To. Thomas, Fresno	.944	9	2	15	1	2
Tr. Thomas, San Jose	.911	73	43	100	14	7
Thompson, Fresno	.813	4	3	10	3	0
Thrower, Modesto	.919	63	44	115	14	18
Utecht, Stockton	.805	17	12	21	8	3
White, Bakersfield	.905	69	37	135	18	18
B. Williams, Bakersfield	.905	6	6	13	2	2
D. Williams, Bakersfield	1.000	2	2	1	0	0
E. Williams, Bakersfield	.887	43	32	62	12	6
Ra. Wilson, San Jose	.833	14	11	14	5	0

Triple Play—Wilson.

SHORTSTOPS

Player and Club	Pct.	G.	PO.	A.	E.	DP.
Abbott, Stockton	.924	18	19	42	5	7
J. Aragon, Visalia	.923	62	102	151	21	25
S. Barton, San Jose	.937	137	223	370	40	65
Bogart, Salinas	1.000	3	6	7	0	2
Butcher, Visalia-Salinas	.889	33	63	65	16	13
Clawson, Reno	.944	41	62	122	11	31
Conklin, Modesto	.878	8	10	26	5	4
Cruz, Modesto	.902	23	44	75	13	17
Damon, Lodi	.927	51	77	127	16	22
Davis, Redwood	.936	129	193	432	43	86
Denton, Lodi	.871	19	28	46	11	9
E. Diaz, Stockton	.934	122	189	381	40	75
Ferraro, Visalia	.891	13	17	24	5	4
Flores, Bakersfield	.922	75	118	202	27	39
Freeman, Reno	.846	13	16	17	6	6
Guinn, Modesto	.913	88	134	246	36	34
Gutierrez, Bakersfield	.908	27	43	65	11	20
Heatherly, Redwood	1.000	1	0	1	0	0
Jacobson, San Jose	1.000	2	1	3	0	0
Long, Fresno	.869	39	55	97	23	14
McDougal, Salinas	.901	62	92	189	31	28
McLemore, Redwood	.929	12	23	29	4	5
Miller, Fresno	.931	82	94	215	23	37
MYERS, Salinas	.948	136	219	395	34	68
Perkins, Stockton	.000	1	0	0	1	0
Rodriguez, Reno	.808	6	7	14	5	3
Rutledge, Lodi	.962	10	13	37	2	6
Saverino, Redwood	1.000	2	1	3	0	0
Shirahata, San Jose	.000	1	0	0	1	0
Stanek, Stockton	.875	3	3	4	1	1
Tarangelo, Visalia	.926	28	48	78	10	16
F. Thomas, Stockton	.931	5	9	18	2	4
To. Thomas, Fresno	.931	20	19	48	5	10
Thompson, Fresno	.917	8	11	22	3	1
Thrower, Modesto	.917	26	36	64	9	8
Tunnell, Salinas	.000	3	0	0	2	0
Ward, Bakersfield	.936	47	82	165	17	37
D. Williams, Visalia	.888	17	22	49	9	9
E. Williams, San Jose	1.000	2	4	4	0	0
Wrona, Reno	.938	89	147	276	28	72

Triple Play—Myers.

OUTFIELDERS

Player and Club	Pct.	G.	PO.	A.	E.	DP.
Allen, Fresno	.982	19	53	3	1	1
Aoyama, San Jose	.943	28	31	2	2	0
Beuerlein, Stockton	.966	15	26	2	1	0
Black, Visalia	.500	2	1	0	1	0
Braddy, Visalia°	1.000	5	6	0	0	0
Bradley, San Jose	.959	40	69	1	3	1
Braggs, Stockton	.964	66	158	4	6	1
Briggs, Salinas	.956	24	40	3	2	0
Brooks, San Jose	.882	19	29	1	4	0
J. Brown, Bakersfield	.972	69	98	7	3	0
R. Brown, Salinas	.964	103	175	12	7	1
Buss, Salinas	.906	33	44	4	5	0

OUTFIELDERS—Continued

Player and Club	Pct.	G.	PO.	A.	E.	DP.	Player and Club	Pct.	G.	PO.	A.	E.	DP.
Butcher, Visalia	.952	10	18	2	1	1	Marte, Visalia☆	.980	126	286	7	6	2
Canseco, Modesto	.963	115	216	17	9	8	E. Miller, Reno	.963	22	50	2	2	0
Cartwright, Stockton☆	.927	31	51	0	4	0	Sc. Miller, Lodi	.981	35	51	2	1	0
Champoux, Modesto	1.000	1	2	0	0	0	Moncrief, Modesto	.962	68	119	6	5	2
Cimo, Fresno	.973	77	135	8	4	2	MONTGOMERY, Redwood	.981	110	152	5	3	3
Cockrell, Fresno	.955	52	96	9	5	1	M. Moran, Bakersfield	.949	59	68	6	4	1
Codinach, Visalia	.833	11	9	1	2	1	Naber, Fresno	1.000	6	1	0	0	0
Coleman, Reno	.949	124	199	6	11	1	Nichols, San Jose	.000	1	0	0	1	0
Colton, Salinas	.962	51	97	5	4	0	O'Dell, San Jose	.960	80	112	7	5	1
Cordner, Lodi	.900	3	8	1	1	0	Penigar, Fresno	.987	36	72	3	1	0
Coyle, Modesto	.972	123	235	10	7	4	Perkins, Stockton	1.000	15	22	0	0	0
Cummings, Modesto	.957	72	106	4	5	1	Peterson, Salinas	1.000	49	69	3	0	0
Davis, Bak.-San Jose☆	.955	106	188	5	9	0	Picart, Bakersfield	1.000	1	1	0	0	0
Dawson, Lodi	.936	77	128	3	9	2	Pitts, San Jose☆	.964	96	203	5	10	3
Diaz, Visalia	.968	29	55	5	2	0	Pott, Reno	.500	2	1	0	1	0
Erdahl, Salinas	.965	87	158	6	6	1	Rhinehart, San Jose	.920	11	20	3	2	0
Everton, San Jose	1.000	10	9	0	0	0	Richie, Visalia	.953	80	117	6	6	1
Farmar, Lodi	.963	130	251	11	10	3	Rodriguez, Reno	1.000	6	3	0	0	0
Francis, Fresno	.957	114	167	10	8	0	Roomes, Lodi	.962	102	194	11	8	1
D. Freeman, Reno	.800	4	4	0	1	0	Roth, Modesto	.963	30	51	1	2	0
L. Freeman, Stockton☆	.946	78	136	5	8	2	Salery, Visalia	.925	22	36	1	3	0
Gibbons, Stockton☆	.978	113	214	4	5	1	Sasser, Fresno	1.000	8	14	0	0	0
Gonzalez, Bakersfield	.969	129	264	13	9	3	Scheer, Visalia	.951	136	253	21	14	2
Graham, Fresno☆	.970	80	150	9	5	6	Sferrazza, Stockton	.920	63	99	5	9	0
Hartsock, Redwood	.952	59	76	4	4	0	Shirahata, San Jose	1.000	13	13	1	0	0
Harvey, Lodi	.973	88	138	7	4	1	R. Smith, Modesto	1.000	2	6	0	0	0
Heatherly, Redwood	1.000	13	14	3	0	0	T. Smith, Redwood	.978	30	41	3	1	1
R. Hill, Salinas	.977	133	282	10	7	1	Sowards, Fresno	1.000	6	7	0	0	0
T. Hill, Bakersfield	.984	45	58	2	1	0	To. Thomas, Fresno	1.000	1	2	0	0	0
Hoskins, Reno	.939	96	180	6	12	1	Tr. Thomas, San Jose	.947	44	69	3	4	1
H. Hubbard, Reno	.939	30	62	0	4	0	Thrower, Modesto	1.000	10	19	1	0	0
Hudson, San Jose	1.000	6	11	0	0	0	Utecht, Stockton	1.000	7	5	1	0	0
Jackson, Stockton☆	.958	47	65	4	3	0	Vanderburg, San Jose☆	.980	44	93	3	2	1
Jeremko, Visalia	1.000	16	32	1	0	0	White, Redwood	.963	138	322	16	13	5
D. Jones, Reno	.916	65	74	2	7	0	Wiggins, Reno☆	.957	99	145	12	7	4
Gl. Jones, Fresno	.944	40	63	4	4	2	B. Williams, Bakersfield	.958	84	150	10	7	3
Kirby, Bakersfield	.786	7	10	1	3	1	D. Williams, Visalia	1.000	2	4	0	0	0
Loscalzo, Modesto☆	1.000	4	3	0	0	0	Wright, Redwood	.923	47	46	2	4	1
Marr, Fresno	.800	2	4	0	1	0							

Triple Play—R. Hill.

CATCHERS

Player and Club	Pct.	G.	PO.	A.	E.	DP.	PB.	Player and Club	Pct.	G.	PO.	A.	E.	DP
Amaya, Salinas	.976	88	570	86	16	7	11	Lane, Fresno	.979	91	586	58	14	5	22
Antonelli, Stockton	.964	98	725	77	30	7	20	Loard, Fresno-San Jose	.993	57	387	40	3	2	21
G. Barton, San Jose	.983	35	263	20	5	0	5	Nichols, San Jose-Redwood	.982	119	769	112	16	11	33
Beuerlein, Stockton	.976	52	296	27	8	3	11	Nittoli, San Jose	.906	4	29	0	3	0	3
Borowsky, Visalia	.983	95	631	79	12	8	7	O'Brien, Modesto	1.000	8	41	8	0	1	0
Bradley, Modesto	.971	54	382	25	12	1	10	Pott, Reno	.973	38	190	29	6	3	5
Brady, Redwood	1.000	9	50	6	0	0	1	Rivera, Bakersfield	.929	2	13	0	1	0	1
Calvert, Visalia	.894	9	35	7	5	1	0	Roadcap, Lodi	.969	62	376	33	13	1	12
Dorsett, Modesto	.978	72	494	73	13	7	15	Robinson, Modesto	.987	14	74	3	1	1	3
Duncan, Salinas	.985	52	350	37	6	5	8	Santiago, Reno	.969	107	692	96	25	5	27
Empting, Lodi	.970	20	118	12	4	3	6	Shirahata, San Jose	1.000	5	13	2	0	0	1
Ferraro, Lodi	.980	56	351	42	8	3	8	Stewart, Lodi	.970	15	58	6	2	0	4
Gatewood, Bakersfield	.978	52	298	56	8	5	9	Strom, San Jose	.917	7	41	3	4	2	5
Gonzalez, Fresno	.982	31	197	26	4	3	6	Su'a, Stockton	1.000	2	12	0	0	0	2
Graupmann, Visalia	.980	44	259	34	6	5	6	Szekely, Bakersfield	.979	98	563	88	14	15	12
Hudson, San Jose	1.000	1	1	0	0	0	0	Vega, Salinas	.963	10	45	7	2	1	0
JIMENEZ, Redwood	.992	72	449	38	4	4	11	Wetzel, Fresno	.991	16	104	6	1	1	1

PITCHERS

Player and Club	Pct.	G.	PO.	A.	E.	DP.	Player and Club	Pct.	G.	PO.	A.	E.	DP.
Abrego, Lodi	.921	23	12	23	3	1	Charley, Lodi☆	.778	14	4	3	2	0
Aldrich, Stockton	.897	54	1	25	3	1	Chestnut, Lodi	.900	12	5	13	2	1
Alfonzo, Visalia	.833	31	7	28	7	3	Christ, Salinas	.947	12	4	14	1	0
Anderson, Visalia☆	.923	26	10	26	3	2	Cobbs, Bakersfield	1.000	21	10	9	0	1
Antunez, Stockton☆	1.000	10	0	5	0	1	Cooper, Salinas	1.000	5	0	2	0	1
Ayers, Lodi☆	1.000	12	2	0	0	0	deChavez, Modesto	.933	25	7	21	2	3
Baker, Lodi-Modesto	.917	25	6	5	1	0	D. Diaz, Stockton	.833	29	5	10	3	0
Baldrick, Salinas☆	.977	27	9	34	1	1	D. Diaz, Visalia	.923	43	3	9	1	0
Bargerhuff, Fresno	1.000	58	5	13	0	2	Dominguez, Visalia	.952	23	6	14	1	0
Barling, Fresno	.880	28	10	12	3	1	Duffy, Bakersfield	.900	12	2	7	1	1
Barnhouse, Salinas	1.000	39	6	16	0	0	Eichhorn, Bakersfield	.962	41	5	20	1	3
Barry, Modesto☆	.904	27	14	33	5	0	Engel, Lodi☆	.979	27	12	34	1	1
Bauer, Modesto	1.000	12	9	14	0	1	Evans, Stockton	.750	8	0	3	1	0
Bautista, Fresno	1.000	19	4	7	0	0	Ma. Ferguson, Modesto	1.000	7	1	2	0	0
Biko, Reno☆	.800	31	1	3	1	0	Mi. Ferguson, Salinas	.900	26	3	6	1	1
Blas, San Jose	1.000	30	5	13	0	2	Forbes, Reno	1.000	12	1	2	0	0
Blevins, Lodi	.935	59	9	20	2	1	Fruge, Lodi	.917	22	6	5	1	0
Borowsky, Visalia	1.000	3	0	1	0	0	Gentle, Bakersfield☆	1.000	10	0	1	0	0
Brahms, Fresno☆	.909	23	2	8	1	1	Gibson, Visalia	.700	24	1	6	3	1
Bryant, Salinas	1.000	33	4	17	0	0	Gladden, Fresno	.862	17	5	20	4	2
Bryden, Redwood	.929	20	2	11	1	1	Gonzalez, Redwood	.941	52	1	15	1	4
Buonantony, Stockton	.919	20	6	28	3	0	Gorman, Modesto	1.000	41	5	20	0	4
Cadaret, Modesto☆	.903	26	3	25	3	0	Goto, San Jose	.833	22	1	4	1	1
Capel, Lodi	.938	20	6	9	1	0	Grachen, Lodi☆	.833	22	6	24	6	1
CARNE, Bakersfield☆	1.000	33	5	20	0	0	Graupmann, Visalia	1.000	1	1	0	0	0

PITCHERS—Continued

Player and Club	Pct.	G.	PO.	A.	E.	DP.	Player and Club	Pct.	G.	PO.	A.	E.	DP.
Groh, Redwood°	.857	35	1	5	1	0	Parmenter, Lodi	.964	27	11	16	1	1
Guerrero, Visalia°	1.000	7	3	2	0	0	Pedersen, Salinas	1.000	23	3	6	0	0
Hall, Lodi°	1.000	8	2	5	0	0	Phillips, Lodi	1.000	13	4	6	0	0
Hallgren, San Jose	.833	15	6	19	5	0	Piper, Bakersfield	1.000	8	3	2	0	0
Hartzell, Stockton	1.000	5	0	3	0	0	Plesac, Stockton°	.909	16	6	14	2	2
Harvey, Modesto°	1.000	12	0	1	0	0	Price, Redwood°	.929	7	5	8	1	1
Hayes, Salinas°	.909	28	0	10	1	0	Psaltis, Redwood°	.857	24	0	6	1	0
Heise, San Jose°	1.000	21	0	1	0	0	Raubolt, Salinas	1.000	7	1	3	0	0
Henning, Fresno	1.000	31	4	11	0	0	Ray, San Jose	.733	19	6	16	8	2
Hobaugh, Visalia	.964	29	10	17	1	2	Raymer, Reno	.930	27	9	31	3	2
Holland, Salinas	.900	11	3	6	1	0	Reece, Stockton°	.840	23	3	18	4	1
M. Hubbard, Reno	.840	43	3	18	4	0	Reinholtz, Salinas	1.000	13	0	4	0	0
Hummel, Fresno°	.953	27	6	35	2	1	Rentschler, Redwood°	1.000	17	2	6	0	0
Innis, Bakersfield	.964	16	15	12	1	1	Rodriguez, Modesto	1.000	2	2	2	0	0
Ishii, San Jose	.923	21	5	7	1	2	Rojas, Visalia	1.000	17	5	13	0	0
James, Reno	.833	30	4	6	2	0	Roma, San Jose	.882	13	4	11	2	1
Jarrett, Salinas	1.000	20	2	4	0	1	Rosenhahn, Lodi	.778	24	3	4	2	0
S. Johnson, Lodi°	.778	18	1	6	2	1	Rowen, Bakersfield°	.767	29	2	21	7	2
Kawamura, San Jose	1.000	21	3	18	0	2	Sanderson, Lodi	1.000	1	0	1	0	0
Kemmerling, Redwood	1.000	18	0	4	0	0	Scherer, Modesto	.865	27	8	24	5	1
Kindred, Visalia	.864	31	2	17	3	0	Scudder, Bakersfield	.917	23	4	7	1	0
King, Redwood	1.000	28	4	5	0	0	Serritella, Bakersfield	1.000	27	3	16	0	2
Kipper, Redwood°	.939	26	11	35	3	4	Sheppard, Visalia	.750	9	0	3	1	0
Kobernus, Modesto-Baker°	.889	21	2	6	1	0	Sierra, Reno	.912	28	9	22	3	3
Kockenmeister, Reno°	.929	46	3	10	1	1	L. Smith, Modesto°	1.000	20	2	3	0	0
Kopf, Lodi	1.000	16	1	2	0	0	S. Smith, Fresno	.818	11	3	6	2	0
Krsnich, San Jose	.789	15	1	14	4	0	Strichek, Modesto	.933	27	2	12	1	0
Kudoh, San Jose°	.875	20	5	9	2	4	Suehr, Redwood	.917	24	8	14	2	2
Kuhn, Fresno-San Jose	.895	19	3	14	2	0	Taft, Fresno°	.750	7	2	1	1	1
Kushihara, San Jose	.941	20	1	15	1	0	Takayama, San Jose	1.000	24	1	3	0	0
Law, Modesto	.903	29	10	18	3	0	Taylor, Salinas	.871	17	5	22	4	1
Lee, Bakersfield	.600	8	0	3	2	0	Tejeda, Bakersfield°	1.000	13	1	5	0	2
Leiper, Modesto°	.900	19	1	8	1	0	Thayer, Lodi	1.000	2	2	0	0	0
Lindquist, Visalia°	.600	14	0	3	2	0	Thomas, Stockton	1.000	1	0	2	0	0
Mancuso, Visalia°	.955	56	4	17	1	1	Thompson, Visalia	.967	27	10	19	1	2
Martin, Salinas	.956	28	12	31	2	3	Timberlake, Redwood	.973	25	10	26	1	2
May, Bakersfield	.912	25	4	27	3	2	Torres, Bakersfield	.789	25	11	19	8	1
Mayberry, Bakersfield	1.000	1	0	2	0	1	Utley, Fresno	1.000	7	0	1	0	0
McCoy, Stockton	1.000	3	2	1	0	0	Wadley, San Jose	1.000	2	0	1	0	0
McKenzie, Redwood	.795	28	9	22	8	0	C. Walker, Stockton	.815	14	7	15	5	0
Mills, Reno	.860	27	11	26	6	2	S. Walker, Bakersfield	.909	20	4	16	2	1
Moore, Salinas	1.000	13	1	1	0	0	Wilburn, Redwood	.842	24	9	23	6	0
Mulholland, Fresno°	.667	9	0	6	3	0	B. Williams, Stockton	.813	36	4	9	3	1
Murtha, Fresno°	.917	18	1	10	1	0	M. Williams, Reno°	.850	26	11	23	6	1
Narita, San Jose	.875	46	1	13	2	0	Williamson, Reno	1.000	56	7	14	0	1
Newman, Salinas°	.930	22	5	35	3	1	Ro. Wilson, San Jose°	.833	15	3	22	5	0
Nieves, Stockton°	.935	24	9	20	2	0	Winters, Stockton°	1.000	25	2	5	0	1
Norman, Fresno	.886	28	7	24	4	0	Yokubaitis, Fresno°	.889	54	4	12	2	1
Norton, Stockton	.979	38	9	37	1	1	Zamba, San Jose	.917	15	3	19	2	1
Oakes, Fresno	1.000	35	7	17	0	0	Zmudosky, Modesto	1.000	10	1	6	0	0
Parks, Reno	.852	25	1	22	4	0							

The following players do not have any recorded accepted chances at the positions indicated; therefore, are not listed in the fielding averages for those particular positions: Aase, p; Abbott, of; Bogart, 1b; Cunningham, p; Delzer, p; Garrett, ss; Gibbons, p; Heatherly, 3b; Kent, of; Meister, p; Palma, ss; Pitts, p; Ruthven, p; Stanek, p; Su'a, p; Westmoreland, of; D. Williams, p.

CLUB PITCHING

Club	ERA.	G.	CG.	ShO.	Sv.	IP.	H.	R.	ER.	HR.	HB.	BB.	Int. BB.	SO.	WP.	Bk.
Redwood	2.82	139	30	21	26	1189.1	1053	483	372	34	30	461	27	814	39	5
Modesto	3.15	139	37	5	31	1195.0	1103	541	418	59	33	497	13	956	73	13
Salinas	3.35	140	27	4	22	1219.1	1123	586	454	54	47	554	32	909	60	13
Lodi	3.56	140	22	12	26	1197.1	1165	622	473	58	45	528	31	882	55	10
Bakersfield	3.70	140	22	9	27	1203.1	1156	644	495	51	18	653	22	840	50	9
Fresno	3.72	140	12	7	48	1209.2	1132	620	500	59	46	567	9	964	94	8
San Jose	3.95	140	22	1	25	1204.1	1220	687	529	44	58	545	21	1040	72	11
Visalia	4.06	140	29	8	25	1200.1	1186	681	541	66	42	688	14	879	80	5
Stockton	4.30	139	16	7	17	1218.2	1207	742	582	71	52	763	31	1014	105	7
Reno	4.54	139	25	9	23	1178.0	1299	745	594	62	45	612	29	870	84	10

PITCHERS' RECORDS
(Leading Qualifiers for Earned-Run Average Leadership— 112 or More Innings)

°Throws lefthanded.

Pitcher—Club	W.	L.	Pct.	ERA.	G.	GS.	CG.	GF.	ShO.	Sv.	IP.	H.	R.	ER.	HR.	HB.	BB.	Int. BB.	SO.	WP.
Kipper, Redwood°	18	8	.692	2.04	26	26	8	0	3	0	185.0	147	61	42	4	3	65	3	98	5
Abrego, Lodi	9	9	.500	2.10	23	23	5	0	3	0	150.1	111	57	35	2	9	66	1	139	4
Law, Modesto	11	2	.846	2.58	29	17	6	7	1	1	143.0	114	47	41	4	4	71	1	105	4
Newman, Salinas°	10	9	.526	2.65	22	21	6	0	1	0	156.1	126	61	46	4	8	61	0	169	4
McKenzie, Redwood	15	6	.714	2.66	28	28	6	0	2	0	186.0	155	69	55	9	3	52	2	144	1
Engel, Lodi°	11	7	.611	2.68	27	27	4	0	2	0	171.0	141	63	51	9	4	78	2	153	3
Hummel, Fresno°	13	6	.684	2.84	27	27	3	0	0	0	146.0	130	64	46	10	5	78	0	92	14
Anderson, Visalia°	12	7	.632	2.86	26	26	8	0	5	0	188.2	152	80	60	3	2	105	1	151	8
Rowen, Bakersfield°	12	5	.706	2.92	29	21	3	3	0	0	166.1	151	70	54	5	1	80	1	140	6
Timberlake, Redwood	15	5	.750	3.04	25	25	5	0	3	0	156.2	149	67	53	7	0	57	3	111	6

Departmental Leaders: G—Blevins, 59; W—Kipper, 18; L—Aldrich, Blevins, Parks, 14; Pct.—Law, .846; GS—Martin, McKenzie, Norman, 28; CG—Scherer, 10; GF—Blevins, 51; ShO—Anderson, 5; Sv.—Bergerhuff, 23; IP—Mills, 194.2; H—Mills, 193; R—Kindred, 113; ER—Parks, 98; HR—Kindred, 18; HB—B. Williams, 13; BB—B. Williams, 168; IBB—Aldrich, Williamson, 10; SO—Newman, 169; WP—B. Williams, 24.

(All Pitchers—Listed Alphabetically)

Pitcher—Club	W.	L.	Pct.	ERA.	G.	GS.	CG.	GF.	ShO.	Sv.	IP.	H.	R.	ER.	HR.	HB.	BB.	Int. BB.	SO.	WP.
Aase, Redwood	0	1	.000	5.11	4	3	0	0	0	0	12.1	9	9	7	2	0	7	0	10	0
Abrego, Lodi	9	9	.500	2.10	23	23	5	0	3	0	150.1	111	57	35	2	9	66	1	139	4
Aldrich, Stockton	11	14	.440	2.90	54	0	0	46	0	8	105.2	107	46	34	8	2	44	10	78	4
Alfonzo, Visalia	7	5	.583	2.96	31	9	2	15	0	2	97.1	82	39	32	4	1	59	3	57	8
Anderson, Visalia°	12	7	.632	2.86	26	26	8	0	5	0	188.2	152	80	60	3	2	105	1	151	8
Antunez, Stockton°	0	3	.000	5.01	10	2	0	2	0	0	32.1	40	25	18	2	0	18	1	17	3
Ayers, Lodi°	0	0	.000	6.32	12	0	0	6	0	0	15.2	21	12	11	1	1	9	1	14	3
Baker, Lodi 21-Modesto 4	0	7	.000	4.74	25	2	0	10	0	1	57.0	60	42	30	10	0	33	3	24	1
Baldrick, Salinas°	8	10	.444	3.14	27	27	8	0	0	0	183.1	184	93	64	8	3	58	3	114	3
Bargerhuff, Fresno	6	7	.462	3.60	58	0	0	44	0	23	90.0	80	41	36	3	5	34	3	85	6
Barling, Fresno	5	4	.556	4.68	28	13	1	2	0	0	100.0	100	61	52	4	4	57	0	87	9
Barnhouse, Salinas	5	3	.625	3.06	39	7	2	23	0	3	82.1	67	34	28	1	1	63	4	64	6
Barry, Modesto°	10	10	.500	4.37	27	25	7	1	0	0	156.2	176	90	76	16	2	44	1	92	6
Bauer, Modesto	6	4	.600	2.94	12	12	3	0	0	0	88.2	74	34	29	7	1	28	0	91	8
Bautista, Fresno	4	4	.500	7.52	19	10	0	6	0	0	46.2	49	48	39	6	5	36	1	32	5
Biko, Reno°	1	1	.500	4.28	31	0	0	19	0	3	27.1	32	18	13	4	0	11	0	18	3
Blas, San Jose	3	3	.500	4.11	30	3	0	10	0	2	76.2	91	46	35	2	2	30	2	61	10
Blevins, Lodi	7	14	.333	3.59	59	0	0	51	0	19	97.2	102	49	39	3	1	35	7	48	4
Borowsky, Visalia	0	0	.000	9.00	3	0	0	3	0	0	6.0	6	7	6	1	1	3	0	2	0
Brahms, Fresno°	3	5	.375	3.00	23	0	0	7	0	3	54.0	51	24	18	1	4	17	1	45	4
Bryant, Salinas	5	6	.455	2.40	33	0	0	29	0	8	63.2	44	17	17	1	1	21	3	55	3
Bryden, Redwood	1	3	.250	2.97	20	0	0	18	0	6	30.1	26	12	10	3	3	10	2	34	0
Buonantony, Stockton	6	7	.462	3.82	20	19	4	0	2	0	129.2	127	61	55	5	8	72	1	121	13
Cadaret, Modesto°	13	8	.619	3.05	26	26	6	0	2	0	171.1	162	79	58	7	1	82	0	138	14
Capel, Lodi	0	7	.000	3.65	20	6	1	3	0	1	69.0	54	38	28	4	1	35	2	46	6
Carne, Bakersfield°	4	7	.364	4.41	33	10	0	11	0	4	112.1	109	70	55	4	0	70	3	76	1
Charley, Lodi°	3	0	1.000	2.34	14	1	1	5	1	0	34.2	31	12	9	0	0	10	1	16	1
Chestnut, Lodi	5	5	.375	4.09	12	12	4	0	0	0	77.0	84	38	35	2	4	29	2	56	2
Christ, Salinas	3	4	.429	3.59	12	12	3	0	1	0	80.1	77	39	32	3	4	39	0	67	5
Cobbs, Bakersfield	4	3	.571	3.52	21	7	2	9	0	1	69.0	82	38	27	4	3	27	2	43	5
Cooper, Salinas	0	0	.000	0.00	5	0	0	4	0	1	7.1	6	1	0	0	0	0	0	3	0
Cunningham, Bakersfield°	1	0	1.000	3.00	1	0	0	0	0	0	6.0	6	2	2	0	1	1	0	4	0
deChavez, Modesto	13	5	.722	3.65	25	25	5	0	1	0	157.2	154	81	64	8	11	67	2	128	8
Delzer, Redwood°	0	0	.000	0.00	1	0	0	0	0	0	1.0	1	0	0	0	0	1	0	0	0
Derksen, Stockton	4	2	.667	4.42	29	2	0	9	0	0	77.1	93	50	38	6	0	34	3	52	7
Diaz, Stockton	2	4	.333	4.32	43	3	0	21	0	1	81.1	79	46	39	6	5	53	5	86	10
Dominguez, Visalia	2	7	.222	4.85	23	8	4	7	0	0	85.1	85	56	46	3	4	54	0	58	13
Duffy, Bakersfield	1	3	.250	6.35	12	2	0	5	0	1	28.1	32	25	20	2	0	18	0	15	0
Eichhorn, Bakersfield	4	4	.500	2.23	41	0	0	30	0	12	68.2	71	25	17	0	0	33	4	46	0
Engel, Lodi°	11	7	.611	2.68	27	27	4	0	2	0	171.0	141	63	51	9	4	78	2	153	3
Evans, Stockton	1	2	.333	6.62	8	1	0	3	0	0	17.2	19	13	13	4	1	9	0	13	0
Ma. Ferguson, Modesto	0	2	.000	7.56	7	0	0	2	0	0	16.2	27	16	14	0	0	8	0	14	2
Mi. Ferguson, Salinas	2	3	.400	4.94	26	6	0	5	0	0	74.2	72	50	41	8	6	57	1	55	2
Forbes, Reno	1	0	1.000	5.50	12	0	0	9	0	0	18.0	24	14	11	1	1	10	0	16	1
Fruge, Lodi	4	3	.571	5.63	22	7	0	8	0	0	56.0	76	42	35	5	4	26	2	32	3
Gentle, Bakersfield°	0	2	.000	2.18	10	0	0	5	0	2	20.2	18	13	5	0	0	19	1	22	2
Gibbons, Stockton°	0	0	.000	0.00	2	0	0	1	0	0	2.0	1	0	0	0	0	1	0	1	0
Gibson, Visalia	6	5	.545	4.35	24	6	2	7	0	1	82.2	91	55	40	2	2	39	1	71	4
Gladden, Fresno	7	2	.778	2.05	17	10	4	4	0	2	92.1	68	30	21	0	3	37	0	68	2
Gonzalez, Redwood	8	6	.571	2.72	52	0	0	39	0	8	72.2	57	25	22	0	4	45	4	54	5
Gorman, Modesto	4	7	.364	2.24	41	0	0	32	0	9	64.1	60	28	16	2	4	22	1	48	6
Goto, San Jose	2	3	.400	4.98	22	7	0	11	0	1	72.1	82	51	40	6	4	29	0	38	5
Grachen, Lodi°	6	12	.333	3.39	22	22	3	0	1	0	138.0	149	76	52	10	4	31	2	85	4
Graupmann, Visalia	0	0	.000	9.00	1	0	0	0	0	0	1.0	1	1	1	0	0	1	0	0	0
Groh, Redwood°	3	1	.750	1.50	35	0	0	16	0	8	42.0	32	11	7	1	2	11	1	43	0
Guerrero, Visalia°	3	1	.750	2.31	7	7	1	0	1	0	46.2	37	15	12	1	0	15	0	36	2
Hall, Lodi°	3	3	.500	4.88	8	8	2	0	0	0	48.0	43	31	26	1	0	44	0	43	7
Hallgren, San Jose	2	8	.200	3.15	15	15	1	0	0	0	103.0	95	59	36	3	1	22	0	91	2
Hartzell, Stockton	0	1	.000	3.14	5	1	0	2	0	1	14.1	15	8	5	1	0	3	0	9	1
Harvey, Modesto°	1	0	1.000	1.85	12	2	0	7	0	2	34.0	33	12	7	2	0	11	1	41	1
Hayes, Salinas°	4	4	.500	2.01	28	0	0	21	0	5	44.2	32	14	10	0	0	27	6	31	3
Heise, San Jose°	3	1	.750	3.13	21	1	0	8	0	3	23.0	22	9	8	0	1	15	3	28	2
Henning, Fresno	4	2	.667	4.27	31	7	0	9	0	1	86.1	87	51	41	3	7	51	0	78	15
Hobaugh, Visalia	4	12	.250	5.49	29	20	2	6	1	2	134.1	179	100	82	9	2	57	3	81	7
Holland, Salinas	2	4	.333	5.18	11	11	0	0	0	0	57.1	58	40	33	2	3	29	1	30	4
Hubbard, Reno	1	6	.143	4.10	43	4	1	10	0	3	94.1	106	56	43	4	2	47	5	70	3
Hummel, Fresno	13	6	.684	2.84	27	27	3	0	0	0	146.0	130	64	46	10	5	78	0	92	14
Innis, Bakersfield	6	2	.750	3.03	16	13	1	3	0	0	89.0	77	36	30	1	3	52	1	46	7
Ishii, San Jose	4	3	.571	3.53	21	0	0	18	0	2	35.2	32	17	14	1	3	19	6	48	0
James, Reno	3	8	.273	6.50	30	14	1	6	0	0	99.2	143	103	72	6	4	55	3	55	2
Jarrett, Salinas	2	3	.400	4.75	20	5	0	7	0	1	60.2	66	37	32	4	1	27	1	31	3
Johnson, Lodi°	0	0	.000	3.86	18	0	0	8	0	1	32.2	35	23	14	2	1	14	1	17	3
Kawamura, San Jose	5	11	.313	3.54	21	18	6	0	1	0	124.2	122	63	49	5	9	45	0	144	1
Kemmerling, Redwood	4	1	.800	2.36	18	1	0	8	0	0	42.0	38	14	11	0	0	8	0	15	2
Kindred, Visalia	9	13	.409	5.20	31	22	6	7	0	1	154.0	161	113	89	18	5	115	1	101	15
King, Redwood	4	1	.800	3.35	28	1	0	15	0	1	51.0	60	28	19	0	2	22	5	21	3
Kipper, Redwood°	18	8	.692	2.04	26	26	8	0	3	0	185.0	147	61	42	4	3	65	3	98	5
Kobernus, Mod. 5-Bak. 16°	2	4	.333	4.35	21	1	0	11	0	1	31.0	41	21	15	3	0	11	2	20	3
Kockenmeister, Reno°	5	0	1.000	3.64	46	0	0	17	0	1	64.1	69	30	26	5	3	19	3	39	0
Kopf, Lodi	1	2	.333	5.49	16	4	0	6	0	0	39.1	35	27	24	1	5	41	0	28	5
Krsnich, San Jose	4	6	.400	2.84	15	12	4	1	0	0	95.0	90	46	30	4	3	31	0	87	6
Kudoh, San Jose°	3	4	.429	1.91	20	0	0	10	0	0	37.2	42	13	8	1	1	14	2	41	3
Kuhn, Fresno 10—S.J. 9	8	8	.111	4.79	19	16	0	0	0	0	97.2	110	64	52	11	3	42	0	56	1
Kushihara, San Jose	2	7	.222	4.52	20	11	0	5	0	0	69.2	73	42	35	2	4	36	0	58	4
Law, Modesto	11	2	.846	2.58	29	17	6	7	1	1	143.0	114	47	41	4	4	71	1	105	4
Lee, Bakersfield	1	3	.250	7.71	8	4	0	2	0	0	23.1	32	24	20	3	1	17	0	22	1
Leiper, Modesto°	5	0	1.000	0.25	19	0	0	17	0	7	35.1	12	2	1	0	0	14	2	30	2
Lindquist, Visalia°	0	0	.000	7.76	14	4	0	5	0	0	29.0	27	29	25	0	4	44	0	30	4
Mancuso, Visalia	12	7	.632	1.86	56	0	0	49	0	18	101.2	78	30	21	2	4	56	2	106	5
Martin, Salinas	12	11	.522	3.59	28	28	6	0	1	0	185.1	177	88	74	14	5	62	2	125	10
May, Bakersfield	8	10	.444	3.83	25	23	7	2	1	0	152.2	128	78	65	7	2	81	1	107	6

Pitcher—Club	W.	L.	Pct.	ERA	G.	GS.	CG.	GF.	ShO.	Sv.	IP.	H.	R.	ER.	HR.	HB.	BB.	Int. BB.	SO.	WP.
Mayberry, Bakersfield	0	1	.000	2.57	1	1	0	0	0	0	7.0	5	2	2	1	0	2	1	7	1
McCoy, Stockton	0	1	.000	4.50	3	2	0	1	0	0	10.0	5	5	5	2	0	8	0	9	0
McKenzie, Redwood	15	6	.714	2.66	28	28	6	0	2	0	186.0	155	69	55	9	3	52	2	144	1
Meister, Salinas	0	0	.000	2.45	2	1	0	0	0	0	3.2	3	1	1	0	0	0	4	1	
Mills, Reno	11	8	.579	3.61	27	26	9	0	1	0	194.2	193	94	78	6	7	89	3	139	9
Moore, Salinas	1	2	.333	3.04	13	0	0	4	0	1	26.2	25	13	9	1	0	14	4	28	4
Mulholland, Fresno°	5	2	.714	2.95	9	9	0	0	0	0	42.2	32	17	14	1	0	36	0	39	1
Murtha, Fresno°	6	1	.857	2.39	18	4	1	6	0	1	60.1	51	20	16	2	1	25	1	47	4
Narita, San Jose	4	4	.500	2.67	46	0	0	39	0	16	77.2	72	34	23	3	10	34	8	80	5
Newman, Salinas°	10	9	.526	2.65	22	21	6	0	1	0	156.1	126	61	46	4	8	61	0	169	4
Nieves, Stockton°	10	3	.769	3.54	24	24	5	0	1	0	139.2	137	75	55	7	11	63	1	133	8
Norman, Fresno	11	6	.647	3.06	28	28	2	0	0	0	167.2	139	76	57	8	5	71	1	108	13
Norton, Stockton	11	7	.611	3.62	38	17	2	16	0	6	144.1	141	87	58	2	4	81	7	94	11
Oakes, Fresno	7	5	.583	4.19	35	10	0	9	0	2	105.1	127	55	49	7	2	23	0	85	6
Parks, Reno	4	14	.222	6.96	25	25	1	0	0	0	126.2	180	112	98	6	7	73	2	75	18
Parmenter, Lodi	8	9	.471	3.83	27	26	2	0	1	0	143.1	152	81	61	6	6	59	2	132	7
Pedersen, Salinas	2	6	.250	4.55	23	5	0	7	0	2	57.1	71	34	29	3	7	23	2	38	2
Phillips, Lodi	1	2	.333	4.63	13	0	0	8	0	3	23.1	31	17	12	2	1	5	1	18	0
Piper, Bakersfield	1	2	.333	3.65	8	0	0	6	0	2	12.1	13	7	5	3	0	7	0	17	1
Pitts, San Jose°	0	0	.000	0.00	1	0	0	1	0	0	1.0	0	0	0	0	0	0	0	0	
Plesac, Redwood	6	6	.500	3.32	16	16	2	0	0	0	108.1	106	51	40	7	2	50	0	101	3
Price, Redwood°	2	2	.500	2.28	7	7	1	0	1	0	51.1	40	18	13	0	3	29	1	43	4
Psaltis, Redwood°	4	0	1.000	2.36	24	2	0	7	0	0	45.2	36	14	12	1	1	25	3	29	1
Raubolt, Salinas	0	0	.000	0.77	7	0	0	3	0	0	11.2	9	2	1	0	0	8	0	3	0
Ray, San Jose	5	10	.333	4.19	19	18	5	1	0	1	118.0	114	71	55	2	3	72	0	96	13
Raymer, Reno	10	12	.455	4.37	27	27	4	0	1	0	160.2	151	97	78	10	5	101	2	118	15
Reece, Stockton°	4	10	.286	4.83	23	22	1	0	1	0	123.0	110	77	66	7	3	92	0	109	7
Reinholtz, Salinas	3	3	.500	5.95	13	0	0	10	0	1	19.2	19	14	13	1	0	10	4	19	0
Rentschler, Redwood°	0	2	.000	2.89	17	1	0	6	0	3	28.0	18	9	9	0	1	9	1	32	0
Rodriguez, Modesto	0	0	.000	2.03	2	2	0	0	0	0	13.1	11	3	3	0	1	5	0	6	0
Rojas, Visalia	6	4	.600	4.34	17	11	0	4	0	1	83.0	88	48	40	9	5	42	0	34	2
Roma, San Jose	6	7	.462	4.33	13	13	2	0	0	0	79.0	90	45	38	1	7	35	0	45	4
Rosenhahn, Lodi	1	2	.333	2.48	24	0	0	10	0	1	36.1	32	15	10	0	2	15	4	27	1
Rowen, Bakersfield°	12	5	.706	2.92	29	21	3	3	0	0	166.1	151	70	54	5	1	80	1	140	6
Ruthven, Lodi	1	0	1.000	4.00	2	1	0	1	0	0	9.0	9	4	4	0	0	2	0	8	0
Sanderson, Lodi	0	1	.000	3.60	1	1	0	0	0	0	5.0	7	2	2	1	0	0	0	2	0
Scherer, Modesto	11	11	.500	3.40	27	25	10	1	0	0	166.2	141	81	63	7	4	83	3	139	11
Scudder, Bakersfield	6	2	.750	2.23	23	2	1	17	1	3	48.1	37	15	12	3	2	18	0	48	2
Serritella, Bakersfield	5	4	.556	3.43	27	10	1	8	0	1	99.2	102	53	38	1	0	47	0	43	3
Sheppard, Visalia	0	1	.000	7.77	9	1	0	5	0	0	22.0	25	23	19	3	3	17	0	15	2
Sierra, Reno	11	4	.733	3.72	28	16	7	6	3	1	135.1	133	67	56	7	6	57	0	106	10
L. Smith, Modesto°	1	1	.500	0.25	20	0	0	16	0	7	35.2	24	5	1	0	0	8	0	38	3
S. Smith, Fresno	3	4	.429	5.66	11	11	1	0	0	0	62.0	68	42	39	5	1	22	0	55	1
Stanek, Stockton	0	0	.000	0.00	1	0	0	1	0	0	1.0	0	0	0	0	1	0	0	0	
Strichek, Modesto	6	3	.667	3.36	27	4	0	11	0	1	72.1	64	36	27	3	4	41	2	62	4
Su'a, Stockton	1	0	1.000	9.00	1	0	0	1	0	0	2.0	2	2	2	0	0	2	0	0	0
Suehr, Redwood	8	7	.533	3.41	24	21	3	0	1	0	129.2	138	68	52	2	5	38	2	84	3
Taft, Fresno°	1	3	.250	7.66	7	4	0	0	0	0	22.1	27	22	19	2	0	17	0	11	4
Takayama, San Jose	4	2	.667	3.93	24	4	2	14	0	7	71.0	70	35	31	2	3	34	0	68	2
Taylor, Salinas	7	6	.538	2.93	17	17	2	0	1	0	104.1	87	48	34	4	8	55	1	73	10
Tejeda, Bakersfield°	5	2	.714	2.82	13	9	2	2	2	0	60.2	57	20	19	1	0	14	1	38	0
Thayer, Lodi	0	0	.000	9.00	2	0	0	2	0	0	4.0	8	4	4	0	0	3	0	0	
Thomas, Stockton	0	1	.000	0.00	1	0	0	1	0	0	2.2	4	1	0	0	0	3	1	0	0
Thompson, Visalia	5	12	.294	3.67	27	26	5	1	0	0	166.2	170	85	68	11	9	80	3	138	10
Timberlake, Redwood	15	5	.750	3.04	25	25	5	0	3	0	156.2	149	67	53	7	0	57	3	111	6
Torres, Bakersfield	4	11	.267	4.46	25	19	5	4	1	0	119.0	112	80	59	4	4	79	3	74	4
Utley, Fresno	0	0	.000	6.59	7	0	0	2	0	0	13.2	14	12	10	0	2	12	0	12	3
Wadley, San Jose	0	0	.000	3.60	2	0	0	0	0	0	5.0	2	3	2	0	1	7	0	3	0
C. Walker, Stockton	3	6	.333	4.34	14	14	2	0	0	0	83.0	97	63	40	6	3	37	0	44	9
S. Walker, Bakersfield	4	8	.333	5.22	20	19	0	0	0	0	98.1	100	76	57	10	1	80	2	76	9
Wilburn, Redwood	9	5	.643	3.53	24	24	7	0	3	0	155.2	147	78	61	4	3	82	1	96	9
B. Williams, Stockton	4	8	.333	8.18	36	16	0	7	0	1	106.2	84	114	97	5	13	168	0	124	24
D. Williams, Visalia	0	0	.000	0.00	1	0	0	1	0	0	2.0	1	0	0	0	1	0	0	0	
M. Williams, Reno°	9	8	.529	4.99	26	26	3	0	1	0	164.0	163	113	91	11	9	127	1	165	19
Williamson, Reno	10	12	.455	2.90	56	1	0	46	0	15	93.0	105	41	30	2	2	23	10	69	4
Wilson, San Jose°	5	5	.500	5.35	15	15	0	0	0	0	69.0	56	53	41	1	1	74	0	72	13
Winters, Stockton°	1	0	1.000	3.35	25	0	0	11	0	0	37.2	40	18	14	1	0	24	2	23	5
Yokubaitis, Fresno°	6	3	.667	2.66	54	0	0	39	0	16	81.1	65	34	24	3	1	35	2	91	6
Zamba, San Jose	3	7	.300	5.17	15	14	2	0	0	0	87.0	101	59	50	4	3	22	0	53	2
Zmudosky, Modesto	2	1	.667	1.37	10	0	0	8	0	4	19.2	11	5	3	1	1	4	0	14	3

BALKS—Hummel, Mills, 4 each; Blevins, Cobbs, Hayes, Law, May, Newman, M. Williams, 3 each; Baldrick, Cadaret, Engel, Ishii, Kawamura, Kindred, Kobernus, Parmenter, Plesac, Reece, Wilburn, 2 each; Anderson, Ayers, Barling, Barnhouse, Barry, Blas, Buonantony, Capel, Charley, Christ, deChavez, Duffy, Mi. Ferguson, Gladden, Gonzalez, Goto, Harvey, Heise, Henning, Hubbard, Jarrett, King, Kudoh, Kuhn, Kushihara, Leiper, McKenzie, Narita, Nieves, Norman, Raymer, Rojas, Rowen, Scherer, Sierra, L. Smith, Takayama, Taylor, Torres, C. Walker, 1 each.

COMBINATION SHUTOUTS—Innis-Scudder, Innis-Kobernus, Rowen-Eichhorn, Tejeda-Eichhorn-Kobernus, Bakersfield; Barling-Brahms, Hummel-Barling-Murtha, Hummel-Bargerhuff, Mulholland-Oakes, Mulholland-Yokubaitis, Norman-Brahms, Norman-Yokubaitis, Fresno; Abrego-Charley-Blevins, Engel-Capel, Engel-Phillips, Parmenter-Baker, Lodi; deChavez-Gorman, Modesto; King-Bryden-Rentschler, Kipper-Kemmerling-Psaltis-King, Kipper-Gonzalez, McKenzie-Groh, Suehr-Bryden, Timberlake-Groh, Timberlake-Kemmerling-Groh, Wilburn-Groh, Redwood; James-Williamson, Mills-Biko-Williamson, Parks-Williamson, Reno; Buonantony-Aldrich, Nieves-Norton, Plesac-Diaz, Stockton; Guerrero-Gibson-Mancuso, Visalia.

NO-HIT GAMES—Scudder, Bakersfield, defeated Reno, 1-0 (seven innings, first game), April 29; Kipper, Redwood, defeated San Jose, 9-0 (seven innings, second game), June 10; Sierra, Reno, defeated Modesto, 2-0 (seven innings, first game), June 15.

Carolina League

CLASS A

CHAMPIONSHIP WINNERS IN PREVIOUS YEARS

1945—Danville .681	1960—Greensboro‡ .636	1971—Peninsula‡ .647
1946—Greensboro .599	Burlington .586	Kinston .623
Raleigh (2nd)† .563	1961—Wilson .594	1972—Salem‡ .657
1947—Burlington .613	1962—Durham .636	Burlington .632
Raleigh (3rd)† .574	Wilson .600	1973—Lynchburg .588
1948—Raleigh .592	Kinston (2nd)† .593	Winston-Salem‡ .557
Martinsville (2nd)† .570	1963—Kinston§ .538	1974—Salem .671
1949—Danville .601	Greensboro§ .590	Salem .582
Burlington (4th)† .500	Wilson (2nd)† .535	1975—Rocky Mount .667
1950—Winston-Salem* .693	1964—Kinston§ .572	Rocky Mount .614
1951—Durham .600	Winston-Salem§† .590	1976—Winston-Salem .618
Wins-Salem (2nd)† .583	1965—Peninsula§ .597	Winston-Salem .551
1952—Raleigh .581	Durham§ .580	1977—Lynchburg .591
Reidsville (4th)† .536	Tidewater† .528	Peninsula‡ .556
1953—Raleigh .593	1966—Kinston§ .547	1978—Peninsula .696
Danville (2nd)† .572	Winston-Salem§ .586	Lynchburg‡ .614
1954—Fayetteville* .628	Rocky Mount† .533	1979—Winston-Salem a .607
1955—HP-Thomasville .580	1967—Durham x (West.) .536	1980—Peninsula‡ .714
Danville (2nd)† .533	Raleigh (East.) .542	Durham .600
1956—HP-Thomasville .591	1968—Salem (West.) .607	1981—Peninsula .522
Fayetteville (4th)† .523	Ral-Dur (East.) .597	Hagerstown‡ .507
1957—Durham .632	HP-Thom. y (W.) .493	1982—Alexandria‡ .597
HP-Thomasville .622	1969—Rocky M (East.) .569	Durham .588
1958—Danville .576	Salem (West.) .542	1983—Lynchburg§ .691
Burlington (4th)† .511	Ral-Dur z (East.) .560	Winston-Salem .529
1959—Raleigh .600	1970—Winston-Salem‡ .586	
Wilson (2nd)† .550	Burlington .597	

*Won championship and four-club playoff. †Won four-club playoff. ‡Won split-season playoff. §League was divided into Eastern, Western divisions. xWon eight-club, two-division playoff. yWon eight-club, two-division playoff against Raleigh-Durham. zWon eight-club, two-division playoff against Burlington. aWon both halves of split-season (no playoffs).

STANDING OF CLUBS AT CLOSE OF FIRST HALF, JUNE 18

NORTHERN DIVISION

Club	W.	L.	T.	Pct.	G.B.
Lynchburg (Mets)	43	27	0	.614	....
Prince William (Pirates)	42	28	0	.600	1
Hagerstown (Orioles)	32	38	0	.457	11
Salem (Rangers)	28	42	0	.400	15

SOUTHERN DIVISION

Club	W.	L.	T.	Pct.	G.B.
Durham (Braves)	39	31	0	.557	....
Winston-Salem (Red Sox)	33	37	0	.471	6
Kinston (Blue Jays)	33	37	0	.471	6
Peninsula (Phillies)	30	40	0	.429	9

STANDING OF CLUBS AT CLOSE OF SECOND HALF, AUGUST 31

NORTHERN DIVISION

Club	W.	L.	T.	Pct.	G.B.
Lynchburg (Mets)	46	22	0	.676	....
Salem (Rangers)	36	32	0	.529	10
Prince William (Pirates)	33	37	0	.471	14
Hagerstown (Orioles)	28	42	0	.400	19

SOUTHERN DIVISION

Club	W.	L.	T.	Pct.	G.B.
Peninsula (Phillies)	43	27	0	.614	....
Kinston (Blue Jays)	38	32	0	.543	5
Durham (Braves)	29	41	0	.414	14
Winston-Salem (Red Sox)	25	45	0	.357	18

COMPOSITE STANDING OF CLUBS AT CLOSE OF SEASON, AUGUST 31

Club	Lyn.	P.W.	Pen.	Kin.	Dur.	Sal.	Hag.	W-S	W.	L.	T.	Pct.	G.B.
Lynchburg (Mets)	....	16	6	9	9	23	18	8	89	49	0	.645	....
Prince William (Pirates)	12	....	7	8	8	16	16	8	75	65	0	.536	15
Peninsula (Phillies)	8	7	....	14	16	6	7	15	73	67	0	.521	17
Kinston (Blue Jays)	5	6	14	....	17	4	7	18	71	69	0	.507	19
Durham (Braves)	5	6	12	11	....	8	8	18	68	72	0	.486	22
Salem (Rangers)	3	12	8	10	6	....	17	8	64	74	0	.464	25
Hagerstown (Orioles)	10	12	7	7	6	11	....	7	60	80	0	.429	30
Winston-Salem (Red Sox)	6	6	13	10	10	6	7	....	58	82	0	.414	32

Peninsula represented Hampton, Va.

Major league affiliations in parentheses.

Playoffs—Durham defeated Peninsula, two games to one; Lynchburg defeated Durham, three games to one, to win league championship.

Regular-Season Attendance—Durham, 157,109; Hagerstown, 114,951; Kinston, 61,204; Lynchburg, 75,034; Peninsula, 27,465; Prince William, 108,818; Salem, 61,623; Winston-Salem, 75,272. Total—681,476. Playoffs, 6,606. All-Star game at Salem, 731.

Managers—Durham, Brian Snitker; Hagerstown, John Hart (to June 20), Grady Little (June 21-24) and Len Johnston; Kinston, Doug Ault; Lynchburg, Mike Cubbage; Peninsula, Ron Clark; Salem, Bill Stearns, Winston-Salem, Bill Slack.

All-Star Team: 1B—Dave Magadan, Lynchburg; 2B—Leon Roberts, Prince William; 3B—Kim Christenson, Prince William; SS—Rey Quinonez, Winston-Salem; OF—Kash Beauchamp, Kinston; Stan Jefferson, Lynchburg; Jason Felice, Lynchburg; C—Barry Lyons, Lynchburg; LHP—Randy Myers, Lynchburg; RHP—Mitchell Cook, Lynchburg; Most Valuable Player—Barry Lyons, Lynchburg; Most Valuable Pitcher—Randy Myers, Lynchburg; Manager-of-the-Year—Mike Cubbage, Lynchburg.

(Compiled by Howe News Bureau, Boston, Mass.)

CLUB BATTING

Club	Pct.	G.	AB.	R.	OR.	H.	TB.	2B.	3B.	HR.	RBI.	GW.	SH.	SF.	HP.	BB.	Int. BB.	SO.	SB.	CS.	LOB.
Lynchburg	.275	138	4522	758	469	1245	1802	195	49	88	679	80	29	34	36	610	29	755	122	55	1031
Kinston	.256	140	4490	623	603	1148	1706	184	46	94	536	55	35	28	44	520	20	907	94	70	947
Peninsula	.253	140	4407	638	656	1117	1619	186	26	88	551	63	38	50	44	534	15	859	98	44	979
Winston-Salem	.249	140	4403	588	662	1096	1639	176	35	99	533	54	36	33	50	505	15	939	148	60	950
Prince William	.249	140	4402	584	604	1095	1505	172	29	60	498	66	54	44	27	500	20	856	217	91	917
Durham	.247	140	4590	604	606	1135	1644	152	21	105	540	62	38	35	30	557	22	809	84	36	1053
Hagerstown	.246	140	4388	596	666	1079	1554	200	28	73	531	52	31	37	28	621	17	808	95	47	1020
Salem	.240	138	4426	628	753	1064	1648	168	22	124	565	54	40	42	61	605	141	072	162	62	1010

INDIVIDUAL BATTING

(Leading Qualifiers for Batting Championship—378 or More Plate Appearances)

°Bats lefthanded.   †Switch-hitter.

Player and Club	Pct.	G.	AB.	R.	H.	TB.	2B.	3B.	HR.	RBI.	GW.	SH.	SF.	HP.	BB.	Int. BB.	SO.	SB.	CS.
Magadan, David, Lynchburg°	.350	112	371	78	130	160	22	4	0	62	7	0	5	6	104	10	43	2	1
Lyons, Barry, Lynchburg	.316	115	412	59	130	189	17	3	12	87	12	1	7	2	45	1	40	1	3
Horn, Samuel, Winston-Salem°	.313	127	403	67	126	217	22	3	21	89	7	1	3	4	76	5	107	5	4
Felice, J. Jason, Lynchburg	.307	125	417	83	128	223	25	5	20	86	11	0	4	1	45	3	74	9	3
Greenwell, Michael, Winston-Salem°..	.306	130	454	70	139	222	23	6	16	84	5	1	1	15	56	4	40	9	5
Roberts, Leon, Prince William†	.301	134	498	81	150	209	25	5	8	77	9	2	5	3	44	3	63	50	13
Brown, Anthony, Peninsula°	.292	132	493	79	144	213	27	3	12	60	7	0	8	2	43	3	84	24	7
Oliva, David, Winston-Salem	.292	94	339	55	99	158	23	6	8	43	6	4	4	1	41	1	55	20	10
Hale, Demarlo, Winston-Salem	.290	134	490	90	142	191	20	1	9	53	4	6	3	6	40	0	77	24	7
Charboneau, Joseph, Prince William	.289	108	342	65	99	143	16	2	8	52	9	0	9	2	49	1	51	4	4
Jefferson, Stanley, Lynchburg	.288	128	493	113	142	195	20	9	5	47	6	0	3	3	84	3	73	45	15

Departmental Leaders: G—Shaddy, 140; AB—Liriano, 512; R—Jefferson, 113; H—L. Roberts, 150; TB—Day, 236; 2B—Quinonez, 30; 3B—Beauchamp, Jefferson, 9; HR—Day, 29; RBI—Day, 103; GWRBI—Day, 13; SH—Haro, 12; SF—Mace, 11; HP—Greenwall, 15; BB—Tumpane, 110; IBB—Magadan, 10; SO—Ben, 135; SB—Crum, 61; CS—Crum, 20.

(All Players—Listed Alphabetically)

Player and Club	Pct.	G.	AB.	R.	H.	TB.	2B.	3B.	HR.	RBI.	GW.	SH.	SF.	HP.	BB.	Int. BB.	SO.	SB.	CS.
Adamczak, James, Lynchburg	.000	45	1	0	0	0	0	0	0	0	0	1	0	0	0	0	0	0	0
Aguilera, Richard, Lynchburg	.200	13	10	1	2	2	0	0	0	0	0	0	0	0	1	0	3	0	0
Aitcheson, James, Kinston°	.293	36	116	17	34	47	4	3	1	11	0	0	0	0	15	1	15	1	2
Assenmacher, Paul, Durham°	.000	26	6	0	0	0	0	0	0	0	1	0	0	0	2	0	4	0	0
Aulenback, James, Prince William	.206	23	34	3	7	13	1	1	1	8	1	0	0	0	11	1	11	0	0
Auten, James, Hagerstown	.172	28	93	6	16	23	7	0	0	15	4	0	1	0	1	0	9	0	0
Aviles, Brian, Durham	.063	26	16	1	1	2	1	0	0	0	0	0	0	0	2	0	6	0	0
Baker, Kerry, Prince William	.175	74	212	24	37	46	4	1	1	12	3	1	1	0	29	0	51	2	1
Barbosa, Rafael, Durham	.231	64	143	20	33	44	5	0	2	15	2	1	3	3	8	0	37	2	1
Beauchamp, J. Kash, Kinston	.266	130	463	63	123	188	23	9	8	58	3	1	3	1	51	0	92	10	9
Ben, Elijah, Salem	.221	113	357	69	79	160	14	2	21	58	6	4	3	13	62	1	135	38	5
Berger, Michael, Prince William	.276	82	279	48	77	102	11	1	4	36	5	3	4	0	44	1	49	15	4
Blasucci, Anthony, Prince William° ..	.500	7	2	0	1	3	0	1	0	2	1	0	0	0	0	0	0	0	0
Borges, George, Prince William	.234	80	248	28	58	72	7	2	1	21	2	3	2	5	17	1	48	1	1
Brown, Anthony, Peninsula°	.292	132	493	79	144	213	27	3	12	60	7	0	8	2	43	3	84	24	7
Brown, Kevin, Lynchburg°	.000	28	17	0	0	0	0	0	0	0	0	4	0	0	2	0	11	0	0
Brown, Samuel, Prince William	.228	71	259	33	59	94	15	1	6	22	1	1	0	1	12	0	65	6	5
Bruno, Angelo, Hagerstown	.244	54	160	15	39	57	7	1	3	17	2	2	1	2	16	0	34	0	2
Buckley, Brian, Prince William	.000	16	2	0	0	0	0	0	0	0	0	0	0	0	0	0	1	0	0
Buckmier, James, Prince William	.167	31	18	2	3	4	1	0	0	0	0	1	0	0	1	0	10	0	2
Bulls, David, Peninsula	.400	11	10	0	4	4	0	0	0	0	0	0	0	0	1	0	4	0	0
Cano, Jose, Durham	.100	21	10	0	1	2	1	0	0	2	0	1	0	0	1	0	2	0	0
Caraballo, Wilmer, Lynchburg	.293	15	41	5	12	16	1	0	1	3	0	0	0	0	2	0	5	0	0
Carlucci, Anthony, Salem	.201	58	144	16	29	45	8	1	2	20	2	1	4	6	23	0	43	1	0
Carmichael, Alan, Lynchburg	.229	11	35	2	8	10	2	0	0	5	0	0	1	0	3	1	6	0	1
Castaneda, Nick, Prince William°	.274	92	266	36	73	135	13	2	15	59	7	1	5	1	56	2	75	3	2
Castro, Edgar, Salem°	.264	121	371	49	98	166	14	0	18	61	4	1	2	3	76	8	99	2	1
Charboneau, Joseph, Prince William	.289	108	342	65	99	143	16	2	8	52	9	0	9	2	49	1	51	4	4
Childress, Willie, Durham	.252	126	457	63	115	161	15	2	9	44	3	3	4	2	55	1	59	8	5
Christenson, Kim, Prince William	.285	105	330	35	94	137	15	5	6	53	10	3	6	2	62	2	51	4	5
Clay, Kenneth, Durham°	.000	4	5	0	0	0	0	0	0	0	0	0	0	0	0	0	2	1	0
Coker, Kevin, Peninsula	.067	24	15	1	1	1	0	0	0	0	0	0	3	0	0	0	6	0	0
Cook, Mitchell, Lynchburg°	.208	27	24	0	5	6	1	0	0	1	1	1	0	0	2	0	7	0	0
Cordoba, Wilfredo, Prince William	.000	38	4	1	0	0	0	0	0	0	0	0	0	0	0	0	1	0	0
Cormack, Terry, Durham°	.189	77	264	20	50	60	4	0	2	19	3	3	2	1	28	1	38	1	0
Coss, David, Prince William	.178	50	107	11	19	21	2	0	0	2	0	4	0	1	9	0	28	11	7
Crum, George, Salem	.268	118	425	68	114	146	10	2	6	47	4	4	3	6	79	0	80	61	20
Cusack, David, Hagerstown	.143	16	35	4	5	8	3	0	0	1	0	0	0	0	5	0	17	0	0
Davis, Douglas, Salem	.268	100	343	48	92	158	20	2	14	57	5	0	4	11	42	2	83	4	4
Day, Randall, Peninsula	.265	132	468	84	124	236	25	0	29	103	13	1	8	3	57	0	108	7	5
DeLaRosa, Nelson, Prince William° ...	.250	35	112	15	28	42	5	0	3	17	3	0	1	0	12	0	21	5	2
Delucchi, Ronald, Prince William	.168	26	95	6	16	22	3	0	1	7	1	0	2	0	4	1	15	2	0
Dennett, James, Winston-Salem	.203	31	79	6	16	27	2	0	3	11	2	0	2	0	9	0	17	0	0
Dennis, Eduardo, Kinston	.263	21	76	5	20	27	3	2	0	4	0	2	0	0	1	0	5	0	0
Derryberry, Timothy, Hagerstown° ..	.145	27	69	12	10	16	0	0	2	11	1	1	0	1	14	2	18	0	0
DeWillis, Jeffrey, Kinston	.236	122	356	47	84	100	11	1	1	31	5	6	1	9	62	0	69	7	3
Dillard, Ronald, Salem	.201	65	209	29	42	54	7	1	1	20	2	6	2	2	21	0	39	17	9
Doerr, Jeffrey, Hagerstown	.164	31	73	10	12	17	2	0	1	12	0	3	0	1	18	0	24	0	1
Doughty, Jamie, Salem	.277	57	206	37	57	85	5	1	7	30	2	5	2	2	23	0	48	6	3
Downs, Dorley, Prince William	.333	47	3	0	1	1	0	0	0	0	0	0	0	0	1	0	1	0	0
Edens, Thomas, Lynchburg	.000	3	2	1	0	0	0	0	0	0	0	0	0	0	1	0	1	0	0
Engram, Graylyn, Peninsula	.000	4	11	2	0	0	0	0	0	1	0	0	0	0	3	0	1	0	0
Estrada, Asdrubal, Winston-Salem	.134	52	134	13	18	22	1	0	1	10	0	1	2	1	11	0	32	1	0
Evetts, Anthony, Peninsula	.417	41	12	7	5	6	1	0	0	2	0	0	3	0	3	0	3	0	0
Faherty, Sean, Prince William°	.000	24	4	0	0	0	0	0	0	0	0	0	0	0	0	0	1	0	0
Felice, J. Jason, Lynchburg	.307	125	417	83	128	223	25	5	20	86	11	0	4	1	45	3	74	9	3
Felt, James, Prince William	.143	42	14	3	2	2	0	0	0	2	0	1	0	0	3	0	1	0	0
Fermin, Felix, Prince William	.246	119	382	34	94	109	13	1	0	41	3	5	2	5	29	0	32	32	10

Player and Club	Pct.	G.	AB.	R.	H.	TB.	2B.	3B.	HR.	RBI.	GW.	SH.	SF.	HP.	BB.	Int. BB.	SO.	SB.	CS.
Fielder, Cecil, Kinston	.284	61	222	42	63	134	12	1	19	49	5	1	3	1	28	7	44	2	1
Fitzgerald, Francis, Hagerstown	.202	44	94	12	19	24	3	1	0	4	0	2	2	2	12	1	23	0	0
Foit, James, Salem	.221	62	190	29	42	65	9	1	4	17	0	2	2	1	27	1	56	2	1
Frishman, Mark, Peninsula	.245	42	102	15	25	32	7	0	0	9	1	1	0	1	18	1	20	1	0
Garcia, Agustin, Lynchburg	.250	35	4	0	1	3	0	1	0	2	0	0	0	0	1	0	0	0	0
Gerhart, H. Kenneth, Hagerstown	.321	47	168	39	54	96	18	3	6	21	1	1	1	1	21	0	35	9	2
Gertz, T. Michael, Hagerstown°	.182	6	22	2	4	4	0	0	0	0	0	0	0	1	0	0	6	0	0
Gile, Mark, Salem°	.247	122	449	56	111	137	15	1	3	42	4	5	4	1	31	2	86	8	6
Glynn, Dennis, Lynchburg	.269	99	238	28	64	81	10	2	1	26	1	3	1	5	30	1	41	3	1
Gonzalez, Otto, Salem	.224	88	308	34	69	115	12	2	10	38	5	0	1	1	43	0	60	0	1
Gordon, Kevin, Prince William	.000	14	1	0	0	0	0	0	0	0	0	0	0	0	0	0	0	0	0
Gordon, Timothy, Winston-Salem	.209	101	306	33	64	86	8	1	4	28	3	1	5	4	34	1	80	0	0
Granger, L. Randle, Hagerstown†	.272	76	246	47	67	119	14	4	10	27	2	1	2	3	43	1	68	23	8
Green, Otis, Kinston°	.259	84	305	40	79	121	18	3	6	34	12	0	1	2	32	1	62	9	3
Greenwell, Michael, Winston-Salem°..	.306	130	454	70	139	222	23	6	16	84	5	1	1	15	56	4	40	9	5
Griffin, D. Alan, Durham	.263	103	327	41	86	130	11	0	11	50	6	0	4	2	34	1	52	0	0
Griffin, Gregory, Kinston	.228	69	232	27	53	76	8	3	3	24	3	1	3	3	24	0	61	13	5
Hale, Demarlo, Winston-Salem	.290	134	490	90	142	191	20	1	9	53	4	6	3	6	40	0	77	24	7
Hansen, Ronald, Salem	.111	14	36	3	4	10	0	0	2	6	1	1	1	0	8	0	13	0	0
Harlow, Larry, Hagerstown°	.258	30	97	9	25	32	3	2	0	14	1	1	0	3	23	0	19	1	1
Haro, Samuel, Prince William†	.242	129	429	71	104	132	17	4	1	31	3	12	3	2	56	4	73	49	10
Harris, Kenneth, Lynchburg	.191	46	131	14	25	37	6	0	2	13	0	1	0	1	18	0	17	3	3
Hatcher, Johnny, Durham	.246	123	471	61	116	150	15	5	3	34	3	2	4	1	46	0	79	24	4
Heller, John, Lynchburg°	.216	60	125	18	27	40	2	1	3	21	1	1	0	0	15	2	24	2	0
Henderson, Ramon, Peninsula	.265	115	378	57	100	149	19	0	10	51	10	1	4	3	51	0	78	2	2
Heyison, Mark, Hagerstown	.200	5	15	1	3	4	1	0	0	1	0	0	0	0	0	0	4	0	0
Hodge, Patrick, Durham°	.262	51	107	22	28	46	3	3	3	10	1	1	1	0	18	0	31	1	0
Holland, John, Kinston	.116	21	43	3	5	8	0	0	1	3	0	0	0	1	5	0	10	0	0
Hollins, Paul, Lynchburg°	.277	118	379	58	105	200	23	3	22	100	11	0	6	2	62	1	84	2	0
Holman, Shawn, Prince William	.167	15	6	0	1	1	0	0	0	0	0	1	0	0	0	0	4	0	0
Hood, Scott, Durham°	.202	63	183	24	37	52	4	1	3	22	3	2	1	0	21	1	29	0	0
Horn, Samuel, Winston-Salem°	.313	127	403	67	126	217	22	3	21	89	7	1	3	4	76	5	107	5	4
Ingle, Randy, Durham	.269	23	67	11	18	26	3	1	1	8	1	1	0	0	8	0	5	0	1
Jackson, Kenneth, Peninsula	.225	71	222	37	50	71	10	1	3	22	3	1	5	4	56	0	56	5	2
Jacobson, Jeffrey, Peninsula	.275	96	309	48	85	118	17	2	4	29	0	3	2	0	59	0	46	7	3
Jacoby, Donald, Hagerstown°	.154	26	78	8	12	15	0	0	1	6	0	0	2	3	0	17	0	0	
Jefferson, Stanley, Lynchburg	.288	128	493	113	142	195	20	9	5	47	6	0	3	3	84	3	73	45	15
Jelks, Patrick, Winston-Salem	.243	97	337	55	82	113	11	4	4	25	2	0	1	2	46	0	110	28	10
Jensen, David, Lynchburg°	.000	9	3	0	0	0	0	0	0	0	0	0	0	0	2	0	3	0	0
Johnson, David, Prince-William	.091	13	11	1	1	2	1	0	0	1	0	3	0	1	0	5	0	0	
Jones, David, Durham	.333	4	3	0	1	1	0	0	0	0	0	0	0	0	0	0	0	0	0
Jones, Ricky, Hagerstown	.100	5	10	0	1	1	0	0	0	0	0	0	0	1	0	0	0	0	
Jose, Manuel, Winston-Salem†	.205	102	370	37	76	93	6	4	1	17	3	5	1	2	30	0	86	27	13
Josephson, Paul, Durham	.000	45	2	0	0	0	0	0	0	0	0	0	0	0	1	0	1	0	0
Kanter, John, Peninsula†	.175	32	80	5	14	26	4	1	2	11	1	0	0	0	3	0	26	1	0
Kenaga, Jeffrey, Hagerstown°	.290	70	272	28	79	120	14	0	9	43	5	2	2	0	12	1	36	4	4
Kennard, David, Peninsula	.238	126	383	39	91	113	12	2	2	28	1	7	5	8	44	0	35	7	4
Kiecker, Dana, Winston-Salem	.000	29	2	0	0	0	0	0	0	0	0	0	0	0	0	0	1	0	0
Knox, Michael, Durham	.271	129	458	48	124	160	16	1	6	62	11	4	1	1	36	1	65	16	6
Labay, Stephen, Peninsula°	.000	14	6	1	0	0	0	0	0	0	0	0	0	1	0	2	0	0	
Laird, Anthony, Prince William°	.305	47	154	22	47	61	11	0	1	18	2	1	1	1	16	2	18	0	4
Lamb, Todd, Durham°	.364	26	22	6	8	9	1	0	0	1	0	2	0	0	2	0	6	0	0
Lance, Mark, Durham	.000	30	1	0	0	0	0	0	0	0	0	0	0	0	0	0	0	0	0
Lawton, Marcus, Lynchburg	.222	3	9	3	2	2	0	0	0	1	0	0	0	0	3	0	3	0	0
Ledbetter, David, Hagerstown	.000	27	1	0	0	0	0	0	0	0	0	0	0	0	0	0	0	0	0
Leggatt, Richard, Durham°	.000	19	2	0	0	0	0	0	0	0	0	0	1	0	0	1	0	0	
Leiter, Kurt, Hagerstown	1.000	25	2	1	2	2	0	0	0	0	0	0	0	0	0	0	0	0	
Leiva, Jose, Peninsula	.210	87	286	42	60	71	6	1	1	12	1	5	2	3	32	0	57	13	7
Leriger, Jeffrey, Hagerstown	.129	41	85	10	11	13	2	0	0	2	0	3	0	1	16	0	13	2	0
Lewis, Herman, Lynchburg†	.269	41	78	16	21	25	4	0	0	7	0	1	0	0	9	0	18	4	2
Linkmeyer, Thomas, Kinston	.200	17	10	2	2	2	0	0	0	2	0	0	0	0	7	0	3	0	0
Liriano, Nelson, Kinston†	.246	132	512	68	126	171	22	4	5	50	2	7	2	4	46	4	86	10	9
Lockwood, Richard, Hagerstown	.237	88	295	49	70	114	12	1	10	40	3	0	2	0	51	0	59	6	4
Lopez, Michael, Hagerstown°	.235	116	383	50	90	133	12	5	7	51	3	2	4	2	31	4	66	9	5
Loy, Darren, Peninsula	.238	59	185	24	44	73	6	1	7	33	3	1	0	2	23	0	43	2	3
Lundgren, Kurt, Lynchburg	.154	33	13	1	2	2	0	0	0	0	0	1	0	0	1	0	7	0	0
Luzon, Robert, Durham	.167	4	6	3	1	1	0	0	0	0	0	0	0	0	3	1	1	0	0
Lyons, Barry, Winston-Salem	.316	115	412	59	130	189	17	3	12	87	12	1	7	2	45	1	40	1	3
Mace, Jeffrey, Salem	.270	131	466	65	126	201	26	2	15	73	8	3	11	6	59	0	101	7	3
Machin, John, Peninsula°	.231	19	13	1	3	4	1	0	0	0	1	0	1	0	1	0	3	0	0
Magadan, David, Lynchburg°	.350	112	371	78	130	160	22	4	0	62	7	0	5	6	104	10	43	2	1
Malave, Omar, Kinston	.265	109	404	56	107	135	11	1	5	52	7	4	1	8	33	0	44	3	8
Martinez, Z. Tomas, Prince William...	.203	25	79	11	16	24	0	1	2	9	2	0	0	1	5	0	19	4	3
McKelvey, Mitch, Prince William	.000	13	11	0	0	0	0	0	0	0	0	0	0	0	1	0	4	0	0
McPhail, Marlin, Lynchburg	.281	77	278	46	78	99	9	3	2	42	12	0	1	4	38	1	36	5	2
Melillo, Gerry, Hagerstown	.243	90	263	34	64	77	6	2	1	21	1	3	0	2	31	1	43	4	1
Menard, Darryl, Peninsula	.111	44	9	1	1	1	0	0	0	1	0	3	0	0	2	0	0		
Miller, N. Keith, Peninsula†	.323	65	226	44	73	91	8	5	0	36	2	2	3	2	38	1	24	7	3
Morel, Nelson, Peninsula°	.000	49	2	0	0	0	0	0	0	0	0	1	0	0	0	1	0	0	
Mortillaro, John, Durham	.000	24	8	0	0	0	0	0	0	0	0	0	0	0	0	0	3	0	0
Morton, William, Peninsula	.111	19	9	1	1	1	0	0	0	0	0	0	1	0	0	2	0	0	
Moscat, Fernando, Lynchburg	.238	55	185	27	44	45	1	0	0	19	2	1	1	1	7	0	36	1	4
Mota, Luis, Peninsula°	.251	92	267	28	67	89	12	2	2	24	2	0	1	1	8	0	47	1	1
Mucha, Keith, Hagerstown	.182	4	11	0	2	2	0	0	0	1	0	0	0	0	0	0	5	0	0
Murray, Scott, Lynchburg	.000	43	2	0	0	0	0	0	0	0	0	0	0	0	0	0	0	0	0
Myers, Randall, Lynchburg°	.200	23	20	1	4	4	0	0	0	1	0	6	0	1	0	2	0	0	
Neuendorff, Tony, Durham	.181	35	83	7	15	18	3	0	0	5	0	1	2	0	11	1	18	0	0
Neufang, Gerald, Salem	.223	31	103	15	23	28	3	1	0	8	1	1	0	0	22	0	15	0	1
Oliva, David, Winston-Salem	.292	94	339	55	99	158	23	6	8	43	6	4	4	1	41	1	55	20	10
Olmedo, Luis, Winston-Salem	.169	51	130	11	22	25	3	0	0	7	0	7	1	2	12	0	28	5	1
Ortega, Raymond, Peninsula	.158	14	38	2	6	12	3	0	1	4	0	0	1	0	4	0	11	1	0
Parkins, Robert, Winston-Salem†	.000	20	1	0	0	0	0	0	0	0	0	0	0	0	1	0	0	0	0

Player and Club	Pct.	G	AB	R	H	TB	2B	3B	HR	RBI	GW	SH	SF	HP	BB	Int. BB	SO	SB	CS
Paula, Julio, Lynchburg†	.252	78	202	37	51	70	7	3	2	26	4	2	2	1	34	0	31	3	1
Pavlik, John, Prince William†	.222	30	63	3	14	16	2	0	0	4	1	2	0	1	3	1	17	0	1
Pettis, Stacy, Prince William°	.229	69	227	31	52	63	6	1	1	9	2	5	0	0	22	1	79	23	16
Piskol, Peter, Prince William	.238	51	151	18	36	44	3	1	1	14	1	3	2	1	13	0	36	5	1
Pruitt, Edwin, Lynchburg°	.000	39	7	0	0	0	0	0	0	0	0	0	0	0	0	0	3	0	0
Quinonez, Rey, Winston-Salem	.279	132	458	53	128	203	30	6	11	69	9	1	4	5	46	1	64	14	5
Reddish, Michael, Hagerstown	.296	66	223	36	66	105	10	1	9	40	7	0	4	2	37	2	33	5	3
Redfield, Joseph, Lynchburg	.269	122	428	80	115	180	18	7	11	58	5	2	3	4	64	1	81	14	7
Reilly, James, Peninsula	.000	23	1	0	0	0	0	0	0	0	0	0	0	0	0	0	1	0	0
Rembielak, Richard, Hagerstown	.140	34	93	9	13	17	4	0	0	6	1	1	1	0	12	1	25	2	0
Richardson, Billy Joe, Winston-Salem	.202	75	223	21	45	74	5	0	8	29	5	3	0	2	22	0	74	5	1
Ripken, William, Hagerstown	.230	115	409	48	94	121	15	3	2	40	3	2	0	4	36	1	64	3	5
Rivas, Rafael, Kinston†	.243	67	202	28	49	80	8	1	7	29	0	2	1	4	18	0	53	1	3
Rivera, James, Durham	.000	45	3	0	0	0	0	0	0	0	0	0	0	0	0	0	2	0	0
Roberts, J. Drexel, Kinston°	.172	22	58	7	10	17	3	2	0	6	0	0	0	0	8	3	14	3	0
Roberts, Leon, Prince William†	.301	134	498	81	150	209	25	5	8	77	9	2	5	3	44	3	63	50	13
Rogers, MacArthur, Durham	.000	13	0	0	0	0	0	0	0	0	0	0	0	0	1	0	0	0	0
Romagna, Randolph, Kinston	.182	13	33	3	6	6	0	0	0	4	0	0	1	0	10	0	8	0	1
Roman, Ray, Peninsula°	.118	10	17	1	2	2	0	0	0	0	0	0	1	3	0	5	0	0
Rosado, Luis, Hagerstown	.571	7	21	5	12	21	7	1	0	11	2	0	0	0	5	0	2	0	0
Rosario, Simon, Durham	.291	100	333	43	97	145	13	1	11	42	6	4	1	0	31	1	32	3	7
Ruiz, Manuel, Durham	.286	12	28	2	8	8	0	0	0	3	0	0	2	0	2	1	2	0	0
Sakowski, Vincent, Salem	.182	62	181	19	33	44	2	0	3	14	2	2	2	1	15	0	25	2	0
Sanchez, Leopoldo, Prince William°	.136	26	22	1	3	4	1	0	0	0	0	2	0	0	1	0	8	0	0
Sarmiento, Ramon, Kinston	.000	3	5	0	0	0	0	0	0	2	0	0	0	0	2	0	4	0	0
Sauveur, Richard, Prince William°	.273	11	11	0	3	3	0	0	0	1	0	0	0	0	1	0	2	0	0
Schexnayder, Wade, Lynchburg	.125	25	72	9	9	16	2	1	1	5	0	0	1	7	0	19	0	1
Schreiber, Martin, Durham°	.000	28	19	1	0	0	0	0	0	1	0	3	0	0	3	0	12	0	0
Seiler, David, Peninsula°	.100	31	10	0	1	1	0	0	0	1	0	0	0	0	1	0	5	0	0
Shaddy, J. Christopher, Kinston	.254	140	449	61	114	190	22	3	16	66	4	4	3	3	56	4	128	4	5
Simpson, Danny, Salem	.232	81	259	39	60	104	13	2	9	31	2	2	1	4	28	0	92	4	3
Skripko, J. Scott, Winston-Salem	.158	25	57	8	9	11	2	0	0	3	0	2	0	0	10	0	18	9	2
Sliwinski, Kevin, Kinston	.308	68	240	34	74	116	15	0	9	41	5	0	3	2	30	0	49	1	1
Soares, J.A. Todd, Peninsula°	.284	61	194	31	55	76	9	3	2	27	3	0	1	3	24	4	44	0	3
Soriano, Hilario, Kinston	.138	13	29	1	4	4	0	0	0	2	0	1	0	0	0	7	1	0
Stefero, John, Hagerstown°	.209	41	134	9	28	34	3	0	1	17	2	0	3	0	24	0	36	0	1
Stewart, H. Wayne, Peninsula	.143	14	14	1	2	2	0	0	0	0	0	0	0	1	0	8	0	0
Stock, Kevin, Salem	.146	42	123	19	18	31	4	0	3	13	2	0	0	3	21	0	46	1	0
Stone, Shawn, Prince William	.000	39	6	0	0	0	0	0	0	0	0	0	0	0	0	5	0	0
Sutton, L. Ricardo, Kinston	.279	103	340	54	95	155	18	6	10	37	4	1	5	2	48	0	80	5	8
Tatis, Bernardo, Kinston†	.253	110	395	65	100	129	6	7	3	31	5	5	1	4	44	0	73	24	12
Taylor, Donald, Prince William	.000	26	17	1	0	0	0	0	0	0	0	1	0	1	0	0	6	0	0
Tejada, Wilfredo, Peninsula	.268	45	127	13	34	48	6	1	2	16	0	0	0	1	8	0	28	0	2
Thielker, David, Hagerstown°	.257	122	370	45	95	130	19	2	4	60	8	3	8	2	81	2	50	1	2
Thomas, Andres, Durham	.263	114	460	64	121	168	18	4	7	44	7	3	3	4	32	2	75	19	6
Thornton, Louis, Lynchburg°	.275	131	505	78	139	196	25	7	6	67	7	0	1	8	29	5	81	28	11
Thoutsis, Paul, Winston-Salem°	.224	90	299	32	67	86	9	2	2	26	2	2	2	4	32	3	55	1	1
Traber, James, Hagerstown°	.358	48	165	33	59	80	15	0	2	29	5	0	3	0	26	1	19	14	3
Tremblay, Gary, Winston-Salem	.196	102	321	37	63	111	11	2	11	39	6	2	4	2	39	0	95	0	1
Triplett, Antonio, Salem	.267	77	251	33	67	99	6	4	6	30	4	3	0	1	23	0	49	8	5
Tumpane, Robert, Durham°	.265	123	373	70	99	193	11	1	27	75	9	1	3	9	110	8	75	1	0
Vanderburg, Michael, Hagerstown†	.226	46	146	18	33	41	5	0	1	9	0	1	1	0	32	0	22	4	2
Vest, James, Peninsula	.261	54	176	17	46	54	6	1	0	15	1	2	2	2	16	0	34	3	0
Wagner, Jeffrey, Durham†	.215	116	386	51	83	134	15	0	12	53	2	1	2	6	55	0	127	5	4
Walters, Kevin, Peninsula†	.253	69	170	21	43	54	5	0	2	28	3	0	3	2	41	3	15	3	2
Ward, Kevin, Peninsula	.261	130	456	84	119	186	18	5	13	69	12	4	7	6	53	3	90	21	3
Warner, Harold, Peninsula†	.143	11	7	0	1	1	0	0	0	0	0	0	0	1	0	3	0	0
Weatherford, Brant, Peninsula	.111	24	9	0	1	2	1	0	0	0	0	1	0	0	0	6	0	0
Weissman, Craig, Lynchburg	.000	25	15	0	0	0	0	0	0	0	0	0	2	0	0	0	6	0	0
Williams, Donald, Prince William	.000	4	3	0	0	0	0	0	0	0	0	0	0	0	0	2	0	0
Williams, Jeffrey, Hagerstown°	.196	23	46	7	9	10	1	0	0	3	1	0	0	0	10	0	15	1	0
Witt, Stephen, Peninsula	.000	16	8	0	0	0	0	0	0	0	0	0	0	0	0	3	0	0
Wright, Scott, Peninsula	.000	17	3	0	0	0	0	0	0	0	0	0	0	0	0	3	0	0
Yastrzemski, C. Michael, Durham†	.264	110	352	46	93	134	13	2	8	50	5	2	1	46	1	43	3	2
Youmans, Floyd, Lynchburg	.200	7	5	0	1	1	0	0	0	0	0	0	0	0	0	0	0	0

The following pitchers, listed alphabetically by club, with games in parentheses, had no plate appearances, primarily through use of designated hitters:

DURHAM—Barger, Vincent (8); Rosario, Maximo (1); Ziem, Stephen (49).

HAGERSTOWN—Alexander, Tommy (33); Arias, Juan (14); Bell, Eric (3); Bianchi, Ben (19); Boyd, Randy (1); Concepcion, Carlos (1); Cratch, Richard (4); Dooner, Glenn (23); Habyan, John (13); Lavelle, William (25); Leiter, Mark (27); Milacki, Robert (15); Moretti, Roy (25); Mulcahy, Timothy (42); Raczka, Michael (8); Rice, Richard (24); Welchel, Donald (4).

KINSTON—Aquino, Luis (53); Castro, Eddy (8); Clemons, Mark (21); Cullen, Michael (16); Elam, Scott (1); Gallagher, Glenn (7); Holbrook, Robert (29); Howard, Dennis (9); Lychak, Perry (44); McKay, Alan (27); Mesa, Jose (10); Robbins, Ronnie (22); Segura, Jose (16); Shanks, William (9); Sprowl, Robert (11); Taylor, Johnny (39); Valenzuela, Guillermo (23); Walsh, David (3); Wells, David (7); Yearout, Michael (8).

PENINSULA—Caraballo, Ramon (1); Ferguson, Billy (6); Hill, John (13); Long, Bruce (1).

PRINCE WILLIAM—Carlie, Aaron (2).

SALEM—Bass, Regan (25); Brosious, Frank (4); Coatney, Rickey (21); Esposito, Nick (18); Hartman, Albert (27); Henry, Timothy (16); Hudson, Anthony (39); Joslin, Christopher (27); Killingsworth, Kirk (46); Kramer, Randall (12); Leach, Martin (21); Maki, Timothy (2); Moses, John (9); Reichard, Clyde (44); Scarpetta, Daniel (25); Smith, Daryl (16).

WINSTON-SALEM—Araujo, Anazario (34); Cappadona, Anthony (35); Corder, Timothy (28); Ellsworth, Steven (26); Greco, George (33); Grubbs, Kevin (34); Lockhart, Bruce (28); Peterson, David (33); Riddle, Larry (13); Stewart, Hector (27).

GRAND SLAM HOME RUNS—Davis, Day, Felice, Horn, Lockwood, 2 each; Ben, Edg. Castro, Cormack, Doerr, Gonzalez, Greenwell, D. Griffin, Henderson, Hollins, Lyons, L. Roberts, Stock, Thornton, Tumpane, 1 each.

AWARDED FIRST BASE ON CATCHER'S INTERFERENCE—Oliva 3 (Borges, Fitzgerald, Melillo); Charboneau 2 (DeWillis, Gonzalez); Felice 2 (Borges, Gonzalez); Day (DeWillis); Gile (Borges); Harris (Baker); Jacoby (Hansen); Ripken (Borges); Rivas (Richardson); Sliwinski (Fitzgerald); Thornton (Aulenback).

CLUB FIELDING

Club	Pct.	G.	PO.	A.	E.	DP.	PB.	Club	Pct.	G.	PO.	A.	E.	DP.	PB.
Durham	.972	140	3590	1526	146	119	19	Prince William	.964	140	3545	1530	190	150	14
Kinston	.965	140	3553	1450	181	124	21	Peninsula	.958	140	3465	1415	214	110	16
Hagerstown	.964	140	3457	1534	184	122	28	Salem	.956	138	3523	1664	240	143	28
Lynchburg	.964	138	3506	1365	184	98	21	Winston-Salem	.953	140	3454	1514	243	117	33

INDIVIDUAL FIELDING

*Throws lefthanded.

FIRST BASEMEN

Player and Club	Pct.	G.	PO.	A.	E.	DP.	Player and Club	Pct.	G.	PO.	A.	E.	DP.
Aulenback, Prince William	1.000	2	12	1	0	1	Lyons, Lynchburg	.971	11	88	14	3	9
Berger, Prince William	.986	60	476	29	7	46	Machin, Peninsula*	1.000	1	3	0	0	1
Borges, Prince William	1.000	3	21	2	0	3	Magadan, Hagerstown	.984	112	896	64	16	69
Castaneda, Prince William	.993	44	371	30	3	42	Mota, Peninsula*	.980	49	349	34	8	32
Castro, Prince William*	.983	100	904	67	17	91	Ortega, Peninsula	.944	5	32	2	2	2
Davis, Salem	.974	45	385	29	11	33	Piskol, Prince William	1.000	2	1	2	0	1
Day, Peninsula	.990	92	733	50	8	56	Reddish, Hagerstown	1.000	1	1	0	0	0
DeLaRosa, Prince William*	.833	2	9	1	2	0	Redfield, Lynchburg	1.000	1	14	5	0	1
Dennis, Kinston	1.000	1	3	0	0	1	Richardson, Winston-Salem	.983	9	57	2	1	4
Derryberry, Hagerstown	.970	8	30	2	1	2	Rivas, Kinston	.983	14	99	14	2	11
Fielder, Kinston	.984	60	533	24	9	38	Sakowski, Salem	1.000	1	2	0	0	0
Fitzgerald, Hagerstown	1.000	3	16	0	0	0	Skripko, Winston-Salem	1.000	1	4	1	0	0
Gertz, Hagerstown*	.955	3	18	3	1	4	Sliwinski, Kinston	.986	68	543	24	8	59
Griffin, Durham	.986	27	260	15	4	18	Thielker, Hagerstown	.988	25	224	21	3	21
Hale, Winston-Salem	.979	19	173	11	4	14	Thornton, Lynchburg	.985	8	64	2	1	1
Hansen, Salem	.976	5	39	1	1	2	Traber, Hagerstown*	.982	44	352	30	7	23
Heller, Lynchburg	.974	7	70	5	2	5	Triplett, Salem	1.000	4	5	0	0	0
Horn, Winston-Salem*	.973	114	978	70	29	87	TUMPANE, Durham*	.995	113	1043	56	5	90
Kenaga, Hagerstown	.994	68	589	59	4	61	Walters, Peninsula	.987	10	65	9	1	9
Laird, Prince William	1.000	41	339	13	0	46							

SECOND BASEMEN

Player and Club	Pct.	G.	PO.	A.	E.	DP.	Player and Club	Pct.	G.	PO.	A.	E.	DP.
Caraballo, Lynchburg	.926	10	12	13	2	4	Lawton, Lynchburg	.917	2	3	8	1	1
Childress, Durham	.947	8	21	15	2	5	Leriger, Hagerstown	1.000	16	20	49	0	10
Christenson, Prince William	.909	2	5	5	1	3	Liriano, Kinston	.967	129	260	357	21	77
Dillard, Salem	.993	26	55	84	1	25	Lockwood, Hagerstown	.972	26	42	64	3	14
Engram, Peninsula	.950	3	8	11	1	2	Martinez, Prince William	.893	7	11	14	3	2
Estrada, Winston-Salem	.935	41	63	81	10	23	McPhail, Lynchburg	.984	45	71	108	3	19
Foit, Salem	.955	7	9	12	1	1	Moscat, Lynchburg	.970	45	97	100	6	24
Gile, Salem	.968	108	226	322	18	64	Neuendorff, Durham	1.000	1	0	2	0	0
Glynn, Lynchburg	1.000	2	3	3	0	0	Olmedo, Winston-Salem	.966	48	85	111	7	28
Gordon, Winston-Salem	.961	73	133	164	12	25	Paula, Lynchburg	.934	46	86	85	12	18
Henderson, Peninsula	.971	40	67	100	5	20	Piskol, Prince William	.963	9	14	12	1	4
Ingle, Durham	1.000	2	6	5	0	3	Redfield, Lynchburg	1.000	9	10	10	0	2
Jackson, Peninsula	.938	5	8	7	1	1	Ripken, Hagerstown	.981	13	21	31	1	4
Jacobson, Hagerstown	.978	89	173	230	9	60	ROBERTS, Prince William	.969	129	282	352	20	91
Jacoby, Hagerstown	.875	6	4	3	1	0	Ruiz, Durham	1.000	2	6	5	0	1
Kanter, Peninsula	.954	18	37	46	4	9	Sakowski, Salem	.978	11	18	27	1	4
Kennard, Peninsula	.984	80	167	198	6	43	Tatis, Kinston	.971	14	21	46	2	7
Knox, Durham	.968	128	265	342	20	70							

THIRD BASEMEN

Player and Club	Pct.	G.	PO.	A.	E.	DP.	Player and Club	Pct.	G.	PO.	A.	E.	DP.
Barbosa, Durham	.920	33	25	55	7	0	Kanter, Peninsula	1.000	1	1	0	0	0
Borges, Prince William	.750	1	1	2	1	0	Kenaga, Hagerstown	.333	1	0	1	2	0
Bruno, Hagerstown	.936	40	24	78	7	11	Leriger, Hagerstown	.950	11	3	16	1	2
Childress, Durham	.959	88	51	184	10	14	Linkmeyer, Kinston	.909	8	2	8	1	0
CHRISTENSON, Prince William	.917	96	55	188	22	19	Lockwood, Hagerstown	.914	58	43	128	16	14
Day, Peninsula	.904	32	26	49	8	3	Malave, Kinston	.891	104	86	167	31	19
Dennis, Kinston	1.000	1	2	3	0	0	Martinez, Prince William	.737	7	0	14	5	0
Dillard, Salem	.902	21	18	65	9	4	McPhail, Lynchburg	.898	25	13	40	6	2
Doerr, Hagerstown	.870	21	12	28	6	4	Miller, Peninsula	.879	36	27	75	14	8
Doughty, Salem	1.000	1	0	6	0	0	Moscat, Lynchburg	.692	6	2	7	4	0
Estrada, Winston-Salem	.833	5	1	4	1	1	Mucha, Hagerstown	1.000	2	2	2	0	0
Frishman, Peninsula	.840	25	14	28	8	2	Neuendorff, Durham	.969	10	5	26	1	1
Gile, Salem	.810	5	7	10	4	0	Olmedo, Winston-Salem	.750	1	0	3	1	0
Glynn, Lynchburg	1.000	1	0	1	0	0	Paula, Lynchburg	1.000	3	2	0	0	0
Gordon, Winston-Salem	.931	20	14	40	4	2	Piskol, Prince William	.919	27	17	40	5	10
Greenwell, Winston-Salem	.869	64	41	125	25	7	Redfield, Lynchburg	.926	82	54	147	16	9
Hale, Winston-Salem	.944	60	52	117	10	7	Rembielak, Hagerstown	1.000	4	3	9	0	1
Haro, Prince William	.868	22	16	30	7	5	Romagna, Kinston	1.000	3	11	18	0	2
Harris, Lynchburg	.897	43	18	60	9	0	Ruiz, Durham	.870	6	5	15	3	1
Henderson, Peninsula	.883	56	31	97	17	10	Sakowski, Salem	.910	36	16	65	8	8
Heyison, Hagerstown	1.000	4	6	4	0	0	Stock, Salem	.864	40	35	73	17	5
Ingle, Durham	.909	13	7	23	3	1	Tatis, Kinston	.897	25	12	40	6	2
Jacobson, Hagerstown	.000	1	0	0	0	0	Thielker, Salem	.462	6	1	5	7	0
Jacoby, Hagerstown	1000	12	2	14	0	0	Triplett, Salem	.906	44	28	88	12	8

SHORTSTOPS

Player and Club	Pct.	G.	PO.	A.	E.	DP.	Player and Club	Pct.	G.	PO.	A.	E.	DP.
Caraballo, Lynchburg	1.000	3	0	8	0	0	Ingle, Durham	1.000	3	6	12	0	3
Childress, Durham	.983	26	36	81	2	13	Jackson, Peninsula	.932	66	100	172	20	24
Christenson, Prince William	1.000	10	11	18	0	7	Jacobson, Hagerstown	.929	7	9	17	2	4
Dillard, Salem	.907	10	14	35	5	7	Jones, Hagerstown	.833	3	1	4	1	1
Doughty, Salem	.912	55	85	174	25	42	Kennard, Peninsula	.974	47	56	131	5	25
FERMIN, Prince William	.960	119	181	376	23	72	Lawton, Lynchburg	.600	1	1	2	2	0
Foit, Salem	.927	58	71	184	20	29	Leriger, Hagerstown	1.000	2	1	2	0	0
Gile, Salem	.865	7	13	19	5	4	Linkmeyer, Kinston	1.000	3	2	1	0	0
Glynn, Lynchburg	.937	95	102	223	22	46	Lockwood, Hagerstown	.875	7	5	9	2	1
Gordon, Winston-Salem	.929	14	12	27	3	4	Martinez, Prince William	.846	4	5	6	2	0

SHORTSTOPS—Continued

Player and Club	Pct.	G.	PO.	A.	E.	DP.	Player and Club	Pct.	G.	PO.	A.	E.	DP.
Miller, Peninsula	.909	32	44	106	15	17	Rembielak, Hagerstown	.937	30	32	72	7	7
Moscat, Lynchburg	.750	4	0	3	1	0	Ripken, Hagerstown	.948	104	166	327	27	61
Paula, Lynchburg	.930	26	22	44	5	8	Shaddy, Kinston	.931	140	192	411	45	79
Piskol, Prince William	.930	18	17	49	5	9	Tatis, Kinston	1.000	2	2	4	0	1
Quinonez, Winston-Salem	.930	132	240	428	50	84	Thomas, Durham	.938	113	156	361	34	64
Redfield, Lynchburg	.926	50	55	107	13	15	Triplett, Salem	.904	19	20	46	7	11

OUTFIELDERS

Player and Club	Pct.	G.	PO.	A.	E.	DP.	Player and Club	Pct.	G.	PO.	A.	E.	DP.
Aitcheson, Kinston	.895	35	47	4	6	0	Laird, Prince William°	1.000	2	3	0	0	0
Auten, Hagerstown	.917	24	30	3	3	1	Leiva, Peninsula	.955	80	180	9	9	1
BEAUCHAMP, Kinston	.979	129	274	10	6	2	Leriger, Hagerstown	1.000	7	7	0	0	0
Ben, Salem	.950	105	200	8	11	2	Lewis, Lynchburg	.930	29	38	2	3	0
Berger, Prince William	.975	26	37	2	1	0	Linkmeyer, Kinston	.333	1	0	1	2	0
A. Brown, Peninsula	.892	117	170	12	22	2	Lopez, Hagerstown°	.942	110	174	6	11	0
S. Brown, Prince William	.975	70	105	11	3	2	Luzon, Durham	1.000	2	6	0	0	0
Bruno, Hagerstown	1.000	1	0	1	0	0	Mace, Salem	.968	127	199	12	7	2
Charboneau, Prince William	.990	76	88	8	1	1	Malave, Kinston	1.000	2	3	0	0	0
Childress, Durham	1.000	3	1	0	0	0	Martinez, Prince William	.857	7	6	0	1	0
Coss, Prince William	.930	45	51	2	4	0	McPhail, Lynchburg	1.000	6	5	1	0	0
Crum, Salem	.962	106	145	5	6	1	Mota, Peninsula°	1.000	8	11	3	0	0
Cusack, Hagerstown	.857	10	6	0	1	0	Oliva, Winston-Salem	.970	94	222	5	7	1
Davis, Salem	.957	18	20	2	1	1	Pavlik, Prince William	.969	23	31	0	1	0
Day, Peninsula	1.000	13	31	1	0	0	Pettis, Prince William	.939	60	120	3	8	0
DeLaRosa, Prince William°	.923	23	34	2	3	0	Reddish, Hagerstown	.968	61	82	8	3	0
Delucchi, Prince William	1.000	25	43	1	0	0	Rivas, Kinston	.966	25	26	2	1	0
Dennis, Kinston	1.000	15	15	0	0	0	Rosario, Durham	.948	68	108	1	6	0
Doerr, Hagerstown	1.000	6	7	1	0	0	Sarmiento, Kinston	1.000	1	1	0	0	0
Felice, Lynchburg	.938	116	111	11	8	3	Simpson, Salem	.959	68	105	12	5	2
Gerhart, Hagerstown	.956	47	108	1	5	1	Skripko, Winston-Salem	.981	22	48	4	1	0
Gertz, Hagerstown°	1.000	1	1	0	0	0	Soares, Peninsula	.946	55	85	2	5	2
Granger, Hagerstown	.966	71	138	3	5	1	Stefero, Peninsula	1.000	3	7	1	0	0
Green, Kinston°	.962	70	120	7	5	0	Sutton, Kinston	1.000	32	46	1	0	0
Greenwell, Winston-Salem	.948	57	85	7	5	0	Tatis, Kinston	.963	65	97	6	4	1
Griffin, Kinston	.993	70	133	10	1	3	Thielker, Hagerstown	.972	24	31	4	1	0
Hale, Winston-Salem	.957	18	20	2	1	0	Thornton, Lynchburg	.952	123	186	11	10	2
Harlow, Hagerstown°	.952	18	19	1	1	1	Thoutsis, Winston-Salem	.921	61	79	3	7	1
Haro, Prince William	.976	109	191	12	5	3	Traber, Hagerstown°	1.000	8	9	0	0	0
Hatcher, Durham	.962	121	220	5	9	1	Triplett, Salem	1.000	7	2	0	0	0
Heller, Lynchburg	.889	7	7	1	1	0	Vanderburg, Hagerstown°	1.000	45	73	2	0	0
Hodge, Durham	.942	25	45	4	3	1	Vest, Peninsula	.927	46	80	9	7	1
Hollins, Lynchburg	.969	36	31	0	1	0	Wagner, Durham	.953	112	133	10	7	3
Jefferson, Lynchburg	.972	127	265	11	8	2	Ward, Peninsula	.957	115	217	4	10	0
Jelks, Winston-Salem	.946	84	134	6	8	1	Williams, Hagerstown°	.947	15	17	1	1	0
Jose, Winston-Salem	.939	97	212	17	15	4	Yastrzemski, Durham	.969	103	176	11	6	2

CATCHERS

Player and Club	Pct.	G.	PO.	A.	E.	DP.	PB.	Player and Club	Pct.	G.	PO.	A.	E.	DP.	PB.
Aulenback, Prince William	.917	3	9	2	1	0	0	Loy, Peninsula	.985	56	306	28	5	2	6
Baker, Prince William	.983	73	457	52	9	4	6	LYONS, Lynchburg	.98973	100	806	72	10	5	17
Borges, Prince William	.970	74	468	43	16	3	8	Melillo, Prince William	.976	87	529	50	14	6	18
Carlucci, Salem	.976	57	308	19	8	2	11	Neuendorff, Durham	.990	22	98	5	1	0	1
Carmichael, Lynchburg	.986	11	69	3	1	0	2	Neufang, Salem	.986	31	185	29	3	2	3
Cormack, Durham	.98970	70	478	47	6	6	11	Ortega, Peninsula	.976	8	37	3	1	0	0
Davis, Salem	.978	16	71	17	2	3	5	Richardson, Winston-Salem	.970	52	232	29	8	4	10
Dennett, Winston-Salem	.972	7	33	2	1	0	3	Roman, Peninsula	.941	6	15	1	1	0	0
DeWillis, Kinston	.984	122	848	69	15	8	19	Rosado, Peninsula	1.000	5	39	2	0	1	0
Fitzgerald, Hagerstown	.981	28	132	21	3	3	6	Schexnayder, Lynchburg	.995	24	171	21	1	3	2
Gonzalez, Salem	.967	36	207	25	8	3	5	Soriano, Kinston	.979	9	43	3	1	0	2
Hansen, Salem	.929	8	50	2	4	0	4	Stefero, Hagerstown	.989	29	164	20	2	0	4
Heller, Lynchburg	1.000	18	72	6	0	0	0	Tejada, Peninsula	.963	44	262	27	11	3	4
Henderson, Peninsula	.961	11	42	7	2	1	5	Thielker, Hagerstown	1.000	6	18	3	0	0	1
Holland, Kinston	.979	21	80	13	2	1	0	Tremblay, Winston-Salem	.986	90	474	70	8	3	20
Hood, Durham	.991	63	386	37	4	3	7	Walters, Peninsula	.990	35	191	15	2	1	1

PITCHERS

Player and Club	Pct.	G.	PO.	A.	E.	DP.	Player and Club	Pct.	G.	PO.	A.	E.	DP.
Adamczak, Lynchburg	.850	45	4	13	3	1	Coatney, Salem	1.000	21	2	7	0	0
Aguilera, Lynchburg	.944	13	6	11	1	1	Coker, Peninsula	.952	24	12	8	1	0
Alexander, Hagerstown	.917	33	3	8	1	0	Cook, Lynchburg	.962	27	13	38	2	2
Aquino, Kinston	.950	53	4	15	1	1	Corder, Winston-Salem	.950	28	3	16	1	1
Araujo, Winston-Salem	.871	34	9	18	4	0	Cordoba, Prince William	.938	36	2	13	1	1
Arias, Hagerstown	1.000	14	0	4	0	0	Cratch, Hagerstown	1.000	3	1	4	0	1
Assenmacher, Durham°	.903	26	4	24	3	2	Cullen, Kinston	1.000	16	1	3	0	0
Aviles, Durham	.913	26	4	17	2	0	Day, Peninsula	1.000	1	1	0	0	0
Barger, Durham°	.833	8	1	4	1	0	Dooner, Hagerstown	.909	23	4	6	1	1
Bass, Salem	.926	25	11	14	2	0	Downs, Prince William	1.000	47	4	13	0	1
Bianchi, Hagerstown	.839	19	8	18	5	1	Edens, Lynchburg	.833	3	1	4	1	0
Blasucci, Prince William°	.500	7	1	1	2	0	Ellsworth, Winston-Salem	.947	26	11	25	2	3
Brosious, Salem	1.000	4	2	1	0	0	Esposito, Kinston	.800	18	1	3	1	0
Brown, Lynchburg°	.914	28	8	24	3	1	Evetts, Peninsula	.933	41	6	22	2	0
Buckley, Prince William	1.000	16	0	1	0	0	Faherty, Prince William°	.923	24	2	10	1	0
Buckmier, Prince William	.905	31	12	26	4	2	Felt, Prince William	.778	35	2	19	6	1
Bulls, Peninsula	1.000	11	2	11	0	1	Ferguson, Peninsula	1.000	6	3	10	0	1
Cano, Durham	1.000	20	5	18	0	1	Gallagher, Kinston	1.000	7	1	3	0	0
Cappadona, Winston-Salem°	.857	35	5	7	2	0	Garcia, Lynchburg	1.000	34	1	3	0	1
Castaneda, Prince William	1.000	4	0	1	0	1	Gordon, Prince William	.800	14	3	1	1	0
Castro, Kinston	.941	8	2	14	1	1	Greco, Winston-Salem°	.915	33	5	38	4	2
Clemons, Kinston	1.000	20	7	15	0	5	Grubbs, Winston-Salem	.938	36	4	11	1	1

PITCHERS—Continued

Player and Club	Pct.	G.	PO.	A.	E.	DP.
Habyan, Hagerstown	1.000	13	3	15	0	3
Hartman, Salem	.906	27	13	35	5	2
Henry, Salem*	.950	16	3	16	1	2
Hill, Peninsula	.833	13	3	2	1	0
HOLBROOK, Kinston	1.000	29	8	22	0	1
Holman, Prince William	.905	15	6	13	2	3
Howard, Kinston	.667	9	0	2	1	0
Hudson, Salem	.938	39	10	20	2	1
Jensen, Lynchburg*	1.000	9	0	3	0	0
Johnson, Prince William	.926	13	5	20	2	3
Jones, Durham	.833	4	1	4	1	0
Josephson, Durham	1.000	45	1	13	0	0
Joslin, Salem*	1.000	27	1	5	0	1
Kennard, Peninsula	1.000	1	1	0	0	0
Kiecker, Winston-Salem	.829	29	8	21	6	1
Killingsworth, Salem	.952	46	4	16	1	3
Kramer, Salem	.917	12	3	19	2	0
Labay, Peninsula*	1.000	10	4	12	0	1
Lamb, Durham	.971	25	9	25	1	3
Lance, Durham*	.800	30	1	3	1	0
Lavelle, Hagerstown	1.000	25	8	15	0	2
Leach, Salem	.980	21	13	36	1	5
Ledbetter, Hagerstown	.875	27	3	11	2	1
Leggatt, Durham	.857	19	1	5	1	2
K. Leiter, Hagerstown	.940	25	14	33	3	1
M. Leiter, Hagerstown	.897	27	7	28	4	2
Lockhart, Winston-Salem*	1.000	28	0	7	0	0
Long, Peninsula	1.000	1	1	0	0	0
Lundgren, Lynchburg	.963	33	13	13	1	2
Lychak, Kinston*	1.000	44	6	20	0	0
Machin, Peninsula	.889	17	4	12	2	0
Maki, Salem	1.000	2	0	1	0	0
McKay, Kinston	1.000	27	2	7	0	0
McKelvey, Prince William	.889	13	4	12	2	0
Menard, Peninsula	1.000	44	9	9	0	2
Mesa, Kinston	1.000	10	1	8	0	1
Milacki, Hagerstown	.824	15	5	9	3	0
Morel, Peninsula*	1.000	49	1	10	0	1
Moretti, Hagerstown	.750	25	1	5	2	0
Mortillaro, Durham*	1.000	24	0	17	0	0
Morton, Peninsula*	.952	19	3	17	1	0
Moses, Salem*	1.000	9	0	2	0	0
Mota, Peninsula*	1.000	1	0	1	0	0
Mulcahy, Hagerstown*	.938	42	1	14	1	0
Murray, Lynchburg	.857	43	5	7	2	1
Myers, Lynchburg*	.923	23	3	21	2	1
Parkins, Winston-Salem	.813	20	6	7	3	0
Peterson, Winston-Salem	1.000	33	3	5	0	1
Pruitt, Lynchburg*	1.000	39	1	13	0	0
Raczka, Hagerstown*	1.000	8	0	4	0	1
Reichard, Salem	.833	44	4	11	3	1
Reilly, Peninsula	1.000	19	1	6	0	0
Rice, Hagerstown	.939	24	8	23	2	1
Riddle, Winston-Salem	1.000	13	4	8	0	0
Rivera, Durham	1.000	45	5	14	0	1
Robbins, Kinston	.955	22	7	14	1	0
Rogers, Durham	1.000	13	1	1	0	0
Rosario, Durham*	1.000	1	0	1	0	0
Sanchez, Prince William*	.895	26	4	30	4	1
Sauveur, Prince William*	.938	10	0	15	1	1
Scarpetta, Salem*	.952	25	5	15	1	2
Schreiber, Durham*	.965	28	7	48	2	1
Segura, Kinston	.893	16	3	22	3	2
Seiler, Peninsula*	.864	31	3	16	3	1
Shanks, Salem	1.000	9	0	9	0	0
Smith, Salem	.895	16	9	25	4	3
Soriano, Kinston	1.000	2	1	1	0	0
Sprowl, Kinston*	.875	11	0	7	1	2
H. Wa. Stewart, Peninsula	.906	14	7	22	3	2
He. Stewart, Winston-Salem*	.929	27	4	22	2	1
Stone, Prince William	1.000	39	8	7	0	2
D. Taylor, Prince William	.875	25	5	23	4	3
J. Taylor, Kinston	.857	39	0	6	1	1
Valenzuela, Kinston	.929	23	3	23	2	2
Warner, Peninsula*	.857	9	1	5	1	0
Weatherford, Peninsula	.875	24	2	5	1	0
Weissman, Lynchburg	.875	25	4	10	2	0
Welchel, Hagerstown	.667	4	0	2	1	0
Wells, Kinston*	.909	7	2	8	1	0
Williams, Prince William	1.000	4	3	0	0	0
Witt, Peninsula	1.000	16	3	9	0	1
Wright, Peninsula	.833	17	3	2	1	0
Yearout, Kinston*	.923	8	4	8	1	1
Youmans, Lynchburg	1.000	7	3	7	0	0
Ziem, Durham	.957	49	7	15	1	0

The following players had no recorded accepted chances at the positions indicated; therefore, are not listed in the fielding averages for those particular positions: Bell, p; Boyd, p; R. Caraballo, p; W. Caraballo, 3b; Carlie, p; Clay, of; Concepcion, p; DeLaRosa, p; Dillard, of; Elam, p; Gile, of; Harris, of; Kenaga, of; Labay, of; Lyons, of; Olmedo, of; Rembielak, of; Rivas, p; Simpson, 1b; Walsh, p; Walters, of.

CLUB PITCHING

Club	ERA.	G.	CG.	ShO.	Sv.	IP.	H.	R.	ER.	HR.	HB.	BB.	Int. BB.	SO.	WP.	Bk.
Lynchburg	2.80	138	28	11	26	1168.2	1020	469	363	68	32	442	14	1092	64	11
Prince William	3.79	140	17	7	34	1181.2	1034	604	498	65	50	724	20	892	90	9
Kinston	3.91	140	13	8	38	1184.1	1094	603	515	87	31	590	20	942	62	9
Durham	4.02	140	19	11	31	1196.2	1129	606	535	133	36	512	17	936	67	13
Winston-Salem	4.03	140	24	13	19	1151.1	1187	662	516	83	26	530	16	702	87	13
Peninsula	4.08	140	21	6	29	1155.0	1155	656	524	99	58	482	30	822	78	7
Hagerstown	4.39	140	31	9	26	1152.1	1142	666	562	78	42	633	22	838	79	4
Salem	4.58	138	14	8	30	1174.1	1218	753	598	118	45	539	13	781	83	6

PITCHERS' RECORDS
(Leading Qualifiers for Earned-Run Average Leadership—112 or More Innings)

*Throws lefthanded.

Pitcher—Club	W.	L.	Pct.	ERA.	G.	GS.	CG.	GF.	ShO.	Sv.	IP.	H.	R.	ER.	HR.	HB.	BB.	Int. BB.	SO.	WP.
Myers, Lynchburg*	13	5	.722	2.06	23	22	7	1	1	0	157.0	123	46	36	7	3	61	0	171	11
Lundgren, Lynchburg	8	1	.889	2.95	33	10	3	9	0	2	113.0	103	48	37	11	2	33	1	83	3
Cook, Lynchburg	16	4	.800	2.97	27	27	6	0	2	0	184.2	174	77	61	9	2	49	0	178	7
Ellsworth, Winston-Salem	13	8	.619	3.29	26	26	7	0	0	0	164.1	158	79	60	6	4	68	2	104	18
D. Taylor, Prince William	11	5	.688	3.40	25	25	6	0	2	0	161.2	133	68	61	10	3	67	2	148	10
Aviles, Durham	9	11	.450	3.43	26	26	6	0	2	0	165.1	161	79	63	19	0	55	1	155	5
Valenzuela, Kinston	11	4	.733	3.61	23	21	4	1	2	1	149.2	133	66	60	13	5	41	0	110	9
Araujo, Winston-Salem	8	8	.500	3.65	34	15	3	8	3	2	125.2	115	61	51	8	4	44	1	61	6
Brown, Lynchburg*	10	7	.588	3.66	28	26	3	0	0	0	160.0	143	80	65	11	1	78	0	163	9
Leach, Salem	8	9	.471	3.67	21	21	6	0	1	0	144.2	136	78	59	12	6	50	1	82	1

Departmental Leaders: G—Aquino, 53; W—Cook, 16; L—Bass, Hartman, M. Leiter, Sanchez, H. Stewart, 13; Pct.—Henry, .818; GS—Cook, Hartman, Schreiber, 27; CG—Ellsworth, K. Leiter, Myers, 7; GF—Aquino, 42; ShO—Aguilera, Araujo, 3; Sv.—Downs, 21; IP—Cook, 184.2; H—Cook, 174; R—Hartman, 109; ER—M. Leiter, 87; HR—Aviles, 22; HB—K. Leiter, 12; BB—M. Leiter, 108; IBB—Evetts, 7; SO—Cook, 178; WP—Buchmier, 20.

(All Pitchers—Listed Alphabetically)

Pitcher—Club	W.	L.	Pct.	ERA.	G.	GS.	CG.	GF.	ShO.	Sv.	IP.	H.	R.	ER.	HR.	HB.	BB.	Int. BB.	SO.	WP.
Adamczak, Lynchburg	2	6	.250	1.17	45	0	0	35	0	11	69.1	56	14	9	1	2	22	5	43	2
Aguilera, Lynchburg	8	3	.727	2.34	13	13	6	0	3	0	88.1	72	29	23	3	6	28	1	101	6
Alexander, Hagerstown	2	2	.500	3.66	33	1	0	13	0	1	71.1	59	34	29	4	4	47	0	53	5
Aquino, Kinston	5	6	.455	2.70	53	0	0	42	0	20	70.0	50	21	21	3	3	37	4	78	2
Araujo, Winston	8	8	.500	3.65	34	15	3	8	3	2	125.2	115	61	51	8	4	44	1	61	6
Arias, Hagerstown	0	1	.000	3.28	14	0	0	6	0	1	24.2	18	12	9	1	1	16	1	12	1

Pitcher—Club	W.	L.	Pct.	ERA	G.	GS.	CG.	GF.	ShO.	Sv.	IP.	H.	R.	ER.	HR.	HB.	BB.	Int. BB.	SO.	WP.
Assenmacher, Durham*	6	11	.353	4.28	26	24	3	1	1	0	147.1	153	78	70	16	4	52	0	147	5
Aviles, Durham	9	11	.450	3.43	26	26	6	0	2	0	165.1	161	79	63	19	0	55	1	155	5
Barger, Durham*	0	4	.000	3.77	8	8	1	0	0	0	45.1	33	22	19	8	3	26	0	48	3
Bass, Salem	7	13	.350	5.96	25	20	2	2	0	0	116.1	156	90	77	15	5	41	1	52	4
Bell, Hagerstown*	0	0	.000	9.82	3	1	0	0	0	0	3.2	6	4	4	0	1	5	0	6	0
Bianchi, Hagerstown	2	8	.200	3.91	19	11	1	4	0	1	76.0	78	44	33	6	3	40	2	57	6
Blasucci, Prince William*	2	2	.500	3.75	7	6	0	1	0	0	24.0	21	13	10	1	0	17	0	22	1
Boyd, Hagerstown*	0	0	.000	18.00	1	0	0	1	0	0	1.0	2	2	2	0	0	1	0	1	2
Brosious, Salem	0	0	.000	5.59	4	0	0	1	0	0	9.2	13	8	6	1	0	4	0	3	3
Brown, Lynchburg*	10	7	.588	3.66	28	26	3	0	0	0	160.0	143	80	65	11	1	78	0	163	9
Buckley, Prince William	1	0	1.000	4.50	16	0	0	8	0	0	20.0	18	15	10	1	1	17	2	9	2
Buckmier, Prince William	9	8	.529	4.81	31	19	2	7	0	2	121.2	109	80	65	6	5	85	0	85	20
Bulls, Peninsula	5	3	.625	2.91	11	10	2	0	0	0	65.0	58	30	21	3	2	23	0	56	6
Cano, Durham	4	5	.444	3.10	20	9	4	6	1	1	81.1	68	35	28	6	4	29	2	53	3
Cappadona, Winston-Salem*	3	4	.429	2.50	35	0	0	28	0	7	57.2	56	18	16	2	0	20	1	35	1
Caraballo, Peninsula	0	0	.000	0.00	1	0	0	1	0	0	1.0	0	0	0	0	0	0	0	0	0
Carlie, Prince William*	0	0	.000	14.73	2	0	0	1	0	0	3.2	10	7	6	1	0	3	0	5	0
Castaneda, Prince William	0	0	.000	10.38	4	0	0	3	0	0	4.1	11	6	5	0	0	4	0	1	0
Castro, Kinston	2	4	.333	5.40	8	7	1	0	1	0	40.0	37	27	24	3	1	26	3	27	1
Clemons, Kinston	6	7	.462	3.50	20	11	1	5	1	3	92.2	93	43	36	7	0	35	1	71	4
Coatney, Salinas	0	1	.000	3.46	21	0	0	6	0	2	41.2	40	19	16	4	1	22	1	39	4
Coker, Peninsula	5	5	.500	3.93	24	19	2	1	1	1	110.0	105	57	48	9	2	60	2	91	6
Concepcion, Hagerstown	0	0	.000	81.00	1	0	0	0	0	0	0.1	0	3	3	0	0	3	0	0	0
Cook, Lynchburg	16	4	.800	2.97	27	27	6	0	2	0	184.2	174	77	61	9	2	49	0	178	7
Corder, Winston-Salem	3	4	.429	3.48	28	2	0	12	0	1	64.2	73	31	25	4	3	27	2	38	2
Cordoba, Prince William	8	2	.800	1.84	36	1	0	23	0	6	78.1	43	23	16	2	2	40	4	78	1
Cratch, Hagerstown	1	1	.500	2.60	3	3	1	0	1	0	17.1	16	6	5	0	2	6	0	9	1
Cullen, Kinston	3	6	.333	8.34	16	10	1	1	1	0	49.2	43	47	46	6	2	76	0	58	12
Day, Peninsula	0	0	.000	0.00	1	0	0	0	0	0	2.0	0	0	0	0	0	2	0	1	0
DeLaRosa, Prince William*	0	0	.000	0.00	1	0	0	1	0	0	0.2	1	0	0	0	0	0	0	1	0
Dooner, Hagerstown	4	1	.800	2.56	23	0	0	21	0	5	31.2	26	16	9	1	3	7	1	18	0
Downs, Prince William	2	4	.333	4.38	47	0	0	40	0	21	61.2	69	34	30	2	0	40	6	31	3
Edens, Lynchburg	1	1	.500	2.51	3	2	0	0	0	0	14.1	11	6	4	1	0	8	0	15	1
Elam, Kinston	0	0	.000	9.00	1	0	0	1	0	0	1.0	0	2	1	0	0	3	0	1	0
Ellsworth, Winston-Salem	13	8	.619	3.29	26	26	7	0	0	0	164.1	158	79	60	6	4	68	2	104	18
Esposito, Peninsula	0	1	.000	6.81	18	0	0	8	0	0	38.1	46	40	29	6	3	18	0	27	1
Evetts, Peninsula	9	9	.500	3.90	41	17	6	13	2	6	140.2	153	73	61	14	4	40	7	86	2
Faherty, Prince William*	2	3	.400	5.34	24	4	0	8	0	1	55.2	53	41	33	4	3	59	1	31	3
Felt, Prince William	8	8	.500	4.73	35	7	1	7	1	0	106.2	99	66	56	9	8	89	0	76	8
Ferguson, Peninsula	4	0	1.000	3.49	6	5	2	1	0	0	38.2	41	17	15	2	1	9	0	25	2
Gallagher, Kinston	1	1	.000	4.91	7	1	0	5	0	0	14.2	17	9	8	1	1	4	1	12	1
Garcia, Lynchburg	5	3	.625	2.65	34	2	0	21	0	2	54.1	45	22	16	3	2	36	2	56	9
Gordon, Prince William	1	0	1.000	4.42	14	0	0	8	0	1	18.1	19	13	9	0	1	18	0	21	3
Greco, Winston-Salem*	7	11	.389	3.87	33	23	3	5	2	0	155.2	165	89	67	11	1	83	2	79	15
Grubbs, Winston-Salem	4	3	.571	3.45	36	1	0	25	0	6	70.1	72	38	27	7	0	22	3	48	4
Habyan, Hagerstown	9	4	.692	3.54	13	13	4	0	0	0	81.1	64	41	32	6	0	33	0	81	5
Hartman, Salem	6	13	.316	4.76	27	27	3	0	0	0	160.2	169	109	85	14	4	75	1	74	13
Henry, Salem*	9	2	.818	3.47	16	16	0	0	0	0	85.2	80	44	33	7	5	65	0	56	2
Hill, Peninsula	0	0	.000	8.10	13	0	0	8	0	0	20.0	28	26	18	2	5	17	2	7	3
Holbrook, Kinston	9	10	.474	4.67	29	25	2	2	0	0	138.2	148	87	72	16	2	65	2	87	1
Holman, Prince William	7	4	.636	4.06	15	14	1	0	0	0	77.2	74	46	35	4	2	49	0	47	9
Howard, Kinston	2	0	1.000	1.99	9	9	0	0	0	0	31.2	25	7	7	3	0	8	0	22	1
Hudson, Salem	7	5	.583	3.71	39	9	2	22	1	6	104.1	102	58	43	6	3	20	2	67	11
Jensen, Lynchburg*	2	1	.667	2.37	9	7	0	2	0	0	38.0	34	10	10	2	1	7	0	32	0
Johnson, Prince William	7	5	.583	1.32	13	13	3	0	1	0	88.1	60	22	13	2	1	35	0	48	3
Jones, Durham	1	1	.500	3.86	4	3	1	1	0	0	18.2	22	9	8	3	0	2	0	13	1
Josephson, Durham	5	9	.357	2.97	45	0	0	28	0	5	88.0	76	32	29	10	3	43	5	69	7
Joslin, Salem*	2	2	.500	2.91	27	0	0	12	0	1	34.0	28	15	11	2	1	21	1	42	6
Kennard, Peninsula	0	1	.000	3.00	1	0	0	0	0	0	3	3	1	1	0	0	1	0	1	1
Kiecker, Winston-Salem	6	11	.353	4.38	29	19	5	8	1	1	137.2	142	86	67	12	1	55	2	82	12
Killingsworth, Salem	4	4	.500	4.28	46	0	0	31	0	7	88.1	87	50	42	7	3	47	3	65	7
Kramer, Salem	2	8	.200	9.85	12	11	0	0	0	0	53.0	63	66	58	14	4	34	0	35	7
Labay, Peninsula*	5	3	.625	2.98	10	10	4	0	1	0	60.1	54	31	20	3	3	14	0	41	1
Lamb, Peninsula	11	7	.611	4.45	25	25	0	0	0	0	147.2	140	78	73	15	2	76	0	90	8
Lance, Durham*	0	2	.000	7.54	30	2	0	9	0	1	37.0	39	34	31	7	3	25	1	23	4
Lavelle, Hagerstown	4	2	.667	3.76	25	4	1	11	0	5	76.2	80	32	32	2	2	30	5	43	1
Leach, Salem	8	9	.471	3.67	21	21	6	0	1	0	144.2	136	78	59	12	6	50	1	82	1
Ledbetter, Hagerstown	4	3	.571	3.06	27	10	4	11	2	2	97.0	90	40	33	3	2	43	1	62	12
Leggatt, Durham	6	0	1.000	2.13	19	0	0	5	0	2	38.0	27	11	9	1	0	15	1	29	1
K. Leiter, Hagerstown	5	10	.333	4.55	25	20	7	1	0	0	140.1	149	88	71	9	12	75	3	76	8
M. Leiter, Hagerstown	8	13	.381	5.62	27	24	5	2	1	0	139.1	132	96	87	13	8	108	2	105	13
Lockhart, Winston-Salem*	2	5	.286	6.16	28	4	0	9	0	0	57.0	80	52	39	6	1	33	0	32	3
Long, Peninsula	0	0	.000	0.00	1	0	0	0	0	0	1.0	1	0	0	0	0	1	0	1	0
Lundgren, Lynchburg	8	1	.889	2.95	33	10	3	9	0	2	113.0	103	48	37	11	2	33	1	83	3
Lychak, Kinston*	5	2	.714	3.15	44	1	0	24	0	7	65.2	68	33	23	3	2	29	2	51	3
Machin, Peninsula*	3	4	.429	4.24	17	14	0	0	0	0	91.1	100	53	43	10	3	37	1	75	1
Maki, Salem	0	0	.000	12.15	2	0	0	0	0	0	6.2	14	16	9	3	0	6	0	5	3
McKay, Kinston*	2	3	.400	2.58	27	1	0	13	0	4	59.1	45	22	17	5	0	26	0	59	0
McKelvey, Prince William	4	3	.571	3.05	13	11	0	1	0	0	59.0	43	24	20	4	10	36	0	68	5
Menard, Peninsula	11	5	.688	3.91	44	8	0	28	0	6	96.2	118	53	42	9	8	23	3	60	10
Mesa, Kinston	5	2	.714	3.91	10	9	0	0	0	0	50.2	51	23	22	2	0	28	0	24	2
Milacki, Hagerstown	4	5	.444	3.36	15	13	1	1	0	0	77.2	69	35	29	2	0	48	0	62	6
Morel, Hagerstown	2	5	.286	4.08	49	1	0	30	0	7	57.1	52	28	26	5	0	23	3	43	7
Moretti, Hagerstown	4	3	.571	4.21	25	0	0	19	0	4	36.1	39	24	17	3	0	19	1	34	3
Mortillaro, Durham	6	6	.500	4.92	24	14	1	1	1	0	93.1	99	54	51	13	0	33	1	73	6
Morton, Peninsula*	2	6	.250	5.14	19	8	1	4	0	0	68.1	70	52	39	11	4	31	1	53	5
Moses, Salem*	0	0	.000	3.65	9	0	0	4	0	0	12.1	11	6	5	3	0	4	0	12	0
Mota, Peninsula*	0	0	.000	0.00	1	0	0	0	0	0	2.0	1	0	0	0	0	1	0	1	0
Mulcahy, Hagerstown*	2	10	.167	5.42	42	8	2	18	0	7	88.0	95	64	53	8	0	53	2	84	7
Murray, Lynchburg	4	4	.500	3.14	43	0	0	29	0	6	57.1	51	32	20	5	2	24	2	41	1
Myers, Lynchburg*	13	5	.722	2.06	23	22	7	1	1	0	157.0	123	46	36	7	3	61	0	171	11
Parkins, Winston-Salem	5	8	.385	4.48	20	17	2	2	1	0	74.1	74	48	37	4	3	54	0	53	7
Peterson, Winston-Salem	0	2	.000	4.40	33	0	0	17	0	1	59.1	58	38	29	8	1	33	2	49	7

Pitcher—Club	W.	L.	Pct.	ERA.	G.	GS.	CG.	GF.	ShO.	Sv.	IP.	H.	R.	ER.	HR.	HB.	BB.	Int. BB.	SO.	WP.
Pruitt, Lynchburg*	6	3	.667	1.88	39	2	0	13	0	5	71.2	53	21	15	3	2	12	2	69	1
Raczka, Hagerstown*	1	5	.167	8.10	8	7	0	0	0	0	36.2	44	35	33	7	0	35	1	36	3
Reichard, Salem	7	4	.636	2.63	44	0	0	36	0	14	82.0	50	29	24	5	5	51	1	98	5
Reilly, Peninsula	0	4	.000	6.75	19	2	0	12	0	5	21.1	26	28	16	2	5	28	0	16	4
Rice, Hagerstown	6	12	.333	5.56	24	21	4	1	0	0	126.1	153	86	78	13	4	57	3	75	5
Riddle, Winston-Salem	1	5	.167	4.43	13	7	1	2	0	1	42.2	39	28	21	1	4	29	0	26	4
Rivas, Kinston	0	0	.000	9.00	1	0	0	1	0	0	2.0	2	2	2	0	2	2	0	0	0
Rivera, Durham	3	3	.500	4.35	45	1	0	21	0	8	82.2	93	44	40	10	5	31	3	72	2
Robbins, Kinston	0	3	.000	5.73	22	3	0	6	0	0	59.2	71	47	38	3	0	46	3	48	5
Rogers, Durham	3	1	.750	4.24	13	0	0	8	0	2	23.1	15	11	11	4	0	10	0	22	3
Rosario, Durham*	1	0	1.000	0.00	1	1	0	0	0	0	7.0	2	0	0	0	0	4	0	5	1
Sanchez, Prince William*	7	13	.350	3.87	26	24	4	1	2	0	146.1	142	72	63	7	8	67	1	95	12
Sauveur, Prince William*	3	3	.500	3.13	10	10	0	0	0	0	54.2	43	22	19	5	1	31	0	54	3
Scarpetta, Salem*	6	9	.400	4.86	25	22	1	1	1	0	129.2	156	85	70	13	3	37	1	86	6
Schreiber, Durham*	8	8	.500	4.32	28	27	2	0	0	0	154.1	152	89	74	14	10	85	2	82	15
Segura, Kinston	7	4	.636	3.98	16	14	2	1	1	0	97.1	88	48	43	7	1	35	1	55	7
Seiler, Peninsula*	6	3	.667	4.65	31	4	0	7	0	2	60.0	64	37	31	1	1	30	2	41	4
Shanks, Kinston	3	1	.750	1.54	9	4	0	2	0	0	41.0	32	9	7	2	1	14	0	24	1
Smith, Salem	6	3	.667	4.30	16	12	0	1	0	0	67.0	67	40	32	6	2	44	1	38	10
Soriano, Kinston	0	0	.000	6.00	2	0	0	2	0	0	3.0	5	2	2	0	0	0	0	2	0
Sprowl, Kinston*	1	5	.167	3.97	11	9	1	1	0	0	47.2	47	29	21	5	3	30	0	27	0
H. Wa. Stewart, Peninsula	9	3	.750	2.27	14	13	2	0	1	0	91.0	67	33	23	6	2	37	2	56	5
He. Stewart, Winston-Salem*	6	13	.316	4.88	27	26	3	0	1	0	142.0	155	94	77	14	4	62	1	95	8
Stone, Prince William	3	4	.429	3.78	39	4	0	13	0	3	85.2	68	40	36	4	4	58	4	70	6
D. Taylor, Prince William	11	5	.688	3.40	25	25	6	0	2	0	161.2	133	68	61	10	3	67	2	148	10
J. Taylor, Kinston	3	3	.500	3.58	39	0	0	19	0	2	73.0	42	33	29	4	6	45	2	90	9
Valenzuela, Kinston	11	4	.733	3.61	23	21	4	1	2	1	149.2	133	66	60	13	5	41	0	110	9
Walsh, Kinston*	1	1	.500	2.35	3	0	0	1	0	1	7.2	8	2	2	0	0	2	0	9	0
Warner, Peninsula*	2	2	.500	3.62	9	3	0	1	0	0	37.1	27	18	15	0	1	11	3	37	6
Weatherford, Peninsula	3	6	.333	4.41	24	11	1	2	0	0	81.2	72	46	40	13	3	45	1	61	10
Weissman, Lynchburg	9	9	.500	3.94	25	20	0	0	0	0	121.0	124	65	53	9	8	57	1	95	12
Welchel, Hagerstown	4	0	1.000	1.01	4	4	1	0	0	0	26.2	22	4	3	0	0	7	0	24	1
Wells, Kinston*	1	6	.143	4.71	7	7	0	0	0	0	42.0	51	29	22	1	1	19	1	44	4
Williams, Prince William	0	1	.000	7.43	4	2	0	2	0	0	13.1	18	12	11	3	1	8	0	2	1
Witt, Peninsula	4	7	.364	6.32	16	14	1	0	0	0	74.0	89	59	52	7	11	35	3	49	5
Wright, Peninsula	3	1	.750	3.62	17	0	0	10	0	2	32.1	26	14	13	2	3	15	0	21	0
Yearout, Kinston*	5	1	.833	2.66	8	8	1	0	0	0	47.1	38	15	14	3	1	19	0	43	0
Youmans, Lynchburg	5	2	.714	3.63	7	7	3	0	0	0	39.2	31	19	16	3	1	27	0	45	2
Ziem, Durham	5	4	.556	3.88	49	0	0	41	0	12	67.1	49	30	29	7	2	26	1	55	3

BALKS—Sanchez, 5; Brown, Schreiber, 4 each; Aviles, Garcia, Greco, H. Stewart, 3 each; Aguilera, Araujo, Esposito, Kiecker, McKelvey, Riddle, Robbins, Valenzuela, Weatherford, Witt, Ziem, 2 each; Aquino, Assenmacher, Bass, Brosious, Buckmier, Cano, Cook, Downs, Elam, Ellsworth, Josephson, Joslin, Labay, Lavelle, K. Leiter, M. Leiter, Mesa, Mortillaro, Morton, Murray, Raczka, Scarpetta, Shanks, Warner, Wells, 1 each.

COMBINATION SHUTOUTS—Lamb-Cano-Ziem, Lamb-Ziem, Schreiber-Leggatt, Schreiber-Rivera-Ziem, Lamb-Rivera-Ziem, Durham; Milacki-Bell-Ledbetter, Rice-Arias-Mulcahey, Rice-Ledbetter, Welchel-Mulcahey, K. Leiter-Dooner, Hagerstown; Clemons-McKay, Shanks-Sprowl, Kinston; Weissman-Pruitt-Garcia, Jensen-Adamczak, Brown-Pruitt-Murray, Myers-Adamczak, Jensen-Garcia, Lynchburg; Warner-Morel-Evetts-Seiler, Peninsula; Sauveur-Felt-Downs, Prince William; Henry-Killingsworth, Bass-Killingsworth, Henry-Hudson, Scarpetta-Hudson, Salem; Ellsworth-Cappadona 2, Stewart-Grubbs, Ellsworth-Grubbs, Parkins-Grubbs, Winston-Salem.

NO-HIT GAME—Parkins, Winston-Salem, defeated Durham, 3-0, June 7.

Florida State League

CLASS A

CHAMPIONSHIP WINNERS IN PREVIOUS YEARS

1919—Sanford°...............................	.605
Orlando°..............................	.703
1920—Tampa	.654
Tampa	.722
1921—Orlando	.635
1922—St. Petersburg	.503
St. Petersburg	.618
1923—Orlando	.667
Orlando	.678
1924—Lakeland	.695
Lakeland	.683
1925—St. Petersburg	.667
Tampa†	.696
1926—Sanford	.647
Sanford	.623
1927—Orlando†	.600
Miami	.661
1928-35—Did not operate.	
1936—Gainesville	.542
St. Augustine (4th)†	.492
1937—Gainesville§	.616
1938—Leesburg	.626
Gainesville (2nd)‡	.615
1939—Sanford§	.787
1940—Daytona Beach	.619
Orlando (4th)‡	.507
1941—St. Augustine	.659
Leesburg (4th)‡	.488
1942-45—Did not operate.	
1946—Orlando§	.681
1947—St. Augustine	.625
Gainesville (2nd)‡	.584
1948—Orlando	.643
Daytona Beach (2nd)‡	.616

1949—Gainesville	.635
St. Augustine (3rd)‡	.556
1950—Orlando	.629
DeLand (3rd)‡	.590
1951—DeLand§	.643
1952—DeLand x	.704
Palatka (3rd)‡	.569
1953—Daytona Beach†	.657
DeLand	.703
1954—Jacksonville Beach.............	.629
Lakeland†	.594
1955—Orlando	.671
Orlando	.643
1956—Cocoa	.614
Cocoa	.671
1957—Palatka	.629
Tampa†	.681
1958—St. Petersburg	.732
St. Petersburg	.681
1959—Tampa	.591
St. Petersburg†	.612
1960—Lakeland	.731
Palatka†	.614
1961—Tampa†	.710
Sarasota	.696
1962—Sarasota	.689
Fort Lauderdale†	.623
1963—Sarasota	.645
Sarasota	.667
1964—Fort Lauderdale†	.629
St. Petersburg	.594
1965—Fort Lauderdale	.627
Fort Lauderdale	.634
1966—Leesburg†	.781
St. Petersburg	.700

1967—St. Petersburg y	.691
Orlando	.638
1968—Miami	.613
Orlando z	.579
1969—Miami a	.606
Orlando	.606
1970—Miami b	.662
St. Petersburg	.600
1971—Miami b	.667
Daytona Beach	.586
1972—Miami c	.562
Daytona Beach	.606
1973—St. Petersburg d	.575
West Palm Beach	.580
1974—West Palm Beach d	.598
Fort Lauderdale	.626
1975—St. Petersburg d	.652
Miami	.581
1976—Tampa	.559
Lakeland d	.536
1977—Lakeland d	.616
West Palm Beach	.583
1978—Lakeland	.565
Miami§	.539
1979—Fort Lauderdale	.643
Winter Haven e	.577
1980—Daytona Beach	.628
Fort Lauderdale d	.606
1981—Fort Myers	.554
Daytona Beach f	.504
1982—Fort Lauderdale f	.621
Tampa	.546
1983—Daytona Beach	.634
Vero Beach f	.515

°Split-season playoff abandoned after each team won three games. †Won split-season playoff. ‡Won four-club playoff. §Won championship and four-club playoff. xWon both halves of split season. yLeague divided into Eastern and Western divisions with split season. St. Petersburg and Orlando won both halves of split season; St. Petersburg won playoff. zLeague divided into Eastern and Western divisions. Miami won regular-season pennant on basis of highest won-lost percentage. Orlando won four-club playoff involving first two teams in each division. aLeague divided into Southern and Central divisions. Miami won playoff between division leaders. (NOTE—Pennant awarded to playoff winner in 1936.) bLeague divided into Eastern and Western divisions. Miami won regular-season pennant on basis of highest won-loss percentage, and also won four-club playoff involving first two teams in each division. cLeague divided into Eastern and Western divisions. Won four-club playoff involving first two teams in each division. dLeague divided into Northern and Southern divisions. Won four-club playoff involving first two teams in each division. eLeague divided into Northern and Southern divisions. Same two clubs won both halves; won playoffs. fWon split-season playoff.

STANDING OF CLUBS AT CLOSE OF FIRST HALF, JUNE 20

NORTHERN DIVISION

Club	W.	L.	T.	Pct.	G.B.
Tampa (Reds)	44	32	0	.579	....
Daytona Beach (Astros)...................	43	34	0	.558	1½
St. Petersburg (Cardinals)	39	38	0	.506	5½
Winter Haven (Red Sox)	36	40	0	.474	8
Lakeland (Tigers)...........................	22	56	0	.282	23

SOUTHERN DIVISION

Club	W.	L.	T.	Pct.	G.B.
Fort Myers (Royals)	48	27	0	.640	....
West Palm Beach (Expos).................	45	33	0	.577	4½
Vero Beach (Dodgers)	40	38	0	.513	9½
Fort Lauderdale (Yankees)	36	40	0	.474	12½
Miami (Padres)	29	44	0	.397	18

STANDING OF CLUBS AT CLOSE OF SECOND HALF, AUGUST 30

NORTHERN DIVISION

Club	W.	L.	T.	Pct.	G.B.
Daytona Beach (Astros)	39	28	0	.582	....
Winter Haven (Red Sox)	34	34	0	.500	5½
St. Petersburg (Cardinals)	32	35	0	.478	7
Tampa (Reds)	30	33	0	.476	7
Lakeland (Tigers)..........................	24	42	0	.364	14½

SOUTHERN DIVISION

Club	W.	L.	T.	Pct.	G.B.
Fort Lauderdale (Yankees).................	38	28	0	.576	....
Vero Beach (Dodgers)	39	29	0	.574	....
Miami (Padres)	35	30	0	.538	2½
Fort Myers (Royals)	33	33	0	.500	5
West Palm Beach (Expos)	27	39	0	.409	11

COMPOSITE STANDING OF CLUBS AT CLOSE OF SEASON, AUGUST 30

Club	FtM.	Day.	V.B.	Tam.	FtL.	WPB	St.P.	WH	Mia.	Lak.	W.	L.	T.	Pct.	G.B.
Fort Myers (Royals)	....	7	13	6	11	13	8	5	12	6	81	60	0	.574	....
Daytona Beach (Astros)...................	2	....	6	13	3	6	13	16	7	16	82	62	0	.569	½
Vero Beach (Dodgers)...................	11	4	....	4	17	11	6	5	13	8	79	67	0	.541	4½
Tampa (Reds)	3	11	6	....	5	5	13	10	4	17	74	65	0	.532	6
Fort Lauderdale (Yankees)...............	13	6	7	4	....	14	6	6	14	4	74	68	0	.521	7½
West Palm Beach (Expos)............	11	4	13	5	8	....	5	8	13	5	72	72	0	.500	10½
St. Petersburg (Cardinals)	2	11	4	11	4	5	....	11	6	17	71	73	0	.493	11½
Winter Haven (Red Sox)	5	8	5	14	4	2	12	....	3	17	70	74	0	.486	12½
Miami (Padres)	9	3	11	3	10	11	3	6	....	8	64	74	0	.464	15½
Lakeland (Tigers).........................	4	8	2	5	6	5	7	7	2	....	46	98	0	.319	36½

Major league affiliations in parentheses.

Playoffs—Fort Lauderdale defeated Fort Myers, two games to none; Tampa defeated Daytona Beach, two games to none, and Fort Lauderdale defeated Tampa, three games to two, to win league championship.

Regular-Season Attendance—Daytona Beach, 102,510; Fort Lauderdale, 50,201; Fort Myers, 137,553; Lakeland, 36,107; Miami, 38,313; St. Petersburg, 144,692; Tampa, 62,776; Vero Beach, 81,453; West Palm Beach, 134,771; Winter Haven, 18,249. Total, 806,625. All-Star Attendance: 3,749.

Managers—Daytona Beach, Dave Cripe; Fort Lauderdale, Barry Foote; Fort Myers, Tom Jones; Lakeland, Bill Fahey; Miami, Steve Smith; St. Petersburg, Jim Riggleman; Tampa, Marc Bombard; Vero Beach, Stan Wasiak; West Palm Beach, Tommy Thompson; Winter Haven, Dave Holt.

All-Star Team: Northern Division—1B—Joe Birriel, Winter Haven; Marty Pevey, St. Petersburg; 2B—Jim Walewander, Lakeland; 3B—Jeff Treadway, Tampa; SS—Nelson Rood, Daytona Beach; OF—Tracy Jones, Tampa; Curtis Burke, Daytona Beach; Dana Williams, Winter Haven; Mike Stellern, Daytona Beach; C—Terry McGriff, Tampa; Robbie Wine, Daytona Beach; Mike Williams, Lakeland; P—Billy Hawley, Tampa; Jeff Sellers, Winter Haven; Chuck Mathews, Daytona Beach; Nelson Torres, Winter Haven; Jeff Montgomery, Tampa. Southern Division—1B—Mike Hocutt, West Palm Beach; Tim Richardson, Fort Myers; 2B—Dave Corman, Miami; 3B—Jeff Hamilton, Vero Beach; SS—Gary Newsom, Vero Beach; Tom Brassil, Miami; OF—Wayne Kirby, Vero Beach; Winston Ficklin, Fort Lauderdale; Bill Moore, West Palm Beach; Vince Beringhele, Vero Beach; C—Frank Castro, Miami; Jim Cecchini, West Palm Beach; P—Mike McClain, Miami; Glenn Kinns, West Palm Beach; Eric Plunk, Fort Lauderdale; Lance McCullers, Miami; Randy Huber, West Palm Beach.

(Compiled by Howe News Bureau, Boston, Mass.)

CLUB BATTING

Club	Pct.	G.	AB.	R.	OR.	H.	TB.	2B.	3B.	HR.	RBI.	GW.	SH.	SF.	HP.	BB.	Int. BB.	SO.	SB.	CS.	LOB.
Daytona Beach	.262	144	4679	760	562	1224	1763	234	52	67	668	72	51	47	40	668	52	878	121	55	1080
Tampa	.258	139	4329	559	507	1117	1447	180	21	36	475	61	52	49	35	592	50	678	104	58	1055
Vero Beach	.257	146	4559	649	605	1172	1481	174	36	21	555	67	71	47	60	716	47	733	192	115	1137
Fort Lauderdale	.256	142	4469	626	591	1143	1636	194	37	75	534	64	35	45	46	651	28	737	168	103	1068
Winter Haven	.255	144	4560	565	634	1165	1543	167	38	45	497	66	36	46	38	608	33	735	110	80	1093
Fort Myers	.252	141	4455	681	608	1124	1481	150	33	47	566	68	69	43	43	624	21	734	211	75	1020
West Palm Beach	.248	144	4619	605	608	1145	1512	167	16	56	533	60	45	39	53	683	57	642	98	79	1134
Miami	.247	138	4344	490	555	1073	1390	147	25	40	421	52	49	42	30	511	35	777	90	80	953
St. Petersburg	.242	144	4491	572	600	1088	1454	171	42	37	494	61	66	52	31	577	36	765	106	49	1061
Lakeland	.236	144	4397	520	757	1037	1303	140	27	24	441	35	47	42	23	596	30	812	151	84	1012

INDIVIDUAL BATTING

(Leading Qualifiers for Batting Championship—394 or More Plate Appearances)

*Bats lefthanded. †Switch-hitter.

Player and Club	Pct.	G.	AB.	R.	H.	TB.	2B.	3B.	HR.	RBI.	GW.	SH.	SF.	HP.	BB.	Int. BB.	SO.	SB.	CS.
Williams, Dana, Winter Haven	.327	135	511	65	167	213	27	8	1	54	10	1	7	5	46	5	44	18	12
Newsom, Gary, Vero Beach	.315	98	330	59	104	137	14	8	1	49	8	8	5	6	53	1	23	17	11
Treadway, H. Jeffrey, Tampa*	.309	119	372	44	115	131	16	0	0	44	3	7	3	5	54	8	40	13	7
Pevey, Marty, St. Petersburg*	.308	128	441	53	136	166	16	4	2	60	6	6	2	1	48	7	47	7	7
Botkin, Michael, Daytona Beach*	.302	131	420	71	127	162	20	6	1	59	8	4	5	1	75	6	35	11	6
Moore, William, West Palm Beach	.300	143	484	102	145	245	26	4	22	94	17	0	4	9	112	11	76	8	4
Cannizzaro, Chris, Winter Haven†	.297	122	438	60	130	158	13	6	1	48	5	2	8	1	69	5	29	14	6
Lombardi, Phillip, Fort Lauderdale	.293	127	393	58	115	163	20	2	8	70	10	6	4	6	85	1	37	22	4
Richardson, Timothy, Fort Myers	.290	133	489	59	142	157	5	5	0	67	8	3	4	2	58	0	27	18	3
Rood, Nelson, Daytona Beach	.289	89	329	84	95	120	12	5	1	28	2	2	0	4	74	1	50	40	10

Departmental Leaders: G—Hocutt, Moore, Ramsey, 143; AB—Ramsey, 529; R—Moore, 102; H—D. Williams, 167; TB—Moore, 245; 2B—Wine, 36; 3B—S. Robinson, 16; HR—Moore, 22; RBI—Hocutt, 100; GWRBI—Moore, 17; SH—Shuffield, 21; SF—Hunt, 10; HP—C. Burke, 11; BB—Moore, 112; IBB—Martin, Moore, 11; SO—Ramsey, 130; SB—Ramsey, 69; CS—Ramsey, 30.

(All Players—Listed Alphabetically)

Player and Club	Pct.	G.	AB.	R.	H.	TB.	2B.	3B.	HR.	RBI.	GW.	SH.	SF.	HP.	BB.	Int. BB.	SO.	SB.	CS.
Abner, Benjamin, West Palm Beach	.232	39	125	7	29	39	7	0	1	9	0	0	2	0	6	3	15	1	0
Allaire, Karl, Daytona Beach*	.232	52	151	24	35	47	6	3	0	14	2	3	2	0	36	3	40	5	4
Allen, Edward, Fort Myers	.257	136	412	64	106	116	4	3	0	42	7	6	1	3	78	2	97	22	20
Amante, Thomas, St. Petersburg	.272	102	235	27	64	81	15	1	0	28	4	1	6	2	26	1	47	1	2
Arce, Lorenzo, Lakeland	.167	34	102	12	17	20	1	1	0	5	0	2	0	1	21	0	10	3	1
Ashkinazy, Allan, Winter Haven	.157	63	115	19	18	19	1	0	0	9	0	5	0	0	22	0	5	3	9
Austin, Terry, Miami	.233	113	386	47	90	108	12	0	2	18	1	5	0	4	46	4	78	16	12
Bachman, Kent, West Palm Beach	.159	14	44	2	7	9	2	0	0	0	0	0	0	0	2	0	10	1	0
Baker, Derrell, West Palm Beach	.300	67	227	39	68	93	11	1	4	36	3	2	4	4	44	2	14	1	3
Baker, Mark, Daytona Beach	.000	17	1	0	0	0	0	0	0	0	0	0	0	0	1	0	0	0	0
Baker, Robert, Lakeland*	.200	18	40	7	8	10	2	0	0	5	1	0	0	2	15	1	9	1	3
Balcomb, Alan, Vero Beach†	.237	90	228	27	54	65	11	0	0	26	1	0	2	3	33	5	25	5	2
Barrett, Timothy, West Palm Beach*	.063	11	16	1	1	2	1	0	0	1	0	0	1	0	2	0	6	0	0
Bartlett, Charles, Vero Beach	.283	41	106	14	30	35	2	0	1	12	2	0	0	0	14	0	19	2	1
Belanger, Barry, West Palm Beach*	.250	48	4	0	1	1	0	0	0	0	0	0	0	0	1	0	1	0	0
Beringhele, Vincent, Vero Beach	.256	124	367	63	94	119	20	1	1	49	6	3	2	3	100	5	52	10	7
Berti, Donald, Daytona Beach	.322	48	121	22	39	57	5	2	3	22	3	1	2	0	13	1	20	1	0
Birriel, Jose, Winter Haven*	.238	129	453	52	108	169	13	0	16	69	12	0	7	3	68	7	76	1	2
Blair, Fred, West Palm Beach	.247	92	247	29	61	83	10	0	4	40	2	1	4	2	44	2	36	2	1
Blair, Michael, Vero Beach	.272	74	246	23	67	76	6	0	1	45	7	0	3	3	18	7	13	1	2
Blaser, Mark, Fort Lauderdale	.242	81	273	36	66	108	12	3	8	44	6	1	4	1	27	2	47	7	0
Boever, Daniel, Tampa	.217	10	23	3	5	5	0	0	0	4	0	0	0	0	4	1	4	0	0
Boever, Joseph, St. Petersburg	.667	48	3	0	2	2	0	0	0	1	0	0	0	0	0	0	1	0	1
Bombard, Richard, Daytona Beach	.000	30	3	0	0	0	0	0	0	0	0	0	0	0	0	0	0	0	0
Bonk, Thomas, Winter Haven*	.251	65	191	13	48	62	6	1	2	32	3	1	1	0	16	1	23	0	1
Botkin, Michael, Daytona Beach*	.302	131	420	71	127	162	20	6	1	59	8	4	5	1	75	6	35	11	6
Boyles, John, Tampa	.125	18	16	0	2	2	0	0	0	1	0	0	0	0	0	0	8	0	1
Brahs, Gary, West Palm Beach	.000	20	24	0	0	0	0	0	0	0	0	0	0	0	1	0	0	0	0
Brassil, Thomas, Miami	.277	126	447	44	124	155	13	3	4	53	6	7	4	1	30	1	42	5	7
Braun, Randall, Daytona Beach*	.271	51	177	26	48	69	6	3	3	28	3	1	4	0	23	2	22	11	1
Brock, Eric, Vero Beach*	.185	37	108	12	20	29	4	1	1	10	1	1	1	1	28	0	28	0	5
Burke, Curtis, Daytona Beach	.265	86	306	68	81	149	22	5	12	70	8	0	3	11	45	5	59	5	0
Burks, Ellis, Winter Haven	.256	112	375	52	96	137	15	4	6	43	5	1	5	4	42	1	68	29	8
Burrell, Kevin, Winter Haven	.248	96	323	27	80	118	15	4	5	31	2	4	0	1	20	2	80	0	4
Burwell, Phil, St. Petersburg	.000	22	1	0	0	0	0	0	0	0	0	0	0	0	1	0	0	0	0
Cadahia, C. Benito, Fort Myers	.279	29	43	12	12	16	4	0	0	10	1	1	3	0	8	0	5	0	0
Caffrey, Robert, West Palm Beach	.132	12	38	4	5	8	0	0	1	3	0	0	1	0	3	0	14	0	1
Cahill, Mark, St. Petersburg	.167	45	6	1	1	1	0	0	0	2	0	1	0	0	2	0	3	0	0

Player and Club	Pct.	G.	AB.	R.	H.	TB.	2B.	3B.	HR.	RBI.	GW.	SH.	SF.	HP.	BB.	Int. BB.	SO.	SB.	CS.
Calvert, Mark, Tampa	.333	10	3	0	1	1	0	0	0	0	0	1	0	1	0	0	1	0	1
Camelo, Peter, West Palm Beach°	.216	103	273	32	59	80	13	1	2	30	3	0	3	3	55	4	45	6	3
Cannizzaro, Chris, Winter Haven†	.297	122	438	60	130	158	13	6	1	48	5	2	8	1	69	5	29	14	6
Carpenter, Glenn, Daytona Beach	.295	83	281	45	83	112	17	0	4	43	2	3	4	3	39	1	40	2	3
Castro, Frank, Miami	.225	124	395	50	89	127	14	0	8	49	7	0	6	2	63	1	70	3	6
Caulfield, Thomas, St. Petersburg	.000	30	1	0	0	0	0	0	0	0	0	0	0	0	0	0	0	0	0
Cecchini, James, West Palm Beach	.236	108	356	34	84	108	15	0	3	40	6	4	2	7	60	3	37	1	2
Cerefin, Michael, Daytona Beach°	.143	23	21	2	3	3	0	0	0	2	0	3	0	0	2	0	14	0	0
Champion, Randall, St. Pete.†	.158	15	19	0	3	4	1	0	0	0	0	0	0	0	2	0	5	0	0
Chapman, Ronald, Fort Lauderdale†	.260	97	281	56	73	88	9	3	0	19	1	5	2	5	45	0	19	31	10
Charlton, Norman, West Palm Beach°	.000	8	6	0	0	0	0	0	0	0	0	0	0	0	0	0	3	0	0
Cherry, Michael, Vero Beach	.333	3	3	0	1	1	0	0	0	0	0	0	0	0	0	0	1	0	0
Cherry, Paul, St. Petersburg°	.103	37	29	2	3	4	1	0	0	0	0	0	0	0	3	0	12	0	0
Childers, Jeffrey, Miami	.111	36	9	1	1	1	0	0	0	1	0	2	0	0	4	0	4	0	0
Citari, Joseph, Fort Myers	.237	59	198	41	47	104	12	0	15	47	6	1	3	4	46	2	56	2	3
Clark, Henry, Daytona Beach	.257	21	70	10	18	22	4	0	0	13	3	2	0	0	9	1	9	1	0
Cloninger, Darin, 3 Mia.-29 Ft.L.	1.000	32	1	2	1	1	0	0	0	0	0	0	0	0	0	0	0	0	0
Cobb, Robert, West Palm Beach°	.233	59	193	21	45	49	4	0	0	15	1	1	1	5	23	4	20	4	4
Corman, David, Miami	.288	127	420	75	121	152	16	6	1	28	2	4	1	2	108	6	69	11	11
Cunningham, Michael, Vero Beach	.167	14	12	0	2	2	0	0	0	0	0	2	0	0	2	0	6	0	0
Cutshall, William, West Palm Beach°	.600	5	5	1	3	3	0	0	0	0	0	0	0	0	0	0	2	0	1
Daggy, Robert, Lakeland°	.234	125	385	54	90	139	19	6	6	35	3	2	3	0	55	2	74	19	11
Daniel, P. Clay, Tampa†	.400	4	5	0	2	2	0	0	0	1	0	0	0	0	0	0	0	0	0
Datz, Jeffrey, Daytona Beach	.217	11	23	5	5	10	2	0	1	5	0	0	0	3	0	0	3	0	0
Davis, Ronald, Lakeland°	.130	28	69	9	9	9	0	0	0	4	0	0	0	4	16	1	13	0	0
Delgado, Juan, Daytona Beach	.268	112	396	52	106	141	16	5	3	41	3	2	4	2	42	5	65	5	6
DelRosario, Manuel, Miami†	.176	25	34	4	6	8	0	1	0	1	0	1	0	0	2	0	4	1	4
Destrade, Orestes, Fort Lauderdale†	.221	95	308	40	68	122	14	2	12	57	5	1	6	2	64	8	82	3	4
Dibble, Robert, Tampa°	.250	15	12	2	3	3	0	0	0	0	0	0	0	0	2	0	5	0	0
Dillard, David, Miami°	.236	116	326	53	77	125	9	6	9	45	3	5	7	5	44	6	76	12	4
Dophied, W. Tracy, Daytona Beach°	.227	41	119	13	27	34	5	1	0	18	1	2	0	1	14	0	29	2	2
Dunlop, David, Miami	.212	87	193	20	41	46	5	0	0	16	1	1	2	2	28	1	39	4	5
Dunn, Gregory, St. Petersburg	.158	30	19	0	3	3	0	0	0	0	0	1	0	0	1	0	7	0	0
Eagar, Stephen, Lakeland	.234	42	124	9	29	34	3	1	0	16	0	0	2	0	18	1	17	2	1
Edmiston, Craig, Lakeland	.188	13	32	2	6	7	1	0	0	5	0	1	0	1	3	0	11	1	0
Epple, Thomas, St. Petersburg†	.100	32	20	1	2	2	0	0	0	1	0	3	1	0	0	0	5	0	0
Erdmann, Frederick, Lakeland	.180	43	122	14	22	25	1	1	0	11	0	1	1	0	16	2	20	0	1
Ergle, Robert, Tampa°	.000	13	2	0	0	0	0	0	0	0	0	0	0	0	0	0	1	0	0
Falls, Robert, Daytona Beach†	.220	84	227	24	50	57	7	0	0	14	3	4	0	2	21	2	44	2	2
Fennell, Michael, Fort Lauderdale°	.236	54	140	10	33	48	6	3	1	11	1	1	1	1	10	3	37	0	2
Ficklin, Winston, Fort Lauderdale†	.279	122	441	72	123	162	18	6	3	36	4	4	5	5	61	3	62	30	20
Flores, David, West Palm Beach	.250	51	12	1	3	3	0	0	0	2	1	0	0	1	0	0	3	0	0
Fortaleza, Raymond, Fort Lauderdale	1.000	1	1	0	1	1	0	0	0	0	0	0	0	0	0	0	0	0	0
Freeman, Martin, Lakeland	.151	51	159	19	24	29	5	0	0	9	1	0	0	1	14	2	37	5	0
Friedrich, Michael, Daytona Beach	.000	25	18	0	0	0	0	0	0	0	0	0	2	0	0	1	0	9	0
Frierson, John, Miami	.223	100	318	29	71	101	12	3	4	39	6	1	2	4	23	2	63	4	4
Fulgencio, Elvin, Tampa	.203	91	207	14	42	47	3	1	0	23	1	1	0	3	12	1	57	2	3
Galvez, Balvino, Vero Beach	.273	28	33	2	9	11	2	0	0	2	1	1	0	0	1	0	7	0	0
Geels, Rob, Winter Haven°	.192	76	182	13	35	37	2	0	0	20	2	2	2	5	53	1	40	0	5
Gentle, Michael, Vero Beach°	.000	12	2	1	0	0	0	0	0	0	0	0	0	0	0	0	2	0	0
Gilcrease, Douglas, Fort Myers	.220	61	182	24	40	56	8	1	2	24	1	3	4	3	22	0	30	4	4
Gjesdal, Brent, Fort Lauderdale	.226	91	292	41	66	107	10	2	9	36	5	1	2	4	52	2	84	6	3
Gleissner, James, Fort Myers	.254	82	193	19	49	68	10	0	3	28	0	4	2	2	33	0	27	2	1
Gomez, Jose, Miami°	.279	91	262	30	73	95	14	1	2	17	2	0	1	0	26	1	56	1	1
Gonzalez, Orlando, Tampa	.253	125	431	41	109	127	13	1	1	47	6	2	3	0	37	1	18	3	1
Graham, Michael, Winter Haven°	.200	3	5	0	1	1	0	0	0	0	0	0	0	0	1	0	2	0	0
Graham, Randle, Fort Lauderdale	.000	12	1	0	0	0	0	0	0	0	0	0	0	0	0	0	0	0	0
Graybill, David, West Palm Beach	.000	10	2	0	0	0	0	0	0	0	0	0	0	0	0	0	1	0	0
Greenlee, Robert, Miami°	.000	11	1	0	0	0	0	0	0	0	0	0	0	0	0	0	1	0	0
Gregory, John, Vero Beach°	.000	8	4	0	0	0	0	0	0	0	0	0	1	0	0	0	0	0	0
Gundelfinger, Matthew, St. Pete.	.208	112	346	55	72	133	13	3	14	51	7	2	0	6	64	2	96	10	2
Haberle, David, Tampa°	.169	37	89	9	15	17	2	0	0	5	0	2	1	0	10	0	14	2	0
Hall, Matthew, Fort Myers°	.198	104	263	40	52	66	9	1	1	17	2	7	3	3	42	3	61	27	3
Hall, R. David, Winter Haven	.167	7	18	1	3	3	0	0	0	1	0	1	0	0	2	0	6	0	0
Hamilton, Alvin, Winter Haven	.249	115	362	47	90	130	16	3	6	43	5	3	3	0	40	5	108	13	3
Hamilton, Jeffrey, Vero Beach	.260	127	466	51	121	172	31	4	4	59	6	2	3	4	41	2	78	7	7
Hamilton, Robert, Vero Beach°	.333	6	6	2	2	2	0	0	0	1	0	0	0	0	2	0	1	0	0
Hamrick, Randy, Vero Beach°	.000	42	1	0	0	0	0	0	0	0	0	0	0	0	1	0	1	0	0
Hansen, Raymond, Winter Haven°	.246	59	199	16	49	65	6	2	2	17	3	0	0	1	12	0	26	1	2
Harkins, James, Miami	.000	40	6	0	0	0	0	0	0	0	0	0	0	0	0	0	4	0	0
Harrison, Brett, St. Petersburg	.213	69	235	27	50	64	10	2	0	21	2	7	5	1	34	1	33	0	2
Hartley, Michael, St. Petersburg	.087	31	23	2	2	2	0	0	0	0	0	0	0	0	1	0	7	0	0
Harvey, Kenneth, Vero Beach	.270	111	318	46	86	101	8	2	1	42	7	16	4	10	59	2	50	21	11
Hatcher, Harold, Fort Myers	.234	61	184	23	43	72	8	0	7	39	4	1	2	2	29	2	29	2	1
Hawkins, Johnny, Fort Lauderdale†	.340	19	53	4	18	21	3	0	0	3	1	0	1	0	1	0	3	0	0
Hawley, G. William, Tampa°	.258	27	31	4	8	9	1	0	0	3	1	1	0	0	3	0	6	1	0
Herrera, Rene, Tampa†	.145	23	55	9	8	11	1	1	0	3	0	1	0	1	9	2	9	1	0
Hess, James, West Palm Beach	.000	13	1	0	0	0	0	0	0	0	0	0	0	0	0	0	0	0	0
Heuer, Mark, Vero Beach	.000	26	19	1	0	0	0	0	0	0	0	2	0	0	1	0	11	0	0
Hilgenkamp, Russell, Lakeland	.182	4	11	0	2	2	0	0	0	0	0	0	0	0	0	0	3	0	0
Hill, Orsino, Tampa°	.276	130	416	69	115	161	19	6	5	45	7	1	4	3	86	5	68	15	13
Hillegas, Shawn, Vero Beach	.056	13	18	1	1	1	0	0	0	0	0	0	0	0	2	0	11	0	0
Hocutt, Michael, West Palm Beach°	.279	143	523	70	146	209	19	4	12	100	10	4	7	3	66	4	68	10	10
Holman, Brian, West Palm Beach	.000	4	1	0	0	0	0	0	0	0	0	0	0	0	0	0	1	0	0
Hoskins, Osbe, Miami	.161	33	87	10	14	15	1	0	0	7	0	3	1	0	5	0	11	3	3
Hough, Stanley, Daytona Beach	.000	4	3	0	0	0	0	0	0	0	0	0	0	0	0	0	1	0	0
Houp, Kenneth, Tampa	.000	1	2	0	0	0	0	0	0	0	0	0	0	0	0	0	2	0	0
Hoyt, David, St. Petersburg	.257	128	373	67	96	141	20	5	5	39	6	6	2	8	84	1	54	17	9
Huber, Randolph, West Palm Beach	.333	43	3	0	1	1	0	0	0	0	0	0	0	0	0	0	3	0	0
Hunt, J. Randy, St. Petersburg	.274	100	336	43	92	128	15	3	5	59	5	1	10	0	30	2	53	8	2
Impagliazzo, Joseph, W. P. Beach	.000	11	1	0	0	0	0	0	0	0	0	1	0	0	0	0	0	0	0
Isaac, Johnny, Daytona Beach†	.463	20	41	11	19	28	3	0	2	12	1	0	0	0	6	0	9	0	1

Player and Club	Pct.	G.	AB.	R.	H.	TB.	2B.	3B.	HR.	RBI.	GW.	SH.	SF.	HP.	BB.	Int. BB.	SO.	SB.	CS.
Jarrell, Joseph, Fort Myers	.255	135	482	66	123	176	20	6	7	62	10	4	5	3	32	0	102	22	7
Jefferson, James, West Palm Beach..	.250	12	12	1	3	3	0	0	0	3	0	0	0	0	2	0	5	0	0
Johnston, J. Mark, Fort Lauderdale°.	.276	80	210	33	58	78	8	3	2	26	5	0	2	●	51	3	13	5	3
Johnston, Jody, Vero Beach	.000	21	2	0	0	0	0	0	0	0	0	1	0	0	0	0	0	0	0
Jones, Kenneth, Tampa	.231	26	26	4	6	7	1	0	0	0	5	0	0	1	0	3	0	1
Jones, Scott, Tampa	.000	12	1	1	0	0	0	0	0	0	0	0	0	1	0	1	0	0
Jones, Tracy, Tampa	.309	86	307	50	95	127	14	3	4	41	8	1	5	2	32	3	30	24	1
Kane, Michael, Winter Haven°	.200	32	100	11	20	21	1	0	0	8	1	0	1	1	15	0	13	0	1
Kasprzak, Michael, Daytona Beach	.000	2	1	0	0	0	0	0	0	0	0	0	0	0	0	0	0	0	0
Keller, David, Tampa	.258	41	62	11	16	23	2	1	1	5	0	1	0	0	21	0	17	1	0
Kinns, Glenn, West Palm Beach	.188	26	16	2	3	4	1	0	0	2	0	2	0	0	1	0	4	0	0
Kirby, Wayne, Vero Beach°	.272	76	224	39	61	73	6	3	0	21	4	5	2	6	21	2	30	11	9
Konderla, Michael, Tampa	.000	20	5	0	0	0	0	0	0	0	0	0	0	0	0	0	2	0	0
Krynitsky, Mark, Fort Myers	.191	52	68	11	13	17	2	1	0	7	1	0	1	3	16	0	14	0	0
Kuilan, Jorge, Winter Haven	.300	6	20	4	6	8	2	0	0	0	0	0	0	1	4	0	5	0	0
Lemon, Ricky, West Palm Beach°	.176	33	68	9	12	15	1	1	0	7	0	2	0	0	10	3	14	3	2
Lindsey, William, Fort Lauderdale	.307	35	101	8	31	37	4	1	0	12	1	1	0	0	14	0	11	1	4
Livingston, Dennis, Vero Beach	.222	13	9	1	2	2	0	0	0	3	0	2	0	0	1	0	2	0	0
Lombardi, Phillip, Fort Lauderdale	.293	127	393	58	115	163	20	2	8	70	10	6	4	6	85	1	37	22	4
Long, Anthony, Lakeland	.262	109	359	57	94	111	10	2	1	43	6	7	3	1	50	1	51	16	11
Lottsfeldt, David, Lakeland°	.118	17	34	4	4	4	0	0	0	3	0	0	0	0	5	0	14	0	0
Lowery, Edward, Fort Myers	.211	80	242	42	51	75	9	3	3	32	4	7	4	2	31	2	45	12	3
Luther, Bradley, St. Petersburg	.194	77	242	23	47	61	11	0	1	21	5	3	1	2	32	3	36	5	1
Machado, Ruben, Tampa	.229	38	105	8	24	34	7	0	1	18	2	0	1	3	6	0	12	1	1
MacKay, Joey, Fort Lauderdale	.167	23	72	9	12	22	4	0	2	8	0	0	0	0	9	0	15	2	1
Madden, Morris, Tampa°	.143	33	21	3	3	3	0	0	0	0	0	3	0	0	3	0	7	0	1
Mahnken, Kenneth, Lakeland°	.333	4	9	0	3	3	0	0	0	2	0	1	0	0	1	0	1	0	1
Martin, Sam, St. Petersburg†	.254	130	393	41	100	106	6	0	0	34	2	7	4	7	40	11	36	8	4
Martinez, Christian, St. Petersburg....	.154	17	13	0	2	5	1	1	0	2	0	1	0	0	1	0	5	0	0
Martinez, Porfirio, Lakeland†	.200	11	20	3	4	4	0	0	0	0	0	0	0	0	1	0	12	2	0
Mathews, Charles, Daytona Beach ...	.179	27	28	2	5	6	1	0	0	1	0	5	0	0	2	0	8	0	0
Mauch, Thomas, St. Petersburg°	.500	5	4	1	2	2	0	0	0	0	0	0	0	0	1	0	0	0	0
McClain, Michael, Miami	.121	27	33	0	4	4	0	0	0	1	0	1	0	2	0	12	0	0
McClure, David, Lakeland	.207	30	92	6	19	25	3	0	1	11	0	2	3	0	21	1	23	1	2
McCullers, Lance, Miami†	.313	22	16	1	5	6	1	0	0	1	1	0	0	0	2	0	2	0	0
McGriff, Terence, Tampa	.278	110	345	48	96	136	19	0	7	41	8	0	5	2	48	4	62	5	4
McLoughlin, Timothy, Miami	.000	24	1	0	0	0	0	0	0	0	0	0	0	0	0	0	0	0	0
McManus, Robert, Lakeland	.100	14	40	1	4	4	0	0	0	2	0	0	1	1	2	1	10	0	0
Meadows, Louie, Daytona Beach°	.302	70	252	49	76	128	14	10	6	44	3	1	4	1	47	7	35	14	5
Meagher, Adrian, Vero Beach	.000	49	4	0	0	0	0	0	0	0	0	0	0	0	0	0	4	0	0
Medina, Pedro, Fort Lauderdale†	.255	29	55	4	14	17	0	0	1	3	1	1	0	0	4	0	8	0	1
Meleski, Mark, Winter Haven°	.333	58	171	31	57	67	8	1	0	18	4	3	1	0	24	1	19	2	1
Merulla, Tony, Fort Lauderdale°	.091	4	11	1	1	1	0	0	0	1	0	0	0	0	1	0	2	0	0
Mielke, M. Shawn, West Palm Beach .	.077	28	13	1	1	1	0	0	0	1	0	1	0	0	0	0	2	0	0
Miller, Michael, Fort Myers	.299	56	201	42	60	83	16	2	1	25	4	1	2	2	43	2	35	15	5
Millis, Joseph, Lakeland	.265	98	343	52	91	107	7	3	1	36	4	3	2	1	44	2	69	17	9
Mills, R. Craig, Lakeland	.286	5	14	2	4	4	0	0	0	1	0	0	0	0	1	0	3	0	0
Mitchell, Thomas, Daytona Beach	.247	64	239	41	59	84	8	4	3	31	5	0	3	5	32	4	54	7	6
Mitchell, William, St. Petersburg	.000	23	5	0	0	0	0	0	0	0	0	0	0	0	0	0	4	0	0
Mize, Gregory, Daytona Beach	.118	30	17	1	2	2	0	0	0	0	0	0	0	1	1	0	6	0	0
Monda, Gregory, Tampa°	.290	105	255	31	74	85	11	0	0	22	2	2	5	3	30	6	36	4	3
Montgomery, Jeff, Tampa	.200	31	5	0	1	1	0	0	0	0	0	0	0	0	0	0	4	0	0
Moore, William, West Palm Beach	.300	143	484	102	145	245	26	4	22	94	17	0	4	9	112	11	76	8	4
Moran, Steven, West Palm Beach°	.188	23	16	2	3	3	0	0	0	0	0	0	0	1	0	8	0	1
Moreno, Jaime, Miami	.237	46	135	9	32	39	4	0	1	18	1	0	1	2	6	1	19	0	0
Morgan, W. Christopher, Lakeland°	.276	68	221	29	61	70	4	1	1	30	3	0	5	0	30	2	43	5	4
Moss, Barry, Tampa†	.333	6	3	1	1	1	0	0	0	1	0	0	1	0	2	1	0	0	0
Mueller, Peter, Daytona Beach°	.186	38	102	20	19	37	7	1	3	21	3	0	3	2	33	4	36	0	1
Newsom, Gary, Winter Haven	.315	98	330	59	104	137	14	8	1	49	8	5	6	53	1	23	17	11
Newsome, Timothy, Lakeland	.300	25	80	9	24	27	3	0	0	10	1	4	1	0	9	0	16	4	0
Nicometi, Anthony, W. P. Beach°	.250	26	16	3	4	4	0	0	0	2	0	3	0	0	2	0	3	0	0
Noble, Rayner, Daytona Beach°	.261	29	23	4	6	8	2	0	0	1	0	3	1	0	3	0	5	0	0
Nunez, Mauricio, St. Petersburg	.240	100	217	36	52	61	9	0	0	17	2	4	3	1	22	0	50	2	0
Oliver, Bruce, Miami	.200	45	5	0	1	1	0	0	0	0	0	0	0	0	0	0	2	0	0
Oruna, Roland, Fort Myers	.236	38	89	13	21	29	4	2	0	16	3	1	1	2	14	0	26	2	2
Padia, Steven, Tampa°	.278	70	223	28	62	96	16	0	6	30	3	0	5	2	28	5	30	0	3
Palacios, R. Rey, Lakeland	.247	107	373	44	92	127	21	4	2	53	5	0	6	2	42	1	56	2	3
Paredes, Johnny, West Palm Beach ...	.253	112	438	64	111	124	11	1	0	32	4	8	2	5	43	2	47	23	11
Paris, Zacarias, Daytona Beach	.111	9	9	0	1	1	0	0	0	0	0	2	0	0	0	0	3	0	0
Parsons, Scott, Miami	.333	7	36	2	12	16	2	1	0	5	0	3	0	0	0	6	1	0
Pate, Brian, Winter Haven	.203	57	192	22	39	59	6	1	4	24	4	2	3	1	24	0	34	0	2
Perdomo, Felix, Fort Lauderdale	.236	72	225	19	53	68	7	1	2	24	3	4	2	2	15	0	47	4	10
Perkins, W. Ray, Daytona Beach	.000	39	6	0	0	0	0	0	0	0	0	0	0	0	0	0	1	0	0
Peruso, Steven, Fort Lauderdale	.244	57	205	27	50	68	12	0	2	24	1	0	2	1	21	1	34	7	4
Pesavento, Michael, Vero Beach°	.125	15	8	0	1	1	0	0	0	0	0	0	0	0	2	0	3	0	0
Pevey, Marty, St. Petersburg°	.308	128	441	53	136	166	16	4	2	60	6	6	2	1	48	7	47	7	7
Phillips, W. Joseph, Fort Myers	.258	114	326	64	84	95	4	2	1	28	3	0	1	5	51	0	35	32	6
Pirruccello, Mark, Fort Myers†	.266	26	79	13	21	31	4	0	2	17	3	1	1	2	12	0	22	0	0
Plesac, Joseph, Miami	.250	9	4	0	1	1	0	0	0	0	0	0	0	0	1	0	0	0	0
Porter, Jason, Miami	.282	90	294	30	83	106	14	0	3	37	4	0	6	1	33	2	54	2	2
Poston, Mark, Miami	.227	30	22	1	5	6	1	0	0	2	0	3	0	0	0	0	7	0	0
Powell, Dennis, Vero Beach°	.500	4	4	0	2	2	0	0	0	0	0	0	0	0	0	0	0	0	0
Pratt, Crestwell, Tampa	.249	57	173	33	43	68	6	2	5	30	6	0	4	3	46	4	54	1	1
Price, David, Vero Beach	.270	109	311	42	84	114	11	5	3	54	2	3	9	5	58	3	51	8	7
Ramler, Steven, West Palm Beach	.152	19	46	2	7	7	0	0	0	4	0	0	0	7	1	15	1	0
Ramsey, Michael, Vero Beach	.263	143	529	99	139	181	16	7	4	46	3	2	3	4	98	5	133	69	30
Raziano, M. Scott, West Palm Beach	.132	15	38	2	5	7	2	0	0	2	0	1	0	4	0	8	1	3
Reed, Jody, Winter Haven	.271	77	273	46	74	90	14	1	0	20	2	6	3	0	52	3	19	9	8
Regalado, J. Uvaldo, Daytona Beach..	.154	24	13	1	2	2	0	0	0	0	0	2	0	0	0	0	7	0	0
Reilly, Edward, Daytona Beach	.667	8	3	1	2	2	0	0	0	0	0	0	0	0	0	0	0	0	0
Rexrode, J. Mark, Vero Beach	.400	43	5	0	2	3	1	0	0	0	0	1	0	0	0	0	2	0	0
Reynolds, C. Timothy, Tampa†	.083	36	24	1	2	2	0	0	0	3	1	3	1	0	1	0	6	0	0

5

Player and Club	Pct.	G.	AB.	R.	H.	TB.	2B.	3B.	HR.	RBI.	GW.	SH.	SF.	HP.	BB.	Int. BB.	SO.	SB.	CS.
Richardson, Timothy, Fort Myers	.290	133	489	59	142	157	5	5	0	67	8	3	4	2	58	0	27	18	3
Richmond, Seth, Daytona Beach°	.146	27	41	6	6	8	2	0	0	4	0	0	1	1	6	0	5	0	1
Riggs, James, Fort Lauderdale°	.270	111	337	38	91	146	21	2	10	58	10	0	9	1	41	2	33	1	5
Rivera, Luis, West Palm Beach	.228	124	439	54	100	141	23	0	6	43	5	0	3	5	50	5	79	14	2
Rivera, Pablo, Miami	.201	110	324	20	65	76	5	3	0	24	9	2	5	4	14	4	69	16	7
Roberts, James, Vero Beach†	.208	37	72	7	15	19	4	0	0	8	1	2	3	1	14	2	15	0	0
Robinson, Brian, Tampa	.238	109	311	44	74	96	7	3	3	28	4	11	2	2	51	3	40	8	5
Robinson, Steven, St. Petersburg	.254	138	445	61	113	174	17	16	4	61	8	8	9	0	52	1	88	11	3
Rodriguez, Aristides, Daytona Beach	.000	2	1	0	0	0	0	0	0	0	0	0	0	0	0	0	1	0	0
Rodriguez, Ramon, Daytona Beach	.246	91	289	38	71	86	8	2	1	32	5	2	0	1	24	5	46	2	1
Rood, Nelson, Daytona Beach	.289	89	329	84	95	120	12	5	1	28	2	2	0	4	74	1	50	40	10
Ross, Carey, Fort Myers	.251	107	335	61	84	97	8	1	1	28	6	6	1	1	50	3	51	26	4
Rosthenhausler, Ramon, Lakeland	.189	59	164	14	31	42	4	2	1	18	0	2	0	0	24	0	67	5	4
Roth, John, Winter Haven	.233	42	120	16	28	37	5	2	0	14	2	0	1	3	14	0	27	0	3
Ruiz, Benny, Lakeland	.206	78	248	22	51	61	8	1	0	20	3	5	0	0	25	0	21	5	4
Russell, Anthony, Fort Lauderdale	.229	131	420	74	96	124	8	7	2	29	2	4	3	6	72	2	84	32	23
Samuels, Roger, Daytona Beach°	.111	13	9	0	1	1	0	0	0	1	0	0	0	0	0	0	4	0	0
Schulz, Jeffrey, Fort Myers°	.314	59	204	23	64	74	10	0	0	26	3	2	2	1	18	0	23	8	5
Scime, Joseph, Lakeland	.294	60	187	16	55	67	6	0	2	14	2	3	3	0	17	3	27	1	0
Scott, Richard, Fort Lauderdale	.245	111	351	43	86	126	20	1	6	37	4	6	2	4	37	0	70	6	5
Seoane, Mitchell, Fort Lauderdale°	.333	17	42	4	14	16	2	0	0	7	2	0	0	0	5	0	4	5	1
Shaab, Douglas, Daytona Beach°	.167	48	6	0	1	1	0	0	0	0	0	0	0	0	0	0	2	0	0
Shade, Michael, St. Petersburg	.500	28	4	1	2	2	0	0	0	2	0	0	1	1	0	1	0	0	0
Sherman, James, Daytona Beach	.254	37	134	24	34	60	8	0	6	28	4	1	1	2	17	1	23	2	1
Shipley, Craig, Vero Beach	.280	85	293	56	82	97	11	2	0	28	3	1	1	4	52	6	44	18	7
Shuffield, Jack, Fort Myers°	.241	130	465	68	112	149	13	6	4	51	2	21	3	3	41	5	45	17	8
Silkwood, Joe, St. Petersburg	.143	8	7	1	1	1	0	0	0	1	0	1	0	0	0	0	1	0	0
Skripko, J. Scott, Winter Haven	.219	35	73	8	16	17	1	0	0	6	1	2	1	0	14	0	15	7	4
Slezak, Robert, Vero Beach	.250	3	4	0	1	1	0	0	0	0	0	0	0	0	0	0	1	0	0
Smith, Daniel, Tampa°	.000	54	3	0	0	0	0	0	0	0	0	0	2	0	0	0	2	0	0
Smith, Gregory, Miami°	.354	52	178	25	63	95	14	0	6	31	7	1	0	0	24	4	24	2	5
Soto, Maximilliano, Lakeland	.286	15	49	7	14	17	3	0	0	3	0	1	0	0	6	0	13	3	1
Spagnola, Glenn, Tampa°	.333	12	3	0	1	1	0	0	0	0	0	2	0	0	0	0	0	0	0
Spisok, Jeffery, Tampa	.160	29	75	6	12	14	2	0	0	7	0	0	1	0	11	0	20	3	1
Starnes, Vance, Fort Lauderdale	.264	47	91	15	24	32	5	0	1	11	1	0	0	0	16	0	9	3	1
Stellern, Michael, Daytona Beach	.278	103	352	49	98	142	23	3	5	55	5	2	4	1	36	1	70	10	3
Stewart, Jeffrey, Miami	.042	32	24	1	1	1	0	0	0	0	0	0	3	0	2	0	18	0	0
Strasser, Richard, Daytona Beach	.000	15	17	1	0	0	0	0	0	1	0	2	0	0	8	0	9	0	0
Strickland, Terry, West Palm Beach	.204	50	162	11	33	35	2	0	0	8	1	0	2	0	11	2	25	3	4
Szajko, Daniel, West Palm Beach	.265	69	196	31	52	61	7	1	0	15	1	4	2	0	43	3	18	7	12
Tejeda, Felix, Vero Beach†	.000	15	6	1	0	0	0	0	0	0	0	0	0	0	1	0	4	0	0
Thiessen, Timothy, West Palm Beach	.322	47	171	29	55	63	5	0	1	11	1	1	0	1	29	2	18	4	5
Thomas, Reginald, Lakeland°	.193	37	119	7	23	36	6	2	1	9	0	1	2	1	10	0	28	1	2
Thompson, Scott, Miami	.478	7	23	7	11	14	1	1	0	6	1	0	1	2	2	0	4	2	1
Toale, John, Winter Haven°	.259	8	27	3	7	8	0	0	0	0	0	0	0	0	1	0	4	0	0
Toler, Gregory, Tampa	.232	35	99	16	23	26	3	0	0	9	2	2	1	0	15	1	21	1	1
Traen, Thomas, West Palm Beach†	.500	1	4	0	2	2	0	0	0	1	0	0	0	0	0	0	0	0	0
Treadway, H. Jeffrey, Tampa°	.309	119	372	44	115	131	16	0	0	44	3	7	3	5	54	8	40	13	7
Turco, Steve, St. Petersburg°	.247	138	446	63	110	131	14	2	1	34	5	6	4	0	55	3	44	20	10
Turgeon, Stephen, St. Petersburg	.221	131	425	43	94	126	12	4	4	46	8	2	3	2	51	2	83	17	4
Valdez, Sergio, West Palm Beach	.000	5	2	0	0	0	0	0	0	0	0	0	0	0	0	0	1	0	0
Vaughn, Michael, St. Petersburg°	.214	49	140	16	30	45	10	1	1	11	1	1	2	0	11	1	28	0	1
Velasquez, I. Javier, Vero Beach	.265	107	313	40	83	98	13	1	0	45	4	6	4	2	57	3	40	5	5
Wade, Scott, Winter Haven	.242	48	157	24	38	54	10	0	2	15	1	0	1	1	26	0	36	3	2
Walewander, James, Lakeland†	.271	137	502	70	136	156	16	2	0	36	2	8	3	6	64	2	40	47	18
Walker, Stephen, Winter Haven†	.216	88	255	35	55	70	5	5	0	25	4	3	5	10	43	2	56	10	7
Wallace, Timothy, St. Petersburg	.139	18	36	5	5	5	0	0	0	3	0	2	0	0	9	1	7	0	1
Walter, Gene, Miami°	.000	9	7	0	0	0	0	0	0	0	0	0	2	0	1	0	2	0	0
Washington, Marc, Lakeland	.190	38	105	7	20	23	3	0	0	5	0	1	0	0	10	0	33	1	4
Watson, K. Steven, Tampa	.000	41	3	0	0	0	0	0	0	0	0	1	0	0	0	0	3	0	0
Wayne, Gary, West Palm Beach°	.000	13	8	2	0	0	0	0	0	0	0	1	0	0	2	0	3	0	0
Weinberger, Gary, West Palm Beach°	.249	117	381	49	95	108	7	3	0	31	5	8	2	6	58	6	33	8	10
Williams, Dana, Winter Haven	.327	135	511	65	167	213	27	8	1	54	10	1	7	5	46	5	44	18	12
Williams, Edward, Tampa	.254	50	138	20	35	49	8	0	2	16	4	0	1	5	25	0	23	0	1
Williams, Mark, West Palm Beach	.125	9	8	0	1	1	0	0	0	0	0	0	0	0	1	0	0	0	0
Williams, Michael, Lakeland	.254	128	394	44	100	140	14	1	8	55	4	3	7	2	76	8	91	10	4
Williams, Reginald, Vero Beach	.239	60	222	31	53	62	5	2	0	19	3	3	1	1	20	2	20	11	7
Wine, Robert, Daytona Beach	.244	124	430	66	105	184	36	2	13	79	8	2	6	2	55	3	114	1	2
Winkler, Brad, Fort Lauderdale°	.297	52	165	32	49	80	11	1	6	18	1	0	5	2	20	1	35	3	2
Wohler, Barry, Vero Beach°	.000	28	30	2	0	0	0	0	0	7	0	1	8	0	17	0	0	0	0
Wolff, Steven, Miami	.232	111	358	31	83	92	9	0	0	22	1	4	5	1	46	2	39	7	8
Woodson, Tracy, Vero Beach	.219	76	256	29	56	77	9	0	4	36	8	0	4	6	27	2	41	7	4
Worrell, Todd, St. Petersburg	.125	10	8	0	1	1	0	0	0	0	0	0	0	0	1	0	4	0	0
Young, Delwyn, Tampa†	.259	129	478	59	124	162	29	3	1	52	3	3	6	1	49	5	73	18	9
Young, Scott, St. Petersburg	.158	22	19	2	3	3	0	0	0	0	0	0	1	0	0	4	0	0	0

The following pitchers, listed alphabetically by club, with games in parentheses, had no plate appearances, primarily through use of designated hitters:

DAYTONA BEACH—Retz, Robert (4).

FORT LAUDERDALE—Armstrong, Michael (8); Beahan, Scot (25); Birtsas, Timothy (11); Byron, Timothy (37); Easley, Logan (32); Frey, Steven (48); Gumbert, Richard (7); Horne, Jeffrey (4); Mathison, Charles (1); Morgan, Stacy (46); Nielson, Scott (4); Plunk, Eric (28); Raftice, Robert (36); Ray, Steven (1); Seitz, John (6); Smalley, David (12); Wever, Stefan (7); Wex, Gary (14); Woodworth, David (19).

FORT MYERS—Bass, Edward (30); Benedict, James (20); Burke, Richard (25); Daniel, Jimmy (12); Davis, John (25); Drizmala, Thomas (26); Goodin, Richard (21); Klein, Gary (22); Martinez, Arthur (9); Mohr, Thomas (28); Sanchez, Israel (14); Snell, David (11); Tuck, Kevin (40); Vanderpohl, Arthur (6); Walberg, Mark (16); Ware, Duane (27); Wong, David (15).

LAKELAND—Barlow, Ricky (26); Cooper, William (7); Dotson, Wayne (18); Duffy, John (9); Dunn, Allen (14); Freeman, Clements (17); Garcia, Alejandro (14); Halley, Michael (2); Harvey, Randall (7); Hinz, William (16); James, Duane (21); Labozzetta, Albert (3); Lara, Luis (33); Melchert, Gregory (17); Minnema, David (2); Moya, Ernest (4); Nilsson, Gary (9); Pena, Ramon (20); Perrotte, Joseph (22); Peterson, Jeffrey (5); Phillion, Gerald (6); Raubolt, Arthur (29); Robinson, Jeffrey (10); Scudero, James (12); Simmons, Glenn (9); Souza, Robert (7); Wheeler, Bradley (5).

MIAMI—Cloninger, Darin (3); Kolotka, Charles (11).

ST. PETERSBURG—Carrasco, Ernest (10).

TAMPA—Owchinko, Robert (7); Soto, Osvaldo (2).

VERO BEACH—Mosher, Peyton (11).

WEST PALM BEACH—Azcona, Manuel (4); Johnson, Gregory (7).

WINTER HAVEN—Bencomo, Omar (41); Dalton, Michael (38); Leister, John (31); Mettler, Bradley (7); Minor, Bruster (30); Mitchell, John (27); Perry, Paul (20); Poindexter, Michael (21); Sellers, Jeffrey (29); Snediker, James (11); Torres, Nelson (35); Weinbrecht, Mark (8); Wheeler, Bradley (24).

GRAND SLAM HOME RUNS—Bonk, Burks, Wine, 2 each; Hatcher, Isaac, Mackay, Moreno, Mueller, Newsome, Palacios, Pevey, Pirruccello, Price, Ramsey, Rosthenhausler, G. Smith, Turco, Woodson, 1 each.

AWARDED FIRST BASE ON CATCHER'S INTERFERENCE—Gundelfinger 12 (Burrell 2, Krynitsky 2, Blair, Eagar, Gleissner, Hawkins, Lombardi, McClure, McGriff, Mi. Williams); Hocutt 3 (Castro, Lombardi, Velasquez); Daggy (Toler); Hill (Cannizzaro); Shipley (Gleissner); Shuffield (Castro); Treadway (Vaughn); Wohler (Cecchini).

CLUB FIELDING

Club	Pct.	G.	PO.	A.	E.	DP.	PB.	Club	Pct.	G.	PO.	A.	E.	DP.	PB.
West Palm Beach	.967	144	3709	1607	182	132	20	Daytona Beach	.961	144	3676	1687	217	167	33
Vero Beach	.966	146	3696	1538	183	134	18	St. Petersburg	.961	144	3596	1394	204	123	27
Miami	.965	138	3524	1614	186	140	26	Tampa	.961	139	3432	1347	193	111	15
Fort Myers	.963	141	3548	1461	195	104	11	Lakeland	.960	144	3508	1361	203	127	28
Winter Haven	.963	144	3625	1752	204	156	26	Fort Lauderdale	.959	142	3567	1529	218	146	20

Triple Plays—Lakeland, Miami, West Palm Beach, Winter Haven.

INDIVIDUAL FIELDING
FIRST BASEMEN

☆Throws lefthanded.

Player and Club	Pct.	G.	PO.	A.	E.	DP.	Player and Club	Pct.	G.	PO.	A.	E.	DP.
Amante, St. Petersburg	.978	15	84	3	2	9	Johnston, Fort Lauderdale	.980	19	137	13	3	13
Berti, Daytona Beach	.974	4	34	3	1	2	Keller, Tampa☆	.987	32	145	10	2	6
BIRRIEL, Winter Haven☆	.988	125	1198	94	16	125	Lombardi, Fort Lauderdale	.975	5	37	2	1	5
Blair, West Palm Beach	.990	33	281	22	3	27	McManus, Lakeland	.963	10	70	8	3	7
Bonk, Winter Haven	1.000	10	94	6	0	6	Meadows, Daytona Beach	.992	26	244	16	2	18
Brock, Vero Beach	.983	35	270	26	5	30	Merulla, Fort Lauderdale	.941	3	16	0	1	2
Burrell, Winter Haven	.991	12	99	7	1	9	Monda, Tampa☆	.982	34	200	17	4	20
Carpenter, Daytona Beach☆	.984	76	719	33	12	92	Moore, West Palm Beach☆	.993	17	128	6	1	16
Castro, Miami	.955	6	61	2	3	10	Moreno, Miami	.979	8	43	3	1	6
Champion, St. Petersburg	1.000	1	1	0	0	0	Morgan, Lakeland	.990	39	283	20	3	28
Citari, Fort Myers	.991	45	400	35	4	22	Mueller, Daytona Beach☆	.994	34	294	12	2	28
Clark, Daytona Beach	.972	12	96	7	3	9	Padia, Tampa	.968	49	313	24	11	37
Datz, Daytona Beach	1.000	1	2	0	0	0	Palacios, Lakeland	.984	31	231	14	4	19
Davis, Lakeland	1.000	3	17	2	0	1	Pevey, St. Petersburg	.985	85	550	47	9	63
Destrade, Fort Lauderdale	.981	93	764	41	16	82	Pratt, Lakeland	.988	52	382	35	5	37
Dillard, Miami☆	.990	36	276	22	3	27	Richardson, Fort Myers	.987	94	794	57	11	58
Dunlop, Miami	1.000	7	48	5	0	8	Scime, Lakeland	.984	47	338	28	6	40
Fennell, Fort Lauderdale	.967	33	225	11	8	24	Smith, Miami	.997	37	372	26	1	34
Gomez, Miami☆	.986	63	508	36	8	43	Starnes, Fort Lauderdale	.974	8	34	4	1	3
Gregory, Vero Beach☆	1.000	2	4	1	0	0	Vaughn, St. Petersburg	.969	10	59	4	2	3
Gundelfinger, St. Petersburg	.988	55	374	23	5	30	Velasquez, Vero Beach	.986	46	333	32	5	30
Hatcher, Fort Myers	.974	7	37	1	1	3	Williams, Lakeland	.976	26	146	16	4	11
Hocutt, West Palm Beach	.986	100	840	73	13	78	Woodson, Vero Beach	.987	74	630	38	9	54
Hunt, St. Petersburg	1.000	2	14	2	0	0							

Triple Plays—Birriel, Blair, Morgan, Smith.

SECOND BASEMEN

Player and Club	Pct.	G.	PO.	A.	E.	DP.	Player and Club	Pct.	G.	PO.	A.	E.	DP.
Ashkinazy, Winter Haven	.970	36	58	103	5	21	Miller, Fort Myers	.969	56	115	132	8	23
Baker, West Palm Beach	1.000	8	12	12	0	2	Millis, Lakeland	.913	6	9	12	2	3
Balcomb, Vero Beach	.940	22	48	62	7	15	Newsom, Vero Beach	.982	29	63	102	3	27
Blaser, Fort Lauderdale	1.000	4	8	6	0	1	Newsome, Lakeland	1.000	1	0	1	0	0
Botkin, Daytona Beach	1.000	2	1	0	0	0	PAREDES, West Palm Beach	.974	111	275	295	15	71
Cannizzaro, Winter Haven	.972	113	263	393	19	82	Perdomo, Fort Lauderdale	.947	40	86	109	11	23
Chapman, Fort Lauderdale	.961	78	166	182	14	47	Phillips, Fort Myers	.950	39	87	102	10	21
Corman, Miami	.969	122	303	374	22	92	Robinson, Tampa	.875	2	5	2	1	0
DelRosario, Miami	.875	10	17	18	5	4	Rodriguez, Daytona Beach	.948	88	168	248	23	44
Falls, Daytona Beach	.973	76	158	205	10	68	Ruiz, Lakeland	1.000	4	5	9	0	3
Gilcrease, Fort Myers	.968	61	115	156	9	37	Seoane, Fort Lauderdale	.923	4	5	7	1	3
Gonzalez, Tampa	.964	90	175	204	14	52	Spisok, Tampa	.920	26	45	35	7	5
Harrison, St. Petersburg	.963	65	122	167	11	35	Strickland, West Palm Beach	.985	27	66	68	2	20
Harvey, Vero Beach	.968	100	213	236	15	45	Szajko, West Palm Beach	1.000	2	2	1	0	0
Johnston, Fort Lauderdale	1.000	20	41	34	0	12	Treadway, Tampa	.966	33	74	66	5	14
Long, Lakeland	.925	12	34	28	5	10	Turco, St. Petersburg	.913	17	28	35	6	2
Martin, St. Petersburg	.963	69	156	182	13	44	Walewander, Lakeland	.968	129	329	316	21	74
Medina, Fort Lauderdale	.957	17	29	38	3	18	Wolff, Miami	.983	9	17	41	1	8

Triple Play—Corman.

THIRD BASEMEN

Player and Club	Pct.	G.	PO.	A.	E.	DP.	Player and Club	Pct.	G.	PO.	A.	E.	DP.
Arce, Lakeland	.929	30	27	51	6	6	Dunlop, Miami	.916	55	24	85	10	10
Balcomb, Vero Beach	.875	20	17	39	8	4	Gonzalez, Tampa	1.000	2	2	2	0	0
Blaser, Fort Lauderdale	.953	76	70	171	12	19	Hall, Winter Haven	1.000	4	1	8	0	0
Botkin, Daytona Beach	.890	28	33	56	11	5	A. Hamilton, Winter Haven	.927	58	32	108	11	9
Brassil, Miami	.937	77	42	137	12	10	J. HAMILTON, Vero Beach	.932	126	109	259	27	25
Clark, Daytona Beach	.909	6	3	7	1	2	Hocutt, West Palm Beach	.871	22	12	49	9	7
Cobb, West Palm Beach	.906	52	43	120	17	11	Jarrell, Fort Myers	.833	2	1	4	1	0
Corman, Miami	.900	3	3	6	1	1	Johnston, Fort Lauderdale	.957	13	9	13	1	1
Delgado, Daytona Beach	.860	32	27	59	14	4	Kane, Winter Haven	.931	22	9	45	4	5
Dophied, Daytona Beach	.800	3	0	4	1	0	Lombardi, Fort Lauderdale	1.000	3	0	2	0	0

THIRD BASEMEN—Continued

Player and Club	Pct.	G.	PO.	A.	E.	DP.
Long, Lakeland	.884	15	13	25	5	2
Lowery, Fort Myers	.908	52	44	94	14	5
Luther, St. Petersburg	1.000	2	2	6	0	0
Machado, Tampa	.918	32	19	48	6	4
Medina, Fort Lauderdale	1.000	4	1	3	0	0
Meleski, Winter Haven	.887	26	17	38	7	2
Mills, Lakeland	.917	5	3	8	1	0
Mitchell, Daytona Beach	.929	63	41	130	13	21
Moreno, Miami	.913	10	3	18	2	2
Newsome, Lakeland	.929	20	21	31	4	4
Palacios, Lakeland	.904	54	51	91	15	6
Pate, Winter Haven	.924	40	41	81	10	8
Pevey, St. Petersburg	1.000	1	1	3	0	1
Porter, Miami	.667	2	0	2	1	0
Raziano, West Palm Beach	.861	11	8	23	5	3
Riggs, Fort Lauderdale	.896	55	41	79	14	10
Robinson, Tampa	.875	7	4	10	2	1
Ross, Fort Myers	.919	90	72	155	20	17

Player and Club	Pct.	G.	PO.	A.	E.	DP.
Ruiz, Lakeland	.980	18	18	32	1	3
Seoane, Fort Lauderdale	.842	8	7	9	3	1
Sherman, Daytona Beach	.932	16	18	23	3	5
Smith, Miami	.833	2	1	4	1	1
Strickland, West Palm Beach	1.000	9	7	7	0	0
Szajko, West Palm Beach	.938	11	6	24	2	2
Thiessen, West Palm Beach	.911	46	33	90	12	10
Toale, Winter Haven	.900	6	3	15	2	2
Toler, Tampa	1.000	4	0	6	0	1
Treadway, Tampa	.896	80	54	118	20	8
Turco, St. Petersburg	.903	72	59	62	13	8
Turgeon, St. Petersburg	.875	81	52	116	24	8
Velasquez, Vero Beach	1.000	3	2	3	0	1
Walewander, Lakeland	.923	6	4	8	1	1
Wallace, St. Petersburg	.900	5	6	3	1	0
E. Williams, Tampa	.861	37	25	43	11	6
M. Williams, Lakeland	1.000	3	0	3	0	0
Wine, Daytona Beach	1.000	1	0	2	0	0

Triple Plays—Palacios, Pate.

SHORTSTOPS

Player and Club	Pct.	G.	PO.	A.	E.	DP.
Allaire, Daytona Beach	.933	52	69	166	17	47
Ashkinazy, Winter Haven	.947	5	7	11	1	2
Bachman, West Palm Beach	.954	14	18	44	3	7
Balcomb, Vero Beach	.970	11	13	19	1	3
Brassil, Miami	.944	49	68	135	12	29
Chapman, Fort Lauderdale	1.000	2	1	0	0	0
DelRosario, Miami	.857	1	3	3	1	1
Dunlop, Miami	1.000	1	0	1	0	0
Falls, Daytona Beach	1.000	9	11	15	0	3
Gonzalez, Tampa	.861	30	31	56	14	8
Hamilton, Vero Beach	.904	48	97	167	28	45
Harrison, St. Petersburg	.889	3	3	5	1	0
Herrera, Tampa	.967	22	26	61	3	12
Jarrell, Fort Myers	.925	132	192	387	47	51
Lowery, Fort Myers	.956	11	14	29	2	7
Luther, St. Petersburg	.938	73	125	207	22	43
Martin, St. Petersburg	.923	64	95	146	20	29
Medina, Fort Lauderdale	.882	8	6	9	2	2
Meleski, Winter Haven	.951	23	27	71	5	8
Miller, Fort Myers	.833	1	1	4	1	0

Player and Club	Pct.	G.	PO.	A.	E.	DP.
Millis, Lakeland	.952	9	16	24	2	4
Newsom, Vero Beach	.928	59	89	167	20	37
Newsome, Lakeland	1.000	5	5	12	0	1
Perdomo, Fort Lauderdale	.921	32	51	88	12	12
Phillips, Fort Myers	1.000	3	5	6	0	1
Reed, Winter Haven	.939	76	128	271	26	56
Rivera, West Palm Beach	.938	124	198	389	39	66
B. ROBINSON, Tampa	.956	100	157	278	20	58
Rood, Daytona Beach	.955	89	154	289	21	53
Rosthenhausler, Lakeland	.947	58	74	140	12	25
Ruiz, Lakeland	.921	59	76	158	20	36
Scott, Fort Lauderdale	.935	111	171	365	37	73
Shipley, Vero Beach	.954	84	137	216	17	46
Soto, Lakeland	.883	15	13	40	7	7
Strickland, West Palm Beach	.923	6	8	16	2	3
Szajko, West Palm Beach	1.000	2	6	5	0	2
Thiessen, West Palm Beach	1.000	2	1	11	0	0
Turco, St. Petersburg	.897	24	27	43	8	12
Walewander, Lakeland	.963	6	9	17	1	4
Wolff, Miami	.961	94	143	325	19	59

Triple Plays—Rosthenhausler, Rivera, Wolff.

OUTFIELDERS

Player and Club	Pct.	G.	PO.	A.	E.	DP.
Abner, West Palm Beach	.987	39	77	1	1	0
Allen, Fort Myers	.984	136	298	10	5	2
Amante, St. Petersburg	.925	30	32	5	3	0
Austin, Miami	.970	109	157	5	5	0
D. Baker, West Palm Beach	.978	52	86	3	2	0
R. Baker, Lakeland	.920	12	23	0	2	0
Balcomb, Vero Beach	1.000	10	23	0	0	0
Beringhele, Vero Beach	.980	100	190	10	4	0
Boever, Tampa	1.000	3	1	0	0	0
Botkin, Daytona Beach	.985	80	127	6	2	3
Braun, Daytona Beach	.988	47	80	5	1	1
Burke, Daytona Beach	.968	83	139	12	5	4
Burks, Winter Haven	.977	107	196	12	5	6
Camelo, West Palm Beach	.994	90	150	6	1	2
Carpenter, Daytona Beach	1.000	4	6	0	0	0
Clark, Daytona Beach	1.000	6	7	0	0	0
Daggy, Lakeland	.979	112	220	9	5	2
Delgado, Daytona Beach	.929	63	88	4	7	0
Dillard, Miami	.980	71	96	3	2	0
Dophied, Daytona Beach	.948	31	53	2	3	1
Dunlop, Miami	1.000	7	17	1	0	0
Erdmann, Lakeland	.988	40	81	2	1	0
Fennell, Fort Lauderdale	1.000	1	2	0	0	0
Ficklin, Fort Lauderdale	.966	118	206	22	8	2
Freeman, Lakeland	1.000	49	90	3	0	1
Frierson, Miami	.931	91	131	3	10	0
Fulgencio, Tampa	.983	72	110	3	2	1
Geels, Winter Haven	1.000	2	1	0	0	0
Gjesdal, Fort Lauderdale	.973	70	102	8	3	1
Gundelfinger, St. Petersburg	.969	25	27	4	1	1
Hall, Fort Myers⬦	.974	79	108	5	3	1
Hansen, Winter Haven⬦	.949	48	70	5	4	0
Hill, Tampa	.975	124	231	4	6	1
Hoskins, Miami	.930	34	38	2	3	0
Hoyt, St. Petersburg	.981	119	296	15	6	0
Hunt, St. Petersburg	1.000	5	2	1	0	0
Isaac, Daytona Beach	.935	20	29	0	2	0
Johnston, Fort Lauderdale	1.000	16	19	0	0	0
Jones, Tampa	1.000	81	150	6	0	1
Kirby, Vero Beach	.954	46	101	3	5	1
Lemon, West Palm Beach⬦	.917	12	22	0	2	0
Lombardi, Fort Lauderdale	.893	25	24	1	3	1
Long, Lakeland	.986	62	140	5	2	2
MacKay, Fort Lauderdale	.960	18	23	1	1	1
Martinez, Lakeland	.833	10	10	0	2	0
McClure, Lakeland	1.000	7	11	0	0	0

Player and Club	Pct.	G.	PO.	A.	E.	DP.
Meadows, Daytona Beach	.964	41	79	1	3	0
Millis, Lakeland	.970	77	183	8	6	2
Monda, Tampa⬦	.970	51	64	1	2	0
Moore, West Palm Beach⬦	.968	119	172	8	6	2
Moreno, Miami	.962	15	23	2	1	0
Morgan, Lakeland	1.000	30	51	1	0	1
Newsome, Lakeland	1.000	3	2	0	0	0
Nunez, St. Petersburg	.966	76	107	8	4	1
Oruna, Fort Myers	.970	31	64	1	2	0
Pate, Winter Haven	1.000	17	17	1	0	0
Peruso, Fort Lauderdale	.945	29	50	2	3	0
Pevey, St. Petersburg	.889	14	6	2	1	0
Phillips, Fort Myers	.956	28	40	3	2	1
Porter, Miami	1.000	26	28	3	0	1
Price, Vero Beach	.967	91	165	10	6	6
Ramsey, Vero Beach⬦	.980	141	379	13	8	5
Richmond, Daytona Beach	.929	15	13	0	1	0
Rivera, Miami	.945	102	200	6	12	0
Robinson, St. Petersburg	.964	143	232	9	9	1
Ross, Fort Myers	1.000	1	3	1	0	0
Roth, Winter Haven	.984	40	59	1	1	0
Russell, Fort Lauderdale	.975	126	225	13	6	3
Schulz, Fort Myers	1.000	62	110	10	0	1
Scime, Lakeland	1.000	1	1	0	0	0
Sherman, Daytona Beach	1.000	19	26	2	0	0
Shuffield, Fort Myers⬦	.979	126	214	14	5	3
Skripko, Winter Haven	1.000	29	80	2	0	1
Smith, Miami	1.000	11	14	1	0	0
Starnes, Fort Lauderdale	1.000	10	5	0	0	0
Stellern, Daytona Beach	.953	65	115	6	6	2
Szajko, West Palm Beach	.979	51	91	4	2	1
Thomas, Lakeland⬦	.979	30	44	2	1	0
Thompson, Miami	1.000	7	17	0	0	0
Toler, Tampa	1.000	3	5	0	0	0
Turco, St. Petersburg	.980	35	45	5	1	0
Turgeon, St. Petersburg	.981	57	95	7	2	0
Vaughn, St. Petersburg	.938	13	15	0	1	0
Wade, Winter Haven	.944	45	64	3	4	0
Walker, Winter Haven	.952	39	57	3	3	1
Washington, Lakeland	1.000	35	38	1	0	0
WEINBERGER, W.P. Beach⬦	.996	104	230	7	1	1
D. Williams, Winter Haven	.967	126	226	12	8	5
R. Williams, Vero Beach	.989	59	87	5	1	0
Winkler, Fort Lauderdale	.974	49	73	2	2	0
Young, Tampa	.957	124	248	18	12	2

CATCHERS

Player and Club	Pct.	G.	PO.	A.	E.	DP.	PB.
Bartlett, Vero Beach	.941	25	97	15	7	3	1
Berti, Daytona Beach	.961	27	129	17	6	2	5
F. Blair, West Palm Beach	.975	17	72	7	2	1	4
M. Blair, Vero Beach	.982	68	335	56	7	3	7
Bonk, Winter Haven	.992	32	106	16	1	0	6
Burrell, Winter Haven	.955	60	276	24	14	8	9
Cadahia, Fort Myers	.974	29	102	12	3	2	2
Caffrey, West Palm Beach	.965	11	76	7	3	0	6
Cannizzaro, Winter Haven	.000	1	0	0	1	0	0
Castro, Miami	.965	95	539	102	23	6	15
Cecchini, West Palm Beach	.980	105	609	74	14	4	8
Champion, St. Petersburg	.957	7	21	1	1	0	0
Datz, Daytona Beach	.961	9	43	6	2	0	3
Eagar, Lakeland	.970	39	170	21	6	2	9
Edmiston, Lakeland	.977	9	38	4	1	0	3
Fennell, Fort Lauderdale	.968	14	57	3	2	1	1
Geels, Winter Haven	.989	72	303	42	4	2	11
Gleissner, Fort Myers	.964	78	338	36	14	3	2
Haberle, Tampa	.986	28	126	15	2	1	5
Hatcher, Fort Myers	.976	46	167	39	5	4	4
Hawkins, Fort Lauderdale	.960	9	40	8	2	1	0
Hilgenkamp, Lakeland	1.000	3	23	1	0	0	0
Hough, Daytona Beach	1.000	3	6	0	0	0	0
Houp, Tampa	1.000	1	6	0	0	0	0
Hunt, St. Petersburg	.974	87	561	75	17	8	19
Krynitsky, Fort Myers	.981	46	140	15	3	0	3
Lindsey, Fort Lauderdale	.967	35	171	31	7	5	6
LOMBARDI, Fort Lauderdale	.985	100	608	56	10	8	13
Lottsfeldt, Lakeland	.931	16	46	8	4	2	1
McClure, Lakeland	.958	21	127	11	6	2	3
McGriff, Tampa	.976	98	576	88	16	6	8
Moreno, Miami	1.000	9	44	6	0	0	1
Padia, Tampa	1.000	1	2	0	0	1	0
Palacios, Lakeland	1.000	2	3	0	0	0	0
Pevey, St. Petersburg	.995	35	174	19	1	3	3
Porter, Miami	.969	41	198	21	7	2	10
Ramler, West Palm Beach	.990	18	89	13	1	1	2
Roberts, Vero Beach	.983	28	105	11	2	0	3
Toler, Tampa	.979	26	167	22	4	0	2
Vaughn, St. Petersburg	.977	26	114	11	3	0	4
Velasquez, West Palm Beach	.988	44	210	27	3	0	7
Wallace, St. Petersburg	1.000	9	44	2	0	1	1
Williams, Lakeland	.964	70	340	40	14	6	12
Wine, Daytona Beach	.976	116	601	124	18	14	25

PITCHERS

Player and Club	Pct.	G.	PO.	A.	E.	DP.
Baker, Daytona Beach	1.000	17	2	3	0	0
Barlow, Lakeland	.926	25	9	16	2	1
Barrett, West Palm Beach	.958	11	5	18	1	1
Bass, Fort Myers	1.000	30	9	15	0	0
Beahan, Fort Lauderdale	.739	25	5	12	6	0
Belanger, West Palm Beach°	.950	48	1	18	1	1
Bencomo, Winter Haven	.938	41	2	13	1	1
Benedict, Fort Myers	1.000	20	0	4	0	0
Birtsas, Fort Lauderdale°	.917	11	2	9	1	1
Boever, St. Petersburg	.909	48	3	7	1	1
Bombard, Daytona Beach	1.000	30	1	10	0	0
Boyles, Tampa	1.000	18	8	8	0	0
Brahs, West Palm Beach°	.913	20	6	15	2	0
Burke, Fort Myers°	.800	25	1	3	1	0
Burwell, St. Petersburg	.923	22	3	9	1	2
Byron, Fort Lauderdale	.865	37	9	23	5	1
Cahill, St. Petersburg	.905	45	6	13	2	0
Calvert, Tampa	.900	10	2	7	1	0
Carrasco, St. Petersburg	.667	10	0	2	1	1
Caulfield, St. Petersburg°	.818	30	1	8	2	0
Cerefin, Daytona Beach	.696	23	2	14	7	1
Charlton, West Palm Beach°	.933	8	5	9	1	0
M. Cherry, Vero Beach	1.000	3	1	3	0	0
P. Cherry, St. Petersburg°	.944	36	5	29	2	0
Childers, Miami	.950	36	2	17	1	0
Cloninger, 3 Mia.-26 Ft.L.	.941	29	19	29	3	1
Cooper, Lakeland	.667	7	2	0	1	0
Cunningham, Vero Beach	1.000	14	6	8	0	0
Cutshall, West Palm Beach	1.000	5	0	4	0	0
Dalton, Winter Haven°	.895	38	3	31	4	1
J. Daniel, Fort Myers	1.000	12	5	6	0	1
P.C. Daniel, Tampa°	1.000	4	0	3	0	0
Davis, Fort Myers	.789	25	13	17	8	0
Dibble, Tampa	.923	15	4	8	1	0
Dotson, Lakeland	.667	18	4	4	4	0
Drizmala, Fort Myers°	.938	26	3	12	1	0
Duffy, Lakeland°	.500	9	0	2	2	0
A. Dunn, Lakeland	.895	14	9	8	2	0
G. Dunn, St. Petersburg	.947	30	5	13	1	0
Easley, Fort Lauderdale	.818	32	6	21	6	2
Epple, St. Petersburg°	1.000	29	4	14	0	1
Ergle, Tampa	1.000	13	2	2	0	1
Flores, West Palm Beach	.800	51	8	12	5	0
Freeman, Lakeland°	1.000	17	1	7	0	0
Frey, Fort Lauderdale°	1.000	48	2	8	0	0
Friedrich, Daytona Beach	.931	25	3	24	2	1
Galvez, Vero Beach	.951	26	13	26	2	1
Garcia, Lakeland°	1.000	14	2	3	0	0
Gentle, Vero Beach°	.917	11	6	5	1	0
Goodin, Fort Myers°	.909	21	6	24	3	0
Graham, Fort Lauderdale	1.000	12	0	3	0	1
Graybill, West Palm Beach	.917	10	2	9	1	1
Greenlee, Miami°	1.000	11	1	2	0	1
Gumbert, Fort Lauderdale	1.000	7	1	0	0	0
Halley, Lakeland	1.000	2	0	1	0	0
A. Hamilton, Winter Haven	1.000	1	0	1	0	0
R. Hamilton, Vero Beach	.857	4	1	5	1	2
Hamrick, Vero Beach°	1.000	40	3	8	0	0
Harkins, Miami°	.938	40	4	11	1	1
Hartley, St. Petersburg	.944	31	11	23	2	4
Harvey, Lakeland°	1.000	7	3	2	0	0
Hawkins, Fort Lauderdale	1.000	1	0	1	0	0
Hawley, Tampa	.976	26	19	22	1	3
Hess, West Palm Beach	1.000	13	2	5	0	0
Heuer, Vero Beach	.941	26	12	20	2	2
Hillegas, Vero Beach	.913	13	4	17	2	1
Hinz, Lakeland	.933	16	6	8	1	0
Holman, West Palm Beach	.500	4	0	1	1	0
Hoyt, St. Petersburg	1.000	4	1	1	0	0
Huber, West Palm Beach	1.000	43	8	15	0	3
Impagliazzo, West Palm Beach..	.750	11	0	3	1	1
James, Lakeland	.684	21	6	7	6	0
Jefferson, West Palm Beach	.917	12	5	6	1	0
Johnson, West Palm Beach	.667	7	0	2	1	0
Johnston, Vero Beach	1.000	21	1	2	0	0
K. Jones, Tampa	.909	20	13	27	4	1
S. Jones, Tampa°	.800	12	5	3	2	1
Kasprzak, Daytona Beach	1.000	2	0	2	0	0
Kinns, West Palm Beach	.955	26	4	17	1	0
Klein, Fort Myers	1.000	11	3	2	0	0
Kolotka, Miami	1.000	11	1	2	0	0
Konderla, Tampa	1.000	20	0	4	0	0
Lara, Tampa	.714	33	2	3	2	0
Leister, Winter Haven	.895	31	12	22	4	2
Livingston, Vero Beach°	.941	13	4	12	1	1
Madden, Tampa°	.889	29	11	29	5	4
A. Martinez, Fort Myers	1.000	9	0	5	0	0
C. Martinez, St. Petersburg	1.000	17	3	8	0	1
Mathews, Daytona Beach	.951	27	9	30	2	1
McClain, Miami	.938	27	21	54	5	4
McCullers, Miami	1.000	22	11	18	0	1
McLoughlin, Miami	.889	24	0	8	1	0
Meagher, Vero Beach	1.000	49	7	11	0	1
Melchert, Lakeland°	.769	17	5	3	1	1
Mettler, Winter Haven	1.000	7	1	2	0	0
Mielke, West Palm Beach	.957	28	10	12	1	1
Minnema, Lakeland	.000	2	0	3	0	0
Minor, Winter Haven	.948	30	21	34	3	1
J. Mitchell, Winter Haven	.930	27	20	33	4	5
W. Mitchell, St. Petersburg	.889	23	3	5	1	0
Mize, Daytona Beach	.810	30	8	9	4	1
Mohr, Fort Myers°	1.000	28	4	1	0	0
Montgomery, Tampa	1.000	31	5	4	0	2
Moran, West Palm Beach°	.842	18	4	12	3	1
Morgan, Fort Lauderdale	.929	46	1	12	1	0
Mosher, Vero Beach	1.000	11	0	2	0	0
Moya, Lakeland	1.000	4	1	3	0	1
Nicometi, West Palm Beach°	.935	25	13	30	3	1
Nielson, Fort Lauderdale	.857	4	2	4	1	2
Nilsson, Lakeland	1.000	9	4	10	0	1
Noble, Daytona Beach°	1.000	24	4	29	0	2
Oliver, Miami	.857	45	9	9	3	1
Owchinko, Tampa°	1.000	7	0	4	0	0
Paris, Daytona Beach	.917	9	3	19	2	2
Parsons, Miami	.912	29	8	23	3	0
Pena, Lakeland	1.000	20	2	6	0	0
Perkins, Daytona Beach	.929	39	6	20	2	1
Perrotte, Lakeland°	1.000	22	4	18	0	0
Perry, Winter Haven	.867	20	4	9	2	1
Pesavento, Vero Beach°	.750	15	4	11	5	0
Peterson, Lakeland°	1.000	5	1	3	0	0
Phillion, Lakeland°	1.000	6	1	5	0	0
Plesac, Miami	1.000	9	1	5	0	1
Plunk, Fort Lauderdale	.892	28	9	24	4	1
Poindexter, Winter Haven	.923	21	5	7	1	3
Poston, Miami	.957	29	16	28	2	2
Powell, Vero Beach°	1.000	4	0	4	0	0
Raftice, Fort Lauderdale°	.818	36	1	8	2	0
Raubolt, Lakeland	1.000	29	1	14	0	2
Regalado, Daytona Beach	.905	24	4	15	2	1
Reilly, Daytona Beach	.667	8	0	4	2	1
Retz, Daytona Beach°	1.000	4	1	1	0	1

PITCHERS—Continued

Player and Club	Pct.	G.	PO.	A.	E.	DP.
Rexrode, Vero Beach	.700	43	4	10	6	0
Reynolds, Tampa	.968	36	6	24	1	2
Robinson, Lakeland	.923	10	5	7	1	2
Samuels, Daytona Beach*	.958	13	3	20	1	0
Sanchez, Fort Myers*	.824	14	5	9	3	0
Scudero, Lakeland*	1.000	12	1	7	0	0
Seitz, Fort Lauderdale	1.000	6	0	7	0	1
Sellers, Winter Haven	.976	29	9	31	1	4
Shaab, Daytona Beach*	.933	48	4	10	1	0
Shade, St. Petersburg	1.000	28	2	6	0	0
Silkwood, St. Petersburg	.929	8	4	9	1	1
Simmons, Lakeland	.625	9	1	4	3	0
Skripko, Winter Haven	1.000	5	5	2	0	0
Slezak, Vero Beach	1.000	3	2	1	0	0
Smalley, Fort Lauderdale*	.833	12	0	5	1	0
Smith, Tampa*	.852	54	6	17	4	3
Snediker, Winter Haven	.923	11	6	6	1	0
Snell, Fort Myers	.923	11	6	6	1	0
Soto, Tampa	.667	2	1	1	1	0
Souza, Lakeland	1.000	7	3	7	0	1
Spagnola, Tampa	.750	12	3	6	3	0
Stewart, Miami	.925	32	6	31	3	0
Strasser, Daytona Beach	.938	15	13	17	2	1
Tejeda, Vero Beach*	1.000	15	2	5	0	0
Torres, Winter Haven	.875	35	2	12	2	0
Traen, West Palm Beach*	1.000	1	0	2	0	0
Tuck, Fort Myers	.929	40	7	6	1	1
Valdez, West Palm Beach	1.000	5	2	1	0	0
Vanderpohl, Fort Myers*	1.000	6	1	0	0	0
Walberg, Fort Myers	.958	16	8	15	1	1
Walter, Miami*	.909	9	4	6	1	0
Ware, Fort Myers	.902	27	13	24	4	2
Watson, Tampa	.875	41	2	5	1	1
Wayne, West Palm Beach*	1.000	13	7	18	0	2
Weinbrecht, Winter Haven*	1.000	8	4	5	0	0
Wever, Fort Lauderdale	1.000	7	1	2	0	0
Wex, Fort Lauderdale	1.000	14	0	10	0	0
Wheeler, 5 Lake. 24 W. Hav.*	.909	29	4	6	1	0
Williams, West Palm Beach	.957	9	9	13	1	1
Wohler, Vero Beach*	.936	28	6	38	3	2
Wong, Fort Myers	.778	15	3	4	2	0
Woodworth, Fort Lauderdale*	.962	19	5	20	1	0
Worrell, St. Petersburg	.727	8	3	5	3	1
YOUNG, St. Petersburg	1.000	22	13	24	0	1

Triple Play—Perry.

The following players do not have any recorded accepted chances at the positions indicated; therefore, are not listed in the fielding averages for those particular positions: Arce, ss; Armstrong, p; Azcona, p; Balcomb, c; Beringhele, 2b; Camelo, p; Chapman, 3b, of; Dunlop, p; Edmiston, of; Fennell, 3b, p; Fortaleza, c; Graham, of; Gregory, p; R.D. Hall, ss; Hawkins, 3b; Horne, p; Hough, p; J.M. Johnston, ss; Labozzetta, p; Mathison, p; Mauch, of; McManus, of; Meleski, 1b; T. Mitchell, 2b; Ray, p; Riggs, of; S. Robinson, ss; A. Rodriguez, c; Wallace, of.

CLUB PITCHING

Club	ERA.	G.	CG.	ShO.	Sv.	IP.	H.	R.	ER.	HR.	HB.	BB.	Int. BB.	SO.	WP.	Bk.
Tampa	3.01	139	36	12	24	1144.0	988	507	383	47	29	581	49	837	69	11
Daytona Beach	3.33	144	25	10	28	1225.1	1112	562	453	41	52	640	29	745	90	5
Fort Lauderdale	3.33	142	18	11	28	1189.0	1103	591	440	37	46	620	32	825	63	17
Miami	3.44	138	36	13	21	1174.2	1037	555	449	32	44	626	54	722	64	17
Vero Beach	3.54	146	35	11	26	1232.0	1172	605	484	41	28	613	41	686	74	17
St. Petersburg	3.56	144	26	11	28	1198.2	1128	600	474	39	28	615	66	841	72	11
West Palm Beach	3.61	144	24	7	32	1236.1	1151	608	496	66	45	615	21	798	61	14
Winter Haven	3.73	144	26	7	30	1208.1	1222	634	501	50	29	636	22	643	87	18
Fort Myers	3.79	141	23	14	20	1182.2	1222	608	498	39	37	537	49	695	43	8
Lakeland	4.74	144	31	7	15	1169.1	1153	757	616	56	61	743	26	699	88	27

PITCHERS' RECORDS
(Leading Qualifiers for Earned-Run Average Leadership — 117 or More Innings)

*Throws lefthanded.

Pitcher—Club	W.	L.	Pct.	ERA.	G.	GS.	CG.	GF.	ShO.	Sv.	IP.	H.	R.	ER.	HR.	HB.	BB.	Int. BB.	SO.	WP.
Hawley, Tampa	18	5	.783	1.87	26	26	12	0	5	0	178.0	151	52	37	4	1	44	3	95	4
Reynolds, Tampa	9	7	.563	2.01	36	14	7	9	1	2	129.2	108	45	29	6	2	29	1	106	8
K. Jones, Tampa	10	7	.588	2.76	20	19	7	1	0	0	133.2	119	50	41	5	4	55	4	93	9
Cloninger, Fort Lauderdale	4	9	.308	2.85	29	17	0	3	0	2	129.1	120	57	41	2	2	66	4	67	6
Plunk, Fort Lauderdale	12	12	.500	2.86	28	28	7	0	1	0	176.1	153	85	56	5	6	123	1	152	17
Cerefin, Daytona Beach	8	8	.500	2.98	23	23	1	0	1	0	139.0	105	59	46	5	7	122	2	106	12
Heuer, Vero Beach	13	5	.722	2.99	26	21	10	1	2	0	162.2	153	61	54	3	4	49	1	76	8
Epple, St. Petersburg	9	7	.563	3.07	29	23	5	3	4	1	137.2	109	56	47	5	3	42	2	105	4
J. Mitchell, Winter Haven	16	9	.640	3.14	27	27	4	0	0	0	183.2	160	84	64	9	5	66	2	109	21
Poston, Miami	14	12	.538	3.23	29	28	7	1	2	0	175.2	156	82	63	3	6	67	4	101	4

Departmental Leaders: G—Smith, 54; W—Hawley, 18; L—Barlow, 17; Pct.—Kinns, .800; GS—Sellers, 29; CG—Hawley, 12; GF—Boever, 38; ShO—Hawley, Parsons, 5; Sv.—Boever, Montgomery, Torres, 14; IP—J. Mitchell, 183.2; H—Mathews, 198; R—Barlow, 116; ER—Barlow, 92; HR—Mielke, 14; HB—James, Watson, 9; BB—Plunk, 123; IBB—Oliver, 13; SO—Plunk, 152; WP—J. Mitchell, 21.

(All Pitchers—Listed Alphabetically)

Pitcher—Club	W.	L.	Pct.	ERA.	G.	GS.	CG.	GF.	ShO.	Sv.	IP.	H.	R.	ER.	HR.	HB.	BB.	Int. BB.	SO.	WP.
Armstrong, Fort Lauderdale	1	0	1.000	0.77	8	0	0	6	0	2	11.2	9	2	1	1	1	5	0	15	0
Azcona, West Palm Beach*	0	0	.000	14.54	4	0	0	2	0	0	4.1	5	7	7	0	0	6	0	4	1
Baker, Daytona Beach	0	1	.000	1.01	17	0	0	12	0	7	26.2	24	14	3	0	0	13	2	12	1
Barlow, Lakeland	1	17	.056	6.79	25	25	4	0	1	0	122.0	134	116	92	6	8	101	2	65	12
Barrett, West Palm Beach	5	4	.556	2.30	11	11	3	0	1	0	78.1	68	25	20	0	1	23	0	64	3
Bass, Fort Myers	7	5	.583	3.41	30	15	3	7	1	0	111.0	121	51	42	4	4	42	5	57	8
Beahan, Fort Lauderdale	9	10	.474	3.71	25	23	3	0	1	0	116.1	117	70	48	6	8	61	7	77	7
Belanger, West Palm Beach*	2	2	.500	4.03	48	0	0	25	0	9	73.2	77	38	33	5	4	22	4	42	4
Bencomo, Winter Haven	5	3	.625	2.89	41	5	0	32	0	6	93.1	100	40	30	0	2	47	4	65	5
Benedict, Fort Myers	5	1	.833	1.27	20	0	0	19	0	7	35.1	26	11	5	0	1	11	2	27	0
Birtsas, Fort Lauderdale*	5	1	.833	3.59	11	10	0	0	0	0	57.2	51	23	23	0	3	37	0	62	2
Boever, St. Petersburg	6	4	.600	3.01	48	0	0	38	0	14	77.2	52	31	26	2	1	45	5	81	1
Bombard, Daytona Beach	2	6	.250	2.35	30	0	0	25	0	12	46.0	38	18	12	0	2	14	1	40	5
Boyles, Tampa	3	9	.250	3.92	18	16	2	2	0	0	85.0	73	42	37	2	0	41	0	65	4
Brahs, West Palm Beach*	7	3	.700	2.27	20	11	3	4	2	1	91.0	69	30	23	4	7	32	2	61	3
Burke, Fort Myers*	2	3	.400	3.97	25	2	0	11	0	0	59.0	58	27	26	4	1	34	2	45	2
Burwell, St. Petersburg	0	0	.000	5.91	6	0	0	0	0	0	35.0	43	28	23	1	2	23	2	14	3
Byron, Fort Lauderdale	11	4	.733	3.50	37	13	3	11	1	0	126.0	106	58	49	0	1	68	1	81	13
Cahill, St. Petersburg	6	6	.500	3.15	45	7	0	15	0	1	91.1	97	44	32	4	1	48	11	38	5
Calvert, Tampa	2	2	.500	2.72	10	7	0	2	0	0	36.1	29	17	11	3	0	23	1	20	1
Camelo, West Palm Beach*	0	0	.000	9.00	1	0	0	1	0	0	2.0	6	5	2	1	0	1	0	0	0
Carrasco, St. Petersburg	1	1	.500	8.38	10	0	0	4	0	0	9.2	12	12	9	1	1	6	2	6	2
Caulfield, St. Petersburg*	1	3	.250	4.46	30	0	0	10	0	1	38.1	33	22	19	1	0	34	2	33	4
Cerefin, Daytona Beach	8	8	.500	2.98	23	23	1	0	1	0	139.0	105	59	46	5	7	122	2	106	12

Pitcher—Club	W.	L.	Pct.	ERA.	G.	GS.	CG.	GF.	ShO.	Sv.	IP.	H.	R.	ER.	HR.	HB.	BB.	Int. BB.	SO.	WP.
Charlton, West Palm Beach*	1	4	.200	4.58	8	8	0	0	0	0	39.1	51	27	20	2	1	22	0	27	1
M. Cherry, Vero Beach	0	2	.000	8.71	3	3	0	0	0	0	10.1	17	12	10	3	0	6	0	5	1
P. Cherry, St. Petersburg*	12	11	.522	3.30	36	28	4	3	2	1	169.0	183	90	62	6	1	73	8	93	6
Childers, Miami	4	7	.364	3.66	36	10	2	18	0	0	108.1	108	54	44	4	8	63	7	52	3
Cloninger, 3 Mia. 26-Ft.L.	4	9	.308	2.85	29	17	0	3	0	2	129.1	120	57	41	2	2	66	4	67	6
Cooper, Lakeland	0	1	.000	4.02	7	0	0	5	0	0	15.2	20	9	7	1	0	14	1	7	2
Cunningham, Vero Beach	4	5	.444	5.77	14	14	0	0	0	0	78.0	93	59	50	2	5	44	1	29	1
Cutshall, West Palm Beach	0	2	.000	5.26	5	5	0	0	0	0	25.2	23	16	15	2	0	19	0	31	1
Dalton, Winter Haven*	5	8	.385	3.18	38	9	2	23	0	6	107.2	115	56	38	2	2	52	4	43	8
J. Daniel, Fort Myers	4	1	.800	4.81	12	8	1	1	0	0	43.0	52	29	23	2	1	17	0	26	0
P.C. Daniel, Tampa*	0	3	.000	7.63	4	3	0	0	0	0	15.1	16	14	13	2	1	6	2	17	4
Davis, Fort Myers	7	11	.389	4.53	25	25	5	0	0	0	153.0	170	91	77	9	6	70	3	84	8
Dibble, Tampa	5	2	.714	2.92	15	11	2	1	0	0	64.2	59	31	21	2	1	29	4	39	3
Dotson, Lakeland	3	7	.300	5.25	18	11	0	5	0	0	60.0	60	45	35	4	4	55	1	34	5
Drizmala, Fort Myers*	5	3	.625	4.76	26	13	1	4	0	0	85.0	94	57	45	2	3	54	3	58	3
Duffy, Lakeland*	0	1	.000	7.90	4	0	0	6	0	1	13.2	19	18	12	4	0	8	1	13	0
Dunlop, Miami	0	0	.000	0.00	1	0	0	1	0	0	0.1	0	0	0	0	0	1	0	0	0
A. Dunn, Lakeland	3	8	.273	5.44	14	14	6	0	0	0	82.2	90	51	50	8	3	43	1	30	6
G. Dunn, St. Petersburg	5	12	.294	4.26	30	23	0	4	0	1	126.2	120	75	60	6	3	90	5	99	8
Easley, Fort Lauderdale	5	7	.417	3.85	32	19	1	5	0	1	131.0	150	76	56	5	5	44	4	57	4
Epple, St. Petersburg*	9	7	.563	3.07	29	23	5	3	4	1	137.2	109	56	47	5	3	42	2	105	4
Ergle, Tampa	1	2	.333	2.56	13	3	0	2	0	0	31.2	23	10	9	1	0	26	0	31	6
Fennell, Fort Lauderdale	0	0	.000	9.00	1	0	0	1	0	0	2.0	2	2	2	0	0	2	0	0	0
Flores, West Palm Beach	8	7	.533	3.32	51	0	0	18	0	3	122.0	108	54	45	10	4	53	3	67	3
Freeman, Lakeland*	4	2	.667	2.97	17	0	0	10	0	3	30.1	23	10	10	2	0	5	1	11	1
Frey, Fort Lauderdale*	4	2	.667	2.09	47	0	0	25	0	4	64.2	46	26	15	2	0	34	2	66	4
Friedrich, Daytona Beach	12	9	.571	3.48	25	24	5	0	1	0	147.1	121	69	57	3	6	94	3	80	17
Galvez, Vero Beach	12	11	.522	3.62	26	26	9	0	3	0	156.2	152	68	63	8	1	62	4	76	3
Garcia, Lakeland*	3	3	.500	3.48	14	4	0	7	0	1	44.0	46	26	17	0	1	23	3	30	0
Gentle, Vero Beach*	2	2	.500	3.78	11	7	1	2	0	0	50.0	48	25	21	2	0	37	0	28	6
Goodin, Fort Myers*	8	6	.571	3.41	21	18	2	2	0	0	116.0	136	61	44	7	3	35	1	67	3
Graham, Fort Lauderdale	2	1	.667	1.96	25	1	0	11	0	5	18.1	16	4	4	0	1	2	1	15	0
Graybill, West Palm Beach	2	2	.500	2.39	10	4	2	2	0	1	37.2	23	11	10	2	1	19	1	16	2
Greenlee, Miami*	0	1	.000	6.28	11	0	0	8	0	0	14.1	17	11	10	1	0	18	0	4	5
Gregory, Vero Beach*	0	0	.000	2.35	5	0	0	2	0	0	7.2	8	4	2	0	1	6	0	5	0
Gumbert, Fort Lauderdale	0	1	.000	13.50	7	0	0	2	0	1	10.2	17	18	16	1	2	12	0	12	0
Halley, Lakeland	0	0	.000	36.00	2	0	0	0	0	0	2.0	9	12	8	0	0	2	0	3	1
A. Hamilton, Winter Haven	0	0	.000	0.00	1	0	0	1	0	0	1.0	2	0	0	0	0	0	0	0	0
R. Hamilton, Vero Beach	3	0	1.000	2.60	4	3	0	0	0	0	17.1	12	6	5	1	0	12	0	8	0
Hamrick, Vero Beach*	1	2	.333	5.73	40	0	0	25	0	3	55.0	44	40	35	2	1	59	5	36	9
Harkins, Miami*	4	3	.571	4.47	40	2	0	9	0	2	86.2	92	53	43	2	4	40	2	58	7
Hartley, St. Petersburg	8	14	.364	4.20	31	23	4	1	1	0	139.1	142	81	65	3	4	84	10	88	16
Harvey, Lakeland*	1	0	1.000	1.98	7	1	0	3	0	0	13.2	12	7	3	0	1	10	0	9	1
Hawkins, Fort Lauderdale	0	0	.000	36.00	1	0	0	0	0	0	1.0	3	4	4	0	1	3	1	0	0
Hawley, Tampa	18	5	.783	1.87	26	26	12	0	5	0	178.0	151	52	37	4	1	44	3	95	4
Hess, West Palm Beach	0	2	.000	4.60	13	0	0	7	0	0	15.2	23	14	8	3	0	5	0	7	0
Heuer, Vero Beach	13	5	.722	2.99	26	21	10	1	2	0	162.2	153	61	54	3	4	49	1	76	8
Hillegas, Vero Beach	5	3	.625	1.83	13	13	4	0	2	0	93.1	71	25	19	1	3	33	3	64	1
Hinz, Lakeland	2	7	.222	5.27	16	16	2	0	0	0	83.2	86	53	49	4	2	61	1	53	6
Holman, West Palm Beach	3	0	1.000	18.00	4	4	0	0	0	0	8.0	14	19	16	0	0	21	0	14	2
Horne, Fort Lauderdale	1	0	1.000	0.00	4	0	0	1	0	0	4.1	7	5	0	1	2	1	0	2	0
Hough, Daytona Beach	0	0	.000	0.00	1	0	0	1	0	0	1.0	2	0	0	0	0	0	0	0	0
Hoyt, St. Petersburg	0	0	.000	24.30	4	0	0	2	0	0	3.1	7	9	9	0	1	5	0	4	1
Huber, West Palm Beach	7	6	.538	3.02	43	0	0	29	0	12	59.2	61	21	20	2	2	32	7	39	3
Impagliazzo, West Palm Beach	1	2	.333	1.32	11	0	0	11	0	3	13.2	8	3	2	0	0	10	1	13	1
James, Lakeland	5	8	.385	3.47	21	10	6	6	1	0	90.2	53	40	35	4	9	70	3	78	9
Jefferson, West Palm Beach	6	4	.600	4.38	12	12	2	0	1	0	76.0	81	48	37	4	2	35	0	60	1
Johnson, West Palm Beach	0	1	.000	4.09	7	0	0	2	0	1	11.0	7	6	5	0	3	7	0	5	2
Johnston, Vero Beach	2	2	.500	2.96	21	0	0	16	0	6	27.1	26	10	9	0	0	13	0	11	2
K. Jones, Tampa	10	7	.588	2.76	20	19	7	1	0	0	133.2	119	50	41	8	0	55	4	93	9
S. Jones, Tampa*	1	3	.250	6.94	12	5	0	3	0	1	35.0	35	35	27	4	2	33	0	20	2
Kasprzak, Daytona Beach	0	0	.000	1.59	2	0	0	2	0	1	5.2	5	1	1	0	0	1	0	5	0
Kinns, West Palm Beach	12	3	.800	3.10	26	14	4	7	1	0	101.2	69	41	35	3	4	76	1	62	6
Klein, Fort Myers	2	0	1.000	5.79	22	0	0	10	0	0	32.2	38	27	21	1	0	27	4	16	1
Kolotka, Miami	1	2	.333	5.11	11	0	0	6	0	0	12.1	7	10	7	0	0	9	3	6	0
Konderla, Tampa	3	1	.750	1.20	20	0	0	15	0	0	30.0	19	10	4	1	0	29	7	38	3
Labozzetta, Lakeland*	0	0	.000	9.82	3	0	0	1	0	1	3.2	6	4	4	0	0	3	1	0	1
Lara, Lakeland	1	4	.200	4.84	33	3	1	17	0	1	74.1	78	52	40	2	4	52	4	79	12
Leister, Winter Haven	12	12	.500	3.39	31	27	7	1	1	0	175.1	173	90	66	4	4	93	1	103	8
Livingston, Vero Beach*	5	3	.625	4.85	13	13	1	0	0	0	68.2	67	42	37	5	0	39	0	61	7
Madden, Tampa*	6	9	.400	4.36	29	21	5	0	1	0	132.0	123	71	64	6	5	98	8	103	15
A. Martinez, Fort Myers	3	2	.600	1.76	9	0	0	6	0	1	15.1	8	3	3	0	2	3	1	9	1
C. Martinez, St. Petersburg	7	0	1.000	1.40	17	7	4	2	3	1	70.2	50	12	11	1	2	31	3	81	5
Mathews, Daytona Beach	13	7	.650	3.54	27	27	5	0	1	0	172.2	190	83	68	10	5	41	0	73	15
Mathison, Fort Lauderdale	0	0	.000	0.00	1	0	0	0	0	0	2.0	3	3	0	0	0	3	0	1	0
McClain, Miami	11	11	.500	3.89	27	26	10	0	2	0	182.2	162	85	79	7	7	83	8	100	5
McCullers, Miami	4	6	.400	2.54	22	13	5	4	1	0	106.1	92	37	30	3	5	45	5	94	5
McLoughlin, Miami	3	3	.500	2.48	24	0	0	15	0	5	40.0	29	11	11	0	2	17	5	31	2
Meagher, Vero Beach	8	7	.533	3.53	49	1	0	35	0	10	81.2	67	47	32	2	2	51	6	84	8
Melchert, Lakeland*	0	8	.000	6.07	17	3	0	6	0	0	46.0	52	35	31	1	1	29	0	25	4
Mettler, Winter Haven	1	0	1.000	3.97	7	0	0	4	0	0	11.1	20	8	5	1	0	7	0	9	2
Mielke, West Palm Beach	5	4	.556	4.29	28	11	0	5	0	1	109.0	116	66	52	14	3	48	1	76	5
Minnema, Lakeland	0	1	.000	14.21	2	2	0	0	0	0	6.1	11	12	10	0	2	4	0	0	0
Minor, Winter Haven	10	13	.435	3.91	30	28	6	0	0	0	182.0	183	95	79	6	2	99	1	65	9
J. Mitchell, Winter Haven	16	9	.640	3.14	27	27	4	0	0	0	183.2	160	84	64	9	5	66	2	109	21
W. Mitchell, St. Petersburg	1	1	.500	5.31	23	0	0	6	0	0	39.0	38	27	23	3	2	28	3	22	2
Mize, Daytona Beach	5	9	.357	6.16	30	12	0	12	0	0	87.2	88	70	60	3	7	73	4	51	8
Mohr, Fort Myers*	6	0	1.000	1.11	28	0	0	26	0	9	40.2	28	8	5	0	0	12	2	31	2
Montgomery, Tampa	5	3	.625	2.44	31	0	0	28	0	14	44.1	29	15	12	1	0	30	6	56	1
Moran, West Palm Beach	2	6	.250	4.12	18	14	0	2	0	1	74.1	69	44	34	2	1	50	0	48	4
Morgan, Fort Lauderdale	3	7	.300	2.42	46	1	0	30	0	7	81.2	50	27	22	4	0	48	4	41	2
Mosher, Vero Beach	0	2	.000	2.03	11	0	0	5	0	1	13.1	16	7	3	0	3	2		8	1

Pitcher—Club	W.	L.	Pct.	ERA.	G.	GS.	CG.	GF.	ShO.	Sv.	IP.	H.	R.	ER.	HR.	HB.	BB.	Int. BB.	SO.	WP.
Moya, Lakeland	0	4	.000	5.57	4	4	1	0	0	0	21.0	27	13	13	0	2	8	0	10	1
Nicometi, W. Palm Beach°	5	8	.385	3.30	25	18	3	3	0	0	136.1	116	55	50	4	7	61	1	70	8
Nielson, Fort Lauderdale	2	1	.667	1.08	4	3	1	0	0	0	16.2	16	8	2	0	1	5	0	7	0
Nilsson, Lakeland	1	4	.200	5.95	9	6	4	3	0	0	39.1	46	31	26	1	1	21	2	16	1
Noble, Daytona Beach°	9	4	.692	2.64	29	13	4	8	1	0	116.0	98	36	34	4	2	44	1	67	1
Oliver, Miami	2	7	.222	2.48	45	2	1	26	1	8	83.1	74	35	23	2	4	39	13	44	4
Owchinko, Tampa°	1	1	.500	0.00	7	0	0	5	0	1	12.2	4	2	0	0	3	1	13	0	
Paris, Daytona Beach	3	3	.500	3.28	9	9	0	0	0	0	57.2	44	27	21	2	6	46	0	45	3
Parsons, Miami	10	9	.526	3.56	29	22	6	5	5	1	134.0	125	69	53	6	4	55	1	66	5
Pena, Lakeland	6	1	.857	1.67	20	0	0	18	0	4	37.2	22	8	7	3	1	14	3	41	3
Perkins, Daytona Beach	4	2	.667	3.06	39	1	0	18	0	6	64.2	57	29	22	2	2	37	2	46	6
Perrotte, Lakeland°	5	10	.333	4.80	22	20	2	1	0	0	114.1	105	73	61	5	7	81	0	62	6
Perry, Winter Haven	1	2	.333	5.32	20	2	0	4	0	0	44.0	32	33	26	5	3	40	0	27	4
Pesavento, Vero Beach°	6	1	.857	1.71	15	8	5	2	0	0	73.2	50	20	14	2	4	37	4	44	3
Peterson, Lakeland°	0	1	.000	5.48	5	1	0	2	0	0	21.1	18	19	13	4	1	19	1	8	5
Phillion, Lakeland°	4	1	.800	3.26	6	6	1	0	1	0	38.2	39	15	14	0	0	18	0	18	2
Plesac, Miami	1	1	.500	3.89	9	5	0	2	0	0	34.2	21	18	15	0	2	39	0	16	4
Plunk, Fort Lauderdale	12	12	.500	2.86	28	28	7	0	1	0	176.1	153	85	56	5	6	123	1	152	17
Poindexter, Winter Haven	1	1	.500	5.19	21	0	0	6	0	1	52.0	65	35	30	4	5	28	0	35	5
Poston, Miami	14	12	.538	3.23	29	28	7	1	2	0	175.2	156	82	63	3	6	67	4	101	4
Powell, Vero Beach°	1	1	.500	1.38	4	4	0	0	0	0	26.0	19	7	4	0	1	12	1	14	3
Raftice, Fort Lauderdale	4	2	.667	2.79	36	0	0	18	0	5	58.0	41	19	18	2	2	27	3	41	3
Raubolt, Lakeland	3	3	.500	3.09	29	1	0	14	0	3	55.1	43	26	19	0	8	38	1	26	4
Ray, Fort Lauderdale°	0	0	.000	0.00	1	0	0	0	0	0	0.0	0	1	1	0	0	3	0	0	0
Regalado, Daytona Beach	6	1	.857	2.91	24	8	1	8	0	1	74.1	65	31	24	4	3	34	3	31	2
Reilly, Daytona Beach	0	1	.000	1.96	8	1	0	3	0	3	23.0	20	5	5	1	0	5	1	9	1
Retz, Daytona Beach°	0	0	.000	20.25	4	0	0	2	0	0	4.0	13	11	9	0	0	8	0	4	2
Rexrode, Vero Beach	5	10	.333	4.15	43	1	0	20	0	5	73.2	81	50	34	1	2	52	10	38	8
Reynolds, Tampa	9	7	.563	2.01	36	14	7	9	1	2	129.2	108	45	29	6	2	29	1	106	8
Robinson, Lakeland	2	3	.400	3.36	10	10	2	0	1	0	61.2	62	30	23	3	1	26	0	33	1
Samuels, Daytona Beach°	5	4	.556	4.21	13	11	3	1	1	0	68.1	67	40	32	3	4	37	0	44	6
Sanchez, Fort Myers°	3	3	.500	3.65	14	10	1	0	1	0	66.2	62	30	27	4	1	29	1	63	1
Scudero, Lakeland°	1	2	.333	4.91	12	0	0	5	0	1	18.1	20	16	10	1	2	10	0	10	2
Seitz, Fort Lauderdale	0	2	.000	5.30	6	4	0	2	0	1	18.2	30	15	11	1	0	8	0	10	0
Sellers, Winter Haven	12	10	.545	3.41	29	29	7	0	1	0	182.0	182	87	69	5	2	80	3	94	13
Shaab, Daytona Beach°	5	4	.556	3.48	48	0	0	27	0	4	77.2	73	35	30	2	1	38	7	77	7
Shade, St. Petersburg	0	2	.000	1.38	28	0	0	23	0	8	45.2	35	12	7	0	3	26	5	43	4
Silkwood, St. Petersburg	3	3	.500	4.24	8	6	2	0	1	0	40.1	42	21	19	0	1	13	2	29	1
Simmons, Lakeland	0	4	.000	4.45	9	4	0	2	0	0	32.1	41	22	16	3	0	11	0	16	2
Skripko, Winter Haven	0	1	.000	3.05	5	4	0	1	0	0	20.2	15	8	7	0	0	11	0	14	1
Slezak, Vero Beach	1	2	.333	3.75	3	3	0	0	0	0	12.0	14	5	5	0	0	6	0	12	1
Smalley, Fort Lauderdale°	1	1	.500	3.32	12	0	0	3	0	1	21.2	17	10	8	1	2	7	0	23	0
Smith, Tampa°	4	4	.500	2.55	54	0	0	23	0	5	77.2	62	33	22	3	2	69	10	63	4
Snediker, Winter Haven	1	3	.250	4.54	11	6	0	2	0	0	33.2	36	20	17	2	1	37	0	12	3
Snell, Fort Myers	4	7	.364	3.27	11	11	3	0	0	0	74.1	91	37	27	1	2	20	2	28	2
Soto, Tampa	0	1	.000	3.48	2	1	0	0	0	0	10.1	13	4	4	1	0	3	0	5	0
Souza, Lakeland	2	2	.500	2.22	7	3	2	1	0	0	28.1	14	10	7	0	2	15	1	14	2
Spagnola, Tampa	2	6	.250	4.05	12	12	0	0	0	0	60.0	55	39	27	4	2	35	0	34	3
Stewart, Miami	5	7	.417	3.78	32	19	2	6	0	0	126.1	104	64	53	3	1	114	5	75	14
Strasser, Daytona Beach	10	3	.769	2.30	15	15	6	0	2	0	113.2	102	34	29	2	7	33	3	55	4
Tejeda, Vero Beach°	2	0	1.000	2.86	15	5	1	1	0	1	50.1	51	24	16	5	1	20	0	27	2
Torres, Winter Haven	2	7	.222	3.55	35	0	0	33	0	14	50.2	55	23	20	1	2	19	3	27	5
Traen, West Palm Beach	1	0	1.000	1.00	1	1	1	0	0	0	9.0	7	1	1	1	0	2	0	4	0
Tuck, Fort Myers	5	2	.714	3.89	40	7	0	15	0	2	85.2	77	45	37	0	5	68	5	55	4
Valdez, West Palm Beach	0	0	.000	8.74	5	0	0	2	0	0	11.1	15	11	11	2	0	8	0	6	1
Vanderpohl, Fort Myers°	1	1	.500	5.40	6	0	0	1	0	0	6.2	9	4	4	0	0	5	1	0	
Walberg, Fort Myers	8	4	.667	3.86	16	12	5	0	2	0	93.1	89	41	40	2	2	31	6	57	1
Walter, Miami°	3	5	.375	2.29	9	9	3	0	0	0	59.0	43	22	15	1	1	27	1	70	4
Ware, Fort Myers	9	11	.450	4.02	27	20	3	4	0	0	134.1	138	71	60	2	1	58	7	53	4
Watson, Tampa	4	0	1.000	3.59	41	1	1	12	0	1	67.2	70	37	27	2	9	28	2	39	2
Wayne, West Palm Beach°	3	5	.375	3.87	13	12	2	0	0	0	74.1	70	38	32	1	3	49	0	46	9
Weinbrecht, Winter Haven°	0	3	.000	10.23	8	4	0	1	0	0	22.0	36	26	25	6	1	30	0	18	2
Wever, Fort Lauderdale	1	3	.250	5.09	7	5	0	0	0	0	23.0	22	15	13	1	0	15	0	13	3
Wex, Fort Lauderdale	4	2	.667	2.14	14	5	1	5	0	1	42.0	35	14	10	2	2	21	1	31	2
Wheeler, 5 Lake.-24 W. Hav.°	4	2	.667	4.26	29	3	0	11	0	3	61.1	65	33	29	5	1	29	4	29	1
Williams, West Palm Beach	5	4	.556	2.74	9	9	4	0	1	0	62.1	65	28	19	4	2	14	0	36	1
Wohler, Vero Beach°	9	9	.500	3.67	28	24	4	2	0	0	174.1	183	93	71	4	3	72	4	60	10
Wong, Fort Myers	2	0	1.000	3.52	15	0	0	11	0	2	30.2	25	15	12	1	5	21	4	18	3
Woodworth, Fort Lauderdale°	5	5	.500	4.47	19	16	2	2	0	0	86.2	99	53	43	3	0	34	3	57	2
Worrell, St. Petersburg	3	2	.600	2.09	8	7	2	0	0	0	47.1	41	22	11	0	0	24	2	33	4
Young, St. Petersburg	9	7	.563	3.60	22	20	5	0	0	0	127.2	124	58	51	6	3	43	4	72	6

BALKS—Nilsson, Plunk, 7 each; Minor, Stewart, 6 each; Hawley, Pesavento, 5 each; G. Dunn, Galvez, James, Sellers, 4 each; Cutshall, Morgan, Perrotte, Poston, Raubolt, 3 each; Byron, Childers, J. Daniel, A. Dunn, Easley, Hartley, K. Jones, Livingston, McClain, J. Mitchell, Moran, Rexrode, Robinson, Strasser, Wayne, 2 each; Barlow, Bass, Beahan, Bencomo, Boever, Boyles, Burwell, Cerefin, Charlton, P. Cherry, Cloninger, Cooper, Dalton, Davis, Dibble, Dotson, Drizmala, Duffy, Flores, Garcia, Gentle, Graybill, Harkins, Hillegas, Holman, Hoyt, Impagliazzo, A. Martinez, C. Martinez, Meagher, Mielke, Parsons, Perry, Plesac, Reynolds, Samuels, Scudero, Shaab, Skripko, Spagnola, Torres, Tuck, Valdez, Walter, Ware, Weinbrecht, Wex, Wohler, 1 each.

COMBINATION SHUTOUTS—Cerefin-Perkins, Friedrich-Bombard, Cerefin-Perkins-Baker, Daytona Beach; Plunk-Graham, Seitz-Frey-Graham, Beahan-Byron-Graham, Woodworth-Armstrong, Byron-Morgan, Birtsas-Cloninger, Beahan-Raftice, Byron-Raftice, Fort Lauderdale; Sanchez-Benedict, Sanchez-Wong, Ware-Wong, Davis-Benedict, Bass-Klein, Davis-Wong, Davis-Mohr, Ware-Drizmala, Goodin-Tuck, Burke-Bass, Fort Myers; Hinz-Duffy, Dotson-Freeman, Garcia-Lara, Lakeland; Parsons-Childers, Poston-Oliver, Miami; K. Jones-Watson-Owchinko; Hawley-S. Jones, Spagnola-Reynolds-Owchinko, Reynolds-Montgomery, Boyles-Konderla, Tampa; Tejeda-Meagher-Johnston, Galvez-Johnston-Meagher, Galvez-Meagher, Slezak-Gregory, Vero Beach; Kinns-Johnson, West Palm Beach; Mitchell-Bencomo, Mitchell-Wheeler-Bencomo, Wheeler-Leister, Skripko-Wheeler-Dalton, Leister-Perry-Snedicker, Winter Haven.

NO-HIT GAMES—Martinez, St. Petersburg, defeated Lakeland, 1-0 (seven innings, first game), June 9; James, Lakeland, defeated Daytona Beach, 1-0 (seven innings, second game), July 18; Epple, St. Petersburg, defeated Tampa, 4-0, August 21.

Midwest League

CLASS A

CHAMPIONSHIP WINNERS IN PREVIOUS YEARS

1947—Belleville	.667
Belleville	.672
1948—West Frankfort*	.708
1949—Centralia	.627
Paducah (4th)†	.454
1950—Centralia‡	.675
1951—Paris§	.700
Danville (4th)†	.432
1952—Danville x	.685
Decatur (3rd)†	.584
1953—Decatur*	.576
1954—Decatur	.587
Danville (2nd)‡	.528
1955—Dubuque*	.587
1956—Paris y	.656
Dubuque	.603
1957—Decatur y	.683
Clinton	.623
1958—Michigan City	.623
Waterloo z	.613
1959—Waterloo	.613
Waterloo	.613
1960—Waterloo	.629
Waterloo	.677
1961—Waterloo	.613
Quincy z	.594
1962—Dubuque z	.667
Waterloo	.625
1963—Clinton	.710
Clinton	.629
1964—Clinton	.667
Fox Cities z	.667
1965—Burlington	.667
Burlington	.677
1966—Fox Cities z	.689
Cedar Rapids	.762
1967—Wisconsin Rapids	.685
Appleton z	.587
1968—Decatur	.656
Quad Cities z	.648
1969—Appleton	.648
Appleton	.690
1970—Quincy z	.691
Quad Cities	.581
1971—Appleton	.642
Quad Cities a	.548
1972—Appleton	.598
Danville a	.584
1973—Wisconsin Rapids a	.562
Danville	.537
1974—Appleton	.593
Danville a	.517
1975—Waterloo a	.727
Quad Cities	.624
1976—Waterloo a	.600
Cedar Rapids	.595
1977—Waterloo	.580
Burlington a	.511
1978—Appleton a	.708
Burlington	.500
1979—Waterloo	.600
Quad Cities a	.579
1980—Waterloo a	.610
Quad Cities	.532
1981—Wausau a	.636
Quad Cities	.570
1982—Madison	.626
Appleton b	.579
1983—Appleton c	.635
Springfield	.576

*Won championship and four-club playoff. †Won four-club playoff. ‡Playoff finals canceled because of bad weather. §Won both halves of split-season. xWon first half of split-season and tied Paris for second-half title. yWon first-half title and four-team playoff. zWon split-season playoff. aLeague divided into Northern and Southern divisions and played split-season. Playoff winner. bLeague divided into Northern, Central and Southern. Playoff winner. cLeague divided into Northern, Central and Southern divisions; regular-season and playoff winner. (NOTE—Known as Illinois State League in 1947-48 and Mississippi-Ohio Valley League from 1949 through 1955.)

STANDING OF CLUBS AT CLOSE OF SEASON, SEPTEMBER 2

NORTHERN DIVISION

Club	W.	L.	T.	Pct.	G.B.
Appleton (White Sox)	87	49	0	.640	....
Madison (A's)	77	61	0	.558	11
Wausau (Mariners)	70	66	0	.515	17
Kenosha (Twins)	70	68	0	.507	18

CENTRAL DIVISION

Club	W.	L.	T.	Pct.	G.B.
Beloit (Brewers)	86	53	0	.619	....
Cedar Rapids (Reds)	75	63	0	.543	10½
Waterloo (Indians)	65	74	0	.468	21
Clinton (Giants)	62	77	0	.446	24

SOUTHERN DIVISION

Club	W.	L.	T.	Pct.	G.B.
Springfield (Cardinals)	70	69	0	.504	....
Peoria (Angels)	66	73	0	.475	4
Burlington (Rangers)	51	88	0	.367	19
Quad Cities (Cubs)	50	88	0	.362	19½

COMPOSITE STANDING OF CLUBS AT CLOSE OF SEASON, SEPTEMBER 2

Club	Apl.	Bel.	Mad.	C.R.	Wau.	Ken.	Spr.	Peo.	Wat.	Cln.	Bur.	Q.C.	W.	L.	T.	Pct.	G.B.
Appleton (White Sox)	....	6	12	10	10	10	7	6	7	6	8	5	87	49	0	.640	....
Beloit (Brewers)	4	....	6	10	5	6	7	7	12	13	8	8	86	53	0	.619	2½
Madison (A's)	8	4	....	7	8	9	7	7	7	6	7	7	77	61	0	.558	11
Cedar Rapids (Reds)	0	10	3	....	4	5	5	6	10	15	9	8	75	63	0	.543	13
Wausau (Mariners)	7	5	12	5	....	9	6	3	5	5	6	7	70	66	0	.515	17
Kenosha (Twins)	10	4	10	4	11	....	5	7	5	5	3	5	70	68	0	.507	18
Springfield (Cardinals)	3	3	3	5	4	5	....	7	6	5	13	16	70	69	0	.504	18½
Peoria (Angels)	4	2	3	4	7	3	13	....	5	6	12	7	66	73	0	.475	22½
Waterloo (Indians)	2	8	3	10	5	4	4	5	....	9	8	7	65	74	0	.468	23½
Clinton (Giants)	4	7	3	5	5	4	4	11	....	7	7	62	77	0	.446	26½
Burlington (Rangers)	2	2	4	1	4	7	7	8	2	3	....	11	51	88	0	.367	37½
Quad Cities (Cubs)	5	2	2	3	2	3	5	4	13	3	3	8	....	50	88	0	.362	38

Quad Cities represented Davenport and Bettendorf, Ia., and Moline and Rock Island, Ill.

Major league affiliations in parentheses.

Playoffs—Springfield defeated Beloit, two games to none; Appleton defeated Madison, two games to one, and Appleton defeated Springfield, three games to two, to win league championship.

Regular-Season Attendance—Appleton, 54,281; Beloit, 92,474; Burlington, 60,528; Cedar Rapids, 134,639; Clinton, 91,872; Kenosha, 87,672; Madison, 118,161; Peoria, 116,473; Quad Cities, 124,788; Springfield, 141,321; Waterloo, 70,878; Wausau, 50,095. Playoff attendance, 7,308. All-Star Game attendance, 2,215.

Managers—Appleton, Sal Rende; Beloit, Tom Gamboa; Burlington, Rudy Jaramillo; Cedar Rapids, Jim Lett; Clinton, Bill Lachemann; Kenosha, Duffy Dyer; Madison, Brad Fischer; Peoria, Joe Madden; Quad Cities, Larry Cox; Springfield, Joe Rigoli; Waterloo, Harold "Gomer" Hodge; Wausau, Greg Mahlberg.

All-Star Team: 1B-Ron Henika, Cedar Rapids; 2B-Greg Steen, Peoria; 3B-Bill Merrifield, Peoria; SS-Kurt Stillwell, Cedar Rapids; OF-Luis Polonia, Madison; Dave Hengel, Wausau; Brian Finley, Peoria; C-Tom Pagnozzi, Springfield; DH-Joe Meyer, Beloit; LHP-Craig Henderson, Kenosha; RHP-Mike Birkbeck, Beloit; LH Reliever-Al Candelaria, Clinton; RH Reliever-Jim Hickey, Appleton; Most Valuable Player-Joe Meyer, Beloit; Manager of the Year-Tom Gamboa, Beloit.

(Compiled by Howe News Bureau, Boston, Mass.)

CLUB BATTING

Club	Pct.	G.	AB.	R.	OR.	H.	TB.	2B.	3B.	HR.	RBI.	GW.	SH.	SF.	HP.	BB.	Int. BB.	SO.	SB.	CS.	LOB.
Wausau	.256	136	4403	642	570	1127	1679	217	16	101	569	63	56	40	36	642	18	858	123	89	1041
Springfield	.254	139	4572	679	650	1161	1745	203	33	105	586	60	44	45	41	484	19	885	97	60	958
Beloit	.254	139	4541	639	568	1155	1630	186	32	75	541	70	41	39	35	616	29	905	167	79	1006
Madison	.253	138	4382	654	594	1108	1569	181	35	70	547	62	51	33	40	654	23	951	186	95	1037
Appleton	.249	136	4335	648	507	1081	1511	181	42	55	544	74	54	33	30	626	13	904	136	56	1003
Peoria	.248	139	4541	598	622	1128	1645	217	24	84	522	56	51	27	55	480	19	939	112	82	956
Waterloo	.246	139	4408	566	624	1084	1594	201	24	87	493	56	55	27	45	476	18	926	102	58	949
Quad Cities	.245	138	4460	531	724	1094	1446	149	25	51	455	41	40	30	38	461	11	845	187	99	910
Cedar Rapids	.243	138	4429	594	517	1078	1609	196	25	95	522	64	47	45	25	553	28	764	137	51	986
Kenosha	.241	138	4347	568	513	1046	1443	188	22	55	482	61	45	34	54	565	25	754	80	43	1020
Burlington	.234	139	4414	586	756	1035	1445	178	20	64	483	41	50	24	49	553	20	1076	150	73	963
Clinton	.230	139	4500	548	608	1033	1410	168	28	51	471	49	59	37	27	517	19	1031	130	51	958

INDIVIDUAL BATTING

(Leading Qualifiers for Batting Championship—378 or More Plate Appearances)

*Bats lefthanded.   †Switch-hitter.

Player and Club	Pct.	G.	AB.	R.	H.	TB.	2B.	3B.	HR.	RBI.	GW.	SH.	SF.	HP.	BB.	Int. BB.	SO.	SB.	CS.
Meyer, T. Joe, Beloit	.320	128	475	73	152	264	22	0	30	102	8	1	8	2	46	5	94	0	2
Clark, David, Waterloo*	.309	110	363	74	112	179	16	3	15	63	2	4	4	10	57	4	68	20	5
Hengel, David, Wausau	.308	120	441	68	136	249	31	2	26	98	10	0	6	6	58	5	65	10	9
Polonia, Luis, Madison†	.307	135	528	103	162	227	21	10	8	64	8	9	2	5	57	7	95	55	24
McLaughlin, David, Appleton*	.305	121	455	70	139	159	11	3	1	41	4	8	3	1	45	2	40	6	5
Henika, Ronald, Cedar Rapids*	.304	95	349	59	106	186	26	3	16	72	10	2	6	2	40	3	38	5	3
Martinez, Edgar, Wausau	.303	126	433	72	131	212	32	2	15	66	10	7	6	3	84	2	57	11	9
Loscalzo, Robert, Madison*	.299	95	321	49	96	129	12	3	5	39	7	2	0	0	64	4	76	28	15
Steinbach, Terry, Madison	.295	135	474	57	140	209	24	6	11	79	9	4	7	1	49	1	59	5	6
Moritz, Thomas, Appleton	.293	112	406	48	119	168	18	5	7	68	9	4	1	3	51	1	90	4	1

Departmental Leaders: G—Merrifield, Sierra, 138; AB—Polonia, 528; R—Finley, 113; H—Polonia, 162; TB—Meyer, 264; 2B—Batista, 35; 3B—Finley, 11; HR—Meyer, 30; RBI—Meyer, 102; GWRBI—Morman, 15; SH—J. Jones, 10; SF—Freytes, 9; HP—Finley, 15; BB—Thornton, 100; IBB—Verkuilen, 10; SO—Nelson, 140; SB—Finley, 66; CS—Polonia, 24.

(All Players—Listed Alphabetically)

Player and Club	Pct.	G.	AB.	R.	H.	TB.	2B.	3B.	HR.	RBI.	GW.	SH.	SF.	HP.	BB.	Int. BB.	SO.	SB.	CS.
Abbott, Ricardo, Beloit	.158	36	95	11	15	16	1	0	0	5	0	2	2	2	13	0	30	1	0
Adams, Bert, Peoria	.165	55	133	16	22	34	7	1	1	10	2	2	0	1	3	0	53	3	0
Alfredson, Thomas, Peoria	.261	28	69	10	18	27	6	0	1	10	0	2	0	1	3	0	24	3	3
Allanson, Andrew, Waterloo	.271	46	144	14	39	44	5	0	0	10	3	1	0	0	20	0	16	6	5
Allen, W. David, Clinton	.220	65	232	38	51	71	8	0	4	24	3	3	0	3	35	0	66	4	4
Amaral, Richard, Quad Cities	.210	34	119	21	25	26	1	0	0	7	1	1	0	0	24	0	29	12	0
Anderson, Kent, Peoria	.224	67	223	24	50	64	9	1	1	16	2	2	0	1	23	1	34	6	3
Anderson, Steven, Beloit	.167	23	72	7	12	16	4	0	0	5	0	0	2	0	4	0	12	0	0
Andrade, John, Burlington	.206	60	170	26	35	41	6	0	0	9	2	4	0	5	29	0	37	5	1
Antle, Michael, Clinton	.000	21	3	0	0	0	0	0	0	0	0	0	0	0	0	0	1	0	0
Aponte, Edwin, Waterloo	.292	35	130	17	38	52	6	1	2	13	2	0	2	0	13	0	10	4	7
Appino, G. Kevin, Beloit	.236	44	106	10	25	29	4	0	0	5	0	3	0	1	17	0	21	3	0
Aquino, Fausto, Burlington*	.191	35	115	12	22	25	3	0	0	3	0	2	0	1	3	0	26	2	3
Artiles, Orlando, Kenosha*	.245	53	159	18	39	51	9	0	1	10	1	0	0	1	23	0	38	0	3
Austin, Terry, Quad Cities	.231	5	13	2	3	3	0	0	0	0	0	1	0	0	2	0	4	1	1
Bailey, Gregory, Burlington	.223	116	363	49	81	129	13	1	11	39	2	9	1	6	46	1	132	18	5
Baker, Jonathan, Quad Cities	.214	8	14	1	3	3	0	0	0	1	0	0	1	0	2	0	4	0	0
Balmer, J. Stephen, Quad Cities	1.000	9	1	0	1	1	0	0	0	1	0	0	0	0	0	0	0	0	0
Barba, Douglas, Cedar Rapids	.250	19	4	1	1	1	0	0	0	0	0	0	0	0	0	0	1	0	0
Barineau, Mark, Waterloo	.137	19	51	7	7	8	1	0	0	4	1	1	1	1	9	0	10	6	0
Bates, Kirk, Burlington*	.214	61	229	25	49	84	11	0	8	24	5	1	0	2	9	1	48	3	3
Batista, Francisco, Springfield	.274	127	470	78	129	197	35	6	7	58	4	4	4	4	45	2	93	6	8
Bayron, Angel, Kenosha*	.279	33	86	9	24	31	4	0	1	17	2	2	0	0	10	0	21	0	0
Beall, Peter, Peoria	.202	45	119	15	24	28	1	0	1	9	0	0	0	1	14	0	20	0	1
Beardman, Lawrence, Madison	.247	109	364	66	90	136	14	4	8	49	4	3	4	1	51	2	65	29	4
Bell, Terence, Wausau	.245	83	253	30	62	77	10	1	1	23	2	7	2	2	33	1	51	7	7
Berge, Jordan, Cedar Rapids*	.253	128	446	70	113	156	23	4	4	51	7	7	7	0	73	1	29	3	3
Berryhill, Damon, Quad Cities	.276	62	217	30	60	74	14	0	0	31	4	1	0	1	16	0	44	4	4
Bethel, Donald, Quad Cities	.000	51	0	0	0	0	0	0	0	0	0	1	0	0	0	0	0	0	0
Blair, Martin, Burlington†	.247	115	392	70	97	127	17	5	1	34	1	8	0	3	70	2	61	23	15
Blunt, Bradley, Springfield	.125	17	16	1	2	2	0	0	0	0	0	1	0	0	1	0	6	0	0
Bocock, Thomas, Springfield	.249	119	394	69	98	147	14	4	9	36	4	3	5	2	65	1	82	9	8
Boderick, W. Stanley, Madison†	.093	25	54	4	5	6	1	0	0	3	1	2	0	0	5	0	11	2	4
Boever, Daniel, Cedar Rapids	.260	66	208	20	54	82	10	0	6	34	4	1	1	0	26	1	41	3	3
Borowski, Richard, Madison	.242	87	293	35	71	85	6	1	2	24	1	4	0	1	22	0	75	7	3
Brahms, Russell, Clinton	.000	14	1	0	0	0	0	0	0	0	0	0	0	0	1	0	0	0	0
Brown, Brian, Springfield	.000	12	3	1	0	0	0	0	0	0	0	0	0	0	1	0	3	0	0
Browne, Jerome, Burlington†	.236	127	420	70	99	111	10	1	0	18	0	7	2	1	71	0	76	31	8
Bruzik, Robert, Wausau	.272	111	437	75	119	162	21	2	6	51	4	10	4	6	48	1	68	12	9
Buchanon, Bobby, Peoria*	.240	107	338	49	81	111	11	2	5	32	6	8	2	2	44	5	76	28	18
Burkett, John, Clinton	.000	20	8	0	0	0	0	0	0	1	0	0	0	0	0	0	3	0	0
Burton, Steven, Quad Cities*	.231	106	316	44	73	110	14	1	7	37	5	0	2	8	25	1	80	19	5
Caianiello, John, Appleton*	.236	81	233	24	55	66	11	0	0	24	5	7	3	0	45	1	55	1	1
Calvert, Mark, Cedar Rapids	.000	20	2	0	0	0	0	0	0	0	0	2	0	0	0	0	2	0	0
Candelaria, Albert, Clinton*	.500	41	2	1	1	1	0	0	0	0	0	1	0	0	0	0	1	0	0
Carrasco, Claudio, Waterloo†	.239	104	368	47	88	108	9	4	1	20	1	4	1	3	28	3	86	16	8
Carter, Richie, Peoria	.000	31	2	0	0	0	0	0	0	0	0	0	0	0	0	0	1	0	0
Castain, Maurice, Madison	.227	73	233	25	53	76	9	1	4	30	2	0	0	5	27	1	72	2	1
Caulfield, Thomas, Springfield	.000	5	3	1	0	0	0	0	0	0	0	1	0	0	1	0	0	0	0
Cesario, James, Burlington	.250	65	216	26	54	76	13	0	3	25	1	0	0	2	22	0	53	3	2
Champion, K. Randall, Springfield*	.255	39	98	18	25	30	3	1	0	9	1	0	1	0	5	18	1	9	1
Clark, David, Waterloo*	.309	110	363	74	112	179	16	3	15	63	2	4	4	10	57	4	68	20	5
Conley, K. Virgil, Cedar Rapids*	.200	43	10	0	2	2	0	0	0	0	0	0	0	0	0	0	5	0	0
Copeland, Thomas, Kenosha*	.262	129	439	70	115	170	24	2	9	50	0	4	4	5	71	3	32	5	2
Corbell, Charles, Clinton	.071	25	14	0	1	1	0	0	0	0	0	4	0	0	1	0	3	0	0
Coughlon, Kevin, Madison	.000	30	5	0	0	0	0	0	0	0	0	0	0	1	0	0	1	0	0

Player and Club	Pct.	G.	AB.	R.	H.	TB.	2B.	3B.	HR.	RBI.	GW.	SH.	SF.	HP.	BB.	Int. BB.	SO.	SB.	CS.
Cox, John, Quad Cities*	.083	17	12	0	1	1	0	0	0	0	0	1	0	0	0	0	4	0	0
Crabtree, Gary, Wausau	.237	116	426	71	101	165	26	1	12	46	6	2	6	2	53	1	107	11	14
Cruz, Luis, Quad Cities	.254	119	418	54	106	127	6	6	1	23	5	4	3	2	40	0	78	33	22
Culberson, Charles, Clinton	.258	70	267	38	69	109	9	5	7	38	3	0	0	4	36	0	56	22	4
Davidson, Jackie, Quad Cities†	.200	27	10	0	2	2	0	0	0	0	0	1	0	0	2	0	3	0	0
Davis, Douglas, Peoria	.220	43	127	15	28	36	2	0	2	14	0	5	2	4	18	0	41	1	3
Davis, Glenn, Burlington*	.220	40	141	17	31	45	5	0	3	18	4	1	4	1	20	0	55	3	2
Day, G. Dexter, Cedar Rapids	.270	61	200	35	54	87	16	1	5	28	5	0	2	3	22	1	37	18	1
Demeter, Todd, Springfield	.000	1	1	0	0	0	0	0	0	0	0	0	0	0	0	0	1	0	0
Denbo, Gary, Cedar Rapids	.195	45	123	19	24	27	1	1	0	4	3	2	1	0	21	1	33	4	2
Derby, Terrence, Beloit†	.121	12	33	6	4	7	0	0	1	3	0	0	0	0	7	0	12	2	1
Devlin, Donald, Appleton	.188	17	64	13	12	17	3	1	0	5	0	0	2	2	12	0	25	3	1
Diaz, Alejandro, Peoria	.219	79	224	28	49	87	6	1	10	37	4	3	1	1	40	0	86	0	1
Diaz, Eduardo, Waterloo	.250	48	116	10	29	37	5	0	1	15	3	3	1	1	7	0	28	1	0
Diaz, Jorge, Kenosha	.222	4	9	2	2	2	0	0	0	1	0	0	0	0	0	0	3	0	0
Diaz, Lazaro, Kenosha†	.286	16	21	4	6	7	1	0	0	0	0	0	0	0	4	0	8	1	2
DiCeglio, Thomas, Kenosha	.227	61	185	15	42	47	5	0	0	20	3	2	2	2	9	0	19	0	1
Dickerson, James, Quad Cities	.277	114	394	56	109	173	20	1	14	64	3	1	4	10	47	1	91	10	8
Digioia, John, Springfield	.223	41	112	14	25	40	7	1	2	19	0	2	1	0	19	0	36	0	2
Ditto, Bradley, Quad Cities	.235	81	166	13	39	44	5	0	0	8	2	2	0	1	21	0	38	13	7
Dodd, Timothy, Cedar Rapids	.125	27	16	0	2	2	0	0	0	1	0	0	4	1	0	0	5	1	0
Doran, Mark, Peoria	.289	119	432	61	125	163	16	2	6	36	3	2	1	13	48	1	95	23	13
Dougherty, Mark, Springfield	.287	100	356	63	102	128	15	1	3	40	1	6	4	1	43	1	56	32	8
Dowless, Michael, Cedar Rapids	.000	33	6	0	0	0	0	0	0	0	0	1	0	0	0	0	2	0	0
Doyle, James, Quad Cities	.500	42	2	0	1	1	0	0	0	0	0	0	0	0	0	0	1	0	0
Dressler, Kenneth, Clinton	.125	19	8	0	1	1	0	0	0	0	0	0	0	0	0	0	5	0	0
Duggan, Thomas, Wausau	.256	99	347	47	89	142	19	2	10	49	3	2	3	2	41	1	88	4	12
Edwards, Glenn, Waterloo	.229	103	327	46	75	123	12	0	12	44	6	8	2	7	31	0	105	6	5
Embser, Richard, Springfield	.143	27	21	3	3	6	0	0	1	1	0	2	0	0	1	0	6	0	0
Epps, Riley, Burlington†	.194	57	170	21	33	49	8	1	2	24	3	1	2	0	24	2	59	0	0
Escobar, Angel, Clinton†	.225	99	311	47	70	96	16	2	2	25	2	7	1	1	57	2	89	15	6
Espinal, Feliz, Clinton	.225	67	209	27	47	62	8	2	1	24	3	4	3	0	18	1	40	6	3
Everett, Kerry, Beloit	.250	137	521	61	130	185	24	2	9	69	9	3	1	0	40	5	87	2	4
Faber, Walter, Clinton	.000	9	6	0	0	0	0	0	0	0	0	0	1	0	0	0	3	0	0
Farley, Brian, Springfield	.200	22	10	1	2	5	0	0	1	2	0	0	0	0	1	0	4	0	0
Felix, Paul, Kenosha†	.274	124	402	62	110	174	26	1	12	57	5	2	3	11	70	7	104	2	3
Ferran, George, Clinton	.000	41	7	0	0	0	0	0	0	0	0	3	0	0	0	0	3	0	0
Fingers, Robert, Beloit	.000	31	1	0	0	0	0	0	0	0	0	0	0	0	0	0	0	0	0
Finley, Brian, Beloit*	.288	137	510	113	147	193	21	11	1	41	4	0	3	15	93	5	71	66	22
Fischer, Bradley, Madison	.200	2	5	1	1	1	0	0	0	0	0	0	0	1	0	0	1	0	0
Forgione, Christopher, Kenosha*	.273	133	473	58	129	169	27	2	3	51	11	2	6	2	46	2	81	6	5
Franko, Philip, Kenosha*	.175	68	212	17	37	45	4	2	0	10	1	4	2	2	23	0	18	1	3
Freeman, Lavel, Beloit*	.294	49	170	29	50	72	14	1	2	33	6	1	3	2	23	1	37	7	2
Freytes, Hector, Quad Cities	.264	117	435	45	115	168	14	6	9	69	4	2	9	3	13	0	62	7	4
Funk, Bryan, Cedar Rapids	.000	46	5	0	0	0	0	0	0	0	0	0	1	0	0	0	0	0	0
Gambeski, Michael, Springfield	.111	8	18	0	2	2	0	0	0	1	0	0	0	0	2	0	6	0	0
Garrett, Eric, Madison	.214	6	14	2	3	4	1	0	0	0	0	0	0	0	5	0	6	0	1
Gherna, Joseph, Kenosha	.183	20	60	6	11	12	1	0	0	3	0	3	0	0	12	0	13	0	1
Giddens, Ronnie, Cedar Rapids	.238	95	319	32	76	107	14	4	3	35	3	3	0	2	39	3	44	8	4
Gill, Gary, Springfield	.300	111	317	52	95	162	20	4	13	54	8	0	5	4	48	2	75	7	4
Gill, Shawn, Madison	.222	51	135	10	30	39	5	2	0	12	2	0	0	0	16	0	26	0	3
Glendening, Robert, Quad Cities	.243	86	239	26	58	79	9	0	4	20	1	3	0	1	20	2	44	3	6
Gobbo, Michael, Beloit	.230	64	178	15	41	52	4	2	1	14	1	0	1	0	38	1	35	1	2
Gomez, Ernesto, Wausau†	.255	115	424	55	108	131	13	2	2	35	7	8	2	5	40	0	64	26	12
Gordon, Carl, Beloit*	.000	13	14	3	0	0	0	0	0	0	0	0	0	0	4	0	9	0	1
Gould, Robert, Madison	.213	54	155	20	33	53	10	2	2	20	2	2	0	6	22	0	44	4	1
Grant, Kenneth, Peoria	.200	37	135	14	27	34	2	1	1	16	1	1	0	3	9	0	26	3	0
Griggs, David, Beloit†	.000	1	1	0	0	0	0	0	0	0	0	0	0	0	0	0	1	0	0
Haberle, David, Cedar Rapids*	.208	12	24	4	5	6	1	0	0	1	0	0	0	0	2	0	6	0	0
Halberg, Eric, Clinton	.167	11	30	0	5	5	0	0	0	0	0	0	0	0	0	0	6	0	1
Haley, Samuel, Wausau	.077	11	39	2	3	4	1	0	0	0	0	0	0	0	2	0	9	1	0
Hamilton, Carlton, Quad Cities*	.267	18	15	1	4	4	0	0	0	1	0	0	0	0	0	0	6	0	0
Hance, William, Burlington*	.348	39	141	25	49	79	9	0	7	38	2	0	0	0	29	2	11	2	4
Hansen, Darel, Madison	.000	23	1	0	0	0	0	0	0	0	0	0	0	0	1	0	1	0	0
Hardamon, Derrick, Quad Cities	.077	7	13	1	1	1	0	0	0	0	0	2	0	0	3	0	8	2	0
Hardwick, Willie, Springfield	1.000	3	1	0	1	1	0	0	0	0	0	0	0	0	0	0	0	0	0
Harper, Milton, Waterloo	.278	110	356	58	99	140	22	2	5	44	2	5	1	1	49	3	56	10	4
Harris, Leonard, Cedar Rapids*	.246	132	468	52	115	154	15	3	6	53	4	2	6	3	42	4	59	31	10
Harrison, Ronald, Madison*	.197	19	66	10	13	17	4	0	0	9	0	1	0	0	3	0	7	5	1
Hayes, Charles, Clinton	.245	116	392	41	96	123	17	2	2	51	4	5	3	1	34	1	110	4	1
Hazard, Richard, Beloit*	.228	40	123	20	28	46	7	1	3	14	3	0	0	0	21	1	30	0	3
Hengel, David, Wausau	.308	120	441	68	136	249	31	2	26	98	10	0	6	8	58	5	65	10	9
Henika, Ronald, Cedar Rapids*	.304	95	349	59	106	186	26	3	16	72	10	2	6	2	40	3	38	5	3
Hickey, James, Appleton	.000	49	1	0	0	0	0	0	0	0	0	0	0	0	0	0	1	0	0
Hill, Gregory, Kenosha	.203	91	295	31	60	86	13	2	3	24	6	4	1	5	25	0	73	0	1
Houston, Barry, Clinton*	.235	122	388	48	91	137	17	1	9	57	5	0	5	2	54	1	121	13	5
Howard, Raymond, Waterloo	.197	41	127	11	25	27	2	0	0	9	1	2	1	0	15	0	22	2	2
Howard, Steve, Madison	.171	44	123	13	21	31	4	0	2	14	1	1	1	7	21	0	56	4	4
Hunsinger, Alan, Springfield	.250	114	412	53	103	155	17	1	11	54	5	3	3	7	34	0	67	8	2
Irvine, Edward, Beloit	.260	111	446	58	116	143	19	4	0	45	5	6	4	0	42	2	57	31	9
Jackson, Larry, Clinton*	.288	72	240	30	69	89	10	2	2	34	10	1	1	2	34	3	38	17	4
Jackson, T. Todd, Burlington	.182	4	11	1	2	2	0	0	0	2	0	0	0	0	1	0	4	0	0
Jensen, Roger, Appleton	.224	121	459	71	103	180	24	7	13	66	10	3	3	1	44	1	96	8	7
Johnson, John H., Quad Cities	.087	32	69	4	6	6	0	0	0	2	0	1	0	2	9	1	30	0	1
Johnson, Richard, Appleton	.172	9	29	2	5	8	1	1	0	2	0	1	0	1	1	0	9	0	0
Johnson, Thomas, Quad Cities	.196	19	51	5	10	12	2	0	0	0	0	2	0	0	11	0	16	3	1
Jones, Anthony, Clinton	.222	105	343	51	76	98	13	0	3	36	6	2	6	4	46	3	95	16	11
Jones, J. Bradley, Burlington	.274	96	325	34	89	126	16	0	7	48	3	1	5	3	35	0	71	4	1
Jones, James, Madison	.260	125	400	66	104	141	16	0	7	52	10	10	3	5	82	1	79	5	5
Jones, Terry, Peoria	.280	77	271	34	76	108	18	1	4	40	4	5	2	2	21	1	23	4	4
Kavanaugh, Timothy L., Springfield	.196	56	143	17	28	35	5	1	0	9	0	1	2	12	1	30	2	4
Kemp, Darrell, Peoria*	.197	24	66	6	13	22	6	0	1	7	1	0	0	1	10	2	14	2	1

Player and Club	Pct.	G.	AB.	R.	H.	TB.	2B.	3B.	HR.	RBI.	GW.	SH.	SF.	HP.	BB.	Int. BB.	SO.	SB.	CS.
Kemp, G. Hubert, Cedar Rapids*	.077	27	13	2	1	1	0	0	0	1	0	1	0	0	2	0	5	0	0
King, Eric, Clinton	.091	35	11	1	1	1	0	0	0	0	0	1	0	0	2	0	5	0	0
Kish, Robert, Springfield	.167	9	6	1	1	1	0	0	0	0	0	0	0	0	0	0	2	0	0
Klein, Larry, Burlington	.196	33	112	6	22	25	1	1	0	12	4	2	0	0	14	1	28	4	4
Kline, Kris, Peoria	.258	133	472	74	122	180	27	8	5	51	5	6	5	6	45	0	73	16	6
Komeiji, Keith, Wausau	.208	66	192	26	40	67	9	0	6	25	1	1	0	0	39	0	66	4	4
Kopf, David, Quad Cities	.000	10	2	0	0	0	0	0	0	0	0	0	0	0	1	0	1	0	0
Kramer, Joseph, Waterloo	.205	48	132	19	27	40	7	0	2	9	0	1	0	2	19	1	31	9	3
Krause, Andrew, Madison*	.179	19	56	5	10	11	1	0	0	5	1	1	0	1	6	0	10	0	1
Kumiega, Peter, Quad Cities	.222	49	153	10	34	52	3	0	5	16	0	0	1	1	13	1	38	1	3
Lamar, Daniel, Cedar Rapids	.294	71	252	52	74	130	14	0	14	40	5	4	2	2	34	1	47	1	1
Langdon, L. Ted, Cedar Rapids	.350	21	20	3	7	7	0	0	0	2	0	0	0	0	1	0	2	0	0
Lee, R. Kurt, Clinton*	.176	27	17	2	3	3	0	0	0	1	0	1	0	0	0	0	5	0	0
Leighton, Brian, Kenosha	.186	34	86	8	16	26	1	0	3	10	1	0	2	1	9	0	29	0	0
Lenderman, David, Quad Cities*	.000	28	7	0	0	0	0	0	0	0	0	0	0	0	0	0	4	0	0
Lewis, Jay, Peoria	.227	48	141	16	32	38	4	1	0	13	3	3	0	0	22	0	34	1	1
Lindeman, James, Springfield	.271	94	354	69	96	169	15	2	18	66	8	2	1	3	47	2	81	6	3
Lopez, Juan, Waterloo	.223	75	215	11	48	61	5	1	2	18	3	5	1	0	3	0	36	1	1
Loscalzo, Robert, Madison*	.299	95	321	49	96	129	12	3	5	39	7	2	0	0	64	4	76	28	15
Loseke, Scott, Cedar Rapids*	.215	97	311	43	67	103	13	1	7	29	2	4	3	2	59	2	51	18	1
Lusby, Steven, Peoria*	.255	32	106	16	27	37	7	0	1	10	2	0	1	1	29	2	21	0	1
Luther, Bradley, Springfield	.236	48	140	14	33	37	4	0	0	8	0	1	2	1	14	0	22	4	5
Madden, Victor, Waterloo*	.241	120	353	54	85	154	26	2	13	51	2	1	2	5	65	0	84	3	4
Manfre, Michael, Cedar Rapids	.232	130	456	65	106	203	26	4	21	62	5	1	5	3	54	4	108	17	7
Manning, Otis, Wausau*	.245	86	245	38	60	73	11	1	0	20	3	5	2	1	55	4	28	4	1
Marquardt, John, Madison	.252	71	242	38	61	78	11	3	0	19	2	5	1	0	46	0	34	8	3
Mart, James, Burlington	.141	22	64	7	9	13	1	0	1	5	1	0	0	0	4	0	24	0	0
Martin, John A., Springfield	.091	20	11	1	1	1	0	0	0	1	0	0	0	0	0	0	3	0	0
Martinez, David, Cedar Rapids*	.220	12	41	6	9	15	2	2	0	5	1	0	0	1	9	0	13	3	4
Martinez, Edgar, Wausau	.303	126	433	72	131	212	32	2	15	66	10	7	6	3	84	2	57	11	9
Martinez, Randy, Springfield*	.400	27	5	1	2	3	1	0	0	1	0	0	0	0	0	0	2	0	0
Martinez, Rey, Waterloo*	.256	131	454	49	116	185	22	7	11	68	13	3	5	3	26	3	98	1	2
Martinez, Robert, Burlington	.239	113	389	59	93	133	14	1	8	46	5	4	3	12	46	4	95	12	2
Mason, Martin, Springfield	.000	17	1	1	0	0	0	0	0	0	0	0	0	0	0	0	1	0	0
McCue, Deron, Clinton	.237	92	295	38	70	87	11	0	2	22	0	5	2	3	42	2	64	13	2
McLaughlin, David, Appleton*	.305	121	455	70	139	159	11	3	1	41	4	8	3	1	45	2	40	6	5
Meadows, Geoffrey, Springfield	.000	5	2	0	0	0	0	0	0	0	0	0	0	0	0	0	1	0	0
Meier, Scott, Appleton	.243	67	206	32	50	76	11	0	5	36	5	2	3	0	55	1	52	1	0
Mejia, Simon, Quad Cities	.252	37	115	8	29	37	5	0	1	11	3	1	1	1	7	0	18	6	3
Menssen, Gary, Kenosha	.169	27	65	7	11	17	3	0	1	6	0	2	0	3	10	0	20	1	2
Merrifield, Billie, Peoria	.272	138	523	78	142	263	34	0	29	97	12	0	4	6	47	2	83	2	4
Meyer, T. Joe, Beloit	.320	128	475	73	152	264	22	0	30	102	8	1	8	2	46	5	94	0	2
Migliore, Brian, Peoria	.000	16	2	0	0	0	0	0	0	0	0	0	0	0	0	0	0	0	0
Mitchell, William, Springfield	.500	17	2	1	1	1	0	0	0	0	0	0	0	0	0	0	1	0	0
Montanari, David, Quad Cities	.258	128	446	47	115	140	19	0	2	37	5	4	2	2	35	0	49	5	4
Moore, Charles, Appleton	.200	90	260	36	52	68	6	2	2	25	3	5	2	1	56	0	82	7	2
Moritz, Thomas, Appleton	.293	112	406	48	119	168	18	5	7	68	9	4	1	3	51	1	90	4	1
Morman, Russell, Appleton	.262	122	424	68	111	163	17	7	7	80	15	4	4	8	80	3	93	29	6
Mosley, Reginald, Burlington	.200	15	45	5	9	16	2	1	1	8	0	0	0	0	9	1	23	0	1
Munson, Jay, Cedar Rapids	.231	48	108	9	25	34	4	1	1	7	2	1	0	0	13	0	32	0	0
Nelson, Robert, Madison*	.246	136	487	71	120	206	25	2	19	85	8	1	8	5	80	6	140	4	6
North, Jay, Springfield	.000	27	12	0	0	0	0	0	0	0	0	0	0	0	0	0	7	0	0
Odom, Joe, Madison	.000	9	1	0	0	0	0	0	0	0	0	0	0	0	0	0	0	0	0
Oliver, Joseph, Cedar Rapids	.218	102	335	34	73	93	11	0	3	29	2	4	3	4	17	1	83	2	2
Oliverio, Stephen, Cedar Rapids	.000	27	3	0	0	0	0	0	0	0	0	2	0	0	0	0	1	0	0
Ortega, Jose, Springfield	.000	9	1	0	0	0	0	0	0	0	0	0	0	0	0	0	0	0	0
Padia, Steven, Cedar Rapids*	.193	50	171	14	33	52	5	1	4	23	2	0	1	1	20	2	31	0	2
Pagnozzi, Thomas, Springfield	.283	114	396	57	112	170	20	4	10	68	9	4	7	4	31	3	75	3	4
Palmer, Douglas, Kenosha	.236	131	437	71	103	112	9	0	0	31	5	3	1	9	83	0	55	31	11
Parrett, Jeffrey, Beloit	.000	30	2	0	0	0	0	0	0	0	0	0	0	0	0	0	1	0	0
Pedraza, Nelson, Waterloo	.252	134	448	52	113	175	33	1	9	53	9	5	2	3	53	4	77	3	2
Pena, Jose, Clinton	.176	70	222	20	39	56	8	0	3	26	5	1	2	3	18	1	62	1	2
Perez, Edgar, Appleton	.212	46	113	13	24	25	1	0	0	10	1	0	1	0	15	0	28	0	0
Perez, Oriol, Wausau	.249	118	417	54	104	144	17	1	7	54	9	5	4	2	50	1	90	12	6
Pettibone, James, Cedar Rapids	.050	26	20	1	1	2	1	0	0	2	0	1	0	1	1	0	12	0	0
Phillips, James, Quad Cities	.167	17	6	0	1	1	0	0	0	0	0	0	0	0	0	0	3	0	0
Phillips, Robert, Cedar Rapids*	.120	12	25	2	3	5	0	1	0	2	0	0	0	1	3	1	14	0	0
Pimentel, Rafael, Springfield	.000	22	2	0	0	0	0	0	0	0	0	1	0	0	0	0	1	0	0
Pino, Rolando, Appleton	.211	103	308	61	65	101	12	3	6	35	6	2	4	4	85	2	84	9	7
Pleis, W. Scott, Springfield	.239	27	46	4	11	12	1	0	0	3	0	1	0	0	0	0	12	0	0
Pobur, Hugh, Quad Cities	.000	30	4	0	0	0	0	0	0	0	0	0	0	0	0	0	2	0	0
Polonia, Luis, Madison†	.307	135	528	103	162	227	21	10	8	64	8	9	2	5	57	7	95	55	24
Powell, Alonzo, Clinton	.248	47	149	22	37	47	3	2	1	10	2	2	0	0	19	0	31	0	0
Quinones, Hector, Beloit	.223	99	309	27	69	75	6	0	0	15	1	9	2	1	22	1	67	4	4
Rainey, Scott, Clinton	.229	78	227	23	52	73	7	1	4	25	3	6	4	0	14	1	38	1	0
Rembielak, Richard, Quad Cities	.249	81	269	37	67	84	8	0	3	23	3	6	1	1	40	2	29	17	7
Richardson, Donald, Quad Cities	.230	118	379	43	87	104	9	4	0	22	1	2	2	2	32	0	56	27	10
Rigos, John, Springfield	.221	127	425	57	94	155	16	6	11	59	9	2	5	1	53	1	88	9	2
Riley, Thomas, Cedar Rapids	.261	43	153	14	40	44	1	0	1	13	2	1	2	0	12	2	23	2	3
Rodriguez, Angel, Beloit	.244	71	242	28	59	105	11	1	11	50	4	2	5	5	15	1	45	1	1
Rodriguez, Jose, Springfield	.239	133	394	46	94	120	11	0	5	39	4	4	3	5	12	1	49	8	6
Roman, Luis, Springfield*	.000	19	5	0	0	0	0	0	0	0	0	0	0	0	0	0	0	0	0
Roman, Miguel, Waterloo	.232	32	82	9	19	30	5	0	2	10	1	1	1	0	2	0	21	0	0
Saatzer, Michael, Peoria*	.264	115	397	44	105	162	26	2	9	47	4	3	2	2	15	3	90	5	2
Sandry, William, Quad Cities	.241	71	220	24	53	82	10	2	5	34	1	1	2	1	30	1	40	4	3
Sasser, Mack, Clinton*	.292	118	428	57	125	173	20	5	6	65	9	4	7	2	30	3	46	15	2
Sauer, Richard, Beloit*	.214	42	112	15	24	29	3	1	0	13	4	1	1	0	16	0	39	0	3
Schmidt, Gregory, Clinton	.000	26	4	0	0	0	0	0	0	0	0	0	0	0	0	0	3	0	0
Schulte, Mark, Springfield*	.257	74	261	40	67	114	13	2	10	38	5	3	4	1	21	2	26	3	3
Schwarz, Jeffrey, Quad Cities	.200	27	10	2	2	2	0	0	0	0	0	0	0	0	0	0	6	0	0
Schwarz, Thomas, Kenosha	.262	115	416	46	109	139	17	2	3	68	11	4	5	4	28	2	49	1	5
Segura, Americo, Peoria	.265	54	147	19	39	51	6	0	2	17	1	0	1	4	10	0	30	0	2

Player and Club	Pct.	G.	AB.	R.	H.	TB.	2B.	3B.	HR.	RBI.	GW.	SH.	SF.	HP.	BB.	Int. BB.	SO.	SB.	CS.
Sheck, Thomas, Clinton°	.078	25	51	3	4	10	1	1	1	5	0	0	0	0	12	1	10	1	0
Sierra, Ruben, Burlington†	.263	138	482	55	127	188	33	5	6	75	5	6	3	1	49	5	97	13	9
Slavin, Timothy, Wausau	.189	34	111	19	21	34	4	0	3	15	1	1	1	2	16	0	33	4	1
Smith, Charles, Peoria°	.189	12	37	3	7	10	1	1	0	4	0	2	0	0	3	0	5	0	0
Smith, James W., Kenosha	.000	3	3	0	0	0	0	0	0	0	0	0	0	0	0	0	1	0	0
Smith, Kelvin, Clinton	.227	98	366	35	83	109	11	3	3	29	2	5	4	3	29	1	69	9	3
Smith, Michael, Beloit	.220	22	41	4	9	9	0	0	0	6	1	1	1	0	7	1	6	0	1
Smith, Paul, Wausau	.202	37	124	18	25	29	2	1	0	14	1	1	2	0	23	1	20	7	2
Smith, Shawn, Kenosha	.200	20	55	9	11	12	1	0	0	6	1	1	0	2	4	0	12	0	0
Smith, Steven, Waterloo	.234	64	209	29	49	66	9	1	2	19	4	5	2	4	16	0	38	7	0
Soper, Michael D., Appleton	.236	128	444	47	105	130	18	2	1	48	5	9	3	3	16	0	60	3	2
Spalt, Steven, Beloit	.143	8	7	1	1	1	0	0	0	1	0	1	1	0	1	0	1	0	0
Spring, James, Clinton°	.213	125	456	49	97	130	16	4	3	28	2	2	0	0	56	2	82	9	6
Steen, Gregory, Peoria	.233	133	481	54	112	145	20	2	3	45	3	6	4	8	49	1	74	10	10
Steinbach, Eugene, Waterloo	.330	28	94	18	31	64	9	0	8	22	2	0	0	2	14	0	32	0	0
Steinbach, Terry, Madison	.295	135	474	57	140	209	24	6	11	79	9	4	7	1	49	1	59	5	6
Stewart, Charles, Quad Cities	.152	16	33	2	5	5	0	0	0	1	0	2	0	0	5	0	11	0	0
Stillwell, Kurt, Cedar Rapids†	.251	112	382	63	96	125	15	1	4	33	7	3	5	1	70	1	53	24	9
Stock, Kevin, Burlington	.168	55	173	21	29	53	3	3	5	21	2	3	2	2	24	1	49	2	4
Tapias, Luis, Kenosha	.250	9	20	1	5	5	0	0	0	3	0	1	0	0	2	0	4	0	0
Tarnow, Greg, Appleton	.174	51	132	12	23	36	7	0	2	15	1	4	1	1	17	0	39	0	2
Taylor, Michael, Appleton	.278	117	435	87	121	168	17	6	6	52	5	3	2	0	66	1	64	49	12
Teahan, James, Clinton	.286	27	7	1	2	3	1	0	0	2	0	0	0	0	0	0	2	0	0
Thornton, John, Beloit	.284	117	342	64	97	165	20	3	14	50	5	1	0	2	100	1	103	19	13
Threadgill, George, Burlington	.255	62	212	26	54	61	7	0	0	13	1	1	1	2	20	0	49	10	4
Tiefenthaler, Dennis, Peoria	.261	17	23	9	6	10	1	0	1	1	1	0	0	1	12	1	8	1	1
Tinoco, David, Wausau	.209	51	153	15	32	43	3	1	2	16	2	5	0	1	18	0	24	2	1
Tolleson, Michael, Waterloo°	.197	45	142	21	28	32	2	1	0	5	0	2	0	2	18	0	41	2	3
Torve, Kenton, Appleton°	.251	66	219	40	55	74	13	3	0	11	1	1	1	3	23	1	38	3	5
Tullier, Michael, Quad Cities°	.276	38	105	13	29	36	5	1	0	15	0	0	1	0	21	0	19	3	3
Turner, John, Quad Cities°	.279	51	165	34	46	53	3	2	0	23	2	2	1	1	30	2	13	13	3
Valera, Alcadio, Waterloo†	.200	5	15	0	3	3	0	0	0	0	0	0	0	0	0	0	8	1	0
VanBurkleo, Tyler, Peoria°	.315	26	73	13	23	35	7	1	1	10	2	0	0	0	15	0	27	4	0
Vargas, Jose, Beloit†	.235	39	102	13	24	31	3	2	0	5	0	3	0	0	5	1	11	5	1
Vasquez, R. Angelo, Clinton°	.209	79	244	31	51	62	6	1	1	21	0	1	0	8	28	0	78	14	5
Vaughn, Michael, Springfield°	.262	46	126	15	33	51	6	0	4	18	2	1	0	1	14	2	26	0	0
Verkuilen, Michael, Kenosha°	.273	133	443	66	121	205	29	5	15	78	11	3	7	3	93	10	74	4	1
Vetsch, David, Kenosha°	.203	26	69	8	14	22	4	2	0	4	0	0	0	0	11	0	18	0	0
Villa, Michael, Clinton°	.167	12	6	0	1	1	0	0	0	0	0	0	0	0	0	0	4	0	0
Walck, Harold, Quad Cities°	.000	17	1	1	0	0	0	0	0	1	0	0	0	0	3	0	1	0	0
Wasem, James, Clinton	.275	15	40	6	11	13	2	0	1	0	1	0	1	0	9	0	8	1	1
Wilder, David, Madison	.251	48	167	28	42	60	10	1	2	25	3	1	1	2	33	1	35	10	4
Wilder, Michael, Madison	.205	101	258	51	53	60	7	0	0	18	1	4	6	1	63	0	57	18	9
Williams, David, Kenosha	.154	8	13	2	2	2	0	0	0	0	0	1	0	1	0	0	8	0	0
Williams, Fred, Beloit	.208	128	399	51	83	103	13	2	1	31	9	6	4	3	68	1	98	8	6
Williams, Kenneth, Appleton	.286	38	147	23	42	72	11	2	5	26	4	1	2	2	15	0	48	13	5
Wilmet, Paul, Springfield	.143	53	7	1	1	1	0	0	0	0	2	1	0	0	1	0	3	0	0
Wilson, Phillip E., Waterloo	.321	17	53	8	17	28	3	1	2	5	0	0	1	3	0	8	3	2	
Wilson, Phillip F., Kenosha	.198	104	399	58	79	109	10	4	4	33	1	7	1	3	32	1	74	28	3
Winfield, M. Steven, Springfield	.000	5	1	0	0	0	0	0	0	0	0	0	0	0	0	0	1	0	0
Wishnevski, William, Wausau°	.266	110	361	52	96	147	18	0	11	57	4	2	2	4	82	1	88	8	2
Wooster, Robert, Waterloo	.157	80	229	12	36	38	2	0	0	11	1	5	1	0	28	0	51	1	5

The following pitchers, listed alphabetically by club, with games in parentheses, had no plate appearances, primarily through use of designated hitters.

APPLETON—Babcock, William (7); Burns, Britt (1); Correa, Edwin (26); Davis, Joel (11); Drabek, Douglas (1); Guzman, Pedro (26); Hickey, Kevin (10); Imig, Paul (30); Johnson, John P. (27); Layton, Thomas (8); Moses, John (6); Phelps, James (5); Schmidt, Eric (21); Simmons, Todd (7); Stacey, Shawn (1); Tanner, Bruce (37); Tanzi, Michael (3); Walker, Kurt (46).

BELOIT—Birkbeck, Michael (26); Bosio, Christopher (26); Candiotti, Thomas (2); Ciardi, Mark (25); Derksen, Robert (6); Gilbert, Jeffrey (16); Madrid, Alexander (22); Morris, James (24); Murphy, Daniel (26); Rice, Woolsey (35); Shamblin, Archie (9); Stapleton, David (48).

BURLINGTON—Allison, James (29); Anderson, Scott (14); Carter, Kendall (13); Cipres, Mark (8); Daniel, Stephen (11); Dersin, Eric (5); Dial, Charles (2); Harman, David (47); Harrington, John (12); Hester, Ricky (32); Hicks, Robert (10); Keathley, Robin (18); Kipper, Bruce (32); Knapp, Richard (33); LoSauro, Carmelo (7); Rech, Edward (13); Rogers, Kenneth (39); Soper, Michael J. (23); Winbush, Michael (7).

CEDAR RAPIDS—Culver, Lanell (6); Konderla, Michael (12); Trujillo, Louie (26).

CLINTON—Tate, Stuart (17); Tavarez, David (5).

KENOSHA—Clay, Danny (26); Cloninger, Michael (8); Galloway, Troy (8); Gomez, Steven (46); Henderson, Craig (28); Iasparro, Donnie (30); Klingbeil, Scott (44); Parham, Terrill (20); Prickett, Scott (7); Rodriguez, Enrique (10); Russell, Gerald (9); Sontag, Alan (20); Wiseman, Timothy (26).

MADISON—Akerfelds, Darrel (24); Baker, Mark (7); Belcher, Timothy (16); Burns, Todd (10); Fulmer, Michael (50); Giddings, Wayne (22); Godwin, Glenn (5); Gonsalves, Dennis (24); Hallas, Robert (8); Heath, Allan (27); Leonette, Mark (9); Ontiveros, Steven (5); Smith, Lawrence (17); Vantrease, Robert (16); Whaley, Scott (44).

PEORIA—Banning, Douglas (15); Cannon, Scott (47); Chadwick, Ray (26); Cozzolino, Paul (56); Delzer, Edwin (39); Gallo, Bernard (15); Gonzales, Jim (19); Kemmerling, Byron (11); Knowles, Kirk (7); Ojeda, Jorge (6); Pruneda, Armando (12); Psaltis, Spiro (28); Reed, Martin (16); Sillivent, Gregory (5); Stanfield, Donald (9); Tinkey, James (27).

QUAD CITIES—Bell, Gregory (17); Hrynko, Lawrence (2); Sain, Joseph (8); Slowik, Thaddeus (5); Volkman, John (42).

SPRINGFIELD—Arnold, Scott (1); Barton, Jeffrey (5); Cherry, Paul (1); Rigoli, Joseph (4).

WATERLOO—Arney, Jeffrey (4); Cisco, Shawn (37); DiFrancisco, Mark (8); Dixon, Ronn (10); Farrell, John (9); Galloway, Kenneth (7); McCullock, Alec (9); Miglio, John (37); Minyard, John (4); Mora, Abraham (3); Murphy, Michael (17); Myles, Rick (8); Pierorazio, Wesley (22); Piphus, Benjamin (19); Reynolds, Thomas (24); Ritter, Reggie (37); Roche, Stephen (5); Santarelli, Calvin (19); Stephenson, Joe (17); Street, Michael (30); Szymczak, David (3); Tamarez, Manuel (6); Whitmyer, Stephen (13).

WAUSAU—Barnes, Tyrone (3); Bergendahl, Wray (27); Bryant, James (9); Burns, Thomas (28); Gunnarsson, Robert (53); Held, Robert (23); Hinson, Robert (24); Malave, Benito (34); Medvin, Scott (40); Moore, Richard (5); Salazar, Edward (20); Schneider, Paul (58); Smith, David W. (21); Spratke, Kenneth (3); Swearingen, Douglas (31); Wilkinson, William (19).

GRAND SLAM HOME RUNS—Edwards, Sierra, 2 each; Berge, Boever, Dickerson, Dougherty, Duggan, S. Howard, Jensen, T. Jones, Komeiji, Lamar, Lopez, Manfre, Ro. Martinez, Merrifield, O. Perez, T. Schwarz, Slavin, T. Steinbach, Thornton, Wishnevski, 1 each.

AWARDED FIRST BASE ON CATCHER'S INTERFERENCE—Beardman 5 (Meier 2, T. Bell, Glendening, Hill); Burton 2 (D. Davis, Segura); Appino (Lamar); Batista (J.H. Johnson); T. Bell (Tarnow); Berryhill (Pena); Gould (Segura); Hengel (Tarnow); A. Jones (St. Anderson); Moritz (Oliver); Pleis (J.H. Johnson); Saatzer (Epps).

CLUB FIELDING

Club	Pct.	G.	PO.	A.	E.	DP.	PB.	Club	Pct.	G.	PO.	A.	E.	DP.	PB.
Madison	.966	138	3499	1448	175	125	22	Springfield	.962	139	3555	1404	195	114	26
Kenosha	.965	138	3458	1494	180	120	31	Waterloo	.962	139	3477	1565	198	124	36
Appleton	.964	136	3485	1372	179	107	16	Cedar Rapids	.961	138	3533	1347	198	101	33
Wausau	.964	136	3512	1525	187	121	28	Quad Cities	.959	138	3538	1530	219	113	29
Peoria	.963	139	3588	1469	197	123	28	Clinton	.954	139	3615	1570	251	150	18
Beloit	.962	139	3676	1406	202	116	36	Burlington	.952	139	3482	1508	254	108	39

Triple Plays—Beloit 2, Kenosha, Peoria, Quad Cities.

INDIVIDUAL FIELDING

☆Throws lefthanded.

FIRST BASEMEN

Player and Club	Pct.	G.	PO.	A.	E.	DP.	Player and Club	Pct.	G.	PO.	A.	E.	DP.
Bates, Burlington	.982	7	50	6	1	1	Meier, Appleton	1.000	7	44	5	0	3
Beall, Peoria	1.000	1	3	0	0	0	Merrifield, Peoria	1.000	4	25	1	0	4
Berryhill, Quad Cities	1.000	2	2	0	0	0	Meyer, Beloit	.982	68	560	34	11	54
Cesario, Burlington	.974	15	111	3	3	6	Montanari, Quad Cities	.986	52	447	38	7	44
Davis, Burlington	.967	40	337	20	12	26	Morman, Appleton	.990	93	809	41	9	65
Demeter, Springfield	1.000	1	5	0	0	3	Mosley, Burlington	1.000	1	2	0	0	0
Diaz, Waterloo	.857	3	6	0	1	2	Nelson, Madison☆	.987	136	1173	89	17	111
Duggan, Wausau	.980	55	471	31	10	46	Padia, Cedar Rapids	.931	4	24	3	2	1
Felix, Kenosha	.982	7	53	2	1	4	Perez, Appleton	1.000	1	2	0	0	0
Freytes, Quad Cities	1.000	2	2	0	0	0	Powell, Clinton	.972	17	132	8	4	10
Gambeski, Springfield	.889	3	22	2	3	2	Saatzer, Peoria	.952	26	223	15	12	26
Gill, Springfield	.985	53	389	16	6	38	Sandry, Quad Cities	.981	36	331	22	7	25
Hazard, Beloit☆	1.000	1	1	0	0	0	Sasser, Clinton	.983	52	498	29	9	49
Henika, Cedar Rapids	.978	92	761	55	18	55	Sauer, Beloit☆	1.000	2	13	1	0	3
Houston, Clinton☆	.983	77	697	39	13	77	Schulte, Springfield	.992	17	123	6	1	5
Hunsinger, Springfield	.987	80	643	48	9	55	C. Smith, Peoria☆	.989	10	80	8	1	8
Johnson, Quad Cities	1.000	1	6	1	0	0	M. Smith, Beloit	1.000	1	5	2	0	0
J. Jones, Madison	1.000	1	2	0	0	0	P. Smith, Wausau	.984	36	338	27	6	28
T. Jones, Peoria☆	.996	70	508	44	2	47	E. Steinbach, Waterloo	1.000	3	19	0	0	1
Komeiji, Wausau	1.000	3	24	1	0	1	T. Steinbach, Madison	1.000	2	15	1	0	1
Kumiega, Quad Cities	.984	44	336	28	6	22	Tarnow, Appleton	.993	23	141	9	1	11
Lamar, Cedar Rapids	1.000	8	45	2	0	3	Thornton, Beloit	.983	75	606	35	11	52
Lusby, Peoria	.987	31	293	16	4	19	Tinoco, Wausau	.991	48	406	27	4	22
Madden, Waterloo	.993	69	556	37	4	55	Turner, Quad Cities☆	.966	10	83	3	3	6
Manfre, Cedar Rapids	.990	38	290	18	3	22	VanBurkleo, Peoria☆	.938	9	59	1	4	8
Re. Martinez, Waterloo☆	.978	77	637	44	15	55	Vaughn, Springfield	.957	3	20	2	1	1
Ro. Martinez, Burlington	.991	83	714	44	7	57	VERKUILEN, Kenosha☆	.991	133	1132	71	11	97
McLaughlin, Appleton	.982	20	161	6	3	12	Wilson, Waterloo	1.000	4	11	1	0	2

Triple Plays—Jones, Meyer, Sandry, Thornton, Verkuilen.

SECOND BASEMEN

Player and Club	Pct.	G.	PO.	A.	E.	DP.	Player and Club	Pct.	G.	PO.	A.	E.	DP.
Abbott, Beloit	.972	6	12	23	1	6	Irvine, Beloit	1.000	2	2	0	0	0
Amaral, Quad Cities	.958	23	49	65	5	13	Jackson, Burlington	.818	3	3	6	2	0
Andrade, Burlington	.949	14	25	31	3	5	Klein, Burlington	1.000	1	1	3	0	0
Barineau, Waterloo	.918	15	14	42	5	9	Kline, Peoria	.958	10	23	23	2	6
Bates, Burlington	.980	41	80	121	4	18	Krause, Madison	1.000	4	1	9	0	0
Beardman, Madison	.953	101	216	226	22	54	Manning, Wausau	.970	13	23	42	2	7
Blair, Burlington	.945	39	82	106	11	18	Montanari, Quad Cities	1.000	2	0	3	0	0
Bocock, Springfield	.970	50	97	128	7	25	Moore, Appleton	.954	26	51	53	5	9
Browne, Burlington	.961	50	128	120	10	29	PALMER, Kenosha	.980	118	269	329	12	76
Bruzik, Wausau	.941	18	41	54	6	11	Pedraza, Waterloo	.972	76	153	228	11	50
Carrasco, Waterloo	.922	19	23	36	5	7	Perez, Appleton	.905	11	17	21	4	7
Cruz, Quad Cities	.957	101	227	285	23	59	Pino, Appleton	.950	103	238	258	26	50
Denbo, Cedar Rapids	.954	41	75	90	8	14	Rembielak, Quad Cities	1.000	2	2	5	0	1
Derby, Beloit	.889	4	8	8	2	1	Riley, Cedar Rapids	.922	13	20	27	4	8
Ditto, Quad Cities	.985	19	25	39	1	6	Smith, Waterloo	.924	29	41	56	8	11
Doran, Peoria	1.000	1	3	2	0	0	Spring, Clinton	.955	116	255	342	28	73
Dougherty, Springfield	.958	100	198	233	19	51	Steen, Peoria	.978	130	280	373	15	76
Espinal, Clinton	.938	24	52	54	7	15	Tapias, Kenosha	1.000	3	5	6	0	2
Franko, Burlington	1.000	2	2	5	0	0	Tiefenthaler, Peoria	1.000	2	4	3	0	0
Gherna, Kenosha	.929	19	38	41	6	5	Vargas, Beloit	.889	13	17	23	5	7
Giddens, Cedar Rapids	.940	90	158	235	25	46	Wasem, Clinton	.923	5	7	5	1	1
Gomez, Wausau	.970	108	250	301	17	66	Wilder, Madison	.966	43	81	88	6	25
Howard, Waterloo	.970	16	26	38	2	5	Williams, Beloit	.969	125	255	310	18	79

Triple Play—Gherna.

THIRD BASEMEN

Player and Club	Pct.	G.	PO.	A.	E.	DP.	Player and Club	Pct.	G.	PO.	A.	E.	DP.
Abbott, Beloit	.875	4	1	6	1	2	Duggan, Wausau	.905	7	5	14	2	1
Andrade, Burlington	.917	41	35	87	11	8	Edwards, Waterloo	.786	21	7	26	9	0
Aponte, Waterloo	.942	35	46	67	7	6	Everett, Beloit	.933	137	79	270	25	29
Barineau, Waterloo	.500	1	0	1	1	0	Franko, Kenosha	.929	8	6	20	2	0
Bates, Burlington	.846	5	5	17	4	1	Freytes, Quad Cities	.917	107	92	216	28	20
Beall, Peoria	1.000	2	2	0	0	0	Gould, Madison	.800	2	1	3	1	1
Beardman, Madison	.000	2	0	0	1	0	Grant, Peoria	.778	4	0	7	2	0
Bocock, Springfield	.976	15	8	32	1	4	Harris, Cedar Rapids	.903	129	111	204	34	12
Borowski, Madison	.875	18	7	21	4	1	Hayes, Clinton	.910	112	68	216	28	17
Carrasco, Waterloo	.851	40	22	58	14	3	Hill, Kenosha	.762	5	3	13	5	0
Cesario, Burlington	.778	3	4	10	4	1	Howard, Waterloo	.881	25	18	41	8	2
Devlin, Appleton	.833	17	8	22	6	1	Hunsinger, Springfield	.931	44	39	55	7	4
Diaz, Waterloo	.500	2	0	1	1	0	Johnson, Appleton	.833	8	5	10	3	2
DiCeglio, Kenosha	1.000	2	1	1	0	0	Klein, Burlington	.920	8	5	18	2	4
Ditto, Quad Cities	1.000	2	0	2	0	0	Kline, Peoria	1.000	7	2	6	0	0

THIRD BASEMEN—Continued

Player and Club	Pct.	G.	PO.	A.	E.	DP.
Lindeman, Springfield	.883	93	68	159	30	13
Madden, Waterloo	1.000	1	1	1	0	0
Manfre, Cedar Rapids	.962	8	8	17	1	1
Manning, Wausau	.972	13	11	24	1	4
E. Martinez, Wausau	.930	118	85	246	25	17
R. Martinez, Burlington	.940	30	27	67	6	6
MERRIFIELD, Peoria	.958	133	122	267	17	22
Montanari, Quad Cities	.947	29	25	47	4	0
Moore, Appleton	.932	54	32	106	10	5
Moritz, Appleton	1.000	1	1	0	0	0
Palmer, Kenosha	.909	13	10	20	3	0
Parrett, Beloit	1.000	1	3	1	0	0
Perez, Appleton	.889	22	15	33	6	4
Rembielak, Quad Cities	1.000	6	2	8	0	0
Riley, Cedar Rapids	.750	2	0	3	1	0
Sandry, Quad Cities	.000	1	0	0	1	0
Sasser, Clinton	.917	34	23	65	8	6
Schwarz, Kenosha	.916	112	87	209	27	26
Smith, Waterloo	.956	18	11	32	2	3
T. Steinbach, Madison	.930	124	91	256	26	31
Stock, Burlington	.907	55	48	98	15	4
Tarnow, Appleton	1.000	6	2	8	0	0
Torve, Appleton	.921	39	32	84	10	9
Vargas, Beloit	.500	2	0	1	1	0
Wilson, Waterloo	1.000	2	1	3	0	0
Wooster, Waterloo	.875	6	3	11	2	0

Triple Play—Montanari.

SHORTSTOPS

Player and Club	Pct.	G.	PO.	A.	E.	DP.
Abbott, Beloit	.936	26	35	53	6	8
Alfredson, Peoria	.737	7	4	10	5	1
Amaral, Quad Cities	.955	5	13	8	1	2
Anderson, Peoria	.946	67	124	189	18	40
Andrade, Burlington	1.000	6	3	8	0	0
Barineau, Waterloo	1.000	2	0	1	0	1
Beardman, Madison	.875	1	1	6	1	1
Blair, Burlington	.857	43	54	120	29	15
Bocock, Springfield	.951	63	55	138	10	27
Borowski, Madison	.941	55	70	136	13	28
Browne, Burlington	.899	76	103	191	33	30
Carrasco, Waterloo	1.000	1	0	1	0	0
CRABTREE, Wausau	.952	108	171	321	25	59
Cruz, Quad Cities	.900	2	6	3	1	1
Denbo, Cedar Rapids	1.000	1	4	4	0	0
DiCeglio, Kenosha	.929	57	78	145	17	26
Ditto, Quad Cities	.932	43	50	114	12	20
Escobar, Clinton	.907	96	175	295	48	71
Espinal, Clinton	.911	39	70	114	18	24
Franko, Kenosha	.915	57	71	154	21	30
Hardamon, Quad Cities	.917	7	12	10	2	3
Hill, Kenosha	1.000	1	0	1	0	0
Howard, Waterloo	.909	2	4	6	1	1
Hunsinger, Springfield	1.000	1	1	1	0	0
Kavanaugh, Springfield	.906	53	86	145	24	30
Klein, Burlington	.920	24	42	73	10	10
Kline, Peoria	.924	69	103	166	22	36
Lindeman, Springfield	1.000	9	10	16	0	2
Luther, Springfield	.916	44	67	118	17	25
Manfre, Cedar Rapids	.947	18	30	41	4	10
Manning, Wausau	.956	37	61	90	7	19
Marquardt, Madison	.949	71	107	191	16	33
Montanari, Quad Cities	.896	26	30	56	10	8
Moore, Appleton	.938	10	14	31	3	5
Pedraza, Waterloo	.956	66	97	207	14	39
Quinones, Beloit	.903	99	119	234	38	59
Rembielak, Quad Cities	.933	73	102	216	23	42
Riley, Cedar Rapids	.919	22	27	64	8	12
Smith, Kenosha	.916	19	31	45	7	8
Soper, Appleton	.949	128	189	350	29	51
Spalt, Beloit	.846	8	7	4	2	1
Steen, Peoria	.833	1	2	3	1	1
Stillwell, Cedar Rapids	.941	99	156	245	25	51
Tapias, Kenosha	.960	6	11	13	1	1
Valera, Waterloo	1.000	5	5	18	0	1
Vargas, Beloit	.874	25	32	44	11	7
Wasem, Clinton	.968	8	6	24	1	1
Wilder, Madison	.895	16	15	36	6	6
D. Williams, Kenosha	.947	7	5	13	1	0
F. Williams, Beloit	.750	2	0	3	1	0
Wooster, Waterloo	.949	74	129	246	20	55

Triple Plays—Quinones 2, Kline, Rembielak.

OUTFIELDERS

Player and Club	Pct.	G.	PO.	A.	E.	DP.
Adams, Peoria	.934	45	67	4	5	1
Allen, Clinton	.955	65	99	7	5	2
Appino, Beloit	.878	38	33	3	5	0
Aquino, Burlington°	.977	33	40	3	1	2
Artiles, Kenosha°	.778	3	6	1	2	0
Austin, Quad Cities	1.000	2	0	1	0	0
Bailey, Burlington	.961	106	140	8	6	3
Batista, Springfield	.964	119	176	12	7	0
Bayron, Kenosha°	.000	1	0	0	1	0
Beall, Peoria	.986	37	65	3	1	0
Beardman, Madison	1.000	1	1	0	0	0
Berge, Cedar Rapids	.982	117	160	5	3	0
Boderick, Madison	1.000	17	15	0	0	0
Boever, Cedar Rapids	.954	63	95	9	5	3
Borowski, Madison	1.000	7	3	1	0	0
Bruzik, Wausau	.978	85	173	8	4	1
Buchanon, Peoria	.957	91	128	4	6	0
Burton, Quad Cities°°	.970	65	95	2	3	1
Carrasco, Waterloo	1.000	5	6	0	0	0
Cesario, Burlington	.979	35	46	1	1	0
Clark, Waterloo	.972	96	128	10	4	1
Copeland, Kenosha°	.967	124	219	19	8	4
Coughlon, Madison	1.000	2	2	0	0	0
Culberson, Clinton	.949	69	104	7	6	2
Day, Cedar Rapids	.938	59	101	5	7	1
Derby, Beloit	.923	7	12	0	1	0
Diaz, Kenosha	.917	9	11	0	1	0
Dickerson, Quad Cities	.955	98	162	9	8	1
Digioia, Springfield	.972	9	35	0	1	0
Doran, Peoria	.980	118	277	13	6	3
Duggan, Wausau	1.000	4	3	0	0	0
Edwards, Waterloo	.978	83	129	5	3	1
Finley, Beloit°	.978	136	261	12	6	4
FORGIONE, Kenosha°	.984	129	245	6	4	4
Freeman, Beloit°	.957	44	65	2	3	0
Garrett, Madison	1.000	1	1	0	0	0
G. Gill, Springfield	1.000	2	2	0	0	0
Glendening, Quad Cities	.929	11	12	1	1	0
Gordon, Beloit	1.000	3	3	0	0	0
Gould, Madison	.961	53	94	4	4	1
Grant, Peoria	.977	21	35	7	1	1
Haley, Wausau	.824	11	12	2	3	0
Harper, Waterloo	.971	107	161	4	5	0
Harrison, Madison	.974	19	36	2	1	1
Hazard, Beloit°	.889	4	7	1	1	0
Hengel, Wausau	.929	89	109	9	9	0
Hill, Kenosha	1.000	2	1	0	0	0
Houston, Clinton°	.500	1	1	0	1	0
Howard, Madison	.900	32	36	0	4	0
Irvine, Beloit	.968	106	175	8	6	0
Jackson, Beloit°	.963	67	77	1	3	0
Jensen, Appleton	.962	121	248	8	10	3
Johnson, Quad Cities	1.000	9	7	0	0	0
A. Jones, Clinton	.910	91	119	2	12	0
T. Jones, Peoria°	1.000	9	16	1	0	0
Kemp, Peoria	1.000	14	22	1	0	0
Kline, Peoria	.919	39	66	2	6	1
Kramer, Waterloo	.950	43	69	7	4	0
Krause, Madison	1.000	16	22	2	0	0
Leighton, Kenosha	.912	27	31	0	3	0
Lewis, Peoria	.988	47	76	8	1	1
Loscalzo, Madison°	.971	92	157	8	5	2
Loseke, Cedar Rapids°	.945	90	153	3	9	0
Manfre, Cedar Rapids	.973	65	100	7	3	2
Mart, Quad Cities	1.000	6	4	0	0	0
D. Martinez, Quad Cities°	.938	12	13	2	1	0
Re. Martinez, Waterloo°	.967	44	56	3	2	1
Ro. Martinez, Burlington	1.000	2	1	0	0	0
McCue, Clinton	.965	78	104	7	4	2
McLaughlin, Appleton	.970	85	126	3	4	1
Mejia, Quad Cities	.967	31	58	1	2	0
Menssen, Kenosha	1.000	22	34	4	0	0
Migliore, Peoria	1.000	1	2	0	0	0
Moore, Appleton	1.000	1	1	0	0	0
Moritz, Appleton	.974	95	144	8	4	3
Morman, Appleton	.941	9	14	2	1	1
Mosley, Burlington	.500	1	1	0	1	0
Munson, Cedar Rapids	.984	41	55	6	1	1
Perez, Wausau°	.961	118	206	13	9	2
Phillips, Cedar Rapids°	.750	9	9	0	3	0
Pleis, Springfield	.929	13	13	0	1	0
Polonia, Madison°	.955	131	202	9	10	3
Powell, Clinton	.972	22	34	1	1	0
Richardson, Quad Cities	.977	114	237	16	6	6
Rigos, Springfield	.977	115	163	7	4	0
Rodriguez, Springfield	.978	127	249	13	6	3

OUTFIELDERS—Continued

Player and Club	Pct.	G.	PO.	A.	E.	DP.
M. Roman, Waterloo	1.000	24	25	2	0	1
Saatzer, Peoria	.824	16	12	2	3	0
Sandry, Quad Cities	.941	26	30	2	2	0
Sasser, Clinton	1.000	2	2	0	0	0
Sauer, Beloit*	.957	30	42	3	2	0
Schulte, Springfield	.971	49	66	1	2	0
Sheck, Clinton*	.857	6	5	1	1	0
Sierra, Burlington	.928	134	239	18	20	2
Slavin, Wausau	.945	33	49	3	3	0
K. Smith, Clinton	.973	97	173	8	5	2
M. Smith, Beloit	1.000	11	11	0	0	0
S. Smith, Waterloo	.970	22	30	2	1	0
Stewart, Quad Cities	.929	7	12	1	1	0
Taylor, Appleton	.981	68	96	5	2	1
Thornton, Beloit	1.000	5	2	0	0	0
Threadgill, Burlington	.958	58	89	3	4	1
Tiefenthaler, Peoria	.923	12	12	0	1	0
Tolleson, Waterloo	.985	45	65	2	1	0
Torve, Appleton	1.000	3	3	0	0	0
Tullier, Quad Cities*	.986	34	64	4	1	1
Turner, Quad Cities*	.926	37	46	4	4	0
VanBurkleo, Peoria*	1.000	16	24	0	0	0
Vasquez, Burlington*	.897	66	96	9	12	2
Vaughn, Springfield	.929	14	12	1	1	0
Vetsch, Kenosha	1.000	16	19	3	0	0
D. Wilder, Madison	.961	49	92	7	4	2
M. Wilder, Madison	.962	21	24	1	1	0
F. Williams, Beloit	1.000	2	9	0	0	0
K. Williams, Appleton	.969	38	58	5	2	2
Wilson, Kenosha	.936	104	210	9	15	3
Wishnevski, Wausau*	.946	83	127	13	8	4

CATCHERS

Player and Club	Pct.	G.	PO.	A.	E.	DP.	PB.
Allanson, Waterloo	.987	15	68	9	1	3	3
Anderson, Beloit	.979	23	173	15	4	0	8
Baker, Quad Cities	.967	4	27	2	1	0	1
BELL, Wausau	.993	83	496	53	4	7	18
Berryhill, Quad Cities	.977	53	312	31	8	3	7
Caianiello, Appleton	.981	75	503	66	11	9	6
Champion, Springfield	.980	34	181	13	4	0	5
Cruz, Quad Cities	1.000	1	1	0	0	0	0
Davis, Peoria	.971	42	273	25	9	1	4
A. Diaz, Peoria	.961	60	322	48	15	2	13
E. Diaz, Waterloo	.951	37	184	11	10	0	6
J. Diaz, Kenosha	.875	3	14	0	2	0	0
Digioia, Springfield	1.000	4	18	3	0	0	0
Epps, Burlington	.976	48	252	27	7	2	7
Felix, Kenosha	.989	75	401	64	5	6	19
Fischer, Madison	.923	2	10	2	1	0	0
Garrett, Madison	1.000	5	34	5	0	0	2
Gill, Madison	.985	36	183	13	3	1	6
Glendening, Quad Cities	.965	63	339	45	14	4	15
Gobbo, Beloit	.979	60	417	43	10	1	12
Griggs, Beloit	1.000	1	1	0	0	0	1
Haberle, Cedar Rapids	1.000	4	20	3	0	0	2
Halberg, Clinton	.982	8	53	3	1	1	0
Hance, Burlington	.991	27	192	27	2	6	5
Hill, Kenosha	.987	64	394	78	6	12	12
Johnson, Quad Cities	.982	31	197	17	4	2	5
J.B. Jones, Burlington	.986	61	381	37	6	8	19
J. Jones, Madison	.987	112	735	73	11	11	14
Komeiji, Wausau	.978	62	384	54	10	10	10
Lamar, Cedar Rapids	.991	28	210	16	2	2	0
Lopez, Waterloo	.988	73	453	58	6	4	17
Mart, Burlington	.974	11	68	8	2	1	8
Meier, Appleton	.984	47	345	20	6	5	8
Montanari, Quad Cities	1.000	2	3	0	0	0	1
Oliver, Cedar Rapids	.985	99	757	85	13	9	30
Padia, Cedar Rapids	1.000	15	93	10	0	3	1
Pagnozzi, Springfield	.984	102	667	90	12	8	16
Pena, Clinton	.970	69	409	40	14	6	11
Rainey, Clinton	.986	74	439	62	7	7	6
Rodriguez, Beloit	.993	66	556	38	4	2	15
Sasser, Clinton	1.000	1	3	1	0	0	1
Segura, Peoria	.983	53	259	36	5	4	11
Steinbach, Waterloo	.987	22	138	15	2	0	8
Stewart, Quad Cities	.950	6	18	1	1	0	0
Tarnow, Appleton	.959	18	124	15	6	0	2
Vaughn, Springfield	.978	12	83	6	2	0	5
Wilson, Waterloo	.986	11	56	15	1	1	2

Triple Play—Berryhill.

PITCHERS

Player and Club	Pct.	G.	PO.	A.	E.	DP.
Akerfelds, Madison	1.000	24	13	29	0	4
Allison, Burlington	.556	29	1	4	4	0
Anderson, Burlington	.938	14	4	11	1	0
Antle, Clinton	.958	21	6	17	1	3
Arney, Waterloo	.800	4	3	1	1	0
Arnold, Springfield	1.000	1	1	0	0	0
Babcock, Appleton*	1.000	7	1	5	0	0
Baker, Madison	1.000	7	0	1	0	0
Balmer, Quad Cities	1.000	9	1	2	0	0
Banning, Peoria	.895	15	5	12	2	0
Barba, Cedar Rapids	.933	19	2	12	1	2
Barnes, Wausau	1.000	3	0	2	0	0
Barton, Springfield	1.000	5	0	1	0	0
Belcher, Madison	.955	16	7	14	1	0
Bell, Quad Cities*	1.000	17	0	5	0	0
Bergendahl, Wausau	.833	27	5	25	6	1
Bethel, Quad Cities	.875	51	2	26	4	1
Birkbeck, Beloit	.964	26	16	37	2	2
Blunt, Springfield	.842	17	10	6	3	0
Bosio, Beloit	.889	26	10	46	7	2
Brahms, Clinton*	1.000	14	5	6	0	1
Brown, Springfield	.750	12	0	6	2	0
Bryant, Wausau	.750	9	1	2	1	0
Burkett, Clinton	.971	20	14	19	1	2
B. Burns, Appleton*	.500	1	0	1	1	0
Th. Burns, Wausau	.976	28	17	24	1	0
To. Burns, Madison	1.000	10	1	3	0	0
Calvert, Cedar Rapids	.893	20	6	19	3	1
Candelaria, Clinton*	.815	41	3	19	5	3
Candiotti, Beloit	1.000	2	2	2	0	0
Cannon, Peoria	.900	47	7	11	2	0
K. Carter, Burlington	1.000	13	2	15	0	1
R. Carter, Peoria	1.000	30	8	15	0	1
Caulfield, Springfield*	1.000	5	0	3	0	0
Chadwick, Peoria	.684	26	10	16	12	2
Ciardi, Beloit	.956	25	16	27	2	0
Cipres, Burlington	.000	8	0	0	1	0
Cisco, Waterloo	.891	37	11	30	5	4
Clay, Kenosha	.895	26	13	38	6	0
Cloninger, Kenosha	1.000	8	4	9	0	0
Conley, Cedar Rapids*	.920	43	8	15	2	1
Corbell, Clinton	.926	25	11	52	5	6
Correa, Appleton	.912	26	10	21	3	1
Coughlon, Madison	1.000	28	3	13	0	0
Cox, Quad Cities*	.956	17	4	39	2	0
Cozzolino, Peoria	1.000	56	2	7	0	0
Culver, Cedar Rapids*	1.000	6	0	1	0	0
Daniel, Burlington	.750	11	0	3	1	0
Davidson, Quad Cities	.952	27	14	26	2	2
Davis, Appleton	.867	11	2	11	2	0
Delzer, Peoria*	.889	39	5	11	2	1
Derksen, Beloit	1.000	6	1	2	0	0
Dersin, Burlington	1.000	5	0	5	0	0
Dial, Burlington	1.000	2	0	1	0	0
DiFrancisco, Waterloo	1.000	8	2	3	0	1
Dixon, Waterloo*	.857	10	2	10	2	0
Dodd, Cedar Rapids	.935	27	5	24	2	0
Dowless, Cedar Rapids	1.000	33	11	14	0	0
Doyle, Quad Cities	.958	42	6	17	1	2
Drabek, Appleton	1.000	1	0	1	0	0
Dressler, Clinton	1.000	19	3	12	0	0
Embser, Springfield*	.926	26	4	21	2	3
Faber, Clinton*	.857	9	2	4	1	0
Farley, Clinton*	.920	22	4	19	2	1
Farrell, Waterloo	.889	9	0	8	1	0
Ferran, Clinton	.952	41	4	16	1	3
Fingers, Beloit	.933	31	2	12	1	0
Fulmer, Madison*	.930	50	8	45	4	2
Funk, Cedar Rapids	.957	46	3	19	1	1
Gallo, Peoria*	1.000	15	0	5	0	1
K. Galloway, Waterloo*	1.000	7	0	3	0	0
T. Galloway, Kenosha*	.923	8	3	9	1	0
GIDDINGS, Madison	1.000	22	10	33	0	0
Gilbert, Beloit	1.000	16	0	11	0	0
Godwin, Appleton*	1.000	5	0	2	0	0
Gomez, Kenosha	.947	46	4	14	1	0
Gonsalves, Madison	.933	24	3	11	1	0
Gonzales, Peoria	.889	19	3	5	1	0
Gunnarsson, Wausau*	.950	53	4	15	1	0
Guzman, Appleton	.929	22	6	7	1	1
Hallas, Madison	.933	8	4	10	1	0
Hamilton, Quad Cities*	.875	18	2	12	2	1
Hansen, Madison	1.000	22	1	20	0	1
Hardwick, Springfield	1.000	3	4	2	0	0
Harman, Burlington	1.000	47	6	16	0	0
Harrington, Burlington	.909	12	6	4	1	0

PITCHERS—Continued

Player and Club	Pct.	G.	PO.	A.	E.	DP.
Heath, Madison*	.882	26	3	27	4	1
Held, Wausau	.704	23	5	14	8	0
Henderson, Kenosha*	.978	28	10	34	1	0
Hester, Burlington	.981	32	15	36	1	3
J. Hickey, Appleton	.893	49	7	18	3	1
K. Hickey, Appleton*	.909	10	1	9	1	1
Hicks, Burlington	.667	10	0	2	1	0
Hinson, Wausau	.941	24	7	25	2	1
Hrynko, Quad Cities	1.000	2	1	0	0	0
Iasparro, Kenosha	.875	30	1	13	2	0
Imig, Appleton	.905	30	5	14	2	1
Johnson, Appleton	.966	27	11	45	2	4
Keathley, Burlington	.909	18	10	20	3	1
Kemmerling, Peoria	.857	11	1	5	1	1
Kemp, Cedar Rapids	.974	27	9	28	1	1
King, Clinton	.950	35	10	28	2	2
Kipper, Burlington*	.950	32	6	32	2	2
Kish, Springfield	1.000	9	2	1	0	0
Klingbeil, Kenosha	.913	44	4	17	2	3
Knapp, Burlington	.889	33	6	26	4	2
Konderla, Cedar Rapids	1.000	12	2	4	0	0
Kopf, Quad Cities	1.000	10	6	7	0	0
Langdon, Cedar Rapids	.741	21	5	15	7	1
Layton, Appleton	.833	8	2	3	1	0
Lee, Clinton*	.882	26	7	23	4	1
Lenderman, Quad Cities	.921	28	7	28	3	2
Leonette, Madison	.833	9	4	6	2	2
LoSauro, Burlington	.750	7	0	3	1	0
Madrid, Beloit	.920	22	4	19	2	1
Malave, Wausau	.900	34	6	12	2	0
Martin, Springfield	.929	20	7	19	2	0
Martinez, Springfield*	.938	27	6	9	1	0
Mason, Springfield	1.000	16	1	1	0	0
McCullock, Waterloo	.000	9	0	0	1	0
Meadows, Springfield	.667	5	0	2	1	0
Medvin, Wausau	.643	40	0	9	5	0
Miglio, Waterloo*	.667	37	3	3	3	0
Migliore, Peoria	.844	15	8	19	5	3
Minyard, Waterloo	1.000	4	2	0	0	0
Mitchell, Springfield	1.000	17	0	3	0	0
R. Moore, Wausau	1.000	5	0	2	0	0
Mora, Waterloo	1.000	3	1	6	0	0
Morris, Beloit*	.917	24	4	18	2	0
Moses, Appleton*	1.000	6	2	0	0	0
D. Murphy, Beloit	.870	26	6	14	3	0
M. Murphy, Waterloo	.960	17	5	19	1	0
Myles, Waterloo*	.846	8	3	8	2	1
North, Springfield	.951	27	8	31	2	2
Odom, Madison	.923	9	4	8	1	1
Ojeda, Peoria	1.000	6	0	1	0	0
Oliverio, Cedar Rapids	.941	27	3	13	1	1
Ontiveros, Madison	.923	5	5	7	1	0
Ortega, Springfield	.800	9	0	4	1	0
Parham, Springfield*	.964	20	6	21	1	2
Parrett, Beloit	.950	29	9	10	1	0
Pettibone, Cedar Rapids	.971	26	14	19	1	1
Phelps, Appleton	.833	5	0	5	1	0
Phillips, Quad Cities	1.000	16	4	20	0	0
Pierorazio, Waterloo*	1.000	22	8	18	0	1
Pimentel, Springfield	1.000	22	4	7	0	0

Player and Club	Pct.	G.	PO.	A.	E.	DP.
Piphus, Waterloo	.885	19	3	20	3	1
Pobur, Quad Cities	.867	30	2	11	2	0
Prickett, Kenosha*	.800	7	1	3	1	1
Pruneda, Peoria	.938	12	6	9	1	2
Psaltis, Peoria*	1.000	28	5	8	0	3
Rech, Burlington*	1.000	13	1	7	0	0
Reed, Peoria*	.880	16	4	18	3	0
Reynolds, Waterloo	.941	24	4	12	1	0
Rice, Beloit	.714	35	0	5	2	0
Rigoli, Springfield	.667	4	0	2	1	0
Ritter, Waterloo	.981	37	12	40	1	2
Roche, Waterloo	1.000	5	3	0	0	0
Rodriguez, Kenosha	1.000	10	2	3	0	0
Rogers, Burlington*	.938	39	10	20	2	1
Roman, Springfield*	1.000	18	2	5	0	0
Russell, Kenosha	1.000	9	0	3	0	0
Saatzer, Peoria	1.000	2	0	1	0	0
Sain, Quad Cities	1.000	8	0	1	0	0
Salazar, Wausau*	1.000	20	1	3	0	0
Santarelli, Waterloo	.870	19	3	17	3	0
E. Schmidt, Appleton	1.000	21	8	23	0	2
G. Schmidt, Clinton	.833	26	7	18	5	2
Schneider, Wausau	.917	58	9	13	2	1
Schwarz, Quad Cities	.793	27	9	14	6	0
Shamblin, Beloit	.833	9	0	5	1	0
Sillivent, Peoria*	.600	5	0	3	2	0
Simmons, Appleton	1.000	7	0	7	0	0
D.W. Smith, Wausau	1.000	21	1	10	0	1
L. Smith, Madison*	1.000	17	1	5	0	0
Sontag, Kenosha	.946	20	10	25	2	3
Soper, Burlington*	1.000	23	3	7	0	0
Spratke, Wausau	.750	3	2	1	1	0
Stanfield, Peoria	1.000	9	2	6	0	0
Stapleton, Beloit*	.964	48	7	20	1	3
Steinbach, Madison	.500	2	1	0	1	0
Stephenson, Waterloo	1.000	17	3	6	0	1
Street, Waterloo	.941	30	6	10	1	0
Swearingen, Wausau*	1.000	31	6	22	0	0
Szymczak, Waterloo	1.000	3	1	3	0	0
Tamarez, Waterloo*	1.000	6	0	2	0	0
Tanner, Appleton	.962	37	5	20	1	3
Tanzi, Appleton*	1.000	3	1	2	0	0
Tate, Clinton	1.000	17	4	1	0	0
Teahan, Clinton	.920	27	7	16	2	0
Tinkey, Peoria	.947	27	7	29	2	1
Trujillo, Cedar Rapids	1.000	26	3	7	0	1
Tullier, Quad Cities*	1.000	1	0	1	0	0
Vantrease, Madison*	.800	16	1	3	1	0
Villa, Clinton	.867	12	4	9	2	1
Volkman, Quad Cities	.692	42	2	7	4	0
Walck, Quad Cities	.818	17	3	6	2	1
Walker, Appleton	1.000	46	1	11	0	1
Whaley, Madison	.962	44	3	22	1	0
Whitmyer, Waterloo	.625	13	4	1	3	0
Wilkinson, Wausau*	.842	19	3	13	3	1
Wilmet, Springfield	.880	53	6	16	3	2
Winbush, Burlington	.769	7	4	6	3	0
Winfield, Springfield	1.000	5	0	1	0	0
Wiseman, Kenosha	.958	26	13	33	2	0

Triple Play—Davidson.

The following players do not have any recorded accepted chances at the positions indicated; therefore, are not listed in the fielding averages for those particular positions: Bocock, of, p; Burton, 3b; R. Carter, of; Cherry, p; Day, 3b; Devlin, 2b; Ditto, p; Dougherty, 3b; Franko, p; S. Gill, of; E. Gomez, of; Hansen, of; T. Jackson, ss; Klein, of; Knowles, p; Luther, 2b; Manning, of; Mart, p; McLaughlin, 3b; C. Moore, p; E. Perez, ss; Pleis, p; Powell, 2b; A. Rodriguez, ss; L. Roman, of; Sandry, p; Slowik, p; Stacey, p; J.W. Smith, c; Steen, of; E. Steinbach, 3b; Tarnow, of, p; Tavarez, p; Taylor, ss.

CLUB PITCHING

Club	ERA.	G.	CG.	ShO.	Sv.	IP.	H.	R.	ER.	HR.	HB.	BB.	Int. BB.	SO.	WP.	Bk.
Kenosha	3.06	138	29	10	25	1152.2	1015	513	392	74	35	513	12	785	73	10
Cedar Rapids	3.09	138	33	14	28	1177.2	967	517	404	80	19	550	30	1043	68	8
Appleton	3.15	136	22	13	33	1161.2	1068	507	406	49	31	469	11	940	82	12
Beloit	3.26	139	32	12	35	1225.1	1097	568	444	69	18	533	17	1090	93	12
Wausau	3.36	136	10	6	31	1170.2	1078	570	437	73	73	541	11	847	84	8
Clinton	3.56	139	20	9	19	1205.0	1083	608	476	65	42	594	19	879	96	8
Madison	3.78	138	30	8	20	1166.1	1107	594	490	52	29	507	23	937	91	11
Springfield	3.91	139	26	14	20	1185.0	1147	650	515	88	37	557	25	916	95	7
Waterloo	3.98	139	24	9	26	1159.0	1114	624	512	84	41	534	30	875	77	13
Peoria	4.01	139	11	4	29	1196.0	1134	622	533	74	43	576	14	811	90	15
Burlington	4.44	139	13	7	19	1160.2	1184	756	573	92	55	588	9	862	101	14
Quad Cities	4.52	138	13	8	20	1179.1	1136	724	592	93	52	665	41	853	97	14

PITCHERS' RECORDS
(Leading Qualifiers for Earned-Run Average Leadership—112 or More Innings)

*Throws lefthanded.

Pitcher—Club	W.	L.	Pct.	ERA.	G.	GS.	CG.	GF.	ShO.	Sv.	IP.	H.	R.	ER.	HR.	HB.	BB.	Int. BB.	SO.	WP.
Tanner, Appleton	12	4	.750	1.96	37	9	6	15	3	2	123.2	96	32	27	0	4	30	1	91	10
Birkbeck, Beloit	14	3	.824	2.18	26	25	6	1	2	0	177.2	134	57	43	5	1	64	3	164	13

Pitcher—Club	W.	L.	Pct.	ERA.	G.	GS.	CG.	GF.	ShO.	Sv.	IP.	H.	R.	ER.	HR.	HB.	BB.	Int. BB.	SO.	WP.
Henderson, Kenosha°	13	7	.650	2.24	28	27	6	1	0	0	197.0	153	73	49	10	1	82	1	160	10
North, Springfield	7	4	.636	2.33	27	19	5	3	5	1	154.1	132	49	40	6	1	40	0	98	6
Corbell, Clinton	9	11	.450	2.64	25	25	7	0	1	0	177.0	148	71	52	7	2	52	3	101	8
Clay, Kenosha	9	8	.529	2.73	26	26	6	0	0	0	171.2	146	73	52	8	11	64	2	96	16
Pettibone, Cedar Rapids	9	8	.529	2.73	26	25	12	0	1	0	165.0	107	61	50	15	3	77	1	159	17
Bosio, Beloit	17	6	.739	2.73	26	26	11	0	2	0	181.0	159	83	55	12	5	56	0	156	17
Sontag, Kenosha	7	7	.500	2.76	20	20	6	0	1	0	143.1	118	51	44	8	4	57	0	110	7
Giddings, Madison	9	8	.529	2.79	22	18	6	4	2	0	122.2	101	48	38	4	1	42	0	89	10
Kemp, Cedar Rapids	11	9	.550	2.79	27	25	8	1	4	0	164.1	139	65	51	12	0	69	5	143	6
J. P. Johnson, Appleton	12	7	.632	2.80	27	26	6	1	2	1	170.1	160	72	53	5	3	55	2	136	8
Whaley, Madison	7	6	.538	2.89	44	9	4	19	0	9	127.2	105	49	41	2	3	35	3	106	6

Departmental Leaders: G—Schneider, 58; W—Bosio, 17; L—Kipper, Schwarz, 14; Pct.—Walker, .900; GS—Davidson, Henderson, Tinkey, 27; CG—Pettibone, 12; GF—Harman, 44; ShO—North, 5; Sv.—J. Hickey, 20; IP—Henderson, 197.0; H—Tinkey, 180; R—Tinkey, 105; ER—Davidson, Tinkey, 95; HR—Davidson, Farley, Lee, 16; HB—Hinson, 16; BB—Schwarz, 111; IBB—Wilmet, 10; SO—Ciardi, 166; WP—Akerfelds, Lee, Martin, 19.

(All Pitchers—Listed Alphabetically)

Pitcher—Club	W.	L.	Pct.	ERA.	G.	GS.	CG.	GF.	ShO.	Sv.	IP.	H.	R.	ER.	HR.	HB.	BB.	Int. BB.	SO.	WP.
Akerfelds, Madison	11	6	.647	4.41	24	24	6	0	1	0	151.0	156	86	74	7	5	74	2	137	19
Allison, Burlington	2	7	.222	5.84	29	8	0	9	0	1	77.0	59	63	50	9	3	101	0	80	10
Anderson, Burlington	3	6	.333	2.50	14	13	2	0	0	0	86.1	79	33	24	8	4	28	0	81	2
Antle, Clinton	0	6	.000	4.57	21	6	1	8	0	1	61.0	56	40	31	7	7	29	1	38	7
Arney, Waterloo	1	2	.333	1.86	4	4	1	0	0	0	29.0	22	7	6	1	0	6	1	16	0
Arnold, Springfield	0	1	.000	9.00	1	1	0	0	0	0	6.0	6	6	6	4	0	0	0	9	0
Babcock, Appleton°	2	1	.667	1.98	7	5	0	2	0	0	27.1	24	9	6	0	2	13	0	22	1
Baker, Madison	1	0	1.000	4.35	7	1	1	3	0	0	20.2	17	13	10	2	0	9	1	14	0
Balmer, Quad Cities	0	1	.000	7.00	9	0	0	0	0	0	18.0	29	18	14	4	2	12	0	13	1
Banning, Peoria	1	6	.143	5.63	15	8	0	2	0	0	54.1	62	40	34	2	1	23	1	34	3
Barba, Cedar Rapids	4	4	.500	4.96	19	14	0	1	0	0	69.0	59	47	38	4	2	64	1	58	9
Barnes, Wausau	0	0	.000	11.57	3	0	0	1	0	0	2.1	0	3	3	0	0	5	0	3	0
Barton, Springfield	1	1	.500	17.36	5	1	0	1	0	0	9.1	18	21	18	3	0	11	0	3	1
Belcher, Madison	9	4	.692	3.57	16	16	3	0	1	0	98.1	80	45	39	6	8	48	1	111	6
Bell, Quad Cities°	1	0	1.000	2.05	17	0	0	4	0	0	22.0	18	9	5	0	1	18	3	28	0
Bergendahl, Wausau	10	8	.556	3.46	27	25	1	0	0	0	151.0	137	78	58	14	7	76	1	113	17
Bethel, Quad Cities	4	6	.400	3.36	51	2	1	36	0	12	80.1	80	36	30	1	3	39	7	61	5
Birkbeck, Beloit	14	3	.824	2.18	26	25	6	1	2	0	177.2	134	57	43	5	1	64	3	164	13
Blunt, Springfield	6	4	.600	2.74	17	17	4	0	1	0	105.0	82	40	32	4	3	59	1	75	12
Bocock, Springfield	0	0	.000	7.11	6	0	0	4	0	0	6.1	11	7	5	0	0	4	0	5	1
Bosio, Beloit	17	6	.739	2.73	26	26	11	0	2	0	181.0	159	83	55	12	5	56	0	156	17
Brahms, Clinton°	1	0	1.000	0.33	14	0	0	9	0	1	27.1	14	1	1	0	1	5	1	21	0
Brown, Springfield	1	2	.333	3.38	12	7	0	3	0	0	37.1	37	21	14	3	1	14	0	39	5
Bryant, Wausau	1	1	.500	12.60	9	0	0	2	0	1	10.0	20	16	14	2	0	3	0	4	1
Burkett, Clinton	7	6	.538	4.33	20	20	2	0	0	0	126.2	128	81	61	5	6	38	1	83	9
B. Burns, Appleton°	1	0	1.000	1.80	1	1	0	0	0	0	5.0	4	1	1	0	0	1	0	5	0
Th. Burns, Wausau	7	10	.412	3.50	28	26	4	2	1	0	167.1	162	88	65	6	12	63	3	90	7
To. Burns, Madison	3	2	.600	2.57	10	0	0	9	0	1	14.0	11	4	4	1	0	3	0	20	0
Calvert, Cedar Rapids	2	8	.200	4.01	20	20	3	0	0	0	114.1	119	63	51	7	2	48	0	58	3
Candelaria, Clinton°	6	6	.500	2.04	41	3	0	23	0	4	84.0	66	34	19	3	3	58	2	94	10
Candiotti, Beloit	0	1	.000	2.70	2	2	0	0	0	0	10.0	12	5	3	1	0	5	0	12	1
Cannon, Peoria	3	6	.333	2.97	47	1	0	14	0	4	69.2	59	30	23	1	3	41	2	45	2
K. Carter, Burlington	2	5	.286	5.53	13	7	0	3	0	0	55.1	62	39	34	4	1	23	0	23	1
R. Carter, Beloit	5	9	.357	3.91	30	17	3	5	0	2	124.1	118	59	54	9	6	56	1	93	6
Caulfield, Springfield°	0	1	.000	5.93	5	1	0	2	0	0	13.2	13	9	9	3	1	10	0	7	0
Chadwick, Peoria	11	9	.550	3.99	26	25	2	0	0	0	153.1	138	87	68	7	7	85	1	133	11
Cherry, Springfield°	0	0	.000	0.00	1	0	0	1	0	0	1.0	1	0	0	0	0	0	0	1	0
Ciardi, Beloit	10	7	.588	3.02	25	25	7	0	1	0	176.0	160	76	59	12	6	41	3	166	9
Cipres, Burlington	2	2	.500	4.42	8	0	0	5	0	1	18.1	18	11	9	0	0	18	0	16	7
Cisco, Waterloo	9	10	.474	3.78	37	8	1	19	0	2	109.2	113	56	46	7	4	34	6	68	4
Clay, Kenosha	9	8	.529	2.73	26	26	6	0	0	0	171.2	146	73	52	8	11	64	2	96	16
Cloninger, Kenosha	4	2	.667	2.91	8	6	2	1	2	0	43.1	36	16	14	2	1	22	1	19	6
Conley, Cedar Rapids°	8	4	.667	2.83	43	1	0	15	0	4	82.2	71	35	26	2	1	27	6	73	3
Corbell, Clinton	9	11	.450	2.64	25	25	7	0	1	0	177.0	148	71	52	7	2	52	3	101	8
Correa, Appleton	10	6	.625	3.44	26	26	1	0	1	0	149.1	127	71	57	7	4	87	0	135	12
Coughlin, Madison	3	0	1.000	3.72	28	1	0	13	0	3	55.2	51	27	23	1	1	25	2	49	9
Cox, Quad Cities	6	8	.429	4.25	17	17	1	0	1	0	95.1	85	57	45	4	0	52	3	65	7
Cozzolino, Peoria	7	3	.700	2.10	56	0	0	39	0	9	77.0	39	21	18	4	4	55	4	88	5
Culver, Cedar Rapids°	0	0	.000	3.52	6	0	0	3	0	0	7.2	6	3	3	0	0	5	0	9	2
Daniel, Burlington	1	3	.250	5.54	11	1	0	3	0	0	26.0	33	21	16	5	1	13	0	16	2
Davidson, Quad Cities	7	13	.350	5.71	27	27	0	0	0	0	149.2	145	102	95	16	6	103	4	109	13
Davis, Appleton	1	2	.333	6.02	11	10	0	0	0	0	40.1	40	27	27	0	0	38	0	38	3
Delzer, Peoria°	5	1	.833	1.34	39	0	0	25	0	9	60.2	46	10	9	0	2	24	1	48	5
Derksen, Beloit	0	0	.000	3.75	6	0	0	2	0	1	12.0	13	8	5	1	0	3	0	10	0
Dersin, Burlington	1	2	.333	7.32	5	4	0	0	0	0	19.2	34	27	16	6	2	8	0	14	5
Dial, Burlington	0	1	.000	4.70	2	1	0	1	0	0	7.2	7	4	4	1	0	5	0	4	1
DiFrancisco, Waterloo	1	3	.250	3.91	8	1	1	5	0	0	23.0	19	13	10	1	0	20	1	15	2
Ditto, Quad Cities	0	0	.000	18.00	1	0	0	1	0	0	1.0	2	2	2	0	0	1	0	0	0
Dixon, Waterloo°	1	4	.200	3.93	10	2	0	0	0	0	34.1	29	19	15	1	2	28	0	31	2
Dodd, Cedar Rapids	12	7	.632	2.98	27	24	6	2	3	1	169.1	148	67	56	9	2	65	1	152	9
Dowless, Cedar Rapids	6	5	.545	2.83	33	9	2	10	0	2	105.0	88	42	33	10	3	41	4	85	2
Doyle, Quad Cities	4	6	.400	4.12	42	0	0	27	0	5	83.0	85	47	38	8	3	35	6	41	3
Drabek, Appleton	1	0	1.000	1.80	1	1	0	0	0	0	5.0	3	1	1	0	0	3	0	6	0
Dressler, Clinton	4	4	.500	3.82	19	7	0	2	0	1	63.2	61	37	27	4	1	30	0	44	0
Embser, Springfield°	10	11	.476	3.97	26	26	8	0	3	0	152.0	135	83	67	7	2	94	2	142	17
Faber, Clinton°	3	0	1.000	2.05	9	5	0	0	0	0	30.2	16	12	7	0	0	30	0	22	1
Farley, Springfield	8	9	.471	5.00	22	22	1	0	0	0	131.1	154	92	73	16	2	62	1	104	9
Farrell, Waterloo	0	5	.000	6.44	9	9	2	0	0	0	43.1	59	34	31	4	1	33	0	29	4
Ferran, Clinton	5	10	.333	2.58	41	3	1	27	1	5	90.2	73	32	26	4	1	42	6	87	1
Fingers, Beloit	4	4	.500	1.57	31	6	0	23	0	8	46.0	42	11	8	2	0	15	5	45	3
Franko, Kenosha	0	0	.000	0.00	1	0	0	1	0	0	1.0	0	0	0	0	0	1	0	1	0
Fulmer, Madison°	6	5	.545	3.48	50	5	2	17	0	5	113.2	112	59	44	6	3	46	5	79	9
Funk, Cedar Rapids	6	6	.500	2.61	46	0	0	34	0	12	72.1	72	35	21	5	2	15	5	51	5

Pitcher—Club	W.	L.	Pct.	ERA.	G.	GS.	CG.	GF.	ShO.	Sv.	IP.	H.	R.	ER.	HR.	HB.	BB.	Int. BB.	SO.	WP.
Gallo, Peoria*	2	2	.500	4.31	15	6	0	3	0	0	39.2	40	22	19	3	2	26	0	36	5
K. Galloway, Waterloo*	2	3	.400	4.91	7	6	1	1	0	0	29.1	27	20	16	3	2	18	2	23	3
T. Galloway, Kenosha*	1	3	.250	6.25	8	8	1	0	0	0	40.1	53	35	28	5	4	21	0	24	1
Giddings, Madison	9	8	.529	2.79	22	18	6	4	2	0	122.2	101	48	38	4	1	42	0	89	10
Gilbert, Burlington	1	2	.333	4.09	16	0	0	8	0	2	22.0	26	12	10	1	0	15	1	16	3
Godwin, Madison*	0	0	.000	4.70	5	0	0	3	0	1	7.2	5	4	4	1	1	3	0	4	0
Gomez, Kenosha	8	10	.444	3.01	46	0	0	39	0	12	83.2	82	36	28	1	2	29	2	54	9
Gonsalves, Madison	4	6	.400	4.69	24	5	1	11	0	0	55.2	58	37	29	1	0	36	2	42	4
Gonzales, Peoria	0	5	.000	5.31	19	4	0	7	0	0	40.2	42	30	24	3	4	26	0	21	6
Gunnarsson, Wausau*	7	4	.636	2.34	53	0	0	42	0	13	61.2	50	21	16	4	2	26	0	55	5
Guzman, Appleton	3	2	.600	4.04	22	1	0	15	0	0	49.0	38	25	22	6	3	40	0	43	4
Hallas, Madison	5	1	.833	4.74	8	7	2	1	0	1	43.2	48	24	23	5	1	6	0	27	1
Hamilton, Quad Cities*	5	7	.417	2.81	18	18	1	0	1	0	109.0	69	48	34	8	7	76	0	104	6
Hansen, Madison	2	5	.286	4.85	22	8	0	7	0	0	65.0	84	42	35	5	3	35	1	39	5
Hardwick, Springfield	2	1	.667	6.59	3	3	0	0	0	0	13.2	14	13	10	0	3	10	0	13	4
Harman, Burlington	13	4	.765	2.08	47	0	0	44	0	10	86.2	71	32	20	5	5	15	4	55	4
Harrington, Burlington	2	4	.333	4.60	12	9	0	0	0	0	43.0	38	28	22	1	1	38	0	48	5
Heath, Madison*	7	9	.438	4.24	26	21	2	5	1	0	119.0	100	64	56	4	1	77	1	90	15
Held, Wausau	5	6	.455	5.03	23	13	0	2	0	1	73.1	83	57	41	6	3	36	0	39	4
Henderson, Kenosha*	13	7	.650	2.24	28	27	7	0	0	0	197.0	153	73	49	10	1	82	1	160	10
Hester, Burlington	5	7	.417	4.43	32	21	3	5	0	1	148.1	162	99	73	4	4	56	1	66	14
J. Hickey, Appleton	13	5	.722	1.81	49	0	0	41	0	20	99.1	88	30	20	2	1	32	5	96	7
K. Hickey, Appleton*	4	3	.571	2.36	10	8	1	2	0	1	49.2	45	18	13	5	0	11	0	41	1
Hicks, Burlington	1	1	.500	9.00	10	0	0	5	0	0	15.0	23	15	15	3	3	6	0	16	1
Hinson, Wausau	9	6	.600	3.16	24	24	2	0	0	0	142.1	133	59	50	8	16	59	0	86	8
Hrynko, Quad Cities	0	0	.000	0.00	2	0	0	1	0	0	3.2	1	1	0	0	0	0	0	5	0
Iasparro, Kenosha	4	4	.500	2.37	30	5	0	13	0	1	79.2	70	31	21	6	3	45	1	56	4
Imig, Appleton	4	7	.364	4.38	30	12	3	7	0	2	111.0	126	63	54	7	2	37	0	82	13
Johnson, Appleton	12	7	.632	2.80	27	26	6	1	2	1	170.1	160	72	53	5	3	55	2	136	8
Keathley, Burlington	5	9	.357	5.18	18	18	0	0	0	0	85.2	99	63	53	7	5	41	0	56	5
Kemmerling, Peoria	1	0	1.000	1.40	11	0	0	5	0	2	19.1	22	4	3	1	0	4	1	8	1
Kemp, Cedar Rapids	11	9	.550	3.79	25	25	8	1	4	0	164.1	139	65	51	12	0	69	5	143	6
King, Clinton	5	10	.333	3.36	35	21	2	12	0	3	147.1	142	74	55	5	1	76	2	124	15
Kipper, Burlington*	3	14	.176	4.16	32	20	0	6	0	1	127.2	124	83	59	7	7	67	0	95	16
Kish, Springfield	2	5	.286	5.26	9	7	1	1	0	0	49.2	66	35	29	5	3	18	4	19	2
Klingbeil, Kenosha	5	7	.417	3.27	44	2	1	35	1	10	82.2	76	37	30	7	3	34	4	56	8
Knapp, Burlington	6	9	.400	3.31	33	18	6	9	3	1	147.0	144	75	54	9	6	39	0	122	7
Knowles, Peoria	0	1	.000	8.49	7	2	0	1	0	0	11.2	13	12	11	1	2	9	0	9	4
Konderla, Cedar Rapids	2	1	.667	1.19	12	0	0	10	0	4	22.2	15	5	3	0	1	8	1	34	2
Kopf, Quad Cities	0	5	.000	6.30	10	7	0	0	0	0	40.0	37	36	28	2	5	43	2	39	6
Langdon, Cedar Rapids	8	6	.571	2.90	21	20	2	0	1	0	114.2	78	51	37	5	3	75	0	132	9
Layton, Burlington	3	0	1.000	1.84	8	4	1	2	1	2	29.1	17	8	6	0	1	10	0	16	1
Lee, Clinton*	13	10	.565	4.87	26	25	4	1	1	0	159.0	157	95	86	16	9	93	0	139	19
Lenderman, Quad Cities	8	9	.471	4.14	28	25	2	1	0	0	158.2	156	83	73	12	6	51	6	91	16
Leonette, Madison	2	5	.286	5.08	9	9	1	0	1	0	44.1	54	32	25	3	0	18	0	33	3
LoSauro, Burlington	0	1	.000	2.60	7	3	0	4	0	0	17.1	19	14	5	2	1	8	0	5	0
Madrid, Beloit	6	7	.462	4.19	22	22	3	0	0	0	118.0	113	59	55	5	3	49	0	92	3
Malave, Wausau	4	8	.333	3.34	34	11	0	10	0	0	107.2	90	47	40	8	3	58	0	79	6
Mart, Burlington	0	0	.000	15.43	1	0	0	0	0	0	2.1	4	4	4	3	1	2	0	1	0
Martin, Springfield	8	7	.533	5.08	20	20	6	0	1	0	129.1	152	92	73	15	2	36	1	97	19
Martinez, Springfield*	1	2	.333	4.30	27	0	0	10	0	2	44.0	39	24	21	3	3	29	1	28	4
Mason, Springfield	4	1	.800	0.59	16	0	0	14	0	4	30.1	22	8	2	2	0	3	0	22	0
McCullock, Waterloo	0	0	.000	1.74	9	0	0	6	0	1	10.1	6	3	2	0	0	5	1	14	1
Meadows, Springfield	0	4	.000	7.65	5	5	0	0	0	0	20.0	27	25	17	4	0	18	0	9	3
Medvin, Wausau	4	2	.667	3.56	40	0	0	13	0	2	65.2	62	36	26	5	12	35	1	53	11
Miglio, Waterloo*	5	3	.625	2.06	37	0	0	28	0	10	56.2	43	21	13	2	2	21	4	57	2
Migliore, Peoria	4	4	.500	4.81	15	15	2	0	0	0	97.1	104	57	52	12	3	28	0	39	5
Minyard, Waterloo	1	2	.333	5.00	4	2	0	1	0	0	9.0	8	5	5	2	1	11	0	4	1
Mitchell, Springfield	1	3	.250	3.56	17	0	0	9	0	2	30.1	22	13	12	2	2	16	1	26	1
C. Moore, Appleton	0	0	.000	18.00	1	0	0	0	0	0	1.0	4	4	2	0	0	0	0	0	0
R. Moore, Wausau	1	0	1.000	0.00	5	0	0	1	0	0	10.2	10	3	0	0	1	3	0	4	0
Mora, Waterloo	0	1	.000	6.75	3	1	0	2	0	0	14.2	19	11	11	2	0	6	0	4	0
Morris, Beloit*	8	9	.471	5.05	24	22	1	0	0	0	112.1	107	80	63	8	1	79	1	109	13
Moses, Appleton*	1	2	.333	1.86	6	0	0	3	0	0	9.2	13	2	2	0	0	2	0	9	1
D. Murphy, Beloit	9	4	.692	3.59	26	12	3	6	1	2	112.2	116	59	45	5	0	44	0	79	5
M. Murphy, Waterloo	6	4	.600	2.41	17	10	6	2	3	1	86.0	64	26	23	6	4	18	1	66	2
Myles, Waterloo	3	2	.600	3.61	8	8	2	0	1	0	47.1	45	23	19	2	2	26	0	27	3
North, Springfield	7	4	.636	2.33	27	19	5	3	5	1	154.1	132	49	40	6	1	40	0	98	6
Odom, Madison	2	2	.500	3.48	9	9	0	0	0	0	44.0	41	21	17	1	1	16	1	30	1
Ojeda, Peoria	0	2	.000	9.00	6	1	0	3	0	0	12.0	14	12	12	3	1	13	1	5	1
Oliverio, Cedar Rapids	5	1	.833	2.71	27	0	0	10	0	2	63.0	45	26	19	7	0	35	4	55	2
Ontiveros, Madison	3	1	.750	2.05	5	5	2	0	0	0	30.2	23	10	7	0	1	6	0	26	1
Ortega, Springfield	1	0	1.000	5.93	9	0	0	6	0	1	13.2	17	9	9	1	0	2	1	12	0
Parham, Springfield*	3	9	.250	3.86	20	17	1	2	1	0	105.0	85	56	45	7	4	67	1	99	6
Parrett, Beloit	4	3	.571	4.52	29	5	1	6	1	2	91.2	76	50	46	8	1	71	1	95	13
Pettibone, Cedar Rapids	9	8	.529	2.73	26	25	12	0	1	0	165.0	107	61	50	15	3	77	1	159	17
Phelps, Appleton	1	2	.333	4.38	5	5	1	0	0	0	24.2	27	15	12	2	0	8	0	14	4
Phillips, Quad Cities	6	5	.545	2.93	16	15	6	1	2	0	98.1	102	36	32	8	3	13	0	67	1
Pierorazio, Waterloo*	7	4	.636	4.48	22	9	1	7	0	1	70.1	59	39	35	8	2	43	2	44	2
Pimentel, Springfield	7	1	.875	2.55	22	8	1	10	1	5	70.2	57	29	20	1	3	39	0	69	4
Piphus, Waterloo	3	7	.300	4.64	19	16	0	0	0	0	66.0	68	41	34	4	6	33	0	64	5
Pleis, Springfield	0	0	.000	0.00	1	0	0	1	0	0	1.0	1	0	0	0	0	0	0	2	0
Pobur, Quad Cities	1	5	.167	6.83	30	3	0	19	0	1	54.0	70	54	41	7	2	36	2	32	11
Prickett, Kenosha*	0	1	.000	8.10	7	1	0	5	0	0	10.0	15	13	9	2	0	7	0	7	2
Pruneda, Peoria	4	2	.667	2.96	12	11	1	1	0	1	76.0	71	26	25	6	0	23	0	52	4
Psaltis, Peoria	6	3	.667	2.64	28	0	0	17	0	2	44.1	34	13	13	2	0	18	1	34	1
Rech, Burlington*	0	2	.000	6.37	13	3	1	3	0	1	29.2	37	26	21	3	0	15	0	24	4
Reed, Peoria*	10	2	.833	3.39	16	16	1	0	0	0	103.2	92	48	39	5	1	45	0	42	13
Reynolds, Waterloo	0	1	.000	4.35	24	0	0	13	0	1	41.1	49	23	20	2	0	13	3	27	2
Rice, Beloit	4	1	.800	2.95	35	0	0	23	0	5	58.0	42	29	19	3	1	41	0	49	9
Rigoli, Springfield	0	0	.000	6.43	4	0	0	4	0	0	7.0	7	5	5	0	1	6	0	2	0
Ritter, Waterloo	6	6	.500	4.76	37	14	1	13	0	9	128.2	145	82	68	11	3	50	2	89	9

Pitcher—Club	W.	L.	Pct.	ERA.	G.	GS.	CG.	GF.	ShO.	Sv.	IP.	H.	R.	ER.	HR.	HB.	BB.	Int. BB.	SO.	WP.
Roche, Waterloo	1	0	1.000	4.19	5	4	0	1	0	0	19.1	18	12	9	1	0	3	0	15	1
Rodriguez, Kenosha	1	2	.333	2.70	10	0	0	8	0	1	16.2	14	8	5	1	1	8	0	13	0
Rogers, Burlington°	4	7	.364	3.98	39	4	1	16	1	3	92.2	87	52	41	9	4	33	3	93	8
Roman, Springfield°	3	4	.429	3.89	18	2	0	8	0	0	44.0	42	27	19	3	3	24	0	32	3
Russell, Kenosha	0	1	.000	5.19	9	0	0	5	0	1	8.2	8	5	5	3	0	8	0	6	1
Saatzer, Peoria	0	0	.000	4.50	2	0	0	2	0	0	2.0	4	1	1	0	0	0	0	1	1
Sain, Quad Cities	0	1	.000	7.62	8	0	0	2	0	0	13.0	18	14	11	2	0	7	0	5	2
Salazar, Wausau°	0	0	.000	3.00	20	0	0	5	0	1	24.0	16	11	8	3	0	13	1	18	0
Sandry, Quad Cities	0	0	.000	6.75	1	0	0	1	0	0	1.1	4	1	1	1	0	0	0	1	0
Santarelli, Waterloo	7	9	.438	3.88	19	18	2	0	0	0	111.1	108	65	48	8	4	47	3	123	11
E. Schmidt, Appleton	9	4	.692	3.21	21	21	2	0	1	0	123.1	124	56	44	5	5	48	1	66	7
G. Schmidt, Clinton	3	3	.500	4.01	26	6	0	11	0	1	74.0	75	47	33	2	4	49	2	38	8
Schneider, Wausau	6	8	.429	2.00	58	0	0	39	0	11	76.1	59	25	17	0	4	35	3	64	6
Schwarz, Quad Cities	4	14	.222	5.05	27	24	2	1	0	0	130.0	106	88	73	11	11	111	2	123	17
Shamblin, Beloit	0	0	.000	5.87	9	0	0	2	0	0	15.1	20	10	10	1	0	15	0	12	2
Sillivent, Peoria°	1	0	1.000	7.45	5	2	0	2	0	0	9.2	9	11	8	1	0	11	0	5	3
Simmons, Appleton	1	3	.250	6.81	7	6	1	0	0	0	37.0	46	30	28	4	0	14	0	22	3
Slowik, Quad Cities	1	1	.500	4.05	5	0	0	5	0	0	6.2	4	4	3	0	1	3	0	5	0
D. Smith, Wausau	1	0	1.000	2.72	21	0	0	3	0	1	43.0	38	15	13	3	6	20	1	31	3
L. Smith, Madison°	2	1	.667	0.83	17	0	0	7	0	0	21.2	18	3	2	1	0	12	2	21	0
Sontag, Kenosha	7	7	.500	2.76	20	20	6	0	1	0	143.1	118	51	44	8	4	57	0	110	7
Soper, Burlington°	0	1	.000	7.25	23	2	0	13	0	0	44.2	57	44	36	4	1	38	1	22	5
Spratke, Wausau	0	0	.000	4.66	3	2	0	0	0	0	9.2	12	5	5	0	0	7	0	4	0
Stacey, Appleton	0	0	.000	4.50	1	0	0	0	0	0	2.0	2	1	1	1	0	1	0	5	1
Stanfield, Peoria	0	5	.000	6.68	9	4	0	2	0	0	33.2	47	34	25	3	4	7	0	11	2
Stapleton, Beloit°	9	6	.600	2.33	48	0	0	36	0	15	92.2	77	29	24	5	0	35	3	85	2
Steinbach, Madison	0	0	.000	9.00	2	0	0	2	0	0	3.0	2	4	3	0	0	4	0	0	0
Stephenson, Waterloo	2	4	.333	3.47	17	2	1	7	0	0	49.1	44	27	19	5	2	23	3	18	5
Street, Waterloo	9	4	.692	3.17	30	15	5	5	1	1	127.2	107	54	45	12	4	55	1	113	9
Swearingen, Wausau°	9	9	.500	3.16	31	17	1	5	0	2	122.1	127	59	43	9	4	50	0	87	9
Szymczak, Waterloo	0	0	.000	13.50	3	1	0	0	0	0	5.1	12	9	8	0	0	4	0	1	1
Tamarez, Waterloo°	0	0	.000	8.44	6	4	0	1	0	0	10.2	14	11	10	1	0	5	0	8	1
Tanner, Appleton	12	4	.750	1.96	37	9	6	15	3	2	123.2	96	32	27	0	4	30	1	91	10
Tanzi, Appleton°	0	0	.000	2.25	3	0	0	1	0	0	4.0	2	1	1	0	0	1	0	5	1
Tarnow, Appleton	0	0	.000	9.00	4	0	0	4	0	0	9.0	14	9	9	1	0	6	0	3	0
Tate, Clinton	1	1	.500	2.92	17	0	0	12	0	1	24.2	22	9	8	0	0	12	0	26	4
Tavarez, Clinton	0	0	.000	10.13	5	0	0	1	0	0	8.0	15	9	9	1	1	12	0	5	1
Teahan, Clinton	3	6	.333	4.41	27	10	2	11	1	2	79.2	77	48	39	5	5	36	1	28	4
Tinkey, Peoria	7	12	.368	5.13	27	27	2	0	1	0	166.2	180	105	95	11	3	82	1	107	12
Trujillo, Cedar Rapids	2	4	.333	5.20	26	0	0	19	0	3	27.2	20	17	16	4	0	21	2	34	1
Tullier, Quad Cities°	0	0	.000	0.00	1	0	0	1	0	0	1.0	0	0	0	0	0	0	0	2	0
Vantrease, Madison°	1	0	1.000	6.11	16	0	0	7	0	0	28.0	41	22	19	2	0	12	2	20	2
Villa, Clinton	2	4	.333	3.86	12	8	1	2	0	0	51.1	33	23	22	5	2	32	0	29	9
Volkman, Quad Cities	2	6	.250	6.32	42	0	0	19	0	1	68.1	79	64	48	7	2	45	4	40	5
Walck, Quad Cities	1	1	.500	4.11	17	0	0	6	0	1	46.0	46	24	21	2	0	20	2	22	4
Walker, Appleton	9	1	.900	1.96	46	1	0	21	0	5	91.2	68	32	20	4	6	32	2	106	5
Whaley, Madison	7	6	.538	2.89	44	9	4	19	0	9	127.2	105	49	41	2	3	35	3	106	6
Whitmyer, Waterloo	1	0	1.000	4.71	13	5	0	4	0	0	36.1	36	23	19	1	2	32	0	20	7
Wilkinson, Wausau°	6	4	.600	3.31	19	18	2	1	1	0	103.1	79	47	38	5	3	52	1	117	7
Wilmet, Springfield	7	7	.500	2.59	53	0	0	34	0	11	107.2	86	38	31	5	6	52	10	95	4
Winbush, Burlington	1	3	.250	5.04	7	7	0	0	0	0	30.1	27	23	17	2	6	34	0	25	4
Winfield, Springfield	1	1	.500	3.68	5	0	0	2	0	0	7.1	6	4	3	1	1	3	0	7	0
Wiseman, Kenosha	15	7	.682	3.30	26	26	5	0	2	0	169.1	159	79	62	14	1	69	0	84	3

BALKS—Chadwick, 5; Bosio, Johnson, 4 each; Cox, Delzer, Gunnarsson, Keathley, Sontag, 3 each; Allison, Banning, Bell, Corbell, Davidson, Dodd, Ember, Farrell, T. Galloway, Giddings, Gomez, Guzman, Hallas, Held, Henderson, Kemp, Kipper, Knapp, Lee, Lenderman, Madrid, Piphus, Rech, Stapleton, Whitmyer, 2 each; Akerfelds, Anderson, Arney, Baker, Barton, Bethel, Birkbeck, Brahms, Brown, Burkett, To. Burns, Candelaria, K. Carter, R. Carter, Caulfield, Ciardi, Cisco, Correa, DiFrancisco, Dowless, Fingers, Godwin, Gonzales, Hamilton, Harrington, J. Hickey, Imig, King, Klingbeil, Kopf, Langdon, Leonette, Martin, Morris, M. Murphy, Myles, Oliverio, Pettibone, Phillips, Psaltis, Ritter, Sain, Salazar, E. Schmidt, Simmons, D.W. Smith, L. Smith, Stanfield, Swearingen, Szymczak, Tinkey, Walker, Whaley, Wilmet, 1 each.

COMBINATION SHUTOUTS—Correa-J. Hickey 2, Tanner-J. Hickey, Johnson-Walker, Correa-Layton, Appleton; Madrid-Stapleton-Rice, Madrid-Murphy, Murphy-Fingers, Bosio-Shamblin, Parrett-Fingers, Beloit; Kipper-Harman, Allison-Knapp, Keathley-Harman, Burlington; Dowless-Funk 2, Barba-Oliverio, Calvert-Funk, Kemp-Oliverio, Cedar Rapids; Lee-Ferran 2, Teahan-Schmidt, Dressler-Candelaria-King, Corbell-King, Clinton; Galloway-Klingbeil, Clay-Gomez, Cloninger-Klingbeil, Kenosha; Giddings-Fulmer-Heath, Heath-Hansen, Madison; Carter-Cozzolino, Reed-Delzer, Reed-Cozzolino, Peoria; Schwarz-Bethel, Lenderman-Bethel, Phillips-Doyle, Cox-Bethel, Quad Cities; Blunt-Mason 2, Blunt-Mitchell, Springfield; Ritter-Miglio, Piphus-Cisco-McCullock, Myles-Cisco, Minyard-DiFrancisco, Waterloo; Malave-Gunnarsson, Hinson-Smith-Gunnarsson, Hinson-Schneider, Swearingen-Schneider, Wausau.

NO-HIT GAME—Martin, Springfield, defeated Wausau, 2-0, August 8.

NY-Pennsylvania League

CLASS A

CHAMPIONSHIP WINNERS IN PREVIOUS YEARS

1939—Olean*	.631	1956—Wellsville*	.617
1940—Olean*	.625	1957—Wellsville	.632
1941—Jamestown	.618	Erie (2nd)†	.598
Bradford (2nd)†	.549	1958—Wellsville	.556
1942—Jamestown*	.672	Geneva (2nd)†	.548
1943—Lockport	.591	1959—Wellsville†	.635
Wellsville (3rd)†	.532	1960—Erie	.643
1944—Lockport	.608	Wellsville (2nd)†	.535
Jamestown (2nd)†	.565	1961—Geneva	.616
1945—Batavia*	.677	Olean (4th)†	.512
1946—Jamestown‡	.672	1962—Jamestown	.580
Batavia‡	.672	Auburn (3rd)†	.521
1947—Jamestown*	.690	1963—Auburn	.585
1948—Lockport*	.603	Batavia (3rd)†	.485
1949—Bradford*	.635	1964—Auburn§	.622
1950—Hornell	.653	1965—Binghamton	.677
Olean (2nd)†	.568	Binghamton	.607
1951—Olean	.622	1966—Auburn x	.620
Hornell (3rd)†	.568	Binghamton	.646
1952—Hamilton	.659	1967—Auburn	.667
Jamestown (2nd)†	.643	1968—Auburn	.645
1953—Jamestown*	.704	Oneonta (2nd)*	.558
1954—Corning*	.621	1969—Oneonta	.662
1955—Hamilton*	.656		

1970—Auburn	.623
1971—Oneonta	.662
1972—Niagara Falls	.686
1973—Auburn	.667
1974—Oneonta	.768
1975—Newark	.688
Newark	.714
1976—Elmira	.727
Elmira	.703
1977—Oneonta y	.671
Batavia	.600
1978—Oneonta	.729
Geneva z	.718
1979—Geneva	.725
Oneonta z	.618
1980—Oneonta y	.662
Geneva	.649
1981—Oneonta y	.658
Jamestown	.649
1982—Oneonta	.566
Niagara Falls y	.553
1983—Utica y	.649
Newark	.649

*Won championship and four-club playoff. †Won four-club playoff. ‡Jamestown and Batavia declared co-champions; Batavia defeated Jamestown in final of four-club playoff. §Won championship and two-club playoff. xWon split-season playoff. yLeague divided into Eastern and Western Divisions; won playoff. zLeague divided into Wrigley and Yawkey Divisions; won playoff. (NOTE—Known as Pennsylvania-Ontario-New York League from 1939 through 1956.)

STANDING OF CLUBS AT CLOSE OF SEASON, SEPTEMBER 3

EASTERN DIVISION

Club	W.	L.	T.	Pct.	G.B.
Little Falls (Mets)	44	31	0	.587	......
Watertown (Pirates)	39	35	0	.527	4½
Auburn (Astros)	38	38	0	.500	6½
Elmira (Red Sox)	35	38	0	.479	8
Utica (Independent)	31	44	0	.413	13
Oneonta (Yankees)	29	45	0	.392	14½

WESTERN DIVISION

Club	W.	L.	T.	Pct.	G.B.
Newark (Orioles)	46	28	0	.622	......
Erie (Cardinals)	43	31	0	.581	3
Batavia (Indians)	41	35	0	.539	6
Geneva (Cubs)	38	36	0	.514	8
Niagara Falls (White Sox)	35	40	0	.467	11½
Jamestown (Expos)	28	46	0	.378	18

COMPOSITE STANDING OF CLUBS AT CLOSE OF SEASON, SEPTEMBER 3

Club	New.	L.F.	Eri.	Bat.	Wat.	Gen.	Aub.	Elm.	N.F.	Uti.	Ont.	Jam.	W.	L.	T.	Pct.	G.B.
Newark (Orioles)	...	2	4	7	3	9	1	2	5	2	4	7	46	28	0	.622	......
Little Falls (Mets)	2	...	3	1	6	2	6	5	2	8	6	3	44	31	0	.587	2½
Erie (Cardinals)	4	1	...	6	2	5	2	2	8	3	3	7	43	31	0	.581	3
Batavia (Indians)	3	3	4	...	2	5	3	3	7	1	3	7	41	35	0	.539	6
Watertown (Pirates)	0	6	2	2	...	2	5	4	3	5	7	3	39	35	0	.527	7
Geneva (Cubs)	5	1	5	4	2	...	2	2	5	3	2	7	38	36	0	.514	8
Auburn (Astros)	3	2	2	1	5	2	...	4	2	8	1	8	38	38	0	.500	9
Elmira (Red Sox)	2	5	1	1	6	2	7	...	2	4	5	0	35	38	0	.479	10½
Niagara Falls (White Sox)	4	2	3	6	1	4	2	2	...	2	2	7	35	40	0	.467	11½
Utica (Independent)	2	4	1	3	4	1	3	6	2	...	2	3	31	44	0	.413	15½
Oneonta (Yankees)	0	4	1	1	3	2	4	4	2	7	...	1	29	45	0	.392	17
Jamestown (Expos)	3	1	5	3	1	2	3	4	2	1	3	...	28	46	0	.378	18

Major league affiliations in parentheses.

Playoffs—Little Falls defeated Newark, two games to one, to win league championship.

Regular Season Attendance—Auburn, 22,392; Batavia, 32,958; Elmira, 57,448; Erie, 35,694; Geneva, 26,392; Jamestown, 30,057; Little Falls, 30,356; Newark, 22,240; Niagara Falls, 38,131; Oneonta, 33,817; Utica, 26,077; Watertown, 61,563. Playoffs—1,667. Total—416,225.

Managers—Auburn, Bob Hartsfield; Batavia, Eddie Bane; Elmira, Dick Berardino; Erie, Rich Hacker; Geneva, Tony Franklin; Jamestown, Moby Benedict; Little Falls, Buddy Harrelson; Newark, Jim Hutto; Niagara Falls, Fred Nelson; Oneonta, Bill Livesey; Utica, Bob McBee; Watertown, Bill Bryk.

All-Star Team—1B-Chuck Lynn, Newark; 2B-Paul Daddario, Batavia; 3B-Paul Birkover, Jamestown; SS-Kevin Elster, Little Falls; OF-Jay Buhner, Watertown; Dave Dahse, Newark; Lance Johnson, Erie; Miguel Roman, Batavia; C-Butch Garcia, Batavia; Tony DeFrancesco, Elmira; DH-Randy Riley, Newark; RHP-Joel Davis, Niagara Falls; Brad Mettler, Elmira; LHP-Steve Hill, Erie; Jamie Moyer, Geneva; Manager of the Year-Buddy Harrelson, Little Falls.

(Compiled by Howe News Bureau, Boston, Mass.)

CLUB BATTING

Club	Pct.	G.	AB.	R.	OR.	H.	TB.	2B.	3B.	HR.	RBI.	GW.	SH.	SF.	HP.	BB.	Int. BB.	SO.	SB.	CS.	LOB.
Utica	.266	75	2407	397	495	640	998	85	9	85	336	25	27	17	20	336	16	512	87	49	538
Erie	.266	74	2588	412	378	688	1004	111	20	55	364	41	13	17	20	309	19	458	88	35	611
Newark	.265	74	2443	450	332	648	967	107	19	58	397	40	32	28	22	377	17	507	76	26	566
Batavia	.260	76	2590	392	406	674	1033	110	9	77	332	38	17	17	21	262	19	526	72	34	547
Watertown	.259	74	2415	366	314	625	884	86	16	47	309	34	26	23	35	319	23	518	85	40	552
Elmira	.256	73	2400	350	358	614	868	108	7	44	300	27	39	25	29	302	22	431	70	18	564

CLUB BATTING

Club	Pct.	G.	AB.	R.	OR.	H.	TB.	2B.	3B.	HR.	RBI.	GW.	SH.	SF.	HP.	BB.	Int. BB.	SO.	SB.	CS.	LOB.
Little Falls	.250	75	2421	334	324	604	788	79	15	25	257	30	21	17	26	312	11	535	123	69	536
Oneonta	.244	74	2415	337	358	588	818	80	12	42	287	23	34	23	18	315	18	498	51	24	542
Geneva	.232	74	2432	319	305	563	761	88	7	32	261	33	35	10	23	334	11	545	67	30	574
Niagara Falls	.230	75	2439	334	341	561	804	93	27	32	282	27	30	20	21	303	9	527	59	27	522
Jamestown	.230	74	2396	283	326	550	773	93	20	30	236	23	24	23	18	262	14	453	65	20	525
Auburn	.220	76	2371	301	338	522	722	77	21	27	228	27	22	21	30	259	8	499	103	25	492

INDIVIDUAL BATTING

(Leading Qualifiers for Batting Championship—205 or More Plate Appearances)

*Bats lefthanded. †Switch-hitter.

Player and Club	Pct.	G.	AB.	R.	H.	TB.	2B.	3B.	HR.	RBI.	GW.	SH.	SF.	HP.	BB.	Int. BB.	SO.	SB.	CS.
Riley, Randall, Newark*	.351	70	248	50	87	126	19	1	6	50	2	1	1	2	41	7	50	2	1
Jacoby, Donald, Utica*	.350	55	203	49	71	133	12	1	16	53	3	0	4	1	30	1	29	3	4
Garcia, Victor, Batavia	.347	60	216	38	75	133	15	2	13	41	5	0	7	16	2	35	1	1
Johnson, K. Lance, Erie*	.339	71	283	63	96	116	7	5	1	28	1	1	3	0	45	0	20	29	10
Buhner, Jay, Watertown	.323	65	229	43	74	123	16	3	9	58	3	0	2	1	42	4	58	3	1
Barnard, Steve, Erie†	.317	74	271	46	86	121	13	2	6	45	3	0	1	2	46	4	37	1	2
Finley, Jackie, Utica	.311	69	235	36	73	109	9	0	9	39	1	1	1	1	33	1	45	6	3
Crabbe, Bruce, Geneva	.307	62	202	30	62	95	13	4	4	26	4	4	2	0	34	1	29	5	4
Gonzalez, Roberto, Watertown	.301	61	196	23	59	70	9	1	0	18	1	3	0	6	7	2	32	4	5
Brito, Bernardo, Batavia	.300	76	297	41	89	171	19	3	19	57	6	2	0	1	14	1	67	3	4

Departmental Leaders: G—B. Brito, Mikulik, Mueller, 76; AB—B. Brito, 297; R—K.L. Johnson, 63; H—K.L. Johnson, 96; TB—B. Brito, 171; 2B—B. Brito, Goff, Lane, Riley, 19; 3B—Winters, 7; HR—B. Brito, 19; RBI—Buhner, Lynn, 58; GWRBI—Blaine, Lynn, 9; SH—Traylor, 10; SF—Wilkinson, 9; HP—Little, 9; BB—Fortner, 63; IBB—Scott, 8; SO—T. Edwards, 92; SB—Little, 34; CS—Westbrook, 13.

(All Players—Listed Alphabetically)

Player and Club	Pct.	G.	AB.	R.	H.	TB.	2B.	3B.	HR.	RBI.	GW.	SH.	SF.	HP.	BB.	Int. BB.	SO.	SB.	CS.
Abner, Shawn, Little Falls	.265	18	68	7	18	23	2	0	1	5	0	0	1	0	5	0	16	3	6
Adams, Gerald, Newark	1.000	13	1	1	1	4	0	0	1	1	0	0	0	0	0	0	0	0	0
Adams, Ralph, Little Falls	.091	18	11	1	1	1	0	0	0	0	0	0	0	0	1	0	4	0	0
Adkins, Terry, Watertown	.000	8	0	0	0	0	0	0	0	0	0	0	1	0	0	0	0	0	0
Adkins, Todd, Utica†	.255	56	161	13	41	42	1	0	0	9	1	7	0	0	14	0	32	7	7
Allaire, Karl, Auburn*	.174	8	23	4	4	9	0	1	1	5	1	0	0	1	6	0	1	1	1
Amaro, David, Geneva	.200	56	150	17	30	37	4	0	1	16	1	1	1	2	26	0	41	0	4
Andersh, Kevin, Watertown*	.000	8	3	0	0	0	0	0	0	0	0	0	0	0	0	0	3	0	0
Andujar, Ramon, Jamestown*	.500	16	2	1	1	1	0	0	0	0	0	0	0	0	1	0	0	0	0
Arrington, Larry, Niagara Falls	.197	52	132	19	26	43	6	1	3	20	0	0	3	1	23	2	42	0	0
Autry, Gene, Little Falls	.233	49	150	19	35	52	3	1	4	20	1	1	2	2	18	1	34	1	2
Azcona, Manuel, Jamestown	.000	7	2	0	0	0	0	0	0	0	0	0	1	0	0	0	0	0	0
Bair, Richard, Newark	.189	31	90	13	17	20	3	0	0	10	0	3	0	2	9	0	9	1	0
Baker, Jonathan, Geneva	.161	36	124	12	20	21	1	0	0	9	1	1	0	3	8	0	11	0	0
Balmer, J. Stephen, Geneva	.000	13	5	1	0	0	0	0	0	0	0	0	2	0	0	0	2	0	0
Barnard, Steve, Erie†	.317	74	271	46	86	121	13	2	6	45	3	0	1	2	46	4	37	1	2
Barnes, Tyrone, Utica	.000	17	1	0	0	0	0	0	0	0	0	0	0	0	0	0	0	0	0
Barringer, Reginald, Watertown	.258	63	221	30	57	74	4	5	1	31	4	4	3	7	29	3	32	15	12
Barrios, E. Gregg, Elmira	.279	62	183	33	51	84	14	2	5	27	6	4	2	3	33	0	31	1	1
Bear, R. David, Utica	.000	29	1	0	0	0	0	0	0	0	0	0	0	0	1	0	1	0	0
Belcik, Keith, Little Falls	.250	6	16	3	4	4	0	0	0	1	0	1	0	1	0	0	4	0	0
Bell, Gregory, Geneva*	.111	19	9	0	1	1	0	0	0	0	0	0	1	0	0	0	2	0	0
Billinger, Jon, Erie	.228	54	123	15	28	49	6	0	5	19	3	2	1	2	26	3	29	1	1
Birkofer, Kevin, Jamestown*	.285	57	207	27	59	80	11	2	2	35	2	2	7	0	16	3	21	9	3
Blackwell, Rex, Niagara Falls	.180	61	172	19	31	49	4	4	2	15	3	3	0	0	17	0	56	1	3
Blaine, Gary, Erie	.279	66	219	43	61	109	16	1	10	45	9	0	1	1	19	1	61	3	1
Blake, Kevin, Oneonta*	.080	14	25	5	2	2	0	0	0	0	0	0	0	0	7	0	8	2	1
Bleckley, S. Lex, Jamestown	.208	60	197	14	41	59	12	0	2	14	2	0	2	1	16	3	47	3	5
Boderick, W. Stanley, Geneva†	.221	49	145	17	32	38	6	0	0	9	0	4	1	1	12	1	41	12	4
Bradley, Ike, Oneonta	.200	33	85	13	17	23	3	0	1	13	1	3	1	0	13	0	26	1	1
Braukmiller, Kurt, Jamestown	.222	11	9	1	2	3	1	0	0	1	0	0	0	0	2	0	0	1	0
Brewer, Jeffrey, Geneva	.167	14	18	0	3	3	0	0	0	0	0	1	0	0	0	0	2	0	1
Brito, Bernardo, Batavia	.300	76	297	41	89	171	19	3	19	57	6	2	0	1	14	1	67	3	4
Brito, Tulio, Elmira	.222	37	81	8	18	20	2	0	0	8	0	2	1	0	7	0	18	1	1
Brock, Norman, Auburn*	.245	56	159	25	39	53	6	1	2	16	1	1	3	1	23	1	34	10	1
Bruno, Angelo, Newark	.231	17	52	8	12	18	4	1	0	6	1	0	1	0	3	0	14	1	0
Brunswick, Mark, Little Falls	.270	46	148	18	40	49	6	0	1	14	2	0	1	1	11	1	37	1	4
Buhner, Jay, Watertown	.323	65	229	43	74	123	16	3	9	58	3	0	2	1	42	4	58	3	1
Byrd, James, Niagara Falls†	.214	51	140	19	30	39	4	1	1	17	1	5	1	2	26	0	26	13	2
Cain, Jerald, Utica	.175	27	63	7	11	11	0	0	0	6	1	0	1	2	11	0	20	4	2
Camilli, Kevin, Elmira*	.140	17	43	2	6	6	0	0	0	1	0	0	0	0	6	1	11	0	1
Campbell, Eric, Niagara Falls	.253	38	75	8	19	20	1	0	0	10	0	5	2	1	7	0	11	0	0
Carganilla, Peter, Batavia	.250	62	168	20	42	49	4	0	1	11	3	2	1	2	10	1	30	7	3
Carter, Scott, Oneonta*	.241	58	141	17	34	45	0	1	3	15	2	1	2	1	17	1	26	1	1
Casteel, A. Brent, Geneva	.240	7	25	5	6	6	0	0	0	3	0	1	0	0	2	1	0	1	0
Castro, Ruben, Geneva	.257	50	175	21	45	65	8	0	4	23	5	0	0	2	23	1	39	3	1
Cathcart, Gary, Oneonta*	.238	74	286	37	68	88	9	1	3	26	2	3	3	2	38	3	49	5	3
Chance, R. Anthony, Watertown	.148	41	115	13	17	28	2	0	3	14	0	2	2	3	17	1	47	5	2
Cheek, Carey, Watertown	.265	58	162	16	43	67	3	0	7	36	2	0	2	0	21	1	34	1	1
Chesnoski, Gary, Auburn	.000	22	3	1	0	0	0	0	0	0	0	0	0	0	1	0	1	0	0
Christy, Alexander, Oneonta	.195	14	41	4	8	14	1	1	1	6	0	0	1	0	0	0	12	3	0
Christy, John, Niagara Falls	.102	24	59	5	6	8	0	1	0	2	0	0	0	1	3	0	20	0	1
Ciszkowski, Jeffrey, Little Falls	.200	15	5	3	1	1	0	0	0	0	0	0	0	0	0	0	1	0	0
Clark, Daniel, Watertown	.190	6	21	2	4	4	0	0	0	0	0	0	0	0	6	0	6	2	1
Claxton, N. Keith, Jamestown†	.205	52	161	11	33	38	5	0	0	9	0	3	2	2	22	0	36	7	3
Coker, Reginald, Batavia	.034	30	29	12	1	3	0	1	0	3	0	0	0	0	8	0	16	8	2
Collins, Allen, Jamestown	.000	8	5	1	0	0	0	0	0	0	0	0	0	0	1	0	3	0	0
Couisnard, Prince, Utica	.281	60	146	20	41	51	4	0	2	16	0	2	1	1	29	0	32	8	5
Crabbe, Bruce, Geneva	.307	62	202	30	62	95	13	4	4	26	4	4	2	0	34	1	29	5	4
Crossley, David, Erie	.250	11	8	0	2	2	0	0	0	2	0	0	0	0	0	0	0	0	0
Cunningham, Herman, Oneonta	.234	20	47	5	11	11	0	0	0	6	0	0	1	2	4	0	18	1	0
Cusack, David, Utica	.286	58	203	45	58	128	13	3	17	48	2	0	1	39	4	53	10	2

Player and Club	Pct.	G.	AB.	R.	H.	TB.	2B.	3B.	HR.	RBI.	GW.	SH.	SF.	HP.	BB.	Int. BB.	SO.	SB.	CS.
Daddario, Paul, Batavia	.293	73	270	48	79	98	7	0	4	27	2	3	0	2	39	0	46	9	5
Dahse, David, Newark	.272	71	283	51	77	103	9	1	5	40	6	5	3	4	21	0	56	18	3
Datz, Jeffrey, Auburn	.197	24	71	2	14	14	0	0	0	8	0	0	2	3	9	0	15	0	2
Davis, Mark, Little Falls	.000	38	7	0	0	0	0	0	0	0	0	0	0	0	1	0	4	0	0
Decker, Thomas, 33 Bat.-11 Utica ...	.202	44	99	5	20	24	4	0	0	11	1	1	2	1	9	2	23	2	0
DeFrancesco, Anthony, Elmira	.299	56	194	26	58	74	8	1	2	24	3	4	1	2	26	2	22	0	0
Delgado, Rumaldo, Watertown°	.125	9	16	2	2	2	0	0	0	0	0	0	0	1	3	0	7	0	0
DelRosario, Manuel, Utica†	.264	55	140	22	37	46	6	0	1	10	1	4	0	1	13	0	24	4	3
Denczi, Edward, Watertown	.200	31	55	7	11	18	4	0	1	4	0	1	1	1	6	0	19	0	0
Depiano, Jeffrey, Jamestown	.210	61	205	25	43	68	9	2	4	24	3	1	1	1	32	0	38	5	1
Dillenberger, David, Erie	.100	15	10	1	1	1	0	0	0	0	0	0	0	0	1	0	5	0	0
Diprimo, John, Elmira	.294	13	34	3	10	10	0	0	0	0	1	0	2	2	0	4	0	1	
Doerr, Jeffrey, Newark	.274	27	95	13	26	.38	4	1	2	15	3	0	1	2	9	0	29	0	0
Dominico, Ronald, Little Falls°	.000	27	4	0	0	0	0	0	0	0	0	0	0	0	2	0	1	0	0
Doorey, Jephrey, Jamestown°	.667	18	3	1	2	2	0	0	0	0	1	0	0	0	0	0	0	0	0
Dunster, Donald, Auburn	.000	15	9	0	0	0	0	0	0	0	0	0	0	0	0	0	2	0	0
Edge, Michael, Watertown	.333	19	6	0	2	2	0	0	0	0	0	0	1	0	0	0	2	0	0
Edwards, John, Auburn	.207	18	29	1	6	6	0	0	0	0	1	1	0	0	0	0	10	0	0
Edwards, Terrence, Geneva	.191	66	225	31	43	61	6	0	4	27	5	2	0	1	42	1	92	15	1
Elliott, John, Auburn	.171	44	152	26	26	35	5	2	0	12	2	1	0	1	21	0	24	9	3
Elster, Kevin, Little Falls	.257	71	257	35	66	88	7	3	3	35	5	0	5	1	35	1	41	13	2
Erickson, Paul, Jamestown	.000	12	7	0	0	0	0	0	0	0	0	0	0	0	0	0	3	0	0
Falkner, Belgee, Watertown	.279	60	165	33	46	91	9	3	10	33	6	0	1	2	18	3	38	8	3
Fansler, Stanley, Watertown	.111	14	18	2	2	3	1	0	0	0	1	0	0	0	4	0	5	0	0
Fernandez, Carlos, Batavia	.130	12	23	2	3	7	1	0	1	3	0	0	0	0	3	0	11	0	0
Fiepke, Scott, Watertown°	.000	18	4	0	0	0	0	0	0	0	0	1	0	0	0	0	3	0	0
Finley, Jackie, Utica	.311	69	235	36	73	109	9	0	9	39	1	1	1	1	33	1	45	6	3
Foley, Keith, Oneonta	.211	21	57	7	12	16	1	0	1	4	0	1	0	1	3	0	5	0	0
Fortner, Dennis, Geneva°	.241	70	237	37	57	63	3	0	1	26	2	4	0	0	63	1	54	9	5
Foyt, Randolph, Oneonta	.257	62	218	28	56	80	5	5	3	21	2	2	1	0	20	2	48	7	2
Franchi, Kevin, Watertown°	.000	61	2	1	0	0	0	0	0	0	0	0	0	0	2	0	1	0	0
Franks, Jeffery, Oneonta°	.243	62	173	32	42	61	7	0	4	27	1	0	1	2	38	2	36	2	0
Friedel, Charles, Little Falls	.333	5	3	0	1	1	0	0	0	1	0	0	0	0	0	0	1	0	0
Frye, Daniel, Utica	.182	16	33	4	6	6	0	0	0	2	0	0	1	0	5	0	2	0	0
Fuentes, Rick, Niagara Falls	.205	45	146	14	30	38	4	2	0	13	0	0	1	0	6	0	33	3	1
Garcia, Victor, Batavia	.347	60	216	38	75	133	15	2	13	41	5	0	0	7	16	2	35	1	1
Garner, Michael, Auburn	.249	53	169	30	42	57	5	5	0	6	0	1	0	4	27	0	33	24	3
Gass, Jeffrey, Erie	.000	22	9	0	0	0	0	0	0	0	0	0	1	0	1	0	7	0	0
Glass, Christopher, Utica°	.125	8	16	1	2	2	0	0	0	0	0	0	0	0	6	0	2	2	0
Goff, Michael, Elmira	.296	62	230	40	68	123	19	0	12	51	6	2	4	6	26	2	25	6	1
Gonzalez, Angel, Elmira	.287	63	202	54	58	88	14	2	4	24	0	3	4	2	41	2	36	9	3
Gonzalez, Roberto, Watertown	.301	61	196	23	59	70	9	1	0	18	1	3	0	6	7	2	32	4	5
Goss, Scott, Niagara Falls	.250	54	184	24	46	70	12	3	2	30	2	1	2	1	31	0	45	2	1
Gozzo, Mauro, Little Falls	.000	26	3	1	0	0	0	0	0	0	0	0	0	0	0	0	3	0	0
Graham, Lewis, Little Falls°	.280	67	207	29	58	73	8	2	1	27	2	2	4	2	23	2	33	6	6
Graham, Michael, Elmira°	.279	23	43	3	12	13	1	0	0	4	0	2	0	1	11	1	10	0	0
Gutierrez, Dimas, Watertown	.254	70	264	33	67	108	14	3	7	33	5	1	5	1	19	0	45	1	1
Gutierrez, Roberto, Newark	.256	67	215	45	55	79	8	2	4	25	3	3	2	0	46	0	44	8	4
Haines, Michael, Jamestown	.250	5	4	0	1	1	0	0	0	2	1	1	0	0	0	0	0	0	0
Hall, R. David, Elmira	.159	55	132	10	21	28	4	0	1	13	0	5	0	0	18	0	48	0	1
Hardee, Amos, Jamestown°	.222	12	9	1	2	2	0	0	0	0	0	0	0	0	0	0	2	0	0
Hayes, Daniel, Newark°	.169	34	83	14	14	16	0	1	0	5	0	1	0	0	17	1	18	3	1
Heise, Larry, Newark°	1.000	18	1	1	1	1	0	0	0	0	0	0	0	0	0	0	0	0	0
Henkel, Mark, Auburn	.125	11	8	2	1	1	0	0	0	0	0	0	0	0	2	0	2	0	0
Heredia, Geysi, Auburn	.000	5	3	0	0	0	0	0	0	0	0	0	0	0	0	0	2	0	0
Higgins, Mark, Batavia	.272	74	279	38	76	112	12	0	8	39	4	0	5	1	26	3	46	5	4
Hill, Stephen, Erie°	.188	16	16	0	3	3	0	0	0	1	0	0	0	0	0	0	0	0	0
Holtz, Gerald, Newark°	.275	71	247	60	68	102	14	4	4	41	4	3	3	1	59	1	50	18	4
Hopkins, Mark, Batavia	.211	30	71	9	15	28	1	0	4	11	0	1	1	1	15	1	21	3	1
Hopkins, Richard, Geneva°	.272	67	235	43	64	93	11	0	6	33	6	5	2	1	49	2	44	4	2
Howard, Raymond, Batavia	.056	8	18	3	1	1	0	0	0	0	0	0	0	0	1	0	4	0	0
Huchingson, Christopher, Auburn	.200	15	5	1	1	3	0	0	0	0	0	0	0	0	6	0	10	1	0
Hudson, Gregory, Jamestown	.100	15	10	0	1	1	0	0	0	1	0	1	0	0	1	0	3	0	0
Humbert, Craig, Utica°	1.000	16	1	1	1	1	0	0	0	0	0	0	0	0	0	0	0	0	0
Jackson, Charles, Auburn	.368	10	38	4	14	21	0	2	1	4	0	0	0	0	6	0	10	1	0
Jackson, Lavern, Elmira	.276	55	170	32	47	54	1	0	2	23	1	2	0	1	18	0	25	20	1
Jacoby, Donald, Utica°	.350	55	203	49	71	133	12	1	16	53	3	0	4	1	30	1	29	3	4
Jenkins, W. David, Batavia	.279	36	104	19	29	42	4	0	3	8	0	2	1	0	4	0	28	4	1
Jimenez, Francisco, Watertown°	.263	48	114	26	30	37	4	0	1	8	1	1	3	0	24	0	17	14	2
Johns, Ronald, Erie	.280	70	257	42	72	116	16	2	8	42	4	1	3	1	28	2	48	1	1
Johnson, John, Geneva	.196	38	112	8	22	23	1	0	0	10	2	1	0	1	12	1	31	2	1
Johnson, K. Lance, Erie°	.339	71	283	63	96	116	7	5	1	28	1	1	3	0	45	0	20	29	10
Johnson, Lindsey, Watertown	.284	50	155	14	44	50	3	0	1	11	0	0	4	0	17	1	31	0	0
Johnson, Richard, Niagara Falls	.292	59	202	35	59	95	13	4	5	37	5	1	4	1	27	2	50	4	1
Johnson, Terence, Little Falls	.232	35	95	12	22	34	3	0	3	10	1	0	0	0	11	0	28	1	1
Jones, Anson, Jamestown	.178	42	107	8	19	31	5	2	1	12	1	0	0	2	17	0	38	0	0
Jones, Barry L., Watertown	.235	14	17	1	4	4	0	0	0	2	0	1	0	0	0	0	6	0	0
Jongewaard, Steven, Elmira	.278	36	108	17	30	37	4	0	1	8	0	0	3	5	12	0	34	1	1
Jordan, A. Rozier, Batavia	.219	67	228	38	50	83	10	1	7	21	4	1	1	2	22	6	47	9	6
Karr, Jeffrey, Little Falls†	.241	9	29	2	7	11	1	0	1	2	1	0	0	0	2	0	7	0	1
Kavanaugh, Timothy L., Erie	.185	47	108	15	20	27	4	0	1	11	0	0	0	1	19	1	19	4	2
Kiley, Craig, Little Falls	.083	10	24	0	2	3	1	0	0	0	0	0	0	0	2	0	13	0	0
Kinard, Charles, Erie	.244	62	221	26	54	76	9	2	3	21	1	1	0	1	22	4	40	9	6
King, Jeffery, Oneonta	.233	47	129	13	30	42	6	0	2	13	1	3	3	2	12	0	16	0	2
Knotts, Ronald, Watertown	.217	60	157	29	34	39	3	1	0	12	2	5	1	1	27	2	23	19	4
Knox, David, Little Falls	.216	53	162	20	35	48	4	0	3	20	3	0	1	0	25	1	29	3	3
Knox, Scott, Watertown	.394	24	99	18	39	46	4	0	1	8	3	1	1	1	7	0	9	3	3
Koch, Bryan, Niagara Falls°	.173	29	52	5	9	12	3	0	0	7	1	3	1	1	15	0	14	2	1
Lane, Phillip Oneonta	.291	66	244	41	71	116	19	1	8	43	1	3	2	2	29	1	56	4	0
Lange, Clarke, Auburn	.333	4	15	2	5	6	1	0	0	5	0	0	3	1	0	3	0	0	
Lelievre, David, Batavia	.200	25	45	3	9	10	1	0	0	1	1	0	0	2	1	0	13	0	0
Leon, Ronald, Erie°	.268	70	276	42	74	109	11	3	6	39	4	0	1	3	23	1	35	4	4

Player and Club	Pct.	G.	AB.	R.	H.	TB.	2B.	3B.	HR.	RBI.	GW.	SH.	SF.	HP.	BB.	Int. BB.	SO.	SB.	CS.
Lezcano, Manuel, Geneva	.245	64	220	29	54	86	8	0	8	33	2	2	1	5	11	0	34	4	1
Lind, Orlando, Watertown	.000	14	2	1	0	0	0	0	0	0	0	0	0	0	0	0	1	0	0
Little, D. Scott, Little Falls	.298	66	225	38	67	81	11	0	1	23	3	2	0	9	27	0	54	34	8
Livin, Jeffrey, Auburn	.250	16	12	0	3	5	2	0	0	2	0	0	0	0	2	0	5	0	0
Lockwood, Richard, Newark†	.267	40	146	28	39	59	8	0	4	25	1	3	6	0	24	1	26	2	4
Lopes, Howard J., Jamestown	.278	69	248	49	69	115	13	3	9	25	2	1	0	0	46	0	33	9	2
Lora, Jesus, Auburn	.263	13	38	3	10	14	4	0	0	5	0	0	1	0	2	0	12	0	0
Loschiavo, Christopher, Oneonta	.199	45	151	14	30	31	1	0	0	15	3	1	1	1	19	1	27	2	5
Lynn, Charles, Newark	.274	64	223	43	61	129	10	2	18	58	9	2	4	6	27	2	49	4	0
Mahler, Gary, Jamestown°	.209	56	177	16	37	52	4	1	3	17	2	1	1	1	18	3	29	1	0
Mahnken, Kenneth, Utica°	.243	73	243	38	59	116	11	2	14	36	5	0	1	1	38	2	57	7	9
Mandel, Darren, Oneonta	.239	69	222	40	53	97	5	0	13	40	4	2	3	1	55	4	58	0	2
Maples, Randall, Utica	.218	40	110	16	24	29	2	0	1	9	2	0	1	1	19	1	28	2	1
Marino, Thomas, Niagara Falls	.168	55	161	20	27	37	4	0	2	12	4	2	1	0	22	0	37	0	0
Mathews, Gregory, Erie°	.333	3	3	0	1	1	0	0	0	0	0	0	0	0	0	0	1	0	0
Maynard, Chris, Oneonta	.274	53	197	21	54	58	2	1	0	15	1	5	1	1	9	0	37	8	1
Mazeroski, Darren, Jamestown°	.237	38	97	10	23	25	2	0	0	8	1	3	0	2	9	0	24	0	0
McCandlish, Robert, Geneva	.000	7	1	0	0	0	0	0	0	0	0	0	0	0	0	0	1	0	0
McMahan, Jimmy, 28 Bat.-10 Uti.†	.157	38	83	7	13	15	2	0	0	2	0	3	0	1	14	0	28	2	0
McPherson, Barry, Erie	.200	9	5	0	1	1	0	0	0	0	0	0	0	0	1	0	2	0	0
Meadows, Geoffrey, Watertown	.000	10	2	0	0	0	0	0	0	0	0	0	0	0	0	0	0	0	0
Meads, David, Auburn°	.000	10	0	0	0	0	0	0	0	0	0	1	0	0	0	0	0	0	0
Mejia, Simon, Geneva	.213	68	249	34	53	75	12	2	2	17	1	2	1	4	27	3	52	9	6
Melendez, Jose, Watertown	.000	15	8	0	0	0	0	0	0	0	0	0	0	0	1	0	6	0	0
Metoyer, Tony, Auburn°	.175	70	217	19	38	45	5	1	0	10	1	1	0	7	18	0	47	5	0
Meyer, Gordon, Oneonta	.276	28	58	14	16	18	0	1	0	8	1	0	1	0	12	1	14	10	1
Mickan, Daniel, Newark	.220	36	91	15	20	22	2	0	0	10	3	1	2	1	19	0	25	3	0
Mieses, Julio, Erie	.000	13	2	0	0	0	0	0	0	0	0	1	0	0	0	0	1	0	0
Mikulik, Joseph, Auburn	.247	76	283	57	70	86	8	1	2	27	5	1	2	3	28	0	55	23	8
Miller, John, Auburn	.252	49	119	18	30	52	4	0	6	24	2	1	5	1	9	1	23	0	0
Moon, Kevin, Erie	.000	20	2	0	0	0	0	0	0	0	0	0	0	0	0	0	0	0	0
Moreland, Oscar, Little Falls	.273	13	11	2	3	3	0	0	0	0	0	2	0	1	3	0	2	0	0
Moritz, Christopher, Elmira	.235	70	230	32	54	77	12	1	3	29	1	9	5	2	15	0	49	14	1
Morris, James, Utica°	.293	73	263	49	77	136	9	1	16	48	4	5	2	2	20	1	54	5	6
Morrow, Benjamin, Watertown	.000	29	7	0	0	0	0	0	0	0	0	0	0	0	0	0	7	0	0
Moyer, Jamie, Geneva°	.250	14	12	1	3	3	0	0	0	0	0	0	0	0	2	0	5	0	0
Mueller, Peter, Auburn°	.262	76	252	40	66	127	14	4	13	54	7	1	3	5	48	5	55	7	2
Murphy, John, Erie	.281	60	185	32	52	74	8	1	4	41	3	1	1	4	25	1	26	22	2
Murray, Michael, Niagara Falls	.155	36	103	7	16	23	4	0	1	10	0	0	0	4	5	0	22	1	0
Nicholson, James, Watertown	.154	34	65	13	10	10	0	0	0	2	0	2	0	0	20	1	15	6	4
Ninneman, Scott, Geneva	.000	15	3	1	0	0	0	0	0	0	0	1	0	0	1	0	3	0	0
O'Connor, James, Erie	.127	29	55	7	7	14	1	0	2	4	0	0	1	0	9	0	21	1	0
Oliveros, Romulo, Jamestown	.218	35	101	6	22	23	1	0	0	8	1	1	1	2	0	0	19	1	0
Ott, Jeff, Oneonta	.195	22	41	5	8	12	4	0	0	3	0	1	0	0	6	1	13	0	0
Pacheco, Ernest, Jamestown	.000	5	1	0	0	0	0	0	0	0	0	1	0	0	0	0	0	0	0
Padget, Chris, Newark°	.373	20	67	15	25	48	6	1	5	26	3	0	0	1	8	1	13	0	0
Paparella, Ray, Auburn	.143	20	35	2	5	6	1	0	0	1	0	0	0	0	3	0	7	0	0
Parker, Christopher, Auburn	1.000	13	2	0	2	2	0	0	0	0	0	0	0	0	0	0	0	0	0
Parker, Robert, Auburn°	.125	20	64	9	8	8	0	0	0	1	0	0	0	0	22	0	8	7	3
Paul, Grady, Newark	.242	14	33	10	8	10	0	1	0	3	0	0	1	0	9	0	10	4	2
Peck, David, Jamestown	.000	23	4	0	0	0	0	0	0	0	0	0	1	0	0	0	1	0	0
Pereira, Ramon, Little Falls	.263	41	95	13	25	31	3	0	1	13	2	1	0	0	12	1	25	0	2
Perez, Hector, Little Falls°	.241	65	199	23	48	63	8	2	1	24	1	0	0	0	21	1	51	3	5
Pitti, Marcelino, Oneonta	.375	5	8	1	3	6	0	0	1	3	0	0	0	0	1	0	1	0	0
Pleis, W. Scott, Erie	.241	44	108	14	26	34	2	0	2	10	4	0	1	0	7	1	30	0	1
Prince, Thomas, Watertown	.203	23	69	6	14	23	3	0	2	13	2	1	0	1	9	0	13	0	0
Pruitt, Darrell, Niagara Falls	.284	70	282	49	80	108	14	1	4	19	0	6	1	4	21	3	52	16	6
Rather, Dody, Oneonta	.000	14	1	0	0	0	0	0	0	0	0	0	0	0	0	0	0	0	0
Rector, Darryl, Niagara Falls°	.189	57	148	14	28	42	4	2	2	18	0	1	1	1	10	0	35	2	2
Reed, Darren, Oneonta	.230	40	113	17	26	39	7	0	2	9	2	1	1	0	10	0	19	2	1
Reid, Timothy, Geneva	.200	17	5	0	1	2	1	0	0	0	0	1	0	0	0	0	1	0	0
Renfroe, Cohen, Geneva	.000	24	1	0	0	0	0	0	0	0	0	0	0	1	0	0	0	0	0
Reyes, Ricardo, Elmira	.105	17	19	0	2	3	0	0	0	0	0	0	0	0	0	0	6	0	0
Riley, Randall, Newark°	.351	70	248	50	87	126	19	1	6	50	2	1	1	2	41	7	50	2	1
Rivera, Carlos, Batavia†	.161	23	31	2	5	6	1	0	0	1	0	0	0	0	4	0	8	1	0
Rivera, Luis, Utica	.287	38	122	16	35	56	6	0	5	24	1	2	1	1	16	2	19	3	2
Rizzo, Charles, Jamestown	.178	41	118	11	21	23	2	0	0	6	0	0	0	0	12	0	22	3	0
Roberts, John, Elmira	.249	69	245	38	61	78	6	1	3	24	2	3	2	1	30	0	19	18	3
Robertson, Bryant, Little Falls	.208	46	106	15	22	33	8	0	1	7	1	0	0	1	12	0	36	2	5
Robinson, Emmett, Watertown	.143	5	7	0	1	1	0	0	0	1	0	0	0	0	1	0	3	0	0
Robles, Aquilino, Jamestown	.111	12	27	1	3	6	1	1	0	3	0	0	0	2	0	10	0	0	0
Rodriguez, Alejandro, Erie	.200	12	5	1	1	1	0	0	0	0	0	0	0	0	0	0	1	0	0
Rodriguez, Manuel, Auburn	.189	38	111	13	21	26	5	0	0	8	1	0	1	2	6	0	33	6	0
Rodriguez, Richard, Little Falls°	.000	25	0	0	0	0	0	0	0	0	0	0	0	0	0	0	0	0	0
Rogers, Marte, Elmira	.053	16	19	2	1	2	1	0	0	1	0	0	0	1	2	1	8	0	0
Roman, Miguel, Batavia	.254	70	283	48	72	135	13	1	16	53	5	0	1	0	16	0	55	7	2
Rooney, James, Newark°	.000	6	1	0	0	0	0	0	0	0	0	0	0	0	0	0	1	0	0
Roque, Omar, Auburn	.050	17	20	0	1	1	0	0	0	1	0	0	0	0	1	0	4	0	0
Rosario, Victor, Elmira	.111	23	27	2	3	3	0	0	0	0	0	0	0	0	3	0	6	0	0
Salinas, Manuel, Niagara Falls°	.261	64	253	35	66	79	8	1	1	36	3	1	2	0	23	1	22	3	3
Santana, Jose, Erie	.142	57	113	12	16	16	0	0	0	9	2	0	2	0	7	1	37	2	1
Satzinger, Jeffrey, Watertown	.286	14	7	3	2	3	1	0	0	0	1	0	0	0	1	0	1	0	0
Scott, Tary, Elmira	.288	57	191	27	55	92	7	0	10	36	8	0	1	2	24	8	32	0	1
Sherlock, Glenn, Auburn°	.226	57	177	13	40	44	4	0	0	16	4	3	1	0	8	1	29	6	1
Slocumb, Heath, Little Falls	.000	5	3	0	0	0	0	0	0	0	0	0	0	0	1	0	1	0	0
Slowik, Thaddeus, Geneva	.000	21	2	0	0	0	0	0	0	0	0	0	0	0	0	0	1	0	0
Smith, David L., Newark	.240	71	229	38	55	69	9	1	1	31	1	4	2	3	39	0	37	3	5
Smith, David W., Newark°	.000	14	1	0	0	0	0	0	0	0	0	0	0	0	0	0	1	0	0
Smith, Richard, Jamestown	.187	46	139	10	26	36	1	3	1	11	1	0	0	1	8	0	39	1	0
Smith, Timothy, Newark	.244	46	156	17	38	58	6	1	4	30	3	1	0	0	24	3	31	3	1
Smith, Todd, Geneva	.252	37	131	15	33	47	6	1	2	19	4	1	1	1	10	0	20	2	0
Spazante, John, Auburn°	.333	15	9	0	3	3	0	0	0	0	0	2	0	0	0	0	3	0	0

Player and Club	Pct.	G.	AB.	R.	H.	TB.	2B.	3B.	HR.	RBI.	GW.	SH.	SF.	HP.	BB.	Int. BB.	SO.	SB.	CS.
Spear, Frank, Geneva*	.000	15	1	4	0	0	0	0	0	0	0	0	0	0	4	0	1	0	0
Steinbach, Eugene, Batavia	.667	1	3	2	2	3	1	0	0	2	0	0	0	0	2	0	1	0	0
Stevenson, Craig, Auburn	.211	60	209	17	44	60	8	1	2	18	1	5	1	1	12	0	35	2	1
Stone, Jerome, Utica†	.000	9	26	3	0	0	0	0	0	0	0	0	0	0	2	0	11	3	0
Sullivan, Daniel, Elmira†	.229	42	105	11	24	31	7	0	0	10	0	1	0	0	16	4	18	0	2
Swain, Steven, Auburn	.234	34	124	10	29	38	5	2	0	4	1	1	0	1	1	0	35	1	0
Syverson, Dain, Batavia	.262	66	225	42	59	76	12	1	1	30	3	4	4	5	43	2	38	7	2
Tarasovitch, Scott, Erie	.000	7	1	0	0	0	0	0	0	0	0	0	0	0	0	0	0	0	0
Tindall, Mark, Jamestown*	.000	14	11	1	0	0	0	0	0	0	1	0	2	0	2	0	6	0	0
Toale, John, Elmira*	.243	50	144	10	35	46	8	0	1	17	0	1	2	1	12	1	29	0	0
Tolleson, Michael, Batavia*	.077	10	26	3	2	2	0	0	0	0	0	0	0	0	10	0	5	3	1
Tostenson, Ronald, Jamestown*	.262	72	275	47	72	95	9	4	2	15	1	1	0	1	37	3	27	24	5
Traylor, Keith, Little Falls	.289	63	204	35	59	83	8	5	2	19	3	10	0	2	34	1	37	25	9
Tuller, Brian, Geneva	.182	14	11	3	2	3	1	0	0	1	0	0	0	1	0	0	1	0	0
Tyson, Marty, Geneva	.239	41	134	10	32	39	7	0	0	9	0	3	0	1	8	0	36	1	0
Ullian, Michael, Auburn*	.000	15	15	2	0	0	0	0	0	0	0	1	0	0	3	0	9	1	0
Valdez, Sergio, Jamestown	.182	13	11	2	2	2	0	0	0	1	0	0	0	0	0	0	4	0	0
Valera, Alcadio, Batavia†	.257	12	35	2	9	10	1	0	0	1	0	0	0	0	5	0	11	0	0
Van Houten, James, Erie	.250	21	4	0	1	1	0	0	0	1	0	0	2	0	0	0	1	0	0
Velleggia, Frank, Newark	.246	55	179	28	44	65	5	2	4	24	1	5	2	0	22	1	43	6	1
Venturini, Peter, Niagara Falls	.189	29	95	15	18	22	4	0	0	7	1	1	1	0	10	0	17	5	1
Vergara, Alberto, Erie*	.100	8	10	0	1	1	0	0	0	0	0	0	0	1	0	4	1	0
Walker, Scott, Watertown*	.275	69	229	50	63	81	6	0	4	25	4	0	4	3	36	5	53	4	1
Washington, Marc, Utica	.265	64	211	46	56	69	6	2	1	17	1	1	1	2	28	1	42	16	2
Weiss, Joel, Utica	.228	53	162	27	37	50	4	0	3	18	3	3	2	3	27	2	41	6	3
West, David, Little Falls*	.471	18	17	3	8	10	0	1	0	5	0	1	0	2	0	3	0	0
Westbrook, Michael, Little Falls*	.263	66	228	43	60	66	4	1	0	15	1	1	2	0	37	1	38	29	13
Whitaker, Kevin, Erie*	.167	15	12	0	2	2	0	0	0	0	0	0	0	0	0	0	4	0	0
Wilkinson, Todd, Jamestown	.274	71	259	40	71	110	17	2	6	42	6	2	9	6	20	2	48	2	1
Williams, Rafael, Batavia	.274	43	124	14	34	38	4	0	0	11	3	0	1	0	5	1	13	2	2
Wilson, Craig, Erie	.294	72	282	53	83	130	18	4	7	46	6	1	2	4	29	0	27	10	4
Wilson, Roger, Newark*	.000	14	1	0	0	0	0	0	0	0	0	0	0	0	0	0	0	0	0
Wilson, W. Allen, Little Falls	.132	32	76	10	10	14	1	0	1	8	2	1	1	2	20	0	22	0	1
Wilson, Wayne, Newark*	.000	1	1	0	0	0	0	0	0	0	0	0	0	0	1	0	0	0	0
Winters, James, Niagara Falls	.298	64	235	46	70	119	8	7	9	29	3	1	0	4	47	1	45	7	5
Woellert, Ronald, Little Falls	.000	18	6	0	0	0	0	0	0	0	0	0	0	0	0	0	1	0	0
Woleslagel, Thomas, Oneonta	.264	64	178	23	47	59	10	1	0	20	2	8	1	2	16	0	29	3	4
Young, M. Shane, Little Falls*	.194	40	62	2	12	16	1	0	1	8	1	0	0	2	7	1	7	2	0

The following pitchers, listed alphabetically by club, with games in parentheses, had no plate appearances, primarily through use of designated hitters:

AUBURN—Baez, Joaquin (7); Cash, Timothy (29); Mallicoat, Robbin (1); Wilmore, Orlando (21).

BATAVIA—Beasley, Christopher (14); Clark, Edward (9); Compres, Fidel (2); DiFrancisco, Mark (1); Encarnacion, Luis (21); Feliciano, Rafael (3); Galloway, Kenneth (9); Greer, Michael (17); Kahler, Christopher (16); Leach, Daniel (2); Mora, Abraham (6); Phillips, Lonnie (1); Robertson, Andrew (14); Sharp, Richard (18); Snyder, Mark (3); Stephenson, Joe (14); Tamarez, Manuel (24); Whitmyer, Stephen (4).

ELMIRA—Abril, Ernest (15); Curry, Stephen (14); Diez, Scott (14); Fenn, Michael (16); Gakeler, Daniel (14); Hines, James (13); Knight, Brock (15); Manzanillo, Josia (14); Mettler, Bradley (15); Sanderski, John (17); Slifko, Paul (19); Stephenson, Joseph (12).

LITTLE FALLS—Howes, Jeff (7); Stiles, William (3).

NEWARK—Bell, Eric (15); Caldwell, Richard (27); Concepcion, Carlos (3); Ennis, Alan (18); Fitzpatrick, Danny (3); Gonzalez, Henry (5); Hixon, Alan (10); King, Randy (6); Kline, Robert (5); Skinner, Michael (11); Whalen, Michael (2); Wirth, Gregory (6).

NIAGARA FALLS—Anderson, Jeffrey (3); Carr, Donald (4); D'Agostino, Robert (12); Davis, Joel (11); Garrick, Darren (17); Gilmore, William (8); Nossek, Scott (15); Oswald, Steven (15); Phelps, James (10); Ruckebeil, Mark (20); Simmons, Todd (8); Wanzer, Scott (14); White, David (1).

ONEONTA—Canseco, Osvaldo (14); Chastain, Dennis (15); Davidson, Robert (24); Davis, Fernando (3); DeLaTorre, Mark (17); Dougherty, Patrick (22); Greenleaf, Daniel (24); Harrison, Matthew (16); Leiter, Alois (10); Pries, Jeffrey (11); Rebiejo, Kenneth (6); Sarno, Anthony (18); Stinnett, James (10).

UTICA—Compres, Fidel (6); Cooper, William (16); DiFrancisco, Mark (4); Giron, Tomas (7); Greenlee, Robert (16); Hoag, Timothy (9); Magyari, John (26); Melchert, Gregory (3); Mora, Abraham (2); Ortiz, Elsis (14); Phillips, Lonnie (11); Reed, Mark (6); Shellnut, Todd (11).

WATERTOWN—Carlie, Aaron (9); Fabre, Stan (8); Mercedes, Guillermo (7); Russell, Robert (4).

GRAND SLAM HOME RUNS—Higgins, 2; B. Brito, Buhner, Cheek, Doerr, Finley, Garcia, Goff, R. Hopkins, Leon, Lezcano, Mahler, Mandell, Murphy, Murray, Pruitt, Riley, Roberts, Velleggia, 1 each.

AWARDED FIRST BASE ON CATCHER'S INTERFERENCE—Roberts 6 (Brunswick, Datz, Franks, Henkel, J. King, Koch); Decker 2 (Franks, Li. Johnson); Hayes 2 (Foley 2); Morris (DeFrancesco).

CLUB FIELDING

Club	Pct.	G.	PO.	A.	E.	DP.	PB.	Club	Pct.	G.	PO.	A.	E.	DP.	PB.
Erie	.963	74	1939	813	105	77	19	Watertown	.953	74	1906	821	135	63	16
Elmira	.961	73	1878	776	109	47	19	Geneva	.951	74	1943	725	137	50	10
Newark	.957	74	1911	845	123	55	20	Batavia	.951	76	1978	902	149	75	26
Jamestown	.957	74	1895	804	122	68	22	Oneonta	.947	74	1910	818	152	56	29
Little Falls	.957	75	1944	777	123	69	21	Niagara Falls	.946	75	1952	875	163	73	5
Auburn	.955	76	1909	828	130	64	19	Utica	.942	75	1853	771	162	62	23

Triple Play—Little Falls.

INDIVIDUAL FIELDING

FIRST BASEMEN

*Throws lefthanded.

Player and Club	Pct.	G.	PO.	A.	E.	DP.	Player and Club	Pct.	G.	PO.	A.	E.	DP.
Amaro, Geneva	.979	46	311	20	7	26	Goss, Niagara Falls	.985	54	471	49	8	45
Arrington, Niagara Falls	1.000	1	3	1	0	0	Gutierrez, Newark*	.750	2	2	1	1	0
Barnard, Erie	1.000	1	4	0	0	0	Hayes, Newark*	.987	19	145	6	2	12
Blaine, Erie	.982	17	102	8	2	11	Higgins, Batavia	.979	73	684	46	16	66
Carter, Oneonta*	.977	40	315	18	8	31	Hopkins, Batavia	1.000	1	3	0	0	0
Castro, Geneva	.986	37	270	21	4	17	Jenkins, Batavia	.833	2	10	0	2	2
Cheek, Watertown	.981	14	97	8	2	8	Johns, Erie	.984	66	583	22	10	54
Crabbe, Geneva	1.000	6	20	1	0	1	R. Johnson, Niagara Falls	.992	12	124	5	1	15
Cusack, Utica	1.000	1	3	0	0	0	T. Johnson, Little Falls	.984	18	115	6	2	7
Decker, Batavia	1.000	1	1	0	0	0	Jones, Jamestown	.986	19	136	9	2	9
DelRosario, Utica	.929	2	12	1	1	1	Jongewaard, Elmira	1.000	6	29	1	0	3
Foyt, Oneonta	1.000	3	14	7	0	0	Knox, Little Falls	.983	15	107	8	2	11

FIRST BASEMEN—Continued

Player and Club	Pct.	G.	PO.	A.	E.	DP.	Player and Club	Pct.	G.	PO.	A.	E.	DP.
Koch, Niagara Falls	1.000	1	1	0	0	1	Rector, Niagara Falls°	.900	1	8	1	1	1
Lynn, Newark	.986	50	417	20	6	29	Riley, Newark	.971	10	97	2	3	8
Mahler, Jamestown	.985	50	426	29	7	38	Scott, Elmira	.969	51	390	21	13	23
Mandel, Oneonta	.953	24	189	14	10	10	Steinbach, Batavia	1.000	1	13	0	0	1
Maples, Utica	.982	26	203	13	4	20	Stevenson, Auburn	1.000	1	0	1	0	0
MORRIS, Utica	.994	54	445	25	3	38	Sullivan, Elmira	.980	31	236	15	5	18
Mueller, Auburn°	.989	76	698	33	8	54	Syverson, Batavia	1.000	1	12	0	0	0
Murray, Niagara Falls	.958	12	88	4	4	5	Walker, Watertown°	.985	68	547	38	9	46
Ott, Oneonta	.947	18	103	4	6	5	Wilkinson, Jamestown	.990	12	87	9	1	11
Perez, Little Falls°	.989	61	402	28	5	40	Young, Little Falls°	1.000	3	10	1	0	2

SECOND BASEMEN

Player and Club	Pct.	G.	PO.	A.	E.	DP.	Player and Club	Pct.	G.	PO.	A.	E.	DP.
Barnard, Erie	1.000	2	0	1	0	0	Johnson, Niagara Falls	1.000	2	5	1	0	0
Barringer, Watertown	.904	17	44	41	9	11	Kinard, Erie	1.000	1	2	4	0	0
Blake, Oneonta	.943	11	19	14	2	2	Lockwood, Newark	.923	2	5	7	1	0
Bruno, Newark	1.000	2	0	2	0	0	Lopes, Jamestown	.969	62	160	180	11	44
Byrd, Niagara Falls	.953	41	82	82	8	25	Loschiavo, Oneonta	.949	42	107	99	11	19
Clark, Watertown	.882	3	7	8	2	2	Mazeroski, Jamestown	.946	13	27	26	3	7
Crabbe, Geneva	.950	4	9	10	1	0	Meyer, Oneonta	.957	21	36	31	3	4
DADDARIO, Batavia	.975	73	186	240	11	60	Mickan, Newark	.952	16	24	36	3	7
DelRosario, Utica	.885	21	42	43	11	14	Nicholson, Watertown	1.000	5	8	7	0	3
Elliott, Auburn	.948	39	86	97	10	19	Paparella, Auburn	.941	12	17	15	2	2
Fortner, Geneva	.926	69	150	152	24	29	Parker, Auburn	.960	20	44	52	4	13
Foyt, Oneonta	.933	4	5	9	1	1	Pereira, Little Falls	.908	19	39	40	8	11
Frye, Utica	1.000	4	7	9	0	3	Pruitt, Niagara Falls	.919	32	73	75	13	23
Garner, Auburn	1.000	3	5	5	0	0	Reyes, Elmira	.850	12	8	9	3	2
Glass, Utica	1.000	4	9	10	0	4	Roque, Auburn	.667	2	0	2	1	0
Goff, Elmira	.943	60	108	158	16	20	Salinas, Niagara Falls	.979	9	17	29	1	2
A. Gonzalez, Elmira	.941	11	22	26	3	6	Santana, Erie	.972	8	17	18	1	6
R. Gonzalez, Watertown	.934	55	98	130	16	22	Smith, Newark	.857	2	2	4	1	0
Graham, Little Falls	.947	63	110	138	14	26	Stevenson, Auburn	1.000	7	18	17	0	5
Hall, Elmira	.875	3	3	4	1	0	Westbrook, Little Falls	1.000	3	4	7	0	1
Holtz, Newark	.927	64	139	165	24	36	Williams, Batavia	1.000	7	8	5	0	0
Hopkins, Geneva	1.000	4	3	6	0	0	Wilson, Erie	.966	69	168	201	13	50
Howard, Batavia	.864	6	8	11	3	1	Woleslagel, Oneonta	.980	9	16	33	1	9
Jacoby, Utica	.959	55	100	134	10	30							

Triple Play—Graham.

THIRD BASEMEN

Player and Club	Pct.	G.	PO.	A.	E.	DP.	Player and Club	Pct.	G.	PO.	A.	E.	DP.
Arrington, Niagara Falls	.872	25	16	25	6	1	Mahnken, Utica	.910	69	56	137	19	12
Autry, Little Falls	.910	48	36	86	12	5	Marino, Niagara Falls	.800	1	3	1	1	0
Barnard, Erie	.905	41	25	80	11	6	McMahan, 10 Bat.-8 Utica°	.912	18	8	23	3	1
Barringer, Watertown	.857	1	3	3	1	0	Mejia, Geneva	.900	6	3	6	1	1
Belcik, Little Falls	.833	4	3	7	2	0	METOYER, Auburn	.945	69	57	151	12	15
Birkofer, Jamestown	.885	56	42	127	22	12	Mickan, Newark	.929	9	8	18	2	1
Bruno, Newark	.981	14	11	42	1	2	Murphy, Erie	.897	15	9	26	4	2
Cheek, Watertown	.900	5	4	5	1	1	Murray, Niagara Falls	1.000	1	1	0	0	0
Crabbe, Geneva	.867	40	25	66	14	4	Nicholson, Watertown	.875	5	0	7	1	2
Cusack, Utica	.667	1	1	1	1	0	Paparella, Auburn	.923	3	5	10	1	0
Denczi, Watertown	.750	4	1	2	1	0	Pereira, Little Falls	1.000	3	0	3	0	0
Doerr, Newark	.903	15	6	22	3	1	Pleis, Erie	1.000	3	2	6	0	1
Foyt, Oneonta	.924	31	31	66	8	4	Prince, Watertown	.667	1	0	2	1	0
Frye, Utica	1.000	7	0	2	0	0	Pruitt, Niagara Falls	.818	18	17	28	10	2
Glass, Utica	.600	2	2	1	2	0	Rivera, Batavia	.667	2	1	1	1	0
Gonzalez, Watertown	.667	6	2	2	2	0	Rizzo, Jamestown	.891	16	11	30	5	3
Gutierrez, Watertown	.933	61	46	120	12	13	Rogers, Elmira	.833	6	2	3	1	0
Hall, Elmira	.898	52	23	74	11	2	Roque, Auburn	.800	7	1	3	1	0
Hopkins, Batavia	.000	1	0	0	1	0	Salinas, Niagara Falls	.818	11	2	25	6	0
Jacoby, Utica	1.000	2	0	1	0	0	Santana, Erie	.959	33	10	37	2	2
Johnson, Niagara Falls	.813	35	21	57	18	6	T. Smith, Geneva	.853	32	25	56	14	5
Jones, Jamestown	.833	2	1	4	1	1	Stevenson, Auburn	.875	2	3	4	1	0
Kinard, Erie	.957	11	7	15	1	1	Syverson, Batavia	.942	61	37	126	10	18
Knox, Little Falls	.864	30	22	54	12	2	Toale, Elmira	.868	42	19	40	9	5
Lane, Oneonta	.870	17	12	35	7	2	Tyson, Geneva	.667	4	2	2	2	0
Lange, Auburn	.778	3	3	4	2	2	Williams, Batavia	.778	9	4	17	6	1
Little, Little Falls	1.000	1	0	1	0	0	Wilson, Erie	1.000	2	1	1	0	1
Lockwood, Newark	.893	38	22	87	13	4	Winters, Niagara Falls°	1.000	2	2	1	0	0
Lopes, Jamestown	.833	2	1	4	1	0	Woleslagel, Oneonta	.917	32	30	80	10	8
Lynn, Newark	.857	3	3	3	1	1							

Triple Play—Autry.

SHORTSTOPS

Player and Club	Pct.	G.	PO.	A.	E.	DP.	Player and Club	Pct.	G.	PO.	A.	E.	DP.
Adkins, Utica	.916	55	63	144	19	24	Gutierrez, Watertown	.981	10	10	41	1	5
Allaire, Auburn	.935	8	15	28	3	4	Hall, Elmira	1.000	2	0	2	0	0
Barringer, Watertown	.896	48	86	154	28	33	Holtz, Newark	.946	11	9	26	2	2
Bleckley, Jamestown	.930	57	97	170	20	37	Hopkins, Geneva	.924	65	91	163	21	25
Carganilla, Batavia	.868	59	59	152	32	23	Jones, Jamestown	.750	3	2	10	4	1
Clark, Watertown	1.000	4	2	6	0	0	Kavanaugh, Erie	.922	16	24	47	6	12
Crabbe, Geneva	.898	15	14	30	5	4	Kinard, Erie	.945	54	82	160	14	29
DelRosario, Utica	.815	24	17	49	15	3	Lora, Auburn	.886	13	22	48	9	10
Elliott, Auburn	.917	6	7	15	2	0	Maynard, Oneonta	.941	53	89	149	15	25
ELSTER, Little Falls	.955	71	128	214	16	45	McMahan, 17 Bat.-2 Utica°	.917	19	22	33	5	6
Frye, Utica	.900	6	6	12	2	6	Metoyer, Auburn	.800	1	1	3	1	0
Glass, Utica	.857	2	5	7	2	2	Moritz, Elmira	.942	70	117	205	20	27

SHORTSTOPS—Continued

Player and Club	Pct.	G.	PO.	A.	E.	DP.
Nicholson, Watertown	.855	17	25	34	10	7
Pereira, Little Falls	.897	11	8	18	3	5
Pitti, Oneonta	.600	5	6	3	6	0
Pruitt, Niagara Falls	1.000	1	0	4	0	0
Reyes, Elmira	1.000	1	0	2	0	0
Rivera, Batavia	.732	20	7	23	11	1
Rizzo, Jamestown	.917	15	19	36	5	4
Robinson, Watertown	1.000	3	5	4	0	0
Roque, Auburn	.333	1	0	1	2	0
Rosario, Elmira	.882	22	8	22	4	3
Salinas, Niagara Falls	.930	48	75	191	20	38
Santana, Erie	.920	12	19	27	4	6
Smith, Newark	.938	68	99	219	21	29
Stevenson, Auburn	.934	51	69	142	15	22
Syverson, Batavia	1.000	3	3	6	0	1
Valera, Batavia	.750	4	0	6	2	0
Venturini, Niagara Falls	.864	28	38	95	21	13
Wilson, Erie	.800	2	0	4	1	1
Woleslagel, Oneonta	.854	21	25	57	14	8

OUTFIELDERS

Player and Club	Pct.	G.	PO.	A.	E.	DP.
Abner, Little Falls	.977	18	40	2	1	0
Arrington, Niagara Falls	1.000	5	6	0	0	0
Barnard, Erie	1.000	11	13	0	0	0
Barrios, Elmira	.978	58	84	4	2	1
Blackwell, Niagara Falls	.930	58	88	5	7	0
Blaine, Erie	.854	33	38	3	7	1
Boderick, Geneva	.907	30	38	1	4	0
Bradley, Oneonta	.920	29	22	1	2	0
B. Brito, Batavia	.931	75	100	8	8	0
T. Brito, Elmira	.932	32	41	0	3	0
Brock, Auburn*	.966	37	54	3	2	0
Buhner, Watertown	.991	64	106	8	1	3
Cain, Utica	.921	19	34	1	3	0
Campbell, Niagara Falls	1.000	2	1	1	0	0
Cathcart, Oneonta*	.959	74	127	12	6	2
Chance, Watertown	.961	34	45	4	2	0
Cheek, Watertown	.250	3	0	1	3	0
A. Christy, Oneonta	1.000	12	12	1	0	0
J. Christy, Niagara Falls	.889	16	15	1	2	0
Claxton, Jamestown	.989	47	86	3	1	1
Coker, Batavia	1.000	7	4	0	0	0
Couisnard, Utica	.864	46	53	4	9	0
Cunningham, Oneonta	.769	17	9	1	3	1
Cusack, Utica	.932	42	52	3	4	0
Dahse, Newark	.949	69	124	5	7	0
Delgado, Watertown*	1.000	6	9	0	0	0
Depiano, Jamestown	.933	55	106	6	8	2
Doerr, Newark	1.000	6	4	1	0	1
Edwards, Geneva	.944	66	118	0	7	0
Falkner, Watertown	.959	40	44	3	2	1
Fernandez, Batavia	1.000	4	1	2	0	0
Finley, Utica	.600	6	3	0	2	0
Foyt, Oneonta	.950	15	18	1	1	0
Fuentes, Niagara Falls	.982	39	54	2	1	0
Garcia, Batavia	.000	1	0	0	1	0
Garner, Auburn	.965	46	78	5	3	0
M. Graham, Elmira	.857	8	6	0	1	0
Gutierrez, Newark*	.925	63	95	3	8	1
Hayes, Newark*	1.000	7	6	2	0	0
Humbert, Utica*	1.000	1	0	1	0	0
C. Jackson, Auburn	1.000	9	9	3	0	0
L. JACKSON, Elmira	1.000	55	54	4	0	0
Jenkins, Batavia	.973	28	30	6	1	0
Jimenez, Watertown*	.943	26	33	0	2	0
K.L. Johnson, Erie*	.960	71	188	5	8	1
T. Johnson, Little Falls	1.000	1	2	0	0	0
Jongewaard, Elmira	.965	31	54	1	2	0
Jordan, Batavia	.959	54	67	4	3	0
Kavanaugh, Erie	1.000	19	25	3	0	0
King, Oneonta	1.000	11	16	0	0	0
Knotts, Watertown	.973	47	70	2	2	0
D. Knox, Little Falls	.667	3	2	0	1	0
S. Knox, Watertown	1.000	23	29	2	0	1
Lane, Oneonta	.937	48	72	2	5	1
Leon, Erie*	.957	65	84	6	4	4
Lezcano, Geneva	.941	49	75	5	5	1
Little, Little Falls	.944	65	107	11	7	1
Lynn, Watertown	.500	1	1	0	1	0
Mahnken, Utica	1.000	9	14	0	0	0
McMahan, Utica*	1.000	1	1	0	0	0
Mejia, Geneva	.979	60	129	8	3	1
Mikulik, Auburn	.961	76	116	8	5	2
Miller, Auburn	.500	1	0	1	1	0
Morris, Utica	.957	21	19	3	1	2
Murphy, Erie	.959	41	68	3	3	1
Padget, Newark	1.000	19	19	2	0	1
Paul, Newark	.900	9	9	0	1	0
Pereira, Little Falls	1.000	8	10	1	0	1
Perez, Little Falls*	.923	5	12	0	1	0
Pleis, Erie	.400	4	2	0	3	0
Pruitt, Niagara Falls	.942	29	47	2	3	0
Rector, Niagara Falls*	.915	40	40	3	4	0
Reed, Oneonta	.952	36	38	2	2	0
Riley, Newark	.960	30	45	3	2	1
Rizzo, Jamestown	1.000	4	5	0	0	0
Roberts, Elmira	.979	67	132	8	3	1
Robertson, Little Falls	.951	33	39	0	2	0
Rodriguez, Auburn	.905	36	53	4	6	3
Rogers, Elmira	1.000	4	3	0	0	0
Roman, Batavia	.945	70	143	11	9	1
Smith, Newark	.976	31	33	7	1	1
Stone, Utica	1.000	8	7	2	0	0
Swain, Auburn	.824	33	40	2	9	0
Tolleson, Batavia	1.000	7	11	2	0	0
Tostenson, Jamestown	.968	71	117	4	4	0
Traylor, Little Falls	.963	63	102	1	4	0
Tyson, Geneva	.943	27	31	2	2	1
Vergara, Erie*	1.000	4	2	0	0	0
Washington, Utica	.908	60	94	5	10	0
Weiss, Utica	.942	50	94	4	6	0
Westbrook, Little Falls	.973	55	67	6	2	2
Wilkinson, Jamestown	.956	49	59	6	3	0
Winters, Niagara Falls	.965	63	104	5	4	1

CATCHERS

Player and Club	Pct.	G.	PO.	A.	E.	DP.	PB.
Arrington, Niagara Falls	1.000	13	50	6	0	0	0
Bair, Newark	.984	28	173	9	3	0	12
Baker, Geneva	.989	35	249	19	3	1	4
BARNARD, Erie	.995	42	169	18	1	3	4
Billinger, Erie	.996	45	205	21	1	1	3
Brunswick, Little Falls	.979	45	291	29	7	0	14
Camilli, Elmira	.985	12	60	4	1	0	1
Casteel, Geneva	.923	5	33	3	3	0	1
Castro, Geneva	.917	1	9	2	1	0	1
Datz, Newark	.976	24	147	18	4	1	5
Decker, 6 Bat.-11 Utica	.944	17	76	9	5	0	2
DeFrancesco, Elmira	.979	54	378	45	9	3	8
Denczi, Watertown	.958	19	79	13	4	1	4
Diprimo, Elmira	1.000	11	58	8	0	0	0
Edwards, Auburn	.842	5	13	3	3	0	3
Finley, Utica	.965	37	228	22	9	0	11
Foley, Oneonta	.963	16	91	13	4	0	6
Franks, Oneonta	.976	37	241	41	7	5	12
Garcia, Batavia	.981	46	271	34	6	3	14
Graham, Elmira	1.000	1	1	0	0	0	2
Henkel, Auburn	.875	4	7	0	1	0	0
Hopkins, Batavia	.972	21	125	16	4	2	8
J. Johnson, Geneva	.982	37	295	30	6	1	4
L. Johnson, Watertown	.977	48	314	32	8	3	8
Karr, Little Falls	.971	9	60	6	2	1	2
King, Oneonta	.976	34	223	22	6	3	11
Koch, Niagara Falls	.993	24	117	20	1	1	0
Lelievre, Batavia	.975	21	106	9	3	1	3
Mahnken, Utica	.875	2	6	1	1	0	0
Maples, Utica	1.000	7	21	1	0	0	3
Marino, Niagara Falls	.981	51	336	33	7	0	5
O'Connor, Erie	.986	24	63	5	1	0	12
Oliveros, Jamestown	.991	32	191	20	2	1	8
Prince, Watertown	.994	22	155	24	1	2	4
Reed, Oneonta	1.000	1	3	0	0	0	0
Rivera, Utica	.979	29	167	18	4	1	8
Robles, Jamestown	.972	7	32	3	1	0	4
Sherlock, Auburn	.965	56	312	46	13	7	11
Smith, Jamestown	.986	44	246	26	4	6	10
Vellegia, Newark	.991	53	383	36	4	5	8
Wilson, Little Falls	.967	30	193	15	7	5	5

Triple Play—Brunswick.

PITCHERS

Player and Club	Pct.	G.	PO.	A.	E.	DP.
Abril, Elmira	.947	15	6	12	1	1
G. Adams, Newark	1.000	12	1	12	0	0
R. Adams, Little Falls	.909	18	7	13	2	0
Adkins, Watertown	1.000	8	3	4	0	0
Andersh, Watertown*	1.000	8	1	3	0	0
Anderson, Niagara Falls	1.000	3	0	6	0	1
Andujar, Jamestown*	1.000	16	1	6	0	0
Azcona, Jamestown	1.000	7	2	5	0	1
Baez, Auburn	1.000	7	1	1	0	0
Balmer, Geneva	1.000	13	5	7	0	0
Barnes, Utica	1.000	16	4	6	0	1
Bear, Utica	1.000	28	1	12	0	1
Beasley, Batavia	.976	14	17	23	1	7
E. Bell, Newark*	1.000	15	6	21	0	1
G. Bell, Geneva*	1.000	19	5	11	0	0
Braukmiller, Jamestown	.917	11	6	16	2	0
Brewer, Geneva	.933	14	6	22	2	4
Bruno, Newark	1.000	1	1	0	0	0
Caldwell, Newark	1.000	27	2	5	0	0
Campbell, Niagara Falls	.889	20	1	7	1	1
Canseco, Oneonta	.769	14	4	6	3	0
Carlie, Watertown*	1.000	9	0	1	0	0
Carr, Niagara Falls	1.000	4	6	2	0	1
Cash, Auburn	.933	29	4	10	1	0
Chastain, Oneonta*	.923	15	1	11	1	1
Chesnoski, Auburn	.667	22	0	4	2	0
Ciszkowski, Little Falls	.833	10	1	4	1	0
Clark, Batavia*	.800	9	0	8	2	0
Collins, Jamestown	.818	8	4	5	2	0
Compres, 2 Bat.-6 Utica	1.000	8	2	5	0	0
Cooper, Utica	.833	16	5	15	4	0
Couisnard, Utica	.500	2	0	1	1	0
Crossley, Erie*	.667	11	0	2	1	0
Curry, Elmira	1.000	14	7	9	0	0
D'Agostino, Niagara Falls	1.000	12	3	7	0	1
Davidson, Oneonta	1.000	24	0	2	0	0
F. Davis, Oneonta*	1.000	3	0	1	0	0
J. Davis, Niagara Falls	.895	11	7	10	2	1
M. Davis, Little Falls	.909	38	2	8	1	1
DeLaTorre, Oneonta*	.750	17	0	6	2	0
Diez, Elmira*	1.000	14	0	3	0	0
DiFrancisco, 1 Bat.-4 Utica	.667	5	0	2	1	0
Dillenberger, Erie	.944	15	4	13	1	0
Doerr, Newark	.000	1	0	0	1	0
Dominico, Little Falls	1.000	27	7	10	0	0
Doorey, Jamestown*	.818	17	1	8	2	0
Dougherty, Oneonta	.933	22	5	9	1	0
Dunster, Auburn	1.000	15	6	12	0	0
Edge, Watertown	.833	19	6	4	2	0
Encarnacion, Batavia	.895	21	8	9	2	0
Ennis, Newark	1.000	18	1	5	0	0
Erickson, Jamestown*	1.000	12	0	4	0	1
Fabre, Watertown*	.667	8	2	2	2	0
Fansler, Watertown	.946	14	5	30	2	3
Fenn, Elmira	1.000	16	4	9	0	0
Fiepke, Watertown*	1.000	18	2	2	0	0
Finley, Utica	1.000	2	0	1	0	0
Franchi, Watertown*	.933	16	1	13	1	1
Gakeler, Elmira	1.000	14	6	23	0	1
Galloway, Batavia*	1.000	9	4	8	0	0
Garrick, Niagara Falls	.909	17	6	14	2	0
Gass, Erie	1.000	22	9	7	0	0
Gilmore, Niagara Falls	1.000	8	4	4	0	1
Giron, Utica	1.000	6	1	6	0	1
Gonzalez, Newark	1.000	5	0	4	0	0
Gozzo, Little Falls	.875	24	2	5	1	0
Greenleaf, Oneonta	1.000	24	3	13	0	0
Greenlee, Utica*	1.000	16	2	5	0	0
Greer, Batavia	.857	17	2	16	3	0
Haines, Jamestown	1.000	5	2	3	0	0
Hardee, Jamestown	.929	12	3	10	1	1
Harrison, Oneonta*	.926	16	5	20	2	0
Heise, Newark*	1.000	17	4	6	0	1
Heredia, Auburn	1.000	5	0	2	0	0
Hill, Erie*	1.000	16	1	16	0	2
Hines, Elmira	1.000	13	1	6	0	1
Hixon, Newark	.947	10	3	15	1	0
Hoag, Utica	.778	9	0	7	2	0
Howes, Little Falls	1.000	6	1	2	0	1
Huchingson, Auburn	.966	15	10	18	1	4
Hudson, Jamestown	.810	15	10	7	4	0
Humbert, Utica*	1.000	14	0	6	0	0
Jones, Watertown	.906	14	7	22	3	0
Kahler, Batavia	.867	16	4	9	2	0
Kavanaugh, Erie	1.000	7	0	9	0	1
King, Newark	.929	6	4	9	1	0
Kline, Newark	.000	5	0	0	1	0
Knight, Elmira	1.000	15	1	6	0	0
Leach, Batavia	.667	2	1	1	1	0
Leiter, Oneonta*	1.000	10	5	7	0	1
Lelievre, Batavia	1.000	4	0	2	0	0
Lind, Watertown	1.000	13	0	7	0	1
Livin, Auburn	.962	16	2	23	1	1
Magyari, Utica	.875	26	0	14	2	0
Mallicoat, Auburn*	1.000	1	0	1	0	0
Manzanillo, Elmira	.909	14	6	4	1	0
Mathews, Erie*	1.000	3	1	3	0	0
McCandlish, Geneva	1.000	7	1	3	0	0
McPherson, Erie	1.000	9	0	4	0	0
Meadows, Watertown	1.000	10	0	2	0	0
Meads, Watertown*	.833	10	0	5	1	0
Melchert, Utica*	.714	3	0	5	2	0
Melendez, Watertown	.875	15	4	10	2	0
Mercedes, Watertown	1.000	7	0	1	0	0
METTLER, Elmira	1.000	15	7	26	0	3
Mieses, Erie	.800	13	2	10	3	1
Moon, Erie	1.000	20	2	9	0	1
Mora, 6 Bat.-2 Utica	1.000	8	0	2	0	0
Moreland, Little Falls	.950	12	4	15	1	2
Morrow, Watertown	1.000	29	2	8	0	0
Moyer, Geneva*	.967	14	8	21	1	2
Ninneman, Geneva	1.000	15	4	6	0	0
Nossek, Niagara Falls*	.933	15	3	11	1	0
Ortiz, Utica	.800	14	1	3	1	0
Oswald, Niagara Falls*	.944	15	1	16	1	0
Pacheco, Jamestown	1.000	5	0	4	0	0
Parker, Auburn	1.000	13	1	2	0	0
Peck, Jamestown	.600	23	0	3	2	0
Phelps, Niagara Falls	.800	10	4	12	4	1
Phillips, 1 Bat.-11 Utica	.625	12	0	5	3	0
Pleis, Erie	1.000	3	0	1	0	0
Pries, Oneonta	.950	11	9	10	1	1
Rather, Oneonta	.800	13	3	5	2	1
Rebiejo, Oneonta	.900	6	1	8	1	3
Reed, Utica	.800	6	1	3	1	1
Reid, Geneva	.875	17	1	6	1	2
Renfroe, Geneva	.947	24	5	13	1	1
Robertson, Batavia	1.000	14	0	10	0	2
A. Rodriguez, Erie	.833	12	1	4	1	0
R. Rodriguez, Little Falls*	.765	25	1	12	4	1
Ruckebeil, Niagara Falls	.900	20	3	6	1	0
Russell, Watertown*	1.000	4	1	3	0	0
Sanderski, Elmira	1.000	7	2	7	0	1
Sarno, Oneonta	.909	18	5	5	1	0
Satzinger, Watertown	.846	14	3	8	2	1
Sharp, Batavia	.939	18	7	24	2	3
Shellnut, Utica	1.000	11	2	3	0	0
Simmons, Niagara Falls	.944	8	4	13	1	2
Skinner, Newark	.889	11	3	13	2	2
Slifko, Elmira	1.000	19	2	13	0	0
Slocumb, Little Falls	1.000	4	0	1	0	0
Slowik, Geneva	1.000	21	2	8	0	0
Smith, Newark	1.000	13	1	6	0	0
Snyder, Batavia	1.000	3	2	6	0	0
Spazante, Auburn	1.000	15	4	9	0	0
Spear, Geneva*	.826	15	3	16	4	1
Stephenson, Batavia	1.000	14	2	5	0	0
Stephenson, Elmira*	1.000	12	0	2	0	0
Stiles, Little Falls	1.000	3	1	0	0	0
Tamarez, Batavia*	1.000	24	0	8	0	0
Tarasovitch, Erie	.500	7	1	0	1	0
Tindall, Jamestown*	.917	14	6	16	2	0
Tuller, Geneva	.923	14	3	9	1	0
Ullian, Auburn*	.857	15	4	14	3	1
Valdez, Jamestown	.923	13	9	15	2	1
Van Houten, Erie	1.000	21	1	4	0	0
Wanzer, Niagara Falls	.864	14	7	12	3	1
West, Little Falls*	.889	13	0	8	1	0
Whalen, Newark	1.000	2	0	1	0	0
Whitaker, Erie*	.938	15	5	10	1	2
White, Niagara Falls	1.000	1	0	1	0	0
Wilmore, Auburn	1.000	21	0	3	0	0
R. Wilson, Newark*	.778	13	0	14	4	1
W. Wilson, Newark	.778	9	3	4	2	0
Wirth, Newark	1.000	6	1	2	0	0
Woellert, Little Falls*	.900	18	3	6	1	0
Young, Little Falls	.944	18	6	11	1	0

The following players had no recorded accepted chances at the positions indicated; therefore, are not listed in the fielding averages for those particular positions: Billinger, p; Bruno, ss; Campbell, c; Concepcion, p; Daddario, ss; Feliciano, p; Fitzpatrick, p; Friedel, p; L. Graham, of; M. Graham, p; Hayes, p; Holtz, p; Howard, 3b; Jenkins, p; Li. Johnson, of; Kavanaugh, 1b; Lane, ss; Mahnken, p; Meyer, 3b; McMahan, 2b; Mickan, of; Moritz, 2b; Murray, of, c; Ott, p; Paparella, ss; Paul, 3b; Pleis, 2b; Reyes, of; Rooney, p; Santana, 1b; D.L. Smith, 3b; Stinnett, p; Sullivan, of; Tyson, 1b; Washington, p; Whitmyer, p; Williams, ss; R. Wilson, of.

CLUB PITCHING

Club	ERA.	G.	CG.	ShO.	Sv.	IP.	H.	R.	ER.	HR.	HB.	BB.	Int. BB.	SO.	WP.	Bk.
Geneva	3.22	74	12	8	21	647.2	558	305	232	48	27	254	28	570	46	8
Niagara Falls	3.42	75	17	5	7	650.2	621	341	247	40	32	248	17	489	36	7
Watertown	3.44	74	10	9	16	635.1	516	314	243	28	35	348	11	546	67	9
Little Falls	3.47	75	6	4	26	648.0	533	324	250	43	19	375	24	528	63	7
Jamestown	3.48	74	22	6	9	631.2	621	326	244	41	20	237	6	440	35	8
Newark	3.66	74	17	9	15	637.0	610	332	259	32	13	305	23	534	64	5
Oneonta	3.72	74	4	4	16	636.2	611	358	263	29	24	306	10	556	42	13
Auburn	3.85	76	7	4	23	636.1	660	338	272	50	20	232	6	472	59	3
Elmira	4.04	73	8	7	12	626.0	564	358	281	44	24	355	23	469	51	6
Batavia	4.26	76	13	5	9	659.1	629	406	312	59	30	357	17	513	56	7
Erie	4.28	74	11	2	16	646.1	658	378	307	68	18	294	7	423	45	10
Utica	5.60	75	5	1	9	617.2	696	495	384	72	21	379	15	469	55	8

PITCHERS' RECORDS
(Leading Qualifiers for Earned-Run Average Leadership — 61 or More Innings)

✩Throws lefthanded.

Pitcher—Club	W.	L.	Pct.	ERA.	G.	GS.	CG.	GF.	ShO.	Sv.	IP.	H.	R.	ER.	HR.	HB.	BB.	Int. BB.	SO.	WP.
Simmons, Niagara Falls	7	1	.875	1.29	8	8	7	0	3	0	70.0	54	14	10	2	1	12	0	53	1
Hudson, Jamestown	6	7	.462	1.72	15	11	7	3	2	0	94.1	86	35	18	7	1	19	0	58	5
G. Bell, Geneva✩	7	1	.875	1.73	19	9	2	7	0	2	78.0	45	15	15	4	3	29	3	81	2
Moyer, Geneva✩	9	3	.750	1.89	14	14	5	0	2	0	104.2	99	27	22	5	5	31	0	120	7
Mettler, Elmira	9	4	.692	1.90	15	15	4	0	2	0	104.0	94	30	22	4	2	36	5	89	9
Braukmiller, Jamestown	5	3	.625	1.95	11	10	4	1	1	1	69.1	61	21	15	2	1	21	1	50	6
Fansler, Watertown	5	1	.833	2.01	14	14	4	0	2	0	98.2	68	32	22	4	6	38	0	78	5
Skinner, Newark	7	2	.778	2.04	11	11	7	0	2	0	79.1	65	25	18	1	0	25	0	55	4
J. Davis, Niagara Falls	3	4	.429	2.35	11	11	2	0	1	0	69.0	57	35	18	1	1	37	0	72	4
Brewer, Geneva	7	2	.778	2.36	14	14	3	0	1	0	91.2	75	30	24	4	4	21	1	71	5

Departmental Leaders: G—M. Davis, 38; W—Bear, Caldwell, Mettler, Moyer, 9; L—Cooper, 9; Pct.—Caldwell, .900; GS—R. Adams, Greer, 16; CG—Hudson, Simmons, Skinner, 7; GF—M. Davis, 36; ShO—Simmons, 3; Sv.—M. Davis, 22; IP—Moyer, 104.2; H—Ullian, 106; R—Greer, 63; ER—Cooper, 49; HR—Beasley, Hill, Kahler, Magyari, 11; HB—Greer, 10; BB—Barnes, 63; IBB—R. Rodriguez, Slowik, 7; SO—Moyer, 120; WP—West, 16.

(All Pitchers—Listed Alphabetically)

Pitcher—Club	W.	L.	Pct.	ERA.	G.	GS.	CG.	GF.	ShO.	Sv.	IP.	H.	R.	ER.	HR.	HB.	BB.	Int. BB.	SO.	WP.
Abril, Elmira	3	6	.333	4.08	15	10	0	3	0	1	68.1	58	39	31	3	1	41	1	63	4
G. Adams, Newark	3	6	.333	5.19	12	12	0	0	0	0	60.2	63	38	35	2	2	38	1	26	3
R. Adams, Little Falls	7	4	.636	2.49	18	16	3	1	0	0	101.1	89	38	28	6	2	40	1	56	2
Adkins, Watertown	3	0	1.000	4.50	8	0	0	3	0	0	18.0	10	9	9	1	1	10	0	13	3
Anderson, Watertown✩	3	3	.500	3.75	8	7	0	1	0	0	36.0	27	18	15	1	1	18	0	36	3
Anderson, Niagara Falls	1	0	1.000	2.75	3	3	0	0	0	0	19.2	18	9	6	1	0	5	0	24	4
Andujar, Jamestown✩	2	2	.500	3.48	16	0	0	9	0	2	33.2	37	23	13	5	0	17	1	26	4
Azcona, Jamestown	0	2	.000	12.00	7	2	0	1	0	0	12.0	13	18	16	2	3	14	0	15	0
Baez, Auburn	0	1	.000	4.05	7	0	0	4	0	0	13.1	13	7	6	1	0	6	0	10	2
Balmer, Geneva	2	4	.333	4.73	13	6	0	3	0	0	51.1	55	39	27	7	1	24	3	43	7
Barnes, Utica	1	6	.143	6.30	16	11	1	5	0	2	50.0	36	42	35	4	7	63	1	49	6
Bear, Utica	9	2	.818	3.49	28	0	0	22	0	5	49.0	52	25	19	1	0	12	1	52	3
Beasley, Batavia	6	5	.545	4.01	14	13	4	0	1	0	89.2	97	54	40	11	1	33	2	70	8
E. Bell, Newark✩	8	3	.727	2.46	15	15	4	0	1	0	102.1	82	40	28	6	2	26	0	114	8
G. Bell, Geneva✩	7	1	.875	1.73	19	9	2	7	0	2	78.0	45	15	15	4	3	29	3	81	2
Billinger, Erie	0	0	.000	36.00	1	0	0	1	0	0	1.0	4	4	4	1	0	1	0	0	1
Braukmiller, Jamestown	5	3	.625	1.95	11	10	4	1	1	1	69.1	61	21	15	2	1	21	1	50	6
Brewer, Geneva	7	2	.778	2.36	14	14	3	0	1	0	91.2	75	30	24	4	4	21	1	71	5
Bruno, Newark	0	0	.000	27.00	1	0	0	0	0	0	1.0	3	3	3	1	0	2	0	0	1
Caldwell, Newark	9	1	.900	0.64	27	0	0	25	0	11	42.0	34	8	3	0	0	17	6	52	4
Campbell, Niagara Falls	3	5	.375	4.58	20	0	0	18	0	3	37.1	41	27	19	2	1	16	4	39	1
Canseco, Oneonta	1	6	.143	3.53	14	4	1	4	1	0	43.1	44	29	17	1	3	21	2	40	5
Carlie, Watertown✩	0	0	.000	3.75	9	0	0	4	0	0	12.0	7	5	5	1	0	8	0	12	5
Carr, Niagara Falls	2	0	1.000	1.57	4	4	0	0	0	0	23.0	19	6	4	0	0	6	0	19	1
Cash, Auburn	2	1	.667	1.65	29	0	0	24	0	15	43.2	30	12	8	1	1	13	0	34	5
Chastain, Oneonta✩	4	4	.500	4.70	15	13	1	2	0	0	67.0	75	41	35	7	5	30	1	45	4
Chesnoski, Auburn	1	1	.500	7.04	22	2	0	10	0	4	47.1	63	45	37	7	1	26	2	42	10
Ciszkowski, Little Falls	3	2	.600	3.33	10	9	0	0	0	0	46.0	37	19	17	3	6	24	0	33	3
Clark, Batavia✩	1	1	.500	7.23	9	3	0	2	0	0	23.2	30	22	19	3	1	24	0	23	3
Collins, Jamestown	1	6	.143	7.28	8	8	0	0	0	0	47.0	57	39	38	8	1	18	0	34	2
Compres, 2 Bat.-6 Utica	2	2	.500	6.97	8	6	1	0	0	0	31.0	35	29	24	8	0	25	0	18	5
Concepcion, Newark	0	0	.000	12.00	3	0	0	1	0	0	3.0	3	4	4	0	1	7	0	4	4
Cooper, Oneonta	2	9	.182	5.54	16	12	2	3	0	1	79.2	81	57	49	9	5	36	1	50	2
Couisnard, Utica	0	0	.000	3.00	2	0	1	0	0	0	6.0	8	2	2	1	0	1	0	1	0
Crossley, Erie✩	4	2	.667	5.02	11	11	1	0	0	0	57.1	66	39	32	7	3	26	0	50	0
Curry, Elmira	6	4	.600	4.00	14	14	3	0	0	0	83.1	83	51	37	6	1	35	4	82	6
D'Agostino, Niagara Falls	3	3	.500	3.83	12	8	1	2	0	1	47.0	29	24	20	1	9	31	1	41	4
Davidson, Niagara Falls	2	5	.286	3.45	24	0	0	19	0	10	28.2	27	18	11	1	4	11	3	26	3
F. Davis, Oneonta✩	0	1	.000	0.00	3	0	0	1	0	0	1.2	7	5	0	0	0	0	0	3	0
J. Davis, Niagara Falls	3	4	.429	2.35	11	11	2	0	1	0	69.0	57	35	18	1	1	37	0	72	4
M. Davis, Little Falls	3	2	.600	2.54	38	0	0	36	0	22	60.1	39	18	17	6	2	18	3	54	1
DeLaTorre, Oneonta✩	0	3	.000	7.13	17	0	0	7	0	3	35.1	44	33	28	3	2	17	0	32	2
Diez, Elmira✩	1	4	.200	7.04	14	8	0	2	0	0	46.0	45	42	36	8	1	42	1	22	3
DiFrancisco, 1 Bat.-4 Utica	2	0	1.000	2.76	5	1	1	3	0	0	16.1	17	5	5	1	0	9	0	14	1
Dillenberger, Erie	3	6	.333	4.97	15	6	1	2	0	1	63.1	68	44	35	8	2	35	0	42	10
Doerr, Newark	0	0	.000	45.00	1	0	0	0	0	0	1.0	3	5	5	0	0	3	0	1	1
Dominico, Little Falls	3	4	.429	2.00	27	0	0	9	0	4	54.0	44	25	12	2	2	37	6	42	13
Doorey, Jamestown✩	1	2	.333	2.94	17	3	0	2	0	0	33.2	32	17	11	4	0	11	1	32	3
Dougherty, Oneonta	5	2	.714	2.86	22	3	0	9	0	1	56.2	54	19	18	4	1	23	1	64	1
Dunster, Auburn	5	7	.417	3.28	15	15	2	0	1	0	90.2	84	38	33	5	8	28	1	55	6
Edge, Watertown✩	1	1	.500	1.97	19	0	0	8	0	2	32.0	22	8	7	0	3	9	2	38	1
Encarnacion, Batavia	5	2	.714	3.12	21	1	0	17	0	6	60.2	48	25	21	7	3	33	2	65	1
Ennis, Newark	2	0	1.000	2.72	18	0	0	6	0	1	36.1	47	17	11	1	1	13	1	19	7

Pitcher—Club	W.	L.	Pct.	ERA	G.	GS	CG	GF	ShO	Sv.	IP	H.	R.	ER.	HR.	HB	BB.	Int. BB.	SO.	WP.
Erickson, Jamestown*	1	3	.250	3.86	12	4	1	4	0	1	39.2	48	23	17	0	0	17	0	18	2
Fabre, Watertown	0	0	.000	9.31	8	0	0	2	0	0	9.2	19	13	10	1	1	11	1	5	4
Fansler, Watertown	5	1	.833	2.01	14	14	4	0	2	0	98.2	68	32	22	4	6	38	0	78	5
Feliciano, Batavia	0	0	.000	2.25	3	0	0	2	0	0	4.0	3	1	1	0	0	7	0	1	0
Fenn, Elmira	2	3	.400	3.28	16	3	0	10	0	2	49.1	39	24	18	4	0	36	2	35	3
Fiepke, Watertown*	8	2	.800	1.38	18	1	1	12	1	2	32.2	14	7	5	0	1	15	1	46	3
Finley, Utica	0	0	.000	6.75	2	0	0	2	0	0	4.0	6	3	3	0	0	4	1	2	0
Fitzpatrick, Newark	0	1	.000	5.06	3	0	0	0	0	0	5.1	9	3	3	0	0	5	1	5	0
Franchi, Watertown*	2	4	.333	4.91	16	7	0	0	0	0	47.2	42	35	26	2	4	39	1	40	4
Friedel, Little Falls	1	1	.500	5.19	5	1	0	0	0	0	8.2	9	8	5	0	0	9	1	10	0
Gakeler, Elmira	4	6	.400	4.11	14	13	0	1	0	0	76.2	67	47	35	9	7	41	3	54	2
Galloway, Batavia*	3	2	.600	3.09	9	6	1	2	1	0	46.2	42	24	16	2	1	25	1	38	1
Garrick, Niagara Falls	3	4	.429	3.47	17	6	1	7	0	0	62.1	62	31	24	4	2	24	5	45	2
Gass, Erie	7	6	.538	3.72	22	7	3	12	0	3	87.0	81	46	36	6	1	30	2	69	3
Gilmore, Niagara Falls	0	2	.000	6.62	8	2	0	3	0	0	17.2	23	15	13	1	3	11	0	16	0
Giron, Utica	1	3	.250	8.84	6	4	0	2	0	0	19.1	34	21	19	6	1	8	0	9	5
Gonzalez, Newark	2	0	1.000	5.19	5	1	0	1	0	1	17.1	17	10	10	3	1	12	1	13	2
Gozzo, Little Falls	4	3	.571	5.63	24	0	0	8	0	2	38.1	40	27	24	3	0	28	4	30	7
Graham, Elmira	0	0	.000	33.75	1	0	0	0	0	0	1.1	0	5	5	0	0	5	0	0	2
Greenleaf, Oneonta	1	3	.250	3.86	24	1	0	10	0	1	46.2	49	27	20	1	1	16	1	34	2
Greenlee, Utica*	3	2	.600	5.65	16	6	0	1	0	0	51.0	50	43	32	7	1	39	1	53	8
Greer, Batavia	4	7	.364	5.93	17	16	1	0	0	0	68.1	63	63	45	3	10	47	0	57	7
Haines, Jamestown	2	3	.400	3.96	5	5	0	0	0	0	25.0	22	15	11	2	1	12	0	10	0
Hardee, Jamestown	3	4	.429	2.08	12	6	1	6	0	2	56.1	38	17	13	2	6	19	1	35	2
Harrison, Oneonta*	4	6	.400	3.05	16	14	1	1	1	0	91.1	83	45	31	4	2	31	0	62	6
Hayes, Newark*	0	0	.000	0.00	1	0	0	1	0	0	0.1	0	0	0	0	0	2	0	0	0
Heise, Newark*	2	3	.400	2.76	17	0	0	8	0	3	32.2	22	11	10	3	0	11	4	34	3
Heredia, Auburn	1	2	.333	6.00	5	4	0	1	0	0	18.0	22	13	12	1	0	16	0	10	6
Hill, Erie*	7	1	.875	3.59	16	13	2	2	1	0	85.1	89	37	34	11	1	19	1	52	3
Hines, Elmira	2	0	1.000	1.15	13	0	0	11	0	4	31.1	16	5	4	2	1	9	0	18	1
Hixon, Newark	6	3	.667	3.39	10	10	4	0	1	0	69.0	70	26	26	1	1	23	2	48	1
Hoag, Utica	2	4	.333	6.21	9	8	0	1	0	0	42.0	58	39	29	3	0	22	3	23	4
Holtz, Newark	0	0	.000	0.00	1	0	0	0	0	0	1.0	1	0	0	0	0	0	0	1	0
Howes, Little Falls	0	0	.000	7.20	6	0	0	2	0	0	5.0	6	8	4	1	1	4	0	1	3
Huchingson, Auburn	6	6	.500	3.99	15	13	2	2	0	1	90.1	103	49	40	7	1	22	1	48	2
Hudson, Jamestown	6	7	.462	1.72	15	11	7	3	2	0	94.1	86	35	18	7	1	19	0	58	5
Humbert, Utica*	2	2	.500	5.01	14	6	0	6	0	0	50.1	57	40	28	5	1	23	0	38	2
Jenkins, Batavia	0	0	.000	0.00	1	0	0	0	0	0	1.0	0	0	0	0	0	0	0	2	0
Jones, Watertown	6	3	.667	3.43	14	14	2	0	1	0	86.2	75	41	33	4	4	49	0	61	8
Kahler, Batavia	6	4	.600	3.24	16	11	3	4	1	0	86.0	70	41	31	11	6	33	2	44	8
Kavanaugh, Erie	3	0	1.000	1.04	7	2	0	2	0	0	26.0	19	3	3	1	1	22	0	12	2
King, Newark	1	2	.333	5.72	6	5	0	0	0	0	28.1	31	25	18	2	2	19	0	16	3
Kline, Newark	2	2	.000	10.45	5	5	0	0	0	0	10.1	18	19	12	1	0	9	0	11	7
Knight, Elmira	0	4	.000	8.10	15	4	0	6	0	1	36.2	41	42	33	1	3	43	2	18	7
Leach, Batavia	0	1	.000	1.42	2	0	0	1	0	0	6.1	2	2	1	0	0	2	0	7	0
Leiter, Oneonta*	3	2	.600	3.63	10	10	0	0	0	0	57.0	52	32	23	1	2	26	0	48	5
Lelievre, Batavia	0	0	.000	6.75	4	0	0	3	0	0	5.1	3	4	4	1	1	4	0	4	0
Lind, Watertown	1	1	.500	2.18	13	1	0	5	0	1	33.0	34	11	8	0	2	11	0	29	3
Livin, Auburn	5	7	.417	3.34	16	15	2	0	0	0	89.0	96	49	33	7	3	19	0	76	5
Magyari, Utica	1	3	.250	6.60	26	4	0	12	0	0	61.1	90	62	45	11	2	30	1	40	4
Mahnken, Utica	0	0	.000	0.00	1	0	0	1	0	0	1.0	1	0	0	0	0	2	0	1	0
Mallicoat, Auburn*	0	0	.000	5.40	1	1	0	0	0	0	5.0	8	3	3	1	0	3	0	6	2
Manzanillo, Elmira	2	3	.400	5.26	14	0	0	7	0	1	25.2	27	24	15	1	1	26	1	15	9
Mathews, Erie*	0	1	.000	9.00	3	3	0	0	0	0	15.0	16	15	15	5	1	8	1	9	1
McCandlish, Geneva	0	1	.000	10.80	7	1	0	5	0	0	15.0	18	23	18	1	1	20	1	9	2
McPherson, Erie	1	2	.333	7.61	9	3	0	1	0	0	23.2	26	25	20	4	0	17	0	11	1
Meadows, Watertown	0	1	.000	2.95	10	0	0	4	0	2	18.1	15	7	6	0	2	7	1	11	1
Meads, Auburn*	5	1	.833	5.14	10	3	0	1	0	0	28.0	31	17	16	4	0	12	1	29	3
Melchert, Utica*	2	0	1.000	2.18	3	3	0	0	0	0	20.2	17	11	5	1	0	13	0	20	1
Melendez, Watertown	5	7	.417	2.77	15	15	3	0	1	0	91.0	61	37	28	6	6	40	0	68	4
Mercedes, Watertown	0	1	.000	7.36	7	0	0	4	0	2	7.1	7	6	6	2	0	9	1	6	2
Mettler, Elmira	9	4	.692	1.90	15	15	4	0	2	0	104.0	94	30	22	4	2	36	5	89	9
Mieses, Erie	3	3	.500	4.88	13	5	1	6	0	0	51.2	54	31	28	6	3	15	0	23	1
Moon, Erie	3	0	1.000	4.60	20	3	0	9	0	1	43.0	42	26	22	5	2	24	0	26	5
Mora, 6 Bat.-2 Utica	1	2	.333	7.97	8	1	0	2	0	0	20.1	25	19	18	5	2	15	0	15	4
Moreland, Little Falls	5	3	.625	3.66	12	10	0	0	0	0	66.1	55	31	27	7	0	17	0	45	0
Morrow, Watertown	2	4	.333	3.93	29	0	0	19	0	6	55.0	41	29	24	4	0	26	4	62	9
Moyer, Geneva*	9	3	.750	1.89	14	14	5	0	2	0	104.2	59	27	22	5	5	31	0	120	7
Ninneman, Geneva	1	3	.250	4.33	15	4	0	3	0	2	54.0	58	30	26	4	1	16	1	41	4
Nossek, Niagara Falls*	1	1	.500	3.26	15	1	1	10	0	2	38.2	37	23	14	4	5	17	2	30	3
Ortiz, Utica	1	0	1.000	8.22	14	0	0	5	0	1	38.1	59	44	35	5	1	17	1	24	7
Oswald, Niagara Falls*	4	3	.571	2.68	15	11	2	2	0	0	84.0	67	30	25	7	1	25	0	53	4
Ott, Oneonta	0	0	.000	3.86	2	0	0	0	0	0	2.1	6	1	1	0	0	3	0	0	0
Pacheco, Jamestown	0	0	.000	2.35	5	0	0	2	0	0	7.2	8	2	2	0	0	6	0	4	0
Parker, Auburn	3	1	.750	2.70	13	3	0	7	0	1	30.0	24	14	9	3	0	14	1	29	2
Peck, Jamestown	1	4	.200	2.54	23	0	0	17	0	3	46.0	39	18	13	3	1	19	2	42	3
Phelps, Niagara Falls	2	6	.250	4.38	10	9	1	1	0	0	63.2	80	43	31	4	2	21	0	38	2
Phillips, 1 Bat.-11 Utica	0	4	.000	9.10	12	5	0	3	0	0	29.2	26	41	30	2	2	46	2	26	5
Pleis, Erie	1	1	.500	6.35	3	0	0	2	0	0	5.2	5	4	4	1	0	4	0	6	0
Pries, Oneonta	3	4	.429	2.48	11	11	0	0	0	0	65.1	50	26	18	2	1	27	0	41	3
Rather, Oneonta	0	4	.000	5.92	13	5	0	5	0	0	38.0	34	29	25	1	1	35	1	59	4
Rebiejo, Oneonta	1	1	.500	2.29	6	6	0	0	0	0	35.1	27	12	9	0	1	21	0	40	3
Reed, Utica	0	2	.000	5.40	6	5	0	0	0	0	25.0	34	19	15	4	0	15	0	15	0
Reid, Geneva	0	6	.000	4.15	17	5	0	10	0	0	47.2	45	32	22	8	0	26	1	37	2
Renfroe, Geneva	3	3	.500	1.38	24	0	0	18	0	10	39.0	34	10	6	1	3	10	5	33	1
Robertson, Jamestown	1	2	.333	5.33	14	10	0	2	0	0	54.0	56	36	32	5	1	29	0	39	4
A. Rodriguez, Erie	3	1	.750	3.98	12	8	0	1	0	0	40.2	37	28	18	3	1	33	0	28	7
R. Rodriguez, Little Falls*	2	1	.667	2.80	25	1	0	6	0	0	35.1	28	21	11	0	1	36	7	27	3
Rooney, Newark*	0	0	.000	13.50	5	0	0	0	0	0	8.2	12	13	13	2	1	11	0	8	1
Ruckebeil, Niagara Falls	4	4	.500	5.16	20	1	0	12	0	1	45.1	46	34	26	5	3	23	2	29	4
Russell, Watertown*	1	0	1.000	0.00	4	1	0	2	0	1	9.1	7	0	0	0	0	4	0	10	0
Sanderski, Elmira	1	1	.500	2.66	7	5	0	2	0	0	23.2	17	8	7	1	0	11	0	14	2

Pitcher—Club	W.	L.	Pct.	ERA.	G.	GS.	CG.	GF.	ShO.	Sv.	IP.	H.	R.	ER.	HR.	HB.	BB.	Int. BB.	SO.	WP.
Sarno, Oneonta	4	3	.571	3.00	18	7	1	5	0	0	57.0	48	32	19	3	1	39	1	46	3
Satzinger, Watertown	2	7	.222	7.50	14	14	0	0	0	0	48.0	57	55	40	2	4	54	0	31	12
Sharp, Batavia	5	4	.556	3.21	18	10	3	5	0	0	89.2	91	44	32	3	3	53	3	53	12
Shellnut, Utica	2	4	.333	3.72	11	3	0	4	0	0	38.2	33	18	16	4	0	25	3	29	4
Simmons, Niagara Falls	7	1	.875	1.29	8	8	7	0	3	0	70.0	54	14	10	2	1	12	0	53	1
Skinner, Newark	7	2	.778	2.04	11	11	7	0	2	0	79.1	65	25	18	1	0	25	0	55	4
Slifko, Elmira	5	2	.714	2.51	19	1	1	15	1	3	57.1	44	19	16	3	4	17	3	44	1
Slocumb, Little Falls	0	0	.000	11.00	4	1	0	0	0	0	9.0	8	11	11	0	1	16	0	10	4
Slowik, Geneva	1	3	.250	3.26	21	0	0	13	0	7	38.2	37	21	14	5	2	16	7	29	4
Smith, Newark	1	0	1.000	5.48	13	0	0	5	0	0	23.0	33	21	14	2	0	9	4	15	1
Snyder, Batavia	0	2	.000	4.05	3	3	0	0	0	0	13.1	21	12	6	1	0	5	0	9	0
Spazante, Auburn	2	4	.333	3.14	15	6	1	7	0	2	57.1	57	26	20	7	4	16	0	47	7
Spear, Geneva*	5	3	.625	2.86	15	7	1	3	0	6	66.0	57	28	21	7	2	25	4	54	5
Stephenson, Batavia	6	0	1.000	1.85	14	0	0	11	0	3	34.0	22	10	7	1	1	6	1	32	1
Stephenson, Elmira*	0	1	.000	8.87	12	0	0	8	0	0	22.1	33	22	22	2	3	13	1	15	2
Stiles, Little Falls	0	0	.000	0.00	3	0	0	2	0	2	6.0	4	1	0	0	0	0	0	10	1
Stinnett, Oneonta	1	1	.500	6.55	10	0	0	7	0	0	11.0	11	9	8	1	0	6	0	16	1
Tamarez, Batavia*	4	4	.500	3.83	24	3	1	9	0	0	49.1	44	27	21	5	1	19	5	48	3
Tarasovitch, Erie	0	1	.000	3.32	7	0	0	6	0	2	21.2	18	10	8	2	1	10	2	15	3
Tindall, Jamestown*	4	3	.571	4.25	14	14	2	0	0	0	91.0	102	51	43	3	5	31	0	70	4
Tuller, Geneva	3	7	.300	5.40	14	14	1	0	1	0	61.2	75	50	37	2	5	36	2	52	7
Ullian, Auburn*	6	6	.500	3.91	15	14	0	0	0	0	89.2	106	45	39	4	0	28	0	65	5
Valdez, Jamestown	2	7	.222	4.03	13	12	5	1	1	0	76.0	78	47	34	3	1	33	0	46	4
Van Houten, Erie	2	2	.500	2.65	21	2	0	18	0	8	37.1	29	13	11	2	1	15	1	31	3
Wanzer, Niagara Falls	2	7	.222	4.42	14	11	2	3	0	0	71.1	85	47	35	8	4	18	3	28	5
Washington, Utica	0	0	.000	0.00	1	0	0	0	0	0	1.0	1	0	0	0	0	1	0	0	1
West, Little Falls*	6	4	.600	3.34	13	11	0	1	0	0	62.0	43	35	23	1	1	62	0	79	16
Whalen, Newark	0	2	.000	5.63	2	2	0	0	0	0	8.0	11	9	5	2	1	4	0	7	0
Whitaker, Erie*	6	5	.545	3.80	15	11	3	1	0	1	87.2	104	53	37	6	1	35	0	49	6
White, Niagara Falls	0	0	.000	10.80	1	0	0	0	0	0	1.2	3	3	2	0	0	2	0	2	1
Whitmyer, Batavia	0	0	.000	10.45	4	0	0	1	0	0	10.1	13	16	12	1	0	10	0	11	1
Wilmore, Auburn	2	1	.667	4.24	21	0	0	13	0	0	34.0	23	20	16	2	2	29	0	21	4
R. Wilson, Newark*	3	1	.750	2.37	13	5	2	4	1	0	57.0	45	25	15	1	0	27	2	69	7
W. Wilson, Newark	2	1	.667	4.53	9	8	0	1	0	0	43.2	34	24	22	2	1	38	0	28	4
Wirth, Newark	0	1	.000	8.10	6	0	0	4	0	0	6.2	7	6	6	2	0	4	1	8	3
Woellert, Batavia	6	2	.750	4.30	18	11	1	2	0	0	69.0	61	35	33	7	1	37	1	49	5
Young, Little Falls*	4	5	.444	3.95	18	15	2	2	1	0	86.2	70	47	38	7	2	47	1	82	5

BALKS—Canseco, 4; Humbert, 3; Barnes, Bear, Brewer, Ciszkowski, Dougherty, Gakeler, Greer, Heise, Huchingson, Hudson, Melendez, Pries, Reid, Satzinger, West, Whitaker, Woellert, 2 each; G. Adams, Anderson, Beasley, E. Bell, G. Bell, Braukmiller, Carr, Cash, Chastain, Clark, Compres, Crossley, Curry, D'Agostino, DeLaTorre, Erickson, Fabre, Fenn, Fiepke, Galloway, Garrick, Gass, Gozzo, Greenleaf, Haines, Hardee, Harrison, Hill, Jones, Knight, Leiter, Lind, Mathews, McCandlish, McPherson, Meadows, Mieses, Moon, Moyer, Ninneman, Oswald, Phelps, Phillips, Sharp, Skinner, Slifko, Tindall, Valdez, Van Houten, Wanzer, 1 each.

COMBINATION SHUTOUTS—Ullian-Cash, Livin-Cash, Parker-Spazante, Auburn; Greer-Stephenson, Robertson-Encarnacion, Batavia; Mettler-Slifko, Sanderski-Slifko, Curry-Slifko, Gakeler-Hines, Elmira; Whitaker-Van Houten, Erie; Spear-Renfroe, Bell-Slowik, Bell-Renfroe, Moyer-Renfroe, Geneva; Hardee-Andujar, Braukmiller-Andujar, Jamestown; Young-Davis, Woellert-Davis, Adams-Davis, Little Falls; Adams-Caldwell, Bell-Heise, Wilson-Caldwell, Adams-Ennis, Newark; Davis-Oswald, Niagara Falls; Pries-Greenleaf, Pries-Sarno-Davidson, Oneonta; Barnes-Humbert-Bear, Utica; Andersh-Morrow, Fansler-Lind, Melendez-Edge, Melendez-Meadows, Watertown.

NO-HIT GAME—None.

Northwest League

CLASS A

CHAMPIONSHIP WINNERS IN PREVIOUS YEARS

1901—Portland .675	1942—Vancouver .594	1965—Lewiston .667
1902—Butte .608	1943-45—Did not operate.	Tri-City* .681
1903—Butte .578	1946—Wenatchee .622	1966—Tri-City .679
1904—Boise .625	1947—Vancouver .566	1967—Medford .607
1905—Vancouver .586	1948—Spokane .614	1968—Tri-City .600
Everett* .667	1949—Yakima .660	1969—Rogue Valley .633
1906—Tacoma .600	Vancouver (2nd)† .615	1970—Lewiston a .538
1907—Aberdeen .625	1950—Yakima .613	Coos Bay-No. Bend .563
1908—Vancouver .578	1951—Spokane .655	1971—Tri-City a .625
1909—Seattle .653	1952—Victoria .631	Bend .538
1910—Spokane .596	1953—Salem .635	1972—Lewiston a .675
1911—Vancouver .628	Spokane* .590	Walla Walla .513
1912—Seattle .600	1954—Vancouver* .636	1973—Walla Walla b .638
1913—Vancouver .600	Lewiston .629	Portland .563
1914—Vancouver .632	1955—Salem .646	1974—Bellingham .619
1915—Seattle .564	Eugene* .639	Eugene c .571
1916—Spokane .622	1956—Yakima .691	1975—Portland .545
1917—Great Falls .592	Yakima .619	Eugene d .684
1918—Seattle .588	1957—Eugene .576	1976—Portland .556
1919—Seattle .590	Wenatchee* .647	Walla Walla d .639
1920—Victoria .600	1958—Lewiston .621	1977—Bellingham e .618
1921—Yakima .710	Yakima* .594	Portland .667
Yakima .660	1959—Salem .623	1978—Grays Harbor f .671
1922—Calgary† .600	Yakima* .563	Eugene .514
1923-36—Did not operate.	1960—Yakima .638	1979—Central Oregon d .606
1937—Wenatchee .603	Yakima .562	Walla Walla .571
Tacoma* .627	1961—Lewiston* .621	1980—Bellingham g .643
1938—Yakima .583	Yakima .600	Eugene g .529
Bellingham (2nd)† .511	1962—Wenatchee* .574	1981—Medford d .600
1939—Wenatchee .601	Tri-City .580	Bellingham .557
Tacoma (2nd)† .533	1963—Lewiston .594	1982—Medford .757
1940—Spokane .587	Yakima* .613	Salem d .486
Tacoma (4th)† .500	1964—Eugene .636	1983—Medford h .735
1941—Spokane .669	Yakima* .611	Bellingham .588

*Won split-season playoff. †Won four-club playoff. §League disbanded June 18. aLeague divided into Northern and Southern divisions, declared champion under league rules. bLeague divided into Eastern and Western divisions, declared champion under league rules. cLeague divided into Eastern and Western divisions; won two-team playoff. dLeague divided into Northern and Southern divisions; won two-team playoff. eLeague divided into Affiliate and Independent divisions; won two-team playoff. fDeclared league champion after winning one-game playoff. Balance of playoff canceled due to rain and wet grounds. gDeclared co-champion after winning one game. Balance of playoff canceled due to rain and wet grounds. hLeague divided into Washington and Oregon divisions; won two-team playoff. (NOTE—Known as Pacific Northwest League 1901-02, Pacific National League 1903-04, Northwestern League 1905-18, Pacific Coast International League 1919-22 and Western International League 1937-54.)

STANDING OF CLUBS AT CLOSE OF SEASON, SEPTEMBER 2
WASHINGTON DIVISION

Club	T.C.	Bell.	Ev.	Spo.	Med.	Bend	Sal.	Eug.	W.	L.	T.	Pct.	G.B.
Tri-Cities (Rangers)	....	9	10	8	5	2	6	6	46	28	0	.622	....
Bellingham (Mariners)	6	....	11	8	2	4	5	6	42	32	0	.568	4
Everett (Giants)	5	5	....	6	5	4	5	6	36	38	0	.486	10
Spokane (Padres)	8	7	9	....	4	1	1	5	35	39	0	.473	11

OREGON DIVISION

Club	T.C.	Bell.	Ev.	Spo.	Med.	Bend	Sal.	Eug.	W.	L.	T.	Pct.	G.B.
Medford (A's)	2	5	2	3	....	13	8	12	45	29	0	.608	....
Bend (Phillies)	5	3	3	6	3	....	7	11	38	36	0	.514	7
Salem (Angels)	1	2	2	6	7	8	....	9	35	39	0	.473	10
Eugene (Royals)	1	1	1	2	3	4	7	....	19	55	0	.257	26

Tri-Cities represented Richland, Pasco and Kennewick, Wash.

Major league affiliations in parentheses.

Playoff—Tri-Cities defeated Medford, one game to none.

Regular-Season Attendance—Bellingham, 15,812; Bend, 32,201; Eugene, 66,738; Everett, 41,442; Medford, 62,905; Salem, 30,800; Spokane, 43,607; Tri-Cities, 52,042. Total, 345,547. Playoff, 921.

Managers—Bellingham, Gary Pellant; Bend, Ramon Aviles; Eugene, Dave Roberts; Everett, Everett Bridges; Medford, Dennis Rogers; Salem, Larry Patterson; Spokane, Jack Maloof; Tri-Cities, Marty Scott.

All-Star Team: 1B—Ron Gideon, Bend; 2B—Greg Litton, Everett; 3B—Brad Pounders, Spokane; SS—Sergio Perez, Bend; OF—Sam Haley, Bellingham; Kevin Bootay, Tri-Cities; Brad Hill, Tri-Cities; C—Dan Winters, Medford; LHP—Greg Brake, Medford; RHP—Jim Walker, Bellingham; DH—Robyn Amble, Tri-Cities; Manager—Marty Scott, Tri-Cities. Most Valuable Player—Sam Haley, Bellingham.

(Compiled by William J. Weiss, League Statistician, San Mateo, Calif.)

CLUB BATTING

Club	Pct.	G.	AB.	R.	OR.	H.	TB.	2B.	3B.	HR.	RBI.	GW.	SH.	SF.	HP.	BB.	Int. BB.	SO.	SB.	CS.	LOB.
Tri-Cities	.267	74	2476	459	351	660	902	100	17	36	386	39	30	24	28	384	15	477	163	52	562
Bend	.245	74	2461	360	301	602	790	88	17	22	269	28	9	20	23	309	14	602	123	60	526
Everett	.236	74	2522	274	325	596	780	94	12	22	226	30	14	9	22	253	9	562	52	30	586
Bellingham	.231	74	2429	337	304	562	723	93	10	16	258	35	29	23	30	414	16	570	175	53	593

CLUB BATTING

Club	Pct.	G.	AB.	R.	OR.	H.	TB.	2B.	3B.	HR.	RBI.	GW.	SH.	SF.	HP.	BB.	Int. BB.	SO.	SB.	CS.	LOB.
Spokane	.230	74	2545	346	339	585	776	81	19	24	288	29	26	29	23	387	8	535	119	31	634
Eugene	.229	74	2467	296	486	564	729	83	14	18	243	16	18	20	29	264	9	592	91	37	509
Medford	.227	74	2440	328	249	553	736	89	11	24	265	34	20	21	35	339	4	569	108	51	561
Salem	.226	74	2495	326	371	564	733	77	19	18	264	29	24	22	31	283	20	598	129	75	523

INDIVIDUAL BATTING

(Leading Qualifiers for Batting Championship—200 or More Plate Appearances)

*Bats lefthanded.　†Switch-hitter.

Player and Club	Pct.	G.	AB.	R.	H.	TB.	2B.	3B.	HR.	RBI.	GW.	SH.	SF.	HP.	BB.	Int. BB.	SO.	SB.	CS.
King, Ronald, Tri-Cities*	.370	57	162	48	60	82	11	1	3	37	4	0	2	3	48	3	22	17	5
Haley, Samuel, Bellingham	.331	67	257	63	85	117	13	2	5	35	5	3	0	1	39	0	33	58	6
Amble, Robyn, Tri-Cities†	.301	65	239	43	72	91	10	0	3	48	6	2	5	5	17	0	44	18	6
Martinez, Reynaldo, Eugene	.301	59	176	18	53	71	12	3	0	26	1	1	0	0	24	2	38	4	4
Pounders, Bradley, Spokane	.297	74	286	46	85	137	16	3	10	55	7	0	1	1	56	2	85	2	3
Hill, Bradley, Tri-Cities*	.295	63	237	38	70	113	12	2	9	59	9	0	1	1	27	0	25	12	4
Paul, Jeffrey, Tri-Cities*	.289	60	190	43	55	62	7	0	0	21	1	9	1	2	44	2	39	8	4
Soto, Fernando, Bend*	.285	65	239	43	71	79	6	1	0	16	1	1	2	0	31	3	47	15	9
Perez, Sergio, Bend	.282	70	294	48	83	104	14	2	1	26	2	1	0	4	17	1	42	23	10
McDonald, Thomas, Everett	.278	58	216	29	60	80	6	1	4	25	2	1	1	2	11	1	41	8	2

Departmental Leaders: G—Pounders, 74; AB—Perez, 294; R—Bootay, 66; H—Haley, Pounders, 85; TB—Pounders, 137; 2B—Pounders, 16; 3B—(Eight tied with 4); HR—Pounders, 10; RBI—Hill, 59; GWRBI—Hill, 9; SH—Paul, 9; SF—Sparks, 6; HP—Bootay, Meggs, 7; BB—Varoz, 69; IBB—Gideon, 6; SO—Howard, 89; SB—Haley, 58; CS—Bootay, 13.

(All Players—Listed Alphabetically)

Player and Club	Pct.	G.	AB.	R.	H.	TB.	2B.	3B.	HR.	RBI.	GW.	SH.	SF.	HP.	BB.	Int. BB.	SO.	SB.	CS.
Ackerman, John, Everett	.222	13	9	0	2	2	0	0	0	0	0	1	0	0	2	0	3	0	0
Alfredson, Thomas, Salem	.214	57	220	18	47	53	3	0	1	20	0	0	0	0	11	0	85	19	5
Alomar, Santos, Spokane†	.215	59	219	13	47	52	5	0	0	21	2	4	2	1	13	0	20	3	0
Amble, Robyn, Tri-Cities†	.301	65	239	43	72	91	10	0	3	48	6	2	5	5	17	0	44	18	6
Anderson, Roy, Medford	.242	40	124	9	30	36	6	0	0	18	3	0	1	0	9	0	25	0	1
Arias, Antonio, Medford	.197	60	203	27	40	67	7	1	6	25	3	0	2	0	20	1	51	3	2
Baker, Gerald, Salem	.143	28	84	11	12	14	2	0	0	8	1	0	0	0	10	0	30	5	2
Barton, Shawn, Bend	.500	13	4	1	2	3	1	0	0	0	0	0	0	0	1	0	1	0	0
Beall, Peter, Salem	.400	1	5	2	2	2	0	0	0	2	0	0	0	0	1	0	2	0	0
Bedell, Jeffrey, Eugene†	.500	1	2	0	1	1	0	0	0	0	0	0	0	0	0	0	0	0	0
Bell, Robert, Eugene	.241	51	145	22	35	42	2	1	1	9	0	1	0	5	8	0	36	7	4
Bennett, Eric, Bend	.268	18	56	6	15	16	1	0	0	9	0	1	1	0	11	1	8	2	2
Bichette, Dante, Salem	.232	64	250	27	58	83	9	2	4	30	4	3	1	3	6	0	53	6	2
Bitker, Joseph, Spokane	.200	14	10	2	2	5	0	0	1	1	0	3	0	0	1	0	1	0	0
Blair, Paul, Everett	.301	41	136	7	41	48	4	0	1	10	3	0	0	1	8	1	18	2	6
Bootay, Kevin, Tri-Cities	.264	68	265	66	70	89	5	4	2	22	0	2	1	7	37	0	38	45	13
Brady, Brian, Salem*	.215	67	242	29	52	72	10	2	2	26	3	2	3	2	29	4	42	19	11
Bresnahan, David, Bellingham†	.259	64	197	29	51	62	6	1	1	28	3	3	3	4	49	4	44	15	6
Brown, Jeffrey, Eugene	.277	54	202	23	56	78	10	0	4	32	2	0	4	1	6	2	42	3	1
Buss, Scott, Bellingham	.217	6	23	5	5	6	1	0	0	4	0	0	0	0	3	0	4	0	0
Byers, Randell, Spokane*	.231	67	273	34	63	92	9	4	4	43	4	1	4	1	27	2	35	13	5
Calzado, Sebastian, Everett	.258	22	66	9	17	22	5	0	0	4	1	0	0	4	0	0	22	0	1
Campbell, Michael, Salem*	.206	44	131	24	27	37	4	3	0	11	1	1	1	0	25	1	33	6	4
Carlson, John, Spokane	.235	57	179	15	42	47	5	0	0	16	2	1	2	2	16	1	31	3	2
Carozza, Michael, Bellingham	.213	55	164	23	35	44	5	2	0	15	2	3	2	3	43	1	46	14	3
Champoux, Anthony, Medford	.333	5	9	1	3	3	0	0	0	1	1	0	0	0	3	0	6	1	0
Cicione, Michael, Everett	.295	47	166	18	49	63	8	3	0	18	2	0	0	2	15	0	23	1	0
Coachman, Bobby, Salem	.260	65	231	44	60	74	10	2	0	21	2	2	3	1	44	3	28	22	8
Cockrell, Alan, Everett	.375	2	8	1	3	3	0	0	0	3	0	0	0	0	1	0	2	0	0
Colpitt, Michael, Bend	.229	68	245	30	56	85	15	1	4	35	5	0	3	2	22	0	83	7	3
Cooper, Kent, Everett	.169	41	124	12	21	26	5	0	0	11	1	1	1	0	33	0	33	0	3
Cosby, Robert, Everett	.125	3	8	1	1	1	0	0	0	0	0	0	0	0	0	0	3	0	0
Costello, Michael, Spokane	.111	15	9	0	1	1	0	0	0	0	0	0	0	0	0	0	5	0	0
Cottrell, Stephen, Everett	.000	14	2	0	0	0	0	0	0	0	0	0	0	0	0	0	1	0	0
Culberson, Charles, Everett	.269	7	26	4	7	8	1	0	0	2	0	1	0	0	3	0	6	2	1
Czyzewski, Tracey, Spokane*	.000	15	3	1	0	0	0	0	0	0	0	1	0	0	1	0	2	0	0
Dantzler, Shawn, Bend	.217	15	46	3	10	14	1	0	1	2	0	0	0	2	8	0	12	1	0
Davila, Victor, Eugene†	.137	20	51	3	7	7	0	0	0	1	0	0	1	1	6	0	16	0	3
Davis, Harry, Everett	.207	48	184	26	38	45	2	1	1	16	1	3	1	1	22	0	36	22	3
Davis, Lee, Bend	.238	62	227	37	54	89	6	4	7	35	4	0	2	2	26	0	58	12	7
DeButch, Michael, Spokane	.238	70	269	48	64	76	8	2	0	25	4	4	3	4	52	0	38	34	5
De La Cruz, Tony, Eugene	.136	19	22	5	3	3	0	0	0	1	0	1	0	1	3	0	13	1	0
de la Rosa, Marino, Bend	.221	21	77	6	17	21	2	1	0	10	3	0	3	0	4	0	17	4	4
De Leon, Rafael, Eugene	.189	64	201	16	38	51	6	2	1	13	3	5	1	2	9	2	44	2	3
de los Santos, Luis, Eugene	.268	67	257	27	69	89	10	2	2	30	0	0	2	1	13	1	33	5	3
Dietrick, Patrick, Medford	.226	69	270	45	61	87	14	0	4	26	2	1	1	3	39	1	84	26	8
Dorsey, Maurice, Eugene	.200	3	5	0	1	1	0	0	0	0	0	0	0	0	0	0	0	0	0
Echavarria, Francisco, Everett	.000	5	11	0	0	0	0	0	0	0	0	0	0	0	0	0	7	0	0
Eddington, Michael, Medford	.150	34	100	12	15	21	3	0	1	10	1	1	0	4	26	0	23	2	2
Fannin, Robert, Bend	.222	16	45	7	10	11	1	0	0	2	0	0	0	0	8	0	8	0	0
Filandino, Joseph, Spokane	1.000	9	2	1	2	2	0	0	0	0	0	0	0	0	0	0	0	0	0
Forbes, Terence, Spokane	.000	8	1	1	0	0	0	0	0	0	0	0	0	0	0	0	0	0	0
Fortenberry, Jimmy, Bend*	.248	30	105	17	26	37	5	0	2	13	0	1	2	0	11	1	19	4	1
Francis, Todd, Bellingham*	.222	10	36	5	8	14	3	0	1	6	0	0	0	0	9	0	9	0	0
Freeman, Marvin, Bend	.000	15	3	1	0	0	0	0	0	0	0	0	0	0	2	0	1	0	0
Frohwirth, Todd, Bend	.667	29	3	0	2	2	0	0	0	1	0	0	0	0	0	0	0	0	0
Fuentes, Louis, Eugene	.204	36	98	8	20	24	4	0	0	7	0	1	0	0	11	0	28	0	0
Gibree, Robert, Bellingham	.171	52	170	15	29	37	5	0	1	21	1	2	4	5	33	0	55	2	1
Gideon, Ronnie, Bend*	.270	66	237	37	64	88	7	4	3	37	5	0	1	2	40	6	70	2	5
Gilbert, Gregory, Everett	.000	13	1	0	0	0	0	0	0	0	0	0	0	0	0	0	1	0	0
Gildehaus, Michael, Spokane*	.000	24	1	0	0	0	0	0	0	0	0	0	0	0	0	0	0	0	0
Grant, Kenneth, Salem	.268	70	269	38	72	102	7	4	5	45	6	5	5	3	16	5	57	14	7
Grayston, Joseph, Tri-Cities	.264	62	201	40	53	91	12	4	6	36	5	0	3	2	31	0	57	14	3
Grimes, Darin, Eugene	.109	26	46	7	5	5	0	0	0	0	0	0	0	0	13	0	22	0	1

Player and Club	Pct.	G.	AB.	R.	H.	TB.	2B.	3B.	HR.	RBI.	GW.	SH.	SF.	HP.	BB.	Int. BB.	SO.	SB.	CS.
Grimes, John, Everett	.256	39	129	10	33	43	4	0	2	16	4	0	0	2	17	3	24	0	3
Grouse, Michael, Tri-Cities°	.325	28	83	11	27	35	2	0	2	18	1	1	0	1	9	2	11	5	0
Guerrero, Jose, Eugene	.250	49	164	17	41	53	12	0	0	18	2	0	1	0	11	0	42	2	3
Haley, Samuel, Bellingham	.331	67	257	63	85	117	13	2	5	35	5	3	0	1	39	0	33	58	6
Hansen, Ronald, Tri-Cities	.173	36	98	11	17	26	1	1	2	10	2	0	2	1	15	0	25	0	0
Harris, Twayne, Medford	.250	14	20	3	5	9	2	1	0	5	1	0	0	0	4	0	4	0	0
Hibbs, Loren, Everett	.220	39	118	18	26	43	3	1	4	10	2	1	0	1	23	2	38	1	0
Higgs, Darrell, Bellingham	.250	27	12	0	3	3	0	0	0	2	0	0	0	1	6	0	3	0	0
Hill, Bradley, Tri-Cities°	.295	63	237	38	70	113	12	2	9	59	9	0	1	1	27	0	25	12	4
Hinnrichs, David, Everett	.000	24	2	0	0	0	0	0	0	0	0	1	0	0	0	0	2	0	0
Hornsby, David, Everett	.120	31	92	6	11	16	2	0	1	7	0	1	0	1	11	0	34	0	0
Howard, Steven, Medford	.211	53	185	26	39	57	4	1	4	24	3	0	1	4	43	1	89	15	6
Howarth, Paul, Eugene	.226	59	199	30	45	59	6	1	2	28	3	5	2	4	31	0	32	15	2
Howie, Mark, Medford	.266	71	256	39	68	80	12	0	0	25	3	0	3	5	45	0	35	14	9
Hyde, Nathan, Medford	.251	51	171	18	43	55	9	0	1	22	3	0	2	2	25	1	55	2	0
Jacas, Andre, Medford	.262	43	107	19	28	33	1	2	0	9	0	4	1	2	14	0	21	23	0
Jackson, A.D., Bellingham	.263	57	179	18	47	58	11	0	0	13	2	3	0	2	7	0	33	14	6
Jackson, Todd, Tri-Cities	.187	40	134	16	25	30	3	1	0	11	1	1	1	1	14	0	36	8	3
James, Darin, Everett	.262	17	42	4	11	12	1	0	0	6	0	0	0	1	4	0	10	0	1
Jennings, Douglas, Salem°	.260	52	173	29	45	57	7	1	1	17	3	1	4	3	40	1	45	12	12
Jester, William, Bend°	.286	13	7	2	2	2	0	0	0	2	0	0	0	0	2	0	3	0	0
Jimenez, Genaro, Salem	.083	20	24	5	2	2	0	0	0	0	0	0	0	0	3	0	13	0	1
Johnson, Thomas, Eugene°	.183	39	71	16	13	14	1	0	0	5	1	0	2	0	15	0	17	1	0
Jones, Carl, Medford	.211	27	95	14	20	30	2	1	2	6	0	0	0	1	6	0	31	1	2
Kazmierski, Mickey, Spokane	.000	24	0	0	0	0	0	0	0	0	0	0	0	0	0	0	0	0	0
King, Ronald, Tri-Cities°	.370	57	162	48	60	82	11	1	3	37	4	0	2	3	48	3	22	17	5
Koslofski, Kevin, Eugene°	.187	53	155	23	29	38	2	2	1	10	2	1	1	0	25	0	37	10	2
Krause, Andrew, Medford°	.227	31	88	18	20	27	4	0	1	11	1	2	2	2	17	0	11	3	3
Krause, Thomas, Bellingham°	.220	62	232	42	51	58	7	0	0	14	5	0	2	1	39	4	27	22	5
Kunz, Kurt, Eugene	.222	5	9	1	2	2	0	0	0	0	0	0	0	0	2	0	3	4	0
Leonard, Andrew, Eugene	.211	57	199	14	42	65	8	0	5	29	1	0	3	3	11	0	60	1	2
Lewis, Kenneth, Bend	.134	29	67	13	9	13	4	0	0	8	0	0	0	0	14	0	26	7	1
Litton, Gregory, Everett	.235	62	243	29	57	85	12	2	4	26	6	0	0	1	27	0	47	2	1
Lora, Jose, Spokane	.190	36	116	12	22	24	2	0	0	7	0	3	0	3	9	0	30	3	1
Lukes, Louis, Bend	.290	26	93	16	27	42	5	2	2	13	2	0	1	0	13	0	23	5	4
Lynds, Mark, Salem	.200	30	95	11	19	25	3	0	1	10	1	1	0	2	12	1	31	4	1
Madden, Scott, Bend	.000	14	3	0	0	0	0	0	0	0	0	0	0	0	0	0	2	0	0
Marquez, Edwin, Salem	.250	22	48	4	12	12	0	0	0	6	0	0	1	2	11	0	10	1	3
Martes, Sixto, Everett	.000	8	15	0	0	0	0	0	0	0	0	0	0	0	0	0	10	0	0
Martin, Lawrence, Spokane	.216	37	97	13	21	27	4	1	0	6	1	2	0	3	20	0	37	4	1
Martinez, Enrique, Bend	.167	12	42	5	7	10	1	1	0	2	0	0	0	0	3	0	12	0	0
Martinez, Reynaldo, Eugene	.301	59	176	18	53	71	12	3	0	26	1	1	0	0	24	2	38	4	4
McCray, Rodney, Spokane	.205	71	244	40	50	61	6	1	1	20	1	0	4	2	65	0	50	25	5
McDevitt, Stephen, Bend	.200	13	5	1	1	1	0	0	0	1	0	0	0	0	0	0	1	0	0
McDonald, Thomas, Everett	.278	58	216	29	60	80	6	1	4	25	2	1	1	2	11	1	41	8	2
Meggs, Lindsay, Eugene	.238	58	168	18	40	47	4	0	1	11	1	2	1	7	28	0	31	10	3
Melrose, Jeffrey, Tri-Cities°	.269	41	108	15	29	44	9	0	2	20	2	1	1	2	12	2	17	3	1
Messier, Thomas, Everett	.500	12	4	1	2	2	0	0	0	0	0	0	0	0	0	0	2	0	0
Middleton, Richard, Bellingham	.186	54	177	22	33	51	9	0	3	17	2	2	1	5	33	1	69	6	3
Miller, David, Bellingham	.184	45	141	15	26	29	1	1	0	6	1	1	2	0	16	0	48	7	5
Miller, Keith, Bend°	.167	3	12	1	2	2	0	0	0	0	0	0	0	0	1	0	3	1	0
Miller, Michael, Bend†	.000	16	8	0	0	0	0	0	0	0	0	0	0	0	0	0	5	0	0
Mitchell, William, Salem	.134	36	112	11	15	26	5	0	2	13	1	2	0	3	13	1	41	0	0
Moriarty, Todd, Everett°	.067	15	15	0	1	1	0	0	0	0	0	0	0	0	0	0	9	0	0
Morris, Manuel, Bellingham	.265	52	181	15	48	66	7	1	3	30	4	2	4	0	17	0	41	6	4
Murray, David, Tri-Cities	.191	42	136	25	26	31	3	1	0	23	0	3	1	0	25	0	16	7	1
Murray, Stephen, Bellingham	.174	60	218	27	38	46	2	3	0	17	1	8	1	3	31	1	46	19	10
Newcombe, Donald, Salem†	.087	19	46	4	4	6	2	0	0	6	0	0	0	1	3	1	21	1	1
Newell, Thomas, Bend	.185	43	135	14	25	32	2	1	1	10	1	0	0	2	14	0	49	4	1
Noble, Ramon, Eugene	.216	40	102	10	22	28	2	2	0	10	0	0	1	0	10	2	40	3	3
Nunez, Dario, Salem	.250	9	20	3	5	5	0	0	0	0	0	0	0	1	0	0	6	2	0
O'Hearn, Robert, Tri-Cities	.330	32	106	13	35	41	6	0	0	19	3	4	1	0	15	3	14	2	2
Olker, Joseph, Everett	.444	13	9	1	4	4	0	0	0	1	0	1	0	0	0	0	1	0	0
Ortega, Raymond, Bend	.248	50	141	18	35	43	5	0	1	13	0	1	1	0	26	0	31	7	2
Osborne, James, Salem	.231	43	143	13	33	45	7	1	1	17	3	2	3	4	9	2	29	1	1
Pappas, Erik, Salem	.243	56	177	24	43	55	3	3	1	15	1	3	1	3	31	0	26	10	5
Paul, Jeffrey, Tri-Cities°	.289	60	190	43	55	62	7	0	0	21	1	9	1	2	44	2	39	8	4
Perez, Sergio, Bend	.282	70	294	48	83	104	14	2	1	26	2	1	0	4	17	1	42	23	10
Perezchica, Antonio, Everett	.193	33	119	10	23	31	6	1	0	10	1	1	2	1	6	0	24	0	0
Perkins, Robert, Spokane	.067	15	30	0	2	2	0	0	0	1	0	0	0	0	2	0	12	0	0
Peterson, Allan, Salem†	.261	6	23	8	6	6	0	0	0	1	0	0	0	0	3	0	3	0	1
Porter, Bradley, Everett	.221	55	190	18	42	61	14	1	1	16	0	1	0	2	21	0	50	0	0
Pottinger, Mark, Bend†	.276	33	98	13	27	28	1	0	0	16	1	2	1	2	16	0	17	14	1
Pounders, Bradley, Spokane	.297	74	286	46	85	137	16	3	10	55	7	0	1	1	56	2	85	2	3
Powell, Alonzo, Everett	.176	6	17	2	3	7	1	0	1	4	0	0	2	0	1	0	3	0	0
Poznanski, Richard, Tri-Cities	.260	43	146	25	38	53	6	0	3	26	1	3	2	1	16	1	22	4	4
Redus, Jeffrey, Eugene	.189	13	37	6	7	11	1	0	1	6	0	0	1	0	9	0	17	1	0
Reilly, Neil, Tri-Cities	.237	31	97	13	23	32	3	0	2	8	2	1	0	1	10	0	39	3	0
Reyes, Orlando, Medford	.215	21	65	7	14	21	3	2	0	12	1	1	0	0	9	0	20	0	0
Robertson, Randy, Spokane	.118	14	17	1	2	2	0	0	0	2	0	0	1	0	2	0	8	0	0
Rosario, Luis, Eugene	.087	23	23	7	2	2	0	0	0	0	0	0	0	1	8	0	13	0	0
Ross, Cordell, Medford†	.209	70	215	27	45	49	4	0	0	20	2	6	2	4	38	4	44	5	9
Rousey, Stephen, Bellingham°	.000	15	1	0	0	0	0	0	0	0	0	0	0	0	0	0	0	0	0
Rush, Rodney, Everett	.282	35	131	15	37	49	4	1	2	12	1	0	0	0	22	2	2	2	2
St. Laurent, James, Tri-Cities°	.233	30	90	14	21	25	4	0	0	4	0	1	1	0	8	1	15	2	2
Sanchez, Juan, Bend	.212	51	156	20	33	41	8	0	0	9	2	2	2	5	15	1	27	3	6
Santos, Fausto, Medford	.219	69	233	25	51	60	9	0	0	14	5	3	1	3	18	0	37	2	1
Scales, Richard, Spokane	.194	58	180	24	35	37	2	0	0	16	0	1	2	1	25	1	31	8	1
Schuessler, John, Tri-Cities	.195	33	82	11	16	24	2	0	2	9	0	1	1	1	14	0	36	1	0
Sciacca, Steven, Salem	.333	1	3	0	1	1	0	0	0	0	0	0	0	0	0	0	1	0	1
Sexton, Matthew, Salem	.246	55	199	21	49	56	5	1	0	16	3	1	0	3	15	1	42	7	10
Shepard, Royce, Bend	.000	17	1	0	0	0	0	0	0	0	0	0	0	0	0	0	1	0	0
Silver, Keith, Everett	.600	8	5	0	3	4	1	0	0	1	0	1	0	0	1	0	1	0	0

Player and Club	Pct.	G.	AB.	R.	H.	TB.	2B.	3B.	HR.	RBI.	GW.	SH.	SF.	HP.	BB.	Int. BB.	SO.	SB.	CS.
Simpson, Gregory, Bend*	.500	17	2	0	1	1	0	0	0	0	0	0	0	0	1	0	0	0	0
Smith, Henry, Bend	.240	39	96	21	23	26	3	0	0	9	2	0	1	2	22	1	33	11	4
Smith, Curtis, Medford	.261	39	115	14	30	36	2	2	0	11	2	1	2	0	12	0	26	6	2
Solomon, Michael, Bellingham	.239	44	142	27	34	46	9	0	1	21	4	1	2	3	34	1	23	9	4
Soto, Fernando, Bend*	.285	65	249	43	71	79	6	1	0	16	1	1	2	0	31	3	47	15	9
Sparks, Gregory, Spokane*	.252	67	270	34	68	101	13	4	4	37	6	1	6	0	17	1	65	1	2
Stangel, Christopher, Everett	.000	17	2	0	0	0	0	0	0	0	0	0	0	0	0	0	2	0	0
Strutton, Michael, Eugene†	.262	30	107	20	28	33	3	1	0	5	0	0	3		13	0	14	12	3
Suris, Jorge, Spokane	.159	33	82	11	13	16	3	0	0	4	0	1	0	2	11	0	22	1	2
Swepson, Lyle, Everett	.158	27	95	12	15	19	4	0	0	4	2	0	1	1	5	0	34	1	0
Tavarez, Davis, Everett	.000	22	4	0	0	0	0	0	0	0	0	0	0	0	0	0	1	0	0
Thomas, Bradley, Bend	.000	10	2	0	0	0	0	0	0	0	0	0	0	0	0	0	1	0	0
Thrift, James, Medford	.081	17	37	1	3	3	0	0	0	3	0	1	2	1	3	0	10	0	0
Tinoco, David, Bellingham	.095	5	21	3	2	2	0	0	0	0	0	0	0	1	0		3	0	0
Toribio, Guadalupe, Medford*	.218	23	55	8	12	15	3	0	0	5	2	0	1	3	9	0	13	1	1
Valdez, Efrain, Spokane*	.000	13	1	0	0	0	0	0	0	0	0	0	0	0	0	0	0	0	0
Vanacore, Derek, Eugene	.179	8	28	5	5	5	0	0	0	2	0	1	0	0	8	0	11	10	1
Vargas, Miguel, Bend	.000	16	2	0	0	0	0	0	0	0	0	0	0	0	0	0	2	0	0
Varoz, Eric, Spokane*	.260	74	254	50	66	94	8	4	4	34	2	3	4	3	69	1	67	21	4
Villa, Michael, Everett*	.500	2	2	0	1	1	0	0	0	0	0	0	0	0	0	0	1	0	0
Visor, Michael, Spokane	.000	17	2	0	0	0	0	0	0	0	0	0	0	0	0	0	0	0	0
Ward, Timothy, Bellingham*	.222	36	108	9	24	29	5	0	0	7	2	1	0	0	29	3	32	1	0
Wasem, James, Everett	.260	33	127	19	33	37	4	0	0	5	0	0	1		10	0	17	7	4
Wesley, Joseph, Tri-Cities†	.225	42	102	27	23	33	4	3	0	15	2	1	1	0	42	1	21	14	4
Wetzel, Thomas, Everett	.239	14	46	2	11	11	0	0	0	5	1	0	1		8	1	3	0	0
Winters, Daniel, Medford	.262	67	263	33	69	102	13	1	6	40	4	0	2	3	24	1	39	6	5
Woodhouse, Kevin, Everett*	.262	49	168	20	44	56	7	1	1	14	3	0	0	4	18	1	38	4	3

The following pitchers, listed alphabetically by club, with games in parentheses, had no plate appearances, primarily through use of designated hitters:

BELLINGHAM—Blanchette, Daniel (22); Jones, Calvin (10); Lewis, Larry (12); Mendek, William (24); Metz, Mark (24); Moore, Richard (2); Neufelder, Donald (15); Osterode, Jeffrey (21); Siegel, Robert (11); Walker, James (14); West, Edwin (8).

BEND—Creekmore, Edward (4); King, Stacey (13); Labay, Stephen (2); Lloyd, Raymond (3).

EUGENE—Bell, Kevin (21); Berrios, Hector (22); Brauchle, Troy (25); Crouch, Matthew (16); Ellis, Roy (15); Koller, David (14); Konruff, Douglas (12); McCormack, Ronald (11); Morales, Edwin (10); Radtke, John (3); Robinson, Henry (14); Rodiles, Jose (11); Rogers, Carl (18); Shook, Thomas (3); Sparling, Donald (16); Van Vuren, Robert (12).

EVERETT—Ewing, James (4); Mulholland, Terence (3); Tate, Stuart (10); Utley, James (1).

MEDFORD—Beaver, Mark (4); Brake, Gregory (14); Burns, Todd (22); Criswell, Brian (10); Edwards, David (11); Figueroa, Victor (6); Hansen, Derel (6); Kibler, Russell (13); Parrish, Scott (6); Puikunas, Edmund (24); Sanchez, Carlos (17); Strong, Joseph (20).

SALEM—Butler, Michael (15); Cedeno, Vinicio (23); Cook, Larry (20); Corbett, Sherman (15); Dacus, Barry (33); Eggertsen, Todd (14); Hernandez, Carlos (18); Horrell, Christopher (3); Martinez, David (15); Ojeda, Jorge (12); Price, Bryan (4); Rivera, Elvin (9); Romanovsky, Michael (13); Ruiz, Franco (5); Sillivent, Gregory (5).

SPOKANE—Ford, Russell (25); Keys, Cornelius (14).

TRI-CITIES—Bridges, James (20); Cipres, Mark (22); Danelson, Dannie (18); Daniel, Stephen (20); Dersin, Eric (14); Fay, Michael (16); Ittner, Lee (6); Kilgus, Paul (14); Kramer, Randall (15); LoSauro, Carmelo (15); Thomas, Steven (21).

GRAND SLAM HOME RUNS—Amble 2; Byers, Gideon, Grouse, King, Ortega, Pappas, Varoz, 1 each.

AWARDED FIRST BASE ON CATCHER'S INTERFERENCE—Hill 2 (Alomar, Bennett); Brady (Winters); D. Grimes (Gibree); Haley (Alomar); Jacas (Pappas); Kazmierski (Hornsby); Lynds (Winters); Morris (Alomar); Peterson (Leonard); Santos (Fannin); H. Smith (Anderson).

CLUB FIELDING

Club	Pct.	G.	PO.	A.	E.	DP.	PB.
Medford	.955	74	1990	842	133	54	11
Everett	.953	74	1959	755	130	57	23
Spokane	.951	74	2022	864	150	75	18
Tri-Cities	.947	74	1952	831	155	60	36
Salem	.941	74	2003	840	179	72	39
Bend	.939	74	1944	815	130	74	39
Bellingham	.938	74	2009	872	192	50	14
Eugene	.930	74	1940	705	199	37	32

Triple Plays—Bellingham, Tri-Cities.

INDIVIDUAL FIELDING

FIRST BASEMEN

*Throws lefthanded.

Player and Club	Pct.	G.	PO.	A.	E.	DP.
Alomar, Spokane	.981	7	44	7	1	6
Anderson, Medford	1.000	1	1	0	0	0
Arias, Medford	.980	44	368	25	8	22
Baker, Salem	.985	8	62	4	1	5
Bedell, Eugene	1.000	1	3	0	0	0
Bichette, Salem	.973	22	175	8	5	15
Blair, Everett	1.000	13	65	3	0	7
Bresnahan, Bellingham	.976	20	187	15	5	16
Brown, Eugene	.985	43	307	19	5	20
Carlson, Spokane	1.000	1	2	0	0	0
Eddington, Medford	.987	29	218	13	3	14
Francis, Bellingham*	.988	7	73	6	1	5
Gibree, Bellingham	.966	4	26	2	1	2
Gideon, Bend*	.965	65	541	46	21	50
Grimes, Everett	1.000	7	70	4	0	8
Grouse, Tri-Cities	.959	24	197	12	9	10
Guerrero, Eugene	.973	32	232	17	7	11
Hansen, Tri-Cities	.989	20	171	12	2	21
Higgs, Bellingham	1.000	4	21	1	0	1
Hill, Tri-Cities	1.000	4	25	3	0	0
Hyde, Bellingham	.959	25	198	12	9	10
Johnson, Eugene*	.800	2	3	1	1	0
Melrose, Tri-Cities*	.984	34	290	25	5	25
Middleton, Bellingham	.960	13	112	8	5	7
Newcombe, Salem*	.960	19	110	9	5	8
Ortega, Bend	1.000	2	11	1	0	1
Osborne, Salem	.981	38	290	18	6	37
Perkins, Spokane	.957	3	20	2	1	0
Porter, Everett	.974	55	440	18	12	32
Powell, Everett	.930	5	38	2	3	4
Redus, Eugene	.964	4	26	1	1	1
Reyes, Medford	.959	8	65	6	3	6
Schuessler, Tri-Cities	1.000	1	1	0	0	0
Sciacca, Salem	1.000	1	5	2	0	0
Smith, Bend	.947	10	85	4	5	10
Solomon, Bellingham	1.000	1	13	1	0	0
SPARKS, Spokane*	.982	66	619	37	12	60
Tinoco, Bellingham	1.000	5	46	5	0	2
Ward, Bellingham	1.000	1	3	0	0	1

Triple Plays—Hansen, Hyde.

SECOND BASEMEN

Player and Club	Pct.	G.	PO.	A.	E.	DP.
Alfredson, Salem	.889	9	15	17	4	3
Blair, Everett	.969	21	40	55	3	13
Campbell, Salem	1.000	3	4	2	0	0
Coachman, Salem	.969	52	128	155	9	35
Davila, Eugene	.958	6	11	12	1	3
DeButch, Spokane	1.000	13	27	28	0	8
De La Cruz, Eugene	1.000	6	5	10	0	0
DeLeon, Eugene	.906	7	14	15	3	0
Howarth, Eugene	1.000	1	0	1	0	0
A.D. Jackson, Bellingham	.902	28	50	69	13	13
T. Jackson, Tri-Cities	.821	10	16	16	7	3
A. Krause, Medford	1.000	7	9	12	0	2
T. Krause, Bellingham	1.000	5	7	13	0	2
Lewis, Bend	.927	25	52	49	8	15
Litton, Everett	.956	58	131	152	13	28
Lora, Spokane	.934	34	64	78	10	19
Meggs, Eugene	.937	49	107	130	16	21
D. Murray, Tri-Cities	.951	40	68	105	9	24
S. Murray, Bellingham	.926	46	110	127	19	20
Pottinger, Bend	.958	32	55	59	5	19
ROSS, Medford	.972	65	157	157	9	30
Sanchez, Bend	.962	28	50	76	5	15
Santos, Medford	1.000	1	0	2	0	0
Scales, Spokane	.953	33	63	101	8	19
Sexton, Salem	.918	12	27	29	5	6
Strutton, Eugene	.882	14	30	30	8	3
Suris, Spokane	.750	1	0	3	1	1
Thrift, Medford	.944	10	16	18	2	4
Wesley, Tri-Cities	.898	35	77	72	17	15

Triple Plays—D. Murray, S. Murray.

THIRD BASEMEN

Player and Club	Pct.	G.	PO.	A.	E.	DP.
Anderson, Medford	1.000	1	1	3	0	0
Beall, Salem	1.000	1	0	2	0	0
Bichette, Salem	.846	4	3	8	2	2
Blair, Everett	.600	1	3	0	2	0
Calzado, Everett	.692	7	4	14	8	0
Champoux, Medford	1.000	1	0	1	0	0
Cicione, Everett	.922	39	30	65	8	8
Coachman, Salem	.889	4	1	7	1	0
Colpitt, Bend	.838	58	39	101	27	11
De La Cruz, Eugene	.556	6	1	4	4	0
de los Santos, Eugene	.879	66	67	93	22	9
GRANT, Salem	.897	68	44	157	23	13
Grayston, Tri-Cities	.925	17	10	52	5	7
Grimes, Eugene	.857	4	3	3	1	0
Harris, Medford	.727	3	4	4	3	1
Kunz, Eugene	.667	1	0	2	1	0
Litton, Everett	.750	5	4	8	4	1
Meggs, Eugene	1.000	5	0	4	0	0
Middleton, Bellingham	.845	30	26	56	15	1
Miller, Medford	.783	9	6	12	5	2
Murray, Bellingham	.897	10	6	29	4	1
Paul, Tri-Cities	.896	59	51	121	20	5
Pounders, Spokane	.873	69	68	145	31	9
Ross, Medford	1.000	2	2	3	0	1
Sanchez, Bend	.918	21	15	41	5	5
Santos, Medford	.892	68	58	148	25	11
Scales, Spokane	.727	8	3	5	3	0
Sexton, Salem	.667	2	0	2	1	0
Smith, Bend	1.000	1	0	2	0	1
Swepson, Everett	.831	27	19	30	10	7
Thrift, Medford	.750	5	6	3	3	0
Ward, Bellingham	.874	32	16	60	11	6

Triple Play—Middleton.

SHORTSTOPS

Player and Club	Pct.	G.	PO.	A.	E.	DP.
Alfredson, Salem	.864	34	57	96	24	23
Blair, Everett	1.000	4	5	9	0	0
Calzado, Everett	.929	6	8	18	2	4
DeButch, Spokane	.914	58	78	198	26	46
De La Cruz, Eugene	1.000	2	1	1	0	0
DeLeon, Eugene	.883	58	97	136	31	17
Grayston, Tri-Cities	.906	46	76	127	21	24
Grimes, Eugene	.843	18	13	30	8	1
Harris, Medford	.667	2	5	1	3	1
HOWIE, Medford	.930	70	107	187	22	27
Jackson, Tri-Cities	.886	31	46	86	17	15
Krause, Bellingham	.894	36	52	109	19	15
Middleton, Bellingham	1.000	1	0	2	0	1
D. Miller, Bellingham	.894	36	45	107	18	15
K. Miller, Bend	.955	3	9	12	1	2
D. Murray, Tri-Cities	.900	3	4	5	1	0
S. Murray, Bellingham	.865	8	14	18	5	3
Nunez, Salem	.939	8	10	21	2	6
Perez, Bend	.926	70	103	237	27	45
Perezchica, Everett	.868	33	45	73	18	14
Pottinger, Bend	.800	3	2	2	1	0
Ross, Medford	.923	5	8	16	2	2
Scales, Spokane	.857	4	8	10	3	3
Sexton, Salem	.918	39	66	103	15	17
Strutton, Eugene	.895	10	15	19	4	2
Suris, Spokane	.984	18	21	42	1	11
Wasem, Everett	.931	33	53	109	12	16

Triple Play—Grayston.

OUTFIELDERS

Player and Club	Pct.	G.	PO.	A.	E.	DP.
Amble, Tri-Cities	.961	44	47	2	2	0
Arias, Medford	1.000	5	3	0	0	0
R. Bell, Eugene	.918	44	102	10	10	0
Bichette, Salem	.931	33	46	8	4	1
Bootay, Tri-Cities	.954	66	141	5	7	1
Brady, Salem*	.945	65	110	10	7	1
Buss, Bellingham	1.000	6	9	0	0	0
Byers, Spokane	.944	66	146	6	9	1
Campbell, Salem	.969	37	58	4	2	0
Carozza, Bellingham	.955	50	80	5	4	1
Cockrell, Everett	1.000	2	6	0	0	0
Colpitt, Bend	.889	6	6	2	1	0
Cooper, Everett	.971	32	30	4	1	1
Culberson, Everett	.944	7	16	1	1	0
Dantzler, Bend	1.000	1	1	0	0	0
H. Davis, Everett	.982	47	104	4	2	0
L. Davis, Bend	.908	56	78	1	8	0
de la Rosa, Bend	.969	20	29	2	1	1
DIETRICK, Medford	.976	67	152	10	4	3
Fortenberry, Bend	1.000	22	29	3	0	2
Guerrero, Eugene	.750	9	9	0	3	0
Haley, Bellingham	.934	64	96	3	7	1
Hibbs, Everett	1.000	24	36	3	0	0
Hill, Tri-Cities	1.000	40	61	4	0	0
Howard, Medford	.919	39	55	2	5	0
Howarth, Eugene	.935	57	95	5	7	1
Hyde, Bellingham	1.000	7	6	0	0	0
Jacas, Medford	.959	33	47	0	2	0
Jackson, Bellingham	.960	21	24	0	1	0
James, Everett	1.000	6	1	0	0	0
Jennings, Salem*	.906	49	82	5	9	1
Jimenez, Salem	1.000	13	2	0	0	0
Johnson, Eugene*	.810	15	15	2	4	0
Jones, Medford	.875	21	18	3	3	0
King, Tri-Cities*	.958	37	45	1	2	0
Koslofski, Eugene	.959	33	46	1	2	1
Krause, Medford	.975	22	37	2	1	1
Lukes, Bend	.920	26	44	2	4	0
Lynds, Salem	.900	22	24	3	3	1
Martes, Everett	.600	5	3	0	2	0
Martin, Spokane	.909	18	19	1	2	0
Martinez, Eugene	.909	49	78	2	8	0
McCray, Spokane	.972	70	124	13	4	3
McDonald, Everett	.988	45	75	9	1	1
Middleton, Bellingham	1.000	1	1	0	0	0
Miller, Bellingham	1.000	2	3	0	0	0
Mitchell, Salem	.931	20	25	2	2	0
Morris, Bellingham	.912	49	77	6	8	0
Newell, Bend	.943	27	46	4	3	2
Noble, Eugene	.927	36	49	2	4	0
Ortega, Bend	1.000	1	1	0	0	0
Peterson, Salem	.900	6	7	2	1	0
Redus, Eugene	1.000	2	3	0	0	0
Rosario, Eugene	.909	12	9	1	1	0
Rush, Everett	.968	30	59	2	2	1
St. Laurent, Tri-Cities	.974	27	35	2	1	1
Scales, Spokane	1.000	2	1	0	0	0
Schuessler, Tri-Cities	.968	29	27	3	1	0
H. Smith, Bend	1.000	16	22	1	0	1
R. Smith, Medford	.978	33	42	2	1	0
Solomon, Bellingham	.964	35	52	2	2	0
Soto, Bend*	.952	62	115	5	6	0
Toribio, Medford*	.818	17	17	1	4	1
Vanacore, Eugene*	.941	8	16	0	1	0
Varoz, Spokane	.957	74	99	11	5	1
Woodhouse, Everett*	.933	44	90	7	7	1

CATCHERS

Player and Club	Pct.	G.	PO.	A.	E.	DP.	PB.
ALOMAR, Spokane	.985	52	421	44	7	5	10
Anderson, Medford	.961	26	173	26	8	3	4
Baker, Salem	.954	13	98	5	5	0	5
Bennett, Bend	.953	12	76	6	4	0	6
Bresnahan, Bellingham	.984	41	328	32	6	3	8
Carlson, Spokane	.984	30	162	19	3	0	8
Cosby, Everett	1.000	3	29	4	0	1	0
Dorsey, Eugene	.833	2	10	0	2	0	2
Fannin, Bend	.947	13	83	7	5	0	8
Fuentes, Eugene	.959	33	200	13	9	1	16
Gibree, Bellingham	.965	40	285	42	12	2	6
Grimes, Everett	.982	32	243	34	5	4	13
Hansen, Tri-Cities	.965	7	50	5	2	1	4
Hornsby, Everett	.968	31	188	26	7	0	8
King, Tri-Cities*	1.000	1	1	0	0	0	0
Leonard, Eugene	.975	50	335	50	10	3	14
Marquez, Salem	.958	21	123	13	6	0	8
Martinez, Bend	.934	12	101	13	8	2	8
O'Hearn, Tri-Cities	.974	25	161	23	5	0	13
Ortega, Bend	.977	45	315	21	8	0	17
Pappas, Salem	.957	52	404	38	20	6	26
Perkins, Spokane	1.000	1	1	0	0	0	0
Poznanski, Tri-Cities	.974	34	221	38	7	1	9
Reilly, Tri-Cities	.957	17	93	17	5	0	10
Smith, Bend	1.000	3	7	0	0	0	0
Wetzel, Everett	.982	14	103	9	2	0	2
Winters, Medford	.981	52	391	62	9	6	7

PITCHERS

Player and Club	Pct.	G.	PO.	A.	E.	DP.
ACKERMAN, Everett	1.000	13	7	16	0	2
Barton, Bend*	.947	13	4	14	1	0
Beaver, Medford	1.000	4	0	2	0	0
K. Bell, Eugene	.938	21	8	7	1	0
Berrios, Eugene*	.909	22	1	9	1	0
Bitker, Spokane	.793	14	4	19	6	1
Blanchette, Bellingham	.706	22	4	8	5	0
Brauchle, Eugene	.947	25	3	15	1	1
Bridges, Tri-Cities*	1.000	20	2	4	0	0
Brake, Medford*	.952	14	8	32	2	1
Burns, Medford	1.000	22	2	4	0	0
Butler, Salem*	.889	15	4	20	3	4
Cedeno, Salem	.750	23	0	3	1	0
Cipres, Tri-Cities	1.000	22	1	5	0	0
Cook, Salem*	.714	20	2	3	2	1
Corbett, Salem*	.893	15	4	21	3	2
Costello, Spokane	.885	15	8	15	3	1
Cottrell, Everett	1.000	14	1	2	0	0
Creekmore, Bend	1.000	4	0	1	0	0
Criswell, Medford*	.778	10	2	5	2	0
Crouch, Eugene	.933	16	5	9	1	0
Czyzewski, Spokane	1.000	15	0	10	0	1
Dacus, Salem	1.000	33	2	5	0	0
Danelson, Tri-Cities	1.000	18	1	3	0	0
Daniel, Tri-Cities	.923	20	5	7	1	0
Dersin, Tri-Cities	1.000	14	5	10	0	0
Edwards, Medford	.889	11	1	7	1	1
Eggertsen, Salem	.824	14	1	13	3	1
Ellis, Eugene	.667	15	0	2	1	0
Ewing, Everett	1.000	4	0	1	0	0
Fay, Tri-Cities	.963	16	5	21	1	0
Figueroa, Medford	1.000	6	3	6	0	0
Filandino, Bend	.600	9	0	3	2	0
Forbes, Spokane	.857	8	1	5	1	0
Ford, Spokane	1.000	25	2	10	0	1
Freeman, Bend	.722	15	2	11	5	0
Frohwirth, Bend	1.000	29	3	12	0	0
Gilbert, Everett	.800	13	2	2	1	0
Gildehaus, Spokane	.870	24	6	14	3	0
Hansen, Medford	1.000	8	0	5	0	0
Harris, Medford	1.000	8	2	10	0	0
Hernandez, Salem	1.000	18	2	5	0	0
Higgs, Bellingham	1.000	22	4	5	0	0
Hinnrichs, Everett	1.000	24	3	10	0	0
Horrell, Salem	1.000	3	0	1	0	0
Ittner, Tri-Cities	1.000	6	1	1	0	0
Jester, Bend*	.889	13	6	18	3	3
Jones, Bellingham	.917	10	2	9	1	0
Kazmierski, Spokane	.909	24	2	8	1	1
Keys, Spokane*	1.000	14	2	2	0	0
Kibler, Medford	.958	13	5	18	1	0
Kilgus, Tri-Cities*	.909	14	5	15	2	1
S. King, Bend	.923	13	1	11	1	0
Koller, Eugene	.571	14	0	4	3	0
Konruff, Eugene	.769	12	4	6	3	0
Kramer, Tri-Cities	.850	15	7	10	3	0
Labay, Bend*	.889	2	1	7	1	0
Lewis, Bellingham	.750	12	0	3	1	0
Lloyd, Bend*	.500	3	0	1	1	0
LoSauro, Tri-Cities	.875	15	3	11	2	0
Madden, Bend*	.800	14	1	3	1	0
Martinez, Salem	.778	15	2	5	2	1
McCormack, Eugene	.800	11	4	4	2	1
McDevitt, Bend	.600	13	3	6	6	0
Melrose, Tri-Cities*	1.000	3	1	0	0	0
Mendek, Bellingham	.857	24	1	17	3	0
Messier, Everett*	1.000	12	1	10	0	0
Metz, Bellingham	.636	24	2	5	4	0
M. Miller, Bend*	.889	16	3	13	2	1
Moore, Bellingham	1.000	2	0	3	0	0
Morales, Eugene	1.000	10	0	1	0	0
Moriarty, Everett*	.905	15	2	17	2	1
Mulholland, Everett*	.857	3	0	6	1	0
Neufelder, Bellingham*	.955	15	5	16	1	1
Ojeda, Salem	1.000	12	0	4	0	0
Olker, Everett*	.857	13	0	6	1	1
Osterode, Bellingham*	1.000	21	4	8	0	0
Parrish, Medford	1.000	6	1	1	0	0
Price, Salem*	.938	4	2	13	1	2
Puikunas, Medford*	.952	24	3	17	1	0
Radtke, Eugene	.750	3	0	3	1	0
Rivera, Salem	1.000	9	0	2	0	0
Robertson, Spokane	.935	14	7	22	2	1
Robinson, Eugene	.800	14	2	10	3	0
Rodiles, Eugene	.700	11	2	5	3	1
Rogers, Eugene	.714	18	2	3	2	0
Romanovsky, Salem*	.875	13	5	9	2	2
Rousey, Bellingham	.850	13	3	14	3	0
Ruiz, Salem	1.000	19	2	7	0	2
Sanchez, Medford	.875	17	1	13	2	1
Shepard, Bend	.750	17	1	5	2	1
Shook, Eugene	1.000	3	0	4	0	0
Siegel, Bellingham	1.000	11	2	12	0	2
Silver, Everett	1.000	8	4	10	0	0
Simpson, Bend*	1.000	17	0	5	0	1
Sparling, Eugene	1.000	16	2	4	0	0
Stangel, Everett	.750	17	0	6	2	1
Strong, Medford	.810	20	2	15	4	1
Tate, Everett	1.000	10	1	0	0	0
Tavarez, Everett	.857	22	0	6	1	0
B. Thomas, Bend	.750	10	2	4	2	2
S. Thomas, Tri-Cities	.909	21	2	8	1	0
Valdez, Spokane*	.500	13	0	1	1	0
Van Vuren, Eugene	.769	12	4	6	3	0
Vargas, Bend	.818	16	2	7	2	0
Visor, Spokane	.556	16	0	5	4	1
Walker, Bellingham	.966	14	7	21	1	0
West, Bellingham	.800	8	3	9	3	0

The following players do not have any recorded accepted chances at the positions indicated; therefore, are not listed in the fielding averages for those particular positions: Arias, p; Champoux, 2b; Echavarria, p; Grouse, 2b; Harris, of; Hyde, p; R. King, p; Kunz, of; Perkins, of; St. Laurent, 2b; Sillivent, p; Utley, p; Villa, p; Winters, of.

CLUB PITCHING

Club	ERA.	G.	CG.	ShO.	Sv.	IP.	H.	R.	ER.	HR.	HB.	BB.	Int. BB.	SO.	WP.	Bk.
Bend	2.65	74	5	4	21	648.0	496	301	191	16	30	310	8	574	41	3
Medford	2.66	74	19	8	12	663.1	559	249	196	28	25	244	8	553	22	5
Bellingham	2.90	74	4	7	25	669.2	516	304	216	19	22	324	9	613	59	4
Everett	3.31	74	9	4	12	653.0	575	325	240	26	24	361	14	556	46	5
Spokane	3.38	74	9	4	9	674.0	650	339	253	17	16	291	20	555	35	3
Tri-Cities	3.40	74	3	5	25	650.2	598	351	246	29	33	340	3	542	65	2
Salem	3.80	74	10	4	19	667.2	610	371	282	21	36	347	10	591	57	11
Eugene	4.79	74	8	3	3	646.2	682	486	344	24	35	416	27	521	73	5

PITCHERS' RECORDS
(Leading Qualifiers for Earned-Run Average Leadership — 59 or More Innings)

*Throws lefthanded.

Pitcher—Club	W.	L.	Pct.	ERA.	G.	GS.	CG.	GF.	ShO.	Sv.	IP.	H.	R.	ER.	HR.	HB.	BB.	Int. BB.	SO.	WP.
Kibler, Medford	6	6	.500	1.74	13	13	5	0	0	0	103.2	79	34	20	1	6	23	1	100	6
Brake, Medford*	12	0	1.000	1.76	14	14	6	0	2	0	112.2	78	27	22	4	1	36	0	97	4
Messier, Everett*	4	5	.444	1.97	12	12	1	0	0	0	77.2	44	28	17	4	1	41	0	116	6
McDevitt, Bend	5	3	.625	1.97	13	13	1	0	1	0	68.2	42	37	15	1	4	46	0	93	7
Sparling, Eugene	4	3	.571	2.06	16	8	3	3	1	1	65.2	59	25	15	2	4	18	3	63	4
Robertson, Spokane	6	3	.667	2.12	14	14	4	0	1	0	106.1	96	36	25	2	1	26	4	51	4
Jester, Bend*	6	3	.667	2.15	13	10	0	2	0	0	71.0	57	23	17	2	1	19	0	57	3
Walker, Bellingham	8	4	.667	2.16	14	14	3	0	1	0	95.2	65	29	23	3	1	28	0	88	4
Ackerman, Everett	6	4	.600	2.34	13	13	3	0	0	0	96.0	97	27	25	3	7	21	2	32	3
Jones, Bellingham	5	0	1.000	2.41	10	9	0	0	0	0	59.2	29	23	16	0	7	36	0	59	8

Departmental Leaders: G—Dacus, 33; W—Brake, 12; L—Robinson, 10; Pct.—Brake, 1.000; GS—(Eight tied with 15); CG—Brake, 6; GF—Frohwirth, 25; ShO—Brake, Corbett, 2; Sv.—Dacus, Frohwirth, 11; IP—Brake, 112.2; H—Ackerman, 97; R—Robinson, 67; ER—Robinson, 50; HR—LoSauro, 7; HB—Hernandez, 11; BB—Kramer, 58; IBB—Ford, 6; SO—Messier, 116; WP—Ellis, Kramer, Rousey, 13.

(All Pitchers—Listed Alphabetically)

Pitcher—Club	W.	L.	Pct.	ERA.	G.	GS.	CG.	GF.	ShO.	Sv.	IP.	H.	R.	ER.	HR.	HB.	BB.	Int. BB.	SO.	WP.
Ackerman, Everett	6	4	.600	2.34	13	13	3	0	0	0	96.0	97	27	25	3	7	21	2	32	3
Arias, Medford	0	0	.000	0.00	1	0	0	1	0	0	1.0	0	0	0	0	0	1	0	0	0
Barton, Bend*	4	5	.444	2.16	13	8	1	1	0	0	58.1	46	28	14	3	4	24	0	47	2
Beaver, Medford	0	2	.000	3.75	4	1	0	1	0	0	12.0	12	6	5	0	0	7	2	14	0
Bell, Eugene	1	3	.250	9.09	21	0	0	6	0	0	33.2	48	39	34	2	1	19	3	23	6
Berrios, Eugene*	1	2	.333	2.53	22	2	0	6	0	0	57.0	52	26	16	1	2	34	5	70	3
Bitker, Spokane	4	4	.500	3.41	14	14	2	0	0	0	87.0	85	48	33	2	2	33	0	60	8
Blanchette, Bellingham	2	4	.333	3.56	22	1	0	12	0	4	43.0	37	28	17	2	2	21	0	36	8
Brake, Medford*	12	0	1.000	1.76	14	14	6	0	2	0	112.2	78	27	22	4	1	36	0	97	4
Brauchle, Eugene	4	6	.400	4.69	25	0	0	19	0	1	40.1	45	28	21	1	2	19	4	28	5
Bridges, Tri-Cities*	2	3	.400	4.36	20	0	0	15	0	5	33.0	34	21	16	4	0	13	1	43	5
Burns, Medford	3	0	1.000	0.50	22	0	0	18	0	8	36.1	21	4	2	0	0	12	1	63	0
Butler, Salem*	8	3	.727	2.91	15	15	1	0	0	0	92.2	82	38	30	2	3	47	0	73	8
Cedeno, Salem	0	1	.000	4.05	23	0	0	8	0	1	33.1	26	23	15	1	3	20	1	37	4
Cipres, Tri-Cities	4	2	.667	0.92	22	0	0	19	0	9	39.1	31	16	4	0	4	21	0	51	4
Cook, Salem*	2	3	.400	3.05	20	1	0	9	0	5	41.1	37	22	14	2	3	20	4	52	5
Corbett, Salem*	7	6	.538	3.14	15	15	3	0	2	0	100.1	75	42	35	5	2	43	0	97	12
Costello, Spokane	7	6	.538	2.72	15	15	3	0	1	0	102.2	85	48	31	3	1	43	1	114	4
Cottrell, Everett	0	2	.000	7.24	14	1	0	7	0	2	32.1	34	36	26	2	4	34	0	32	7
Creekmore, Bend	0	0	.000	5.40	4	0	0	3	0	0	6.2	13	4	4	1	0	1	0	6	1
Criswell, Medford*	3	2	.600	2.90	10	8	1	2	0	1	49.2	48	26	16	6	3	29	0	19	1
Crouch, Eugene	3	6	.333	2.81	16	9	1	5	1	0	57.2	45	28	18	4	2	34	1	42	6
Czyzewski, Spokane	3	9	.250	4.72	15	14	0	0	0	0	76.1	87	47	40	1	2	38	0	91	4
Dacus, Salem	5	3	.625	1.56	33	0	0	22	0	11	52.0	44	15	9	0	2	22	2	39	5
Danelson, Tri-Cities	2	1	.667	2.45	18	0	0	13	0	3	36.2	31	17	10	2	4	13	0	33	3
Daniel, Tri-Cities	1	1	.500	3.29	20	0	0	8	0	3	52.0	45	26	19	3	3	31	1	49	4
Dersin, Tri-Cities	10	1	.909	2.58	14	13	2	0	0	0	90.2	80	37	26	0	2	35	0	80	9
Echavarria, Everett	0	0	.000	7.88	5	0	0	4	0	0	8.0	12	8	7	1	1	6	0	2	2
Edwards, Medford	0	1	.000	2.91	11	4	0	2	0	0	43.1	45	16	14	1	2	14	0	21	2
Eggertsen, Salem	3	7	.300	3.68	14	14	1	0	0	0	73.1	59	46	30	6	4	57	0	62	9
Ellis, Eugene	0	0	.000	8.38	15	0	0	9	0	0	19.1	12	20	18	0	0	31	2	20	13
Ewing, Everett	0	0	.000	7.50	4	0	0	3	0	0	6.0	10	6	5	0	0	4	1	4	1
Fay, Tri-Cities	7	2	.778	3.74	16	13	0	1	0	0	77.0	61	45	32	2	4	57	0	44	8
Figueroa, Bend	1	3	.250	4.83	6	6	1	0	0	0	31.2	29	18	17	3	4	15	0	23	0
Filandino, Spokane	2	3	.400	4.32	9	7	0	2	0	0	41.2	47	24	20	0	1	19	0	22	5
Forbes, Spokane	2	1	.667	5.23	8	1	0	4	0	0	20.2	22	15	12	0	3	10	1	13	0
Ford, Spokane	2	3	.400	3.57	25	0	0	19	0	5	40.1	28	19	16	2	2	28	6	48	2
Freeman, Bend	8	5	.615	2.61	15	15	2	0	1	0	89.2	64	41	26	1	1	52	0	79	7
Frohwirth, Bend	4	4	.500	1.63	29	0	0	25	0	11	49.2	26	17	9	0	3	31	4	60	1
Gilbert, Everett	1	3	.250	5.95	13	0	0	3	0	0	39.1	42	30	26	0	0	30	2	39	7
Gildehaus, Spokane	2	2	.500	2.27	24	0	0	12	0	2	47.2	43	21	12	4	2	12	5	44	3
Hansen, Medford	0	0	.000	2.13	6	0	0	4	0	1	12.2	9	4	3	1	1	4	0	12	0
Harris, Medford	3	3	.500	2.90	8	5	2	1	0	0	40.1	41	16	13	2	0	9	0	26	2
Hernandez, Salem	0	0	.000	7.84	18	0	0	1	0	0	31.0	30	35	27	0	11	27	1	32	1
Higgs, Bellingham	3	1	.750	2.09	22	1	0	12	0	2	43.0	26	12	10	0	0	15	2	47	0
Hinnrichs, Everett	4	3	.571	1.92	24	0	0	17	0	4	51.2	43	15	11	0	1	28	5	49	2
Horrell, Salem	0	0	.000	10.13	3	0	0	2	0	0	2.2	6	6	3	0	0	3	0	3	0
Hyde, Bellingham	0	0	.000	9.00	1	0	0	1	0	0	1.0	0	1	1	0	0	2	0	1	0
Ittner, Tri-Cities	0	0	.000	4.15	6	3	0	1	0	0	13.0	16	8	6	1	0	10	0	13	0
Jester, Bend*	6	3	.667	2.15	13	10	0	2	0	0	71.0	57	23	17	2	1	19	0	57	3
Jones, Bellingham	5	0	1.000	2.41	10	9	0	0	0	0	59.2	29	23	16	0	7	36	0	59	8
Kazmierski, Spokane	2	3	.400	2.72	24	0	0	10	0	2	53.0	42	24	16	2	1	22	2	38	1
Keys, Spokane*	1	0	1.000	4.62	14	1	0	7	0	0	25.1	20	13	13	0	0	23	1	18	0
Kibler, Medford	6	6	.500	1.74	13	13	5	0	0	0	103.2	79	34	20	1	6	23	1	100	6
Kilgus, Tri-Cities*	7	5	.583	2.87	14	14	0	0	0	0	78.1	87	38	25	1	3	31	0	60	4
R. King, Tri-Cities*	0	0	.000	0.00	2	0	0	2	0	0	2.0	1	0	0	0	0	3	0	3	0
S. King, Bend	2	1	.667	3.20	13	5	0	1	0	0	39.1	43	24	14	0	4	23	1	13	1
Koller, Eugene	1	3	.250	6.43	14	7	0	3	0	0	49.0	50	43	35	0	10	53	0	50	10
Konruff, Eugene	0	3	.000	5.28	12	4	0	4	0	0	29.0	35	33	17	3	4	26	0	19	3
Kramer, Tri-Cities	5	6	.455	5.04	15	15	0	0	0	0	84.0	83	62	47	6	5	58	1	74	13
Labay, Bend*	0	1	.000	0.79	2	2	0	0	0	0	11.1	6	4	1	0	0	3	0	4	0
Lewis, Bellingham	0	0	.000	4.09	12	3	0	3	0	2	33.0	32	20	15	1	1	26	0	27	4
Lloyd, Bend*	2	0	1.000	3.29	3	1	0	2	0	0	13.2	14	5	5	2	1	2	0	13	2
LoSauro, Tri-Cities	6	6	.500	4.93	15	15	1	0	1	0	80.1	73	57	44	7	6	46	0	59	12
Madden, Bend*	1	1	.500	4.24	14	3	0	5	0	1	23.1	23	13	11	0	1	17	0	21	1
Martinez, Salem	3	8	.273	4.30	15	15	3	0	0	0	90.0	88	53	43	1	4	43	1	62	7
McCormack, Eugene	0	6	.000	6.23	11	6	0	1	0	0	43.1	50	40	30	4	1	27	3	21	4
McDevitt, Bend	5	3	.625	1.97	13	13	1	0	1	0	68.2	42	37	15	1	4	46	0	93	7
Melrose, Tri-Cities*	0	0	.000	2.70	3	0	0	2	0	0	6.2	4	2	2	0	0	4	0	3	2
Mendek, Bellingham*	2	3	.400	1.37	24	0	0	19	0	10	39.1	24	14	6	0	0	18	2	59	6
Messier, Everett*	4	5	.444	1.97	12	12	1	0	0	0	77.2	44	28	17	4	1	41	0	116	6
Metz, Bellingham	4	2	.667	4.25	24	1	0	13	0	3	48.2	47	31	23	3	1	22	4	40	2

Pitcher—Club	W.	L.	Pct.	ERA.	G.	GS.	CG.	GF.	ShO.	Sv.	IP.	H.	R.	ER.	HR.	HB.	BB.	Int. BB.	SO.	WP.
Miller, Bend°	1	7	.125	4.53	16	8	0	6	0	0	55.2	60	40	28	2	1	24	1	29	5
Moore, Bellingham	1	0	1.000	0.00	2	1	0	0	0	0	8.0	5	0	0	0	0	0	0	8	0
Morales, Eugene	0	0	.000	5.73	10	0	0	4	0	0	11.0	13	12	7	0	0	14	0	7	2
Moriarty, Everett°	7	4	.636	2.66	15	15	4	0	1	0	105.0	92	41	31	4	1	43	1	83	5
Mulholland, Everett°	1	0	1.000	0.00	3	3	0	0	0	0	19.0	10	2	0	0	1	4	0	15	0
Neufelder, Bellingham°	3	3	.500	4.18	15	14	1	0	1	0	79.2	78	46	37	5	3	33	0	80	7
Ojeda, Salem	2	2	.500	4.35	12	4	0	5	0	1	31.0	25	20	15	1	2	18	0	24	2
Olker, Everett°	4	4	.500	2.64	13	11	0	2	0	1	58.0	27	26	17	3	3	53	1	64	3
Osterode, Bellingham°	1	5	.167	3.19	21	1	0	10	0	4	42.1	35	18	15	1	1	23	1	33	3
Parrish, Medford	1	1	.500	2.05	6	4	0	2	0	0	22.0	19	6	5	2	0	7	0	19	0
Price, Salem°	0	2	.000	3.71	4	4	0	0	0	0	26.2	32	14	11	0	0	14	0	29	2
Puikunas, Medford°	8	2	.800	2.84	24	3	0	13	0	0	63.1	54	28	20	1	4	18	2	56	3
Radtke, Eugene	0	0	.000	0.96	3	2	0	0	0	0	18.2	11	5	2	0	0	8	0	19	0
Rivera, Salem	0	0	.000	9.35	9	0	0	5	0	0	8.2	15	9	9	0	0	5	0	6	1
Robertson, Spokane	6	3	.667	2.12	14	14	0	0	1	0	106.1	96	36	25	2	1	26	4	51	4
Robinson, Eugene	2	10	.167	6.05	14	14	1	0	0	0	74.1	85	67	50	4	2	44	4	52	2
Rodiles, Eugene	1	5	.167	3.58	11	10	2	0	1	0	55.1	58	39	22	1	2	26	0	36	4
Rogers, Eugene	0	1	.000	7.20	18	0	0	6	0	1	30.0	43	36	24	0	2	22	2	22	5
Romanovsky, Salem°	4	2	.667	3.29	13	6	2	4	1	1	54.2	50	25	20	2	1	19	0	56	0
Rousey, Bellingham	3	6	.333	2.64	13	12	0	0	0	0	75.0	66	38	22	2	2	43	0	58	13
Ruiz, Salem	1	2	.333	4.13	19	0	0	6	0	0	24.0	30	13	11	1	1	7	1	16	0
Sanchez, Medford	3	3	.500	4.02	17	7	1	1	1	0	62.2	60	31	28	5	2	33	0	37	0
Shepard, Bend	2	0	1.000	3.48	17	0	0	6	0	3	41.1	29	20	16	0	2	17	1	37	3
Shook, Eugene	0	0	.000	3.68	3	0	0	0	0	0	7.1	9	4	3	0	0	2	0	7	1
Siegel, Bellingham	6	1	.857	2.50	11	9	0	0	0	0	54.0	33	23	15	1	4	41	0	50	2
Sillivent, Salem°	0	0	.000	15.00	5	0	0	3	0	0	6.0	11	10	10	0	0	5	0	3	1
Silver, Everett°	2	4	.333	4.44	8	8	1	0	0	0	46.2	47	31	23	1	2	33	1	33	5
Simpson, Bend°	1	1	.500	2.18	17	2	0	7	0	4	41.1	14	14	10	1	0	27	0	53	3
Sparling, Eugene	4	3	.571	2.06	16	8	3	3	1	1	65.2	59	25	15	2	4	18	3	63	4
Stangel, Everett	1	3	.250	3.86	17	2	0	7	0	1	49.0	50	31	21	1	1	27	1	34	1
Strong, Medford	5	6	.455	3.88	20	9	3	10	0	2	72.0	64	33	31	2	2	36	2	66	4
Tate, Everett	1	2	.333	6.10	10	0	0	9	0	3	10.1	9	7	7	1	0	10	0	15	1
Tavarez, Everett	5	3	.625	4.60	22	2	0	12	0	1	43.0	47	28	22	3	1	21	0	28	1
B. Thomas, Bend	1	4	.200	3.26	10	6	1	3	0	2	38.2	34	18	14	2	2	13	1	23	4
S. Thomas, Tri-Cities	2	1	.667	2.50	21	0	0	10	0	5	57.2	52	22	16	3	2	18	0	30	1
Utley, Everett	0	0	.000	0.00	1	0	0	1	0	0	2.1	3	2	0	0	1	1	0	3	0
Valdez, Spokane°	1	2	.333	7.56	13	1	0	6	0	0	16.2	26	18	14	1	0	8	0	15	0
Van Vuren, Eugene	2	7	.222	5.56	12	12	1	0	0	0	55.0	67	41	34	2	3	39	0	42	5
Vargas, Bend	1	1	.500	1.60	16	1	0	8	0	0	39.1	25	13	7	1	6	11	0	39	1
Villa, Everett	0	1	.000	6.23	2	2	0	0	0	0	8.2	8	7	6	2	0	4	0	7	2
Visor, Spokane	3	3	.500	3.36	16	7	0	5	0	0	56.1	69	26	21	0	1	29	0	41	4
Walker, Bellingham	8	4	.667	2.16	14	14	3	0	1	0	95.2	65	29	23	3	1	28	0	88	4
West, Bellingham	4	3	.571	3.04	8	8	0	0	0	0	47.1	39	21	16	1	0	16	0	27	2

BALKS—Hernandez, 4; Eggertsen, Figueroa, 3 each; Rodiles, Tavarez, 2 each; Barton, Berrios, Bridges, Cedeno, Costello, Czyzewski, Edwards, Filandino, Hyde, Jones, Kibler, LoSauro, McCormack, McDevitt, Mendek, Moriarty, Neufelder, Ojeda, Olker, Price, Ruiz, Stangel, Van Vuren, Vargas, 1 each.

COMBINATION SHUTOUTS—Jones-Higgs, Neufelder-Higgs, Neufelder-Metz-Higgs, Siegel-Osterode, Walker-Neufelder-Higgs-Mendek, Bellingham; Barton-Simpson, Freeman-Jester-Shepard-Barton, Bend; Olker-Tavarez, Messier-Stangel, Messier-Tate, Everett; Kibler-Burns, Kibler-Strong, Criswell-Hansen, Puikunas-Sanchez-Strong, Brake-Burns, Medford; Butler-Dacus-Romanovsky, Salem; Czyzewski-Forbes-Valdez, Visor-Ford, Spokane; Dersin-Cipres, Ittner-Daniel, Kilgus-Daniel, Kramer-Thomas, Tri-Cities.

NO-HIT GAMES—None.

South Atlantic League

CLASS A

CHAMPIONSHIP WINNERS IN PREVIOUS YEARS

1948—Lincolnton* .627	1965—Salisbury .641	1975—Spartanburg .543
1949—Newton-Conover .667	Rock Hill‡ .603	Spartanburg .614
Ruth'ford Co. (2nd)† .627	1966—Spartanburg .682	1976—Asheville .544
1950—Newton-Conover .627	Spartanburg .767	Greenwood‡ .600
Lenoir (2nd)† .626	1967—Spartanburg .730	1977—Greenwood .557
1951—Morganton .645	Spartanburg .567	Gastonia‡ .590
Shelby (2nd)† .604	1968—Spartanburg .597	1978—Greenwood .614
1952—Lincolnton .649	Greenwood‡ .597	Greenwood .565
Shelby (2nd)† .645	1969—Greenwood‡ .587	1979—Greenwood‡ .565
1953-59—League inactive.	Shelby .565	Spartanburg .525
1960—Lexington .707	1970—Greenville .576	1980—Greensboro .590
Salisbury (2nd)† .650	Greenville .619	Charleston .561
1961—Salisbury .627	1971—Greenwood .631	1981—Greensboro‡ .695
Shelby (4th)† .481	Greenwood .759	Greenwood .549
1962—Statesville .563	1972—Spartanburg‡ .788	1982—Greensboro‡ .681
Statesville .700	Greenville .652	Florence .546
1963—Greenville† .576	1973—Spartanburg‡ .646	1983—Columbia .620
Salisbury .631	Gastonia .619	Gastonia‡ .587
1964—Rock Hill .672	1974—Gastonia .606	
Salisbury‡ .631	Gastonia .672	

*Won championship and four-club playoff. †Won four-club playoff. ‡Won split-season playoff. (NOTE—Known as Western Carolina League from 1948 through 1962 and known as Western Carolinas League through 1979.)

STANDING OF CLUBS AT CLOSE OF FIRST HALF, JUNE 20

NORTHERN DIVISION

Club	W.	L.	T.	Pct.	G.B.
Greensboro (Yankees)	44	28	0	.611	......
Gastonia (Expos)	38	34	0	.528	6
Spartanburg (Phillies)	37	34	0	.521	6½
Asheville (Astros)	31	41	0	.431	13
Anderson (Braves)	24	48	0	.333	20

SOUTHERN DIVISION

Club	W.	L.	T.	Pct.	G.B.
Charleston (Royals)	45	26	0	.634	......
Columbia (Mets)	42	29	0	.592	3
Savannah (Cardinals)	37	34	0	.521	8
Macon (Pirates)	30	42	0	.417	15½
Florence (Blue Jays)	29	41	0	.414	15½

STANDING OF CLUBS AT CLOSE OF SECOND HALF, AUGUST 31

NORTHERN DIVISION

Club	W.	L.	T.	Pct.	G.B.
Asheville (Astros)	42	29	0	.592	......
Anderson (Braves)	37	34	0	.521	5
Spartanburg (Phillies)	33	36	0	.478	8
Greensboro (Yankees)	31	41	0	.431	11½
Gastonia (Expos)	29	41	0	.414	12½

SOUTHERN DIVISION

Club	W.	L.	T.	Pct.	G.B.
Savannah (Cardinals)	41	27	0	.603	......
Columbia (Mets)	40	28	1	.588	1
Florence (Blue Jays)	36	32	0	.529	5
Charleston (Royals)	33	38	1	.465	9½
Macon (Pirates)	27	43	0	.386	15

COMPOSITE STANDING OF CLUBS AT CLOSE OF SEASON, AUGUST 31

Club	Col.	Sav.	Char.	Gbr.	Ash.	Spar.	Gas.	Flo.	And.	Mac.	W.	L.	T.	Pct.	G.B.
Columbia (Mets)	....	6	7	8	11	10	11	7	14	8	82	57	1	.590	......
Savannah (Cardinals)	4	....	13	6	4	8	7	13	8	15	78	61	0	.561	4
Charleston (Royals)	4	11	....	8	7	8	6	12	8	14	78	64	1	.549	5½
Greensboro (Yankees)	10	6	4	....	11	9	13	8	8	6	75	69	0	.521	9½
Asheville (Astros)	7	8	5	7	....	15	7	4	12	8	73	70	0	.510	11
Spartanburg (Phillies)	8	3	4	9	9	....	11	6	12	8	70	70	0	.500	12½
Gastonia (Expos)	7	4	6	11	11	7	....	8	7	6	67	75	0	.472	16½
Florence (Blue Jays)	3	11	4	7	4	4	4	....	7	14	65	73	0	.471	16½
Anderson (Braves)	10	3	4	10	6	6	11	5	....	6	61	82	0	.427	23
Macon (Pirates)	4	9	10	6	4	3	5	10	6	....	57	85	0	.401	26½

Major league affiliations in parentheses.

Playoffs—Asheville defeated Greensboro, two games to one; Charleston defeated Savannah, two games to one, and Asheville defeated Charleston, three games to none, to win league championship.

Regular-Season Attendance—Anderson, 24,935; Asheville, 66,597; Charleston, 117,185; Columbia, 76,650; Florence, 44,217; Gastonia, 60,832; Greensboro, 183,646; Macon, 32,059; Savannah, 37,897; Spartanburg, 40,223. Total, 684,241. Playoff attendance, 7,640. All-Star attendance, 1,677.

Managers—Anderson, Rick Albert; Asheville, Tom Spencer; Charleston, Duane Gustavson; Columbia, Rich Miller; Florence, Dennis Holmberg; Gastonia, Junior Miner; Greensboro, Carlos Tosca; Macon, Joe Frisina; Savannah, Lloyd Merritt; Spartanburg, Jay Ward.

All-Star Team: 1B—Andy Lawrence, Columbia; 2B—Ramon Sambo, Spartanburg; 3B—Kevin Seitzer, Charleston; SS—Manuel Lee, Columbia; OF—Wayne Dannenberg, Spartanburg; George Chadwick, Gastonia; Dave Dyrek, Asheville; Brad Winkler, Greensboro; C-Sal D'Alessandro, Anderson; DH—Maurice Ching, Greensboro; RHP—Jeff Hull, Charleston; LHP-Cliff Young, Gastonia; RH Rel Pit—Ramon Caraballo, Spartanburg; LH Rel Pit—Joe Klink, Columbia; Most Valuable Player—Kevin Seitzer, Charleston; Most Outstanding Pitcher—Ramon Caraballo, Spartanburg; Manager of the Year-Rich Miller, Columbia.

(Compiled by Howe News Bureau, Boston, Mass.)

CLUB BATTING

Club	Pct.	G.	AB.	R.	OR.	H.	TB.	2B.	3B.	HR.	RBI.	GW.	SH.	SF.	HP.	BB.	Int. BB.	SO.	SB.	CS.	LOB.
Florence	.256	138	4399	670	671	1125	1686	209	35	94	583	55	22	37	29	535	10	809	122	57	951
Columbia	.255	140	4385	714	586	1118	1578	200	34	64	578	63	49	38	33	646	28	793	196	46	994
Spartanburg	.249	140	4572	689	703	1137	1566	190	40	53	575	59	24	43	33	602	24	890	182	61	1035
Charleston	.243	143	4618	746	672	1120	1552	171	45	57	628	67	21	50	38	816	16	904	227	72	1148
Asheville	.242	143	4390	647	606	1064	1576	192	25	90	572	63	41	37	34	677	19	853	135	54	1051
Greensboro	.236	144	4449	647	610	1051	1467	146	33	68	536	64	24	43	33	669	24	882	225	63	1004
Gastonia	.235	142	4332	586	595	1019	1412	184	10	63	488	53	62	41	25	675	18	603	91	36	1041
Macon	.228	142	4453	526	714	1017	1387	150	29	54	436	49	30	35	45	473	18	895	133	58	936
Anderson	.225	143	4302	517	672	969	1346	171	40	42	432	50	61	40	35	607	17	964	107	39	1059
Savannah	.224	139	4327	642	555	970	1379	149	16	76	544	67	33	42	38	623	11	678	202	54	954

INDIVIDUAL BATTING

(Leading Qualifiers for Batting Championship—389 or More Plate Appearances)

*Bats lefthanded.   †Switch-hitter.

Player and Club	Pct.	G.	AB.	R.	H.	TB.	2B.	3B.	HR.	RBI.	GW.	SH.	SF.	HP.	BB.	Int. BB.	SO.	SB.	CS.
Lee, Manuel, Columbia†	.329	102	346	84	114	142	12	5	2	33	1	1	4	0	60	2	42	24	6
Sambo, Ramon, Spartanburg†	.300	96	353	75	106	119	9	2	0	29	4	0	0	1	64	2	55	57	14
Ching, Mauricio, Greensboro*	.298	110	325	52	97	162	17	3	14	62	9	0	3	1	67	2	93	7	3
Seitzer, Kevin, Charleston	.297	141	489	96	145	205	26	5	8	79	9	1	6	3	118	2	70	23	5
Caraballo, Wilmer, Columbia	.296	110	398	65	118	207	27	1	20	81	11	2	8	2	17	0	74	2	3
Jordan, Paul, Spartanburg	.292	128	490	72	143	204	23	4	10	76	7	0	5	4	32	2	63	8	2
Dennis, Eduardo, Florence	.289	105	380	53	110	163	22	5	7	55	4	3	4	15	0	17	4	0
Kauil, Kurtis, Savannah	.287	128	453	67	130	188	24	2	10	85	16	1	4	3	54	0	47	25	3
Mabe, Todd, Charleston†	.286	123	447	86	128	157	10	5	3	43	6	7	2	1	92	1	69	32	17
Harrison, Wayne, Anderson	.284	134	391	50	111	166	17	4	10	56	10	2	5	9	73	2	58	3	1

Departmental Leaders: G—Petersen, Seitzer, 141; AB—Garrison, 502; R—Seitzer, 96; H—Seitzer, 145; TB—Lawrence, 208; 2B—Nipper, 37; 3B—Tenacen, Van Blaricom, Wallace, 9; HR—W. Caraballo, Digioia, 20; RBI—Borders, Kauil, 85; GWRBI—Lawrence, 18; SH—Soto, 10; SF—Longenecker, 13; HP—Tenacen, 13; BB—Seitzer, 118; IBB—Dannenberg, 6; SO—Hill, 150; SB—Reboulet, 62; CS—Mabe, Thurman, 17.

(All Players—Listed Alphabetically)

Player and Club	Pct.	G.	AB.	R.	H.	TB.	2B.	3B.	HR.	RBI.	GW.	SH.	SF.	HP.	BB.	Int. BB.	SO.	SB.	CS.
Adkins, Terry, Macon	.500	13	2	0	1	1	0	0	0	0	0	0	0	0	0	0	0	0	0
Afenir, M. Troy, Asheville	.193	115	358	44	69	133	16	0	16	69	2	0	4	6	2	39	1	125	1	2
Agostinelli, Salvatore, Savannah	.234	67	175	30	41	48	7	0	0	17	2	0	0	4	40	1	13	6	3
Akers, Howard, Florence*	.253	104	292	52	74	104	14	5	2	27	3	2	1	1	69	2	84	20	7
Allaire, Karl, Asheville*	.219	9	32	4	7	9	0	1	0	7	2	0	0	0	4	1	9	1	0
Angelo, Mark, Savannah	.230	118	395	47	91	147	18	1	12	61	5	0	5	2	41	1	69	4	4
Anglin, Russell, Anderson	.150	11	20	0	3	3	0	0	0	1	0	0	0	0	1	0	1	0	0
Antone, Ralph, Gastonia	.253	128	419	56	106	160	24	0	10	64	7	3	2	3	64	2	43	1	0
Bachman, Kent, Gastonia	.204	51	157	17	32	54	8	1	4	24	3	1	2	4	14	0	49	3	1
Baird, Christopher, Anderson*	.182	56	165	20	30	43	9	2	0	13	0	0	3	0	29	1	53	6	2
Baker, Derrell, Gastonia	.303	70	238	51	72	107	12	1	7	31	4	4	1	49	1	20	5	4
Ballou, Gary, Anderson	.214	49	145	14	31	41	7	0	1	13	1	0	0	19	0	36	1	2
Barger, Vincent, Anderson*	.429	4	7	0	3	3	0	0	0	0	0	2	0	1	0	0	0	0
Barrett, Timothy, Gastonia*	.091	13	22	2	2	2	0	0	0	0	0	2	0	2	0	10	0	0
Bautista, Jose, Columbia	.357	24	42	5	15	19	1	0	1	6	0	0	2	1	10	4	0
Behrend, Michael, Savannah	.125	34	8	0	1	1	0	0	0	0	0	0	0	2	0	3	0	0
Belcik, Keith, Columbia	.200	20	40	4	8	10	2	0	0	6	1	0	1	1	5	0	9	0	0
Belen, Lance, Macon	.274	74	281	35	77	127	12	4	10	40	4	1	0	3	24	1	48	2	2
Blasucci, Anthony, Macon*	.111	14	9	2	1	1	0	0	0	2	0	0	1	0	3	0	0
Bolivar, Esteban, Florence	.267	5	15	3	4	5	1	0	0	2	0	0	0	1	0	4	0	0
Bombard, Richard, Asheville	.000	5	5	0	0	0	0	0	0	0	0	0	0	0	2	0	0
Borders, Patrick, Florence	.276	131	467	69	129	207	32	5	12	85	11	0	3	1	56	0	109	3	4
Brahs, Gary, Gastonia*	.200	3	5	1	1	1	0	0	0	0	0	0	0	2	0	1	0	0
Braukmiller, Kurt, Gastonia	.333	2	3	0	1	2	1	0	0	2	0	0	0	0	0	0	0	0
Brisco, Jamie, Savannah	.071	26	14	1	1	1	0	0	0	0	0	0	0	3	0	5	0	0
Butters, David, Macon	.190	17	42	3	8	11	3	0	0	2	1	1	0	1	5	0	12	0	0
Callahan, Michael, Asheville	.200	29	10	2	2	2	0	0	0	0	0	0	0	4	0	0	0
Canseco, Osvaldo, Greensboro	.000	8	1	0	0	0	0	0	0	0	0	0	0	0	0	0	0
Caraballo, Ramon, Spartanburg	.125	52	8	0	1	1	0	0	0	0	0	0	0	1	0	5	0	1
Caraballo, Wilmer, Columbia	.296	110	398	65	118	207	27	1	20	81	11	2	8	2	17	0	74	2	3
Carmichael, Alan, Columbia	.179	42	123	14	22	33	5	0	2	4	2	1	1	21	3	34	1	0
Carpenter, Douglas, Greensboro	.211	122	365	58	77	121	17	3	7	44	4	2	5	7	72	0	90	27	4
Carrasco, Ernest, Savannah	.000	46	5	0	0	0	0	0	0	0	0	0	0	0	0	4	0	0
Carson, Henry, Savannah	.063	25	32	2	2	2	0	0	0	3	1	0	0	2	0	4	0	0
Chadwick, George, Gastonia	.278	139	450	71	125	167	28	1	4	52	6	7	5	2	106	1	36	12	6
Chestna, Mark, Greensboro	.000	4	3	0	0	0	0	0	0	0	0	0	0	1	0	1	0	1
Ching, Mauricio, Greensboro*	.298	110	325	52	97	162	17	3	14	62	9	0	3	1	67	2	93	7	3
Clark, T. Kennedy, Anderson	.209	78	225	30	47	58	7	2	0	16	2	1	1	1	49	0	39	6	3
Clawson, Christopher, Anderson	.186	46	118	21	22	31	4	1	1	5	0	1	1	1	26	0	45	1	0
Cobb, Robert, Gastonia*	.274	69	248	40	68	82	8	0	2	19	3	3	1	1	28	1	27	10	1
Coffman, Kevin, Anderson	.250	7	4	0	1	1	0	0	0	1	0	1	0	0	2	0	0	0
Coleman, Jerome, Gastonia*	.212	87	208	31	44	50	4	1	0	15	4	6	3	2	24	0	13	11	3
Collins, Allen, Gastonia	.063	14	16	1	1	1	0	0	0	0	0	0	1	0	7	0	0
Cooke, John, Macon	.091	47	11	0	1	1	0	0	0	0	0	0	0	0	4	0	0
Cooper, Mark, Florence	.227	31	97	13	22	36	8	0	2	13	2	0	0	10	0	7	0	1
Coss, David, Macon	.276	66	210	37	58	72	7	2	1	19	0	3	0	30	0	27	22	6
Costello, John, Savannah	.097	26	31	3	3	3	0	0	0	2	0	2	0	1	0	9	0	0
Creekmore, G. Edward, Spartanburg	.000	23	2	0	0	0	0	0	0	0	0	0	0	0	0	0	0
Cuevas, Angelo, Columbia*	.130	8	23	2	3	4	0	0	1	0	0	0	2	0	3	0	0
Cunningham, Charles, Macon	.444	36	9	2	4	4	0	0	0	1	0	1	0	0	2	0	3	0	0
Cutshall, William, Gastonia*	.273	8	11	0	3	3	0	0	0	0	0	0	2	0	1	0	0
D'Alessandro, Salvatore, Anderson	.222	113	342	36	76	108	14	3	4	45	7	1	5	2	51	2	59	5	0
Dannenberg, Wayne, Spartanburg*	.270	120	444	66	120	179	21	7	8	69	8	1	8	1	43	6	89	10	1
Davis, Robert, Charleston	.173	39	110	8	19	22	3	0	0	10	2	1	3	0	11	1	20	0	0
Dearth, Ronald, Gastonia	.197	83	218	20	43	55	6	0	2	19	2	2	4	0	26	1	43	5	0
DeLaRosa, Marino, Spartanburg	.174	19	46	2	8	9	1	0	0	2	1	0	0	3	0	10	2	1

Player and Club	Pct.	G.	AB.	R.	H.	TB.	2B.	3B.	HR.	RBI.	GW.	SH.	SF.	HP.	BB.	Int. BB.	SO.	SB.	CS.
DelRosario, Maximo, Anderson	.000	28	13	0	0	0	0	0	0	0	0	0	0	1	1	0	11	0	0
Delucchi, Ronald, Macon	.240	99	338	37	81	119	14	3	6	45	6	1	3	5	33	0	49	5	3
Dennis, Eduardo, Florence	.289	105	380	53	110	163	22	5	7	55	4	6	3	4	15	0	17	4	0
Diaz, Jose, Florence	.188	36	85	11	16	19	3	0	0	8	1	1	0	1	11	0	17	4	1
Digioia, John, Savannah	.282	68	216	40	61	133	12	0	20	57	10	0	5	2	37	0	57	1	1
Dinkel, Jeffrey, Columbia	.272	103	309	47	84	114	19	1	3	56	3	2	3	6	59	1	42	2	4
Dobie, Reginald, Columbia	.075	26	40	5	3	4	1	0	0	2	0	5	0	0	3	0	7	1	0
Dombek, Damon, Spartanburg†	.071	28	28	0	2	2	0	0	0	0	0	0	0	0	3	0	7	0	0
Dophied, W. Tracy, Asheville°	.240	76	242	45	58	96	15	1	7	33	6	2	0	1	46	4	48	13	5
Drummond, Timothy, Macon	.120	27	25	2	3	4	1	0	0	0	0	2	0	0	4	0	12	0	0
Dube, Gregory, Asheville	.103	23	29	3	3	4	1	0	0	2	0	2	2	0	0	0	13	0	0
Durocher, Francois, Macon	.000	35	6	1	0	0	0	0	0	0	0	1	0	0	1	0	3	0	0
Dyrek, David, Asheville°	.275	130	411	69	113	147	19	3	3	32	2	2	2	0	113	2	67	31	10
Edens, Thomas, Columbia	.235	16	17	0	4	4	0	0	0	1	0	0	0	1	0	0	2	0	0
Edwards, David, Asheville	.224	58	116	9	26	33	7	0	0	10	0	0	0	0	8	0	20	3	0
Englehart, William, Greensboro°	.282	100	326	53	92	138	11	1	11	55	6	0	3	6	61	5	50	3	1
Engram, Graylyn, Spartanburg	.237	102	325	51	77	105	11	4	3	43	6	2	3	1	47	1	46	8	7
Escobar, Santiago, Florence	.195	59	164	16	32	34	2	0	0	8	0	1	1	1	8	0	26	8	1
Foley, Keith, Greensboro	.098	21	61	1	6	9	3	0	0	3	0	0	0	0	3	0	7	1	0
Fortaleza, Raymond, Greensboro	.173	78	220	21	38	48	5	1	1	20	4	0	6	1	19	0	53	5	2
Fredymond, Juan, Anderson	.254	92	307	40	78	97	7	6	0	34	4	3	1	4	28	0	79	12	6
Friedel, Charles, Columbia	.143	5	7	0	1	2	1	0	0	0	0	0	0	1	0	1	0	0
Fulgencio, Jose, Florence	.282	73	234	28	66	78	7	1	1	33	4	1	0	5	29	0	39	2	3
Funk, Thomas, Asheville°	.222	54	9	1	2	3	1	0	0	2	0	1	0	0	1	0	4	1	0
Gant, Ronnie, Anderson	.237	105	359	44	85	120	14	6	3	38	8	0	6	1	29	0	65	13	5
Garrison, Webster, Florence	.239	129	502	80	120	134	14	0	0	33	6	2	2	1	57	0	44	16	7
Gass, Jeffrey, Savannah	.000	9	3	2	0	0	0	0	0	0	0	0	0	0	3	0	3	0	0
Gay, Steven, Columbia	.071	31	14	1	1	2	1	0	0	1	0	0	1	0	2	0	4	0	0
George, Nathaniel, Greensboro	.285	108	267	54	76	104	13	3	3	35	3	1	2	2	55	1	46	24	6
Gil, Jose, Spartanburg	.299	81	288	34	86	108	19	0	1	52	5	0	4	2	20	1	30	2	1
Gillermo, Carlos, Florence	.189	41	111	13	21	27	0	0	2	17	2	2	0	0	5	0	16	3	2
Glynn, Dennis, Columbia	.250	14	44	8	11	12	1	0	0	7	0	2	0	0	8	0	8	2	1
Gonzales, Robinson, Gastonia	.174	77	184	19	32	38	6	0	0	15	0	1	0	0	15	0	30	2	3
Gonzalez, Fredi, Greensboro	.196	85	250	21	49	69	11	0	3	33	4	1	4	3	27	2	72	4	1
Gordon, Kevin, Macon	.000	27	2	0	0	0	0	0	0	0	0	0	0	0	0	0	0	0	1
Green, Otis, Florence°	.266	43	158	31	42	71	6	4	5	26	1	0	2	0	19	1	32	9	1
Grosdidier, William, Anderson	.400	19	5	0	2	2	0	0	0	0	0	0	0	0	0	0	2	0	0
Groves, Jeffrey, Anderson	.000	4	5	0	0	0	0	0	0	0	0	0	0	0	0	0	5	0	0
Grudzinski, Gary, Macon	.143	25	14	1	2	5	0	0	1	2	0	0	0	0	1	0	4	0	0
Gutierrez, Dimas, Macon	.248	66	242	26	60	80	13	2	1	19	0	3	0	7	2	45	3	3
Hall, D. Andrew, Macon	.190	73	189	16	36	52	9	2	1	10	1	1	0	1	10	0	60	0	1
Hall, Gary, Anderson	.206	44	136	16	28	32	4	0	0	5	0	0	1	1	17	1	33	7	1
Hammond, Randy, Asheville	.000	46	6	0	0	0	0	0	0	0	0	0	0	0	0	0	2	0	0
Hardee, Amos, Gastonia°	.333	7	6	0	2	2	0	0	0	1	0	0	0	0	0	0	1	0	0
Harris, Glenn, Asheville°	.223	115	291	37	65	85	6	1	4	28	3	1	4	0	40	2	43	4	1
Harrison, Wayne, Anderson	.284	134	391	50	111	166	17	4	10	56	10	2	5	9	73	2	58	3	1
Hartshorn, R. Kyle, Columbia°	.233	24	30	6	7	12	2	0	1	6	1	4	1	0	6	0	10	0	0
Hazlett, James, Anderson°	.000	6	1	0	0	0	0	0	0	0	0	0	0	0	0	0	0	0	0
Helton, Kevin, Macon	.286	9	7	1	2	3	1	0	0	3	0	0	0	0	0	0	1	0	0
Hernandez, Juan M., Greensboro	.162	20	68	4	11	12	1	0	0	3	0	2	0	0	5	0	13	3	0
Herzog, Hans, Savannah°	.000	46	5	0	0	0	0	0	0	0	0	0	0	0	2	0	0	0	0
Hicks, Robert, Spartanburg	.200	19	5	0	1	1	0	0	0	0	0	0	0	0	0	0	2	0	0
Hill, Glenallen, Florence	.239	129	440	75	105	182	19	5	16	64	10	0	6	3	63	3	150	30	15
Hinson, Bobby Joe, Asheville	.244	91	225	38	55	59	4	0	0	18	0	3	2	2	35	1	13	6	0
Holman, Brian, Gastonia	.154	20	13	0	2	3	1	0	0	4	1	1	0	0	0	0	10	0	0
Holman, Shawn, Macon	.125	9	8	1	1	1	0	0	0	0	0	1	0	0	2	0	4	0	0
Houp, Scott, Asheville	.200	107	170	26	34	46	6	0	2	13	2	2	4	25	0	55	4	4
Householder, Brian, Spartanburg	.000	40	9	1	0	0	0	0	0	0	0	2	0	0	1	0	6	0	0
Huth, Kenneth, Savannah	.199	48	156	20	31	50	7	0	4	26	3	0	3	1	26	0	33	5	2
Impagliazzo, Joseph, Gastonia	.100	42	10	0	1	2	1	0	0	2	0	0	0	0	1	0	7	0	0
Isaac, Johnny, Asheville†	.256	31	82	9	21	33	6	0	2	9	2	0	1	8	0	26	4	2
Isner, Donald, Savannah	.144	36	90	10	13	20	1	0	2	6	0	0	1	0	18	0	26	1	0
Jackson, Charles, Asheville	.261	59	199	42	52	79	12	0	5	32	7	1	2	1	40	0	28	12	2
Jackson, Michael, Spartanburg	.368	14	19	4	7	10	3	0	0	7	0	1	0	0	1	0	1	0	0
James, Richard, Savannah	.228	112	307	45	70	96	11	3	3	40	6	0	3	3	39	1	20	11	7
Jimenez, Francisco, Macon°	.219	10	32	3	7	10	1	1	0	4	0	0	0	0	4	0	7	0	0
Job, Ryan, Asheville	.250	134	480	64	120	146	19	2	1	43	4	3	4	7	49	0	47	18	5
Johnson, M. Gregory, Gastonia	.000	9	1	0	0	0	0	0	0	0	0	0	1	0	0	0	0	0	0
Johnson, Todd, Spartanburg	.235	96	268	36	63	92	10	2	5	35	1	2	1	3	35	0	88	16	3
Johnston, J. Mark, Greensboro°	.111	9	27	2	3	6	0	0	1	4	1	0	1	2	6	0	3	0	0
Jones, David, Anderson	.222	23	36	2	8	10	2	0	0	5	0	6	1	0	1	0	10	1	0
Jordan, Paul, Spartanburg	.292	128	490	72	143	204	23	4	10	76	7	0	5	4	32	2	63	8	2
Karr, Jeffrey, Columbia	.213	26	80	10	17	21	1	0	1	2	0	0	0	10	1	7	0	0
Kaull, Kurtis, Savannah	.287	128	453	67	130	188	24	2	10	85	16	1	4	3	54	0	47	25	3
Kelley, Anthony, Asheville	.053	26	38	2	2	3	1	0	0	3	0	6	1	0	2	0	16	0	0
Kelly, Roberto, Greensboro	.238	111	361	68	86	106	13	2	1	26	4	1	3	1	57	0	49	42	10
Kiernan, T. Michael, Macon	.000	21	1	0	0	0	0	0	0	0	0	0	0	0	0	0	0	0	0
Kingsley, Ross, Anderson°	.226	14	31	3	7	7	0	0	0	0	0	0	0	5	1	4	0	0
Kish, Robert, Savannah	.091	12	11	1	1	1	0	0	0	0	0	1	0	0	0	0	4	0	0
Klink, Joseph, Columbia°	.167	31	6	1	1	1	0	0	0	0	0	0	0	0	0	0	2	0	0
Knox, David, Columbia	.243	59	185	28	45	59	8	0	2	25	3	1	1	0	27	0	31	2	1
Kolb, Jonathan, Macon	.167	11	6	0	1	1	0	0	0	0	0	2	0	0	0	0	1	0	0
Kraft, Kenneth, Spartanburg	.251	136	490	91	123	142	17	1	0	47	6	4	6	1	95	1	57	24	8
Krupa, Thomas, Gastonia°	.228	106	263	32	60	95	14	0	7	42	6	3	1	0	38	3	47	0	0
Kunz, Kurt, Charleston	.143	22	49	5	7	8	1	0	0	6	1	2	1	1	9	0	18	2	1
LaCava, Tony, Macon	.153	46	118	8	18	19	1	0	0	6	1	2	1	1	19	0	0
Lajszky, Werner, Columbia	.200	22	50	7	10	18	2	0	2	9	1	0	2	5	0	12	0	0
Landrith, David, Charleston	.211	49	171	13	36	39	3	0	0	14	1	0	1	0	11	1	38	6	1
Lange, Clarke, Anderson	.193	62	187	26	36	53	9	1	2	14	1	1	3	5	39	0	42	2	2
Lauck, Jeffrey, Savannah†	.203	81	197	24	40	49	3	0	2	14	1	0	2	1	30	0	51	4	0
Lawrence, Andy, Columbia	.269	138	484	73	130	208	35	5	11	83	18	1	3	6	61	3	96	2	4
Ledezma, C. Julio, Anderson	.208	57	149	8	31	42	4	2	1	12	1	2	1	1	18	0	35	1	1

Player and Club	Pct.	G.	AB.	R.	H.	TB.	2B.	3B.	HR.	RBI.	GW.	SH.	SF.	HP.	BB.	Int. BB.	SO.	SB.	CS.
Lee, Manuel, Columbia†	.329	102	346	84	114	142	12	5	2	33	1	1	4	0	60	2	42	24	6
Lemke, Mark, Anderson†	.149	42	121	18	18	20	2	0	0	5	1	0	2	1	14	0	14	3	1
Lemon, Ricky, Gastonia°	.221	39	95	10	21	28	7	0	0	6	0	0	0	0	5	1	10	4	0
Lind, Jose, Macon	.207	121	396	39	82	91	5	2	0	30	6	2	3	0	29	3	48	17	7
Llewellyn, Paul, Anderson	.216	99	245	34	53	74	7	1	4	21	0	1	2	2	32	0	72	2	3
Lloyd, Raymond, Spartanburg°	.188	12	16	2	3	3	0	0	0	1	0	0	0	1	0	6	0	1	
Long, Bruce, Spartanburg	.190	24	42	1	8	9	1	0	0	3	0	2	1	0	2	0	16	0	0
Longenecker, Jere, Charleston	.268	134	497	90	133	192	28	2	9	84	8	1	13	4	60	4	57	29	4
Lopes, Howard J., Gastonia	.238	49	143	20	34	43	7	1	0	10	1	5	1	2	16	0	22	2	2
Lopez, Saul, Macon	.211	14	19	3	4	9	0	1	1	4	0	1	1	0	1	0	3	0	0
Lora, Jesus, Asheville	.205	16	44	2	9	11	2	0	0	0	0	0	0	0	3	1	11	0	0
Lowe, Dion, Spartanburg°	.231	93	264	40	61	79	9	0	3	32	0	1	2	0	41	2	59	5	6
Lucas, Arbrey, Asheville	.000	45	12	1	0	0	0	0	0	0	0	1	0	1	0	10	0	0	
Lucas, David, Gastonia	.158	50	114	15	18	21	3	0	0	11	1	2	3	0	19	1	9	9	3
Lyden, Mitchell, Greensboro	.219	14	32	3	7	11	1	0	1	2	1	0	0	0	1	1	9	0	0
Mabe, Todd, Charleston†	.286	123	447	86	128	157	10	5	3	43	6	7	2	1	92	1	69	32	17
MacKay, Joey, Greensboro	.210	84	248	27	52	66	9	1	1	25	2	3	3	1	32	1	38	8	4
Magrann, Thomas, Spartanburg	.222	68	203	32	45	61	4	3	2	28	4	1	2	0	34	0	33	1	0
Mallicoat, Robbin, Asheville°	.176	13	17	1	3	3	0	0	0	0	0	2	0	1	0	4	0	0	
Maloney, J. Christopher, Columbia†	.324	56	173	27	56	77	12	0	3	24	3	0	1	1	41	3	23	1	1
Martin, Charles, Anderson	.000	19	2	0	0	0	0	0	0	0	0	0	0	0	0	0	2	0	0
Massiah, Omar, Macon	.198	101	268	33	53	76	9	1	4	20	0	1	2	6	24	0	63	8	1
Mathews, Gregory, Savannah†	.000	6	5	0	0	0	0	0	0	0	1	0	0	0	0	2	0	0	
Mattocks, Richard, Greensboro	.208	133	442	77	92	104	4	4	0	22	4	4	1	0	99	0	84	54	11
McAllister, Steven, Macon	.266	106	346	51	92	118	13	2	3	37	5	3	4	4	53	2	50	16	4
McClain, Gregory, Macon	.234	59	197	26	46	72	11	0	5	32	4	0	3	5	26	1	40	8	1
McCulla, Henry, Savannah	.222	55	176	33	39	69	9	0	7	28	3	1	1	3	43	2	32	1	1
McGrath, Charles, Savannah	.174	25	23	1	4	4	0	0	0	1	0	3	0	0	2	0	10	0	0
McKnight, Jefferson, Columbia°	.255	95	251	31	64	79	10	1	1	27	2	1	1	1	26	2	17	9	1
McLarnon, John, Spartanburg	.143	30	7	1	1	1	0	0	0	0	0	0	0	0	1	0	4	0	0
McPherson, Barry, Savannah	.167	12	6	2	1	1	0	0	0	1	0	1	0	0	3	0	1	0	0
Meacham, Timothy, Anderson	.000	18	3	1	0	0	0	0	0	0	0	0	0	0	1	0	3	0	0
Medina, Pedro, Greensboro†	.163	65	221	26	36	44	6	1	0	21	4	3	3	2	20	1	35	5	2
Mehalko, Andrew, Anderson°	.000	29	10	0	0	0	0	0	0	0	0	6	0	0	1	0	4	0	0
Milner, Theodore, Savannah°	.195	97	226	49	44	54	3	2	1	20	3	1	2	7	55	1	38	25	5
Mitchell, Thomas, Asheville	.291	66	237	37	69	116	14	6	7	43	2	1	0	3	27	0	53	13	4
Moore, Bryant, Macon	.249	58	193	24	48	56	4	2	0	13	1	1	1	5	25	2	45	10	5
Moore, Sam, Asheville	.143	30	28	0	4	4	0	0	0	0	0	1	0	0	3	0	9	0	0
Morelock, J. Charles, Anderson	.111	30	18	0	2	2	0	0	0	0	0	0	0	0	0	0	10	0	0
Morris, Angel, Macon	.259	91	251	30	65	93	11	1	5	32	0	1	3	1	35	1	55	0	0
Morris, David, Anderson	.333	11	3	0	1	1	0	0	0	0	0	1	0	0	1	0	0	0	0
Morton, William, Spartanburg	.091	11	11	2	1	1	0	0	0	0	0	0	0	0	1	0	1	0	0
Neidlinger, James, Macon	.065	25	31	1	2	2	0	0	0	1	1	2	0	0	4	0	10	0	0
Nichols, Howard, Spartanburg	.267	107	318	52	85	134	22	0	9	56	5	0	5	3	63	1	67	8	2
Niemann, Tom, Charleston	.270	87	259	37	70	82	7	1	1	40	5	6	2	5	45	0	25	6	1
Nipper, R. Michael, Anderson	.248	135	451	56	112	177	37	2	8	71	6	7	7	5	56	3	99	7	4
Norton, Randy, Gastonia	.273	35	11	1	3	3	0	0	0	0	0	2	0	0	2	0	3	0	0
Norwood, Jeffrey, Spartanburg°	.333	5	3	0	1	1	0	0	0	0	0	1	0	0	1	0	1	0	0
O'Dell, James, Asheville°	.244	136	450	76	110	190	21	1	19	78	10	1	8	2	70	5	45	3	2
O'Donnell, Steven, Greensboro†	.154	12	26	3	4	4	0	0	0	1	0	1	0	7	0	7	0	0	
Oates, Paul, Savannah°	.333	3	3	0	1	1	0	0	0	1	0	0	0	0	0	0	0	0	0
Odgers, Daniel, Spartanburg	.214	103	285	33	61	83	10	3	2	35	3	1	3	3	27	2	37	10	3
Ortega, Jose, Savannah	.000	18	3	0	0	0	0	0	0	0	0	0	0	0	1	0	1	0	0
Pacheco, Jose, Macon°	.246	117	414	52	102	110	8	0	0	25	3	2	1	2	34	1	71	29	14
Packer, William, Savannah	.138	18	58	6	8	9	1	0	0	4	1	1	0	0	5	0	13	1	0
Palmer, David, Asheville°	.286	17	21	5	6	9	0	0	1	1	0	0	0	0	6	0	6	0	0
Parker, Marvin, Columbia°	.316	8	19	5	6	8	2	0	0	4	0	0	0	0	8	0	5	1	0
Parker, Robert, Asheville°	.303	53	155	17	47	52	3	1	0	17	2	1	0	0	36	2	18	2	1
Pascho, David, Gastonia	.125	41	8	0	1	1	0	0	0	1	0	1	0	0	0	0	4	0	0
Paulino, Victor, Savannah†	.248	63	210	25	52	60	6	1	0	16	2	1	0	1	11	0	5	8	3
Perdomo, Cristobal, Charleston	.333	2	6	1	2	2	0	0	0	0	0	0	0	0	2	0	3	1	0
Perdomo, Felix, Greensboro	.263	53	160	18	42	49	5	1	0	24	4	1	1	2	19	0	32	6	2
Perry, Jeff, Savannah	.000	24	24	1	0	0	0	0	0	0	0	2	0	0	3	0	17	0	0
Peruso, Steven, Greensboro	.286	58	203	31	58	87	10	5	3	42	3	0	4	1	23	2	40	3	3
Petersen, Geoff, Charleston	.204	141	481	76	98	137	23	2	4	64	5	1	3	4	109	4	95	10	7
Phillips, Stephen, Columbia°	.249	127	389	88	97	146	18	8	5	38	2	6	3	1	74	4	102	39	7
Posey, Robert, Anderson°	.226	67	208	30	47	69	8	4	2	23	0	3	2	0	36	3	42	2	1
Powell, John, Spartanburg	.040	35	25	2	1	1	0	0	0	1	0	2	0	0	8	0	12	0	0
Rasnick, James, Spartanburg	.273	22	22	2	6	9	3	0	0	1	0	3	0	0	0	0	6	0	0
Ratliff, Daniel, Gastonia	.100	40	20	1	2	2	0	0	0	0	0	3	0	0	1	0	6	0	0
Raziano, M. Scott, Gastonia	.239	43	117	16	28	44	5	1	3	21	5	1	0	0	25	1	13	3	0
Reboulet, James, Savannah	.244	122	427	88	104	128	10	1	4	43	2	3	5	2	53	0	35	62	9
Reed, Kenneth, Columbia	.167	38	6	2	1	1	0	0	0	0	0	3	0	0	0	0	4	0	0
Reilly, Edward, Asheville	.000	34	2	0	0	0	0	0	0	0	0	0	0	0	1	0	0	0	0
Reynolds, Mark, Asheville°	.305	49	118	21	36	70	7	0	9	32	5	1	0	0	23	0	19	1	0
Richmond, Seth, Asheville	.167	7	18	1	3	3	0	0	0	1	0	0	0	0	2	0	5	0	0
Robair, Michael, Columbia	.000	13	4	0	0	0	0	0	0	0	0	0	0	0	2	0	3	0	0
Roberts, J. Drexel, Florence°	.227	47	150	29	34	55	8	2	3	13	1	0	1	0	31	2	29	6	3
Roberts, R. Jay, Anderson	.203	43	138	13	28	42	7	2	1	2	0	0	1	5	0	50	6	0	
Rogers, MacArthur, Anderson	.000	29	4	0	0	0	0	0	0	0	0	2	0	0	2	0	2	0	0
Romagna, Randolph, Florence	.250	92	272	36	68	93	12	2	3	28	0	1	3	2	25	0	25	6	2
Rooker, David, Charleston	.167	61	180	17	30	48	6	0	4	25	4	0	2	0	18	0	55	4	0
Roque, Gustavo, Macon	.172	67	180	20	31	41	3	2	1	16	2	1	1	0	36	1	43	1	2
Rosario, Maximo, Anderson°	.133	25	30	2	4	4	0	0	0	0	0	4	0	0	3	0	23	0	0
Ross, Keith, Spartanburg°	.197	88	254	41	50	79	7	5	4	22	4	0	0	1	48	4	94	20	5
Rowe, Mathew, Anderson	.125	12	16	0	2	2	0	0	0	1	0	2	0	0	0	0	3	0	0
Rupp, Michael, Gastonia	.246	128	406	54	100	141	20	0	7	54	6	4	7	5	86	2	45	2	0
Russo, Anthony, Asheville	.111	21	27	4	3	4	1	0	0	1	0	0	0	1	0	9	0	1	
Rypien, Timothy, Florence	.138	10	29	0	4	4	0	0	0	1	0	0	0	0	4	0	4	0	0
Saccocia, Michael, Gastonia	.228	114	311	44	71	99	7	0	7	28	2	3	1	1	47	1	37	11	5
Salisbury, James, Anderson	.000	7	6	0	0	0	0	0	0	0	0	0	0	0	0	0	2	0	0
Sambo, Ramon, Spartanburg†	.300	96	353	75	106	119	9	2	0	29	4	0	0	1	64	2	55	57	14

Player and Club	Pct.	G.	AB.	R.	H.	TB.	2B.	3B.	HR.	RBI.	GW.	SH.	SF.	HP.	BB.	Int. BB.	SO.	SB.	CS.
Samuels, Roger, Asheville°	.059	15	17	1	1	1	0	0	0	0	0	2	0	0	3	0	7	0	0
Sanchez, Jose, Savannah	.200	15	20	2	4	4	0	0	0	1	0	0	0	0	0	0	1	0	0
Sanchez, Zoilo, Columbia	.167	5	12	2	2	3	1	0	0	1	0	0	0	0	0	0	3	1	0
Sarmiento, Ramon, Florence	.258	81	240	38	62	117	12	2	13	31	0	0	2	3	38	1	84	6	3
Schuler, Mark, Gastonia	.000	14	1	0	0	0	0	0	0	0	0	0	0	0	0	0	1	0	0
Schulz, Jeffrey, Charleston°	.336	69	265	52	89	124	14	3	5	54	6	0	2	1	34	3	20	4	2
Seitzer, Kevin, Charleston	.297	141	489	96	145	205	26	5	8	79	9	1	6	3	118	2	70	23	5
Seoane, Mitchell, Greensboro°	.246	97	342	43	84	87	1	1	0	21	3	5	1	3	36	3	36	23	10
Sepanek, Robert, Anderson°	.219	52	128	21	28	47	6	2	3	21	4	1	1	1	34	3	30	1	0
Shaheed, Daraka, Asheville°	.282	86	188	29	53	72	10	3	1	28	4	1	1	3	30	1	33	8	7
Sherlock, Glenn, Asheville°	.244	31	82	9	20	32	4	1	2	13	3	2	0	1	7	1	11	2	1
Shields, J. Douglas, Gastonia	.237	63	173	32	41	55	5	3	1	6	0	0	2	2	40	0	20	5	4
Shirley, W. Eric, Anderson	.000	26	6	1	0	0	0	0	0	0	0	0	2	0	0	1	0	2	0	0
Simon, Kelly, Macon	1.000	7	1	1	1	1	0	0	0	0	0	0	0	0	0	0	0	0	0
Sliwinski, Kevin, Florence	.335	69	242	44	81	145	19	0	15	54	5	1	4	3	29	0	29	0	2
Smiley, John, Macon°	.242	24	33	4	8	12	2	1	0	3	1	0	1	0	1	0	10	0	0
Smith, Richard, Gastonia	.200	8	10	2	2	2	0	0	0	1	0	0	0	0	1	0	2	0	0
Smith, William, Greensboro°	.136	18	44	5	6	9	0	0	1	3	0	0	0	0	5	0	24	1	1
Snyder, Doug, Asheville°	.269	117	316	50	85	141	13	5	11	60	9	3	4	1	48	0	71	10	6
Soma, Charles, Gastonia	.000	19	6	1	0	0	0	0	0	0	0	1	0	0	2	0	1	0	0
Soto, Miguel, Savannah	.187	109	347	23	65	74	7	1	0	36	6	10	3	1	19	0	26	8	9
Spurlin, Robert, Macon	.162	29	74	5	12	14	0	1	0	3	1	0	2	1	13	0	10	0	1
Stampfl, Eric, Columbia	.250	7	8	2	2	3	1	0	0	4	0	1	0	1	0	3	0	2	0	0
Stark, Matthew, Florence	.224	69	205	24	46	64	7	1	3	27	1	2	2	1	39	1	25	1	2
Stevens, J. Michael, Macon	.236	88	288	41	68	125	11	2	14	50	10	0	5	5	30	2	95	9	4
Stewart, H. Wayne, Spartanburg	.056	11	18	1	1	1	0	0	0	0	0	0	0	0	0	0	7	0	0
Stiles, William, Columbia	.000	18	1	0	0	0	0	0	0	0	0	0	0	0	0	0	0	0	0
Strickland, Terry, Gastonia	.230	38	139	14	32	45	8	1	1	18	2	0	1	1	6	1	20	3	0
Swain, Steven, Asheville	.364	11	22	3	8	12	1	0	1	7	0	0	0	1	0	0	7	0	0
Sweeney, Michael, Greensboro	.243	36	115	10	28	44	5	1	3	14	0	1	0	0	12	2	11	0	0
Swindell, Daniel, Columbia°	.167	16	30	3	5	5	0	0	0	2	0	0	0	0	8	1	6	0	1
Takach, David, Columbia	.000	2	3	0	0	0	0	0	0	0	0	1	0	0	0	0	2	0	0
Tenacek, Francisco, Spartanburg	.231	103	308	48	71	126	19	9	6	34	5	0	2	13	29	2	79	11	6
Teno, Todd, Columbia†	.353	21	17	4	6	7	1	0	0	0	2	0	0	1	0	4	0	0
Thomas, Kevin, Anderson	.143	9	7	0	1	1	0	0	0	1	0	0	0	0	0	0	3	0	0
Thurman, Gary, Charleston	.228	129	478	71	109	149	6	8	6	51	4	1	3	8	81	1	127	44	17
Tomsick, Troy, Anderson	.238	18	21	0	5	6	1	0	0	6	1	2	0	0	0	0	2	0	0
Torres, Rudy, Anderson	.000	13	5	0	0	0	0	0	0	0	0	0	0	0	0	0	5	0	0
Tostenson, Ronald, Gastonia°	.171	23	35	7	6	7	1	0	0	5	0	0	1	1	6	0	8	1	1
Traen, Thomas, Gastonia†	.077	25	26	1	2	2	0	0	0	3	0	1	0	0	25	0	11	0	0
Tubbs, Gregory, Anderson	.305	50	174	25	53	68	5	2	2	11	0	3	0	1	27	0	29	19	6
Tunison, Mark, Spartanburg	.214	19	14	0	3	3	0	0	0	1	0	0	0	0	1	0	7	0	0
Valliant, Robert, Gastonia†	.077	30	13	0	1	1	0	0	0	0	0	0	0	0	1	0	6	0	0
Vanacore, Derek, Charleston	.216	57	194	36	42	53	3	1	2	12	1	0	1	1	42	1	40	19	3
Van Blaricom, Mark, Charleston	.232	115	362	61	84	143	14	9	9	59	8	2	5	1	71	0	83	8	1
Van Horn, David, Anderson	.170	17	53	5	9	10	1	0	0	1	0	0	0	0	6	0	1	1	1
Vargas, Miguel, Spartanburg	.333	17	3	0	1	1	0	0	0	1	0	1	0	0	0	0	0	0	0
Verrone, Stephen, Asheville	.161	21	31	6	5	8	0	0	1	4	0	0	0	3	0	12	0	0
Vizcaino, Jorge, Asheville°	.333	11	6	0	2	2	0	0	0	0	0	0	0	0	0	0	0	0	0
Vogel, George, Savannah	.239	134	410	83	98	151	24	4	7	52	3	1	4	7	90	3	108	36	6
Walker, Darcy, Gastonia°	.284	91	201	25	57	89	8	0	8	31	0	2	2	0	38	2	26	1	0
Walker, Scott, Macon°	.201	63	209	21	42	56	11	0	1	17	2	0	1	2	19	1	46	3	4
Wallace, Thomas, Charleston	.210	134	466	79	98	158	24	9	6	63	7	1	5	6	94	1	134	31	11
Wayland, Jeffrey, Macon	.000	8	1	0	0	0	0	0	0	0	0	0	0	0	0	0	1	0	0
Weatherford, Brant, Spartanburg	.250	6	4	0	1	2	1	0	0	1	0	0	0	0	0	0	2	0	0
Welch, Billy, Columbia	.250	83	248	36	62	76	9	1	1	29	3	0	4	2	42	2	33	5	2
Wellman, Phillip, Anderson†	.222	68	194	27	43	59	8	1	2	25	5	8	1	2	38	1	31	10	2
West, David, Columbia°	.100	12	10	0	1	1	0	0	0	0	0	0	0	0	1	0	4	0	0
Weston, Michael, Columbia	.000	32	11	0	0	0	0	0	0	0	0	0	1	0	0	0	6	0	0
Whitehurst, Willis, Charleston	.183	56	164	18	30	33	3	0	0	25	1	0	2	3	19	0	50	8	2
Whitfield, Kenneth, Florence	.282	102	316	55	89	148	23	3	10	58	4	0	7	3	26	0	68	4	3
Williams, Edward, Columbia	.184	43	152	17	28	45	4	2	3	24	3	1	0	4	15	2	31	1	0
Wilson, John, Columbia°	.258	129	395	62	102	137	9	7	4	46	5	3	2	3	47	3	84	56	8
Winkler, Brad, Greensboro°	.298	71	262	50	78	142	13	6	13	59	6	1	0	1	38	4	79	6	2
Worden, William, Greensboro	.363	22	80	19	29	45	1	0	5	17	2	0	1	0	5	0	10	3	0
Wyatt, David, Columbia	.364	13	22	6	8	9	1	0	0	3	1	2	0	0	3	0	2	0	0
Young, Clifford, Gastonia°	.161	24	31	2	5	5	0	0	0	3	0	3	0	0	5	0	10	1	1
Young, Gerald, Columbia†	.212	124	396	69	84	107	14	3	1	52	4	5	3	2	84	1	69	43	7

The following pitchers, listed alphabetically by club, with games in parentheses, had no plate appearances, primarily through use of designated hitters:

ANDERSON—Parker, Darren (3); Santiago, Michael (10).

ASHEVILLE—Wilmore, Orlando (4).

CHARLESTON—Burke, Richard (11); Davis, Bradley (34); George, Phillip (25); Hull, Jeffrey (27); Klein, Gary (21); McCormack, Ronald (10); Mohr, Thomas (14); Morales, Edwin (2); Nunez, Jose (25); Perez, Melido (16); Perez, Valerio (5); Shook, Thomas (15); Snell, David (19); Velazquez, Jose (27); Walter, Craig (38); Yowler, John (23).

FLORENCE—Anthony, Dane (17); Burgess, Christopher (20); Burgos, Enrique (2); Castillo, Antonio (25); Clemons, Mark (4); Dickman, Mark (34); Emerson, Robin (9); Ferlenda, Gregory (28); Gallagher, Glenn (6); Johnson, Ronald (20); Lounello, Stephen (5); McKay, Alan (13); Mesa, Jose (7); Peraza, Oswald (31); Reyes, Pablo (24); Robbins, Ronnie (22); Sprowl, Robert (4); Tejada, Henry (22); Turano, Robert (8); Yearout, Michael (21).

GASTONIA—Fedor, Francis (8).

GREENSBORO—Armstrong, Douglas (5); Arnsberg, Bradley (23); Browne, Richard (1); Davis, Fernando (4); Devlin, Robert (39); Fedor, Francis (40); Ferguson, Mark (10); Fulton, William (10); George, Stephen (24); Horne, Jeffrey (33); Mathison, Charles (14); Parent, Eric (22); Ray, Steven (4); Rebiejo, Kenneth (6); Rodriguez, Yonis (27); Smalley, David (5); Torres, Ricardo (20); Williams, Timothy (33).

SAVANNAH—Sinclair, Kenneth (20).

SPARTANBURG—Ghelfi, Anthony (2).

GRAND SLAM HOME RUNS—Dophied, Magrann, Seitzer, 2 each; Antone, W. Caraballo, Ching, Delucchi, Digioia, Dinkel, Huth, James, Maloney, McClain, Mitchell, O'Dell, Odgers, Reynolds, Rupp, Vogel, 1 each.

AWARDED FIRST BASE ON CATCHER'S INTERFERENCE—Baker 3 (Carmichael, Landrith, Niemann); Ching 2 (Gil, Nichols); Dyrek 2 (Carmichael, A. Morris); Krupa 2 (Carmichael, Edwards); Belen (Niemann); Chadwick (Gil); Massiah (Rypien); Niemann (Nichols); O'Dell (Carmichael); Petersen (Welch); Rupp (R. Davis); Wellman (A. Morris).

CLUB FIELDING

Club	Pct.	G.	PO.	A.	E.	DP.	PB.	Club	Pct.	G.	PO.	A.	E.	DP.	PB.
Savannah	.964	139	3495	1548	186	139	30	Columbia	.955	140	3480	1429	229	113	26
Asheville	.964	143	3481	1525	188	123	40	Anderson	.954	143	3433	1465	239	132	26
Gastonia	.963	142	3506	1336	186	118	29	Macon	.952	142	3529	1488	251	114	42
Spartanburg	.957	140	3554	1537	230	102	43	Charleston	.950	143	3674	1553	274	107	23
Greensboro	.956	144	3588	1427	232	110	43	Florence	.943	138	3387	1336	284	89	23

Triple Plays—Asheville, Macon.

INDIVIDUAL FIELDING

Throws lefthanded.

FIRST BASEMEN

Player and Club	Pct.	G.	PO.	A.	E.	DP.	Player and Club	Pct.	G.	PO.	A.	E.	DP.
Afenir, Asheville	1.000	1	8	1	0	2	Kelly, Greensboro	1.000	2	9	0	0	2
Akers, Florence	1.000	1	3	0	0	1	Knox, Columbia	1.000	7	20	0	0	1
Angelo, Savannah	.977	47	405	18	10	30	Krupa, Gastonia	.984	77	251	28	9	48
Anglin, Anderson	1.000	2	9	0	0	0	Lawrence, Columbia	.982	134	1050	81	21	93
Antone, Gastonia	.981	44	303	12	6	26	Ledezma, Anderson	1.000	2	5	0	0	1
Belen, Macon	.985	74	644	60	11	50	Longenecker, Charleston	.941	5	45	3	3	6
Borders, Florence	.983	75	602	38	11	48	Maloney, Columbia*	.956	10	63	2	3	5
Ching, Greensboro*	.970	54	386	32	13	39	McCulla, Savannah	.991	11	99	6	1	10
Coleman, Gastonia*	.986	25	70	3	1	4	McKnight, Columbia	1.000	5	9	0	0	0
Dyrek, Asheville*	.929	3	13	0	1	0	Morris, Macon	.970	10	63	2	2	4
Edwards, Asheville	1.000	13	84	7	0	9	Nichols, Spartanburg	.982	19	158	4	3	11
Englehart, Greensboro*	.983	70	638	48	12	49	O'DELL, Asheville*	.992	135	1139	62	10	96
Fortaleza, Greensboro	.957	13	85	5	4	5	Petersen, Charleston	.985	138	1270	67	21	90
Gonzalez, Greensboro	.977	5	40	3	1	0	Rooker, Spartanburg	1.000	3	13	0	0	1
Harris, Savannah*	.990	95	727	30	8	78	Sepanek, Anderson*	.992	45	345	23	3	30
Harrison, Anderson	.981	100	802	44	16	87	Sherlock, Savannah	1.000	1	5	0	0	1
Johnston, Greensboro	1.000	3	25	4	0	0	Sliwinski, Florence	.983	64	499	37	9	28
Jordan, Spartanburg	.988	125	1129	69	14	85	D. Walker, Gastonia*	.996	35	234	3	1	15
Kaull, Savannah	.992	14	112	8	1	8	S. Walker, Macon*	.966	63	515	22	19	49

Triple Plays—O'Dell, S. Walker.

SECOND BASEMEN

Player and Club	Pct.	G.	PO.	A.	E.	DP.	Player and Club	Pct.	G.	PO.	A.	E.	DP.
Baker, Gastonia	.960	21	42	54	4	5	Mattocks, Greensboro	.945	129	271	343	36	69
Caraballo, Columbia	.950	10	22	16	2	1	McKnight, Columbia	.978	28	66	65	3	18
Clark, Anderson	1.000	3	1	6	0	1	Medina, Greensboro	.957	5	9	13	1	5
Cobb, Gastonia	.983	53	95	133	4	28	O'Donnell, Greensboro	1.000	1	3	0	0	0
Dennis, Florence	.954	63	139	153	14	31	Odgers, Spartanburg	1.000	2	7	7	0	0
Diaz, Florence	.959	32	59	58	5	11	Paulino, Savannah	.941	25	57	55	7	10
Edwards, Asheville	1.000	8	10	17	0	3	Perdomo, Greensboro	1.000	6	15	13	0	5
Engram, Spartanburg	.956	52	109	132	11	30	Phillips, Columbia	.949	110	224	260	26	62
Escobar, Florence	.928	53	101	119	17	29	REBOULET, Savannah	.980	121	281	364	13	82
Fulgencio, Florence	.900	9	12	15	3	2	Roque, Macon	.936	56	92	129	15	23
Gant, Anderson	.943	100	248	263	31	75	Russo, Asheville	1.000	8	5	17	0	4
Gonzales, Gastonia	.667	3	1	1	1	0	Sambo, Spartanburg	.945	93	185	264	26	45
Hinson, Asheville	.963	71	119	165	11	31	J. Sanchez, Savannah	1.000	5	3	2	0	1
Job, Asheville	.972	74	124	185	9	37	Z. Sanchez, Columbia	.941	4	8	8	1	1
Johnston, Greensboro	1.000	1	1	1	0	0	Seoane, Greensboro	1.000	6	15	13	0	2
Kaull, Savannah	1.000	1	4	2	0	2	Shaheed, Asheville	.826	5	10	9	4	3
LaCava, Macon	.955	18	34	30	3	8	Strickland, Gastonia	.983	26	51	63	2	17
Lee, Columbia	1.000	1	1	1	0	0	Swindell, Columbia	.966	6	15	13	1	3
Lemke, Anderson	.980	30	67	81	3	24	Van Horn, Anderson	.952	13	31	29	3	8
Lind, Macon	.977	79	200	184	9	44	Wellman, Anderson	1.000	3	1	0	0	0
Lopes, Gastonia	.974	45	90	97	5	30	Whitehurst, Charleston	.973	25	49	61	3	15
Mabe, Charleston	.935	120	256	323	40	64							

Triple Plays—Hinson, Roque.

THIRD BASEMEN

Player and Club	Pct.	G.	PO.	A.	E.	DP.	Player and Club	Pct.	G.	PO.	A.	E.	DP.
Borders, Florence	.855	22	14	39	9	1	McClain, Macon	.921	53	43	108	13	11
Caraballo, Columbia	.886	96	55	162	28	16	McKnight, Columbia	.714	10	1	9	4	1
Cobb, Gastonia	.907	15	11	28	4	0	Medina, Greensboro	.946	17	12	23	2	4
Dearth, Gastonia	.869	70	37	109	22	6	Mitchell, Asheville	.921	62	38	138	15	10
Dennis, Florence	1.000	10	7	13	0	3	Nichols, Spartanburg	.780	47	25	60	24	5
Dophied, Asheville	.923	6	2	10	1	0	Nipper, Anderson	.903	131	94	223	34	26
Edwards, Asheville	.875	10	4	10	2	0	O'Donnell, Greensboro	.800	10	1	11	3	0
Engram, Spartanburg	.957	29	24	66	4	3	Odgers, Spartanburg	.917	93	65	166	21	10
Fortaleza, Greensboro	1.000	5	0	4	0	1	Paulino, Savannah	1.000	4	2	8	0	0
Fulgencio, Florence	.870	34	18	62	12	5	Perdomo, Greensboro	.875	28	23	33	8	4
Gutierrez, Macon	.895	66	40	122	19	11	Raziano, Gastonia	.933	38	24	60	6	3
Hernandez, Greensboro	1.000	6	4	6	0	0	Romagna, Florence	.925	88	66	155	18	11
Hinson, Asheville	.857	12	1	17	3	0	Roque, Macon	.900	7	3	15	2	0
James, Savannah	.894	40	24	77	12	8	Rupp, Gastonia	.909	22	9	31	4	4
Johnston, Greensboro	.889	4	2	6	1	1	Russo, Asheville	.769	5	2	8	3	0
KAULL, Savannah	.919	116	70	248	28	19	Seitzer, Charleston	.878	127	80	279	50	22
Kingsley, Anderson	.800	1	1	3	1	0	Seoane, Greensboro	.857	19	8	28	6	1
Knox, Columbia	.000	1	0	0	1	0	Shields, Gastonia	1.000	1	1	1	0	0
Kunz, Charleston	.853	16	5	24	5	1	Smith, Greensboro	.913	18	5	16	2	2
LaCava, Macon	.877	22	15	42	8	0	Strickland, Gastonia	.813	6	3	10	3	0
Lange, Asheville	.881	62	37	103	19	9	Sweeney, Charleston	.864	28	19	57	12	1
Lemke, Anderson	.667	2	0	2	1	0	Walker, Gastonia*	1.000	1	0	1	0	0
Longenecker, Charleston	.846	10	4	18	4	2	Wellman, Anderson	.853	13	5	24	5	4
Lucas, Gastonia	.000	1	0	0	1	0	Williams, Columbia	.862	41	24	76	16	10
MacKay, Greensboro	.833	3	1	4	1	0	Worden, Greensboro	.870	21	16	44	9	1

SHORTSTOPS

Player and Club	Pct.	G.	PO.	A.	E.	DP.
Allaire, Asheville	.925	9	11	26	3	9
Bachman, Gastonia	.919	47	44	127	15	24
Clark, Anderson	.899	53	66	147	24	35
Dennis, Florence	.893	6	3	22	3	3
Engram, Spartanburg	.833	8	5	10	3	2
Fredymond, Anderson	.908	83	84	241	33	41
Fulgencio, Florence	.885	7	10	13	3	1
Garrison, Florence	.869	127	192	339	80	50
Glynn, Columbia	.952	12	21	39	3	8
Gonzales, Gastonia	.913	63	57	143	19	24
Hernandez, Greensboro	.955	14	22	37	10	4
Job, Asheville	.927	69	83	171	20	33
Kaull, Savannah	.871	12	12	15	4	6
Kingsley, Anderson	.867	8	12	14	4	3
Kraft, Spartanburg	.938	136	184	438	41	71
Lee, Columbia	.922	98	125	276	34	41
Lind, Macon	.894	44	71	122	23	23
Longenecker, Charleston	.909	10	17	23	4	2
Lora, Asheville	.973	16	13	60	2	10
Lucas, Gastonia	938	42	48	104	10	30
McAllister, Macon	938	106	139	333	31	48
McKnight, Columbia	.875	28	28	70	14	9
Medina, Greensboro	.926	43	68	132	16	28
Mitchell, Asheville	1.000	1	0	1	0	0
O'Donnell, Greensboro	.889	2	4	4	1	2
Odgers, Spartanburg	1.000	2	0	2	0	0
Parker, Asheville	.931	53	62	139	15	27
Paulino, Savannah	.921	34	29	76	9	12
Perdomo, Greensboro	.949	17	21	35	3	6
Phillips, Columbia	.902	10	14	32	5	5
Seoane, Greensboro	.944	72	94	210	18	35
Shaheed, Asheville	.839	13	8	18	5	1
SOTO, Savannah	.944	109	154	349	30	63
Strickland, Gastonia	.885	6	5	18	3	2
Van Blaricom, Charleston	.922	115	148	373	44	44
Wellman, Anderson	1.000	3	5	7	0	1
Whitehurst, Charleston	.848	24	38	57	17	16

OUTFIELDERS

Player and Club	Pct.	G.	PO.	A.	E.	DP.
Akers, Florence	.946	82	136	4	8	1
Angelo, Savannah	.909	58	60	0	6	0
Antone, Gastonia	.974	28	35	2	1	0
Baird, Anderson	.970	50	92	4	3	1
Baker, Savannah	.956	52	63	2	3	0
Ballou, Anderson	.933	46	66	4	5	1
Belcik, Columbia	1.000	9	11	0	0	0
Borders, Florence	.872	19	34	0	5	0
Canseco, Greensboro	1.000	1	1	0	0	0
Carpenter, Greensboro	.984	115	231	10	4	1
Chadwick, Gastonia	.966	138	264	16	10	6
Chestna, Greensboro	1.000	2	2	0	0	0
Clawson, Anderson	.988	42	82	1	1	0
Cobb, Gastonia	1.000	1	2	0	0	0
Coleman, Gastonia°	.975	62	113	3	3	2
Coss, Macon	.936	56	99	3	7	1
Cuevas, Columbia	1.000	6	8	0	0	0
Dannenberg, Spartanburg°	.974	115	210	11	6	2
DeLaRosa, Spartanburg	1.000	15	23	1	0	0
Delucchi, Macon	.969	78	116	8	4	3
Dennis, Florence	1.000	10	8	0	0	0
Digioia, Savannah	1.000	39	40	2	0	0
Dinkel, Columbia	.979	98	134	3	3	1
Dophied, Asheville	.950	69	92	4	5	1
Dyrek, Asheville°	.976	113	192	10	5	1
Engram, Spartanburg	.882	11	13	2	2	0
George, Greensboro	.923	44	60	0	5	0
Green, Florence°	.974	42	70	4	2	1
Hall, Anderson	.946	40	87	1	5	1
Harris, Savannah°	.933	11	13	1	1	1
Hill, Florence	.948	127	281	9	16	2
Houp, Asheville	.922	91	92	2	8	0
Huth, Savannah	.921	45	76	6	7	2
Isaac, Asheville	.893	18	25	0	3	0
Isner, Savannah	1.000	1	2	0	0	0
Jackson, Asheville	.963	57	98	6	4	4
James, Savannah	.988	75	82	2	1	0
Jimenez, Macon°	.857	9	17	1	3	1
Johnson, Spartanburg	.930	82	166	6	13	0
Kelly, Greensboro	.982	100	219	5	4	1
Knox, Columbia	.931	47	49	5	4	2
Lajszky, Columbia	1.000	10	21	0	0	0
Lauck, Savannah°	.947	47	52	2	3	0
Lemon, Gastonia°	.918	29	44	1	4	1
Llewellyn, Anderson	.951	93	168	8	9	2
Longenecker, Charleston	1.000	32	46	3	0	1
Lowe, Spartanburg	.990	65	100	4	1	0
Lucas, Gastonia	1.000	1	1	0	0	0
MacKay, Greensboro	.983	69	110	3	2	1
Maloney, Columbia°	1.000	33	34	0	0	0
Massiah, Macon	.935	79	134	9	10	1
McCulla, Savannah	1.000	6	7	1	0	1
McKnight, Columbia	1.000	8	11	0	0	0
Milner, Savannah°	.959	85	133	7	6	3
Moore, Macon	.959	53	88	5	4	1
Pacheco, Macon°	.922	110	206	7	18	1
Parker, Columbia	1.000	7	9	1	0	0
Perdomo, Charleston	.750	1	3	0	1	0
Peruso, Greensboro	.960	56	93	4	4	1
Posey, Anderson	.949	66	89	4	5	0
Reynolds, Asheville	1.000	16	31	1	0	1
Richmond, Asheville	1.000	5	5	0	0	0
J.D. Roberts, Florence	1.000	1	1	0	0	0
R.J. Roberts, Anderson	.911	33	51	0	5	0
Romagna, Florence	.667	1	1	1	1	0
Rooker, Charleston	.967	42	84	5	3	1
Ross, Spartanburg	.928	71	87	3	7	0
SACCOCIA, Gastonia	.986	100	140	2	2	1
Sarmiento, Florence	.896	56	109	3	13	0
Schulz, Charleston	.969	67	115	12	4	1
Shaheed, Asheville	.980	42	45	3	1	1
Shields, Gastonia	.990	59	96	4	1	2
Snyder, Asheville	.986	83	126	10	2	1
Stevens, Macon	.939	64	91	2	6	1
Swain, Asheville	1.000	10	4	2	0	0
Tenacen, Spartanburg	.952	85	153	4	8	0
Thurman, Charleston	.960	124	311	5	13	3
Tostenson, Gastonia	1.000	12	8	0	0	0
Tubbs, Anderson	.969	50	88	7	3	3
Vanacore, Charleston°	.986	51	131	6	2	2
Vogel, Savannah	.985	131	254	17	4	4
Wallace, Charleston	.947	115	224	6	13	0
Wellman, Anderson	.932	46	67	2	5	0
Whitfield, Florence	.929	100	148	10	12	0
Wilson, Columbia	.953	128	212	10	11	2
Winkler, Greensboro	.951	61	94	3	5	2
Young, Columbia	.985	122	254	7	4	3

CATCHERS

Player and Club	Pct.	G.	PO.	A.	E.	DP.	PB.
Afenir, Asheville	.983	105	648	60	12	8	32
Agostinelli, Savannah	.985	65	298	35	5	1	10
Anglin, Anderson	1.000	1	7	0	0	0	0
Antone, Gastonia	.981	48	344	26	7	4	10
Belcik, Columbia	1.000	4	7	1	0	0	0
Butters, Macon	.987	15	70	6	1	0	4
Carmichael, Columbia	.978	42	284	32	7	2	10
Cooper, Florence	.986	30	192	17	3	0	0
D'Alessandro, Anderson	.982	103	571	89	12	7	20
Davis, Charleston	.966	33	126	16	5	0	9
Edwards, Asheville	.963	14	50	2	2	2	1
Foley, Greensboro	.992	21	114	17	1	4	5
Fortaleza, Greensboro	.974	57	303	38	9	3	18
Gil, Spartanburg	.972	77	416	38	13	1	23
Gillermo, Florence	.972	41	191	16	6	2	9
GONZALEZ, Greensboro	.994	76	437	58	3	3	18
Hall, Macon	.975	67	347	47	10	2	24
Isner, Savannah	.963	35	164	16	7	1	10
Karr, Columbia	.980	22	138	12	3	0	3
Landrith, Charleston	.953	41	224	19	12	3	6
Ledezma, Anderson	.977	49	228	31	6	2	6
Lyden, Greensboro	.971	5	28	5	1	0	2
Magrann, Spartanburg	.978	67	389	57	10	0	14
Maloney, Columbia°	1.000	2	3	0	0	0	0
McCulla, Savannah	.988	39	224	28	3	2	6
Morris, Macon	.983	56	264	30	5	3	11
Nichols, Spartanburg	.917	7	32	1	3	0	6
Niemann, Charleston	.977	84	409	62	11	5	8
Packer, Savannah	.968	13	56	4	2	0	4
Reynolds, Asheville	.992	16	110	16	1	1	1
Rupp, Gastonia	.986	100	695	77	11	14	18
Rypien, Florence	.953	10	56	5	3	0	1
Sherlock, Asheville	.993	22	122	12	1	1	6
Smith, Gastonia	.750	1	3	0	1	0	1
Spurlin, Macon	.988	25	139	20	2	2	3
Stark, Florence	.972	67	383	36	12	1	13
Welch, Columbia	.980	79	481	57	11	5	13
Worden, Greensboro	1.000	1	8	0	0	0	0

PITCHERS

Player and Club	Pct.	G.	PO.	A.	E.	DP.
Adkins, Macon	1.000	13	4	3	0	0
Anthony, Florence	.957	17	5	17	1	1
Armstrong, Greensboro	1.000	5	0	4	0	0
Arnsberg, Greensboro	.977	23	15	27	1	0
Barger, Anderson°	1.000	4	0	4	0	0
Barrett, Gastonia	.920	13	10	13	2	2
Bautista, Columbia	.861	19	7	24	5	0
Behrend, Savannah	.813	34	2	11	3	0
Blasucci, Macon°	.909	14	2	8	1	0
Bombard, Asheville	1.000	5	0	4	0	1
Brahs, Gastonia°	1.000	3	0	3	0	0
Braukmiller, Gastonia	1.000	2	0	1	0	0
Brisco, Savannah	1.000	26	7	17	0	0
Browne, Greensboro°	.750	1	0	3	1	1
Burgess, Florence	.778	20	2	5	2	0
Burke, Charleston°	1.000	11	2	4	0	0
Callahan, Asheville	.800	28	2	6	2	1
Canseco, Greensboro	.600	6	2	1	2	0
Caraballo, Spartanburg	.867	52	6	20	4	4
Carrasco, Savannah	.917	46	5	17	2	0
CARSON, Savannah	1.000	25	7	30	0	1
Castillo, Florence°	.917	25	1	21	2	1
Clark, Anderson	1.000	1	1	0	0	0
Clemons, Florence	1.000	4	4	9	0	0
Coffman, Anderson	.933	7	1	13	1	2
Collins, Gastonia	.875	14	4	17	3	1
Cooke, Macon	.864	46	6	13	3	2
Costello, Savannah	.931	26	9	18	2	0
Creekmore, Spartanburg	1.000	23	2	6	0	0
Cunningham, Macon	.968	35	11	19	1	0
Cutshall, Gastonia	.818	8	0	9	2	0
B. Davis, Charleston	1.000	34	3	12	0	0
F. Davis, Greensboro°	1.000	4	1	0	0	0
DelRosario, Anderson	.808	28	4	17	5	0
Devlin, Greensboro	1.000	39	5	3	0	0
Dickman, Florence	.850	34	4	13	3	1
Dobie, Columbia	.931	25	11	16	2	0
Dombek, Spartanburg°	.857	28	3	9	2	0
Drummond, Macon	.903	27	10	18	3	1
Dube, Asheville	.941	23	4	12	1	1
Durocher, Macon	.839	35	9	17	5	0
Edens, Columbia	.917	16	5	17	2	0
Emerson, Florence	.667	9	0	2	1	0
Engram, Spartanburg	1.000	1	1	0	0	0
Fedor, 40 Gr'nboro-8 Gas	.889	48	7	17	3	1
Ferguson, Greensboro	1.000	10	2	9	0	1
Ferlenda, Florence	.750	28	3	9	4	0
Friedel, Columbia	1.000	5	0	5	0	0
Fulton, Greensboro	.889	10	3	5	1	0
Funk, Asheville°	.917	54	4	7	1	0
Gallagher, Florence	1.000	6	3	0	0	0
Gass, Savannah	.800	9	2	2	1	1
Gay, Columbia	1.000	31	7	9	0	0
P. George, Charleston°	.971	25	8	25	1	0
S. George, Greensboro°	.818	24	3	6	2	0
Ghelfi, Spartanburg	1.000	2	0	1	0	0
Gordon, Anderson	1.000	27	1	5	0	0
Grosdidier, Anderson	1.000	19	1	6	0	0
Groves, Anderson	.750	4	0	3	1	0
Grudzinski, Macon	1.000	25	9	10	0	0
Hammond, Asheville	1.000	46	2	9	0	3
Hardee, Gastonia	1.000	7	1	1	0	0
Hartshorn, Columbia	.942	24	15	34	3	2
Helton, Macon	.923	9	4	8	1	0
Herzog, Savannah	.929	46	3	10	1	2
Hicks, Spartanburg	1.000	19	3	6	0	0
B. Holman, Gastonia	1.000	20	5	8	0	1
S. Holman, Macon	.889	9	4	12	2	3
Horne, Greensboro	.875	33	6	15	3	1
Houp, Asheville	1.000	2	1	0	0	0
Householder, Spartanburg°	.889	40	3	13	2	1
Hull, Charleston	.906	27	11	18	3	2
Impagliazzo, Gastonia	.800	42	4	12	4	1
Jackson, Spartanburg	1.000	14	5	10	0	0
M.G. Johnson, Gastonia	.500	9	1	0	1	0
R. Johnson, Florence	1.000	20	1	5	0	0
Jones, Anderson	.972	23	9	26	1	0
Kelley, Asheville	.966	26	10	46	2	2
Kiernan, Macon	1.000	21	7	1	0	0
Kish, Savannah	.929	12	3	10	1	2
Klein, Charleston	1.000	21	3	8	0	0
Klink, Columbia°	1.000	31	2	5	0	0
Kolb, Macon	1.000	11	2	10	0	0
Llewellyn, Anderson	1.000	2	0	1	0	0
Lloyd, Spartanburg	.917	12	3	8	1	0
Long, Spartanburg	.950	24	10	28	2	1
Lopez, Macon	.826	14	4	15	4	1
Lounello, Florence	1.000	5	0	2	0	0
Lucas, Asheville	.964	45	6	21	1	0
Mallicoat, Asheville°	.950	11	2	17	1	1
Martin, Anderson	1.000	19	1	3	0	0
Mathews, Savannah°	1.000	6	0	5	0	0
Mathison, Greensboro	.933	14	4	10	1	1
McCormack, Charleston	.929	10	4	9	1	1
McGrath, Savannah	.907	25	9	30	4	4
McKay, Florence°	1.000	13	1	5	0	0
McLarnon, Spartanburg	.905	30	4	15	2	1
McPherson, Savannah	1.000	12	1	1	0	0
Meacham, Anderson	.875	18	0	7	1	0
Mehalko, Anderson°	.960	29	2	22	1	0
Mesa, Florence	1.000	7	2	6	0	1
Mohr, Charleston°	1.000	14	0	8	0	0
Moore, Asheville	.879	30	6	23	4	2
Morales, Charleston	1.000	2	1	2	0	1
Morelock, Anderson	.875	30	7	14	3	0
Morris, Anderson	1.000	9	2	3	0	0
Morton, Spartanburg°	1.000	11	2	9	0	1
Neidlinger, Macon	.972	25	12	23	1	3
Norton, Gastonia	.900	35	1	17	2	0
Norwood, Spartanburg°	1.000	5	3	3	0	0
Nunez, Charleston	.891	25	8	33	5	1
Oates, Savannah°	1.000	3	0	3	0	2
Ortega, Savannah	1.000	18	2	2	0	0
Palmer, Asheville°	1.000	16	5	11	0	2
Parent, Greensboro	.880	22	8	14	3	2
Parker, Anderson	.750	3	0	3	1	0
Pascho, Gastonia	.786	41	1	10	3	0
Peraza, Florence	.778	31	6	8	4	1
M. Perez, Charleston	.692	16	5	4	4	0
V. Perez, Charleston	1.000	5	0	3	0	0
Perry, Savannah	.882	24	5	10	2	1
Powell, Spartanburg	.963	35	6	20	1	0
Rasnick, Spartanburg	.958	22	10	13	1	2
Ratliff, Gastonia	.964	40	6	21	1	5
Rebiejo, Greensboro	.750	6	4	2	2	0
Reed, Columbia	.800	38	2	10	3	0
Reilly, Asheville	.917	34	2	9	1	0
Reyes, Florence°	1.000	24	7	23	0	0
Robair, Columbia	1.000	13	2	2	0	0
Robbins, Florence	1.000	22	0	5	0	0
Rodriguez, Greensboro	.778	27	7	14	6	1
Rogers, Anderson	1.000	29	5	6	0	0
Rooker, Charleston	1.000	8	3	2	0	0
Rosario, Anderson°	.933	25	11	17	2	0
Rowe, Anderson	.952	12	4	16	1	0
Salisbury, Anderson	1.000	7	0	1	0	0
Samuels, Asheville°	.946	15	5	30	2	1
Santiago, Anderson°	1.000	10	2	3	0	0
Schuler, Gastonia	.800	14	1	3	1	1
Shirley, Anderson	1.000	26	3	1	0	0
Shook, Charleston	.900	15	4	5	1	0
Simon, Macon	1.000	7	0	6	0	0
Sinclair, Savannah	.600	20	0	3	2	0
Smalley, Greensboro°	.667	5	3	3	3	0
Smiley, Macon°	.852	21	13	10	4	1
Snell, Charleston	.947	19	5	13	1	1
Soma, Gastonia	1.000	19	6	8	0	2
Sprowl, Florence°	1.000	4	0	1	0	0
Stampfl, Columbia	1.000	7	3	6	0	2
Stewart, Spartanburg	.864	11	4	15	3	0
Stiles, Columbia	1.000	18	1	3	0	0
Takach, Columbia°	1.000	2	2	2	0	1
Tejada, Florence	1.000	22	5	13	0	0
Teno, Columbia°	.842	21	4	12	3	1
Thomas, Anderson	1.000	8	3	12	0	1
Tomsick, Anderson	.867	17	3	23	4	4
H.R. Torres, Greensboro	.857	20	11	13	4	0
R. Torres, Anderson	.889	13	2	6	1	0
Traen, Gastonia	.926	24	7	18	2	2
Tunison, Spartanburg	1.000	19	5	7	0	2
Turano, Florence	1.000	8	3	10	0	1
Valliant, Gastonia°	1.000	30	1	16	0	1
Vargas, Spartanburg	.900	17	3	6	1	0
Velazquez, Charleston	.973	27	8	28	1	0
Verrone, Asheville	.896	21	13	30	5	1
Vizcaino, Asheville°	.889	11	1	7	1	0
Walter, Charleston	1.000	38	4	8	0	0
Wayland, Macon	.800	7	1	3	1	0
Weatherford, Spartanburg	.800	6	1	3	1	0
West, Columbia	.846	12	4	18	4	0
Weston, Columbia	.950	32	5	14	1	1
Williams, Greensboro	.893	33	10	15	3	2
Wilmore, Asheville	1.000	4	0	3	0	0
Wyatt, Columbia	.957	13	8	14	1	2
Yearout, Florence°	.905	21	5	14	2	1
Young, Gastonia°	.917	24	4	18	2	0
Yowler, Charleston°	.867	23	7	6	2	0

The following players do not have any recorded accepted chances at the positions indicated; therefore, are not listed in the fielding averages for those particular positions: Bachman, p; Burgos, p; Carpenter, ss; Chadwick, p; Clawson, c; Dennis, 1b; Diaz, of; Dyrek, p; Edwards, of; Escobar, 3b; Gonzales, p; G. Hall, p; Harris, p; Hazlett, p; Issac, 1b; James, p; Kaull p; Lemke, of; Mabe, ss; Milner, ss; Nichols, of; O'Dell, p; Pacheco, 2b; Phillips, 3b; Ray, p; Romagna, 2b, p; Roque, ss; Russo, ss.

CLUB PITCHING

Club	ERA.	G.	CG.	ShO.	Sv.	IP.	H.	R.	ER.	HR.	HB.	BB.	Int. BB.	SO.	WP.	Bk.
Savannah	3.21	139	23	13	34	1165.0	1050	555	416	64	33	608	27	706	44	7
Columbia	3.54	140	31	15	30	1160.0	954	586	456	56	22	689	26	880	78	11
Greensboro	3.60	144	39	12	18	1196.0	1059	610	478	58	27	631	26	857	84	14
Charleston	3.64	143	26	12	28	1224.2	1199	672	495	77	39	413	9	709	57	7
Florence	3.78	138	24	10	26	1129.0	1051	671	474	85	34	579	7	800	101	11
Gastonia	3.82	142	27	12	22	1168.2	1031	595	496	56	23	664	9	1018	97	16
Asheville	3.86	143	18	15	34	1160.1	1050	606	498	69	41	669	24	903	101	17
Anderson	4.05	143	21	9	26	1144.1	1065	672	515	51	29	699	11	779	143	12
Macon	4.12	142	15	7	28	1176.1	1078	714	538	66	45	660	21	782	63	10
Spartanburg	4.27	140	11	9	36	1184.2	1053	703	562	79	50	711	25	837	121	15

PITCHERS' RECORDS
(Leading Qualifiers for Earned-Run Average Leadership — 115 or More Innings)

*Throws lefthanded.

Pitcher — Club	W.	L.	Pct.	ERA.	G.	GS.	CG.	GF.	ShO.	Sv.	IP.	H.	R.	ER.	HR.	HB.	BB.	Int. BB.	SO.	WP.
Hartshorn, Columbia	14	4	.778	2.48	24	24	10	0	4	0	160.0	126	64	44	7	3	83	2	100	4
Kelley, Asheville	14	9	.609	2.58	26	26	7	0	4	0	174.2	160	68	50	14	3	56	1	121	6
Neidlinger, Macon	9	8	.529	2.77	25	25	2	0	0	0	166.0	138	65	51	6	0	85	2	113	4
Hull, Charleston	16	5	.762	2.84	27	23	3	2	2	0	164.2	147	73	52	13	7	57	0	105	9
Arnsberg, Greensboro	12	5	.706	2.95	23	23	10	0	4	0	158.2	121	61	52	9	4	59	2	112	10
Dobie, Columbia	10	9	.526	3.03	25	25	6	0	2	0	172.1	123	75	58	11	0	119	3	128	7
Traen, Gastonia*	8	5	.615	3.08	24	20	2	2	1	0	125.2	120	63	43	3	0	54	0	89	3
Bautista, Columbia	13	4	.765	3.13	19	18	5	0	3	0	135.0	121	52	47	10	0	35	3	96	3
Carson, Savannah	14	9	.609	3.17	25	25	8	0	3	0	167.1	131	72	59	10	3	76	1	93	3
Brisco, Savannah	9	7	.563	3.23	26	18	6	3	1	0	128.1	128	64	46	5	3	57	1	77	3

Departmental Leaders: G—Funk, 54; W—Hull, 16; L—Drummond, 15; Pct.—Hartshorn, .778; GS—Velazquez, 127; CG—Arnsberg, Hartshorn, 10; GF—Caraballo, 46; ShO—Arnsberg, Hartshorn, Kelley, 4; Sv.—Carrasco, 23; IP—Kelley, 174.2; H—Nunez, 167; R—Velazquez, 98; ER—Velazquez, 80; HR—P. George, 15; HB—Dobie, 119; IBB—Fedor, 7; SO—Dobie, 128; WP—Long, 22.

(All Pitchers — Listed Alphabetically)

Pitcher — Club	W.	L.	Pct.	ERA.	G.	GS.	CG.	GF.	ShO.	Sv.	IP.	H.	R.	ER.	HR.	HB.	BB.	Int. BB.	SO.	WP.
Adkins, Macon	2	0	1.000	1.54	13	0	0	8	0	3	23.1	19	12	4	2	1	7	2	30	2
Anthony, Florence	6	3	.667	1.59	17	8	3	8	2	1	73.2	53	21	13	5	1	21	1	59	0
Armstrong, Greensboro	1	3	.250	6.41	5	3	0	2	0	0	19.2	20	17	14	5	0	20	2	10	0
Arnsberg, Greensboro	12	5	.706	2.95	23	23	10	0	4	0	158.2	121	61	52	9	4	59	2	112	10
Bachman, Gastonia	0	0	.000	0.00	1	0	0	1	0	0	0.2	1	0	0	0	0	0	0	1	0
Barger, Anderson*	4	0	1.000	0.39	4	4	0	0	0	0	23.1	15	1	1	0	0	8	0	19	3
Barrett, Gastonia	7	2	.778	1.94	13	13	3	0	2	0	88.1	63	25	19	4	4	31	0	96	2
Bautista, Columbia	13	4	.765	3.13	19	18	5	0	3	0	135.0	121	52	47	10	0	35	3	96	3
Behrend, Savannah	7	5	.583	3.07	34	2	1	17	0	2	85.0	68	41	29	4	2	42	5	54	6
Blasucci, Macon*	2	7	.222	6.16	14	14	0	0	0	0	68.2	67	60	47	6	1	43	0	57	2
Bombard, Asheville	2	0	1.000	0.00	5	1	1	4	1	2	15.1	6	0	0	0	6	1	0	7	0
Brahs, Gastonia*	1	1	.500	3.63	3	3	0	0	0	0	17.1	19	7	7	0	1	4	0	16	0
Braukmiller, Gastonia	2	0	1.000	3.21	2	2	2	0	0	0	14.0	12	5	5	1	1	4	0	11	1
Brisco, Savannah	9	7	.563	3.23	26	18	6	3	1	0	128.1	128	64	46	5	3	57	1	77	3
Browne, Greensboro*	1	0	1.000	1.80	1	1	0	0	0	0	5.0	5	5	1	0	0	2	0	2	1
Burgess, Florence	0	2	.000	3.91	20	1	0	6	0	0	53.0	58	33	23	6	1	16	1	41	9
Burgos, Florence*	0	0	.000	18.00	2	0	0	0	0	0	1.0	2	2	2	0	0	1	0	1	0
Burke, Charleston*	0	0	.000	3.12	11	1	0	4	0	1	17.1	10	7	6	0	1	13	0	9	1
Callahan, Asheville	2	2	.500	5.51	28	2	0	14	0	3	50.2	42	35	31	5	3	52	2	34	10
Canseco, Greensboro	1	1	.500	4.86	6	2	0	1	0	0	16.2	19	13	9	1	1	22	1	9	2
Caraballo, Spartanburg	6	2	.750	2.19	52	0	0	46	0	21	70.0	55	24	17	0	3	18	3	44	4
Carrasco, Savannah	5	5	.500	1.98	46	0	0	40	0	23	63.2	49	28	14	2	5	29	5	42	5
Carson, Savannah	14	9	.609	3.17	25	25	8	0	3	0	167.1	131	72	59	10	3	76	1	93	3
Castillo, Florence*	11	8	.579	3.41	25	24	4	0	1	0	137.1	123	71	52	11	0	50	0	96	4
Chadwick, Gastonia	0	0	.000	0.00	1	0	0	1	0	0	1.0	1	0	0	0	1	0	0	2	0
Clark, Anderson	0	0	.000	18.00	1	0	0	1	0	0	2.0	4	5	4	0	0	5	0	0	0
Clemons, Florence	1	2	.333	1.38	4	4	1	0	0	0	26.0	17	6	4	1	0	6	0	25	2
Coffman, Anderson	1	4	.200	4.68	7	7	0	0	0	0	32.2	37	23	17	1	0	26	0	23	8
Collins, Gastonia	3	7	.300	6.01	14	14	2	0	1	0	73.1	84	58	49	5	4	42	1	47	7
Cooke, Macon	6	7	.462	2.40	46	2	2	27	0	7	90.0	77	51	24	5	3	40	1	54	9
Costello, Savannah	13	9	.591	3.36	26	26	2	0	0	0	166.0	142	80	62	9	5	86	1	114	5
Creekmore, Spartanburg	3	2	.600	6.38	23	0	0	10	0	0	36.2	42	32	26	4	1	24	3	22	4
Cunningham, Macon	0	2	.000	5.01	35	2	0	11	0	0	79.0	67	49	44	5	8	65	4	37	2
Cutshall, Gastonia	2	3	.400	2.08	8	8	0	0	0	0	43.1	28	10	10	1	0	30	0	57	1
B. Davis, Charleston	7	2	.778	2.31	34	0	0	23	0	7	66.1	56	23	17	7	2	14	3	44	0
F. Davis, Greensboro*	0	0	.000	4.15	4	0	0	1	0	0	8.2	10	8	4	0	0	11	0	6	2
DelRosario, Anderson	7	8	.467	3.84	28	8	0	10	0	0	89.0	87	51	38	3	4	45	1	43	10
Devlin, Greensboro	6	5	.545	3.36	39	0	0	19	0	2	69.2	59	33	26	2	3	35	3	69	4
Dickman, Florence	5	3	.625	3.34	34	5	0	19	0	4	72.2	58	40	27	3	4	61	0	61	11
Dobie, Columbia	10	9	.526	3.03	25	25	6	0	2	0	172.1	123	75	58	11	0	119	3	128	7
Dombek, Spartanburg*	6	4	.600	6.55	28	15	0	2	0	0	103.0	97	90	75	6	4	103	1	80	14
Drummond, Macon	7	15	.318	3.90	27	26	4	0	1	0	154.2	139	93	67	8	9	81	2	76	3
Dube, Asheville	9	9	.500	4.55	23	23	4	0	2	0	122.2	108	71	62	6	5	84	1	106	15
Durocher, Macon	6	5	.545	2.67	35	2	1	22	0	9	67.1	53	27	20	3	5	26	2	58	2
Dyrek, Asheville*	0	0	.000	0.00	1	0	0	1	0	0	1.0	0	0	0	0	0	0	0	0	0
Edens, Columbia	7	4	.636	3.12	16	15	4	1	1	0	95.1	65	44	33	1	1	58	1	60	10
Emerson, Columbia	0	1	.000	6.75	9	0	0	4	0	1	18.2	27	21	14	3	3	7	0	13	3
Engram, Spartanburg	0	0	.000	0.00	1	0	0	1	0	0	3.0	3	0	0	0	0	1	0	1	0
Fedor, 40 Gr'nboro-8 Gas.	8	5	.615	2.55	48	1	1	33	0	5	88.1	60	39	25	0	4	57	7	87	13
Ferguson, Greensboro	4	4	.500	2.49	10	9	5	0	0	0	68.2	54	24	19	2	0	22	0	58	1
Ferlenda, Florence	2	11	.154	5.72	28	13	3	8	0	3	89.2	92	74	57	12	5	67	2	70	7
Friedel, Columbia	1	1	.500	1.80	5	3	1	1	1	0	20.0	15	7	4	0	3	10	0	22	0
Fulton, Greensboro	2	3	.400	4.15	10	8	3	0	0	0	52.0	45	26	24	1	2	26	1	29	4
Funk, Asheville*	6	2	.750	2.77	54	1	0	26	0	9	74.2	56	26	23	3	0	33	4	80	5
Gallagher, Florence	1	2	.333	0.51	6	1	1	4	0	2	17.2	9	3	1	0	0	3	0	14	1
Gass, Savannah	0	0	.000	3.74	9	0	0	1	0	1	21.2	23	15	9	0	0	17	1	19	1

Pitcher—Club	W.	L.	Pct.	ERA.	G.	GS.	CG.	GF.	ShO.	Sv.	IP.	H.	R.	ER.	HR.	HB.	BB.	Int. BB.	SO.	WP.
Gay, Columbia	8	5	.615	4.04	31	5	0	15	0	1	82.1	84	44	37	2	0	32	6	65	3
P. George, Charleston°	8	8	.500	4.07	25	24	3	0	0	0	159.1	162	91	72	15	0	41	0	84	8
S. George, Greensboro°	2	4	.333	5.18	24	3	0	8	0	0	48.2	30	31	28	0	1	55	1	46	8
Ghelfi, Spartanburg	0	1	.000	3.00	2	2	0	0	0	0	6.0	5	3	2	1	1	2	0	5	1
Gonzales, Gastonia	0	1	.000	4.76	3	0	0	1	0	0	5.2	9	4	3	0	0	2	0	3	0
Gordon, Macon	2	3	.400	4.02	27	0	0	21	0	3	31.1	20	16	14	0	3	31	3	42	1
Grosdidier, Anderson	0	5	.000	5.97	19	1	0	11	0	0	37.2	45	29	25	3	1	20	1	27	8
Groves, Anderson	3	1	.750	3.54	4	4	0	0	0	0	20.1	17	8	8	0	0	13	0	14	3
Grudzinski, Macon	5	6	.455	6.84	25	15	0	6	0	0	96.0	103	85	73	7	3	76	1	67	17
Hall, Anderson	0	0	.000	13.50	1	0	0	1	0	0	2.2	7	5	4	0	0	3	0	0	0
Hammond, Asheville	4	7	.364	3.46	46	1	0	28	0	5	78.0	73	45	30	5	1	38	4	60	3
Hardee, Gastonia	1	1	.500	5.40	7	3	1	1	0	0	18.1	18	13	11	1	1	15	0	12	3
Harris, Savannah°	0	0	.000	0.00	1	0	0	0	0	0	1.0	0	0	0	0	0	3	0	0	0
Hartshorn, Columbia	14	4	.778	2.48	24	24	10	0	4	0	160.0	126	64	44	7	3	83	2	100	4
Hazlett, Anderson°	0	0	.000	7.62	6	0	0	4	0	1	13.0	12	12	11	0	2	12	0	18	2
Helton, Macon	1	4	.200	7.32	9	9	1	0	0	0	35.2	34	34	29	3	1	34	0	14	2
Herzog, Savannah°	2	4	.333	2.43	46	0	0	27	0	4	66.2	61	25	18	5	0	28	4	46	0
Hicks, Spartanburg	3	2	.600	3.38	19	1	0	16	0	0	37.1	31	18	14	3	4	15	0	20	1
B. Holman, Gastonia	5	8	.385	4.76	20	20	1	0	0	0	90.2	76	58	48	5	1	98	0	94	14
S. Holman, Macon	3	2	.600	1.93	9	6	1	2	1	0	46.2	48	19	10	1	1	25	0	32	3
Horne, Greensboro	6	6	.500	3.12	33	12	4	16	3	3	106.2	97	51	37	7	1	56	2	80	8
Houp, Asheville	0	0	.000	4.50	2	0	0	1	0	0	2.0	3	3	1	1	0	1	0	3	0
Householder, Spartanburg°	5	5	.500	4.70	40	3	0	20	0	8	69.0	55	42	36	2	4	64	1	82	9
Hull, Charleston	16	5	.762	2.84	27	23	3	2	2	0	164.2	147	73	52	13	7	57	0	105	9
Impagliazzo, Gastonia	3	8	.273	4.69	42	0	0	32	0	12	71.0	62	38	37	7	1	50	1	87	9
Jackson, Spartanburg	7	2	.778	2.68	14	14	0	0	0	0	80.2	53	35	24	8	5	50	0	77	4
James, Savannah	0	0	.000	9.00	1	0	0	0	0	0	1.0	2	1	1	0	0	0	1	1	0
M.G. Johnson, Gastonia	2	1	.667	5.19	9	0	0	5	0	0	8.2	7	6	5	0	0	8	0	11	0
R. Johnson, Florence	3	1	.750	4.15	20	3	1	10	0	1	52.0	47	29	24	5	1	19	0	35	7
Jones, Anderson	7	9	.438	3.24	23	23	8	0	0	0	147.0	127	68	53	6	3	66	1	75	6
Kaull, Savannah	0	0	.000	0.00	1	0	0	1	0	0	1.0	1	0	0	0	0	0	0	1	1
Kelley, Asheville	14	9	.609	2.58	26	26	7	0	4	0	174.2	160	68	50	14	3	56	1	121	6
Kiernan, Macon	0	5	.000	6.68	21	0	0	17	0	5	31.0	37	34	23	0	2	22	2	25	6
Kish, Savannah	4	3	.571	4.50	12	12	2	0	0	0	66.0	66	37	30	6	1	35	3	22	5
Klein, Charleston	1	1	.500	3.98	21	1	0	13	0	3	40.2	52	28	18	1	0	11	1	19	2
Klink, Columbia°	5	4	.556	3.49	31	0	0	27	0	11	38.2	30	19	15	1	1	28	0	49	5
Kolb, Macon	1	3	.250	5.73	11	5	0	3	0	0	37.2	42	30	24	4	2	26	1	20	1
Llewellyn, Anderson	0	0	.000	13.50	2	0	0	2	0	0	1.1	2	2	2	0	0	2	0	1	1
Lloyd, Spartanburg	4	3	.571	4.12	12	9	1	1	0	0	54.2	43	28	25	2	2	38	1	38	3
Long, Spartanburg	9	9	.500	3.62	24	24	4	0	2	0	149.1	118	68	60	11	5	103	3	93	22
Lopez, Macon	6	6	.500	3.96	14	14	2	0	0	0	86.1	83	50	38	2	3	47	0	61	3
Lounello, Florence	1	0	1.000	12.00	5	0	0	3	0	1	12.0	17	16	16	3	0	10	0	5	1
Lucas, Asheville	5	2	.714	2.88	45	4	0	21	0	5	90.2	77	35	29	0	4	49	5	74	6
Mallicoat, Asheville°	3	4	.429	3.92	11	11	2	0	0	0	64.1	49	30	28	5	4	36	0	57	7
Martin, Anderson	4	0	1.000	3.12	19	0	0	13	0	4	26.0	21	10	9	1	2	20	1	24	1
Mathews, Savannah°	1	0	1.000	2.96	6	3	0	0	0	0	27.1	24	10	9	1	1	15	0	21	3
Mathison, Greensboro	7	3	.700	3.55	14	13	0	1	0	0	71.0	68	31	28	4	0	44	0	61	7
McCormack, Charleston	2	1	.667	3.30	10	2	0	4	0	0	30.0	24	14	11	0	2	10	0	16	3
McGrath, Savannah	10	10	.500	3.25	25	25	0	0	0	0	146.2	143	66	53	6	4	75	3	57	2
McKay, Florence°	1	3	.250	5.08	13	6	0	5	0	1	33.2	34	27	19	2	0	24	0	29	5
McLarnon, Spartanburg	4	4	.500	3.03	30	0	0	16	0	5	59.1	45	27	20	7	0	19	0	56	5
McPherson, Savannah	3	1	.750	2.59	12	5	1	4	0	0	48.2	45	22	14	2	2	26	0	42	1
Meacham, Anderson	1	2	.333	4.67	18	0	0	11	0	5	27.0	28	15	14	0	0	17	0	22	4
Mehalko, Anderson°	4	10	.286	4.10	29	13	3	10	0	3	90.0	85	55	41	5	2	54	2	60	8
Mesa, Florence	4	3	.571	3.76	7	7	0	0	0	0	38.1	38	24	16	3	0	25	0	35	2
Mohr, Charleston°	1	2	.333	2.23	14	1	1	8	1	3	32.1	26	10	8	0	0	8	0	36	1
Moore, Asheville	5	14	.263	5.11	30	20	1	2	0	1	132.0	124	89	75	6	10	101	2	125	16
Morales, Charleston	1	0	1.000	1.69	2	2	1	0	1	0	10.2	5	6	2	1	0	8	0	3	0
Morelock, Anderson	4	6	.400	4.76	30	11	2	8	0	2	87.0	75	59	46	5	2	72	0	57	16
Morris, Anderson	2	0	1.000	5.03	9	0	0	4	0	1	19.2	15	11	11	2	0	21	0	18	4
Morton, Spartanburg°	6	3	.667	3.48	11	11	2	0	1	0	72.1	61	39	28	5	2	36	0	55	3
Neidlinger, Macon	9	8	.529	2.77	25	25	2	0	0	0	166.0	138	65	51	6	0	85	2	113	4
Norton, Gastonia	4	4	.500	3.15	35	6	3	11	2	3	94.1	73	40	33	4	0	58	2	69	9
Norwood, Spartanburg°	1	3	.250	5.48	5	5	0	0	0	0	21.1	22	14	13	0	1	12	1	12	2
Nunez, Charleston	14	8	.636	3.28	25	25	8	0	1	0	170.0	167	91	62	8	3	54	1	106	8
O'Dell, Asheville°	0	0	.000	0.00	1	0	0	1	0	0	1.0	0	0	0	0	0	0	0	1	0
Oates, Savannah°	0	2	.000	3.65	3	0	0	0	0	0	12.1	7	7	5	0	1	18	1	7	1
Ortega, Savannah	2	0	1.000	4.60	18	0	0	7	0	0	31.1	34	18	16	2	1	23	2	23	1
Palmer, Asheville°	6	5	.545	5.10	16	16	1	0	0	0	77.2	92	50	44	6	2	50	0	35	8
Parent, Greensboro	1	4	.200	6.47	22	7	1	6	0	0	64.0	79	53	46	4	3	35	2	39	4
Parker, Anderson	0	1	.000	5.25	3	3	0	0	0	0	12.0	12	12	7	0	2	15	0	8	1
Pascho, Gastonia	2	6	.250	4.24	41	3	1	13	0	0	74.1	71	46	35	4	2	35	2	61	7
Peraza, Florence	8	7	.533	3.41	31	13	4	14	0	1	137.1	108	67	52	7	5	62	0	104	7
M. Perez, Charleston	5	7	.417	4.35	16	15	0	0	0	0	89.0	99	52	43	9	2	19	0	55	4
V. Perez, Charleston	0	0	.000	5.68	5	0	0	5	0	0	6.1	5	5	4	0	1	4	0	0	1
Perry, Savannah	7	5	.583	3.21	24	20	3	1	1	0	109.1	102	50	39	8	5	59	0	64	7
Powell, Spartanburg	4	8	.333	5.21	35	13	1	7	0	0	129.2	134	93	75	8	9	67	3	83	10
Rasnick, Spartanburg	4	9	.308	5.53	22	16	1	1	0	0	97.2	95	71	60	11	4	54	3	53	14
Ratliff, Gastonia	8	6	.571	3.25	40	9	0	20	0	0	121.2	113	52	44	4	5	57	1	87	11
Ray, Greensboro°	0	1	.000	3.97	4	2	0	0	0	0	11.1	10	7	5	0	0	12	0	8	2
Rebiejo, Greensboro	3	2	.600	4.33	6	6	2	0	0	0	35.1	30	22	17	2	1	16	0	30	0
Reed, Columbia	4	0	1.000	5.83	38	2	1	20	1	6	63.1	57	45	41	6	3	61	1	70	7
Reilly, Asheville	3	0	1.000	3.63	34	0	0	26	0	8	39.2	39	18	16	4	1	19	0	31	1
Reyes, Florence°	7	11	.389	4.42	24	23	5	1	0	1	128.1	136	96	63	10	1	56	0	59	14
Robair, Columbia	0	3	.000	5.34	13	2	0	3	0	0	32.0	25	24	19	2	2	29	1	21	4
Robbins, Florence	1	1	.500	3.14	22	0	0	18	0	3	28.2	27	20	10	0	0	19	1	29	3
Rodriguez, Greensboro	7	7	.500	2.98	27	12	4	7	1	4	108.2	109	50	36	4	1	46	1	46	3
Rogers, Anderson	6	1	.857	4.68	29	0	0	17	0	6	50.0	47	30	26	3	0	18	1	54	4
Romagna, Florence	0	0	.000	9.00	1	0	0	1	0	0	1.0	1	1	1	0	0	1	0	3	0
Rooker, Charleston	1	3	.250	3.80	8	4	0	3	0	0	23.2	27	26	10	0	0	18	0	14	0
Rosario, Anderson°	7	12	.368	3.27	25	24	5	0	3	0	151.1	125	76	55	11	2	75	1	119	12
Rowe, Anderson	2	4	.333	4.71	12	11	1	1	0	1	65.0	64	38	34	1	3	43	0	29	12
Salisbury, Anderson	0	4	.000	8.72	7	7	0	0	0	0	21.2	22	31	21	0	0	39	0	16	9

Pitcher—Club	W.	L.	Pct.	ERA.	G.	GS.	CG.	GF.	ShO.	Sv.	IP.	H.	R.	ER.	HR.	HB.	BB.	Int. BB.	SO.	WP.
Samuels, Asheville*	4	5	.444	3.36	15	14	1	0	1	0	88.1	82	38	33	7	0	44	1	82	10
Santiago, Anderson*	1	1	.500	3.31	10	0	0	6	0	2	16.1	16	13	6	0	0	9	1	14	2
Schuler, Gastonia	1	1	.500	4.91	14	0	0	11	0	3	14.2	19	8	8	2	0	2	0	14	1
Shirley, Anderson	1	4	.200	5.09	26	0	0	14	0	1	53.0	62	37	30	4	1	27	2	41	9
Shook, Charleston	3	3	.500	3.67	15	3	0	7	0	1	41.2	43	21	17	1	1	17	1	27	2
Simon, Macon	1	1	.500	5.02	7	2	0	2	0	0	14.1	12	9	8	1	1	5	0	15	1
Sinclair, Savannah	1	1	.500	3.90	20	0	0	13	0	2	27.2	24	19	12	3	0	19	0	23	0
Smalley, Greensboro*	1	2	.333	3.03	5	5	0	0	0	0	29.2	25	15	10	2	1	16	0	14	1
Smiley, Macon*	5	11	.313	3.95	21	19	2	2	0	1	130.0	119	73	57	12	2	41	1	73	4
Snell, Charleston	3	8	.273	3.80	19	11	4	4	0	0	83.0	89	53	35	4	3	29	2	44	3
Soma, Gastonia	0	7	.000	4.50	19	9	2	4	0	0	60.0	60	36	30	2	1	44	0	43	4
Sprowl, Florence*	1	0	1.000	3.07	4	2	0	0	0	0	14.2	12	8	5	0	2	13	0	10	0
Stampfl, Columbia	3	0	1.000	3.02	7	7	2	0	1	0	44.2	34	18	15	1	1	26	0	33	4
Stewart, Spartanburg	4	5	.444	2.76	11	11	1	0	0	0	65.1	55	29	20	2	1	34	1	52	6
Stiles, Columbia	0	4	.000	2.49	18	0	0	18	0	8	21.2	20	13	6	0	0	10	0	18	3
Takach, Columbia*	0	0	.000	3.60	2	2	0	0	0	0	10.0	15	5	4	2	1	6	0	6	0
Tejada, Florence	2	11	.154	4.54	22	12	0	5	0	0	77.1	89	55	39	8	8	53	1	29	10
Teno, Columbia*	2	5	.286	5.02	21	11	1	4	0	2	86.0	71	57	48	6	2	72	1	57	6
Thomas, Anderson	1	4	.200	4.20	8	8	0	0	0	0	40.2	41	25	19	3	0	25	0	27	6
Tomsick, Anderson	5	4	.556	2.05	17	17	2	0	2	0	92.1	76	34	21	1	2	42	0	47	7
H.R. Torres, Greensboro	8	4	.667	3.69	20	19	3	1	0	0	117.0	97	59	48	11	2	49	0	110	9
R. Torres, Anderson	1	2	.333	6.17	13	2	0	9	0	0	23.1	23	22	16	2	3	22	0	23	7
Traen, Gastonia*	8	5	.615	3.08	24	20	2	2	1	0	125.2	120	63	43	3	0	54	0	89	3
Tunison, Spartanburg	3	5	.375	5.12	19	13	0	2	0	0	70.1	70	52	40	4	1	45	3	37	13
Turano, Florence	4	1	.800	3.70	8	8	0	0	0	0	41.1	41	27	17	1	1	34	0	19	2
Valliant, Gastonia*	10	3	.769	3.93	30	8	3	10	1	0	89.1	74	45	39	3	0	56	0	80	12
Vargas, Spartanburg	0	1	.000	2.92	17	0	0	12	0	1	37.0	44	21	12	5	1	13	2	17	3
Velazquez, Charleston	11	12	.478	4.42	27	27	6	0	2	0	163.0	152	98	80	8	13	69	0	85	4
Verrone, Asheville	10	7	.588	3.95	21	21	1	0	1	0	118.1	113	66	52	9	6	64	0	65	6
Vizcaino, Asheville*	0	3	.000	5.68	11	3	0	1	0	1	25.1	23	23	16	1	0	25	2	19	7
Walter, Charleston	5	2	.714	2.92	38	0	0	34	0	12	71.0	70	31	23	8	1	26	1	33	2
Wayland, Macon	1	0	1.000	2.45	8	1	0	7	0	0	18.1	20	7	5	1	0	6	0	8	1
Weatherford, Spartanburg	1	2	.333	6.14	6	3	0	2	0	0	22.0	25	17	15	0	0	12	0	10	3
West, Columbia	3	5	.375	6.23	12	12	0	0	0	0	60.2	41	47	42	2	2	68	1	60	14
Weston, Columbia	6	5	.545	1.84	32	2	0	20	0	2	63.2	58	27	13	2	2	27	6	40	5
Williams, Greensboro	5	11	.313	3.65	33	18	6	13	1	4	128.1	125	69	52	4	3	54	4	58	9
Wilmore, Asheville	0	1	.000	18.00	4	0	0	0	0	0	4.0	5	9	8	1	2	10	1	3	1
Wyatt, Columbia*	6	4	.600	3.63	13	12	1	0	1	0	74.1	69	45	30	3	1	25	1	55	3
Yearout, Florence*	7	3	.700	2.29	21	8	2	8	1	2	74.2	62	30	19	5	2	31	1	63	13
Young, Gastonia*	8	10	.444	4.18	24	24	7	0	2	0	144.1	117	77	67	10	1	68	2	121	9
Yowler, Charleston*	0	2	.000	5.66	23	4	0	10	0	1	55.2	65	43	35	2	3	15	0	29	5

BALKS—Traen, 6; Powell, 4; Arnsberg, Coffman, Dobie, Moore, Samuels, Yearout, 3 each; Canseco, Carson, Collins, Cunningham, DelRosario, Dube, Durocher, Funk, P. George, Horne, Hull, Impagliazzo, Kolb, Lucas, Mallicoat, Peraza, Rasnick, Reyes, Rogers, Stampfl, H.R. Torres, Valliant, 2 each; Bautista, Brisco, Burgess, Caraballo, Costello, Cutshall, Dickman, Dombek, Drummond, Edens, Ferguson, Gay, S. George, Gonzales, Grudzinski, Herzog, B. Holman, Jackson, Klink, Lloyd, Long, Lounello, Mathews, Mehalko, Mesa, Morelock, Morton, Neidlinger, Ortega, Palmer, Parent, M. Perez, Ratliff, Reed, Rodriguez, Rowe, Smiley, Stewart, Thomas, Tomsick, Tunison, Vargas, Velazquez, Verrone, Vizcaino, West, Williams, Yowler, 1 each.

COMBINATION SHUTOUTS—Jones-Grosdidier-Mehalko, Mehalko-Rogers, Tomsick-Morelock, Groves-Santiago, Anderson; Moore-Lucas-Hammond, Samuels-Bombard, Kelley-Reilly, Verrone-Funk, Funk-Moore, Palmer-Reilly-Funk, Asheville; Hull-Walter-Davis, Nunez-Walter, Velazquez-Yowler, George-Shook-Walter, Perez-Davis-Walter, Charleston; Dobie-Gay, Columbia; Mesa-Dickman, Tejada-McKay, Yearout-Dickman, Castillo-Yearout, Yearout-Anthony, Dickman-Reyes, Florence; Barrett-Schuler, Cutshall-Impagliazzo, Soma-Valliant, Gastonia; Mathison-Fedor, Smalley-Devlin-Fedor, Mathison-Horne, Greensboro; Smiley-Durocher, Neidlinger-Gordon-Durocher, Holman-Cooke, Drummond-Cooke, Wayland-Cooke, Macon; Costello-Carrasco 2, Costello-Herzog, Costello-Brisco, Carson-Herzog-Ortega, McGrath-Herzog-Carrasco, Kish-Carrasco, Perry-Carrasco, Savannah; Rasnick-Caraballo, Stewart-McLarnon, Tunison-McLarnon, Jackson-Householder, Jackson-Caraballo, Spartanburg.

NO-HIT GAMES—Arnsberg, Greensboro, defeated Savannah, 5-0, May 24; Castillo-Yearout, Florence, defeated Charleston, 4-0, June 7; Norton, Gastonia, defeated Anderson, 1-0 (seven innings), August 15.

Appalachian League

SUMMER CLASS A CLASSIFICATION

CHAMPIONSHIP WINNERS IN PREVIOUS YEARS

1921—Greenville	.608	1947—Pulaski	.648	1967—Bluefield	.627
Johnson City°	.627	New River (3rd)†	.516	1968—Marion	.583
1922—Bristol	.557	1948—Pulaski‡	.680	1969—Pulaski a	.576
1923—Knoxville	.635	1949—Bluefield‡	.721	Johnson City	.544
1924—Knoxville°	.642	1950—Bluefield	.600	1970—Bluefield	.638
Bristol	.607	Bluefield z	.745	1971—Bluefield a	.609
1925—Greenville	.667	1951—Kingsport‡	.659	Kingsport	.559
1926-36—Did not operate.		1952—Johnson City	.595	1972—Bristol a	.588
1937—Elizabethton	.559	Welch (3rd)†	.509	Covington	.586
Pennington Gap°	.580	1953—Welch°	.705	1973—Kingsport	.757
1938—Elizabethton	.664	Johnson City	.672	1974—Bristol a	.754
Greenville (3rd)†	.571	1954—Bluefield‡	.619	Bluefield	.536
1939—Elizabethton‡	.597	1955—Salem°°	.689	1975—Marion	.515
1940—Johnson City§	.726	1956—Did not operate.		Johnson City a	.603
Elizabethton	.750	1957—Bluefield	.701	1976—Johnson City a	.714
1941—Johnson City	.614	1958—Johnson City	.662	Bluefield	.600
Elizabethton°	.661	1959—Morristown	.603	1977—Kingsport	.623
1942—Bristol	.667	1960—Wytheville	.614	1978—Elizabethton	.594
Bristol x	.660	1961—Middlesboro	.591	1979—Paintsville	.800
1943—Bristol	.755	1962—Bluefield	.671	1980—Paintsville	.657
Bristol y	.617	1963—Bluefield	.652	1981—Paintsville	.657
1944—Kingsport‡	.575	1964—Johnson City	.662	1982—Bluefield a	.681
1945—Kingsport‡	.670	1965—Salem	.614	Johnson City	.478
1946—New River‡	.675	1966—Marion	.623	1983—Paintsville	.653

°Won split-season playoff. †Won four-team playoff. ‡Won championship and four-team playoff. §Johnson City, first-half winner, won playoff involving six clubs. xWon both halves and defeated second-place Elizabethton in playoff. yWon both halves, but Erwin won four-team playoff. zWon both halves, but Bristol won two-club playoff. °°Salem and Johnson City declared playoff co-champions when weather forced cancellation of final series. aLeague was divided into Northern, Southern divisions; declared league champion, based on highest won-lost percentage.

STANDING OF CLUBS AT CLOSE OF SEASON, AUGUST 30

NORTHERN DIVISION

Club	W.	L.	T.	Pct.	G.B.
Pulaski (Braves)	37	32	0	.536	......
Paintsville (Brewers)	37	33	0	.529	½
Pikeville (Cubs)	34	34	0	.500	2½
Bluefield (Orioles)	32	38	0	.457	5½

SOUTHERN DIVISION

Club	W.	L.	T.	Pct.	G.B.
Elizabethton (Twins)	40	29	0	.580	......
Bristol (Tigers)	37	33	0	.529	3½
Kingsport (Mets)	31	38	0	.449	9
Johnson City (Cardinals)	29	40	0	.420	11

COMPOSITE STANDING OF CLUBS AT CLOSE OF SEASON, AUGUST 30

Club	Eliz.	Pul.	Pvl.	Bri.	Pike.	Blu.	Kng.	J.C.	W.	L.	T.	Pct.	G.B.
Elizabethton (Twins)	....	1	6	7	4	4	10	8	40	29	0	.580	......
Pulaski (Braves)	6	....	6	4	6	6	4	5	37	32	0	.536	3
Paintsville (Brewers)	2	6	....	4	7	10	4	4	37	33	0	.529	3½
Bristol (Tigers)	7	4	4	....	4	6	5	7	37	33	0	.529	3½
Pikeville (Cubs)	4	6	7	4	....	5	3	5	34	34	0	.500	5½
Bluefield (Orioles)	4	8	2	2	7	....	4	5	32	38	0	.457	8½
Kingsport (Mets)	2	4	4	7	4	4	....	6	31	38	0	.449	9
Johnson City (Cardinals)	4	3	4	5	2	3	8	....	29	40	0	.420	11

Major league affiliations in parentheses.

Playoffs—Elizabethton defeated Pulaski, 7-4, to win league championship.

Regular Season Attendance—Bluefield, 25,100; Bristol, 10,114; Elizabethton, 12,063; Johnson City, 12,263; Kingsport, 34,007; Paintsville, 7,595; Pikeville, 5,511; Pulaski, 17,533. Total, 124,186. Playoff attendance, 379.

Managers—Bluefield, Greg Biagini; Bristol, Hal Dyer; Elizabethton, Fred Waters; Johnson City, Chuck Hiller; Kingsport, Dan Radison; Paintsville, Ron Hansen; Pikeville, Jim Fairey; Pulaski, Buddy Bailey.

All-Star Team—1B—Gene Larkin, Elizabethton; 2B—Bryan House, Pikeville; 3B—Craig Mills, Bristol; SS—Jay Bell, Elizabethton; OF—Shawn Abner, Kingsport; Dave Vetsch, Elizabethton; Tim Casey, Paintsville; C—Kurt Beamesderfer, Bluefield; DH—Mike Fitzgerald, Johnson City; RHP—Alfredo Cardwood, Elizabethton; LHP—Tim Rice, Pikeville; Player of the Year—Dave Vetsch, Elizabethton; Manager of the Year—Fred Waters, Elizabethton.

(Compiled by Howe News Bureau, Boston, Mass.)

CLUB BATTING

Club	Pct.	G.	AB.	R.	OR.	H.	TB.	2B.	3B.	HR.	RBI.	GW.	SH.	SF.	HP.	BB.	Int. BB.	SO.	SB.	CS.	LOB.
Kingsport	.257	69	2228	358	420	572	825	89	16	44	297	27	7	20	16	256	2	461	112	23	456
Paintsville	.254	70	2309	384	336	587	937	108	13	72	334	27	7	15	24	274	10	536	32	18	495
Elizabethton	.252	69	2234	354	293	563	823	123	10	39	294	37	4	25	14	358	5	381	77	25	552
Bluefield	.250	70	2254	373	381	563	816	111	11	40	303	27	10	26	31	339	6	495	101	27	525
Johnson City	.248	69	2328	341	373	578	878	113	14	53	294	27	10	22	22	283	7	425	40	26	515
Bristol	.242	70	2208	390	358	535	820	89	20	52	339	33	6	22	15	360	6	482	58	23	512
Pulaski	.239	69	2226	340	341	533	741	86	4	38	279	25	26	28	26	352	6	507	96	22	540
Pikeville	.222	68	2127	302	340	473	662	80	11	29	245	26	14	21	23	361	7	552	142	54	496

INDIVIDUAL BATTING
(Leading Qualifiers for Batting Championship—189 or More Plate Appearances)

*Bats lefthanded.   †Switch-hitter.

Player and Club	Pct.	G.	AB.	R.	H.	TB.	2B.	3B.	HR.	RBI.	GW.	SH.	SF.	HP.	BB.	Int. BB.	SO.	SB.	CS.
Fitzgerald, Michael, Johnson City	.345	51	171	31	59	91	11	0	7	31	2	0	2	5	18	0	25	2	0
Larkin, Eugene, Elizabethton†	.326	57	193	29	63	96	13	1	6	37	5	0	3	2	29	1	18	1	1
Vetsch, David, Elizabethton*	.309	63	217	55	67	115	22	1	8	49	9	1	4	2	41	0	41	11	3
Beamesderfer, Kurt, Bluefield	.302	65	222	32	67	88	12	0	3	44	3	0	3	1	35	1	32	6	2
Mills, R. Craig, Bristol	.300	60	200	51	60	85	14	1	3	30	4	0	1	6	46	1	33	4	4
Lawton, Marcus, Kingsport	.298	54	191	43	57	72	10	1	1	15	2	0	0	0	25	0	22	38	4
Silver, Roy, Johnson City†	.294	57	211	33	62	95	15	0	6	35	3	0	3	0	31	5	24	4	2
Casey, Timothy, Paintsville*	.292	70	250	55	73	144	11	3	18	52	5	0	2	4	54	4	68	4	1
Baird, Christopher, Pulaski*	.291	54	182	43	53	76	11	0	4	30	3	0	4	1	46	0	50	23	3
Gaeta, Christopher, Bluefield	.286	49	161	44	46	65	12	2	1	22	1	2	1	5	29	0	23	16	3

Departmental Leaders: G—Casey, 70; AB—Infante, 252; R—Mack, 56; H—Casey, 73; TB—Casey, 144; 2B—Vetsch, 22; 3B—Hermann, 6; HR—Casey, 18; RBI—Casey, 52; GWRBI—Vetsch, 9; SH—Williams, 5; SF—Dunn, 8; HP—Sjoberg, 7; BB—Casey, Mack, 54; IBB—Silver, 5; SO—Mack, 79; SB—J.D. Smith, 39; CS—Mandeville, 10.

(All Players—Listed Alphabetically)

Player and Club	Pct.	G.	AB.	R.	H.	TB.	2B.	3B.	HR.	RBI.	GW.	SH.	SF.	HP.	BB.	Int. BB.	SO.	SB.	CS.
Abner, Shawn, Kingsport	.273	46	183	32	50	88	8	0	10	35	6	0	2	2	10	1	24	9	6
Arnold, Scott, Johnson City	.000	14	14	0	0	0	0	0	0	0	0	4	0	0	2	0	3	0	0
Atkinson, Timothy, Johnson City	1.000	14	2	0	2	2	0	0	0	0	0	1	0	0	0	0	0	0	0
Bailey, Brandon, Kingsport	.213	62	202	28	43	72	8	0	7	29	3	1	3	0	20	0	50	0	0
Baird, Christopher, Pulaski*	.291	54	182	43	53	76	11	0	4	30	3	0	4	1	46	0	50	23	3
Ballou, Gary, Pulaski	.115	8	26	3	3	3	0	0	0	1	0	0	0	0	7	1	13	3	0
Bates, J. Douglas, Pulaski*	.000	20	3	0	0	0	0	0	0	1	0	1	0	0	2	0	1	0	0
Bautista, Angel, Johnson City	.000	13	2	0	0	0	0	0	0	0	0	0	0	0	0	0	1	0	0
Bautista, Bienvenido, Bluefield	.261	65	218	38	57	70	5	1	2	18	1	1	1	1	22	0	57	20	4
Bautista, Hector, Pikeville	.118	28	68	3	8	10	2	0	0	2	1	0	1	0	5	0	31	1	2
Bayron, Angel, Elizabethton*	.154	6	13	2	2	3	1	0	0	0	0	0	0	0	5	0	2	0	0
Beamesderfer, Kurt, Bluefield	.302	65	222	32	67	88	12	0	3	44	3	0	3	1	35	1	32	6	2
Beer, Steven, Pulaski	.000	12	7	0	0	0	0	0	0	0	0	3	0	0	0	0	4	0	0
Belen, Rolando, Kingsport	.167	17	12	1	2	2	0	0	0	0	0	1	0	0	1	0	2	0	0
Bell, Jay, Elizabethton	.220	66	245	43	54	86	12	1	6	30	1	0	2	1	42	0	50	4	2
Blackwell, Larry, Elizabethton	.233	63	227	44	53	64	7	2	0	14	3	1	1	1	46	0	41	27	6
Blauser, Jeffrey, Pulaski	.249	62	217	41	54	71	6	1	3	24	2	3	1	3	38	0	47	14	2
Bowens, Howard, Paintsville	.248	60	202	24	50	58	6	1	0	21	0	3	2	11	1	35	1	3	
Brooks, Desmond, Kingsport	.278	31	79	19	22	28	1	1	1	10	0	0	1	3	24	0	14	2	1
Brooks, Samuel, Kingsport	.000	13	1	0	0	0	0	0	0	0	0	0	0	0	0	0	0	0	0
Burke, Keith, Pulaski†	.244	55	172	22	42	57	10	1	1	21	3	4	1	1	30	1	61	5	0
Burton, Kelly, Bristol*	.230	55	161	24	37	43	3	0	1	17	2	2	2	0	30	0	20	3	1
Calley, Robert, Elizabethton	.239	12	46	7	11	16	2	0	1	9	2	0	0	0	4	0	5	0	0
Calvert, K. Christopher, Elizabethton.	.250	17	56	9	14	19	2	0	1	2	0	0	0	0	6	0	8	0	1
Camara, David, Pulaski*	.264	62	208	44	55	67	12	0	0	17	0	0	2	1	45	1	22	6	5
Carter, Dennis, Johnson City	.296	38	135	33	40	67	7	1	6	34	5	0	2	1	26	0	37	5	2
Cartwright, Timothy, Johnson City†	.227	41	132	20	30	44	7	2	1	13	1	1	1	0	30	1	16	5	2
Casey, Timothy, Paintsville*	.292	70	250	55	73	144	11	3	18	52	5	0	2	4	54	4	68	4	1
Casteel, A. Brent, Pikeville	.202	49	168	20	34	54	11	0	3	24	4	0	6	0	17	0	24	4	1
Castillo, David, Bristol	.238	43	126	18	30	45	4	1	3	22	4	1	2	2	12	1	20	3	2
Castro, Genaro, Kingsport	.241	40	116	19	28	37	3	3	0	11	0	0	1	2	10	0	32	2	0
Cepero, Edwin, Johnson City	.000	5	7	1	0	0	0	0	0	0	0	0	0	0	0	0	3	0	0
Cijntje, Sherwin, Bluefield*	.255	61	200	38	51	66	7	1	2	22	4	1	1	3	22	0	33	19	5
Clark, Isaiah, Paintsville	.175	15	57	9	10	15	2	0	1	6	1	0	2	4	6	0	8	3	0
Clossen, William, Pulaski	.100	14	10	2	1	1	0	0	0	1	0	0	0	0	1	0	2	0	0
Coffman, Kevin, Pulaski	.000	11	3	1	0	0	0	0	0	0	0	2	0	0	0	0	0	0	0
Colbert, Cary, Bristol	.279	62	219	45	61	103	15	0	9	50	3	0	3	2	34	1	29	0	0
Colescott, Robert, Kingsport	.239	54	180	23	43	62	10	3	1	21	1	0	2	1	17	0	43	5	2
Cornwell, Curtis, Bristol*	.261	53	184	32	48	68	6	1	4	25	3	1	1	1	35	1	22	4	2
Creech, Kevin, Bristol	.188	31	80	9	15	25	5	1	1	10	2	0	0	1	11	0	41	0	0
Crews, Marty, Kingsport	.266	31	94	11	25	45	5	0	5	18	2	0	0	0	9	1	35	0	1
Cron, Christopher, Pulaski	.368	32	114	22	42	71	8	0	7	37	5	0	0	2	6	17	1	20	2	0
Crosby, Patrick, Elizabethton*	.356	24	73	8	26	33	4	0	1	10	1	0	3	0	5	0	10	3	1
Cuevas, Angelo, Kingsport*	.299	45	154	27	46	78	7	2	7	30	0	0	2	0	18	0	6	8	3
Cunningham, Joseph, Johnson City	.247	55	174	27	43	71	8	1	6	17	2	0	3	3	31	0	31	3	3
Dalton, James, Elizabethton	.270	36	111	20	30	38	6	1	0	9	1	0	1	0	30	0	22	8	2
Danek, William, Pikeville	.200	21	5	0	1	1	0	0	0	0	0	0	0	0	0	0	0	0	0
DeGroot, Kenneth, Elizabethton	.161	34	112	13	18	25	4	0	1	7	2	0	0	0	19	0	15	0	2
DeWolf, Robert, Paintsville*	.216	56	167	24	36	50	11	0	1	15	0	0	1	1	29	1	34	6	2
Diaz, Esteban, Bluefield	.271	39	133	25	36	65	14	0	5	29	7	0	3	4	13	1	33	1	1
Diaz, Lazaro, Elizabethton†	.286	8	21	3	6	6	0	0	0	3	0	0	0	1	0	4	0	0	
Dunn, Victor, Bluefield	.253	56	162	41	41	66	10	0	5	32	1	0	8	3	53	1	34	13	2
Edmiston, Craig, Bristol	.226	45	133	18	30	40	4	0	2	11	0	1	2	1	16	1	40	5	1
Erdmann, Frederick, Bristol*	.237	10	38	10	9	19	1	0	3	12	4	0	1	0	7	0	4	0	0
Espinoza, Andres, Kingsport*	.249	51	169	16	42	55	8	1	1	16	3	0	1	2	6	0	24	0	0
Fassero, Jeffrey, Johnson City*	.063	13	16	3	1	2	1	0	0	1	0	0	0	2	0	9	0	0	
Fitzgerald, Michael, Johnson City	.345	51	171	31	59	91	11	0	7	31	2	0	2	5	18	0	25	2	0
Fugatt, W. Troy, Bristol*	.259	31	81	17	21	32	5	0	2	10	1	0	0	0	17	0	12	1	0
Gaeta, Christopher, Bluefield	.286	49	161	44	46	65	12	2	1	22	1	2	1	5	29	0	23	16	3
Gardner, Jimmie, Pikeville	.000	18	2	0	0	0	0	0	0	0	0	0	0	0	0	0	1	0	0
Givens, Brian, Kingsport	.000	15	8	2	0	0	0	0	0	0	0	1	0	0	3	0	4	0	0
Gomez, Carlos, Kingsport	.333	7	3	1	1	1	0	0	0	0	0	0	0	0	0	0	1	0	1
Gomez, Sixto, Elizabethton	.182	9	22	1	4	4	0	0	0	0	0	0	0	0	5	0	10	0	0
Gordon, Carl, Paintsville*	.300	5	10	4	3	4	1	0	0	1	0	0	0	0	6	0	3	1	0
Grosdidier, William, Pulaski	.000	26	3	0	0	0	0	0	0	0	0	0	0	0	0	0	1	0	0
Guilliams, Gregory, Pulaski	.224	28	85	14	19	26	2	1	1	12	0	0	2	19	0	18	1	0	
Guthrie, Kelly, Pulaski	.261	65	249	33	65	93	8	1	6	36	3	0	2	3	28	0	58	12	2
Hamrick, F. Dale, Pikeville	.190	55	184	19	35	52	5	0	4	16	0	2	3	0	9	0	53	3	0
Hanza, Antonio, Pikeville	.262	55	183	33	48	76	4	3	6	23	1	0	0	1	35	0	57	13	5
Hardamon, Derrick, Pikeville	.164	42	122	25	20	24	2	1	0	6	0	1	2	0	21	1	38	16	3
Hayes, Christopher, Kingsport	.000	16	2	0	0	0	0	0	0	0	0	0	0	0	0	0	2	0	0

Player and Club	Pct.	G.	AB.	R.	H.	TB.	2B.	3B.	HR.	RBI.	GW.	SH.	SF.	HP.	BB.	Int. BB.	SO.	SB.	CS.
Hayes, Daniel, Bluefield°	.313	7	16	3	5	6	1	0	0	4	1	1	0	0	0	0	3	1	0
Haynes, J. Kevin, Johnson City	.200	20	5	1	1	1	0	0	0	0	0	0	0	0	0	0	3	0	0
Hazlett, James, Pulaski°	.000	9	1	0	0	0	0	0	0	0	0	0	0	0	0	0	0	0	0
Hennessy, Michael, Johnson City°	.200	17	5	0	1	1	0	0	0	2	0	1	0	0	1	0	1	0	0
Hermann, Jeffrey, Bristol°	.262	62	183	37	48	77	8	6	3	37	4	0	3	1	47	0	40	10	2
Hernandez, Juan B., Bristol	.169	51	136	13	23	32	3	0	2	18	1	0	1	3	15	0	56	2	1
Hightower, Barry, Kingsport	.200	14	5	0	1	1	0	0	0	0	0	1	0	0	0	0	1	0	0
Hosie, Christopher, Pikeville	.111	26	54	6	6	7	1	0	0	2	1	0	0	1	18	1	27	2	1
House, Bryan, Pikeville†	.270	68	241	41	65	99	14	1	6	37	5	1	2	2	41	1	37	19	8
Howes, Jeff, Kingsport	.133	9	15	1	2	4	0	1	0	0	0	0	0	0	1	0	5	0	0
Hubbard, Jeffrey, Bluefield	.239	45	142	12	34	44	5	1	1	16	2	0	1	0	19	0	23	3	0
Hunter, Myron, Pikeville°	.000	10	2	0	0	0	0	0	0	0	0	0	0	0	0	0	0	0	0
Husband, L. Perry, Elizabethton°	.211	65	247	28	52	70	10	1	2	22	3	1	4	2	21	0	27	12	0
Iglesias, Luis, Johnson City	.232	31	82	11	19	32	6	2	1	4	0	0	1	0	8	0	9	0	2
Infante, Kennedy, Johnson City	.274	61	252	34	69	101	12	1	6	28	3	0	3	4	8	0	57	1	2
James, Scott, Pulaski	.202	39	119	12	24	30	3	0	1	10	1	1	3	2	8	0	18	0	0
James, Troy, Kingsport	.000	26	4	0	0	0	0	0	0	0	0	0	0	0	0	0	2	0	0
Jimenez, Raul, Johnson City	.185	42	124	12	23	29	6	0	0	17	2	1	2	1	20	0	24	0	2
Johnson, Everton, Kingston°	.330	46	106	22	35	54	2	1	5	27	1	0	1	1	22	0	16	4	1
Johnson, Greg, Pulaski	.000	20	2	0	0	0	0	0	0	0	0	0	0	0	0	0	2	0	0
Jones, Daniel, Elizabethton	.167	8	18	2	3	4	1	0	0	2	1	0	0	0	4	0	5	0	0
Jundy, Lorin, Kingsport	.000	11	3	0	0	0	0	0	0	0	0	0	1	0	0	0	1	0	0
Kent, M. Bernard, Paintsville°	.264	65	220	36	58	105	15	1	10	37	4	0	3	0	35	1	52	1	2
Kilner, John, Pulaski°	.000	14	13	0	0	0	0	0	0	0	0	0	0	0	2	0	6	0	0
LaMarche, Michel, Pikeville	.000	13	1	0	0	0	0	0	0	0	0	0	0	0	0	0	1	0	0
Lara, Crucito, Johnson City°	.173	36	104	13	18	27	3	0	2	8	0	0	1	0	13	0	20	1	0
Larkin, Eugene, Elizabethton†	.326	57	193	29	63	96	13	1	6	37	5	0	3	2	29	1	18	1	1
Larsen, James, Paintsville	.195	17	41	2	8	8	0	0	0	4	0	1	1	1	5	0	8	0	0
Lawton, Marcus, Kingsport	.298	54	191	43	57	72	10	1	1	15	2	0	0	0	25	0	22	38	4
Lee, Anthony, Pikeville	.000	6	6	0	0	0	0	0	0	0	0	0	0	0	0	0	1	0	0
Lewis, John, Pikeville°	.181	50	149	16	27	30	1	1	0	5	0	0	0	0	24	0	44	5	7
Liddell, David, Pikeville	.065	22	46	3	3	4	1	0	0	1	1	0	0	1	9	0	21	0	0
Lopez, Anthony, Elizabethton	.207	30	87	10	18	26	5	0	1	11	1	1	0	0	13	0	14	0	0
Mack, Jeremiah, Bristol	.221	67	244	56	54	105	11	5	10	36	1	0	1	6	54	0	79	13	7
Maddux, Gregory, Pikeville	.000	14	14	1	0	0	0	0	0	0	0	0	0	0	1	0	9	0	0
Mandeville, Robert, Pikeville	.283	67	247	38	70	86	12	2	0	34	4	1	0	2	46	1	36	20	10
Marte, Roberto, Johnson City	.000	8	16	0	0	0	0	0	0	0	0	0	0	0	0	0	8	0	0
Martinez, Jose, Elizabethton°	.218	19	55	5	12	20	0	1	2	8	1	0	0	0	10	2	7	1	2
Martinez, Porfirio, Bristol†	.217	44	129	12	28	47	2	4	3	22	2	0	1	1	5	0	33	1	0
Mathews, Gregory, Johnson City†	.000	5	2	1	0	0	0	0	0	0	0	0	0	0	0	0	1	0	0
Mathews, Thomas, Johnson City°	.270	59	200	32	54	98	13	2	9	36	3	0	1	2	29	1	30	2	1
Mattox, Frank, Paintsville†	.270	45	178	33	48	59	6	1	1	27	4	1	0	0	22	0	19	3	3
Mauch, Thomas, Johnson City°	.219	63	228	21	50	65	10	1	1	23	3	0	2	1	8	0	32	0	5
Maye, Stephen, Pikeville	.222	14	9	1	2	2	0	0	0	1	0	0	0	0	1	0	5	0	0
Mica, Christopher, Bluefield	.192	27	73	7	14	21	1	0	2	6	0	2	0	3	12	0	27	0	0
Mills, R. Craig, Bristol	.300	60	200	51	60	85	14	1	3	30	4	0	1	6	46	1	33	8	4
Mitchell, Joseph, Paintsville	.205	42	132	19	27	55	4	0	8	24	1	0	2	2	8	1	29	1	1
Natera, Luis, Kingsport	.279	19	43	6	12	15	1	1	0	7	0	1	0	1	2	0	8	1	0
Newsome, Timothy, Bristol	.268	36	112	23	30	48	3	0	5	25	2	0	3	1	22	1	20	1	0
Nichols, Ty, Bluefield	.207	63	213	24	44	62	10	1	2	11	0	2	2	1	20	0	46	1	0
Nicholson, Keith, Bristol	.000	16	1	0	0	0	0	0	0	0	0	0	0	0	1	0	1	0	0
Nunley, Angelo, Johnson City	.261	53	184	31	48	57	5	2	0	13	1	1	0	1	31	0	33	16	3
O'Brien, Kyle, Pulaski	.234	12	47	5	11	14	3	0	0	3	0	0	0	1	4	0	8	0	0
O'Connor, Michael, Pikeville	.227	39	110	14	25	39	5	0	3	18	4	0	2	1	17	0	27	2	0
Oates, Paul, Johnson City°	.250	14	12	1	3	6	1	1	0	3	0	0	0	0	1	0	0	0	0
Olson, Warren, Paintsville	.200	23	65	11	13	23	2	1	2	5	0	0	0	0	5	0	26	0	0
Padget, Chris, Bluefield°	.308	34	117	23	36	60	5	2	5	20	4	1	1	4	19	2	22	1	0
Page, W. Kelvin, Kingsport	.000	19	2	0	0	0	0	0	0	0	0	0	0	0	0	0	2	0	0
Paul, Grady, Bluefield	.186	21	43	4	8	14	3	0	1	8	1	0	0	0	9	0	13	2	1
Pena, Nelson, Johnson City	.229	54	179	27	41	67	5	0	7	22	1	0	1	3	19	0	43	1	2
Perry, Parnell, Pikeville	.134	36	67	8	9	10	1	0	0	1	0	1	0	1	12	0	25	2	1
Piazza, Nicholas, Bluefield	.000	4	6	0	0	0	0	0	0	0	0	0	0	0	1	0	5	0	0
Pico, Jeffrey, Pikeville	.250	13	4	1	1	1	0	0	0	0	0	1	0	0	1	0	1	0	0
Picota, Lenin, Johnson City	.111	15	9	1	1	1	0	0	0	2	0	0	1	0	0	0	3	0	0
Pohle, Walter, Paintsville	.299	39	147	26	44	55	6	1	1	12	1	0	0	1	15	0	13	4	1
Powers, F. Scott, Pulaski	.244	52	168	24	41	74	6	0	9	27	4	0	2	0	37	0	27	5	2
Ramon, Ernesto, Kingsport	.219	29	64	13	14	14	0	0	0	3	0	0	0	1	13	0	22	5	0
Reed, Matthew, Pikeville	.000	28	5	0	0	0	0	0	0	0	0	0	1	0	0	0	0	0	0
Reese, R. Kyle, Pulaski	.228	39	123	11	28	34	3	0	1	15	2	0	2	1	12	0	29	3	1
Ricciani, Robert, Bluefield†	.283	23	53	5	15	23	5	0	1	7	1	0	1	0	3	0	7	0	1
Rice, Timothy, Pikeville	.333	14	9	0	3	3	0	0	0	0	0	3	0	0	0	0	3	0	0
Ricketts, P. Erick, Kingsport	.276	48	123	17	34	44	5	1	1	11	1	0	1	0	14	0	27	10	1
Riley, Steven, Elizabethton	.200	23	65	8	13	21	5	0	1	8	2	0	1	1	13	1	18	0	0
Robertson, Bryant, Kingsport	.455	4	11	2	5	7	2	0	0	3	0	0	1	0	1	0	3	0	0
Robertson, Michael, Johnson City	.000	21	4	0	0	0	0	0	0	0	0	0	0	0	0	0	2	0	0
Rodgers, Rodney, Kingsport	.000	14	7	1	0	0	0	0	0	0	0	0	0	0	1	0	3	0	0
Rodriguez, Ulisses, Elizabethton	.317	48	164	20	52	75	17	0	2	28	2	0	2	0	16	0	29	0	2
Salisbury, James, Pulaski	.000	10	3	0	0	0	0	0	0	0	0	0	0	0	0	0	3	0	0
Sanchez, Zoilo, Kingsport	.259	50	158	25	41	61	8	0	4	30	6	0	2	1	18	0	28	9	2
Sanders, David, Kingsport	.200	16	5	0	1	1	0	0	0	0	0	0	0	0	2	0	4	0	0
Santiago, Michael, Pulaski°	.500	12	2	0	1	1	0	0	0	2	0	0	0	0	0	0	1	0	0
Schafer, L. Russell, Paintsville	.220	41	123	16	27	38	3	1	2	20	3	1	2	0	10	0	31	0	0
Shockman, Mark, Bluefield°	.228	62	193	28	44	80	10	1	8	37	1	0	2	4	32	1	52	1	1
Siebert, Richard, Pulaski	.333	14	9	1	3	3	0	0	0	0	0	2	0	0	0	0	2	0	0
Silver, Roy, Johnson City†	.294	57	211	33	62	95	15	0	6	35	3	0	3	0	31	5	24	4	2
Simonson, Robert, Paintsville	.248	48	153	36	38	72	6	2	8	23	1	0	0	4	18	0	58	4	2
Sisney, Lorenzo, Kingsport	.143	30	70	11	10	14	1	0	1	7	0	0	2	0	11	0	26	1	0
Sjoberg, Jeffrey, Pikeville	.233	58	180	22	42	58	10	0	2	32	2	1	5	7	29	1	47	13	4
Smith, Dana, Bluefield	.200	3	5	0	1	1	0	0	0	0	0	0	0	0	1	0	2	0	0
Smith, J. Dwight, Bluefield	.236	61	195	42	46	59	6	2	1	17	0	2	0	4	52	1	47	39	7
Smith, Jeffrey, Elizabethton°	.179	21	39	8	7	9	0	1	0	5	0	0	0	3	0	10	2	0
Smith, Lyle, Pulaski	.333	19	3	0	1	1	0	0	0	0	0	0	1	0	0	0	0	0	0

Player and Club	Pct.	G.	AB.	R.	H.	TB.	2B.	3B.	HR.	RBI.	GW.	SH.	SF.	HP.	BB.	Int. BB.	SO.	SB.	CS.
Solz, Mark, Pikeville°	.268	59	205	25	55	88	7	1	8	39	3	0	3	2	25	1	68	3	2
Soto, Maximilliano, Bristol	.227	51	181	25	41	51	5	1	1	14	0	1	1	0	8	0	32	7	3
Steinbach, Thomas, Paintsville	.250	47	144	17	36	50	8	0	2	18	2	1	1	0	3	1	35	0	2
Stuart, Jervis, Bluefield°	.282	51	149	37	42	60	8	2	2	12	0	0	0	0	25	0	45	15	3
Tackett, Jeffrey, Bluefield	.163	34	98	9	16	18	2	0	0	12	0	0	2	0	23	0	28	1	1
Takach, David, Kingsport	.250	4	4	1	1	1	0	0	0	0	0	0	0	1	0	0	1	0	0
Tapias, Luis, Elizabethton	.375	4	8	1	3	3	0	0	0	1	0	0	0	0	3	0	0	0	0
Thompson, Anthony, Kingsport	.260	39	104	20	27	33	6	0	0	10	1	1	0	1	15	0	34	12	1
Tucker, John, Johnson City	.200	19	45	6	9	16	2	1	1	4	0	0	0	0	4	0	7	0	0
Tullier, Michael, Pikeville°	.235	10	34	3	8	9	1	0	0	2	0	0	0	0	8	0	2	3	3
Turner, James R., Pulaski	.216	48	111	19	24	27	0	0	1	9	1	2	1	2	28	2	23	10	3
Van Heyningen, E. Patrick, Bluefield°	.120	17	50	3	6	7	1	0	0	3	0	0	0	1	1	0	10	1	3
Vargas, Jose, Paintsville†	.294	6	17	4	5	6	1	0	0	1	0	0	0	2	2	0	3	0	0
Vetsch, David, Elizabethton°	.309	63	217	55	67	115	22	1	8	49	9	1	4	2	41	0	41	11	3
Villanueva, Juan, Kingsport	.273	37	110	17	30	36	4	1	0	13	1	1	1	1	10	0	19	6	0
Wagner, Gerald, Pulaski	.000	22	3	1	0	0	0	0	0	0	0	1	0	0	0	0	2	0	0
Walters, Darryel, Paintsville	.279	60	219	39	61	116	15	2	12	39	2	0	2	0	18	0	67	3	1
Whitford, Larry, Pikeville	.000	14	1	0	0	0	0	0	0	0	0	0	0	0	0	0	0	0	0
Williams, Charles, Pulaski	.195	56	159	23	31	40	9	0	0	18	1	5	3	4	19	0	35	9	4
Wilson, William, Johnson City°	.308	21	13	2	4	5	1	0	0	1	1	0	0	1	0		4	0	0
Yanes, Edward, Elizabethton	.256	64	215	38	55	90	12	1	7	41	3	0	4	3	42	1	45	8	3
Zeratsky, Rodney, Paintsville	.272	55	184	29	50	79	11	0	6	30	3	0	3		27	1	47	1	0

The following pitchers, listed alphabetically by club, with games in parentheses, had no plate appearances, primarily through use of designated hitters:

BLUEFIELD—Burroughs, Anthony (3); Carter, Charles (6); Duval, John (13); Egelston, Christopher (4); Gannon, Justin (16); Gonzalez, Henry (9); King, Randy (6); Kline, Robert (15); Llanes, Pedro (13); Newton, Robert (9); Rohan, Edward (11); Sanchez, Geraldo (15); Skinner, Michael (3); Talamantez, Gregory (12); Thorpe, Paul (25); Whalen, Michael (5); Wirth, Gregory (8).

BRISTOL—Boling, John (13); Burduan, Rafael (8); Duffy, John (15); Goetz, Alan (19); Kline, Allan (10); Labozzetta, Albert (10); McHugh, Charles (16); Minnema, David (8); Phillion, Gerald (5); Poissant, Rodney (11); Roddy, John (12); Schultz, Scott (13); Scudero, James (19); Simmons, Glenn (13); Stock, Ronald (15).

ELIZABETHTON—Budke, Todd (19); Campos, Marcos (5); Cardwood, Alfredo (12); Cloninger, Michael (6); Galloway, Troy (10); Garcia, Angel (7); Honeycutt, Brian (7); Landmark, Neil (13); Lee, Robert (12); Malec, Jason (12); Perez, Yorkis (1); Prickett, Scott (13); Richards, Jon (1); Rodriguez, Enrique (6); Velasquez, Raymond (19); Yancof, Juan (1).

KINGSPORT—Encarnacion, Jose (7); Overcash, Martin (6); Slocumb, Heath (1); Woellert, Matthew (1).

PAINTSVILLE—Ames, Richard (6); Anderson, Steven (4); Eskildsen, Kurt (22); Freeland, Dean (10); Frew, Michael (12); Gilbert, Jeffrey (21); Montano, Martin (17); Sadler, Alan (11); Serviente, Michael (5); Simmons, Gregory (13); Taylor, Robert (16); Watkins, Gregory (7); Watkins, Troy (26).

PIKEVILLE—Kranitz, Richard (1).

GRAND SLAM HOME RUNS—Bailey, Beamesderfer, D. Carter, Hernandez, Z. Sanchez, Silver, Steinbach, 1 each.

AWARDED FIRST BASE ON CATCHER'S INTERFERENCE—Steinbach 8 (Tackett 2, Calvert, Edmiston, S. Gomez, Lopez, O'Connor, Riley); P. Martinez 2 (Crews 2); Blackwell (Edmiston); Colbert (Reese); Cornwell (Crews); Pohle (S. James); Simonson (Sisney); J. Dw. Smith (S. James).

CLUB FIELDING

Club	Pct.	G.	PO.	A.	E.	DP.	PB.
Johnson City	.962	69	1790	747	99	58	16
Elizabethton	.961	69	1744	741	102	77	12
Pikeville	.950	68	1749	746	132	66	20
Bristol	.949	70	1733	753	133	68	18
Pulaski	.949	69	1787	672	132	36	18
Paintsville	.947	70	1765	739	140	47	12
Kingsport	.944	69	1698	705	142	57	32
Bluefield	.939	70	1758	689	160	58	19

Triple Play—Paintsville.

INDIVIDUAL FIELDING
FIRST BASEMEN

°Throws lefthanded.

Player and Club	Pct.	G.	PO.	A.	E.	DP.
Bailey, Kingsport	.984	40	278	25	5	26
Bautista, Pikeville	.986	10	67	4	1	7
Beamesderfer, Bluefield	.951	7	37	2	2	4
Camara, Pulaski°	.991	23	195	14	2	9
Colbert, Bristol	.975	30	216	14	6	23
Cron, Pulaski	.981	30	241	18	5	15
Cunningham, Johnson City	.982	34	305	17	6	25
DeGroot, Elizabethton	1.000	1	2	0	0	0
Dunn, Bluefield	.986	8	67	4	1	6
Espinoza, Kingsport°	.979	37	256	25	6	23
Hamrick, Pulaski	.962	19	116	9	5	9
Hayes, Bluefield°	1.000	1	2	0	0	0
Hermann, Bristol	.985	38	295	32	5	32
Hernandez, Bristol	1.000	3	10	0	0	0
Hubbard, Bluefield	1.000	2	8	0	0	0
Kent, Paintsville°	.980	64	510	33	11	35
LARKIN, Elizabethton	.988	55	478	19	6	54
Liddell, Pikeville	1.000	1	3	0	0	1
Mathews, Johnson City	.991	36	308	21	3	23
Mitchell, Paintsville	1.000	6	37	7	0	2
Newsome, Bristol	1.000	8	70	2	0	6
Paul, Bluefield	1.000	2	21	2	0	1
Piazza, Bluefield	1.000	1	2	0	0	1
Rodriguez, Elizabethton	.965	14	128	9	5	19
Shockman, Bluefield°	.982	59	443	35	9	38
Sjoberg, Bluefield	.974	5	35	3	1	2
Solz, Pikeville	.972	57	468	27	14	46
Steinbach, Paintsville	1.000	1	5	2	0	0
Zeratsky, Paintsville	.941	2	15	1	1	3

Triple Play—Kent.

SECOND BASEMEN

Player and Club	Pct.	G.	PO.	A.	E.	DP.
B. Bautista, Bluefield	.911	64	106	150	25	31
H. Bautista, Pikeville	1.000	2	1	2	0	0
Bowens, Paintsville	.931	29	56	66	9	14
Cartwright, Johnson City	.965	33	66	98	6	17
Castillo, Bristol	.939	9	13	18	2	5
Castro, Kingsport	.941	35	65	79	9	14
Dalton, Elizabethton	1.000	2	0	3	0	0
Diaz, Bluefield	.500	2	0	1	1	0
Dunn, Bluefield	.909	8	10	20	3	3
Hermann, Bristol	1.000	1	0	1	0	0
House, Pikeville	.954	68	159	171	16	36
HUSBAND, Elizabethton	.966	64	124	161	10	49
Iglesias, Johnson City	.952	14	22	38	3	9
Mack, Bristol	.937	53	107	132	16	34
Mandeville, Pikeville	1.000	2	4	3	0	2
Martinez, Elizabethton	.885	8	8	15	3	5
Mattox, Paintsville	.954	45	64	123	9	13
Mitchell, Paintsville	1.000	1	1	0	0	0
Natera, Kingsport	.889	5	3	5	1	1
Newsome, Bristol	.958	14	31	38	3	12
Nunley, Johnson City	.945	15	25	44	4	7
Powers, Pulaski	.944	4	12	5	1	1
Sanchez, Kingsport	.986	20	33	37	1	9
Tucker, Johnson City	.976	15	19	22	1	6
Turner, Pulaski	.914	33	54	74	12	7
Villanueva, Kingsport	.934	23	36	63	7	10
Williams, Pulaski	.940	39	81	106	12	16

THIRD BASEMEN

Player and Club	Pct.	G.	PO.	A.	E.	DP.
Bautista, Pikeville	.917	9	7	15	2	0
Bowens, Paintsville	.930	23	21	32	4	2
Burton, Bristol	.750	1	0	3	1	0
Calley, Elizabethton	.882	6	5	10	2	0
Cartwright, Johnson City	.500	2	0	1	1	0
Castillo, Bristol	.950	6	9	10	1	3
Colescott, Kingsport	.876	41	37	76	16	6
Cornwell, Bristol°	1.000	1	1	1	0	0
Creech, Bristol	.853	15	5	24	5	2
Cunningham, Johnson City	.952	7	7	13	1	1
Dalton, Elizabethton	.925	28	25	61	7	9
DeGroot, Elizabethton	.927	34	23	66	7	9
Diaz, Bluefield	.868	22	15	31	7	7
Dunn, Bluefield	.889	33	20	44	8	4
Gomez, Kingsport	.000	1	0	0	1	0
Hamrick, Pulaski	.918	29	33	45	7	5
Hubbard, Bluefield	.800	22	14	30	11	3
Iglesias, Johnson City	1.000	5	0	1	0	0
INFANTE, Johnson City	.947	61	46	133	10	17
Lara, Johnson City	1.000	1	0	1	0	0
Mandeville, Pikeville	.978	16	14	31	1	3
Mills, Bristol	.917	51	34	98	12	7
Mitchell, Paintsville	.897	16	16	19	4	0
Natera, Kingsport	.500	2	1	0	1	0
Newsome, Bristol	.923	4	3	9	1	1
O'Brien, Pulaski	.935	12	8	21	2	1
Paul, Bluefield	1.000	6	6	5	0	0
Piazza, Bluefield	.714	3	1	4	2	0
Powers, Pulaski	.875	34	26	51	11	5
Sanchez, Kingsport	.863	29	33	55	14	2
Schafer, Paintsville	.821	40	19	45	14	4
Sjoberg, Pikeville	.913	50	38	88	12	10
Smith, Bluefield	.667	1	2	0	1	0
Tapias, Elizabethton	1.000	3	4	5	0	0

SHORTSTOPS

Player and Club	Pct.	G.	PO.	A.	E.	DP.
B. Bautista, Bluefield	.571	1	2	2	3	1
Bell, Elizabethton	.929	64	109	218	25	43
Blauser, Pulaski	.903	58	61	162	24	15
Bowens, Paintsville	.882	11	17	28	6	4
Cartwright, Johnson City	.955	7	6	15	1	3
Castillo, Bristol	.913	20	20	53	7	14
Clark, Paintsville	.857	15	33	39	12	6
Creech, Bristol	.889	2	2	6	1	1
Dalton, Elizabethton	.839	6	7	19	5	2
Hardamon, Pikeville	.878	22	22	50	10	9
Hubbard, Bluefield	.964	9	6	21	1	1
Lara, Johnson City	.934	33	55	87	10	13
Lawton, Kingsport	.914	52	86	126	20	27
MANDEVILLE, Pikeville	.932	52	82	180	19	33
Mills, Bristol	.882	5	7	8	2	1
Natera, Kingsport	.896	13	23	20	5	4
Nichols, Bluefield	.883	63	90	182	36	36
Nunley, Johnson City	.896	36	37	66	12	18
Pohle, Paintsville	.945	39	60	128	11	19
Powers, Pulaski	.929	13	18	34	4	4
Smith, Bluefield	1.000	1	0	1	0	0
Soto, Bristol	.887	51	62	119	23	26
Tapias, Elizabethton	1.000	1	1	1	0	0
Vargas, Paintsville	.885	6	3	20	3	2
Villanueva, Kingsport	.927	14	16	35	4	12

Triple Play—Clark.

OUTFIELDERS

Player and Club	Pct.	G.	PO.	A.	E.	DP.
Abner, Kingsport	.989	46	87	1	1	0
Bailey, Kingsport	1.000	1	1	0	0	0
Baird, Pulaski	.964	53	123	9	5	1
Ballou, Pulaski	1.000	8	7	3	0	0
Bayron, Elizabethton°	1.000	2	1	0	0	0
Beamesderfer, Bluefield	.962	36	46	4	2	1
Blackwell, Elizabethton	.969	61	120	7	4	1
Burke, Pulaski	.913	47	77	7	8	0
Burton, Bristol	.934	53	80	5	6	1
Camara, Pulaski°	1.000	31	53	1	0	0
Carter, Johnson City	1.000	36	60	2	0	1
Casey, Paintsville°	.928	65	78	12	7	1
Cepero, Johnson City	1.000	4	5	3	0	1
Cijntje, Bluefield°	.940	56	91	3	6	0
Colescott, Kingsport	1.000	1	1	0	0	0
Cornwell, Bristol°	.943	53	95	5	6	0
Crosby, Elizabethton	.944	10	14	3	1	1
Cuevas, Kingsport°	.979	44	88	4	2	1
Cunningham, Johnson City	1.000	6	8	0	0	0
DeWolf, Paintsville°	.950	45	72	4	4	1
Diaz, Bluefield	.875	6	7	0	1	0
Diaz, Elizabethton	1.000	5	5	3	0	0
Erdmann, Bristol°	1.000	9	18	0	0	0
Fitzgerald, Johnson City	.818	7	8	1	2	0
Gaeta, Bluefield	1.000	40	42	3	0	0
Gomez, Elizabethton	1.000	1	3	0	0	0
Gordon, Paintsville	1.000	4	6	0	0	0
Guilliams, Bristol	.882	13	14	1	2	1
Guthrie, Pulaski	.941	59	89	7	6	2
Hanza, Pikeville	.961	43	66	7	3	0
Hardamon, Pikeville	.851	20	36	4	7	2
Hayes, Bluefield°	.857	4	6	0	1	0
Hermann, Bristol	1.000	5	5	0	0	0
Hernandez, Bristol	.909	48	47	3	5	0
Hosie, Pikeville	.969	22	29	2	1	1
Hubbard, Bluefield	1.000	2	2	0	0	0
Johnson, Kingsport	.923	38	42	6	4	1
Larsen, Paintsville	.947	13	14	4	1	0
Lewis, Pikeville	.961	45	73	1	3	1
Mack, Bristol	.971	17	31	2	1	0
Martinez, Bristol	.895	45	63	5	8	1
Mauch, Johnson City	.970	58	94	2	3	0
Newsome, Bristol	1.000	8	7	1	0	0
Padget, Bluefield	1.000	29	35	6	0	2
Paul, Bluefield	1.000	4	6	0	0	0
Pena, Johnson City	.964	50	74	6	3	2
Perry, Pikeville	.958	26	21	2	1	1
Powers, Pulaski	1.000	1	1	1	0	0
Ramon, Kingsport	.907	25	38	1	4	0
Ricciani, Bluefield	.333	4	1	0	2	0
Ricketts, Kingsport	.902	39	43	3	5	2
Robertson, Kingsport	1.000	4	3	1	0	1
SILVER, Johnson City	.980	57	97	2	2	1
Simonson, Paintsville	.750	1	3	0	1	0
J.D. Smith, Pikeville	.904	60	77	8	9	3
Je. Smith, Elizabethton°	1.000	11	15	0	0	0
Steinbach, Paintsville	.967	37	57	2	2	1
Stuart, Bluefield°	.883	42	64	4	9	1
Thompson, Kingsport	.922	35	57	2	5	0
Tullier, Pikeville	1.000	9	18	0	0	0
Van Heyningen, Bluefield°	.923	14	12	0	1	0
Vetsch, Elizabethton	.969	62	116	10	4	3
Walters, Paintsville	.963	59	71	7	3	1
Wilson, Johnson City°	1.000	3	0	0	0	0
Yanes, Elizabethton	.949	63	89	5	5	1

CATCHERS

Player and Club	Pct.	G.	PO.	A.	E.	DP.	PB.
Beamesderfer, Bluefield	.970	22	143	17	5	2	7
Brooks, Kingsport	.988	30	152	15	2	2	2
Calvert, Elizabethton	.955	14	69	15	4	0	1
Casteel, Pikeville	.971	37	269	35	9	3	13
Colbert, Bristol	1.000	2	10	0	0	0	2
Crews, Kingsport	.949	29	158	28	10	2	19
Edmiston, Bristol	.971	45	243	26	8	1	9
Fitzgerald, Johnson City	.961	33	237	34	11	4	7
Fugatt, Bristol	.980	16	82	17	2	2	2
Gomez, Elizabethton	.941	8	43	5	3	0	1
Hamrick, Pulaski	1.000	2	9	0	0	0	1
Hermann, Bristol	.992	26	118	3	1	1	5
James, Pulaski	.983	37	277	15	5	0	7
JIMENEZ, Johnson City	.987	42	275	22	4	3	9
Jones, Elizabethton	1.000	8	49	2	0	1	1
Liddell, Pikeville	.953	13	78	4	4	0	3
Lopez, Elizabethton	.985	28	179	19	3	0	7
Mica, Bluefield	.981	27	197	14	4	1	3
Mitchell, Paintsville	.991	12	101	10	1	1	0
O'Connor, Pikeville	.965	21	151	15	6	3	4
Olson, Paintsville	.952	17	94	6	5	3	4
Reese, Pulaski	.971	37	256	12	8	2	10
Ricketts, Kingsport	1.000	2	7	0	0	0	1
Riley, Elizabethton	.966	19	109	4	4	0	2
Sisney, Kingsport	.969	20	110	15	4	0	10
Tackett, Bluefield	.979	30	215	22	5	1	9
Zeratsky, Paintsville	.974	47	359	48	11	3	8

PITCHERS

Player and Club	Pct.	G.	PO.	A.	E.	DP.	Player and Club	Pct.	G.	PO.	A.	E.	DP.
Ames, Paintsville	1.000	6	2	6	0	0	A. Lee, Pikeville	1.000	6	0	2	0	0
Anderson, Paintsville	1.000	4	0	1	0	0	R. Lee, Elizabethton	1.000	12	1	7	0	1
Arnold, Johnson City	.960	14	8	16	1	1	Llanes, Bluefield	.833	13	6	9	3	0
Atkinson, Johnson City	.875	14	5	9	2	0	Maddux, Pikeville	.957	14	5	17	1	2
Bates, Pulaski*	.833	20	4	6	2	0	Malec, Elizabethton*	1.000	12	0	3	0	1
Bautista, Johnson City	1.000	13	1	5	0	0	Mathews, Johnson City*	.941	5	2	14	1	1
Beer, Pulaski	.750	12	2	4	2	0	Maye, Pikeville	.733	14	4	7	4	0
Belen, Kingsport	.914	17	11	21	3	2	McHugh, Bristol	1.000	16	1	5	0	1
Boling, Bristol*	1.000	13	2	10	0	0	Minnema, Bristol	.947	8	6	12	1	2
Brooks, Kingsport	.714	13	1	4	2	0	Montano, Paintsville*	.923	17	6	18	2	1
Budke, Elizabethton	1.000	19	2	9	0	1	Newton, Bluefield	.625	9	0	5	3	0
Burduan, Bristol	.750	8	1	2	1	1	Nicholson, Bristol	.929	14	3	10	1	1
Campos, Elizabethton*	1.000	5	0	4	0	0	Oates, Johnson City*	.880	14	5	17	3	1
Cardwood, Elizabethton	1.000	12	2	10	0	0	Overcash, Kingsport	1.000	6	2	1	0	0
Carter, Bluefield	1.000	6	1	0	0	0	Page, Kingsport	1.000	19	2	3	0	0
Cloninger, Elizabethton	1.000	6	2	9	0	1	Phillion, Bristol*	.900	5	2	7	1	0
Classen, Pulaski	.833	14	4	6	2	0	Pico, Pikeville	.960	13	7	17	1	2
Coffman, Pulaski	.944	11	6	11	1	0	Picota, Johnson City	.800	15	3	9	3	0
Danek, Pikeville	.727	21	0	8	3	0	Poissant, Bristol	.800	11	8	4	3	1
Duffy, Bristol*	1.000	15	1	5	0	0	Prickett, Elizabethton*	1.000	13	4	5	0	1
Duval, Bluefield	1.000	13	4	5	0	1	Reed, Pikeville	1.000	28	5	8	0	2
Egelston, Bluefield	.800	4	2	6	2	0	RICE, Pikeville*	1.000	14	3	21	0	0
Encarnacion, Kingsport	1.000	7	0	3	0	0	Richards, Elizabethton	1.000	1	0	1	0	0
Eskildsen, Paintsville	.625	22	3	2	3	0	Robertson, Johnson City	.786	21	4	7	3	0
Fassero, Johnson City*	.947	13	2	16	1	2	Roddy, Bristol	.889	12	1	7	1	1
Freeland, Paintsville	.938	10	5	10	1	1	Rodgers, Kingsport	.950	13	9	10	1	0
Frew, Paintsville	.826	12	9	10	4	1	Rodriguez, Elizabethton	1.000	6	0	3	0	0
Galloway, Elizabethton*	1.000	10	2	9	0	0	Rohan, Bluefield	1.000	11	4	6	0	1
Gannon, Bluefield*	.917	16	4	7	1	0	Sadler, Paintsville	.931	11	8	19	2	2
Garcia, Elizabethton*	.833	7	0	5	1	0	Salisbury, Pulaski	.750	10	1	2	1	1
Gardner, Pikeville	.800	18	2	6	2	0	Sanchez, Bluefield	.947	15	3	15	1	1
Gilbert, Paintsville	1.000	21	4	7	0	2	Sanders, Kingsport	1.000	16	1	1	0	0
Givens, Kingsport*	.800	14	1	7	2	1	Santiago, Pulaski*	1.000	10	2	0	0	0
Goetz, Bristol	1.000	19	2	5	0	0	Schultz, Bristol	1.000	13	4	5	0	0
Gonzalez, Bluefield	1.000	9	1	6	0	0	Scudero, Bristol*	1.000	19	4	8	0	0
Grosdidier, Pulaski	.778	26	1	6	2	0	Serviente, Paintsville	.800	5	1	3	1	0
Hayes, Kingsport	.889	16	4	4	1	1	Siebert, Pulaski	1.000	14	4	6	0	0
Haynes, Johnson City	.800	20	2	6	2	1	Gl. Simmons, Bristol	.818	13	3	6	2	1
Hazlett, Pulaski*	1.000	9	2	2	0	0	Gr. Simmons, Paintsville	.938	13	6	9	1	1
Hennessy, Johnson City*	.941	17	3	13	1	0	Skinner, Bluefield	1.000	3	4	0	0	0
Hightower, Kingsport*	1.000	14	1	6	0	0	Smith, Pulaski	.800	19	1	7	2	0
Honeycutt, Elizabethton	1.000	7	1	1	0	0	Stock, Bristol*	.917	15	4	7	1	1
Howes, Kingsport	.769	8	5	5	3	0	Takach, Kingsport*	1.000	4	4	4	0	0
Hunter, Pikeville*	.667	10	0	2	1	0	Talamantez, Bluefield	.875	12	8	6	2	1
James, Kingsport	.800	26	1	7	2	0	Taylor, Paintsville	.750	16	3	3	2	0
Johnson, Pulaski	1.000	20	2	6	0	0	Thorpe, Bluefield	.750	25	2	4	2	0
Jundy, Kingsport	.900	11	2	7	1	0	Velasquez, Elizabethton	.917	19	2	9	1	1
Kilner, Pulaski*	.909	14	3	7	1	0	Wagner, Pulaski*	1.000	22	4	14	0	1
King, Bluefield	1.000	6	1	4	0	0	G. Watkins, Paintsville	.714	7	2	3	2	0
A. Kline, Bristol	1.000	10	2	12	0	1	T. Watkins, Paintsville	.842	26	4	12	3	0
R. Kline, Bluefield	1.000	5	1	0	0	0	Whalen, Bluefield	1.000	5	0	1	0	0
Labozzetta, Bristol*	1.000	10	5	12	0	0	Whitford, Pikeville	.900	14	5	4	1	0
LaMarche, Pikeville	1.000	13	0	2	0	0	Wilson, Johnson City*	1.000	18	1	5	0	0
Landmark, Elizabethton	.800	13	2	6	2	1	Wirth, Bluefield	1.000	8	2	6	2	1

The following players do not have any recorded accepted chances at the positions indicated; therefore, are not listed in the fielding averages for those particular positions: H. Bautista, ss; Burroughs, p; Casteel, of; Castillo, of; Castro, 3b; Creech, of; Crews, p; Dunn, of; C. Gomez, p; Hernandez, 3b; Kranitz, p; Larsen, 2b; Marte, c; T. Mathews, of; Padget, 2b; Perez, p; Ricciani, 2b; Rodgers, of; Slocumb, p; Da. Smith, 2b; Tucker, of; Turner, 3b, of; Woellert, p; Yancof, p.

CLUB PITCHING

Club	ERA.	G.	CG.	ShO.	Sv.	IP.	H.	R.	ER.	HR.	HB.	BB.	Int. BB.	SO.	WP.	Bk.
Elizabethton	3.82	69	19	5	16	581.1	482	293	247	48	11	300	4	433	40	8
Paintsville	3.98	70	10	6	17	588.1	539	336	260	36	27	335	7	524	43	6
Pulaski	4.05	69	1	1	20	595.2	536	341	268	57	13	308	3	512	49	9
Pikeville	4.09	68	12	5	7	583.0	507	340	265	43	36	310	17	476	48	8
Bluefield	4.38	70	14	2	10	586.0	577	381	285	49	25	291	0	538	41	7
Bristol	4.57	70	2	5	20	577.2	632	358	293	36	23	289	1	444	40	11
Johnson City	4.65	69	12	2	8	596.2	582	373	308	50	20	334	8	489	42	10
Kingsport	5.14	69	7	1	14	566.0	549	420	323	48	26	416	9	423	91	5

PITCHERS' RECORDS
(Leading Qualifiers for Earned-Run Average Leadership — 56 or More Innings)

*Throws lefthanded.

Pitcher—Club	W.	L.	Pct.	ERA.	G.	GS.	CG.	GF.	ShO.	Sv.	IP.	H.	R.	ER.	HR.	HB.	BB.	Int. BB.	SO.	WP.
Sadler, Paintsville	9	1	.900	1.91	11	11	2	0	2	0	70.2	43	21	15	1	3	29	0	78	1
Freeland, Paintsville	5	2	.714	2.04	10	9	0	0	0	0	61.2	50	24	14	2	2	27	0	51	9
Cardwood, Elizabethton	7	3	.700	2.31	12	12	7	0	1	0	93.1	59	27	24	11	5	40	0	93	1
Rice, Pikeville	6	4	.600	2.53	14	10	5	1	1	0	78.1	63	28	22	6	5	20	3	57	2
Maddux, Pikeville	6	2	.750	2.63	14	12	2	1	2	0	85.2	63	35	25	2	8	41	2	62	4
Maye, Pikeville	7	2	.778	2.90	14	13	2	0	0	0	87.0	69	37	28	4	0	24	1	90	2
Arnold, Johnson City	4	5	.444	3.05	14	13	4	1	0	0	91.1	80	38	31	8	4	38	0	90	8
Belen, Kingsport	4	2	.667	3.11	17	7	1	3	0	1	72.1	57	33	25	4	1	22	0	46	4
Montano, Paintsville*	3	1	.750	3.14	17	6	2	3	1	2	63.0	59	32	22	3	2	28	0	47	5
Pico, Pikeville	2	3	.400	3.31	13	13	1	0	1	0	73.1	65	35	27	0	6	29	3	46	2

Departmental Leaders: G—Reed, 28; W—Sadler, 9; L—Rodgers, 10; Pct.—Sadler, .900; GS—(Nine tied with 13); CG—Cardwood, 7; GF—Reed, Thorpe, 21; ShO—Cloninger, Maddux, Sadler, 2; Sv.—James, 8; IP—Cardwood, 93.1; H—Picota, 81; R—Llanes, 72; ER—Rodgers, 51; HR—Cardwood, 11; HB—Maddux, 8; BB—Rodgers, Gr. Simmons, 53; IBB—Reed, 5; SO—Cardwood, Talamantez, 93; WP—Givens, 20.

(All Pitchers—Listed Alphabetically)

Pitcher—Club	W.	L.	Pct.	ERA.	G.	GS.	CG.	GF.	ShO.	Sv.	IP.	H.	R.	ER.	HR.	HB.	BB.	Int. BB.	SO.	WP.
Ames, Paintsville	1	1	.500	3.03	6	4	1	0	0	0	29.2	20	11	10	1	1	11	0	22	0
Anderson, Paintsville	0	0	.000	5.19	4	0	0	3	0	1	8.2	11	5	5	0	0	2	0	13	1
Arnold, Johnson City	4	5	.444	3.05	14	13	4	1	0	0	91.1	80	38	31	8	4	38	0	90	8
Atkinson, Johnson City	3	3	.500	5.25	14	9	2	1	1	0	61.2	57	38	36	6	3	36	1	36	3
Bates, Pulaski°	3	5	.375	4.95	20	9	0	7	0	1	60.0	65	47	33	8	0	25	0	42	6
Bautista, Johnson City	0	0	.000	7.76	13	0	0	7	0	1	26.2	35	24	23	3	1	13	1	17	6
Beer, Pulaski	3	3	.500	4.23	12	10	0	0	0	0	55.1	56	31	26	8	1	20	0	24	5
Belen, Kingsport	4	2	.667	3.11	17	7	1	3	0	1	72.1	57	33	25	4	1	22	0	46	4
Boling, Bristol°	6	3	.667	5.98	13	10	0	0	0	0	52.2	58	40	35	7	4	35	0	46	5
Brooks, Kingsport	2	0	1.000	5.20	13	2	0	4	0	0	27.2	26	29	16	3	4	30	1	16	2
Budke, Elizabethton	3	1	.750	1.71	19	0	0	14	0	6	31.2	15	6	6	0	0	23	2	27	5
Burduan, Bristol	0	1	.000	18.36	8	0	0	4	0	0	8.1	23	19	17	2	0	7	0	7	3
Burroughs, Bluefield	0	0	.000	6.23	3	0	0	2	0	0	4.1	5	4	3	0	1	8	0	2	0
Campos, Elizabethton°	1	1	.500	4.87	5	2	0	1	0	0	20.1	16	12	11	1	0	12	0	12	2
Cardwood, Elizabethton	7	3	.700	2.31	12	12	7	0	1	0	93.1	59	27	24	11	5	40	0	93	1
Carter, Bluefield	0	0	.000	3.38	6	0	0	4	0	0	10.2	10	6	4	0	1	7	0	7	3
Cloninger, Elizabethton	4	2	.667	3.60	6	6	3	0	2	0	35.0	19	15	14	2	1	11	0	20	1
Clossen, Pulaski	5	4	.556	3.80	14	13	1	1	1	0	73.1	49	37	31	10	5	48	0	73	5
Coffman, Pulaski	1	4	.200	4.13	11	7	0	2	0	0	48.0	41	26	22	4	1	33	1	41	5
Crews, Kingsport	0	0	.000	0.00	1	0	0	0	0	0	0.1	0	0	0	0	1	1	0	0	1
Danek, Pikeville	3	2	.600	2.54	21	0	0	17	0	5	46.0	40	15	13	2	1	19	1	58	1
Duffy, Bristol°	0	1	.000	1.65	15	0	0	11	0	5	27.1	20	8	5	1	0	7	1	28	1
Duval, Bluefield	4	4	.500	4.20	13	9	3	0	0	0	60.0	59	34	28	3	3	32	0	51	1
Egelston, Bluefield	3	0	1.000	3.00	4	4	0	0	0	0	27.0	25	12	9	1	0	6	0	26	2
Encarnacion, Kingsport	0	0	.000	7.84	7	0	0	4	0	0	10.1	11	10	9	2	3	11	0	1	0
Eskildsen, Paintsville	0	2	.000	5.68	22	1	0	6	0	0	38.0	53	34	24	2	4	18	0	27	1
Fassero, Johnson City°	4	7	.364	4.59	13	11	2	0	1	0	66.2	65	42	34	2	0	39	0	59	1
Freeland, Paintsville	5	2	.714	2.04	10	9	0	0	0	0	61.2	50	24	14	2	2	27	0	51	9
Frew, Paintsville	1	9	.100	6.49	12	12	2	0	0	0	68.0	73	60	49	6	4	51	1	45	3
Galloway, Elizabethton°	5	4	.556	3.57	10	9	1	0	0	0	68.0	60	31	27	5	1	15	0	46	3
Gannon, Bluefield°	2	4	.333	3.96	16	4	2	5	0	2	52.1	49	34	23	1	1	29	0	59	2
Garcia, Johnson City°	2	0	1.000	3.68	7	1	1	1	0	0	29.1	20	13	12	3	0	22	0	16	3
Gardner, Pikeville	1	4	.200	5.28	18	5	0	4	0	0	44.1	36	40	26	5	3	51	2	44	14
Gilbert, Paintsville	1	5	.167	2.94	21	0	0	20	0	7	33.2	28	13	11	0	0	18	2	34	1
Givens, Kingsport°	4	1	.800	6.50	14	10	0	2	0	0	44.1	41	36	32	2	5	52	0	51	20
Goetz, Bristol	0	2	.000	7.40	19	0	0	5	0	1	24.1	31	23	20	3	1	15	0	21	2
Gomez, Kingsport	1	0	1.000	0.00	1	0	0	0	0	0	0.0	1	2	2	0	0	1	0	0	0
Gonzalez, Bluefield	2	1	.667	3.97	9	2	0	6	0	0	34.0	35	21	15	5	1	13	0	24	1
Grosdidier, Pulaski	2	4	.333	2.94	26	0	0	19	0	6	33.2	24	18	11	1	1	10	0	35	4
Hayes, Kingsport	1	4	.200	3.70	16	5	0	7	0	0	41.1	55	30	17	6	0	17	0	31	6
Haynes, Johnson City	2	2	.500	3.44	21	0	0	8	0	1	36.2	32	19	14	2	0	20	0	20	2
Hazlett, Pulaski°	0	0	.000	5.40	9	0	0	2	0	0	11.2	14	8	7	1	0	12	0	9	0
Hennessy, Johnson City°	3	2	.600	4.22	17	4	0	10	0	4	49.0	41	32	23	5	1	29	2	56	3
Hightower, Kingsport°	1	3	.250	8.19	14	6	0	3	0	1	40.2	52	45	37	3	0	48	2	38	6
Honeycutt, Elizabethton	1	0	1.000	5.52	7	1	0	5	0	0	14.2	13	11	9	6	0	9	0	18	1
Howes, Kingsport	4	3	.571	3.53	8	8	2	0	0	0	51.0	45	26	20	4	7	32	0	35	9
Hunter, Pikeville°	0	0	.000	7.64	10	0	0	2	0	0	17.2	13	20	15	2	2	30	0	11	9
James, Kingsport	4	4	.500	4.14	26	0	0	19	0	8	45.2	42	30	21	4	1	19	4	40	5
Johnson, Pulaski	3	1	.750	2.98	20	0	0	3	0	3	45.1	43	20	15	3	0	14	0	35	4
Jundy, Kingsport	3	5	.375	5.55	11	10	2	0	1	0	58.1	61	49	36	5	0	43	0	37	8
Kilner, Kingsport	4	3	.571	3.38	14	13	0	1	0	1	72.0	66	35	27	5	2	40	0	72	3
King, Bluefield	2	2	.500	4.64	6	4	0	2	0	0	33.0	28	20	17	7	0	12	0	30	2
A. Kline, Bristol	2	0	1.000	5.68	10	6	0	2	0	0	31.2	33	22	20	1	2	22	0	30	3
R. Kline, Bluefield	1	2	.333	3.99	5	5	0	0	0	0	29.1	23	16	13	1	2	20	0	37	2
Kranitz, Pikeville	0	0	.000	13.50	1	0	0	1	0	0	2.0	3	3	3	1	0	1	0	2	0
Labozzetta, Bristol°	3	2	.600	3.06	10	8	0	0	0	0	53.0	55	25	18	3	1	16	0	32	0
LaMarche, Pikeville	0	2	.000	8.87	13	2	0	7	0	0	23.1	29	24	23	4	3	9	0	18	2
Landmark, Elizabethton	5	3	.625	5.97	13	13	1	0	0	0	69.1	79	54	46	5	0	38	2	44	4
A. Lee, Pikeville	1	3	.250	6.11	6	6	1	0	0	0	28.0	25	22	19	4	3	19	0	16	3
R. Lee, Elizabethton	3	6	.333	5.68	12	9	2	2	0	0	57.0	60	43	36	9	2	30	0	41	5
Llanes, Bluefield	1	9	.100	6.52	13	13	1	0	0	0	58.0	78	72	42	6	6	44	0	35	0
Maddux, Pikeville	6	2	.750	2.63	14	12	2	1	2	0	85.2	63	35	25	2	8	41	2	62	4
Malec, Elizabethton°	2	0	1.000	3.42	12	0	0	7	0	1	23.2	27	12	9	0	0	13	0	15	1
Mathews, Johnson City°	2	3	.400	2.59	5	5	2	0	1	0	31.1	27	12	9	2	1	13	0	21	0
Maye, Pikeville	7	2	.778	2.90	14	13	2	0	0	0	87.0	69	37	28	4	0	24	1	90	2
McHugh, Bristol	4	3	.571	3.48	16	2	0	14	0	3	33.2	34	18	13	3	0	15	0	41	4
Minnema, Bristol	5	2	.714	2.82	8	7	0	0	0	0	38.1	29	14	12	1	3	24	0	30	2
Montano, Paintsville°	3	1	.750	3.14	17	6	2	3	1	2	63.0	59	32	22	3	2	28	0	47	5
Newton, Bluefield°	1	0	1.000	3.41	9	0	0	2	0	0	29.0	23	15	11	2	2	14	0	29	5
Nicholson, Bristol	6	2	.750	2.95	14	7	1	2	0	2	55.0	59	28	18	1	1	28	0	43	4
Oates, Johnson City°	2	6	.250	5.42	14	12	1	2	0	0	73.0	70	53	44	4	4	51	0	56	7
Overcash, Kingsport	0	0	.000	3.12	6	0	0	2	0	1	8.2	7	3	3	1	1	7	0	2	0
Page, Kingsport	3	2	.600	5.74	19	2	0	10	0	1	26.2	12	19	17	1	4	35	1	31	8
Perez, Elizabethton°	0	0	.000	0.00	1	0	0	0	0	0	1.1	1	0	0	0	0	1	0	1	1
Phillion, Bristol°	1	1	.500	4.09	5	5	0	0	0	0	22.0	21	10	10	3	2	14	0	14	0
Pico, Pikeville	2	3	.400	3.31	13	13	1	0	0	0	73.1	65	35	27	0	6	29	3	46	2
Picota, Johnson City	3	5	.375	4.44	15	10	1	4	0	0	79.0	81	46	39	7	3	43	3	53	8
Poissant, Bristol	4	4	.500	5.76	11	10	1	0	0	0	54.2	71	39	35	3	2	25	0	37	4
Prickett, Elizabethton°	5	4	.556	3.32	13	13	3	0	0	0	78.2	67	42	29	4	1	47	0	44	8
Reed, Pikeville	6	7	.462	4.18	28	1	0	21	0	7	56.0	50	34	26	3	5	26	5	46	2
Rice, Pikeville	6	4	.600	2.53	14	10	5	1	1	0	78.1	65	28	22	6	5	20	3	57	2
Richards, Elizabethton	0	0	.000	9.00	1	0	0	1	0	0	1.0	2	1	1	0	0	0	0	0	0
Robertson, Johnson City	4	3	.571	5.66	21	4	0	11	0	0	47.2	59	42	30	6	0	25	1	35	4
Roddy, Bristol	4	3	.571	7.23	12	7	0	2	0	0	37.1	40	32	30	3	1	25	0	29	6
Rodgers, Kingsport	3	10	.231	6.12	13	13	1	0	0	0	75.0	78	63	51	5	1	53	0	49	13
Rodriguez, Elizabethton	0	0	.000	2.84	6	0	0	5	0	2	6.1	5	2	2	0	1	2	0	8	1
Rohan, Bluefield	0	1	.000	4.97	11	2	1	4	0	0	29.0	36	23	16	4	2	20	0	19	3
Sadler, Paintsville	9	1	.900	1.91	11	11	2	0	2	0	70.2	43	21	15	1	3	29	0	78	1
Salisbury, Pulaski	2	4	.333	12.76	10	5	0	3	0	0	18.1	25	30	26	2	0	31	0	19	5
Sanchez, Bluefield	4	4	.500	4.24	15	8	2	7	0	1	63.2	60	32	30	5	2	21	0	58	6
Sanders, Kingsport	0	3	.000	6.68	16	1	0	8	0	2	32.1	31	27	24	5	0	24	0	24	7

Pitcher—Club	W.	L.	Pct.	ERA.	G.	GS.	CG.	GF.	ShO.	Sv.	IP.	H.	R.	ER.	HR.	HB.	BB.	Int. BB.	SO.	WP.
Santiago, Pulaski°	3	0	1.000	1.59	10	0	0	7	0	2	11.1	11	5	2	0	0	5	0	15	0
Schultz, Bristol	0	1	.000	6.16	13	2	0	6	0	0	30.2	43	25	21	3	4	17	0	17	4
Scudero, Bristol°	0	2	.000	3.12	19	0	0	14	0	7	26.0	26	17	9	0	1	9	0	14	0
Serviente, Paintsville	3	2	.600	4.67	5	5	0	0	0	0	27.0	21	16	14	1	1	20	0	24	7
Siebert, Pulaski	4	3	.571	3.84	14	12	0	0	0	0	68.0	66	39	29	6	2	30	0	78	6
Gl. Simmons, Bristol	2	5	.286	4.44	13	6	0	3	0	0	46.2	62	27	23	1	1	18	0	31	1
Gr. Simmons, Paintsville	7	3	.700	4.58	13	12	2	0	0	0	74.2	62	44	38	10	3	53	0	72	3
Skinner, Bluefield	1	1	.500	4.50	3	3	0	0	0	0	14.0	25	13	7	4	1	7	0	13	2
Slocumb, Kingsport	0	0	.000	0.00	1	0	0	0	0	0	0.1	0	1	0	0	0	1	0	0	0
Smith, Pulaski	1	0	1.000	5.05	19	0	0	12	0	4	46.1	41	30	26	5	1	21	0	30	3
Stock, Bristol°	0	1	.000	1.75	15	0	0	5	0	2	36.0	27	11	7	1	0	12	0	24	1
Takach, Kingsport°	2	0	1.000	3.24	4	4	1	0	0	0	25.0	28	13	9	3	0	13	1	21	2
Talamantez, Bluefield	6	4	.600	3.48	12	12	4	0	1	0	75.0	57	36	29	4	2	31	0	93	5
Taylor, Paintsville	2	1	.667	4.37	16	4	0	7	0	0	47.1	59	31	23	5	0	21	2	42	5
Thorpe, Bluefield	4	2	.667	2.67	25	0	0	21	0	7	30.1	20	10	9	0	1	18	0	28	2
Velasquez, Elizabethton	3	4	.429	3.86	19	3	1	13	0	7	49.0	38	24	21	2	0	36	0	48	4
Wagner, Pulaski°	6	1	.857	2.24	22	0	0	11	0	3	52.1	35	15	13	4	0	19	2	39	3
G. Watkins, Paintsville	1	1	.500	7.63	7	2	0	4	0	0	15.1	12	17	13	0	2	19	1	17	2
T. Watkins, Paintsville	4	5	.444	3.91	26	4	1	17	0	7	50.2	48	28	22	5	5	38	1	52	5
Whalen, Bluefield	0	2	.000	9.69	5	2	0	2	0	0	13.0	18	16	14	4	0	6	0	8	1
Whitford, Pikeville	2	5	.286	8.27	14	6	1	2	0	0	41.1	49	'47	38	10	0	41	0	26	7
Wilson, Johnson City°	2	4	.333	6.68	18	1	0	11	0	1	33.2	35	27	25	5	3	27	0	46	0
Wirth, Bluefield	1	2	.333	5.79	8	2	1	1	0	0	23.1	26	17	15	2	0	3	0	19	4
Woellert, Kingsport	0	0	.000	6.00	1	1	0	0	0	0	6.0	2	4	4	0	0	7	0	1	0
Yancof, Elizabethton	0	0	.000	0.00	1	0	0	1	0	0	2.2	1	0	0	0	0	1	0	3	1

BALKS—Kilner, 4; Gardner, Haynes, Scudero, 3 each; Egelston, Hennessy, Labozzetta, Maye, Minnema, Prickett, Rodgers, Sadler, Wagner, 2 each; Bates, Boling, Budke, Burduan, Burroughs, Cardwood, Carter, Encarnacion, Fassero, Freeland, Galloway, Garcia, Givens, Hayes, Hazlett, LaMarche, Landmark, R. Lee, Maddux, Mathews, Montano, Oates, Picota, Roddy, Rohan, Siebert, Gr. Simmons, Stock, Talamantez, Thorpe, G. Watkins, Whitford, Wilson, 1 each.

COMBINATION SHUTOUTS—Duval-Carter-Rohan, Bluefield; Minnema-Nicholson-Scudero, Roddy-Nicholson, Boling-McHugh, Nicholson-McHugh, Kline-Stock-Burduan, Bristol; Prickett-Rodriguez, Cardwood-Rodriguez, Elizabethton; Sadler-Anderson, Watkins-Eskildsen-Gilbert, Freeland-Eskildsen-Gilbert, Paintsville; Maye-Reed, Pikeville.

NO-HIT GAMES—None.

Gulf Coast League

SUMMER CLASS A CLASSIFICATION

CHAMPIONSHIP WINNERS IN PREVIOUS YEARS

1964—Sarasota Braves .610	1972—Chicago N.L. a .651	1979—Houston .635
1965—Bradenton Astros .632	Kansas City a .651	1980—Kansas City-Blue .635
1966—New York A.L. .667	1973—Texas .732	1981—Kansas City-Gold .688
1967—Kansas City .614	1974—Chicago N.L. .702	1982—New York-A.L. .667
1968—Oakland .650	1975—Texas .774	1983—Texas .645
1969—Montreal .585	1976—Texas .704	Los Angeles b .617
1970—Chicago A.L. .600	1977—Chicago-A.L .731	
1971—Kansas City .755	1978—Texas .600	

(Note—Known as Sarasota Rookie League in 1964 and Florida Rookie League in 1965.) aDeclared co-champions; no playoff. bLeague divided into Northern and Southern divisions; won one-game playoff for league championship.

STANDING OF CLUBS AT CLOSE OF SEASON, AUGUST 31

NORTHERN DIVISION

Club	W.	L.	T.	Pct.	G.B.
Rangers	36	27	0	.571	......
Dodgers	34	29	0	.540	2
Braves	31	32	0	.492	5
Blue Jays	29	34	0	.460	7
Pirates	21	42	0	.333	15

SOUTHERN DIVISION

Club	W.	L.	T.	Pct.	G.B.
White Sox	41	22	0	.651	......
Astros	36	27	0	.571	5
Reds	32	31	0	.508	9
Yankees	28	35	0	.444	13
Phillies	27	36	0	.429	14

COMPOSITE STANDING OF CLUBS AT CLOSE OF SEASON, AUGUST 31

Club	W.S.	Rng.	Ast.	Dod.	Rds.	Brv.	B.J.	Yan.	Phi.	Pir.	W.	L.	T.	Pct.	G.B.
White Sox	....	5	4	5	4	4	5	4	4	6	41	22	0	.651	......
Rangers	2	....	6	4	2	4	5	6	3	4	36	27	0	.571	5
Astros	3	1	...	4	6	5	3	5	2	7	36	27	0	.571	5
Dodgers	2	3	3	....	3	4	4	4	7	4	34	29	0	.540	7
Reds	3	5	1	4	....	4	4	3	3	5	32	31	0	.508	9
Braves	3	3	2	3	3	....	4	6	3	3	31	32	0	.492	10
Blue Jays	2	2	4	4	3	1	....	5	4	4	29	34	0	.460	12
Yankees	3	1	2	3	4	2	.....	5	4	28	35	0	.444	13
Phillies	3	4	5	4	2	3	2	....	4	27	36	0	.429	14
Pirates	1	3	0	3	2	4	2	3	3	....	21	42	0	.333	20

Games played at Bradenton and Sarasota, Fla.

Club names are major league affiliations.

Playoffs—Rangers (Northern Division winner) defeated White Sox (Southern Division winner) 6-5 to win league championship.

Regular Season Attendance—4,361 total paid for 16 openings (only games for which admission was charged).

Managers—Astros, Jose Tartabull; Blue Jays, Ramon Webster; Braves, Pedro Gonzalez; Dodgers, Jose Alvarez; Phillies, Rollie Dearmas; Pirates, Woody Huyke; Rangers, Mike Bucci; Reds, Sam Mejias; White Sox, Steve Dillard; Yankees, Jack Gillis.

All-Star Team: 1B—Luis Peraza, White Sox; 2B—Mark Lemke, Braves; 3B—Norm Santiago, White Sox; SS—Santiago Garcia, Blue Jays; OF—Andrew Denson, Braves; Jerry Bertolani, White Sox; Tim McMillan, Pirates; C—Jorge Alcazar, White Sox; Starter—Jim Filippi, White Sox; Reliever—Jeff Gray, Phillies; Manager—Steve Dillard, White Sox.

(Compiled by Howe News Bureau, Boston, Mass.)

CLUB BATTING

Club	Pct.	G.	AB.	R.	OR.	H.	TB.	2B.	3B.	HR.	RBI.	GW.	SH.	SF.	HP.	BB.	Int. BB.	SO.	SB.	CS.	LOB.
White Sox	.270	63	2121	326	260	573	720	91	19	6	261	31	10	26	22	241	9	372	92	42	481
Dodgers	.253	63	2051	269	281	519	647	68	15	10	215	29	24	14	21	224	12	281	83	31	447
Rangers	.251	63	2100	288	269	528	672	76	16	12	221	26	31	15	22	180	10	446	102	56	421
Pirates	.246	63	2124	269	333	522	693	67	25	18	208	15	17	16	30	148	5	444	86	38	405
Braves	.242	63	2088	287	255	506	717	73	21	32	241	27	19	20	19	209	3	417	43	26	441
Astros	.240	63	2111	299	294	506	637	71	15	10	232	32	21	20	33	200	10	362	64	30	455
Reds	.236	63	2036	279	241	480	630	67	22	13	217	27	27	21	9	191	5	402	88	42	391
Blue Jays	.235	63	2085	277	286	490	637	91	10	12	214	23	9	15	18	163	11	330	71	40	382
Phillies	.225	63	2096	253	293	471	622	62	22	15	211	21	17	17	19	229	9	444	60	34	457
Yankees	.219	63	2029	208	243	445	550	49	13	10	167	22	33	16	26	196	10	436	66	35	444

INDIVIDUAL BATTING

(Leading Qualifiers for Batting Championship—170 or More Plate Appearances)

*Bats lefthanded.　†Switch-hitter.

Player and Club	Pct.	G.	AB.	R.	H.	TB.	2B.	3B.	HR.	RBI.	GW.	SH.	SF.	HP.	BB.	Int. BB.	SO.	SB.	CS.
Denson, Andrew, Braves	.322	62	239	43	77	133	20	3	10	45	5	0	1	3	17	0	41	5	2
Santiago, Norman, White Sox	.315	53	203	30	64	86	10	3	2	32	1	0	3	0	13	0	18	4	4
Dorsey, Craig, Dodgers*	.301	47	153	26	46	61	6	3	1	16	0	0	0	2	19	2	21	8	1
Mitchell, Reginald, Reds*	.295	51	173	38	51	69	5	5	1	19	1	0	0	0	20	0	22	19	5
Alcazar, Jorge, White Sox	.292	50	171	29	50	67	10	2	1	35	7	0	2	3	26	0	41	5	4
Farmer, Albert, Rangers	.282	46	156	27	44	52	4	2	0	26	2	0	2	1	12	0	10	7	5
Martinez, Joseph, White Sox*	.281	46	167	36	47	50	3	0	0	16	1	1	0	2	17	1	20	12	4
Aquino, Diego, Astros	.278	50	176	24	49	62	11	1	0	21	6	1	0	1	8	0	19	4	2
Kopetsky, Brian, Dodgers	.277	49	166	11	46	56	4	3	0	16	2	1	2	1	8	1	23	7	0
Peraza, Luis, White Sox	.277	56	195	32	54	69	10	1	1	38	7	1	8	1	22	1	20	12	5
Garcia, Santiago, Blue Jays	.276	58	210	31	58	70	12	0	0	25	2	0	1	0	24	2	22	8	5
Lemke, Mark, Braves†	.276	63	243	41	67	87	11	0	3	32	4	2	4	2	29	0	14	2	2

Departmental Leaders: G—Campusano, Lemke, J. Reyes, 63; AB—Lemke, 243; R—Bertolani, 49; H—Denson, 77; TB—Denson, 133; 2B—Denson, 20; 3B—McMillan, 9; HR—Benson, Smiciklas, 10; RBI—Denson, 45; GWRBI—Alcazar, Peraza, 7; SH—Jagnow, 8; SF—Peraza, 8; HP—Hampton, 7; BB—Bertolani, 46; IBB—Boyd, Green, 4; SO—McMillan, 83; SB—Campusano, Wheeler, 21; CS—Glasker, 10.

(All Players—Listed Alphabetically)

Player and Club	Pct.	G.	AB.	R.	H.	TB.	2B.	3B.	HR.	RBI.	GW.	SH.	SF.	HP.	BB.	Int. BB.	SO.	SB.	CS.
Acevedo, Ernesto, Dodgers	.188	28	69	6	13	13	0	0	0	6	0	0	0	1	2	0	5	0	0
Acosta, Carlos, Reds	.213	30	61	6	13	17	1	0	1	3	0	1	0	1	0	0	17	5	3
Adams, F. Steven, Pirates	.400	13	5	0	2	2	0	0	0	0	0	1	0	0	0	0	2	0	0
Alcantara, Agapito, Rangers	.260	40	104	12	27	35	1	2	1	12	1	1	3	1	3	0	32	2	2
Alcantara, Julio, Braves	.222	24	63	9	14	18	0	2	0	6	1	1	1	9	0	18	1	0	
Alcazar, Jorge, White Sox	.292	50	171	29	50	67	10	2	1	35	7	0	2	3	26	0	41	5	4
Aquino, Diego, Astros	.278	50	176	24	49	62	11	1	0	21	6	1	0	1	8	0	19	4	2
Aquino, Fausto, Rangers*	.395	32	124	22	49	55	4	1	0	22	3	1	0	2	3	0	11	17	3
Arias, Cornelio, Dodgers	.246	33	122	20	30	36	2	2	0	13	2	0	0	1	12	0	22	18	3
Bacon, Ernest, Reds	.286	18	7	1	2	2	0	0	0	0	0	1	0	0	0	0	1	0	0
Baker, Mark, Astros	.000	9	2	0	0	0	0	0	0	0	0	0	0	0	0	0	1	0	0
Barringer, Reginald, Pirates	.350	6	20	6	7	12	1	2	0	1	1	0	0	0	5	0	1	2	0
Basora, Edward, Dodgers†	.286	17	21	5	6	6	0	0	0	3	0	2	0	0	4	0	3	0	1
Benitez, Manuel, Dodgers	.333	22	72	11	24	33	4	1	1	9	0	0	0	3	4	0	9	0	0
Benitez, Wolfgang, Reds	.204	30	103	5	21	25	2	1	0	8	2	1	1	1	0	0	17	4	3
Bennett, Eric, Phillies	.000	3	2	0	0	0	0	0	0	0	0	0	0	1	1	0	2	0	0
Berezo, Lalo, Reds*	.263	41	118	15	31	39	2	0	2	20	2	2	1	0	15	2	24	8	4
Berlin, Steven, Astros*	.000	7	1	0	0	0	0	0	0	0	0	0	0	0	0	0	1	0	0
Berroa, Geronimo, Blue Jays	.251	62	235	31	59	86	16	1	3	34	2	0	2	2	12	2	34	2	3
Berroa, Henry, Reds	.500	3	2	0	1	1	0	0	0	0	0	0	0	0	0	0	1	0	0
Bertolani, Jerry, White Sox	.274	58	208	49	57	65	8	0	0	24	5	0	2	1	46	0	20	19	5
Blankenship, Kevin, Braves	.000	19	3	0	0	0	0	0	0	0	0	0	0	0	0	0	2	0	0
Blethen, Charles, Reds	.000	14	4	0	0	0	0	0	0	0	0	0	0	0	0	0	1	0	0
Bolivar, Esteban, Blue Jays	.229	39	131	22	30	48	7	1	3	14	1	0	1	9	0	19	2	2	
Bolling, Eric, Pirates	.182	3	11	1	2	4	0	1	0	5	1	0	0	1	0	0	0	0	
Borras, Juan, Pirates	.111	3	9	0	1	1	0	0	0	0	0	0	0	0	0	0	5	0	0
Boyd, Mark, Dodgers	.269	54	171	24	46	62	10	0	2	18	4	1	2	0	28	4	16	5	0
Brock, Norman, Astros*	.208	8	24	5	5	8	1	1	0	0	0	2	0	0	7	1	1	1	0
Brodsky, Daniel, Yankees†	.500	1	2	0	1	1	0	0	0	0	0	0	0	1	1	0	1	0	0
Broussard, Woodrow, Phillies†	.000	13	3	0	0	0	0	0	0	0	0	0	3	0	0	0	1	0	0
Brown, Steven, Pirates	.184	19	38	5	7	8	1	0	0	1	0	0	1	0	1	0	14	1	0
Brown, Wayman, Yankees	.224	54	196	35	44	59	7	1	2	8	0	4	1	4	30	1	43	12	7
Burton, Jay, Yankees	.250	4	12	2	3	3	0	0	0	1	0	1	0	0	2	0	1	1	0
Butler, C. Gilbert, Reds	.203	26	74	12	15	15	0	0	0	6	1	2	1	0	7	0	20	4	4
Butters, David, Pirates	.188	4	16	2	3	3	0	0	0	1	0	0	0	1	0	0	4	0	0
Caceres, Edgar, Dodgers†	.299	20	77	11	23	28	3	1	0	11	3	0	0	0	10	0	6	5	2
Campbell, Curtis, Dodgers	.290	44	100	14	29	31	2	0	0	6	0	1	0	1	3	0	12	6	4
Campusano, Silvestre, Blue Jays	.267	63	236	42	63	84	17	2	0	22	3	0	1	3	20	0	40	21	4
Carrion, Jesus, Astros	.221	27	86	6	19	24	3	1	0	5	1	0	0	0	7	0	9	1	0
Casellas, Rolando, Yankees	.111	3	9	0	1	1	0	0	0	0	0	0	0	0	0	0	3	0	0
Cash, Johnny, Braves	.000	12	7	1	0	0	0	0	0	0	0	0	0	0	0	0	2	1	0
Castro, Felix, Blue Jays†	.152	31	66	8	10	10	0	0	0	1	1	1	0	4	3	0	20	2	0
Cepeda, Octavio, Pirates	.000	10	5	0	0	0	0	0	0	0	0	0	0	0	0	0	2	0	0
Chance, R. Anthony, Pirates	.218	16	55	9	12	13	1	0	0	10	0	0	0	1	0	5	0	11	2	2
Charles, Juan, Dodgers	.545	14	11	2	6	6	0	0	0	3	1	1	0	0	1	0	0	0	0
Chestna, Mark, Yankees	.262	32	107	12	28	33	1	2	0	11	3	1	1	0	13	0	24	7	4
Cieslak, Mark, Reds†	.200	13	15	3	3	3	0	0	0	1	0	1	0	1	2	0	1	0	0
Clark, Daniel, Pirates	.251	45	175	19	44	56	6	3	0	9	0	3	1	1	5	1	24	7	1
Clemente, Roberto, Phillies	.167	35	96	7	16	20	2	1	0	5	0	1	0	0	5	0	27	3	1
Clifton, Darrell, Phillies*	.242	48	165	18	40	44	2	1	0	21	4	1	4	1	20	0	18	3	6
Cochran, Arnold, Rangers	.236	50	182	19	43	58	4	1	3	24	4	1	1	0	14	2	60	3	2
Constanzo, Fernando, Braves	.216	25	74	6	16	18	2	0	0	5	1	0	1	0	11	0	2			
Contrera, Jose, Blue Jays	.182	5	11	0	2	3	1	0	0	0	0	0	0	0	1	0	1	0	2
Covington, Rodney, Rangers*	.235	40	102	7	24	38	6	1	2	10	1	0	1	2	9	1	34	4	0
Crispin, Alberto, Phillies	.188	32	96	11	18	24	1	1	1	5	1	2	0	3	4	1	19	1	0
Criswell, Timothy, Dodgers	.333	8	9	0	3	3	0	0	0	1	0	0	0	0	0	0	0	0	0
Cruz, Marino, Dodgers	.235	51	136	12	32	36	2	1	0	12	0	3	1	2	4	0	8	1	1
Cuba, Angel, Dodgers	.273	13	11	3	3	3	0	0	0	1	0	1	0	0	1	0	2	0	0
Cueva, Johnny, Braves	.240	42	129	18	31	47	3	2	3	18	3	0	1	7	0	28	3	2	
Cullers, Steven, Rangers	.202	33	89	7	18	20	2	0	0	8	1	3	0	2	6	0	12	3	1
Cunningham, Derrick, Yankees*	.196	51	168	7	33	36	3	0	0	13	0	2	2	1	16	1	41	2	5
Darretta, David, Rangers	.241	52	191	35	46	63	8	3	1	19	3	3	2	1	22	0	50	11	6
Davins, James, Pirates	.000	1	4	0	0	0	0	0	0	0	0	0	0	0	0	0	1	0	0
DeLaCruz, Hector, Blue Jays	.227	56	181	28	41	45	2	1	0	10	3	4	1	2	24	1	33	11	6
DeLaCruz, Laito, Astros	.279	42	154	17	43	47	4	0	0	17	3	0	3	1	6	1	17	3	3
DeLeon, Pedro, Astros	.000	13	8	0	0	0	0	0	0	0	0	1	0	0	1	0	5	1	0
Denczi, Edward, Pirates	.513	10	39	7	20	30	5	1	1	9	0	0	1	1	5	1	3	0	2
Denson, Andrew, Braves	.322	62	239	43	77	133	20	3	10	45	5	0	1	3	17	0	41	5	2
Dilone, Ivan, Dodgers	.000	14	1	0	0	0	0	0	0	0	0	0	0	0	0	0	1	0	0
Dorsey, Craig, Dodgers*	.301	47	153	26	46	61	6	3	1	16	0	0	2	19	2	21	8	1	
Dorsey, William, Pirates	.213	31	108	13	23	25	2	0	0	12	2	3	0	0	11	0	19	7	2
Duffy, Thomas, Dodgers	.000	10	6	0	0	0	0	0	0	0	0	0	0	0	0	0	3	0	0
Edwards, Jovon, Dodgers*	.210	57	176	21	37	41	4	0	0	13	3	0	0	3	16	2	22	11	2
Elliott, John, Astros	.250	18	60	14	15	18	3	0	0	7	2	2	0	1	13	0	10	5	3
Ethridge, Gregory, Rangers	.128	20	39	7	5	6	1	0	0	1	0	1	0	0	5	0	13	5	1
Evans, Daryl, Phillies	.000	14	2	0	0	0	0	0	0	0	0	0	0	0	0	0	2	0	0
Eveline, William, White Sox*	.252	41	135	14	34	44	4	3	0	15	1	1	0	2	10	0	18	1	3
Farmer, Albert, Rangers	.282	46	156	27	44	52	4	2	0	26	2	0	2	1	12	0	10	7	5
Fernandez, Jose, Rangers*	.230	28	61	10	14	18	4	0	0	6	0	0	0	1	11	0	17	0	0
Ferreiras, Salvador, Pirates	.210	26	81	4	17	18	1	0	0	5	1	0	1	0	3	0	29	0	1
Fick, Barry, Reds	.000	14	5	1	0	0	0	0	0	0	0	0	0	0	0	0	1	0	0
Fidanza, John, Yankees	.500	2	4	2	2	2	0	0	0	0	0	0	0	0	2	0	0	0	0
Fiepke, Scott, Pirates*	.500	1	2	1	1	1	0	0	0	1	0	0	0	0	0	0	0	0	0
Fitzpatrick, David, Braves	.188	9	16	1	3	3	0	0	0	1	0	0	0	0	0	0	5	0	0
Fortenberry, Jimmy, Phillies*	.347	27	101	20	35	54	7	3	2	16	2	0	1	2	13	0	15	6	6
Fraser, Glendon, Astros	.176	26	68	11	12	15	0	0	1	6	1	0	1	0	9	0	21	2	1
Frazier, Heath, Phillies	.215	41	130	17	28	35	5	1	0	12	1	0	0	1	10	0	32	6	2

Player and Club	Pct.	G.	AB.	R.	H.	TB.	2B.	3B.	HR.	RBI.	GW.	SH.	SF.	HP.	BB.	Int. BB.	SO.	SB.	CS.
Frazier, J. Shawn, Braves	.273	46	150	24	41	52	6	1	1	13	2	1	1	1	7	0	33	11	4
Frias, Santo, Blue Jays	.182	8	22	2	4	6	2	0	0	3	0	0	0	0	1	0	3	0	0
Fuentes, Roberto, Pirates	.162	13	37	5	6	7	1	0	0	2	0	0	0	0	2	0	1	0	0
Fumarola, Nicolas, Pirates°	.000	4	1	0	0	0	0	0	0	0	0	0	0	0	0	0	2	0	0
Garcia, Carlos, Blue Jays	.179	44	95	11	17	18	1	0	0	6	1	0	0	0	7	0	26	7	3
Garcia, Cornelio, White Sox°	.266	54	192	29	51	67	5	4	1	21	3	0	3	2	16	2	53	4	4
Garcia, Santiago, Blue Jays	.276	58	210	31	58	70	12	0	0	25	2	0	1	0	24	2	22	8	5
Gibbs, Austis, Dodgers°	.188	46	69	10	13	20	1	0	2	11	3	1	1	1	15	1	28	0	0
Gilles, Thomas, Yankees	.241	42	145	14	35	49	4	2	2	13	3	2	1	1	10	2	16	4	1
Glasker, Stephen, Rangers°	.240	55	208	31	50	65	9	3	0	15	0	3	0	0	11	2	43	11	10
Glavine, Thomas, Braves°	.000	8	2	2	0	0	0	0	0	0	0	1	0	0	1	0	1	0	0
Gonzalez, Andres, Yankees	.115	26	78	12	9	17	1	2	1	3	1	1	0	2	3	0	30	5	0
Gray, Jeffrey, Phillies	.333	26	3	0	1	1	0	0	0	0	0	0	0	0	1	0	1	0	0
Green, Terry, Astros	.261	61	234	35	61	76	6	3	1	36	4	1	2	0	20	4	21	10	5
Gregory, John, Dodgers°	.000	10	16	2	0	0	0	0	0	1	1	1	0	1	4	0	4	0	0
Groves, Jeffrey, Braves	.000	10	2	0	0	0	0	0	0	0	0	0	0	0	0	0	2	0	0
Gsellman, Bob, Phillies	.103	26	68	5	7	13	3	0	1	4	0	0	1	2	12	0	28	2	0
Guance, Julio, Reds	.500	6	2	0	1	1	0	0	0	0	0	0	0	0	0	0	0	0	0
Guante, Enrique, Yankees	.176	6	17	2	3	3	0	0	0	0	0	0	0	1	3	0	2	0	0
Guerrero, Epifano, Blue Jays	.227	55	185	24	42	49	5	1	0	20	1	0	0	1	22	1	20	5	3
Guerrero, Jonas, Astros	.232	54	177	23	41	65	9	0	5	24	2	0	1	6	19	0	59	3	1
Guerrero, Sixto, Astros	.145	28	62	8	9	10	1	0	0	7	0	2	0	3	4	0	14	1	1
Guzman, Rudolfo, Braves	.000	10	4	0	0	0	0	0	0	0	0	5	0	0	0	0	2	0	0
Hammonds, Reginald, Pirates	.235	44	149	22	35	51	4	0	4	24	2	0	4	5	8	0	26	8	3
Hampton, Anthony, Astros°	.233	61	227	46	53	69	7	3	1	32	5	2	4	7	25	0	30	14	6
Hansen, Todd, Pirates°	.125	14	8	1	1	1	0	0	0	0	0	1	0	0	0	0	3	1	0
Hardaker, Guy, Phillies†	.166	50	157	14	26	34	3	1	1	13	1	0	2	4	25	1	33	3	1
Hartley, Thomas, White Sox	.250	59	204	23	51	63	10	1	0	21	0	1	2	3	21	1	52	12	3
Heeney, Joseph, Yankees	.272	42	158	24	43	57	8	0	2	19	3	1	1	3	18	0	19	9	2
Hendricks, Kenneth, White Sox	.157	39	102	5	16	21	3	1	0	9	0	0	0	0	6	1	38	1	1
Hendrix, James, Phillies	.000	16	2	1	0	0	0	0	0	0	0	1	0	0	1	0	1	0	0
Heredia, Geysi, Astros°	.000	12	3	0	0	0	0	0	0	0	0	0	0	0	0	0	3	0	0
Hern, John, Braves	.000	7	3	0	0	0	0	0	0	0	0	0	0	0	3	0	0	0	0
Hernandez, Pedro, Dodgers°	.167	10	6	0	1	1	0	0	0	0	0	1	0	0	1	0	1	0	0
Herrenbruck, Todd, Phillies	.222	34	117	14	26	32	1	1	1	12	1	0	1	0	15	0	26	0	0
Hibberd, Huck, Rangers	.000	16	2	1	0	0	0	0	0	0	0	0	0	0	0	0	1	0	0
Hicks, Robert, Phillies	.000	8	1	0	0	0	0	0	0	0	0	0	0	0	0	0	0	0	0
Hood, Dennis, Braves	.200	49	155	16	31	41	7	0	1	18	0	1	2	0	15	0	40	4	2
Hornacek, Jay, Dodgers	.274	47	146	18	40	55	7	1	2	20	2	2	2	0	13	0	30	0	3
Houp, Kenneth, Reds	.250	35	96	17	24	30	3	0	1	5	1	0	0	3	19	0	12	3	0
Hufford, Scott, Phillies	.226	53	177	22	40	69	12	1	5	32	5	1	2	2	18	1	47	1	0
Hurtado, Jose, Phillies	.250	45	140	18	35	48	3	2	2	9	0	0	1	0	10	2	35	4	2
Jagnow, James, Rangers	.271	52	170	26	46	57	8	0	1	17	3	8	0	1	10	0	22	13	7
James, Rodney, Pirates	.500	11	6	1	3	3	0	0	0	2	0	0	0	0	0	0	1	0	0
Jimenez, Cesar, Braves	.000	12	7	0	0	0	0	0	0	0	0	1	0	0	0	0	2	0	0
Jimenez, Francisco, Pirates°	.231	6	13	5	3	5	0	1	0	0	0	0	0	1	1	0	6	2	1
Johnson, Isaac, Phillies	.242	18	62	5	15	15	0	0	0	8	0	0	1	0	5	2	9	0	2
Johnson, Jason, Astros°	.250	12	12	2	3	3	0	0	0	1	0	0	0	0	2	0	5	0	0
Johnson, John, Pirates	.328	20	67	10	22	27	5	0	0	8	2	0	1	3	6	0	16	5	3
Johnson, Roger, Phillies	.201	42	134	12	27	38	6	1	1	16	2	2	0	1	10	0	18	0	1
Jones, Carl, Yankees	.176	5	17	0	3	4	1	0	0	0	0	0	0	0	1	0	5	0	0
Jones, J. Keith, Braves	.000	18	2	0	0	0	0	0	0	0	0	0	0	0	0	0	0	0	0
Jones, Labarry, Braves°	.291	21	55	9	16	24	0	1	2	9	0	0	1	1	4	1	8	3	0
Kaiser, Bart, Phillies°	.294	25	85	9	25	31	6	0	0	9	0	0	1	0	6	2	13	1	2
Karmeris, Joseph, Dodgers	.500	2	2	0	1	1	0	0	0	0	0	0	0	0	0	0	0	0	0
Keller, David, Reds	.328	21	58	16	19	38	5	1	4	19	1	0	1	1	16	0	12	3	1
Kelley, Thomas, Rangers°	.206	45	131	16	27	34	4	0	1	9	1	1	1	1	21	2	29	2	1
Kennelley, Steve, Reds	.260	36	123	16	32	45	9	2	0	13	1	1	0	2	11	0	24	4	3
King, Darrell, Braves†	.260	47	131	12	34	41	1	3	0	15	0	0	2	3	17	0	32	1	1
King, William, Astros	.123	26	73	6	9	10	1	0	0	3	0	0	1	3	7	0	20	0	2
Klein, Larry, Rangers	.329	25	82	19	27	36	5	2	0	6	0	2	1	0	10	0	8	12	1
Knox, Jeffrey, Phillies	.500	13	2	1	1	1	0	0	0	0	0	0	0	0	0	0	1	0	0
Knox, Scott, Pirates	.267	5	15	3	4	7	0	0	1	4	1	0	0	1	1	0	3	4	0
Kopetsky, Brian, Dodgers	.277	49	166	11	46	56	4	3	0	16	2	1	2	1	8	1	23	7	0
Kovach, Douglas, Reds	.186	31	86	10	16	22	2	2	0	7	3	0	1	0	4	0	13	4	1
Krepp, Robert, Astros	.000	22	4	1	0	0	0	0	0	0	0	0	0	0	1	0	2	0	0
Kwolek, Joseph, Astros	.211	46	147	13	31	40	4	1	1	14	3	2	2	1	13	2	17	2	0
Laboy, Jose, Yankees	.262	51	191	15	50	60	6	2	0	18	0	0	1	1	9	0	40	4	3
Laird, Anthony, Pirates°	.385	4	13	2	5	7	0	1	0	2	0	0	1	0	0	0	1	0	0
Lanik, Dale, Rangers°	.257	44	144	20	37	50	8	1	1	18	4	0	1	5	13	2	44	6	2
Leger, Fernando, Braves	.196	25	56	5	11	11	0	0	0	2	1	2	0	0	3	0	9	3	0
Lemke, Mark, Braves†	.276	63	243	41	67	87	11	0	3	32	4	2	4	2	29	0	14	2	2
Litwin, Christopher, Braves°	.333	9	3	0	1	1	0	0	0	1	0	1	0	0	0	0	1	0	0
Lopez, Ignacio, Yankees	.265	26	83	4	22	31	2	2	1	11	3	2	4	1	3	1	20	0	0
Luna, Jose, Braves	.194	33	62	9	12	14	2	0	0	2	0	0	0	0	13	0	19	3	4
Lyden, Mitchell, Yankees	.235	54	200	21	47	54	4	0	1	21	2	1	2	4	13	1	36	3	1
Mangham, Donald, Astros	.143	10	7	1	1	1	0	0	0	0	0	0	0	0	2	0	2	1	0
Markert, James, White Sox	.290	33	100	11	29	34	3	1	0	5	1	2	1	1	8	1	13	2	3
Marston, Tod, Yankees	.250	4	12	1	3	3	0	0	0	1	0	0	0	2	0	0	2	0	0
Martin, Norberto, White Sox†	.273	56	205	36	56	71	8	2	1	30	2	1	4	4	21	0	31	18	5
Martinez, Carlos, Yankees	.154	31	91	9	14	17	1	1	0	4	1	2	1	0	6	0	15	3	0
Martinez, Joseph, White Sox°	.281	46	167	36	47	50	3	0	0	6	1	1	0	2	17	1	20	12	4
Mathews, Edward, Braves	.250	15	4	1	1	1	0	0	0	0	0	0	0	0	0	0	1	0	0
McClain, Gregory, Pirates	.273	6	22	3	6	6	0	0	0	1	0	0	0	0	3	0	5	1	0
McMillan, L. Timothy, Pirates	.244	60	221	32	54	93	6	9	5	30	2	0	0	1	13	2	83	8	3
Meads, David, Astros°	.000	7	0	0	0	0	0	0	0	0	0	0	0	0	0	0	0	0	0
Mercedes, Guillermo, Pirates	1.000	12	1	0	1	2	1	0	0	0	0	0	0	0	0	0	0	0	0
Mesa, Narciso, Dodgers	.000	14	4	0	0	0	0	0	0	0	0	0	0	0	0	0	2	0	0
Michel, Domingo, Dodgers	.261	43	142	25	37	44	5	1	0	12	2	2	2	1	21	0	21	10	7
Mirabito, Timothy, Reds	.000	12	11	0	0	0	0	0	0	0	0	0	0	0	0	0	4	0	0
Mitchell, Darryl, Reds	.222	12	9	1	2	2	0	0	0	3	0	2	0	0	1	0	1	0	0
Mitchell, Reginald, Reds°	.295	51	173	38	51	69	5	5	1	19	1	0	0	0	20	0	22	19	5

Player and Club	Pct.	G.	AB.	R.	H.	TB.	2B.	3B.	HR.	RBI.	GW.	SH.	SF.	HP.	BB.	Int. BB.	SO.	SB.	CS.
Monson, Steven, Phillies	.273	17	44	6	12	21	2	2	1	7	1	0	0	0	7	0	8	1	1
Monte, Louis, Yankees	.000	12	2	0	0	0	0	0	0	0	0	0	0	0	0	0	0	0	0
Moore, Bryant, Pirates°	.261	7	23	5	6	7	1	0	0	1	0	0	0	0	7	0	1	4	2
Morales, Osvaldo, Dodgers°	.169	46	89	17	15	20	1	2	0	4	1	0	0	2	25	0	14	0	3
Morban, Domingo, Pirates	.000	8	10	0	0	0	0	0	0	0	0	0	0	0	0	0	0	0	0
Morris, David, Braves	.300	10	10	2	3	3	0	0	0	2	0	1	0	0	0	0	2	0	0
Morse, Michael, White Sox	.267	11	30	3	8	11	3	0	0	1	0	0	0	0	0	0	6	0	0
Mosquera, David, Dodgers	.000	21	2	0	0	0	0	0	0	0	0	0	0	0	0	0	6	0	1
Natera, Antonio, Braves°	.167	13	6	1	1	1	0	0	0	0	0	0	0	0	0	0	3	0	0
Nesbit, Walter, Phillies	.143	12	7	0	1	1	0	0	0	0	0	0	0	0	1	0	3	0	0
Newsome, Louis, Braves	.333	8	3	1	1	3	0	0	0	0	0	0	0	0	0	0	0	0	0
Nina, Hector, Reds	.197	25	61	5	12	14	0	1	0	3	0	1	0	0	7	0	16	1	2
O'Brien, Kyle, Braves	.196	47	148	18	29	37	4	2	0	11	0	1	2	1	20	0	13	0	1
Obando, German, Pirates	.151	21	53	2	8	8	0	0	0	2	0	0	1	0	3	0	15	0	0
Ottino, William, White Sox	.303	34	99	12	30	36	6	0	0	16	2	2	0	3	10	1	17	0	0
Owen, Timothy, Rangers	.237	45	139	13	33	46	7	0	2	20	3	2	2	2	14	1	14	1	2
Paredez, Juan, Astros	.000	18	3	0	0	0	0	0	0	0	0	0	0	0	1	0	3	0	0
Parker, Darren, Braves	.000	5	1	0	0	0	0	0	0	0	0	0	0	0	0	0	0	0	0
Patterson, Glenn, Rangers	.000	15	0	1	0	0	0	0	0	0	0	0	0	0	0	0	0	0	0
Pena, Hipolito, Pirates°	.000	10	2	0	0	0	0	0	0	0	0	1	0	0	0	0	2	0	0
Pena, Luis, Rangers	.259	26	54	5	14	14	0	0	0	1	0	1	0	2	7	0	18	2	6
Pender, Shawn, Phillies	.267	30	86	12	23	24	1	0	0	1	0	1	0	0	1	0	10	7	1
Pequignot, Jonathan, Dodgers°	.250	39	108	10	27	39	6	0	2	17	1	0	2	0	20	2	15	2	0
Peraza, Luis, White Sox	.277	56	195	32	54	69	10	1	1	38	7	1	8	1	22	1	20	12	5
Perdomo, Rigoberto, Dodgers	.000	4	7	0	0	0	0	0	0	0	0	0	0	0	0	0	2	0	0
Perez, Alfredo, Astros	.299	29	97	14	29	31	2	0	0	12	0	2	2	1	4	0	6	4	0
Perez, Freddy, Phillies	.247	36	81	7	20	20	0	0	0	6	0	0	1	1	3	0	27	1	0
Perez, J. Manuel, Pirates°	.000	12	2	0	0	0	0	0	0	0	0	1	0	0	0	0	1	0	0
Pfaff, Robert, Braves	.182	21	66	8	12	16	1	0	1	5	1	0	0	1	3	0	25	0	0
Phillips, William, Dodgers°	.000	31	1	0	0	0	0	0	0	0	0	0	0	0	1	0	0	0	0
Picart, Juan, Dodgers	.246	33	114	15	28	35	7	0	0	14	2	0	2	0	4	0	4	10	3
Picht, Keith, Pirates†	.500	4	2	0	1	2	1	0	0	0	0	0	0	0	0	0	0	0	0
Pitti, Marcelino, Yankees	.167	33	108	7	18	19	1	0	0	9	3	2	1	0	3	0	14	1	1
Polanco, Carlos, Phillies	.200	31	105	6	21	24	3	0	0	13	2	0	0	0	6	0	21	0	1
Polledo, Santiago, Yankees	.208	9	24	0	5	5	0	0	0	8	1	0	1	2	3	0	7	0	0
Pottinger, Mark, Phillies†	.314	12	35	5	11	11	0	0	0	4	0	1	1	0	5	0	5	2	0
Prince, Thomas, Pirates	.229	18	48	4	11	14	0	0	1	6	0	0	0	1	8	0	10	1	0
Pujols, Ramon, Rangers	.196	25	56	3	11	11	0	0	0	6	0	3	0	0	3	0	14	0	0
Ramirez, Victor, Phillies	.000	13	3	0	0	0	0	0	0	0	0	0	0	0	0	0	0	0	0
Remigio, Jose, Pirates	.333	14	3	0	1	1	0	0	0	0	0	0	0	0	0	0	2	0	0
Reyes, Carlos, Astros	.235	8	17	3	4	7	1	1	0	3	0	0	0	0	2	0	4	0	0
Reyes, Joselito, Blue Jays	.240	63	242	34	58	82	12	3	2	20	2	3	2	3	16	1	50	10	8
Reyna, Luis, Blue Jays°	.242	57	194	28	47	70	12	1	3	29	4	0	5	0	14	3	21	2	3
Rivas, Juan, Yankees	.273	34	128	16	35	38	1	1	0	6	1	7	0	1	10	0	32	8	5
Rivas, R. Manuel, Yankees	.158	8	19	0	3	3	0	0	0	1	0	1	0	0	0	0	5	2	0
Robinson, Emmett, Pirates	.271	43	170	23	46	57	6	1	1	15	2	2	0	1	16	0	29	7	5
Rodriguez, Aristides, Astros	.268	47	142	22	38	50	7	1	1	23	3	0	1	4	23	1	32	3	0
Rojas, Miguel, Blue Jays	.220	56	191	14	42	49	4	0	1	20	1	1	2	2	8	1	25	1	0
Roque, Gustavo, Pirates	.230	21	74	10	17	20	3	0	0	5	0	0	2	0	10	0	11	0	0
Roque, Omar, Astros	.444	10	27	2	12	14	2	0	0	6	2	0	0	2	1	0	2	1	0
Rosario, Danilo, Astros	.267	32	105	9	28	34	2	2	0	5	0	0	2	1	3	0	19	4	1
Russell, Robert, Pirates°	.500	9	6	0	3	3	0	0	0	0	0	0	0	0	0	0	0	0	0
Russell, Ronald, Astros	.254	40	134	28	34	41	5	1	0	7	0	0	0	2	16	1	19	4	5
Russell, Scott, Rangers	.197	28	66	7	13	14	1	0	0	2	0	1	1	1	6	0	14	3	6
Russo, Francis, Reds	.000	15	6	3	0	0	0	0	0	0	1	0	2	1	0	0	1	1	0
Ryder, Gerald, Reds	.000	13	1	0	0	0	0	0	0	0	0	1	0	0	0	0	0	0	0
Salinas, Manuel, White Sox°	.382	9	34	7	13	17	4	0	0	5	1	0	1	0	2	0	4	1	0
Santana, Carlos, Blue Jays	.198	33	86	2	17	17	0	0	0	10	2	0	1	0	2	0	16	0	1
Santana, Ernesto, Pirates	.000	9	5	0	0	0	0	0	0	0	0	0	0	0	0	0	2	0	0
Santana, Leonel, Astros	.156	18	32	4	5	7	2	0	0	2	0	0	0	0	3	0	10	0	0
Santiago, Norman, White Sox	.315	53	203	30	64	86	10	3	2	32	0	0	3	0	13	0	18	4	3
Scanlan, Robert, Phillies	.400	13	5	1	2	3	1	0	0	0	0	0	0	0	1	0	1	0	0
Sehlhorst, Daniel, White Sox	.171	26	76	10	13	19	4	1	0	3	0	1	0	0	17	1	21	1	0
Sepulveda, Jorge, Dodgers	.000	11	1	0	0	0	0	0	0	0	0	0	0	0	0	0	1	0	0
Serrano, Luis, Reds†	.264	61	201	26	53	64	6	1	1	26	5	0	5	0	29	1	27	6	3
Siblerud, Daniel, Phillies	.000	12	6	0	0	0	0	0	0	1	0	3	0	0	2	0	2	0	0
Silverio, Francisco, Reds	.228	51	162	15	37	53	8	1	2	24	3	2	1	0	6	1	49	3	3
Smiciklas, Michael, Braves	.222	61	216	28	48	92	8	3	10	36	6	1	1	3	25	0	75	1	3
Smith, Michael, Reds	.267	11	15	3	4	9	1	2	0	3	0	0	0	0	0	0	6	0	0
Smith, Peter, Phillies	.000	8	5	0	0	0	0	0	0	0	0	0	0	0	0	0	2	0	0
Smith, Terrance, Pirates	.148	18	54	4	8	13	2	0	1	4	0	0	0	0	5	1	12	0	1
Smith, Todd, Pirates	.271	38	118	9	32	46	9	1	1	10	0	2	1	4	7	0	29	12	4
Smith, William, Yankees°	.195	25	82	7	16	24	5	0	1	8	1	3	0	2	9	2	22	1	4
Spotts, Ralph, Reds	.230	50	148	20	34	49	6	3	1	16	0	1	4	0	9	0	38	15	3
Stading, Gregory, Reds	.167	12	12	1	2	2	0	0	0	0	0	1	0	0	1	0	7	0	0
Stewart, Anthony, Pirates	.253	49	166	23	42	57	5	2	2	18	1	2	2	3	22	0	23	1	3
Stone, Jerome, Phillies†	.277	26	65	16	18	30	2	5	0	3	0	1	0	1	11	0	18	4	0
Taveras, Rafael, Pirates	.253	49	166	25	42	56	5	3	1	19	0	0	1	5	17	0	25	6	4
Toler, Gregory, Reds	.271	13	48	11	13	18	1	2	0	5	0	0	0	2	0	0	5	0	0
Torre, Michael, Reds	.153	42	118	10	18	21	3	0	0	5	1	4	1	0	8	0	41	1	1
Truzzolino, Gary, Yankees	.067	5	15	4	1	1	0	0	0	0	0	0	0	0	3	0	5	0	0
Tubbs, Gregory, Braves	.362	18	58	13	21	31	4	3	0	3	0	0	0	1	15	0	5	5	2
Ubiera, Andres, Pirates	1.000	8	1	0	1	1	0	0	0	0	0	0	0	0	0	0	0	0	0
Valenzuela, Victor, Astros	.125	12	8	1	1	1	0	0	0	0	0	2	0	0	0	0	4	0	0
Vargas, Jose, Astros	.100	14	10	2	1	1	0	0	0	1	0	1	0	0	0	0	2	0	0
Velazquez, Juan, Dodgers	.320	15	25	2	8	10	2	0	0	4	1	2	0	0	4	0	2	0	1
Victor, Miguel, Astros	.375	13	8	3	3	3	0	0	0	1	0	0	0	0	0	0	0	0	0
Villalobos, Juan, Pirates	.000	5	2	0	0	0	0	0	0	0	0	0	0	0	0	0	1	0	0
Viltz, Corey, Yankees	.168	48	149	14	25	28	3	0	0	12	0	2	0	1	35	2	53	4	2
Vizcaino, Jorge, Astros°	.000	16	3	0	0	0	0	0	0	0	0	0	0	0	1	0	1	0	0
Watts, Leonard, Phillies°	.000	7	1	0	0	0	0	0	0	0	0	0	0	0	0	0	1	0	0
Westmoreland, W. Anthony, Reds	.181	28	83	3	15	17	2	0	0	5	1	1	0	0	2	0	15	0	2

Player and Club	Pct.	G.	AB.	R.	H.	TB.	2B.	3B.	HR.	RBI.	GW.	SH.	SF.	HP.	BB.	Int. BB.	SO.	SB.	CS.
Wheeler, Rodney, Phillies*	.243	55	189	38	46	53	3	2	0	15	1	0	1	0	36	0	24	21	9
White, Calvin, Phillies	.000	13	7	0	0	0	0	0	0	0	0	1	0	1	0	0	3	0	0
Wilcox, Leon, Reds	.255	53	184	29	47	57	10	0	0	17	5	2	3	0	17	0	26	4	2
Wilson, Dino, Braves	.375	12	8	2	3	3	0	0	0	1	0	0	0	0	1	0	0	0	0
Winfield, Stephen, Pirates	.000	10	0	0	0	0	0	0	0	0	0	0	0	0	1	0	0	0	0
Wright, Leon, Braves	.204	48	162	17	33	40	4	0	1	16	3	2	2	2	14	0	23	1	1
Zapolski, Timothy, Dodgers	.278	10	18	4	5	7	2	0	0	4	0	0	1	5	0	3	0	0
Zielinski, Glenn, Reds	.258	37	62	13	16	19	1	1	0	8	0	1	0	12	1	6	3	2
Zink, Christopher, Yankees*	.083	4	12	0	1	2	1	0	0	0	0	0	0	2	0	0	0	0

The following pitchers, listed alphabetically by club, with games in parentheses, had no plate appearances, primarily through use of designated hitters:

BLUE JAYS—Bautista, Camilo (4); Burgos, Enrique (12); Diaz, Victor (14); Hightower, Daniel (22); Miller, Duane (13); Monaco, Larence (23); Nunez, Juan (13); Rutledge, Guy (9); Santana, Fernando (17); Winter, Thomas (17).

BRAVES—Leonardi, Anthony (2); Thomas, Kevin (1).

DODGERS—Mena, Andres (18); Nelson, Jeffrey (9); Williams, Jimmy (2).

PHILLIES—Garces, Robinson (17); Garcia, Danielo (10); Jenkins, Clint (12).

PIRATES—Almonte, Eduardo (9); DeLaCruz, Pedro (3); Helton, Kevin (1); Hill, Christopher (4); Kiernan, Michael (1); Kolb, Jonathan (1); Mondesi, Nelson (1); Wayland, Jeffrey (4); Welch, Jack (4).

RANGERS—Aviles, Luis (9); Baker, Matthew (16); Ballista, Johnny (12); Dial, Charles (11); Edwards, Richard (8); Harden, Ty (11); Jones, Ross (6); Meadows, Jimmy (10); Pardo, Lawrence (13); Rogers, Stuart (15); Schofield, John (15); Sheeks, Billy (2); Whitaker, Darrell (20); Winbush, Michael (7).

REDS—Jones, Scott (5).

WHITE SOX—Babcock, William (4); Carr, Donald (19); Filippi, James (11); Jefferson, Byron (16); Jefts, Christopher (12); Lahrman, Thomas (11); Lampkin, Steven (14); Menendez, Antonio (6); Morgan, Bradford (18); Mullen, Thomas (1); Peterson, Adam (12); Renz, Kevin (1); White, David (13); York, Michael (5).

YANKEES—Armstrong, Douglas (10); Azocar, Oscar (11); Carreno, Amalio (9); Davis, Fernando (5); Gibbs, James (13); Guercio, Maurice (9); Heckard, Thom (8); Lane, Derek (7); Lewis, Donald (1); McClear, Michael (11); Robinson, Elmer (1); Shamie, Frank (6); Simmons, Michael (2); Starling, James (10); Thomas, Tony (10); Trudeau, Kevin (10); Yeager, Charles (17).

GRAND SLAM HOME RUNS—Cochran, Denson, Guerrero, Hood, McMillan, Stewart, 1 each.

AWARDED FIRST BASE ON CATCHER'S INTERFERENCE—Hansen (Cueva).

CLUB FIELDING

Club	Pct.	G.	PO.	A.	E.	DP.	PB.	Club	Pct.	G.	PO.	A.	E.	DP.	PB.
Yankees	.955	63	1638	711	111	41	15	Blue Jays	.939	63	1627	730	154	43	12
Rangers	.953	63	1654	764	120	52	12	White Sox	.939	63	1639	713	153	38	15
Braves	.947	63	1632	745	133	54	19	Astros	.938	63	1637	776	160	56	25
Pirates	.943	63	1630	702	142	42	19	Phillies	.936	63	1654	735	162	54	22
Reds	.943	63	1615	652	137	28	8	Dodgers	.934	63	1625	724	165	45	14

Triple Play—Yankees.

INDIVIDUAL FIELDING

*Throws lefthanded.

FIRST BASEMEN

Player and Club	Pct.	G.	PO.	A.	E.	DP.	Player and Club	Pct.	G.	PO.	A.	E.	DP.
Alcantara, Rangers	.953	16	158	3	8	14	Keller, Reds*	1.000	15	109	9	0	8
Alcazar, White Sox	1.000	1	8	1	0	1	King, Astros	.969	14	119	8	4	8
Berezo, Reds*	1.000	3	12	0	0	1	Laird, Pirates*	1.000	4	31	0	0	4
Berroa, Blue Jays	1.000	6	29	0	0	2	LANIK, Rangers*	.995	43	385	18	2	26
Boyd, Dodgers	.981	51	429	26	9	29	Lopez, Yankees	.986	23	206	11	3	9
Carrion, Astros	1.000	2	18	1	0	2	Obando, Pirates	.972	20	131	8	4	12
Castro, Blue Jays	.993	21	138	7	1	13	Ottino, White Sox	1.000	12	84	3	0	4
Clifton, Phillies	1.000	1	2	0	0	0	Pena, Rangers*	.981	10	51	1	1	3
Constanzo, Braves	1.000	5	50	6	0	5	Peraza, White Sox	.974	45	387	22	11	23
Cullers, Rangers	.961	7	47	2	2	5	Perez, Astros	.983	12	109	9	2	11
Denczi, Pirates	.971	3	34	0	1	0	Polanco, Phillies	.979	26	224	11	5	21
Dorsey, Pirates	.988	27	235	20	3	15	Polledo, Yankees	1.000	5	26	0	0	1
Edwards, Dodgers*	1.000	1	9	2	0	1	Prince, Pirates	.867	3	12	1	2	1
Fraser, Astros	.981	10	92	13	2	7	Reyna, Blue Jays*	.970	48	436	19	14	27
Garcia, White Sox*	.977	6	40	2	1	4	Rosario, Astros	.989	29	245	17	3	24
Gibbs, Dodgers*	.971	26	126	9	4	8	Serrano, Reds	.969	47	389	21	13	14
Gilles, Yankees	1.000	34	333	20	0	27	Smiciklas, Braves*	.974	58	545	20	15	45
Hendricks, White Sox	.971	6	32	2	1	2	Spotts, Reds	.750	1	3	0	1	0
Herrenbruck, Phillies	.977	30	271	20	7	19	Truzzolino, Yankees	.971	5	33	1	1	2
Hornacek, Dodgers	1.000	1	5	0	0	1	Zapolski, Dodgers	1.000	1	3	0	0	0
Johnson, Pirates	.975	13	109	9	3	3	Zielinski, Reds	1.000	2	9	0	0	0
Kaiser, Phillies	.980	11	93	5	2	6							

Triple Play—Lopez.

SECOND BASEMEN

Player and Club	Pct.	G.	PO.	A.	E.	DP.	Player and Club	Pct.	G.	PO.	A.	E.	DP.
Aquino, Astros	.932	17	48	48	7	12	Garcia, Blue Jays	.902	11	16	21	4	4
Barringer, Pirates	.917	2	8	3	1	2	Guerrero, Blue Jays	.909	50	99	121	22	17
Basora, Dodgers	.853	10	10	19	5	2	Heeney, Yankees	.958	34	76	85	7	17
Benitez, White Sox	1.000	26	60	51	0	8	Jagnow, Rangers	.939	48	104	110	14	20
Bertolani, White Sox	.958	5	8	15	1	3	Kennelley, Reds	.895	35	65	72	16	6
Bolling, Pirates	1.000	2	2	6	0	0	King, Astros	.920	5	8	15	2	3
Butler, Reds	1.000	5	5	7	0	1	Klein, Rangers	1.000	1	2	6	0	1
Caceres, Dodgers	.959	20	54	62	5	10	Kovach, Reds	1.000	3	3	5	0	1
Clark, Pirates	.971	14	40	28	2	6	Leger, Braves	1.000	2	1	0	0	0
Contrera, Blue Jays	1.000	3	7	5	0	1	LEMKE, Braves	.977	63	175	207	9	39
Crispin, Phillies	.947	29	54	72	7	16	Martinez, White Sox	.818	5	8	10	4	1
Elliott, Astros	.903	17	44	49	10	9	Michel, Dodgers	.911	22	48	64	11	6
Eveline, White Sox	.934	36	80	76	11	11	Pender, Pirates	.940	23	43	36	5	3
Farmer, Rangers	.972	23	43	60	3	19	Picart, Dodgers	.852	18	26	43	12	5
Fidanza, Yankees	1.000	2	2	1	0	0	Pitti, Yankees	.905	3	4	15	2	1
Frazier, Phillies	.941	41	74	102	11	24	Pottinger, Phillies	1.000	2	4	9	0	1
Fuentes, Pirates	.895	3	10	7	2	1	Reyes, Blue Jays	.821	7	9	14	5	1

SECOND BASEMEN—Continued

Player and Club	Pct.	G.	PO.	A.	E.	DP.	Player and Club	Pct.	G.	PO.	A.	E.	DP.
J. Rivas, Yankees	.908	22	40	49	9	7	Stone, Phillies	1.000	1	6	4	0	1
R.M. Rivas, Yankees	1.000	1	3	3	0	0	Taveras, Pirates	.936	8	21	23	3	6
Roque, Pirates	.951	18	48	50	5	7	Wilcox, Reds	.786	3	6	5	3	1
Russell, Astros	.937	26	65	69	9	18	Wilson, Braves	.857	8	2	4	1	0
Salinas, White Sox	1.000	5	14	13	0	0	Zink, Yankees	.929	4	7	6	1	0
Santiago, White Sox	.953	17	45	37	4	10							

THIRD BASEMEN

Player and Club	Pct.	G.	PO.	A.	E.	DP.	Player and Club	Pct.	G.	PO.	A.	E.	DP.
Alcantara, Rangers	.917	8	3	8	1	1	Klein, Rangers	.946	13	11	42	3	1
Aquino, Astros	.903	13	5	23	3	1	Kovach, Reds	.913	10	8	13	2	2
Benitez, Dodgers	.733	4	4	7	4	0	Kwolek, Astros	.883	41	29	84	15	4
Bennett, Phillies	1.000	1	0	2	0	0	Laboy, Yankees	.894	40	24	86	13	10
Bertolani, White Sox	.868	20	26	40	10	2	Leger, Braves	1.000	2	0	1	0	0
Bolling, Pirates	.750	1	0	3	1	0	McClain, Pirates	.889	6	1	15	2	1
Castro, Blue Jays	.900	10	6	12	2	0	Michel, Dodgers	1.000	5	1	11	0	1
Clark, Pirates	.864	20	20	37	9	3	Morales, Dodgers	.829	19	8	21	6	1
Cochran, Rangers	.892	43	32	100	16	8	Morse, White Sox	.824	8	5	9	3	0
Contrera, Blue Jays	.500	2	1	0	1	0	Nina, Reds	.852	25	11	35	8	3
Cruz, Dodgers	.750	2	1	2	1	0	O'Brien, Braves	.894	42	25	76	12	4
Denczi, Pirates	1.000	1	2	0	0	0	Ottino, White Sox	.879	23	15	36	7	0
Farmer, Rangers	.829	11	7	22	6	1	Picart, Dodgers	.625	3	2	3	3	1
Fraser, Astros	1.000	1	0	2	0	0	Reyes, Blue Jays	.854	54	40	100	24	7
Fuentes, Pirates	.923	4	4	8	1	0	G. Roque, Pirates	.800	2	3	5	2	2
Garcia, Blue Jays	.778	6	3	11	4	0	O. Roque, Astros	.762	9	6	10	5	1
Gilles, Yankees	.939	7	9	22	2	0	Russell, Astros	.944	6	4	13	1	3
Hardaker, Phillies	.910	37	38	83	12	9	Salinas, White Sox	.500	3	0	2	2	0
Heeney, Yankees	.900	5	1	8	1	1	Santiago, White Sox	.870	23	10	50	9	3
HORNACEK, Dodgers	.896	46	35	85	14	5	Smith, Yankees	.893	13	16	34	6	3
Hurtado, Phillies	.822	29	24	50	16	5	Stone, Phillies	1.000	2	2	1	0	0
D. King, Braves	.897	28	20	58	9	7	Taveras, Pirates	.885	34	31	77	14	7
W. King, Astros	.800	2	0	4	1	2	Wilcox, Reds	.835	38	27	79	21	3

SHORTSTOPS

Player and Club	Pct.	G.	PO.	A.	E.	DP.	Player and Club	Pct.	G.	PO.	A.	E.	DP.
Aquino, Astros	.862	11	17	39	9	6	Lemke, Braves	1.000	1	0	2	0	1
Barringer, Pirates	.913	4	2	19	2	0	Martin, White Sox	.852	48	64	149	37	17
Bertolani, White Sox	.909	7	14	16	3	3	Martinez, Yankees	.918	31	53	103	14	14
Clark, Pirates	.895	12	22	29	6	2	Mitchell, Reds	.944	18	24	43	4	3
Clifton, Phillies	.838	43	66	110	34	21	Morales, Dodgers	.925	18	24	50	6	9
Cochran, Rangers	.867	5	2	11	2	2	Morse, White Sox	.818	2	5	4	2	1
Covington, Rangers	.800	1	0	4	1	0	O'Brien, Braves	.909	5	3	7	1	1
DARRETTA, Rangers	.914	51	64	170	22	25	Perdomo, Dodgers	.667	4	2	2	2	0
Ethridge, Rangers	.500	1	1	0	1	0	Pitti, Yankees	.860	30	38	85	20	12
Fuentes, Pirates	.952	5	5	15	1	2	Pottinger, Phillies	.750	8	5	16	7	2
Garcia, Blue Jays	.898	58	85	205	33	30	Reyes, Blue Jays	.889	6	7	17	3	1
Green, Astros	.881	54	78	182	35	27	Robinson, Pirates	.903	42	79	126	22	18
Heeney, Yankees	.931	4	13	14	2	2	Roque, Pirates	.750	1	1	2	1	0
Jagnow, Rangers	1.000	1	2	1	0	0	Salinas, White Sox	.800	2	1	3	1	0
Johnson, Phillies	.883	16	25	58	11	7	Santiago, White Sox	.915	8	12	31	4	4
Klein, Rangers	.900	8	12	33	5	4	Taveras, Pirates	.778	3	1	6	2	1
Kopetsky, Dodgers	.871	49	72	130	30	18	Torre, White Sox	.889	42	65	111	22	11
Kovach, Reds	.971	12	15	18	1	2	Wright, Braves	.847	48	46	131	32	25
Laboy, Yankees	.842	4	8	8	3	0	Zapolski, Dodgers	1.000	1	0	1	0	0
Leger, Braves	.891	22	39	43	10	8							

Triple Play—Heeney.

OUTFIELDERS

Player and Club	Pct.	G.	PO.	A.	E.	DP.	Player and Club	Pct.	G.	PO.	A.	E.	DP.
Acosta, Reds	1.000	19	20	2	0	1	Edwards, Dodgers*	.963	49	75	2	3	1
A. Alcantara, Rangers	1.000	11	11	0	0	0	Ethridge, Rangers	.917	12	9	2	1	0
J. Alcantara, Braves	.958	20	20	3	1	0	Fernandez, Rangers*	1.000	19	18	2	0	0
D. Aquino, Astros	.750	5	3	0	1	0	Fortenberry, Phillies	1.000	27	60	4	0	0
F. Aquino, Rangers*	1.000	28	38	4	0	0	Fraser, Astros	1.000	1	1	0	0	0
Arias, Dodgers	.969	33	60	3	2	1	Frazier, Braves	.924	39	60	1	5	0
Benitez, Dodgers	.958	16	22	1	1	0	Ca. Garcia, Blue Jays	.944	14	14	3	1	0
Berezo, Reds*	.912	26	26	5	3	0	Co. Garcia, White Sox*	.948	42	52	3	3	0
Berroa, Blue Jays	.939	56	75	2	5	0	GLASKER, Rangers*	.988	55	82	3	1	0
Bertolani, White Sox	.962	30	44	6	2	0	Guante, Yankees	.909	6	9	1	1	0
Brock, Astros*	.900	7	9	0	1	0	J. Guerrero, Astros	.932	51	79	3	6	0
S. Brown, Pirates	.846	11	10	1	2	0	S. Guerrero, Astros	.864	27	36	2	6	0
W. Brown, Yankees	.963	51	96	7	4	0	Hammons, Pirates	1.000	21	35	3	0	0
Burton, Yankees	1.000	4	7	0	0	0	Hampton, Astros*	.963	61	140	15	6	3
Butler, Reds	.933	18	25	3	2	1	Hartley, White Sox	.974	59	102	9	3	0
Campbell, Dodgers	1.000	37	48	2	0	1	Hendricks, White Sox	.950	33	36	2	2	1
Campusano, Blue Jays	.944	63	128	7	8	1	Hibberd, Rangers	1.000	2	1	0	0	0
Casellas, Yankees	.750	2	3	0	1	0	Hood, Braves	.971	49	96	3	3	0
Chance, Yankees	.862	14	24	1	4	0	Hufford, Phillies	.932	49	63	5	5	0
Chestna, Yankees	1.000	31	67	2	0	0	Jimenez, Pirates*	1.000	3	6	0	0	0
Clemente, Phillies	1.000	28	41	2	0	0	Johnson, Pirates	1.000	5	10	0	0	0
Covington, Rangers	.929	32	26	0	2	0	C. Jones, Yankees	1.000	2	3	0	0	0
Cruz, Dodgers	1.000	3	2	0	0	0	L. Jones, Braves	.906	17	27	2	3	1
Cunningham, Yankees	.984	48	57	3	1	0	Kaiser, Phillies	.824	10	13	1	3	0
Davins, Pirates	1.000	1	2	0	0	0	Keller, Reds*	1.000	1	1	1	0	0
H. DeLaCruz, Blue Jays	.973	56	101	6	3	1	Kelley, Rangers	.978	36	42	2	1	0
L. DeLaCruz, Astros	.958	40	66	3	3	1	Knox, Pirates	1.000	5	6	1	0	0
Denson, Braves	.973	47	65	6	2	0	Luna, White Sox	.972	29	34	1	1	0
C. Dorsey, Dodgers*	.935	37	68	4	5	0	Martin, White Sox	1.000	1	2	0	0	0
W. Dorsey, Pirates	1.000	1	1	0	0	0	Martinez, White Sox	.967	39	55	3	2	1

OUTFIELDERS—Continued

Player and Club	Pct.	G.	PO.	A.	E.	DP.
McMillan, Pirates*	.958	58	128	9	6	2
Mitchell, Reds	.933	29	41	1	3	0
Moore, Pirates	1.000	7	10	0	0	0
Pena, Rangers*	.889	10	8	0	1	0
Pequignot, Dodgers	.933	37	52	4	4	0
A. Perez, Astros	1.000	5	2	2	0	0
F. Perez, Phillies	.929	26	35	4	3	1
Picart, Dodgers	.889	6	6	2	1	1
Polledo, Yankees	1.000	3	3	0	0	0
Reyna, Blue Jays*	.900	8	9	0	1	0
Rodriguez, Astros	.938	11	15	0	1	0
Roque, Astros	1.000	1	2	1	0	0
S. Russell, Rangers	.938	25	28	2	2	0
Serrano, Pirates*	.750	5	3	0	1	0
Silverio, Reds	.955	48	80	5	4	0
T. Smith, Pirates	.968	31	57	3	2	0
W. Smith, Yankees	.750	2	3	0	1	0
Spotts, Reds	.938	47	59	2	4	0
Stewart, Pirates	.932	41	78	4	6	0
Stone, Phillies	.967	17	27	2	1	1
Tubbs, Braves	1.000	18	24	2	0	1
Viltz, Yankees*	.968	48	59	2	2	0
Wheeler, Phillies*	.934	53	85	0	6	0
Wilcox, Reds	1.000	9	8	1	0	0
Zapolski, Dodgers	.933	7	13	1	1	0
Zielinski, Reds	1.000	26	32	3	0	0

CATCHERS

Player and Club	Pct.	G.	PO.	A.	E.	DP.	PB.
Acevedo, Dodgers	.973	27	127	18	4	1	5
Alcazar, White Sox	.974	28	190	31	6	1	8
Borras, Pirates	1.000	3	13	1	0	0	1
Brodsky, Yankees	1.000	1	1	0	0	0	0
Butters, Pirates	1.000	4	30	1	0	0	3
Carrion, Astros	.973	20	100	9	3	2	8
Constanzo, Braves	.957	16	69	21	4	1	2
Cruz, Dodgers	.969	43	217	35	8	4	6
Cueva, Braves	.973	37	191	28	6	1	7
Cullers, Rangers	.974	27	167	23	5	3	4
Denczi, Pirates	.920	4	20	3	2	0	0
Dorsey, Pirates	1.000	2	18	2	0	1	0
Ferreiras, Pirates	.934	25	102	11	8	0	6
Gonzalez, Yankees	.978	19	121	13	3	1	5
Gsellman, Phillies	.976	19	110	11	3	0	8
Hern, Braves	1.000	7	8	0	0	0	4
Houp, Reds	.978	35	241	27	6	0	3
Johnson, Phillies	.970	37	225	36	8	3	10
Lyden, Yankees	.977	41	254	49	7	2	3
Markert, White Sox	.990	24	173	24	2	0	4
Marston, Yankees	.964	3	23	4	1	0	2
Monson, Phillies	.957	13	79	10	4	2	4
OWEN, Rangers	.981	33	173	35	4	2	2
Perez, Astros	.972	11	59	10	2	1	2
Pfaff, Braves	1.000	20	98	18	0	0	6
Prince, Pirates	.975	14	63	15	2	0	3
Pujols, Rangers	.991	22	103	8	1	2	6
Reyes, Astros	.944	7	29	5	2	0	5
Rivas, Yankees	1.000	5	9	1	0	0	5
Rodriguez, Astros	.973	28	129	17	4	0	8
Rojas, Blue Jays	.977	53	319	55	9	1	6
C. Santana, Blue Jays	.965	16	69	14	3	0	6
L. Santana, Astros	.976	13	34	6	1	0	2
Sehlhorst, White Sox	.973	16	95	12	3	2	3
Silverio, Reds	1.000	1	2	0	0	0	0
Smith, Pirates	.954	18	90	14	5	0	6
Toler, Reds	.978	12	77	12	2	1	1
Velazquez, Dodgers	.909	10	36	4	4	1	3
Westmoreland, Reds	.970	25	166	25	6	3	4

PITCHERS

Player and Club	Pct.	G.	PO.	A.	E.	DP.
Adams, Pirates	1.000	13	1	8	0	1
Almonte, Pirates	1.000	9	1	3	0	0
Armstrong, Yankees	.875	10	4	10	2	0
Aviles, Rangers*	.667	9	0	2	1	0
Azocar, Yankees*	1.000	11	2	7	0	2
Babcock, White Sox*	1.000	4	1	4	0	0
Bacon, Reds	.917	18	2	9	1	0
Mar. Baker, Astros	1.000	9	0	3	0	0
Mat. Baker, Rangers	.667	16	2	2	2	0
Ballista, Rangers	.800	12	1	3	1	1
Bautista, Blue Jays	.875	4	1	6	1	0
Berlin, Astros*	.000	7	0	0	1	0
Blankenship, Braves	.909	19	4	6	1	0
Blethen, Braves	.875	14	1	6	1	0
Broussard, Phillies*	.800	13	3	13	4	0
Burgos, Blue Jays*	.967	12	5	24	1	1
Carr, White Sox	1.000	19	2	5	0	0
Carreno, Yankees	.833	9	0	5	1	0
Cash, Braves	.923	12	1	11	1	0
Cepeda, Pirates	.889	10	2	6	1	0
Charles, Dodgers	.800	14	1	7	2	0
Cieslak, Reds*	.875	13	3	18	3	1
Criswell, Dodgers	.964	8	7	20	1	2
Cuba, Dodgers	.913	13	4	17	2	1
Davis, Yankees*	1.000	5	1	2	0	0
DeLaCruz, Pirates*	1.000	3	0	1	0	0
DeLeon, Astros	.875	13	3	11	2	1
Dial, Rangers	1.000	11	5	9	0	1
Diaz, Blue Jays*	1.000	14	1	6	0	0
Dilone, Dodgers	.500	14	0	1	1	0
Duffy, Dodgers	.923	10	6	6	1	1
Edwards, Rangers	1.000	8	1	3	0	0
Evans, Phillies	.727	14	1	7	3	2
Fick, Reds*	.667	14	0	2	1	0
Filippi, White Sox	.833	11	3	17	4	1
Garces, Phillies*	1.000	17	2	2	0	0
Garcia, Phillies	.875	10	0	7	1	2
Gibbs, Yankees	1.000	13	6	12	0	0
Glavine, Braves*	1.000	8	3	6	0	0
Gray, Phillies	1.000	26	1	18	0	0
Gregory, Dodgers*	1.000	7	5	15	0	6
Groves, Braves	.818	13	0	4	5	2
Guance, Reds	1.000	6	1	0	0	0
Guercio, Yankees	1.000	9	2	1	0	0
GUZMAN, Braves	1.000	10	4	16	0	0
Hansen, Pirates*	.852	14	4	19	4	2
Harden, Rangers	.917	11	1	10	1	1
Heckard, Yankees	1.000	8	0	3	0	0
Helton, Pirates	1.000	1	0	1	0	0
Hendrix, Phillies	.857	16	1	5	1	0
Heredia, Astros	1.000	12	2	9	0	2
Hernandez, Dodgers	.923	9	4	8	1	0
Hibberd, Rangers	.800	12	1	7	2	0
Hightower, Blue Jays*	1.000	22	6	11	0	1
Hill, Pirates	1.000	4	0	3	0	0
James, Pirates	1.000	11	5	12	0	1
Jefferson, White Sox	.909	16	3	7	1	0
Jefts, White Sox	.800	12	6	14	5	0
Jenkins, Phillies	1.000	12	3	5	0	0
Jimenez, Braves	.833	12	2	13	3	0
Johnson, Astros	.938	12	4	11	1	0
J.K. Jones, Braves	.923	18	3	9	1	1
M.R. Jones, Rangers	1.000	6	1	3	0	0
S. Jones, Rangers*	.778	5	1	6	2	0
Kiernan, Pirates	.000	1	0	0	1	0
Knox, Phillies	1.000	13	0	4	0	0
Kolb, Pirates	1.000	1	0	1	0	0
Krepp, Astros	.957	22	8	14	1	0
Lahrman, White Sox	.833	11	1	4	1	0
Lampkin, White Sox*	1.000	13	3	10	0	1
Leonardi, Braves	.000	2	0	0	1	0
Lewis, Yankees	.000	1	0	0	1	0
Litwin, Braves*	1.000	9	2	4	0	1
Mangham, Astros	.800	10	4	12	4	1
Mathews, Braves	.917	15	3	8	1	0
McClear, Yankees	1.000	11	6	5	0	0
Meadows, Rangers	1.000	10	2	11	0	1
Meads, Astros*	1.000	7	1	4	0	0
Mena, Dodgers	.900	18	6	12	2	0
Menendez, White Sox	.750	6	2	4	2	0
Mercedes, Pirates	1.000	12	5	3	0	0
Mesa, Dodgers	1.000	14	1	6	0	0
Miller, Blue Jays	.900	13	4	14	2	2
Mirabito, Reds	.960	12	2	22	1	1
Mitchell, Reds	.923	12	3	9	1	0
Monaco, Blue Jays	.944	23	3	14	1	1
Monte, White Sox	1.000	12	3	7	0	0
Morban, Pirates	1.000	8	1	7	0	0
Morgan, White Sox	1.000	18	4	5	0	0
Morris, Braves	.895	8	4	13	2	0
Mosquera, Dodgers	.750	20	2	7	3	0
Natera, Braves*	.667	13	1	7	4	0
Nelson, Dodgers	1.000	9	0	1	0	0
Nesbit, Phillies	.926	12	5	20	2	1
Newsome, Braves	.700	8	1	6	3	0
Nunez, Blue Jays	.765	13	6	7	4	0
Pardo, Rangers	.818	13	4	5	2	0
Paredes, Astros	1.000	18	3	4	0	1
Parker, Braves	1.000	5	0	1	0	0
Patterson, Rangers	.667	12	1	7	4	0

PITCHERS—Continued

Player and Club	Pct.	G.	PO.	A.	E.	DP.	Player and Club	Pct.	G.	PO.	A.	E.	DP.
Pena, Pirates*	1.000	10	0	2	0	0	Stading, Pirates	.909	12	4	6	1	0
Perez, Pirates*	1.000	12	0	2	0	0	Starling, Yankees	.875	10	2	5	1	0
Peterson, White Sox	.667	12	1	7	4	0	Thomas, Braves	1.000	1	2	0	0	2
Phillips, Dodgers	.688	31	2	9	5	1	Thomas, Yankees	1.000	10	1	4	0	0
Picht, Pirates	.750	4	1	8	3	0	Trudeau, Yankees	.889	10	2	6	1	0
Ramirez, Phillies	1.000	13	1	1	0	0	Ubiera, Pirates	1.000	8	1	2	0	1
Remigio, Pirates	1.000	14	0	1	0	1	Valenzuela, Astros	.840	12	6	15	4	0
Renz, White Sox	1.000	1	0	1	0	0	Vargas, Astros	.966	14	11	17	1	3
Rogers, Rangers*	.909	15	1	9	1	0	Victor, Astros	.875	13	3	4	1	0
Russell, Pirates*	1.000	9	0	2	0	0	Villalobos, Pirates	1.000	5	1	4	0	0
Russo, Reds	.947	15	3	15	1	0	Vizcaino, Astros*	.933	16	1	13	1	0
Rutledge, Blue Jays	1.000	9	1	7	0	0	Watts, Phillies*	1.000	7	0	1	0	0
Ryder, Reds	.857	13	1	5	1	0	Wayland, Pirates	1.000	4	1	2	0	0
Santana, Pirates	1.000	8	4	5	0	1	Welch, Pirates	1.000	4	0	2	0	0
Santana, Blue Jays	.917	16	8	14	2	2	Whitaker, Rangers	1.000	20	0	10	0	0
Scanlan, Phillies	.917	13	3	8	1	0	White, Phillies	1.000	13	6	7	0	0
Schofield, Rangers	1.000	15	4	6	0	0	White, White Sox	.962	13	6	19	1	0
Sepulveda, Dodgers	.800	10	2	2	1	1	Williams, Dodgers*	.000	2	0	0	0	0
Shamie, Yankees	1.000	6	0	5	0	0	Winbush, Rangers	1.000	7	0	3	0	0
Sheeks, Rangers	.667	2	0	2	1	0	Winfield, Pirates	1.000	10	1	0	0	0
Siblerud, Phillies	.769	12	1	9	3	0	Winter, Blue Jays*	1.000	17	1	8	0	0
Simmons, Yankees	1.000	2	0	1	0	0	Yeager, Yankees*	1.000	17	2	5	0	0
Smith, Reds	.800	11	4	4	2	0	York, White Sox	.833	5	0	5	1	0
Smith, Phillies	.846	8	1	10	2	0	Zielinski, Reds	.667	6	2	0	1	0

The following players do not have any recorded accepted chances at the positions indicated; therefore, are not listed in the fielding averages for those particular positions: Alcazar, of; Bennett, c; H. Berroa, 3b, ss; Bolivar, of; Boyd, of; Eveline, of; Fiepke, p; Fumarola, p; A. Gibbs, c; Hicks, p; Jagnow, 3b; Kovach, of; Lane, p; Marston, p; Mondesi, p; Morales, 2b, c; Mullen, p; Polanco, of; El. Robinson, p; Rosario, 3b; Ron. Russell, of; E. Santana, of; Tubbs, 2b; Wilson, 3b.

CLUB PITCHING

Club	ERA.	G.	CG.	ShO.	Sv.	IP.	H.	R.	ER.	HR.	HB.	BB.	Int. BB.	SO.	WP.	Bk.
White Sox	2.72	63	9	3	18	546.1	504	260	165	13	17	169	4	456	36	3
Yankees	2.82	63	6	10	13	546.0	475	243	171	6	9	215	0	400	30	14
Braves	2.86	63	5	6	14	544.0	500	255	173	9	17	170	12	364	64	7
Blue Jays	2.89	63	5	2	12	542.1	530	286	174	22	22	156	3	384	51	5
Reds	2.89	63	9	4	11	538.1	476	241	173	16	22	179	15	469	28	6
Dodgers	2.97	63	9	6	14	541.2	518	281	179	11	27	161	11	368	30	8
Astros	3.02	63	7	5	13	545.2	510	294	183	17	19	206	17	348	45	7
Phillies	3.23	63	2	5	11	551.1	536	293	198	17	26	213	11	389	37	8
Rangers	3.31	63	0	5	18	551.1	449	269	203	7	34	268	9	438	47	9
Pirates	3.99	63	2	1	12	543.1	542	333	241	20	26	244	2	318	33	16

PITCHERS' RECORDS
(Leading Qualifiers for Earned-Run Average Leadership — 50 or More Innings)

*Throws lefthanded.

Pitcher—Club	W.	L.	Pct.	ERA.	G.	GS.	CG.	GF.	ShO.	Sv.	IP.	H.	R.	ER.	HR.	HB.	BB.	Int. BB.	SO.	WP.
Filippi, White Sox	10	1	.909	0.61	11	11	3	0	1	0	74.0	46	14	5	1	2	19	0	74	5
Dial, Rangers	6	1	.857	1.13	11	8	0	3	0	0	56.0	39	10	7	0	2	11	0	36	0
Azocar, Yankees*	4	1	.800	1.28	11	10	2	1	0	0	56.1	37	12	8	1	2	17	0	60	1
Hernandez, Dodgers	3	3	.500	1.30	9	9	3	0	1	0	55.1	42	16	8	1	1	12	0	33	1
Blankenship, Braves	3	1	.750	1.34	19	2	0	14	0	5	53.2	48	20	8	0	0	16	4	27	3
Cieslak, Reds	7	2	.778	1.49	13	13	0	0	0	0	84.2	60	28	14	2	6	34	1	76	2
Cash, Braves	7	0	1.000	1.57	12	10	2	2	0	0	69.0	53	17	12	1	5	6	0	54	6
Hightower, Blue Jays*	4	2	.667	1.84	22	3	1	16	0	8	63.2	53	22	13	1	1	13	3	50	4
Morris, Braves	2	3	.400	2.16	8	7	0	1	0	0	50.0	38	20	12	0	0	23	3	39	7
Jefts, White Sox	6	1	.857	2.20	12	11	3	0	0	0	69.2	55	25	17	1	5	19	1	63	6

Departmental Leaders: G—Phillips, 31; W—Filippi, 10; L—F. Santana, 8; Pct.—Filippi, .909; GS—F. Santana, 16; CG—Filippi, Hernandez, Jefts, Mitchell, D. White, 3; GF—Phillips, 28; ShO—Gregory, 2; Sv.—Carr, Phillips, 9; IP—F. Santana, 105.1; H—F. Santana, 112; R—F. Santana, 58; ER—F. Santana, 39; HR—Diaz, F. Santana, Valenzuela, 5; HB—Hibberd, 10; BB—Hibberd, 48; IBB—Gray, Krepp, Phillips, 5; SO—Cieslak, 76; WP—Glavine, 12.

(All Pitchers—Listed Alphabetically)

Pitcher—Club	W.	L.	Pct.	ERA.	G.	GS.	CG.	GF.	ShO.	Sv.	IP.	H.	R.	ER.	HR.	HB.	BB.	Int. BB.	SO.	WP.
Adams, Pirates	1	4	.200	4.96	13	6	0	1	0	0	45.1	59	27	25	3	1	17	0	21	6
Almonte, Pirates	0	0	.000	3.46	9	0	0	5	0	0	13.0	10	8	5	1	0	3	0	4	1
Armstrong, Yankees	1	3	.250	3.68	10	8	0	2	0	0	51.1	49	25	21	1	0	19	0	28	2
Aviles, Rangers*	0	2	.000	4.97	9	0	0	5	0	0	12.2	11	14	7	0	3	12	0	4	2
Azocar, Yankees*	4	1	.800	1.28	11	10	2	1	0	0	56.1	37	12	8	1	2	17	0	60	1
Babcock, White Sox*	3	1	.750	1.13	4	4	0	0	0	0	24.0	18	11	3	0	0	4	0	37	1
Bacon, Reds	2	5	.286	3.63	18	1	1	17	0	4	34.2	35	18	14	1	2	17	3	23	2
Mar. Baker, Astros	1	1	.500	1.13	9	0	0	9	0	4	16.0	7	3	2	0	0	6	2	16	0
Mat. Baker, Rangers	2	3	.400	6.29	16	1	0	10	0	3	24.1	32	26	17	1	1	12	2	11	2
Ballista, Rangers	1	2	.333	1.86	12	1	0	7	0	1	19.1	17	10	4	1	0	9	0	14	3
Bautista, Blue Jays	1	1	.500	2.57	4	2	0	1	0	0	21.0	20	9	6	1	1	5	0	11	1
Berlin, Astros*	1	0	1.000	5.40	7	1	0	2	0	0	6.2	8	11	4	0	2	13	0	3	5
Blankenship, Braves	3	1	.750	1.34	19	2	0	14	0	5	53.2	48	20	8	0	0	16	4	27	3
Blethen, Reds	2	2	.333	4.28	14	1	0	9	0	1	33.2	32	21	16	2	2	18	3	31	6
Broussard, Phillies*	3	6	.333	4.42	13	12	0	0	0	0	57.0	49	36	28	1	4	39	1	62	3
Burgos, Blue Jays*	4	5	.444	2.39	12	10	1	0	0	0	71.2	74	37	19	1	1	22	0	38	9
Carr, White Sox	1	2	.333	2.83	19	0	0	19	0	9	28.2	24	12	9	0	2	17	0	38	2
Carreno, Yankees	1	6	.143	4.91	19	7	1	2	0	0	33.0	37	28	18	1	0	26	0	31	4
Cash, Braves	7	0	1.000	1.57	12	10	2	2	0	0	69.0	53	17	12	1	5	6	0	54	6
Cepeda, Pirates	2	3	.400	4.78	10	4	0	0	0	0	32.0	24	21	17	1	5	22	0	17	5
Charles, Dodgers	3	1	.750	3.66	14	5	0	2	0	0	39.1	43	29	16	1	1	13	1	29	3
Cieslak, Reds*	7	2	.778	1.49	13	13	0	0	0	0	84.2	60	28	14	2	6	34	1	76	2
Criswell, Dodgers	5	1	.833	2.25	8	8	2	0	1	0	60.0	57	19	15	2	1	4	0	41	1

Pitcher—Club	W.	L.	Pct.	ERA.	G.	GS.	CG.	GF.	ShO.	Sv.	IP.	H.	R.	ER.	HR.	HB.	BB.	Int. BB.	SO.	WP.
Cuba, Dodgers	4	6	.400	3.68	13	12	1	0	1	0	66.0	75	49	27	0	4	17	1	30	2
Davis, Yankees°	1	2	.333	1.61	5	4	1	1	0	0	28.0	23	11	5	0	1	9	0	36	0
DeLaCruz, Pirates°	0	0	.000	11.25	3	0	0	1	0	0	4.0	5	6	5	0	0	5	0	3	2
DeLeon, Astros	3	3	.500	2.45	13	6	2	5	1	0	55.0	47	24	15	3	4	13	0	29	4
Dial, Rangers	6	1	.857	1.13	11	8	0	3	0	0	56.0	39	10	7	0	2	11	0	36	0
Diaz, Blue Jays°	0	3	.000	4.57	14	3	1	9	0	0	41.1	48	28	21	5	0	14	0	38	4
Dilone, Dodgers	0	1	.000	3.71	14	0	0	11	0	1	17.0	15	7	7	2	2	8	1	25	1
Duffy, Dodgers	2	2	.500	3.23	10	10	0	0	0	0	53.0	48	24	19	0	3	17	0	28	4
Edwards, Rangers	2	1	.667	4.82	8	0	0	1	0	0	18.2	19	11	10	0	0	20	1	8	4
Evans, Phillies	1	0	1.000	3.09	14	1	0	3	0	0	23.1	24	12	8	0	0	7	0	11	1
Fick, Reds°	3	1	.750	0.76	14	0	0	10	0	2	35.1	23	8	3	0	0	2	0	35	2
Fiepke, Pirates°	1	0	1.000	0.00	1	0	0	0	0	0	2.0	0	0	0	0	0	3	0	2	1
Filippi, White Sox	10	1	.909	0.61	11	11	3	0	1	0	74.0	46	14	5	1	2	19	0	74	5
Fumarola, Pirates°	0	0	.000	3.52	4	0	0	1	0	0	7.2	9	3	3	0	1	0	1	0	0
Garces, Phillies°	1	1	.500	1.01	17	0	0	9	0	1	26.2	24	7	3	0	0	6	0	20	2
Garcia, Phillies	0	3	.000	7.80	10	1	0	2	0	0	15.0	22	26	13	1	1	17	1	11	7
Gibbs, Yankees	3	2	.600	3.86	13	3	0	3	0	0	44.1	45	25	19	0	2	12	0	28	2
Glavine, Braves°	2	3	.400	3.34	8	7	0	1	0	0	32.1	29	17	12	0	1	13	0	34	12
Gray, Phillies	6	4	.600	1.31	26	0	0	24	0	7	41.1	35	9	6	0	1	10	5	26	0
Gregory, Dodgers	6	0	1.000	1.46	7	7	2	0	2	0	49.1	41	11	8	0	1	11	0	30	4
Groves, Braves	2	0	.000	3.34	10	3	0	5	0	2	29.2	26	18	11	0	0	12	0	33	4
Guance, Reds	0	1	.000	8.03	6	0	0	3	0	0	12.1	20	14	11	1	0	1	0	11	0
Guercio, Yankees	1	3	.250	4.96	9	0	0	8	0	3	16.1	17	14	9	1	0	10	0	24	3
Guzman, Braves	3	3	.500	2.32	10	8	2	0	1	0	54.1	48	20	14	1	2	15	1	24	6
Hansen, Pirates°	4	6	.400	3.06	14	12	1	1	1	0	61.2	65	41	21	2	2	34	1	32	1
Harden, Rangers	1	1	.500	4.28	11	7	0	3	0	0	40.0	35	26	19	0	3	25	0	31	7
Heckard, Yankees	0	2	.000	1.54	8	0	0	6	0	0	11.2	16	5	2	0	0	6	0	3	0
Helton, Pirates	0	0	.000	18.00	1	1	0	0	0	0	1.0	0	2	2	0	0	5	0	0	1
Hendrix, Phillies	2	2	.500	1.39	16	0	0	2	0	1	32.1	25	15	5	0	2	10	1	31	4
Heredia, Astros	5	1	.833	1.25	12	3	2	7	0	4	36.0	25	10	5	0	0	12	1	25	1
Hernandez, Dodgers	3	3	.500	1.30	9	9	3	0	1	0	55.1	42	16	8	1	1	12	0	33	1
Hibberd, Rangers	1	3	.250	4.24	12	11	0	0	0	0	51.0	24	29	24	1	10	48	0	46	6
Hicks, Phillies	1	0	1.000	0.75	8	0	0	6	0	1	12.0	9	1	1	0	0	6	0	9	1
Hightower, Blue Jays°	4	2	.667	1.84	22	3	1	16	0	8	63.2	53	22	13	1	1	13	3	50	4
Hill, Pirates	0	1	.000	3.79	4	3	0	1	0	1	19.0	15	10	8	0	1	7	0	12	0
James, Pirates	3	3	.500	5.18	11	8	0	1	0	0	48.2	46	34	28	1	1	25	0	22	4
Jefferson, White Sox	1	2	.333	3.56	16	1	0	9	0	5	48.0	50	25	19	1	0	22	1	28	3
Jefts, White Sox	6	1	.857	2.20	12	11	3	0	0	0	69.2	55	25	17	1	5	19	1	63	6
Jenkins, Phillies	1	3	.250	4.66	12	0	0	5	0	0	19.1	29	19	10	2	3	7	0	14	4
Jimenez, Braves	2	2	.500	2.35	12	10	1	2	1	0	57.1	52	22	15	1	1	7	0	39	2
Johnson, Astros	4	5	.444	3.48	12	12	0	0	0	0	62.0	60	37	24	0	2	27	1	39	7
J.K. Jones, Braves	3	1	.250	4.24	18	0	0	14	0	4	34.0	38	19	16	2	1	10	1	13	2
M.R. Jones, Rangers	2	0	1.000	2.84	6	0	0	3	0	0	19.0	16	8	6	0	2	6	1	25	3
S. Jones, Reds°	3	1	.750	2.10	5	5	2	0	1	0	34.1	22	9	8	0	1	16	1	36	2
Kiernan, Pirates	0	1	.000	13.50	1	0	0	0	0	0	2.0	4	4	3	0	0	2	0	2	0
Knox, Phillies	2	2	.500	3.65	13	5	0	1	0	0	37.0	39	21	15	3	0	12	1	25	1
Kolb, Pirates	1	0	1.000	4.50	1	0	0	1	0	0	2.0	2	1	1	0	0	1	0	3	0
Krepp, Astros	4	2	.667	2.50	22	0	0	13	0	2	36.0	37	16	10	1	1	11	5	26	4
Lahrman, White Sox	2	2	.500	1.15	11	2	0	7	0	2	31.1	22	11	4	0	2	4	0	22	1
Lampkin, White Sox°	3	3	.500	3.93	13	7	0	1	0	0	55.0	74	41	24	1	2	20	0	34	5
Lane, Yankees	1	0	1.000	7.04	7	0	0	6	0	0	7.2	10	9	6	0	0	4	0	5	2
Leonardi, Braves	1	0	1.000	6.75	2	0	0	1	0	0	4.0	7	3	3	0	0	3	0	0	0
Lewis, Yankees	0	1	.000	0.00	1	0	0	1	0	0	3.0	3	2	0	0	1	0	0	4	1
Litwin, Braves°	1	4	.200	8.55	9	1	0	4	0	0	20.0	23	21	19	1	2	11	0	17	4
Mangham, Astros	4	2	.667	3.96	10	9	0	1	0	0	52.1	51	42	23	2	1	24	1	33	8
Marston, Yankees	0	1	.000	9.00	1	0	0	0	0	0	1.0	2	3	1	0	1	0	0	1	1
Mathews, Braves	3	2	.600	2.35	15	2	0	7	0	2	38.1	39	18	10	0	2	14	2	22	10
McClear, Yankees	3	2	.600	2.35	11	10	2	1	1	0	65.0	49	22	17	0	0	19	0	43	3
Meadows, Rangers	6	1	.857	1.29	10	9	0	1	0	1	49.0	34	11	7	0	0	8	0	29	1
Meads, Astros°	2	2	.500	1.23	7	4	1	3	1	2	29.1	22	11	4	1	1	2	0	28	1
Mena, Dodgers	3	6	.333	4.76	18	7	1	4	0	3	51.0	60	40	27	2	4	9	1	30	3
Menendez, White Sox	3	2	.600	3.16	6	6	0	0	0	0	37.0	26	19	13	2	0	13	0	30	2
Mercedes, Pirates	2	2	.500	0.42	12	0	0	10	0	3	21.2	14	8	1	2	0	4	0	18	1
Mesa, Dodgers	2	2	.500	5.40	14	2	0	3	0	0	30.0	32	20	18	0	2	11	0	24	2
Miller, Blue Jays	4	4	.500	2.92	13	13	0	0	0	0	64.2	67	41	21	4	4	16	0	40	6
Mirabito, Reds	4	4	.500	2.27	12	12	2	0	0	0	75.1	68	27	19	0	4	12	3	52	0
Mitchell, Reds	4	4	.500	5.50	12	12	3	0	1	0	55.2	61	40	34	3	1	25	0	50	1
Monaco, Blue Jays	4	3	.571	2.23	23	0	0	19	0	3	48.1	48	26	12	1	1	9	0	36	1
Mondesi, Pirates°	0	0	.000	9.00	1	0	0	0	0	0	1.0	2	1	1	0	0	0	0	0	0
Monte, Yankees	3	4	.429	3.99	12	4	0	6	0	2	38.1	37	20	17	0	1	18	0	20	5
Morban, Pirates	1	4	.200	3.83	8	8	0	0	0	0	42.1	43	28	18	2	2	21	0	25	2
Morgan, White Sox	1	1	.500	3.89	18	0	0	14	0	2	34.2	36	20	15	0	2	15	0	19	4
Morris, Braves	2	3	.400	2.16	8	7	0	1	0	0	50.0	38	20	12	0	0	20	3	39	7
Mosquera, Dodgers	2	2	.500	2.72	20	0	0	3	0	1	36.1	29	18	11	1	1	21	2	31	2
Mullen, White Sox	0	0	.000	9.00	1	1	0	0	0	0	1.0	3	1	1	0	0	0	0	2	0
Natera, Braves°	4	4	.500	2.75	13	7	0	3	0	0	52.1	52	28	16	2	1	16	1	36	0
Nelson, Dodgers	0	0	.000	1.35	9	0	0	3	0	0	13.1	6	3	2	0	1	6	0	7	1
Nesbit, Phillies	3	2	.600	2.90	12	12	1	0	1	0	68.1	60	32	22	3	6	23	0	28	3
Newsome, Braves	0	4	.000	6.86	8	1	0	4	0	1	21.0	22	22	16	1	1	22	0	9	4
Nunez, Blue Jays	3	5	.375	3.59	13	11	0	1	0	0	62.2	58	36	25	1	5	30	0	36	9
Pardo, Rangers	1	5	.167	4.72	13	8	0	3	0	2	47.2	37	30	25	0	2	34	0	38	2
Paredez, Astros	3	1	.750	2.93	18	0	0	8	0	1	30.2	34	19	10	0	2	14	1	16	3
Parker, Braves	1	1	.500	3.68	5	4	0	0	0	0	22.0	24	10	9	0	1	6	0	10	4
Patterson, Rangers	2	1	.667	3.65	12	4	0	5	0	2	37.0	31	16	15	0	3	24	1	33	6
Pena, Pirates°	1	1	.500	2.76	10	0	0	5	0	2	16.1	12	8	5	0	1	9	0	15	0
Perez, Pirates	0	0	.000	4.68	12	0	0	5	0	1	25.0	21	16	13	1	3	10	1	12	0
Peterson, White Sox	1	4	.200	5.44	12	8	0	3	0	0	43.0	49	39	26	4	1	19	1	31	5
Phillips, Dodgers	4	3	.571	2.23	31	0	0	28	0	9	44.1	46	24	11	1	3	13	5	31	3
Picht, Pirates	0	1	.000	6.11	4	3	0	0	0	0	17.2	26	13	12	3	0	4	0	12	0
Ramirez, Phillies	2	1	.667	0.91	13	0	0	3	0	0	29.2	25	4	3	1	1	4	1	21	0
Remigio, Braves	2	2	.500	4.74	14	0	0	7	0	1	19.0	21	11	10	0	2	7	0	8	2
Renz, White Sox	0	0	.000	0.00	1	1	0	0	0	0	3.0	2	1	0	0	0	1	0	1	0
Robinson, Yankees	0	0	.000	3.00	1	0	0	0	0	0	3.0	3	1	1	0	0	5	0	0	1

Pitcher—Club	W.	L.	Pct.	ERA.	G.	GS.	CG.	GF.	ShO.	Sv.	IP.	H.	R.	ER.	HR.	HB.	BB.	Int. BB.	SO.	WP.
Rogers, Rangers⊕	4	3	.571	3.83	15	6	0	4	0	4	47.0	46	24	20	2	2	8	1	47	1
Russell, Pirates⊕	0	1	.000	1.16	9	1	0	3	0	1	23.1	15	8	3	1	0	4	0	16	1
Russo, Reds	5	5	.500	2.82	15	8	1	4	1	3	60.2	55	29	19	3	1	17	0	54	5
Rutledge, Blue Jays	1	1	.500	1.65	9	2	0	5	0	1	27.1	19	11	5	0	3	9	0	22	3
Ryder, Reds	1	2	.333	2.20	13	0	0	8	0	1	32.2	28	12	8	1	0	8	2	26	1
E. Santana, Pirates	1	5	.167	4.91	8	4	0	1	0	0	25.2	30	22	14	0	2	12	0	14	4
F. Santana, Blue Jays	5	8	.385	3.33	16	16	2	0	0	0	105.1	112	58	39	5	5	16	0	71	10
Scanlan, Phillies	0	2	.000	6.48	13	6	0	2	0	0	33.1	43	31	24	0	0	30	0	17	4
Schofield, Rangers	3	1	.750	3.83	15	4	0	4	0	1	42.1	36	21	18	1	2	24	0	23	5
Sepulveda, Dodgers	0	2	.000	3.80	10	3	0	0	0	0	23.2	20	17	10	1	3	15	0	24	3
Shamie, Yankees	1	0	1.000	3.06	6	0	0	3	0	0	17.2	14	7	6	0	0	8	0	10	0
Sheeks, Rangers	0	0	.000	4.50	2	0	0	0	0	0	8.0	10	6	4	0	1	3	0	4	1
Siblerud, Phillies	2	5	.286	4.15	12	11	0	1	0	0	60.2	62	33	28	4	7	11	0	33	3
Simmons, Yankees	0	0	.000	1.80	2	0	0	0	0	0	5.0	3	1	1	0	0	0	0	1	0
M. Smith, Reds	2	4	.333	3.63	11	11	0	0	0	0	67.0	65	33	27	3	5	24	1	65	7
P. Smith, Phillies	1	2	.333	1.46	8	8	0	0	0	0	37.0	28	11	6	0	0	16	0	35	2
Stading, Pirates	1	4	.200	2.58	12	11	1	1	0	1	69.2	66	29	20	2	4	16	0	57	2
Starling, Yankees	1	4	.200	2.43	10	2	0	3	0	0	37.0	25	16	10	1	0	13	0	19	2
K. Thomas, Braves	1	0	1.000	0.00	1	1	0	0	0	0	6.0	1	0	0	0	0	2	0	4	0
T. Thomas, Yankees	1	2	.333	4.37	10	7	0	2	0	1	35.0	34	24	17	0	1	27	0	21	3
Trudeau, Yankees	2	1	.667	1.96	10	8	0	0	0	0	46.0	37	13	10	0	1	15	0	35	0
Ubiera, Pirates	0	2	.000	6.17	8	2	0	2	0	0	11.2	16	10	8	0	0	7	0	8	0
Valenzuela, Astros	0	3	.000	3.18	12	8	0	1	0	0	56.2	58	26	20	5	2	18	3	31	6
Vargas, Astros	2	1	.667	4.06	14	10	0	1	0	0	75.1	80	46	34	3	4	25	1	46	4
Victor, Astros	4	3	.571	3.42	13	7	2	2	1	0	52.2	50	31	20	1	0	22	1	28	0
Villalobos, Pirates	0	0	.000	3.86	5	0	0	3	0	1	9.1	9	4	4	1	0	3	0	2	0
Vizcaino, Astros⊕	4	2	.667	2.92	16	3	0	4	0	0	37.0	31	18	12	1	0	19	1	28	2
Watts, Phillies⊕	0	0	.000	4.63	7	0	0	1	0	0	11.2	12	8	6	1	0	5	1	13	0
Wayland, Pirates	0	0	.000	0.00	4	0	0	3	0	1	4.2	4	1	0	0	0	2	0	5	0
Welch, Pirates	0	0	.000	8.31	4	0	0	3	0	0	4.1	4	4	4	0	2	6	0	3	0
Whitaker, Rangers	2	2	.500	2.38	20	1	0	12	0	3	53.0	45	21	14	1	2	14	3	56	3
C. White, Phillies	2	3	.400	3.86	17	1	2	0	1	46.2	50	28	20	1	1	10	0	33	2
D. White, White Sox	9	3	.750	2.51	13	10	3	1	0	0	82.1	81	32	23	2	1	7	1	58	2
Williams, Dodgers⊕	0	0	.000	0.00	2	0	0	0	0	0	3.0	4	4	0	0	0	4	0	1	0
Winbush, Rangers	3	1	.750	2.05	7	3	0	2	0	1	26.1	17	6	6	0	1	10	0	33	1
Winfield, Pirates	1	2	.333	6.75	10	0	0	6	0	0	13.1	20	13	10	0	0	14	0	4	0
Winter, Blue Jays⊕	3	2	.600	3.22	17	3	0	7	0	0	36.1	31	18	13	3	1	22	0	42	4
Yeager, Yankees⊕	5	1	.833	0.58	17	0	0	12	0	7	46.1	34	5	3	1	0	6	0	34	1
York, White Sox	1	0	1.000	3.68	5	1	0	0	0	0	14.2	18	9	6	1	0	9	0	19	0
Zielinski, Reds	0	0	.000	0.00	6	0	0	3	0	0	12.0	7	2	0	0	0	5	1	10	0

BALKS—Azocar, Hansen, Mena, Perez, Vargas, 3 each; Mat. Baker, Broussard, Carreno, Fick, Mathews, Monte, Morris, Nunez, Pardo, Pena, E. Santana, T. Thomas, Victor, Winbush, 2 each; Armstrong, Blankenship, Burgos, DeLeon, Diaz, Garcia, Guance, Guercio, Guzman, Heredia, Hernandez, Hibberd, Hill, James, Jefts, Jenkins, Lampkin, Litwin, McClear, Mesa, Miller, Mitchell, Morban, Mosquera, Nelson, Patterson, Peterson, Phillips, Ramirez, Remigio, Russo, Scanlan, Sheeks, Siblerud, Simmons, M. Smith, Stading, Trudeau, C. White, Winfield, 1 each.

COMBINATION SHUTOUTS—Mangham-Baker, Johnson-Heredia, Astros; Santana-Hightower, Winters-Hightower, Blue Jays; Jiminez-Newsome, Guzman-Jimenez, Thomas-Groves, Natera-Jones, Braves; Duffy-Phillips, Dodgers; Broussard-Hendrix-Evans-Gray, Smith-Knox-Gray, White-Scanlan, Smith-Evans-Siblerud, Phillies; Hibberd-Dial, Meadows-Patterson, Dial-Rogers, Pardo-Whitaker-Ballista, Dial-Schofield-Baker, Rangers; Cieslak-Bacon, Reds; Filippi-Jefferson-Morgan, Filippi-Carr, White Sox; Azocar-Monte 2, McClear-Yeager 2, Trudeau-Yeager 2, Armstrong-Carreno, Thomas-Yeager, Gibbs-Yeager, Yankees.

NO-HIT GAMES—None.

Pioneer League

SUMMER CLASS A CLASSIFICATION

CHAMPIONSHIP WINNERS IN PREVIOUS YEARS

1939—Twin Falls° .581	1954—Salt Lake City .595	1969—Ogden .620
1940—Salt Lake City .608	Great Falls (4th)° .530	1970—Idaho Falls .629
Ogden (4th)° .492	1955—Boise .588	1971—Great Falls .643
1941—Boise .623	Magic Valley (4th)° .489	1972—Billings .694
Ogden (2nd)° .598	1956—Boise .561	1973—Billings .629
1942—Pocatello† .690	1957—Salt Lake City .650	1974—Idaho Falls .569
Boise .683	Billings† .582	1975—Great Falls .577
1943-44-45—Did not operate.	1958—Great Falls .582	1976—Great Falls .577
1946—Twin Falls‡ .585	Boise† .615	1977—Lethbridge .629
Salt Lake City† .585	1959—Boise .633	1978—Billings x .735
1947—Salt Lake City .618	Billings (2nd)° .523	1979—Helena .623
Twin Falls† .600	1960—Boise† .686	Lethbridge y .559
1948—Pocatello .611	Idaho Falls .650	1980—Lethbridge y .743
Twin Falls (2nd)° .595	1961—Boise .638	Billings y .629
1949—Twin Falls .624	Great Falls° .571	1981—Calgary .657
Pocatello (3rd)° .595	1962—Boise§ .565	Butte y .557
1950—Pocatello .635	Billings† .706	1982—Medicine Hat y .629
Billings (3rd)° .571	1963—Idaho Falls .702	Idaho Falls .600
1951—Salt Lake City .618	Magic Valley† .643	1983—Billings y .614
Great Falls (3rd)° .559	1964—Treasure Valley .615	Calgary .600
1952—Pocatello .595	1965—Treasure Valley .530	
Idaho Falls (2nd)° .573	1966—Ogden .591	
1953—Ogden .679	1967—Ogden .621	
Salt Lake C. (4th)° .527	1968—Ogden .609	

°Won four-club playoff. †Won split-season playoff. ‡Ended first half in tie with Salt Lake City and won one-game playoff. §Ended first half in tie with Billings and Great Falls and won playoff. xBillings (first place) defeated Idaho Falls (second place) in First Place-Second Place playoff. yLeague divided in Northern and Southern divisions; won two-club playoff.

STANDING OF CLUBS AT CLOSE OF SEASON, AUGUST 31

NORTHERN DIVISION

Club	Hel.	G.F.	M.H.	Cal.	Bil.	But.	I.F.	Poc.	W.	L.	T.	Pct.	G.B.
Helena (Independent)	....	5	5	8	3	7	7	9	44	24	0	.647	......
Great Falls (Dodgers)	5	....	8	5	4	4	4	7	37	31	0	.544	7
Medicine Hat (Blue Jays)	5	2	....	5	2	6	6	6	32	38	0	.457	13
Calgary (Expos)	2	5	5	....	4	3	5	4	28	42	0	.400	17

SOUTHERN DIVISION

Club	Hel.	G.F.	M.H.	Cal.	Bil.	But.	I.F.	Poc.	W.	L.	T.	Pct.	G.B.
Billings (Reds)	5	6	8	6	....	4	8	10	47	21	0	.691	......
Butte (Mariners)	3	6	4	7	6	....	6	6	38	32	0	.543	10
Idaho Falls (A's)	3	4	4	5	2	4	....	5	27	41	0	.397	20
Pocatello (Co-op)	1	3	4	6	0	4	5	....	23	47	0	.329	25

Major league affiliations in parentheses.

Playoff—Helena defeated Billings, three games to one, to win league championship.

Regular-Season Attendance—Billings, 96,670; Butte, 25,766; Calgary, 32,562; Great Falls, 64,309; Helena, 20,199; Idaho Falls, 18,043; Medicine Hat, 51,401; Pocatello, 26,346. Playoffs, 6,589.

Managers—Billings, Larry Barton; Butte, Manuel Estrada; Calgary, Talcott Creech; Great Falls, Kevin Kennedy; Helena, Harry Gurley; Idaho Falls, Jim Nettles; Medicine Hat, Duane Larson; Pocatello, Ron Mihal.

All-Star Team: 1B—John Daugherty, Helena; 2B—Daniel Clark, Butte; 3B—Ruben Machado, Billings; SS—Brooks Shumake, Billings; OF—Darryl Landrum, Medicine Hat; Jonathan Groth, Billings; Evan Evans, Pocatello; C—Mark Berry, Billings; DH—Edward Jacobo, Great Falls; P—Gregory Brinkman, Butte; Gregory Mayberry, Great Falls; John Dodd, Calgary; Manager—Larry Barton, Billings.

(Compiled by William J. Weiss, League Statistician, San Mateo, Calif.)

CLUB BATTING

Club	Pct.	G.	AB.	R.	OR.	H.	TB.	2B.	3B.	HR.	RBI.	GW.	SH.	SF.	HP.	BB.	Int. BB.	SO.	SB.	CS.	LOB.
Billings	.306	68	2444	522	326	749	1104	130	36	51	443	41	12	30	23	323	7	449	58	24	561
Helena	.303	68	2402	556	398	728	1042	132	25	44	462	38	25	25	20	418	13	424	97	36	571
Great Falls	.301	68	2332	447	441	701	971	105	36	31	374	31	28	18	22	306	12	348	85	23	515
Medicine Hat	.281	70	2494	456	504	700	1063	112	22	69	390	26	14	20	12	350	6	554	86	35	579
Butte	.275	70	2370	449	422	652	929	126	35	27	379	36	19	34	27	360	7	511	111	30	529
Calgary	.275	70	2443	404	525	671	915	108	23	30	333	20	32	13	13	309	10	504	84	49	549
Idaho Falls	.265	68	2330	357	446	617	813	91	24	19	300	24	12	22	18	276	10	417	67	31	540
Pocatello	.260	70	2317	394	523	602	826	93	19	31	326	15	21	17	23	306	4	573	87	27	509

INDIVIDUAL BATTING

(Leading Qualifiers for Batting Championship—189 or More Plate Appearances)

°Bats lefthanded.   †Switch-hitter.

Player and Club	Pct.	G.	AB.	R.	H.	TB.	2B.	3B.	HR.	RBI.	GW.	SH.	SF.	HP.	BB.	Int. BB.	SO.	SB.	CS.
Daugherty, John, Helena†	.402	66	259	77	104	179	26	2	15	82	6	0	2	2	52	10	48	16	3
Machalec, Mark, Butte	.366	65	235	60	86	112	13	2	3	40	2	1	4	1	45	2	21	10	3
Reid, Patrick, Helena	.363	55	212	57	77	101	9	6	1	41	3	5	2	0	31	0	38	11	5
Shumake, Brooks, Billings°	.348	56	204	52	71	106	10	5	5	38	6	2	5	2	31	0	37	9	5
Jacobo, Edward, Great Falls	.346	63	231	51	80	128	18	3	8	48	3	0	2	2	41	0	39	4	0
Bryant, John, Billings	.345	46	165	32	57	79	12	2	2	23	3	1	0	7	25	1	28	5	4
Flores, Norberto, Great Falls°	.333	65	237	53	79	113	14	7	2	31	3	2	1	0	51	2	36	19	3

Player and Club	Pct.	G.	AB.	R.	H.	TB.	2B.	3B.	HR.	RBI.	GW.	SH.	SF.	HP.	BB.	Int. BB.	SO.	SB.	CS.
Evans, Evan, Pocatello	.331	67	257	56	85	135	13	5	9	56	1	3	4	1	22	1	82	17	1
Holcomb, Ted, Great Falls°	.330	60	203	46	67	82	8	2	1	33	1	7	3	0	31	2	27	6	2
Berry, Mark, Billings	.330	52	191	53	63	105	15	3	7	43	3	1	1	4	20	1	22	4	0

Departmental Leaders: G—Munford, 70; AB—Yelding, 304; R—Daugherty, 77; H—Daugherty, 104; TB—Daugherty, 179; 2B—Daugherty, 26; 3B—Flores, 7; HR—Landrum, 17; RBI—Daugherty, 82; GWRBI—Munford, 8; SH—Graf, Heist, Holcomb, 7; SF—Riley, 6; HP—Bryant, Patterson; 7; BB—Daugherty, Groth, 52; IBB—Daugherty, 10; SO—Landrum, 94; SB—Anderson, 35; CS—Yelding, 11.

(All Players—Listed Alphabetically)

Player and Club	Pct.	G.	AB.	R.	H.	TB.	2B.	3B.	HR.	RBI.	GW.	SH.	SF.	HP.	BB.	Int. BB.	SO.	SB.	CS.
Anderson, John, Butte°	.316	59	209	47	66	95	11	6	2	24	2	3	0	1	39	0	56	35	7
Armstrong, Eldridge, Idaho Falls	.258	59	198	27	51	70	8	1	3	24	1	1	3	2	26	1	45	3	0
Batista, Juan, Calgary†	.270	69	252	48	68	97	21	1	2	28	1	5	3	2	49	0	43	7	7
Beltre, Esteban, Calgary	.200	18	20	1	4	4	0	0	0	2	0	0	0	2	0	0	8	1	0
Berry, Mark, Billings	.330	52	191	53	63	105	15	3	7	43	3	1	1	4	20	1	22	4	0
Boyer, Mickey, Idaho Falls	.273	43	139	36	38	51	4	0	3	26	0	0	3	1	27	0	23	7	2
Brito, Adan, Idaho Falls	.239	40	134	16	32	39	3	2	0	18	0	2	4	0	18	0	24	5	4
Bryant, John, Billings	.345	46	165	32	57	79	12	2	2	23	3	1	0	7	25	1	28	5	4
Cabrera, Antonio, Idaho Falls	.268	42	168	22	45	54	5	2	0	17	3	3	1	0	20	2	11	7	0
Cacciaguida, Michael, Medicine Hat°..	.331	41	121	33	40	60	8	0	4	17	1	2	0	0	35	2	13	5	2
Campbell, Michael, Billings	.250	18	4	1	1	2	1	0	0	0	0	0	0	0	1	0	0	0	0
Carlucci, David, Great Falls	.316	63	237	34	75	109	8	4	6	40	5	1	4	3	19	0	42	1	1
Chetock, Mark, Helena	.297	65	202	44	60	77	9	1	2	40	3	3	5	2	47	0	29	6	5
Chewey, Franklin, Billings	.185	12	27	2	5	5	0	0	0	3	0	0	0	1	0	0	6	0	1
Cisco, Jeffrey, Calgary†	.227	39	119	16	27	30	1	1	0	7	1	0	0	0	16	0	19	5	4
Clark, Daniel, Butte	.308	52	185	46	57	99	11	5	7	59	5	0	5	0	45	1	47	7	0
Coates, Terry, Idaho Falls°	.257	16	35	6	9	13	4	0	0	6	0	0	1	0	10	0	9	0	0
Conte, Michael, Pocatello	.207	56	164	27	34	49	7	1	2	24	0	0	2	1	37	2	52	0	0
Cook, Michael, Calgary	.000	10	0	0	0	0	0	0	0	0	0	0	0	0	1	0	0	0	0
Cooper, Mark, Medicine Hat	.152	11	33	3	5	5	0	0	0	2	0	0	0	0	2	0	4	0	0
Cummins, Mark, Helena	.281	65	224	51	63	93	16	1	4	36	2	2	1	2	44	0	35	2	2
Cupples, Michael, Idaho Falls	.310	61	245	38	76	101	12	2	3	36	2	0	1	0	25	0	24	2	1
Daniel, Clay, Billings†	.000	9	4	1	0	0	0	0	0	1	0	0	1	0	0	0	1	0	0
Daugherty, John, Helena†	.402	66	259	77	104	179	26	2	15	82	6	0	2	2	52	10	48	16	3
David, Amin, Helena	.265	42	117	24	31	42	6	1	1	19	0	1	1	2	17	1	15	0	0
Delgado, Jose, Idaho Falls	.324	65	275	55	89	132	16	3	7	50	5	0	1	1	31	0	53	11	8
Diaz, Jose, Medicine Hat	.164	40	140	25	23	31	2	0	2	18	1	0	4	3	14	0	32	4	1
Diaz, Serafin, (Tony), Butte°	.216	50	148	28	32	53	12	3	1	14	1	1	0	1	28	1	26	5	3
Dodd, John, Calgary°	.200	15	15	0	3	3	0	0	0	0	0	0	0	0	1	0	4	0	0
Donahue, Charles, Billings°	.280	30	75	19	21	25	2	1	0	14	3	1	2	1	10	0	13	1	1
Dorsey, Craig, Great Falls°	.250	1	4	0	1	1	0	0	0	0	0	0	0	0	0	0	2	0	0
Ducey, Robert, Medicine Hat°	.302	63	235	49	71	123	10	3	12	49	0	1	1	1	41	0	61	13	6
Edwards, Jeffrey, Great Falls°	.125	13	8	0	1	1	0	0	0	0	0	0	0	0	3	0	3	0	0
Estes, Marcus, Great Falls°	.000	14	1	0	0	0	0	0	0	0	0	0	0	0	0	0	1	0	0
Evans, Evan, Pocatello	.331	67	257	56	85	135	13	5	9	56	1	3	4	1	22	1	82	17	1
Fair, Douglas, Pocatello°	.280	64	182	31	51	64	13	0	0	14	0	1	1	0	32	0	39	1	1
Ferreira, Arturo, Idaho Falls	.400	13	5	0	2	2	0	0	0	2	0	0	0	0	2	0	1	0	0
Flores, Norberto, Great Falls°	.333	65	237	53	79	113	14	7	2	31	3	2	1	0	51	2	36	19	3
Fonville, Charlie, Butte	.272	47	162	26	44	57	8	1	1	28	2	1	3	3	19	0	23	6	2
Francois, Manuel, Great Falls	.299	51	174	37	52	68	7	3	1	22	4	1	1	3	18	0	32	10	2
Francour, James, Great Falls	.000	16	0	0	0	0	0	0	0	0	0	0	0	0	0	0	0	0	0
Frazier, Andre, Pocatello	.176	35	108	14	19	25	1	1	1	9	0	0	1	0	13	0	40	5	1
Freitas, John, Helena	.330	35	97	19	32	50	3	0	5	30	4	0	3	0	15	1	12	1	1
Fritz, Jack, Helena	.157	25	51	11	8	10	0	1	0	6	1	0	1	0	10	0	15	1	0
Fulgencio, Jose, Medicine Hat	.211	26	90	8	19	22	3	0	0	14	0	1	2	0	9	0	22	2	0
George, Timothy, Calgary	.375	21	8	0	3	3	0	0	0	3	1	0	0	0	2	0	2	0	0
Germann, Mark, Billings†	.292	61	212	44	62	81	3	5	2	36	0	1	3	1	20	1	23	5	3
Goedde, Michael, Billings	.182	13	11	2	2	2	0	0	0	0	0	1	0	0	6	0	0	0	0
Gould, Robert, Idaho Falls	.375	6	24	4	9	14	0	1	1	2	1	0	0	0	4	0	5	2	0
Graf, Steven, Calgary	.299	60	214	26	64	83	9	5	0	19	2	7	0	0	18	0	42	9	5
Griffin, Danny, Pocatello	.205	56	156	28	32	45	7	0	2	21	2	5	0	5	24	0	66	12	3
Groth, Jonathan, Billings	.317	48	167	57	53	102	14	4	9	38	3	0	1	1	52	2	52	14	4
Guenther, Robert, Medicine Hat	.000	17	1	0	0	0	0	0	0	0	0	0	0	0	0	0	1	0	0
Hayashi, Ross, Pocatello	.667	34	3	2	2	2	0	0	0	0	0	0	0	0	1	0	1	0	0
Hayden, Richard, Butte	.111	6	18	1	2	3	1	0	0	1	0	0	1	0	2	0	7	0	0
Heist, Charles, Helena°	.322	64	245	62	79	103	13	4	1	31	2	7	4	3	33	0	32	30	3
Hilgenberg, Scott, Billings°	.314	64	245	47	77	111	13	3	5	65	4	1	1	0	28	1	32	2	1
Hilton, Charles, Calgary†	.286	13	7	2	2	3	1	0	0	4	1	1	0	0	2	0	1	0	0
Holcomb, Ted, Great Falls°	.330	60	203	46	67	82	8	2	1	33	3	7	3	0	31	2	27	6	2
Holmes, Darren, Great Falls	.000	18	3	0	0	0	0	0	0	0	0	1	0	0	0	0	3	0	0
Hornacek, Jay, Great Falls	.100	4	10	2	1	1	0	0	0	2	0	0	0	0	3	0	3	0	1
Howard, James, Medicine Hat	.294	44	177	38	52	79	11	2	4	30	2	1	1	2	26	0	34	8	5
Ifverson, Ronald, Helena°	.291	59	213	42	62	78	8	1	2	39	4	4	3	2	20	0	32	16	5
Jackson, James, Idaho Falls°	.231	53	182	25	42	66	7	4	3	28	3	0	2	1	24	3	39	2	0
Jacobo, Edward, Great Falls	.346	63	231	51	80	128	18	3	8	48	3	0	2	2	41	0	39	4	0
Jacobsen, Robert, Great Falls	.000	24	1	0	0	0	0	0	0	0	0	0	0	0	0	0	1	0	0
Johnson, Anthony, Idaho Falls	.226	45	146	21	33	40	7	0	0	15	2	0	1	1	21	0	30	3	3
Johnson, John, Pocatello	.325	15	40	12	13	17	1	0	1	7	2	1	0	1	7	0	9	4	0
Jones, Christopher, Billings	.151	21	73	8	11	19	2	0	2	13	1	0	1	0	2	0	24	4	0
Jose, Felix, Idaho Falls†	.217	45	152	16	33	42	6	0	1	18	1	0	2	1	18	1	37	5	1
Kampsen, Douglas, Billings°	.000	23	0	0	0	0	0	0	0	0	0	0	0	0	0	0	0	0	0
Karmeris, Joseph, Great Falls	.295	15	44	8	13	16	1	1	0	11	1	0	0	0	7	0	9	0	0
Kennelley, Steve, Billings	.154	9	26	6	4	5	1	0	0	1	0	0	0	0	5	0	10	0	0
Kijurna, Daniel, Calgary	.283	61	219	38	62	112	13	2	11	44	2	2	3	3	24	0	52	5	2
Kirby, Wayne, Great Falls°	.310	20	84	19	26	35	2	2	1	11	0	1	1	0	12	2	9	19	3
Klopp, Francis, Pocatello	.318	57	211	43	67	110	14	1	9	47	2	2	0	2	15	0	30	4	3
Kopetsky, Brian, Great Falls	.000	2	2	0	0	0	0	0	0	0	0	0	0	0	0	0	0	0	0
Krause, Aaron, Calgary	.000	14	9	0	0	0	0	0	0	0	0	0	0	0	4	0	0	0	0
Lamarr, Jeffrey, Calgary	.304	43	125	28	38	51	5	4	0	11	1	2	0	0	29	2	3	4	3
Landrum, Darryl, Medicine Hat	.237	64	249	49	59	125	9	3	17	55	4	0	2	3	45	1	94	14	5
Larson, Daniel, Butte	.298	49	171	51	51	64	7	3	0	27	0	1	2	4	34	0	25	8	2

Player and Club	Pct.	G.	AB.	R.	H.	TB.	2B.	3B.	HR.	RBI.	GW.	SH.	SF.	HP.	BB.	Int. BB.	SO.	SB.	CS.
Lewis, David, Pocatello	.281	52	203	43	57	63	2	2	0	21	0	2	1	3	16	0	25	12	2
Lewis, Roger, Pocatello	.000	17	0	1	0	0	0	0	0	0	0	0	0	0	0	0	0	0	0
Lono, Joel, Billings*	.333	21	6	1	2	2	0	0	0	1	0	1	0	0	0	0	2	0	0
Lopez, Luis, Great Falls	.327	68	275	60	90	133	15	5	6	61	7	1	2	5	27	1	15	4	4
Lutz, John, Pocatello*	.237	61	194	22	46	53	3	2	0	20	2	0	2	2	19	0	51	11	3
Machado, Ruben, Billings	.319	62	254	49	81	122	19	5	4	43	6	0	3	0	23	0	24	3	1
Machalec, Mark, Butte	.366	65	235	60	86	112	13	2	3	40	2	1	4	1	45	2	21	10	3
Malone, Scott, Helena*	.242	31	66	10	16	19	3	0	0	12	0	0	0	0	17	0	17	0	1
Marston, Tod, Pocatello	.260	57	177	40	46	70	8	5	2	15	0	3	0	3	33	0	42	0	2
Matos, Rafael, Butte†	.220	26	82	13	18	32	6	1	2	16	3	2	0	2	6	0	20	4	1
Mayberry, Gregory, Great Falls*	.143	13	14	1	2	2	0	0	0	0	0	2	0	0	1	0	3	0	0
McCarter, Edward, Helena	.000	16	0	1	0	0	0	0	0	0	0	0	0	0	0	0	0	0	0
Meert, Timothy, Pocatello	.179	44	84	13	15	16	1	0	0	9	1	1	0	0	17	0	24	2	0
Meinhold, Donald, Billings	.295	27	61	11	18	27	3	0	2	7	0	0	0	0	10	0	13	1	0
Monceratt, Pablo, Butte*	.305	47	154	24	47	65	10	1	2	24	2	2	0	1	26	0	32	2	1
Moran, Jorge, Great Falls	.200	10	10	4	2	2	0	0	0	0	0	0	0	1	2	0	2	1	0
Morfin, Arvid, Butte	.192	36	120	13	23	29	2	2	0	8	1	2	2	1	12	0	39	1	1
Morrison, Brian, Medicine Hat	.267	63	232	34	62	92	8	2	6	32	1	1	0	2	25	0	90	0	3
Mulvey, Edward, Calgary	.500	21	2	0	1	1	0	0	0	0	0	0	0	0	0	0	0	1	0
Munford, Willie, Medicine Hat	.318	70	280	53	89	123	14	1	6	53	8	0	0	0	48	2	28	4	1
Myers, Gregory, Medicine Hat*	.316	38	133	20	42	57	9	0	2	20	3	3	1	0	16	1	6	0	0
Neves, Kevin, Pocatello	.314	11	35	3	11	11	0	0	0	3	0	1	0	0	2	0	4	0	2
Nowakowski, Joseph, Medicine Hat	.331	42	133	19	44	63	6	2	3	22	1	0	3	0	8	0	21	1	0
Nunez, Dario, Pocatello	.256	35	129	7	33	36	3	0	0	16	1	3	0	0	9	0	16	3	4
O'Leary, William, Butte	.279	43	147	26	41	52	9	1	0	25	2	1	3	4	16	0	34	2	1
Pace, George, Billings*	.329	39	170	31	56	86	8	5	4	29	2	0	2	1	12	0	35	1	0
Pacheco, Ernest, Calgary	.000	7	1	0	0	0	0	0	0	0	0	0	0	0	1	0	1	0	0
Patterson, Kenneth, Idaho Falls	.313	59	217	40	68	94	12	4	2	31	2	0	2	7	20	0	40	13	6
Perez, Javier, Calgary	.269	18	26	3	7	9	0	1	0	5	1	0	1	0	3	0	6	0	0
Petit, Rolando, Butte	.154	11	26	5	4	6	2	0	0	1	0	0	0	0	1	0	7	0	0
Picart, Juan, Great Falls	.306	16	62	12	19	21	2	0	0	9	0	2	0	0	5	0	5	6	1
Pierce, Troy, Calgary	.000	9	1	0	0	0	0	0	0	0	0	0	0	0	0	0	1	0	0
Pregon, David, Calgary*	.310	67	252	43	78	119	18	4	5	51	2	0	0	1	43	6	57	1	3
Ramont, Shaye, Calgary	.000	19	3	0	0	0	0	0	0	0	0	0	0	0	0	0	3	0	0
Ray, Bregg, Butte	.275	43	131	20	36	51	2	5	1	17	4	1	3	1	15	0	25	7	0
Reburn, Scott, Billings	.100	13	10	1	1	2	1	0	0	1	0	1	0	0	0	0	7	0	0
Reid, Patrick, Helena	.363	55	212	57	77	101	9	6	1	41	3	5	2	0	31	0	38	11	5
Riedl, Jordan, Helena	.232	61	177	46	41	66	4	3	5	32	4	1	1	0	42	0	48	1	3
Reilly, John, Calgary	.214	26	84	10	18	19	1	0	0	12	1	0	0	0	5	0	15	2	1
Reynolds, Dennis, Calgary*	.000	14	0	0	0	0	0	0	0	0	0	0	0	0	0	0	0	1	0
Riley, Darren, Billings*	.312	65	247	47	77	94	8	0	3	47	4	1	6	2	34	0	42	4	2
Rise, David, Helena*	.262	52	168	34	44	58	12	1	0	19	2	3	1	2	30	0	27	1	0
Ritch, Harris, Great Falls	.324	55	185	28	60	82	11	4	1	36	1	2	1	4	17	3	25	4	3
Robles, Daniel, Great Falls*	.210	41	119	18	25	31	4	1	0	10	0	1	0	1	14	0	27	2	2
Rodriguez, Ignacio, Calgary	.279	60	215	34	60	72	9	0	1	32	0	3	1	1	27	1	52	6	5
Rogers, Sebastian, Billings	.188	13	16	1	3	4	1	0	0	0	0	0	0	0	0	0	2	0	0
Rosario, Melvin, Great Falls	.143	8	7	0	1	1	0	0	0	1	0	0	0	0	0	0	4	0	0
Rowan, Paul, Helena*	.229	46	96	23	22	34	7	1	1	25	2	0	4	0	19	1	23	1	0
Russ, Kevin, Idaho Falls	.255	63	239	55	61	81	7	5	1	31	2	1	1	1	14	3	45	11	8
Rypien, Timothy, Medicine Hat	.292	31	106	14	31	41	4	0	2	13	1	3	2	1	15	0	18	1	0
St. Claire, Steven, Calgary	.000	13	9	0	0	0	0	0	0	0	0	0	0	0	0	0	3	0	0
Samples, Van, Calgary	.303	65	238	53	72	110	9	1	9	47	3	0	2	2	45	2	59	19	9
Sanchez, Miguel, Medicine Hat	.500	13	2	0	1	2	1	0	0	0	0	0	0	0	0	0	1	0	0
Santana, Osvaldo, Butte	.138	38	109	13	15	23	5	0	1	9	2	0	0	4	13	0	51	1	0
Satnat, Dale, Great Falls*	.000	22	1	0	0	0	0	0	0	0	0	0	0	0	1	0	1	0	0
Schlichting, John, Great Falls	.316	46	190	35	60	78	10	1	2	35	2	1	1	0	15	0	17	5	0
Scott, Shell, Pocatello	.239	65	222	36	53	83	14	2	4	46	4	1	1	4	35	1	48	15	4
Scott, Timothy, Great Falls	.429	13	7	1	3	6	0	0	1	1	0	0	0	1	0	0	3	0	0
Shumake, Brooks, Billings*	.348	56	204	52	71	106	10	5	5	38	6	2	5	2	31	0	37	9	5
Sigler, Allen, Billings*	.297	56	175	43	52	82	12	3	4	33	6	0	3	2	35	1	48	1	1
Silva, Jose, Calgary	.279	41	140	25	39	48	3	0	2	20	2	0	0	1	17	0	23	9	2
Slover, Robert, Calgary*	.257	66	230	42	59	68	5	2	0	23	2	5	3	2	26	1	47	10	4
Spisok, Jeffrey, Billings	.280	16	50	6	14	15	1	0	0	3	0	1	1	0	7	0	10	3	1
Stender, Scott, Pocatello*	.000	14	1	0	0	0	0	0	0	0	0	0	0	0	0	0	1	0	0
Stis, Douglas, Calgary	.000	12	2	0	0	0	0	0	0	0	0	0	0	0	0	0	1	0	0
Tavarez, Alfonso, Calgary	.262	65	252	35	66	83	13	2	0	25	0	6	0	1	3	0	32	6	4
Tengan, Kyle, Pocatello	.269	38	93	12	25	29	4	0	0	10	0	2	2	19	0	21	1	1
Toler, Gregory, Billings	.347	16	49	8	17	27	4	0	2	4	0	0	0	1	9	0	11	1	0
Tonucci, Norman, Medicine Hat	.264	69	258	50	68	108	13	3	7	36	2	2	2	0	40	0	83	3	2
Torres, Philip, Great Falls	.500	29	2	1	1	1	0	0	0	0	0	0	0	0	0	0	1	0	0
Trasacco, Francesco, Billings	.500	19	2	0	1	1	0	0	0	0	0	0	0	0	0	0	1	0	0
Treadway, Douglas, Great Falls	.500	15	2	0	1	1	0	0	0	2	0	0	0	0	0	0	0	0	0
Tucker, Preston, Pocatello	.224	21	58	4	13	18	2	0	1	8	0	1	1	1	5	0	22	0	2
Uribe, Jorge, Butte	.227	52	176	31	40	61	6	3	3	29	3	3	3	3	23	1	45	17	8
Valiente, Nestor, Butte	.301	47	166	29	50	80	14	2	4	35	3	1	4	1	18	1	22	2	0
Vega, Luis, Butte	.302	27	86	9	26	31	5	0	0	18	2	0	3	0	15	1	23	2	1
Veras, Camilo, Idaho Falls	.235	35	115	17	27	41	6	1	2	16	2	1	0	0	12	0	23	1	3
Vizquel, Omar, Butte	.311	15	45	7	14	16	2	0	0	4	1	0	1	0	3	0	8	2	0
Walker, Michael, Idaho Falls	.275	57	211	37	58	70	8	2	0	20	2	2	1	4	20	0	40	6	2
Warren, Mark, Idaho Falls	.275	40	120	17	33	35	2	0	0	10	3	2	0	0	15	0	21	1	1
Williams, Jimmy, Great Falls	.000	8	1	0	0	0	0	0	0	0	0	0	0	0	0	0	1	0	0
Yelding, Eric, Medicine Hat	.309	67	304	61	94	132	14	6	4	29	2	0	2	0	26	0	46	31	11
Young, Raymond, Great Falls	.000	13	4	0	0	0	0	0	0	0	0	0	0	0	0	0	1	0	0
Zapolski, Timothy, Great Falls	.196	18	51	8	10	15	0	1	1	9	0	0	0	2	11	0	18	0	0
Zehr, Theodore, Great Falls	.196	51	163	29	32	44	5	2	1	14	2	6	2	0	29	2	16	4	1

The following pitchers, listed alphabetically by club, with games in parentheses, had no plate appearances, primarily through use of designated hitters:

BILLINGS—Driver, Frank (9); Neuberger, James (6); Soto, Osvaldo (12).

BUTTE—Bowden, James (14); Brinkman, Gregory (15); French, Steven (18); Kinney, Bradley (17); Ochs, Kevin (19); Reinholtz, Jack (2); Steinert, Paul (17); Thienpont, Gregory (17); Vilella, Lazaro (13); White, Logan (25); Wood, Michael (21).

CALGARY—Guilbe, Victor (8); Morales, Nicolas (7); Thesken, Randy (3).

GREAT FALLS—Criswell, Timothy (5); Nelson, Jeffrey (1).

HELENA—Helton, Charles (12); Macko, Bradley (13); Manweiler, Steven (12); Plumleigh, Charles (17); Poppe, Steven (14); Roth, Michael (12); Smith, James (5); Smith, Marc (8); Strickland, Lonnie (8); Tetreault, Michael (1); Trautwein, John (19); Wolin, Harry (17); Young, Bruce (14).

IDAHO FALLS—Applegate, Russell (26); Balsley, Darren (14); Figueroa, Victor (7); Gillespie, Mark (20); Gonzalez, John (13); Hassel, Robert (11); Leonette, Mark (4); Levander, Scott (6); Nunez, Ramon (19); Reyes, Basilio (13); Sabo, Scott (14); Vantrease, Roberts (8); Wilridge, James (12).

MEDICINE HAT—Blake, Bruce (25); Burgess, Christopher (6); Englund, Timothy (13); Johnson, Dane (10); Lounello, Stephen (10); Moyer, Richard (12); Provence, Todd (12); Richardson, Jeffrey (18); Rutledge, Guy (12); Saitta, Patrick (14); Shanks, William (12); Turano, Gerald (5); Wasilewski, Thomas (21).

POCATELLO—Anderson, Stephen (18); Hanna, David (17); Hill, Christopher (14); Horrell, Christopher (3); Lindquist, Dan (3); Lipson, Stefan (2); Neal, Scott (21); Schultz, Timothy (24); Spector, Douglas (14); Swain, Gregory (20); Weatherly, John (11); Werner, Michael (1).

GRAND SLAM HOME RUNS—Boyer, Clark, Daugherty, Freitas, Groth, Hilgenberg, Munford, Ritch, Shumake, Valiente, 1 each.

AWARDED FIRST BASE ON CATCHER'S INTERFERENCE—Rowan 2 (Conte, Valiente); Evans 2 (Rypien, Warren); Scott 2 (Carlucci, Warren); Boyer (Cooper); Cooper (Cisco); Flores (Rise); Heist (Berry); Machado (Vega); Munford (Conte).

CLUB FIELDING

Club	Pct.	G.	PO.	A.	E.	DP.	PB.	Club	Pct.	G.	PO.	A.	E.	DP.	PB.
Billings	.9498	68	1793	780	136	73	28	Butte	.942	70	1836	824	163	55	22
Helena	.9497	68	1789	778	136	62	23	Great Falls	.940	68	1753	666	155	57	25
Calgary	.943	70	1845	817	160	80	23	Idaho Falls	.935	68	1745	797	177	69	17
Medicine Hat	.943	70	1840	850	163	62	19	Pocatello	.930	70	1753	800	192	54	34

INDIVIDUAL FIELDING

*Throws lefthanded.

FIRST BASEMEN

Player and Club	Pct.	G.	PO.	A.	E.	DP.	Player and Club	Pct.	G.	PO.	A.	E.	DP.
Coates, Idaho Falls	1.000	5	39	1	0	4	Meinhold, Billings	.984	8	60	2	1	9
Conte, Pocatello	.982	29	262	18	5	16	Monceratt, Butte*	.980	40	381	22	7	30
Daugherty, Helena*	.987	63	583	33	8	47	Munford, Medicine Hat	.986	57	503	52	8	49
Ducey, Medicine Hat	.965	16	132	6	5	12	PREGON, Calgary	.9904	60	483	34	5	52
Fair, Idaho Falls	.971	18	125	7	4	12	Riedl, Helena*	1.000	4	21	2	0	2
Fonville, Butte	.969	35	274	12	9	16	Reilly, Calgary	1.000	2	3	0	0	1
Griffin, Pocatello	.943	8	49	1	3	3	Rowan, Helena*	1.000	5	38	0	0	1
Hilgenberg, Billings*	.9903	62	565	45	6	55	Schlichting, Great Falls	1.000	10	63	6	0	5
Jackson, Idaho Falls	.974	51	461	25	13	40	Veras, Idaho Falls	.900	1	9	0	1	2
Kijurna, Calgary	.977	17	119	9	3	14	Warren, Idaho Falls	.938	14	115	7	8	8
Lopez, Great Falls	.966	55	418	32	16	39	Zapolski, Great Falls	.981	7	49	3	1	1
Marston, Pocatello	.962	25	171	6	7	13							

SECOND BASEMEN

Player and Club	Pct.	G.	PO.	A.	E.	DP.	Player and Club	Pct.	G.	PO.	A.	E.	DP.
Batista, Calgary	.962	14	28	22	2	5	Kennelley, Billings	.893	7	11	14	3	2
Boyer, Idaho Falls	.913	6	6	15	2	3	Larson, Butte	.900	40	83	108	22	13
Brito, Idaho Falls	.950	13	25	32	3	10	D. Lewis, Pocatello	.916	32	68	84	14	11
Bryant, Billings	1.000	1	3	2	0	1	Machado, Billings	.964	5	11	16	1	5
Cabrera, Idaho Falls	.970	36	98	125	7	27	Matos, Butte	.900	17	40	41	9	8
Cacciaguida, Medicine Hat	.965	36	64	129	7	21	Nunez, Pocatello	.893	9	21	29	6	6
Clark, Butte	.925	17	27	47	6	9	Picart, Great Falls	.824	7	13	15	6	1
Cummins, Helena	.952	65	143	194	17	46	Reid, Helena	.905	3	10	9	2	4
David, Helena	1.000	1	2	3	0	1	Ritch, Great Falls	.970	11	22	43	2	7
Diaz, Medicine Hat	1.000	1	6	9	0	2	Scott, Pocatello	.927	17	39	50	7	11
Donahue, Billings	1.000	1	0	1	0	0	Spisok, Billings	.877	15	29	21	7	8
Fritz, Helena	.926	10	9	16	2	3	Tavarez, Calgary	.948	64	136	193	18	48
GERMANN, Billings	.967	50	105	133	8	35	Tengan, Pocatello	.978	17	47	40	2	12
Howard, Medicine Hat	.949	38	88	118	11	24	Vizquel, Butte	1.000	1	0	4	0	1
Johnson, Idaho Falls	.917	15	34	32	6	4	Zehr, Great Falls	.946	51	102	126	13	31

THIRD BASEMEN

Player and Club	Pct.	G.	PO.	A.	E.	DP.	Player and Club	Pct.	G.	PO.	A.	E.	DP.
Batista, Calgary	1.000	1	1	2	0	0	Neves, Pocatello	1.000	1	0	2	0	0
Berry, Billings	.500	1	0	1	1	0	Nowakowski, Medicine Hat	.750	2	0	3	1	0
Boyer, Idaho Falls	.868	33	19	73	14	6	O'Leary, Butte	.939	43	28	95	8	6
Cabrera, Idaho Falls	1.000	2	0	3	0	0	Perez, Calgary	.737	13	10	4	5	1
Chetock, Helena	.833	17	8	27	7	2	Petit, Butte	.600	2	1	2	2	0
Clark, Butte	.925	25	22	52	6	1	Picart, Great Falls	.824	7	13	15	6	1
Conte, Pocatello	.857	3	2	4	1	0	Pregon, Calgary	.875	9	12	16	4	1
David, Helena	.804	21	8	33	10	1	Ray, Butte	.905	5	3	16	2	1
Fair, Idaho Falls	.950	8	3	16	1	0	Reid, Helena	.859	29	21	58	13	5
Ferreira, Idaho Falls	.750	2	3	1	1	1	Reilly, Calgary	.778	4	1	6	2	0
Fritz, Helena	.808	14	4	17	5	2	Ritch, Great Falls	.843	32	21	38	11	3
Holcomb, Great Falls	.808	32	19	40	14	3	Scott, Pocatello	.900	8	4	14	2	2
Hornacek, Great Falls	.750	2	1	5	2	1	Shumake, Billings	.800	4	5	7	3	0
Johnson, Idaho Falls	.738	27	18	41	21	10	SLOVER, Calgary	.946	60	35	122	9	6
Jones, Billings	.868	16	6	27	5	5	Tengan, Pocatello	.909	7	2	8	1	1
Lutz, Pocatello	.864	51	51	95	23	5	Tonucci, Medicine Hat	.903	69	47	121	18	6
Machado, Billings	.912	51	49	116	16	11	Walker, Idaho Falls	.750	6	6	6	4	0
Matos, Butte	1.000	1	0	3	0	0	Zapolski, Great Falls	1.000	5	7	9	0	1

SHORTSTOPS

Player and Club	Pct.	G.	PO.	A.	E.	DP.	Player and Club	Pct.	G.	PO.	A.	E.	DP.
Batista, Calgary	.920	61	89	199	25	53	D. Lewis, Pocatello	.833	10	14	26	8	2
Beltre, Calgary	.722	15	13	13	10	5	Morfin, Butte	.867	36	55	101	24	16
Brito, Idaho Falls	.871	25	32	69	15	9	Nunez, Pocatello	.917	26	35	86	11	15
Chetock, Helena	.901	49	59	132	21	26	Ray, Butte	.932	32	47	104	11	20
Diaz, Medicine Hat	.914	39	78	124	19	31	Reid, Helena	.925	27	37	87	10	14
Donahue, Billings	.840	21	25	59	16	9	Scott, Pocatello	.911	37	55	120	17	21
Francois, Great Falls	.833	46	70	114	37	24	Shumake, Billings	.914	56	80	166	23	36
Fulgencio, Medicine Hat	.895	25	58	70	15	18	Slover, Calgary	.921	14	21	37	5	8
Germann, Billings	1.000	2	0	5	0	1	Vizquel, Butte	.884	10	13	25	5	4
Holcomb, Great Falls	.891	26	32	74	13	15	WALKER, Idaho Falls	.944	50	75	160	14	26
Howard, Medicine Hat	.914	6	12	20	3	3							

OUTFIELDERS

Player and Club	Pct.	G.	PO.	A.	E.	DP.	Player and Club	Pct.	G.	PO.	A.	E.	DP.
Anderson, Butte	.942	49	61	4	4	0	Lutz, Pocatello	.400	3	2	0	3	0
Armstrong, Idaho Falls	.973	53	67	6	2	2	Machalec, Butte	.975	64	116	3	3	0
Bryant, Billings	.878	39	33	3	5	0	Morrison, Medicine Hat	.886	44	60	2	8	0
Cisco, Calgary	1.000	4	4	1	0	0	Neves, Pocatello	.917	10	10	1	1	0
Coates, Idaho Falls	1.000	3	3	0	0	0	Nowakowski, Medicine Hat	.938	17	15	0	1	0
Delgado, Helena	.970	61	63	2	2	0	Pace, Billings*	.896	33	42	1	5	0
Diaz, Butte	.974	29	34	3	1	0	Patterson, Idaho Falls	.847	42	56	5	11	1
Ducey, Medicine Hat	.983	31	53	5	1	0	Picart, Great Falls	.833	4	4	1	1	0
Evans, Pocatello	.946	66	115	7	7	2	Reilly, Calgary	1.000	6	6	0	0	0
Fair, Pocatello	.903	24	27	1	3	0	Riedl, Helena*	.969	49	59	3	2	0
Flores, Great Falls*	.976	63	116	6	3	3	Riley, Billings	.966	64	107	7	4	0
Frazier, Pocatello	.895	26	46	5	6	2	Robles, Great Falls*	.982	26	50	4	1	1
Gould, Idaho Falls	.875	5	7	0	1	0	Rodriguez, Calgary	.884	57	99	15	15	5
Graf, Calgary	.944	59	128	7	8	1	Rowan, Helena*	.938	15	13	2	1	0
Griffin, Pocatello	.898	42	87	1	10	0	Russ, Idaho Falls*	.913	63	112	4	11	2
Groth, Billings	.975	45	75	4	2	1	Samples, Calgary	.931	64	91	4	7	1
Heist, Helena	.929	59	112	6	9	1	Santana, Butte	.911	35	51	0	5	0
Ifverson, Helena*	.915	45	50	4	5	0	Schlichting, Great Falls	.948	36	52	3	3	2
JACOBO, Great Falls	1.000	51	82	4	0	1	Scott, Pocatello	1.000	5	7	0	0	0
Johnson, Pocatello	1.000	4	3	0	0	0	Shumake, Billings	1.000	1	1	0	0	0
Jose, Idaho Falls	.982	31	48	6	1	3	Sigler, Billings	.961	30	47	2	2	1
Karmeris, Great Falls	1.000	4	1	0	0	0	Silva, Calgary	.833	2	4	1	1	0
Kijurna, Calgary	.976	33	37	3	1	1	Uribe, Butte	.889	52	74	6	10	1
Kirby, Great Falls	.950	20	35	3	2	0	Veras, Idaho Falls	.925	21	36	1	3	0
Klopp, Pocatello	.962	46	68	7	3	0	Warren, Idaho Falls	1.000	1	1	0	0	0
Landrum, Medicine Hat	.879	62	81	6	12	1	Yelding, Medicine Hat	.893	64	99	9	13	1
D. Lewis, Pocatello	.500	1	1	0	1	0	Zapolski, Great Falls	1.000	5	6	0	0	0

CATCHERS

Player and Club	Pct.	G.	PO.	A.	E.	DP.	PB.	Player and Club	Pct.	G.	PO.	A.	E.	DP.	PB.
Berry, Billings	.968	46	325	34	12	4	15	Meert, Pocatello	.946	20	92	14	6	1	12
Carlucci, Great Falls	.975	55	436	39	12	3	19	Meinhold, Billings	.973	13	33	3	1	0	1
Chewey, Billings	.981	12	46	7	1	1	6	Myers, Medicine Hat	.984	35	216	24	4	1	10
Cisco, Calgary	.977	27	162	10	4	2	4	Nowakowski, Medicine Hat	.962	7	43	7	2	0	5
Conte, Pocatello	.949	26	124	24	8	3	13	Rise, Helena	.982	50	336	45	7	2	14
Cooper, Medicine Hat	.951	8	52	6	3	1	0	Rosario, Great Falls	1.000	4	4	0	0	0	1
CUPPLES, Idaho Falls	.986	50	308	54	5	4	8	Rypien, Medicine Hat	.977	27	182	26	5	1	4
David, Helena	1.000	6	41	4	0	0	1	Silva, Calgary	.958	25	166	18	8	0	7
Fair, Pocatello	1.000	1	1	0	0	0	2	Spisok, Billings	1.000	1	6	1	0	0	4
Hayden, Butte	.962	6	46	4	2	1	0	Toler, Billings	.981	16	94	12	2	2	2
Lamarr, Calgary	.951	26	154	19	9	2	12	Tucker, Pocatello	.923	11	51	9	5	0	3
Lopez, Great Falls	.992	14	109	10	1	1	6	Valiente, Butte	.978	45	276	40	7	3	11
Malone, Helena	.988	25	143	17	2	1	8	Vega, Butte	.974	27	173	17	5	0	5
Marston, Pocatello	.953	29	144	20	8	2	4	Warren, Idaho Falls	.960	21	144	24	7	2	9

PITCHERS

Player and Club	Pct.	G.	PO.	A.	E.	DP.	Player and Club	Pct.	G.	PO.	A.	E.	DP.
Anderson, Pocatello	1.000	18	4	4	0	0	Hassel, Idaho Falls*	1.000	11	0	2	0	0
Applegate, Idaho Falls	.833	26	4	11	3	1	Hayashi, Pocatello	1.000	32	1	8	0	0
Balsley, Idaho Falls	.875	14	5	9	2	1	Helton, Helena*	1.000	12	2	5	0	1
Blake, Medicine Hat*	1.000	25	4	5	0	0	Hill, Pocatello	.625	14	0	5	3	0
Bowden, Butte*	1.000	14	5	12	0	1	Hilton, Calgary	.933	17	10	18	2	2
Brinkman, Butte	.893	15	3	22	3	2	Holmes, Great Falls	.867	18	2	11	2	1
Burgess, Medicine Hat	1.000	6	0	4	0	1	Horrell, Pocatello	1.000	3	1	1	0	0
Campbell, Billings	.842	18	4	12	3	1	Jacobsen, Great Falls	.857	24	2	4	1	0
Cook, Calgary	.500	10	1	0	1	0	Johnson, Medicine Hat	.905	10	6	13	2	1
Criswell, Great Falls	1.000	5	2	6	0	0	Kampsen, Billings	.889	23	1	7	1	2
Daniel, Billings*	1.000	8	2	6	0	1	Kinney, Butte	.846	17	4	7	2	1
Dodd, Calgary*	.875	14	7	14	3	1	Krause, Calgary	.909	14	8	2	1	0
Driver, Billings	.857	9	2	4	1	1	Leonette, Idaho Falls	.667	4	1	3	2	0
Edwards, Great Falls*	.875	13	1	6	1	1	Levander, Idaho Falls	.667	6	0	2	1	0
Englund, Medicine Hat	.947	13	7	11	1	0	R. Lewis, Pocatello	.750	16	2	7	3	0
Estes, Great Falls*	1.000	14	0	1	0	0	Lipson, Pocatello	1.000	2	0	1	0	0
Ferreira, Idaho Falls	.818	11	3	6	2	0	Lono, Billings*	1.000	21	2	12	0	0
Figueroa, Idaho Falls	.813	7	2	11	3	1	Lounello, Medicine Hat	.667	10	2	2	2	1
Francour, Great Falls	1.000	16	2	8	0	1	Macko, Helena*	.800	13	0	4	1	0
French, Butte	1.000	18	3	15	0	2	Manweiler, Helena*	.813	12	3	10	3	1
George, Calgary*	1.000	21	2	8	0	0	Mayberry, Great Falls	.957	13	14	8	1	1
Gillespie, Idaho Falls*	.917	20	0	11	1	1	McCarter, Helena	.920	15	8	15	2	0
Goedde, Billings	.895	13	5	12	2	1	Morales, Calgary	.667	7	0	2	1	0
Gonzalez, Idaho Falls	.889	13	1	15	2	1	Moyer, Medicine Hat	.900	12	3	6	1	0
Guenther, Medicine Hat	1.000	17	4	5	0	0	Mulvey, Calgary	1.000	20	7	7	0	0
Guilbe, Calgary	1.000	8	0	2	0	1	NEAL, Pocatello*	1.000	20	3	23	0	1
Hanna, Pocatello	.917	17	9	13	2	1	Neuberger, Billings	.000	6	0	0	1	0

PITCHERS—Continued

Player and Club	Pct.	G.	PO.	A.	E.	DP.	Player and Club	Pct.	G.	PO.	A.	E.	DP.
Nunez, Idaho Falls	.818	19	1	8	2	1	Soto, Billings	.786	12	7	4	3	1
Ochs, Butte	.882	19	3	12	2	0	Spector, Pocatello	.833	14	1	4	1	0
Pacheco, Calgary	1.000	7	1	1	0	0	Steinert, Butte	.909	17	3	7	1	1
Pierce, Calgary	.500	9	1	0	1	0	Stender, Pocatello*	.895	13	0	17	2	1
Plumleigh, Helena	.909	16	4	6	1	0	Stis, Calgary	.875	12	1	6	1	0
Provence, Medicine Hat	.958	12	5	18	1	1	Strickland, Helena	.800	8	0	4	1	1
Ramont, Calgary	.700	19	2	12	6	0	Swain, Pocatello*	.882	20	1	14	2	0
Reburn, Billings	.958	13	9	14	1	0	Tetreault, Helena	1.000	1	0	1	0	0
Reinholtz, Butte*	1.000	2	0	3	0	0	Thesken, Calgary	1.000	3	1	2	0	1
Reyes, Idaho Falls	.762	13	2	14	5	3	Thienpont, Butte*	.947	17	3	15	1	2
Reynolds, Calgary	1.000	13	0	1	0	0	Torres, Great Falls	.857	29	0	6	1	0
Richardson, Medicine Hat	.769	18	8	12	6	0	Trasacco, Billings*	1.000	19	1	6	0	0
Rogers, Billings*	1.000	13	2	13	0	0	Trautwein, Helena	1.000	19	3	5	0	0
Roth, Helena	.889	12	1	7	1	0	Treadway, Great Falls	.875	15	4	10	2	0
Rutledge, Medicine Hat	.667	12	0	2	1	0	Turano, Medicine Hat	.889	5	1	7	1	2
Sabo, Idaho Falls*	.929	14	3	10	1	0	Vantrease, Idaho Falls*	.667	8	0	2	1	0
St. Claire, Calgary	.750	13	2	7	3	0	Vilella, Butte*	.846	13	2	9	2	0
Saitta, Medicine Hat	.759	14	5	17	7	1	Wasilewski, Medicine Hat	.667	21	3	7	5	0
Sanchez, Medicine Hat	1.000	13	1	1	0	0	Weatherly, Pocatello	.500	11	2	0	2	0
Satnat, Great Falls*	.667	22	3	5	4	2	White, Butte	.800	25	2	6	2	0
Schultz, Pocatello	.733	24	3	8	4	1	Wilridge, Idaho Falls	.667	12	1	3	2	0
Scott, Great Falls	.905	13	8	11	2	0	Wolin, Helena	.667	17	1	1	1	0
Shanks, Medicine Hat	1.000	12	2	3	0	0	Wood, Butte	.833	21	3	7	2	0
Shumake, Billings	1.000	1	0	1	0	0	B. Young, Helena	.909	14	4	16	2	1
J.E. Smith, Helena	.833	5	2	3	1	1	R. Young, Great Falls	.933	13	2	12	1	0
J.M. Smith, Helena*	1.000	8	1	7	0	0							

The following players do not have any recorded accepted chances at the positions indicated; therefore, are not listed in the fielding averages for those particular positions: Cacciaguida, 3b; Cisco, p; Dodd, p; Francois, 2b; Frazier, p; Freitas, 3b; Griffin, p; Jackson, p; Kennelley, 3b; Lindquist, p; Lutz, 2b; Moran, of; Nelson, p; Perez, 2b; Poppe, p; Rosario, p; Samples, c; Spisok, of; Werner, p; Williams, p.

CLUB PITCHING

Club	ERA.	G.	CG.	ShO.	Sv.	IP.	H.	R.	ER.	HR.	HB.	BB.	Int. BB.	SO.	WP.	Bk.
Billings	3.72	68	13	2	18	597.2	589	326	247	34	12	257	3	494	38	11
Butte	4.47	70	8	1	14	612.0	653	422	304	22	19	314	5	483	54	11
Helena	4.64	68	14	2	13	596.1	667	398	307	38	14	251	9	515	57	11
Idaho Falls	4.92	68	6	1	11	581.2	645	446	318	37	25	339	6	434	40	9
Great Falls	5.02	68	12	7	11	584.1	661	441	326	39	19	332	7	537	47	15
Pocatello	5.48	70	9	2	10	584.1	736	523	356	33	21	377	19	387	89	7
Medicine Hat	5.99	70	4	1	14	613.1	719	504	408	50	24	372	8	472	71	14
Calgary	6.41	70	14	3	7	615.0	750	525	439	49	24	406	12	458	80	8

PITCHERS' RECORDS
(Leading Qualifiers for Earned-Run Average Leadership — 56 or More Innings)

*Throws lefthanded.

Pitcher—Club	W.	L.	Pct.	ERA.	G.	GS.	CG.	GF.	ShO.	Sv.	IP.	H.	R.	ER.	HR.	HB.	BB.	Int. BB.	SO.	WP.
Daniel, Billings*	7	0	1.000	2.56	8	8	3	0	1	0	56.1	46	18	16	4	1	8	0	60	1
Plumleigh, Helena	7	1	.875	3.20	16	3	0	8	0	1	56.1	56	27	20	4	0	28	4	70	6
Mayberry, Great Falls	7	4	.636	3.22	13	13	5	0	1	0	89.1	75	47	32	9	3	39	0	89	5
Soto, Billings	5	1	.833	3.27	12	12	3	0	0	0	77.0	79	44	28	3	0	23	0	69	3
Edwards, Great Falls*	4	5	.444	3.55	13	13	2	0	2	0	66.0	83	42	26	2	0	26	0	75	5
Reburn, Billings	7	4	.636	3.66	13	13	2	0	0	0	86.0	84	50	35	4	2	32	0	59	10
Brinkman, Butte	10	2	.833	3.75	15	15	5	0	0	0	98.1	101	56	41	1	4	35	0	76	11
Rogers, Billings*	6	2	.750	3.87	13	13	0	0	0	0	72.0	64	38	31	4	3	57	0	61	6
Gonzalez, Idaho Falls	2	6	.250	3.96	13	12	2	1	0	0	77.1	78	47	34	5	2	40	0	61	5
McCarter, Helena	5	4	.556	4.03	15	14	6	1	1	1	98.1	92	56	44	2	3	31	2	79	6

Departmental Leaders: G—Hayashi, 32; W—Brinkman, 10; L—Neal, 9; Pct.—Daniel, Manweiler, 1.000; GS—Brinkman, 15; CG—McCarter, 6; GF—Hayashi, 27; ShO—Dodd, Edwards, Scott, 2; Sv.—Jacobsen, 8; IP—Brinkman, McCarter, 98.1; H—Krause, Swain, 104; R—St. Claire, 69; ER—Krause, 58; HR—Saitta, 12; HB—Provence, 8; BB—St. Claire, 61; IBB—Schultz, 7; SO—Mayberry, 89; WP—Ramont, 15.

(All Players—Listed Alphabetically)

Pitcher—Club	W.	L.	Pct.	ERA.	G.	GS.	CG.	GF.	ShO.	Sv.	IP.	H.	R.	ER.	HR.	HB.	BB.	Int. BB.	SO.	WP.
Anderson, Pocatello	0	1	.000	7.43	18	0	0	7	0	0	40.0	58	55	33	3	2	38	3	13	12
Applegate, Idaho Falls	7	3	.700	3.23	26	0	0	21	0	4	47.1	53	29	17	4	3	13	0	35	4
Balsley, Idaho Falls	3	6	.333	5.59	14	13	0	1	0	0	77.1	84	63	48	7	5	40	1	68	7
Blake, Medicine Hat*	4	2	.667	5.70	25	1	0	13	0	2	42.2	59	41	27	2	0	22	0	47	2
Bowden, Butte*	5	2	.714	4.09	14	12	1	2	0	0	72.2	70	56	33	4	1	49	0	59	4
Brinkman, Butte	10	2	.833	3.75	15	15	5	0	0	0	98.1	101	56	41	1	4	35	0	76	11
Burgess, Medicine Hat	2	0	1.000	9.28	6	0	0	2	0	0	10.2	16	11	11	1	1	5	0	14	1
Campbell, Billings	4	3	.571	4.42	18	6	0	2	0	1	59.0	60	36	29	5	1	26	0	39	1
Cisco, Calgary	0	0	.000	162.00	1	0	0	0	0	0	.1	3	6	6	2	1	2	0	0	1
Cook, Calgary	0	0	.000	5.93	10	0	0	6	0	0	13.2	22	11	9	0	0	6	0	6	2
Criswell, Great Falls	2	0	1.000	6.95	5	4	1	1	1	0	22.0	28	18	17	2	1	9	1	17	1
Daniel, Billings*	7	0	1.000	2.56	8	8	3	0	1	0	56.1	46	18	16	4	1	8	0	60	1
Dodd, Calgary*	9	2	.818	4.04	14	11	3	2	2	0	91.1	94	49	41	7	0	33	1	69	6
Driver, Billings	1	0	1.000	5.40	9	0	3	0	1	0	23.1	26	16	14	2	1	14	0	16	2
Edwards, Great Falls*	4	5	.444	3.55	13	13	2	0	2	0	66.0	83	42	26	2	0	26	0	75	5
Englund, Medicine Hat	3	2	.600	4.67	13	10	1	1	0	1	71.1	86	43	37	5	1	17	0	61	4
Estes, Great Falls*	0	1	.000	10.89	14	0	0	6	0	0	20.2	39	28	25	5	1	11	0	23	4
Ferreira, Idaho Falls	2	2	.000	3.12	11	3	1	2	0	0	40.1	39	16	14	0	2	17	1	31	1
Figueroa, Idaho Falls	2	2	.500	2.09	7	7	0	0	0	0	43.0	35	22	10	2	2	26	0	29	3
Francour, Great Falls	1	1	.500	3.86	16	1	0	0	0	0	35.0	40	21	15	0	3	27	1	35	3
Frazier, Pocatello	0	0	.000	9.00	1	0	0	0	0	0	1.0	1	1	1	0	0	2	0	1	1
French, Butte	1	2	.333	4.80	18	2	0	7	0	1	50.2	63	42	27	1	2	19	0	27	5
George, Butte	2	2	.500	4.89	21	3	0	5	0	0	53.1	44	35	29	1	2	59	2	44	3
Gillespie, Idaho Falls*	1	4	.200	3.99	20	3	1	12	0	1	38.1	47	27	17	3	0	24	2	32	2
Goedde, Billings	4	4	.500	4.64	13	13	3	0	0	0	75.2	88	54	39	4	1	38	0	45	6
Gonzalez, Idaho Falls	2	6	.250	3.96	13	12	2	1	0	0	77.1	78	47	34	5	2	40	0	61	5
Griffin, Pocatello	0	0	.000	9.00	1	0	0	0	0	0	2.0	2	2	2	1	0	1	0	1	0
Guenther, Medicine Hat	1	2	.333	8.32	17	1	0	2	0	1	44.1	69	48	41	6	1	34	1	48	9
Guilbe, Calgary	0	2	.000	9.92	8	1	0	1	0	0	16.1	20	29	18	2	6	33	0	8	6
Hanna, Pocatello	3	5	.375	4.62	17	7	2	0	1	0	64.1	67	52	33	3	1	45	0	27	12

Pitcher—Club	W.	L.	Pct.	ERA.	G.	GS.	CG.	GF.	ShO.	Sv.	IP.	H.	R.	ER.	HR.	HB.	BB.	Int. BB.	SO.	WP.
Hassel, Idaho Falls*	0	0	.000	12.89	11	0	0	4	0	0	14.2	21	22	21	2	0	14	0	8	3
Hayashi, Pocatello	3	4	.429	3.66	32	0	0	27	0	6	32.0	28	21	13	0	3	24	1	22	2
Helton, Helena*	3	0	1.000	5.09	12	5	0	2	0	0	40.2	46	24	23	1	0	19	0	45	10
Hill, Pocatello	0	6	.000	11.47	14	3	0	2	0	0	24.1	45	37	31	0	3	27	2	15	5
Hilton, Calgary	4	5	.444	5.05	13	13	4	0	0	0	87.1	94	62	49	6	3	46	0	66	9
Holmes, Great Falls	2	5	.286	6.65	18	6	1	4	0	0	44.2	53	41	33	5	2	30	1	29	3
Horrell, Pocatello	0	0	.000	15.43	3	0	0	0	0	0	4.2	9	9	8	0	1	5	0	1	0
Jackson, Idaho Falls	0	0	.000	0.00	1	0	0	1	0	0	1.0	0	0	0	0	0	0	0	0	0
Jacobsen, Great Falls	3	1	.750	2.16	24	0	0	23	0	8	33.1	21	11	8	1	1	12	1	45	3
Johnson, Medicine Hat	1	5	.167	8.42	10	10	0	0	0	0	41.2	43	48	39	2	1	59	0	15	9
Kampsen, Billings	4	3	.571	3.58	23	0	0	20	0	6	32.2	27	18	13	4	1	18	1	37	2
Kinney, Butte	2	7	.222	4.60	17	8	0	5	0	0	60.2	80	49	31	4	1	25	1	59	5
Krause, Calgary	2	8	.200	7.15	14	13	1	1	0	0	73.0	104	66	58	5	1	29	0	67	7
Leonette, Idaho Falls	0	1	.000	2.21	4	4	0	0	0	0	20.1	18	12	5	0	0	10	0	16	1
Levander, Idaho Falls	0	4	.000	9.00	6	0	0	1	0	0	7.0	12	11	7	0	1	8	1	5	0
Lewis, Pocatello	4	6	.400	4.76	16	11	1	3	0	1	81.1	103	56	43	2	0	44	1	63	10
Lindquist, Pocatello*	0	1	.000	21.60	3	1	0	0	0	0	1.2	6	8	4	0	0	5	0	3	3
Lipson, Pocatello	0	1	.000	11.25	2	1	0	1	0	0	4.0	5	5	5	0	0	7	0	1	2
Lono, Billings*	5	4	.556	3.33	21	2	1	18	0	3	46.0	45	21	17	1	0	12	1	38	2
Lounello, Medicine Hat	0	1	.000	5.87	10	0	0	5	0	1	23.0	25	17	15	2	0	19	0	15	1
Macko, Helena*	1	2	.333	8.10	13	2	0	5	0	1	30.0	50	31	27	2	2	22	1	24	6
Manweiler, Helena*	9	0	1.000	4.17	12	11	2	0	0	0	82.0	92	55	38	9	1	27	0	70	3
Mayberry, Great Falls	7	4	.636	3.22	13	13	5	0	1	0	89.1	75	47	32	9	3	39	0	89	5
McCarter, Helena	5	4	.556	4.03	15	14	6	1	1	1	98.1	92	56	44	2	3	31	2	79	6
Morales, Calgary	0	0	.000	10.80	7	0	0	5	0	0	8.1	12	15	10	0	0	13	0	6	4
Moyer, Medicine Hat	3	2	.600	3.40	12	7	1	3	0	0	47.2	36	21	18	4	2	24	2	47	6
Mulvey, Calgary	3	4	.429	7.94	20	0	0	10	0	1	34.0	54	33	30	1	1	21	6	15	5
Neal, Pocatello*	3	9	.250	5.04	20	14	3	1	0	0	85.2	94	68	48	4	4	49	3	88	4
Nelson, Great Falls	0	0	.000	54.00	1	0	0	0	0	0	.2	3	4	4	1	1	3	0	1	0
Neuberger, Billings	0	0	.000	6.91	6	0	0	2	0	1	14.1	20	14	11	1	2	13	0	8	3
Nunez, Idaho Falls	3	3	.500	6.34	19	2	0	7	0	1	38.1	46	37	27	2	1	26	1	35	1
Ochs, Butte	3	2	.600	3.86	19	3	0	9	0	2	51.1	45	28	22	0	3	18	1	37	5
Pacheco, Calgary	1	2	.333	10.00	7	5	0	2	0	0	18.0	27	21	20	1	1	16	0	11	1
Pierce, Calgary	0	1	.000	8.56	9	0	0	6	0	1	13.2	22	14	13	4	0	10	1	8	1
Plumleigh, Helena	7	1	.875	3.20	16	3	0	8	0	1	56.1	56	27	20	0	0	28	4	70	6
Poppe, Helena*	1	2	.333	1.88	14	0	0	9	0	2	14.1	10	7	3	0	0	8	0	17	3
Provence, Medicine Hat	4	5	.444	4.68	12	12	2	0	0	0	67.1	79	48	35	2	8	27	0	31	4
Ramont, Medicine Hat	3	4	.429	5.82	19	8	2	8	0	2	72.2	81	54	47	7	4	38	0	68	15
Reburn, Billings	7	4	.636	3.66	13	13	2	0	0	0	86.0	84	50	35	4	2	32	0	59	10
Reinholtz, Butte*	0	1	.000	5.00	2	2	0	0	0	0	9.0	10	5	5	1	0	0	0	6	1
Reyes, Idaho Falls	2	5	.286	6.11	13	13	1	0	0	0	70.2	84	64	48	6	4	48	0	34	9
Reynolds, Calgary	0	0	.000	11.00	13	0	0	4	0	0	18.0	31	23	22	3	0	19	2	20	2
Richardson, Medicine Hat	4	6	.400	7.20	18	7	0	4	0	0	70.0	96	67	56	7	1	32	1	39	8
Rogers, Billings*	6	2	.750	3.87	13	13	0	0	0	0	72.0	64	38	31	4	3	57	0	61	6
Rosario, Great Falls	0	0	.000	0.00	1	0	0	1	0	0	.1	0	0	0	0	0	0	0	0	0
Roth, Helena	4	4	.500	5.01	12	12	1	0	0	0	50.1	62	50	28	3	1	19	0	42	8
Rutledge, Medicine Hat	2	2	.500	5.52	12	0	0	8	0	3	14.2	15	11	9	0	2	10	1	12	4
Sabo, Idaho Falls*	5	3	.625	4.92	14	11	1	1	0	0	71.1	84	50	39	1	1	44	0	57	4
St. Claire, Calgary	2	7	.222	6.69	13	13	3	0	1	0	72.2	88	69	54	4	2	61	0	44	14
Saitta, Medicine Hat	2	5	.286	7.83	14	13	0	0	0	0	64.1	84	66	56	12	1	48	0	39	6
Sanchez, Medicine Hat	0	0	.000	6.08	13	0	0	12	0	0	13.1	14	9	9	1	2	11	0	12	4
Satnat, Great Falls*	4	2	.667	2.73	22	0	0	8	0	0	33.0	32	20	10	1	0	9	0	20	3
Schultz, Pocatello	1	1	.500	4.89	24	0	0	9	0	3	35.0	32	31	19	4	1	34	7	20	7
Scott, Great Falls	5	4	.556	4.38	13	13	3	0	2	0	78.0	90	58	38	4	2	38	1	44	5
Shanks, Medicine Hat	1	0	1.000	3.66	12	0	0	8	0	5	19.2	14	8	8	1	2	8	1	17	0
Shumake, Billings	0	0	.000	0.00	1	0	0	1	0	1	1.2	0	0	0	0	0	1	0	1	0
J.E. Smith, Helena	0	2	.000	7.07	5	1	0	0	0	0	14.0	19	13	11	0	1	12	1	7	3
J.M. Smith, Helena*	0	1	.000	6.82	8	3	0	2	0	0	30.1	44	27	23	1	1	12	0	22	2
Soto, Billings	5	1	.833	3.27	12	12	3	0	0	0	77.0	79	44	28	3	0	23	0	69	3
Spector, Pocatello	0	1	.000	2.70	14	0	0	8	0	0	30.0	41	33	9	0	0	15	0	17	3
Steinert, Butte	3	5	.375	4.11	17	8	1	8	1	2	65.2	55	42	30	1	4	46	0	61	7
Stender, Pocatello*	4	3	.571	4.91	13	13	0	0	0	0	69.2	95	51	38	6	3	33	1	49	9
Stis, Calgary	2	3	.400	4.84	12	0	0	6	0	2	35.1	39	23	19	4	1	13	0	24	4
Strickland, Helena	1	1	.500	4.61	8	0	0	2	0	0	13.2	13	11	7	1	0	8	0	7	1
Swain, Pocatello*	5	6	.455	4.91	20	13	3	2	0	0	77.0	104	57	42	6	1	28	1	47	8
Tetreault, Helena	0	0	.000	0.00	1	0	0	0	0	0	2.2	3	3	0	0	0	2	0	2	0
Thesken, Calgary	0	2	.000	18.00	3	3	0	0	0	0	7.0	14	15	14	2	2	7	0	2	0
Thienpont, Butte*	3	1	.750	4.82	17	6	1	3	0	1	56.0	50	35	30	2	0	40	1	32	7
Torres, Great Falls	4	3	.571	4.07	29	0	0	11	0	2	48.2	48	25	22	3	1	27	0	53	8
Trasacco, Billings*	4	0	1.000	2.35	19	1	1	8	0	5	53.2	48	17	14	2	0	15	1	61	2
Trautwein, Helena	3	4	.429	3.28	19	0	0	17	0	7	35.2	27	14	13	1	1	14	1	39	3
Treadway, Great Falls	2	2	.500	7.79	15	10	0	0	0	0	54.1	86	66	47	2	2	39	1	50	3
Turano, Medicine Hat	1	2	.333	3.55	5	5	0	0	0	0	25.1	20	16	10	0	1	16	0	16	3
Vantrease, Idaho Falls*	2	1	.667	5.79	8	0	0	6	0	0	14.0	12	10	9	1	2	9	0	8	0
Vilella, Butte*	6	2	.750	5.59	13	13	0	0	0	0	67.2	94	54	42	5	0	31	0	47	4
Wasilewski, Medicine Hat	4	4	.500	5.81	21	4	0	7	0	1	57.1	66	50	37	5	1	40	2	59	10
Weatherly, Pocatello	0	3	.000	7.11	11	7	0	0	0	0	31.2	43	35	25	4	2	20	0	22	11
Werner, Pocatello*	0	0	.000	......	1	0	0	0	0	0	0.0	3	2	2	0	0	0	0	0	0
White, Butte	3	3	.500	2.52	25	0	0	19	0	6	35.2	37	13	10	1	0	14	1	38	1
Williams, Great Falls*	0	1	.000	9.00	8	0	0	3	0	0	11.0	10	14	11	0	0	16	0	9	1
Wilridge, Idaho Falls	0	1	.000	9.58	12	0	0	5	0	3	20.2	32	36	22	4	2	20	0	15	0
Wolin, Helena	3	1	.750	6.55	17	5	0	7	0	0	45.1	56	34	33	10	2	27	0	38	4
Wood, Butte	2	5	.286	6.70	21	4	0	7	0	0	44.1	48	42	33	2	4	37	1	41	4
B. Young, Helena	7	2	.778	4.03	14	12	5	1	0	1	82.2	97	46	37	4	2	22	0	53	2
R. Young, Great Falls	3	2	.600	7.23	13	8	0	0	0	0	47.1	53	46	38	4	2	46	0	47	3

BALKS—McCarter, Turano, B. Young, 4 each; Bowden, Campbell, Ferreira, Holmes, Provence, St. Claire, Swain, R. Young, 3 each; Blake, Dodd, Goedde, Mayberry, Ochs Reyes, Richardson, Rogers, Sabo, Saitta, Scott, Steinert, Vilella, Weatherly, 2 each; Balsley, Cook, Edwards, Estes, Francour, George, Gonzalez, Jacobsen, Kampsen, Kinney, Lewis, Lono, Macko, Manweiler, Moyer, Ramont, Schultz, J.M. Smith, Soto, Torres, Trasacco, White, 1 each.

COMBINATION SHUTOUTS—Rogers-Lono, Billings; Edwards-Jacobsen, Great Falls; Helton-Poppe, Helena; Sabo-Applegate, Idaho Falls; Johnson-Englund, Medicine Hat; Weatherly-Swain, Pocatello.

NO-HIT GAME—Daniel, Billings, defeated Pocatello, 6-1, July 30.

DON MATTINGLY
● YANKEES ●
BATTING CHAMPION (.343)
HITS (207)
DOUBLES (44)

TONY ARMAS
● RED SOX ●
HOME RUNS (43)
RBIs (123)
TOTAL BASES (339)

EDDIE MURRAY
● ORIOLES ●
GAME-WINNING RBIs (19)
WALKS (107)
ON-BASE PCT. (.410)

1984 A.L. LEADERS

MIKE BODDICKER
● ORIOLES ●
WINS (20)
ERA (2.79)

MARK LANGSTON
● MARINERS ●
STRIKEOUTS (204)

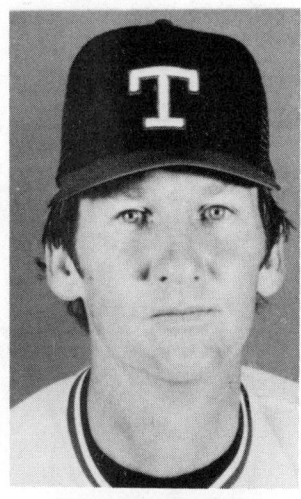

CHARLIE HOUGH
● RANGERS ●
COMPLETE GAMES (17)
GAMES STARTED (36—tie)

1985 A.L. EAST DIVISION SLATE . . .

1985	EAST						
	AT MILWAUKEE	AT DETROIT	AT CLEVELAND	AT TORONTO	AT BALTIMORE	AT NEW YORK	AT BOSTON
MILWAUKEE ...		April 16*, 17 Aug. 2*, 3, **4-4**	May 20*, 21*, 22* Aug.23*,24*,**25**,26*	June 25*, 26*, 27 Sept.20*,21,**22**,23*	June 13*,14*,15*,**16** Sept. 17*, 18*, 19*	June 28*, 29*, **30** Oct. 1*, 2*, 3*	June 10*, 11*, 12* Oct. 4*, 5, **6**
DETROIT	April 25*, 26*, 27, **28** Aug. 12*, 13*, 14*		April 22, 23, 24 Aug. 9*, 10*, **11**	June 6*, 7*, 8, **9** Sept. 9*, 10*, 11*	July 1*, 2*, 3* Oct. 4*, 5*, **6**	June 14*, 15*, **16** Sept. 24*, 25*, 26*	June 24*, 25*, 26* Sept.20*,21,**22**,23*
CLEVELAND ...	May 27, 28*, 29* Aug. 30*, 31* Sept. **1**	April 8, 10, 11 Aug. 15*,16*,17*,**18**		May 31* June 1, **2-2** Sept. 2, 4*	April 25*,26*,27*,**28** Aug. 12*, 13*, 14*	April 19*, 20, **21** Aug. 6*, 7, 8*	June 3*, 4*, 5* Sept. 5*, 6*, 7, **8**
TORONTO	June 17*, 18*, 19 Sept. 27*, 28, **29**	June 28*, 29*, **30** Oct. 1*, 2*, 3*	May 23*, 24*, 25, **26** Aug. 19*, 20*, 21*		April 12*, 13*, **14** July 29*, 30*, 31* Aug. 1*	June 10*, 11*, 12* Sept. 12*,13*,14*,**15**	June 13*,14*, 15,**16** Sept. 17*, 18*
BALTIMORE	June 21*, 22*, **23** Sept. 24*, 25*, 26*	June 10*, 11*, 12* Sept. 13*,14,**15**,16*	April 16, 17, 18 Aug. 2*, 3*, **4**	April 19*, 20, **21** Aug. 6*, 7*, 8*		June 24*, 25*, 26* Sept.27*,28,**29**,30*	June 28*, 29, **30** Sept.9*,10*,11*,12*
NEW YORK	June 6*, 7*, 8, **9** Sept. 9*, 10*, 11*	June20*,21*,22*,**23** Sept. 17*, 18*, 19*	April 13, **14** July29*,30 (Tn),31* Aug. 1*	July 1, 2*, 3 Oct. 4*, 5, **6**	June 17*, 18*, 19* Sept. 20*, 21*, **22**		April 8, 10, 11 Aug. 9*, 10, **11**
BOSTON	July 1*, 2*, 3 Sept. 13*,14*,**15**,16*	June 17*, 18*, 19* Sept. 27*, 28, **29**	May 17*, 18, **19** Aug. 27*, 28*, 29*	June 20*, 21*, 22, **23** Sept. 24*, 25*, 26*	June 7*, 8*, **9** Oct. 1*, 2*, 3*	April 23*, 24*, 25* Aug. 16*, 17*, **18**, 19	
SEATTLE	May 7*, 8* July 18*, 19*, 20*, **21**	June 3*, 4*, 5* Sept. 6*, 7*, **8**	June 6*, 7*, 8*, **9** Oct. 1*, 2*	May 10*, 11, **12** July 22*, 23*, 24*	May 29*, 30* Aug. 29*, 30*, 31* Sept. 1*	May 31* June 1*, **2** Sept. 2, 3*, 4*	May 14*, 15* July 25*, 26*, 27, **28**
OAKLAND	May 14*, 15 July 25*, 26*, 27*, **28**	May 29*, 30 Aug. 29*, 30*, 31* Sept. **1**	June 14*, 15, **16-16** Sept. 17*, 18*	May 7*, 8* July 18*, 19*, 20, **21**	May 31* June 1*, **2** Sept. 2, 3*, 4*	June 3*, 4*, 5* Sept. 6*, 7*, **8**	May 10*, 11, **12** July 22*, 23*, 24*
CALIFORNIA ...	May 10*, 11*, **12** July 22*, 23*, 24	May 31* June 1*, **2** Sept. 2, 3*, 4*	June 18*, 19*, 20* Sept. 27*, 28, **29**	May 14*, 15* July 25*, 26*, 27, **28**	June 3*, 4*, 5* Sept. 6*, 7*, **8**	May 29*, 30* Aug. 29*, 30*, 31* Sept. **1**	May 7*, 8* July 18*, 19*, 20, **21**
TEXAS	April 19*, 20, **21** July 29*, 30*, 31	May 13*, 14* July 18*, 19*, 20*, **21**	May 3*, 4, **5** July 8*, 9*, 10*	April 16, 17, 18 Aug. 2*, 3, **4**	April 8, 10* Aug. 15*,16*,17*,**18**	May 15*, 16 July 11*, 12*, 13, **14**	May 31* June 1, **2** Aug. 20*, 21*, 22*
KANSAS CITY ...	May 17*, 18, **19** Aug. 27*, 28*, 29	April 19*, 20, **21** July 29*, 30*, **31**	May 15*, 16* July 11*, 12*, 13*, **14**	April 22*, 23*, 24 Aug. 16*, 17, **18**	May 13*, 14* July 18*, 19*, 20*, **21**	May 3*, 4, **5** July 8*, 9*, 10	April 26*, 27, **28** Aug. 12*, 13*, 14*
MINNESOTA ...	May 24*, 25*, **26** Aug. 19*, 20*, 21	April 30* May 1 July 11*, 12*, 13, **14**	June 10*, 11*, 12* Sept. 13*, 14, **15**	June 4*, 5* Sept. 5*, 6*, 7, **8**	May 10*, 11*, **12** July 8*, 9*, 10*	May 13*, 14* July 4*, 5*, 6*, 7	May 27, 28*, 29* Aug. 23*, 24, **25**
CHICAGO	April 9, 11* Aug. 15*, 16*, 17, **18**	May 3*, 4, **5** July 8*, 9*, 10*	May 7*, 8* July 4*, 5*, 6*, 7	May 20, 21*, 22* Aug. 30*, 31 Sept. **1**	April 30* May 1* July 11*, 12*, 13*, **14**	April 16, 18* Aug. 2*, 3*, **4**, 5*	April 13, **14**, 15 July 30*, 31* Aug. 1*
1985	81 HOME DATES 53 NIGHTS	80 HOME DATES 53 NIGHTS	79 HOME DATES 54 NIGHTS	80 HOME DATES 45 NIGHTS	81 HOME DATES 66 NIGHTS	81 HOME DATES 58 NIGHTS	81 HOME DATES 50 NIGHTS

* NIGHT GAME
NIGHT GAME: Any game starting after 5:00 p.m.
HEAVY BLACK FIGURES DENOTE SUNDAY

AND COMPLETE WEST SCHEDULES

1985	WEST						
	AT SEATTLE	**AT OAKLAND**	**AT CALIFORNIA**	**AT TEXAS**	**AT KANSAS CITY**	**AT MINNESOTA**	**AT CHICAGO**
MILWAUKEE...	April 29*, 30* July 4, 5*, 6*, **7**	May 1*, 2 July 11, 12*, 13, **14**	May 3*, 4, **5** July 8*, 9*, 10*	April 12*, 13*, **14** Aug. 6*, 7*, 8*	June 3*, 4*, 5* Sept. 6*, 7*, **8**	May 31* June 1*, **2** Sept. 2*, 3*, 4*	April 22*, 23*, 24* Aug. 9*, 10*, **11**
DETROIT.........	May 24*, 25*, **26***, 27 Aug. 26*, 27*	May 17*, 18, **19** Aug. 20*, 21, 22*	May 20*, 21*, 22* Aug. 23*, 24*, **25**	May 7*, 8* July 4*, 5*, 6*, **7***	April 13, **14** Aug. 5*, 6*, 7*, 8*	May 15*, 16 July 25*, 26*, 27*, **28**	May 10*, 11, **12*** July 22*, 23*, 24*
CLEVELAND ...	June 28*, 29*, **30** Sept. 9*, 10*, 11*	June 21*, 22, **23** Sept 23*, 24*, 25	June 24*, 25*, 26* Sept. 20*, 21*, **22**	May 10*, 11*, **12** July 22*, 23*, 24*	April 29*, 30* May 1* July 26*, 27*, **28**	July 1*, 2*, 3* Oct. 4*, 5, **6**	May 13*, 14* July 18, 19*, 20*, **21**
TORONTO	May 3*, 4*, **5** July 8*, 9*, 10*	April 29*, 30* July 4*, 5*, 6, **7**	May 1*, 2* July 11*, 12*, 13*, **14**	April 26*, 27*, **28** Aug. 12*, 13*, 14*	April 8, 10*, 11* Aug. 9*, 10*, **11**	May 17*, 18, **19** Aug. 26*, 27*, 28	May 27*, 28*, 29* Aug. 23*, 24*, **25**
BALTIMORE....	May 17*, 18*, **19** Aug. 20*, 21*, 22*	May 21*, 22*, 23 Aug. 23*, 24, **25**	May 24*, 25, **26**, 27 Aug. 26*, 27*	April 22*, 23*, 24* Aug. 9*, 10*, **11***	May 7*, 8* July 4*, 5*, 6, **7**	May 3*, 4*, **5** July 22*, 23*, 24*	May 15*, 16* July 25*, 26*, 27*, **28**
NEW YORK	May 21*, 22*, 23* Aug. 23*, 24*, **25**	May 24*, 25, **26**, 27* Aug. 26*, 27*	May 17*, 18*, **19** Aug. 20*, 21*, 22*	April 29*, 30* May 1* July 26*, 27*, **28***	May 10*, 11*, **12** July 22*, 23*, 24*	May 7*, 8* July 18, 19*, 20*, **21**	April 26*, 27, **28** Aug. 12*, 13*, 14*
BOSTON	May 1*, 2* July 11*, 12*, 13*, **14**	May 3*, 4, **5** July 8*, 9*, 10	April 29*, 30* July 4*, 5*, 6*, **7**	May 23*, 24*, 25*, **26*** Sept. 2*, 3*	April 16*, 17*, 18* Aug. 2*, 3*, **4**	May 20*, 21*, 22* Aug. 30*, 31* Sept. 1	April 19, 20, **21** Aug. 6*, 7*, 8*
SEATTLE........		April 15*, 16*, 17 Aug. 2*, 3, **4**	April 19*, 20, **21** Aug. 5*, 6*, 7	June 18*, 19*, 20* Sept. 20*, 21*, **22***, 23*	June 21*, 22*, **23** Sept. 16*, 17*, 18*	April 22*, 23*, 24 Aug. 15*, 16*, 17, **18**	July 1*, 2*, 3* Oct. 3*, 4*, 5*, **6**
OAKLAND	April 9*, 10*, 11* Aug. 8*, 9*, 10*, **11**		April 22*, 23*, 24 Aug. 16*, 17*, **18**, 19*	June 28*, 29*, **30*** Sept. 30* Oct. 1*, 2*	July 1*, 2*, 3* Oct. 4*, 5*, **6**	April 25*, 26*, 27, **28** Aug. 12*, 13*, 14	June 18*, 19*, 20* Sept. 20*, 21*, **22**
CALIFORNIA ...	April 25*, 26*, 27*, **28** Aug. 12*, 13*, 14	April 12*, 13, **14** July 30*, 31* Aug. 1		July 1*, 2*, 3* Oct. 4*, 5*, **6**	June 28*, 29*, **30** Sept. 30* Oct. 1*, 2*, 3*	April 15*, 17*, 18 Aug. 8*, 9*, 10*, **11**	June 21*, 22, **23** Sept. 17*, 18*, 19*
TEXAS	June 24*, 25*, 26 Sept. 27*, 28*, **29**	June 7*, 8, **9-9** Sept. 9*, 10*, 11	June 10*, 11*, 12* Sept. 12*, 13*, 14*, **15**		May 27*, 28*, 29* Aug. 23*, 24*, **25**, 26*	June 21*, 22*, **23** Sept. 16*, 17*, 18	May 17*, 18*, **19** Aug. 27*, 28*, 29*
KANSAS CITY	June 13*, 14*, 15*, **16** Sept. 24*, 25*, 26*	June 10*, 11*, 12 Sept. 13, 14, **15-15**	June 7*, 8*, **9** Sept. 9*, 10*, 11*	May 20*, 21*, 22* Aug. 30*, 31* Sept. 1*		June 24*, 25*, 26* Sept. 27*, 28, **29**	May 30*, 31* June 1*, **2** Aug. 20*, 21*, 22*
MINNESOTA ...	April 12*, 13*, **14** July 29*, 30*, 31	April 19*, 20, **21** Aug. 5*, 6*, 7	April 9*, 10*, 11* Aug. 2*, 3*, **4**	June 13*, 14*, 15*, **16***, 17* Sept. 24*, 25*, 26*	June 17*, 18*, 19*, 20* Sept. 20*, 21*, **22**		June 28*, 29*, **30** Sept.9*, 10*, 11*, 12*
CHICAGO........	June 10*, 11*, 12* Sept. 13*, 14*, **15**	June 24*, 25*, 26 Sept. 26*, 27*, 28, **29**	June 13*, 14*, 15*, **16** Sept. 23*, 24*, 25*	June 3*, 4*, 5* Sept. 5*, 6*, 7*, **8***	May 24*, 25, **26** Sept. 2*, 3*, 4*	June 7*, 8*, **9** Sept. 30* Oct. 1*, 2*	
1985	81 HOME DATES 64 NIGHTS	79 HOME DATES 40 NIGHTS	81 HOME DATES 62 NIGHTS	81 HOME DATES 77 NIGHTS	81 HOME DATES 64 NIGHTS	81 HOME DATES 56 NIGHTS	81 HOME DATES 63 NIGHTS

JULY 16—ALL STAR GAME AT MINNEAPOLIS
JULY 29—HALL OF FAME GAME AT COOPERSTOWN, N.Y. (Houston Astros vs. Boston Red Sox)

1985 N.L. EAST DIVISION SLATE...

1985	EAST					
	AT **CHICAGO**	**AT** **MONTREAL**	**AT** **NEW YORK**	**AT** **PHILADELPHIA**	**AT** **PITTSBURGH**	**AT** **ST. LOUIS**
CHICAGO........		April 19, 20, **21** June 10*, 11*, 12*, 13* Sept. 16*, 17*	June 17*, 18*, 19*, 20 Aug. 9*, 10, **11** Sept. 18*, 19*	April 26*, 27*, **28** July 1*, 2*, 3* Sept. 20*, 21, **22**	April 22*, 23*, 24* June 28*, 29*, **30** Sept. 10*, 11*, 12*	June 21*, 22*, **23** Aug. 6*, 7*, 8* Oct. 4*, 5, **6**
MONTREAL	April 12, 13, **14** Aug. 12, 13, 14, 15 Sept. 23, 24		June 21*, 22*, **23** July 29, 30*, 31 Oct. 4*, 5, **6**	April 29*, 30* May 1* June 7*, 8*, **9** Sept. 10*, 11*, 12*	June 25*, 26*, 27* Aug. 2*, 3*, **4**, 5* Sept. 25*, 26*	April 15*, 17*, 18 Aug. 16*, 17*, **18** Sept. 20*, 21*, **22**
NEW YORK	June 25, 26, 27 Aug. 2, 3, **4**, 5 Sept. 25, 26	June 14*, 15*, **16** Aug. 6*, 7*, 8* Sept. 13*, 14*, **15**		April 19*, 20, **21** June 10*, 11*, 12*, 13* Sept. 23*, 24	April 15*, 16*, 17* Aug. 16*, 17*, **18** Sept. 27*, 28*, **29**	April 22*, 23*, 24 June 28*, 29*, **30** Oct. 1*, 2*, 3*
PHILADELPHIA	April 15, 16, 17 Aug. 16, 17, **18** Sept. 27, 28, **29**	April 22, 23, 24 June 28*, 29, **30** Oct. 1*, 2*, 3*	May 10*, 11, **12** Aug. 12*, 13*, 14*, 15 Sept. 16*, 17*		June 14*, 15*, **16** July 30*, 31* Aug. 1* Sept. 13*, 14*, **15**	June 18*, 19*, 20* Aug. 2*, 3*, **4**, 5* Sept. 25*, 26*
PITTSBURGH..	April 9, 11 June 6, 7, 8, **9** Oct. 1, 2, 3	June 17*, 18*, 19*, 20* Aug. 9*, 10*, **11** Sept. 18*, 19*	April 26*, 27, **28** July 1*, 2*, 3* Sept. 20*, 21, **22**	June 21*, 22*, **23** Aug. 6*, 7*, 8 Oct. 4*, 5*, **6**		April 19*, 20*, **21** Aug. 12*, 13*, 14*, 15 Sept. 23*, 24*
ST. LOUIS	June 14, 15, **16** July 30, 31 Aug. 1 Sept. 13, 14, **15**	April 25, 26, 27, **28** July 1, 2* Sept. 27*, 28*, **29**	April 9, 11 June 7*, 8, **9-9** Sept. 10*, 11*, 12	June 25*, 26*, 27 Aug. 9*, 10 (Tn), **11** Sept. 18*, 19*	April 12*, 13*, **14** June 10*, 11*, 12*, 13* Sept. 16, 17*	
ATLANTA.......	June 4, 5 Aug. 29, 30, 31 Sept. **1**	May 10*, 11, **12** July 22*, 23*, 24*	May 7*, 8* July 18*, 19*, 20, **21**	April 9*, 11* July 25*, 26*, 27*, **28**	May 31* June 1*, **2** Sept. 2, 3*, 4*	May 20*, 21*, 22 Sept. 6*, 7*, **8**
CINCINNATI ...	May 20, 21, 22 Sept. 6, 7, **8**	May 15*, 16* July 25*, 26*, 27*, **28**	April 12*, 13, **14** July 22*, 23*, 24	May 7*, 8* July 4, 5*, 6*, **7**	May 17*, 18*, **19** Aug. 20*, 21*, 22*	May 31* June 1, **2** Sept. 2*, 3*, 4*
HOUSTON.......	May 24, 25, **26** Sept. 2, 3, 4	May 7*, 8* July 18*, 19*, 20*, **21**	April 30* May 1* July 25*, 26*, 27*, **28**	May 3*, 4*, **5** July 22*, 23*, 24*	May 20*, 21*, 22* Aug. 23*, 24*, **25**	June 3*, 4*, 5* Aug. 30*, 31 Sept. **1**
LOS ANGELES ..	May 6, 7 July 11, 12, 13, **14**	May 20, 21*, 22* Aug. 23*, 24*, **25**	May 24*, 25, **26**, 27* Aug. 26*, 27*	May 17*, 18*, **19** Aug. 20*, 21*, 22*	May 3*, 4, **5** July 8*, 9*, 10*	April 30* May 1 July 4*, 5*, 6, **7**
SAN DIEGO.....	May 3, 4, **5** July 8, 9, 10	May 17*, 18, **19** Aug. 20*, 21*, 22*	May 20*, 21*, 22* Aug. 23*, 24*, **25**	May 24*, 25*, **26**, 27 Aug. 26*, 27*	April 30* May 1* July 4, 5*, 6*, **7**	May 6*, 7 July 11*, 12*, 13*, **14**
SAN FRAN......	April 30 May 1 July 4, 5, 6, **7**	May 24*, 25, **26**, 27* Aug. 26*, 27*	May 17*, 18*, **19** Aug. 20*, 21*, 22*	May 20*, 21*, 22* Aug. 23*, 24*, **25**	May 6*, 7 July 11*, 12*, 13, **14**	May 3*, 4*, **5** July 8*, 9*, 10*
1985	81 HOME DATES 0 NIGHTS	81 HOME DATES 54 NIGHTS	80 HOME DATES 51 NIGHTS	80 HOME DATES 60 NIGHTS	81 HOME DATES 62 NIGHTS	81 HOME DATES 59 NIGHTS

*NIGHT GAME
NIGHT GAME: Any game starting after 5:00 p.m.
HEAVY BLACK FIGURES DENOTE SUNDAY

AND COMPLETE WEST SCHEDULES

1985	WEST					
	AT ATLANTA	AT CINCINNATI	AT HOUSTON	AT LOS ANGELES	AT SAN DIEGO	AT SAN FRANCISCO
CHICAGO........	May 17*, 18, **19** Aug. 20*, 21*, 22*	May 27*, 28*, 29 Aug. 23*, 24*, **25**	May 31* June 1*, **2** Aug. 26*, 27*, 28	May 14*, 15* July 25*, 26*, 27, **28**	May 10*, 11*, **12** July 22*, 23*, 24*	May 8*, 9 July 18, 19*, 20, **21**
MONTREAL	May 3*, 4*, **5** July 8*, 9*, 10*	April 8, 10 July 11*, 12*, 13*, **14**	May 13*, 14* July 4*, 5*, 6*, **7***	May 31*, June 1*, **2** Sept. 2*, 3*, 4*	May 28*, 29*, 30 Aug. 29, 31* Sept. 1	June 3, 4, 5 Sept. 6*, 7, **8**
NEW YORK	May 13*, 14* July 4*, 5*, 6, **7**	May 3*, 4, **5** July 8*, 9*, 10*	May 15*, 16* July 11*, 12*, 13*, **14***	June 3*, 4*, 5* Sept. 6*, 7, **8**	May 31* June 1*, **2** Sept. 2*, 3*, 4*	May 29, 30 Aug. 29, 30*, 31 Sept. 1
PHILADELPHIA	May 15*, 16* July 11*, 12*, 13*, **14**	May 13*, 14 July 18*, 19*, 20*, **21**	April 12*, 13*, **14** July 8*, 9*, 10*	May 29*, 30* Aug. 29*, 30*, 31* Sept. 1	June 3*, 4*, 5* Sept 6*, 7, **8**	May 31* June 1, **2** Sept. 2, 3, 4
PITTSBURGH..	May 24*, 25*, **26** Aug. 26*, 27*, 28*	June 4*, 5* Aug. 29*, 30*, 31* Sept. 1	May 27*, 28*, 29* Sept. 5*, 6*, 7*	May 10*, 11, **12** July 22*, 23*, 24*	May 8*, 9 July 18, 19*, 20, **21**	May 14, 15 July 25*, 26*, 27, **28**
ST. LOUIS	May 28*, 29*, 30* Aug. 23*, 24*, **25**	May 24*, 25*, **26** Aug. 26*, 27*, 28*	May 17*, 18*, **19** Aug. 20*, 21*, 22*	May 8*, 9* July 18*, 19*, 20*, **21**	May 14*, 15* July 25*, 26*, 27*, **28**	May 10*, 11*, **12** July 22, 23, 24
ATLANTA.......		April 30* May 1 June 21 (Tn), 22, **23** Sept. 24*, 25*, 26	April 25*, 26*, 27*, **28*** June 25*, 26*, 27* Sept 30* Oct. 1	June 28*, 29, **30** Aug. 12*, 13*, 14*, 15 Oct. 2*, 3*	April 22*, 23*, 24* Aug. 16*, **18-18** Sept. 20*, 21*, **22**	July 1, 2 Aug. 8, 9*, 10, **11** Oct. 4*, 5, **6**
CINCINNATI ...	April 15*, 16*, 17* June 13*, 14*, 15*, **16** Sept. 18*, 19*		April 22*, 23*, 24 Aug. 16*, 17*, **18*** Sept. 20*, 21, **22***	July 1*, 2* Aug. 8*, 9*, 10*, **11** Oct. 4*, 5, **6**	June 28*, 29*, **30** Aug. 12*, 13*, 14*, 15 Oct. 2*, 3	April 25, 26*, 27*, **28** June 17, 18, 19 Sept. 30 Oct. 1
HOUSTON.......	April 19*, 20*, **21** June 17*, 18*, 19*, 20* Sept. 16*, 17*	May 10*, 11*, **12** July 30*, 31* Aug. 1* Sept. 27*, 28, **29**		April 15*, 16*, 17* June 21*, 22*, **23**, 24* Sept. 18*, 19*	July 1*, 2* Aug. 8*, 9 (Tn), **11** Oct. 4*, 5, **6**	June 28*, 29, **30-30** Aug. 13, 14, 15 Oct. 2, 3
LOS ANGELES	June 7*, 8, **9** Aug. 5*, 6*, 7* Sept. 10*, 11*, 12*	June 10*, 11*, 12 Aug. 2*, 3*, **4** Sept. 13*, 14*, **15**	April 9*, 10*, 11 June 14*, 15, **16*** Sept. 23*, 24*, 25*		April 18, 19*, 20*, **21** June 25*, 26*, 27 Sept. 16*, 17*	April 22*, 23, 24 Aug. 16*, 17, **18** Sept. 20*, 21, **22**
SAN DIEGO.....	April 12*, 13, **14** July 30*, 31* Aug. 1* Sept. 27*, 28*, **29**	June 7 (Tn), 8*, **9** Aug. 5*, 6*, 7 Sept. 10*, 11*	June 10*, 11*, 12* Aug. 2*, 3*, **4*** Sept. 13*, 14, **15***	April 25*, 26*, 27*, **28** June 17*, 18*, 19* Sept. 30* Oct. 1*		April 9, 10 June 13*, 14*, 15, **16-16** Sept. 18*, 19
SAN FRAN......	June 10*, 11*, 12* Aug. 2*, 3*, **4** Sept. 13*, 14*, **15**	April 18*, 19*, 20, **21** June 25*, 26*, 27 Sept. 16*, 17	June 7*, 8*, **9*** Aug. 5*, 6* Sept. 9*, 10*, 11*, 12*	April 12, 13*, **14** July 29*, 30*, 31* Sept. 27*, 28, **29**	April 15*, 16* June 20, 21*, 22, **23** Sept. 23*, 24*, 25*	
1985	81 HOME DATES 64 NIGHTS	79 HOME DATES 54 NIGHTS	81 HOME DATES 72 NIGHTS	81 HOME DATES 60 NIGHTS	79 HOME DATES 53 NIGHTS	79 HOME DATES 17 NIGHTS

JULY 16—ALL STAR GAME AT MINNEAPOLIS
JULY 29—HALL OF FAME GAME AT COOPERSTOWN, N.Y. (Houston Astros vs. Boston Red Sox)

TONY GWYNN
● PADRES ●
BATTING CHAMPION (.351)
HITS (213)
ON-BASE PCT. (.410—tie)

MIKE SCHMIDT
● PHILLIES ●
HOME RUNS (36—tie)
RBIs (106—tie)

TIM RAINES
● EXPOS ●
STOLEN BASES (75)
DOUBLES (38—tie)

1984 N.L. LEADERS

JOAQUIN ANDUJAR
● CARDINALS ●
WINS (20)
INNINGS (261.1)
SHUTOUTS (4—tie)

DWIGHT GOODEN
● METS ●
STRIKEOUTS (276)

ALEJANDRO PENA
● DODGERS ●
ERA (2.48)
SHUTOUTS (4—tie)

Index to Contents

1984 All-Star Game 219
Baseball Writers' Awards
  (MVP, Cy Young, Rookie of Year)............... 256
Directory of Organized Ball.......................... 286
Farm Systems for 1985 317
Five-Hit Games 239
Hall of Fame 259
Home Runs, Grand-Slam 237
Home Runs by Parks 247
Home Runs, Three in One Game 236
Low-Hit Games 230
Major League Draft 267
Most Valuable Player and
  Cy Young voting for 1984 27-28
Necrology 275

No-Hit Games 227
No. 1 Men Selections 315
1-0 Games 235
Pinch-Hitting 241
Player Deals 268
Player Debuts 244
Players' Association, Major League 316
Presidents of Minor Leagues, 1985 318
Re-Entry Draft 265
Relief Pitcher Ratings 233
Review of Year   3
Strikeout Performances, Top 232
THE SPORTING NEWS Awards 251
1984 World Series 203

AMERICAN LEAGUE

Attendance, 1984 267
Batting Averages, 1984 87
Batting Statistics, Miscellaneous, 1984 92
Championship Series 189
Designated Hitting, 1984 94
Directory for 1985 300
Fielding Averages, 1984 97
Pennant Winners Each Year 86
Pitchers vs. Individual Clubs 109
Pitching Averages, 1984 103
Schedule, 1985 490
Standings, 1984 86
Team Reviews 33

NATIONAL LEAGUE

Attendance, 1984 267
Batting Averages, 1984 161
Batting Statistics, Miscellaneous, 1984 168
Championship Series 195
Directory for 1985 287
Fielding Averages, 1984 172
Pennant Winners Each Year 160
Pitchers vs. Individual Clubs 183
Pitching Averages, 1984 177
Schedule, 1985 492
Standings, 1984 160
Team Reviews 115

1984 Game Scores

Baltimore 50   Milwaukee 58
Boston 46   Minnesota 70
California 66   New York 42
Chicago 78   Oakland 74
Cleveland 54   Seattle 82
Detroit 34   Texas 84
Kansas City 62   Toronto 38

1984 Game Scores

Atlanta 120   New York 142
Chicago 138   Philadelphia 150
Cincinnati 132   Pittsburgh 158
Houston 124   St. Louis 146
Los Angeles 128   San Diego 116
Montreal 154   San Francisco 135

NATIONAL ASSOCIATION (MINOR LEAGUE) AVERAGES

American Association 320   Gulf Coast 472   Pacific Coast 351
Appalachian 464   International 329   Pioneer 482
California 392   Mexican 338   South Atlantic 453
Carolina 402   Midwest 422   Southern 371
Eastern 362   New York-Pennsylvania 434   Texas 382
Florida State 411   Northwest 445

Index to Minor League Clubs, Cities

Aguascalientes, Mexico 338
Albany, N.Y. 362
Albuquerque, N.M. 351
Anderson, S.C. 453
Appleton, Wis. 422
Arkansas 382
Asheville, N.C. 453
Auburn, N.Y. 434

Bakersfield, Calif. 392
Batavia, N.Y. 434
Beaumont, Tex. 382
Bellingham, Wash. 445
Beloit, Wis. 422
Bend, Ore. 445
Bettendorf, Ia.
(see Quad Cities) 422
Billings, Mont. 482
Birmingham, Ala. 371
Bluefield, W.Va. 464
Bradenton, Fla. 472
Bristol, Va. 464
Buffalo, N.Y. 362
Burlington, Ia. 422
Burlington, Vt.
(see Vermont) 362
Butte, Mont. 482

Calgary, Alberta, Can. 482
Campeche, Mexico 338
Cedar Rapids, Ia. 422
Charleston, S.C. 453
Charlotte, N.C. 371
Chattanooga, Tenn. 371
Clinton, Ia. 422
Columbia, S.C. 453
Columbus, Ga. 371
Columbus, O. 329
Cordoba, Mexico 338

Davenport, Ia.
(see Quad Cities) 422
Daytona Beach, Fla. 411
Denver, Colo. 320
Des Moines, Ia. (see Iowa) 320
Durham, N.C. 402

Edmonton, Alberta, Can. 351
Elizabethton, Tenn. 464
Elmira, N.Y. 434
El Paso, Tex. 382
Erie, Pa. 434
Eugene, Ore. 445
Evansville, Ind. 320
Everett, Wash. 445

Florence, S.C. 453
Fort Lauderdale, Fla. 411
Fort Myers, Fla. 411
Fresno, Calif. 392

Gastonia, N.C. 453
Geneva, N.Y. 434
Glens Falls, N.Y. 362
Great Falls, Mont. 482
Greensboro, N.C. 453
Greenville, S.C. 371

Hagerstown, Md. 402
Hampton, Va.
(see Peninsula) 402

Hawaii 351
Helena, Mont. 482
Honolulu, Hawaii
(see Hawaii) 351

Idaho Falls, Ida. 482
Indianapolis, Ind. 320
Iowa 320

Jackson, Miss. 382
Jacksonville, Fla. 371
Jamestown, N.Y. 434
Johnson City, Tenn. 464
Juarez, Mexico 338

Kennewick, Wash.
(see Tri-Cities) 445
Kenosha, Wis. 422
Kingsport, Tenn. 464
Kinston, N.C. 402
Knoxville, Tenn. 371

Lakeland, Fla. 411
Las Vegas, Nev. 351
Leon, Mexico 338
Little Falls, N.Y. 434
Little Rock, Ark.
(see Arkansas) 382
Lodi, Calif. 392
Louisville, Ky. 320
Lynchburg, Va. 402

Macon, Ga. 453
Madison, Wis. 422
Maine 329
Medicine Hat, Alberta, Can. 482
Medford, Ore. 445
Memphis, Tenn. 371
Mexico City, Mex. Reds 338
Mexico City, Mex. Tigers 338
Miami, Fla. 411
Midland, Tex. 382
Modesto, Calif. 392
Moline, Ill.
(see Quad Cities) 422
Monclova, Mexico 338
Monterrey, Mexico 338

Nashua, N.H. 362
Nashville, Tenn. 371
Newark, N.Y. 434
New Britain, Conn. 362
Niagara Falls 434
Norfolk, Va.
(see Tidewater) 329
Nuevo Laredo, Mexico 338

Oklahoma City, Okla. 320
Old Orchard Beach, Me.
(see Maine) 329
Omaha, Neb. 320
Oneonta, N.Y. 434
Orlando, Fla. 371

Paintsville, Ky. 464
Pasco, Wash.
(see Tri-Cities) 445
Pawtucket, R.I. 329
Peninsula 402
Peoria, Ill. 422
Phoenix, Ariz. 351

Pikeville, Ky. 464
Pocatello, Ida. 482
Portland, Ore. 351
Portsmouth, Va.
(see Tidewater) 329
Prince William, Va. 402
Pulaski, Tenn. 464

Quad Cities 422

Reading, Pa. 362
Redwood, Calif. 392
Reno, Nev. 392
Richland, Wash.
(see Tri-Cities) 445
Richmond, Va. 329
Rochester, N.Y. 329
Rock Island, Ill.
(see Quad Cities) 422

St. Petersburg, Fla. 411
Salem, Ore. 445
Salem, Va. 402
Salinas, Calif. 392
Saltillo, Mexico 338
Salt Lake City, Utah. 351
San Antonio, Tex. 382
San Jose, Calif. 392
Sarasota, Fla. 472
Savannah, Ga. 371
Shreveport, La. 382
Spartanburg, S.C. 453
Spokane, Wash. 445
Springfield, Ill. 422
Stockton, Calif. 392
Syracuse, N.Y. 329

Tabasco, Mexico 338
Tacoma, Wash. 351
Tampa, Fla. 411
Tampico, Mexico 338
Tidewater 329
Toledo, O. 329
Toluca, Mexico 338
Tri-Cities 445
Tucson, Ariz. 351
Tulsa, Okla. 382

Utica, N.Y. 434

Vancouver, B.C., Can. 351
Veracruz, Mexico 338
Vermont 362
Vero Beach, Fla. 411
Villahermosa, Mexico
(see Tabasco) 338
Visalia, Calif. 392

Waterbury, Conn. 362
Waterloo, Ia. 422
Watertown, N.Y. 434
Wausau, Wis. 422
West Palm Beach, Fla. 411
Wichita, Kan. 320
Winston-Salem, N.C. 402
Winter Haven, Fla. 411

Yucatan, Mexico 338